KU-251-724

# The Blackwell Companion to Major Social Theorists

# BLACKWELL COMPANIONS TO SOCIOLOGY

The *Blackwell Companions to Sociology* provide introductions to emerging topics and theoretical orientations in sociology as well as presenting the scope and quality of the discipline as it is currently configured. Essays in the Companions tackle broad themes or central puzzles within the field and are authored by key scholars who have spent considerable time in research and reflection on the questions and controversies that have activated interest in their area. This authoritative series will interest those studying sociology at advanced undergraduate or graduate level as well as scholars in the social sciences and informed readers in applied disciplines.

*The Blackwell Companion to Social Theory*, Second Edition
Edited by Bryan S. Turner

*The Blackwell Companion to Major Social Theorists*
Edited by George Ritzer

**Forthcoming:**
*The Blackwell Companion to Sociology*
Edited by Judith Blau

*The Blackwell Companion to Political Sociology*
Edited by Kate Nash and Alan Scott

*The Blackwell Companion to Organizations*
Edited by Joel Baum

*The Blackwell Companion to Sociology of the Family*
Edited by Jackie Scott, Judith Treas, and Martin Richards

*The Blackwell Companion to Criminology*
Edited by Colin Sumner and William Chambliss

UNIVERSITY OF
WOLVERHAMPTON

WP 2206982 8

# The Blackwell Companion to Major Social Theorists

*Edited by*

## George Ritzer

UNIVERSITY OF WOLVERHAMPTON
LIBRARY

ACC NO. 2206982  CLASS
301.

CONTROL
063l207l04  01

DATE  SITE
26. JUN 2000  DY  BLA

BLACKWELL
*Publishers*

Copyright © Blackwell Publishers Ltd 2000; editorial introduction and organization
copyright © George Ritzer 2000

First published 2000

2 4 6 8 10 9 7 5 3 1

Blackwell Publishers Inc.
350 Main Street
Malden, Massachusetts 02148
USA

Blackwell Publishers Ltd
108 Cowley Road
Oxford OX4 1JF
UK

All rights reserved. Except for the quotation of short passages for the purposes of criticism and
review, no part of this publication may be reproduced, stored in a retrieval system, or
transmitted, in any form or by any means, electronic, mechanical, photocopying, recording, or
otherwise, without the prior permission of the publisher.

Except in the United States of America, this book is sold subject to the condition that it shall
not, by way of trade or otherwise, be lent, resold, hired out, or otherwise circulated without
the publisher's prior consent in any form of binding or cover other than that in which it is
published and without a similar condition including this condition being imposed on the
subsequent purchaser.

*Library of Congress Cataloging-in-Publication Data*

The Blackwell companion to major social theorist / edited by George Ritzer
        p. cm.—(Blackwell companions to sociology)
    Includes bibliographical references and index.
    ISBN 0–631–20710–4 (alk. paper)
    1. Sociologists—Biography. 2. Social sciences—Philosophy. I. Ritzer, George. II.
Series.

HM478 .B583 2000
301'.092'2—dc21
[B]                                                                                        99–049624

*British Library Cataloguing in Publication Data*
A CIP catalogue record for this book is available from the British Library.

Typeset in 10.5/12pt Sabon
by Kolam Information Services Pvt Ltd, Pondicherry, India
Printed in Great Britain by
MPG Books, Bodmin, Cornwall

This book is printed on acid-free paper.

# Contents

# Preface

---

As anyone who has ever edited a volume like this one knows, it can be a very frustrating experience. This *Companion* was no exception, but having just finished proofreading the nearly 800 pages of text, I can truthfully say that in the end it was worth all the effort. Other than the co-authored introductory essay, I can claim little credit for what follows and what does follow is a remarkable set of essays on 25 of the leading social theorists, both classic and contemporary. I have written about many of these thinkers myself and I found that I learned a great deal from these essays. The 25 original essays in this volume may well constitute the best available introduction to the leading social theorists, and taken together they do an excellent job of telling us where we have come from in social theory, where we are at the start of a new millennium, and in many cases where social theorists need to think about going in the coming years.

The authors were presented with a set of guidelines about the topics to be covered in each essay. Although all of the authors received the same guidelines, they were encouraged to cover them in their own ways. Thus, while the essays have a number of similarities in terms of coverage, there is great variation from one essay to another. A few authors chose to cover all of the recommended topics in the order suggested. Others dealt with all of the topics but in a variety of idiosyncratic ways. Still others chose to focus on a few of the topics and to downplay or even ignore others. While I suggested a format, I did not want it to be a straitjacket. The authors have employed the guidelines in diverse ways and the result is a set of essays that reflects not only those guidelines, but also the interests and strengths of the authors, and the distinctive orientations and contributions of the theorists they analyze so well.

Beyond the contributors, there are a number of other people to thank. I begin with Blackwell's sociology editor, Susan Rabinowitz, who proposed that I undertake this project and was of great help throughout its creation and development.

I could not have done this book without the help of Douglas Goodman, who not only co-authored the introductory essay, but read and commented on all of the essays and helped with the innumerable details involved in bringing this project to fruition. Finally, I would like to thank my undergraduate assistants, Zinnia Cho and Jan Geesin, for their invaluable help.

George Ritzer

# Contributors

**Robert J. Antonio** is Professor of Sociology at the University of Kansas. He works in classical, critical, and contemporary social theory. Among his publications are: "Nietzsche's Antisociology: Subjectified Culture and the End of History," *American Journal of Sociology*; "The Normative Foundations of Emancipatory Theory: Evolutionary vs. Pragmatic Perspectives," *American Journal of Sociology*; and "Mapping Postmodern Social Theory," in *What Is Social Theory?*

**Christopher G. A. Bryant** is Professor of Sociology, and Dean of the Faculty of Arts, Media and Social Sciences, at the University of Salford. He is the author of *Sociology in Action* (1976), *Positivism in Social Theory and Research* (1985), and *Practical Sociology: Postempiricism and the Reconstruction of Theory and Application* (1995) and co-editor of five other books, including two with David Jary: *Giddens' Theory of Structuration* (1991) and *Anthony Giddens: Critical Assessments* (four volumes, 1997). In addition to social theory, he has research interests in: the post-communist transformation of Eastern Europe; George Soros and the Central European University; and the nations of Britain.

**Craig Calhoun** is President of the Social Science Research Council and Professor of Sociology and History at New York University. Among his books are *Nationalism* (1997), *Critical Social Theory: Culture, History, and the Challenge of Difference* (1995), and *Neither Gods nor Emperors: Students and the Struggle for Democracy in China* (1994). He was the editor of the ASA journal *Sociological Theory* from 1994 to 1999, and is the editor-in-chief of the *Oxford Dictionary of the Social Sciences*.

**Patricia T. Clough** is Professor of Sociology, Women's Studies and Intercultural Studies at Queens College and The Graduate Center of CUNY. She is author of

*The End(s) of Ethnography: from Realism to Social Criticism* (second edition 1998), *Feminist Thought: Desire, Power and Discourse* (1994), and *Autoaffection: Unconscious Thought in the Age of Teletechnology* (in the press). Clough is interested in the transformation of sociality, subjectivity, and political economy in relationship to changes in technology. She is presently working on a book on psychoanalysis, mass media, and trauma.

**Karen S. Cook** is the Ray Lyman Wilbur Professor of Sociology at Stanford University. She is currently conducting research on social exchange, social networks, trust, and physician referral networks. Her recent publications include work on social psychology, social exchange, distributive justice (with K. Hegtvedt), and trust in the USA and Japan (with T. Yamagishi and M. Watabe, *American Journal of Sociology*, July 1998).

**Gary Alan Fine** is Professor of Sociology at Northwestern University. He received a PhD in social psychology from Harvard University in 1976. He is most recently the author of *Morel Tales: the Culture of Mushrooming* (1998) and *Kitchens: the Culture of Restaurant Work* (1996). His current research is an examination of the creation of a market for self-taught art.

**Doug Goodman** is completing his dissertation, "The Sociology of Freedom," at the University of Maryland at College Park. He has published pieces on Lacan, Luhmann, and Habermas, and has written on the sociology of consumption and postmodernism.

**Susan Hoecker-Drysdale** is Adjunct Professor of Sociology, Department of Sociology and Anthropology, Concordia University, Montreal, Quebec; Visiting Fellow, School of Advanced Study, University of London, 1997–8. Her publications include: *Harriet Martineau: First Woman Sociologist* (1992); "Harriet Martineau (1802–1876): Kritische Sozialforschung: Theorie und Praxis," in *Frauen in der Soziologie: Neun Porträts* (edited by Claudia Honegger and Theresa Wobbe, 1998); "The Enigma of Harriet Martineau's Letters on Science," *Women's Writings: the Elizabethan to Victorian Period* (1995); "Sociologists in the Vineyard: the Careers of Everett Cherrington Hughes and Helen MacGill Hughes," in *Creative Couples in the Sciences* (edited by Helena Pycior et al., 1996); "Women Sociologists in Canada: the Careers of Helen MacGill Hughes, Aileen Dansken Ross and Jean Robertson Burnet," in *Despite the Odds: Essays on Canadian Women and Science* (edited by Marianne G. Ainley, 1990). Her current research and writing focuses on Harriet Martineau, selected women in the historical emergence of sociology, and the history of feminist sociological theory. She is a founding member of the British Martineau Society and the Harriet Martineau Sociological Society.

**David Jary** is Professor of Sociology and Dean of the Graduate School at Staffordshire University, UK. Previously, he was Senior Lecturer in Sociology at the University of Salford, UK. His writings include *The Middle Class in Politics* (with J. Garrard et al.), *Sport, Leisure and Social Relations* (with J. Horne and A Tomlinson), *The New Higher Education* (with M. Parker), *Giddens's Theory of Structuration* (with C. Bryant) and recently *Anthony Giddens: Critical Assessments* (four volumes, with C. Bryant).

**Robert Alun Jones** is Professor of Religious Studies, History, and Sociology at the University of Illinois in Urbana-Champaign. He also has an appointment with the Graduate School of Library and Information Science and is a member of the Campus Honors Faculty. He was the founder and director of the Advanced Information Technologies Laboratory, and is Senior Research Scientist for the Humanities at the National Center for Supercomputing Applications. His research interests include the French philosopher and social theorist Émile Durkheim and his intellectual context, the methodology of the history of ideas, and the scholarly use of electronic documents and networked information systems. He is the author of *Emile Durkheim: an Introduction to Four Major Works* (1986), *The Development of Durkheim's Social Realism* (1999), several edited volumes, and numerous journal articles on Durkheim. He has been editor of *Études durkheimiennes*, and is also responsible for the Durkheim site on the Internet. He is writing a book on the study of primitive religion between 1865 and 1914.

**Stephen Kalberg** is Associate Professor of Sociology, Boston University. His major publications include *Max Weber's Comparative-Historical Sociology* (1994), *Max Weber's Sociology of Civilizations* (forthcoming), and, as editor, *Max Weber* (forthcoming). His research interests include classical and contemporary sociological theory, comparative-historical sociology, political sociology, and comparative political cultures, especially German and American.

**Douglas Kellner** is George Kneller Chair in the Philosophy of Education at UCLA and is author of many books on social theory, politics, history, and culture, including *Herbert Marcuse and the Crisis of Marxism, Critical Theory, Marxism, and Modernity, Jean Baudrillard: from Marxism to Postmodernism and Beyond, Postmodern Theory: Critical Interrogations* (with Steven Best), *Television and the Crisis of Democracy, The Persian Gulf TV War, Media Culture,* and *The Postmodern Turn* (with Steven Best).

**Richard Kilminster** is Senior Lecturer in Sociology at the University of Leeds, where he also gained his PhD under Zygmunt Bauman in 1976, having previously studied sociology at the Universities of Essex and Leicester. In the 1980s he worked with Norbert Elias at the University of Bielefeld and in Amsterdam, and edited his last major work, *The Symbol Theory* (1991). He is author of *Praxis and Method* (1979) and *The Sociological Revolution: from the Enlightenment to the Global Age* (1998), and editor (with Ian Varcoe) of *Culture, Modernity and Revolution: Essays in Honour of Zygmunt Bauman* (1995). His research interests are in the fields of sociological theory, the sociology of knowledge, and psychoanalysis. He is currently researching social identity.

**Charles Lemert** teaches sociology at Wesleyan University. He has written many books and articles on various subjects, most recently *Postmodernism Is Not What You Think* and *Social Things*. He is completing *Dark Thoughts*, a study of the troubles race has caused in social thought and culture over the course of the past century.

**Victor Lidz** was taught by Talcott Parsons at Harvard, and, after graduation in 1962, entered the Department of Social Relations there as a graduate student to continue studies in sociological theory. From 1963 to 1968, he served as Parsons's research assistant. In the 1970s, he taught seminars on new developments in the theory of social action with Parsons at both the University of Chicago and the University of Pennsylvania. Lidz received his doctorate in sociology from Harvard University in 1976. He is presently Acting Director of the Institute for Addictive Disorders, Department of Psychiatry, MCP Hahnemann University in Philadelphia.

**Siegwart Lindenberg** holds a chair of theoretical sociology at the University of Groningen, the Netherlands, and is co-director of the Interuniversity Center for Social Science Theory and Methodology (ICS). He received his PhD from Harvard University in 1971 and is a member of the Royal Netherlands Academy of Arts and Sciences. His research interests focus mainly on developing a sociological approach to rational choice and applying it to questions of contracting, solidarity in groups and organizations, and quality of life. Some recent publications are: "Contractual Relations and Weak Solidarity: the Behavioral Basis of Restraints on Gain-maximization," *Journal of Institutional and Theoretical Economics* (1988); "An Extended Theory of Institutions and Contractual Discipline," *Journal of Institutional and Theoretical Economics* (1992); "Framing, Empirical Evidence, and Applications," in *Jahrbuch für Neue Politische Ökonomie, volume 12* (1993); "Alternatives, Frames, and Relative Prices: a Broader View of Rational Choice," *Acta Sociologica* (with B. Frey, 1993); "Grounding Groups in Theory: Functional, Cognitive, and Structural Interdependencies," in *Advances in Group Processes volume 14* (1997); "Solidarity: Its Microfoundations and Macro/dependence," in *The Problem of Solidarity: Theories and Models* (1998).

**Philip Manning** is Associate Professor of Sociology at Cleveland State University. Recent publications include "The Deinstitionalization and Deinstitutionalization of the Mentally Ill: Lessons from Goffman," in *Counseling and Therapeutic State* (1999) and "Ethnographic Coats and Tents," in *Goffman and Social Organization: Studies in a Sociological Legacy* (1999). He is presently working on a study of Freud's impact on American sociology.

**Stephen Mennell** has been Professor of Sociology and Head of Department at University College Dublin (National University of Ireland, Dublin) since 1993. He read economics at the University of Cambridge and spent the year 1966–7 as a Frank Knox Memorial Fellow in the Department of Social Relations at

Harvard University. Between 1967 and 1990 he taught in the Department of Sociology at the University of Exeter, England, and was awarded the degree of Doctor in de Sociale Wetenschappen by the University of Amsterdam in 1985. From 1990 to 1993 he was Professor of Sociology and Head of the Department of Anthropology and Sociology at Monash University, Melbourne, Australia. His book *All Manners of Food* was awarded the Grand prix international de littérature gastronomique and the Prix Marco Polo. He is a Trustee of the Norbert Elias Foundation, Amsterdam. He has written and edited a number of other books

**William Outhwaite,** born in 1949, studied at Oxford and Sussex Universities and is Professor of Sociology in the School of European Studies at Sussex, where he has taught since 1973. His research interests include the philosophy of social science (especially realism), social theory (especially critical theory and contemporary European social theory), political sociology, and the sociology of knowledge. He is the author of *Understanding Social Life: the Method Called Verstehen* (1975; 2nd edn 1986), *Concept Formation in Social Science* (1983), *New Philosophies of Social Science: Realism, Hermeneutics and Critical Theory* (1987), and *Habermas: A Critical Introduction* (1994). He edited *The Habermas Reader* (1996), *The Blackwell Dictionary of Twentieth-Century Social Thought* (1993, with Tom Bottomore), and *The Sociology of Politics* (with Luke Martell, 1998). He is currently working on books on social theory and post-communism, contemporary Europe and Germany. He has been a deputy editor of *Sociology,* editor of *Current Sociology,* and chair of the International Sociological Association's Publications Committee, and is now an associate editor of the *European Journal of Social Theory.*

**Mary Pickering** is an associate professor of history at San Jose State University. She received a DEA from the Institut d'Etudes Politiques in 1984 and a PhD from Harvard in 1988. Cambridge University Press published in 1993 the first volume of her major work, *Auguste Comte: an Intellectual Biography.* Thanks to a NEH fellowship, she has almost completed the second volume.

**Anne Warfield Rawls** is an Associate Professor of Sociology at Wayne State University. Her interests are in the areas of social theory and interaction. In that regard she has published papers that attempt to connect various writings on interaction with issues developed by classical social theorists. This synthesis has in turn been applied to the analysis of "race" and intercultural communication. Publications include "The Interaction Order *Sui Generis*: Goffman's Contribution to Social Theory," "Durkheim's Epistemology: the Neglected Argument," and "'Race' as an Interaction Order Phenomenon: W. E. B. Du Bois' Double Consciousness Thesis Revisited." She is currently completing books on Durkheim's epistemology and on interaction between "races" in the United States. For the past ten years Professor Rawls has worked closely with Harold Garfinkel, preparing several edited volumes of his collected works for publication.

**George Ritzer** is Professor of Sociology at the University of Maryland, where he has been a Distinguished Scholar-Teacher and won a Teaching Excellence Award. He has chaired the American Sociological Associations's sections on Theoretical Sociology and Organizations and Occupations. George Ritzer has held a Fulbright-Hays Fellowship, has been a Fellow at the Netherlands Institute for Advanced Study and the Swedish Collegium for Advanced Study in the Social Sciences, and has held the UNESCO Chair in Social Theory at the Russian Academy of Sciences. His major areas of interest are sociological theory and metatheory, as well as the application of theory to the sociology of consumption. In the former, his major publications are *Sociology: a Multiple Paradigm Science* (1975/1980), *Toward an Integrated Sociological Paradigm* (1981) and *Metatheorizing in Sociology* (1991). In the latter, he has written *The McDonaldization of Society* (1993, 1996), *Expressing America: a Critique of the Global Credit Card Society* (1995), *The McDonaldization Thesis: Explorations and Extensions* (1998) and *Enchanting a Disenchanted World: Revolutionizing the Means of Consumption* (1999). His work has been translated into many languages: *The McDonaldization of Society* alone has been, or is being, translated into more than a dozen languages. He is currently co-editing the *Handbook of Social Theory* with Barry Smart.

**Mary Rogers** is Professor of Sociology at the University of West Florida. Her publications include *Barbie Culture* (1999), *Contemporary Feminist Theory: a Text/Reader* (1998), *Multicultural Experiences, Multicultural Theories: a Text/Reader* (1996), *Novels, Novelists, and Readers: toward a Phenomenological Sociology of Literature* (1993), and *Sociology, Ethnomethodology, and Experience: a Phenomenological Critique* (1983).

**Lawrence A. Scaff** is Professor of Political Science and Dean of the College of Liberal Arts at Wayne State University, Detroit. He teaches political and social theory, and he is the author of *Fleeing the Iron Cage: Culture, Politics and Modernity in the Thought of Max Weber*. He has published numerous essays in modern social theory, including recent work on Weber, Simmel, the problem of historicism, and issues in cultural sociology. He has also served on the faculty of the University of Arizona, Pennsylvania State University, and as a Fulbright scholar at the University of Freiburg.

**Dmitri Shalin** is Professor of Sociology at the University of Nevada, Las Vegas, and received his first PhD from the Institute of Sociology, Russian Academy of Science, and the second from Columbia University. He has published extensively in the areas of sociological theory, the history of sociology, and Russian society. He was the editor of special issues of *Symbolic Interaction*, on "Self in Crisis: Identity and the Postmodern Condition" and "Russian Society in Transition."

**Barry Smart** is Professor of Sociology in the School of Social and Historical Studies. He is the author of a number of books, including *Michel Foucault, Modern Conditions, Postmodern Controversies*, and *Postmodernity*. Recent publications include *Facing Modernity* and *Resisting McDonaldization*. He is also the co-editor (with George Ritzer) of *The Handbook of Social Theory* (forthcoming).

**Piotr Sztompka** is a Professor of Theoretical Sociology at the Jagiellonian University in Krakow, Poland. He has taught at several American and European universities, most often at Columbia and UCLA. He has been a fellow at the Institutes for Advanced Study at Uppsala, Berlin, Vienna, and Stanford. He was a recipient of the New Europe Prize 1995, is a Member of Academia Europaea (London), the American Academy of Arts and Sciences (Cambridge, MA) and the Polish Academy of Sciences, and Vice-President of the International Sociological Association. His twelve books published in English include *System and Function* (1974), *Sociological Dilemmas* (1979), *Robert Merton: an Intellectual Profile* (1986), *Society in Action* (1991), *The Sociology of Social Change* (1993), and *Trust: a Sociological Theory* (1999). He has also edited a number of volumes, including *Robert Merton on Social Structure and Science* (1996). He is currently working on a book on cultural trauma in post-communist societies.

**Jonathan H. Turner** is Distinguished Professor of Sociology at the University of California at Riverside. He is the author of twenty-four books and many articles on sociological theory, ethnic relations, institutional systems, stratification dynamics, and evolutionary processes. His most recent research has been on the biology and sociology of human emotions.

**Malcolm Waters** is Professor of Sociology and Dean of Arts at the University of Tasmania, Australia. He is the author or co-author of *Postmodernization*, *Modern Sociological Theory*, *The Death of Class*, *Globalization*, and *Daniel Bell*. Waters is a Fellow of the Academy of the Social Sciences in Australia.

**Joseph M. Whitmeyer** is Associate Professor of Sociology at the University of North Carolina at Charlotte. He is interested in developing actor models and using them deductively to analyze social phenomena such as associational networks, reputation systems, social power, and nationalism. A recent article in *Rationality and Society* presents an experimental test of how negatively connected exchange networks produce power inequality.

# Introduction: Toward a More Open Canon

## GEORGE RITZER AND DOUGLAS GOODMAN

This introduction is an exercise in metatheorizing in sociology. This seems harmless and academic, at least until one realizes that neither theories about society nor theories about theories of society are confined to professional academics. Pragmatic agents engaged in changing their society cannot avoid thinking about how society works and how society affects the way that individuals think. It is but a short step from there to considering how others have thought a society works and how they were affected by their society.

This essay employs one of three types of metatheorizing – "metatheorizing as a means of attaining a deeper understanding of sociological theory."[1] More specifically, it involves the use of the typology of ways of doing such metatheoretical work shown in figure 1.

The first section of this chapter involves an external-intellectual approach, in which ideas derived from philosophy are used to better understand the chapters presented in this volume. More specifically, Richard Rorty's genres of historiography are used to analyze four types of narrative histories of social theory represented in these chapters. Focusing on one of Rorty's types, we then employ a typology derived from Donald Levine's work (an internal-intellectual approach, since it was created by a sociologist) to analyze several of the ways in which sociological narratives connect the past to the present in order to suggest progress and continuity. This section closes with the case for the addition of a fifth type of narrative – critical and effective histories (derived from the work of Michel Foucault) – to be added to Rorty's typology.

The second half of this introduction takes as its objective the better understanding of the theorists and theories covered in the chapters in this volume. To that end, all four types of metatheorizing detailed in figure 1 will be employed. At the same time, this section performs the function of introducing the reader to at least some aspects of each of the chapters to be found in this book.

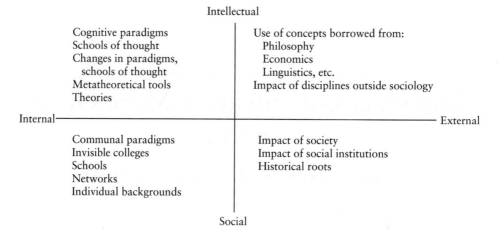

**Figure 1**   Major types of metatheorizing in order to attain a better understanding of social theory.

We conclude with the argument that the goal of such metatheoretical analysis is the creation of new theoretical (and metatheoretical) perspectives. Thus, while this book involves largely a look back into the ancient and recent history of theory, it is also oriented to the future and the creation of new theoretical perspectives.

## NARRATIVES, *GEISTESGESCHICHTES*, AND THE HISTORY OF SOCIAL THEORY

One of the purposes of this volume is to contribute to the narrative history of social theory. It serves this purpose in at least three ways. First, and most obviously, the chapters themselves are narratives about social theorists. They are biographies related to tales of intellectual disputes set within epic social histories. The stories move from the theorists' social and intellectual context to present-day impacts and assessments. Second, the selection of the twenty-five theorists covered in this volume implies a narrative of social theory because, certainly, this cast of characters was selected to fit if not a specific plot, then at least a *mise en scène*. Finally, and perhaps most importantly, this volume is meant to be a source book for constructing not only new theories, but also new narratives of social theory. Retellings and reinterpretations, such as those in this volume, have always been more than a resource for present controversies. They have been an intrinsic part of most of social theory's paradigmatic shifts. Therefore, although any list of theorists covered in a collection such as this one can be read as an official canon, this book is intended to be used as "canon fodder" in an open, contestable process of theory construction and reconstruction.

To say, however, that these are narratives, or that they are meant to contribute to narrative reinterpretations, is not to say enough, because there are many ways in which the story of social theory can be told and not all of them fit the intention of this collection. Richard Rorty[2] discusses four genres of historiography and, although he is dealing with narrative histories of philosophy, his typology can be applied to social theory.

Let us begin with the genre that Rorty refers to as "most familiar and dubious," *doxography*. In social theory, this would be an approach that enumerates what various authors traditionally called sociologists have had to say about topics traditionally defined as sociological. This type of narrative takes a list of supposedly timeless sociological issues such as order, control, organization, etc., and cites the exemplary contributions made by an equally timeless list of social theorists. It makes the mistake of taking both central sociological issues and exemplary social theorists as natural rather than contestable constructions. Rorty sees this genre as a degenerate form fit only for the most basic pedagogical purposes.

It would be easy, in a collection such as this, to accept a timeless list of social theorists and simply offer new interpretations of these people and their contributions. While there are certainly a number of such essays here, there are also essays on thinkers who would traditionally not be covered in such a volume – Martineau, Gilman, Du Bois, Emerson, Coleman, Elias, Baudrillard, and Butler. There has been a conscious effort to extend the net and include thinkers who have not heretofore been considered part of the canon. More importantly, the idea that there can be such a timeless list is rejected. *All* such lists are provisional and it is our expectation that future collections will offer somewhat different rosters. The list of thinkers dealt with in this book tells us much about the state of social theory at the beginning of the twenty-first century (and undoubtedly about the person doing the selecting), but in a decade or two, the list of authors covered will almost certainly look very different.

The idea that there is a timeless list of social theorists can become a straitjacket. At the very least, it quickly becomes dated, because both the social world and social theory are continually changing. For example, a similar book a few decades ago would almost certainly have included an essay on George Homans. However, looking at work in exchange theory today, it seems clear that the work of Richard Emerson has replaced that of Homans as the major theoretical resource. While this particular choice – indeed all choices – is open to debate and disagreement, what is indisputable is the fact that lists of our centrally important social theorists are open to continual change.

Although it may offend the sacred priests of what Robert Alun Jones calls the Nacirema Tsigoloicos, the work of *no* theorist is timeless.[3] Marx, Weber, Durkheim, and a few others have been of great importance for a century or more, but the time will come when they, too, will be relegated to the prehistory of social theory. At some point in the future, the social world will be so different that even Marx, Weber, and Durkheim will prove to be of little relevance in thinking about it. In fact, were this not to be the case, one would be forced to reconsider the whole enterprise of social theory. Changes in both society and social theory are inevitable and necessary. Doxographies obscure this fact.

Similarly, a belief in a timeless list of sociological problems restricts our vision to a horizon defined by a wish to remain still. It obscures the vistas opened up by unpredictable historical movements. For example, the topics of industrialization and modes of production were among the founding problems of modern sociology, but many have argued that the continued focus on them has led to the neglect of important changes in modes of consumption.[4] A recent sociological theory text organized around subjects begins with rationality because it "has been at the foundation of dominant conceptions of modernity."[5] However, even where the topic appears to be abiding, as rationality certainly has, a closer look reveals that its meaning is not. The Kantian concept of reason that structured the debates around rationality at the end of the eighteenth century bears only a genealogical relation to postmodern contestations. The current controversy around rationality has inherited the name and a faint family resemblance, but it is not at all clear that the previous participants – for example, Durkheim and Kant or Weber and Marx – would recognize their progeny. Furthermore, there are certainly a number of theorists, especially those associated with a postmodern approach, who would argue that it is irrationality rather than rationality that characterizes large portions of contemporary society.

The second genre discussed by Rorty is called *rational reconstructions*. This is a presentist project that treats predecessors as contemporaries with whom one can exchange views. However, since the "founders" of sociology often had little to say about the problems we now regard as fundamental, this approach usually involves imagining what they would have said if only they had understood the importance of these issues. For example, Lemert, in his chapter on Charlotte Perkins Gilman, reconstructs some of her writings as an intervention in the debate around essentialism, even though the ambiguity of Lemert's citations from her work suggest that this was an issue that held little interest for her. It is not that Lemert is arguing that Gilman really meant to assert a position on essentialism, but rather that her approach can provide a resource for a move in this current debate in which Lemert is himself involved. Another example would be Hoecker-Drysdale calling Harriet Martineau's analysis an "immanent critique," thereby locating Martineau's method within the debate over the relative ground of normative criticism, although Martineau clearly had no such intent. But, of course, simply because Martineau's naturalistic assumptions did not require a critique that emerged from the system being examined does not mean that her reasoning cannot contribute to our current discussions.

For the purpose of rational reconstructions, it must be assumed that debates as well as concepts are more or less stable. In order to reconstruct the answers of past theorists, we must assume that they would understand today's questions. Furthermore, engaging in a rational reconstruction often means correcting what appear to us now to be their obvious mistakes; for example, reconstructing Durkheim's sacred/profane dichotomy in light of our present anthropological knowledge (see the discussion in chapter 6). This, of course, assumes that we now know better than them. While this can often be said in the natural sciences, it is not always so obvious in social theory. The primary difference is that in social theory – Rorty makes this same point with regard to philosophy – the people that we assume we know better than are not just predecessors, but include our colleagues. To reconstruct what Marx would say about capitalist classes now that the proletariat revolution looks less than inevitable is to call not just Marx mistaken but also a number of our colleagues who are still waiting for the proletariat to cast off their chains.[6]

The presentism, and assumptions of stable concepts and of knowing better than our predecessors are all serious problems with this approach, but Rorty argues that they are not fatal as long as we are aware of them. These assumptions contribute to a certain necessary reassurance that there is the possibility of progress because the problems we are working on are part of a tradition and not just trivial ephemera. Also, these rational reconstructions provide what disciplinary structures there are in sociology. Without rational reconstructions there would be no neo-Weberians, neo-Marxists, neofunctionalists, or any of the schools of sociology, since they all derive their vitality from reconstructing their received traditions.

There is one final point to be made regarding rational reconstructions, and this has an impact on the cohesiveness of sociological schools. Rational reconstructions do not necessarily converge. Parsons's rational reconstruction of Weber is radically different from Marcuse's.[7] This means that some neo-Weberians may have more in common with neo-Marxists than with other neo-Weberians. Furthermore, since reconstructions are always to some extent fictions, it is not possible to say that one is wrong and it is even difficult to say that one is better than another.

The third genre is *historical reconstructions*. Here, rather than trying to understand what theorists might have said about our present controversies, the goal is to try to understand what they did say in the context of their contemporary controversies. Theoretical pronouncements are situated in their dialogic context and placed in relation to other texts of the period that address similar issues and use comparable rhetorical strategies. Doing a historical reconstruction usually means bracketing later developments and suspending judgments about what we now know better. Although a historical reconstruction is analytically distinct from a rational reconstruction, they are regularly conjoined in practice. The rational reconstruction of what sociologists would have said usually begins with what they did say and involves an interpretation of our present context based upon their reconstructed historical context.

From the historical reconstructor's viewpoint, exemplary theorists may be most valuable where they seem most strange and alien. In other words, they are most useful when they are most difficult to rationally reconstruct. Such extraordinary ideas expose our "essential" questions and "timeless" issues as contingent socio-historical products. Historical reconstructions help us to recognize that there are other conversations than those we think are important today. Rather than assuring us of our progress, the historical reconstruction contributes to understanding our own socio-historical embeddedness.

One of the leading advocates of this approach in social theory has been Robert Alun Jones, author of the chapter on Durkheim in this volume. As he points out, it is a difficult undertaking, since it requires "a considerable breadth of knowledge of economic, political and social as well as intellectual history; a reading knowledge of relevant foreign languages; and at least some understanding of the principles of the philosophy of social science."[8] It is, as Alan Sica notes, "risky for the most able scholars, foolhardy for many others."[9] Even where successful, it can, as Sica points out, be professionally counterproductive. Mary Pickering, for example, argues in her chapter that our understanding of Comte is much too simplistic. However, the revelation of Comte's ambiguous relation to modernity may simply remove him from the canon, thereby devaluing Pickering's cultural capital. This is why a scholar may prefer to do a rational reconstruction such as Jonathan Turner's chapter on Spencer in order to increase the value of his or her intellectual investment.

Jones's chapter on Durkheim demonstrates that historical reconstructions are far from reductionist. Rather than seeing Durkheim's ideas as determined by social forces that are working behind the back of the theorist, Durkheim is presented as involved in debates with his contemporaries and as pursuing specific and concrete projects. Consequently, for example, Jones is able to argue that it is absurd to read the *Division of Labor* as a challenge to Marx, since it is unlikely that Durkheim would have thought Marx to be a serious antagonist. The question as to whether we should take it as a challenge to Marx despite Durkheim's intent is not raised in this approach.

Kalberg's chapter on Weber demonstrates how important a historical reconstruction can be for understanding the limits of the theorist's concepts. While Weber is often portrayed as a theorist of a universal process of rationalization, Kalberg's historical reconstruction reveals rationalization to be a concept that Weber developed in order to explain the uniqueness of Western culture rather than as a universal drive. Weber's major works analyze specific and complex developments through a historical-comparative approach. Weber never intended his analysis to be applied to world-historical universals.

Finally, we come to the genre that Rorty champions and which he calls *Geistesgeschichte*. Like a rational reconstruction, it involves the idea of progress, but here progress is not simply assumed; instead it is narrated as an explicit part of the story. In addition, it is a narrative of continuity. Our connection to a set of predecessors gives us hope that our project will be continued by our intellectual descendants. It provides the field with a necessary self-assurance and legitimacy without concealing its constructed nature.

A *Geistesgeschichte* works at the level of paradigms and problematics. It gives plausibility to a certain image of social theory rather than a particular solution of a given sociological problem. It defines which projects are sociological and distinguishes them from, for example, social philosophy. A *Geistesgeschichte* would argue for (rather than simply assume) a list of exemplary contributors to this reinterpreted project and it would narrate a story of progress and continuity in that endeavor.

Parsons's *The Structure of Social Action* includes a *Geistesgeschichte*, even though his professed intent was to provide a rational reconstruction. In the second edition of that book, Parsons insisted that it "was intended to be primarily a contribution to systematic social science and not to history, that is the history of social thought."[10] But in order to legitimate his focus on the problem of social action and to be able to refer to economists, philosophers, and, at that time, marginal sociologists, Parsons had to construct a *Geistesgeschichte* which became more influential and enduring than his particular theories.

In fact, both rational and historical reconstructors rely upon an assumed *Geistesgeschichte* even when they do not find it necessary to construct one themselves. Rational reconstructors do not really want to bother reconstructing, and engaging with, minor sociologists. Historical reconstructors would like to reconstruct sociologists who are currently relevant or who, they argue, can be. In both cases, there needs to be a narrative that constructs a connection between what was important and what is important. For example, Pickering is most persuasive when she places her historical reconstruction within a *Geistesgeschichte* that connects Comte's complexity to present sociological problems.

A *Geistesgeschichte* is intrinsically related to canon formation. The fight over who fits into the history of a discipline is connected to controversies over the image of the field. It is not just a question of who is discerning enough or original enough to be an exemplary figure, but, more importantly, who is sociological enough. For instance, one of Lemert's chapters makes the argument that Du Bois's ideas are important, but we could still question whether they are social theory. Even though such debates seem to be about the honor of the designation, they are more prescriptive than is usually acknowledged. It is not about who deserves the honor of belonging to a predefined category, but about what the definition of the category should be. First, what criteria should distinguish a social theorist; second, what are the criteria that mark a classic in that field?

Unlike rational reconstructions, *Geistesgeschichtes* must concern themselves with anachronisms. The question of who belongs in the canon cannot be decided merely by present concerns. And unlike historical reconstructions, they cannot stay within the context of the past. *Geistesgeschichtes* must narrate a bridge to the present. Most importantly, this connection between the past and the present cannot be simply assumed. When that occurs, when the *Geistesgeschichte* no longer appears to be controversial, we have degenerated into doxology.

To the list of drawbacks associated with living in our present age must be added this one advantage: *Geistesgeschichtes* are less likely to degenerate into doxologies. The narratives, the canon, and the image of the field seem, in our current condition, to be incorrigibly unstable. Rorty presents a view that could be seen as the invitation that this book offers to its readers. "He or she should be free to create a new canon, as long as they respect the right of others to create alternative canons.... They should be urged to try it, and to see what sort of historical story they can tell when these people are left out and some unfamiliar people are brought in."[11]

## A typology of *Geistesgeschichtes*

Of the narrative forms that Rorty delineates, *Geistesgeschichtes* are those that explicitly construct a story of progress and continuity that connects the past to the present. Its central trope is a specific image of the field and its illocutionary effect is to create a canon. Since so many of the chapters in this collection offer this type of narrative, it may be useful to refine the typology. We don't intend to use this to pigeonhole these essays, since, like all good stories, they use multiple narrative techniques. Rather, we will use the refined typology as "sensitizing concepts" for the analysis of theoretical narratives.[12]

We see in the essays five different ways in which the past is connected to the present in order to suggest progress and continuity: (a) classical; (b) positivist; (c) pluralist; (d) convergent; and (e) contextualist. Donald Levine's perceptive book *Visions of the Sociological Tradition* is the source of some of these labels, if not of the precise formulation that we give them here.[13]

In a classical approach, past theorists are seen as foundational for the discipline and current theoretical approaches are built upon traditions that can rarely be completely superseded. Progress is recognized in the refinement and development of this foundation. A classic has been defined as "a book to be read partly because it is regarded as having been widely read."[14] Put this way, the status of the classic appears circular, but this in no way diminishes its importance. There is a circular relation between the present and the past. What is important in the past is a function of our present questions, but our present questions are, to a significant degree, determined by our past. Such, for example, is our relation with Marx. As Antonio's chapter in this volume makes clear, Marx is still a vital resource for our current theoretical problems. But, just as clearly, Marx's relevance for current controversies has as much to do with his prescience as it does with the fact that he helped to delineate what the controversies are – he defined them and brought them to our attention as social theorists. Just as it has been said that all of philosophy is a series of footnotes on Plato, it could be said that social theory, to date, consists of a series of footnotes on Marx.

Continuity and progress is guaranteed by the founding traditions of our field. According to the classical approach, these traditions will be criticized, but they are difficult to entirely supplant, because the criticism usually ends up taking a form which is profoundly influenced by the tradition that is the target of criticism. For example, Marx's theories are sometimes criticized as a reflection of the early industrialized capitalist mode of production of his society, and therefore of less relevance to our current mode of production. Whatever its intent, this type of criticism does more to perpetuate Marx's ideas by demonstrating their potential for self-criticism than any so-called orthodox appropriation.

With the second type, the positivist approach, past theories are seen as containing dispersed true empirical knowledge mixed in with virtually useless speculation. Progress is seen in the identification, collection, and systematization of this empirical knowledge. The positivist *Geistesgeschichte* tells the story of social theory's progression from a speculative philosophy through a plurality of theoretical approaches and finally entering or about to enter its true phase of rigorously empirical investigations. Classical theories represent either speculative philosophy (Comte, Spencer) or one-sided theoretical viewpoints (Durkheim, Simmel, Weber) that have been absorbed and surpassed by a coherent body of scientifically grounded theoretical conceptions. These previous theorists represent a transitional stage on the way to the subordination of ideas to controlled observation.

Merton is often taken as a model for a positivist approach, especially since he began his much cited work on the classics with a quote from Whitehead that seemed to sum up the positivist view. "A science which hesitates to forget its founders is lost."[15] However, Merton interprets this warning somewhat differently than his positivist followers. In the foreword to the second edition of Coser's *Masters of Sociological Thought*, Merton argues that engagement with the classics must include more than simply distilling verifiable hypothesis: "The direct study of masterworks helps us to acquire intellectual taste and style, a sense for the significant problem and for the form of its solution."[16] Consequently, it is quite appropriate that Sztompka's chapter on Merton does not fit him within a positivist narrative that attempts to extract only his verifiable ideas, but instead refers to "his exemplary style of doing sociology."

We do, however, see other theorists in this collection located within a positivist narrative. Cook was a colleague of Emerson, and she and Whitmeyer are able to bracket the historical situation which they shared. They rely primarily upon a rational reconstruction of his work to separate out his theoretical approach from the particular content of the theories. This, however, is performed within an implicit positivist *Geistesgeschichte*. In Cook and Whitmeyer's chapter, the story of progress and continuity is found not in the accumulation of specific theoretical formulations, but in an approach that takes previously vague notions and rigorously defines them so that they can be quantified and measured. The essay suggests that even if all of his particular theories are proven wrong, Emerson's approach would still make him a central character within the story of social theory.

Even an apparently non-positivist theorist can be presented in a positivist narrative. For example, while many have viewed Garfinkel as an antipositivist,[17] Rawls, relying on interviews with Garfinkel, tells a positivist story of the progressive discovery of order in what had previously been the chaos of everyday interactions. In this narrative, Garfinkel takes the empirical position against Parsons's speculative approach. Like all *Geistesgeschichtes*, Rawls's rewrites the progressive history of social theory, starting with Durkheim and here passing through Mead, Husserl, Heidegger, Mills, and Schutz to its zenith in Garfinkel.

A third type is the pluralist narrative. This approach views the past as a repository of diverse ideas and theoretical standpoints that can contribute to the manifold theories necessary for analyzing a pluralistic society. Here progress is identified with the growth of multiple perspectives which are necessary for analyzing something as complex and multilayered as society. Social theory is viewed as a collection of paradigms with differing methodological, philosophical, and political assumptions.[18] Often these paradigms are seen as having intimate and necessary relations with other disciplines, such as psychology, literature, philosophy. In this narrative, exemplary theorists are paradigm builders who provide incisive summaries of alternative approaches. What makes their work classic is its inherent plurality and openness to rereadings.

In this collection, Waters celebrates Bell's contribution to social theory's pluralism. His "central legacy to sociology is the role he played in fracturing the holistic hegemony" of Marx and Parsons. In addition, Bell's ideas are valuable not for their consistency, which is admittedly lacking, but for putting forward big provocative ideas. In keeping with the pluralist viewpoint, Bell's intellectual predecessors are less academic sociologists than a group of interdisciplinary intellectuals. Similarly, in Rogers's chapter, Schutz is presented as a kind of translator who enables a non-reductive dialogue between a European philosophical tradition and an increasingly scientized American sociology.

Simmel is, in many ways, the pluralist *par excellence*. Consequently, it is only from the pluralist approach that his contribution to sociology can be appreciated. As Scaff notes, Simmel never founded a school or movement and never intended to. Instead he contributed daring, impressionistic perspectives. These are practically useless from the classical viewpoint and contain only the faint possibility of providing positivistic hypotheses, but for a pluralist, "it is precisely these alleged deficiencies that have once again made Simmel an engaging presence" (chapter 7).

Convergence is the fourth type of narrative. From this viewpoint, pluralism represents an early stage of partial attempts that we are now able to see as contributing to a coherent totality. Exemplary early theorists are those who identified problems and offered partial solutions that now converge and are surpassed.

Parsons's convergence thesis is a famous example of this, but he is not the only theorist treated in this collection who is described as bringing together theoretical diversity in order to create "a coherent conceptual scheme" (chapter 12). Habermas, as with so many things, follows Parsons in seeing his predecessors as offering partial solutions that now converge. Outhwaite specifically mentions Kant, Hegel, Marx, Weber, Simmel, Pierce, Husserl, Lukács, Adorno, Horkheimer, Goffman, Garfinkel, and Gadamer, but there are certainly many others whom Habermas's brilliant reinterpretation fit into his new convergent theory.

Kilminster and Mennell argue for convergence in Elias. However, while Parsons and Habermas provided their own *Geistesgeschichte*, Elias's must be constructed on the basis of clues in his work. While this makes the constructed nature of a convergent narrative more obvious, it does not make it any less convincing. In our skeptical, post-Freudian age, the repressed influence has become more credible than the overt reference. Hence, the importance attached by Bryant and Jary in their chapter to the debate over Elias's influence on Giddens. It can still be contested, despite the fact that Giddens flatly denies it.

Shalin's chapter on Mead shows most clearly the importance of the convergence of acknowledged and unacknowledged influences. Mead explicitly engaged the theories of Kant and Hegel in order to show that they were partial solutions that now converged in a new pragmatist social philosophy. Driving this theoretical convergence, as well as driving the convergence between theory and political reform, was the influence of Mead's religious upbringing. Shalin suggests that Mead's social theories were, in many ways, an attempt to transform a failed religious belief into a partial solution that converged with some of the very ideas (e.g. Darwinism) that originally contradicted it.

Again, the narrative can assume this form even if the theorist's work does not. Baudrillard's influences rarely converge for more than a chapter before he moves on to another, often contradictory, convergence. Nevertheless, Kellner's comparisons of Baudrillard's ideas and the Frankfurt School's imply a kind of stable convergence.

A fifth narrative type is a contextual approach that sees the history of theory and the status of classics as primarily due to forces that are external to their intellectual content. Social theories are seen as tightly connected to the social context from which they emerge and which they try to describe. Progress and continuity are guaranteed by society – the subject and context of the theories – rather than the theories themselves. In many cases, the contextual approach is not a *Geistesgeschichte*; that is, it is not a progressive, self-assuring story that connects what was important in the past to what is important in the present. Instead it functions as an ideology critique, revealing the way in which the cognitive substance of the social theory is subordinate to its political context – whether that political context is a macro one of industrial rationalism[19] or the micro situation of academic reputation at Harvard.[20]

Nevertheless, there are two ways that a contextualist approach can be used within a *Geistesgeschichte*. First, a contextualist analysis can help to explain historical facts that seem to contradict a progressive and self-assuring story. For instance, although Pickering points out the originality of Comte's sociology, which seems to transcend his sociohistorical position, she invokes the "binary logic of his times," and his fragile mental health to explain his views on women. Second, what was important in the past and what is important now can be connected through their relation to an evolving social context. For example, Scaff argues that Simmel is an important representative of *fin de siècle* Vienna. This would seem to make him of merely historical interest, except that Scaff makes the further argument that the type of intellectual whirl in Vienna – which was marginal to Western society one hundred years ago – has become central to ours.

This typology suggests the variety of forms that a *Geistesgeschichte* can take. They all have in common the themes of self-assurance and progress that Rorty argues is necessary. Natural scientists can look to increased control of the natural environment as evidence of progress and be assured that they participate in an endeavor that is going somewhere. Funding agencies can be similarly assured that they are making a good investment. Disciplines that can cure illness, provide energy, and feed people may have little need of legitimating narratives, but Rorty suggests that social theory does need *Geistesgeschichtes* both for the psychological well-being of those who devote their lives to such a suspect pursuit and to continue receiving even the slight institutional support that they do. This is a persuasive argument until we notice that Rorty's own historical studies cannot be located in his typology. *Philosophy and the Mirror of Nature*, for example, could hardly be called a *Geistesgeschichte*. It pursues no theme of progress and self-assurance. Let us then use the phrase that Mitchell Dean[21] borrows from

Foucault to describe a fifth genre of narrative, effective and critical histories, to put alongside Rorty's doxologies, rational reconstructions, historical reconstructions, and *Geistesgeschichte*.

## Effective and critical histories

Instead of a self-assuring narrative of progress, an effective and critical history is problematizing. Furthermore, it is pragmatic, using historical analysis to understand the basis for practical transgressive experiments. Its goal is to discover what ideas, traditions, and practices are still necessary and what can now be seen as merely contingent. For example, Foucault's *History of Sexuality*, discussed in Smart's chapter, investigated whether the connection between identity and sexuality was still necessary and what new experimental practices involving bodies and pleasure are now possible. We do not find in Foucault the notion that the new experiments represent progress over the old regime. The aim of his historical analysis is to open up novel possibilities, not to establish advancements.

Like the *Geistesgeschichte*, an effective and critical history is related to both historical and rational reconstructions. Historical reconstructions are used to challenge our present concerns, while rational reconstructions allow historical reconstructions their greatest impact. It is, after all, not a general history, but a history of the present that is being pursued by effective and critical histories – one that traces the tricks, ruses, and reversals that have led to what we now consider to be necessary.

This is what makes Bourdieu's metaphor of the game, discussed in Calhoun's chapter, such a powerful one. Bourdieu is able to analyze academic sociology as a contest for stakes defined by an autonomous field, with its idiosyncratic strategic maneuvers based upon embodied styles. This is a game to be taken seriously within sociology because of its structural effects and because of the powerful analogies between the institutionally rewarded style of theorizing and the inculcated inclinations of those who are attracted to the field. Yet for all of its serious consequences, moves within this game are improvisations that could be otherwise.

An effective and critical history of sociology is not simply a response to a more pluralist, more postmodern, or even more cynical social context. Dean argues that it is a project that is internal to sociology, "a strategic reformation of the complex relations between sociology and history that are the conditions of existence of sociology as a discipline."[22] In this narrative, the study of exemplary theorists is used to oppose, undermine, or qualify present directions instead of support them. Theorists will find little assurance here, since their own contributions will be similarly opposed, undermined, and qualified, just as Clough's chapter describes Butler doing to Foucault. How fitting it would have been if Clough had been equally subversive of Butler.

Nevertheless, Clough's chapter is an example of a critical and effective history. The stories of sociology, psychoanalysis, and feminism are told using the rhetoric of progress – for example, we see a progressive revelation of social construction expanding from gender to sex to bodies to materiality. However, this always functions as a challenge to present beliefs rather than an attempt to establish a new paradigm. Notions such as the "sociality of matter" are used only to deconstruct previous understandings and are never spelled out explicitly enough to found a new discourse.

This ultimately is the genre to which we would like to dedicate this volume. Not the critical and effective histories contained here, but the critical and effective histories that are created by the reader using these essays as a resource.

## METATHEORIZING IN ORDER TO ACHIEVE BETTER UNDERSTANDING

As indicated in the introduction to this chapter, the objective in this second section is to analyze the essays in this volume in order to better understand them, as well as the theorists covered in them. The typology in figure 1 will be employed to highlight some of the most important conclusions to be derived from the following chapters. There is no attempt at completeness here; far too much is covered in each of the essays, as well as the book as a whole, to be covered in this brief section. Furthermore, there is a great deal of selectivity in what is discussed in the chapters themselves as well as in those theorists who are covered and those who are not. Much of what is dealt with in the book is familiar to many readers and generally need not be repeated here. Rather, the focus is on matters that are far less known about the theorists covered here and their theories. In the course of the following discussion some very familiar matters will be raised, but when they are it is to link them to other issues, or to make some more general point about social theory and social theorists.

### Internal-social influences

Here the focus is on social factors internal to the lives of social theorists that have had an impact on them and their theories. The most obvious and important is the impact of a wide range of biographical factors. Of course, such influences, at least as they involve the most famous social theorists, are well known. Thus, Durkheim's rabbinical background and his rejection of it, the relationship between Weber's fight with his father (Comte also had problems with his father) and the subsequent development of his mental illness, and Marx's relationship with Engels are known to most and repeated in these pages. However, the contribution of this volume is to make visible less well known facts about the giants, and virtually all biographical details about the lesser known and more contemporary theorists are new to most readers.

Antonio tells us of Marx's strenuous work habits and this immediately brings to mind Weber's similar commitment to work. Similarly parallel are Marx's various illnesses, many of them psychosomatic (see also Hoecker-Drysdale on Martineau and Turner on Spencer and his physical problems and insomnia), and Weber's mental illness. Pickering offers us insight into Comte's recurring mental illnesses and we learn of the psychotherapy undergone by Parsons and Giddens.

Gilman's mental problems and her lifelong battle with depression are played out in her famous short story, "The Yellow Wallpaper." Since this issue is not systematically covered in each chapter, one wonders just how many major theorists have experienced some form of mental illness and how that might relate to the nature of their theories. For example, it is clear that Giddens's psychotherapy helped lead him away from the abstractions of structuration theory and toward more concrete and personally meaningful topics like self, identity, love, and sexuality. On the other hand, the main effect of Parsons's therapy seems to have been to move him to add Freudian abstractions to the other abstract notions that went into making up his theoretical perspective. This all says nothing of the mental illnesses of those close to theorists, as exemplified by Erving Goffman's wife's mental illness and eventual suicide and their impact on his scholarly interest in mental illness.

Social experiences of various types lead theorists to new insights and new directions. Giddens's trips to California and his exposure to the alternative lifestyles of hippies are said to have opened his eyes to the limitations (characteristic of British sociology) of looking at the social world largely through the lens of social class. Rawls makes it clear that the courses that Garfinkel took as an undergraduate played a major role in shaping his theory of accounts. Emerson was an avid and skilled mountain climber and this helped lead to the study of groups of climbers and ultimately of small groups more generally.

Family is a key factor for everyone, and social theorists are no exception. The story not only of Weber's fight with his father, but also of being torn between his father's hedonism and his mother's Calvinist asceticism, is well known. Similarly famous is Marx's relationship with his wife and children and his struggles in supporting them. Disasters such as the early death of Mead's father, Gilman's bad first marriage, and the suicides of Parsons's daughter and of Goffman's first wife had powerful effects. Emerson is depicted as being profoundly shaken and affected by the death of his son in a mountaineering accident. While family can have an adverse effect, it can also have a positive impact, as is the case with Gilman's family background (and despite her painful relationship with her father), involving a long line of abolitionists, feminists, suffragists, as well as the famous writer Harriet Beecher Stowe. On a completely different tack, one is struck by Rogers's description of Schutz's loyal wife typing his manuscripts, and led to wonder how many other male theorists were similarly advantaged, as well as how many female theorists suffered for lack of a "wife."

The race, class, and/or gender of theorists clearly have a powerful impact on them and their theories. The absence of blacks and women from the generally accepted canon is reflective of that and, in fact, led to the inclusion of Harriet Martineau, Charlotte Perkins Gilman, Judith Butler, and W. E. B. Du Bois in this volume. Gender and race affected all of their careers (adversely) and, especially in the cases of Gilman and Du Bois, had a profound effect on their theories. Judith Butler's sexual orientation is certainly a factor in her work (and may have been one in Gilman's), especially her contribution to queer theory. A number of theorists (Garfinkel, Bell, and Merton, for example) are depicted as coming from the lower social classes, but there are some (e.g. Simmel and Spencer) who seem to have been helped by a more comfortable class position. Religion is also important in shaping a theorist's career and theoretical orientation. Durkheim's rejection of Judaism, the antisemitism that confronted Simmel, the impact of Christianity on the thinking of Mead and Parsons, and Weber's "unmusicality" as far as religion is concerned, to say nothing of Comte's positivistic religion, are all manifestations of the importance of this factor. A striking number of the theorists discussed on this book have a Jewish background, including (in addition to Durkheim), Marx, Simmel, Goffman, Merton, Schutz, Garfinkel, Bell, and Butler. Particularly formative is Bell's involvement in a circle of wide-ranging Jewish intellectuals.

Also important in internal-social analysis is the theorist's ties to networks, schools, invisible colleges, and communities of thinkers. Starting negatively, some thinkers seem to be near-isolates and that isolation does not seem to have adversely affected their ability to theorize creatively. From Kellner's account (and other sources), Baudrillard, for example, seems to have little contact with other social thinkers and is certainly not deeply enmeshed in a community of like-minded theorists. Although he was surrounded by first-rate scholars at Chicago and Berkeley, Goffman is depicted by Fine and Manning as alienated from most of his colleagues at the University of Pennsylvania. Schutz's lack of a permanent position served to isolate him, although he maintained contact with scholars through letters and other means. While she was not lacking in intellectual contacts, Gilman's position as an outsider also isolated her from those in academia working on similar scholarly issues (although she was able to publish in the *American Journal of Sociology*). Perhaps the most notorious of isolates (at least in terms of formal scholarly contacts) in the history of sociology was Herbert Spencer, who held no academic posts and seemed to absorb much of what he knew from interaction at clubs with intellectuals of the day. While not excluded from contact with sociologists, Daniel Bell, as we have seen, is largely out of mainstream sociological communities, but he is deeply enmeshed in the circles of New York Jewish intellectuals. Of course, no matter how isolated socially they are, theorists are always able to interact with the minds and works of the forebears, even if they are deceased. Rogers makes this point in her discussion of Schutz, and it is certainly true of all other theorists, as well. As Mead points out, the mind is simply an internal conversation and in it one can communicate with every theorist who ever lived.

Then there are those who are deeply embedded in mainstream intellectual communities, such as is the case with Parsons and followers such as Merton. But Parsons and Merton were not just members of communities, they were also their leaders, and the same can be said of other social theorists, such as Durkheim and Weber. Merton was deeply involved with not only Parsons at Harvard, but also others such as Sorokin and George Sarton (a philosopher of science). When he achieved fame at Columbia, Merton became the center of a community of his own. And, as Sztompka makes clear, Merton sought systematically to develop contacts among scholars throughout the world through regular trips abroad. A similar picture emerges from the life of James Coleman, who was part of the Columbia community where he was trained and became the center of the worldwide movement toward rational choice theory in sociology. Some came to occupy such a position early in their careers, but others (e.g. Elias) only acceded to such a position late in their lives. Still others, like Simmel, Goffman, Baudrillard, and perhaps even Foucault, eschewed such a position and ambition. Then there are those like Schutz, Gilman, and Du Bois, who, because they were outsiders, could never have become deeply enmeshed in communities of sociologists, although that certainly did not preclude their involvement in intellectual communities of other types.

Personal relationships with fellow theorists are similarly important. Comte's thinking was clearly affected by his relationship, and ultimate break, with Saint-Simon. The multifaceted relationship between Marx and Engels is well known, as are the ways in which Engels both furthered and distorted Marx's work. John Dewey clearly played a key role in the career and theorizing of Mead. Norbert Elias was strongly shaped by his position as assistant to Karl Mannheim and his personal relationship with Mannheim. Talcott Parsons's well known conflict with the chair of his department, Pitirim Sorokin, impeded his career, at least for a time. Alfred Schutz is depicted as being sustained in his isolation by his correspondence with Aron Gurwitsch, and others. Richard Emerson had close ties with Karen Cook, and she has played a central role in not only extending his work, but being sure that he receives the credit he deserves for transforming exchange theory. Theorists like Emerson have been advantaged by having loyal and capable followers, but others, like Simmel and Goffman, have grown influential without a group of disciples. Then there are important collaborative relationships such as those between Merton and Paul Lazarsfeld, although in the main important social theorists tend to work and publish on their own.

How theorists do their work has a profound effect on its reception. Grand theory seems to increase the likelihood of acceptance, with the result that Simmel's essayistic style tended to limit his impact. Being very serious also seems to help. Thus, even though he was primarily an essayist, Robert Merton's seriousness and the care with which he crafted his essays seemed to help him succeed. Goffman's "sardonic, satiric, jokey" style has had a negative effect on the legitimacy of his ideas.

Impact is strongly related to a theorist's professional ties. Thus, people like Weber, Durkheim, Mead, Parsons, Merton, and Coleman seem to have been helped by being deeply enmeshed in professional circles. However, it is heartening to know that work can have important effects without such ties, and this is clearest in the case of Schutz. Formerly excluded thinkers like Martineau, Gilman, and Du Bois are beginning to get a hearing even though they were largely excluded from the discipline. Ideas count, even if the social ties are absent, but it helps enormously to have those linkages.

## External-social influences

The broadest interest here is the impact of the sociohistorical context on a theorist's work. Clearly, there is a wide range of such factors that are identified throughout these chapters and that have had an impact on the theorists discussed. The French Revolution and its chaotic aftermath are well known for their impact on the thinking of Comte and Durkheim. The Industrial Revolution had a powerful impact on Marx's thinking, as well as that of others, such as Spencer and Martineau. Marx was also affected by, and influenced, the revolutionary movements of his day. Much later developments in the economy animated others, such as Bell, who theorized the post-industrial economy. The shift from the centrality of the economy to the growing importance of culture led Bell to theorize the cultural contradictions of capitalism and, more extremely, Baudrillard to argue that we have moved into a society dominated by signs and simulations. While Baudrillard leads us into (and out of) the postmodern world, others (e.g. Giddens and his "juggernaut of modernity") continue to think about contemporary developments in modern terms. Of course, this continues a long-running effort to come to grips with the essence of modernity in the work of such luminaries as Weber (rationalization) and Simmel ("tragedy of culture"). The feminist movement of the late nineteenth and early twentieth centuries certainly had a strong impact on Gilman's thinking. More contemporaneously, Butler's theorizing has been affected by changes in the relationship between gays and lesbians and the larger society. In fact, she has been active in social movements on behalf of lesbians.

Economic depressions and wars have affected most social theorists. Many of the thinkers discussed in this book had their lives disrupted by the Second World War (Weber, Durkheim, and Simmel were similarly affected by the First World War), and Elias and Schutz (as well as many others) were forced to emigrate. Garfinkel taught small arms warfare against tanks during the war on a golf course in Miami without any real tanks. As Rawls puts it, "He had to train troops to throw explosives into the tracks of imaginary tanks; to keep imaginary tanks from seeing them by directing fire at imaginary tank ports. This task posed in a new and very concrete way the problems of the adequate description of action and accountability." The post-Second World War environment had a strong effect on a number of theorists, including the graduate program at the University of Chicago, in which Goffman and many other sociologists who were later to become important were trained. The Great Depression had an effect on Bell, Garfinkel, and others.

Theorists are not only reflections of cross-national developments, but also of their national contexts. Weber's thinking was shaped by the Germany in which he lived and worked, and the same can be said of Martineau, Gilman, Mead (the social gospel movement and American pragmatism), and Coleman, among others. Waters feels that Bell's Americanism is a source of problems in his thinking. In other cases, theorizing was shaped by visits to other nations, with the most notable example being Weber's trip to America in 1904 and its role in shaping his thinking on the Protestant Ethic. Visits to America also profoundly affected the thinking of Martineau, Baudrillard, and Foucault. Then, there are instances where travels by Americans to other areas of the world (Emerson's trip to Mount Everest, for example) helped shape their theories.

The existence of support in the larger society for a theorist's work can be important. For example, Emerson was able to do his work because of the existence of funding for such work after the Second World War. Of course, most theorists do not need external funding and function quite well without it. But what of a more subtle kind of support within society for one's work? In the main, society has been largely unaware of the work of social theorists. Furthermore, many social theorists adopt positions that are at odds with the thinking in the larger society. Thus, most theorists function in at best a benign, and more often hostile, social environment.

## External-intellectual influences

Here the focus shifts to the impact of ideas outside of sociology on social theorists. Of course, in the early days of social theory there were no clear lines between sociology and neighboring disciplines; in many cases, there was, as yet, no sociology. Thus, in the case of the early giants of the field (Comte, Spencer), all influences were "external" in the sense of the term used here. However, the thinkers were embedded in other fields; for example, Marx was enmeshed in political economy, philosophy, utopian socialism, etc. Most of Martineau's influences were external (e.g. political economy), but she was powerfully affected by the work of a figure (Comte) who was to become central to sociology. Even more recent theorists (e.g. Bell) are more engaged in fields outside of sociology than they are in that field. Giddens is legendary for cobbling together a theory out of many inputs from both in and out of sociology. Then, there are those whose association with sociology is, at best, marginal (Foucault, Baudrillard), and their theories are far greater reflections of debates in an array of other domains: existentialism, structuralism, Marxism, Bataille on excess, etc.

An interesting figure in this context is Erving Goffman. While Goffman's thinking was certainly shaped by his background in symbolic interactionism and his association with the major figures involved in it, his work generally eschewed reference to them, or to most other social theorists. He was more prone to cite popular sources, such as a baseball umpire, than scholarly ones. Of course, this does not mean that such scholarly work did not play a central role in his thinking.

## Internal-intellectual influences

The norm in more recent years is for theorists to be most powerfully influenced by ideas internal to sociology, but to have a smattering of external inputs as well. Over the course of his career, the inputs into Parsons's work became increasingly internal to sociology and he, himself, became a powerful internal force in shaping other sociological theories, both positively and negatively. Thus, Merton's thinking was strongly and largely positively shaped by Parsons's structural functionalism, but in the case of Garfinkel, Parsons was a largely negative influence. Emerson was strongly influenced by behaviorism and George Homans and he, in turn, has become an increasingly central figure in exchange and network theory.

Perhaps of greatest importance in this context is the fact that many of the thinkers discussed in this book are famous for playing a major role in the creation of a perspective that has shaped sociological thinking. Pride of place in this must go to Comte, who both named and defined the field as a whole and, along with Spencer, set in motion the development of structural functionalism. Durkheim played a central role in this, but his influence was far greater and broader within both sociological theory (his impact on structural sociology, for example) and the discipline as a whole (his impact on research methods and statistics). The structural functional mantle was, of course, picked up by Parsons (and Merton), and he was clearly the key figure in the development and solidification of that theory in the mid-twentieth century. No one had more impact in (and out of) sociology than Karl Marx and the development of the various neo-Marxian perspectives, and almost as strong has been the effect of Weber on the neo-Weberians. Symbolic interactionism would not be what is without the pioneering work of Mead.

More recently, one must point to the role played by Emerson in the recent directions taken by exchange and network theory. Dramaturgical sociology is not as clearly defined as some of the others, but many people accept that approach as pioneered by Goffman. Rational choice theory would clearly not have anything approaching the role that it now has were it not for the impact of the work of James Coleman. Structuration theory owes much of its strength to the work of Giddens (and, relatedly, Bourdieu) and those who follow a post-modern line in sociology owe a most powerful debt to Jean Baudrillard.

In surveying the range of factors discussed above, it is clear that innumerable factors have served to shape social theorists. And, of course, the coverage of theorists in this volume, to say nothing of the factors affecting theorists, barely scratches the surface of those that could be covered. Other theorists need to be analyzed in this way, and such studies will uncover many other factors affecting the nature of social theory.

In this section we have employed a metatheoretical perspective in order to better understand the theorists and theories to be discussed in this book. However, we have said, and will say, little here about the topic that occupies most of the attention of the authors of the essays in this book – the theories themselves. We have summarized some of the background for understanding these theories, and theory more generally. However, it is far beyond the scope of this chapter to summarize the theories themselves. In any case, there is no need to do so: the authors of the ensuing chapters do it for the readers and they do it far better than we could.

## Conclusion

While this chapter is divided into two sections, a common interest in the metatheoretical analysis of theorists and theories unifies them. There is also a unifying conclusion. The first section closed with a call for effective and critical histories that seek openings, not closure. Similarly, the second section on metatheorizing as a means of gaining greater understanding leads naturally to the view that metatheoretical work is a prerequisite for Ritzer's other two types of metatheorizing, which are oriented to the creation of new theory and new overarching theoretical perspectives (or metatheories). Thus, the metatheoretical insights to be derived from these essays would be of greatest utility if they provide readers with ideas useful in the creation of new theories or metatheories. The real payoff of reading this book comes not from simply understanding past and present theorists better, but in using that understanding to create new theoretical and metatheoretical orientations.

Of course, each of these essays does little more than touch on on the life, work, and context of the thinkers covered here. Thus, they should be seen as invitations to read much more by and about them. However, this set of essays with strong commonalities among them in terms of topic coverage permit a comparative analysis of theorists and theories that would be more difficult if one relied on a set of diverse original and secondary sources. This comparative analysis may permit some deductions about how to proceed in new theory creation that would not have arisen if one was immersed, let's say, in the life and work of a particular theorist.

Thus, this volume should be seen as a periodic report; there will be many similar reviews in the coming years. As we write this, the canon is being rewritten and it is hoped that volumes like this one will aid in that rewrite. In fact, the hope is that this volume will help spur readers to play a role in rewriting the canon. Canons are always open and it is to that openness that this volume is dedicated.

## Notes

1  George Ritzer (1991) *Metatheorizing in Sociology*. Lexington, MA: Lexington Books, pp. 17–34. The other two types are as a prelude to new theory development and as a source of perspectives that overarch theory.
2  Richard Rorty (1984) The Historiography of Philosophy: Four Genres. In R. Rorty, J. Schneewind, and Q. Skinner (eds), *Philosophy in History: Essays on the Historiograpy of Philosophy*. Cambridge: Cambridge University Press, pp. 49–76.
3  Robert Alun Jones (1980) Myth and Symbol Among the Nacirema Tsigoloicos: a Fragment. *American Sociologist*, 15, 207–12.
4  For an excellent overview see Don Slater (1997) *Consumer Culture and Modernity*. Cambridge: Polity Press. For an application see George Ritzer (1999) *Enchanting a Disenchanted World: Revolutionizing the Means of Consumption*. Thousand Oaks, CA: Pine Forge Press.
5  Shane O'Neill (1999) Rationality. In F. Ashe, A. Finlayson, M. Lloyd, I. Mackenzie, J. Martin, and S. O'Neill (eds), *Contemporary Social and Political Theory*. Philadelphia: Open University Press.
6  See, for example, Ellen Meiksins Wood (1995) *Democracy Against Capitalism*. Cambridge: Cambridge University Press; E. M. Wood (1997) Modernity, Postmodernity or Capitalism? *Review of International Political Economy*, 4, 539–60; E. M. Wood and J. B. Foster (eds) (1997) *In Defense of History: Marxism and the Postmodern Agenda*. New York: Monthly Review Press.

7   See for example, the essays by Parsons, Marcuse, and others in O. Stammer (ed.) (1971) *Max Weber and Sociology Today*. New York: Harper & Row.

8   Robert Alun Jones (1983) On Merton's "History" and "Systematics" of Sociological Theory. In L. Graham, W. Lepenies, and P. Weingart (eds), *Functions and Uses of Disciplinary Histories*. Dordrecht: D. Reidel, p. 126.

9   Alan Sica (1997) Acclaiming the Reclaimers: the Trials of Writing Sociology's History. In C. Camic (ed.), *Reclaiming the Sociological Classics: the State of Scholarship*. Malden, MA: Blackwell, p. 296.

10  Talcott Parsons (1969) Preface to Second Edition. In *The Structure of Social Action*. New York: Free Press, pp. xv–xvi.

11  Rorty, op. cit., n. 2, p. 67.

12  Herbert Blumer (1969) What Is Wrong with Social Theory? In H. Blumer, *Symbolic Interaction: Perspective and Method*. Englewood Cliffs, NJ: Prentice Hall, p. 148. Another characteristic of sensitizing concepts is that they are designed to do less violence to the world being studied than traditional sociological concepts.

13  Donald Levine (1995) *Visions of the Sociological Tradition*. Chicago: University of Chicago Press.

14  Michael Levin (1973) What Makes a Classic in Political Theory? *Political Science Quarterly*, 88(3), 469.

15  Robert K. Merton (1967) On the History and Systematics of Sociological Theory. In *On Theoretical Sociology*. New York: Free Press, p. 1.

16  Robert K. Merton (1977) Foreword to L. Coser, *Masters of Sociological Thought: Ideas in Historical and Social Context*. New York: Harcourt Brace Jovanovich, p. viii.

17  John Heritage (1976) *Garfinkel and Ethnomethodology*. Cambridge: Cambridge University Press.

18  George Ritzer (1975) *Sociology: a Multiple Paradigm Science*. Boston: Allyn and Bacon.

19  Bruce Mazlish (1989) *A New Science: the Breakdown of Connections and the Birth of Sociology*. New York: Oxford University Press.

20  Charles Camic (1992) Reputation and Predecessor Selection. *American Sociological Review*, 57, 421–45.

21  Mitchell Dean (1994) *Critical and Effective Histories: Foucault's Methods and Historical Sociology*. New York: Routledge.

22  Ibid., p. 10.

# Part I
## Classical Social Theorists

# 1

## Auguste Comte

### Mary Pickering

Love for the principle and Order for the
base; Progress for the goal.
*Auguste Comte,* Système de politique
positive

In our postmodern world, where doubts about the inevitability of progress and
the value of rationalism have weakened utopian impulses, Auguste Comte
appears at first glance to be a quaint, outmoded figure. The "founder" of
sociology and positivism seems to evoke a faraway era, when the benefits of
social planning and the validity of knowledge went largely unquestioned. Yet as
Robert Scharff (1995, p. 6) has recently suggested, the theories of this important
nineteenth-century French philosopher have perhaps never been so relevant.
Comte foreshadowed many issues that contemporary thinkers are grappling
with today: the basis of truth, the role of politics in modern society, the root of
moral crises, the significance of memory, and the problem of gender, class, and
racial identities. More complex than is commonly assumed, Comte's contribution to social theory bears renewed examination.

### THE THEORY

Comte's reputation rests on his dual achievement of establishing a new discipline, sociology, and closely connecting it to a novel philosophical system, which
he called positivism. In the *Cours de philosophie positive,* published in six
volumes between 1830 and 1842, Comte argued that because theory always
precedes practice, the reconstruction of the post-revolutionary world could be

accomplished only by extending the scientific, or "positive," method to the study of politics and society, the last stronghold of theologians and metaphysical philosophers. To adopt the positive method meant tying scientific laws to the observation of concrete facts, especially by avoiding speculations, which were invariably "metaphysical" in nature. In his *Discours sur l'esprit positif* of 1844, Comte further explained that "the positive" designated the real, the useful, the certain, the precise, the relative, and the constructive (as opposed to the "negative") (Comte, 1963, pp. 126–30). Once the positive science of society was established, positivism, the system embracing scientific knowledge, would be unified and complete because all our ideas would be scientific and thus homogeneous. Moreover, the science of society would unite all knowledge because it would focus people's attention on humanity, which was also the object of study of the natural sciences. As a result, everyone would agree on the most essential intellectual and moral principles. Eliminating the anarchy that had ruled since 1789, the new social consensus would become the basis of a stable industrial order.

The science of society was thus the keystone of positivism. Comte asserted that because it would be based solely on the observation of social facts, without reliance on theological and metaphysical dogmas, it would have the certainty and unquestionable authority of the natural sciences. Following Francis Bacon's precept that knowledge is power, Comte assumed that a firm grasp of the scientific laws of society would lead to greater control over this organism. Like other scientific laws, sociological laws would allow one to predict social phenomena and thus formulate suitable social policies. Comte gave the new science of society a specific mission to provide the principles necessary to end the moral, social, and political turmoil caused by the French Revolution of 1789.

To prove that the coming of the positive study of society was inevitable, Comte invented the classification of the sciences. This schema demonstrated that the order in which the sciences were created depended on the simplicity of their phenomena and the distance of these phenomena from man. Astronomy first became a science because it studied the simplest phenomena, those that were farthest from man. The positive method was then extended to disciplines whose subjects were increasingly complex and closer to man: physics, chemistry, and biology, in that order. Each more complex science depended on knowledge provided by the simpler sciences, which had to become positive first. Comte maintained that now that astronomy, physics, chemistry, and biology were positive sciences, it was time for the positive method to be applied to the study of society, which was the most complex science and focused entirely on man. He rejected the arguments of those who sought to reduce the study of society completely to another science, whether it be mathematics (especially statistics), biology, or political economy. To mark the birth of this new independent science, Comte coined a new term for it in 1839: "sociology" (Comte, 1975, volume 2, p. 88).

In keeping with his skepticism regarding metaphysics, he warned sociologists that they could not discover the source or nature of society; they could explain only the way its phenomena were related in space and time. For this reason, sociology comprised two parts, social statics and social dynamics. Both stressed the interconnectedness of the members of the human species in order to counter the egoism of the modern age.

Social statics was the study of the social order. It focused on what kept society together. One crucial aspect of the social order was the family, which taught the importance of love as the basis of moral self-improvement. This love was transferred later to one's family and finally to humanity as a whole. Thus social statics cultivated a person's feelings of solidarity with other members of society. Although his atheism was unorthodox for the early nineteenth century, Comte's views on the sanctity of the family and other moral issues were conventional – in contrast to those of the Saint-Simonians and Fourierists who questioned social institutions.

Giving people a sense of connection with past and future generations of the human species, social dynamics analyzed social development, which Comte represented as continuous, necessary, orderly, and limited. Each social state grew out of the preceding one and generated the next social configuration. The salient feature of this development was that, through exercise, the unique characteristics of the human species – intelligence and sociability – became more dominant within both the individual and society.

Besides delineating the two divisions of sociology, Comte outlined the methods of this new science: observation, comparison, and experimentation. Because every aspect of society had multiple connections, Comte believed the areas of sociological observation were very diverse. Sociologists should study ordinary events, common customs, diverse types of monuments, languages, and other mundane social phenomena. Comte's insights into the significance of everyday life have been verified by recent social and cultural history.

As for experimentation, the second means of scientific investigation, Comte felt its use was problematic in sociology because of the impossibility of isolating any of the circumstances or consequences of a phenomenon's actions. He maintained that like a biologist, a sociologist must study pathological cases, which were forms of indirect experimentation. Because the pathological was simply a variation of the ordinary, examining periods of chaos, such as a revolution, provided clues to normality. The study of social disorder was an important means of gaining insights into the laws of social harmony and history.

Comparison was sociology's third method of scientific investigation. In sociology, there were three types of comparison. One could compare human and animal societies, different existing states of human society (i.e. savage and civilized peoples), or consecutive social states. The latter involved the historical method, which was related to social dynamics and constituted sociology's chief means of scientific investigation. History gave people a sense of social solidarity and continuity, in short a feeling for humanity in the world and their own role in its evolution.

The principal scientific law of sociology was a historical one: the law of three stages. Comte first "discovered" this law in 1822 and revealed its intricacies in his "fundamental opuscule," the *Plan des travaux scientifiques nécessaires pour réorganiser la société* of 1824 (Comte, 1929, volume 1, p. 1). According to this law, each branch of knowledge (e.g. each science) and the mind itself passed through three modes of thinking: the theological, metaphysical, and positive. Such paradigms arose because all aspects of knowledge were interrelated and the mind naturally sought to make all ideas homogeneous.

Each of the three theoretical systems affected politics and society, for in Comte's view all of society represented an organic being in the process of a development influenced by intellectual progress. Intellectual evolution – especially scientific development – was the most advanced form of progress and served as the stimulus to historical change. In an important passage reflecting his idealism, Comte pointed out "that ideas govern and overturn the world, or in other words, that the entire social mechanism rests ultimately on opinions." Like Hegel, he believed that history was the story of the "emancipation of human reason" (Comte, 1975, volume 1, pp. 38, 379). Moreover, as all aspects of society were interrelated, a change in one feature, such as intellectual life, led to changes in other facets of the social organism. Comte wrote, "In effect . . . all the classes of social phenomena develop simultaneously and under each other's influence" (Comte, 1929, volume 4, "Appendice," p. 135).

In short, the law of three stages was a global one; it referred not only to intellectual evolution but to social and political developments as well. It depicted the different stages of progress that every civilization had to experience as well as a future positive age of social cooperation that was definitive, but not perfect. (Although society would see an increase in both intelligence and altruism, Comte believed ordinary man's moral and intellectual weaknesses – his natural egoism and mental lethargy – would never completely disappear.) The law of three stages also pertained to the intellectual trajectory of every person as he or she went through life. In addition, Comte recognized that the three stages actually represented three mentalities that could coexist at various times in a person's or civilization's history.

In the theological stage, man untangled the mystery of natural occurrences by relating them to supernatural beings, whose character was like his own. The notion that gods represented the first cause of all happenings and were in complete control of the universe was the theory that the mind needed in its infancy to link its observations. There were three substages in this first era of history: the fetishist, polytheistic, and monotheistic. In the first, gods resided in concrete objects. In the second, the gods became independent of the objects. In the third, a single god became the ruling principle. In a society that embraced the theological mode of explanation, priests and military men ruled. The theory of divine right was the reigning political doctrine.

The metaphysical stage of history, which began in the fourteenth century, was a transitional period. In searching for first and final causes, people started to connect observed facts with personified essences or abstractions, such as Nature, which were neither supernatural nor scientific. In the process, metaphysicians replaced priests as the spiritual power. Military men ceded their role as the temporal power to lawyers, for society began to direct its activities toward production, not simply conquest. The state of politics was embodied in the doctrines of popular sovereignty and natural rights.

In the positive stage of history, no discussion of first causes or origins was allowed because the existence of supernatural beings and essences could not be proved. Instead, intellectual discourse was characterized by scientific laws explaining how, not why, phenomena worked. These descriptive laws expressed the "relations of resemblance and succession that facts have among themselves" (Comte, 1929, volume 4, "Appendice," p. 144). Moreover, because production replaced conquest as the goal of society, social relations were based entirely on industry. Politically, industrialists constituted the temporal leaders of this secular, peaceful society. Positive philosophers held the spiritual power.

Contrary to scholarly opinion, Comte did not argue that there should be a dictatorship of scientists in control of the future positive republic. He feared that if the mind grew too powerful, it would stifle progress, for it needed stimulation from the active life. Though an idealist, Comte never maintained that intellectual progress could be separated from material development. Furthermore, he recognized that practical enterprises would always remain most important in society because most men were drawn to the active life, not the intellectual one. If a minority of intellectuals took over the material realm, they would oppress society, lose all motivation, and wallow in admiration of the society they produced. Borrowing a term from his close friend John Stuart Mill, Comte called a technocratic society governed purely by philosophers or intellectuals a "pedantocracy" (Comte, 1975, volume 2, p. 656).

The rise of such a regime could be prevented only by the separation of powers. The industrialists would control the practical, material activities of society, which were dangerous because the requisite specialization led to pride and egoism. These men would be checked by positive philosophers, who would be in charge of ensuring morality and encouraging the growth of ideas and feelings.

Positive philosophers were not necessarily scientists, whose tendency to specialize made them as uncaring and socially indifferent as industrialists. Comte wanted positive philosophers to be men who had a general knowledge of all the sciences, especially sociology. In this way, they would understand the impact of the natural environment and human nature on society and the application of the positive method to social phenomena. Moreover, Comte assumed that intellectual well-roundedness was linked to "altruism," a word he also coined. Thus, because positive philosophers possessed general knowledge and consequently had the widest views and sympathies, they would have the interests of all of society at heart. The breadth of their knowledge and sympathies gave them the legitimacy to speak for the entire community.

Forbidden to rule directly, they would especially advise the industrialists on how to solve the "social question"; that is, the difficulties faced by the working class. Although critics contend that Comte was an apologist for the status quo, he was in truth extremely critical of capitalism for promoting a selfish and materialistic culture. Like Marx, he argued that the appalling class struggle was not due to the workers but to "the political incapacity, social indifference, and especially blind egoism of the entrepreneurs" (Comte, 1975, volume 2, p. 620). Calling for the "personal liberation of workers," he campaigned to resolve the class question by incorporating the proletariat into society

(Comte, 1929, volume 3, p. 402). The positive philosophers would be their biggest allies.

These philosophers would also take control of the educational system to improve people's intellectual development and to give them common ideas and values. Countering man's natural egoism, which was exacerbated by the specialization of the modern age, they would persuade people to develop their inherent sociability and contribute to the common welfare. In short, positive philosophers would direct ideas, feelings, and images toward the improvement of Humanity, which would replace God and Nature as the object of people's respect. Serving humanity would be an imperative for everyone, from housewives to scholars. The idea of humanity would thus hold society together. Comte wrote that the principal result of history was "the spontaneous convergence of all modern conceptions toward the great notion of humanity" (Comte, 1975, volume 2, p. 785).

Though highly schematic, the law of three stages allowed Comte to pull together the natural and social sciences. Unlike Saint-Simon, he rejected the conventional approach of basing the sciences on a single method or on universal logical principles; to him, scientific knowledge itself had to be regarded as a historical process (Heilbron, 1990, pp. 155, 161). Indeed, Comte was the only philosopher of the sciences who was more concerned with their social and political ramifications than their theoretical success and practical results (Grange, 1996, p. 17). In his view, the most effective way to consider the sciences and their consequences was to place them in a historical perspective.

Together with Comte's classification of the sciences, the law of three stages ultimately demonstrated the triumph of sociology and completion of positivism. By providing a program ensuring intellectual rigor and encouraging social cooperation, positivism would lead to a political and social revolution that would be far more efficacious than a mere change in the form of government in bringing about a new, harmonious order. To Comte, practical, institutional reforms could never launch a new era, for they were ineffective and often premature. They did not take into account the fact that the disorganization of postrevolutionary society was due primarily to intellectual and moral anarchy.

Although Comte believed that a firm grounding in the sciences was essential to proper reasoning, he did not support a purely scientistic interpretation of positivism. Indeed, Comte would never recognize the simplistic version of positivism that exists today as his own formulation. For years, scholars have commonly equated positivism with scientism; that is, a naive faith in science's ability to solve all problems through the use of empirical, experimental, and quantitative methods of research. Jürgen Habermas claimed that "positivism stands and falls with the principle of scientism" (Habermas, 1971, p. 67). Gertrud Lenzer accused positivism of being naively reductionist: "The triumph of the positive spirit consists in the reduction of quality to quantity in all realms of existence – in the realm of society and man as well as in the realm of nature" (Lenzer, 1975, p. xxi).

Yet Comte never displayed an excessive faith in the power of the sciences to modify nature and society in a boundless fashion. Respectful of the environment and of the slow pace and direction of change, he argued against using the sciences to satisfy man's love of power and conquest. As suggested above, he was more of a historicist in his approach to the sciences than an enthusiast of scientism (Grange, 1996, p. 139).

The *Cours* is therefore a paradoxical work. It called for a social philosophy based upon the sciences, but as reflected in his concept of the spiritual power, Comte deeply distrusted the regenerative capabilities of the purely scientific spirit. His disillusionment is evident at the end of the *Cours*, where he condemned "the prejudices and passions of our deplorable scientific regime" (Comte, 1975, volume 2, p. 791). The *Cours*, an apparently scientistic tract, was intended to counter the scientific spirit – that is, the "positivity" – of the modern age, whose specialization, egoism, and social indifference caused immeasurable moral harm.

In his hatred of the hubris of scientists, Comte always maintained that even in the realm of what was understandable, scientific knowledge was deficient. He opposed, for example, the statistical approach to scientific research, which he believed overlooked the complexity of human existence and threatened the autonomy and individuality of each science. To him, the power of reason was limited. He wrote that "it was necessary to recognize that...our means for conceiving new questions...[was] much more powerful than our resources for solving them, or in other words the human mind...[was] far more capable of imagining than of reasoning" (Comte, 1975, volume 1, p. 99).

In fact, Comte did not believe in absolute truth, for he was a relativist: "It is no longer a question of expounding interminably in order to know what is the best government; speaking in an absolute sense, there is nothing good, there is nothing bad; the only absolute is that everything is relative; everything is relative especially when social institutions are concerned" (Comte, 1970, p. 71). His relativism was connected to his belief that "exact reality can never, in any way, be perfectly unveiled" to our weak mind (Comte, 1975, volume 2, pp. 103–4). It was particularly impossible to have a complete grasp of social reality, which was extremely complex and involved men's prejudices.

Comte never lost sight of the fact that the emotions were of utmost importance in human existence. This realization was partly due to his recognition that he suffered from depression and could not work if he had emotional troubles. Since his youth, he had considered the emotions the motor of existence; their dominance was necessary to rouse the intellect from its natural torpor and give it moral direction. Indeed, he maintained that love, not reason, was the basic principle of social existence. In the *Cours*, he wrote that:

universal love, such as Catholicism conceived it, is certainly far more important than the intellect itself in...our individual or social existence, because love spontaneously uses even the lowest mental faculties for the profit of everyone, whereas egoism distorts or paralyzes the most eminent dispositions, which consequently are more often disturbing than efficacious in regard to true private or public happiness. (Comte, 1975, volume 2, p. 362)

Realizing that reason could not satisfy all human needs, Comte also emphasized that the imagination was crucial to both the creation and propagation of scientific theories. Although he recommended observation as a method of sociological research, he pointed out that complete empiricism was impossible and sterile, for accumulating discrete observable facts about a reality that could not be fully grasped was unproductive. To him, facts could not be perceived or connected without first formulating an *a priori* theory, which required imaginative work. Revealing an awareness of the mind's limitations, he wrote:

> Man is incapable by his nature not only of combining facts and deducing from them several consequences, but of even simply observing them with attention and retaining them with certainty if he does not attach them immediately to some explanation. He cannot have connected observations without some theory any more than [he can have] a positive theory without regular observations. (Comte, 1929, volume 4, "Appendice," p. 144)

Social facts were the most difficult to observe. Because social scientists lived in society, it was impossible for them to notice the significance of familiar social phenomena and to be impartial. To be creative, scientific investigation of all phenomena, especially social phenomena, had to rest on the use of both induction and deduction, rely on rationalism as well as experimentation, and employ man's imaginative capacities.

Moreover, for laws to be scientific, they had to be predictive; that is, they had to display the capability to go from the present to the future and from the known to the unknown (Laudan, 1971, pp. 37–40). Comte wrote, "from science comes prediction; from prediction comes action" (Comte, 1975, volume 1, p. 45). Facts in themselves with no connection to general laws had no predictive value. They were thus not useful.

Comte advocated the use of provisional hypotheses as convenient, artificial devices to link facts and formulate natural laws. These hypotheses could not be considered scientific theories until they were verified by induction and deduction. Comte's representation of hypotheses as useful and respectable tools that serve a crucial function in scientific discovery was an influential idea. His appreciation of the aesthetic considerations in scientists' construction of hypotheses anticipated the work of Thomas Kuhn.

To free scientists from being slaves to direct evidence, Comte also advocated the use of imagination in creating types of "scientific fiction" – hypothetical cases – to elucidate tentatively different scientific problems until the discovery of better evidence. For example, a biologist could insert "purely fictive organisms" between already known organisms in order to make the biological series more homogeneous, continuous, and regular (Comte, 1975, volume 2, p. 728). As reflected in his approach to hypotheses and scientific fictions, Comte intended to offer imagination the "most vast and fertile" field for discovering, observing, and coordinating facts (Comte, 1975, volume 2, p. 102). To avoid giving reason excessive importance in scientific research, he deliberately refused to offer elaborate, universal, ahistorical rules of scientific procedure; he never produced an organon of proof. To him, purely abstract rationalist rules not only made scientific research less flexible but came dangerously close to metaphysical practices (Scharff, 1995, pp. 7, 65). Indeed, a few months before he died in 1857, Comte wrote, "The present...evolution of positivism...depends on sentiment and imagination, and reasoning will henceforth be secondary" (Comte, 1973–90, volume 8, p. 502). His point was to offer scientists of society the widest possible variety of resources that would allow them to construct theories that did not require them tediously to observe facts to no purpose. They must be allowed to go beyond direct evidence without forgetting that ultimately every positive theory had to refer to real, concrete phenomena. Comte's call to resist relying excessively on rationalism to grasp a "real" world has been recently echoed by Jean Baudrillard, who shows a similar appreciation of the symbolic and the poetic (Gane, 1991, pp. 201–2).

Humanity was the most fundamental component of reality. In a famous passage, Comte wrote: "Considered from the static and dynamic points of view, man properly speaking is at heart a pure abstraction; there is nothing real except humanity, especially in the intellectual and moral order" (Comte, 1975, volume 2, p. 715). Comte reinforced the importance of all people being socialized and educated to work for this "real" phenomenon by constructing the Religion of Humanity, whose roots were evident in his early writings. He discussed this religion and introduced the final science of morality in his four-volume *Système de politique positive*, published between 1851 and 1854. Many scholars have asserted that this book was a repudiation of his previous scientific program. Yet in reality there was no significant break in his intellectual evolution. The Religion of Humanity was foreshadowed in the *Cours*, where Comte referred specifically to the need to create a "Positive Church" (Comte, 1975, volume 2, p. 696). The *Système* merely carried forth the program for the intellectual, moral and political regeneration of society that Comte had formulated in the early 1820s.

Whereas the *Cours* dealt with the systematization of ideas and provided a common belief-system, the *Système* covered the organization of feelings as well as the political restructuring of society that would result from the intellectual and moral revolution he hoped to achieve. He explained that because he had already established "fundamental ideas," he now had to describe their "social application," which would consist of "the systematization of human sentiments, [which was] the necessary consequence of that of ideas and the indispensable basis of that of institutions" (Comte, 1973–90, volume 3, p. 61). In view of the fact that the needs of society were not only intellectual but emotional, its spiritual reorganization had to involve the heart at least as much as the mind. As Donald Levine has written, "Comte's positive philosophy...eliminates theology...but retains religion," thus bridging the gap "between the rational imperatives of modern science and the emotional imperatives of societal order" (Levine, 1995, pp. 163, 165). Convinced that a general doctrine and institutional networks were not sufficient to ensure social cohesion, Comte believed that his religion would provide the moral adhesive necessary to hold society together. Ultimately, human unity rested on the sympathies, for it was clear to him that the "essential principle of modern anarchy" consisted of "raising reason against sentiment" (Comte, 1855, p. 10). The positive philosophy would bring about the intellectual and emotional consensus necessary to end anarchy and build the stable industrial society of the future.

The main task of the Religion of Humanity would be to cultivate altruism; replacing Christianity with "a system of terrestrial morality," it was a secular religion of love (Comte, 1970, p. 40). Defending his choice of names for his moral system, Comte explained in 1849 that he had "dared to join...the name [religion] to the thing [positivism], in order to institute directly an open competition with all the other systems" (Comte, 1973–90, volume 5, p. 22). He wanted a clear-cut doctrinal battle with Catholicism to precipitate the triumph of positivism and the start of a new order.

To challenge Catholicism, Comte invented positivist sacraments for baptism, marriage, and death. He also created a special commemorative calendar, with primarily secular saints (Aristotle, Caesar, and Dante), one of whom was to be glorified each day as a servant of Humanity. Comte's theory anticipated the ideas of the sociologist Maurice Halbwachs, who underscored the importance of collective memory in unifying society. Private and public acts of commemoration in the form of worshipping important figures from one's own past and that of Western civilization (highlighted in the calendar) would create a sense of continuity between past and present generations. Such a system of commemoration would also satisfy people's natural "need for eternity" and stimulate them to contribute to the progress of humanity, especially through "benevolent actions" and "sympathetic emotions" (Comte, 1975, p. 778). As Henri Gouhier pointed out, "The Religion of Humanity is essentially a cult of dead people" (Gouhier, 1965, p. 212).

The *Système* also described rituals that would rejuvenate people's emotional life, bring them back into contact with the concrete, and stimulate the arts. Comte was creating an entirely new religious culture, which he felt was crucial for holding society together. He recognized that political action in the new age would consist of using religion, the arts, and education to form collective sentiments, beliefs, and representations.

In outlining the Religion of Humanity, Comte particularly aspired to revive the concreteness, intense emotional spontaneity, and poetic aptitudes of the earliest stage of religious life, that of fetishism (Pickering, 1998, pp. 57–66). Of all the intellectual systems, fetishism, according to Comte, most encouraged the growth of sociability because it inspired "toward all beings, even inert, dispositions [such as veneration, trust, and adoration] that were eminently proper to cultivating...our best affections" (Comte, 1929, volume 3, p. 108). This growth of the emotions destroyed man's animal instincts and fortified his basic sense of humanity.

Although Comte is known as an apostle of progress, he feared the effects of science and abstract thought, which made people proud and egoistic, and he believed the West needed an injection of primitive religion to continue to advance. He was one of the first thinkers to celebrate fetishism, which he connected with the black race and hoped to incorporate into positivism. To him, "the humble thinkers of central Africa" were more rational about human nature and society than the "superb German doctors," with their "pompous verbiage." Comte maintained "The touching logic of the least negroes is ... wiser than our academic dryness, which, under the futile pretext of an always impossible impartiality usually strengthens suspicion and fear" (Comte, 1929, volume 3, pp. 99, 121). Unlike modern men, the fetish worshippers admired what was concrete and useful and respected the natural world. Comte tried to replicate this kind of worship by encouraging people to devote themselves to Humanity, the "Great Being." The purpose of his neo-fetishist religion was to stress the importance of humility and self-effacement by demonstrating that all peoples were related to each other and to the earth, which at the end of his life he called the "Great Fetish." Positivism had to emulate fetishism by recognizing what was beneficial to others in a concrete sense in this world. In 1855, Comte wrote to a friend to explain the "absorption of fetishism by positivism."

> There exists essentially for us only two *beings*, both of which are eminently composite: the Earth, including the stars as appendices, and Humanity, of which the animals capable of association and even the useful vegetables are auxiliaries.... These are our two masters, which are closely connected at least to us; one is superior in power, the other in dignity, but both are worthy of our continual respect. (Comte, 1973–90, volume 8, p. 39)

In Comte's mind, the highest stage of civilization represented a return to the beginning. "Human reason" at the height of its "virility" must include a "degree of poetic fetishism" (Comte, 1973–90, volume 3, p. 212). Comte was thus one of the first philosophers to contend that fetishism did not belong exclusively to the primitive age and did not always represent a type of false consciousness or prelogical mindset. Condemning racism and imperialism for dividing humanity instead of uniting it, he challenged racial stereotypes when he asserted that one day a "negro thinker" might study his works and lend him his support (Comte, 1929, volume 3, p. 156).

Comte imagined that the chief auxiliaries of the positive philosophers, who epitomized reason, would be women, who embodied feeling, and workers, who represented activity. These two oppressed groups had interested Comte since he was a young man. Unlike the ruling male bourgeoisie, whom he called "extremely gangrenous," women and workers were preserved from the artificial, materialist culture of the day (Comte, 1973–90, volume 6, p. 188). He increasingly appealed to them for support, after being rebuffed by scientists and other luminaries of his day.

In the aftermath of the Revolution of 1848, Comte joined the issues of class and gender; he maintained that the liberation of both the proletariat and women was necessary for the advent of positivism. But once he discovered the strength of the proletariat's loyalty to socialism, Comte decided in 1851 that the most "important work of positivism" was to persuade women to join him (Comte, 1973–90, volume 6, p. 188). He was weary of the "depressing regime" of men, who were shallow and narrow-minded (Comte, 1973–90, volume 7, p. 158).

Repelled by the "disorders of male reason" and its futile political machinations, Comte found women to represent the best way to unify an increasingly fragmented society (Comte, 1973–90, volume 6, p. 183).

Scholars frequently accuse Comte of being a "phallocrat" desirous only to preserve the current outlines of the patriarchal society (Kofman, 1978, p. 233). He certainly did not approve of feminism and repeatedly condemned bluestockings and the "liberated woman" as aberrant, sexless creatures. Nevertheless, having read Mary Wollstonecraft's *Vindication of the Rights of Woman* as a young person, he criticized men who employed "the horrible law of the strongest" to lord it over women, whom they regarded as a "domestic animal" or "toy destined for all eternity for the good pleasure and usage of his Majesty *Man*" (Comte, 1973–90, volume 1, p. 56). In the 1840s, he finally recognized that the problem of anarchy would not be resolved "as long as the revolution does not become feminine" (Comte, 1973–90, volume 6, p. 108). He feared his own reform movement would be discredited without female support. He begged women not to misunderstand the gist of his thought:

> The fatal antagonism... between the mind and the heart can be resolved only by the positive regime; no other is capable of subordinating in a dignified fashion, reason to sentiment.... In its vain present supremacy, the mind is ultimately our principal trouble maker.... Better judges than we in moral understanding, women will feel in several regards that the affective superiority of positivism... is even more pronounced than its speculative preeminence, which is henceforth incontestable. They will soon come to this conclusion when they have stopped confusing the new philosophy with its scientific preamble. (Comte, 1929, volume 1, 224)

Trying to take advantage of "the feminine revolution" that he believed was about to begin, and appropriating aspects of the contemporary women's movement for his own purposes, Comte put woman at the center of his schemes for renovation in two of his last works, the *Système de politique positive* and the *Catéchisme positiviste* (Comte, 1973–90, volume 6, p. 109). Whereas in the *Cours* he had declared that women were far from the "ideal type of the race" – the male – he declared in the *Système* the need to establish a "cult of Woman," which would make her into a kind of goddess (Comte, 1929, volume 1, p. 259). The *Catéchisme*, which consisted of a dialogue between a woman and a positivist priest, specifically addressed a female audience. It aimed to develop the alliance between positive philosophers and women that Comte was certain would spur the regenerative process.

Although Comte never supported the notion of the equality of the sexes, he did give women a positive identity; they were not simply harlots or housewives as Pierre Proudhon proclaimed, or permanent invalids as Jules Michelet contended. Comte referred to the "feminine genius" in terms of its important function not solely to propagate but to participate in the public sphere and aid the spiritual power in reorganizing society along moral lines (Comte, 1975, volume 2, p. 300). Experts in the emotions, women made men more sociable, complete human beings. To fulfill this mission, they needed to be able to mold public opinion, preferably in the salons, whose revival he favored. Women also required freedom from economic and sexual exploitation. Comte envisioned the "utopia of women," where they would gain "independence" from men, even in their "physical role," by taking control of their own bodies and having children without any male participation whatsoever (Comte, 1929, volume 4, pp. 66–7, 286). Moreover, because they were endowed with the best human characteristic, that of sociability, women, he insisted, should represent Humanity itself. In the positivist temples, Humanity would be always depicted as a woman accompanied by her son. This daring displacement of God the Father in the positivist system reflects Comte's conviction that women were morally superior and would be "in first place in the normal society" of the future (Comte, 1973–90, volume 7, p. 160). Agents of social unity, women were the key to completing the positive revolution and saving the increasingly fragmented West from complete dissolution. Their role illustrates Comte's goal of placing nurturing and empathy at the center of public life in order to create a new, more compassionate and harmonious society.

In his effort to make feeling of paramount importance, Comte also developed a greater interest in art. In the *Système*, he argued that art's power of idealization encouraged the growth of feeling and social solidarity; because it developed the sympathies, art should have a higher place in society than science, whose work was primarily preparatory. He wrote, "Art corresponds better than science to our most intimate needs. It is both more sympathetic and more synthetic" (Comte, 1929, 51). Ideally, it would be possible to blend the scientific spirit with the aesthetic spirit.

Comte tried to fuse the two in his last work, *Synthèse subjective* (1856), which was devoted to mathematics. Here he argued that the scientific spirit was considered dry because the modern specialization that it engendered hurt moral and aesthetic growth. To him, the "abstract habits of clarity, precision, and consistency, which are normally acquired in the mathematical domain," could be fruitfully applied to religious institutions and art (Comte, 1856, p. xi). To demonstrate his principle, Comte set down rules to ensure that future positive philosophers would be poets celebrating Humanity in verse. The poetic age of his doctrine could then commence. In some respects, Comte's views seem to foreshadow those of Max Weber, who also considered rationalization a global process and lamented the "disenchantment" of the modern world.

In sum, Comte's positivist system was never morally neutral or value-free as some scholars have asserted in equating positivism with a quest for objectivity. From the beginning, Comte embraced social activism and a moral goal, for he was convinced that impartiality was inappropriate and indeed impossible in studying society, whose phenomena were close to us; a viable social theory had to depict a better form of social organization. Comte sought to shape the world of action indirectly by molding people's ideas and opinions. Because he believed that intellectual well-roundedness was linked to altruism, he declared that the adoption of the positivist mental outlook would lead first to a new moral order marked by the bonding together of individuals through sympathy, and then to a political transformation that would launch a new positivist era of social consensus, association, and stability.

# THE PERSON

Comte was eager for this new era to begin, for he was profoundly disenchanted with his own period. Throughout his life, he had trouble fitting into the society around him and always felt he was an outsider. He later admitted that he sought in "public life the noble but imperfect compensation of the unhappiness of his private life" (Comte, 1973–90, volume 3, p. 36).

In his youth he experienced the disruptive effects of civil war within both his family and his native city. He was born in 1798 in Montpellier, which was one of the southern centers of the Counter-Revolution, the movement that resisted the reforming zeal of the French Revolution of 1789. Comte's bourgeois parents were Catholic royalists also opposed to the Revolution. His childhood was thus full of bitter memories caused by the ordeals of this tumultuous period. In the "Personal Preface" to the sixth volume of the *Cours*, which included an auto-biographical sketch, he pointed out that the French Revolution made a profound impression on him, especially because it was rejected by his family. Comte did not get along with his father, who was a bureaucrat in the tax collection office. Though he was closer to his mother, he alienated her by his unconventional beliefs and behavior. Like many members of his generation with whom he studied at the new Montepellier *lycée*, established by Napoleon, Comte was eager to display his defiance and rebelliousness – a questioning attitude encouraged by his republican teachers. At thirteen or fourteen he announced that he no longer believed in God or Catholicism. Soon afterward, rejecting his parents' royalism and following the example set by the revolutionaries, he became a republican.

A brilliant student with a phenomenal memory, Comte in 1814 gained admission to the École Polytechnique, the prestigious Parisian engineering school. Taught by the best scientists of the day, he learned the importance of the sciences in improving social conditions. He also imbibed the republican, reform-oriented atmosphere of the school. Yet in April 1816 the new royalist government had him expelled for his republicanism and insubordinate behavior. Despite his abridged stay at the École Polytechnique, he remained forever marked by its scientific mindset.

After his expulsion, Comte took courses in biology at the famous medical school in Montpellier, studied history, and read the works of Condorcet and Montesquieu on the "moral and political sciences" (Comte, 1973–90, volume 1, p. 19). In June 1816, he wrote his first essay, which was never published: "Mes Réflexions: Humanité, verité, justice, liberté patrie. Rapprochements entre le régime de 1793 et celui de 1816, adressés au peuple français." Horrified at the royalists' vengeful series of massacres, he condemned the new Bourbon monarchy as well as other oppressive despotisms, namely those of Robespierre and Napoleon, which had had their own share of atrocities. Like other liberal republicans of this period, Comte called for a government based on the "national will"; that is, popular consent (Comte, 1970, p. 421). In his view, enlightened men, such as philosophers and scientists, should lead the way. From the start, there was a certain tension between his elitist and populist impulses.

A year later, back in Paris, Comte began working for Henri de Saint-Simon, an older social reformer, whose "liberalism was . . . well known" (Comte, 1973–90, volume 1, p. 27). The extent of Saint-Simon's influence on Comte is still controversial today. It is undoubtedly true that in his many works published during the Napoleonic Empire, Saint-Simon had shown that the creation of a new unified system of scientific knowledge – a "positive philosophy" – centered on the study of society would lead to a new stage of history, where industrialists and scientists would replace military leaders and the clergy. Yet he scattered such critical seminal ideas haphazardly throughout his various writings, along with other less viable notions, such as the necessity of unifying society by means of a single natural law, Newton's law of gravity, which would replace God as "the sole cause of all physical and moral phenomena" (Saint-Simon, 1966, volume 6, pp. 121n1, 154). When Comte started working for him in 1817, Saint-Simon had grown less interested in establishing the theoretical basis of social reconstruction and was turning toward the practical, industrial reorganization of society. He had dropped his faith in scientists and increasingly praised *industriels* (people involved in productive work) for preparing the new order. Comte, however, took up Saint-Simon's original mission of founding the scientific system – that is, the positive philosophy – together with its keystone, the science of society.

It is evident that Saint-Simon gave Comte's thought a certain direction. Although he later denied Saint-Simon's influence, immediately after their break-up Comte was more forthright: "I certainly owe a great deal intellectually to Saint-Simon, that is to say, he has powerfully contributed to launching me in the philosophical direction that I have clearly created for myself today and that I will follow without hesitation all my life" (Comte, 1973–90, volume 1, p. 90). Gifted with a disciplined, methodical mind, Comte built on the legacy given to him by Saint-Simon and achieved an originality of his own. While Saint-Simon was an incoherent autodidact who constantly revised his concept of the science of humanity, Comte had a talent for system-building and synthesis, which he used to develop sociology as a coherent discipline.

Intellectual differences as well as generational tensions soon led to a rupture. Comte broke with Saint-Simon in 1824 after accusing his mentor of trying to take credit for his seminal essay, the *Plan des travaux scientifiques nécessaires pour réorganiser la société*. In this work, Comte had revealed his latest "discovery" – the law of three stages. This law was in fact indebted to Saint-Simon's view that each science passed through three stages – a conjectural stage, a half-conjectural and half-positive stage, and a positive stage – according to its degree of complexity. Yet unlike Saint-Simon, Comte gave this law a new role as the basis of sociology. It was the key to understanding humanity's development in the past, present, and future. Excited about his findings, Comte felt ready to launch his own career.

Despite this rupture, Comte wrote for *Le Producteur*, the journal founded by Saint-Simon's disciples after the old reformer's death in May 1825. He did not join the Saint-Simonian sect, for he maintained purely literary relations with its members. In the two series of articles that he wrote for the journal in 1825 and early 1826, Comte developed his concept of the spiritual power. He was prescient in claiming that the key to power in modern society lay in controlling opinions and ideas. As soon as natural scientists and social scientists took over the educational system, he believed, they would exert enormous influence over society. They would be especially important in checking the corrupt "administrative despotism" that marked the modern age (Comte, 1929, volume 4, "Appendice," p. 187). Henceforth Comte devoted himself to founding the positivist priesthood.

In early 1826 he offered a course on positive philosophy at his apartment, which was attended by many of the great scientists of the day. Yet after the third lecture, he went mad. A paranoid manic depressive, he spent eight months in an asylum. As a result, he could never completely eliminate the suspicion that he was "crazy" – a term often used by his critics to discredit him. Finally recovering with the help of Caroline Massin, an administrator of a reading room who had married him in 1824, he was henceforth always concerned about preserving his mental well-being. His struggles with mental illness made him distrust skepticism as corrosive and strengthened his conviction that a "normal," sane existence necessitated a certain prescribed harmony and a rigid order.

After his convalescence, Comte worked as a mathematics tutor and journalist. Then in 1832 he procured a subordinate teaching and administrative position at the École Polytechnique. He was a *répétiteur* (teaching assistant) and admissions examiner. This non-taxing work left him time to finish the *Cours de philosophie positive* in 1842. Its purpose was to establish sociology, to stimulate the reorganization of society, and to create the foundation for the reform of the sciences to meet the educational needs of modern civilization. One of the founders of the history of science, Comte analyzed the development of each science and its close relationship to the growth of other sciences. The first three volumes covered the history of mathematics, astronomy, physics, chemistry, and biology. The last three volumes treated his new science of sociology. All in all, the *Cours* set down the basic program of study that he had undergone and that he believed the new spiritual power had to master in order to lead society to a new ethic of cooperation.

When Comte began volume 4 in 1838, he experienced another prolonged period of mental illness, which he ascribed not only to the immense intellectual effort required to introduce sociology but to his wife's infidelity. To improve his mental health, Comte underwent an "aesthetic revolution": he suddenly developed an interest in music and poetry. He hoped to use the arts to cultivate his feelings and thereby enlarge his comprehension of society, the new object of his studies. At the same time, he adopted a regime of "cerebral hygiene." To preserve his ego from attacks from critics and to maintain his sense of originality, he abstained from reading newspapers, books, and journals. He allowed himself only the pleasures of great poetry. Cutting himself off from other scholars, whom he accused of disregarding his work, he increasingly retreated from the world. This tendency toward isolation was strengthened when his wife suddenly left him in 1842 after he neglected her advice not to publish the "Personal Preface" to the sixth volume of the *Cours*, which viciously attacked his colleagues at the

École Polytechnique for slighting him. Her departure almost caused another mental breakdown.

Several years later another woman entered his life. In early 1845 Comte fell in love with Clotilde de Vaux, the sister of one of his students. She was seventeen years younger than Comte. Having been abandoned by her husband, she was an aspiring writer trying to gain independence from her parents, who were struggling to support her. Comte pursued her in a very calculated fashion to develop his feelings, which he worried were stunted due to his poor relations with his family and wife. Now that he was about to write the *Système*, which dealt with the emotional side of human existence, he believed he needed more depth in this arena.

Comte represented Vaux as a perfect lady, an angel who made him more virtuous. Moral improvement, he asserted, was imperative for a philosopher because "no great intellect" could develop "in a suitable manner without a certain amount of universal benevolence," the source of lofty goals (Comte, 1975, volume 2, p. 181). He maintained that his adoration for Vaux made him love all of Humanity.

Although Comte now prided himself on being a model of both intellectual and moral strength, he lusted ironically after her body. Considering him only a close friend, Vaux resisted his advances. Yet she was forced to increase her reliance on his good will and financial resources as she began to lose her battle against tuberculosis. In April 1846, she died. During this period, from mid-1845 to 1846, Comte again almost went mad. To immortalize her name, he decided to dedicate to her his next significant work, the *Système de politique positive* (1851–4).

The extent of Vaux's influence on Comte is controversial. Comte claimed she was responsible for his "second career." Scholars from John Stuart Mill to Raymond Aron have usually agreed that there was indeed a break in his intellectual evolution. Yet they considered what he wrote after her death to be far inferior to the *Cours*. The Religion of Humanity, which he erected in her honor, allegedly discredited his earlier scientistic program. Yet just as Comte's earlier work was not completely scientistic, his later career was not entirely sentimental and illogical. His last work, the *Synthèse subjective* (1856), focused almost entirely on the sciences, especially mathematics; it reinterpreted their role from the perspective of the kind of moral education and logic required during the positive age. All of Comte's works form a consistent whole; from the beginning, his concerns were "spiritual" in that he was trying to create a credible general doctrine that would replace Catholicism and still satisfy the human need for beliefs and values.

Although Vaux did not change the direction of Comte's thought, she did reinforce his growing interest in the feelings, and her struggles to establish herself revived his interest in the "woman question," which his bitter relationship with Massin had squelched. The alliance between women and positive philosophers that he had promoted in the closing volume of the *Cours* now became central to his doctrine, as reflected in the *Catéchisme positiviste*.

When the Revolution of 1848 broke out, Comte became eager to gain greater popularity with the common people. Prompted by the belief that every educated person had a duty to enlighten those who wanted to learn, he had given since

1831 a highly successful public course on astronomy to workers. Now seeking to entice the workers from socialism, especially the "communist" doctrines of Etienne Cabet, he founded the Positivist Society to launch the positivist movement and wrote a manifesto, the *Discours sur l'ensemble du positivisme*. In this work, which later formed the opening section of the *Système*, he argued that although positivism did not seek to abolish private property, it absorbed and strengthened the basic principles of communism, in that it agreed that the community should "intervene to subordinate [property] to the needs of society" (Comte, 1929, volume 1, p. 155). Comte also supported the workers' demands for the right to work and a republic where they would hold the reins of power.

However, he soon feared the revolutionaries were becoming too violent and anarchic, and he ended by preferring the dictatorial regime of Louis Napoleon. In 1855 he wrote *Appel au Conservateurs* to persuade all conservatives, including Catholics, to unite with positivists against the Left. Comte's growing conservatism cost him the support of liberals, such as Emile Littré, a leading scholar who had been his most important French supporter. Nevertheless, Comte still had fifty or so faithful disciples in the Positivist Society, which continued to meet once a week. They supported him financially. Such assistance was especially necessary after Comte lost his last job at the École Polytechnique in 1851. His resentment at not being promoted to mathematics professor had led to friction with his colleagues, who finally dismissed him. He depended on his disciples until his death in 1857.

In the last years of his life, Comte ruled the positivist movement in a dictatorial manner, refusing to allow any dissension, especially in matters pertaining to the Religion of Humanity, whose cult he meticulously organized. He also wrote his *Testament*, which enclosed a "Secret Addition"; it was to be used against his wife if she challenged his will and tried to downplay the importance of this religion. The note accused Massin of having been a prostitute – an allegation that has been generally accepted as true. Yet Comte was falling into the binary logic of his time. If Vaux was an angel, Massin, whom he now hated, had to be the opposite, a demonic force, whose representation in the mid-nineteenth century was a prostitute. When Massin did challenge the will and the case went to court, she was shocked to read the "Secret Addition," whose truth she vigorously denied. Just as Comte succeeded in marrying his name with that of Vaux, he forever sullied the reputation of Massin.

Auguste Comte was a brilliant visionary but a difficult, egoistic person. The certainty that he was right, his intolerance of criticism, and his paranoia led to one rupture after another. He lost many important friends, such as Saint-Simon, François Guizot, Emile Littré, and John Stuart Mill. He broke with his wife and his family. He alienated his colleagues. He had difficulty retaining disciples. It is paradoxical that the man who founded the science that specialized in social relations could not get along with other people. And yet, perhaps because of his manic depressive condition, he imagined himself the savior of the world, the "Great Priest" of Humanity, to which he claimed to be devoted. In a sense, he sought in his social philosophy the stability, harmony, and love that eluded him in his private life.

## The Social Context

Generating a series of dramatic transformations, the French Revolution seemed to make dreams of salvation plausible. Comte's aspirations cannot be entirely understood without a proper appreciation of the social context in which he wrote. His sociological theory was a direct response to the upheavals caused by the French and Industrial Revolutions, two turning points in Western history that rendered social conditions uncertain and unstable.

The French Revolution was a cataclysmic event that threw into question the legitimacy of the government and the religion upon which traditional society rested. Henceforth, the basis and ends of power were matters of debate. During the sixty-odd years that Comte lived, France experienced nine different governments and revolutions. In their search for a new government, the French people seemed unsuccessful at avoiding the twin problems of mob rule and dictatorship. The various constitutions setting down the rules of government were discarded one right after another. Different social groups, impelled by the new forces of financial and industrial capitalism, manipulated events to their own advantage and to the detriment of the lower classes, who were trying to adjust to a new machine-based economy that threatened their traditional, artisanal ways of life. Having watched political experimentations wreak havoc in his country, Comte, like many of his countrymen, had little faith in purely political solutions to the anarchy of his time and looked with skepticism on such conventional abstractions as the "rights of man" and "popular sovereignty," which he believed had led to this confusion. Like others, from traditionalists on the Right to republicans on the Left, he craved a moral community.

For him, as for the revolutionaries, the idea of regeneration had to be a global program that touched on politics, the economy, morality, philosophy, and religion. Commending the revolutionaries for presiding over the necessary work of destruction, he looked forward to the day when there would be a new, more profound revolution, a *constructive* one instituting a more virtuous society, not just in France but everywhere. By the mid-nineteenth century, he was well aware that all parts of the world were interconnected. Partaking of the Eurocentrism of his time, he assumed that the other areas of the globe would follow European patterns of development. Deeply affected by the disunity and anarchy surrounding him, he created sociology and positivism to give the world the stability, order, and harmony it needed in an industrial, secular age that he recognized would no longer be dominated by nobles and clergymen.

Eliminating the questionable abstractions of both religion and conventional philosophy, positivism would serve as the basis of a new social consensus. To create a grand philosophical synthesis that would appeal to both the Left and Right and thus transcend party politics, Comte drew from many intellectual traditions. Despite his embrace of "cerebral hygiene," he was also deeply affected by developments going on around him. Comte wanted his system to represent not only the completion of the French Enlightenment but the endpoint of a more wide-ranging, European intellectual evolution as well. To him, this great comprehensiveness made his work even more serious and significant. As a result, his doctrine represents a delicate balancing act.

## THE INTELLECTUAL CONTEXT

Comte's approach to epistemology and the scientific method was influenced by Francis Bacon, René Descartes, Immanuel Kant, and David Hume. In scientific investigations, Comte recommended achieving a balance between Bacon's stress on induction and Descartes's emphasis on rationalism (or deduction) in order to come up with useful laws. Such laws were to be limited to describing facts, for they had to be constructed in accordance with Hume's warning to avoid the absurd pursuit of first and final causes. Like Kant, who, Comte believed, had elaborated on the British philosopher's conclusions, Hume had stressed the "fundamental dualism between the spectator and spectacle" and had brought mankind closer to the triumph of relativism and nominalism (Comte, 1929, volume 3, p. 588). By showing that an artificial logic provisionally linked our thoughts, both Hume and Kant had taught Comte that people could never know more than what appeared to them through their senses and categories. They thus contributed to Comte's theory of the subjective synthesis, which maintained that knowledge was not comprehensive or objective but rested on the nature of man.

Comte also took a great interest in biology, a science that was in a crucial era of development during his lifetime. It deeply influenced his conception of sociology, especially his idea that society formed an organism. Comte frequently used biological terms, such as "social illness," "pathological case," and "chronic epidemic," to characterize French society (Comte, 1975, volume 2, pp. 16, 48, 50). Four biologists in particular had a large impact on Comte. François Broussais's theory that the pathological was simply a variation of the normal was the source of Comte's concept of the use of experimentation in social studies. Henri Ducrotay de Blainville interested Comte in the influence of the environment on living bodies and turned his attention to the difference between statics and dynamics. Marie François Xavier Bichat's concept that there were three types of human skills – rational, emotive, and motor – inspired Comte's idea that the spiritual power consisted of philosophers, women, and workers. The phrenological doctrine of Franz Gall offered Comte a materialist replacement for the religious explanation of the world and human existence. Comte enthusiastically embraced Gall's principle that sympathy, or sociability, was an innate disposition in every individual because this theory strengthened the positivist argument that people simply needed to be socialized to become more altruistic. Both Gall and Bichat were considered by Comte to be his main scientific predecessors.

A wide variety of social thinkers and philosophers in France and abroad also influenced Comte's development. Montesquieu, Saint-Simon, Johann Gottfried Herder, and Georg Wilhelm Friedrich Hegel taught him that society ultimately represented an application of ideas, particularly moral principles, because a common world view united people. Once the dominant philosophy changed, so did morality and politics. Montesquieu inspired Comte to look for social laws. Saint-Simon recommended the scientific study of society based on *a priori* and *a posteriori* ideas and the history of progress. Making Comte aware that they were living in an age of transition requiring a radical new approach to reconstruction, Saint-Simon also delineated the new temporal and spiritual elites that would take over the emerging industrial-scientific society and direct it toward working productively for the happiness of man on earth. Herder emphasized the importance of a feeling of humanity, and Hegel reinforced Comte's organicism and deterministic approach to history.

Political economists, such as Adam Smith and J. B. Say, turned Comte's attention to the problems associated with industrialization and made him see both the benefits and disadvantages of the division of labor. Comte recognized that the division of labor was crucial to progress. However, he lamented that specialization, which was one of its components, led to a withering of the spirit and a breakdown of the community.

The Scottish Enlightenment philosophers (Hume, William Robertston, Adam Ferguson, and Adam Smith) and the Idéologues (Condorcet, Pierre-Jean-Georges Cabanis, Antoine-Louis Claude de Destutt de Tracy, and J. B. Say) also were influential because of their respective efforts to launch a scientific study of society. Comte appreciated the Scottish philosophers' attempt to establish moral principles on a secular, empirical basis in order to reinforce the progress of the human species from rudeness to civilization. They stressed the importance of studying how government and society developed gradually from man's inherently social nature, not from a contract between strong individualists. Contradicting social contract theory, this emphasis on man's natural feeling of sympathy for others, which was also found in Gall's phrenological doctrine, had a large impact on the positivist concept of human nature. As a means of combating "egoistic metaphysics" – that is, doctrines of individualism – the Scottish theory of man's natural sociability as the basic unifying force in society contributed to Comte's own doctrine of altruism and to the establishment of morality as a seventh science based on the social psychology of man.

Carrying on the legacy of the Enlightenment in the early nineteenth century, the Idéologues tried to develop a social science that would lead to social stability while remaining faithful to the essence of liberalism, the movement that had been salient during the first stages of the Revolution. They imagined a secular, educated elite leading a republic according to the findings of a rational, all-encompassing science of man, not according to vague, potentially dangerous political principles, such as inalienable natural rights. Comte was most impressed by the philosopher who inspired this movement: Condorcet. He admired Condorcet's attempt to establish the science of society on the basis of history, particularly the law of progress of the mind, which was the source of the improvement of humanity. Moreover, Comte acknowledged that he borrowed Condorcet's concept of humanity as a single people experiencing the various stages of history. He thus considered Condorcet his "essential precursor" (Comte, 1966, p. 32).

Comte regarded Joseph de Maistre as "the only thinker" after Condorcet and Gall to whom he owed "something important" (Comte, 1973–90, volume 6,

p. 325). Maistre was part of the "reactionary" or counter-revolutionary school of social thought, which included Louis de Bonald. In the pursuit of a synthesis that would transcend stale ideological debates and appeal to people tired of party politics, Comte staked his claim to the liberal tradition by linking his philosophy to that of Condorcet and the Idéologues. Recognizing the force of the Catholic revival that occurred in France after the end of the Napoleonic Empire, Comte also felt obliged to appeal to the conservative sector of the population. He frequently acknowledged his great debt to the doctrine of the theocrats. He agreed with their assessment that "moral anarchy" was the "great scourge" of the nineteenth century and stemmed from the absence of a general unifying doctrine. Inspired by the conservative thinkers' romanticization of the Middle Ages and their organicism, he looked back fondly on the dogmas and structured spiritual order that he believed formed the basis of medieval social unity. Though a severe critic of Catholicism, Comte conceded that the decline of religion had destroyed this harmonious society and had led to "the most abject" individualism and social fragmentation (Comte, 1973–90, volume 1, pp. 147, 156). He blamed the Protestant Revolution in particular for this state of affairs. It had embraced individualism, which influenced the Enlightenment thinkers and the French revolutionaries and formed the basis of liberalism. According to Maistre, the concept of the autonomous, free individual endowed with natural rights was alarming because man could not be understood apart from the organic society in which he lived. Comte concurred with Maistre's arguments against liberalism, finding it an anti-social doctrine, one that contributed to the atomization, materialism, and corruption of modern society. Impressed by Maistre's assessment that the stress on the sovereignty of reason had left people suffering in an abnormal state of unbelief, Comte agreed that to fulfill the "spiritual condition for the continued existence of human society," people needed "fixed, positive, and unanimous principles," which had to be firmly established by a strong spiritual authority ruling a hierarchial society (Comte, 1973–90, volume 1, p. 147). Maistre argued in particular that social solidarity rested on the unlimited power of the Pope, the source of all valid authority. Appreciating his demonstration of the importance of an institution to the power of a religion, Comte strongly endorsed Maistre's concept that a powerful spiritual authority had to remain independent of the temporal government to ensure a moral order. In short, Comte's system reflected Maistre's stance that a unifying spiritual doctrine and structure represented the key to social cohesion.

Yet Comte by no means adopted Maistre's system in its entirety, for he did not wish to return to the past as the theocrats did. Comte recognized the benefits of progress and the new needs of the future industrial-scientific society. He was deeply influenced by contemporary movements promoting change. As a young man, he had been influenced by liberalism and belonged to various republican organizations before he lost faith in political solutions to the anarchy of his times. Despite his turn to the Right, he was a critic of the status quo and remained an opponent of traditional religion and a monarchical form of government. As mentioned previously, he was also much affected by the women's movement and socialism.

Moreover, Comte was touched by the contemporary romantic movement, many of whose themes came to him through the Saint-Simonians, whom he closely watched. Like the romantics, he despised the bourgeois commercialism of his age, argued in favor of spontaneity, and revelled in his eccentricity, which he considered a source of creativity. At the same time, he shared the romantics' interest in the spiritual aspect of human nature and participated in their celebration of women and the emotions. Comte believed that although the intellectual faculties would become stronger with the advance of civilization and would exert more influence on the emotions, they would still need the superior power of the affections to rouse them from their habitual torpor, give them direction, and subject them to the control of reality. Finally, like the romantics, he looked favorably on the Middle Ages. For this reason, he was most drawn to Sir Walter Scott and Alexander Manzoni, who idealized the medieval period in historical epics. The two writers seemed to epitomize the power of the poet or artist to enchant and ennoble. Such aesthetic power would be important in the positivist republic.

## IMPACT

With such a rich, all-encompassing doctrine predicting a harmonious future, Comte attracted numerous followers on both the Left and the Right in France, Britain, the United States, and Latin America. Pierre Laffitte, one of Comte's disciples, became head of the international positivist movement after his master's death. The "orthodox" disciples in the movement compelled him to develop the religious strain of positivism that had preoccupied Comte at the end of his life. Yet the "unorthodox" Littré rejected Comte's religious construction and transformed positivism into a powerful scientific manifesto for a new generation of anti-clerical republicans, who sought legitimacy for their materialist beliefs and hoped to remake the world with the help of science. In this guise, the doctrine became very compelling to Latin American republicans, especially in Brazil, whose flag displays Comte's motto "Order and Progress."

In France, positivism became the semi-official doctrine of the Third Republic. It was a significant weapon in the republic's battle against the Catholic Church, especially in the struggle surrounding the control of schools. Both Jules Ferry and Léon Gambetta, who were leaders in the Third Republic, were enthusiasts, as was Emile Zola, the famous writer. However, another devotee of positivism was Charles Maurras, who in 1898 founded the Action Française, a proto-fascist movement that denounced "un-French" elements such as Protestants and Jews and claimed support for its authoritarian nationalism on the basis of a scientific study of the "facts."

In England, John Stuart Mill actively corresponded with Comte from 1841 to 1847 and came close to becoming his disciple. He absorbed the essential aspects of Comte's conception of a social science, including the positive method and the law of history. He also responded to Comte's call for educated men to provide constructive leadership to a society undergoing a period of transition. Mill and

George Henry Lewes helped to popularize the positivist doctrine, as did Harriet Martineau, who wrote an abridged translation of the *Cours* (1853), which Comte preferred to his own book. The effects of his theories can be seen in the novels of George Eliot, Thomas Hardy, and George Gissing. Richard Congreve and Frederic Harrison set up rival centers of worship dedicated to the Religion of Humanity, whose secular, scientific principles and humanism had wide appeal as an alternative to Christianity. The Fabian Socialists Beatrice and Sidney Webb were taken with Comte's scientific approach to the study of society, his notion of altruism, and his stress on the role of enlightened leaders of opinion (Wright, 1986).

Comte's concern for the common good and his elitism also proved tantalizing to many American liberals, who found in positivism a new naturalistic philosophy that could replace religion as the foundation of society. In the midst of the professionalization of society, these educated elites appreciated the large role that Comte's new science of society entrusted to well-rounded intellectuals to correct the social problems caused by the concentration of corporate power. Henry Edger, David Croly, Thaddeus Wakeman, Edward Bellamy, Herbert Croly, and Lester Ward were some of the American reformers of the Gilded Age and Progressive Era who were influenced by Comte. They turned liberal ideology away from its traditional libertarian, *laissez-faire* position and made it far more receptive to the idea that an organic community could be created by an interventionist state managed by a professional elite of experts devoted to serving humanity (Harp, 1995).

Comte's influence extended to the science he created, sociology. His interest in preserving social cohesion and harmony was echoed by Émile Durkheim, who adopted Comte's idea that society itself is a reality with its own laws and should be studied in a scientific manner. As reflected in his concept of "anomie," he too measured social health in terms of social solidarity. Durkheim's functionalist approach in the end triumphed over alternative schools of sociology, such as those of his competitors Gabriel Tarde and René Worms, and thus ensured the further diffusion of Comte's ideas in the social sciences (Levine, 1995, p. 168). Lucien Lévy-Bruhl introduced positivist ideas into anthropology. His studies of the primitive mentality may have been inspired by Comte's interest in fetishism, for Comte was the first European thinker to look favorably upon this religion. Other social scientists influenced by Comte include Alfred Espinas, Thomas Buckle, Herbert Spencer, Hippolyte Taine, Ernest Renan, Charles Booth, Patrick Geddes, Leonard Hobhouse, and Lewis Mumford.

Scientists and philosophers, especially philosophers of science, have been affected by Comte's explanation for the uniqueness of science, especially its difference from metaphysics. Comte's recognition of the importance of hypotheses as useful, convenient devices to be used in scientific research foreshadowed the later work of Hans Vaihinger and Henri Poincaré and may have also influenced Claude Bernard, Marcelin Berthelot, Paul Janet, Ernst Mach, Wilhelm Ostwald, and Pierre Duhem. Indeed, in the early twentieth century, the philosophy of science was almost thoroughly positivist (Manicas, 1987, p. 185).

There was in particular a connection between Comte's positivism and logical positivism; both took a similar approach to the problems of determining meaningfulness, distinguishing scientific from nonscientific knowledge, and using the principle of verifiability to criticize metaphysicians. Both argued that the natural and social sciences share common logical bases and a superiority to other forms of knowledge. The leading logical positivists included A. J. Ayer, Otto Neurath, Rudolf Carnap, Moritz Schlick, and Hans Reichenbach.

In many respects, the influence of positivism has been more widespread than that of either Marxism or Freudianism. A great many people today are unknowingly positivists in that they claim to believe only statements supported by tangible evidence. Yet the name of Comte is not a household word, for he has always been subject to severe criticism.

## ASSESSMENT

Comte is easy to ridicule. He was pedantic, dogmatic, and authoritarian. His treatment of others was invariably harsh and egotistical. His writing is dry, austere, and convoluted, which makes reading his work a struggle. As for sociology, many of Comte's ideas are not very scientific and seem to be merely assumptions. For example, there is no basis for his schema that there are three stages of history, each of which is rigidly determined and inevitable everywhere in the world. He supported this law of three stages by carefully selecting only those facts that would demonstrate it. His depiction of the third stage of history, the positive one, seems fanciful and "utopian," a reflection of his love of system-building. His epistemology has been criticized for not providing a formal logic of proof; however, Comte's omission was deliberate, for he did not believe one could adequately or usefully define facts, scientific observation, or rules of verification. His rejection of psychology has also been regarded as unwarranted, although critics again have failed to see that his remarks were directed against the speculations of Victor Cousin (Scharff, 1995, p. 11).

Comte's basic impulse to synthesize seems misguided in many respects. In his embrace of French, English, and German philosophical traditions, he betrayed a certain eclecticism, simplicity, and even superficiality. He appeared anxious to synthesize philosophical movements no matter how different they might be. Like his contemporary François Guizot, Comte was trying to find a *"juste milieu"* which would accommodate all opinions. Positivism, in Comte's eyes, would triumph because it would present a doctrine that was even "more organic" than that espoused by the reactionaries and "more progressive" than that advocated by the revolutionaries (Comte, 1975, volume 2, p. 40). In other words, it would create social harmony by combining the traditionalism of the Right and the rationalism of the Left. Comte believed that the Left would be attracted by his hostility toward the Church and established religions; his republicanism; his faith in reason, relativism, and progress; his emphasis on the importance of freedom of discussion to change the world; his concept of radical social reconstruction in the interest of the working class; and his vision of a new industrial and secular order. The Right would allegedly approve of his promotion of traditional values; his stress on a strong spiritual power, duties, hierarchy, order, and stability; and his opposition to equality, popular sovereignty, and individualism. In the end, his synthesis made him highly vulnerable; because he did not cater to one specific group as Marx did, he had no inherent supporters. The Right attacked his anti-religious, anti-monarchical views and his worship of a secular abstraction, Humanity. The Left criticized his brand of illiberalism, which disregarded the rights of the individual and egalitarian impulses.

As a careful reader of Jean-Jacques Rousseau, Comte made the needs of society paramount. The society that he depicted was a highly regimented one, where people were forced to conform to the Religion of Humanity, an artificial creation that substituted Humanity for God as an object of worship, while keeping most of the ceremonies of Catholicism. Consensus would be achieved through uniformity, not by working out differences of opinion. To a certain extent, Comte sacrificed freedom and pluralism for social control, thus exacerbating the problem of the abuse of power. Yet considering his preoccupation with uniting humanity through the recognition of its manifestations in different singularities (individuals, nations, cultures, and religions), Juliette Grange has argued that Comte was not a proto-totalitarian intent on eliminating individualism; indeed, in an effort to reconcile pluralism and holism, he maintained that humanity developed only through the individual. Humanity was a spiritual or moral community, not an institutionalized political construct demanding blind submission and conformity from each member. The unity of humanity rested on the participation of all its individual members, who were necessarily diverse and specialized (Grange, 1996, pp. 270–6).

Despite the defects in Comte's semi-authoritarian solution to the turmoil of the modern era – defects that reflect the tensions of his own time and his fragile personality – his attempt to cure society of its ills continues to be a central objective of the science of society. Comte's admonitions about the dangers of sociology succumbing to the "positivity" of the scientific age are still highly relevant today, when the model of the physical sciences continues to hold great appeal and some sociologists and other scholars remain attracted to an empirical, jargon-laden discourse, one fearful of grand theories. Sociology has become a fragmented discipline that Comte would never recognize as his own, considering his repeated condemnation of modern specialization. Nor would he approve of the direction that philosophy has taken. As Robert Scharff has shown, the so-called "post-positivists," such as Richard Rorty and Hilary Putnam, err today in fostering a detachment from history in their desire to proclaim the beginning of a new era; they never question the legitimacy of their belief in their own maturity, originality, and correctness. They would benefit from taking a new look at Comte's suggestions about the relativism and tentativeness of knowledge – especially the impossibility of validating epistemological proofs – and his demonstration of the importance of reflecting on prescientific practices and their kinship with positivism. Emphasizing Comte's statement that "no conception can be fully understood without its history" (Comte, 1975, volume 1, p. 21), Robert Scharff has maintained that Comte promoted a "historico-critical reflectiveness" among philosophers that is highly relevant today (Scharff, 1995, p. 16). Put into its historical context in a Comtean fashion, the postmodern world may not be as innovative as it prides itself on being. It may well heed Comte's call for moral commitments to the other members of humanity and to the earth, and his recognition of the power of religion. As Juliette Grange suggests, Auguste Comte may well be *the* sociologist for the twenty-first century (Grange, 1996, p. 15).

## Bibliography

### Writings of Auguste Comte

*Ecrits de jeunesse 1816–1828: Suivis du Mémoire sur la Cosmogonie de Laplace 1835* (ed. Paulo E. de Berrêdo Carneiro and Pierre Arnaud). Paris: Ecole Pratique des Hautes Etudes (1970).
*Cours de philosophie positive* (ed. Michel Serres, François Dagognet, Allal Sinaceur, and Jean-Paul Enthoven), 2 volumes. 1830–42. Paris: Hermann (1975).
*Discours sur l'esprit positif*. 1844. Paris: Union Générale d'Editions (1963).
*Système de politique positive ou Traité du sociologie instituant la religion de l'Humanité*, 4 volumes. 1851–4. 5th edn, Paris: Au Siège de la Société Positiviste (1929).
*Catéchisme positiviste, ou Sommaire exposition de la religion universelle en treize entretiens systématiques entre une femme et un prêtre de l'humanité*. 1852. Paris: Garnier-Flammarion (1966).
*Appel aux Conservateurs*. 1855.
*Synthèse subjective ou Système universel des conceptions propres à l'état normal de l'humanité*, volume 1. 1856.
*Testament d'Auguste Comte avec les documents qui s'y rapportent: Pièces justificatives, prières quotidiennes, confessions annuelles, correspondance avec M$^{me}$ de Vaux*. 1884; 2nd edn, 1896.
*Correspondance générale et confessions* (ed. Paulo E. de Berrêdo Carneiro, Pierre Arnaud, Paul Arbousse-Bastide, and Angèle Kremer-Marietti), 8 volumes. 1973–90. Paris: Ecole des Hautes Etudes en Sciences Sociales.

### Further reading

Aron, Raymond (1968) *Main Currents in Sociological Thought*, volume 1, trans. Richard Howard and Helen Weaver. Garden City, NY: Doubleday, Anchor Books.
Gane, Mike (1991) *Baudrillard: Critical and Fatal Theory*. London: Routledge.
Gouhier, Henri (1933–41) *La Jeunesse d'Auguste Comte et la formation du positivisme*, 3 volumes. Paris: J. Vrin.
Gouhier, Henri (1965) *La Vie d'Auguste Comte*, 2nd edn. Paris: J. Vrin.
Grange, Juliette (1996) *La Philosophie d'Auguste Comte: Science, politique, religion*. Paris: Presses Universitaires de France.
Haac, Oscar (ed. and trans.) (1995) *The Correspondence of John Stuart Mill and Auguste Comte*. New Brunswick, NJ: Transaction Publishers.
Habermas, Jürgen (1971) *Knowledge and Human Interests*, trans. Jeremy J. Shapiro. Boston: Beacon Press.
Harp, Gillis J. (1995) *Positivist Republic: Auguste Comte and the Reconstruction of American Liberalism, 1865–1920*. University Park, PA: Penn State University Press.
Heilbron, Johan (1990) Auguste Comte and Modern Epistemology. *Sociological Theory*, 8, 153–62.
Kofman, Sarah (1978) *Aberrations: Le Devenir-Femme d'Auguste Comte*. Paris: Aubier Flammarion.

Kremer-Marietti, Angèle (1982) *Entre le Signe et l'histoire: L'Anthropologie d'Auguste Comte*. Paris: Klincksieck.

Laudan, Larry (1971) Towards a Reassessment of Comte's "Méthode Positive." *Philosophy of Science*, 38, 35–53.

Lenzer, Gertrud (ed.) (1975) *Auguste Comte and Positivism: the Essential Writings*. New York: Harper & Row.

Levine, Donald N. (1995) *Visions of the Sociological Tradition*. Chicago: University of Chicago Press.

Manicas, Peter T. (1987) *A History and Philosophy of the Social Sciences*. Oxford: Basil Blackwell.

Manuel, Frank E. (1962) *The Prophets of Paris*. Cambridge, MA: Harvard University Press.

Petit, Annie (1999) *Le Système positiviste: La Philosophie des sciences d'Auguste Comte et de ses premiers disciples 1820–1900*. Paris: Vrin.

Pickering, Mary (1993) *Auguste Comte: an Intellectual Biography*. Cambridge: Cambridge University Press.

Pickering, Mary (1996) Angels and Demons in the Moral Vision of Auguste Comte. *Journal of Women's History*, 8, 10–40.

Pickering, Mary (1997) Rhetorical Strategies in the Works of Auguste Comte, *Historical Reflections/Réflexions Historiques*, 23, 151–75.

Pickering, Mary (1998) Auguste Comte and the Return to Primitivism. *Revue Internationale de Philosophie*, 52, 51–77.

Saint-Simon, Claude-Henri de (1966) *Oeuvres de Claude-Henri de Saint-Simon*, 6 volumes. Paris: Anthropos.

Scharff, Robert C. (1995) *Comte after Positivism*. Cambridge: Cambridge University Press.

Wright, T. R. (1986) *The Religion of Humanity: the Impact of Comtean Positivism on Victorian Britain*. Cambridge: Cambridge University Press.

# 2

# Harriet Martineau

## Susan Hoecker-Drysdale

In the preface to her condensation and translation of August Comte's *Positive Philosophy*, Harriet Martineau states that she was motivated to produce the English edition out of her "deep conviction of our need for this book in my own country." Two years later, in her *Autobiography*, she went so far as to state that among all her writings she considered her translation of Comte's major work, which introduced French positivism into English thought, to be the best reflection of her direction and influence. The point of her self-appraisal, written shortly after mid-century, was not so much to identify herself with a specifically Comtean world view as to profess her commitment to science as the source of new knowledge and to sociology and the "moral" (social) sciences as the basis for social progress and reform.

Harriet Martineau (1802–76) subscribed to a broadly conceived science of society, a science which, in her view, would offer the key to understanding societal change and the "uncertainties of the age." As a sociologist, historian, journalist, and public educator, Martineau had a significant impact during her lifetime on the thinking of the British public, and through her publications, in English and in translation into numerous other languages, she advanced the sociological understanding of her readers in Britain, America, and many countries around the globe. From her first publications at age 19 to her last major writings at age 74, Martineau addressed a wide range of subjects and issues in a variety of genres to diverse audiences, publishing over 70 volumes, dozens of periodical articles, and nearly 2,000 newspaper leaders and letters. Her ideas were not only consonant with, but influential for, those of succeeding social theorists.

## THE THEORY

Martineau's achievements fall within a number of theoretical perspectives and levels of social analysis, both macro- and microsociological. The theoretical perspectives and epistemological concerns reflected and developed in her major works can be identified as political economy, historical-comparative analysis, theories of history, feminist theory, social stratification theory (including race, class, and gender theory), metamethodology, and the philosophy of science. Although influenced by certain aspects of sociological positivism as well as by sociological organicism, she drew from them selectively. Her work is most clearly compatible with the historical and comparative perspectives and substantive concerns of Weber, Marx, and Durkheim.

In both her theoretical and empirical work Martineau assumes a critical sociological approach, seen particularly in her "immanent critique" of American society. Her strategy is to focus particularly on societal principles, morals and values in relation to the institutional structures, social relationships, and behavioral patterns in which they are concretized, analyzing the inconsistencies, conflicts, and incongruities. Her empiricism is informed by a critical metamethodology, which takes nothing for granted and sets the foundation for a systematic, informed, and reflexive sociological methodology. In a convergence of theory and method Martineau utilizes typological analysis in an innovative manner to examine and compare types of suicide, religion, marriage and family structures, governments, segments of the economy, and occupations. Finally, in her role as a public educator, she contributes in no small measure to the interpretation and communication of theory in political economy, philosophy, politics, sociology, and science.

## Interpreting theory: political economy

Martineau began her career in social science with a project designed to serve the aspirations of society toward progress and improvement, and, in so doing, began to realize her self-defined role as a public educator. It was in fact the endeavor of interpreting political economy which constituted her first major theoretical study in 1832–4, an undertaking which developed her nascent interests in theories about society and was responsible for her entry into the public sphere. Her keen interest in theories of political economy shaped her later original sociological work, which systematically recognized the significance of the economy in the social order. This first major work is important in the sense that it involved the interpretation, rather than creation, of theory.

Having absorbed the ideas of Adam Smith, Thomas Malthus, Dugald Stewart, and Francis Bacon, Martineau wrote reviews of works on political economy in the *Monthly Repository* and then a few "eightpenny stories" in pamphlet form, which dealt, somewhat unintentionally, with such political economy issues as the impact of machinery on wages, the identity of economic interests, and social imperatives in a changing division of labor. In 1831 she conceived the idea of writing a series of stories which would illustrate the principles of political economy for the public, facilitate an understanding of the economic laws at work, and thereby foster social progress. The result was her 25-volume *Illustrations of Political Economy*, a monthly series of tales which illustrated the principles of production, distribution, consumption, and exchange, drawn from James Mill's *Elements of Political Economy* (1821). Convinced that the public would not be attracted to Mill's rather academic and somewhat dull exposition of the science, Martineau skillfully utilized the genre of the novelette to inspire some understanding of the principles. She could thereby dramatize the network of class interests and the increasingly complex interconnections of industrial capitalism and the market economy.

Martineau's purpose was to present didactic stories comprehensible to all classes: "all classes bear an equal relation to the science." In this instance, fiction became a means to interpret theory, to communicate principles of political economy as yet inaccessible to the general reader. Martineau seems to have shared Spencer's view that increasingly complex societies are more vulnerable precisely because of the growing interdependence of a multifarious division of labor. Hence the duty of members of all classes to understand the principles and relationships of this complicated social organism.

> If it concerns rulers that their measures should be wise, if it concerns the wealthy that their property should be secure, the middling classes that their industry should be rewarded, the poor that their hardships should be redressed, it concerns all that Political Economy should be understood. If it concerns all that the advantages of a social state should be preserved and improved, it concerns them likewise that Political Economy should be understood by all. (*Illustrations of Political Economy*, volume 1, p. xvi)

The topics in the tales included: labor as the basis of wealth and capital; the growing division of labor and the effects of machinery; the relation between wages, prices, and profits; the importance of individual initiative and labor and the negative effects of state support; the necessity to limit population growth; the principles of a market economy and free competition; supply and demand; the function and supply of money; the advantages of free trade; the positive and negative roles played by unions; productive and unproductive consumption; the requirement of public expenditure for defense, public order, and social improvement; the importance of just taxation and avoidance of public indebtedness (Hoecker-Drysdale, 1992, pp. 21–48).

The work reflected her nominalist view of society as a collection of individuals who are informed and act in consonance out of their rational understanding and belief in the principles or fundamental laws operating therein. Martineau's illustrative narratives caught the public imagination at the time, although, as often happens with first works, in later years she was quite critical of her early efforts.

## Theorizing empiricism: Martineau's metamethodology

Following her *Illustrations of Political Economy* series, Martineau turned toward another challenging and more original project. Partly as relief from two years of intensive work and partly out of burning curiosity, she embarked in 1834 on a trip to America. This was to be a mission on behalf of an improved

British understanding of American society: "If I am spared to come back, this country shall know something more than it does of the principles of American institutions. I am tired of being kept foundering among the details.... It is urged upon me ... that I should go and see for myself." During the six-week sea voyage to America and in anticipation of the research ahead, she wrote a methodological treatise, the earliest explicit treatment of sociological methods and social research. It remains a landmark in the development of the art and science of social investigation. *How to Observe Morals and Manners* (1838) includes discussions of metamethodological considerations, principles of social investigation, research strategies and methods, and a framework for the study of a total society which she applied in the three-volume *Society in America* (1837).

Martineau emphasizes that studies in the science of morals must be based on disciplined observation, impartiality, a theoretical framework, and systematic research methods used consistently and self-consciously. The treatise emphasizes the necessity of tracing the impact of societal phenomena on one another and of developing a critical view, in order to understand, for example, the corruptive elements of the "marital status," or the overreliance on public opinion. *How to Observe Morals and Manners* is organized into three parts: "Requisites for Observation," "What to Observe," and "Mechanical Methods."

Following a discussion of metamethodology, Martineau presents her macrosociological framework for studying a total society. The institutional areas which must be examined include:

1  Religion (churches, clergy, superstitions, suicide).
2  General moral notions (national character, popular culture, stories, idols, songs, literature, treatment of criminals, the aged and children).
3  The domestic state (topography and geography, economics and occupations, family, marriage and children, health).
4  The idea of liberty (police, law, social classes, servitude, communications, education, public opinion).
5  Progress (cultural, economic and technological change).
6  Discourse.

"Wise inquiry into Morals and Manners [will] begin with the study of *things*, using the *discourse of persons* as a commentary upon them" (*How to Observe Morals and Manners*, p. 63). Facts must be gained from the "records" of a society: "architectural remains, epitaphs, civic registers, national music, or any other of the thousand manifestations of the common mind which may be found among every people" (ibid., p. 64). In a later chapter she elaborates on discourse as the indispensable commentary upon the classes of national facts which are observed; it gives meaning and illustration to the evidence of facts. In the study of discourse the traveller or investigator "must seek intercourse with all classes of the society ... not only the rich and the poor, but those who may be classes by profession, pursuit, habits of mind, and turn of manners.... He must study little ones at their mothers' knees, and flirtations in ballrooms, and dealings in the market-place.... Wherever there is speech, he must devote himself to hear."

Martineau felt a real advantage as a woman investigator, for it gave her access to the kitchens, the nurseries, the boudoirs, where much of the "inner life" of a people is revealed. Discourse is important precisely because it exhibits a certain character of its own and expresses the distinct national character and values of a society, from which we can derive *types* of societies. But discourse in itself is limited and can be deceptive, particularly because it may not, and often does not, coincide with the facts, nor does it represent an appropriate sample of views and opinions.

The danger always exists that every observer assumes he or she can understand, apart from all other phenomena, human behavior. Martineau emphasizes the need for the observer to refrain from premature conclusions, to be self-conscious of his or her own biases, to examine all sides and perspectives on issues, situations, and practices, to use a variety of methods in obtaining information, and to immerse oneself, as a true participant observer, enough to know and understand, while maintaining self-checks of distance and objectivity. For these reasons she advocates the use of three specific methodological tools for the corroboration of facts and observations: a diary, to record one's personal reactions; a journal, to record impressions, incidents, anecdotes, descriptions; and a notebook, to record the facts of daily life. These were mechanisms for systematization and self-monitoring.

Martineau utilizes typological analysis, at once a theoretical and methodological approach, in a number of instances in her work to organize historical/empirical data and to analyze their contents theoretically. Particularly effective is her examination of religion and suicide in society. Reflecting the methodological influence of Montesquieu, she develops a typology of religion – Licentious, Ascetic, and Moderate – distinguished by the degrees of ritualism, physical or spiritual self-indulgence, and individual liberty, and emphasis on interpersonal sentiment. While all societies hold religious sentiments of key importance in understanding them, she concludes that despotic governments can only prevail where licentious or ascetic religions are dominant. On the other hand, democratic government is possible only under a moderate form of religion. At the same time, religious freedom is the highest expression of democracy. "Religion is the highest fact in the Rights of Man from its being the most exclusively private and individual, while it is also a universal concern. . . . Religion is, in its widest sense, the tendency of human nature to the Infinite . . . [to] the pursuit of perfection" (*Society in America*, volume 3, p. 224).

Likewise, in her analysis of suicide, she designates types of suicide which are indicative of the character of social relationships and the sentiments of the social order. "Every society has its suicides, and much may be learned from their character and number, both as to the notions on morals which prevail, and the religious sentiment which animates to or controls the act." In an analysis not dissimilar from Durkheim's, which appeared more than a half century later, she derives the following types of suicide: (a) suicide as duty, as with soldiers; (b) suicide out of devotion to others; (c) suicide when hope of honor is gone; (d) suicide to protect the virtue of chastity; (e) martyrdom for truth, ranging from veneration to fanatical self-seeking. Martineau linked the prevalence of suicide to a group or society's view of future life, to enslavement as opposed to freedom, to religious practices such as the Suttee, to imitation within certain groups, and to religious beliefs, suggesting that considerations of purgatory, for example, might discourage the Irish and the French from such acts. Suicide out of devotion to others generally carries cultural approbation and martyrdom (*How to Observe Morals and Manners*). Having analyzed the sociological relevance of religion and suicide, she proceeds to an inquiry into the moral and cultural values of a society.

Martineau was so convinced of the importance of suicide for understanding societal relations that she returned to the subject, not only in her America studies but also in an article which appeared in Charles Dickens's *Household Words* and later in one of her collections (*Health, Husbandry, and Home*), in which she developed a somewhat different typology: suicides based upon shame, complete devotion to others, preservation of honor, and withdrawal from duty and expectations of others. She concluded that suicide was more frequent among men, was linked to intemperance, varied according to occupation, district, and education, was related to weak imagination and strong egoism, and probably had a hereditary component. In these discussions she also advocated more enlightened attitudes toward the treatment of mental illness.

Martineau's approach in *How to Observe Morals and Manners* is to insist that, in the study of a society, consideration must be given, as in the work of Montesquieu, to the totality of society, including its geographical, climatic, and economic bases; to civilization, as examined by Condorcet, particularly the degree of freedom and equality of its members, especially women; to class structures and cultures and their consequences, as we see later in Marx; and to morals and values, the culture and consequences of religion, as in Weber and Durkheim, as well as the phenomenon of suicide as perhaps a crisis in values or relationships. This important sociological treatise was overshadowed by her other "America studies" and, unlike her other books, was not reprinted for a century and a half, perhaps because it *was* a metamethodological treatise, actually, if not intentionally, aimed at the researcher and epistemologist. There is little doubt, however, that this remarkable piece was of enormous aid to Martineau herself and to those travellers and students of societies who availed themselves of it.

## Theorizing America: Martineau's macrosociology

Martineau's macrosociological investigation of America in the 1830s, including the methodological treatise and her analysis of American society, comprise her most significant sociological work in terms of both empirical investigation and theoretical analysis. The study itself, done in the same decade as de Tocqueville's *Democracy in America*, is equally perspicacious, more clearly rooted in empirical fact, and more self-consciously theoretically ordered. In the analysis a systematic framework for the study of social structures, social institutions and their interrelations, and social dynamics is complemented by attention to the idiographic and the ethnographic. The investigation explores empirically, and analyses theoretically:

1   Politics, parties and government.
2   The morals of politics (political office, newspapers, citizenship, sectional prejudice, citizenship of people of color, the political nonexistence of women).
3   The economy, of various regions, including agriculture, transport, markets, manufactures, commerce.
4   The morals of economy, including the morals of slavery, the morals of manufacture, the morals of commerce.
5   "Civilization," her nomenclature embracing the idea of honor, caste and classes, property and intercourse, women, marriage, occupation, health, children, sufferers, utterance.
6   Religion, the science (principles) of religion, spirit, and administration of religion.

Throughout Martineau's analysis of these institutions in America and their interconnections there are several implicit theoretical foci: (a) the discrepancies between normative structures and social behavior; (b) structural inequalities; (c) conflicts and incongruities of values and value systems; (d) the meaning and motives, and their contradictions, of social actors. These foci are woven into the fabric of the study, accompanied by observations, interviews, narratives, anecdotes, descriptions, and statistical and documentary facts. The following analysis attempts to show these theoretical convergences as well as to provide something of the tenor of her own research narratives.

**SETTING AND FRAMEWORK** Martineau spent two years (September 19, 1834 to August 1, 1836) exploring American society, travelling close to 10,000 miles throughout the United States, visiting many areas more than once, talking with and interviewing people of all ages, classes, races, religions, and political parties. She interviewed and interacted with a wide range of the population, from the highly placed, including the President of the United States, Andrew Jackson, to ordinary persons. She observed and interviewed slaves, mill girls, Indian tribes, members of experimental communities, abolitionists, farmers, workers, and feminists. She visited prisons, hospitals, mental asylums, literary and scientific institutions, factories, plantations, and farms, and lived in all sorts of dwellings, from stately homes to log cabins. She used all possible means of transportation, walked a great deal as she felt that that was the best means of learning about a people, and studied all aspects of the young society. In the manner of de Tocqueville, she brought with her a companion and research assistant, Louisa Jeffrey, to aid her in observation and collection of material and to serve as a second set of eyes and ears (Martineau being by then quite deaf).

Martineau's particular interest in her investigation of America was in the "theory and practice of society," which in fact was Martineau's original title for the book. The theoretical stance of *Society in America* can best be understood as immanent critique; that is, an understanding and assessment of the structures and practices of a society on its own terms, not by external criteria, particularly in the relationship between cultural norms and societal practices. In this context, morals and values become the center point for understanding social behavior. She explained at the outset that her purpose was "to compare the existing state of society in America with the principles on which it was professedly founded; thus testing Institutions, Morals and Manners by an indisputable, instead of an arbitrary standard, and securing to myself the same point of view with my readers of both nations" (*Society in America*, volume 1, p. viii). To compensate for the possibility of omission and misinterpretation and in full recognition of the tentativeness of any interpretation, Martineau used immanent critique to scrutinize social behavior in terms of the principles, beliefs, and values articulated in the society's formal documents: the American Constitution, the Bill of Rights, the Declaration of Independence and other institutionalized creeds. The true test of a nation's success, according to Utilitarian standards to which she at least in part subscribed, is the general happiness of its members. She was concerned, therefore, to assess the extent to which happiness or general well-being could be seen to characterize the lives of people in various social groups. Her analysis and conclusions remain solidly in the tradition of early critical sociology.

Her investigation is descriptive, analytical, and critical. As she conducts her empirical research, her methodological self-consciousness is apparent. She is able to capture the richness and variety, as well as dynamism, of life in a thriving, exciting new society, precisely because she adhered to her own dicta, presented earlier, to "seek intercourse with all classes of society" and to search for the "inner life" of society. At the same time, Martineau integrates her observations into more general theoretical analysis within a historical and comparative perspective.

Martineau observed and analyzed critically the complexities of the plantation as a site of contradictions between the ideology of freedom and the practices of slavery, the New England town hall as a cradle of both democracy and bigotry, the prevalence of political apathy within the world's first modern democracy, the legal freedoms enjoyed but social shackles endured by women, and the disastrous societal consequences of the enslavement of a part of the population by the privileged few.

**THE MORALS OF POLITICS** The analysis is structured around three general concerns: politics and government, the economy, and culture and social institutions. Observations and analyses of the structures, functions, and norms of each are followed by close examination of the morals of politics and the morals of economy. Here Martineau explores the dynamics of power, conflict, and control which occur in everyday life in these arenas. In examining government and politics, for example, Martineau emphasizes the strengths of the system – its principles – and the potential for genuine democracy. "Politics are morals, all the world over; that is, politics universally implicate the duty and happiness of man" (ibid., p. 6). It is in the arena of politics, she maintains, that the theory and practice of a nation's principles intersect, where material realities and the highest ideals confront one another.

The theory that "the majority are in the right" requires that basic principles be secured and that the citizenry have the liberty to ensure a correspondence between the principles and their institutional forms. Inconsistencies arise out of human fallibility rather than political design. Martineau identifies crucial contradictions within American society, in examining, for example, the dynamics of office-holding (e.g. that holding office means the end of one's moral independence), the role of the press (e.g. that it exercises arbitrary power through control of content and perspective), failure of citizenship (through apathy, fear of opinion, or lack of the franchise), significant class, race, and gender differences in observing the law, and the absence of any political and economic power and participation for negroes and women. The flagrant violations of the law by mobs of "white gentlemen" in the North as well as the South left it to the (disenfranchised) women to take responsibility for seeking peaceful means of resolving these conflicts and contradictions. This meant that women abolitionists were suspect in both regions and were frequently harassed, jailed, or, especially if black, beaten or killed as they challenged the corruptions of society.

Martineau found that this new "nation of equals," based upon Enlightenment ideals and lacking a feudal history, created its own hierarchy and class distinctions, exemplifying the "tenacity of rank." She analyzed the many practices which sustained structured inequalities in American society. Although "the law, in a republic, is the embodiment of the will of the people," she noted that the public, commonly uninformed and indifferent, ignored the horrendous treatment of the abolitionists with rationalizations about the respectability of the anti-abolitionists ("the gentlemen of Boston would do nothing improper") and condemned the meddlesomeness and trouble-making of the abolitionists (ibid., 176). Although the citizenship of all society's members was a legal reality, constitutionally, people of color were badly treated. "They are protected as citizens when the public service requires their security; but not otherwise treated as such" (ibid., 195). She noted that prejudice against color was on the increase. Likewise, the democratic principle that "governments derive their just powers from the consent of the governed" is entirely violated given the "political non-existence of women" (ibid., 199). "Indulgence is given her [every woman] as a substitute for justice" (*Society in America*, volume 3, p. 106). Martineau concluded that the denial to negroes and women of the ability to exercise their rights as free citizens within the society constituted the greatest injustice and contradiction in American society. Nonetheless, there were many instances, she reported, of strong-minded and remarkable women and blacks who overcame all odds to free themselves and others.

**THE MORALS OF THE ECONOMY** The morals of the economy likewise revealed serious problems in the values and goals of the society. Martineau emphasized the high priority given to mercenary rather than human values. Indeed, the pursuit of wealth as possible for all and the reduction of all values to mercenary ones lay at the heart of America's cultural malady. In her analysis of work and honor, she showed that in regions of slavery and/or systems of rank, labor was regarded as degrading; work was debased. In the North and particularly in the rugged but free and open western regions, work was seen as necessary, honorable, and an exercise of one's freedom. She predicted that in this new nation eventually labor would be honored. "America is in the singular position of being nearly equally divided between a low degree of the ancient barbarism in relation to labor, and a high degree of the modern enlightenment."

The culturally accepted notion that women do not work is utterly untrue, she demonstrated, as married or single women did indeed work, enduring low pay or no pay, while being charged with enormous responsibility in holding the society together. In her discussions of the economics of stratification, including race, gender, and class, she drew attention to the "mean whites" of the South, who worked with their hands, had no prospects and few positive life chances, and took the harshest attitudes toward negroes. (A similar discussion is found eighty years later in Max Weber's discussions of class in America.) By contrast, there were white plantation women who taught the slaves to read, in relationships of respect and friendship.

The morals of slavery revealed the horrendous degradations of negroes and women, particularly black women, the disregard for human rights, and the hypocrisies of mistreatment and exploitation of men, women, and children within a declared system of honor. Contrarily, the morals of manufactory and commerce showed that, in a democratic society, work was of a higher calibre, resulting, for instance, in improvements in manufacture. In that context, there existed a concern, if rather paternalistic, of employers for employees and a spirit of enterprise emerging from a "sordid love of gain," a love of art, and the practice of benevolence and philanthropy. Again, however, practices of speculation, greed, and support for the profitable institution of slavery created the problematics of this free and open economy.

CIVILIZATION "The degree of civilisation of any people corresponds with the exaltation of the idea which is the most prevalent among that people" (*Society in America*, volume 3, p. 1). Martineau examined "civilization," which in the old world still corresponded with the low idea that "the generality of men live for wealth, ease and dignity and lofty reputation," rather than with inner values. Although the new world was forged out of the fundamental human values of truth and justice – as expressed in the Revolution and the Declaration of Independence – its members remained captivated by the old world's pursuit of wealth rather than social and political freedoms.

These economic realities and accompanying values resulted in peculiar and perhaps destructive conceptions of social honor. "It is true that it is better to live for honour than for wealth: but how much better, depends upon the idea of honour" (ibid., p. 10). While moralists, scholars, professionals, and even some merchants were dissatisfied with the importance attached to wealth, general lifestyle and consumption practices as well as the American idea of honor seemed solidly based on obvious signs of consumption and leisure and an exaggerated concern with reputation and the opinions of others. Tensions existed, therefore, between the tendency toward maintaining an aristocratic European-derived culture, on the one hand, and an obsession with wealth and the real opportunities of economic freedom and mobility within a republic, on the other. In the absence of an established class system, according to Martineau, patterns of consumption, leisure and accumulation of a most conspicuous and self-conscious nature became crucial social indicators. In that context, women became vehicles of display and consumption (ibid., pp. 37–53). These value incongruities posed significant problems for American society as it attempted to both profess and practice its cultural ideals.

According to Martineau, these contradictions were exhibited in the intercourse and discourse of the members of society: a good-natured, friendly, and hospitable people who nevertheless engaged in duelling; a population generous in time and money in the service of others who held a preoccupation with the practice of flattery; and an enterprising and idealistic society which allowed itself to be dominated by the pressures of public opinion. Martineau included within her analysis an examination of the mechanisms which supported the class system, as, for instance, in her discussions of the rules and distinctions in socializing, anticipating Simmel's concept of sociation, where classes establish their own rules for interaction and inclusion. Rules of imitation paralleled rules of anti-commensality in relations between negroes and whites. The class, and even caste, system challenged the very authenticity of the ideology of equality. Nevertheless, even within the context of materialistic, superficial and anti-democratic behavior, Americans were distinguished in the honor given to the intellect and the intellectual as well as in their desire to be open and to communicate on a variety of subjects.

**RELIGION** After exploring the status of women, children and sufferers, and those marginalized by virtue of being criminal, mentally ill, disabled, poor, or alcoholic, she explored the literary life of the society, completing her study of American society with an analysis of religion. With particular sociological finesse, she distinguished the science of religion from its spirit and practice, and dealt specifically with the history, theology, and current status of religion, the spiritual ethic and meaning of religion, and the "administration" or social organization of religion. She emphasized the need to separate the role of theological research ("the science of religion") and the open pursuit of ideas from the function of preaching and administering to the religious needs of the population. Martineau had written considerably about religion early in her writing career; she was well informed on the subject. Examining American society, she was struck by the lack of diversity in religious beliefs in a country exalting freedom of conscience, by religious intolerance, by hypocrisies among the clergy, and by practices of churches as agents of stratification, sometimes helpful but usually ineffectual challengers to the system of slavery. Throughout, the sociological significance of religion was emphasized.

**HER CONCLUSIONS** Martineau concluded her macrosociological study of America with the suggestion of the tentativeness of her observations, but noting that American society had a smaller amount of crime, poverty, and mutual injury of every kind than any known society. "They have realised many things for which the rest of the world is still struggling" (ibid., p. 298). She held high hopes for this new nation founded upon the principle of equality. Americans were self-governing, she noted, and had avoided an aristocracy, a link between church and state, excessive taxation, and the irresponsibility of any class. Any evils arising out of the legislative or executive branches of government could be remedied by the people themselves. However, her final and most general conclusion was that "the civilisation and the morals of the Americans fall far below their own principles" (ibid., p. 299), that there were severe contradictions between the principles and practices of American social life. Resolution of the two great contradictions of slavery and of women's suppressed condition was required before the republic could realize its true goals and morals. Martineau continued to monitor both issues and analyzed them in periodicals and newspaper leaders until well through the 1860s. The issue of slavery, which she had thought earlier would be resolved, had precipitated a challenge to the very existence of the nation.

A rich ethnography of American society is to be found in the second three-volume work, *Retrospect of Western Travel* (1838), which, though less analytical, contains excursions into the microsociological: occurrences and sites which express something of the quintessence of American social and cultural character.

## Interpreting theory: the Comtean system

Martineau declared the rationale for her 1853 translation and condensation of Auguste Comte's *Positive Philosophy* thus: "While our science is split up into arbitrary divisions...and while the researches of the scientific world are presented as mere accretions to a heterogeneous mass of facts, there can be no hope of a scientific progress" (*The Positive Philosophy of Auguste Comte*, volume 1, p. v). The book, she wrote, would be recognized as "one of the chief honours of the century" and must be "rendered accessible to the largest number of intelligent readers." The six volumes of Comte's *Cours de Philosophie Positive*, written and published between 1830 and 1842, were intended to outline the hierarchy of the sciences, to show their development historically and the methods and findings in each as relevant to the whole positive system, and to show that the sciences of observation now needed a new science – social physics or sociology. Undoubtedly, it was Martineau's sense of the urgent need for both a system of the sciences and specifically a science of society which drew her to the task. Human perfectibility and social progress, Enlightenment values fundamental to Martineau's thinking, required knowledge and understanding, not just for the educated few, but for the population as a whole. Martineau believed human beings to be situated in a critical situation in history:

> We find ourselves suddenly living and moving in the midst of the universe, – as a part of it, and not as its aim and object. We find ourselves living, not under capricious and arbitrary conditions, unconnected with the constitution and movements of the whole, but under great, general, invariable laws, which operate on us as a part of the whole. (ibid., p. x)

The six volumes of rather turgid style, repetition, and ennui had to be translated, condensed, and revised into a final version of two volumes. Aware of the obtuseness of Comte's original work, she made clear that hers "is a very free translation." However, she sought the expertise of Professor John Nichol of Glasgow for the sections on mathematics, astronomy, and physics, only the last of which required revision in the form of condensation. As she explored each part of Comte's "rich and diffuse" text, filled as it was with "wearisome epithets," she simultaneously studied the subjects and disciplines discussed in full preparation for the work. She had cultivated a knowledge of science, social science, and philosophy, as seen from her first published essays in the *Monthly Repository*. Her education in languages, classics, philosophy, history, literature, and sciences fully prepared her for the task. Positive philosophy, she was convinced, was the only remedy for the "uncertainties of the age" which haunted and disoriented even the most enlightened and progressive of minds. "The supreme dread of every one who cares for the good of the nation or race is that men should be adrift for want of an anchorage for their convictions...a large proportion of our people are now so adrift" (ibid., p. 5).

Both her interests in science and her indefatigable desire to bring scientific knowledge to the public ("the growth of a scientific taste among the working classes of this country is one of the most striking of the signs of the times") were from her youth integral to her life and work. If society had entered a "critical" period from which regeneration and a new order would emerge, science itself, she believed, would facilitate the "growth of knowledge and the evolution of philosophy." The social sciences, yet to be developed, would be the new basis of "intellectual and moral convictions" not simply for middle-class academics and intellectuals but for the general public – the working classes as well as the bourgeoisie. Her task was to make the public aware of the "great, general, invariable laws" through Positive Philosophy.

Martineau disagreed with Comte's patriarchal, even misogynist, perspective on women, his idea of a hierarchical society with centralized planning and control, and, most certainly, his advocacy of a secular religion with sociologists as high priests and Comte himself as the Pope. While his presentation of a new science of society seemed exactly what was needed, Martineau seems to have regarded the accompanying ideology as regressive, if not reactionary. Nevertheless, she refused to criticize his ideas in the context of the translation, implying in the preface, as in her autobiography written a few years later, that, though she had serious disagreements with Comte, it would be inappropriate to raise them in that context. In fact she did not publish any kind of criticism of Comte's ideas and writings during his lifetime, although some critique appears in later letters and in her article "The Religion of Positivism" of 1858 (see Arbuckle, 1983, pp. 164–5; Sanders, 1990, p. 233).

Comte himself was so pleased with Harriet's translation that he informed her that he would replace the original with her version in his *Bibliotheque positiviste du proletaire au dixneuvieme siecle*. He was convinced that Martineau's version should be translated into French, which was ultimately done by C. Avezac-Lavigne in 1871–2. Later, however, Comte was less enthusiastic about Martineau's work when, in his religious phase, he became aware of Martineau's agnosticism.

## Other aspects of Martineau's theory

The works just presented remain among Martineau's most salient contributions to sociology in interpreting theory, theorizing empiricism, and analyzing society at the macrosociological level. Nevertheless, her theoretical achievements extend considerably beyond these and include feminist theory, social evolutionary theory, historical sociology, theories of religion, microsociology (socialization, childhood, the sociology of illness and disability, for example), law and citizenship, the sociology of work and occupations, and sociological journalism. Elaboration on these theoretical and empirical works is not possible here. The reader should consult the primary and secondary sources in the accompanying bibliography.

## The Person

Harriet Martineau was born on June 12, 1802 in Norwich, England, the sixth of eight children in a Unitarian family of Huguenot descent, significant in shaping the emotional and intellectual lives of Harriet and her siblings. Descendants of the forced migration of Protestants from France in 1686 following the Revocation of the Edict of Nantes, generations of the Martineau family endured minority status as Dissenters but cherished their religious freedoms in the new land, and preserved their French heritage, ensuring that all children were bilingual and educated in the rich historical, philosophical, and literary legacy of England and the Continent. This included most importantly Enlightenment values related to natural rights, respect for the individual, freedom of self-realization, equality of men and women in most matters, and the individual's obligation to serve society. A rather Calvinist posture pervaded this culture.

The primary profession for generations of Martineaus had been medicine, but Thomas Martineau, Harriet's father, became a textile manufacturer. The financial fate of his factory as it endured the consequences of recessions and speculation had serious consequences for the Martineau family, and became, as we shall see, the challenge to which Harriet responded successfully. Her mother, Elizabeth Rankin, was the daughter of a wholesale grocer and sugar-refiner in Newcastle upon Tyne – an intelligent woman of limited education who, in addition to her devotion to the household ("a true nineteenth-century matriarch"; Pichanick, 1980), saw to it that her children were properly educated by tutors at home and in Unitarian schools. She was, nonetheless, stern, with seriously high expectations for the children and sharp reprimands for those who disobeyed. Harriet saw it as "a tyranny of the mind," accompanied by little affection or care for the emotional well-being of her children, particularly Harriet, who became increasingly defiant toward her mother.

The major fact of Harriet's childhood was her poor health. She was passed to a wet-nurse as an infant, was sickly as a child, spent several periods away from the family in "recuperative" situations, and suffered her mother's "cures," which generally exacerbated the problem. Out of fear, physical instability, and emotional deprivation, Harriet responded to family interaction and expectations with trepidation and anxiety. She had been deprived of the senses of taste and smell since childhood and by early adolescence began to suffer from a significant hearing loss. She had largely lost her hearing by the age of twenty and was soon forced to resort to the use of ear trumpets. As the deafness encroached she felt increasingly isolated and unhappy; her family accused her of being stubborn and deliberately difficult. Withdrawal and a sense of unworthiness resulted from negative comments by her mother and other relatives. She prayed in chapel for the angels in heaven to come down to take her away; at one point she contemplated suicide. Harriet's strategy for coping was a turn to religious faith and a precocious study of the Bible. She found sanctuary in books and ideas. Like her siblings, Harriet, an avid reader and learner, studied languages, classics, mathematics, music, literature, biography, history, and religion, and developed a passion to write.

Particularly influential in Harriet's intellectual development were the writings of Shakespeare, Bunyan, and Milton, initially, and later Bacon, Condorcet, Montesquieu, Hegel, Lessing, Smith, Wollstonecraft, Godwin, Wordsworth, Anna Barbauld, and Hannah More. David Hartley, Dugald Stewart, Thomas Malthus, Joseph Priestley, and, by 1830, Saint-Simon, whose work she was introduced to by Gustav D'Eichtal, figured predominantly in the formation of Harriet's interests and ideas in philosophy, political economy, and sociology. She read with enthusiasm the fiction and poetry of such literary figures as Austen, Goethe, Wordsworth, and others. As an adolescent she studied logic, rhetoric, and poetry, extended her learning in Latin, Greek, and Italian, and enjoyed translating Tacitus and Petrarch, and later German and French authors. Harriet nearly married a college friend of her brother James, but the prospective bridegroom became ill and died within a year. She never married, and considered herself to be "the happiest single woman in England."

In 1822 Martineau began her career as a published author in the Unitarian *Monthly Repository*, edited by William J. Fox, with articles on the feminist perspective on religion and on women's education, and by 1832 had published nearly 100 articles, stories and poems in the Unitarian publication. They reveal her literary and analytical skills and her thorough education and breadth of interests, and most importantly anticipate many of her later concerns, as she moved from topics in religion to philosophy, literature, political economy, social issues (slavery, education, women's condition), natural rights, natural theology, science, and the works of Socrates, Godwin, Lessing, Doddridge, and Crombie. Her intellectual and social perspective emerges in, for example, "Essays on the Art of Thinking" (1829) and "Essays on the Proper Use of Retrospective and Prospective Faculty" (1830). In "Theology, Politics and Literature" (1832), she develops a rationale for the moral sciences (the study of Man) and discusses: the importance of positioning knowledge in past, present, and future; induction and analogy as methods of reasoning; and the problems of the ambiguity of terms. In fact, throughout these essays she outlines a scientific epistemology.

Physical science is advancing steadily, and with an accelerating rapidity, under the guidance of philosophical principles. Moral science is lagging behind, blinded, thwarted, led astray by a thousand phantoms of ancient ignorance and error... Let it be ascertained what are the true objects of research, and what is their natural connexion, instead of proposing to split men into parties whose object will be... but to magnify one science at the expense of another... moral and physical science are to [Man] connected in an indissoluble union.

Martineau's first major project was *Illustrations of Political Economy*, discussed above. Criticized for oversimplification and incautiousness in her direct approach, she did not shun controversial and complex issues. The popularity of the tales is attested by extremely high sales (on average 10,000 copies per month), and the fact that, even at moderate royalty rates, Martineau thereby secured not only her financial independence but her reputation as a public educator and interpreter of scientific doctrines.

Harriet's trip to America in 1834–6 resulted in three multi-volume works on American society, as we have seen, and established her as a major social investigator, critic, and travel writer. As after so many such major projects, she sought relief from the hard work of writing and publishing by turning to fiction. In 1839 she published the novel *Deerbrook*, in which the protagonists are a doctor and a governess whose experiences centre on issues of science, work, and occupation.

Martineau endured illnesses throughout her life, which occasionally resulted in a complete withdrawal from daily affairs. In 1839, while on a trip to Italy, she became very ill with gynaecological disorders, returned to England, and spent six years, 1839–44, in Tynemouth as an invalid. Released from the pressures of her regular schedule, she found time and energy to write a historical novel about the Haitian hero Toussaint l'Ouverture (*The Hour and the Man*, 1841), a four-part series of moralistic children's stories (*The Playfellow*, 1841), and a sociological analysis of illness and the patient–caretaker relationship (*Life in the Sickroom*, 1844). In 1844 she was "cured" by mesmerism, of which she wrote in a series *Letters on Mesmerism* (1844), thereby alienating her family and many friends. But Martineau continued to live life as she saw fit, and, upon her recovery, moved to Ambleside in the Lake District, where she designed and built her home, and then left immediately for a seven-month tour of the Middle East. The result of that journey was the three-volume *Eastern Life: Past and Present* (1848), in which she demonstrated the influence of religion on culture and the evolution of religion from magic and superstition to monotheism, from hierarchical godheads to personal belief, from the goal of immortality to a rationalized life of duty and asceticism. Religion had become, for her, a subject for investigation, in which she concluded that an increasingly rational or "intelligent" world had precipitated the growth of rationality in religion within the context of a world-historical evolution of religions.

The 1850s was perhaps the most productive decade of this prolific writer/social investigator, involving the publication, among other works, of a history of England, a book on Ireland, a book on the family and socialization, and her most controversial *Letters on the Laws of Man's Nature and Development* (1851) with Henry George Atkinson. While this exchange between the two was meant to promote the application of scientific method to social life, Martineau was critical of predicating ideas on evidence from the five senses only. She explored other forms of perception, including mesmerism, which she believed united the subjective and intuitive with the rational inductive approach of science. Its materialism and avowed agnosticism, interpreted by many as atheism, made the book her most controversial, and cost her many friendships, including the close relationship with her brother James. The two in fact neither saw nor spoke to one another again.

Soon after becoming a regular contributor of leaders to the London *Daily News* (1852–66), Martineau took up the task of translating and condensing Comte's *Cours de Philosophie Positive* (1853), seeing the potential of Comtean positivism to systematize science and perhaps knowledge in general. In 1855 Martineau became ill again, and this time she was convinced that she was entering the final stage of her life. As someone who had worked diligently throughout her life and who wished to retain control over her own reputation and ideas, she wrote her *Autobiography*, an account of her life, thought, and work, in which she characterized her own intellectual development as having followed the Law of Three Stages: Theology, Metaphysics, and Science. Having had it printed and stored to await her demise, she appointed her American friend Maria Weston Chapman executor of her papers and the *Autobiography*. In releasing the book posthumously Chapman added a volume of *Memorials*, extracts from letters and documents of Martineau and her correspondents. After 1855, however, Martineau once again recovered and entered an extremely busy and productive period of her life. During her last two decades she published compilations of her writings in periodicals and newspapers, as well as major works on India, on Ireland, on health and the military, and on continuing developments in America.

Hers was a life of thinking and writing, but also of investigation, exploration and education. Her journalism allowed her to apply sociological skills to current history in more than 1,600 *Daily News* articles over fourteen years. She continued to publish periodical articles, sustained her voluminous correspondence, and communicated with many individuals and groups regarding major legal and social debates on such women's issues as the Contagious Diseases Act, laws against women, suffrage, and the Salem witchcraft controversy. But she became increasingly weak and by the mid-1870s was ailing considerably. She died on June 27, 1876 at her home, The Knoll, in Ambleside.

The historical and sociological perspective of Harriet Martineau over a lifetime was shaped by and helped to shape the social context. Her life and writings, in fact, reflect the issues, debates, crises, signs of progress, and changing material life in Victorian England. As a known and respected writer and journalist, she played a significant role in influencing social and political change. Yet she recognized her own marginality as a woman, a Dissenter, a disabled person, someone deprived of higher education, a single woman who had to be self-reliant for her livelihood, a woman in the male worlds of writing and science, an agnostic, and a private person who worked in the public sphere. Thus situated, her experiences, education, and precociousness produced an intense sensitivity and astuteness to the public issues, problems, and societal complexities of her age.

## The Social Context

The increased fate of change in all spheres, particularly technological and scientific, led to an emerging and substantial Victorian belief in progress. People responded enthusiastically to signs of the modern age: the expansion of railways, the Crystal Palace (emblem of modernity), discoveries in science and medicine, experimentation in many fields, the increasing mechanization of work, new practices in agriculture, and a modern economy of reorganized production which replaced traditional family business practices – some of the many indicators of the promise of progress.

But accompanying these changes were doubts, skepticism, questioned beliefs, and the resistances of patriarchy and empire. Optimism coexisted with anxiety, enthusiasm and adventurousness with anti-intellectualism and dogmatism. The class system was being challenged, while the poor, much discussed in the context of the Poor Laws, were increasing in numbers. Martineau was asked by Lord Brougham to write some Poor Law tales in anticipation of changes by the Poor Law Commission (1834), which in fact established workhouses, much deplored by Dickens, in place of outdoor relief. The state of the workers in terms of housing, literacy, skills, and cultural development became a popular topic of discussion. Wages, hours, and safety in industrial production became issues of polarization, pitting factory owners against unionists speaking for workers' rights and welfare. Women's rights were much discussed, but social, political, and economic freedoms became legal realities only very slowly, especially regarding married women's property, legal rights, sexuality, suffrage, occupation, education, etc. Slavery had been formally abolished in Britain and was widely criticized but survived as a system in the West for two-thirds of the century. The traditional practices of medicine were supplanted in some circles by mesmerism and phrenology.

Agriculture brought both increased production and the disasters of famine. The Malthusian thesis created general concern about the issue of food production in relation to population needs. With her pen Martineau joined those who fought against the Corn Laws, which prohibited imports and kept the prices of corn artificially high and therefore unaffordable to many.

Travel itself as a leisure activity of the middle and upper classes was increasing and becoming redefined. Although the rising middle classes were fascinated with travel to "exotic" cultures, from the Caribbean islands, the Middle East, and African nations to the young American democracy, few popular writers were able to present objective analyses of their journeys. Martineau, however, was able to contribute to new and more sophisticated ethnographical and sociological perspectives on other cultures and to show that travel could serve the sphere of scientific investigation. Issues of colonialism and empire became increasingly interrogated, resulting in serious examinations by some of the consequences of empire for peoples around the globe. In that context, particular attention was directed toward India. Martineau spent considerable journalism and two books questioning the role of the British Empire in India and the country's future.

This was the age of reform: reform in public institutions such as prisons, the military, the factory, agricultural policy, education, health, medicine, and government. Martineau participated in the discourse of reform and influenced courses of action taken. She was keenly interested in prisons and prison reform, visited prisons in America and interviewed men in solitary confinement, wrote a novel (never published) on the life of prison reformer John Howard, and ironically shared a common birthplace with Elizabeth Fry (1780–1845), pioneer in English prison reform. In the areas of military and health reform, Martineau collaborated with her friend Florence Nightingale in convincing the government, politicians, and the public of the need for reform and for the advancement of the profession of nursing. On the issue of factory legislation and in no small degree out of her enthusiasm for new technologies, Martineau often found herself on the side of factory owners, sometimes holding workers responsible for carelessness in the workplace; but she was not beyond publicly criticizing conditions in the workplace and worker exploitation.

Above all, women in all classes were participating to a greater extent in the public sphere, through work, travel, publishing, and reform movements. Martineau was among those bringing women's issues into the public discourse and women's contributions into societal spheres.

## THE INTELLECTUAL CONTEXT

As already suggested, Martineau reflects not only the ideas and values of the Enlightenment – natural law, natural rights, liberty, equality, individual self-realization, and societal progress – but also the Victorian frame of mind, embracing the tensions and ambivalences with which Victorians confronted modernity. These perspectives can be best seen, perhaps, in terms of a fundamental tension between the rational and the irrational within the post-Enlightenment milieu. Certainly the clashes between science and religion were significant in the lives of Martineau and her contemporaries. Views on this particular confrontation often determined one's relations with family, friends, colleagues, and the public in general. The Unitarian perspective embraced Enlightenment values while insisting on the importance of religious study and pious self-discipline.

The intellectual world of Martineau's youth was filled with the imposing figures of William Wordsworth, Thomas Carlyle, William J. Fox, and the heady influence of *Pilgrim's Progress* and *Paradise Lost*. In Unitarian circles the works of Newton, Hartley, Priestley, Bacon, Kant, and Stewart were widely read; fascination with the potential of science was prevalent. Among the most attractive and influential intellectual theories were necessarianism, associationism, and later positivism. Necessarianism maintained that natural and unchangeable laws in the universe determine the basis of human action and are beyond the control, if not the understanding, of human beings. This was essentially a theory of causation, but, like a Calvinist version of human conduct, it also carried the message of the "importance of moral habits, the never-failing consequences of moral discipline," as she phrased it in an 1824 article on the study of metaphysics in *The Monthly Repository*. Individual moral responsibility was taken very seriously among the Dissenters, who emphasized particularly one's obligation to serve society, perhaps the Dissenters' first rule of life.

Theories of moral conduct did not suffice, for the inquiring mind, to explain human nature and human behavior *per se*. Hence the turn toward theories of the mind, such as the associationism of David Hartley. Hartley's explanation of the mind, an expansion of Locke's *tabula rasa*, was essentially a process whereby impressions or ideas stimulate related vibrations and associations (Pichanik, 1980). Its limitations prompted many like Martineau to go beyond Hartley to theories of phrenology and mesmerism. Phrenology seemed to provide a more detailed and scientific explanation of the structure and functions of the brain, with little consideration of nonmaterialist or spiritual factors. The influence of materialism grew as Victorians searched for explanations of facts, of the concrete, the verifiable. Phrenology could be translated into practice, into situations of treatment. It led, therefore, into the examination of human nature and the impact of social environment on the individual, of social psychology and sociological questions.

If phrenology broke the barrier toward an understanding of the interconnections between the individual and social influences, mesmerism helped to destroy the other polarity, the mind–body bifurcation. Here materialism is expressed in the context of magnetic force. "Animal-magnetism," expounded by Anton Mesmer (1734–1815), involved the notion that magnetic force could be transmitted from one person to another, with the effect of changing or "curing" certain symptoms. Mesmerists developed the practice of artificial somnambulism, later called hypnosis, a state in which the practitioner could assess the ailment and therefore devise a treatment. Martineau and many of her generation used mesmerism, often quite successfully, to treat symptoms deemed untreatable by medical doctors. Such practices aroused both intrigue and scandal, reflecting Victorians' enormous ambivalence about theories and practices which challenged traditional medicine.

Nevertheless, these theories and practices derived from the intellectual quest for certainty, for proof, for useful facts, for a reconstruction of life based on logical, rational principles. This quest gathered momentum and led to the attraction of positivism for thinkers like Martineau, Mill, Whewell, Comte, and others. Saint-Simon and Comte outlined the sciences, assigned them functions and spheres of study, and showed that science could become the source of social reorganization, mental hygiene, and new knowledge. The controversial nature of these discourses can be seen, for example, in the fact that Martineau and Atkinson's *Letters on the Laws of Man's Nature and Development* (1851), in which they simply reiterated the empirical and materialist discourse and made the case for scientific paradigms, scandalized the British public.

Several intellectual developments and movements in the late eighteenth and early nineteenth centuries significantly shaped the discourse of Martineau's generation. Among the most influential were political economy, the equality and human rights issue, Malthusian theory, and socialism. Here again, ambivalence regarding the merits and costs of industrial capitalism, its effects on population trends, the uncertainties of democratic revolutions, and, finally, the increase of both profits and the proportion of poor in society created theories and opinions which linked, in sometimes peculiar ways, traditional attitudes and institutions with modern goals and practices. This can be seen particularly with regard to issues of political economy and in socialism around such issues as the Poor Laws, Chartism, factory legislation, trade unionism, the class system, and the portrayal of the classes in literature.

## IMPACT

In the context of the history of sociological theory and methodology, Harriet Martineau was not only more creative and innovative but also more influential than has previously been assumed. As a member of a generation of Victorian intellectuals, writers, politicians, artists, and professionals attempting to understand and come to terms with the impact of modernity on British society, still imbued with traditionalism, she lent a special voice to the discourse. As a woman situated outside of academic life, as a self-educated and independent scholar, she is not unlike her male contemporaries and predecessors whose education and backgrounds were diverse and, in twentieth-century terms, unorthodox.

By the fact of the popularity of her writings and the breadth of her reputation, however controversial at times, she was a significant author in the Victorian period. With her forays into literature, particularly given her talent for moralistic tales and novels and novelettes of social realism, she inspired her contemporaries: Charlotte Brontë, George Eliot, Matthew Arnold, for example. Her depiction of community dynamics and the culture of social classes in *Deerbrook*, for instance, made an enormous impression on authors and readers alike. Her tales for children, most specifically in *The Playfellow* series, were read to and by British children for many generations. These tales and most of her fictional work were translated into many other languages (German, French, Swedish, Japanese, and Russian, for example) as well, so that she took on a kind of international reputation and presence.

In matters of government legislation regarding the Poor Laws, the Corn Laws, public education, property laws, and individuals' rights and freedoms, Martineau's ideas as expressed in fiction or in periodicals and newspapers exercised considerable influence. The fact that politicians frequently called upon Martineau to help them in proffering a particular political stance on controversial issues offers important commentary on the value placed by the public on her points of view. She effectively used the didactic mode to convince the public of the rectitude of her particular perspective, particularly on the issues of slavery, women, work, and education, as we have seen. But she also exerted considerable authority on issues of the empire, and its impact on colonials and on British society itself. Martineau became recognized as a social critic and authority on American society, India, Ireland, and the Middle East.

In scientific concerns, particularly on the need for the moral or social sciences, Martineau participated in the discourse of science and scientific epistemology and in an examination of the nature and goals of science as a social enterprise. Clearly she was concerned with the practical as well as theoretical and empirical uses of science. She participated in a circle of dialogue and influence which included Charles Darwin, Herbert Spencer, William Whewell, John Stuart Mill, and William G. Sumner. Even in the context of the "scandal" of her book with Atkinson, she brought to the public discourse the idea of a scientific study of the brain and the mind–body problem.

Nowhere was she more influential than in her writings on slavery and on the condition of women. She wrote extensively and over her lifetime on the whole moral question of slavery and demonstrated that societies dependent on that form of domination were bound for failure and crisis. In addition to her novel about l'Ouverture, her extensive analyses of American slavery and the Civil War were read widely and helped to shape the moral positions of many in Europe and America. "A source of much controversy in both Britain and America, it [*Society in America*] played a major role in forming English opinion, particularly among the liberal left of her day" (Lipset, 1981, p. 10). The other instance of her focus on subordination and repression concerned the status of women, in England, Ireland, America, India, and the Middle East, as we have seen. She was the first to sign a petition on behalf of suffrage for women to John Stuart Mill for presentation in the House of Commons. She took up the cause for reform of the Married Women's Property Act, and for women's right to work at a decent wage under humane and acceptable conditions. She lectured the British public on the issue of gender equality in education.

Even early in her career, Martineau's reputation as a social analyst was already rather significant, as indicated by the fact that, shortly after returning from America, she was offered by Saunders and Otley Publishers the opportunity to become editor of a proposed new periodical "to treat of philosophical priniciples, abstract and applied, of sociology." She would have accepted the invitation enthusiastically but for the intervention of her brother James, who strongly discouraged her formal involvement in such secular scientific work, so Harriet missed an unusual opportunity to move into more academic circles.

Martineau's impact on later sociological theory and sociologists and social scientists has been underexamined and underestimated. Her contributions in many instances have been unacknowledged. But when we examine the intellectual backgrounds of leading figures, as well as some of the most innovative and renowned theories and empirical studies, we find the presence of Martineau. Some of these instances have been pointed out above. It can be shown that Martineau was read and appreciated by not only Comte, Spencer, Durkheim, Marx, and Veblen, but also Herkner, Myrdal, Beatrice Webb, Charlotte Gilman, Alice Clark, Edith Abbott, and Annie Besant. Martineau's ideas and original theories, as well as investigatory innovations, converge with their work. The road was not smooth, however. She was criticized and slandered by Karl Marx and Frederic Harrison, and unacknowledged by Émile Durkheim (theories on suicide and on religion), Alexis de Tocqueville (studies of America), Thorstein Veblen, and Gunnar Myrdal.

Evaluation of Martineau's work has been complicated by the scope of her writings and of the issues she engaged with. Like Weber, she is interested in the motivational structures underlying behavior, particularly as they are shaped by cultural and historical contexts and expressed in value systems. Like Durkheim, she understands that the morals and values expressed in religion and translated into politics, for example, lie at the centre of social cohesion, and that the interconnection between the individual and larger social structures is complex and compelling, as studies of suicide reveal. Like Marx, Martineau explored various aspects of work, such as the social organization of work, alienation, and the impact of gender and class on work.

Within the third wave of feminism and, in the last part of the twentieth century, the search for sociology's roots, women's contributions to the emergence of sociology are being recognized, although much remains to be done. Seymour Martin Lipset, in his introduction to the 1961 republication of *Society in America*, stated "Harriet Martineau's *Society in America* is one of the most important of the early efforts to describe and account for these seemingly constant aspects of American society" (Lipset, 1981, p. 9). "Harriet Martineau...belongs in the annals of those who carved out a niche for a science of society. Moreover, she was one of the first to apply explicitly a sociological approach to comparative analysis" (ibid., p. 37). In the sesquicentennial publication of *How to Observe Morals and Manners*, Michael Hill (1989, p. xxii) asserted that "Martineau undertook pioneering studies – substantive, theoretical, and methodological studies – in what is now called sociology." "In her maturity she was an astute sociological theorist, methodologist, and analyst of the first order" (Hill, 1991, p. 289). Simon Dentith maintained that Martineau was a central figure in the nineteenth-century attempt to "make immediately and practically recognizable principles [political economy] which were widely thought to be abstract and difficult to understand." Deegan stated that Martineau "dared to write her views on society and in support of a daring young discipline: sociology" (Deegan, 1991, p. 14). In *Women Founders of the Social Sciences*, McDonald (1994) shows Martineau's significant contributions to sociology, particularly to methodology. Lengermann and Niebrugge-Brantley (1998, p. 39) have demonstrated that, "Martineau represents in the founding generation both the interpretive paradigm...and the feminist paradigm."

## ASSESSMENT

Undoubtedly, Harriet Martineau merits recognition of her contributions to the field of sociology in terms of her philosophy of science and epistemology, her innovations in methodology and empirical investigation, and her theoretical work, conceptual contributions, and critical analyses. Expressing her vision of a science of society, she engaged in the timely education of both academics and the public regarding the need for such an enterprise. The perspectives she brought to her arguments and analyses were singular in their stance and impact. Singular as well was her ability not only to communicate with the public in her role as public educator, but also to connect sociological knowledge to public issues, to demonstrate the important ways in which knowledge can and must be useful, and to utilize journalism to transmit sociological understandings on local, national, and international subjects. The quality of her work stands well against the standards of the nineteenth century and therefore she clearly can be recognized as the first woman sociologist.

Obviously criticisms can be made of the theoretical sociology of Harriet Martineau. She was creative and original in her theoretical analyses but somewhat incomplete, perhaps a reflection of a proliferation of projects, subjects, and genres in which she worked. Her sociological concepts and typologies are innovative and enlightening, as in the cases of types of religion and suicide, but more elaborate analysis is needed. In the case of her critique of positivism, it is clear that she has a nuanced position but she does not provide us with an explication, which would have been informative and important in the context. Martineau addressed the subject of investigator bias as well as the problem of her own biases (*How to Observe Morals and Manners*); indeed, she frequently indulged in self-criticism and even self-effacement. But her own class origins and personal background influenced her work, often creating serious contradictions, as in her analysis of societal power relations, where she consistently supports the interests of women and slaves but not necessarily of workers or the British poor.

Martineau was an opinionated woman, although a similar male contemporary might have been described as having "definite and profoundly held views." Webb and others refer to her as dogmatic. She was seen as an apologist for industrial capitalism and bourgeois power, considered by some to be an "ultra *laissez-faire*" liberal, at least in her early years. In fact, politically she was quite ambivalent, vacillating between the values and goals of liberalism and socialism and reflecting the mixed attitude toward the Enlightenment of her generation's "Victorian frame of mind" (Houghton, 1957).

On the other hand, she was a master of the didactic, which she used effectively to educate and convince. Martineau was an extremely skilled empirical investigator. Her methodological treatise provides a clear guide to maximizing objectivity and clarity in gathering facts, views, attitudes and opinions, and the life experiences of one's subjects. However, she could be extremely moralistic, critical of others' relationships and ethics. Throughout her life she promoted the social usefulness of knowledge, but she was not beyond using knowledge for purposes of promoting a particular political agenda.

Perhaps a singular characteristic of Harriet Martineau as a sociologist was her ability to see the interconnections of theory, empiricism, and social policy. Her work flowed easily among these three intellectual functions, because she was keenly aware that a science of society had to operate on the three levels of social knowledge to validate its own *raison d'être* and societal relevance.

# Bibliography

## Writings of Harriet Martineau

*Illustrations of Political Economy*, 9 volumes. 1832–4. London: Charles Fox.

*Poor Laws and Paupers Illustrated*, 4 parts. 1833. London: Charles Fox.

*Illustrations of Taxation*, 5 parts. 1834. London: Charles Fox.

*Miscellanies*, 2 volumes. 1836. Boston: Hilliard Grey.

*Society in America*, 3 volumes. 1837. London: Saunders and Otley (edited by Seymour Martin Lipset, New York: Doubleday; New Brunswick, NJ: Transaction Books, 1981).

*How to Observe Morals and Manners*. 1838. London: Charles Knight (paperback edition, New Brunswick, NJ: Transaction Publishers, 1989; introduction by Michael R. Hill).

*Retrospect of Western Travel*, 3 volumes. 1838. London: Saunders and Otley.

Domestic Service. 1838. *London and Westminster Review*, 29, August, 405–32.

The Martyr Age of the United States. 1838. *The London and Westminster Review*, 32, December, 1–59.

*The Guide to Service: the Housemaid, the Lady's Maid, the Maid of All Work*. 1838, 1839. London: Charles Knight.

*Deerbrook, a Novel*, 3 volumes. 1839. London: Edward Moxon.

*The Martyr Age of the United States*. 1839. New York: S. W. Benedict.

*The Playfellow: Settlers at Home; The Peasant and the Prince; Feats on the Fjord*, 4 volumes. 1841. London: Charles Knight.

*The Hour and the Man: an Historical Romance*, 3 volumes. 1841. London: Cassell.

*Letters on Mesmerism*. 1844. London: Edward Moxon.

*Life in the Sickroom: Essays by an Invalid*. 1844. London: Edward Moxon.

*Eastern Life: Past and Present*, 3 volumes. 1848. London: Edward Moxon.

*The History of England During the Thirty Years' Peace 1816–1846*, 2 volumes. 1849. London: Charles Knight.

*Household Education*. 1849. London: Edward Moxon.

*Introduction to the History of the Peace, from 1800 to 1815*. 1851. London: Charles Knight.

*Letters on the Laws of Man's Nature and Development*, with Henry G. Atkinson. 1851. London: John Chapman (Boston: Josiah Mendum, 1889).

*Letters from Ireland*. 1852. London: John Chapman.

*The Positive Philosophy of Auguste Comte* (freely translated and condensed by Harriet Martineau), 2 volumes. 1853. London: John Chapman.

Results of the Census of 1851. 1854. *Westminster Review*, 61, April, 323–57.

*The Factory Controversy: a Warning Against Meddling Legislation*. 1855. Manchester: National Association of Factory Occupiers.

*A History of the American Compromises*. 1856. London: John Chapman.

*British Rule in India: a Historical Sketch*. 1857. London: Smith, Elder.

"Manifest Destiny" of the American Union. 1857 *Westminster Review*, 68, July, 1–25.

*The "Manifest Destiny" of the American Union*. 1857. Boston: American Anti-Slavery Society.

Female Dress in 1857. 1857. *Westminster Review*, 68, October, 315–40.

*Suggestions towards the Future Government of India*. 1858. London: Smith, Elder.

The Religion of Positivity. 1858. *Westminster Review*, 69, April, 305–50.

The Slave-trade in 1858. 1858. *Edinburgh Review*, 108, October, 276–99.

*Endowed Schools of Ireland.* 1859. London: Smith, Elder.
*England and Her Soldiers.* 1859. London: Smith, Elder.
Female Industry. 1859. *Edinburgh Review,* 109, April, 151–73.
*Health, Husbandry, and Handicraft.* 1861. London: Bradbury and Evans.
Modern Domestic Service. 1862. *Edinburgh Review,* 115, April, 409–39.
Convict System in England and Ireland. 1863. *Edinburgh Review,* 117, January, 241–68.
Middle-class Education in England: Boys. 1864. *Cornhill Magazine,* 10, October, 409–26.
Middle-class Education in England: Girls. 1864. *Cornhill Magazine,* 10, November, 549–68.
Life in the Criminal Class. 1865. *Edinburgh Review,* 122, October, 337–71.
Salem Witchcraft. 1868. *Edinburgh Review,* 128, July, 1–47.
*Biographical Sketches.* 1869 (new edition, London: Macmillan, 1877).
*Harriet Martineau's Autobiography, with Memorials by Maria Weston Chapman,* 3 volumes. 1877. London: Smith, Elder.

## Further reading

Arbuckle, Elisabeth Sanders (ed.) (1983) *Harriet Martineau's Letters to Fanny Wedgwood.* Stanford, CA: Stanford University Press.
Arbuckle, Elisabeth Sanders (ed.) (1994) *Harriet Martineau in the London Daily News: Selected Contributions, 1852–1866.* New York: Garland.
Blaug, Mark (1958) Political Economy to Be Read as Literature. In *Ricardian Economics: a Historical Study.* New Haven, CT: Yale University Press, chapter 7.
Cawelti, John G. (1963) Conformity and Democracy in America: Some Reflections Occasioned by the Republication of Martineau's *Society in America. Ethics,* 73 (April), 208–13.
David, Deirdre (1987). *Intellectual Woman and the Victorian Patriarchy: Harriet Martineau, Elizabeth Barrett Browning, George Eliot.* Ithaca, NY: Cornell University Press.
Deegan, Mary Jo (ed.) (1991) *Women in Sociology: a Bio-bibliographical Sourcebook.* New York: Greenwood Press.
Durkheim, Émile (1951) *Suicide: a Study in Sociology,* trans. by John A. Spaulding and George Simpson. New York: The Free Press.
Durkheim, Émile (1995) *Elementary Forms of Religious Life,* trans. by Karen E. Fields. New York: The Free Press.
Frawley, Maria H. (1992) Harriet Martineau in America: Gender and the Discourse of Sociology. *The Victorian Newsletter,* Spring, 13–20.
Freedgood, Elaine (1995) Banishing Panic: Harriet Martineau and the Popularization of Political Economy. *Victorian Studies,* Autumn, 33–53.
Frost, Cy (1991) Autocracy and the Matrix of Power: Issues of Propriety and Economics in the Work of Mary Wollstonecraft, Jane Austen, and Harriet Martineau. *Tulsa Studies in Women's Literature,* 10 (Fall), 253–71.
Harrison, Frederic (1896) Introduction. In *The Positive Philosophy of Auguste Comte,* trans. and condensed by Harriet Martineau, 3 vols. London.
Hill, Michael (1989) Empiricism and Reason in Harriet Martineau's Sociology. In Michael Hill (ed.), *How to Observe Morals and Manners.* New Brunswick, NJ: Transaction.
Hill, Michael (1991) Harriet Martineau (1802–1876). In Mary Jo Deegan (ed.), *Women in Sociology: a Bio-bibliographical Sourcebook.* New York: Greenwood Press, pp. 289–97.

Hoecker-Drysdale, Susan (1992) *Harriet Martineau: First Woman Sociologist.* Oxford: Berg.

Hoecker-Drysdale, Susan (1995) The Enigma of Harriet Martineau's Letters on Science. *Women's Writing: the Elizabethan to Victorian Period,* 2, 155–65.

Hoecker-Drysdale, Susan (1998) Harriet Martineau (1802–1876): Kritische Sozial-forschung: Theorie und Praxis. In Claudia Honegger und Theresa Wobbe (eds), *Frauen in der Soziologie: Neun Porträts.* Munich: Verlag C. H. Beck, pp. 28–59.

Houghton, Walter (1957) *The Victorian Frame of Mind, 1830–1870.* New Haven, CT: Yale University Press.

Hunter, Shelagh (1995) *Harriet Martineau: the Poetics of Moralism.* Hants: Scolar Press.

Hutcheon, Pat Duffy (1996) *Leaving the Cave: Evolutionary Naturalism in Social-scientific Thought.* Waterloo: Wilfrid Laurier University Press.

Lengermann, Patricia Madoo and Niebrugge-Brantley, Jill (1996) Early Women Socio-logists and Classical Sociological Theory: 1830–1930. In George Ritzer (ed.), *Classical Sociological Theory,* 2nd edn. New York: McGraw-Hill, pp. 294–328.

Lengermann, Patricia Madoo and Niebrugge-Brantley, Jill (1998) *The Women Founders: Sociology and Social Theory, 1830–1930.* Boston: McGraw-Hill.

Lipset, Seymour Martin (1981) Harriet Martineau's America. In *Society in America* by Harriet Martineau, abridged and edited by S. M. Lipset. New York: Doubleday, pp. 5–42.

Logan, Deborah (1997) Harem Life, West and East. *Women's Studies,* 26, 449–74.

McDonald, Lynn (1994) *Women Founders of the Social Sciences.* Ottawa: Carleton University Press.

Marx, Karl (1887) *Capital: a Critical Analysis of Capitalist Production,* the English edition, edited by Frederick Engels, Vol. I. London: S. Sonnenschein, Lowry & Co.

Melman, Billie (1992) *Women's Orients: English Women and the Middle East, 1718–1918.* Ann Arbor: University of Michigan.

Myrdal, Gunnar (1944) *An American Dilemma: the Negro Problem and Modern Democracy.* New York: Harper.

O'Donnell, Margaret G. (1983) Harriet Martineau: a Popular Early Economics Educa-tor. *Journal of Economic Education,* Fall, 59–64.

Peterson, Linda (1990) Harriet Martineau: Masculine Discourse, Female Sage. In Thais E. Morgan (ed.), *Victorian Sages and Cultural Discourse: Renegotiating Gender and Power.* New Brunswick, NJ: Rutgers University Press.

Pichanik, Valerie Kossew (1980) *Harriet Martineau: the Woman and Her Work, 1802–1876.* Ann Arbor: University of Michigan.

Postlethwaite, Diana (1984) New Faiths – the Philosophy of Necessity, "Force," and Mesmerism: Charles Bray and Harriet Martineau. In *Making It Whole: a Victorian Circle and the Shape of Their World.* Columbus: Ohio University Press.

Postlethwaite, Diana (1989) Mothering and Mesmerism in the Life of Harriet Martineau. *Signs: Journal of Women in Culture and Society,* 14, 583–609.

Reinharz, Shulamit (1989) Teaching the History of Women in Sociology: or Dorothy Swaine Thomas, Wasn't She the Woman Married to William I? *The American Socio-logist,* 20 (Spring), 87–94.

Reinharz, Shulamit (1992) *Feminist Methods in Social Research.* New York: Oxford University Press.

Riedesel, Paul L. (1981) Who *Was* Harriet Martineau? *Journal of the History of Socio-logy,* 3 (Spring/Summer), 63–80.

Rivenburg, Narola (1932) Harriet Martineau: an Example of Victorian Conflict. PhD dissertation, Columbia University.

Rivlin, Joseph B. (1947) *Harriet Martineau: a Bibliography of Her Separately Printed Books*. New York: The New York Public Library.

Rossi, Alice (1973) The First Woman Sociologist: Harriet Martineau. In A. Rossi (ed.), *The Feminist Papers: from Adams to de Beauvoir*. New York: Columbia University Press, pp. 117–34.

Sanders, Valerie (1986) *Reason over Passion: Harriet Martineau and the Victorian Novel*. Brighton: Harvester Press.

Sanders, Valerie (ed.) (1990) *Harriet Martineau: Selected Letters*. Oxford: Clarendon Press.

Smith, Sidonie (1987) Harriet Martineau's Autobiography. In *A Poetics of Women's Autobiography: Marginality and the Fictions of Self-representation*. Bloomington: Indiana University Press.

Spender, Dale (1982) Harriet Martineau. In *Women of Ideas and What Men Have Done to Them, from Aphra Behn to Adrienne Rich*. London: Routledge & Kegan Paul, pp. 125–35.

Terry, James L. (1983) Bringing Women in: a Modest Proposal. *Teaching Sociology*, 10, 251–61.

Thomas, Gillian (1985) *Harriet Martineau*. Boston: Twayne Publishers.

Thomson, Dorothy (1973) Harriet Martineau. In *Adam Smith's Daughters*. Hicksville, NY: Exposition.

Tocqueville, Alexis de (1969) *Democracy in America*, trans. by George Lawrence, ed. by J. P. Mayer. New York: Doubleday.

Walters, Margaret (1976) Mary Wollstonecraft, Harriet Martineau and Simone de Beauvoir. In J. Mitchell and A. Oakley (eds), *The Rights and Wrongs of Women*. Harmondsworth: Penguin, pp. 304–78.

Webb, Robert K. (1959) *A Handlist of Contributions to the Daily News by Harriet Martineau, 1852–1866*. Photocopy, published in Elisabeth Sanders Arbuckle (1994) *Harriet Martineau in the London Daily News: Selected Contributions, 1852–1866*. New York: Garland.

Webb, Robert Kiefer (1960) *Harriet Martineau: a Radical Victorian*. New York: Columbia.

Weiner, Gaby Harriet (1983) Martineau: a Reassessment. In Dale Spender (ed.), *Feminist Theorists: Three Centuries of Key Women Thinkers*. New York: Pantheon Books.

Winter, Alison (1995) Harriet Martineau and the Reform of the Invalid in Victorian England. *The Historical Journal*, 38(3), 597–616.

# 3

# Herbert Spencer

## Jonathan H. Turner

Most introductory sociology texts mention Herbert Spencer, usually as a proponent of such theoretical blunders as organismic analogies, unilinear evolution, and functional analysis. He is one of those "founding fathers" whose methodological and substantive works are less prominent than those of other founders. Yet Spencer was far more widely read in his time than either Émile Durkheim or Max Weber; he rivaled Marx in intellectual influence in the nineteenth century; and he was one of the most respected scholars of his time. Why, then, do we give so little thought to this founding father, whose influence in the latter half of the nineteenth century extended far beyond the narrow confines of academia?

Part of the answer is ideological. Spencer's phrase "survival of the fittest" as it inspired Social Darwinists and his staunch support for what would today be viewed as a "right-wing" and "libertarian" moral and political philosophy make him highly suspect in a field whose ideological sympathies are more collectivistic. Another part of the answer is that, though he had died a decade earlier, his works still represented the most prominent evolutionary scheme at the time when evolutionary thought in general fell into disfavor for its ethnocentricism and racism. Yet another part of the answer is that Spencer thought "big" and across disciplines at a time when science was beginning to specialize and partition itself. Still another part of the answer is that one of sociology's emerging icons, Émile Durkheim, was able to portray Spencer as a crude utilitarian and individualist (Perrin, 1975) – an unfair assessment of Spencer's sociology which, surprisingly, continental and American sociology have tended to accept uncritically. And so when Talcott Parsons (1937) asked "who now reads Spencer?" the answer was clear: very few.

The goal of this chapter, then, is to indicate why Spencer should be given another reading as an important sociological theorist.[1] We will begin with his methodological statements and arrangement of data; then, we will turn to the theory that he developed and so copiously illustrated with the data that he had arrayed; finally, we will turn to Spencer the person and the context of his time in order to get a better understanding of why he produced his theory and why this theory continues to be relevant to contemporary sociology.

## THE METHODOLOGY

### The Study of Sociology

Between 1872 and 1873, Spencer published the serialized essays that would become his *The Study of Sociology* (1873). In this book, Spencer makes a strong case for developing a science of human organization. Spencer opens *The Study of Sociology* with two important observations. First, people in general and policy-makers in particular implicitly assume that there are generic forces operating in the universe; otherwise, they could not so confidently proclaim that this or that policy would eliminate a particular social problem. Such proclamations, Spencer argued, reveal an implicit view that the social universe operates in a law-like manner. What lay persons implicitly assume, and what scientific sociologists must pursue, are the laws of human organization. For, if "no effect can be counted upon – everything is chaotic," and so "it behooves us to use all diligence in ascertaining what the forces are, what are their laws, and what are the ways in which they cooperate" (Spencer, 1873, pp. 45, 47). However, and this is the second introductory observation in *The Study of Sociology*, those who argue that the laws of sociology cannot be like those of the "exact sciences" fail to recognize that many of the insights in these sciences are not stated mathematically but, instead, qualitatively; and this fact does not make such laws any less scientific. When scientists must work with natural systems, the precise values of variables and their interactions pose problems of exact measurement and easy quantification. Indeed, as Spencer stressed, there are "factors so numerous and so hard to measure, that to develop our knowledge of their relations into the quantitative form will be extremely difficult, if not impossible" (ibid., p. 45).

The bulk of *The Study of Sociology* is devoted to the methodological problems involved in collecting and analyzing sociological data. Spencer argues that data should be collected and observations made primarily with respect to generic forces rather than to time-bound, particular, and contextual events. Making such observations is, however, difficult for a number of reasons (ibid., pp. 74–92): (a) research problems are often selected for their currency as dictated by public and political moods; (b) research problems are often defined by those who finance research, and these benefactors always have their own self-serving agenda; (c) particular research techniques often come to dominate and skew the nature of the research questions asked and the data collected; (d) research problems can be distorted by commitments to research paradigms and to particular ideologies; and (e) research problems are often biased by the position of investigators in social structures (inside and outside of academia).

These problems are compounded by biases inherent in data gathering and analysis: (a) scholars rarely wish to see their "cherished hypothesis" disproved, so they skew data collection and analysis in conformity with their hypothesis; (b) scholars will rarely accept observations and conclusions that go against their ideological commitments; (c) scholars will often have difficulty in understanding the "meaning" of situations among those they study and will, therefore, miss important dynamics; and (d) scholars rarely collect data longitudinally, and, as a consequence, data and conclusions are often based upon cross-sections of processes at one point in time.

For Spencer, an awareness of these problems and a "mental discipline" can militate against them (ibid., pp. 314–15). Moreover, and this is an extremely important point for contemporary sociology, a division of labor between theory and research can help to overcome these biases. For "men [and women also, one presumes] who have aptitudes for accumulating observations are rarely men given to generalization; while men given to generalizing are men who mostly [use] the facts of others" (ibid., p. 315). There must exist a "kindred antagonism" between theory and research, each working to militate against sources of bias in the other. For as researchers test theories and as theorists call into question the relevance and significance of data, a natural corrective is built into the cumulation of knowledge.

## Descriptive Sociology

When reading Spencer's *The Principles of Sociology* (1874–96), one is struck by the immense amount of descriptive detail from historical and ethnographic sources. In fact, *The Principles of Sociology* is such a long work, numbering some 2,200 pages, because it is filled with data. So we should ask: where did Spencer get these data?

In 1873, Spencer published the first volume of his *Descriptive Sociology* (1873–1934).[2] In this and the subsequent volumes Spencer hired professional scholars to array historical and ethnographic data into common categories. The goal was to record the features of past and present societies in ways that facilitated comparisons, and toward this end, each oversized volume contains tabular presentations of data in addition to more discursive summaries. Volumes on societies with a written history record data into the categories from different historical epochs, whereas those on preliterates group societies by geographical region and record the available data for each society into the categories (see Turner, 1985; Turner and Maryanski, 1988; Turner et al., 1998, for reviews of the exact categories used to organize presentation of data).

This project was initiated in 1867 and ended long after Spencer's death in 1934 (Spencer had left money in his will for completion and updating of the descriptions recorded under each category and subcategory). Thus, by 1873, Spencer had introduced his own "human relations area files," some sixty years before the idea was resurrected by George P. Murdock (1953, 1965), who, no doubt, got the inspiration from his teacher, Albert G. Keller, who had been well acquainted with Spencer's *Descriptive Sociology* (because he and William Graham Sumner used the data of *Descriptive Sociology* in their four volume *The Science of Society* (1927), as had Sumner in his *Folkways* (1907)). But by the time that Murdock had begun to assemble ethnographic data in the late 1920s into the Human Relations Area Files (HRAF), most of these preliterate societies had been dramatically transformed by Western exploration and colonial expansion. Moreover, the ethnographies were often specialized, focusing on one theme or topic and, hence, failing to record crucial information.

The great loss in this chain of events is that, as Spencer's star declined in the late 1880s and 1890s, his category system, which is almost equal to that of HRAF today, was lost, with the result that the chance to record critical information on fast-disappearing preliterate societies was gone forever (Turner and Maryanski, 1988). Hence, both sociology and anthropology today suffer from an inadequate database for assessing general theoretical principles; and this inadequacy, along with a growing anti-science movement, has led to a disillusionment with the comparative method in anthropology. Surprisingly, the revival of evolutionary thinking in sociology during the 1960s (e.g. Lenski, 1966; Parsons, 1966, 1971) and again in the 1990s (e.g. Sanderson, 1996; Turner, 1996) has increased interest in societal comparisons, and the fact that Spencer's early lead was never pursued systematically only makes this interest in comparative sociology more difficult to realize. The data are gone, forever; and if Spencer's categories had been used as a basic system for recording ethnographic information on preliterates, comparative sociology would stand on a much firmer empirical base.

In terms of methodology, then, Spencer recognized that systematic comparisons among data assembled from very different types of societies were essential to developing inductively, and assessing deductively, abstract theoretical principles. In the end, Spencer recognized that a science is only as good as its theoretical principles, assessed against a broad spectrum of data.

## THE THEORY

### The general systems approach

Long before Spencer turned to sociological analysis in the 1870s, he had written treatises on biology and psychology. Along with his sociological works, these treatises were part of what today we might term a "general systems" approach, where the goal is to articulate a few abstract principles from which the scientific laws of various domains of the universe can be deduced. Thus, the laws of biology, psychology, sociology, and, in Spencer's eye, ethics could be deduced from a few "first principles." In 1862, Spencer wrote these principles down in a book titled *First Principles*, which represented his effort to adopt ideas from Newtonian physics to the analysis of social and ethical phenomena. Indeed, much of the strange vocabulary of Spencer's law of evolution as "an integration of matter and concomitant dissipation of motion, during which the matter passes from an indefinite and incoherent homogeneity to a definite heterogeneity, and during which the retained motion undergoes a parallel transformation," must be seen in this light. For Spencer really believed that he had found the basic principles that guide all domains of the universe – physical, organic, social, and ethical. The details of this analysis are less important than the vision that he had: to unify the sciences with a few fundamental principles, a goal that contemporary general systems theorists still seek to accomplish (e.g. Bailey, 1994).

The basic "general systems" principles in Spencer's grand scheme revolve around a vision of the social world as involving aggregation of individuals, differentiation of their activities into specialized roles and structures, integration of these differentiated roles and structures, and, potentially, disintegration of the social mass when bases of integration prove inviable. The core of Spencerian sociology thus represents an effort to develop general sociological laws on aggregation, differentiation, integration of increased complexity, and pressures for dissolution or disintegration.

## The sociological laws of evolution

Spencer is the founder of functional sociology. True, Auguste Comte had employed organismic analogies where the function of a part for the larger "body social" was to be discovered, but it was Spencer who converted Comte's vague analogies into a rigorous sociology. Thus, as Spencer sought to develop the laws of sociology, he couched them in an evolutionary and functionalist framework. The evolutionary portion of this framework emphasized aggregation, growth, differentiation, integration, and disintegration, whereas the functionalist portion stressed the need to examine differentiating social structures in terms of their consequences for meeting the fundamental needs of the social whole.

The functional part of Spencer's scheme begins with his famous organismic analogy, where he compares the properties of organisms to super-organic structures involving relations among organisms. Both organic and super-organic reveal, Spencer (1874–96, volume 1, p. 448) argued, a "parallelism of principle in the arrangement of components" along several lines: both differentiate structure as they grow, both differentiate functions to sustain the life of the whole, both achieve integration through mutual dependence of parts, both are composed of more elementary forms of life, and both can live on for a while after destruction of the systemic whole. If this were all Spencer had to offer sociology, there would be little reason to consider his work important; yet, unfortunately, it is this organismic analogy that still guides contemporary understandings of Spencer.

Far more important than this simple analogy are the functional and evolutionary ideas developed by Spencer. The functional approach pursued by Spencer was analytical: what basic needs or imperatives must all super-organic systems meet if they are to remain viable in their environments? Although Spencer's vocabulary varies somewhat, the substance of his answer to this question remained constant: all systems must regulate their relations with the environment in terms of protection from enemies and from the vicissitudes of the nature; all systems must secure and transform resources necessary to sustain life forms; all systems must reproduce their constituent members and the structural forms and symbols necessary to sustain individuals and the structural units of the larger super-organic whole; all systems must regulate and coordinate activities of constituent parts of the system; and all systems must be able to distribute resources, information, and individuals throughout the systemic whole. Hence, as social systems grow and differentiate, they develop distinctive structures to meet basic functions (ibid., pp. 498–519). This kind of functional analysis anticipates, of course, the functional schemes that became so prominent at the midpoint of the twentieth century, but Spencer did not stop here. Rather, he used this functional scheme to articulate abstract laws about the dynamics of differentiating social systems as they evolve from simple to more complex forms. Indeed, the functionalism soon recedes into the background as an implicit analytic framework for guiding the development of true scientific principles. Yet, for better or worse, we must give Spencer credit for founding functional analysis in sociology; for all who followed him – Durkheim, A. R. Radcliffe-Brown, Bronislaw Malinowski, Parsons, and others who are identified with functionalism – built upon the foundations laid by Spencer (Turner and Maryanski, 1979).

To convert his analytical functionalism into a true theory, Spencer turned to the analysis of evolution. Spencer analyzed evolution in two ways: (a) as a description of stages as societies become ever more complex (Spencer, 1874–96, volume 1, pp. 549–87); and (b) as a set of models and principles about the dynamics of population growth and social system differentiation (ibid., pp. 463–597). It is this second sense of evolution that we will explore here.

Let us begin by discursively summarizing Spencer's argument; then, we can convert this review into more formal principles in table 3.1. For Spencer, the key driving force of human evolution, or the building up of social structure, is population growth, which, in turn, increases with (a) escalated birth rates, (b) conquest or annexation of other populations, and (c) immigration. As a population grows from any or all of these sources, segmentation or the creation of additional social structures like those already in place will increase, but eventually, segmentation and proliferation of older structural forms can no longer accommodate the increased social mass. The reason for this is that logistical loads for sustaining, regulating, and coordinating activities increase to the point where new kinds of social structures will have to be created, or the population will disintegrate.

**Table 3.1**  The abstract laws of Spencer's theory

---

*The Law of Differentiation*

As a population grows, and the greater the rate of this growth, the greater will be the logistical loads facing this population and the greater will be the selection pressures for differentiation and elaboration of productive, reproductive, regulatory, and distributive structures and associated cultural symbols.

*The Law of Production*

The differentiation and elaboration of productive structures are a multiplicative function of:

A   The size and rate of growth of a population

B   The level of technology available to productive units
C   The skill of labor or human capital
D   The availability of natural resources
E   The differentiation of distributive structures
F   The differentiation of centers of political-legal authority and moderate levels of regulation

## The Law of Reproduction

The differentiation and elaboration of reproductive structures are a multiplicative function of:

A   The size and rate of growth of a population
B   The differentiation of productive, regulatory, and distributive structures and associated cultural symbols

## The Laws of Regulation

The differentiation and elaboration of regulatory structures (consolidation and concentration of power) are an additive function of:

A   The size and rate of growth of a population
B   The level of material surplus generated by productive forces
C   The volume and velocity of exchange transactions
D   The level of inequality and associated internal threat
E   The level of external threat from surrounding populations

The intensity of selection pressures for centralization of power and its use in regulation of internal activities are an additive function of:

A   The level of internal and external threat
B   The duration and extent to which differentiation of operative and distributive processes have remained unregulated by political authority
C   The intensity of conservative ideological mobilization for increased social control by political authority

The intensity of selection pressures for decentralization of power and its less restrictive use are:

A   An inverse function of the level of internal threat stemming from inequalities
B   An inverse function of the level of external threat from other populations
C   A cumulative function of the duration and extent of restrictive regulation by political authority
D   A positive function of the intensity of liberal ideological mobilization for lessened social control by political authority

## The Law of Distribution

The differentiation and elaboration of distributive infrastructures and market structures are:

A   A positive function of the level of production
B   A positive curvilinear function of the level of regulatory authority
C   A positive function of liberal ideological mobilization

At this point in Spencer's argument, an implicit idea contained in all types of functional analysis is introduced: the notion of "selection," but selection of a very special type. Unlike natural selection, which occurs when there is a high level of niche density and a corresponding increase in competition among members of a population for resources, Spencer argues that there is another kind of selection pressure to create new kinds of social structures in order to overcome mounting logistical loads. Such selection can occur alongside more Darwinian selection processes, but this kind of selection does not come from density, *per se*, but from the absence of necessary structures to meet escalating problems of generating sufficient production, reproduction, regulation, distribution, and other key functions that a population must meet if it is to remain viable in its environment. Spencer emphasized that selection processes among human organisms in super-organic systems differ from natural selection, because in human social systems, individuals and the social structures in which they are organized can "think," "plan," and "experiment" with new social forms that can reduce logistical loads; and in deference to Spencer, we might term this "Spencerian selection" to distinguish it from "Darwinian selection." For in Spencer's view, what distinguishes human super-organic structures is their potential flexibility and their capacity to change in order to meet new challenges; and for Spencer, the most fundamental challenges come from the pressures of escalating logistical loads.

Under conditions of escalated logistical loads, both Spencerian and Darwinian selection may be operating; and if a population is to avoid dissolution or disintegration, then differentiation along three axes must occur (ibid., pp. 498–548): (a) production–reproduction, (b) regulation, and (c) distribution. Spencer did not assume that mounting logistical loads and selection pressures would inevitably lead to their resolution; indeed, populations often dissolve and disintegrate when faced with increased selection pressure. He only argued that, if the population is to remain viable in its environment, it will differentiate structures along these three axes.

As selection increases the level of production, it becomes possible to support a larger population. To do so, however, requires differentiation of roles and structures, which, in turn, resolves one set of logistical loads for gathering resources and converting them into usable goods and commodities, while creating new kinds of logistical loads for coordinating the differentiated units. These latter loads increase Spencerian selection for market exchange and interdependence among productive units, and, as we will see shortly, for expanded regulatory authority as well. Differentiation of production creates new logistical loads for reproduction, as older forms of socialization and cultural production prove inadequate for preparing individuals and placing them in the specialized roles of differentiated social structures. Thus, Spencerian selection works to differentiate new forms of reproduction, such as school systems, religious and communal systems, laws and customs, and family systems.

Increased production leads to the expansion of regulatory authority, or the consolidation and concentration of power to coordinate social activity, via two routes. First, increased production generates a larger material surplus that can be usurped through taxation and used to support political decision-makers. Second, increased production generates logistical loads for coordination and control that cannot be met solely by exchange and interdependence. If expanded and concentrated power does not emerge, then evolution is arrested, and, potentially, the population will dissolve under rising logistical loads for coordination and control. Once concentrated power exists, however, it tends to be used to consolidate ever more power and to extract even more of the productive surplus of a society. As a result, inequalities increase, and as inequality grows, the stratification system creates internal threats which force polity to concentrate additional power to suppress dissent and conflict – a tactic which only escalates inequality and internal threat. As a consequence, a society may dissolve under the pressures of this escalating cycle of internal threat, political consolidation and repression, increased inequality, and further escalation of internal threat.

This cycle becomes interrelated with another cycle between what Spencer (1874–96, volume 2, pp. 568–643) termed "militant" societies, relying on concentrated power to coordinate and control activities, and "industrial" societies, employing less concentrated power and a reliance on exchange to control and coordinate activities. Much as Vilfredo Pareto was later to argue, Spencer (1874–96, volume 1, pp. 549–81; volume 2, pp. 568–643) saw societies as fluctuating between concentrated and less concentrated forms of political regulation. As resentments build against concentrated power, then rates of internal conflict, waves of ideological mobilization, and organized social movements become more prevalent and work to reduce the concentration of power and the degree of regulation, thereby transforming a militant system to an industrial one. Yet, as militant control is relaxed, the reduced level of political regulation and the increased reliance on exchange and interdependence as mechanisms of integration eventually begin to generate problems of ineffective coordination and to increase disintegrative pressures, thereby creating selection pressures for a more centralized political system to regain control. For Spencer, all political systems fluctuate back and forth between these two profiles; and so, in Spencer's eye, power reveals a dialectical quality, with its more concentrated and less concentrated forms generating pressures for transformation to their respective opposites.

Geopolitics also plays an important part in power dynamics. Spencer argued that war had been a great force of human evolution, for the simple reason that more organized societies usually win wars and, as a result, the outcome of war selects out less organized populations and ratchets up the level of human organization as the conquered are absorbed into the new, more organized social system. This kind of argument was Darwinian, but a Darwinian analysis that emphasizes the unit of selection as the group or social structure rather than the phenotype of the individual. Yet war also tends to concentrate power in order to mobilize and coordinate resources for the pursuit of the conflict, thereby setting off the disintegrative and dialectical dynamics outlined above. Moreover, success at war tends to expand territories and increase both the size and diversity of a population in these territories, which, in turn, escalates logistical loads for coordination and control as well as for expanded production and for new reproductive structures (if only to integrate the conquered into a society). If these logistical loads cannot be resolved, then internal threats increase, thereby setting polity off on the self-destructive cycle of concentrating more power, increasing inequality, and raising the level of internal threat.

Thus, growth in a population initially leads to differentiation along two axes: production–reproduction (what Spencer sometimes termed "operation" or "operative" processes) and consolidation and concentration of power (what Spencer often termed "regulation" or "regulatory" processes). Lagging some-what behind differentiation of operative and regulatory processes is the third axis of differentiation under escalated logistical loads and increased Spencerian selection pressure: distribution. For Spencer, distribution operates on two levels. First, there is a distributive infrastructure, such as roads, ports, canals, commun-ication facilities, and the like, for moving people, information, and resources about a territory. If a population grows, especially if its territory expands via war, conquest, and annexation, then infrastructural needs expand, setting into motion Spencerian selection for their development. Such development can only occur with productive surplus and some degree of encouragement from political authority. Second, there is exchange distribution, in which goods and commod-ities are transferred through market process. Such market forces depend upon a certain degree of development of distributive infrastructure as well as political regulation via a legal system, but as the population grows and differentiates, exchange distribution becomes an ever more prominent feature of the social system. In fact, Spencer went so far as to argue that in the modern era exchange processes had become so well developed that they could reduce the need for governmental regulation. And in some very modern-sounding passages, he argued against the pursuit of war and conflict by polity because such pursuit creates a military establishment and political system that undermine the dynamic forces of a market economy (Spencer, 1874–96, volume 1, pp. 519–48; volume 2, pp. 603–43). In fact, Spencer argued against British colonialism because it would generate, he felt, an ever more "militant" society in which the concentra-tion of coercive power would limit individual freedom, suppress economic innovation, hinder market dynamics, and distort political decision-making toward military rather than diplomatic solutions.

In table 3.1, Spencer's ideas on evolution are stated as abstract theoretical principles – a mode of representation that is consistent with the title of his major theoretical work in sociology (Turner, 1981, 1984a, 1985). The propositions introduce several additional elements to Spencer's theoretical argument, and thus we should pause to review these. The law of differentiation emphasizes that cultural symbols are an important part of differentiation and elaboration of social structures. Unlike Durkheim's inaccurate portrayal of Spencer as a crude utilitarian, Spencer did stress in all of his work the importance of cultural symbols; and, like Durkheim, he saw such symbols as connected to material structural arrangements. Moreover, he recognized that the differentiation and elaboration of cultural symbols add an additional layer and dimension to struc-tural differentiation; and it is this elaboration of cultural symbols that often imposes additional problems of integration and, most particularly, reproduction of members into the increased diversity of not only structural positions but also new systems of symbols.

The law of production lists forces normally considered to be part of production – population size, technology, natural resources, human capital – but this law also communicates some important feedback effects of regulatory and distributive structures. On the one hand, production increases the likelihood that regulatory and distributive structures will differentiate and elaborate, but on the other hand, once in place, these latter structures will have reverse causal effects on production. Thus, as distributive infrastructures and dynamic markets emerge, they feed back and encourage expanded production. Similarly, the existence of moderate degrees of political authority provides the legal framework and regulatory capacities for expanded production and distribution.

The law of reproduction stresses that as populations grow and differentiate new structures and systems of cultural symbols, the processes of reproduction become more complex. At first, kinship systems become more elaborate, but eventually new kinds of reproductive structures must emerge to impart the skills, dispositions, and knowledge necessary for assuring that individuals and collective units can sustain themselves. Spencer's (1860) work on education indicates his interest in reproductive structures, but equally importantly, he stressed that reproduction is a more inclusive process, involving knowledge of the arts, religious dogmas, tenets of law, and other cultural systems. As systems become more complex, the diversity of these cultural systems increases, and it becomes necessary for reproductive structures to be capable of imparting at least some of this broader cultural content.

The laws of regulation summarize Spencer's view that several forces influence the level of political centralization. External and internal threat will generate highly centralized power, and, to a lesser degree, so will prolonged periods of deregulation during which problems of coordination and control accumulate. When these conditions do not prevail, however, a less centralized system of political regulation will be more likely. Production and distribution are critical to the differentiation of political authority, in that each generates the resources necessary to support polity while also increasing logistical loads for some degree of political intervention into productive and exchange processes. Indeed, as production and exchange velocity accelerate, problems of coordination and control generate selection pressures for bodies of law backed by the authority of government; and as a result of these pressures, the polity inevitably grows (even though Spencer was, in his more purely ideological statements, suspicious of all government).

The law of distribution adds a related refinement. For Spencer, the development of a distributive infrastructure and dynamic markets depends upon the level of production, but it also requires some degree of political–legal regulation. Thus, in the proposition in table 3.1, the relation between polity and distribution is curvilinear: some degree of political authority encourages distributive processes, whereas high degrees of regulation will inhibit distributive dynamics and, in turn, production as well.

## The laws of institutional evolution

The passages from which we can glean the general theory of evolution summarized in table 3.1 constitute a relatively small portion of *The Principles of Sociology* (roughly, pp. 463–558 of volume 1). In contrast, nearly two-thirds of *The Principles* is devoted to the analysis of social institutions. As noted earlier, Spencer had assembled a vast amount of data on other societies in the present and past; and he used these data to make generalizations about the dynamics of social institutions. Most of his analysis concerns why an institution emerged in the first place, as well as how it differentiated and elaborated its structure during social evolution, but these more descriptive tasks were always accompanied by more abstract theoretical principles.

Spencer's analysis is always functional – that is, what are the consequences of an institution for the larger social whole – but this functionalism is simply a shorthand way to make a selectionist argument. Social institutions emerge and evolve under selection pressures generated by persistent problems facing a population, and as populations grow, these problems become more intense and require elaboration of distinctive institutional systems. Indeed, his selectionist argument is highly sophisticated, far exceeding any other scholar of the nineteenth century.

Spencer's (1874–96, volume 1, pp. 603–776) analysis of "domestic institutions" or kinship systems illustrates this sophistication. He begins with the question of why this institution would evolve. His answer is selection pressures to assure a stable environment for reproduction, to avoid conflicts among males over access to females, and to reduce promiscuity; and then, he turns to the question of why kinship elaborated beyond the nuclear structures typical of hunter-gathering bands. Again, his analysis invokes a selectionist argument: as populations grow, there are pressures to organize larger numbers of individuals, and kinship is the easiest structure to elaborate toward this end, at least initially in human evolution. Kinship can provide a system for sustaining cohesion among larger numbers of individuals; it can provide a basis for political organization through the descent rule; and it can offer a structural unit within which solidarity-producing religious rituals can be practiced. Those growing populations, then, that could elaborate kinship systems would have selective advantages because they could provide for systematic reproduction of new members, organize members politically, organize worship, and, thereby, generate a sense of loyalty and cohesion. And if such populations found themselves in conflict with other populations, the kinship system could become centralized around male authority, although Spencer argued that such centralization would subordinate women. (As an important footnote: Spencer had, by far, the most progressive views on gender issues of any of sociology's founding figures; see Beeghley (1983) for documentation of this point.) Table 3.2 summarizes some of the most interesting theoretical ideas emerging from Spencer's analysis of kinship systems.

After describing the evolution and dynamics of humans' first institution – kinship – Spencer turned to what he termed "ceremonial institutions" in

**Table 3.2** Spencer's generalizations on kinship

1   In the absence of alternative ways of organizing societal activities, kinship will become the major organizing principle in a society.
2   The greater the size of a society without alternative ways to organize societal activity, the more elaborate the structure of kinship and the more it will reveal explicit rules of endogamy/exogamy, marriage, and descent.
3   All other things being equal, the greater the conflict, or potential for conflict, the more elaborate the structure of kinship and the more it will reveal explicit rules of exogamy/endogamy, marriage, and descent.
4   All other things being equal, societies in conflict will reveal a strong tendency to be patriarchal (and patrilineal).
5   The more patriarchal a kinship system and the more it exists in a state of conflict, the less is the equality between the sexes, and the more likely are women to be defined and treated as property.

**Table 3.3** Spencer's generalizations on ceremony and ritual

1   The greater is the level of political centralization in a system, the greater is the level of inequality and the greater is the concern for ceremonial activities demarking ranks.
2   The greater is the concern over ceremonial activities demarking ranks in a system of inequality:
    (a) the more likely are people in different ranks to reveal distinctive objects and titles to mark their respective ranks;
    (b) the more are interactions among people in different ranks to be ritualized by standardized forms of address and stereotypical patterns of deference and demeanor.
3   The less is the level of political centralization, the less is the level of inequality; and, therefore, the less is the concern with ceremonial activities demarking ranks and regulating interaction among people in different ranks.

volume 2 of *Principles of Sociology* (pp. 3–228). Spencer saw ceremonies as subinstitutional; and he viewed them as a major micro-level force of social control and regulation because they signify the mutual respect of individuals toward each other and, thereby, contribute to the maintenance of social relations. In passages that are reminiscent of Erving Goffman's (1967) analysis of interaction ritual, Spencer analyzed the components of rituals: trophies symbolizing relations, mutilations of body to signify position and self-presentation, exchanges of gifts, visits, forms of address, titles, fashion, and deference-demeanor. In particular, he was concerned with the effects of inequalities in power and authority on ceremonial activity, arguing that the greater the power differentials among individuals the greater will be individuals' attention to all components of ceremonies. Some of the more interesting propositions from his analysis are summarized in table 3.3.

Despite Spencer's reputation as a *laissez-faire*, anti-government ideologue, he developed a sophisticated theory of politics (Spencer, 1874–96, volume 1, pp. 519–48; volume 2, pp. 229–643). Arguing much as current rational choice theorists, he emphasized that government exists to provide utilities not possible by tit-for-tat bargaining or market exchange alone, especially highly valued utilities such as mobilizing for conflict and defense. He viewed government as always revealing a tripart structure, consisting of a head, leaders, and followers, but he also stressed that this structure cannot exist without legitimating ideologies lodged in tradition. Even then, he argued, government generates a number of inherent tensions that can delegitimate political authority and lead to its collapse. Among these tensions are: the tendency of political systems engaged in conquest to overreach their capacity to control expanded territories and diverse populations; the dilemma that all traditional polities face in trying to balance staffing positions with the most qualified against the demands of elites for patronage and for inherited privilege; the tension between preserving the status quo and the need to change under new circumstances; the tendency of government to use its taxation powers to expand polity and thereby burden the society with unnecessary and resource-draining administrative overhead; and the creation of privileged and less privileged social classes, with inequalities generating internal threats and potential class conflict. For simple societies, Spencer argued, kinship, ceremony, and tradition are sufficient to regulate a population, but as a population grows, and especially if it engages in conflict with other populations, polity emerges as a differentiated institutional system, consisting of the tripart structure of head, leaders, and followers. As this structure elaborates, the bureaucracy of government expands; and as the scale of political bureaucracy expands, new systems for generating revenue emerge. At some point, pressures for more representative political bodies mount, especially as individuals become subject to revenue collection systems, and these pressures are most likely to be successful under certain conditions: the lack of war; a decline of strict adherence to religious beliefs; the dispersion of a population geographically; the existence of well organized subgroups; resentments associated with prolonged oppression; the expansion of markets; and the emergence of liberal ideologies. Much of Spencer's analysis provides detail to his more general theoretical statements on the differentiation of regulatory structures, as is evident in table 3.4, where some of the more interesting generalizations from Spencer's discussion are summarized.

At the beginning of *The Principles of Sociology* (volume 1, pp. 145–442), Spencer analyzed primitive religions, or the elementary forms of religion. Some ten years later, in volume 3 of *The Principles*, he examined the evolution of religion from simple to more complex forms and, then, to monotheism (pp. 3–178). For Spencer, all religions reveal three basic elements: beliefs in supernatural beings and forces, organized groupings who share these beliefs, and explicit activities directed toward supernatural forces. The emergence of religion was the result of selection for structures and cultural symbols to reinforce cultural values and patterns of social relations, especially those revolving around power. Spencer believed that religion emerged from dreams about ancestors, evolving into ancestor worship, which, in turn, supported the integrity of the kinship system. As societies became more complex, however, polytheistic religions emerged in response to this complexity; and as political authority became

**Table 3.4** Spencer's generalizations on polity and power

### Intrasocietal Processes

1 The degree of stability in government is a positive and additive function of its capacity to balance:
 (a) the needs for efficiency and stable succession;
 (b) the creation of privileged classes and potential class antagonisms;
 (c) the expansion of governmental overhead and nongovernmental productivity.
2 The degree of political centralization in a society is a positive function of its level and length of conflict with other societies.
3 The degree of differentiation of subsystems in the government of a society is a positive and additive function of that society's:
 (a) size;
 (b) volume of internal transactions;
 (c) volume of external transactions.
4 The level of inequality and class formation in a society is a positive function of the degree of centralization of political power.

### Intersocietal Processes

5 The degree of political centralization among a population of societies in a region is a positive function of the overall rate of conflict among these societies.
6 The degree of political unification among a population of societies in a region is a positive and additive function of:
 (a) the capacity of one society to coerce others;
 (b) the degree of structural similarity and cultural homogeneity among societies;
 (c) the need for a common defense among societies.

 It is a negative and additive function of:
 (d) the size of the territory that a population of societies encompasses;
 (e) the extent to which barriers in the natural habitat reduce transportation, communication, and migration.
7 The extent to which political unification among a population of societies reveals a highly centralized, bureaucratic profile is a positive function of the length and intensity of the conflicts that unified them politically.
8 The extent to which political unification among a population of societies reveals a less centralized and more colonial profile is a positive and additive function of:
 (a) the size of the territory to be governed;
 (b) the size of the population to be governed;
 (c) the level of structural and cultural heterogeneity among the people to be governed.

consolidated, the pantheon of supernatural forces became hierarchically ordered to reflect inequality and hierarchical social relations in society. Once the principle of hierarchy was established and built into bureaucratized ecclesiastic structures, a trend toward monotheism was initiated, since, in Spencer's view, monotheism simplified the hierarchy and made legitimation of centralized power more efficient. Yet, despite the symbiotic relationship between the state and religion, tension between the two inevitably increases, for several reasons: the claims of

**Table 3.5**  Spencer's generalizations on religion

---

1   The complexity of religious beliefs and ecclesiastical structures is a function of the complexity of social structures, particularly regulatory structures.
2   When kinship is the organizational basis of a population, ancestor worship will be the dominant form of religion, mediated by rituals directed at totems.
    (a) Early religious specialization in systems of ancestor worship involves a medicine man (who drives away evil ghosts) and priests (who make appeals to supernatural forces).
    (b) Subsequent institutional differentiation removes the medicine man and reinstitutionalizes this function in a new medical institutional system.
3   When regulation is increasingly transferred from kinship to polity, religion becomes hierarchical in both its pantheon of supernatural beings and its bureaucratized ecclesiastical structure.
4   Monotheism becomes possible once the principle of hierarchy is established and is used to legitimate the growing regulatory authority of the state.
5   Elites in the state and church eventually come into conflict over their respective capacities to control and regulate taxation, property, privilege, appeals to the supernatural, and rights to control legitimation of regulatory authority, with the state winning out when:
    (a) markets and trade are dynamic;
    (b) production is high and provides adequate resources to support the state;
    (c) law and courts provide alternative bases of legitimation for the state.

---

religious elites to exclusive rights to legitimate centers of political power; the contention of priests and others in the ecclesiastic system as being the only conduit to the supernatural; the assertion of the priestly class as the center of culture, knowledge, literacy, and art; and efforts of the church to create an independent tax system and claim on economic surplus. For these reasons, the church becomes a self-serving bureaucracy which increasingly comes into conflict with a self-serving state bureaucracy. At various points in history, the state seeks to control the power and privilege of religion; and it is aided in this process by the expansion of markets and by the development of law and other alternative structures that can legitimate the state. These ideas were well developed in the 1880s, and they represent important insights for the time. Table 3.5 summarizes some of the interesting generalizations emerging from Spencer's analysis of religion.

The last section in *The Principles of Sociology* (volume 3, pp. 327–608) is on "industrial institutions," or the economy. Spencer had intended to write on other social phenomena that revealed an institutional quality – linguistics, intellectual activity, morals, and aesthetics – but age and health made this the end of his purely sociological work. This is perhaps the most ideologically biased of the sections in *The Principles*, for it contains many of Spencer's diatribes against unions and guilds. Still, as table 3.6 delineates, a number of interesting generalizations can be culled from these flawed pages. Most of these provide some elaboration on his more general statements on productive processes. Spencer saw a basic feedback relation between primary and secondary production, with the emergence of a service sector generating new forms of production and marketing but also facilitating the operation of primary productive processes and distributive structures in ways increasing the overall level of production. Another feedback relation is the division of labor, which, once specialized, accelerates production because of the efficiencies that it introduces; and Spencer, like Max Weber after him, argued that a complex division of labor is only possible with a labor market unrestricted by kinship, community, guilds, and other forces that limit labor's willingness to sell itself in a market. Again, Spencer returned to a theme present throughout his work: the negative effects of war on a dynamic economy and market system. For while war had been an important force in the evolution of more complex societies, conflicts in the modern era deplete capital for private investment, remove human capital from the labor market, bias technological innovation toward military ends, dampen wants and needs that might translate into market demand for domestic goods and services, and undermine the feedback effects of markets on production. Another theme pursued in Spencer's analysis of industrial institutions is the effects of money and credit in market systems, for without a stable medium of exchange and without the ability to secure credit, capital formation is difficult, market exchanges are restricted, and free labor cannot exert its positive effects on production. Moreover, the use of money allows for the pooling of capital beyond any one individual or kin unit, thereby greatly expanding the capacity to form capital in a wide variety of pursuits. These and other interesting insights are summarized in table 3.6.

**Table 3.6**  Spencer's generalizations on economy

1   As productive structures are differentiated and elaborated:
   (a) the relationship between work and products is severed as the division of labor forces specialization of work activities;
   (b) the production of services increases as a proportion of total productivity;
   (c) the scale and velocity of market dynamics increase.
2   The processes delineated in (1) above are reciprocal and self-escalating, but only under conditions of relative peace with other societies, since the pursuit of war depletes capital, suppresses wants and needs for domestic products, mobilizes human capital for nonproductive activities, stagnates technological innovation or biases it for only military ends, and reduces the dynamic feedback between markets and production.
3   Relative peace will also increase population size which, in turn, will create selection pressures for expanded production and distribution.
4   Until market exchanges can create a stable medium of value for establishing equivalences, distributive processes will be limited, as will the productive processes stimulated by distribution.
   (a) The more media for establishing equivalences are, themselves, not valuable but instead only valuable for the equivalences that they symbolize, the more dynamic will market processes become.
   (b) The more stable and trustworthy a medium of exchange, the more it will stimulate market dynamics.
5   When credit systems can be created as a natural extension of stable monetary systems, the dynamism of markets is increased dramatically.
6   Until the evolution of money, capital formation was limited and inflexible, but with the development of money and instruments of credit, it becomes possible to invest in diverse and flexible forms of production.

**Table 3.6** (*Contd.*)

7 The more money can be pooled from diverse sources, the greater is the level of capital formation, the more flexible is the use of capital, and, hence, the greater are its effects on production.
8 The more labor is freed from kinship, community, guilds, unions, and other restrictive forms, the more able is labor to sell itself in a labor market and the more flexible will be the division of labor.

## THE PERSON

If one wandered through Spencer's study after his death, there would be few books on shelves, and the atmosphere would appear spartan, if not bleak. How could the library of a man who wrote treatises on ethics, science, sociology, psychology, and biology be so barren? The answer to this question takes us to Spencer's background and how it shaped the development of a very unusual – indeed, rather odd – man (Turner, 1985, pp. 9–15).

Spencer was born in Derby, England, in 1820. Until the age of thirteen he was given private instruction by his father at home, and then he moved to his uncle's home in Bath, where the private tutelage continued. Thus, Spencer never went to school as a young man, and when it came time to go to college, he felt himself unfit because of his lack of formal education. His father and uncles had, however, taught him mathematics and science; so Spencer was far from ignorant. After working as an engineer in the construction of a railroad, he began to write articles for what were then considered radical presses; and after a few years on the fringes of radical politics and journalism, he landed a position in 1848 on the London *Economist*. In 1850, he published *Social Statics*, which championed the cause of *laissez-faire* and the need for restrictions on the power of government. And it is here that his most famous phrase – "survival of the fittest" – reached a wide audience.

In 1853, Spencer's uncle died and left him sufficient money to pursue a career as a private scholar. Soon, major works began to flow from Spencer's pen: *Principles of Psychology* (1855), *First Principles* (1862), *Principles of Biology* (1864–7), *The Study of Sociology* (1873), *The Principles of Sociology* (1874–96), and *Principles of Ethics* (1892–8). In all, Spencer sold more than 400,000 copies of his books, which, then, was an astounding figure; and when one considers that most of Spencer's works were first serialized in popular magazines and periodicals before being bound into books, the scale and scope of his readership was truly enormous.

Spencer was not, however, a traditional scholar. He did not hold an academic position, and so he was not bound by its standards of scholarship. Instead, he frequented London clubs where he associated with the brightest and most famous scientists and intellectuals of his time; and in these associations, he simply absorbed knowledge which would eventually find its way into his works. And when he needed data, as was the case for his *Descriptive Sociology* (1873–1934), he simply hired academics to produce it.

Outside of his club circles, Spencer was an intensely private and neurotic person. It is unclear if he ever consummated sex, although he was a long time friend of George Eliot (a female novelist writing under a male name). He lived alone with housekeepers, wrote for a portion of the day, visited his clubs or consulted with his research assistants; but he did so under enormous psychic strain, for he was often sick, or at least thought that he was, and he was frequently unable to sleep. Thus, when Spencer died, he did so virtually alone in his spartan living space; and because his ideas were beginning to lose their currency, he died a somewhat bitter and sad man.

## THE SOCIAL CONTEXT

England at the time that Spencer was writing was the most prosperous nation on earth. Indeed, England seemed to confirm Adam Smith's faith in free markets and competition as the best way to organize society. As the first nation to industrialize and, then, use its colonial empire to further trade and commerce, it was difficult not to be impressed with the power of free trade in markets. Karl Marx and Frederick Engels, of course, saw the downside of this kind of economic system in England and elsewhere in Europe: the ruthless exploitation of workers and the abject misery of the masses. Yet Spencer, like so many of his time, saw the upside: the capacity of capitalism to generate wealth and prosperity for many. Moreover, he firmly believed that unbridled competition in markets unencumbered by excessive government intervention and, more generally, in all arenas of life would indeed promote the fitness of individuals and society.

Spencer also existed in a narrower social context of the lone intellectual writing science and philosophy outside confines of academia but within the broader intellectual circles of London – circles that were soon to die out. He was one of the last such private thinkers, for the intellectual world and especially the scientific wing of this world was fast moving into academia, where specialization and partitioning of intellectual activity would be encouraged. Spencer never was a part of this ivory tower world; he was a general intellectual and philosopher, writing for the literate lay public and the broader community of scientists as well.

He was by the time of his death one of the last of his breed. In the end, the growing compartmentalization of thought was to work against Spencer, along several fronts: he was to have no students to carry on his work; he was not sufficiently scholastic in terms of references and footnotes and, as a consequence, academics were soon to turn on him; he was a generalist in a world rapidly specializing not only between the major sciences but within them as well; and he held no academic credentials at a time when such credentials were increasingly seen as the sign of expertise. So, when Spencer died, his legacy appeared to die with him, only to be rediscovered generations later as scholars grappled with the same problems that had stimulated Spencer.

## THE INTELLECTUAL CONTEXT

Spencer walked in elite circles, dining and debating with the leading biologists, physical scientists, and philosophers of his day. From these dialogues he absorbed an enormous amount of knowledge, which, as noted earlier, filtered into his work. This kind of intellectual context is now gone, for can we imagine in the contemporary era leading scientists from many diverse fields gathering informally to discuss and debate their discoveries and ideas?

Aside from this day-to-day interaction with the great thinkers in England, Spencer's theories were influenced by a number of distinct traditions. One was his engineering background, from where comes the basic idea that an increase in size requires an exponential increase in structure to support the larger mass. This idea was developed in *Principles of Biology* and, then, imported into Spencer's sociology in the form of arguments about population size and sociocultural differentiation to support the larger mass.

Spencer borrowed from biology the view that competition among individuals and collective units is critical to formation of social forms, an idea that he initially saw in Thomas Malthus (who obviously was not a biologist) and later in Darwin (who obviously was). He also took from Harvey's embryological studies and Von Baer's physiology the idea that evolution and development involve movement from undifferentiated to differentiated structures marked by interrelated functions. And he took from Darwin the view that differences among individuals and social systems are the result of having to adapt to different environmental conditions.

Spencer drew from the physical sciences the substance of his first principles and the view of science as developing abstract laws. Isaac Newton had shown the power of elegant principles to explain the dynamics of solar systems, and Spencer like so many in this post-Newtonian era felt that the same could be done for all the other sciences, including sociology, where the law of size-differentiation was seen as like Newton's law of gravitation. Moreover, Spencer borrowed the vocabulary of Newtonian physics, and his general law of evolution is couched in the language of physics: matter, motion, force, and the like.

Finally, we need to mention the relation between Auguste Comte and Spencer. Spencer (1864) went to great pains to claim that he was not just following Comte, and he appears to "protest too much" on their relation. But his most intimate intellectual companions, George Elliot and George Lewes, were well versed in Comte's philosophy, so it can be reasonably assumed that he took the idea of the organismic analogy and functionalism from Comte's writings, although he made them far more sophisticated.

Thus, while we can discern some fairly straightforward lines of influence, we must return again to the most unique characteristic of Spencer the lone intellectual: he was an intellectual sponge who absorbed all ideas in which he came into contact; so his sociology reflects a constant engagement with virtually all lines of scientific thought in the second half of the nineteenth century.

## THE IMPACT OF SPENCER'S IDEAS

Spencer had an enormous impact on the broader arena of social thought and philosophy in the late nineteenth and early twentieth centuries, along a number of fronts. First, his moral philosophy continued to resonate with the dynamics of free-market capitalism; and, in America, Spencer was hailed as the most import-ant philosopher by early industrialists such as Andrew Carnegie. Second, his famous phrase – "survival of the fittest" – and the underlying argument against government welfare became the rallying cry to Social Darwinism, an unfortunate event in our retrospective evaluation of Spencer. And doubly tragic, his ideas were used by well known geneticists (e.g. Fisher, 1930) to make arguments in favor of eugenics.

Within narrower circles of sociology proper, Spencer influenced Durkheim's analysis in *The Division of Labor*. For Durkheim's basic model is borrowed from Spencer, and to the degree that Durkheim's analysis remains influential, so must Spencer's, since, despite Durkheim's criticisms of Spencer, he took many of the key ideas in *The Division of Labor* from Spencer (Turner, 1984a). For example, the notion in Durkheim's work that population growth increases population density and, hence, the competition leading to a division of labor comes right out of Spencer's *The Principles of Biology* and *The Principles of Sociology*. In addition to influencing Durkheim, Spencer's ideas and methodology exerted considerable influence on William Graham Sumner and Albert Keller in Amer-ica. Both borrowed from Spencer's data in *Descriptive Sociology* and from his analysis of social evolution of societies from simple to complex forms. In the case of Sumner, Spencer's moral philosophy was borrowed as well.

When we move to the more contemporary era, the impact of Spencer's ideas becomes more difficult to discern. The Human Relations Area Files developed by George P. Murdock (1953, 1965) represent a straightforward adaptation of Spencer's *Descriptive Sociology*, although Spencer is hardly given much credit for the basic idea. The general model of stage evolution is also lost, even as evolutionary thinking has enjoyed a revival (e.g. Lenski, 1966; Turner, 1984b, 1996; Sanderson, 1996). Spencer's model of the evolutionary stages of society is equal to contemporary formulations; so it is a double tragedy that his ideas are ignored by contemporary evolutionary thinkers (exceptions include Carneiro, 1970; Turner, 1996). Spencer's most important ideas on size, differentiation, and modes of integration have been rediscovered in a number of important fields, especially the study of complex organizations, but it is not so clear that thinkers on organizational size and administrative intensity recognize that they are employing Spencerian principles. Spencer's views on selection processes exerted considerable influence on Chicago School urban ecology, and this tradition continues to use Spencerian ideas but few within this tradition realize that they are working with Spencerian theory. Other theorists working within a more purely biological framework, however, have recently recognized the genius of Spencer's work on selection processes and have incorporated his ideas into their theories (e.g. Turner, 1996). Even the impact of Spencer's functionalism remains obscured, despite the fact that Malinowski's (1964) and Parsons's (Parsons et al., 1953) functional imperatives are virtually the same as Spencer's.

Thus, we are left with a curious legacy: everywhere one can see Spencerian ideas in sociology, but in only a few instances are the authors of these ideas aware that they have rediscovered Spencer's sociology. Thus, Spencer's direct impact or, at least, acknowledged impact on modern sociology has been minimal, with a few exceptions.

## AN ASSESSMENT OF SPENCER'S WORK

Spencer's work was brilliant for its time. Spencer was the first to see the relationship between system size and differentiation; he was the first to develop a sophisticated functionalism that saw systems as differentiating along production, reproduction, regulation, and distribution; he was the first to develop a sophisticated selectionist argument, in both the Darwinian sense and the sense of decision-making in the face of escalated logistical loads; he was the first to develop a multidimensional theory of power in terms of dialectical cycles, geopolitics, and internal threats; he was the first to enumerate modern-sounding generalizations describing the dynamics of fundamental human institutions; he was the first to array and use a large body of comparative data on societies; he was the first to enumerate in detail the methodological problems facing the social sciences; and he was the first to fully recognize the importance of distributive dynamics on production and to develop theoretical generalizations about these dynamics.

Spencer was, therefore, the pioneer of many important ideas and approaches in sociology. But Spencer's sociology offers more; it continues to be relevant to contemporary sociologists. His methodological analysis of the forms of bias in sociology still ranks among the best statements on this topic ever written; his understanding that the social universe involves many selection processes can continue to inform ecological and functional analysis; his recognition of the relationship among size, competition, selection, and differentiation is relevant for many meso-level and macro-level analyses of social systems; his view that many of the sciences can perhaps be unified, at least to some degree, with an evolutionary–ecological framework is clearly an idea that should not be abandoned; his descriptions of the stages of evolutionary development can inform similar stage models in present-day sociology; and his institutional analysis of religion, kinship, and polity contains many ideas that offer new ideas to specialists in these areas of institutional analysis. Thus, it is clear not only that Spencer was an important theorist in his own time, but that he continues to be an important theorist at the close of the twentieth century.

## Notes

1  Fortunately, Robert Perrin (1993) has compiled the most exhaustive primary and secondary bibliography on Spencer. The reader is advised to consult this work for Spencer's complete works and for important secondary works on Spencer.

2 Like all of Spencer's work, *The Principles of Sociology* is a compilation of work issued serially, from 1874 to 1896. Rather than cite the exact years of specific sections of *The Principles*, it is better to cite the entire work, 1874–96, with the volume and page numbers following.

## Bibliography

### Writings of Herbert Spencer

*Social Statics*. 1850. New York: D. Appleton (1892).
*The Principles of Psychology*, two volumes. 1855. New York: Appleton (1898).
*Education: Intellectual, Moral, and Physical*. 1860. New York: D. Appleton (1888).
*First Principles*. New York, 1862. New York: A. L. Burt (1880).
*Reasons for Dissenting from the Philosophy of M. Comte and Other Essays*. 1864. Berkeley, CA: Glendessary Press (1968).
*The Principles of Biology*, 2 volumes. 1864–7. New York: D. Appleton (1887).
*The Study of Sociology*. 1873. London: Kegan Paul.
*Descriptive Sociology, or Groups of Sociological Facts*. 1873–1934. Published with Spencer's personal funds by various publishers.
*The Principles of Sociology*, three volumes. 1874–96. New York: D. Appleton (1898).
*Principles of Ethics*. 1892–8. New York: D. Appleton.

### Further reading

Bailey, K. D. (1994) *Sociology and the New Systems Theory*. New York: SUNY Press.
Beeghley, L. (1983) Spencer's Analysis of the Evolution of the Family and the Status of Women: Some Neglected Considerations. *Sociological Perspectives*, 26, 299–313.
Carneiro, R. L. (1970) A Theory of the Origin of the State. *Science*, 169, 733–8.
Comte, A. (1896) *The Positive Philosophy of Auguste Comte*, translated and condensed by H. Martineau. London: George Bell.
Fisher, R. A. (1930) *The Genetical Theory of Natural Selection*. Oxford: Clarendon Press.
Goffman, E. (1967) *Interaction Ritual*. Garden City, NY: Anchor Books.
Lenski, G. (1966) *Power and Privilege: a Theory of Stratification*. New York: McGraw-Hill.
Malinowski, B. (1964) *A Scientific Theory of Culture and Other Essays*. London: Oxford University Press.
Murdock, G. P. (1953) Social Structure. In S. Tax, L. Eiseley, I. Rouse, and C. Voegelin (eds), *An Appraisal of Anthropology Today*. Chicago: University of Chicago Press.
Murdock, G. P. (1965) *Culture and Society*. Pittsburgh, PA: University of Pittsburgh Press.
Parsons, T. (1937) *The Structure of Social Action*. New York: McGraw-Hill.
Parsons, T. (1966) *Societies: Evolutionary and Comparative Perspectives*. Englewood Cliffs, NJ: Prentice Hall.
Parsons, T. (1971) *The System of Modern Societies*. Englewood Cliffs, NJ: Prentice Hall.
Parsons, T., Bales, R. F., and Shils, E. A. (1953) *Working Papers in the Theory of Action*. New York: Free Press.
Perrin, R. G. (1975) Durkheim's Misrepresentation of Spencer: a Reply to Jones' "Durkheim's Response to Spencer." *Sociological Quarterly*, 16, 544–50.
Perrin, R. G. (1993) *Herbert Spencer: a Primary and Secondary Bibliography*. New York: Garland.

Sanderson, S. K. (1996) *Social Transformations*. Oxford: Blackwell.

Sumner, W. G. (1907) *Folkways*. New York: Ginn and Co.

Sumner, W. G. and Keller, A. G. (1927) *The Science of Society*, 4 volumes. New Haven, CT: Yale University Press.

Turner, J. H. (1981) The Forgotten Giant: Herbert Spencer's Models and Principles. *Revue Europeene Des Sciences Sociales*, 19, 79–98.

Turner, J. H. (1984a) Durkheim's and Spencer's Principles of Social Organization. *Sociological Perspectives*, 27, 21–32.

Turner, J. H. (1984b) *Societal Stratification: a Theoretical Analysis*. New York: Columbia University Press.

Turner, J. H. (1985) *Herbert Spencer: a Renewed Appreciation*. Newbury Park, CA: Sage.

Turner, J. H. (1996) *Macrodynamics: toward a Theory on the Organization of Human Populations*. New Brunswick, NJ: Rutgers University Press.

Turner, J. H., Beeghley, L. and Powers, C. (1998) *The Emergence of Sociological Theory*. Belmont, CA: Wadsworth.

Turner, J. H. and Maryanski, A. (1979) *Functionalism*. Menlo Park, CA: Benjamin-Cummings.

Turner, J. H. and Maryanski, A. (1988) Sociology's Lost Human Relations Area Files. *Sociological Perspectives*, 31, 19–34.

# 4

# Karl Marx

## Robert J. Antonio

Perhaps no social theorist has generated more intense feelings among more widely dispersed audiences than Karl Marx. His name is identified with some of the twentieth century's major emancipatory struggles and worst forms of repression. As capitalism spread throughout the world from its original centers in Europe and North America, his ideas were appropriated in nearly every corner of the globe, and were revised, blended with other traditions, and applied in heterodox ways. Different Marxisms bear the imprints of highly divergent cultures, times, and sociopolitical aims. The importance of Marx's thought for labor movements and other forms of resistance and insurgency, as well as for various socialist and communist parties and regimes, has made it a topic of intense debate on the left and right. However, his mature work is as analytical and sociological as it is political. For this reason, his ideas have generated diverse lines of social research and social theory. Also, like Nietzsche, Marx provided alternative presuppositions and concepts to other modern social theories, stimulating numerous attempts to refute or dismiss his ideas. Thus, he has been an oppositional reference point for very diverse types of theory (e.g. from functionalism to postmodernism). Although pronounced dead on many occasions, he always seems to rise again from the ashes. Even after the late twentieth century, neoliberal revival, and the politics of 1989, his ideas still pose poignant questions about fundamental issues. Arguably, they may have increased force, free of the weight of communism, in a world where capitalism has triumphed. Because the matters of class, property, exploitation, ideology, alienation, and capitalism are as important as ever, Marx retains his place as one of the main founders of the sociological tradition.

## MARX'S LIFE AND CONTEXTS

### Young Marx: Hegelianism and method

In 1815, three years before Marx was born, his Rhineland birthplace of Trier was ceded back to Prussia. Previously, the town had been annexed by France; Napoleon's regime opposed semi-feudal institutions and extended individual and constitutional rights. Because many townspeople supported the French Revolution, reimposition of conservative Prussian rule generated tensions. Erosion of the economy and increased poverty made matters worse. Consequently, the region was politically active and the utopian socialists Saint-Simon and Fourier drew followers there during the revolutionary years of 1830 and 1848. Marx was born into a comfortable middle-class household, the oldest male of six surviving children. His father, a successful lawyer, embraced Enlightenment ideals and liberal democratic politics. Both sides of Marx's family had Jewish origins and rabbis as recent ancestors. Facing prejudicial restrictions, his parents converted to Protestantism. Jewish ancestry, however, still made them outsiders to some degree, and it would have been a major impediment had Marx attempted to pursue an academic career in Germany (McLellan, 1973, pp. 1–8; Seigel, 1993, pp. 38–44).

In high school, Marx received a mostly liberal humanist or Enlightenment-oriented education. The liberal headmaster and two other teachers were threatened by police authorities for their progressive views. Although several teachers were excellent, the students were mediocre. Even among this group, Marx was hardly an exceptional student, graduating eighth in a class of thirty-two. Ironically, he did poorly in history. Although he was a playful and energetic child, well liked by many of his fellow students, he was also feared by the targets of his sarcastic wit (his lifelong talent for cleverly skewering opponents earned him enemies). At school, Marx embraced Enlightenment ideals and social views, which were nurtured further by his tie to the progressive Baron Ludwig von Westphalen, his future father-in-law. Taking a liking to the young Marx, the Baron helped to stir his interests in romanticism and socialism (McLellan, 1973, pp. 9–16).

In 1835, Marx became a student at the University of Bonn. Although supposedly studying law, he specialized in "drinking and dueling," overspending, and writing poetry. Unhappy with these activities, his father forced him to transfer to the University of Berlin the following year. In a much more serious intellectual environment, Marx soon became a highly committed scholar. His extremely intense study habits probably contributed to his contracting a respiratory disorder so serious that he was released from military obligations. Maintaining very strenuous work habits as an adult, he suffered recurrent bouts of illness. Marx joined the left-Hegelian "Berlin Doctors' Club," engaging ideas that shaped his later intellectual path. He completed a doctoral dissertation on the philosophies of Epicurus and Democritus in 1841, submitting it successfully at Jena. Marx gave up work on a second thesis, required for entry into German academe, when

Bruno Bauer, his associate and leading left-Hegelian, lost his academic position for political reasons (McLellan, 1973, pp. 16–40; Seigel, 1993, pp. 65–75). Engels (1842, p. 336) portrayed, in rhyme, the young-Hegelian Marx:

> A swarthy chap of Trier, a marked monstrosity,
> He neither hops nor skips, but moves in leaps and bounds,
> Raving aloud. As if to seize and then pull down
> To Earth the spacious tent of heaven up on high,
> He opens wide his arms and reaches for the sky.
> He shakes his wicked fist, raves with a frantic air,
> As if ten thousand devils had him by the hair.

Marx became a journalist and soon editor at the progressive *Rheinische Zeitung* in Cologne. A sharp social critic, he focused on political abuses and socio-economic inequality. Attacking new laws that forbade peasants from gathering wood, Marx decried the monopolization of property by the rich and declared the poor as "the elemental class of human society" (Marx, 1842, pp. 234–5). Also, he began to criticize Hegelian political theory, which portrayed the state as a neutral mediator and rational manifestation of the general will (a position that divided right- and left-Hegelians). Marx turned Hegel's "idea" of the state against the "reality" of Prussian bureaucracy, attacking the official's crass pursuit of self-interest and slavish service to aristocratic and bourgeois interests. He also lambasted state censorship and authoritarianism, defending the free press and nascent public sphere and inveighing against the chilling effect of the police state's dragging vocal citizens into court for alleged "excesses" or "insolence" to officials. Favoring a free society that allows open discussion, he held that citizens often know more about sociopolitical problems than officials and should be encouraged to speak up about them, including official corruption. He saw authoritarian bureaucracy producing "passive uninformed citizens who are the object of administration" (Marx, 1843a, pp. 343–51). Marx's early views about free speech, local knowledge, and active citizens anticipated later ideas of "discursive democracy" (e.g. by Dewey, Habermas, Giddens). The circulation of *Rheinische Zeitung* expanded substantially under Marx's leadership. A skilled editor and writer, he continued journalistic endeavors, on a part-time basis, throughout much of his life. However, in 1843, the Prussian government shut down his newspaper, in part because of his sharp attacks on the monarchy and bureaucracy. That same year he married Jenny von Westphalen, and took another editorial position in Paris. There Marx was exposed to the working class and to socialist and communist ideas (McLellan, 1973, pp. 62–6; Seigel, 1993, pp. 65–75).

In *On the Jewish Question* (1843), Marx criticized Bauer's argument to deny Jews political rights, but his own ambiguous and even negative comments about them indicate that he had not come to terms with this aspect of his identity. Overall, however, he moved in a radical direction, away from his earlier progressive liberalism. Opposing the capitalist celebration of "egoistic" or "abstract" persons and the free pursuit of "self-interest" by "isolated monads,"

Marx held that bourgeois "freedom" dissolves feudal ties and extends formal rights, but neither sustains community nor provides adequate opportunities for those below the middle class. Propertyless peasants, artisans, and workers are left without means to activate their new rights. In his view, political freedom, although not meaningless, falls far short of "human" or "social emancipation." Looking for a sweeping transformation of civil society far beyond liberal reform, Marx called for "ruthless criticism of all that exists", "practical struggles," and "communism." Revolutionary rhetoric aside, he distinguished between substantive freedom and formal freedom, arguing that radical democratic or "true" liberty requires socio-economic equality as well as legal rights. This fundamental issue of genuine inclusion remains a most pressing problem for current democracies (Marx, 1843c, pp. 141–5; 1843d, pp. 162–74).

In the *Critique of Hegel's Philosophy of Law*, Marx attacked Hegel's equation of the actuality of the Prussian state with its democratic constitution, arguing that he justified the repressive monarchy by attributing a more abstract "logic" to an already abstract document that had little to do with political reality. In his view, Hegel sanctified the real as rational (Marx, 1843b). In the *Economic and Philosophical Manuscripts* of 1844, Marx accused Hegelians of not starting with "real corporeal" people in their actual "social" relations, but with "abstract nature" and "thought entities." He held that their "idealism" confuses legitimations with reality, and, thereby, encourages passive acceptance of existing political conditions. Marx implied that all bourgeois thought is prone to this fatal error. Stressing consciousness and its appearances, Hegel addressed human development in the idiom of "spirit." By contrast, left-Hegelians followed Ludwig Feuerbach's "inversion" of Hegel, or shift to materialist explanations of theology and philosophy. This reversal of the primacy of spirit was aimed to avert the alienation that Hegel himself decried. After initially embracing this view, Marx broke with Feuerbach, arguing that he was too philosophical, dwelled too much on the critique of religion, viewed the material realm too inertly, and focused too exclusively on generic "man" or the human "essence" (Marx, 1845). Overall, Marx believed that the Hegelians' abstract philosophical approach, even in materialist form, was ahistorical and, thus, ignored truly important human problems.

Earlier, Marx said, in a letter to his father, announcing his conversion to Hegelianism: "I arrived at the point of seeking the idea in reality itself. If previously the gods had dwelt above the earth, now they became its center" (Marx, 1837, p. 18). This statement expresses a Hegelian methodological theme that Marx retained long after his "break" with the Hegelians. He saw Hegelian "historicism" as a bridge between the "is" and "ought," which were split in Western religion and philosophy. For Hegel, normative ends, which guide and give meaning to action, originate entirely within historical experience. Rejecting transcendental views of values and the related epistemological dualism between "subject" and "object," Hegel argued that we are the authors of our world; as historical beings, we negate existing conditions, create new ones, and make ourselves in the process. However, he held that our self-creation is estranged, because we see our own objectifications as alien objects and, thus, lose our agency. Yet, in the long run, he argued, we gradually overcome this alienation by mediating contradictory facets of experience through heightened self-consciousness, struggle, and labor. In this regard, his argument about masters and slaves was especially important for Marx. Hegel held that masters seek self-recognition by dominating slaves, but languish in the contradiction that coerced recognition is worthless. By contrast to the master's falsity and inactivity, Hegel contended, struggles and labor cause slaves to grow wiser and stronger and to ultimately triumph. In his view, through the same striving, humanity eventually will discover its authorship of the world, creating a state where each person's particularity is recognized by all others, and achieving the condition of "Absolute Spirit," or total freedom and rationality (Hegel, 1807).

Focusing on capitalism and wage workers' "estranged labor," Marx broke with Hegel's "abstract" emphasis on consciousness and equation of objectification with alienation. However, Hegel's idea of self-constitutive labor remained at the center of Marx's thought. At the very moment of his "break" with Hegelianism, he argued that socialist humanity and world history are "nothing but the creation of man through human labor" (Marx, 1844, pp. 305, 332–3). He also called for "determinate negation" of capitalism's contradictions, hoping to preserve its progressive facets, yet create a new socialist world that moves toward a terminus of freedom and rationality. Marx pitted what he considered to be the progressive facets of capitalist production against its backward features, and universalistic aspects of modern democratic ideology against bourgeois repression and inequality. Reframing Hegel's method of "immanent critique," he sought to anchor his theory in specific historical bases rather than philosophical historicism. This move began the broader tradition of "critical theory," which roots theory and critique in concrete historical contradictions, actual social movements, and nascent developmental directions. Although shifting from speculative philosophy to materialism, Marx's theory contained a strong Hegelian residue that animated its emancipatory themes, linkage of theory and practice, and most fruitful empirical questions. But this core aspect of his lineage is also the ultimate source of the distinct tensions between the sociological and political facets of his thought.

## The move to materialism: capitalism and modernity

In the middle and late 1840s, Marx framed the historical and analytical foci of his mature theoretical program. Responding to growing class tensions, inhering in rapid industrialization and proletarianization, fellow young-Hegelians Moses Hess and Frederick Engels addressed political economy critically and became communists. Marx followed their path, and Engels became his lifelong collaborator. Although Engels understated his role in the partnership, he contributed very substantially to Marx's thought and their common project through his editorial capacities and critiques and his own ideas and works. Also, he financially supported the spendthrift Marx and his family. With the help of Engels, Marx broke with Hegelian philosophy and developed his materialist approach to history and sociology. Although political upheavals were an immediate stimulus to Marx's work during this period, accelerating capitalist development became more and more his chief concern. Marx's most decisive context was the Second Industrial Revolution, or the appearance of the complex of mechanized industry, mass labor organizations, interventionist state, modern urbanism, and world market, and profound alteration of almost all traditional modes of association, thought, and everyday life, which he inscribed together under the sign of "modernity."

In the *1844 Manuscripts*, Marx began to transform Hegel's idea of estranged objectification into a historically explicit materialist theory of social development and of the rise of the capitalist "mode of production." In this unfinished text, clear signs exist of his later views about class struggle, proletarian revolution, and abolition of private property. Implying a fundamental contradiction in the heart of capitalism, he portrayed the division of labor as a fusion of repressive class hierarchy with progressive socio-technology. In his view, capitalist development "fetters" progress in the same stroke that it advances it. He also held that we are *social beings* and that modernity's "economic" transformation has a "*social* character"; even monadic, atomized, liberal individualist humanity arises from capitalism's social matrix (Marx, 1844, pp. 298–9, 317–22).

After expulsion from turbulent Paris in 1845, Marx made his decisive break from philosophy in an unfinished collaborative effort with Engels, *The German Ideology*. They turned the Hegelian primacy of ideas and passive view of the material domain "right-side up." This text articulated much more explicitly the bases for their later views of materialism, capitalism, and revolution. Marx considered the work the start of their mature program (Marx and Engels, 1845–6; Seigel, 1993, pp. 177, 181). Marx and Engels described how "large-scale industry" was overturning the premodern world and creating a new global order. They saw hypermodern factories, markets, and capitalist class relations supplanting traditional forms of production, social ties, and hierarchies and replacing local autonomy and particularity with centralized interdependence and homogeneity. In their view, the Second Industrial Revolution was creating "world history for the first time, insofar as it made all civilized nations and every individual member of them dependent for their satisfaction of their wants on the whole world, thus destroying the former natural exclusiveness of separate nations" (Marx and Engels, 1845–6, p. 73). Engaging political economy even more directly, Marx's *Poverty of Philosophy* (1847) provided an early published version of this nascent materialist point of view.

Marx's and Engels's publicly important political pamphlet *The Communist Manifesto* (1848) probed similar themes more dramatically and eloquently. Originally the party platform of the German "Communist League," the essay became a political catechism for later communist movements. Writing in the revolutionary climate sweeping across Europe, Marx and Engels hoped that the capitalist class would soon smash the remains of the old order and elites, attain complete political power, and create global capitalism and liberal democracy, which they saw as the stage for proletarian revolution. They expressed their materialism lucidly and succinctly, applied it to capitalism, and located it *vis-à-vis* other socialist and anticapitalist approaches. In their immanent critique, they detected nascent crises, revolutionary tendencies, and seeds of postcapitalism. Holding that they were amplifying historical tendencies that favor the determinate negation of capitalism, they argued that competition drives the bourgeoisie to constantly revolutionize the productive forces and radically and untiringly transform society and culture. Marx and Engels asserted that the entirety of premodernity's "fixed, fast-frozen relations, with their train of ancient and venerable prejudices" were being "swept away" and "all new-formed ones" were becoming "antiquated before they can ossify." Regardless of unparalleled material progress, they saw capitalism to be "like the sorcerer, who is no longer able to control the powers of the nether world...called up by his spells." They were optimistic, however, that after "all that is solid melts into air," people will come to their "sober senses," see things clearly, take self-conscious collective agency, and shape history rationally in an emancipatory direction (Marx and Engels, 1845, pp. 487–9).

## The mature project: irrational surface and rational depth

Marx was expelled from Belgium in 1848, was invited back to France, and then went to Germany as editor of the radical *Neue Rheinsiche Zeitung*. When politics shifted rightward in 1849, he was expelled from Germany with a passport good only for Paris. Because the new, reactionary French regime restricted him to Brittany, he fled to London. Living the rest of his life in the belly of the beast, the great anticapitalist theorist experienced directly advanced modernity in the seat of liberal individualism and the first nation to undergo the Second Industrial Revolution. Marx was often active in working-class movements (leading the First International 1864–72), but, at other times, withdrew from politics. Although continuing journalism, he and his family depended on regular, generous financial support from Engels. Marx fathered eight children; four died before reaching adolescence. He and the family maid had a son who was given to foster parents and kept secret. But Marx was generally an attentive and loving father, very supportive of his three daughters' intellectual and cultural development. The Marx family apparently was closely knit and warm. Residing first in a poor neighborhood of London, they later moved to a middle-class section and lifestyle. But Marx suffered from his children's deaths, and from recurrent, painful, and probably work-related health problems (concerning his eyes, stomach, liver, lungs, inflammations, headaches, and boils). Although Marx left an enormous corpus of collected works, he was tormented by his inability to finish projects, especially his magnum opus, *Capital*. Finally, he regretted his constant trouble with creditors and financial dependency, and their impact on his family. In a letter to Engels, he lamented that, at 50 years old, he was "still a pauper," recalling his mother's earlier admonition that he should have "made capital" instead of merely writing about it (Marx, 1868, p. 25; McLellan, 1973, pp. 189–225; Seigel, 1993, pp. 195–9, 253–89, 375–87).

Although reactionary forces held sway by mid-century, Marx, at first, remained optimistic that bourgeois revolution would succeed on the Continent and that England's liberal democracy and advanced bourgeoisie and working class had swept away all the precapitalist detritus or main blocks to proletarian revolution. In 1850, Marx and Engels declared that a "new revolution can no longer be very far away." Yet Marx's *Class Struggles in France* (1850) departed from the *Manifesto's* linear scenario, reporting counter-revolutionary paralysis and internecine class and subclass conflict (Marx, 1850, pp. 71–145; Marx and Engels, 1850b, p. 377). His *Eighteenth Brumaire* (1852) was much more pessimistic. At the start of this scalding report on the rise of the second Napoleonic dictatorship, Marx recalled Hegel's point that major historical "facts and personages" happen twice, asserting that he "forgot to add: the first time as tragedy, the second time as farce." The work's opening paragraphs, among the most beautifully written and circumspect in all of Marx's corpus, state disappointedly that we do not make our history just as we please. Rather,

> The tradition of all the dead generations weighs like a nightmare on the brain of the living. And just when they seemed engaged in revolutionizing themselves and things, in creating something that never yet existed, precisely in these times of revolutionary crisis they anxiously conjure up the spirits of the past to their service and borrow from them names, battles-cries and costumes in order to present the new scene of world history in this time-honored disguise and this borrowed language.

After the "revolution," Marx held, the French state returned "to its oldest form," based on "the shamelessly simple domination of the sabre and the cowl" (Marx, 1852a, pp. 103–4, 106).

In the *Brumaire*, Marx reported how Louis Bonaparte became dictator, aided by the Parisian lumpenproletariat, or underclass mob of easily bribed riffraff. In his view, the new regime echoed previous absolutism, but concentrated power much more totally, sweeping both bourgeoisie and proletariat from center stage. Anticipating Weber, Marx held that the earlier parliamentary democracy's modernized, centralized, rationalized bureaucracy was an ideal means for carrying out a *coup d'état* and asserting total power. He blamed the bourgeoisie for creating the conditions of their own demise; their manifestly selfish, one-sided pursuit of short-term, material interest created a Frankenstein's monster, or total state, that appeared to be "completely independent" of the material base and leading classes. Arguing that "state power" could not really be "suspended in mid air," Marx stated that the dictatorship represented the class interests of "small-holding peasantry." He considered this stratum to be the most backward in French society, living in what he considered to be "stupefied seclusion," isolated by their proto-feudal productive forces, lack of cooperative and communicative links to modern classes, and backward lifestyle, culture, and interests. Although still claiming that proletarianization and commodification of rural life would eventually undermine the new regime, the *Brumaire* illustrated dramatically that capitalism's rationalizing locomotive could lead to nightmare fusions of modernity and tradition (portending fascism and Nazism) as well as to socialism's promised land (Marx, 1852a, pp. 147–51, 181–97).

During the same period, Engels provided an even more pessimistic report about the complete failure of the bourgeois revolution in Germany, which he attributed to its backward and complexly split class structure. He argued that the bourgeoisie were more soundly defeated there than anywhere else in Europe and that the dissolution of the provincial and national assemblies and restoration of aristocratic power constituted the death of political liberalism in that nation. Rather than decisive bourgeois hegemony and liberal democracy on the Continent, the revolutions of 1848 stirred counter-revolution and fresh fusions of aristocratic and capitalist power. Moreover, Marx observed that Britain's prosperity was creating "political indifference," neutralizing the progressive possibilities of its highly developed bourgeois institutions and advanced working class and generating a conservative drift away from progressive democracy (Engels, 1851–2, pp. 5–13, 91–6; Marx, 1852b, c).

Although Marx stuck to his materialist agenda, he was no longer optimistic about capitalist modernization bringing us to our senses and making capitalism transparent at the surface level of simple empirical observation. In the *Brumaire*, he spoke about the Napoleonic regime's "superficial appearance" (i.e. state autonomy) as a veil covering the underlying logic of capitalism. This idea of the blinding, fettering effects of ideological illusion can be found in his earlier work, but he now held that immanent critique must dig much more deeply and theoretically to grasp the factors that shape capitalism's highly distorted sociopolitical surface. Marx implied that these conditions stalled completely emancipatory possibilities, which seemed to be at hand a few years before (Marx, 1852a, pp. 127–8). As Seigel argues, the reversals of the 1850s caused Marx to doubt his former belief that "empirical experience" provided direct access to the "real truth" (Seigel, 1993, p. 362; also see pp. 193–216).

In the early 1850s, Marx started to amass a great deal of "economic" information, but it was not until 1857, spurred by an international economic crisis and rekindled revolutionary hopes, that he began to refine his mature theory of capitalism in the *Grundrisse* (1857–8) and in *Contribution to the Critique of Political Economy* (1859). Stressing relations of surface and depth, Marx held that everyday appearances and understandings of capital circulation are characterized by fundamental "mystification"; money and commodities are treated as an independent realm of "things" rather than "a social relation." Although "monetary crises" draw out "immanent" contradictions of capitalism, Marx argued, the money form's illusory independence "shrouds" the tensions at the same time that it manifests them. He said that "in the process of exchange, as it emerges on the surface of bourgeois society, each gives only while taking, and takes only while giving," yet both roles depend on "having" or ownership. In his view, basic property and class inequalities are seen as external to circulation's "free" and "equal" exchange. Marx saw the unequal exchange between workers and capitalists (i.e. wages for labor power) to be capitalism's most profoundly mystified and pivotal social relation. His counterfactual theory of value explained capitalism's surface by transposing the apparent relation between things into an unequal relation between persons. Overall, however, Marx held that the "semblance of simplicity disappears in more advanced relations of production" (Marx, 1859a, pp. 275–6, 289; 1859b, pp. 433, 462).

The first volume of *Capital* (1867) appeared about a decade after Marx began his major effort to theorize capitalist political economy. He planned originally to complete six books of his magnum opus. Although filling many notebooks for the broader study, he never finished it. After Marx's death in 1883, Engels edited and assembled the two unfinished core volumes, completing them in 1885 and 1894. Karl Kautsky later edited the three volumes of *Theories of Surplus Value* (1905–10), or Marx's critical history of economic theory. Engels held that Marx's various illnesses and political activism slowed the project, but the fact that his theoretical work often had to be left to the dim light of the night was also a factor (his daytime hours were occupied with journalistic, polemical, and letter writing and with family affairs). Seigel raises other possible factors: unresolved tensions between Marx's Hegelian residue and his materialism, reservations about core aspects of his theory, and psychological problems originating from his childhood experiences (Engels, 1885, pp. 1–5; Seigel, 1993, pp. 329–92).

Stressing the deadly serious, dogged pursuit of an enormous project, Engels described Marx's "unparalleled conscientiousness and strict self-criticism," leading to constant broadening of the scope of issues, searching for ever more historical support, and doing "incessant study" (Engels, 1885, p. 2). In this light, the effort to fully develop his theory was perhaps more important to him than publication. This normative orientation and tendency to leave major corpora of unfinished work to be published posthumously characterized certain other first-generation modern social theorists (e.g. Max Weber and George Herbert Mead). The material and cultural climate of later twentieth-century, professionally specialized, intellectual spheres is an entirely different terrain. Here, unpublished work is considered stillborn or a dead letter. Although earlier modern theorists' sunny ideas of "science" and "truth" are now seen as passé or misguided, their practices should be read in the context of the different ethical and social meaning that "doing theory" had in their time. Reflection on the matter might provide insight into some of the weaknesses as well as strengths of contemporary social theory.

## Marx's Social Theory

### Contra liberal individualism: discovery of the social

Adam Smith's liberal individualism provides an excellent departure point for moving to explicit consideration of Marx's social theory (Smith, 1776, pp. 3–5, 13–17, 423). Opening the *Wealth of Nations*, Smith illustrated his core concept of the "division of labor" with his famous pinmaker example: a single worker, carrying out all steps of production alone, would be hard pressed to make twenty pins, or possibly even one pin, a day, while ten specialized producers, working together, could produce 48,000 a day or about 4,800 each. Smith suggested that the division of labor increases productivity geometrically, but he saw the market as the ultimate source of progress, rather than labor's complex cooperation. He held that the division of labor originates unintentionally from individual human nature or the universal "propensity to truck, barter, and exchange one thing for another" and the "natural" inclination to pursue individual interests. In his view, capitalist markets unleash heretofore repressed free choice and self-interest, generating an ever more dynamic, efficient, abundant division of labor and, overall, a freer, more rational society. Smith contended that competitive individualism and spontaneous association, based on fleeting contractual relations and consumer choices, produce social harmony, and that the magic of the market's "invisible hand" would be destroyed by socio-political regulation and planning.

Paralleling Smith, Marx held that twelve cooperating masons accomplish much more than one mason working alone for the same number of hours. But he argued that this difference manifests "the creation of a new power, namely, the collective power of the masses." Describing the cooperating masons to be "omnipresent" and to have "hands and eyes before and behind," Marx implied *sui generis* social capacities that inhere in cooperative activity, but do not exist at the individual level per se. He stated that:

> Just as the offensive power of a squadron of cavalry... is essentially different from the sum of the offensive... powers of the individual cavalry... taken separately, so the sum total of the mechanical forces exerted by isolated workmen differs from the social force that is developed when many hands take part simultaneously by one and the same undivided operation. (Marx, 1867, pp. 325–6)

Whereas Smith stressed individual powers released by capitalist markets and bourgeois individualism, Marx emphasized social capacities already present in the "simple cooperation" of premodern or primal humanity. In his view, "different but connected [cooperative] processes," such as joint hunts or harvests, exist everywhere, along with individual activity and independent production. Marx held that even "mere social contact" and consequent "emulation" and "stimulation" enhance existent individual powers and generate new ones, while active cooperation overcomes the "fetters of... individuality" and harnesses the "capabilities of the species" (Marx, 1867, pp. 325–9).

Although he agrees that market growth stimulates expansion of the division of labor, Marx's view of the process differs sharply from Smith's position. Marx saw modern industry's spectacular productive advances as deriving from its quantitative extension and qualitative transformation of *sui generis* social powers, especially tacit knowledge flowing through complex cooperative networks and becoming overt in technology and planning. But he held that the capitalist system, which brings the new ultra-powerful "combined organism" into being, also tears producers from their communities, imposes Darwinian competitive struggles among capitalists, and destroys sociocultural regulation. By contrast to premodern cooperation and communal property, Marx held, capitalism separates individual producers from their means of production (i.e. productive forces), concentrates them in the hands of capitalists, and fuses cooperative activity fully with coercion. In his view, unrestrained pursuit of self-interest generates a profound tension between individual activity and complex cooperation, rather than the spontaneous harmony predicted by Smith. As

Engels said, this "contradiction" appears as the "antagonism" between bourgeoisie and proletariat (Engels, 1892, p. 311; Marx, 1867, pp. 325–35, 355–61).

Marx's presuppositions about human nature reverse Smith's vision of the self-interested individual as prior to society. Marx held that the human being is "at all events a social animal" or an "ensemble of the social relations" (Marx, 1845, p. 4; 1867, p. 326). He saw individuality to be an emergent property of "definite" social relationships within historical communities; it is constituted by our patterns of association, cooperation, and language (Marx, 1845, pp. 43–5). Marx argued that claims about an "inherent" split between the individual and society universalize possessive individualism and hypostatize capitalism's primary contradiction between private productive property and complex social cooperation. However, he also saw capitalism as the matrix for a richer, freer social individuality aware of its ties and responsibilities to others and both product and agent of the emergent highly differentiated, reflexive sociocultural order. By contrast to Smith, Marx saw publicly planned production and distribution as enhancing rather than impeding progress. In his view, self-conscious collective agency arises from complex cooperation, and provides seeds of an emancipated post-capitalist order.

## Marx's theory of history: historical materialism

The aim of specifying and qualifying earlier Enlightenment conceptions of science and knowledge and of forging new sciences, designed to capture differentiated forms of life in their particularity, connect Marx and certain other first-generation modern social theorists with Darwin. Engels held that, "Just as Darwin discovered the law of development of organic nature, so Marx discovered the law of development of human history" (Engels, 1883, p. 467). Marx called for a "historical" or "social" materialism to go beyond early modern ideas of a general and abstract "science of Man." He embraced Hegel's idea of human historicity, but rejected his "abstract" emphasis on spirit (which he believed retained taints of religion and metaphysics and stopped short of a new understanding of history). Although crediting classical economists for bringing material matters into view, Marx attacked their "abstract," individualistic idea of human nature. His materialism was an attempt to transcend dialectically these points of view, retaining key features, yet ultimately breaking with them and creating a new framework.

In an early statement of the materialist conception of history, Marx and Engels (1845–6, p. 37) held that "It is not consciousness that determines life, but life that determines consciousness." Responding to critics and rigid interpreters, Engels asserted, after Marx's death, that "the *ultimately* determining element in history is the production and reproduction of real life. More than this neither Marx nor I ever asserted" (Engels, 1890, pp. 397–8). Like Darwin, they stressed the centrality of material activities and struggles. In particular, they held that human development must be seen in light of the species' uniquely creative, powerful, and diverse ways of producing for its basic animal needs and how the exercise of these capacities generates distinctly new human needs and human history. Friends and foes, alike, have often interpreted this position in narrow ways, even though Marx and Engels stressed that their "standpoint" is "human society, or social humanity." They saw the "historical life-process" as "twofold," or as both "natural" and "social"; our relationship to nature is mediated by  social processes (e.g. cooperation, language, ideas, and customs) that "fetter" productive powers in certain ways, but that also enhance them progressively and make possible eventual emancipation from our original subservience to nature, including our "second nature" or human domination (Marx and Engels, 1845–6, pp. 31–2, 36–7, 41–5; Marx, 1845, p. 5).

Marx stressed "real, active," or "definite individuals," entering "definite social and political relations," producing themselves in specific ways, and, thus, acting as agents of their own history. As stated above, however, he argued that we do not create ourselves of our own accord; instead, people operate under "definite material limits, presuppositions, and conditions independent of their will" (Marx and Engels, 1845–6, pp. 35–6; Marx, 1852b, p. 103). We are born into ready-made, hierarchical sociocultural worlds, which track our ideas and actions in innumerable ways. Stressing the most pervasive source of this systematic social constraint, Marx saw class as an aggregate of people sharing a wide range of limits and possibilities, flowing from their common location *vis-à-vis* societal property relations. He contended that class has an "independent existence against . . . individuals" or that it frames the conditions under which we make ourselves regardless of our consciousness, identity, will, or striving (Marx and Engels, 1845–6, pp. 77–9). For example, feudal class relations (i.e. peasant producers tied to plots and hegemonic lords that controlled landed wealth by military means) reproduced, generation after generation, distinct types of superordinate and subordinate lives, which neither lords nor serfs freely chose. This view of class as a *sui generis* entity gives Marx's thought its distinctive "structural" thrust.

Marx held that as soon as productive powers are advanced to a level where surpluses are large enough to free a significant portion of the adult populace from labor, a fundamental class split arises between "ruling classes" (e.g. feudal lords), who govern politically and culturally and exert effective control over productive forces, and subordinate "direct producers" (feudal serfs), who operate the productive forces and create basic goods and services. He saw these two deeply contradictory class locations as all-important sites of structural advantage and disadvantage and "class struggle." Marx stressed that "class conscious," politically organized class struggle sometimes forges new class structures and reshapes social life *in toto*, but he was also aware that it is usually haphazard, local, and disconnected from overt class identity and conscious collective agency. He saw classes and subclasses engaging in internecine conflict, obscured by complex splits between opposed fragments in single classes and by cross-class alliances between different legal "orders" and status groups. Thus, class struggles are often refracted through ethnic, racial, gender, religious, and other forms of sociocultural conflict. Marx frequently portrayed extremely fragmented class relations. His admission that, in advanced capitalist societies, "middle and intermediate strata . . . obliterate lines of demarcation everywhere" and deflect class consciousness belies his linear hopes about a final showdown between the bourgeoisie and proletariat (Marx, 1894, p. 885). Thus, his declaration that "The history of all hitherto existing society is the history of class struggles" does not mean that they are readily visible or must move history forward (Marx and Engels, 1845, p. 484).

In long-term human history, Marx contended, productive forces, despite many temporary setbacks, advance progressively so that the level of "surplus product" (i.e. exceeding bare subsistence) increases relative to "necessary product" (i.e. required for subsistence). The consequent availability of growing levels of "surplus labor," devoted to overall social development, generates enhanced powers of production, higher standards of subsistence, more differentiated sociocultural orders, and more varied and distinctive human needs. As implied above, however, Marx held that this materially driven civilizing process has been mediated by class and, thus, has operated in a highly unequal way. For example, spectacular built environments and elaborate symbolic cultures of the "great civilizations" were based on a huge divide between "mental" and "physical" labor and relentless extraction of the surplus labor and product of peasants and slaves by ruling political, military, and religious elites. In Marx's view, material and social progress has been and continues to be thoroughly entwined with class domination.

According to Marx's materialist "guiding principle," knowledge about production is necessary to understand the fates of individuals as well as the development of social orders (Marx, 1859a, pp. 262–4). In particular, he stressed the need to study how ruling classes appropriate surplus, seeing this as the most important and veiled social process. Marx considered the historically specific way "in which unpaid surplus labor is pumped out of direct-producers" to be the "hidden basis of the entire social structure" (Marx, 1894, p. 791). He argued that ruling classes and their allied intermediate strata (e.g. priests, scribes, politicians) create ideologies that mystify exploitation as "divinely sanctioned," "natural," "inevitable," and "just," or conceal it completely. For Marx, ideology is the unintended result of parochial class situations as well as an outcome of conscious, strategic political efforts to distort reality. Overall, Marx saw his materialism as a counterhegemonic method that strips away ideology, laying bare the "real bases" of society and posing critical questions about its dynamics and reproduction, which are otherwise systematically suppressed.

Marx saw societies as "social formations," having interrelated parts, governed by systematic internal relations. The most central concept in his materialist framework is *mode* of production, which includes "productive forces" (i.e. natural resources, tools, labor power, technology/science, modes of cooperation), or those factors that contribute directly to the creation of necessary and surplus product, and "property relations," or class-based social relationships that determine who has effective control over the productive forces and the disposition of product and who must engage in productive labor. Marx considered the mode of production as the "base," or ultimate determinant, of social formations. However, as explained above, he held that the "material factor" included sociocultural facets; even the simplest productive forces (e.g.

prehistorical stone tools) require application of rudimentary technical ideas and social cooperation. Arguably, Marx's own materialist analyses stress most centrally class struggles over the forms of property. Overall, his materialism focuses more on social relationships oriented to material factors than on material conditions *per se*.

In Marx's framework, *superstructure* entails nonproductive "modes of intercourse" and "ideology" that help to reproduce the social conditions necessary to maintain the mode of production. Marx saw the state's coercive powers and other control mechanisms as the most vital means of perpetuating productive forces and property relations. He considered the legal, administrative, military, and ideological arms of complex states to be overtowering sources of class power. But he also argued that other organizations and associations (e.g. families or voluntary groups) help to control, socialize, indoctrinate, or otherwise fashion people to fit into or comply with the existing system of production. Marx contended that "ruling ideas" contribute centrally to this process. Although he did not clarify the exact scope of ideology, he usually implied delimited areas rather than culture *per se*. He knew that, in liberal societies, even counter-hegemonic ideas, like his own, could find their way into public life. Marx saw all social life as bearing the imprints of material conditions. Yet he held that certain facets of culture play a very direct role in the reproduction of the mode of production, while others have little to do with the process.

Marx's materialism points to likely structuring and transforming conditions. It holds that productive forces are usually the "ultimate causal agent" of major change, but treats class struggle as its immediate "motor." Referring to conditions that either muffle or intensify class struggle, Marx spoke of relations of "correspondence" and "contradiction," which occur within the mode of production or between it and superstructure. For example, he held that early capitalist labor organization, technology, and markets "contradicted" the feudal manor's and medieval guild's forms of production and property relations and their related complex of laws, economic ethics, and customs. In his view, the "fettering" of nascent capitalism's superior productive forces by exhausted feudal remnants opened the way for political class conflict between the bourgeoisie and feudal strata. The victorious capitalists eventually captured the state, creating "corresponding" political, legal, and sociocultural forms that fit the emergent mode of production.

The issue of the "primacy" of the material factor, or its status as the "ultimate determining" force, has been one of the most enduring and intense topics of Marxist debate. However, Marx himself was somewhat ambiguous about the topic. Following Adam Smith and other early economists, his "soft" position implied that overall sociocultural development depends on the level of material production and types of appropriation. For example, today's mass culture could not be grasped without reference to the advanced capitalist mode of production. But the fact that it determines the overall sophistication, quantity, and diversity of goods and complexity of culture tells us relatively little about any specific commodity or facet of culture. Treating material forces as a matrix that sets broad limits, this soft position provides sociocultural phenomena relative autonomy. In this regard, Marx's view that epochal social transitions must be rooted in qualitative transformations of production is now repeated by many non-Marxist anthropologists and comparative sociologists, theorizing shifts between hunting and gathering, horticultural, agricultural, and industrial societies.

However, Marx also suggested, at times, a "hard" type of material determination. For example, asserting that "social relations are very closely bound to productive forces," he held that technological transformations "change all" our "social relations" ("The hand-mill gives you society with the feudal lord; the steam-mill, society with the industrial capitalist"). He also asserted that a social formation is never "destroyed before all the productive forces for which it is sufficient have been developed, and new superior relations of production never replace older ones before the material conditions for their existence have matured within the framework of the old society" (Marx, 1847, p. 166; 1859a, p. 263). Hard determinism also appears in his claims about the "inevitability" of certain tendencies of capitalist development or of proletarian victory and socialism. Such points imply that politics and culture are epiphenomenal "reflections" of material dynamics. Hard determinism and counterclaims about the relative autonomy of political and cultural factors have constituted a major boundary separating "scientific," "mechanical," or "orthodox" Marxism from "critical," "Western," or "revisionist" Marxism. Anti-Marxist and post-Marxist critics, stressing a more sweeping or even complete autonomy of politics and culture, usually see Marx as a hard materialist, and, on that basis, reject his ideas *in toto*.

Although hard determinist passages exist in Marx's texts, he suggested much more often a complex, historically contingent materialism, which ought not to be reduced to "technological determinism" (i.e. social change arises from technical change) or to "reflection theory" (i.e. ideas are mere emanations of material reality). He frequently pointed to changes arising from diverse sources (e.g. ideological and political as well as material), which deflect class struggles and blur their outcomes. After Marx's death, Engels criticized the hard determinism of younger Marxists. Although admitting that heated debates with opponents led Marx and him to sometimes rhetorically overstate "the economic side," he insisted that their intent was to create "above all a guide to study, not a lever for construction after the manner of the Hegelian." Embracing a softer view of material primacy, he held that the various facets of culture and society exert their own effects. Engels insisted that Marx and he always believed that "history must be studied afresh," that different societies must be "examined individually," and that the relations between the various structural facets are contingent and cannot be deduced in advance (Engels, 1890a, p. 396; 1890b).

The later split over determinism has been primarily between views that treat materialism as a strict or total ontology giving warrants about "inevitable" patterns of change or indubitable historical truths and approaches that employ it as a heuristic principle pointing to likely sources of tension, conflict, and change and to distinctive types of questions about contingent historical processes. Engels argued unequivocally that he and Marx intended the second or more open-ended, undogmatic form of materialism. Although sometimes making hard ontological claims, Marx employed materialism primarily as a heuristic device. His ideas about the shaping force of the material realm were bound up with emergent capitalism's unparalleled materialist powers and agendas, which led even Weber to speak of their "inexorable" determining force. The rationalizing power of later capitalism, especially that of today's neoliberal structure of accumulation, has produced more narrowly tracked, exactly calculated, and global forms of material determination than even Marx could have imagined. Overall, however, he was prescient about materialist trends that his contemporaries did not see. Yet he still implied mainly an open *historical* materialism posing foci, problems, and issues for a distinctly Marxian sociology.

Even in highly complex, premodern civilizations, productive forces tended to develop incrementally over hundreds or even thousands of years and to diffuse slowly between different regions. By contrast, modern capitalism generated, with lightning speed, a nascent "world market," a "global division of labor," and a greater variety of powerful productive forces than all preceding civilizations put together. Marx's materialism bore the marks of this peculiar time, and, perhaps, is best understood as an effort to come to terms with its unique, new capitalist world, rather than with history *in toto*. The primacy that he gave to material factors arose from his experience of the radical changes wrought by the revolution in productive forces, which, as at no previous time, advanced sweepingly and altered everyday life profoundly.

## Marx's theory of capitalism: labor, value, and extraction

Marx's main contribution to social theory derives from his effort to explain capitalism and overall social modernity through the lens of his materialism. He held that the dynamic of all previous class societies was ongoing; capitalism's developmental tendencies are still shaped by the appropriation of unremunerated labor and product and patterns of resistance to this extractive process. He considered the relationship between the historically specific ruling class and subaltern class of direct producers as the most fundamental social site and center of his inquiry. Rather than entrepreneurship, supply and demand, and consumer choices, Marx saw capitalism's most basic facet to be its complex fusion of advanced technical means of production with highly rationalized means of extraction, which, he held, generate the aforementioned radical disturbance and transformation of social life – "modernity." Thus, he also pointed to conditions that distinguish capitalism from all earlier modes of production.

Marx held that the primary modern class relation, between capitalists and workers, lacks the transparency of precapitalist ties between ruling classes and direct producers. In the simpler orders, he argued, goods are generally produced and consumed locally and productive relations are mostly with one's family and neighbors. Patriarchal domination of women and children and aristocratic exploitation of slaves, serfs, and free peasants employ direct forms of personal dependence, unfreedom, and extraction, which contrast starkly with uncoerced cooperation and production. Holding that "every serf knows" that the lords extract "a definite quantity of his own personal labor power," Marx contended that precapitalist modes of appropriation are visible and understand-able to producers (Marx, 1867, p. 77).

By contrast, Marx held that capitalist modes of cooperation and exploitation are obscured by a highly complex and gravely distorted sociocultural surface. He argued that "the specific social character of each producer's labor does not show itself except in the act of exchange" (Marx, 1867, p. 73). In his view, the exceptionally extensive, impersonal productive and extractive networks are "invisible" to average people. Competitive market relations occlude further capitalism's cooperative side, while ruling ideas, equating wage labor and for-mal-legal equality with substantive freedom and equality, veil its extractive processes. Marx saw the bourgeois interpretation of the capital–labor relation (i.e. a voluntary contract and commensurable exchange between equals) to be a gross distortion. He thought that wealth and ready access to political, police, and cultural means of control provided capitalists with an enormous advantage over single unaffiliated workers. Also, he held that mechanization and deskilling rob workers of the market leverage formerly held by artisans. While the capital-ist's livelihood does not ride on the contract with any single worker, semiskilled operatives usually lack the savings to sustain them in a strike or long search for a "good job," and are easily replaced by individuals from the "reserve army" of unemployed. Overall, Marx saw the contractual view of wage labor (i.e. "free labor") as a central means of ideological domination, shoring up and reducing the costs of the coercive power relation between capitalists and workers.

Marx held that prices, wages, profits, and other capitalist "economic" factors are profoundly "mystified"; they are treated as if they have a life of their own detached from socially organized production and the all-important extractive relation between capitalists and workers. Historicizing Hegel's idea of alienated objectification, Marx referred to the "fetishism of commodities," whereby they are transformed into "independent beings" with their own extrahuman, inherent motions, impacts, and interrelations. In this regard, "a definite social relation ... assumes ... the fantastic form of a relation between things." Marx argued that economists conceal the role of capitalist property relations and appropriation by analyzing prices and wages as manifestations of subjective choice and supply and demand. He compared this view to that of idealist medieval historians, who equate "the middle-ages with spirituality" and, thus, hide the "secret history ... of its landed property." While the young Marx saw capitalist dynamics to be transparent or immediately given, he now treated them as distorted refractions of forces operating below the surface. Probing the depths, the mature Marx fashioned a counterfactual social theory aiming to "discover" underlying, shap-ing "conditions and relations of a definite, historically determined mode-of-production" (Marx, 1867, pp. 72–3, 76, 80–3).

Revising earlier ideas of Smith and Ricardo, Marx framed his "labor theory of value" to explain commodity production and capital accumulation. By contrast to his concepts of class and ideology, his view of value is sometimes treated as "economic theory" and, therefore, separate from his sociology. However, his main point is precisely that economic phenomena are not mere emanations of an independent realm of technical conditions or of an individual psychology of self-interest. Rather, they are "social relations." Marx challenged the bourgeois view of capital as a "mysterious and self-creating source of interest," which he considered to be an "automatic fetish." He wanted to expose such ideas as reifications, arising from the matrix of capitalism's sweeping commodification of sociocultural life (Marx, 1894, p. 392). He intended his labor theory of value to identify the very heart or engine of commodification and, especially, to shed light on the central, yet highly mystified, historically specific form of unpaid labor and related mechanisms of class control.

Marx saw the "immense accumulation of commodities" to be capitalism's most distinctive surface feature, arguing that only recently have people become so dependent on commodity production that "growth," or ever-expanding markets and money-making, is now experienced as a "end in itself" and purpose of social life (Marx, 1867, pp. 35, 151–2). He defined the "commodity" as any object that has "use value" (i.e. provides for some want or need) and "exchange value" (i.e. trades systematically against other goods). While individual preferences are central for use values, Marx held, exchange value is a crystallization of "social substance," or the "labor time" that it took to find, mine, refine, or make the object. In his view, bourgeois economists mystify capitalism by reifying its surface phenomena, or treating the proportions at which various commodities exchange against each other as happenstance outcomes of subjective consumer choices. By contrast, he argued that prices are "simply the form under which certain social relations manifest themselves," and that, as all commodity forms, they are "the material envelope of the human labor spent upon it." Thus, for Marx, the "definite," capitalist social process of appropriating labor time operates beneath the flux of market prices and, ultimately, determines their overall pattern (Marx, 1867, pp. 35–70, 91–2).

Marx qualified his theory of value in a number of ways. Rather than labor time *per se*, he stipulated that the exchange value of commodities reflect "socially necessary" labor time, or the average intensity of labor reflecting an industry's level of development. From this vantage point, a subsection of producers, employing very inefficient or backward processes, do not shape overall exchange values in an industry. Also, Marx held that subjective preferences and supply and demand have substantial effects on the "market prices" of individual commodities. For example, when particular goods are in great oversupply or have gone out of style, they can be priced at far less than their labor values or be worthless. The converse occurs when a highly desired or essential commodity is in short supply. Marx saw use value to be highly historically variable and, thus, to exert powerful multicausal effects on market prices. Although conceding that bourgeois economists provide reasonably effective tools for analyzing these "accidental" price movements, Marx believed that their theories fail to grasp the causes of systematic or overall price patterns. Finally, Marx's theory of value itself presumed conditions approximating the free market. He held that monopoly and other bureaucratic manipulations can distort value relations. Depending on the situation, monopoly prices may be set far below or far above their labor values. Surface fluctuations aside, Marx argued, aggregate prices in an entire capitalist industry or economy gravitate toward an average price set by socially necessary labor time or labor value (Marx, 1867, pp. 35–70, 270; 1885, p. 292; 1894, pp. 190–9, 437–8). Most importantly, however, Marx's main aim was not to predict price formations, but to lay bare the "social" or extractive process underlying them.

Seeing the commodification of labor or rise of wage labor as the heart of developing capitalism, Marx stressed labor power's unique characteristics as a commodity. He held that the value of "labor power," as other commodities, is set by the labor time needed to reproduce it; in this case, "the means of subsistence necessary for the maintenance of the laborer" (Marx, 1867, pp. 167–76). Although class struggles between capital and labor determine just how close wages are to subsistence, Marx argued, workers usually produce much more value than is returned to them in wages. Accordingly, by contrast to all other commodities, labor power produces systematically more value than it commands in exchange. This "surplus labor time" is crystallized in the objects produced by workers and realized in the money-form when capitalists sell the items as commodities. Marx contended that overall capitalist profitability depends on the unequal wage exchange, deriving ultimately from systematic appropriation of surplus labor time and consequent "surplus value." Thus, accumulation depends on proletarianization and rationalization of labor processes. The fate of individual capitalists rides on their capacity to maintain high "rates of exploitation" or to minimize paid labor time and maximize surplus value. Darwinian economic competition requires them to employ strategies such as increasing labor discipline, reducing real wages, extending work hours without added compensation, finding new pools of workers accustomed to lower levels of subsistence, and engineering the work process and overall factory regime to maximize the speed and intensity of labor per time unit. In this fashion, Marx attempted to theorize capitalism's specific form of unpaid labor and most basic site of ideological distortion and class conflict.

Expressing contradictory facets of capitalism, Marx posed binary oppositions, related to the commodity's "two-sidedness" (i.e. use value and exchange value). He pitted "concrete labor," or specialized activities that produce use values, against "abstract labor," or the "homogeneous human labor" crystallized in exchange value, and, especially, *real wealth*, or the various use values created by concrete labor, against *abstract wealth*, or the profits and accumulated capital based on surplus value or expropriated labor. Marx used these polar ideas to draw out the tensions between capitalism's distorted surface and depth determinants and between its exploitative facets (i.e. modes of appropriation) and its progressive aspects (i.e. revolutionary capacities for producing use values). Most importantly, he held that bourgeois ideology conflates creation of abstract wealth, or capitalist accumulation, with production of real wealth. In Marx's view, the claim that investors or entrepreneurs "create wealth" *per se* is a gross lie that equates private fortune with the overall social wealth that provides for basic human needs. Although conceding that these contradictory sides of economic growth are entwined inextricably under capitalism, Marx held that the two dimensions have fundamentally different qualities and, thus, should be decoupled analytically. He also thought that the two could be decoupled socially in a future postcapitalist order. Marx hoped that his labor theory of value enhanced the historical possibility for separating abstract wealth from real wealth and for creating a society where use value is the primary or even exclusive goal of production and surplus labor is deployed for communal purposes, rather than for private appropriation.

## Manufacture to modern industry: "science" enters production

Countering Smith's scenario of a "diligent, intelligent, and . . . frugal elite" organizing "lazy rascals" into a responsible workforce (i.e. "primitive accumulation"), Marx contended that capitalism emerged from the dissolution of feudal society and, especially, from expropriation of serf and guild producers, who were "robbed" of their means of production and forced to live by the sale of their labor (Marx, 1867, pp. 713–15). Bringing the complete demise of the old regime, Marx argued, two phases of industrial transformation instituted full capitalist domination and modernity: an initial proletarianization or expansion of *manufacture* (i.e. factory production with limited specialization and simple technologies) and a later move to hyperspecialized and hypertechnical *modern industry*. Marx held that mechanization and, especially, automation magnify greatly the tensions, or contradictory relations, between use value and exchange value and initiate a social decoupling of the production of real wealth from capitalist accumulation. Because "science" replaces "living labor" as the key source of use value and real wealth, Marx argued, modern industry provides the material basis for an ephocal transcendence of capitalism and all earlier class-based social orders dependent on the appropriation of unpaid labor.

According to Marx, manufacture arose gradually from the mid-sixteenth through the late eighteenth centuries in highly developed parts of Europe, especially England. Many propertyless peasant and craft producers were re-employed in small factories. Although seeing manufacture to be anchored in handicraft, Marx held that the beginnings of specialized cooperation advanced "productive power" substantially. Most importantly, separating workers from their means of production, removing labor from the household and family, and employing it within a factory regime of impersonal authority forged a distinct, specialized, "economic" social space for "work" of unparalleled intensity and systematic appropriation of surplus labor time. Money compensation per time unit, or wage labor, provided capitalists with a precise system for calculating rates of extraction. Never before had labor been subjected to such rational appropriation. Marx also argued that increased linkages to wider, more fully monetarized markets intensified competition among capitalists, pressing them into untiring efforts to increase labor coordination, continuity, and discipline. The escalating pace of rationalization centered on maximizing rates of exploitation or surplus-value extraction by increasing the efficiency of production and accelerating the intensity of labor. Because technological change was limited and craft labor was still central, manufacture generated hierarchies based on the relative complexity of functions and a major split between skilled and unskilled labor (Marx, 1867, pp. 336–68).

Marx stressed emphatically that the most important facet of manufacture is the "complete separation" of direct producers from their means of production (Marx, 1867, pp. 714–15). He saw capitalist development "continually" extending and absolutizing this split, stripping workers of their intelligence as well as their property. Marx contended that manufacture initiates the transferal of the individual worker's "knowledge," "judgment," "will," and "cunning" (e.g. formerly basic for hunters and gatherers, peasants, and artisans) to the "workshop as a whole." He argued that modern industry radicalizes this displacement by eliminating remaining pockets of craft workers to overcome bottlenecks and advance rationalization. While manufacture imposes partial, uneven deskilling, Marx held, modern industry's hyperspecialization and mechanization level workers into a homogeneous deskilled mass, or "mere appendage," to the machine. Believing that the industrial operative degenerates into a broken "monstrosity," Marx decried the insouciant bourgeois view of worker stupefaction and marginalization as acceptable costs of "progress" (Marx, 1867, pp. 360–5). Marx held that modern industrial workers suffer terrible work conditions, minimal subsistence, and extreme expendability and that the "reserve army" of unemployed multiplies. Although he noted the appearance of a "superior class" of technical workers (e.g. "engineers" and "mechanics"), he thought that their numbers would remain "unimportant," compared to the massive expansion of proletarian and subproletarian ranks (Marx, 1867, p. 420). However, rejecting utopian ideas of a return to agrarian or artisan production, Marx treated modern industry's mechanization and overall technical rationalization as progressive events. Yet he wanted workers to reap the benefits of the collective intelligence that inheres in the new type of complexly associated labor.

Marx held that modern capitalism's "war of all-against-all" maximizes workshop "despotism" and threatens to "turn all society into one immense factory" (Marx, 1867, pp. 270, 356). Yet he also contended that mass homogenization would stir growing class consciousness and political class struggles, already visible in increased union membership and sociopolitical reform (e.g. the "tenhour day"). However, he was highly critical of the modest nature of labor's "gains," in a context where human drudgery, misery, and poverty grew explosively and unparalleled productive powers served private fortunes. Marx held that extreme class polarization will eventually generate proletarian revolution. He was aware that such collective agency depends on historically contingent political struggles, but he thought that emancipatory possibilities inhere in capitalism's structural contradiction between rapidly mounting technical capacities for the production of use value, or real wealth, and the fettering force of the ever more frenzied capitalist drive for expanded exchange value. Marx argued that applied science, by reducing reliance on "living labor," diminishes the source of abstract wealth in the same stroke that it revolutionizes the means to produce real wealth. He claimed that mechanization erodes the very basis of capitalist profitability and creates material grounds for socialism.

In Marx's core argument about the "general law of capitalist accumulation," he contended that modern industry produces a trend toward automation among the largest, most advanced producers, increasing sharply the "organic composition of capital" (Marx, 1867, pp. 612–712). In other words, the proportion of "fixed capital," or machines, tools, and other purely technical aspects of production, rises, and the proportion represented by living labor shrinks. Seeing "exchange value" to derive only from the unequal wage labor relation or specifically the unpaid portion of living labor, Marx argued that the popular idea, articulated by classical economists, that "profit" derives from fixed capital or technology obscures "the entire secret of capitalist production" (Marx, 1885, p. 199). Marx saw machinery as a form of "crystallized labor" that cannot create surplus value, even though it greatly speeds up the transfer of value from labor to commodities and contributes even more fundamentally to the creation of use value or real wealth. Marx acknowledged that mechanization can raise profits sharply for individual producers, increasing productivity and market-leverage. Gaining competitive advantages and barriers to entry (i.e. massive fixed capital costs keep out all but the richest competitors), modern industrial firms, using advanced technology, can attain monopoly or oligopoly control of their markets and windfall profits from bureaucratic manipulation of prices. According to Marx, however, such producers employ a perverted form of social power and social planning that goes beyond capitalist accumulation (which is predicated on competition) (Marx, 1894, p. 880).

Marx deduced his "law" of the falling rate of profits from his overall theory of capitalist accumulation and labor theory of value (Marx, 1894, pp. 211–66). Although mechanization initially increases the absolute numbers of factory workers and overall mass of surplus value, Marx held, proportionally less living labor is employed in the productive process and is crystallized in commodities. Thus, he believed that the rate of surplus value and, ultimately, profits must fall. However, he pointed out capitalist strategies that counter the process, e.g. intensifying labor, sinking wages below subsistence, and seeking surplus profits by moving production to "backward" regions with much lower living standards and wages. Marx saw profitability crises to be a major impetus of uneven capitalist globalization. Referring to Western colonialism, he warned of a "new international division of labor" refashioning the globe according "to the requirements of the chief centers of modern industry," and, thus, retarding or instituting one-sided development in peripheral regions (Marx, 1867, p. 451). Marx knew that verifying empirically his law of falling profits would be extremely difficult, or impossible, because of "counteracting influences," partial and unreliable data on profits, and myriad technical problems in computing overall rates of profit. However, he pointed to what he believed to be observable social effects of the process, and, on the basis of his theory, predicted trends toward "overpopulation" of "disposable," or "unemployed," workers, vastly concentrated capital, huge centralized firms, great imbalances of wealth and poverty, overaccumulation and underconsumption of capital, and financial speculation spurring deeper, ever more socially disruptive, cyclical economic crises.

Marx first hinted at this gloomy scenario in his youthful metaphor about capitalism being a "sorcerer" that weds vast productive power to equally vast destructive power and that conjures up enormously powerful, uncontrollable forces (Marx and Engels, 1845, p. 489). However, Marx's optimistic side was not limited to his ideas about proletarian revolution. He also argued that the beginnings of progressive sociopolitical transformation were already visible in advanced capitalism, interpreting trends that appeared with modern industry (i.e. monopoly, managerial control, and state interference) as constituting "the abolition of the capitalist mode-of-production within the capitalist mode-of-production itself" (Marx, 1894, p. 438). Anticipating Berle's and Means's progressive-liberal vision of corporate capitalism's socializing tendencies, Marx contended that emergent corporate planning, separation of management from ownership, employment of knowledge-based technologies, interfirm cooperation, and increased government regulation were "transitional forms" to an emergent postcapitalist order. His vision of late capitalism as "a self-dissolving contradiction" implies the possibility of a peaceful socialist transition (Marx, 1894, pp. 266, 436–41).

Marx suggested that his capitalist "laws of motion" were rooted ultimately in labor-intensive manufacture and age-old class dynamics. Like all previous class systems, early capitalism was still centered on the appropriation of unpaid labor. For this reason, Marx claimed that capitalism, at least in a figurative sense, replays human "prehistory." But he also detected something entirely new or the seeds of a fundamentally different historical dynamic. In *Capital*, he stated that "modern industry...makes science a productive force distinct from labor and presses it into the service of capital" (Marx, 1867, p. 361). His 1857–8 notebooks (*Grundrisse*) for his *magnum opus* traced the long evolution away from independent production to a future state of fully developed capital, where "the creation of real wealth becomes less dependent on labor time and the quantity of labor employed," and "depends, rather, upon the general development of science and the progress of technology or application of science in production." Marx believed that, here, the combined powers of "general scientific work" and an intricate system of cooperation begin an active dissolution of capital (Marx, 1871, pp. 86, 90–1). He held that, in this late stage, capitalist accumulation would be based on a profoundly contradictory, vestigial property relation, while use value or real wealth would depend primarily on the ascendent science/technology form. In this climate, Marx argued, efforts to perpetuate capitalism and wage labor will produce increasingly extreme irrationalities, especially as the biggest industries approach automation and monopoly. At this point, Marx held that the system, even if monopolies continued to dominate, would not operate in accord with the logic of capital.

According to Marx, a fusion of collective intelligence and exploitation inheres in advanced capitalist societies. However, the gradual separation of mental and physical labor and later application of science to production increases the contradictory tendencies. Although driven by capitalist competition, scientific and technological development becomes an increasingly autonomous force, undermining the class relations that originally conjured it up. Marx thought that modern industry refined and suffused, more widely than ever before, the tacit knowledge of associated producers. Moreover, in his view, applied science rationalizes this knowledge, making it more reflective and deliberate. He believed, however, that only a complete severing of the ties with capitalism could control science's destructive tendencies and, finally, decouple production from extraction, coercion, and domination. Pointing to a future moment when "production based upon exchange value collapses," Marx stated:

> Free development of individualities, and hence not the reduction of necessary labor time in order to posit surplus labor, but in general the reduction of necessary labor of society to a minimum, to which corresponds the artistic, scientific, etc., development of individuals made possible by the time thus set free and the means produced for all of them. (Marx, 1871, p. 92)

According to Marx, science domesticated by communal democratic ends would be deployed to help guide an epochal, emancipatory, sociocultural rupture with all pre-existing modes of production.

## After capitalism: how soon democracy?

Marx's theories of materialism and capitalism constitute his core legacy in social theory. His enormous public significance, however, derives mainly from his impact on politics, i.e. communist, socialist, and social democratic movements, parties, and regimes, left-leaning labor movements, anticolonial or nationalist insurgencies, liberation struggles, and revolutionary regimes, and even certain "post-Marxist" movements. Marx advocated the unity of theory and praxis, but his political thought is fragmentary and less developed than his other social theory. Although normatively embracing communism, he never elaborated a detailed theory of postcapitalism. According to his historicist method of immanent critique, the prospects for revolution depend on the ability to assess and respond to constraints and resources of specific historical situations and levels of development. Thus, divergent social contexts require different types of agency and forbid a comprehensive, general blueprint of postcapitalism in advance. This emphasis on "local knowledge" has been ignored by later twentieth-century critics.

However, images of postcapitalism can still be gleaned from Marx's polemics, programmatic political points, and theoretical asides about communism. In his view, the new order will be "a spontaneous product of a long, painful process of development" and of very advanced material conditions. He asserted that "freely associated" producers will "consciously" regulate their activity according to "a settled plan" in this demystified, postcapitalist world. He contended that capitalist investment and profits would be eliminated, that communities would decide collectively what needs and wants must be provided for and plan ways to meet them, and that depoliticized public administration will perform the key functions formerly provided by capitalist states, firms, and markets. Treating labor and its products as "social" entities, Marx argued, communist planning would return part of the surplus to producers and retain the rest for public purposes (Marx, 1867, pp. 78–80). Engels held that "systematic, definite organization" would end the anarchy of production and war of all-against-all, raising society above "mere animal conditions of existence into really human ones" (Engels,

1892, p. 323). Weber and neoclassical economists demurred, arguing that social-ist planning is doomed to bureaucratic inefficiency and that only competitive markets could effectively process vastly complicated information about produc-tion and consumption and mesh supply and demand. These critics were prescient about Soviet-style, total-planning regimes, but they failed to anticipate the successes of twentieth-century mixed regimes. Marx implied that a science of planning will arise in the new postcapitalist orders, but he did not attempt to confront the broad range of complex technical and political issues concerning socialist planning.

At the start, Marx argued, a new communist society would "in every respect, economically, morally, and intellectually, [be] still stamped with the birth-marks of the old society from whose womb it emerges" (Marx, 1875, p. 85). He contended that sweeping planning capacities cannot be created *de novo*, but must draw on resources of the pre-existing regime. Planners would have to appropriate methods employed by capitalist states and firms, especially their uses of science and technology in production, distribution, crisis management, and overall administration. As explained above, Marx thought that these facets were capitalism's richest, most socialized resources and that their utility would be greatly enhanced after capitalists were expropriated and productive property was socialized. But he argued that communism would still face the hard task of remaking science and technology incrementally and experimentally to fit the emergent conditions.

Marx scolded the German Social-Democrats for exaggerating the immediate benefits to workers from a possible communist takeover (Marx, 1875, pp. 83–8). Arguing that effusive promises would be deflated and cause political failure, Marx's realist stance followed directly from his historicism and materialism. For example, he argued that a major portion of communist workers' surplus product would have to be held back to maintain productive forces, deal with crises, and pay for improved administration, schools, welfare, and other public services. Also, he contended that a new communist regime, attempting to create a mater-ial base for social progress, would reinvest much surplus in technical develop-ment and expanded production. Thus, he felt that the new regime's increased costs would forbid an immediate radical transformation of the conditions of labor and that work would still be remunerated unequally to address unequal effort, skills, and needs. Although implying that the old system's worst abuses would be altered relatively quickly, he stressed that the new society would retain many capitalist facets and problems of life.

In a coldly realistic tone, Marx held that the "first phase of communist society" would carry the "defects" of capitalism's limited "economic" and "cul-tural development." Wanting to avert counter-revolution, he contended that "the first step in the revolution . . . is to raise the proletariat to the position of ruling-class to win the battle for democracy." In his view, the state's coercive apparatus must, at first, remain intact or even be rationalized. He argued that in this phase of "revolutionary transformation . . . the state can be nothing but *the revolution-ary dictatorship of the proletariat*" (Marx, 1875, pp. 87, 95; Marx and Engels, 1845, pp. 504–6). Marx held that the proletariat's politically organized wing would expropriate the bourgeoisie and centralize primary means of production and infrastructure (e.g. banking, communication, transport). They would also "increase the total productive forces as rapidly as possible," and create "industrial armies" in agriculture. Although suggesting some progressive reform (e.g. free education), Marx implied a near total centralization of power by a much enlarged state, which would employ "despotic" force, when necessary, to implement its modernization plan. Speaking of the need for the "strictest centralization," Marx and Engels held that communist state authorities would need to monopolize power and ignore calls for "freedom for the communities" or "self-government." The main aim would be to create productive and sociocultural infrastructure for a later, more complete break with bourgeois society (Marx and Engels, 1845, pp. 504–6; 1850a, pp. 284–5).

Marx also spoke in a utopian manner about a "higher phase" of communism, which would stress "all-round development of the individual" and the ideal of "From each according to his abilities, to each according to their needs." He held that the old "bourgeois society, with its classes and class antagonisms," will be replaced by "association, in which the free development of each is the condition for the free development of all." In the new communal order, Marx contended, people will be freed from labor, and "public power" will "lose its political character" (i.e. the state, as we know it, will fade away). Expressing the same point, Engels stated that "the government of persons is replaced by the administration of things....The State is not abolished. *It dies out*" (Engels, 1892, p. 321). Marx thought that full communism requires a radical rupture with capitalism and an ephocal transformation of institutions, culture, and selves. All this presumes a much higher level of material and sociocultural development, requiring a very, very long period of gestation.

Marx never articulated all-important political constraints on the proposed proletarian "dictatorship." Moreover, his mature scathing views about the repressiveness of bourgeois states and rights suggest a dismissive attitude to liberal institutions, and his passages about the need for bureaucratic centralism, *carte blanche* power, and productivist reorganization, during the transition to communism, imply a possible authoritarian regime or broad suspension of democracy and individual rights in the name of the future communist utopia. Although few and brief, Marx's unqualified passages about proletarian dictatorship were later used to justify forced modernization, stultifying bureaucracy, and overall repression under actually existing communism.

However, Marx's report on the Paris Commune, *The Civil War in France*, offered an opposing scenario (Marx, 1871, pp. 328–43). Embracing enthusiastically the radical democratic, two-month insurgency, he celebrated the Commune's decentralized, participatory features, which proletarian dictatorship seemed to rule out. He held that the Communard working class did not expect "miracles" and that their greatest achievement was the regime's "working existence," which was forged pragmatically by average people employing participatory means, rather than by a political vanguard and scientific-planning elite asserting total power. Marx described how the Commune reduced economic inequality, dismantled capitalist and clerical power, instituted short terms of office, extended suffrage, governed by participatory assembly, and even created "cheap government" by disbanding the army and debureaucratizing administration. Contradicting his idea that radical democracy requires a long gestation, he portrayed "plain" working people, who lacked experience in governance, rising to the occasion quickly, harmonizing prudence with ideals, and undergoing personal transformation in the process. He implied that they became committed to their duties, motivated by social ends, rather than private interests. Marx reported similar tendencies among "all the healthy" elements of other classes and functionaries. Finally, he described graphically the "self-sacrificing heroism" of "men, women, and children," defending their new democracy against the national army and paying with "heaps of corpses" (Marx, 1857–8, pp. 348–55). Leaving aside questions of historical accuracy, Marx's comments about the Commune express a side of his mature political thought (appearing in scattered places in his later work) that expands his youthful view of democracy and clashes with his passages on dictatorship. The Paris Commune essay raises basic theoretical questions. Was the Commune initiating an immediate leap to the "higher stage" of communism? Could radical democracy have been sustained? Regrettably, the Commune was too short lived to address these questions, being crushed brutally by the army.

In the second preface to the *Manifesto*, written shortly after the Commune, Marx and Engels (1872, pp. 174–5) stated that new historical conditions (i.e. "gigantic strides" in industry and working-class party organization) led them to question the work's programmatic section on the transition to communism. They said that they would have reworded it, had they decided to revise the document. However, they did not retract the idea of proletarian dictatorship. Overall, their idea of a postrevolutionary centralization of power has a basis in their broader thought, following, in part, from their stress on "determinate negations." Accordingly, revolution must build on elements of earlier conditions and create new institutions incrementally. Moreover, Marx did not see capitalism providing distinct sociopolitical resources for democratic reconstruction. In his view, the modern state and civil society were perverted totally by bourgeois power and culture, and modern industry and capital evaporated all former bases of communal identity and association. As exemplified by his view of Judaism, he welcomed capitalist leveling of traditional groups as a necessary step in bourgeois rationalization and political consolidation, paving the way for proletarian solidarity, revolution, and ultimate "total emancipation" (Marx, 1843c). Treating the bourgeois revolution as a clearing mechanism, Marx located resources for revolutionary change mostly in economic organization and closely related aspects of science/technology and associated labor. His view of communist transition inhering in and accentuating late-capitalist rationalization does not articulate determinate bases for wider democratic association and culture. It is unclear how such a centralized regime and leveled populace could forge the types of citizenship, groups, values, and selves needed for Marx's ultimate goal of a self-regulating, emancipated society of "associated producers," which he saw, however briefly, emergent in the Paris Commune. In this light, his "higher stage" of communism would, at some point, have to be created *de novo*.

Regardless of the shortcomings, Marx's political theorizing was prescient in ways that many critics ignore. First, twentieth-century labor movements, especially in northern Europe, achieved substantial class solidarity and refashioned capitalism. However, post-Second World War era advances in social rights, substantive equality, and living standards, ironically, weakened the impetus of labor's struggle for socialism. Similar taming of labor's political goals occurred in many advanced capitalist societies (Przeworski, 1985). Reconfigured capitalist workplaces and complexly segmented labor forces, as well as communism's dismal repression and inefficiency, also eroded socialist aspirations and class-based movements. The late twentieth-century neoliberal revival ended the post-war trend toward more robust social states and decreased class inequality, but recommodification began to generate new class-based conflicts. Marx, himself, saw class struggle and dynamics as episodic affairs. Overall, however, working-class movements have had an enormous political impact on twentieth-century capitalism, as Marx predicted. Second, Marx held that state administration could be depoliticized, and even detected this trend in the Paris Commune. Rather than quiescence, he implied that, after the class issue is defused, conflicts over decommodified public goods would shift from challenges about their overall legitimacy to value questions about the relative importance of different issues and to instrumental matters of cost, efficiency, and patterns of public resource allocation. Although recently challenged by global neoliberalism, social democracy, at its postwar height, decommodified many public goods and generated widespread belief in their legitimacy.

Polar political scenarios in Marx's work (i.e. dictatorship versus radical democracy) foreshadowed fundamental splits in the twentieth-century left and contrary directions in Marxist theory. Alvin Gouldner (1980) identified "two Marxisms": determinist positions that legitimate party discipline and state administration versus voluntaristic approaches that affirm spontaneous, radical, or revolutionary actions. The dynamics of twentieth-century Marxism, socialism, and communism were shaped largely by the interplay of these two chief traditions. By the end of the century, however, decline, dilution, or failure of communist regimes and parties, as well as of "wars of national liberation," once again brought forward the problematical issue of democracy and made postwar political agendas seem moribund. By contrast, global neoliberalism, growing inequality, and failing social welfare programs made Marx's core theoretical arguments about socio-economic issues seem relevant again (Cassidy, 1997).

## Four areas of tension in Marx's social theory

Of course, like any major theoretical effort, Marx's thought has been criticized on many different fronts. I will not attempt a comprehensive summary of these highly varied critiques, but will point to four important areas of tension in his thought.

THE POLITICAL DEFICIT Smashing Hegel's claims about state neutrality, Marx's early work stressed bureaucracy's gross materialism, toadyism, careerism, formalism, pseudo-meritocracy, and rigid hierarchy. Later, in the *Brumaire*, he anticipated a new form of total power, independent of the leading capitalist class. But he never used these rich insights to theorize a possible dark side to communism. Although celebrating, at times, radical democracy, Marx affirmed late-capitalist industrialism, seeing its complex cooperation and technology as *the* primary social resources of modernity. Even putting aside his comments about proletarian dictatorship, Marx did not attend adequately to the huge problems entailed in state appropriation of productive forces and highly centralized administration. Overall, he implied that expropriation of the bourgeoisie insured that democracy and administrative neutrality would eventually be realized in a very advanced stage of postcapitalism. As Marx predicted, twentieth-century communism suffered the privations of an early social state. However, adding greatly to the anticipated problems of planning, management, and distribution, communist officials became primarily a self-interested privileged stratum, and intransigent political interests and power struggles produced arbitrariness, clientalism, and authoritarianism. Regardless of recent neoliberal trends, the possibilities for socialism or mixed regimes are still an open historical question, likely to arise again in the next serious capitalist crisis. But Marx provides few resources for resolving the complex political and technical problems of such regimes.

**THE MISSING EMANCIPATORY SUBJECT** Marx's claims about the revolutionary proletariat and inevitability of the conditions that will bring them to power are another deeply problematical theme of his political thought. His hopes about the proletariat bear the imprint of the early phase of the Second Industrial Revolution, when workers were being deskilled and homogenized to fit emergent, Fordist mass production. Shortly after Marx's death, labor began to be segmented much more complexly than he ever imagined; various levels and types of managerial and wage labor positions were differentiated according to divergent educational grades and by gender, race, ethnicity, and other ascriptive criteria. Many writers have analyzed the consequent splits that blocked the type of proletarian solidarity that Marx hoped for. Later twentieth-century restructuring transformed workplaces even more radically, and forged far more complex, globally dispersed segmentation and disjunctive, cross-cutting class, subclass, and status group hierarchies. Thus, Marxian ideas about the revolutionary proletariat or even an alternative unified emancipatory subject appeared moribund. However, in the United States, highly paid technical, financial, and "infotainment" positions increased, while low-wage, part-time service work expanded much more rapidly. Late-century growth polarized jobs, income, and wealth. The professional middle class flourished and the stock market soared, but lower middle and lower segments of the American workforce suffered stagnating wages, increasing insecurity, and eroding health care and benefits. Poverty grew rapidly among female-headed families, minorities, and poorly paid workers. In Europe, "jobless growth" resulted in postwar highs in unemployment. Polarization of income and wealth grew on a global basis, reflecting neoliberal free market and free trade policies and recommodification of public goods. Industrial expansion in "the developing countries" was reminiscent of nineteenth-century capitalism, with wages sometimes below subsistence levels, terrible work conditions, state repression, and a new "labor movement...struggling to be born" (Greider, 1997, p. 34). Although unionized, blue-collar, labor declined in many rich countries, restructuring, globalization, and polarization generated class compression and new forms of homogeneity of material fate among many workers. Although Marx's theory of the revolutionary proletariat does not hold under current conditions, his broader ideas about class consciousness and political class struggle are still open questions that may soon be tested again.

**OBJECTIONABLE TOTALITIES** The idea of "totality" has been a much debated topic in the history of Marxism (e.g. Jay, 1984). Marx created a basis for a historically specific materialist sociology that puts aside wistful illusions, but it is entwined with an impassioned emancipatory ideal that has had divergent directions and impacts. Although Marx's normative project inspired his effort to unify theory and praxis and much of his best sociological work, it has also been the source of totalizing claims about inevitable progress and about how materialism offers *the* explanation of history, *the* correct understanding of the contemporary situation, and *the* single route to emancipation. As many critics have argued, the presumption of grasping history in a total indubitable way has affinity for centralized authority, elite decision-making, and top-down planning. Marxist academic and party politics have often been plagued by this rigidity, taking on the quality of dogmatic religious belief or even an authoritarian catechism. But the counter themes to this rigidity dominate in Marx's overall corpus. Today, new cultural theorists often express a reverse type of dogmatism, universalizing "local knowledge" and conflating totalities with "broad" historical discourses or theories (Fraser, 1989, p. 13n2). Putting the totalizing tendencies aside, Marx's type of broad historical theory is needed more than ever to grasp the global system.

**TARNISHED FAITH IN SCIENCE AND MODERNIZATION** Marx did not live to experience the application of science to the means of mass destruction or recent threats of overdevelopment, chemical contamination, and global warming. Many theorists' optimistic hopes about science and rationality were shattered or, at least, sobered greatly by the First World War. Moreover, the Second World War era's advanced military technologies, propaganda machines, and fascism, Nazism, Stalinism, the Holocaust, and Hiroshima appeared to be industrial modernization gone mad. The postwar economic expansion once again fueled high hopes about science and technology, but vapid mass consumption, high-tech wars, mass surveillance, major environmental crises and risks, planning failures, and numerous other problems, relating to private and public sector applications of technical knowledge, stimulated strong challenges to the legitimacy of science and modernization. Reminiscent of the Frankfurt School's mid-century "dialectic-of-Enlightenment" critique, new challenges to rational culture reappeared in the form of postmodernism and cultural theory. The

Enlightenment project was reinscribed with the domination of nature, restless instrumentalism, environmental degradation, colonialism, racism, sexism, and even the Holocaust. The cultural left often saw Marx as the prototypical representative of Enlightenment hubris and error. And diverse thinkers heralded a new era, where concern for "risk" and "local knowledge" makes obsolescent deployment of science and planning to solve big public problems and seek socioeconomic justice. Is the era of such intervention over? Will the problems be left to fester? Could planning be pacified, or must the old defects always reappear? If planning is exhausted, what options remain? What threats arise from re-enchantment and aestheticized tribal politics? Although Marx's view of science must be rethought, he framed the idea that grossly uneven, unjust, uncontrolled, and unsustainable development arises from a distinctive fusion of science *and capitalism*, rather than from science or rationality *per se*. This question remains a pressing one. In this regard, antimodern critics are amnesiac about the irrationalist and mythic side of fascism. Science and rational culture are major resources of modernity, and will likely be crucial areas of contestation and struggle in the new millennium.

## Marx's Place in Modern Social Theory

### Crisis of Marxism? Post-Marxism and postmodernism

In the late twentieth century, especially after the 1989 collapse of Eastern European communism and the erosion of Chinese communism from official corruption, the repression in Tiananmen Square, and economic liberalization, many thinkers once again pronounced an end to socialism and the death of Marx. Riding the wave of the politics of 1989, Francis Fukuyama held that Hegel's argument that the liberal state would resolve the contradiction between liberty and equality and end history had been vindicated by "the monumental failure of Marxism as a basis for real-world societies" and by global neoliberal hegemony. Fukuyama held that it is Marx, rather than Hegel, that should be stood "right-side up" (Fukuyama, 1992, pp. 64–5). His neoconservative celebration of ascendent minimalist, free-market democracy and the triumphant defeat of postwar trends toward increased regulation and redistribution was widely covered in the US press. However, many progressive theorists, such as Anthony Giddens, also held that class politics are dead, or have been replaced by the postmaterialist new social movements and "life politics." Taking a more centrist position, "beyond left and right," they were open to engaging liberal views of the market, civil society, and planning. In this context, Giddens stated: "The Promethean outlook which so influenced Marx should be more or less abandoned in the face of the insuperable complexity of society and nature. A drawing back from the ambitions of the Enlightenment is surely necessary" (Giddens 1994, p. 79; Aronson 1995; Boynton 1997).

Even prior to 1989, Marxist and socialist thinkers began to suggest that their tradition was losing vitality. For example, Perry Anderson (1983) held that "Western Marxist" social theory was at an "end"; Martin Jay (1984) chronicled the decline in detail the following year; Ernesto Laclau and Chantal Mouffe (1985) held that materialism and class politics were exhausted, calling for a "post-Marxist" shift to "discursive democracy" and plural new social movement politics; and the Marxist Ellen Meiksins Wood (1986) countered their move vigorously, yet still implied that the new cultural politics were ascendent and had gravely weakened left politics and theory. In the 1990s, many Marxists and former Marxists spoke in pessimistic tones. For example, Habermas (Habermas and Michnik, 1994, p. 11) argued that the left has given up criticizing capitalism at the very moment when economic problems have mounted enormously. He contended that the current situation cries out for increased action from the state, but that political and sociocultural conditions forbid such a move. Similarly, Claus Offe (1996) asserted that the socialist ideal has been emptied of content and that European welfare states are rapidly losing legitimacy. He held that the very idea of progressive modernization, central to Marx's Enlightenment project, is now moribund. Ironically, Offe's claims about "zero options" and "no alternatives" converge unhappily with Fukuyama's cheery view of neoliberal dominance.

A century ago, Georg Simmel (1900, p. 484) spoke about the rise of tragic cultural sensibilities, pointing to a "secret restlessness" and "helpless urgency" that drive people "from socialism to Nietzsche, from Böcklin to impressionism, from Hegel to Schopenhauer and back again." In mid-century, Max Horkheimer and Theodore Adorno held that mass consumption and propaganda neutralized the cultural bases of immanent critique and emancipatory social movements. They held that a new approach was needed to address the nearly complete foreclosure of critical thought by "total administration" and "one-dimensional" culture. Breaking with left-historicism, they shifted from Marxism to a quasi-Nietzschean critique of Western culture. Following Henri Lefebvre's (1962, p. 206) Nietzschean declaration of the exhaustion of Marxism, later thinkers, such as Foucault, Derrida, Lyotard, and Baudrillard, fashioned a postmodern turn. Many late twentieth-century, left-leaning theorists, saw a growing futility in the Marxian program of theory and praxis, and refocused both accordingly. In this regard, recent North American theorists, such as Linda Nicholson and Donna Haraway, or Europeans, such as Anthony Giddens, Alberto Mellucci, Ulrich Beck, and Zygmunt Bauman, applaud many of the same tendencies that Marxists bemoan (Antonio, 1998). They see their breaks from Marxism and fresh theoretical paths as rescuing critical thought and politics from cultural exhaustion. In a sense, they follow Marx's historicist method, which calls for change in response to new conditions, especially when the emancipatory prospects appear bleak or new progressive forces appear on stage. But the recent trends that lead many theorists to the new cultural politics lead others back to political economy and Marx. Paradoxically, revivals of Marxian theory spring from the same climate; fresh critiques, in light of new conditions and exhaustion of older ideas, produce new fusions and possible renewal of the tradition. This "critical" side of the Enlightenment and Marxism gives them multiple lives.

Perhaps the wake of the movements of 1989 will decouple the association of Marx with authoritarian, Soviet-style regimes. Moreover, the antitotalizing themes of recent cultural theories could have a beneficial impact on Marxist theory. Indeed, these sensibilities can already be detected in the plural undogmatic formats of the best Marxist journals (e.g. *New Left Review*). In the same text in which Perry Anderson (1983, pp. 20–7) declared that Western Marxist grand theory was exhausted, he noted the growing body of Marxian empirical-historical work by scholars such as Harry Braverman, Guglielmo Carchedi, Robert Brenner, Immanuel Wallerstein, James O'Connor, and Erik Olin Wright. At the end of the twentieth century, this type of research flourished among Marxian scholars. For example, Erik Olin Wright's (1997) cross-national class project illustrates the period's Marxist sociology, combining comprehensive empirical inquiry with conceptual innovation. In the 1990s, Marxist theorists, such as Ellen Meiksins Wood (1995) and Moishe Postone (1993), produced major interpretive studies, rereading Marx's mature project in a contemporary fashion. Other Marxist scholars, such as David Harvey (1989), Fredric Jameson (1991), and Terry Eagleton (1996), engaged cultural issues and postmodernism. Senior scholars, such as Eric Hobsbawm (1996), Göran Therborn (1995), Jürgen Habermas (1996), and Immanuel Wallerstein (1991), produced major new works. There were also signs of a Marx revival within cultural theory (e.g. Derrida, 1994). Other thinkers produced important Marxian influenced public issue books (e.g. Harrison and Bluestone, 1990; Davis, 1992; Harrison, 1994; Gordon, 1996).

## Marx's enduring contribution to social theory

To many thinkers, Marx's view of the capitalist locomotive flattening traditional structures is a troublesome and, perhaps, naive idea. Marx himself had doubts about the scenario near the end of his life, restricting it to Western Europe (Marx, 1881, p. 370). Yet a case could be made that later twentieth-century globalization manifests some of his main expectations about capitalist leveling. Trends toward global markets, an international division of labor, and substantially increased class inequalities correspond to what Marx implied would be imminent toward the end of the nineteenth century. Although his political thought should not be discounted entirely, his critique of capitalism has most relevance for the current scene. The more capitalism triumphs globally, especially in its current highly unregulated and unequal neoliberal form, the more likely Marx's theory will have renewed critical value. Countering this trend, his theory poses basic questions about loosening restrictions on property rights, disembedding economic affairs from political and sociocultural regulation, and recommodifying public goods. Treated as a heuristic tool, his materialist approach need not preclude attention to or diminish the importance of cultural theory, domination, and movements.

Numerous contemporary critics of Marx have argued that "multicausal" theories are superior to his materialism. In their frameworks, capitalism and class inequality are, at best, segmented parts of a multifaceted sociocultural complex and plural field of diverse problems and competing interests. In particular, the cultural left, attacking Marxian totality and economism, oppose what they see as an improper "privileging" of class. Although the new cultural theories have had definite critical value (i.e. raising cultural questions and pointing to sites of domination that were ignored by the postwar left), their emphatic emphases on difference, locality, and multiplicity lose a bit of their edge in a world where the dominant ideology stresses decentered plurality and niche markets. An argument could be made that these views have a strong affinity for the reigning type of liberalism. In this regard, Richard Rorty (1998, p. B5) holds that the cultural left has been largely silent about economic polarization and misery and has no reply to neoliberal claims that the current form of capitalism is the "only alternative." Similarly, Terry Eagleton (1996, p. 23) says that:

> The power of capital is now so drearily familiar, so sublimely omnipotent and omnipresent, that even large sections of the left have succeeded in naturalizing it, taking it for granted as such an unbudgeable structure that it is as though they hardly have the heart to speak of it....With Darwinian conformity, much of the cultural left has taken on the colour of its historical environs: if we live in an epoch in which capitalism cannot be successfully challenged then . . . it does not exist.

The power of Marx's theory is the compelling case that it makes for the view that capitalism is the most fateful and decisive force in the modern world. It swims against the current tide.

Max Weber argued that "one-sided" theory programs can have great heuristic value if they isolate factors that have decisive impact and are not reified as the single explanation of history. Such theories raise unambiguous questions about vital public matters, generating wide-ranging discussion and oppositional arguments and inquiries. Because theoretical advances and innovations often arise from engagements between contrasting positions, both Marxism and cultural theory could benefit from a climate where they stand beside one another. Marx spelled out the assumptions and provided a systematic rationale for an integrated program of social theory, empirical-historical inquiry, and normative sociopolitical critique. Along with Nietzsche, he remains one of the primary poles of social theory today, as is illustrated by the frequent references to him in the intense battles over modernism and postmodernism and over the value of rational culture and science. While Nietzsche began the current cultural turn, Marx initiated the effort to theorize global, deregulated, unequal capitalism, countering tendencies that render it invisible by treating it as a benign entity, an overwhelmingly affirmative force, or a behemoth beyond change.

In particular, Marx's emphasis on the tension between "abstract" and "real wealth" has renewed pertinence in the current climate of polarization of material and sociocultural life chances, deregulation and disembedding, and expansion of the inequality, power, and privileges of propertied wealth. His core argument that the vast benefits of real wealth, generated by capitalism's scientifically mediated powers of production, should be extended in a much wider and more just fashion poses sharp critical questions about the current tendency to treat as tolerable and even inevitable the increasing misery, drudgery, and insecurity of less advantaged people, while private wealth grows explosively for the fewer fortunate ones in an increasingly "gated" world. During the late 1990s, some thinkers began to question whether the trend toward a "shareholders' society" ought to be shifted in the direction of the "stakeholder" or citizenry. In this climate, Marx's specter becomes visible again. His social theory remains a vital departure point for an alternative way of seeing, thinking, and inquiring in these "postmodern" times.

## Bibliography

Unless otherwise indicated, references to works by Marx and/or Engels are to *Karl Marx Frederick Engels: Collected Works*, 50 volumes, published by International Publishers, New York, from 1975 on.

### *Writings of Karl Marx*

Letter from Marx to His Father: in Trier. 1837. In *Collected Works, volume 1*, pp. 10–21.
Proceedings of the Sixth Rhine Province Assembly. 1842. In *Collected Works, volume 1*, pp. 224–63.
Justification of the Correspondent from Mosel. 1843a. In *Collected Works, volume 1*, pp. 332–58.
Letters from the Deutsche–Französische Jahrbücher. 1843b. In *Collected Works, volume 3*, pp. 133–45.
*On the Jewish Question*. 1843c. In *Collected Works, volume 3*, pp. 146–74.
*Contribution to the Critique of Hegel's Philosophy of Law*. 1843d. In *Collected Works, volume 3*, pp. 3–129.
*Economic and Philosophical Manuscripts of 1844*. In *Collected Works, volume 3*, pp. 229–346.
Theses on Feuerbach. 1845. In *Collected Works, volume 5*, pp. 3–5.
*The Poverty of Philosophy*. 1847. In *Collected Works, volume 6*, pp. 105–212.
*The Class Struggles in France: 1848–1850*. 1850. In *Collected Works, volume 10*, pp. 43–145.
*The Eighteenth Brumaire of Louis Bonaparte*. 1852a. In *Collected Works, volume 11*, pp. 99–197.
Political Consequences of the Commercial Excitement. 1852b. In *Collected Works, volume 11*, pp. 364–8.
Political Parties and Prospects. 1852c. In *Collected Works, volume 11*, pp. 369–72.
*Outlines of the Critique of Political Economy (Rough Draft of 1857–58) [First Installment]*. In *Collected Works, volume 28*, pp. 3–537.
*Outlines of the Critique of Political Economy (Rough Draft of 1857–58) [Second Installment]*. In *Collected Works, volume 29a*, pp. 307–55.
*A Contribution to the Critique of Political Economy*. 1859a. In *Collected Works, volume 29b*, pp. 257–429.
The Original Text of the Second and the Beginning of the Third Chapter of *A Contribution to the Critique of Political Economy*. 1859b. In *Collected Works, volume 29b*, pp. 430–507.
*Capital: a Critique of Political Economy. Volume 1, The Process of Capitalist Production*, ed. Frederick Engels. 1867. New York: International Publishers (1967a).
Letter from Marx to Engels: in Manchester. 1868. In *Collected Works, volume 43*, pp. 20–5.

*The Civil War in France: Address of the General Council of the International Working Men's Association*. 1841. In *Collected Works, volume 22*, pp. 3–537.
*Critique of the Gotha Program*. 1875. In *Collected Works, volume 24*, pp. 75–99.
*Letter to Vera Zasulich*. 1881. In *Collected Works, volume 24*, pp. 370–1.
*Capital: a Critique of Political Economy. Volume 2, The Process of Circulation of Capital*, ed. Frederick Engels. 1885. New York: International Publishers (1967).
*Capital: a Critique of Political Economy. Volume 3, The Process of Capitalist Production as a Whole*, ed. Frederick Engels. 1894. New York: International Publishers (1967).
*Theories of Surplus Value*, 3 volumes, ed. Karl Kautsky. 1905–10. Moscow: Progress Publishers (1963–71).

## Writings of Karl Marx and Frederick Engels

*The German Ideology*. 1845–6. In *Collected Works, volume 5*, pp. 19–608.
*Manifesto of the Communist Party*. 1845. In *Collected Works, volume 6*, pp. 477–519.
Address of the Central Authority to the League: March 1850. 1850a. In *Collected Works, volume 10*, pp. 277–87.
Address of the Central Authority to the League: June 1850. 1850b. In *Collected Works, volume 10*, pp. 371–7.
Preface to the 1872 German Edition of the Manifesto of the Communist Party. In *Collected Works, volume 23*, pp. 174–5.

## Further reading

Anderson, Perry (1983) *In The Tracks of Historical Materialism*. London: Verso.
Antonio, J. Robert (1998) Mapping Postmodern Social Theory. In *What Is Social Theory? The Philosophical Debates*. Oxford and Cambridge, MA: Blackwell.
Aronson, Ronald (1995) *After Marxism*. New York and London: The Guilford Press.
Boynton, Robert S. (1997) The Two Tonys: Why Is the Prime Minister So Interested in What Anthony Giddens Thinks? *The New Yorker*, October 6, 66–74.
Cassidy, John (1997) The Return of Karl Marx. *The New Yorker*, October 20 and 27, 248–52, 254–6, 259.
Davis, Mike (1992) *City of Quartz: Excavating the Future in Los Angeles*. New York: Vintage Books.
Derrida, Jacques (1994) *Specters of Marx: the State of Debt, the Work of Mourning and the New International*. New York and London: Routledge.
Eagleton, Terry (1996) *The Illusions of Postmodernism*. Oxford and Cambridge, MA: Blackwell.
Engels, Frederick (1842) The Insolently Threatened yet Miraculously Rescued Bible or: the Triumph of Faith. In *Collected Works, volume 2*, pp. 313–51.
Engels, Frederick (1851–2) *Revolution and Counter-revolution in Germany*. In *Collected Works, volume 11*, pp. 3–96.
Engels, Frederick (1883) Karl Marx's Funeral. In *Collected Works, volume 24*, pp. 467–71.
Engels, Frederick (1885) Preface. In *Capital: A Critique of Political Economy. Volume 2, The Process of Circulation of Capital*. New York: International Publishers (1967), pp. 1–19.
Engels, Frederick (1890a) Engels to Conrad Schmidt. In Lewis S. Feuer (ed.), *Marx and Engels: Basic Writings on Politics and Philosophy*. Garden City, NY: Anchor Books (1959a), pp. 395–7.

Engels, Frederick (1890b) Engels to Joseph Bloch. In Lewis S. Feuer (ed.), *Marx and Engels: Basic Writings on Politics and Philosophy*. Garden City, NY: Anchor Books (1959b), pp. 397–400.

Engels, Frederick (1892) *Socialism: Scientific and Utopian*. In *Collected Works, volume 24*, pp. 281–325.

Fraser, Nancy (1989) *Unruly Practices: Power, Discourse, and Gender in Contemporary Social Theory*. Minneapolis: University of Minnesota Press, 1989.

Fukuyama, Francis (1992) *The End of History and the Last Man*. London and New York: Penguin Books.

Giddens, Anthony (1994) *Beyond Left and Right: the Future of Radical Politics*. Stanford, CA: Stanford University Press.

Gordon, David M. (1996) *Fat and Mean: the Corporate Squeeze of Working Americans and the Myth of Managerial "Downsizing"*. New York: The Free Press.

Gouldner, Alvin W. (1980) *The Two Marxisms: Contradictions and Anomalies in the Development of Theory*. New York and Toronto: Oxford University Press.

Greider, William (1997) Why the Global Economy Needs Worker Rights. *Working USA*, May/June, 32–44.

Habermas, Jürgen (1996) *Between Facts and Norms: Contributions to a Discourse Theory of Law and Democracy*. Cambridge, MA and London: MIT Press.

Habermas, Jürgen and Michnik, Adam (1994) Overcoming the Past. *New Left Review*, 103, 3–16.

Harrison, Bennett (1994) *Lean and Mean: the Changing Landscape of Corporate Power in the Age of Flexibility*. New York: Basic Books.

Harrison, Bennett and Bluestone, Barry (1990) The *Great U-turn: Corporate Restructuring and the Polarizing of America*. New York: Basic Books.

Harvey, David (1989) *The Condition of Postmodernity: an Inquiry into the Origins of Cultural Change*. Oxford and Cambridge, MA: Blackwell.

Hegel, G. W. F (1807) *The Phenomenology of Mind*. New York: Harper & Row (1967).

Hobsbawm, Eric (1996) *The Age of Extremes: a History of the World, 1914–1991*. New York: Vintage.

Jameson, Fredric (1991) *Postmodernism, or, The Cultural Logic of Late Capitalism*. Durham, NC: Duke University Press.

Jay, Martin (1984) *Marxism and Totality: the Adventures of a Concept from Lukács to Habermas*. Berkeley and Los Angeles, University of California Press.

Laclau, Ernesto and Mouffe, Chantal (1985) *Hegemony and Socialist Strategy: towards a Radical Democratic Politics*. London and New York: Verso.

Lefebvre, Henri (1962) *Introduction to Modernity: Twelve Preludes September 1959–May 1961*. London and New York: Verso (1995).

McLellan, David (1973) *Karl Marx: His Life and Thought*. New York: Harper & Row.

Offe, Claus (1996) *Modernity and the State: East, West*. Cambridge, MA: MIT Press.

Postone, Moishe (1993) *Time, Labor, and Social Domination: a Reinterpretation of Marx's Critical Theory*. Cambridge and New York: Cambridge University Press.

Przeworski, Adam (1985) *Capitalism and Social Democracy*. Cambridge and New York: Cambridge University Press.

Rorty, Richard (1998) The Dark Side of the Academic Left. *Chronicle of Higher Education*, April 3, B4–B6.

Seigel, Jerrold (1993) *Marx's Fate: the Shape of a Life*. University Park: Pennsylvania State University Press.

Simmel, Georg (1900) *The Philosophy of Money*. London and Boston: Routledge & Kegan Paul (1978).

Smith, Adam (1776) *An Inquiry into the Nature and Causes of the Wealth of Nations*. New York: Modern Library (1937).

Therborn, Göran (1995) *European Modernity and Beyond: the Trajectory of European Societies 1945–2000*. London and Thousand Oaks, CA: Sage.

Wallerstein, Immanuel (1991) *Unthinking Social Science: the Limits of Nineteenth-century Paradigms*. Cambridge: Polity Press.

Wood, Ellen Meiksins (1986) *The Retreat from Class: a New "True" Socialism*. London and New York: Verso.

Wood, Ellen Meiksins (1995) *Democracy against Capitalism: Renewing Historical Materialism*. Cambridge and New York: Cambridge University Press.

Wright, Erik Olin (1997) *Class Counts: Comparative Studies in Class Analysis*. Cambridge and New York: Cambridge University Press.

# 5

# Max Weber

## STEPHEN KALBERG

> Simple intellectual integrity [involves giving
> account to oneself] of the final meaning of
> one's own actions.
>
> *Max Weber*

Widely recognized as one of the major founding fathers of sociology, Max Weber (1864–1920) is perhaps today best known for his attempts to define the uniqueness of the modern West and to offer causal explanations for its specific historical development. However, far from offering a justification for industrial societies, his sociological and political writings both evidence a profound ambivalence toward them: although impressed by their capacity to sustain high standards of living, Weber feared that many of their foundational elements opposed the further unfolding of human compassion, ethical action, and individual autonomy. At the dawning of the twentieth century, he asked "where are we headed" and "how shall we live with dignity in this new age?" He worried that it might become an "iron cage" of impersonal, manipulative, and harsh relationships lacking binding values and noble ideals.

His search for answers to these burning questions drove Weber to pursue, even by the ambitious standards of scholarship in his day, an extraordinarily broad and deep comparative agenda. Standing near the end of a long line of distinguished German scholars who undertook "universal-historical" investigations and convinced that the uniqueness of any particular society could be isolated only through rigorous comparisons, Weber's quest led to a series of massive studies. Remarkably, his empirical research spanned the civilizations of the ancient world, China, and India; they moved as well, with full sovereignty, across each century of the West's 2,600-year development. Along the way he explored, in detailed studies, for example, Old Testament prophecy and the Bible, the medieval origins of Western music, the rise of the caste system in India, Confucianism in China, and monotheism in ancient Israel, the salvation doctrines of Buddhism, Hinduism, ancient Judaism, early Christianity, medieval Catholicism, and ascetic Protestantism, the decline of the Roman Empire, the accounting practices of medieval trading companies, the possibilities for democracy in Russia, and the many methodological questions at the foundation of the social sciences.

Weber's approach to these investigations proved unique. He abjured on the one hand a focus upon single factors – such as economic, political, or religious forces – and sought to offer multidimensional analyses that evaluated the causal weight of both "ideas" and "interests." He attempted on the other hand to *understand* the ways in which persons in various civilizations, in light of varieties of demarcated contextual and indigenous social configurations, attributed meaning on a regular basis to certain "types of action" and not to others. How do persons in different civilizational settings create *meaning* in their lives? Weber sought to investigate this question impartially even though the action of persons across the globe at times appeared to him, from the point of view of his own values, as odd and even bizarre.

## THE PERSON

Max Weber was born in Erfurt, Germany, into a distinguished and cosmopolitan family of entrepreneurs, scholars, politicians, and strong women. Most of his younger years were spent in Berlin, where he attended an excellent school that required a strenuous regimen of study. Recognized early on as an exceptional student, he developed a precocious love of learning and a particular fondness for philosophy, literature, and ancient and medieval history. His teenage letters comment upon, among many others, the merits of Goethe, Kant, Hegel, Spinoza, and Schopenhauer. They also demonstrate, as the eldest child, a concern for his overworked, devout mother. Although influenced strongly by his work-obsessed father, a central figure in the city government of Berlin and the state government of Prussia, he deplored his patriarchal ways and insensitive treatment of his wife.

Weber studied economic history, law, and philosophy at the universities of Heidelberg, Berlin, and Goettingen. His letters indicate a keen awareness of the varying quality of instruction in his lectures and seminars, as well as an inability to curtail rather free-wheeling spending habits. He became the protégé in Berlin of the legal historian Goldschmidt and the Roman historian Mommsen. In 1893 he was appointed to a chair in commercial law at the Humboldt University in Berlin at an unusually young age, and in 1894 he accepted a chair in economics and finance in Freiburg. At the age of thirty-three, having recently married a distant cousin, Marianne Schnitger, Weber evicted from their home his father, who had mistreated his mother. The father's death soon afterwards served as the catalyst for a paralyzing mental illness that endured for more than five years.

During much of this time Weber passively pondered the fate of persons living in the new world of secularism, urbanism, and capitalism.

A trip to the United States in 1904 played a part in his recovery. Journeying across much of the East and Midwest, he gained an appreciation for America's dynamism, energy, and uniqueness, as well as for the self-reliance and distrust of authority widespread in the United States. His most famous work, *The Protestant Ethic and the Spirit of Capitalism* (PE), appeared soon after his return to Germany. Although unable to teach until 1918, Weber began once again to publish on a broad array of topics.

His interest in the "ascetic Protestantism" of the American Quaker, Methodist, Presbyterian, Calvinist, Baptist, and Congregationalist churches derived in part from the religiosity of his mother, Helene, and her sister, Ida Baumgarten. As Christian social activists and admirers of mid-century American Unitarianism, the pious sisters transmitted to the young Weber a heightened sensitivity to moral questions, an appreciation of the ways in which the life of dignity and meaning must be guided by ethical standards, and a respect for the worth and uniqueness of every person. Marianne reaffirmed these values, although they opposed the lessons taught by Max's father: the necessity to avoid "naive idealism," to confront the ways of the world in a pragmatic, even amoral fashion, and to avoid personal sacrifice.

Nonetheless, Weber waged impassioned battles throughout his life on behalf of ethical positions and scolded relentlessly all who lacked a rigorous sense of justice and social responsibility. As his student Paul Honigsheim reports, Weber became a man possessed whenever threats to the autonomy of the individual were discussed (see Weber, 1968, pp. 6, 43) – whether to mothers seeking custody of their children, women students at German universities, or bohemian social outcasts and political rebels. Not surprisingly, his concerns for the fate of the German nation, and for the future of Western Civilization, led him perpetually into the arena of politics. Vigorously opposed to the definition of this realm as one of *Realpolitik*, "sober realism," or wheeling and dealing, he called out vehemently for politicians to act by reference to a stern moral code: an "ethic of responsibility" (*Verantwortungsethik*).[1]


## THE INTELLECTUAL CONTEXT


Long before Weber formulated his sociology, many seventeenth- and eighteenth-century thinkers in the West had sought to discover, through the systematic investigation of the natural and social worlds, proof of the existence of an all-powerful supernatural Being. If the centipede's 100 legs moved in a coordinated fashion, this extraordinary achievement must itself indicate the intelligence of a superior Being as its creator (Weber, 1946d, p. 142). The "hand of God" must be at work, it was believed, as in the social world's "natural laws." Once proven, God's existence implied the necessity for "His children" to follow His Commandments. Hence, the investigation of the natural and social worlds held out the promise of embattled Christianity's renascence. The "divine order" would appear on earth and the triumph of Christian compassion and universal love would then banish the danger of a Hobbesian "war of all against all."

Although the nineteenth century brought these hopeful and optimistic investigations to a close, social thinkers in the West only grudgingly set aside an idea prominent in all salvation religions: all history and all activities of the human species possess a higher meaning and direction. Even as openly theological explanations for the purpose of life and history waned, the notion that a component more majestic than mundane everyday activity is bestowed upon human life remained. Whether Utilitarians in England at the beginning of the century or Spencerian Social Darwinists at its end; whether Hegelians or Marxists in Germany; whether followers of Saint-Simon or Comte in France: all these schools of thought, although otherwise so different, articulated the idea that history moved in a lawful manner and in an evolutionary direction. It thus contained a meaning all its own. In his expansive historical studies, the distinguished mid-century historian Ranke discovered the values of Christian Humanism at work through the ages, and the idealist philosopher Hegel charted the history of the West as a progressive realization of the idea of freedom. Even thoroughly secularized German intellectuals at the end of the century – the philosopher Heinrich Rickert, for example – argued that history offered evidence for a firm hierarchy of true values, indeed ones capable of guiding our lives today. The economic historian Gustav Schmoller sought to discover, through historical research, the underlying moral justification for the development of modern capitalism.

History retained a teleology and an "objective meaning" for all these thinkers. Conformity with its unified value system would ensure progress, as well as, in the end, the just ordering of society. Throughout the nineteenth century, and despite the turning by Marx of ethereal Hegelian thought "on its head," a rearguard reluctance to abandon the notion of a transcendental guiding force – now in a sublimated and impersonal form rather than understood as the direct Will of a monotheistic God – prevailed. Even Marx's "scientific socialism" formulated "dialectical laws of history"; the present, he argued, must be understood as only one of many historical stages, all of which lead along a predestined route toward more advanced societies. Protestant Christianity's optimistic view regarding man's capacity to master his sinful human nature and to improve earthly existence constituted the facilitating cultural background for a flourishing of the secular ideas of Progress, Reason, and Freedom, as well as for all ideals of natural justice and all value hierarchies.

Max Weber's works stand directly antagonistic to these ideas of the seventeenth, eighteenth, and nineteenth centuries. With his sociology a new *position* for the human species crystallized, one steadfastly opposed to the notion that history possessed an independent meaning: *persons* now existed as the unequivocal makers of their destinies and as the center and cause of their activities. At the dawning of the twentieth century, Weber insisted that meaning could arise only out of their struggles to mold "meaningful lives" and the choices they made on this behalf: "Every single important activity and ultimately life as a whole, if it is not to be permitted to run on as an event in nature but is instead to be consciously guided, is a series of ultimate decisions through which the soul ... *chooses* its own destiny; i.e., the meaning of its activity and existence" (Weber, 1949, p. 18 translation altered, original emphasis; see also p. 81; 1946d, pp. 148, 151–2). Several currents of thought that placed the individual in the forefront came here to a synthesis: the Enlightenment's individual endowed with Reason and Rationality, the creative and introspective individual of the German Romantics (mainly Goethe and Schiller), and ascetic Protestantism's activity-oriented individual.[2]

The same antagonism to the notion that the flow of history contained a transcendental meaning accounts as well for Weber's principled opposition to the grounding of knowledge and activity beyond the empirical realm. With the prominent exception of Nietzsche, he saw more acutely than his contemporaries that, once the axial turn from theocentrism and quasi-theocentrism to anthropocentrism had been taken, a unifying set of religious values, the "course of history," or the Idea of Progress could no longer offer the ultimate foundation for the social sciences. The study of the meaning-seeking person must now be firmly rooted in reality: "The type of social science in which we are interested is an *empirical science of concrete reality*" (*Wirklichkeitswissenschaft*) (Weber, 1949, p. 72, original emphasis).

Although the secular and industrial character of turn-of-the-century Germany directly influenced the formation of this central tenet of Weber's sociology, as he himself acknowledged, it must not be concluded that his works are empowered to investigate only those few epochs and civilizations in which individualism had come to the fore and unified constellations of values had vanished. On the contrary, a radically comparative and historical reach characterizes his research. He knew well that subjective meaning may be created in a *vast* variety of ways; indeed, his research revealed that for millennia the overriding beacon of light and guiding force for persons had originated from diverse orientations to the supernatural realm (see Weber, 1946, p. 149). Even though subjective meaning stands at the core of Weber's sociology, and hence the individualism dominant in his own epoch's "value ideas" (*Wertideen*) is manifest in its fundamental axioms, Weber's methodology emphatically leaves open – to be studied empirically – the extent to which the formation of subjective meaning is influenced by the mundane world or the supernatural realm.

This monumental shift to a radically empirical sociology rooted in subjective meaning must be acknowledged as foundational to Weber's entire sociology. Cognizance of this turn allows its central features to become more easily comprehensible.

## The rejection of the search for true values, general laws, and objective facts

Weber's rejection of values rooted in religions and quasi-supernatural ideas as the basis for his sociology, and his focus upon empirical reality and subjective meaning, led him to oppose unequivocally the many attempts at the end of the nineteenth century to define the aim of science as the creation of new constellations of values appropriate to the industrial society. His distinguished colleagues Rickert, Dilthey, Schmoller, Roscher, and Knies had all agreed that investigations of social life must be carried out *in order to* substantiate ideals and norms – indeed, even in the name of science. They feared that secular, capitalist, and industrial societies would be devoid of values, and this abhorrent vacuum must be filled by values discovered by science. Their nightmare vision would otherwise soon become reality: persons would become mere drifting "atoms" devoid of reflectivity, a sense of deep obligation to others, and – not least – a sense of true community (*Gemeinschaft*). As religion declined, a new source for desperately needed values must be found. Science offered new hope.

The notion that science should be viewed as the legitimate source of personal values was more than Weber could bear. He saw in such proposals yet another clandestine intrusion of quasi-religious legacies – now into a domain appropriately defined as exclusively involving empirical investigation. Moreover, he denied the possibility that science could serve as the source of values, for an "objective science" *cannot* exist. Even the hope for such a science is a deception, one rooted ultimately in a bygone world of unified values. It has now become clear, Weber asserts, that *each* epoch – perhaps even every generation or decade – calls forth its *own* "culturally significant value-ideas." Invariably, he insists, our observations of empirical reality take place *in reference to these*. The empirical ground upon which science is based "changes" continually (see Weber, 1949, pp. 72–8).

This unavoidable "value-relevance" (*Wertbeziehung*) of our observations always renders certain events and occurrences visible to us and occludes others. Only *some* "realities" are thrown into relief by the culturally significant values of any specific age: those today, for example, are embodied by terms such as equality for all, freedom, individual rights, equal opportunity, globalization, etc., and dichotomies such as capitalism/socialism and First World/Third World. The specific vantage points dominant in any era *allow* its inhabitants to see only a selected slice of the past and present. Consequently, our search today for knowledge cannot take the same form – as a search for concealed *absolutes* – as in the seventeenth and eighteenth centuries, for the ultimate precondition for such a quest no longer exists: a widespread belief in a set of unified values. For the same reason, our knowledge can no longer be anchored in the quasi-supernatural ideas of the nineteenth century. Furthermore, owing to the invariably perspectival character of our knowledge, we can hope neither to find "general laws" in history nor to write history as Ranke proposed: "as it actually occurred." Thus, in the famous "debate over methods" (*Methoden-streit*), Weber opposed both the "nomothetic" position held by Menger – the formulation of general laws must be the task of the social sciences – and the "ideographic" position held by Schmoller's "historical school of economics": to offer exact and full descriptions of specific cases must be the goal.[3]

Weber admonished vehemently and repeatedly that all attempts to create values through science must now be seen as illusions. All such deceptions must be cast aside in the new post-religion and post quasi-religion epoch:

> The fate of a cultural epoch which has eaten from the tree of knowledge is that it must know that, however completely we may investigate history, we cannot learn its real *meaning* from the results of our research. Rather, we must be able to create

this meaning ourselves. Moreover, we must acknowledge that "Weltanschauungen" never can be the product of the advance of empirically based knowledge. Finally, we must recognize that the highest ideals – and those which move us most deeply – become effective influences upon us only as a consequence of their struggle with other ideals. These ideals are just as sacred to others as ours are to us. (Weber, 1949, p. 57; translation altered, original emphasis; see also p. 18)

We know of no ideals that can be demonstrated scientifically. Undoubtedly, the task of pulling them out of one's own breast is all the more difficult in an epoch in which culture has otherwise become so subjective. But we simply have no fool's paradise and no streets paved with gold to promise, either in this world or the next, either in thought or in action. It is the stigma of our human dignity that the peace of our souls can never be as great as the peace of those who dream of such a paradise. (Weber, 1909, p. 420)

## The embrace of multicausality

The search for a single "guiding hand," whether that of a monotheistic God, Adam Smith's "laws of the market," or Karl Marx's class conflict as the "engine of history," remained anathema to Weber. He perceived all such overarching forces as residuals of now-antiquated world views characterized by religious and quasi-religious ideas. Indeed, Weber's adamant refusal to define the "general laws of social life" (Menger), the "stages of historical development" (Buecher, Marx), or Evolution[4] as the central point of departure for his causal explanations[5] paved the way for a focus upon empirical reality and subjective meaning; as importantly, it also provided the underlying precondition for his embrace of radically *multicausal* modes of explanation. Having abandoned reference to all forms of "necessity" as history's moving force, the innumerable actions and beliefs of persons rose to the fore in Weber's sociology as the causal forces that determine the contours of past and present.

His empirical research convinced him that historical change required on the one hand great charismatic figures and on the other hand "carrier" strata and organizations. Moreover, these carriers were, for example, at times political and rulership organizations, at other times status groups or economic organizations, and at still other times religious organizations. His investigations across a vast palette of themes, epochs, and civilizations yielded in this respect a clear conclusion: rather than a causal "resting point," he found only continuous movement across, above all, political, economic, religious, legal, social strata, and familial groupings (see, for example, Weber, 1968, p. 341). Without powerful carriers, even Hegel's "spirit" or Ranke's Christian Humanism could not move history; nor could ideas, world views, or the problem of unjust suffering.

## From Eurocentrism to a comparative sociology of subjective meaning

However weakened by secularization, capitalism, and urbanization, the West's overarching set of values remained viable in the nineteenth century and formed a measuring rod against which European social scientists evaluated societies around the globe with respect to their relative "evolution" and "rationality." Had they experienced the same degree of "advancement" as the modern West? Weber's rejection of the twentieth century's quasi-religious value constellations implied both a skepticism regarding the widespread belief in "progress" and an awareness of its contingency. It also laid the foundation for his sociology's radically comparative character and its break from Eurocentric ideas.

The shift to a fully anthropocentric sociology of subjective meaning and empirical reality had the effect of delegitimizing all Western-centric value configurations. As the underlying justification for a social science oriented exclusively to the "ideas of the West" disappeared, firm standards in terms of which other cultures could be observed and evaluated vanished as well. While his colleagues viewed this development with extreme trepidation and correctly perceived Weber's methodology as threatening at its core the "superiority of the West," as well as the very essence of their being, Weber noted an overriding advantage for research: social scientists were now set free to investigate "the other" on its *own* terms. This liberation from a fixed point of orientation meant to him that unconstrained empirical explorations of *subjective meanings* in Eastern and Western, ancient and modern, civilizations could now be conducted.

However, Weber advocated such a radical swing of the pendulum not only owing to advantages he saw for a social science methodology. Rather, an even larger dynamic induced him to bestow an unqualified legitimacy upon decentered, intercivilizational research. "Unconstrained" comparative studies were now urgently *needed* in order effectively to address immediate questions in his own civilization: in what precise ways can the modern West be said to be unique, what are the *parameters* of possible social change in the West, and how does the orientation of actions to values and the *formation* of subjective meaning as such take place? Whereas these same questions deeply troubled his colleagues as well, Weber alone comprehended the potential achievements of a sociology that, through rigorous comparative-historical studies, would be capable of isolating the boundaries of cases and developments, defining significant causal forces, and drawing conclusions regarding the circumstances under which social change occurs, action becomes oriented to values, and subjective meaning is formed. Such a sociology would cast a sharp beam of light upon the modern West's unique dilemmas and crises – and persons would then be more able to make independent, *informed* decisions and to take clear *ethical* positions (see Weber, 1946, pp. 151–2; Kalberg, forthcoming). The massiveness and extreme thoroughness of his comparative studies cannot be understood without cognizance of this burning motivating concern.[6]

## Conflict and ethical action

Weber's mode of research was decentered in a further manner. In breaking unequivocally from all schools of thought that stressed unifying constellations of values, transcendentally anchored value hierarchies, and – through Progress and Evolution – humanity's common and peaceful future, his sociology banished an array of presuppositions that tended to place obstacles against the empirical analysis of reality. Importantly, having done so, his research could better assess the extent to which mundane conflict appears, as well as its contours and causes. For him, the "struggle for existence" did not take place on the grand stage of "human evolution" and in response to a "survival of the fittest" law, as for Social Darwinists, but exclusively as a result of the hard choices that accompany every-day activity. History unfolded out of these decisions, yet not in a unilinear or directed fashion. Paradox, irony, and unforeseen consequences, Weber insists, were manifest perpetually,[7] as well as restless, undirected conflict. The various domains of life that uniquely constitute the modern world (the economic, polit-ical, rulership, and legal), he argues, rather than congealing into a synthesis to drive Progress or to propel a Parsonsian "value-generalization" process, follow their *own* laws of development and very often stand in relations of irreconcilable conflict to one another (see Weber, 1946, pp. 147–54, 323–59; 1949, p. 18).

In formulating "an empirical science of concrete reality" and emphasizing that persons rather than God, natural laws, or Evolution endow history with mean-ing, several pivotal questions unavoidably confront Weber's sociology. How will our action be oriented? How do we act responsibly? How is ethical action grounded? The liberation from religion-based world views and their legacies led naturally to a degree of freedom, yet just this development called forth the question of how individuals, in industrialized, bureaucratized, and capitalist societies, make choices. Weber's rejection of all schools that defined the modern person's freedom as simply the "philistine freedom of private convenience" (Löwith, 1970, p. 122) rendered these queries all the more urgent, as did his opposition to Nietzsche's answers: his insistence that activity occurs embedded within contexts prevented Weber from placing faith in prophets and great "supermen" (Weber, 1946d, p. 155). Moreover, he argued that secularism, industrialism, and the Enlightenment had already empowered "the people" with rights to such an extent that Nietzsche's call for authoritarian heroes went too far: they would inevitably circumscribe the open, public space now so indispensable for ethically based choices by individuals.

Weber knew well that the social science he proposed failed to offer ethical guidance to individuals. He remained acutely aware that this position disap-pointed in particular the younger generation of his time (see Weber, 1946d, pp. 141–55). Would the elevation of subjective meaning and "concrete empirical reality" to the forefront work out in the end? Or would the modern individual, cast adrift from all directing and obligatory values and traditions, and now forced to locate meaning by reference to his own "demons," become either an opportunistic actor or psychologically paralyzed? Weber rejected the loud calls for "a romantic irrational heroism which sacrifices itself amidst the delirium of self-decomposition" (Salomon, 1935b, p. 384), and scorned, as utopian, all hopes that a politicized proletariat would usher in a more just society. Would configurations of *binding* values capable of anchoring ethical decisions remain? Would the person oriented to and *unified* by values survive? These crucial questions can best be addressed by turning first to Weber's sociology and then to the social context in which he wrote.

## THE THEORY

Some interpreters view Weber as a "theorist of ideas," yet others see him as a "theorist of interests." While the former focus upon *PE* and emphasize the strong role in his sociology of values, religion, and culture, the latter take his analytic opus, *Economy and Society* (*E&S*), as their main source and assert that Weber offers a non-Marxist conflict theory rooted in domination, power, conflict, and individual interests. Still others understand him mainly as a gifted taxonomist engaged in the creation of a vast armament of "ideal types" intended to establish the discipline of sociology on a secure conceptual foundation. In fact, each of these interpretations flows legitimately from the rich vein of his sociological writings (see Kalberg, 1998, pp. 208–14).

However, these commentaries all run astray both by denying the plausibility of opposing interpretations and by casting their focus too narrowly. The broader themes that overcome the seeming fragmentation of Weber's sociology and offer a degree of unity are too often neglected: the ways in which he links ideas and interests, his concern to define the uniqueness of the modern West and to provide a causal explanation of its origins, his search to understand which constellations of social forces give rise to widespread notions of compassion, ethical action, and individual autonomy, his attempt to analyze how action becomes oriented to values, and his focus upon the manner in which persons, in different social settings, create meaning for their lives.

This discussion of Weber's sociology seeks to articulate these central themes while calling attention to the forceful ways in which values, culture, and religion come to the fore in his sociology; domination, power, individual interests, and conflict remain central; and "clear concepts" serve as indispensable foundational cornerstones. This large task can best be pursued by a brief scrutiny of his three major works: *PE*, *E&S*, and *The Economic Ethics of the World Religions* (*EEWR*). Before we do so, a turn to central aspects of the methodology underlying his sociology is indispensable.

### Weber's methodology

Weber's sociology departs from a critique of all approaches that view societies as quasi-organic, holistic units and their separate "parts" as components fully integrated into a larger "system" of objective structures. All organic schools of thought understand the larger collectivity within which the individual acts as a delimited structure, and social action and interaction as merely particularistic expressions of this "whole." German romantic and conservative thought at the beginning of the nineteenth century, as well as Comte and Durkheim in France, fall within this tradition.

Organic theories generally postulate a degree of societal integration questionable to Weber. He never viewed societies as clearly formed and closed entities with delineated boundaries. Seeing the likelihood for fragmentation, tension, open conflict, and the use of power, Weber rejects the notion that societies can be best understood as unified. Moreover, according to him, if organic theories are utilized *other than* as a means of facilitating preliminary conceptualization, a high risk of "reification" arises: "society" and the "organic whole" may become viewed as the fundamental unit of analysis rather than the individual (Weber, 1968, pp. 14–15). This may occur to such an extent that persons are incorrectly understood as simply the "socialized products" of societal forces. Weber argues, to the contrary, that persons are capable of *interpreting* their social realities, bestowing "subjective meaning" upon certain aspects of it, and initiating independent action: "[We are] *cultural* beings endowed with the capacity and will to take a deliberate stand toward the world and to lend it *meaning (Sinn)*" (Weber, 1949, p. 81, translation altered, original emphasis). There *is*, to Weber, a realm of freedom and choice.

Many of the pivotal axioms of his methodology remain central to sociology even today. Only a few of its foundational components can be examined: interpretive understanding, the four types of social action, subjective meaning, value-neutrality, and ideal types. Finally, the aim of Weber's sociology will be discussed.

**INTERPRETIVE UNDERSTANDING AND SUBJECTIVE MEANING** At the core of Weber's sociology stands the attempt by sociologists to "understand interpretively" (*verstehen*) the ways in which persons view their own "social action." This subjectively meaningful action constitutes the social scientist's concern rather than merely reactive or imitative behavior (as occurs, for example, when persons in a crowd expect rain and simultaneously open their umbrellas). Social action, he insists, involves *both* a "meaningful orientation of behavior to that of others" *and* the individual's interpretive, or reflective, aspect (Weber, 1968, pp. 22–4). Persons are social, but not only social. They are endowed with the ability to actively interpret situations, interactions, and relationships by reference to values, beliefs, interests, emotions, power, authority, law, customs, conventions, habits, ideas, etc.

> Sociology...is a science that offers an interpretive understanding of social action and, in doing so, provides a causal explanation of its course and its effects. We shall speak of "action" insofar as the acting individual attaches a subjective *meaning* to his behavior – be it overt or covert, omission or acquiescence. Action is "social" insofar as its subjective meaning takes account of the behavior *of others* and is thereby oriented in its course. (Weber, 1968, p. 4, translation altered, original emphasis)[8]

This central position of meaningful action separates Weber's sociology fundamentally from all behaviorist, structuralist, and positivist schools.

Sociologists can understand the meaningfulness of others' action either through "rational understanding," which involves an intellectual grasp of the meaning actors attribute to their actions, or through "intuitive," or "empathic," understanding, which refers to the comprehension of "the emotional context in which the action [takes] place" (Weber, 1968, p. 5). Thus, for example, the motivation behind the orientation of civil servants to impersonal statutes and laws can be understood by the sociologist, as can the motivation behind the orientation of good friends to one another. To the extent that this occurs, a *causal* explanation of action, Weber argues, is provided. Because it attends alone to external activity, stimulus/response behaviorism neglects the issues foremost to Weber: the *diverse* possible motives behind an observable activity, the manner in which the subjective meaningfulness of the act varies accordingly, and the significant differences that follow in respect to action.

**THE FOUR TYPES OF SOCIAL ACTION AND SUBJECTIVE MEANING** Social action can be best conceptualized as involving one of "four types of meaningful action": means–end rational, value-rational, affectual, or traditional action. Each type refers to the ideal typical (see below) motivational orientations of actors.

Weber defines action as *means–end* rational (*zweckrational*) "when the end, the means, and the secondary results are all rationally taken into account and weighed. This involves a rational consideration of alternative means to the end, of the relations of the end to the secondary consequences, and finally of the relative importance of different possible ends." Similarly, persons possess the capacity to act *value-rationally*, even though this type of action has appeared empirically in its pure form only rarely. It exists when social action is "determined by a conscious belief in the value for its own sake of some ethical, aesthetic, religious, or other form of behavior, independently of its prospects of success.... Value-rational action always involves 'commands' or 'demands' which, in the actor's opinion, are binding (*verbindlich*) on him." Notions of honor involve values, as do salvation doctrines. In addition, "determined by the actor's specific affects and feeling states," *affectual* action, which involves an emotional attachment, must be distinguished clearly from value-rational and means–end rational action. *Traditional* action, "determined by ingrained habituation" and age-old customs, and often merely a routine reaction to common stimuli, stands on the borderline of subjectively meaningful action. Taken together, these constructs – the "types of social action" – establish an analytic base that assists conceptualization of diffuse action-orientations. Rational action in reference to interests constitutes, to Weber, only one possible way of orienting action (see Weber, 1968, pp. 24–6).[9]

Each type of meaningful action can be found in all epochs and all civilizations. The social action of even "primitive" peoples may be means–end rational and value-rational (see, for example, Weber, 1968, pp. 400, 422–6), and modern man is not endowed with a greater inherent capacity for either type of action than his ancestors. However, as a result of identifiable social forces, some epochs may tend predominantly to call forth a particular type of action. Weber is convinced that, by utilizing the types of social action typology, sociologists can understand – and hence explain causally – even the ways in which the social action of persons living in radically different cultures is subjectively meaningful. Assuming that, as a result of intensive study, researchers have succeeded in becoming thoroughly familiar with a particular social context and thus capable of imagining themselves "into" it, an assessment can be made of the extent to which actions approximate one of the types of social action. The subjective meaningfulness of the motives for these actions – whether means–end rational, value-rational, traditional, or affectual – then becomes *understandable*.[10] Weber's "interpretive sociology" in this manner seeks to help sociologists to comprehend social action in terms of the actor's *own* intentions.[11]

This foundational emphasis upon a pluralism of motives distinguishes Weber's sociology unequivocally from all schools of behaviorism, all approaches that place social structures at the forefront (for example, those rooted in Durkheim's "social facts" or Marx's classes), and all positivist approaches that endow norms, roles, and rules with a determining power over persons. Even when social action seems tightly bonded to a social structure, a heterogeneity of motives must be recognized. A great array of motives within a single "external form" is, Weber argues, both analytically and empirically possible *and* sociologically significant. The subjective meaningfulness of action varies even within the firm organizational structure of the political or religious sect. Yet just this reasoning leads Weber to a conundrum: for what subjective reasons do persons orient their social action in common, such that demarcated groupings are formulated? This question assumes a great urgency, for he is convinced that the absence of such orientations – toward, for example, the state, bureaucratic organizations, traditions, and values – means that "structures" cease to exist. The state, for example, in the end is *nothing more* than the patterned action-orientations of its politicians, judges, police, civil servants, etc.[12]

Far from formal methodological postulates only, these foundational distinctions directly anchor Weber's empirical studies, as will become apparent. The investigation of the subjective meaning of action stood at the very center, for example, of his famous "Protestant ethic thesis." Yet Weber engaged in a massive empirical effort to understand the subjective meaning of "the other" on its own terms throughout his comparative-historical sociology, whether, for example, that of the Confucian scholar, the Buddhist monk, the Hindu Brahmin, the prophets of the Old Testament, feudal rulers, monarchs and kings, or functionaries in bureaucracies. For what subjective reasons do people render obedience to authority? Weber wished to understand the diverse ways in which persons subjectively "make sense" of their activities. He argued that sociologists should attempt to do so even when the subjective "meaning-complexes" they discover seem strange or odd to them.

**VALUE-FREEDOM AND VALUE-RELEVANCE** Hence, Weber's sociology does not seek to discover "an objectively 'correct' meaning or one which is 'true' in some metaphysical sense" (Weber, 1968, p. 4).[13] Moreover, neither empathy toward nor hostility against the actors under investigation is central here. Researchers are obligated, with respect to the research process, to set aside their ideological preferences, personal values, likes, and dislikes (of ascetic Protestants, for example, or the bureaucracy's functionaries) as much as humanly possible and to make every effort to remain fair and impartial. Clear standards of inquiry as well as an unbiased observation, measurement, comparison, and evaluation of the sources must be the prescriptive ideal of social scientists. Even if the habits, values, and practices of the groups under investigation are discovered to be repulsive, researchers must strive to uphold this ideal.

To maintain such an "objective" and "value-free" (*Wertfreiheit*) posture with respect to the gathering and evaluation of data, Weber knew, is not an easy task. We are all "cultural beings," and hence values remain inextricably intertwined with our thinking and action; a thin line separates "facts" from "values," and values intrude even into our modes of observation. Indeed, modern Western science itself *arose* as a consequence of a series of specific historical and cultural developments. Nonetheless, the social scientist must make a concerted effort to distinguish empirically based arguments and conclusions from normative – or value-based – arguments and conclusions. The latter should be minimized.

However, with regard to a foundational aspect of the research process, values remain appropriately central, Weber insists: the *selection* of topics. Far from "objective" in some metaphysical or predetermined sense, our choice – unavoidably so, for him – is directly related to our values (*Wertbezogenheit*) and our interests. A sociologist, for example, who strongly believes that persons of different ethnic groupings should be treated equally, may well decide – as a result of this *value* – to study how civil rights movements have assisted heretofore excluded groupings to acquire basic rights.

Yet, with respect to the overall task of the social sciences, Weber again argues that researchers must strive to exclude values: all value-judgments that pronounce, in the name of science, a particular activity or way of life as noble or base, ultimately rational or irrational, provincial or cosmopolitan, must be avoided. The social sciences will not – and should not – assist us to decide with certainty which values are superior. Those of the Sermon on the Mount cannot be proven scientifically to be "better" than those of the Rig Vedas. Nor can social scientists argue that specific values *should* guide our lives. Science provides knowledge and insight, and informs us regarding the various effects of utilizing a certain means to reach a specified goal, yet it must never be allowed to take responsibility for our decisions (Weber, 1946d, 1949).

Weber pronounced such an ethos of "value-neutrality" as indispensable to the definition of sociology – if it wished to be a social science rather than a political endeavor: "Science today is a 'vocation' organized in special disciplines in the service of self-clarification and knowledge of interrelated facts. It is not the gift of grace of seers and prophets dispensing sacred values and revelations, nor does it partake of the contemplation of sages and philosophers about the meaning of the universe" (Weber, 1946d, p. 152). How does the sociologist best proceed to ascertain subjective meaning in the groups under investigation, and to do so in an unbiased fashion? An answer to this question requires a brief discussion of Weber's *ideal typical* mode of analysis.

**IDEAL TYPES** Although Weber takes the meaningful action of individuals as his basic unit of analysis, his interpretive sociology never views social life as an "endless drift" of solitary and unconnected action-orientations. The diverse ways in which persons act *in concert* in groupings captures his attention, rather than the social action of the isolated individual. Indeed, he defines the sociological enterprise as oriented to the investigation of the subjective meaning of persons in delimited groups and the identification of *regularities of action*: "There can be observed, within the realm of social action, actual empirical regularities; that is, courses of action that are repeated by the actor or (possibly also: simultaneously) occur among numerous actors because the subjective *meaning* is typically *meant* to be the same. Sociological investigation is concerned with these *typical* modes of action" (Weber, 1968, p. 29, translation altered, original emphasis). Such patterned action can result, he argues, from an orientation not only to values, but also to affectual, traditional, and even means–end rational action. The various ways in which merely imitative and reactive behaviors are *uprooted* from their random flow and transformed into *meaning*-based regularities anchored in one of the four types of social action constitute one of his sociology's fundamental themes.

Weber's major heuristic concept – the ideal type – "documents" these regularities of meaningful action. Each of these *research tools* charts the action-orientations of individuals – and nothing more. Weber's ideal type "the Reform Calvinist," for example, identifies the regular action of these believers (for example, an orientation toward methodical work and an ascetic style of life). Hence, in seeking to capture patterned action through the formation of ideal types, his sociology steers away from a focus upon isolated action on the one hand and society, societal evolution, social differentiation, and "the question of social order" on the other hand. This level of analysis prevails throughout Weber's texts rather than detailed historical narrative or global concepts. How are ideal types formed?

Not simply a summarization or classification of social action is involved. Instead, and although construction of the ideal type is rooted thoroughly in empirical reality and depends upon the immersion of sociologists in the particular case under investigation, it is formulated, first, through a conscious exaggeration of the *essential* features of a pattern of action of interest to the sociologist, and, second, through a synthesis of these characteristic action-orientations into an internally unified and logically rigorous concept: "An ideal type is formed by the one-sided *accentuation of one or more* points of view and by the synthesis of a great many diffuse, discrete, more or less present and occasionally absent *concrete individual* phenomena, which are arranged according to those one-sidedly emphasized viewpoints into a unified *analytical* construct. In its conceptual purity, this construct cannot be found empirically anywhere in reality" (Weber, 1949, p. 90, original emphasis). While inductive procedures from empirical observations are first followed, deductive procedures then guide the logical ordering of the separate patterns of action into a unified and precise *construct*. Nonetheless, the anchoring of ideal types empirically precludes their understanding as "abstract" or "reified" concepts (see Weber, 1949, pp. 92–107).

Above all, according to Weber, ideal types serve *to assist* empirical, cause-oriented inquiry rather than to "replicate" and directly comprehend the external world (an impossible task, owing to the unending flow of events as well as the infinite diversity and complexity of even a particular social phenomenon) or to articulate an ideal, hoped-for development. Thus, the "Reform Calvinist" portrays accurately the subjective meaning of neither a particular Calvinist nor all Calvinists (Weber, 1968, pp. 19–22). The same holds for ideal types of bureaucracies, brothels, prophets, intellectuals, or charismatic leaders. As he notes, "Concepts are primarily analytical instruments for the intellectual mastery of the empirically given and can be only that" (Weber, 1949, p. 106, translation altered).

Once formed as clear concepts that capture regular action-orientations, ideal types anchor Weber's entire causal sociology in a fundamental fashion: they enable the precise definition of empirical action-orientations. As a logical construct that documents patterned social action, the ideal type establishes clear points of reference – or standards – against which regularities of subjective meaning in a particular case can be compared and "measured." The uniqueness of cases can be defined clearly through an assessment of their approximation to or deviation from the theoretically constructed type. "Ideal types such as Christianity... are of great value for research and of high systematic value for expository purposes when they are used as conceptual instruments for *comparison* and the *measurement* of reality. They are indispensable for this purpose" (Weber, 1949, p. 97, original emphasis; see also pp. 43, 90–3).[14]

**THE AIM OF WEBER'S SOCIOLOGY** Commentaries upon Weber's works have frequently failed to note that he orients his research to discrete problems and the causal analysis of specific cases and developments. He proposes that the causal explanation of this "historical individual" should serve as sociology's primary aim: "We wish to understand the reality that surrounds our lives, in which we are placed, *in its characteristic uniqueness*. We wish to understand on the one hand its context (*Zusammenhang*) and the cultural *significance* of its particular manifestations in their contemporary form, and on the other the causes of it becoming historically so and not otherwise" (Weber, 1949, p. 72, translation altered, original emphasis; see also p. 69; 1968, p. 10).

Hence, Weber opposed strongly the numerous positivist schools of thought in his day that sought, following the method offered by the natural sciences, to define a set of general laws of history and social change and then to explain all specific cases and developments by deduction. He rejected forcefully the position that the social sciences should aim "to construct a closed system of concepts which can encompass and classify reality in some definitive manner and from which it can be deduced again" (Weber, 1949, p. 84), and expressed his clear opposition to the view that laws themselves comprise causal explanations. Because concrete realities, individual cases and developments, and subjective meaning cannot be deduced from them, laws are incapable of providing the knowledge of reality that would offer causal explanations. To Weber, individual cases can be explained causally only by "other equally individual configurations" (Weber, 1949, pp. 75–6; see Kalberg, 1994b, pp. 81–4).[15]

These pivotal components of Weber's methodology will be better understood after a consideration of his major sociological investigations: *PE*, *EEWR*, and *E&S*.

## The Protestant Ethic and the Spirit of Capitalism

Weber wrote much of *PE* (1904–5) after returning from a three-month trip to the United States. Its thesis regarding the important role played by values in the development of modern capitalism set off an intense debate that has continued to this day. A genuine classic, *PE* is both his best known and most accessible work. Although Weber comes prominently to the fore in this study as a theorist who attends alone to values and ideas, its methodology exemplifies a variety of foundational procedures utilized throughout his sociology (see Kalberg, 1996). *PE* also offers a profound commentary upon American society, both past and present. Finally, this study constitutes Weber's first attempt to isolate the uniqueness of the modern West and to define its causal origins.

THE BACKGROUND A number of historians and economists in Weber's time emphasized the importance for economic development of technological innovations, the influx of precious metals, and population increases. Others were convinced that the greed, economic interests, and "desire for riches" of all – but especially of great "economic supermen" (the Carnegies, Rockefellers, and Vanderbilts) and the bourgeoisie in general – pushed economic development past the agrarian and feudal stages to mercantilism and modern capitalism. Disagreeing with all these explanations, evolutionists argued that the expansion of production, trade, banking, and commerce could best be understood as the clear manifestation of a general, societal-wide unfolding of "progress."

None of these forces could offer, Weber insisted, an explanation for that which distinguished *modern* capitalism from capitalism as it had existed throughout the ages: relatively free market exchange, separation of the business from the household, sophisticated bookkeeping, formally free labor, *and* a specific "economic ethos." This ethos stood behind the rigorous organization of work, the methodical approach to labor, and the systematic pursuit of profit typical of this form of capitalism. It was constituted from an "idea of a *duty* of the individual toward the increase of his profits, which is assumed as an end in itself" (Weber, 1930b, p. 51, original emphasis); the notion that "labor [must be] performed as if it were an absolute end in itself" (ibid., p. 62); "the earning of more and more money, combined with the strict avoidance of all spontaneous enjoyment of life" (ibid., p. 53); the view that the "earning of money...is...the result and the expression of virtue and proficiency in a calling" (ibid., p. 54); and "an attitude (*Gesinnung*) that, *in a calling*, seeks profit rationally and systematically" (ibid., p. 64, translation altered, original emphasis). Embodied in these ideas was a *spirit* of capitalism, and Weber argues vehemently that a full understanding of the origins of modern capitalism requires an identification of the sources of this "modern economic ethos" (Weber, 1930b, pp. 64, 91–2).

Hence, an investigation of the specific ancestry of this spirit, rather than the sources in general of either modern capitalism or capitalism, was the comparatively modest project of *PE* (see Weber, 1930b, pp. 51, 55, 74–5, 78, 91). After citing numerous passages from Benjamin Franklin, whose values represent to

Weber the spirit of capitalism in a pure form (see ibid., pp. 48–51), he asserts that he has here discovered an *ethos*, "the violation of [which] is treated not as foolishness but as forgetfulness of *duty*" (ibid., p. 51, original emphasis).[16] However, in seeking to unravel the "causal origins" of this new *set of values* and "ordered way of life," this "positive critique of historical materialism" rejects the view that capitalism's dominant class gave birth to this spirit (see ibid., pp. 26–7, 55–75; Kalberg, 1996, p. 56). It opposes as well the argument that social structures – status groups, or churches and sects themselves – stand at its origin (see Weber, 1930b, pp. 75, 98–154; 1946, p. 292). Instead, Weber wanted to explore, against strong opponents, the "idealist side" (see, for example, Weber, 1930b, p. 183).

**THE ARGUMENT**[17] After observing various ways in which Protestants seemed attracted to business-oriented occupations and organized their daily lives in an especially rigorous fashion, Weber began to explore Protestant doctrine. He discovered a "world-oriented ethos" typically represented in the Westminster Confession (1647) and the sermons of a seventeenth-century Puritan successor of John Calvin, Richard Baxter. For Weber, Baxter's revisions of Calvin's teachings sought above all to banish the bleak conclusions rationally implied by his "Doctrine of Predestination": if the question of salvation constituted *the* burning question to believers (see Weber, 1930b, pp. 110–11), if the "salvation status" of the faithful was preordained from the very beginning, and if God had selected only a tiny minority to be saved, massive fatalism, despair, loneliness, and anxiety among the devout logically followed (ibid., pp. 98–100, 104–8, 232n). Recognizing that the harshness of this decree precluded its continued endorsement by most believers (ibid., p. 110), Baxter undertook doctrinal alterations that, according to Weber, launched the Protestant ethic.

Along with Calvin, Baxter acknowledged that the mortal and weak devout cannot know God's judgment, for the motives of this majestic, distant, and all-mighty Deity of the Old Testament remain incomprehensible to lowly terrestrial inhabitants (ibid., pp. 101–4). However, Baxter emphasized that "the world exists to serve the glorification of God" and that God wishes His Kingdom to be one of wealth, equality, and prosperity, for abundance among "His children" would surely serve to praise His goodness and justice (see ibid., pp. 108, 157–8, 170, 265–6n). Understood as a means toward the creation of God's community on earth, regular and dedicated work – or work in a "calling" – now acquired a *religious* significance among the devout. Believers comprehended their worldly economic activity as in service to a demanding God, and they could view themselves as noble instruments – or tools (ibid., p. 125) – of His Commandments and His Divine Plan: "labor in the service of impersonal social usefulness appears to promote the glory of God and to be willed by Him" (ibid., p. 109; see also pp. 159–62, 178, 265n, 282n). Indeed, those believers capable of systematic work on behalf of God's Plan could convince themselves that their strength to do so emanated from the favoring Hand of an omnipotent God – *and*, the faithful could further conclude, God would favor only those he had chosen to be among the predestined (see ibid., p. 172).

Moreover, continuous and systematic work possessed an undeniable virtue for the good Christian, according to Baxter: it *tames* the creaturely and base side of human nature and thereby facilitates the concentration of the mind upon God and the "uplifting of the soul" (ibid., pp. 158–9). Finally, "intense worldly activity" also effectively counteracts the penetrating doubt, anxiety, and sense of unworthiness induced by the Predestination Doctrine and instills the self-confidence that allows believers to consider themselves among the chosen (see ibid., pp. 111–12). In this manner systematic work, and as well the "systematic rational ordering of the moral life as a whole" (ibid., p. 126), became hallowed.

However, the singular power of the Protestant ethic to upset the "traditional economic ethic" that had existed from time immemorial originated, Weber argues, not simply in these ways, especially if one wishes to understand the "constant self-control" and "methodical rationalization of life" of Calvinist entrepreneurs (ibid,, pp. 126, 128). A further adjustment by Baxter proved significant as well. According to the Predestination Doctrine, believers could never *know* their salvation status; however, in light of God's desire to see the creation of an earthly Kingdom of abundance to serve His glory, they could logically conclude that the production of great wealth for a community by an individual could be viewed as a *sign* that God favored this individual. In effect, personal wealth itself became to the faithful actual *evidence* of their salvation status. Omnipotent and omniscient, God surely would never allow one of the condemned to praise His Glory: "the attainment of [wealth] as a *fruit* of labour in a calling was a sign of God's blessing" (ibid., p. 172, original emphasis). In His universe, nothing happened by chance.

Thus, and although the devout could never be absolutely certain of their membership among the elect, more business-oriented believers could seek to *produce* the evidence – literally, wealth and profit (see ibid., p. 162) – that enabled them to convince themselves of their "chosen" religious status. In view of the unbearable anxiety provoked by the central religious question – "am I among the saved?" – in sixteenth- and seventeenth-century England, a psychological certainty of a favorable salvation status was the crucial issue, Weber emphasizes. Baxter's revisions allowed the faithful to understand their successful accumulation of wealth, and its reinvestment for the betterment of God's community, as tangible proof of their chosen status (see ibid., pp. 177, 281n). Uniquely, riches now acquired among believers a *religious* significance: they constituted signs that indicated one's membership among the elect, thereby losing their traditionally suspect character and becoming endowed with a positive "psychological premium." Methodical work became viewed as the most adequate means toward great wealth.

In this manner, a set of work-oriented values heretofore scorned (see ibid., pp. 56, 75) became of utmost centrality in the lives of the devout. Not the desire for riches alone nor the efficient adaptation to economic forces, but only work motivated "from within" by an "internally binding" set of religious values was empowered to introduce, Weber argues, a "systematization of ethical conduct" (ibid., p. 123) and a "deliberate regulation of one's own life" on behalf of work and the pursuit of wealth (ibid., p. 126; see also pp. 125–8). Only this ethically[18] *ordered way of life rooted in values* was endowed with the methodicalness and intensity requisite for an uprooting and banishing of the traditional economic ethic.

A "Protestant ethic" originated in this manner. Carried by ascetic Protestant and, above all, Reform Calvinist sects and churches, this ethic spread throughout several New England, Dutch, and English communities in the sixteenth and seventeenth centuries. Both the disciplined, hard labor in a calling and the wealth that followed from a steadfast adherence to its religious values marked a person as "chosen." One century later, by the time of Benjamin Franklin's more secularized America, the Protestant ethic had spread beyond churches and sects and into entire communities. As it did so, however, its specifically religious component became weakened and transformed into a "utilitarian-colored ethos" (ibid., pp. 52, 176–7, 180), namely a *spirit* of capitalism.[19] Rather than believed to be among the "chosen elect," adherents of this ethos, such as Franklin, were viewed simply as upright, respectable, community-oriented citizens of good moral character.

*PE* investigates the "causal origins" of the spirit of capitalism in this way. The subjective meaning of believers, as captured through religious sources and values rather than by reference to social structural factors, rational choices, economic interests, domination and power, specific classes, or evolutionary progress, remains central throughout. The spirit of capitalism gave a decisive – although in the end imprecise – push to the development of modern capitalism. Nonetheless, when Weber turns briefly in his conclusion to our present era, he calls attention to an altogether different dynamic. Once the spirit of capitalism has assisted the growth of modern capitalism and this "economic form" has become firmly entrenched amidst massive industrialism, modern capitalism sustains itself, he argues, on the basis alone of *means–end* rational action carried out in reference to external and pragmatic necessities. If present at all, "the idea of a 'duty in one's calling' prowls about in our lives [today] like the ghost of dead religious beliefs" (ibid., p. 182; see pp. 176–7, 180). The Puritan "*wanted* to work in a calling...we *must* do so" (ibid., p. 181; translation altered, original emphasis).

This case study of the spirit of capitalism's origins stands as a powerful demonstration of the ways in which social action may be influenced by non-economic forces. Sociological analysis must not focus exclusively upon material interests, power, structural forces, and "economic forms" to the neglect of cultural forces and "economic ethics," Weber insists. Yet sociologists must also reject a focus alone upon "ideal" forces. "*Both* sides" must be given their due and a "single formula" must always be avoided: "But it is, of course, not my aim to substitute for a one-sided 'materialistic' an equally one-sided spiritualistic causal interpretation of culture and of history. *Both* are *equally possible*, but each, if it serves as the conclusion of an investigation rather than the preparation, accomplishes equally little in the interest of historical truth" (ibid., p. 183; translation altered, original emphasis).

Hence, and although *PE* demonstrates the ways in which values influence the playing out of economic interests and provide the "content" for social structures,

Weber recognized that a series of broad-ranging *multicausal and comparative* investigations would be necessary for a full understanding of the origins of modern capitalism. "Ideas" *and* "interests" must be scrutinized. If the spirit of capitalism is to have an impact upon the development of modern capitalism, constellations of political, economic, stratification, legal, and other factors must congeal, he was convinced, to formulate a conducive context (see ibid., pp. 183, 172n84; Marshall, 1980). *PE* comprised simply the first step in Weber's grand scheme to investigate the causal origins of modern capitalism. *EEWR* took up this theme[20] and, indeed, broadened it to the question of the origins of "modern Western rationalism."

The other major work of his mature sociology – a systematic treatise that lays out the conceptual tools and research procedures for his wide-ranging comparative-historical sociology, *E&S* – provided the theoretical framework for the *EEWR* studies. This analytic opus must first be addressed. In both works, Weber renounced any search for a single, encompassing causal equation: "That sort of thing remains better left to that type of dilettante who believes in the 'unity' of the 'social psyche' and its reducibility to a *single* formula" (ibid., p. 284n, translation altered, original emphasis).

## *Economy and Society*

Incomplete and published posthumously by his wife, *E&S* addresses, as does *EEWR*, the ways in which the West must be understood as unique. Frequently, by reference to configurations of both "ideal" and "material" patterns of action, it also explores the causal origins of the West's specific developmental pathway. However, unlike *EEWR* and *PE*, *E&S* seeks mainly to provide a systematic grounding for the discipline of sociology as distinguished from the fields of history and economics. This three-volume work constitutes the analytic treatise for Weber's comparative-historical, interpretive sociology.

Written over a period of eleven years (1909–20), *E&S* ranges across an astonishingly broad comparative palette. Weber examines, for example, status groups, the state, classes, ethnic groups, the family, the clan, and political organizations on the one hand, and a vast array of types of economies, cities, salvation religions, and rulership and legal organizations on the other hand – and does so not by reference to the twentieth century or a single society, but in "universal-historical" perspective. His strokes are at times broad and encompass developmental trends and patterns over centuries, even millennia, in a variety of civilizations, yet thorough historical research anchors his analysis throughout. Perhaps herein lies its claim to be one of the twentieth century's most remarkable contributions to the social sciences: while "a sociologist's world history... [that] raises some of the big questions [regarding] the modern world" (Roth, 1968, p. xxix), it also rigorously attends to details. Weber is engaged in a breathtaking project: a *systematization* of his vast knowledge of the ancient, medieval, and modern epochs in China, India, and the West, as well as of the ancient Middle Eastern civilizations, into a theoretical treatise that will serve to guide the practice of his comparative-historical, interpretive sociology. He wishes to do so, however, without moving to an abstract level of analysis devoid of a solid empirical foundation.

This attention to detail, combined with the continuous formulation of analytic generalizations, renders *E&S* a difficult, even tortuous, work. Models heuristically useful to researchers are created again and again, yet only after a painstaking examination of numerous historical cases. Some ideal types are of more limited scope and pertain to a specific period, others range broadly and even universally; some are more static, and serve as conceptual yardsticks to assist the definition of empirical cases; others are more dynamic and include sets of hypotheses; still others are "developmental models" comprised of many stages. While the shorter part I (written later) emphasizes model building, and indeed often appears as simply a compendium of concepts, the longer part II focuses more upon historical cases, as well as upon brief (and incomplete) causal analyses of particular developments, before formulating models. The sheer dryness of the definitions in part I and the disjointed, back and forth movement between the historical evidence and the construction of ideal types in part II repeatedly tests the patience of even the most enamored reader. Unfortunately, Weber never provides a summary statement of his aims, themes, or procedures.

Not surprisingly, interpreters of this opus have generally examined only those discussions that have become classic statements and *de rigueur* reading for both theorists and sociologists engaged in specialized research: the chapters on law, status groups, prophets, religion, charisma, rulership in general, the bureaucracy, and the city. Although these sections deserve careful scrutiny (see below), a focus upon them alone fails to reveal the true originality and enduring usefulness of this treatise. An exploration of the five axes that dominate this labyrinthine work will articulate its underlying trajectories. In the process, the major modes of analysis and research procedures of Weber's comparative-historical, interpretive sociology will be delineated. A brief perusal of each must suffice.

## "LOCATING" SOCIAL ACTION: SOCIETAL DOMAINS AND IDEAL TYPES

Convinced that the crystallization of social action into patterns is not random, yet also not to be grasped by reference to a "social system," "cultural order," "social fact," or "generalized other," Weber aims throughout *E&S* to specify *where* such regularities are likely to arise. The foundation for his entire agenda has been laid to the extent that he succeeds in *locating*, analytically, meaningful action. Indeed, this task must be undertaken if his interpretive sociology – the understanding by the sociologist of the subjective meaning persons in diverse groups attribute to their action – is to constitute more than an empty, formalistic enterprise.

Based on massive comparative historical research, Weber argues in *E&S* that social action – largely though not exclusively – congeals in a number of "societal domains" (*gesellschaftliche Ordnungen*): the economy, rulership, religion, law, status groups, and universal organizations (family, clan, and traditional neighborhood) domains.[21] To him, persons are "placed into various societal domains, each of which is governed by different laws" (Weber, 1946a, p. 123). *E&S* undertakes the huge task of delimiting the major domains within which social action significantly crystallizes. It then identifies the themes, dilemmas, or sets of questions indigenous to each domain. For example, a focus upon explanations for suffering, misfortune, and misery distinguishes the domain of religion, while the domain of rulership is concerned with the reasons why persons attribute legitimacy to commands and their motives for rendering obedience. The status groups domain involves social honor and defined ways of leading a life (*Lebensführung*). In this manner, analytic boundaries for each domain become established.

With a significant likelihood, action in these domains becomes uprooted from its random, reactive flow and becomes characterized by a directedness. Weber argues that a good probability exists for this action to become *social* action, and most *E&S* chapters discuss the particular features of domain-specific social action. For example, with respect to economic activity, action becomes social action "if it takes account of the behavior of someone else . . . [and] in so far as the actor assumes that others will respect his actual control over economic goods" (Weber, 1968, p. 22; see also p. 341); and action oriented to status becomes social action wherever a specific way of leading a life is acknowledged and restrictions on social intercourse become effective (ibid., p. 932). *Here* we find, with societal domains, a major heuristic tool for the research of the interpretive sociologist. In Weber's terminology, each domain is a domain of subjective meaning (*Sinnbereich*) within which social action and social groupings are likely to arise.

Nonetheless, and however conceptually pivotal to his entire interpretive agenda, Weber concludes that domains remain too global to anchor his empirically based sociology. With respect to this *E&S* task – locating social action – they constitute only a beginning. Patterned orientations of subjectively meaningful action can be far more rigorously conceptualized, he argues, by reference to *ideal types*. These constructs capture social action with great precision. As an analytic treatise, *E&S* takes the formulation of ideal types as one of its main tasks.

When Weber forms an ideal type of, for example, the prophet, the functionary in a bureaucracy, the market or natural economy, the feudal aristocrat, the peasant, or the intellectual, he is in each case conceptualizing regular orientations of social action. Thus, the "bureaucratic functionary" identifies patterned orientations toward the disciplined organization of work, punctuality, reliability, specialized tasks, and a hierarchical chain of command; and the "charismatic leader" outlines orientations toward persons viewed as extraordinary and a willingness to follow them even if a violation of convention and custom is necessary. Each ideal type signifies an uprooting of action from its amorphous flow and a demarcation of constellations of social action. In the case of most ideal types formulated in *E&S*, Weber sees a likelihood for the congealing of such meaningful action: regular orientations of action with a degree of endurance and firmness – a continuity – are implied. Furthermore, the action-orientations delineated by ideal types imply the possibility that an indigenous causal thrust and staying power may exist empirically. Each ideal type – the patterned action-orientations it implies – retains the potential, depending upon the push and pull of the context of further action-orientations within which it exists, to assert an autonomous (*eigengesetzliche*) influence. Thus, on a broad scale, the ideal types of this wide-ranging treatise chart the "direction" of patterned social action in a far more specific manner than do its societal domains.

The location of meaningful action in *E&S* by reference to ideal types and societal domains fulfills the important task of conceptualizing empirical meaningful action. However, it performs a further crucial service in Weber's interpretive sociology: on a wide-ranging, comparative historical scale, *E&S* assists sociologists *to understand* how a vast variety of social action *can become* subjectively meaningful to persons. In other words, it facilitates the understanding of social action *contextually*: on its own terms, or "from within." In doing so, this analytic opus accomplishes for Weber's *verstehende* project another pivotal task: it opposes all tendencies for sociologists engaged in research to explore meaningful social action solely from the vantage point of their *own* accustomed (and perhaps unexamined) presuppositions. Whenever this occurs, a greater likelihood exists that social scientists will, Weber is convinced, see "unusual action" as odd, irrational, and incomprehensible rather than as subjectively meaningful.

Hence, in locating subjective meaning with the assistance of numerous ideal types and societal domains, *E&S* facilitates comprehension of how values, interests, emotions, and traditions in many empirical settings provide meaning to persons and thereby formulate the foundation for social groupings (see Kalberg, 1994b, pp. 30–46). By enabling an understanding of the putatively "irrational" actions of others as indeed meaningful, it *expands* the imagination of sociologists. For example, the ideal type "missionary prophet" assists "we moderns" to comprehend the ways in which this charismatic figure, who views the cosmos as internally unified by God's Commandments and intentions (Weber, 1968, pp. 450–1), attributes meaning to his actions – however "irrational" they may appear from the point of view of today's scientific and secularized presuppositions. Under some circumstances, action-orientations may "line up" in a concerted fashion and form the foundation for internally consistent and even methodical "ways of leading a life." Several of Weber's ideal types chart just such systematically directed action.[22]

**IDEAL TYPES AS "STANDARDS"** As noted, the ideal types of *E&S*, as conceptual tools, "document" patterned social action and demarcate its "location." In addition, when utilized as "standards" against which the patterns of action under investigation can be compared and "measured," they enable the clear definition of this action. A vast diversity of ideal types of varying scope are formulated in this analytic treatise (for example, feudalism, patriarchalism, missionary prophecy, priests, the Oriental city, natural law, canon law, asceticism, warriors). Perhaps most influential in sociology have been two of Weber's ideal types: "types of rulership"[23] and "status groups."[24]

Rather than a "social fact," an expression of natural laws, or an inevitable culmination of historical evolutionary forces, *rulership* implies for Weber nothing more than the probability that a definable group of individuals (as a result of various motives) will orient their social action to giving commands, that another definable group will direct their social action to obedience (as a result of various motives), and that commands are in fact, to a sociologically relevant degree, carried out.[25] In his famous formulation, rulership refers "to the probability that a command with a given specific content will be obeyed by a given group of persons" (ibid., p. 53). It may be ascribed to diverse individuals, such as judges, civil servants, bankers, craftsmen, and tribal chiefs. All exercise rulership wherever obedience is claimed and in fact called forth (ibid., pp. 941, 948).

Weber's major concern focuses upon *legitimate* rulership, or the situation in which a degree of legitimacy is attributed to the rulership relationship. For this reason, obedience, importantly, acquires a voluntary element. Whether anchored in unreflective habit or custom, an emotional attachment to the ruler or fear of him, values or ideals, or purely material interests and a calculation of advantage, a necessary minimum of compliance, unlike sheer *power*, always exists in the case of legitimate rulership (ibid., p. 212).

To Weber, the establishment of a rulership relationship's legitimacy through material interests alone is likely to be relatively unstable. On the other hand, purely value-rational and affectual motives can be decisive only in "extraordinary" circumstances. A mixture of custom and a means–end rational calculation of material interest generally provides the "motive for compliance" in everyday situations (ibid., pp. 213–14, 943). Yet, in his analysis, these motives alone never form a reliable and enduring foundation for rulership. A further element is crucial: at least a minimum belief on the part of the ruled in the legitimacy of the rulership: "In general, it should be kept clearly in mind that the basis of every rulership, and correspondingly of every kind of willingness to obey, is a *belief*, a belief by virtue of which persons exercising rulership are lent prestige" (ibid., p. 263).[26]

In essence, rulers seek to convince themselves of their *right* to exercise rulership and attempt to implant the notion among the ruled that this right is deserved. If they succeed, a willingness to obey arises that secures their rule far more effectively than does force or power. The character of the typical belief, or claim to legitimacy, provides Weber with the criteria he utilizes to classify the major *types* of legitimate rulership into ideal-typical models (see ibid., p. 953). Why do people obey authority? From the vantage point of his broad-ranging comparative and historical studies, Weber argues that all ruling powers, "profane or religious, political as well as unpolitical," can be understood as appealing to *rational-legal*, *traditional*, or *charismatic* principles of legitimation. What typical beliefs establish the "validity" of these three "pure types" of legitimate rulership?

1   Rational grounds – resting on a belief in the legality of enacted rules and the right of those elevated to rulership under such rules to issue commands (legal rulership).
2   Traditional grounds – resting on an established belief in the sanctity of immemorial traditions and the legitimacy of those exercising rulership under them (traditional rulership).

3   Charismatic grounds – resting on devotion to the exceptional sanctity, heroism, or exemplary character of an individual person, and of the orders revealed or ordained by him (charismatic rulership) (ibid., p. 215). Under the motto, "it is written – but I say unto you," this mission opposes all existing values, customs, laws, rules, and traditions (ibid., pp. 1115–17).[27]

These issues define the "rulership" domain and distinguish action oriented to it from action in the other domains.

Weber's widely discussed model of "rational-legal" rulership is manifest in the bureaucratic organization. In industrial societies, he argues, this type of rulership becomes all-pervasive. It is legitimated by a belief in properly enacted rules and "objective" modes of procedure, rather than by persons or reference to the legitimacy of traditions established in the past. Thus, bureaucratic administration stands in radical opposition to both charismatic rulership and all types of traditional rulership (patriarchalism, feudalism, patrimonialism). The subsumption of diverse social action under stable prescriptions, regulations, and rules accounts for its *comparative* technical superiority *vis-à-vis* traditional and charismatic rulership. Rights and duties are defined and, by virtue of a position in a hierarchy, empower "a superior" to issue commands and expect obedience: "Orders are given in the name of an impersonal norm rather than in the name of a personal authority; and even the giving of a command constitutes obedience toward a norm rather than an arbitrary freedom, favor, or privilege" (Weber, 1946e, pp. 294–5; see also 1968, pp. 229, 945, 1012).

Moreover, in a systematic fashion, bureaucracies orient labor toward general rules and regulations. Work occurs in offices, on a full-time basis, and involves the formulation of written records and their preservation; employees are appointed and rewarded with a regular salary as well as the prospect for advancement. And work procedures maximize calculation: through an assessment of single cases in reference to a set of abstract rules or a weighing of means and ends, decisions can be rendered in a predictable and expedient manner. Compared to the traditional forms of rulership, such decisions occur with less equivocation: arenas of jurisdiction, task specialization, competence, and responsibility for each employee are delimited on the one hand by administrative regulations and on the other hand by technical training. This technical training can be most effectively utilized not only when realms of competence are defined, but also if an unquestioned hierarchy of command reigns in which "each lower office is under the control and supervision of a higher one." Rulership, including a superior's access to coercive means, is distributed in a stable manner and articulated by regulations (Weber, 1968, pp. 223, 975).

Weber's model emphasizes that a "formal rationality" reigns in bureaucracies: problems are solved and decisions made by the systematic and continuous means–end rational orientation of action to abstract rules, which are enacted through discursively analyzable procedures and applied universally. Because decision-making and the giving of commands takes place in direct reference to these rules, bureaucracies typically imply – compared to the traditional and charismatic types of rulership – the reduction of affectual and traditional action.

He repeatedly calls attention to the extremely impersonal character of bureaucratic rulership. For example, "Bureaucracy develops the more perfectly the more it is 'dehumanized,' the more completely it succeeds in eliminating from official business love, hatred, and all purely personal, irrational, and emotional elements which escape calculation" (ibid., p. 975).

This "pure model," Weber argues, can be utilized as a standard against which the particular empirical case under investigation – the American, English, or German bureaucracy, for example, or the state bureaucracy *vis-à-vis* the bureaucracy in private industry – can be compared. Through an assessment of deviation from this heuristic tool, the main features of the particular case will then become defined and its distinctiveness precisely demarcated.[28] His other widely discussed ideal type, "status group," serves the same purpose.

Weber contends that *status groups* – and not only classes, as for Marx – constitute an independent foundation for social stratification. Viewed through the lens of universal history, the dominant mode of stratification varies across civilizations and epochs. In the modern West, for example, "*class* situation" has become a more central organizing principle than "*status* situation" (see Weber, 1946, p. 301). Stratification by status is favored, he insists, whenever relationships of production and distribution are stable, and naked class situation becomes prominent in eras of great technological and economic change. When the tempo of such transformations recedes, a reinvigoration of status structures occurs, as well as an enhancement of the salience of social honor (Weber, 1968, p. 938). How does Weber define "status group" and how does this ideal type, as a conceptual yardstick, assist research?

"Status situation" implies "every typical component of the life of men that is determined by a specific, positive or negative, social estimation of honor" (ibid., p. 932). Thus, social esteem – claims to it and acknowledgment of it – orient social action in this domain. A person's way of leading a life, which in turn rests upon discrete socialization processes and hereditary and occupational prestige, comes here to the fore (ibid., pp. 305–6; see also Weber, 1946, pp. 300, 306).

A status group (*Stand*) appears when persons share a style of life, consumption patterns, common conventions, specific notions of honor, and, conceivably, economic and particular status monopolies. For Weber, status situations, due to an implied evaluation of one's own situation relative to that of others as well as a subjective awareness of common conventions, values, and styles of life, may often lead to the formation of groups. This remains the case even if such groups are at times amorphous (Weber, 1968, p. 932). Status differences become apparent whenever social interaction is restricted or lacking. Stratification by status always implies the "monopolization of ideal and material goods or opportunities," as well as social distance and exclusiveness (ibid., pp. 935, 927; Weber, 1946e, p. 300).

Weber emphasizes that a subjective sense of social honor and esteem may have a significant impact. "Stratification by status" stands in opposition to and may restrict *even* action oriented to classes, material interests, the development of the free market, class conflicts, and hard bargaining. Guilds in the Middle Ages, for example, now and then struggled more fervently over questions of precedence in festival processions than over economic issues. Distinguished families through-out the world permit courtship of their daughters only by status peers, and members of "old families" have frequently cultivated a variety of techniques of exclusiveness, as have the descendants of the Pilgrim fathers, Pocahontas, and the First Families of Virginia (Weber, 1958, pp. 34, 125; 1968, pp. 933, 937). Court nobles and humanist literati influenced greatly the character of education in the seventeenth century, and various "carrier strata" have prominently placed their imprint upon the formation of religious doctrines and ethical teachings (see below). This has occurred to such an extent that belief systems undergo pro-found alterations whenever they acquire a new carrier stratum (see Weber, 1946c, pp. 267–9, 279–85; 1968, pp. 490–2, 1180–1). A single status group might occasionally set its stamp upon the entire development of a civilization, as did intellectuals in China, the samurai warriors in Japan, the Brahmin priests in India, and the business class in the United States.

As ideal types, status groups can be employed as standards against which the particular case under investigation can be "measured." Its uniqueness can be defined in this manner. Without these constructs to assist conceptualization, it is not possible, Weber argues, to conduct the comparative "mental experiments" (*Gedankenbild*) central for the rigorous isolation of significant causal patterns of action.

These yardstick ideal types – status groups and the types of rulership – from *E&S*, as well as many others that could be addressed, place Weber in direct opposition to Marx: material interests do not *alone* constitute the single "engine" of change. On the contrary, Weber's sociology repeatedly contends that a variety of causal forces are effective in history and that social change occurs in a non-linear, complex fashion (see below).

**IDEAL TYPES AS HYPOTHESIS-FORMING MODELS** Many of Weber's ideal types not only facilitate the clear conceptualization of specific cases or develop-ments, but also delineate hypotheses that can be tested against specific empirical cases and developments – indeed, in such a manner that discrete and significant causal regularities of social action can be isolated. Ideal types are employed in *E&S* as hypothesis-forming models in four major ways.

Their *dynamic* character is the focus of Weber's first type of model. Rather than being static, ideal types are constituted from an array of regular action-orientations. Relationships – delimited, empirically testable hypotheses – among these action-orientations are implied. Second, *contextual* models that articulate hypotheses regarding the impact of specific social contexts upon patterned action are constructed in *E&S*. Third, when examined in reference to one another, ideal types may articulate *logical interactions* of patterned, meaning-ful action. Hypotheses regarding "elective affinity" and "antagonism" relation-ships across ideal types abound in *E&S*. Fourth, Weber utilizes ideal types to chart analytic *developments*. Each model hypothesizes a *course* of regular action, or a "developmental path."

By erecting a delineated theoretical framework, every model facilitates a conceptual grasp upon otherwise diffuse realities and formulates causal hypotheses regarding patterned action-orientations. In doing so, each model assists attainment of the overall goal of Weber's sociology: the causal explanation of cases and developments. A strongly theoretical dimension is also injected by each model into the very core of Weber's comparative historical sociology. Only a few of his elective affinity, antagonism, and developmental models can be noted here.[29]

Weber informs us explicitly that he is concerned in *E&S* with the ideal typical relationships between the economy and "society" – that is, the interactions between the economy and "the general structural *forms* (Struktur*formen*) of human groups" (1968, p. 356)[30] in the major societal domains. In great detail and on a universal-historical scale, he charts out, through constellations of ideal types, the diverse ways in which the various stages in the development of the economy (the agricultural and industrial organization of work; the natural, money, planned, market, and capitalist types of economies) relate to – and influence – the various major stages in these domains: for example, the traditional, natural, and logical-formal types of law; the paths to salvation in the religion domain (through a savior, an institution, ritual, good works, mysticism, and asceticism; see Kalberg, 1990); the charismatic, patriarchal, feudal, patrimonial, and bureaucratic types of rulership; the family, clan, and traditional neighborhood; and an array of major status groups (such as intellectuals, civil servants, and feudal nobles).

Nonetheless, this attention to the interactions between the economy and the other domains never implies its elevation to a position of causal dominance. On the contrary, in distinguishing a *series* of realms, Weber wishes, against Marx, to argue that questions of causality cannot be addressed by reference primarily to economic forces, material interests, or *any* single domain. As he notes, "The connections between the economy and the societal domains are dealt with more fully than is usually the case. This is done deliberately so that the autonomy (*Eigengesetzlichkeit*) of these domains *vis-à-vis* the economy is made manifest" (Weber, 1914, p. vii). Each domain, Weber contends, as manifest through its ideal types, implies the possibility of empirically significant patterns of action; many passages in *E&S* are devoted to demonstrations of how this takes place in reference to the indigenous themes, dilemmas, or sets of questions specific to each domain. The elevation of a particular realm to a position of general causal priority, Weber insists, must not occur.

Moreover, and despite an orientation to the economy domain, *E&S* charts much more than the relationships between the various groupings in this realm and the various groupings in the other domains. This opus cannot accurately be depicted as addressing only the manner in which diverse groups influence – and are influenced by – the economy. Instead, Weber examines thoroughly the ideal typical relationships, for example, between clan and religious groupings, legal and rulership organizations, groupings in the domain of religion and organizations in the domain of law, the family and rulership organizations, and religious groups and rulership organizations. More specifically, he scrutinizes the relation of logical-formal law to bureaucratic rulership, the family to various salvation paths, and the "ethics" of various status groups to the major salvation paths on the one hand and the types of law and rulership on the other hand. How, then, do the various domains relate analytically to one another? *E&S* proclaims that they do so in patterned ways.

Two concepts in this treatise capture cross-domain relationships: relations of "elective affinity" and "relations of antagonism." While elective affinity relationships imply a compatible intermingling – a non-deterministic though typical and reciprocal interaction of regular social action – of two or more ideal types that share internal features, antagonistic relationships indicate hypotheses of "inadequacy" and a clash, a hindering, even an excluding of the patterned action-orientations implied by each ideal type.

These "logical interactions" of regular action constitute, to Weber, hypothesis-forming models. For example, the intensely personal character of relationships in the family and clan are viewed as *antagonistic* to the impersonal relationships characteristic of the marketplace (an orientation of meaningful action to the "laws of the market" over persons) and bureaucratic rulership (an orientation to statutes, regulations, and laws over persons). Similarly, the relationships of compassion and brotherhood typically cultivated by the great salvation religions are seen as opposing the formal rationality that appears in the later developmental stages of the economy (capitalism), rulership (bureaucracy), and law (logical-formal) domains. And charismatic rulership stands in a relationship of antagonism to all routine economic action: "From the point of view of rational economic activity, charismatic want satisfaction is a typical anti-economic force" (Weber, 1968, p. 245; see Kalberg, 1994b, pp. 102–17).

On the other hand, innumerable cross-domain *affinity* relationships abound as well in *E&S*. For example, and despite wide diversity, Weber detected a series of elective affinities between the status ethic of intellectuals and certain salvation paths. Due to their typical tendency to ponder the world passively, to search for a comprehensive meaning to life, and to deplore the meaninglessness of empirical reality, rather than to undertake "tasks" and act regularly *in* the world as "doers," intellectuals are generally predisposed to formulate notions of salvation "more remote from life, more theoretical and more systematic than salvation from external need, the quest for which is characteristic of non-privileged strata" (Weber, 1968, p. 506; translation altered). Weber also sees logical interactions of elective affinity as typically occurring between the universal organizations and both magic-based and salvation-based religions. Magical religions simply appropriated the general virtues practiced in the family, kin group, and traditional neighborhood (such as fraternity, truthfulness, loyalty to the sibling, respect for older generations, and reciprocal assistance), and salvation religions typically bestowed distinctly positive premiums upon the brotherhood ethic. In all cases, personal relations and person-oriented values predominated. Similarly, Weber discovered elective affinity relations between traditional types of law and patriarchal rulership, as well as bureaucratic rulership and logical-formal law (see Kalberg, 1994b, pp. 108–16).

In this manner, *E&S* articulates a series of cross-domain analytic relationships, all of which are formulated as hypotheses.[31] Indeed, this opus constructs a broad-ranging analytic – one that can be utilized as a theoretical framework to facilitate the clear conceptualization of empirical relationships, as well as their analytical location.[32] One further type of hypothesis-forming model central in *E&S* must be examined: the developmental model.

Weber's *E&S developmental models* hypothesize a *course* of patterned action. In doing so, they (a) facilitate the clear conceptualization of the particular development under investigation, as well as its significant causal forces, and (b) postulate delineated, empirically testable developmental courses of patterned action. In effect, as "technical aids" constructed with a "rational consistency . . . rarely found in reality" (Weber, 1946c, p. 323), each model charts paths that will be taken if certain "irrational" empirical disturbances do not intervene (Weber, 1949, pp. 101–3). "Even developments," according to Weber, "can be constructed as ideal types, and these constructs may have quite considerable heuristic value" (ibid., p. 101).

In formulating these models, Weber repeatedly notes their basically "unhistorical" character. As ideal typical constructions, each captures the *essence* of a development, presenting it in a manner more internally consistent and systematically unified than ever occurred empirically. Hence, because the stages of his developmental models should never be viewed either as accurate renderings of the course of history or as themselves constituting "effective forces," *E&S* diverges distinctly from all evolutionary schools of thought in search of either society's "scientific laws" or history's "invariable stages" – thereby placing Weber in opposition to social theorists as diverse as Comte, Marx, and Spencer. His models serve a more modest task: they aim to provide the researcher with a clear and practical "means of orientation" on the one hand and an array of hypotheses regarding the course of history with respect to a particular theme on the other hand. Whether the analytic path of development laid out by a specific model is followed always remains an issue for detailed empirical investigation by specialists (ibid., p. 103). Thus, these developmental models again testify to the centrality of model-building and hypothesis-formation procedures in Weber's comparative-historical sociology. Only one example can be offered here: the routinization of charisma model.

Charismatic rulership is exercised by a person over disciples and followers who believe that he possesses supernatural powers of divine origin. This leader, who arises in emergency situations, may be, for example, a prophet, a war hero, a politician, a leader of the hunt, a demagogue, an oracle-giver, or a magician. In all cases, the rulership attributed to him derives from a recognition of extraordinary qualities, ones not accessible to the ordinary person. Once its genuineness is acknowledged, disciples and followers feel duty-bound to devote themselves completely to the charismatic leader, and he demands a strict obedience. They obey his commands as a result of an immense affection and the conviction that a genuinely personal relationship exists. Indeed, Weber sees an "emotional conviction" as central to the belief of disciples and followers in the charismatic leader's right to rule, one that "internally" revolutionizes their entire personalities: "Charisma . . . manifests its revolutionary power from within, from a central *metanoia* [change] of its followers' attitudes" (Weber, 1968, p. 1117; see also pp. 241–4, 1112–17).

The highly personal character of charismatic rule, as well as its lack of concern for everyday routine, leads it to reject all "external order." The "objective" law received by the possessor of charisma as a gift of God bestows upon him a unique and new mission. For this reason, Weber sees charisma as standing in fundamental and revolutionary opposition to all means–end rational action as well as to all existing and stable forces of daily life (see ibid., pp. 291, 1112–20).

He also stresses, however, the fragility of charismatic rulership. As a consequence of its location strictly in the "supernatural qualities" of great leaders and the necessity for the "superhuman" personality repeatedly to demonstrate unusual powers and a "right to rule," "charismatic authority is naturally unstable" (ibid., pp. 1112–14). Even the greatest intensity of personal devotion to the charismatic leader cannot guarantee the perpetuation of the extraordinary figure's teachings in their pure form. Instead, Weber's "routinization" model proclaims that charisma follows a developmental path characterized by its weakening: it becomes repeatedly absorbed into the permanent institutions of everyday life. Such a transformation of charisma has always been sought by followers in the hope that, in the process, a *permanent* protection against sickness, disease, and natural catastrophe will be acquired (see, for example, ibid., pp. 1131–3, 1146–9, 1156).

The material and power interests of the charismatic community of followers and disciples constitute, in Weber's routinization of charisma construct, an important driving force in institutionalizing the "transitory gift of grace ... into a permanent possession of everyday life."[33] Preserved by followers in depersonalized (*versachlichte*) form, a weakened charisma becomes attached to the community of disciples and plays, his model hypothesizes, an indispensable role in attracting new followers, in establishing the legitimacy of new status groups, forms of rulership, and religious doctrines, and in facilitating ascent to positions of dominance in status, rulership, and religious hierarchies. Now as a part of everyday life and capable, often through ceremonies involving magic, of being transmitted to family members, offices or institutions, "hereditary," "institutionalized," and "office" charisma serves to legitimize "acquired rights." Altered into these impersonal and routinized forms, charisma, according to this model, is upheld in all these stages in particular by persons with an economic interest in doing so, as well by all those in possession of power and property who see their position of advantage as legitimated by its authority – for example, court officials, priests, parliamentary monarchs, high dignitaries, and party leaders[34] (ibid., pp. 251, 1122–7, 1139–41, 1146–8; Weber, 1946, p. 297).

Weber's yardstick, affinity, antagonism, and developmental models appear throughout *E&S* and contribute decisively to its rigor, analytic power, and uniqueness. As "constructed schemes," all models alone "serve the purpose of offering an ideal-typical means of *orientation*" (Weber, 1946c, p. 323, original emphasis). With respect to antagonisms across domains, for example, "the theoretically constructed types of conflicting 'societal domains' are merely intended to show that at certain points such and such internal conflicts are *possible* and 'adequate'" (ibid., original emphasis). Yet, in performing this modest task, each model provides a purchase upon ceaselessly flowing realities, thereby facilitating clear conceptualization of the particular patterned social action under investigation. Each hypothesized interaction can then be tested through in-depth investigation. Because viewed alone as mechanisms to facilitate causal analysis, Weber fully expects these "logical constructs" to be "dislocated" when confronted by complex empirical realities. Concrete circumstances and contexts will invariably strengthen or weaken particular analytic relationships. Nonetheless, he emphasizes that sociology, unlike history, *must* include a rigorous theoretical framing – through models – of the problem under investigation.

This remains the case if only because models constitute for Weber the indispensable first step toward his all-important goal of causal analysis. He insists that the typical immersion of sociologists deeply in empirical realities *requires* such constructs if significant causal action-orientations are to be identified, all the more owing to the fundamental character of empirical reality – for him, an unending flow of events and happenings – and the continuous danger that all causal inquiry all too easily becomes mired in an endless description-based regression. By constructing arrays of models in *E&S* that conceptualize patterned, meaningful action, Weber aims to draw sociology *away* from an exclusive focus upon delineated social problems on the one hand and historical narrative on the other hand. Nonetheless, he steadfastly avoids the other side of the spectrum: grounded empirically, his models never move to the level of broad, diffuse generalizations. Rather, these research tools offer limited hypotheses that can be tested against specific cases and developments. To Weber, unique to the sociological enterprise is always a back and forth movement between conceptualization – the formulation of models and theoretical frameworks – and the detailed investigation of empirical cases and developments. If the goal of offering causal explanations of the "historical individual" is to be realized, *both* the empirically particular and conceptual generalization are indispensable.

**DRIVING FORCES: THE MULTICAUSALITY OF *E&S* AND POWER** Although *E&S* gives priority to the task of model building over causal analysis, Weber's unequivocal embrace of multicausal modes of procedure is apparent. Throughout this treatise, as noted, he focuses upon the patterned social action within the status group, universal organizations, religion, law, rulership, and economy domains. An array of ideal types is connected analytically to each domain, and each indicates the empirical possibility of *regular* action-orientations with a degree of endurance. Thus, each ideal type implies an indigenous causal thrust and staying power or, to Weber, an *autonomous* aspect. Nonetheless, and even though the meaningful action of individuals anchors his sociology, the question "within what *carrier* grouping action occurs" remains fundamental to him. Social action becomes sociologically significant action *only* in demarcated groupings of individuals.

In every society, only *certain* traditional, affectual, value-rational, and means-end rational patterns of meaningful action acquire strong exponents and become important aspects of the social fabric. For Weber, status groups, classes, and organizations serve as the most prominent bearers of action. Each "carries" a configuration of delineated action-orientations. He calls attention, for example, to the ideal typical "status ethic" of functionaries in bureaucracies (duty, punctuality, the orderly performance of tasks, disciplined work habits, etc.; Weber, 1968, pp. 956–1003), the ethos of the neighborhood organization (mutual assistance and a "sombre economic 'brotherhood' practised in case of need"; ibid., pp. 363), and the class ethos of the bourgeoisie (opposition to privileges based upon birth and status, a favoring of formal legal equality; ibid., pp. 477–80; see Kalberg, 1985). Attention to such carriers is characteristic of Weber's sociology.

As he notes, "Unless the concept 'autonomy' is to lack all precision, its definition presupposes the existence of a bounded group of persons which, though membership may fluctuate, is determinable" (Weber, 1968, p. 699; translation altered). In introducing his chapters on traditional and charismatic rulership in E&S, for example, Weber summarizes his aims as involving not only an evaluation of the extent to which the "developmental chances" of the major "structural principles" of each rulership type can be said to be subject to "economic, political or any other external determinants," but also an assessment of the degree to which the developmental chances of the types of rulership instead follow "an 'autonomous' logic inherent in their technical structure" (ibid., p. 1002). He insists that this "logic" must be *conceptualized as capable* of exerting an independent effect even upon economic factors (ibid., pp. 578, 1002, 654–5), and discovers – whenever a "bounded group" crystallizes as its social carrier – many empirical cases when it does. Weber is especially aware of the extent to which the attribution of legitimacy to rulership sets an independent driving force into motion. Hence, even while remaining cognizant of the frequent centrality of economic factors, he emphasizes the necessity for multicausal approaches (see ibid., pp. 341, 935). In arguing on behalf of the autonomous potential of action-orientations in the economy, law, rulership, religion, status groups, and universal organizations domains, Weber aims in E&S to conceptualize economic action within a broad theoretical framework and to treat "both sides" of the causal nexus (see Kalberg, 1994b, pp. 50–78).

The "level of analysis" in E&S – an array of societal domains, constellations of domain-specific ideal types, and social carriers – itself further demonstrates his broad multicausality. It is clear as well by Weber's frequent reference to the importance of a further variety of causal forces: historical events, technological innovations, and geographical forces. Moreover, conflict and competition, as well as interests generally and economic interests in particular, constitute, to him, effective causal forces – as does, not least, power. In his classical formulation, Weber defines power thus: "Within a social relationship, power means any chance (no matter whereon this chance is based) to carry through one's (individual *or* collective) own will (*even* against resistance)" (Weber, 1968, p. 53).[35]

New action-orientations frequently fade or become the victims of suppression by opposing coalitions if power is lacking and alliances fail to take place. Rulers are particularly adept, he insists repeatedly, at forming alliances with the sole purpose of maintaining and aggrandizing power. They seek to balance classes, status groups, and organizations against one another as a matter of course. Power plays a central role in Weber's multicausal analyses of how new patterns of social action arise, spread, and set historical developments into motion, as well as in his investigations of how action-orientations become circumscribed and rendered less influential. Finally, *E&S* also endows *ideas* with a causal efficacy. *Religious* ideas, especially those that address the conundrum of frequent and seemingly random human suffering, might cast an influence across centuries and even millennia. Just the attempts to explain misery and injustice, Weber argues, played a significant role in the development of religions from ones anchored in magic to ones rooted in notions of salvation, ethical action, and an "other-world." Ideas regarding the stubborn persistence of misfortune, as articulated by prophets, priests, monks, and theologians, pushed this development, rather than economic and practical interests alone. Repeatedly, ideas were formulated that clarified the relationship of believers to the transcendent realm – and these ideas implied modes of new meaningful action "pleasing to the gods." Eventually, doctrines were formulated that offered broad-ranging views of the universe, explained suffering in a comprehensive sense, and defined action that promised to bring an end to suffering (see ibid., pp. 399–439, 349–50, 577–9; Weber, 1946, pp. 122–3, 269–76, 280–5, 324; Kalberg, 1990, 2000b).

In sum, attention to a diversity of causal forces characterizes *E&S*, as does Weber's unwillingness to elevate particular forces to positions of general causal priority.[36]

THE INTERWEAVING OF PAST AND PRESENT Weber's attempts to define and explain the uniqueness of a particular present always acknowledge the many ways in which the past perpetually interweaves with the present. This remains the case despite the heroic capacity he sees in charismatic leaders: to sever, given constellations of facilitating conditions, abruptly past and present. Even drastic metamorphoses and the abrupt advent of "the new" never fully ruptures ties to the past (see Weber, 1968, pp. 29, 577), and "that which has been handed down from the past becomes everywhere the immediate precursor of that taken in the present as valid" (ibid., translation altered). Even the monumental structural transformations called forth by industrialization fail to sweep away the past. Viable legacies live on.

Weber's orientation in *E&S* to societal domains and ideal types stands at the foundation not only of its multicausality, but also of its capacity to analyze the multiple and subtle ways in which the past interlocks with the present. As noted, to him, the various societal domains are endowed with an independent, or autonomous, capacity rooted in indigenous questions and problems – and they develop in a non-parallel manner and at their own pace. And each ideal type, in "documenting" patterns of meaningful action, implies the possibility of an autonomous sustaining power. Moreover, Weber endows further forces – historical events, geographical constellations, power, social carriers, conflict, competition, and technology – with a viable causal capacity. The patterned social action of persons in groupings is conceptualized as having many and diverse origins.

Thus, *E&S* offers a "view of society" as constituted from an array of moving, even dynamically interacting, "parts." All "general axiom" schools of sociological analysis that depart from encompassing dichotomies (*Gemeinschaft/ Gesellschaft*, tradition/modernity, particularism/universalism), broad themes (the question of social order), or assumptions regarding the "organic unity" and "lawfulness of society" stand radically in opposition to Weber's "open" theoretical framework rooted in ideal types and societal domains. These fundamental features of *E&S* allow conceptualization across an entire spectrum of empirical cases, ranging from those characterized more by flux, competition, conflict, tension, and disintegration, to others characterized more by internal unity and harmony. Furthermore, the familiar concepts at the center of many sociological theories – "class," "the state," "society," for example – are never elevated in *E&S* to a position of special status. Even the dichotomy frequently interpreted by commentators as capturing Weber's "view of history" – his contrast of the stable and routine character of tradition to the revolutionary character of charisma – fails to render the complex relationship in his sociology between past and present.

The wide variety of causal forces articulated in *E&S*, their "open" interaction, and their variable degree of closure enables Weber forcefully to demonstrate that the past and present intimately interweave in many ways. Regularities of social action in some groupings can be recognized as becoming firm and acquiring powerful carriers, even to the extent of developing in terms of their indigenous problematics and penetrating deeply into subsequent epochs; others fail to do so and prove fleeting; still others cast their imprint vigorously and then fade away. The "view of society" that flows out of this systematic opus – as constructed from numerous causally effective, competing, and reciprocally interacting patterns of social action – easily takes cognizance of the "survival" of some patterns of action from the past and their significant influence, as legacies, upon patterns of action in the present.

Weber often charts legacies, for example, from the religion domain. In the United States, central values from Protestant asceticism – disciplined and routine work in a profession, the regular giving to charity organizations, the perpetual formation by persons of goals, the orientation to the future and the attempt to "master" the world's challenges (*Weltbeherrschung*), an optimism regarding the capacity to shape personal destinies, and a strong intolerance of "evil" – remain integral in American life today, despite the fact that most who act by reference to these values have no awareness of them as linked intimately to a religious heritage (Weber, 1968, p. 1187).[37] Moreover, the "direct democratic administration" by the congregation, as it took place in the Protestant sects in the United States, left a legacy crucial for the establishment of democratic forms of government, as did the unwillingness of sect members to bestow a halo of reverence upon secular authority. The Quakers in particular, in advocating freedom of conscience for others as well as for themselves, paved the way for political tolerance (see ibid., pp. 1204–10; Kalberg, 1997).

The interweaving of past and present constitutes a major organizational axis in *E&S*. All present-oriented, functionalist modes of analysis stand in strict opposition to Weber's sociology. To him, the past always penetrates deeply into the present, even molding its core contours. He is especially convinced that an identification of the modern West's uniqueness and its possible course of further development *requires* investigations of its historical development.[38]

These five axes remain central throughout *E&S*, the analytic treatise for Weber's comparative-historical, interpretive sociology. In this opus, as well as in his methodological writings, his modes of analysis and research strategies are demarcated, albeit in a poorly organized fashion. Owing to its explicit attention to "both sides of the causal equation" – ideas and interests – *The Economic Ethics of the World Religions* offers a better example of these modes of analysis and research strategies than *PE*. This massive study can be discussed only briefly.

## The Economic Ethics of the World Religions

Weber's universal-historical studies on China (1951), India (1958), and ancient Israel (1952) expand upon a theme first explored in *PE* in 1904: the relationship between the "economic ethics" of religions and the rise of modern capitalism.[39] Through a series of rigorous comparisons to these civilizations, he sought after 1910 to define the uniqueness of modern capitalism and the modern West more generally, and to offer a causal explanation for its particular path of development.

Moreover, whereas *PE*, in tracing the origins of a spirit of capitalism back to ascetic Protestantism, examined only "one side" of the causal equation, the *EEWR* volumes forcefully articulate a *multicausal* methodology. In exploring the question of why modern capitalism failed to develop before the twentieth century in non-Western civilizations, they investigate "ideas *and* interests." Weber notes the complex ways in which "both sides" are intertwined in a central passage in the *EEWR* introduction:

> Every... attempt at explanation must, recognizing the fundamental significance of the economic factors, above all take account of economic conditions. However, the opposite line of causation should not be neglected. This is the case if only because the origin of economic rationalism depends not only upon an advanced development of technology and law, but also upon the capability and disposition of persons to lead specific types of practical-rational lives. Wherever religious forces have inhibited the unfolding of this way of leading a life, the development of a way of leading a life oriented systematically toward *economic* activity has confronted broad-ranging internal resistance. Magical and religious powers, and the ethical notions of duty that have been based upon them, have been in the past among the most important formative influences upon the way of leading a life. (Weber, 1930, pp. 26–7, translation altered, original emphasis; see also 1968, p. 341)

Weber calls attention to a number of causal forces important to him in this pivotal statement. He emphatically rejects, for example, both greed and a material interest in becoming wealthy; these forces have been universal, yet modern capitalism developed only in a few specific regions and during a part-cular historical epoch. The putative "general evolutionary sweep of history" is omitted, for Weber insists on focusing upon empirical factors. Although acknowledging unequivocally the importance of the economy and classes, he rejects all explanations that view belief systems alone as the "superstructure" of economic interests. Similarly, "a class of formally trained jurists should not be understood as crystallizing simply from capitalistic interests," for then the question arises of why such "interests did not lead to the same development in China or India" (Weber, 1930, p. 25). Furthermore, organizations – and even extremely tightly knit sects – do not, he contends, uniformly lead to the same values: "Structurally identical religious sects . . . existed in Hinduism as well as in Christianity, yet their sacred values pointed [the social action of believers] in radically different directions" (Weber, 1946, p. 292).

Weber's complex multicausality also leads him away from the conclusion that modern capitalism failed to develop first in Asia owing to an absence of inner-worldly asceticism. Although his concern, when he examines Confucianism, Taoism, Hinduism, Buddhism, Jainism, and ancient Judaism, remains focused upon an assessment of whether devoutness bestowed "religious premiums" upon methodical economic activity, he insists that single factors never determine historical development. Rather, *constellations* of forces are always central, as well as the manner in which they interact conjuncturally in delineated contexts and thereby formulate unique configurations.[40] By "applying" the domains-based, *multi*causal theoretical framework developed in *E&S*, Weber identifies vastly different constellations of action-orientations to rulership, religion, the economy, social honor, the family, and the law in each civilization.[41] The many clusters of social action conducive to the unfolding of modern capitalism in China, India, and ancient Israel were, he found, in the end outweighed by a series of opposing patterns of action.

For example, he notes a variety of nonreligious obstacles to economic development in China, such as extremely strong sibling ties and an absence of "a formally guaranteed law and a rational administration and judiciary" (Weber, 1951, p. 85; see also pp. 91, 99–100), and in India, such as constraints placed upon migration, the recruitment of labor, and credit by the caste system (Weber, 1958, pp. 111–17, 52–3, 102–6). He discovers as well, however, an entire host of conducive material forces that nonetheless failed to bring about modern capitalism – such as, in China, freedom of trade, an increase in precious metals, population growth, occupational mobility, and the presence of a money economy (Weber, 1951, pp. 243, 54–5, 99–100, 243, 12).

Weber was quite convinced that modern capitalism could be *adopted* by – and would flourish in – a number of Eastern civilizations. Indeed, he identified the forces that would allow this to occur (on Japan, see Weber, 1958, p. 275). Yet adoption, he insisted, involved different processes than his concern: the *origin* in a specific region of a *new* economic ethos and a *new* type of economy. Furthermore, Weber's analysis identifies great variation across civilizations in the extent to which significant regularities of social action with strong carriers tended to line up and "complement" one another or, conversely, stand in opposition to one another. Pluralistic conflict between relatively independently developing domains arose in the latter case, as well as a societal openness that facilitated regular social change. This "model," Weber argues, significantly distinguishes the Western developmental path (Weber, 1968, pp. 1192–3; see Kalberg, forthcoming).

However, these volumes provide not only a complex causal explanation for modern capitalism's appearance first in the West; Weber also attempts to demarcate the uniqueness of *each* of the *EEWR* civilizations: he defines "Chinese rationalism," "Indian rationalism," and the "rationalism of ancient Israel." He then seeks, first, to offer comparisons and contrasts to "Western rationalism" and, second, to provide explanations for the particular routes of development followed by each great civilization. In doing so, his investigations allowed demarcation of a number of further ways in which the West proved unique: it called forth a systematic science based upon the experimental method and carried out by trained and specialized personnel; a more wide-ranging societal significance was assumed by organized and trained civil servants and managers than elsewhere; and a state based upon a "rational, written constitution, rationally ordained law" arose, as did "an administration bound to rational rules or laws, administered by trained officials" (Weber, 1930, pp. 13–17).

Hence, through his *EEWR* studies Weber acquired essential insight, clarity, and knowledge regarding the specific "tracks" within which a number of major civilizations had developed (see Weber, 1946e, p. 280). These tracks called forth in the West in the twentieth century, he argued, the dominance of formal rationality in the domains of law, rulership, and the economy, and "theoretical rationality" in the domain of science. Great ramifications followed, he insisted repeatedly, regarding the "type of person" (*Menschentyp*) that *could* live under "modern Western rationalism." Yet these volumes also assisted Weber to answer three further burning questions, all of which originated from his skepticism regarding Western civilization's "progress." First, given its distinct features, what is the nature of the social change that *can* take place in the modern West? Second, how do persons in different social contexts – and in different civilizations – formulate meaning in their lives? Finally, what patterned orientations of social action – means–end rational, value-rational, and traditional – have become meaningful in each of the major civilizations, and how did this occur? Because he viewed compassion, ethical action, and a reflective individualism as now endangered in the West, answers to these queries became especially urgent. Would *values* continue to orient social action? The immediacy of these questions itself served to call forth the Herculean motivation required to conduct the *EEWR* investigations.

Although innumerable scholars over the past decades have examined in depth Weber's intense political activities, his volcanic personality, the intellectual origins of his ideas, and his relationships with his many colleagues, we read Weber today owing to the rigor of his sociological writings. Yet *PE*, *E&S*, *EEWR*, and the methodological writings are complex and often extremely difficult to comprehend. Each interpreter of Weber seems to discover a different "Weber" (see Kalberg, 1998, pp. 208–12).

Perhaps this problem is to some extent inevitable in light of the immense scope and complexity of Weber's project. He sought to investigate entire civilizations through interpretive, empirical, multicausal, and context-sensitive procedures, to trace out the unique developmental paths each followed to the present, and to understand the ways in which persons living in diverse epochs and circumstances create meaning in their lives. However, he attempted to fulfill a further daunting task: he wished to define the heuristic tools, modes of analysis, and research procedures for a comparative-historical, interpretive sociology. Indeed, he sought to offer concepts and strategies that could be utilized alike by *verstehende* sociologists engaged in intercivilizational research and others investigating more specialized topics.

As already apparent, Weber's sociology arose in reference to a specific historical background. A turn now to a sketch of the social context in which he lived and wrote will further assist comprehension of its purposes, procedures, and boundaries.

## THE SOCIAL CONTEXT

Very rapid industrialization was occurring in Max Weber's Germany. Moreover, compared to the United States, England, and Holland, industrialization began very late, and hence was accompanied by a sense of urgency. Yet Germans were convinced that, if the powers of the state were harnessed comprehensively, their nation would soon surpass its competitors.

However, this "industrialization from above" tended to place in motion a number of forces that curtailed the unfolding of a democratic political culture on German soil. It implied above all that Germany's business elites would be more closely aligned with the state than was the case in most other industrializing nations. A strong and independent class capable of standing against state power – as a countervailing force to open a public arena of participation and the free exchange of views – failed to arise. Economic development occurred more under the hegemony of a caste of government functionaries than occurred elsewhere.

Three further features of German society characterized this "German model." Although it was largely a secularized country by the middle of the nineteenth century, legacies of Luther's political ideas, now in the form of commonly accepted conventions and values rather than explicitly religious belief, endured. They took the form of a deep respect for authority in general and for the state in particular, even to such a degree that, in many regions, the state, its laws, and its functionaries acquired a "halo" of trust and legitimacy. In addition, the particular character of feudalism in much of Germany – innumerable small principalities and kingdoms – rendered the authoritarian rulership of the feudal master so direct and immediate that notions of self-rule, individual rights, and representative government never found fertile ground. Finally, and as a result of all these forces, the German working class remained politically weak. Unlike the French, the Germans failed in their attempt to introduce modern forms of egalitarianism and democratic self-governance. Prussian troops crushed the Revolution of 1848.

All these features of its political culture erected significant obstacles to the monumental tasks Germany confronted at the turn of the century. Whereas a stable democracy existed in the United States *before* the onset of industrialization, Germany faced the burdensome task of cultivating and extending region-based democratic traditions in the midst of industrialization. In many important ways, these two nations were located at opposite ends of the "modernization" spectrum (see Kalberg, 1987).

Although Chancellor Bismarck had molded a variety of small German principalities and feudal kingdoms into a unified nation in 1871, a "modernizing ideology" – an embrace of democracy and individual freedoms – never accompanied his nation-building. Furthermore, Bismarck's rulership precluded an assertive and independent role for the German parliament, as well as for the population as a whole. In the face of an overwhelming centralization of power, an active, participatory citizenry could scarcely arise. Politics was dominated by the Chancellor, his functionaries, and an antiquated class of agrarian petty aristocrats motivated exclusively by narrow class interests. While successful at calling forth rapid industrialization, as well as a notion of social trust grounded in respect for the state and its laws on the one hand and hierarchical, quasi-feudal social conventions on the other, the German model stood against all developments in the direction of a democratic political culture.

Public sphere ideals that could be nourished failed to appear on a widespread basis. By the turn of the century, massive segments of the population had either turned to introspective endeavors (scholarship, education, art, music, philosophy)[42] or simply withdrawn into private sphere relationships. Others condemned unequivocally the modern, "impersonal and harsh" *Gesellschaft* and sought a return to the putatively stable and compassionate *Gemeinschaft* of the pre-industrial epoch. Varieties of Romanticist movements oriented to the past arose. Still others found refuge in fulfillment of the old Lutheran notion of "vocation": the reliable and dutiful performance of one's workday obligations provided dignity and self-worth. Industrialization rapidly occurred, rooted in part in just this diligent Lutheran work ethic, yet it took place devoid of an internal dynamism or an optimism regarding the future. Compared to most other industrializing nations and despite traditions of parliamentary government and local citizen activism in a number of regions, a severely restricted civic sphere in Germany prevented the widespread development of social egalitarianism and representative democracy.

Not surprisingly, "cultural pessimism" became widespread in the 1890s. Despair, doubt, and a sense of crisis extended throughout much of German society (see Mosse, 1964; Ringer, 1969). Many asked repeatedly, what standards can guide persons in the industrial society? How do we live in this new era? *Who* will live in the modern world? How can ethical and compassionate action survive? "Where are to be found," Dilthey asked, "the instruments for surmounting the spiritual chaos which threatens to engulf us?" (see Salomon, 1934, p. 164).

These questions were also Weber's questions. However, unlike many intellectuals of the time, he refused to withdraw from political activism; nor did he become a resigned cultural pessimist.[43] A tireless actor and lifelong player on the stage of German politics, Weber proved an indefatigable critic – marshalling his relentless and piercing ammunition in innumerable speeches and newspaper articles, directing it alike against nearly all major classes and groupings. He condemned Bismarck for crushing all independent leadership; the German monarchy for blatant incompetence and dilettantism; the bourgeoisie for its weak class consciousness and unwillingness to struggle for political power against the state bureaucracy; the agrarian aristocrats for their militarism, authoritarianism, attempts to deny citizenship rights to the working class, and inability to place the nation's interests above their own concerns for material gain; and the German civil servants for their slavish conformity, obsessive adherence to rules and regulations, meekness, and general unwillingness to take responsibility for their decisions. Weber seemed to admire only the German workers, yet he criticized them as well: while appreciating their competence and notion of duty, he lamented their general passivity in the face of authority (especially compared to their counterparts in France).

Major components of his political and social commentary can only be understood as a complex, even convoluted, attempt to address glaring internal weaknesses in the German political culture and to offer sober and realistic mechanisms to overcome them. He wished to retain high standards of living and efficient modes of organizing work and producing goods – and capitalism, he was convinced, offered the best opportunity for the realization of these aims. Yet the many dehumanizing components of this economic system were apparent to him. Weber's thoroughly sociological analysis of his epoch, and the ways in which he responded to its dilemmas with strategies for action, must be examined briefly.

## Weber's analysis

*Formal* rationality appeared in a nearly omnipresent manner, Weber argued, in the bureaucracies of the industrial society. In its major domains – law, the economy, and the state – decision-making occurs "without regard to persons" and by reference to sets of universally applied rules, laws, statutes, and regulations. Favoritism is precluded as well in hiring, promotion, and recertification: an adherence to the dictates of abstract procedures holds sway over all concerns for distinctions in respect of status or personality. The "logical-formal" law of our day is implemented by trained jurists who insure that "only unambiguous general characteristics of the case are taken into account in terms of purely processual and legal factors" (Weber, 1968, pp. 656–7), and formal rationality increases in the economy domain to the degree that all technically possible calculations within the "laws of the market" are carried out. Those who would seek to acquire a mortage are treated by a bank's specialists in reference alone to impersonal criteria: credit reports, savings, monthly income, etc. (see ibid., pp. 346, 585, 600, 1186; Weber, 1946c, p. 331).[44]

Weber sees a different type of rationality as dominant in daily life in the industrial epoch: *practical* rationality. The individual's egoistic interests and merely adaptive capacities come here to the fore, and pragmatic, calculating – means–end rational – strategies are typically employed in order to deal with the common obstacles of everyday life in the most expedient manner. As a consequence of their normal activities, all business-oriented strata in particular exhibit a strong tendency to order their ways of life in a self-interested, practical rational manner (see Weber, 1930, p. 77; 1946e, pp. 279, 284, 293).

Finally, Weber understands modern societies as pervaded by *theoretical* rationality; in fact, their new "world view" – science – cultivates this type of rationality. An abstract confrontation with reality comes here to the fore, and rigorous experiments, precise concepts, and logical deduction and induction become the tools to address and master reality. Whereas theologians and priests in an earlier age adjusted and refined inconsistencies in religious doctrines through theoretical rationalization processes, the same systematic, cognitive search for explanations takes place today – yet now alone in reference to an *empirical* reality. In both cases, reality is mastered through systematic thought and conceptual schemes. Because it requires a step beyond that which can be observed – "a leap of faith" – religion becomes, to the same degree that a scientific world view ascends to a dominating position, defined as "irrational" (Weber, 1946e, pp. 154, 350, 355).[45]

Formal, practical, and theoretical rationality invariably play central roles in industrial societies, Weber argues, forcefully pushing aside arrays of values as well as traditions from the past. However, none is capable of calling forth and giving sustenance to new sets of *noble* values, he contends. The modern-day functionary in bureaucracies orients his action alone to duty, caution, security, conformity, order, reliability, and punctuality. Laws and regulations must be implemented according to procedures of formal correctness and precedent rather than by reference to higher substantive issues: justice, freedom, and equality. Calculations of interests and advantage dominate the practical rationality of daily life. And the scientist of today is engaged in an enterprise that calls to the fore, as the locus of "truth," empirical observation, description, and abstract synthesizing. Knowledge, insight, clarity, and the "tools and the training for thought" (see Weber, 1946d, pp. 150–1) result from satisfactory scientific work, rather than values. What domains of modern life "carry" and cultivate compassion, a brotherhood ethic, binding values, ethical responsibility, and charity? Weber searches, but finds none. On the contrary, now unconstrained by constellations of values such as those in the doctrines of the great salvation religions, formal, practical, and theoretical rationality develop more and more freely and unhindered.

To Weber, cold, impersonal, non-binding, and merely conventional relationships more and more rise to the forefront in this "cosmos." While once firmly anchored and given direction by a "devotion to a cause" – a calling – rooted ultimately in coherent and meaningful configurations of values, social relationships are now largely adrift, blowing back and forth according to momentary interests, strategic calculations, cognitive processes, power, rulership orientations, and interpretations of statutes and laws. An uninterrupted flow of activity more and more holds sway, and the life methodically *directed* toward a set of ideals becomes less and less possible. Whereas the motivation to join an ascetic Protestant church or sect could once be explained by reference to sincere belief, the external benefits of membership – acquisition of an entire community's trust and hence its business – often now become central (ibid., pp. 304–5).

In this historically unique epoch in which "material goods have gained an increasing and finally an inexorable power over the lives of [persons]" (Weber, 1930, p. 181), the "interests of daily life" are becoming empowered even to such an extent that they consistently manipulate and exploit values, Weber proclaims. A clear *disjunction* between firm values and ideals held dear on the one hand and the empirical flow of life on the other hand is lessening. Without such standards, the "pragmatic approach to life" more and more reigns, not only pushing aside ethical ideals and all notions of responsibility, but also the autonomous and integrated – or "unified" – personality "directed from within" on the basis of beliefs and values (Weber, 1949, p. 18; 1946c, pp. 323–59). Massive conformity will result and individual autonomy will disappear. Values, ideals, and ethical action must not become, Weber insists, simply dead legacies from the past, for in the end means–end rational calculations will neither offer *dignity* to persons as unique individuals nor prevent the rule of force. *Who* will live in this "iron cage" of "mechanized petrification"?[46] Will only "specialists without spirit" and "sensualists without heart" inhabit the new cosmos (Weber, 1930, p. 182)? As Albert Salomon, in his classic interpretation of Weber, asks: "Can man – . . . conceived as molded by the passions and tensions of a lofty human soul – still find a place for himself in the modern world" (Salomon, 1934, p. 153)?

In what ways did Weber's sociology offer a response to this "crisis of Western Civilization"? What strategies of action remained available to confront these fundamental dangers and dilemmas?

## Weber's response

Weber wished to see a constellation of values and ideals in place that would both effectively orient action and offer dignity to individuals. As a self-conscious defender of Western traditions, these were the values of individual autonomy, responsibility, the unified personality, ethical action, brotherhood, compassion, charity, and a sense of honor. Yet his sweeping comparative studies had convinced him that values die out whenever denied their means of sustenance: strong social carriers *and* vigorous competition with other values. As persons develop loyalties and defend their chosen values against others, values become viable and strong. They then more and more guide action and persons formulate, on the basis of them, a sense of dignity and honor. They also provide a firm grounding for initiative-taking and leadership. However, only particular societies nourish values to the point where they become binding upon persons, even at times despite opposing material interests: namely, *dynamic and open* societies in which pluralistic values struggle against one another. In these societies, persons become "responsible" in reference to a set of values and increasingly able to become ethical beings.

Owing to ubiquitous bureaucratization in industrial societies and the rise of formal, practical, and theoretical types of rationality, Weber feared that the contending arenas indispensable for a flourishing of competing values and a realm of freedom were losing their distinct boundaries and collapsing. As this occurred, society would become closed and leaders – defending values – would fade from the social landscape. Societal ossification, driven by the managerial rule of technical efficiency and not unlike the extreme stagnation that had long ago afflicted Egypt and China, more and more appeared to be the fate of "advanced" societies. Indeed, Weber saw an ominous "passion for bureaucratization" that would lead only to "a parcelling out of the soul" (Weber, 1909, p. 414) and a societal-wide passivity in which people are "led like sheep" (Weber, 1978, p. 282). How would it be possible "to save *any remnants* of 'individual' freedom of movement" (Weber, 1968, p. 1403, original emphasis)? "We 'individualists' and partisans of 'democratic' institutions," he proclaimed, "are swimming 'against the tide' of materialist constellations" (Weber, 1978, p. 282, translation altered), and "everywhere the *house of bondage* is already in place" (ibid., p. 281, translation altered, original emphasis; see also pp. 281–2; 1968, pp. 1402–3). Only an outline of the elaborate and complex strategies he proposed can be offered here.[47]

**STRONG PARLIAMENTS** Weber argued vehemently that modern societies need institutions capable of cultivating leadership qualities on a regular basis. This could occur in parliaments, for here the aggressive articulation of political positions and the hard competition of political parties are accepted as the normal course of affairs. In the process of open debate and conflict over values and interests, yet also negotiation and compromise, leaders with the "three pre-eminent qualities" for politicians would emerge: passion, responsibility, and a sense of proportion (Weber, 1946a, p. 115–16). Perhaps even leaders with "inner charismatic qualities" would appear (ibid., p. 113), though also leaders with the sense of detachment that allows judgment. Thus, this institution cultivates leadership characterized by an "ethic of responsibility" and a "passionate devotion to a cause" (ibid., p. 115), and prepares leaders to undertake an indispensable task: on the basis of their values and policies, they are empowered to stand against the formal rationality of functionaries, managers, and technocrats. In doing so, they contribute to the expansion of a societal "free space" within which citizens can debate, make responsible decisions, exercise political rights, and defend values. However, for parliaments to serve as such viable "training grounds" for leaders, this institution must stand strong against other branches of government. Weak parliaments, dominated on the one hand by the state's civil servants and on the other hand by authoritarian politicians, such as Bismarck, will not attract persons capable of becoming leaders.

**THE SUPPORT FOR DEMOCRACY** Parliamentary democracies, Weber believed, far more than other forms of governing, are capable of calling forth the societal dynamism indispensable for the creation of a viable public sphere within which decisions can be rendered in reference to values. Moreover, like strong parliaments, strong democracies would assist the development of strong leaders, as would democracy's ideals: freedom of speech, individual rights, the rule of law, and the right of assembly. "It is a gross self-deception," Weber argued, "to believe that without the achievements of the age of the Rights of Man any one of us, including the most conservative, can go on living" (Weber,

1968, p. 1403). The contesting of power and rulership monopolies, he is convinced, occurs more effectively in democracies.[48]

**THE SUPPORT FOR CAPITALISM** Ambivalence characterizes Weber's attitude to capitalism. On the one hand he laments repeatedly the ways in which the "laws of the open market" introduce a merciless struggle, formal rationality, and merely functional relationships that cannot realistically be influenced by a brotherhood ethic or ideas of compassion and charity (see Weber, 1946c, pp. 331–3; 1968, pp. 584–5, 635–40). The introduction of such humanitarian concerns into economic relationships taking place in competitive markets almost always leads to economic inefficiencies and economic ruin – "and this would not be helpful in any way" (Weber, 1968, pp. 1186–7). On the other hand, capitalism's open competition and private enterprise call forth energetic entrepreneurs and vigorous risk-takers; these heroic actors, just like the sheer irregularity and unpredictability of market forces, introduce societal dynamism (ibid., pp. 1403–4). Socialism not only fails to do so, but also implies a further large step in the direction of a closed and stagnant society: it calls forth, to manage the economy, yet another "caste" of functionaries and administrators.

**THE NECESSARY CONSTRICTION OF SCIENCE** If defined as an endeavor empowered to prescribe values, Weber believed, science posed a threat to the individual's autonomy and, ultimately, to ethical action. Wherever understood as offering "objectively valid" conclusions and wherever a "caste of experts" becomes perceived, in the name of science, as legitimately erecting norms for conduct, science becomes capable of elevating decision-making even out of that domain where it rightfully belongs: the individual's conscience, values, and "demons." Science cannot – and *must* not – inform us how we *should* live (Weber, 1949, p. 58). Notions of ethical responsibility, honor, dignity, and devotion to a cause can be developed, Weber argues, only when persons are starkly aware of their own values – and this takes place alone when individuals are confronted repeatedly with the necessity of making decisions *for themselves*. Moreover, if a science – understood as prescribed norms – becomes broadly institutionalized, decision-making by "specialists" poses a threat to a society's dynamism and capacity for pluralistic conflict.

Hence, the domain of science must be circumscribed by firm boundaries. Its tasks must remain limited to "methods of thinking, the tools and the training for thought," and clarity: assessment of the suitability of the means to reach the given end (including an ethical ideal) and the unintended consequences of action in reference to particular ideals (see Weber, 1946d, pp. 150–1). By fulfilling even these delimited tasks, science can promote self-awareness and enhance a sense of self-responsibility with respect to a set of values:

> *If* you take such and such a stand, then, according to scientific experience, you have to use such and such a *means* in order to carry out your conviction practically.... Does the end "justify" the means?...Figuratively speaking, you serve this god and you offend the other god when you decide to adhere to [a paricular]

position.... Thus, if we [as social scientists] are competent in our pursuit...we can force individuals, or at least we can help [them], to give [themselves] an *account of the ultimate meaning of [their] own conduct*....I am tempted to say of teachers who succeed in this: [they] stand in the service of "moral" forces; [they] fulfill the duty of bringing about self-clarification and a sense of responsibility. (Weber, 1946, pp. 151–2; original emphasis)

Accordingly, Weber insists that professors in university classrooms must not offer to students value judgments, personal views, and political opinions. "So long as [they wish] to remain teacher[s] and not to become demagogue[s]" (ibid., p. 151), they must refrain from discussing the conclusions of their research as "truth."[49] Owing to their high prestige *vis-à-vis* students, doing so presents a great danger: an excessive influence upon them might occur and hence a constriction of their autonomous decision-making powers. In turn, students should not expect leadership and guidance from their professors, for science, unlike politics, excludes the activity – the clash of values – on the basis of which leaders arise.

## The support for a strong national state

Weber is well known as a proponent of a strong nation. Some interpreters view him as an unreconstructed nationalist who favored the power of the German state for its own sake.

This interpretation evidences little understanding of Weber's sociology, his appreciation of the underlying dilemmas confronted by industrial societies, and his own ultimate ideals and values.[50] As noted, Weber perceived Western values as threatened by a specter of societal stagnation and ossification. Yet he was convinced that neither the smaller states of Europe, nor England or the United States, were capable of defending them. He saw a crass materialism and an exploitative commercialism in these nations as having whittled away Western values, particularly the notion of an autonomous individual. These nations, he argued, remained incapable of mobilizing internally to resist threatening forces effectively. In addition, Weber saw the West as under attack from the East: Russian authoritarianism, civil servant rulership, and economic underdevelopment had failed to call forth either the values of the Enlightenment on the one hand – Reason and Rationality – or those of the "Rights of Man" of the French and American Revolutions on the other.

In this crisis situation, Weber and the vast majority of his colleagues perceived the German state as a bulwark against the loss of the Western tradition's noble values. A *strong* state would be best equipped to make a stand in defense of action on behalf of these values: individual autonomy, self-responsibility, the unified personality, ethical action, brotherhood, compassion, charity, and a sense of honor. Furthermore, according to him, the German state would not, if it acted alone on behalf of German nationalism, fulfill its "responsibility before history," Rather, Germany now must undertake a far more monumental task: to defend Western values for *all* Western countries. The advance of formal, practical, and theoretical rationality, as well as the functionary's caution, conformity, and striving for security, he argued, was occurring in all industrializing countries, even in the United States.[51]

Weber hoped that strong parliaments, a dynamic democracy, a vigorous capitalism, a modern science lacking a legitimacy to pronounce "correct" values for persons, and a strong national German state would forestall the advance of bureaucratization on the one hand and formal, practical, and theoretical types of rationality on the other. To the extent that this occurred, a series of forces would crystallize to oppose societal ossification and to construct the dynamic *civic* arena so woefully lacking in Germany. As this took place, the fundamental precondition for the nourishing of values would come to the fore: a societal openness that allowed – even fostered – perpetual conflicts over values (*Wertkämpfe*).

Wherever noble values became empowered to orient action, all those aspects of the West Weber held dear, he was convinced, would be defended. The random push and pull of daily life interests and mundane concerns, and the mere "sterile excitation" they give rise to, would then be counterbalanced. Life could become *directed* on behalf of ethical ideals and a passion for "causes" would be awakened: "For nothing is worthy of man as man unless he can pursue it with passionate devotion" (Weber, 1946, p. 135). And individuals would then practice an "ethic of responsibility" and assume accountability for their own actions. Finally, and of pivotal significance to Weber, the ethical ideal itself places a thrust toward community into motion: "The ethical norm and its 'universal validity' create a community, or at least in so far as an individual might reject the act of another on moral grounds and yet still face it and participate in the common life. Knowing his own creaturely weakness, the individual places himself under the common norm" (ibid., p. 342).

Yet Weber remains alternately pessimistic about the future and unwilling to predict its contours: "No one knows who will live in this cage in the future, or whether at the end of this tremendous development entirely new prophets will arise, or there will be great rebirth of old ideas and ideals, or, if neither, mechanized ossification, embellished with a sort of convulsive self-importance" (Weber, 1930, p. 182).[52] Nonetheless, precisely these overarching concerns drove his scholarly research far and wide. Only comparative investigations could assist Weber to define clearly the ways in which the economies, laws, rulership forms, and religions of the West were unique, to assess possibilities regarding social change, and to understand better the social constellations that assisted an anchoring of meaningful action in values and ethical ideals.

## WEBER'S IMPACT

Weber has been acclaimed universally as a sociologist of sweeping range, insight, and conceptual powers, and his works have had a significant impact upon sociology.[53] Remarkably, his influence has resulted more from several of his pivotal essays than from a wide-ranging acceptance of his sociology (see Kalberg, 1996, 1998, pp. 209–14).

Although best known as an "idealist," or an advocate of the power in history of ideas and values, he firmly rejected this position. This odd turn resulted in part from the search by American critics of Karl Marx in the 1940s and 1950s for a strong advocate for their cause, in part from the misleading interpretation by Weber's earliest proponent, Talcott Parsons, and in part from the early translation of *PE* (1930) and the late translation of *E&S* (1968). Weber's "idealism" could be seen throughout the 1940s and 1950s in the works of innumerable "modernization" theorists, all of whom had noted his emphasis upon the importance of a set of values for the rise of the spirit of capitalism and expanded upon it. These theorists argued on behalf of the central significance of values for the unfolding of modern democracies and economies.[54]

Yet Weber's impact expanded far beyond the modernization theorists. As early as the 1930s *PE* had begun to influence empirical research in the sociology of religion, especially with regard to comparisons between Protestants and Catholics. In the 1940s and 1950s his essay on the bureaucracy became hotly debated by students of modern organizations,[55] and in the 1950s and 1960s "Class, Status, Party" (Weber, 1968, pp. 926–40) became widely viewed as offering a necessary correction to Marxian stratification theory. During this same period his writings on the sociology of law and urban sociology became acknowledged as core contributions to these subdisciplines (see Weber, 1968, pp. 641–900, 1212–372). As a consequence of his emphasis upon power and rulership, Weber became understood in the 1960s and 1970s as a major contributor to "conflict theory" and to political sociology. In the 1970s his attention to the ways in which the state may develop autonomously played a role in the rise of "state-centered theory," and his essay on charismatic leadership and its routinization stimulated research in the area of social movements. In the 1970s and 1980s *E&S* indirectly influenced the new field of comparative-historical sociology. Weber's notion that the social sciences must practice an ethos of value neutrality, although articulated by many others as well, gained full acceptance in the 1950s and has remained to this day a central cornerstone in American sociology. The impact of his work has been a sustained one and a variety of subdisciplines have claimed him as their founder.

Nonetheless, a coherent school of disciples has failed to crystallize – a fact explained only partly by the unavailability, until recently, of major segments of Weber's works in English or by the great complexity and breadth of his writings. Rather, foundational tenets of his sociology stand in opposition to the predominantly Durkheimian orientation of macrosociology in the United States, and powerful barriers resisted a *Weberian sociology*: the central place of organic holism, social structure, institutions, "society," and functional explanations conflicts with his attention to subjective meaning, ideal types, societal domains, power, conflict, an intimate interlocking of past and present, and a radical multicausality that stresses *both* "ideas and interests"; the aim in American sociology to formulate general laws resists Weber's value-relevance axiom and his goal to offer causal explanations of unique cases. Furthermore, the widespread focus among sociologists in the USA upon the "question of social order" in specific societies stands against the intercivilizational and outward-looking thrust of his works; the advocacy in America of a "naturalistic" understanding of concepts – as fully capturing reality – opposes the value-relevance axiom and Weber's anchoring of sociology in ideal types; the broad orientation of sociologists in the USA to social roles remains incompatible with his stress upon subjective meaning, organizations, status groups, and societal domains; and the frequent emphasis in the USA upon evolution and unilinear progress conflicts with Weber's cognizance of paradox, historical accident, unforeseen consequences, and the routinization of charisma, as well as his insistence upon the contextual embeddedness of action and the ubiquitous penetration of the past into the present.

To Weber, the present can be comprehended only by reference to an array of historical backdrop forces, yet the forward-looking orientation of American sociology downplays just such influences. In the United States, sociology has only rarely formulated theories capable of conceptualizing the many ways in which cultural forces, for example, stand behind and influence the contours of interest- and power-based struggles and, conversely, power and interests stand behind value-based conflicts – indeed, to such a degree that a dynamism rooted in the tensions between these contending forces frequently characterizes social life. Moreover, Weber's forceful acknowledgment of the significance, for causal explanations, of the manner in which *configurations* of forces crystallize in unique ways places his sociology firmly in opposition to all diffusion theories and all analyses rooted in historical analogies (see Kalberg, 1994a, 1994b, pp. 168–92, 1999).

These major tenets of his sociology lead Weber frequently to a "perspectival" mode of procedure in which related ideal types are compared and contrasted in respect of the subjective meaning each implies (such as asceticism–mysticism, Confucianism–Puritanism, feudalism–patrimonialism). However, his mode of analysis, rooted in ideal types, places his sociology strictly against all schools that utilize *global* dichotomies (such as tradition–modernity and particularism–universalism), as well as all evolutionary, Social Darwinist, and "universal stage" theories. Thus, it is not surprising that major recent currents in American sociology have opposed Weber: largely rooted in survey research methods, comparative sociology today lacks a notion of subjective meaning and an acknowledgment of the importance of historical forces; state-centered theory and world systems theory both downplay cultural forces, as well as subjective meaning; neo-functionalism opposes Weber's insistence upon the omnipresence of power, rulership, and conflict; and rational choice theory utilizes only one of Weber's four "types of social action" and abjures all situating of individual action within contexts of traditions and values (see Kalberg, 1996).

## AN ASSESSMENT

Large questions about the modern world drove Weber's sociology. What is the fate of ethical action, the unique individual, the personality unified by reference to a constellation of values, and compassion in the industrial society? What does the rise of modern capitalism imply for the "type of person" who will live within this new cosmos? What defines the particularity of the West? How have we arrived at our present situation? How do persons in different social contexts formulate subjective meaning in their lives? What sets of social forces lead persons to attach meaning to specific activities? How can we understand the subjectively meaningful action of persons in other civilizations and epochs on their own terms rather than by reference to a hierarchy of Western values? What are the parameters for social change in the West?

Sociologists today only rarely ask questions of this magnitude. Very delimited themes guide research and broad queries are confined to the misty, non-scientific realms of social philosophy. As Weber himself noted, the social sciences require specialized skills and involve specialized research questions. Moreover, if he had not "translated" these wide-ranging questions in his own investigations into rigorous concepts, research strategies, modes of analysis, and methodological axioms, his writings would be understood today as simply a set of commentaries upon the rapidly changing era in which he lived – and only intellectual historians would study them. A *Weberian sociology* would not exist.

Weber created a rigorous and distinct approach that combined concrete, empirical description with theoretical generalization. Distinguished by its staggering comparative and historical breadth, his sociology investigates the social action of persons by reference to values, traditions, interests, and emotions. It seeks to offer causal analyses of unique cases and proceeds by reference to ideal types, societal domains, social contexts, and the exploration of subjective meaning. His studies emphasize that the past is ineluctably intertwined with the present and assert that the orientation of social action to religious, economic, rulership, legal, familial, and status group factors *all* must be acknowledged as causally significant; geographical forces, power, social carriers, historical events, competition, conflict, and technology must also be recognized as viable causal forces. While Weber remains fully cognizant that some societies may become, in certain epochs and as a result of multiple identifiable action-orientations, more closed or even ossified, he scorns organic holism and takes omnipresent conflict and power for granted. However, he also sees that the regularities of action – continuities and patterns – arise ubiquitously on the basis of values, traditions, interests, and even emotions.

Moreover, he is convinced that persons repeatedly view rulership as legitimate and render obedience, yet they also from time to time overthrow established ruling groups – only then to erect further authorities. Social change is inevitable, even though it never follows an evolutionary or lawful pathway. Yet it cannot be comprehended by reference *alone* to "material" or "ideal" factors, and least of all to transcendent forces, mysterious causes, or "ultimate" determinants. And while material interests possess a strong grip upon everyday activities, persons are also capable of orienting their action to values, conventions, customs, habits, and emotions, even when doing so flies in the face of their economic well-being. Meaning is formulated in a vast variety of ways, though internally consistent sets of values that address ultimate questions – world views – have congealed in the major civilizations to set the "tracks" within which meaningful action becomes defined (see Kalberg, forthcoming). In studying relationships, groups, organizations, epochs, and civilizations of interest to them, sociologists take as their task the interpretive understanding of meaningful action. However, they also seek to understand the social dynamics that give birth to specific meaningful patterns of action and sustain them, and the further social forces that lead to their alteration.

Although impressive in many ways, Weber's ambitious approach is not without weaknesses. Its sheer complexity and frequent lack of clarity have led often to the charge of inconsistency. For example, while subjective meaning stands at the center of his methodological writings, the language Weber utilizes in his comparative-historical works frequently leaves the impression that structural forces constitute his concern.[56] The translations have constituted a longstanding problem in just this respect, and many Anglo-Saxon readers have accused Weber of becoming, in violation of his own methodological premises, a structural sociologist. Other interpreters have found the concept at the foundation of Weber's approach troublesome: the ideal type. Guidelines for its formation and application, it is argued, have remained imprecise and insufficient. These same opponents have generally rejected Weber's view that sociological generalization is appropriately limited to the conceptual level only.

Further common criticisms have cut to the core of Weber's sociology. Many have faulted his orientation to subjective meaning as such, questioning the viability of an approach that takes motives as pivotal. A number of more recent sociologists insist that interaction, creativity, identity formation, and narrative accounts must constitute the fundamental level of analysis. Moreover, while subjective meaning rooted in means–end rational action may be identifiable, critics contend further that value-based subjective meaning will always remain amorphous and problematic. Indeed, some have questioned whether an analytic armament that includes traditions and values is at all necessary for sociologists: persons act, they argue, by reference on the one hand to pragmatic interests and on the other hand to external constraints and power.

Not surprisingly, organic holists have attacked Weber's elevation of ideal types and subjective meaning to the center of his methodology and lamented the absence of their major explanatory concepts – "society" and "institutions" – as well as Weber's indifference to "the problem of social order." Many of these same commentators have viewed his definition of sociology's aim – to offer causal explanations of unique cases – as exceedingly modest. In rejecting Weber's view of theory as an endeavor in the service of heuristic ends only and hence as always provisional, and his value-relevance axiom, they seek to establish a sociology empowered to articulate the general "laws of social life," to offer predictions about the future, and, in the name of science, to assist policy-makers and confront injustice. Remarkably, Marxists and neo-Marxists have on these points agreed with the organic holism tradition: the principled incapacity of Weber's sociology to formulate clear-cut mechanisms for social change, let alone avenues of emancipation from modern capitalism, renders his works, they contend, in the end too beholden to the status quo. Weber's critics from the Left argue as well that this "bourgeois" character of his sociology is apparent in its putative "idealism," its failure to elevate material interests to the level of a pre-eminent causal force, and its unwillingness to recognize the "laws of history." The strengths and weaknesses of Weber's rich sociology will undoubtedly be debated for many years to come. Even as an array of his essays continues to be widely discussed, the opposition by many schools to the core features of his approach will endure. Nonetheless, as the microchip and globalization revolutions reach into the twenty-first century and continue to bring diverse nations into direct contact, a place remains for a comparative-historical sociology oriented to the investigation and understanding – on its own terms – of the subjective meaning of persons near and far.

## Acknowledgment

I would like to thank Abdullah Al-Wagdani, Robert J. Antonio, Mathias Bös, Lewis A Coser, Guenther Roth, Konstanze Senge, and Kurt H. Wolff for very helpful criticisms and suggestions.

## Notes

1  A number of studies examine Weber's life. See Gerth and Mills (1946, pp. 3–44), Loewenstein (1966, pp. 91–104), Honigsheim (1968), Coser (1971, pp. 234–43), Marianne Weber (1975), Kaesler (1979, pp. 1–23) and Roth (1997).

2  That these major currents of thought remained otherwise so difficult to render into a unity laid the foundation for tensions that run throughout Weber's sociology, as will become apparent.

3  His rejection of these positions led him to adopt the ideal type as his major research tool. This construct cut through the middle of the *Methodenstreit* and addressed several of its seemingly irreconcilable conflicts: (a) although "general" and "synthetic," it constitutes only a heuristic tool rather than a historical law; and (b) although formulated in reference to the researcher's interests and values rather than an "objective" reality, the knowledge it provides is verifiable.

4  The frequent translation of Weber's term *Entwicklung* (development) as "evolution" has caused a great deal of confusion.

5  Although nowhere discussed, Weber surely saw Durkheim's elevation of "social facts" to the core of his sociology in the same manner: as a manifestation of a mode of thought still penetrated by the secularized legacies of Western religions.

6  It is also inconceivable that Weber's sociology would have acquired one of its major strengths without having taken this epistemological turn away from a Eurocentric social science, as well as from all quasi-religious and organismic schools: its relentless "perspectivalism," or its capacity to "rotate" factors. This procedure holds a single ideal type (e.g. asceticism) "up to the light" from the perspective of a radically varying ideal type (e.g. mysticism), and then systematically examines the differences with respect to the influence of each upon social action. The "angle of vision" (*Gesichtspunkt*) remains central; "actual reality" – all absolutism – is omitted. Weber is especially fond of noting that a particular phenomenon (e.g. the mystic's withdrawal from the world) is fully "irrational" from the point of view of a second phenomenon (e.g. the "inner-worldly" ascetic's orientation to worldly activity). See Weber (1946c, p. 326), Jaspers (1946, pp. 37–8).

7    "It is ... a fundamental fact of all history that the ultimate result of political activity often – no, actually regularly – stands in a completely inadequate and often even paradoxical relation to its original meaning" (Weber, 1946a, p. 117).

8    Following Weber, I will be using the terms "meaningful action" and "social action" synonymously. Despite his emphasis upon the *capacity* of the human species to bestow subjective meaning upon action, Weber nonetheless argues that this often does not occur: "In the great majority of cases *actual* action goes on in a state of inarticulate half-consciousness or actual unconsciousness of its 'subjective meaning.' Actors are more likely to 'feel' this meaning in a vague sense than to 'know' it or explicitly to 'make themselves' aware of it. In most cases action is governed by impulse or habit; the subjective meaning of the action (whether rational or irrational) is only occasionally elevated into consciousness. This occurs in the uniform action of large numbers only in the case of a few individuals. Meaningful action that is actually effective – that is, when the meaning is fully conscious and apparent – is in empirical reality a marginal case. Every sociological or historical investigation that analyzes empirical reality must acknowledge this situation. However, sociology should not, for this reason, hesitate to construct its *concepts* through a classification of possible 'subjective meanings'; in other words, as if action consciously oriented to meaning actually occurs" (Weber, 1968, pp. 21–2; translation altered, original emphasis). For this reason, as well as his stress upon *four* types of action (see below), Weber cannot be understood simply as a "rationalist" thinker, as many critics have asserted (see, for example, Eder, 1999, pp. 202–3).

9    He points out that his classification does not seek to exhaust all possibilities, "but only to formulate in conceptually pure form certain sociologically important types to which actual action is more or less closely approximated" (Weber, 1968, p. 26). Weber does not expect to discover *empirical* cases in which social action is oriented *only* to one of these types of action.

10   Motives for Weber are causes of action: "A motive is a complex of subjective meaning which seems to the actor himself or to the observer an adequate ground for the conduct in question" (Weber, 1968, p. 11).

11   Of the four types of social action, Weber found means–end rational action to be the most easily understandable by the sociologist (see Weber, 1968, p. 5). In all cases, the interpretation of subjective meaning by the researcher must be based upon empirical evidence and rigorous procedures. Nonetheless, it may be quite difficult, Weber acknowledges, for the social scientist to understand certain action as subjectively meaningful. He notes that values "often cannot be understood completely" (ibid.). Yet this problem does not prevent him from formulating an ideal toward which researchers should strive. And, again, in-depth exploration of the contexts within which action occurs will, he argues, assist understanding. Finally, Weber notes: "The more we ourselves are capable of such emotional reactions as anxiety, anger, ambition, envy, jealousy, love, enthusiasm, pride, vengefulness, loyalty, devotion, and appetites of all sorts, and of the 'irrational' reactions which grow out of them, the more readily can we empathize with them. Even when such emotions are found in a degree of intensity of which the observer himself is completely incapable, he can still have a significant degree of emotional understanding of their meaning and can interpret intellectually their influence on the direction of action and the selection of means" (ibid., p. 6, translation altered).

12   "For the subjective interpretation of action in sociological work these collectivities must be treated as *solely* the resultants and modes of organization of the particular

acts of individual persons, since these alone can be treated as agents in a course of subjectively understandable action" (Weber, 1968, p. 13).

13 This distinguishes the "empirical sciences of action," according to Weber, from jurisprudence, logic, ethics, and aesthetics, all of which aim to ascertain "true" and "valid" meanings (Weber, 1968, p. 4).

14 Weber makes this general point further in the chapter on rulership (*Herrschaft*) in part I of *E&S*: "Hence, the kind of terminology and classification set forth above has in no sense the aim – indeed, it could not have it – to be exhaustive or to confine the whole of historical reality in a rigid scheme. Its usefulness is derived from the fact that in a given case it is possible to distinguish what aspects of a given organized group can legitimately be identified as falling under or approximating one or another of these categories" (Weber, 1968, pp. 263–4; Kalberg, 1994b, pp. 84–91).

15 "The existence of a connection between two historical occurrences cannot be captured abstractly, but only by presenting an internally consistent view of the way in which it was concretely formed" (Weber, 1968, p. 2).

16 Weber makes this point even more vividly in a later essay: "The origin of economic rationalism [of the type which, since the sixteenth and seventeenth centuries, has come to dominate the West], just as it is dependent upon a rational technology and rational law, is also dependent upon the capacity and disposition of people to engage in a certain kind of practical-rational *way of leading a life*" (Weber, 1930, p. 26, translation altered, original emphasis; see also 1946, p. 293).

17 Only an abbreviated version of my earlier interpretation can be offered here (see Kalberg, 1996, e.g. pp. 58–63; 2001).

18 Weber defines an "ethical" standard as "a specific type of value-rational *belief* among individuals which, as a consequence of this belief, imposes a normative element upon human action that claims the quality of the 'morally good' in the same way that action which claims the status of the 'beautiful' is measured against aesthetic standards" (Weber, 1968, p. 36, translation altered, original emphasis). Social action, Weber contends, can be influenced by an ethical standard even if "external" support for it is lacking and even, at times, despite opposing "external" forces.

19 Rather than a "determinative" relationship, Weber sees an "elective affinity" (*Wahl-verwandtschaft*) between the Protestant ethic and the spirit of capitalism. (Parsons's translation of *Wahlverwandtschaft* as "correlation" is inadequate; see Weber, 1930, e.g. p. 91.) This "weak causal" manner of stating the relationship results in part from Weber's position that the sources of the spirit of capitalism are many and that religious sources constitute *only one* – however significant and not to be neglected – possible source (see ibid., pp. 91–2; Weber, 1927, pp. 352–67): "We only wish to ascertain whether and to what extent religious influences *co*-participated in the qualitative formation and the quantitative expansion of [the spirit of capitalism] over the world" (Weber, 1930, p. 91, translation altered, original emphasis). He notes: "One of the fundamental elements of the spirit of modern capitalism – rational conduct on the basis of the *idea of the calling* – was born . . . from the spirit of *Christian asceticism*" (ibid., p. 180; original emphasis).

20 This theme is also prominent in a massive, more historical work by Weber; see *General Economic History* (1927).

21 For this reason, *E&S* is organized around these domains. The unfortunate title of this opus, which stems from Weber's wife, leaves the impression that his sociology is organized around a notion of "society." The title Weber gave to *E&S*'s major section – "The Economy and the Societal Domains and Powers" – points to the centrality of societal domains.

22  Weber saw a particular "methodical rational way of leading a life" as having a significant impact upon the development of the modern West: the ascetic Protestant.

23  *Herrschaft* is normally translated as either "authority" or "domination." Neither of these terms captures *Herrschaft*'s *combination* of both authority and domination, and hence I am using Benjamin Nelson's translation: "rulership."

24  On this usage of the ideal type, see generally Kalberg (1994b, pp. 87–91).

25  Weber emphasizes explicitly the character of rulership as nothing more than meaningful action-orientations: "Rulership does not mean that a superior elementary force asserts itself in one way or another; it refers to a meaningful interrelationship between those giving orders and those obeying, to the effect that the expectations toward which action is oriented on both sides can be reckoned upon" (Weber, 1968, p. 1378).

26  And: "Experience shows that in no instance does rulership voluntarily limit itself to the appeal to material or affectual or ideal motives as a basis for its continuance. In addition, every such system attempts to establish and to cultivate the belief in its legitimacy" (Weber, 1968, p. 213).

27  For Weber's earlier formulations in part II, see p. 954; more generally, see pp. 262–3, 953–4, 947. In empirical reality, of course, rulership always appears in some mixture of these pure types. These three models do not represent an attempt by Weber to capture an "evolutionary" drift of history up to the contemporary era (see below).

28  Charismatic rulership is examined below. With regard to traditional rulership, Weber emphasizes: "The validity of a social order by virtue of the sacredness of tradition is the oldest and most universal type of legitimacy" (Weber, 1968, p. 37). On traditional rulership generally, see Weber (1946, p. 296; 1968, pp. 1041, 958, 1006–7, 216, 226–7).

29  On Weber's dynamic models, see Kalberg (1994b, pp. 95–8); on his contextual models, see ibid. (pp. 39–46, 98–102).

30  As opposed to "culture" (literature, art, science, etc.).

31  For further examples, see Kalberg (1994b, pp. 102–17). These pages also include a discussion of *intra*-domain relationships of antagonism (e.g. the antagonism of charismatic rulership to traditional and bureaucratic rulership).

32  *E&S* also constructs numerous models of antagonism *within* domains. For a discussion of these models, see Kalberg (1994b, pp. 106–8).

33  To Weber, the purity of charisma can be preserved against everyday interests only by the "common danger of military life or a love ethos of an unworldly discipleship" (Weber, 1968, p. 1120).

34  Weber's attention in this model to the role played by pragmatic interests reveals the "sober realism" side of his sociology neglected in the reception of his works influenced by Parsons. Weber also formulates developmental models that chart the closure of social relationships and the monopolization of resources in the economy, rulership, and religion domains (see Kalberg, 1994b, pp. 120–4). Further developmental models outline the rise of formal rationality in regard to the free market and the state, and a "theoretical" rationalization process in the domain of religion (see ibid., pp. 128–40). Qualitatively different "rationalization processes" are charted, as developmental models, in the rulership, law, religion, and economy societal domains. In investigating the economy in relation to the rulership, religion, and law domains, as well as these spheres of life in relationship to one another, *E&S* formulates a vast *rationalization of action theoretical framework*. These developmental models arrange ideal types along an analytic *course* of increasingly rationalized social action. See Kalberg (forthcoming).

35 This is the translation given by Walliman et al. (1980).

36 I have discussed Weber's multicausality, as well as his "conjunctural" mode of establishing causality, in detail in Kalberg (1994b, pp. 32–5, 50–77, 143–92).

37 See also Weber (1927, pp. 368–9; 1930, pp. 72, 181, 282n108) and Kalberg (1996, pp. 52–4, 62).

38 On the exceedingly complex relationship between past and present in Weber's sociology, see further Kalberg (1994b, pp. 158–67; 1996, pp. 57–64; 1998, pp. 233–5).

39 *EEWR* also includes two synoptic essays ("Religious Rejections of the World" and "The Social Psychology of the World Religions"), a general introduction in which Weber lays out his major themes, and his classical essay on the centrality of the ascetic Protestant sects and churches for an understanding of the social dynamics and political culture of the United States ("The Protestant Sects and the Spirit of Capitalism") (see Kalberg, 1997). The major themes in *EEWR* can be only hinted at here. Weber's analyses, for example, of the origins of salvation religions (see Kalberg, 1990, 2000b) and the location of ideas and values in social contexts (see Kalberg, 1994b, pp. 39–46, 98–102; 2000b, forthcoming), as well as his analyses of the rise of monotheism (see Kalberg, 1994a), the caste system (see Kalberg, 1994b), and Confucianism (see Kalberg, 1999), must be fully omitted. Weber's masterful analysis of the major tensions in modern Western societies is examined in the "Social Context" section below.

40 Even great charismatic figures, such as prophets, are not viewed by Weber a-contextually. Their influence requires a pre-existing "certain minimum of intellectual discourse" (see Weber, 1968, pp. 486–7).

41 Hence, the common understanding of *EEWR* as a study that utilizes experimental design procedures to isolate the centrality of a particular economic ethic for the development of modern capitalism in the West does not correspond to the methodology Weber actually utilizes in these volumes. On his context-based mode of establishing causality, see Kalberg (1994b, pp. 98–102, 143–92).

42 Although many engaged in these endeavors viewed their activities as ultimately "political" in a broader sense: they sought to prepare Germans to become citizens (see Jenkins, 1996).

43 Many commentators have attended to the famous phrases that conclude some of his books or stand at the center of his political writings and then painted Weber as a bleak and despairing cultural pessimist. These interpreters have focused upon Weber's most prominent image of the future: as an "iron cage" and "house of bondage." Indeed, he remains unequivocally pessimistic in a famous passage in "Politics as a Vocation": "Not summer's bloom lies ahead of us, but rather a polar night of icy darkness and hardness, no matter which group may triumph eternally now" (Weber, 1946a, p. 128). While Weber surely was not an optimistic believer in the unending progress of civilization, as were many American and English social thinkers of his generation, he also cannot be characterized as a dour pessimist. Nor was he a seeker after an idealized past, as his frequently used phrase – "disenchantment (*Entzauberung*) of the world" – has implied to many; his sociological analyses convinced him that this route remained closed. If truly a cultural pessimist or romantic, Weber would have withdrawn into fatalism and passivity, and perhaps even into one of Germany's many "cults of irrationality." Instead, he scorned such cults, mocked the romantics as delusional, and remained an endlessly combative political commentator and actor. The values acquired from his stern Protestant mother precluded any other course.

44  Weber is here formulating ideal types. He is well aware of the many ways in which rule-bound efficiency can be diminished by "red tape."

45  I have addressed these "types of rationality" in greater detail (see Kalberg, 1980).

46  The centrality of individualism (however differently understood) in three schools of thought – the French Enlightenment, German Romanticism, and ascetic Protestantism – again becomes apparent in Weber's analysis.

47  I am here focusing upon his sociological thinking rather than, as is often the case, Weber's own political activity. In this regard, Weber was a peripatetic defender of individual rights (see Coser, 1971, pp. 242–3, 254–6; Beetham, 1974).

48  Several commentators have argued that Weber's commitment to democracy was not one in principle, but was rooted in his view that modern industrial societies confronted a great danger of societal ossification. It is apparent that Weber, in distrusting the citizenship skills of the Germans, did not break from the tenor of his times in Germany (see Jenkins, 1996). A long period of tutelege in the practices of democracy would be necessary.

49  Weber continues: "Whether, under such conditions, science is a worthwhile 'vocation' for somebody, and whether science itself has an objectively valuable 'vocation' are again value judgments about which nothing can be said in the lecture-room" (Weber, 1946, p. 152).

50  The extreme cosmopolitanism of his own family (see Roth, 1997) also speaks against the interpretation that sees Weber as a virulent nationalist.

51  Albeit, in light of an array of forces, at a slower pace than in the European societies (Weber, 1946, pp. 106–14).

52  Weber nearly always qualifies his statements regarding the future in his sociological writings by the use of terms such as "might," "perhaps," and "potentiality."

53  This section discusses Weber's impact upon American sociology. For an examination of his influence upon British sociology, see Albrow (1989).

54  Many proponents of this school misunderstood Weber. In asserting that modernization took place only if certain "functional prerequisites" were fulfilled, Parsons, for example, sought to formulate "laws" and a "general theory of society" – thereby violating Weber's axiom of value-relevance. Other modernization theorists, arguing that economic development would occur only in those countries where a "functional equivalent" of the Protestant ethic existed, viewed their research as under the direct influence of Weber – all the while neglecting the fundamental *multi*causal, contextual, and case study orientation of his sociology (see Eisenstadt, 1968).

55  However, rather than as an ideal type useful as a "standard" against which empirical cases could be compared, Weber's bureaucracy was understood as a depiction of the actual workings of this type of organization – and hence criticized as inaccurate (mainly for omitting the influence of informal groupings).

56  For example, on behalf of clarity, he should use phrases such as "action oriented to feudalism" or "action oriented to Calvinist doctrine." Abjuring such awkward phraseology, Weber generally prefers simply "feudalism" and "Calvinism."

# Bibliography

## Writings of Max Weber

Die Römische Agrargeschichte in Ihrer Bedeutung für das Staats-und Privatrecht [The Significance of Roman Agrarian History for Civil and Private Law]. 1899. Amsterdam: Verlag P. Schippers (1966).

The Prospects for Liberal Democracy in Tsarist Russia. 1906. In W. G. Runciman (ed.), *Weber: Selections in Translation*. Cambridge: Cambridge University Press (1978), pp. 269–84.

Debattenreden auf der Tagung des Vereins fuer Sozialpolitik [Debates from the Conference of the Association for Social Policy]. 1909. In Marianne Weber (ed.), *Gesammelte Aufsaetze zur Soziologie und Sozialpolitik*. Tübingen: Mohr, pp. 412–23.

Vorwort [Introduction]. 1914. In K. Buecher, J. Schumpeter, and Fr. Freiherr von Wieser (eds), *Grundriss der Sozialoekonomik, 1. Abt. Wirtschaft und Wirtschaftswissenschaft*. Tübingen: Mohr, pp. vii–ix.

*General Economic History*. 1927. New York: Free Press.

Author's Introduction. 1930a. In Max Weber, *The Protestant Ethic and the Spirit of Capitalism*, translated by Talcott Parsons. New York: Scribner's, pp. 13–31.

*The Protestant Ethic and the Spirit of Capitalism*, translated by Talcott Parsons. 1930b. New York: Scribner's (1958).

Politics as a Vocation. 1946a. In H. H. Gerth and C. Wright Mills (eds and trans.), *From Max Weber: Essays in Sociology*. New York: Oxford, pp. 77–128.

The Protestant Sects and the Spirit of Capitalism. 1946b. In *From Max Weber*, pp. 302–22.

Religious Rejections of the World. 1946c. In *From Max Weber*, pp. 323–59.

Science as a Vocation. 1946d. In *From Max Weber*, pp. 129–56.

The Social Psychology of the World Religions. 1946e. In *From Max Weber*, pp. 267–301.

*The Methodology of the Social Sciences* (edited and translated by Edward A. Shils and Henry A. Finch). 1949. New York: Free Press.

*The Religion of China* (edited and translated by Hans H. Gerth). 1951. New York: The Free Press.

*Ancient Judaism* (edited and translated by Hans H. Gerth and Don Martindale). 1952. New York: Free Press.

*The Religion of India* (edited and translated by Hans H. Gerth and Don Martindale). 1958. New York: The Free Press.

*Economy and Society* (edited by Guenther Roth and Claus Wittich). 1968. New York: Bedminster Press.

## Further reading

Albrow, Martin (1989) Die Rezeption Max Webers in der britischen Soziologie [The Reception of Max Weber in British Sociology]. In Johannes Weiss (ed.), *Max Weber Heute*. Frankfurt: Suhrkamp, pp. 165–86.

Beetham, D. (1974) *Max Weber and the Theory of Modern Politics*. London: George Allen & Unwin.

Coser, Lewis A. (1971) *Masters of Sociological Thought*. New York: Harcourt Brace Jovanovich.

Eder, K. (1999) Societies Learn and yet the World Is Hard to Change. *European Journal of Social Theory*, 2, 195–216.

Eisenstadt, S. N. (ed.) (1968) *The Protestant Ethic and Modernization*.

Gerth, Hans H. and Wright Mills, C. (1946) Introduction. In *From Max Weber*. New York: Oxford University Press, pp. 3–74.

Honigsheim, Paul (1968) *On Max Weber*. New York: The Free Press.

Jaspers, Karl (1946) *Max Weber: Politiker, Forscher, Philosoph* [*Max Weber: Politician, Researcher, and Philosopher*]. Bremen: Johs. Storm Verlag.

Jenkins, J. (1996) The Kitsch Collections and *The Spirit in the Furniture*: Cultural Reform and National Culture in Germany. *Social History*, 21, 123–41.

Kaesler, Dirk (1988) *Max Weber: an Introduction to His Life and Work*. Chicago: University of Chicago Press.

Kalberg, Stephen (1980) Max Weber's Types of Rationality: Cornerstones for the Analysis of Rationalization Processes in History. *American Journal of Sociology*, 85(3), 1145–79.

Kalberg, Stephen (1985) The Role of Ideal Interests in Max Weber's Comparative Historical Sociology. In Robert J. Antonio and Ronald M. Glassman (eds), *A Weber–Marx Dialogue*, Lawrence, KS: University Press of Kansas, pp. 46–67.

Kalberg, Stephen (1987) The Origins and Expansion of *Kulturpessimismus*: the Relationship Between Public and Private Spheres in Early Twentieth Century Germany. *Sociological Theory*, 5, 150–64.

Kalberg, Stephen (1990) The Rationalization of Action in Max Weber's Sociology of Religion. *Sociological Theory*, 8(1), 58–84.

Kalberg, Stephen (1994a) Max Weber's Analysis of the Rise of Monotheism: a Reconstruction. *British Journal of Sociology*, 45(4), 563–83.

Kalberg, Stephen (1994b) *Max Weber's Comparative-Historical Sociology*. Chicago: University of Chicago Press.

Kalberg, Stephen (1996) On the Neglect of Weber's *Protestant Ethic* as a Theoretical Treatise: Demarcating the Parameters of Post-war American Sociological Theory. *Sociological Theory*, 14(1), 49–70.

Kalberg, Stephen (1997) Tocqueville and Weber on the Sociological Origins of Citizenship: the Political Culture of American Democracy. *Citizenship Studies*, 1 (July), 199–222.

Kalberg, Stephen (1998) Max Weber's Sociology: Research Strategies and Modes of Analysis. In Charles Camic (ed.), *Reclaiming the Argument of the Founders*. Cambridge, MA: Blackwell, pp. 208–41.

Kalberg, Stephen (1999) Max Weber's Critique of Recent Comparative-Historical Sociology and a Reconstruction of His Analysis of the Rise of Confucianism in China. In J. M. Lehmann (ed.), *Current Perspectives in Social Theory*. Stamford, CT: JAI Press, pp. 207–46.

Kalberg, Stephen (2000a) Americanization, Converging and Diverging Societal Developments, 1968–1990. In Detlef Junker (ed.), *Germany and the US in the era of the Cold War, 1945–1990*. Cambridge: Cambridge University Press.

Kalberg, Stephen (2000b) Ideen und Interessen: Max Weber über den Ursprung Ausserweltliche Erlösungsreligionen [Ideas and Interests: Max Weber on the Origins of Salvation Religions]. *Zeitschrift für Religionsgeschichte*, 7, forthcoming.

Kalberg, Stephen (2001) Editor's Introduction. In *Max Weber: the Protestant Ethic and the Spirit of Capitalism*. Los Angeles: Roxbury Publishing Co.

Kalberg, Stephen (forthcoming) *Max Weber's Sociology of Civilizations*.

Loewenstein, K. (1966) *Max Weber's Political Ideas in the Perspective of Our Time*. Amherst: University of Massachusetts Press.

Loewith, Karl (1970) Weber's Interpretation of the Bourgeois-capitalistic World in Terms of the Guiding Principle of "Rationalization." In Dennis Wrong (ed.), *Max Weber*. Englewood Cliffs, NJ: Prentice Hall, pp. 101–23.

Marshall, Gordon (1980) *Presbyteries and Profits: Calvinism and the Development of Capitalism in Scotland, 1560–1707*. Oxford: Clarendon Press.

Mitzman, Arthur (1970) *The Iron Cage*. New York: Knopf.

Mosse, George (1964) *The Crisis of German Ideology*. New York: Grosset & Dunlap.

Ringer, Fritz (1969) *The Decline of the German Mandarins.* Cambridge, MA: Harvard University Press.

Roth, Guenther (1968) Introduction. In Guenther Roth and Claus Wittich (eds and trans.), Max Weber, *Economy and Society.* New York: Bedminster Press, pp. xxvii–ciii.

Roth, Guenther (1997) The Young Max Weber: Anglo-American Religious Influences and Protestant Social Reform in Germany. *International Journal of Politics, Culture and Society,* 10, 659–71.

Salomon, Albert (1934) Max Weber's Methodology. *Social Research,* 1 (May), 147–68.

Salomon, Albert (1935a) Max Weber's Sociology. *Social Research,* 2 (February), 60–73.

Salomon, Albert (1935b) Max Weber's Political Ideas. *Social Research,* 2 (February), 369–84.

Walliman, Isidor, Rosenbaum, Howard, Tatsis, Nicholas and Zito, George (1980) Misreading Weber: the Concept of "Macht." *Sociology,* 14(2), 261–75.

Weber, Marianne (1975) *Max Weber,* translated by Harry Zohn. New York: Wiley.

# 6

## Émile Durkheim

### Robert Alun Jones

### The Theory

It is useful to think of social theories as "languages" or "vocabularies" – i.e. ways of thinking or speaking about social phenomena – that are cobbled together by theorists to serve their own, quite concrete interests and purposes. Sociologists whose interest is in the explanation, prediction, and control of human behavior, for example, typically prefer vocabularies containing "thin," abstract, statistical, and mathematical terms. By contrast, those who want to praise or condemn certain behaviors or institutions, establish relations with other cultures or sub-cultures, understand different languages, or grasp the nature of others' suffering will quite naturally prefer "thicker" descriptions, and more interpretive or hermeneutic vocabularies. Sociologists of the first kind tend to view themselves as "discovering facts" about the nature of societies, thus carrying on the tradition of Plato, Kant, Enlightenment rationalism, and modern science. Sociologists of the second type see their allies in Hegel, the Romantics, Nietzsche, Heidegger, James, and Dewey, and are more likely to describe themselves as "constructing narratives" like those of a writer or poet.

Durkheim was clearly a theorist of the first type, i.e. he saw himself as a scientist, "discovering" causal and functional explanations for social facts, which he viewed as a part of nature. But Durkheim's preference for this "scientific" vocabulary, by contrast with its more "literary" counterpart, was still a consequence of his own interests and purposes. The specific nature of these interests and purposes is most obvious in Durkheim's writings on the history and theory of education, and this is where my account of his socio-logical theory will begin. From there, I will move on to a discussion of his sociological method, i.e. the "tool" he used in the effort to realize these interests and purposes. Finally, I will discuss the substantive application of this tool to the study of social facts, including the division of labor, suicide, religion, knowledge, and science itself.

## The history and theory of moral education

Shortly after assuming his position at the Sorbonne in 1902, Durkheim began offering a lecture course on the history of educational theory, later published as *The Evolution of Educational Thought* (1938; translated 1977). Throughout history, he observed, the principal aim of education had never been to provide children with "pieces of knowledge," but rather to imbue them with "some deep and internal state of mind, a kind of orientation of the soul which points it in a definite direction, not only during childhood but throughout life" (Durkheim, 1977, p. 30). The Scholastics, for example, evinced an almost superstitious respect toward books, not because they believed these books contained demonstrable truths, but rather because they contained resources useful in *dialectic*, i.e. in scholastic debate. During the Renaissance, this "cult of the book" gave way to a preoccupation with elegance and style, and a form of aesthetic education that Durkheim loathed. But in the seventeenth and eighteenth centuries, this concern for style was in turn replaced by the "pre-eminence of things" – the modern, scientific study of concrete natural phenomena, in all their diversity and complexity. Necessarily secular, Durkheim observed, this modern education must still acknowledge our moral and spiritual needs and, in particular, help us to understand our place in nature, and the extent of our dependence upon it (Durkheim, 1977, pp. 337–8).

A second lecture course on education, published posthumously as *Moral Education* (1925; translated 1961), described the nature of this modern form of education in greater detail. Opposing the Enlightenment notion that there is a single, constant "human nature," Durkheim began by insisting that a society's ideal conception of a person – the kind of moral agent its educational system strives to produce – is relative to each historical period. Educational ideals thus express not the proclivities of individual human nature, but the real needs of real societies; and far from eliciting hidden potentialities within each of us, education actually creates within each of us a new person. Although an ardent supporter of the Third Republic's policies of laicizing the primary and secondary schools, therefore, Durkheim insisted that the historic process of secularizing education could not be simply negative: "It is not enough to cut out," he argued, "we must replace" (Durkheim, 1961, p. 11).

But what kind of person does modern society require? Durkheim's answer comprised three elements. Convinced that the decline of religious authority had left society without any rule or order, Durkheim insisted that the first element of moral education was the "spirit of discipline," i.e. an authoritative constraint existing outside of us, to which our wills and inclinations are subject. This in itself was hardly original, for "discipline" already held an important place in the moral philosophies of Kant and the utilitarians, where it identified and then directed the behavior required by either the categorical imperative or the law of utility. Discipline, in this sense, was necessary to thwart and constrain an otherwise recalcitrant human nature. The distinctive feature of Durkheim's argument – reflecting his more mature understanding of Rousseau – was that discipline was good *intrinsically*, that it was *natural* to human beings because the constraints *themselves* were a part of nature (Durkheim, 1961, pp. 50–1).

Turning to the content of moral education, Durkheim reminded his students that no "egoistic act" – i.e. behavior directed only to the self-interest of the person performing it – had ever been considered moral by any society. But again, Durkheim's point wasn't simply that "moral" acts, by definition, look to the interest of others; on the contrary, a morality elevating the interest of others above those of the self would be self-contradictory, for no person could then accept the other's self-denial. By definition, moral acts must be common and accessible to all, yet at the same time addressed to a living, sentient being outside the self. The only empirically observable entity fitting this definition was the being created by individuals through their association. In this way, Durkheim smoothly folded a major part of the traditional morality of the Church – good works done for others, but ultimately for God – within the secular morality of the Republic, and "the attachment to social groups" thus became the second element of moral education.

As we shall see, this distinction between the "spirit of discipline" and the "attachment to groups" was analogous to a more famous discussion in *Suicide* (1897) – between "regulation" and "integration" – as well as to the more traditional philosophic opposition of "duty" and the "good." But in more traditional usage, Durkheim observed, there is a tension between them: Kantians and rationalists habitually deduce the good from the imperative nature of moral commands, while utilitarians and empiricists frequently derive the sense of duty of the desirability of the consequences of morally obligatory acts. With his typical enthusiasm for the resolution of antinomies, Durkheim insisted that his conception of society as the sole, necessary, and sufficient object of moral conduct contained the means to resolve this contradiction. "Duty" and the "good" are simply two equally appropriate ways of speaking of the same concrete reality: society. There is no genuinely moral act that is not guided by both (Durkheim, 1961, p. 99).

To these two elements of morality, Durkheim then added a third – the autonomy of the individual. For Kant, such autonomy had been the product of the will, guided by a law of pure, transcendent reason (the categorical imperative), imposing itself on the more sensual, inferior aspects of our nature. But our experience of the moral law, Durkheim argued, suggests that it dominates not just our senses, but our reason as well – indeed, our whole nature. Moreover, if the autonomy which Kant would grant us is *logically* possible, it has nothing to do with *reality*, for as creatures both rational and sensual, we would be at war with ourselves.

Instead of a logical autonomy, therefore, Durkheim demanded an effective, progressive autonomy assured only by the study and practice of science. In so far as we *understand* the laws of things – why things are the way they are – we no longer conform out of external constraint, but voluntarily, because it is good to do so, and because we have no more rational alternative. "Conforming to the order of things because one is sure that it is everything it ought to be," Durkheim observed, "is not submitting to a constraint. It is freely desiring this order, assenting through an understanding of the cause" (Durkheim, 1961, p. 115). But the "science" that yields an understanding of these laws is not the product of *individual* reason, any more than *individual* reason created the laws which science understands; rather, science is the *collective* activity dreamed of by Bacon, in which one aspect of nature (society) progressively comprehends another (the physical world).

Durkheim's vocabulary was an attempt to extend this "collective activity" to the understanding of the laws of society. By investigating the degree to which the moral order is founded on the nature of things, he felt that we could learn the extent to which it is as it ought to be, i.e. "normal" rather than "pathological" (see below); and in so far as it is normal, we "freely" (i.e. knowledgeably and consciously) conform. So, henceforth, morality had to be taught by explaining the reasons for things, the causes underlying the particular duties of individuals and groups, and the specific ideals which emerged at certain stages of social evolution. The original element in this argument was not his insistence that this could be done, but his insistence that it could be done without diminishing the dignity and authority of moral rules. As an element of morality itself, the rational comprehension of the reasons for moral rules and ideals became a condition of moral agency itself. For Durkheim, therefore, the study of science – including social science – was itself morally edifying. To produce generations of students capable of such edification was the function not of the Church, but of the School, and, more particularly, of the nascent but rapidly growing discipline of sociology.

## Social facts

For Durkheim, sociology was thus an instrument to a larger purpose – the creation of the "new man" of the Republic, to be achieved by confronting generations of French schoolchildren with a moral power greater than themselves, and thus worthy of their respect and dedication. In *The Rules of Sociological Method* (1895; translated 1982), therefore, Durkheim described sociology as the study of a reality *sui generis*, a group of phenomena different from those studied by any other science. For these phenomena, Durkheim reserved the term *social facts*: "manners of acting, thinking, and feeling external to the individual, which are invested with a coercive power by virtue of which they exercise control over him" (Durkheim, 1982, p. 52). Since these facts consisted of actions, thoughts, and feelings, they could not be confused with biological phenomena; but neither were they the province of psychology, for they existed outside the individual *conscience*.

In addition to defining the subject matter of sociology, *The Rules* was explicit on how social facts were to be recognized and observed. Because the essential trait of social facts is their external coercive power, for example, they could be recognized by the existence of some predetermined legal sanction or, in the case of moral and religious beliefs, by their reaction to forms of individual belief and action perceived as threatening; and where the exercise of social constraint was less direct, as in those forms of economic organization which give rise to anomie (see below), their presence was more easily ascertained by their "generality combined with objectivity," i.e. by how widespread they are within the group, while also existing independently of any particular forms they might assume. Like Francis Bacon, Durkheim also warned us of the quite natural tendency to take our *ideas* of things – what Bacon called *notiones vulgares, praenotiones*, or "idols" – for the *things themselves*. So the most basic rule of all sociological method is *to treat social facts as things*. Other rules followed. As we will see in the discussion of *Suicide* (1897) and *The Elementary Forms of the Religious Life* (1912), for example, the subject matter of research was to include a group of phenomena defined beforehand by certain common external characteristics, and all phenomena corresponding to this definition had to be included; and Durkheim also insisted that sociologists consider social facts from a perspective independent of their individual manifestations.

## Normal and pathological

It is by following such rules, as we have seen, that the sociologist can learn the degree to which the moral order is founded on the nature of things, and thus the extent to which it is as it ought to be. This meant that the sociologist must be able to distinguish between the "normal" and "pathological" forms of social facts. "Normal" social facts are simply those found in many, if not all, cases, most of the time, while social facts are "pathological" if they are encountered only in a minority of cases, and for brief periods.

Despite centuries of effort at its annihilation, for example, crime has increased with the growth of civilization. A certain rate of crime, Durkheim thus argued, is a normal social fact, intimately bound up with the conditions of social life. Durkheim wasn't simply saying that crime is a necessary evil. On the contrary, he was arguing that crime is both *necessary* and *useful*. If we consider "crime" as Durkheim did – i.e. as an action that offends strong, well defined collective feelings – then such actions could be eliminated in a society only by a dramatic increase in the strength of these feelings; but if this occurred, those weaker states of collective sentiment, whose milder reactions previously acknowledged mere "breaches of convention," would also be strengthened, and what was merely "unconventional" would automatically become criminal. Moreover, for sentiments to change, they can be only moderately intense, while the only condition under which crime could cease – as we have just seen – must be one in which collective sentiments had attained an unprecedented intensity. The criminal thus becomes the price we pay for the idealist and the reformer.

By contrast with the "normality" of crime, Durkheim described the "forced" and "anomic" forms of the division of labor, as well as the extraordinarily high rates of "egoistic" and "anomic" suicide, as pathological. Consistent with his notion that the sociologist was a kind of physician, he then called for "therapeutic treatment," which – as Durkheim despaired of the modern state to perform such a regulative function – meant an increased role for occupational groups in the supervision of insurance, welfare, and pensions, the settling of contractual disputes, the regulation of working conditions, but above all exercising moral authority over the aspirations of upwardly mobile citizens of the Republic (Durkheim, 1893, translated 1984, pp. 291–328; 1897, translated 1951, pp. 378–84).

## Causal and functional explanation

Durkheim was careful to avoid any "teleological" confusion of the *function* of a social fact (the role it plays with regard to individual or social needs) with its *cause* (the fact which brought it into existence). For once we recognize that social facts are real things, external to and coercive upon human beings, it becomes clear that no human need or desire, however imperious, could be sufficient to such an effect. Needs and desires might intervene to hasten or retard social development, but they cannot themselves create any social fact. The association of individual human beings creates a social reality of a new kind, and it is in the facts of that association rather than the needs and interests of the associated elements that the explanation for social facts is to be found.

This led Durkheim to some rules of sociological explanation. When the sociologist attempts to explain a social phenomenon, for example, the efficient cause which produces it and the function it fulfills must be investigated separately. Second, the determining cause of a social fact must he sought among the antecedent social facts, and not among the states of the individual consciousness. Durkheim went so far as to insist that "every time a social phenomenon is directly explained by a psychological phenomenon, we may rest assured that the explanation is false" (Durkheim, 1982, p. 129). Finally, while Durkheim did not deny that a social fact may serve individual needs and interests, sociologists should still seek its function in its socially useful effects (Durkheim, 1982, pp. 134–5).

To demonstrate that one phenomenon is the cause of another, we can only compare those cases where both are simultaneously present (or absent), and ask whether the variations they display in these different circumstances suggest that one depends upon the other. Where the two phenomena are produced artificially by the observer, we call this method *experimentation*; and where the artificial production of phenomena is impossible, we compare them as they have been produced naturally, a procedure called *indirect experimentation*, or the *comparative method*. Here Durkheim embraced J. S. Mill's theory of "concomitant variation" – the notion that phenomena that vary together are connected through some fact of causation. For the manner in which a phenomenon develops reveals its internal nature, and where two phenomena develop in the same way, there must thus be some internal connection between the natures thus revealed.

## The function of the division of labor

Durkheim's purpose in *The Division of Labor in Society* (1893, translated 1984) was to show that the increasing rate of occupational specialization in Western societies is a social fact which can be explained, both causally and functionally, by following the principles just described. Beginning with the functional explanation, Durkheim pointed out that, while we like those who resemble us, we are also drawn toward those who are different. But if difference is thus as much a source of mutual attraction as likeness, only *certain kinds* of differences attract, i.e. where we seek in others what we lack in ourselves. Associations are formed wherever there is such a true exchange of services – in short, wherever there is a division of labor. Durkheim thus argued that the economic services rendered by the division of labor are trivial by comparison with its *moral* effect. The true function of the division of labor is that feeling of solidarity in two or more persons which it creates, rendering possible societies which, without it, would not exist.

To determine the extent to which modern societies depend upon this kind of solidarity, Durkheim classified different types of law according to the sanctions associated with them: *repressive* sanctions (characteristic of criminal law) consist of some loss or suffering inflicted on the agent; *restitutive* sanctions (characteristic of civil, commercial, procedural, administrative, and constitutional law) consist only of "the re-establishment of troubled relations to their normal state" (Durkheim, 1984, p. 69). Durkheim was thus able to define two types of solidarity. The first was *mechanical solidarity*, that type of solidarity characterized by the repressive sanctions imposed upon crimes. Since all crimes have one element in common – i.e. they shock sentiments which, "for a given social system, are found in all healthy consciences" – Durkheim was led directly to his important concept of the *conscience collective*: "the totality of beliefs and sentiments common to the average citizens of the same society" (Durkheim, 1984, p. 79). Durkheim endowed the *conscience collective* with quite distinctive characteristics: it forms a determinate system with its own life; it is "diffuse" in each society and lacks a "specific organ"; it is independent of the particular conditions in which individuals find themselves; it is the same in different locations, classes, and occupations; it connects successive generations rather than changing from one to another; and it is different from individual *consciences*, despite the fact that it can be realized only through them.

Durkheim thus introduced an idea which would assume increasing importance in his later work – the duality of human nature. Briefly, in each of us there are two *consciences*: one containing states personal to each of us, representing and constituting our individual personality; the other containing states common to all, representing society, and without which society would not exist. When our conduct is determined by the first, we act out of self-interest; but when it is determined by the second, we act morally, in the interest of society. Thus the individual, by virtue of his resemblance to other individuals, is linked to the social order. This is mechanical solidarity, which, as we have seen, is manifested through repressive law; and the greater the number of repressive laws, the greater the number of social relations regulated by this type of solidarity. The nature of *restitutive* sanctions, however, indicates that there is a different type of social solidarity which corresponds to civil law; for the restitutive sanction is not punitive, vengeful, or expiatory at all, but consists only of a return of things to their previous, normal state. This is the type of solidarity that Durkheim called *organic*, i.e. where mechanical solidarity presumes that individuals resemble one another, organic solidarity presumes their difference; again, where mechanical solidarity is possible only in so far as the individual personality is submerged in the collectivity, organic solidarity becomes possible only in so far as each individual has a sphere of action peculiar to him. For organic solidarity to emerge, therefore, the *conscience collective* must leave untouched a part of the individual *conscience*, so that special functions, which the *conscience collective* itself cannot tolerate, may be established there; and the more this region of the individual *conscience* is extended, the stronger is the cohesion which results from this particular kind of solidarity.

Durkheim thus postulated two distinct types of social solidarity (mechanical and organic), each with its distinctive form of juridical rules (repressive and restitutive). To determine their relative importance in any given societal type, he simply compared the respective extent of the two kinds of rules. The preponderance of repressive rules over their restitutive counterparts, for example, should be just as great as the preponderance of the *conscience collective* over the division of labor; inversely, in so far as the individual personality and the specialization of tasks is developed, the relative proportion of the two types of law ought to be reversed. On the basis of these comparisons, Durkheim was then able to argue that primitive societies are held together primarily by the *conscience collective*, while more advanced societies enjoy that type of solidarity associated with the division of labor.

As we have seen, Durkheim always distinguished the causes of a social fact from its functions. So the causes of the division of labor could not possibly consist in some anticipation of its moral effects, for, as we have seen, those effects could hardly be foreseen. Instead, Durkheim's explanation referred to something he called *dynamic* or *moral density*. First, the real, material distance between members of a society is gradually reduced both spatially (e.g. the growth of cities) and technologically (e.g. advances in communications and transportation); second, this effect is reinforced by the sheer "social volume" of a society (the total number of its members). Durkheim thus claimed to have discovered a law of human societies, i.e. the division of labor varies in direct ratio to the dynamic or moral density of society, which is itself an effect of both material density and social volume.

## Defining suicide

Durkheim defined "suicide" as any death which is the immediate or eventual result of a positive or negative act accomplished by the victim himself, when the victim *knows* that death will be the result of his act (regardless of whether or not death is his goal). This definition was subject to two immediate objections. The first was that such foreknowledge is a matter of degree, varying considerably from one person or situation to another. At what point, for example, does the death of a professional daredevil or that of a man neglectful of his health cease to be an "accident" and start to become "suicide"? But for Durkheim, to ask this question was less to raise an objection to his definition than to correctly identify its greatest advantage: that it indicates the place of suicide within moral life as a whole. Suicides, according to Durkheim, do not constitute a wholly distinctive group of "monstrous phenomena" unrelated to other forms of behavior; on the contrary, they are related to other acts, both courageous and imprudent, by an unbroken series of intermediate cases. Suicides, in short, are simply an exaggerated form of common practices. The second objection was that such practices are individual practices, with individual causes and consequences, which are thus the proper subject matter of psychology rather than sociology. In fact, Durkheim never denied that suicide could be studied by the methods of psychology, but he did insist that suicide could also be studied independent of its individual manifestations, as a social fact *sui generis*. Each society, Durkheim argued, has a "definite aptitude" for suicide, the relative intensity of which can be measured by the proportion of suicides per total population, or what Durkheim called "the rate of mortality through suicide, characteristic of the society under consideration" (Durkheim, 1977, p. 48). This rate was both *permanent* (the rate for any individual society was less variable than that of most other leading demographic data, including the general mortality rate) and *variable* (the rate for each society was sufficiently peculiar to that society as to be more characteristic of it than its general mortality rate). Each society, Durkheim thus concluded, is predisposed to contribute a definite quota of suicides; and it was this predisposition which Durkheim studied sociologically.

## The four types of suicide

Durkheim acknowledged that there were two kinds of extrasocial causes sufficiently general to have a possible effect on the social suicide rate: *individual-psychological* factors (race, heredity, insanity, neurasthenia, alcoholism, etc.) which, varying from country to country, might explain variations in the suicide rates for those societies; and those aspects of the *external physical environment* (climate, temperature, etc.) which might have the same effect. When neither psychology nor the environment seemed to explain much of the social suicide rate, Durkheim turned to "states of the various social environments" – religious confessions, familial and political society, occupational groups, etc. – across which the variations in suicide rates occurred, and within which their causes might be found. If we look at a map of Western Europe, for example, we see that where Protestants are most numerous the suicide rate is highest, that where Catholics predominate it is much lower, and that the aptitude of Jews for suicide is lower still, though to a lesser degree, than that of Catholics. How are these data to be explained? Again Durkheim considered various causes (minority status, the religious doctrine, the Protestant "spirit of free inquiry," etc.), ultimately concluding that the lack of a common, collective *credo* among Protestants – the more limited extent of their social integration – explains their greater proclivity for suicide.

But if religion thus preserves men from suicide because it is a society, Durkheim reasoned, other "societies" (e.g. the family and political society) ought to have the same effect; and, in fact, Durkheim showed that, while marriage alone has a preservative effect against suicide, this is limited and benefits only men, while the addition of children provides an immunity which husband and wife share. When one marital partner dies, the survivor loses a degree of suicidal immunity, while the immunity to suicide increases with the size of the family, a fact Durkheim attributed to the greater number and intensity of collective sentiments produced and repeatedly reinforced by the larger group. Similarly, the examination of political societies showed that suicide, quite rare in a society's early stages, increases as that society matures and disintegrates. During social disturbances or great popular wars, by contrast, the suicide rate declines, because these disturbances arouse collective sentiments. Suicide thus varies inversely with the degree of integration of the religious, domestic, and political groups of which the individual forms a part; in short, as a society weakens or "disintegrates," the individual depends less on the group, depends more upon himself, and recognizes no rules of conduct beyond those based upon private interests. Durkheim called this state of "excessive individualism" *egoism*, and the type of self-inflicted death it produces *egoistic suicide*.

But if excessive individualism (insufficient integration) thus leads to suicide, so does excessive integration. In primitive societies, religious groups, and the military, we find several kinds of suicide – men on the threshold of old age, women upon the deaths of their husbands, martyrs to religious persecution, servants upon the deaths of their chiefs, soldiers in the heat of battle – in which the person kills himself *because it is his duty*. Such a sacrifice, Durkheim argued, is imposed by society for social purposes; and for society to be able to do this, the individual personality must have little value, a state Durkheim called *altruism*, and whose corresponding mode of self-inflicted death was called *obligatory altruistic suicide*. Altruistic suicide thus reflects that crude morality which disregards the individual, while its egoistic counterpart elevates the human personality beyond collective constraints; and their differences thus correspond to those between primitive and advanced societies.

Egoistic and altruistic suicide are thus the respective consequences of the individual's insufficient or excessive integration within the society to which he belongs. But quite aside from integrating its members, a society must control and regulate beliefs and behavior as well; and Durkheim insisted that there is a relation between a society's suicide rate and the way it performs this important regulative function. Where such constraints are excessive, for example, the individual becomes vulnerable to a type of suicide that Durkheim called *fatalistic*, although he considered it of little contemporary significance, and devoted only a footnote to its discussion. Far more interesting were those instances in which economic prosperity – and thus a weakening of social constraints – was accompanied by dramatic increases in the suicide rate.

How can something generally understood to improve a person's life, Durkheim asked, serve to detach him from it? The answer – which reveals how much he had learned from Rousseau (see below) – was that no living being can be happy unless its needs are sufficiently proportioned to its means; for if needs surpass the capacity to satisfy them, the result can only be a weakening of the impulse to live. In Rousseau's state of nature, of course, the desired equilibrium between needs and means is established and maintained by the laws of nature, e.g. an animal cannot imagine ends other than those implicit within its own physiology, and these are ordinarily satisfied by its purely material environment. Among human beings in more advanced societies, however, "a more awakened reflection" suggests better conditions and more desirable ends; and the aspirations implied by such reflections are inherently unlimited, and thus insatiable. "To pursue a goal which is by definition unattainable," Durkheim concluded, "is to condemn oneself to a state of perpetual unhappiness" (Durkheim, 1951, pp. 247–8). For human beings to be happy, therefore, their individual needs and aspirations must be constrained; and this regulatory function must thus be performed by an external, moral agency superior to the individual – in other words, by society. Durkheim used the term anomie to describe this temporary condition of social deregulation, and anomic suicide to describe the resulting type of self-inflicted death. In the sphere of trade and industry, Durkheim insisted that anomie is less a temporary disruption than a chronic condition. "From top to bottom of the ladder," Durkheim argued, "greed is aroused without knowing where to find ultimate foothold. Nothing can calm it, since its goal is far beyond all it can attain" (Durkheim, 1951, p. 256). Like Rousseau, therefore, Durkheim presents us with a devastating picture of the ambitious, indefatigable bourgeois.

## Collective representations

The terms that Durkheim employed in making this argument – "collective tendencies," "collective passions," etc. – were not mere metaphors for average individual psychological states; on the contrary, they were "things," *sui generis* forces which dominate the consciousnesses of individuals. Such an argument, Durkheim admitted, suggests that collective thoughts are of a different nature from individual thoughts, and that the former have characteristics which the latter do not. Individual human beings, by associating with one another, form a psychical existence of a new species, which has its own manner of thinking and feeling. Social life, Durkheim thus admitted, is essentially made up of *representations*; but *collective* representations are quite different from their individual counterparts. In fact, these three currents of opinion – that the individual has a certain personality (egoism), that this personality should be sacrificed if the community required it (altruism), and that the individual is sensitive to ideas of social progress (anomie) – coexist in all societies, turning individual inclinations in three different and opposed directions. Where these currents offset one another, the individual enjoys a state of equilibrium which protects him from suicide; but where one current exceeds a certain strength relative to others, it becomes a cause of self-inflicted death.

## Totemism as the most elementary form of religion

Durkheim's primary purpose in *The Elementary Forms* was to describe and explain the most primitive religion known to man, not for its own sake, but in order to better understand "the religious nature of man" (Durkheim, 1915, p. 13). As he had in *Suicide*, Durkheim began *The Elementary Forms* with the problem of defining his subject matter, including a rejection of earlier attempts to define religion as a belief in the "mysterious," "unknowable," "supernatural," "spiritual beings," etc. The difficulty with all such attempts, Durkheim observed, is that these ideas are frequently absent not only in primitive religions, but even in their more advanced counterparts. Emphasizing that religion is less an indivisible whole than a complex system of parts, and that magic – though similar to religion in certain respects – lacks a "church," Durkheim arrived at his own definition: "A religion is a unified system of beliefs and practices relative to sacred things, that is to say, things set apart and forbidden – beliefs and practices which unite into one single moral community called a Church, all those who adhere to them" (Durkheim, 1915, p. 62).

If this is "religion," what is religion's most elementary form? Some writers, like E. B. Tylor and Herbert Spencer, had argued that the earliest form of religion was animism: the worship of the souls of dead ancestors, whose existence was inferred from primitive dream experience. Others, including Max Müller, insisted that the earliest objects of religious belief were the phenomena of nature. But if the animistic hypothesis is true, Durkheim objected, it would mean not only that religious symbols provide an inexact expression of the realities on which they are based (something Durkheim believed), but also that religious symbols are products of the vague, ill-conceived hallucinations of dream-experience – and thus have no foundation in reality at all (something Durkheim most certainly did *not* believe). The naturistic hypothesis seemed to avoid this objection, by basing primitive religious ideas on the *real* forces of nature. But religion itself begins, Durkheim objected, only when these natural forces are transformed into personal spirits or gods, to whom the "cult of nature" might then be addressed. These forces and the reflections upon them could hardly be the source of religious ideas, for such ideas would provide a misleading conception of those natural forces upon which people depend for their very survival. Any course of practical activity based upon them would be unsuccessful, and this would surely undermine faith in the ideas themselves. In effect, Durkheim's objection to both hypotheses was the same – the importance of religious ideas throughout history and in all societies is evidence that they must correspond to some reality.

Durkheim thus considered totemism – the worship of animals and plants – as the most elementary form of religion. The members of totemic clans consider themselves bound together by a special kind of kinship, based not on blood, but on the mere fact that they share the same name. This name is taken from a determined species of material objects (an animal, less frequently a plant, and in rare cases an inanimate object) with which the clan members are assumed to enjoy the same relations of kinship. But this "totem" is not simply a name; it is also an emblem, which is carved, engraved, or drawn upon other objects belonging to the clan, and even upon the bodies of the clan members themselves. These designs seem to render otherwise common objects "sacred," and their inscription upon the bodies of clan members indicates the approach of the most important religious ceremonies. Since the same religious sentiments aroused by these designs are aroused by the members of the totemic species themselves, clan members are forbidden to kill or eat the totemic animal or plant except at certain mystical feasts, and the violation of this interdiction is assumed to produce death instantaneously.

## The explanation of totemic beliefs

Durkheim explained these beliefs by appealing to the Melanesian belief in *mana* – a diffused, impersonal "force" that could be invested in certain objects, rendering them sacred. To explain totemism was thus to explain the belief in this impersonal religious principle. How could such a belief be explained? Obviously not from sensations aroused by the totemic objects themselves, for these objects – the caterpillar, the ant, the frog, etc. – are hardly of a kind to inspire powerful religious emotions; on the contrary, these objects appear to be the symbols or material expressions of something else. Of what, then, are they the symbols? Durkheim's answer was that the totemic animal symbolized the clan itself, and that god is nothing more than society apotheosized (Durkheim, 1915, p. 236). In support of this extraordinary claim, Durkheim insisted that society, whether primitive or advanced, has everything necessary to arouse the idea of the divine, e.g. it is both physically and morally superior to individuals, and thus individuals both fear its power and respect its authority. Like the gods, society cannot exist except in and through the individual *conscience*, and thus it both demands our sacrifices and periodically strengthens and elevates the divine "principle" within each of us – especially during periods of collective enthusiasm. It is during such extremely rare gatherings of the entire Australian clan, for example, that the religious idea itself seems to have been born, a fact which explained why its most important religious ceremonies continue to be observed only periodically, when the clan as a whole is assembled. It is this succession of intense periods of "collective effervescence" with much longer periods of dispersed, individualistic economic activity, Durkheim suggested, which gives rise to the belief that there are two worlds – the sacred and the profane – both within us and within nature itself. Most important, the sense thus inspired is not an illusion, but is based on reality; for however misunderstood, there actually is a *real* moral power – society – to which these beliefs correspond, and from which the worshipper derives strength.

## The sociology of knowledge

The secondary purpose of *The Elementary Forms* was by far the most ambitious of Durkheim's attempts to provide sociological answers to philosophical questions. At the base of all our judgments there are a certain number of ideas which philosophers since Aristotle have called "the categories of the understanding": time, space, class, number, cause, substance, personality, and so on. When primitive religious beliefs are analyzed, Durkheim observed, these "categories" are found, suggesting that they are the product of religious thought; but as we have seen, religious thought itself is composed of collective representations, the products of real social groups.

These observations suggested to Durkheim that the "problem of knowledge" might be posed in new, sociological terms. Previous efforts to solve this problem had taken one of two philosophical positions: the *empiricist* doctrine that the categories are constructed out of human experience, and that the individual is the artisan of this construction; and the *a priorist* doctrine that the categories are logically prior to experience, and are inherent in the nature of the human intellect itself. The difficulty for the *empirical* thesis, according to Durkheim, was that it deprives the categories of their most distinctive properties: *universality* (they are the most general concepts we have, are applicable to all that is real, and are independent of every particular object) and *necessity* (we literally cannot think without them). For it is in the very nature of empirical data that they be both particular and contingent. The *a priorist* thesis, by contrast, has more respect for these properties of universality and necessity; but by asserting that the categories simply "inhere" in the nature of the intellect, it begs the question of where these categories come from. In sum, if reason is simply a variety of individual experience, it no longer exists; but if its distinctive properties are recognized but not explained, it is set beyond the bounds of nature and thus of scientific investigation.

If we admit the social origin of the categories, Durkheim argued, these problems go away. First, the basic proposition of the *a priorist* thesis is that knowledge is composed of two elements – perceptions mediated by our senses, and the categories of the understanding – neither of which can be reduced to the other. By viewing the first as *individual* representations and the second as their *collective* counterparts, this proposition is left intact (Durkheim, 1915, p. 28). Second, this hypothesis is equally consistent with the duality of human nature – just as our moral ideals are irreducible to our utilitarian motives, so our reason is irreducible to our experience. In so far as we belong to society, therefore, we transcend our individual nature both when we *act* and when we *think*. Finally, this distinction explains both the *universality* and the *necessity* of the categories: they are universal because man has always and everywhere lived in society, which is their origin; and they are necessary because, without them, all contact between individual minds would be impossible, and social life would be destroyed altogether (Durkheim, 1915, p. 30). One might still object that, since the categories are now mere representations of social realities, there is no guarantee of their correspondence to any of the realities of nature. Durkheim's rationalist and rather metaphysical reply was that society itself is a part of nature, and "it is impossible that nature should differ radically from itself" (Durkheim, 1915, p. 31).

## Religion and science

Religion reflects on nature, man, and society, attempts to classify things, relates them to one another, and explains them; and as we have just seen, even the most essential categories of scientific thought are religious in origin. Scientific thought, in short, is but a more perfect form of religious thought; and Durkheim thus felt that the latter would gradually give way before the inexorable advances of the former, including those advances in the social sciences extending to the scientific study of religion itself. But religion is also a form of *action* – the religious believer is not just someone who sees new truths, but one who is more joyful, peaceful, and/or strong for being with his god. Durkheim thus agreed with William James, who, in *The Varieties of Religious Experience* (1902), had argued that religious beliefs rest upon real experiences whose demonstrative value, though different, is in no way inferior to that of scientific experiments. As with such experiments, Durkheim added, it does not follow that the reality which gives rise to these experiences precisely corresponds to the ideas that believers (or scientists) form of it; but it is a reality just the same, and for Durkheim, the reality was society. Durkheim also felt that all societies need such periodic reaffirmations of their collective sentiments, and that there is thus something "eternal" in religion, destined to outlive the particular symbols – totemic, Christian, or otherwise – in which it had been previously embodied.

Like Kant, therefore, Durkheim denied any conflict between science, on the one hand, and morality and religion, on the other; for, also like Kant, he felt that both were directed toward universal principles, and that both thus implied that, in thought as in action, man can lift himself above the limitations of his private, individual nature to live a rational, impersonal life. What Kant could not explain (indeed, he refused to do so) is the cause of this dual existence that we are forced to lead, torn between the sensible and intelligible worlds which, even as they seem to contradict each other, seem to presume and even require each other as well. But to Durkheim the explanation was clear: we lead an existence which is simultaneously both individual and social, and as individuals we can live without society no more than society can live without us.

## THE PERSON

David Émile Durkheim was born on April 15, 1858 in Epinal, in Lorraine, France. His mother was a merchant's daughter, and his father had been rabbi of Epinal since the 1830s. Part of his early education was thus spent in a rabbinical school; and while his later religious beliefs are best described as agnostic, he remained the product of a close-knit, orthodox Jewish family, as well as that long-established Jewish community of Alsace-Lorraine that had been occupied by Prussian troops in 1870, and suffered the resulting antisemitism of the French citizenry. An outstanding student at the Collège d'Epinal, Durkheim skipped two years, obtaining his *baccalauréats* in letters (1874) and sciences (1875) and distinguishing himself in the *Concours Général*. Intent on becoming a teacher, he left Epinal for Paris to prepare for admission to the prestigious École Normale Supérieure. Installed at a *pension* for non-resident students, however, he became utterly miserable: his father's illness left him anxious over his family's financial security; he was an utter *provincial* alone in Paris; and his intellectual predilections, already scientific rather than literary, were ill-fitted to the study of Latin and rhetoric essential for admission to the École. After failing in his first two attempts at the entrance examination (in 1877 and 1878), Durkheim was at last admitted near the end of 1879.

Despite constant fears of failure, which plagued him throughout his life, Durkheim became an active participant in the high-minded political and philosophical debates that characterized the École. He was soon a staunch advocate of the republican cause, with special admiration for Léon Gambetta, the brilliant orator and "spiritual embodiment" of the Third Republic, and the more moderate Jules Ferry, whose anticlerical educational reforms would soon lead to a national system of free, compulsory, secular education. Though ill through much of 1881 and 1882, Durkheim successfully passed his *agrégation* (the competitive examination required for admission to the teaching staff of state secondary schools, or *lycées*), and began teaching philosophy in 1882; and though his thesis preparation gradually focused on the relationship of the individual and society, it is clear that – until his fateful trip to Germany – he still thought like a philosopher rather than a sociologist.

Responding to intellectuals who blamed the humiliations of the Franco-Prussian War (1870–1) on the superiority of German education, the Ministry of Public Education in France had long made a point of awarding scholarships to the brightest young *agrégés* to visit Germany and become acquainted with recent scientific achievements. With this support, Durkheim was able to visit the universities of Marburg, Berlin, and Leipzig in 1885–6, and returned to publish two articles expressing his admiration for German philosophy and social science. In particular, he praised the "socialists of the chair" for their insistence on the social context of economic phenomena; the Germans' "organic" conception of the relationship between the individual and society, the generally Kantian philosophy and, above all, the scientific study of morality, particularly as pursued in the psychological laboratory of Wilhelm Wundt. For Wundt, according to Durkheim, had simultaneously recognized both the importance of independent social causes and the triviality of individual premeditation. The introduction of such a science of morality into the *lycées*, Durkheim thought, would create precisely that liberal, secular, republican ideology essential to the preservation of the Third Republic.

Fortuitously, an instrument for this purpose already existed. In 1882, the Faculty of Letters at Bordeaux had established France's first course in pedagogy for prospective school teachers, and in 1884 the state had begun to support it as part of its drive for a new system of secular, republican education. The course was first taught by Alfred Espinas, whose *Les Sociétés animales* (1877) Durkheim greatly admired, but who had soon been elevated to Dean of the Faculty. But Durkheim's articles on German philosophy and social science had caught the attention of Louis Liard, the Director of Higher Education in France. A devoted republican, Liard both resented the German pre-eminence in social science and was intrigued by Durkheim's suggestions for the reconstruction of a secular, scientific French morality. At the instigation of Espinas and Liard, therefore, Durkheim was appointed in 1887 as "Chargé d'un Cours de Science Sociale et de Pédagogie" at Bordeaux.

Throughout his years at Bordeaux (1887–1902), Durkheim's primary responsibility was to lecture on the theory, history, and practice of education. Each Saturday morning, however, he also taught a public lecture course on "social science," devoted to "specialized studies of particular social phenomena." It was in these public courses, some repeated several times in both Bordeaux and Paris, that Durkheim's major sociological ideas received their earliest expression, and also changed as he assimilated new ideas and intellectual influences. Durkheim's early approach to the study of social phenomena, for example, was largely evolutionary, historical, and comparative, and focused on law and custom as the best indices of change in social structure; gradually, he came to recognize the importance of ethnographic data, a trend epitomized in his focus on the "crucial experiment" of Australian aboriginal religion in *The Elementary Forms of the Religious Life* (1912). Again, Durkheim's early work exhibited a naive evolutionary optimism common to many Victorian social scientists, suggesting that advanced industrial societies (after a brief period of "pathological" disorganization) would be almost mechanically self-regulating; later, in part under the delayed influence of Albert Schaeffle's *Die Quintessenz des Sozialismus* (1875), he pointed to the need for external regulation by occupational groups, and would embrace socialism, not so much for its economic or political advantages, but because of its "morally regenerative" possibilities. And again, Durkheim's early discussion of the *conscience collective* suggested that shared ideas and beliefs are derivative features of forms of social organization; later, the concept itself virtually disappeared from Durkheim's writing, to be replaced by collective *représentations*, more complex, differentiated states of a society's consciousness, which were also granted increased autonomy and independent explanatory power.

The results of this shift became immediately evident in one of Durkheim's most important achievements: the founding of *l'Année sociologique* (1898–1913), the first social science journal in France. Supported by a brilliant group of young scholars, the *Année* was to provide an annual survey of the strictly sociological literature, to provide additional information on studies in other specialized fields (history of law, history of religion, ethnography, social statistics, economics, etc.), and to publish original monographs in sociology. And while he encouraged his contributors and collaborators simply to work within the general, impersonal framework established in his *Rules of Sociological Method* (1895), there is no doubt that Durkheim, whose own inclination was anti-eclectic if not dogmatic, and who revised virtually all copy and even supervised proofs, imposed his own, powerful personality on the publication.

In general, Durkheim was reluctant to enter the realm of politics, the two notable exceptions being the Dreyfus Affair and the First World War. A Dreyfusard from an early date, Durkheim considered the Affair "un moment de la conscience humaine." He was an active member of the Ligue pour la Défense des Droits de l'Homme, a Dreyfusard group, and when Ferdinand Brunetière, a staunch anti-Dreyfusard, published a defense of the army and the Church against the anarchistic "individualism" of French intellectuals, Durkheim responded with "Individualism and the Intellectuals" (1898), an important, sociologically based argument that modern individualism, unlike that of Rousseau and Kant, was a product of society, a secular "religion" that derived from Christianity, sanctified liberalism, and pointed in the direction of socialism. In 1902, when the successful resolution of the Dreyfus Affair had left both sociology and socialism with a more respectable public image, Durkheim was appointed *chargé d'un cours* in science and education at the Sorbonne. Four years later, he was made professeur by a unanimous vote, and in 1913 assumed the prestigious chair of "Science of Education and Sociology."

Durkheim arrived in Paris with a reputation as a powerful intellect pursuing an aggressively scientific approach to all problems (everything else was mysticism, dilettantism, and irrationalism). His "science of morality" offended philosophers, his "science of religion" offended Catholics, and his appointment to the Sorbonne (which, in the wake of the Dreyfus Affair, appeared not above political considerations) offended those on the Right. The appointment also gave Durkheim enormous power. His lecture courses were the only required courses at the Sorbonne, obligatory for all students seeking degrees in philosophy, history, literature, and languages; in addition, he was responsible for the education of successive generations of French schoolteachers, on whom he impressed his sociological theory of secular ethics. The sociology of morality had been an interest as early as his visit to Germany; and though his earliest conception of moral rules emphasized their external, obligatory character, this gradually shifted to an emphasis on the desirable, "eudaemonic" quality of moral actions. The development and deepening of this interest can be traced in both *The Division of Labor* (1893) and *Suicide* (1897); but Durkheim planned to recast these earlier views on morality in a major work entitled *La Morale*. Unfortunately, this went no further than a theoretical introduction, written in the last weeks of Durkheim's life and published three years later; but a sense of its projected content, which relies on a Kantian, "dualistic" conception of human nature, can be gathered from "The Determination of Moral Facts" (1906), "Value Judgments of and Judgments of Reality" (1911), and the discussion of morality in *The Elementary Forms of the Religious Life* (1912).

Of all Durkheim's works, none has afforded such sheer intellectual excitement as *The Elementary Forms*. This is all the more remarkable in light of the fact that, as Durkheim himself later admitted, his earlier treatment of religion was relatively mechanical and unimaginative. The significant change seems to have occurred as a consequence of a lecture course on religion given at Bordeaux in 1894–5, during which Durkheim became familiar with the work of Robertson Smith and James Frazer. Durkheim attempted a provisional statement of these new insights in "Concerning the Definition of Religious Phenomena" (1899); but he had not yet had the opportunity fully to digest the growing body of ethnography on primitive religions, and especially the important accounts of Australian aborigines published by Baldwin Spencer and F. J. Gillen in 1899 and 1904. When these data were combined with the seminal ideas of Robertson Smith's *Religion of the Semites* (1889) and Durkheim's own Kantian and neo-Kantian preconceptions, the result was *The Elementary Forms* – a work which, by any standard, remains a "classic" in the history of sociological thought.

The last course of lectures Durkheim offered before the war also stemmed from a question raised, but not answered, in *The Elementary Forms*: if, as Durkheim at least seemed to imply, all religions are "true in their own fashion," is truth itself "relative" to human interests and purposes? This question acquired a particular urgency in light of the affirmative answer given to it by William James, the increasing interest in James's pragmatism in France, and the use of James's works as a philosophical rationale for what Durkheim considered the anti-intellectualism of the time. Durkheim thus presented a series of lectures in 1913–14 which dealt not only with James but with the elaboration of James's ideas by the Oxford philosopher F. C. S. Schiller, their refinement by John Dewey (whom Durkheim greatly admired), and their extension in the works of Durkheim's life-long rival, Bergson.

With the outbreak of the First World War in August 1914 – despite poor health already induced by overwork – Durkheim devoted himself to the cause of national defense. But when his son, André, a gifted linguist and among the most promising of the younger *Année* circle, died in action, Durkheim withdrew into a "ferocious silence," eventually suffering a stroke. On November 15, 1917, he died at the age of 59.

## THE SOCIAL CONTEXT

"When a people has achieved a state of equilibrium and maturity," Durkheim observed in his seventh lecture on moral education, "then the preference for rule and order is naturally preponderant." But "in times of flux and change," the spirit of discipline "cannot preserve its moral vigor since the prevailing system of rules is shaken, at least in some of its parts. At such times, it is inevitable that we feel less keenly the authority of a discipline that is, in fact, attenuated." Durkheim had no illusions about the type of society or historical period he was living in: "We are going through precisely one of these critical phases," he emphasized. "Indeed, history records no crisis as serious as that in which European societies have been involved for more than a century" (Durkheim, 1961, p. 101).

The crisis was in part the consequence of demographic changes. As the birth rate steadily declined and the death rate remained stable, the traditional, fertile, Roman Catholic family confronted its modern, Malthusian counterpart. Parents, concerned to rise socially and to provide a good future for their children, calculated and looked ahead, reflecting the aspirations of individualism and egalitarianism – a movement which particularly affected the lower middle class (Mayeur and Rebérioux, 1984, p. 43). In 1897, Durkheim insisted that both the decrease in births and the increase in suicides were the consequence of a decline in domestic feelings, an increase in migration from the country to the towns, the break-up of the traditional family, and the "cold wind of egoism" which had ensued (Durkheim, 1951, pp. 198–202). Yet economic growth, rapid before 1860 and steady if unspectacular for the twenty years thereafter, slowed dramatically after 1880, a consequence of the decreasing per capita productivity of the labor force and the declining rate of urbanization. Once the second largest industrial power in the world, France quickly slipped to fourth (Mayeur and Rebérioux, 1984, p. 46). With a stable currency and no income tax, however, an urban bourgeois with an annual income of 20,000 francs paid as little as 2 percent in taxes; thus a doctor, lawyer, or engineer who had been prudent under the prosperity of the Second Empire could retire in his fifties with no decline in his standard of living, a prospect which gave rise to the unregulated aspirations symptomatic of Durkheim's "economic anomie." "Conservatives of the time," Mayeur and Rebérioux warn us, "like to assert that the individualism bred by the Revolution had undermined the family, but in fact family feeling had changed rather than weakened. The bourgeois family looked inward, concentrating on the child and his future. It was a family of limited births, anxious to rise in the world through birth control and saving" (Mayeur and Rebérioux, 1984, p. 71). The working class was primarily agricultural, and remained so until the end of the century; but the living conditions, manners, and mentality of the peasants had changed. Railways, especially the little cross-country lines, and improvements in local roads, went far to break down provincial isolation. The town was easier to reach, and its culture was felt through the schools, compulsory military service, mail-order catalogues, and cheap newspapers. If not for themselves, the agricultural working class could at least anticipate an easier, less trying life for their children.

In short, from the early days of the Third Republic until the end of the century, French society was to change very little, and least of all in its traditional social and economic inequalities. Durkheim's consistently uniformitarian view that revolutions were as rare as unicorns thus reflected not only his deeply conservative nature, but a keen perception of the realities of his own society. In fact, those who made the Republican victory possible – the peasantry and the rising middle class – expected no profound transformation of social relations. What they did expect was the end of the political influence of the traditional aristocracy, as well as the Roman Catholic Church, for this would provide them with the opportunity to rise socially.

These expectations would be intimately bound to the precarious future of the Third French Republic. But historically, the French – and especially the peasantry – had held strong reservations about republicanism. Suspected of bellicosity abroad and instability at home, of opposition to the Church, and of egalitarian and even socialist tendencies, republicans won only 200 seats in the National Assembly elected after the fall of the Paris Commune. "So now we have a republic?" observed Zola's peasant-hero Jean Macquart, in *La Débâcle* (1892, p. 403). "Oh well, all to the good if it helps us beat the Prussians"; but then Macquart shook his head, "for he had always been led to fear a republic when he worked on the land. And besides, in the face of the enemy he didn't think it was a good thing not to be all of one mind." Ironically, the Assembly's ruthless suppression of the Commune – 38,000 were taken prisoner, 20,000 executed, 13,450 sentenced to various prison terms, 7,500 deported to New Caledonia – gave the Third French Republic one of its few reasons for optimism. The proscription and exile of so many "extremists" provided the nascent and extremely precarious Republic an opportunity to evolve in a more peaceful, orderly fashion, and even to attain a degree of constitutional legitimacy; and the absence (or at least quiescence) of these same elements helped to remove the long-held association of Republicanism with violence, instability, and disorder – something essential if the Republic were to win the allegiance of its hard-working, law-abiding, and largely provincial citizenry.

Within the context of the larger European community, such moderation was essential, for in just fifteen years, the position of France had declined precipitously. At the conclusion of the Crimean War (1854–6), Great Britain was an ally, Russia had been firmly defeated, Italy and Germany were simply "geographical expressions," and France was incontestably the foremost power in continental Europe. By the spring of 1871, Britain was no longer an ally, for France had no allies; Russia had gained a modification of the Black Sea clauses of the Treaty of Paris; without any *quid pro quo*, France had been forced to withdraw her troops from Italy, allowing the Italian government to occupy Rome, complete the unification of Italy, imprison Pius IX in the Vatican, and end the temporal power of the papacy; and Germany, whose population already outnumbered France's by more than four million people, had achieved national unity, declared itself an Empire, and would soon become the greatest industrial power on the Continent.

For the French, the natural consequences of this situation included a revulsion for war, a powerful desire for peace and order, the constant affirmation and reaffirmation of patriotism, the elevation of the "sacred" French army to a status beyond political argument altogether, and an utter indifference to the restoration of the temporal power of the Pope. Henceforth, public opinion would favor those like Durkheim, whose republican zeal was tempered by opposition to insurrection and revolution. Even Gambetta became more moderate, acknowledging the imminent rise of what he called "a new social stratum" – *petits bourgeois*, shopkeepers, clerks, and artisans – the class which had profited from the prosperity of the Second Empire, swelled the ranks of investors in the provisional Republic, and thus accelerated the work of postwar reconstruction; and now, given the appropriate education and opportunity, this class would surely support the Republic and strengthen its institutions. Gambetta thus became what he himself described as an "Opportunist" – a name which would characterize the moderate Left to the end of the century. Doctrinaire tenets were shelved in the interest of practical ends, and the electorate was increasingly reassured that, if Gambetta remained a Republican and an anticlerical, he was no revolutionary.

Those who insist on reading *De la division du travail social* as a "dialogue" with Marx's ghost should thus be reminded that revolutionary socialism was virtually non-existent at the parliamentary level of French politics during the period in which that work was conceived. The first series of Jules Guesde's *L'Égalité* appeared only in November 1877, and the second in January 1880. Between the two, the Socialist Workers' Congress of France was held at Marseilles (October 1879), denouncing Gambetta's followers and adopting a Marxist program. But the actual texts of Marx and Engels were almost unknown, and only in 1885 did Guesde's Parti ouvrier publish a complete translation of the *Communist Manifesto*. France, as we have seen, was still a country of peasants rather than urban–industrial workers, and those Paris revolutionaries who had survived the suppression of the Commune were either in prison or in exile, not to be pardoned until 1879.

This helps to explain the central place of laicization within the Republican agenda. To the Opportunists, the Church seemed a growing and increasingly threatening presence. In the syllabus of 1864 which accompanied the encyclical *Quanta Cura*, Pius IX startled the modern world by condemning propositions that seemed self-evident to reasonable people, including the suggestion that the Roman pontiff should reconcile himself to "progress, liberalism and modern civilization." On July 18, 1870, the bishops assembled in St Peter's voted the constitution *Pater aeternus*, declaring the Pope preserved from error when he speaks *ex cathedra* in matters of faith and morals. However ambiguous the Syllabus, and however limited the definition in *Pater aeternus*, in the eyes of other Christians as well as unbelievers, the Church seemed "irretrievably set on the path of absolutism in ecclesiastical government and, by analogy and from the experience of the present pontificate, of reaction in matters social and political" (McManners, 1972, p. 1).

Despite this reactionary posture, the Church enjoyed at least an ephemeral rise in popularity as a consequence of the Franco-Prussian War. Official statistics of the 1870s list 35,000,000 people as Catholics, by contrast to 600,000 Protestants, 50,000 Jews, and only 80,000 "free-thinkers" (McManners, 1972, p. 5). In addition to the sheer numbers of Catholics and the strength of their clergy, a variety of social services were almost entirely in Church hands. But it was in education that the power of the Roman Catholic Church in France seemed to be at its height. Despite the anticlericalism which survived the First Empire and continued into the 1830s and 1840s, the Church had repeatedly tried to improve its position by undermining the university monopoly of higher and secondary education. By 1870, almost 40 percent of the nation's children were educated in Church schools (McManners, 1972, p. 21–2). "Au point de vue sociologique," Durkheim would say in 1905, "l'Église est un monstre" (Durkheim, 1905, p. 369). If so, in 1870 it was a very large *monstre* indeed, and one which threatened to grow still further.

Still, the Catholic Church in France was a deeply troubled institution. Not least among its difficulties, for example, was its lack of a central organization or a distinctive French voice, which made the Church in France dependent on the Vatican, leading to calls – most of which fell upon deaf republican ears – for the "liberation" of the Pope. A second difficulty was that French clergy themselves varied in the degree of their support for Rome. The parish clergy came consistently from the less-educated classes, while the bishops typically possessed literary and classical educations, and were utter strangers to the parochial ministry. Enjoying a salary twenty times that of a *curé*, a bishop inevitably appeared to those below as an aloof, superior figure. By contrast, only one secular priest in ten enjoyed security of tenure; the others could be moved by the bishop at will and, if accused of offences, disciplined without due process.

The aristocracy and bourgeoisie were still interested in the religious orders for their daughters, but nine out of ten candidates for the ministry came from the families of peasants and artisans. As the intellectual foundations of Christian belief came under increasing attack from biblical criticism, natural science, and the comparative study of religion, it is understandable that a ministry thus recruited would be found wanting; and to compound the problem, the educational program of the seminaries was limited to meditation, pious exercises, and the rehearsal of antiquated dogma. McManners finds only two diocesan prelates who, in the 1870s and 1880s, had any first-hand knowledge of the new German biblical criticism that had already inspired Robertson Smith and, largely through Smith, would influence Durkheim.

To this, one must add the indifferent knowledge of an urban, working-class world possessed by a clergy of rural origins, whose language, values, and morals were largely those of an earlier age. The city, Mayeur and Rebérioux (1984, p. 104) emphasize, "a modern Babylon which the Church distrusted, was the citadel of religious indifference," and comparisons of the new districts in Paris with "heathen lands afar" were not uncommon (McManners, 1972, p. 7). The Church was no more apt to appeal to the middle classes. The old, "Voltairean" bourgeoisie of the provinces had largely been reconciled to a vague kind of faith; but Gambetta's "new stratum" was utterly indifferent if not hostile. As for the peasantry, thanks to the invention of the rotary press, post-free railway distribution, and the mass appeal of advertising, the penny newspaper easily reached the countryside (Mayeur and Rebérioux, 1984, p. 116). To this was added the local weekly or bi-weekly newspapers, and the illustrated magazines and catalogues from major Parisian stores. Quite aside from manifestly anticlerical publications, these carriers of a new, popular, Parisian culture, together with military service and improvements in transportation, broadened the horizons of the French people and undermined local, traditional values.

Nor was Roman Catholicism the only religious confession in late nineteenth-century France. There were 580,000 Protestants in France in 1872, and their economic standing and intellectual significance far transcended their numbers (Bury, 1985, p. 156). After the synod of 1872, a division in the Reformed Church produced a liberal Protestant minority which practiced ecclesiastical democracy, rejected theological dogma, reduced religion to a rational morality, encouraged freedom of inquiry, and thus became another component of the secular, republican idea. Protestants like Ferdinand Buisson (whom Durkheim replaced at the Sorbonne in 1902), Félix Pécaut, J. Steeg, and Elie Rabier played important roles in Ferry's educational reforms, and the neo-Kantian philosopher Charles Renouvier, whom Durkheim called "mon educateur," encouraged republicans to become Protestants (Mayeur and Rebérioux, 1984, pp. 107–8). The Jewish minority comprised 50,000 by 1870, most of them living in Paris (McManners, 1972, p. 5). While those who had recently immigrated from Eastern Europe remained isolated by their language and retained their religious traditions, Jews of Alsatian origin (like Durkheim) were largely assimilated. Granted citizenship and the right to vote in the Civil Constitution of the Clergy (1790), these assimilated Jews remained attached to the tradition of the French Revolution, and consistently supported the progressive, secular Republic. Finally, the majority of the brilliant young men trained at the École Normale Supérieure after 1848, as well as the majority of the Republican leaders, were simply agnostics, for whom "the cult of the Great Revolution had become almost a religion, and, in so far as it affected their political thinking, intensified the political offensive of the Left against the Church" (Bury, 1985, p. 156).

French anticlericalism, of course, can be traced back to the literate sensibilities of the Enlightenment, the jest books of the Renaissance, and even the sullen resentments of the Middle Ages. But the "new anticlericalism" that emerged after 1870 bore ironic similarities to Catholicism. In each case, a determined core of "true believers" was outnumbered by a wider circle of occasional conformists and nominal adherents. Moreover, the spheres of nominal Catholicism and ambiguous anticlericalism overlapped, as those Catholics who resented clerical domination and right-wing politics mingled with anticlericals (like Durkheim) whose hatred for priests was not unmixed with a respect and even nostalgia for the moral uniformity of the medieval community. It was in this context that the possibility of a purely lay morality, based on a "science of ethics," was first conceived; and it is the belief in this possibility, as well as the quasi-religious belief in science and progress generally, which distinguishes this anticlericalism from that of earlier ages. "Many of the opponents of the Church," McManners reminds us, "had a reluctant admiration for the system of moral influence they were proposing to destroy, and a vision of a faith to replace it. It was not écrasez l'Infâme, but a different sort of bitterness, compounded of attraction and repulsion, a love-hate relationship" (McManners, 1972, p. 17). The Opportunists who came to power in 1879 thus confronted a Church afflicted with serious internal and external difficulties, whose values were largely if not unambiguously discordant with the middle-class, quasi-religious belief in positivism and social progress, and whose political candidates they had repeatedly (and now decisively) defeated at the polls; but it was also a Church which had the respect and even affection of the majority of the population, one whose moral authority the Opportunists envied and longed to replace with their own, equally fervent brand of secular ethics.

Republican administrators thus turned quite naturally to the Church's educational establishments – "the surest guarantee of its continued influence" – as the focal point for their reforms. In such establishments, McManners (1972, p. 45) emphasizes, "so many young minds were imprinted with a permanent allegiance to religion, or a subconscious residual respect for its practices." Such establishments also bore the weight of accumulated resentments: they were patronized by the upper classes, administered corporal punishment, taught children to admire unrevolutionary mendicant saints, and emphasized impractical subjects to the children of a class with rising social aspirations. "A frontal attack on religion," McManners emphasizes, "on the ceremonies by which wives set so much store, the consolations available in the hour of death, the curé and all his supporters," would surely have failed. But a "flank attack" on clerical education, which left the Church undisturbed in the private sphere of the family, would surely receive political support. Laicization was also seen as the means to repair the negative consequences of an elitist, humanist, and increasingly impractical form of education, to eradicate differences of geographic region and social class, and to unite the French people and restore their sense of national pride (McManners, 1972, p. 47). Secularism, in short, became synonymous with patriotism, and the removal of clerical control over French education became less a neutral political posture than a "civil religion" of its own.

The laicizing movement grew rapidly. The Ligue de l'enseignement, founded in 1866 by Jean Macé, served as an umbrella for a variety of disparate groups unified in defining free, compulsory, secular education as the overriding national necessity. From 1870 to 1877, it grew from 18,000 to 60,000 members. Similarly, the Société pour l'étude des questions de enseignement supérieur, founded in 1879, sought to influence sympathetic ministers to reform higher education on the model of Protestant Germany; and the *Revue internationale de l'enseignement*, which began to appear in 1881, presented a series of studies of both German and French education – including the important products of Durkheim's 1885–6 visit to Berlin, Marburg, and Leipzig – which created the theoretical foundations for public policy.

On February 4, 1879, the Waddington ministry was formed, with Jules Ferry as Minister of Education. During the period of remarkable political stability which followed, Ferry would be Minister of Education for five years and Prime Minister for three; and it was during this period, undisturbed by opposition from both left and right, that the governing Republicans constructed their system of free, compulsory, secular education. Not surprisingly, Ferry's primary intellectual inspiration came from Condorcet and Comte, whose belief in science, progress, and the power of education he embraced without reservation. But much like Durkheim, Ferry also held a deep respect for the medieval Church, whose schools unified society, mitigated inequalities, taught morality, and thus provided the ethical foundations for an entire social order.

Laicization, in short, was the reform that contained all other reforms. It became the obligation of the state to provide for the education of every child in France. The decisive measure was a law of March 28, 1882, which made education compulsory from six to thirteen years, and eliminated religious instruction from the timetable. The teacher, insisted Buisson, "confines himself to inculcating in his pupils the fundamental ideas which recur in all religious denominations and even outside them." With the appearance of the "Goblet law" of October 30, 1886, members of the religious orders were explicitly denied further recruitment into the state's primary schools, and their replacement with exclusively lay personnel was required within the next five years. In secondary education, the timetable was reformed in 1880 to reduce the role, so prominent in Jesuit pedagogical method, of memorization, composition, and Latin recitation. The classical humanistic subjects retained their primacy, but science and modern languages were given a larger place, and an underlying philosophy of educational realism became perceptible: "The observation of things," Ferry emphasized, "is the basis of everything" (Mayeur and Rebérioux, 1984, p. 88).

## THE INTELLECTUAL CONTEXT

At the École Normale, one of the first great minds Durkheim encountered was the French historian Numa Denis Fustel de Coulanges (1830–89). Fustel's classic study of the religious foundations of ancient Rome, *La Cité antique* (1864), was literally awash with ideas that a later generation would automatically recognize as "Durkheimian," e.g. a Cartesian emphasis on doubting preconceptions, the comparative method, a preoccupation with the family as the most elementary form of society, the dismissal of explanations appealing to individual reason or will, the discovery of the origin of religion in a primitive form of sacrificial communion with a god, a rejection of the concern for religious doctrine combined with an emphasis on the stability of ritual practices, the religious origins of institutions like private property, law, and the state, and the identification of "religion" with "society" itself. *La Cité antique* enjoyed an almost instantaneous celebrity, inspiring new interest in the history of institutions among Fustel's followers, including Camille Jullian, who was Durkheim's classmate and edited Fustel's manuscripts. During the time Durkheim was at the École Normale, Fustel was at work on the six volumes of his *Histoire des institutions politiques de l'ancienne France* (1874–93), which included a detailed articulation and defense of the comparative method he had followed in writing *La Cité antique*. "From his time at the Ecole normale," Jullian later recalled, Durkheim "was profoundly affected by the influence of La Cité antique, and by the lectures and examples of its author. He himself has recognized this, and proclaims it openly" (Lukes, 1972, p. 60). Durkheim even dedicated his Latin thesis on Montesquieu to Fustel; but the historian's influence on Durkheim's work seems to have been delayed at least until the mid-1890s, when Durkheim achieved a new understanding of religious phenomena through the study of James Frazer and William Robertson Smith.

The second important influence at the École Normale was the philosopher Émile Boutroux (1845–1921), a disciple of the neo-spiritualist philosopher Jules Lachelier (1832–1918). Boutroux's first major work was *De la Contingence des lois de la nature* (1874), an attack on determinism in its relation to physical and psychological science that ultimately proved to be his *magnum opus*. A devout Roman Catholic, Boutroux argued that phenomenal existence comprises "several worlds, forming, as it were, stages superposed on one another," each studied by a science irreducible to that preceding it (Boutroux, 1916, pp. 151–2). Durkheim dedicated *The Division of Labor* to Boutroux, and in 1907, explaining the origin of his important distinction between sociology and psychology, tried to make his debt clear:

> I owe [this distinction] first to my master, Boutroux, who, at the École normale supérieure, repeated frequently to us that each science must, as Aristotle says, explain [its own phenomena] by "its own principles" – e.g. psychology by psychological principles, biology by biological principles. Most impressed by this idea, I applied it to sociology. (Durkheim, 1907, pp. 612–13)

But if the influence is undeniable, it is not unambiguous. For Durkheim's claims for sociology went far beyond anything Boutroux would have accepted, including a defense of necessary laws of social behavior. Hearing that Durkheim's thesis had been dedicated to him, Boutroux grimaced and then attacked Durkheim's mechanical, necessitarian mode of explanation in *De l'idée de loi naturelle dans la science et la philosophie contemporaines* (1895, translated 1914, p. 198; see Lukes, 1972, pp. 297–8).

Another philosopher Durkheim was reading during these years was the French neo-Kantian Charles Renouvier (1815–1903). Educated at the École Polytechnique, where he specialized in mathematics and natural science, Renouvier had studied under Comte, who was then an instructor in higher mathematics. Influenced by Saint-Simon in the early 1830s, he became a socialist propagandist until, in 1851, the *coup d'état* of Louis-Napoleon destroyed Renouvier's political ambitions. Renouvier became a private scholar, and never held an academic position; but the views expressed in his books and journal articles – uncompromising rationalism, the central concern with ethics and the determination to study it "scientifically," the compatibility of determinism in nature with the freedom presupposed by moral action, concern for the dignity and autonomy of the individual, preference for justice over utility, advocacy of associations independent of the state and public, secular education – exerted a powerful influence on intellectuals of the Third Republic. "If you wish to mature your thought," Durkheim later said to René Maublanc, "devote yourself to the study of a great master; take a system apart, laying bare its innermost secretes. That is what I did and my educator was Renouvier" (Lukes, 1972, pp. 54–5).

Near the end of his studies at the École Normale, Durkheim began to read the works of Auguste Comte (1798–1857), although lecture notes from his philosophy course at the Lycée de Sens suggest that, as late as 1883, he was still not a social realist or even particularly interested in Comte or sociology. It was as he was working on the first draft of *The Division of Labor* between 1884 and 1886, therefore, that he came to see that the solution to his problem might be found in "a new science: sociology" (Lukes, 1972, pp. 66–7). By the time he wrote the introduction to the Latin thesis on Montesquieu (1892), Durkheim could complain that "we have forgotten that this science started up in our own country," for "it was Comte who established it on a sound basis, described its different elements and gave it its own – if somewhat barbarous – name of sociology" (Durkheim, 1997, p. 7e). In particular, Durkheim praised Comte for insisting that social phenomena are natural things and thus subject to natural laws, for his emphasis on careful observation, his resistance to the reduction of sociological explanations to psychological causes, his recognition that the division of labor is a source of solidarity, and his emphasis on the interrelatedness of social phenomena (Lukes, 1972, pp. 67–9, 80–1). Despite Comte's implicit social realism, however, Durkheim found his application of it wanting. "It is ideas which he too takes as the object of his study," Durkheim complained. "Comte has taken his own notion of [social reality], which is one that does not differ greatly from that commonly held...if one proceeds down this path," Durkheim concluded, "one not only remains in the realm of ideology, but assigns to sociology as its object a concept which has nothing peculiarly sociological about it" (1982, pp. 63–4).

At approximately the same time, Durkheim was reading Herbert Spencer (1820–1903), who – despite his methodological individualism – provided Durkheim's social realism with a "treasure of insights and hypotheses" based on analogies between social institutions and biological organisms. By contrast with Comte's sweeping "law of the three stages," Spencer applied these analogies to different social types, themselves classified into genera and species, and subjected them to powerful functional explanations (Lukes, 1972, pp. 82–4). But if Spencer thus discarded Comte's abstract concept, he simply replaced it "with another which is none the less formed in the same way. He makes societies, and not humanity, the object of his study, but immediately gives to societies a definition which causes the thing of which he speaks to disappear and puts in its place the preconception he has of them. . . . What is defined in this way," Durkheim again complained, "is not society but Spencer's idea of it. If he feels no scruples in proceeding in this fashion it is because for him also society is only, and can be only, the realisation of an idea, namely that very idea of cooperation by which he defines society" (Durkheim, 1982, pp. 64–5).

The resources Durkheim needed to construct his social realist vocabulary, therefore, had to be sought in German writers. Durkheim wrote favorable notices of the first volume of Albert Schaeffle's *Bau und Leben des sozialen Körpers* (1885), for example, as well as his *Die Quintessenz der Sozialismus* (1886). In the first paragraph of his review of Ludwig Gumplowicz's *Grundriss der Soziologie* (1885), Durkheim added that this work was further evidence of the German effort to advance sociological studies in every possible direction. "How regrettable it is," he added, that "this interesting movement is so little known and so little followed in France. So it is that sociology, French in origin, becomes more and more a German science" (Durkheim, 1885, p. 627). In 1885 and 1886, Durkheim visited the German universities of Berlin, Marburg, and Leipzig, praising them for their sense of community and corporate life, in sharp contrast to the French taste for "individual distinction and originality"; and he admired still more the German emphasis on the "positive science of ethics," which he wanted to transplant to the French universities so it might then be disseminated through the *lycées*. The so-called "socialists of the chair" – Adolf Wagner (1835–1917) and Gustav Schmoller (1838–1917) – were praised for their social realism, their connection of economics to ethics, and their critique of the Manchester School, which ignored the social context of economic behavior; the leading representatives of the German "historical school of jurisprudence" – Rudolf von Ihering (1818–92) and Albert-Hermann Post (1839–95) – were lauded for relating the study positive law and ethics to customs (Durkheim, 1887, p. 58); and proponents of the German *Völkerpsychologie* – Theodor Waitz (1821–64), Heymann Steinthal (1823–99), and Moritz Lazarus (1824–1903) – were praised for their study of phenomena which, though psychological in nature, "do not have their source in individual psychology, since they infinitely transcend the individual" (Durkheim, 1888, p. 63).

By far the most important German influence, however, was the philosopher and psychologist Wilhelm Wundt (1832–1920). Despite the attractions of the University of Berlin, Durkheim recalled in 1887, "it is always Leipzig that is preferred by foreigners who come to Germany to complete their philosophical education. It is to Wundt and his teachings that this persistent vogue is due. It is this same cause," he added, "which led us to Leipzig, and kept us there longer than anywhere else" (Durkheim, 1887, pp. 313–14). Durkheim described the experiments conducted in Wundt's Psychologische Institut in endless detail, adding that "nothing is more capable of raising in young minds the love of scientific precision, to divest them of vague generalizations and metaphysical possibilities, and finally to make them understand how complex are psychological facts and the laws which govern them" (Durkheim, 1887, p. 433) – an early hint of his notion that the study of science could be morally edifying (see above). Most important, Wundt's great *Ethik* (1886) had offered a genuinely scientific alternative to the French approach to the study of ethics. According to the French tradition, Durkheim complained, moral laws are universally valid in all times and places, the method of ethics is deduction from axiomatic first principles, the individual is an autonomous whole, society is formed by the establishment of relations between these autonomous wills, and the purpose of morality is the perfecting of these individuals. Against this tradition, Wundt and his colleagues argued that moral "laws" are relative to particular times and places, the method is inductive generalization, the "autonomous individual" is an abstraction unknown to science, society penetrates the individual "in every part," and "morality has, as its consequence, to make society possible" (Durkheim, 1887, pp. 336–8, 138).

These issues were foremost in Durkheim's mind as he prepared his Latin thesis on Montesquieu (1892). In a sense, *De l'esprit des lois* became the perfect forge in which Durkheim would shape the tools to be applied in *The Division of Labor* and later works. For Montesquieu (1689–1755), no less than Durkheim, had been troubled by the legacy of Cartesian metaphysics and, no less than Durkheim, sought to temper its emphasis on "clear and distinct ideas" with a language more responsive to the concrete complexity of things. So Durkheim used his Latin thesis on Montesquieu as a way of exploring his own ambivalence about the Cartesian tradition, while also praising Montesquieu's recognition of the real, concrete diversity of societal types, his refusal to deduce "rules valid for all peoples" from artificial first principles, and – anticipating *The Division of Labor* – his explanation of the *esprit* of each societal type as the natural consequence of its structural features. At least equal praise was given to Montesquieu's refusal – so unusual among his Enlightenment contemporaries – to reduce explanations of civil and political law to the principles of human nature, or to some putative, original contract or covenant. Durkheim lamented the extent to which Montesquieu was still bound by the legacy of Aristotle and by the traditions of natural law, not to mention the disturbing element of contingency which leavened the causal explanations of *De l'esprit des lois*. But, recognizing that Montesquieu's "greatest achievement" – the extension of the idea of law to the realm of social phenomena – reflected an undeniable, continuing attachment to the rationalist belief in a determinate order of nature, Durkheim still emphasized how "unique" it was for an eighteenth-century social philosopher to insist that these laws were neither fixed nor immutable. Finally, the notion that "social volume" affects the structures of law and society, which plays so large a role in *The Division of Labor*, was found in Montesquieu's discussion of the conditions of republican government.

It was shortly after the publication of *The Division of Labor* that Durkheim confronted his most formidable intellectual adversary, the French sociologist and philosopher Gabriel Tarde (1843–1904). In his best-known work, *Les lois de l'imitation* (1890), Tarde had advanced a more psychologically based sociology that explained social phenomena as the consequence of the imitation of individual beliefs and desires. Tarde's otherwise generous and respectful review of *The Division of Labor* criticized Durkheim for ignoring the function of the division of labor "in multiplying the objects of [intellectual and moral community] and singularly facilitating their diffusion" – in effect, for ignoring imitation. Durkheim responded in *The Rules of Sociological Method*, insisting that social facts become generalized and diffused because they are obligatory – not the reverse; and in "Les deux éléments de la sociologie" (1894), Tarde responded still more aggressively, denouncing the entire foundation of Durkheim's social realism in Boutroux's distinction between successive, irreducible phenomenal "worlds." In the most fundamental way, Tarde had attacked the very heart of Durkheim's social theory. But by the time Durkheim responded, in the third book of *Suicide*, he had a new weapon – a deeper and more sophisticated understanding of the figure to whom his sociology would owe more than anyone else, Jean-Jacques Rousseau (1712–78).

Rousseau had figured in Durkheim's work from the start, of course, typically as a thinker with an asocial concept of human beings and an artificial concept of society. Undeniably provoked by Tarde, however, Durkheim took another, longer look, giving a lecture course on *Le Contrat social* at Bordeaux after 1896, and another course on *Emile* at Paris after 1902. Transcripts of both sets of lectures have been published, and they reveal a breadth of reading well beyond the two works in question, and a depth of understanding that clearly transformed Durkheim's social theory. Most importantly, these lectures quite literally set out new philosophical foundations for Durkheim's social realism. The dependence on *things*, Durkheim paraphrased Rousseau, is no obstacle to freedom; but "the dependence on *other human beings* – willful, unstable, avaricious, deceitful, etc. – produces the mutual corruption and depravity of master and slave." And then Durkheim confronted the passage in *Emile* that must surely have stopped him cold:

> If there is any means of remedying this ill in society, it is to substitute law for man and to arm the general will with a real strength superior to the action of every particular will. If the laws of nations could, like those of nature, have an inflexibility that no human force could ever conquer, dependence on men would then become dependence on things again; in the republic all of the advantages of the natural state would be united with those of the civil state, and freedom which keeps

man exempt from vices would be joined to morality which raises him to virtue. (Durkheim, 1979, p. 85)

To paraphrase in more Durkheimian terms, if the laws of society could become like those of nature, dependence on individual human wills would again become dependence on things. This new understanding of Rousseau was immediately reflected in Durkheim's discussion of anomic suicide, i.e. the pathological symptom of individual human willfulness, whose only solution was the regulation and constraint provided by society.

As we have already seen, Durkheim himself acknowledged that his early treatment of religion was relatively mechanical and unimaginative. The pivotal influence here seems to have been William Robertson Smith (1846–94), whose works Durkheim encountered while teaching a lecture course on religion at Bordeaux in 1894–5:

> it was not until 1895 that I achieved a clear view of the essential role played by religion in social life. It was in that year that, for the first time, I found the means of tackling the study of religion sociologically. This was a revelation to me. That course of 1895 marked a dividing line in the development of my thought, to such an extent that all my previous researches had to be taken up afresh in order to be made to harmonize with these new insights.... [This reorientation] was entirely due to the studies of religious history which I had just undertaken, and notably to the reading of the works of Robertson Smith and his school. (Durkheim, 1911, pp. 402–3).

There is no doubt that Smith's fascinating *Religion of the Semites* (2nd edn, 1894) – with its comparative approach to the "unconscious religious tradition" preceding and surrounding that of the Old Testament Hebrews, insistence on the temporal priority of ritual over myth, strong distinction between religion and magic, emphasis on the ideas of taboo and sacredness, suggestion that totemism was the earliest form of religion, and that the earliest religious act was one of sacramental communion in which the god and worshippers jointly participated – contained much that would interest the author of *The Elementary Forms of the Religious Life*. But neither is there any evidence, in the years immediately after 1895, that Durkheim knew quite what to do with these ideas – by contrast, for example, with those of Smith's *protégé*, Sir James Frazer (1854–1941), whose *Golden Bough* (1890), with its powerful myth of the "man-god" sacrificed so that his spirit might be passed on unimpaired to his successor, plays a large role in Durkheim's account of altruistic suicide. Even Durkheim's 1899 essay "Concerning the Definition of Religious Phenomena," which defines religion as "obligatory beliefs, connected with clearly defined practices which are related to given objects of those beliefs," has been aptly described by Steven Lukes as "a first, rather groping attempt" (Lukes, 1972, p. 240).

What really caught Durkheim's attention was the publication of Baldwin Spencer and F. J. Gillen's *Native Tribes of Central Australia* (1899) – which would become the primary source of ethnographic data for *The Elementary Forms* – and its almost immediate Frazerian, economic, and utilitarian interpretation.

In fact, Frazer had been corresponding with Baldwin Spencer for several years, and his essay on "The Origin of Totemism" (1899) appeared almost simultaneously with *Native Tribes*. First, Frazer denied the universality of totemism and its long-undisputed connection with exogamy (Durkheim had firmly committed himself to both just a year earlier, in his *Année sociologique* essay on incest). Second, Frazer suggested that some of society's most powerful interdictions had been rationally and purposefully constructed following an earlier period of permissiveness. That the origin of such interdictions lay in the collective unconscious, and that primitive societies could hardly be characterized as "permissive," had been among Durkheim's arguments in *The Division of Labor*. Third, and most alarmingly, Frazer had suggested that the essential function of totemism was to provide for economic needs, and that this was also its sufficient explanation. The fifth chapter of *The Rules of Sociological Method* had been written to oppose such "teleological" confusions of the function of a social fact with its cause, and to insist that needs and desires, while they might hasten or retard social development, cannot themselves *create* social facts at all. Durkheim responded powerfully in "On Totemism" (1902), where Smith proved as useful against Spencer, just as Rousseau had proved so useful against Tarde; and by the time of his lecture course on "La Religion: Origines" at the Sorbonne (1906–7), a rudimentary outline of *The Elementary Forms* had begun to emerge.

Finally, no account of the major intellectual influences on Durkheim would be complete without mentioning the pragmatists. James's *A Pluralistic Universe* had appeared in French in 1910, to be followed by translations of his *Pragmatism* (1911) and *The Meaning of Truth* (1913), at least one with a preface by Bergson; and as we have seen, Durkheim's discussion of science and religion in the conclusion of *The Elementary Forms* had embraced at least one of the ideas in *The Varieties of Religious Experience*. In 1913–14, therefore, Durkheim offered a new course on "Pragmatism and Sociology," and in his first lecture gave two reasons for having chosen this topic. First, pragmatism was "almost the only current theory of truth, and is of topical interest"; second, pragmatism had "in common with sociology, a sense of life and action" (Durkheim, 1983, p. 1). From this point on, however, Durkheim made it abundantly clear that he disagreed with virtually all of the pragmatists' specific arguments (see Lukes, 1972, pp. 485–96). For all of his tampering with the old Cartesian vocabulary, in the end Durkheim fell back on the language of rationalism, realism, natural law, necessary relations of cause and effect, and the correspondence theory of truth.

## IMPACT

Durkheim's impact on modern sociological thought has been so great that, to paraphrase one recent commentator, the reiteration of his importance has become something of a ritual performance. The sociological vocabulary he constructed – e.g. social facts as "things," the comparative method, the normal versus the pathological, sacred versus profane, mechanical versus organic solidarity, egoism, altruism, and anomie, the *conscience collective*, collective representations, collective effervescence – is adopted almost unconsciously whenever social theorists talk about what is most important and distinctive in their discipline.

Durkheim's most immediate disciple was his nephew, Marcel Mauss (1872–1950), with whom he collaborated on "Some Primitive Forms of Classification" (1903), on the statistical tables for *Suicide* (1897), and on numerous reviews published in *l'Année sociologique*. In their collaboration, Mauss seems to have had the better sense for concrete social facts, while Durkheim provided the more general theoretical interpretation. Working with Henri Hubert (1872–1927), Mauss published important studies of sacrifice (1899) and magic (1904), but his masterpiece was *The Gift* (1925), a study of systems of exchange as "total social phenomena," including their religious, legal, moral, economic, and aesthetic expressions. In general, however, the Durkheim School suffered a decline after the First World War, reviving significantly only in the early 1970s with the emergence of the Groupe d'études durkheimiennes and a series of articles in the *Revue française de sociologie*, edited by Philippe Besnard. In Britain, the identification of Durkheim with a conservative, functionalist view of society delayed his influence for a comparable period; but Steven Lukes's *Durkheim* (1972) stimulated renewed interest, and the Institute for Social and Cultural Anthropology at Oxford University is currently the home of the Centre for Durkheimian Studies. Even in the United States, Durkheim (like Marx and Weber) was less interesting to sociologists than Comte, Spencer, and Simmel, at least until Talcott Parsons's *Structure of Social Action* (1937) introduced American social science to Durkheim, Weber, and Pareto. Parsons's structural functionalism later made great use of Durkheimian concepts like *conscience collective* and collective representations; and in *Social Theory and Social Structure* (1949), Parsons's student, Robert Merton, made equally significant use of the concept of anomie.

In the 1960s, structural functionalism came under a withering attack, from conflict theorists like Alvin Gouldner and social behaviorists like George Homans, neither of whom was particularly attracted to the Durkheimian vocabulary. But if structural functionalism was the midwife that brought Durkheim to the attention of American sociology, it was by no means the only theoretical perspective that found Durkheim's ideas useful. In *The Social Construction of Reality* (1967), for example, Peter Berger and Thomas Luckmann extended the concerns of phenomenological social theory to structural issues, thus integrating the individual and societal levels. In the same year, Berger's *The Sacred Canopy* provided a brilliant synthesis of Durkheim and Weber's approaches to the sociology of religion, particularly emphasizing what Berger called the *choseité* (literally, "thingness") of external, coercive social facts, including language, collective beliefs, and ritual actions.

Several years later, in his Presidential Address before the American Sociological Association, Lewis Coser attacked many of his colleagues for succumbing to "a veritable orgy of subjectivism" in their adoption of theories like phenomenology and ethnomethodology. Coser's address thus marked the beginning of what George Ritzer has called "the rebirth of interest in structural theory – that is, a return to the roots of sociology in Emile Durkheim's concept of social facts" (Ritzer, 1992, p. 523). Coser urged sociologists not to give in to "the subjectivists," and to return instead to the study of large-scale social structures as the ultimate determinants of other aspects of social reality. Sociologists responding to Coser's call have included Robert Merton, William Goode, Seymour Martin Lipset, and – most important – Peter Blau, whose deterministic brand of structural sociology eliminated values and norms as explanatory variables altogether.

Despite Claude Lévi-Strauss's observation, in *Tristes Tropiques* (1955), that he early arrived at "a state of open revolt against Durkheim and against any attempt to use sociology for metaphysical purposes," one must also agree with his claim (in the same work) that he has been "more faithful than anyone else to the Durkheimian tradition" (Lévi-Strauss, 1973, p. 52). Structuralist anthropology thus owes a large debt to Durkheim, although not to Durkheim's notion of the externality of social facts, but to the later work of Durkheim and Mauss as well as *The Elementary Forms*. Lévi-Strauss's actors are constrained, of course, but by the structures of the human mind rather than by external social things. Similarly, one of the foundational hypotheses of Pierre Bourdieu's sociology has been the insistence that there is a "correspondence between social structures and mental structures, between the objective divisions of the social world...and the principles of vision and division that agents apply to it" (Bourdieu, 1989, p. 7). Loïc Wacquant has characterized this as a reformulation and generalization of Durkheim and Mauss's argument that the cognitive systems operative in primitive societies are derivations of their social systems. Bourdieu extends this thesis into advanced societies, emphasizing the role of the school; providing a causal mechanism for the social determination of classification with his notion of "genetic links"; revealing how such symbolic systems function, not just as instruments of knowledge, but politically, as instruments of domination; and showing how systems of classification constitute a "stake in the struggles" that oppose individuals and groups (Bourdieu and Wacquant, 1992, pp. 12–14).

While Durkheim has been criticized (see below) for neglecting some aspects of social conflict, theorists like Randall Collins have argued that the Durkheimian tradition provides a kind of infrastructure to conflict theory. On the microlevel of interaction, Collins insists, Durkheim provides an explanatory theory of the varieties of class cultures, then building out of these interactions a stratified network that constitutes the macrostructure of domination and power in the society as a whole. "The conflict tradition," Collins concludes, "can be permeated with the deeper explanatory mechanisms revealed by the Durkheimians" (Collins, 1985, p. 173).

Durkheim's sociology of law and crime has received considerable attention. In *Wayward Puritans* (1966), for example, taking up Durkheim's functional theory of crime, Kai Erikson further developed the theory that societies actually create deviance at those times when they are undergoing a boundary-maintaining crisis. As we have seen, Durkheim argued that even a society of saints would create its own "deviants" by magnifying small faults into significant transgressions. Erickson applied this notion to a real society of "visible saints" – i.e. the Puritan settlers of New England – showing how colonial society as a whole (not the "witches," "heretics," and "deviants" within it) created periodic waves of crisis, thus reaffirming social and cultural boundaries. Similarly, in *The Behavior of Law* (1976), Donald Black has extended Durkheim's theory of crime into a more general theory of social control, showing how public complaints about "crime in the streets" and police violence are part of a larger process of the ritual imposition of social order.

Social theories of religious phenomena have depended heavily on Durkheim's ideas. In books like *Purity and Danger* (1966) and *Natural Symbols* (1973), for example, Mary Douglas – like Lukes, a student of Evans-Pritchard – has explored the way symbols maintain group boundaries and social control. In a classic article, "Civil Religion in America" (1967), Robert Bellah explained the beliefs and ceremonies that unite Americans in their devotion to their country, as celebrated in great public rituals like presidential inaugurations and Thanksgiving. While Bellah acknowledged that there is less unanimity on the location of the "sacred" in modern societies than among Australian aborigines, he effectively demonstrates how such a "civil religion" functions at the national level, where the modern state presents its mission and purpose in sacred, transcendent terms. Again, in *The Birth of the Gods* (1960), Guy Swanson developed the controversial view that belief in a high god or monotheistic deity only tends to occur in those societies containing three or more different types of hierarchically ordered sovereign groups. According to Swanson, such complex hierarchies of temporal authority, with one group dominating the others, establish the social conditions that a high god represents or expresses.

Durkheim's view that the fundamental categories of human reason are collective representations has also had a powerful impact on the sociology of knowledge and science. In a famous article published in 1982, for example, David Bloor has attempted to defend a relativist interpretation of Durkheim and Mauss's essay on primitive classification; and other representatives of the so-called "Strong Programme" in the sociology of scientific knowledge have drawn antirealist implications from that essay and *The Elementary Forms*. This has in turn provoked a realist response, most recently articulated by Warren Schmaus: "Although he believed that there are sociological explanations for the very concepts scientists use," Schmaus emphasizes, Durkheim "thought that the social origins of such concepts in no way undermine the reality of that which scientists describe with them" (Schmaus, 1994, p. 256).

Feminist theory has recently been enriched by Durkheim, primarily through a series of articles and a book, *Durkheim and Women* (1994), written by Jennifer Lehmann. Durkheim's views on women are scattered through a surprisingly small number of his works, and Lehmann's reconstruction of a coherent, consistent, and systematic sociological theory of women from these fragmentary remains has been a significant contribution. Durkheim clearly considered women (by contrast with men) more in touch with nature, and less in touch with society, and he used this to account for the differential immunity to suicide enjoyed by men and women under marriage and divorce. Durkheim also considered sexual anomie (suffered more by men) a far greater threat than fatalism (suffered more by women), and this reflects his patriarchal attitudes as well as his policy recommendations.

Finally, it would be a mistake to ignore Durkheim's powerful influence outside of sociology altogether. In the first number of *l'Année sociologique* (1898), for example, Durkheim was outspoken in his disdain for that kind of historiography that focused on individual political figures or military heroes, or on chronological sequences of dynasties, wars, and elections. By 1929, the historians Marc Bloch and Lucien Febvre had founded the journal *Annales: Economies, sociétés, civilisations*, thereby establishing the famous Annales School of French historiography. The School's most distinguished representative, Fernand Braudel, later praised the "completely new sociology" that "rose like a sun" with Durkheim and *l'Année sociologique*, the latter providing "a favourite reading matter for an entire generation of young historians" (see Thompson, 1982, p. 18). Braudel's *The Mediterranean and the Mediterranean World in the Age of Philip II* (1949) – by many lights the single greatest work of history in the twentieth century – is deeply Durkheimian, systematically embracing long-term changes in agriculture, demography, economy, and society that constitute the infrastructure of more short-term political and military events.

## ASSESSMENT

Recalling that social theories are vocabularies contrived to serve specific interests and purposes, we should not expect that Durkheim's language would appeal equally to all. Despite his undeniable impact on the development of sociology, therefore, his ideas have been subject to a number of criticisms. The concept of the "social fact" itself must be described as extraordinarily capacious if not downright indiscriminate, incorporating the full range of potentially explanatory social phenomena – population size and distribution, social norms and rules, collective beliefs and practices, currents of opinion – from material to immaterial, and from infrastructural to superstructural levels; and as Durkheim's willingness to focus on the latter rather than the former increased over the course of his career, *The Rules* appeared to straddle an equivocal, intermediate stage (Jones, 1986, p. 78).

It might be argued, of course, that these ambiguities are somewhat relieved by Durkheim's insistence that social facts may be distinguished from their biological and psychological counterparts by their "externality" and powers of "constraint"; but here similar difficulties persist. The suggestion that social facts are external to any particular individual, for example, raises few objections, though a concern for balanced statement might add (as Durkheim increasingly did) that they are also internal to particular individuals; but the suggestion that social facts are external to all individuals can be justified only in the limited sense that they have a prior temporal existence, and any extension beyond these limits is subject (as Durkheim frequently was) to charges of hypostatizing some metaphysical "group mind" (Lukes, 1972, pp. 3–4). The term "constraint" seems to have enjoyed a still greater elasticity, for Durkheim used it variously to refer to the authority of laws as manifested through repressive sanctions; the need to follow certain rules in order to successfully perform certain tasks; the influence of the structural features of a society on its cultural norms and rules; the psychological pressures of a crowd on its members; and the effect of socialization and acculturation on the individual. The first of these usages, Lukes has observed, seems more felicitous than the second (which is perhaps better described as a "means–end" relation), and the last three seem something else altogether: far from being cases of "constraint" or "coercion," they describe how people are led to think and feel in a certain way, to know and value certain things, and to act accordingly (Lukes, 1972, p. 4). It was these latter usages, moreover, which Durkheim increasingly adopted as his interests shifted from the structural emphases of *The Division of Labor* to the focus on collective representations characteristic of *The Elementary Forms*; as he did so, "constraint" became less an "essential characteristic" than a "perceptible sign," and, eventually, disappeared altogether.

Like his definition of social facts, Durkheim's rules for their explanation represent the effort to establish sociology as a science independent of psychology. But here again, "psychology" seems to have meant several different things to Durkheim: explanation in terms of "organico-psychic" factors like race and/or heredity; explanation by "individual and particular" rather than "social and general" conditions; and, most frequently, explanation in terms of "individual mental states or dispositions." In each instance, Durkheim discovered logical or empirical shortcomings; but if social facts thus cannot be *completely* explained by psychological facts, it is at least equally true that even the most determinedly "sociological" explanations necessarily rely upon certain assumptions, explicit or otherwise, about how individual human beings think, feel, and act in particular circumstances. Durkheim's insistence that social facts can be explained only by other social facts was thus both excessive and naive (Jones, 1986, p. 79).

Durkheim's effort to find objective criteria by which "normal" might be distinguished from "pathological" social facts was a rather transparent attempt to grant scientific status to the social and political preferences we identified in the discussion of social context (above). In addition to the logical difficulties of inferring "social health" from the "generality" of a phenomenon, Durkheim himself recognized the practical obstacles to drawing such inferences in "transition periods" like his own; but since economic anarchy, anomie, and rapidly rising suicide rates were all "general" features of "organized" societies, Durkheim's second criterion – that this generality be related to the general conditions of the social type in question – could render them "pathological" only by reference to some future, integrated society which Durkheim somehow considered "latent" in the present. Durkheim, in short, tended to idealize future societies, while dismissing present realities and, like many rationalists, thus appears to have been oblivious to the sheer historical contingency of all social arrangements (Lukes, 1972, p. 29).

The example chosen to illustrate these criteria – the "normality" of crime – reflects the same preconceptions. Even if we accept the argument that the punishment elicited by crime reaffirms that solidarity based on shared beliefs and sentiments, for example, we must still ask a series of more specific questions. Which beliefs and sentiments? Shared by whom? What degree of punishment?

Which "criminal" offenses? Committed by whom? For in the absence of specific answers to such questions (Durkheim's treatment of these issues is unrelievedly abstract), the claim that crime is functional to social integration could be used to justify *any* favored set of beliefs and practices, and *any* type or degree of punishment, simply by arguing that the failure to punish would be followed inevitably by social disintegration. Durkheim's additional claim – that crime is functional to social change – was a simple extension of the view discussed earlier, that law is the direct reflection of the *conscience collective*. But as Tarde was quick to point out, there is no *necessary* connection between the violation of these laws constituting crimes and the sources of moral and social innovation (Lukes and Scull, 1983, pp. 15–19).

As we have seen, Durkheim was a social realist and rationalist: he believed that society is a reality independent of individual minds, and that the methodical elimination of our subjective preconceptions will enable us to know it as it is. As we have also seen, this vocabulary had the advantage of providing young people of the Third Republic with a moral authority worthy of their submission (the "spirit of discipline") and an ideal to which they might commit themselves (the "attachment to groups"); but it is equally true that social facts are themselves constituted by the meanings given to them by those agents whose acts, thoughts, and feelings they are, and that such subjective interpretations are thus a part of the reality to be "known." The question of what religion *is*, for example, is hardly one which can be settled aside from the meanings attached to it by those whose "religion" is under investigation; and any effort to study it independent of such meanings runs the risk not merely of abstracting some "essentialist" definition of religion bearing no relation to the beliefs and practices in question, but also of unconsciously imposing one's own subjective interpretation under the guise of detached, scientific observation (Jones, 1986, pp. 80–1).

Politically, Durkheim maintained that scholars make poor activists, abstained from participation in socialist circles, and generally presented himself as a sociological expert advising his contemporaries on their "true" societal interests; but it is difficult to see how theories which so consistently and emphatically endorsed the secular democratic, egalitarian, antiroyalist, and antirevolutionary values of the Third Republic could reasonably be regarded as devoid of political interests and objectives. The point here is not simply that these theories served political ends, or even that these ends were Durkheim's own; it is rather that here the distinction between social thought and social action becomes elusive to the point of non-existence; for Durkheim's entire social science, including choice and formulation of problems, definition of terms, classification of social types, explanatory hypotheses, methods of proof – indeed, even the denial of all philosophical and political commitments itself – was deeply political (Lukes, 1982, pp. 22–3).

In *The Division of Labor*, Durkheim's early suggestion that social solidarity is an exclusively "moral" phenomenon, of which law is the "externally visible symbol," ignores the frequent conflict of some moral principles with others, some laws with other laws, and morality with legality generally. Durkheim did not deny the existence of such conflict, of course, but he did suggest that it was "pathological," not a part of the "normal" functioning of society, and thus placed it beyond the central focus of his sociological vision. Similarly, Durkheim implied that the state is merely an instrument whose authority reflects the disposition of the *conscience collective*, an implication which excludes most of the concerns so brilliantly explored by Max Weber: the means by which one group in a society achieves asymmetrical control over another; the personal, subjective standards by which the first judges the behavior of the second and renders it consequential; and so on. The point here is not simply that Durkheim did not choose to discuss these issues; rather, the point is that he *could* not, given the reasons why he chose to study law in the first place – as an "external index" of the more fundamental moral conditions of the social order (Lukes and Scull, 1983, pp. 5–8).

Durkheim clearly overstated the role of repressive law relative to the institutions of interdependence and reciprocity (kinship, religious ritual, economic and political alliance, etc.) in primitive societies. Malinowski's *Argonauts of the Western Pacific* (1922), for example, has provided ample evidence of the significance and complexity of relations of exchange among the Trobriand Islanders. In part, this may be attributed to Durkheim's ignorance of the ethnographic literature on primitive peoples, for his pronouncements on "primitive" legal systems in *The Division of Labor* are largely based on inferences drawn from the Hebrew Torah, the Twelve Tables of the ancient Romans, and the laws of early Christian Europe; but he seems to have got these wrong as well. The religious and moral exhortations of the Torah, for example, are largely devoid of "penal" sanctions, and coexisted with a predominantly secular legal system maintained by their "restitutive" counterparts; the sanctions attached to the Twelve Tables were almost equally restitutive; and the gradual emergence of the state as the pre-emptive legal institution of early modern Europe witnessed an *increase* in the relative proportion of repressive laws. Indeed, Durkheim understated the role of repressive law even in advanced industrial societies, in part because he ignored the fact that the nineteenth-century system of penal incarceration replaced the custom of compensating the victims of some crimes financially, and in part because he disregarded the punitive, stigmatizing aspect of many civil laws (Lukes and Scull, 1983, pp. 10–15).

It is also difficult to share Durkheim's confidence in the self-regulating quality of organic solidarity. Durkheim's account of the "anomic" division of labor alone, for example, exposed all the evils of unregulated capitalism: commercial and industrial crises, class conflict, meaningless, alienated labor, etc. (Lukes, 1972, p. 174). But his analysis of these evils was notoriously uncritical: because organic solidarity has evolved more slowly than its mechanical counterpart has passed away, the Third Republic endures a "pathological, disintegrative void"; an analysis which simultaneously implies that these evils are not endemic to modern societies (and thus eviscerates any criticism of them), and conveniently locates the conditions for the successful functioning of "organized" societies in some unspecified, Utopian future. As his work developed, however, Durkheim gradually relinquished the evolutionary optimism which underlay this mechanical, self-regulating, conception of the division of labor, became increasingly attracted to socialism and the potentially regulatory function of occupational groups, and granted greater emphasis to the independent role of collective beliefs in social life.

As the first systematic application of the methodological principles set out in 1895, *Suicide* reveals their limitations as well as their advantages, and thus provides an occasion for considering a number of difficulties – argument by elimination, *petitio principii*, an inappropriate and distortive language, etc. – which, though typical of Durkheim's work as a whole, are perhaps most clearly seen here. Durkheim's characteristic "argument by elimination," for example, pervades both *The Division of Labor* and *The Elementary Forms*, but there is no better example of its power to both persuade and mislead than Durkheim's discussion of "extrasocial causes" in Book One of *Suicide*. Briefly, the argument consists of the systematic rejection of alternative definitions or explanations of a social fact, in a manner clearly intended to lend credibility to the sole remaining candidate – which is Durkheim's own. Durkheim's use of this technique, of course, does not imply that his candidate does not deserve to be elected, but as a rhetorical device, argument by elimination runs at least two serious risks: first, that the alternative definitions and/or explanations might not be jointly exhaustive (other alternatives may exist); and, more seriously, that the alternative definitions and/or explanations might not be mutually exclusive (the conditions and causes they postulate separately might be conjoined to form perfectly adequate definitions and/or explanations other than Durkheim's "sole remaining" candidates). Durkheim's persistent use of this strategy can be attributed to his ineradicable belief, clearly stated in *The Rules*, that a given effect must always have a single cause, and that this cause must be of the same nature as the effect (Lukes, 1972, pp. 31–3).

*Petitio principii* – the logical fallacy in which the premise of an argument presumes the very conclusion yet to be argued – is, again, a feature of Durkheim's work as a whole. In *The Elementary Forms*, for example, Durkheim first defined religion as a body of beliefs and practices uniting followers in a single community, and later he concluded that this is one of religion's major functions. But there is no clearer instance of this style of argument than Durkheim's "etiological" classification of the types of suicide, which of course presupposes the validity of the causal explanations eventually proposed for them. The point, again, is not that this automatically destroys Durkheim's argument; but it does make it impossible to entertain alternative causes and typologies, and thus to evaluate Durkheim's frequently ambitious claims (Lukes, 1972, p. 31).

Durkheim's repeated insistence that sociology is a science with its own, irreducible "reality" to study also led him to adopt a language that was both highly metaphorical and systematically misleading. This is first evident in *The Division of Labor*, where abundant biological metaphors continuously suggest that society is "like" an organism in a variety of unspecified and unqualified ways; and it is still more pernicious in *The Elementary Forms*, where the real themes of the work – the social origin of religious beliefs and rituals, their symbolic meanings, etc. – are frequently disguised beneath the obfuscatory language of "electrical currents" and "physical forces." *Suicide* combines elements of both; and in particular, this language made it difficult if not impossible for Durkheim to speak intelligibly about the way in which individual human beings perceive, interpret, and respond to "suicido-genic" social conditions (Lukes, 1972, pp. 34–6).

Finally, it might be argued that Durkheim's central explanatory hypothesis – that when social conditions fail to provide people with the necessary social goals and/or rules at the appropriate levels of intensity their socio-psychological health is impaired, and the most vulnerable among them commit suicide – raises far more questions than it answers. Aren't there different kinds of "social goals and rules," for example, and aren't some of these disharmonious? What is socio-psychological "health"? Isn't it socially determined, and thus relative to the particular society or historical period in question? Why are disintegrative, egoistic appetites always described as individual, psychological, and even organic in origin? Aren't some of our most disruptive drives socially generated? And if they are, aren't they also culturally relative? Why are some individuals rather than others "impaired"? And what is the relationship (if, indeed, there is one) between such impairment and suicide? The fact that these questions and others are continuously begged simply reiterates an earlier point: that Durkheim's macro-sociological explanations all presuppose some social-psychological theory, whose precise nature is never made explicit (Lukes, 1972, pp. 213–22).

Even *The Elementary Forms* – Durkheim's greatest work – is not without flaws; indeed, it contains most of the problems discussed earlier, and a few others besides. In sharp contrast to Max Weber, for example, Durkheim largely ignores the role of individual religious leaders, as well as the way religion functions in social conflict and asymmetrical relations of power. The "collective effervescence" stimulated by religious assemblies presumes a social psychology never made explicit, and Durkheim's account of how such gatherings generate totemic symbols is dubious, to say the least. His definition of religion, preceded by an extended argument by elimination and containing a massive *petitio principii*, bears little relation to anything that the central Australians themselves understand by their beliefs and behavior; and students of aboriginal religion like W. E. H. Stanner have spent months looking for instances of the sacred–profane dichotomy, even to the point of questioning their own competence, before admitting that the Australian facts simply do not fit (Stanner, 1967, p. 229).

If there is a single feature of the work more disturbing than any other, it is Durkheim's treatment of the ethnographic evidence. The choice of the "single case" of central Australia has an intrinsic appeal to anyone familiar with the "scissors and paste" method of comparative religion epitomized in *The Golden Bough*; but in practice this focus led Durkheim to ignore counter-instances among the neighboring Australian tribes, or to interpret them arbitrarily according to some *ad hoc*, evolutionary speculations, or to "correct" them in light of the more advanced, and hence allegedly more edifying, American tribes. In fact, there is no evidence that Australian totemism is the earliest totemism, let alone the earliest religion; and, though technically less advanced than the North American Indians, the Australians have a kinship system which is far more complex. But then, *pace* Durkheim, there is no necessary relationship between the "simplicity" of a society (however that is defined) and that of its religious beliefs and practices; nor, for that matter, is there any necessary relationship between religion and totemism generally (*wakan* and *mana* have no discernible relationship to the "totemic principle"). Even if we limit ourselves to Australian tribes, we find that the central tribes are atypical; that the major cohesive force among aborigines is the tribe rather than the clan; that there are clans without totems (and totems without clans); and that most totems are not represented by the carvings and inscriptions on which Durkheim placed so much weight. Finally, we may choose to circumvent the details of Durkheim's interpretation of the ethnographic literature altogether, observing that its *raison d'être* – the notion that the "essence" of religion itself may be found among the Arunta – is, in Clifford Geertz's (1973, p. 22) words, "palpable nonsense." What one finds among the Arunta are the beliefs and practices of the Arunta, and even to call these "religious" is to impose the conventions of one's own culture and historical period.

Criticisms such as these have led some scholars to suggest that the Australian data were introduced simply to illustrate Durkheim's theories, rather than the theories being constructed or adopted to account for the data. But this suggestion requires at least one major qualification in the light of what we know about the historical development of Durkheim's ideas on religion. The rather formal, simplistic conception of religion characteristic of Durkheim's early work, for example, persisted at least until the appearance of Baldwin Spencer and F. J. Gillen's *Native Tribes of Central Australia* (1899); and it was the largely psychologistic and utilitarian interpretation of these ethnographic data proposed by Frazer (and endorsed by Spencer himself) which led Durkheim back to the more determinedly sociological (even mystical) views of Robertson Smith, and to the contrived and even grotesque evolutionary interpretation of these data found in "Sur le totémisme" (1902). If the theories of *The Elementary Forms* do not "explain the facts" of Australian ethnography, therefore, it is because so much of their original purpose was to explain them away (see Jones, 1985).

The most ambitious claim of *The Elementary Forms*, of course, is that the most basic categories of human thought have their origin in social experience; but this claim, Steven Lukes has argued, is not one but six quite different claims which Durkheim did not consistently and clearly distinguish: the *heuristic* claim that concepts (including the categories) are collective representations; the *causal* claim that society produces these concepts; the *structuralist* claim that these concepts are modeled upon, and are thus similar to, the structures of society; the *functionalist* claim that logical conformity is necessary to social stability; the *cosmological* claim that religious myth provided the earliest systems of classification; and the *evolutionary* claim that the most fundamental notions of modern science have primitive religious origins. The structuralist, cosmological, and evolutionary claims, Lukes observed, have been both challenging and influential. But the heuristic claim, by conflating the categories with concepts in general, confuses a capacity of mind with what is better described as its content. In so far as society is literally defined in terms of collective representations (as the later Durkheim increasingly did), both the causal and the functionalist claims seem simply to restate the heuristic claim, and are vulnerable to the same objection; but, in so far as society is construed in structural terms (as in *The Division of Labor*), the causal claim in particular is open to serious objections. The very relations proposed between the structures of primitive societies and their conceptual apparatus, for example, would seem to presuppose the primitives' possession of precisely those concepts. Finally, Durkheim's sociology of knowledge seems susceptible to at least as many empirical objections as his sociology of religion (Needham, 1963, pp. vii–xlviii).

## CONCLUSION

At the outset, I suggested that we think of social theories as "languages" or "vocabularies" – ways of thinking or speaking about social phenomena – that are cobbled together by theorists to serve their own, quite concrete, interests and purposes. As we have seen, Durkheim's interests and purposes were intertwined with those of the Third French Republic, with producing the kind of citizen who would not simply obey its laws, but would also respect and revere its institutions. For this purpose, he found the traditional vocabulary of Cartesian rationalism – with its emphasis on "clear and distinct ideas" – utterly inadequate. For he was convinced that the notion of society as an "idea" would always remain insufficient to guarantee the veneration of future citizens of the Republic. Instead, relying heavily on writers like Boutroux, Fustel, Espinas, Schäffle, Wundt, Montesquieu, and especially Rousseau, Durkheim constructed the vocabulary of "social realism" – with its insistence that social facts are complex and concrete *things* – and then demonstrated its utility in the study of social differentiation, morality, education, crime, suicide, religion, knowledge, and science. Like all vocabularies, Durkheim's was limited in its capacity to deal with certain kinds of questions; but unlike its seventeenth-century antecedent, it has proved extremely powerful for the kinds of things that twentieth-century people want to do.

## Bibliography

### Writings of Émile Durkheim

Gumplowicz, Ludwig, *Grundriss der Soziologie*. 1885. *Revue Philosophique*, 20, 627–34.

La Science positive de la morale en Allemagne. 1887. *Revue Philosophique*, 24, 33–58, 113–42, 275–84.

Course in Sociology: Opening Lecture. 1888. In Mark Traugott (ed.), *Émile Durkheim on Institutional Analysis*. Chicago: University of Chicago Press (1978), pp. 43–70.

Individualism and the Intellectuals. 1898. In Robert N. Bellah (ed.), *Émile Durkheim on Morality and Society*. Chicago: University of Chicago Press (1973), pp. 43–57.

Concerning the Definition of Religious Phenomena. 1899. In W. S. F. Pickering (ed.), *Durkheim on Religion: a Selection of Readings with Bibliographies*. London and Boston: Routledge & Kegan Paul, pp. 74–99.

On Totemism. 1902. *History of Sociology*, 5 (1985), 79–121.
Sur la séparation des églises et de l'état. 1905. *Libres entretiens*, 1ère série, 369–71, 496–500.
The Determination of Moral Facts. 1906. In Émile Durkheim (ed.), *Sociology and Philosophy*. New York: Macmillan (1974), pp. 35–62.
Lettres au Directeur de la *Revue Néo-Scholastique*. 1907. *Revue Néo-Scholastique*, 14, 606–7, 612–14.
Value Judgments and Judgments of Reality. 1911. In Émile Durkheim (ed.), *Sociology and Philosophy*. New York: Macmillan (1974).
*The Elementary Forms of the Religious Life*, translated by Joseph Ward Swain. 1915. New York and London: Free Press.
*Suicide: a Study in Sociology*, translated by John A. Spaulding and George Simpson. 1951. Glencoe, IL: Free Press of Glencoe.
Rousseau's Social Contract. 1960. In Émile Durkheim (ed.), *Montesquieu and Rousseau: Forerunners of Sociology*. Ann Arbor, Michigan: University of Michigan Press, pp. 65–138.
*Moral Education: a Study in the Theory and Application of the Sociology of Education*, translated by Everett K. Wilson and Herman Schnurer. 1961. New York: Free Press of Glencoe.
*Primitive Classification*, translated by Edward Sagarin. 1963. Chicago: University of Chicago Press.
Individual and Collective Representations. 1974. In *Sociology and Philosophy*. New York: Macmillan, pp. 1–34.
*The Evolution of Educational Thought: Lectures on the Formation and Development of Secondary Education in France*. 1977. London and Boston: Routledge & Kegan Paul.
Rousseau on Educational Theory. 1979. In W. S. F. Pickering (ed), *Durkheim: Essays on Morals and Education*. London and Boston: Routledge & Kegan Paul, pp. 162–94.
The Rules of Sociological Method. 1982. In Steven Lukes (ed.), *The Rules of Sociological Method and Selected Texts on Sociology and Its Method*. London and Basingstoke: Macmillan, pp. 29–163.
*Pragmatism and Sociology*, translated by J. C. Whitehouse. 1983. Cambridge: Cambridge University Press.
*The Division of Labor in Society*, translated by W. D. Halls. 1984. New York: Free Press.
*Quid Secondatus Politicae Scientiae Instituendae Contulerit (Montesquieu's Contribution to the Rise of Social Science)*, translated by W. Watts Miller and Emma Griffiths. 1997. Oxford: Durkheim Press.

## Further reading

Alexander, Jeffrey C. (1983) *Theoretical Logic in Sociology, Volume 2. The Antinomies of Classical Thought: Marx and Durkheim*. Berkeley and Los Angeles: University of California Press.
Alexander, Jeffrey C. (ed.) (1988) *Durkheimian Sociology: Cultural Studies*. Cambridge: Cambridge University Press.
Bellah, Robert N. (ed.) (1973) *Émile Durkheim: On Morality and Society*, translated by Mark Traugott. Chicago and London: University of Chicago Press.
Berger, Peter (1967) *The Sacred Canopy*. New York: Doubleday.
Berger, Peter and Luckman, Thomas (1967) *The Social Construction of Reality*. New York: Doubleday.

Besnard, Philippe (ed.) (1983) *The Sociological Domain: the Durkheimians and the Founding of French Sociology*. Cambridge: Cambridge University Press.

Black, Donald (1976) *The Behavior of Law*. New York: Academic Press.

Bloor, David (1982) Durkheim and Mauss Revisited: Classification and the Sociology of Knowledge. *Studies in the History and Philosophy of Science*, 13, 267–97.

Bourdieu, Pierre (1989) *La Noblesse d'État: Grands Corps et Grandes Écoles*. Paris: Minuit.

Bourdieu, Pierre and Wacquant, Loïc J. D. (1992) *An Invitation to Reflexive Sociology*. Chicago: University of Chicago Press.

Boutroux, Émile (1895) *Natural Law in Science and Philosophy*, translated by Fred Rothwell. London: D. Nutt (1914).

Boutroux, Émile (1916) *The Contingency of the Laws of Nature*, translated by Fred Rothwell. Chicago and London: Open Court.

Braudel, F. (1949) *The Mediterranean and the Mediterranean World in the Age of Philip II*. Glasgow: Collins (1966).

Bury, J. P. T. (1985) *France, 1814–1940*. London: Methuen.

Cladis, Mark S. (1992) *A Communitarian Defense of Liberalism: Émile Durkheim and Contemporary Social Theory*. Stanford, CA: Stanford University Press.

Clark, T. N. (1973) *Prophets and Patrons: the French University and the Emergence of the Social Sciences*. Cambridge, MA: Harvard University Press.

Collins, Randall (1985) *Three Sociological Traditions*. New York and Oxford: Oxford University Press.

Coser, Lewis A. (1971) *Masters of Sociological Thought*. New York: Macmillan.

Douglas, Mary (1966) *Purity and Danger: an Analysis of Concepts of Pollution and Taboo*. London: Routledge  Kegan Paul.

Douglas, Mary (1973) *Natural Symbols: Explorations in Cosmology*. London: Barrie and Rockcliff.

Erikson, Kai (1966) *Wayward Puritans: a Study in the Sociology of Deviance*. New York: Wiley.

Fenton, S. (1984) *Durkheim and Modern Sociology*. Cambridge: Cambridge University Press.

Frazer, James (1890) *The Golden Bough*. New York: Macmillan.

Frazer, James (1899) The Origin of Totemism. *Fortnightly Review*, 68, 657–65, 835–52.

Gane, Mike (1988) *On Durkheim's Rules of Sociological Method*. London: Routledge & Kegan Paul.

Geertz, Clifford (1973) Thick Description: toward an Interpretive Theory of Culture. In *The Interpretation of Cultures*. New York: Basic Books, pp. 3–30.

James, William (1902) *The Varieties of Religious Experience*. Harmondsworth: Penguin (1983).

Jones, Robert Alun (1985) Durkheim, Totemism and the Intichiuma. *History of Sociology: an International Review*, 5(2), 79–121.

Jones, Robert Alun (1986) *Émile Durkheim. An Introduction to Four Major Works*. Beverly Hills, CA and London: Sage.

LaCapra, D. (1972) *Émile Durkheim: Sociologist and Philosopher*. Ithaca, NY and London: Cornell University Press.

Lehmann, Jennifer M. (1994) *Durkheim and Women*. Lincoln and London: University of Nebraska Press.

Lévi-Strauss, Claude (1955) *Tristes Tropiques*. Paris: Librarie Plon.

Lukes, Steven (1972) *Émile Durkheim: His Life and Work. A Historical and Critical Study*. New York: Harper & Row.

Lukes, Steven (1982) Introduction. In Steven Lukes (ed.), *Durkheim: the Rules of Sociological Method and Selected Texts on Sociology and Its Method.* New York: Macmillan, pp. 1–27.

Lukes, S. and Scull, A. (eds) (1983) *Durkheim and the Law.* Oxford: St Martin's Press.

McManners, John (1972) *Church and State in France, 1871–1914.* London: Church Historical Society.

Malinowski, Bronislaw (1922) *Argonauts of the Western Pacific.* London: Routledge & Kegan Paul.

Mauss, Marcel (1925) *The Gift.* New York: Free Press (1954).

Mayeur, Jean-Marie and Rebérieux, Madeleine (1984) *The Third Republic from Its Origins to the Great War, 1871–1914.* Cambridge: Cambridge University Press.

Merton, R. K. (1949) *Social Theory and Social Structure.* New York: Free Press; revised edition, 1957; enlarged and revised edition, 1968.

Needham, Rodney (1963) Introduction. In Rodney Needham (ed.), *Primitive Classification.* Chicago: University of Chicago Press, pp. vii–xlviii.

Parsons, Talcott (1937) *The Structure of Social Action.* New York: Free Press.

Pickering, W. S. F. (1984) *Durkheim's Sociology of Religion: Themes and Theories.* London, Boston and Melbourne: Routledge & Kegan Paul.

Pickering, W. S. F. and Martins, H. (eds) (1994) *Debating Durkheim.* London and New York: Routledge.

Pope, Whitney (1976) *Durkheim's Suicide: a Classic Analyzed.* Chicago and London: University of Chicago Press.

Ritzer, George (1992) *Sociological Theory.* New York: McGraw-Hill.

Robertson, Smith, William (1889) *The Religion of the Semites.* 2nd edn 1894. New York: Schocken (1972).

Schmaus, Warren (1994) *Durkheim's Philosophy of Science and the Sociology of Knowledge: Creating an Intellectual Niche.* Chicago and London: University of Chicago Press.

Spencer, Baldwin and Gillen, F. J. (1899) *The Native Tribes of Central Australia.* London: Macmillan.

Stanner, W. E. H. (1967) Reflections on Durkheim and Aboriginal Religion. In M. Freedman (ed.), *Social Organization: Essays Presented to Raymond Firth.* Chicago: Aldine, pp. 217–40.

Swanson, Guy (1960) *The Birth of the Gods: the Origin of Primitive Beliefs.* Ann Arbor: University of Michigan Press.

Thompson, Kenneth (1982) *Émile Durkheim.* London and New York: Tavistock/Routledge.

Traugott, Mark (ed. and trans.) (1978) *Émile Durkheim on Institutional Analysis.* Chicago: University of Chicago Press.

Wallwork, Ernest (1972) *Durkheim, Morality and Milieu.* Cambridge, MA: Harvard University Press.

Zola, Émile (1892) *La Débâcle.* Chester Springs, PA: Dufour (1969).

# 7

# Georg Simmel

## LAWRENCE A. SCAFF

## LIFE, WORK AND ORIENTATION

As one of the most important modern social theorists, Georg Simmel has always presented an impressive yet ambiguous face to the world. A prescient and brilliant diagnostician of our times, as Habermas has acknowledged, he has also been seen as more interested in the suggestive *aperçu* than in systematic science (Habermas, 1991, p. 158). Simmel was a key founder of sociology in Germany, and his essays received international recognition during his lifetime, but his work as a whole has nevertheless been treated as an ambivalent "experiment" with "impressionist" leanings (Lukács, 1918, cited in Gassen and Landmann, 1993, p. 175; Frisby, 1992). Conflicting judgments about Simmel should not be surprising, however, considering the task that he set for himself to write as both a philosopher and sociologist, ignoring the usual disciplinary fetters, while probing the dynamics of modern social and individual experience in all of its aspects, from economics to art, with an uncompromising earnestness and originality. Much of what remains engaging and instructive in Simmel's work has to do with the reach, depth and risks of his intellectual journey. In an ironic twist that Simmel would have appreciated, the very marginality of his daring seems to have ensured his centrality in our own times.

Simmel was an intellectual of the *fin de siècle*. Born in the very heart of old Berlin in 1858, he lived in the city nearly all his life, experiencing its rise from a modest and sleepy provincial capital to a teeming, industrialized metropolis and center of world power. Only in 1914 did he move to a chair in philosophy at Strasbourg, Alsace, dying of liver cancer in that disputed city four years later as the Great War ground to a halt outside its gates. The intellectual, cultural, and political life of Berlin was essential for Simmel. He was a man of the city, a close observer of its dynamic social life, and a devotee of its varied sociocultural milieu. In one of his rare autobiographical statements, he commented that "Berlin's development from a city to a metropolis in the years around and after the turn of the century coincides with my own strongest and extensive development" (quoted in Frisby, 1992, p. 19).

That personal development took place most importantly within the Philosophical Faculty of the Humboldt University, where Simmel was a student and lecturer for nearly forty years, though never gaining a regular professorial appointment – a source of bitter disappointment. The problems, topics, and themes of his many writings over these decades breathe the spirit of this most urban of universities and its powerful intellectual traditions and profoundly unsettled environment of sublime spectacle and dynamic pace. Contemporaries understood this fact. As the philosopher Karl Joël observed in reviewing *The Philosophy of Money*, the work some regard as Simmel's major achievement, it could only have been "written in these times and in Berlin" (Frisby, 1992, pp. 11, 19). It was in this urban center also that Simmel moved from philosophy to sociology, delivering the first lectures on sociological subjects in a German university in 1893–4. His sociological commitments were underscored later when, with Max Weber and Ferdinand Tönnies, he founded the German Sociological Society, inaugurating its first meeting in 1910 with his important paper on "sociability."

Georg Simmel was the youngest of seven children in a family of Jewish heritage from Silesia, now in southern Poland. Both parents had converted to Christianity, his mother to Protestantism as a teenager, and his father to Catholicism during a business trip to Paris. The son followed his mother's example, though he never entirely lost his Jewish identity and thus felt the sting of antisemitism. Simmel's father, Edward, a successful businessman and founder of the firm "Felix and Sarotti" (later the well known chocolate company), died when young Georg was sixteen, leaving him in the care of a family friend, Julius Friedländer. This tragic event proved fortuitous, however, as Friedländer had successfully established the "Edition Peters" music publishing firm, and the generous inheritance he left Simmel allowed the promising young scholar to pursue an academic career, despite years spent without a regular salaried position. Simmel's life path thus paralleled those of others in his generation, such as Weber, Sombart, or slightly later Robert Michels, in which the sons fled the comfortable confines of the *Besitzbürgertum*, the wealthy upper middle class, for the speculative fields of science – a flight made possible in part by inherited wealth or the condition Weber ironically labeled his "miserable *rentier* existence."

One of the most significant aspects of Simmel's upbringing and university years was his introduction not simply to philosophy and social theory, but also to artistic circles in Berlin. Supported by Friedländer, Simmel continued a musical education begun in his youth, studying both piano and violin. But even more importantly he became acquainted with the Graef family, home of the famous painter, and through the members of the family came into contact with artistic circles, the figures of the Berlin *Secession*, and eventually the symbolist poet Stefan George and his circle. It was also through the daughter, Sabine, that he met his future wife, Gertrud Kinel, who with Sabine had studied painting at the celebrated *Académie Julien* in Paris.

By the 1880s and 1890s the interest in these circles in the inner life, emotions, the psyche, and artistic expression had congealed in a new aesthetic "culture of feeling" in urban centers like Berlin, Vienna, and Paris – a cultural movement, as historians have pointed out, that was sharply set off from the dominant liberal, politically oriented, moralizing, and philosophical culture of the era. Simmel was immersed in both cultures, associating with the poets attracted to Stefan George and composing experimental verse and prose for the art nouveau journal *Jugend*. Yet he was also dedicated to the rigors of Kantian philosophy, while publishing in Karl Kautsky's socialist publication, *Die neue Zeit*, and also becoming active in the politically engaged Social Science Students Association (the *Sozialwissenschaftliche Studentenvereinigung*). He thus bridged the great cultural divisions of his times, showing an inclination to multiple perspectives and group affiliations. His work can be seen as an effort to understand the different and opposed sides of these divisions, to rethink the problems of each through the new science of "sociology" and the modes of inquiry characteristic of "philosophical culture," as he titled one of his most important collections of essays.

Critical synthesis of contradictory viewpoints, system building, or reconciliation between opposing forces in the world was not Simmel's ambition, however. For again and again he presents himself to us as a man of ideas having an uncommon will to originality, adopting an "experimental" stance, a mode of writing, and a "style" that reveals the unique grammar of his thinking. His emphasis is on maintaining the dualisms, the dyadic tensions, rather than imposing a new synthesis or schematic "master narrative." Today some would call such a view "postmodern," though for Simmel himself it was merely "modern." If as a modernist he singled out a particular moral-political problem, then it had to do with individuality: how can our individuality be preserved in the face of the dominating forces external to us? Or, as he notes in the idiom of *The Philosophy of Money*, it is "the discrepant relationship between objective and subjective culture, which forms our specific problem" (Simmel, 1990, p. 450). Simmel's social theory and sociology represent an effort to address this assertion.

## YOUNG SIMMEL: THE EARLY WRITINGS

"I began with epistemological and Kantian studies, which went hand in hand with historical and social scientific studies," wrote Simmel about his own starting points (Gassen and Landmann, 1993, p. 9). This self-appraisal referred quite obviously to the neo-Kantian movements of the time, represented in Berlin by Wilhelm Dilthey, and also to Simmel's participation in lectures and seminars offered by famous historians like Theodor Mommsen and Heinrich von Treitschke. But the "social scientific" reference is more obscure. In part because of the detailed recent work of Klaus Köhnke (1996), we now know considerably more about this aspect of the intellectual point of departure and its significance for Simmel's mature work.

As a budding social scientist in his early twenties, Simmel in his earliest writte work actually dealt with a field of social psychology known as *Völkerpsycholc gie* or ethnopsychology, founded by one of his most important teachers, Morit Lazarus. His first effort at a dissertation, subsequently rejected by his committee bore the striking title "Psychological and Ethnographic Studies on the Origins c Music," and incorporated an evolutionary perspective informed generally b Spencer and Darwin. Indeed, Dilthey himself later commented appropriately o the early Simmel that his "standpoint is Spencer's evolutionary theory" (Köhnke 1996, pp. 65, 77; Gassen and Landmann, 1993, p. 22). The reason for thi assessment had to do with an effort to postulate mechanisms and stages c evolutionary change with regard to the production of human culture – in thi case, musicality. But Simmel was also fascinated by problems in the less con troversial field of Kantian philosophy, where much of his early work wa centered. Kant was the subject of his successfully defended dissertation o 1881, and problems in Kantian ethics and logic formed the subject matter fo his habilitation four years later. When he began lecturing at the University o Berlin in 1885 the subjects revolved around philosophical and ethnopsycholo gical problems: ethics, Kant, and the significance of Darwinism.

It took Simmel a decade to shift "from ethnopsychology to sociology," as h noted himself – a transition that went hand-in-hand with the gradual substitu tion of evolutionary theory by a more "formal" approach. When the transitio was completed he began offering the first sociology lectures in a Germai university. So whereas his good friend Max Weber came to sociology by wa of political economy, Simmel developed his perspective through engagemen with ethnography, psychology, and philosophy. This particular intellectua path had important implications for the form and content of the Simmeliai sociological field, in contrast to what has come to be called a "Weberian perspective.

We see something of Simmel's developing intellectual perspective in the highl varied work leading up to the *Philosophy of Money* (1900). Many of Simmel' lifelong themes are evident in essays and lectures on: epistemological problems the philosophy of history; pessimism and culture; the nature of sociology; the psychology and social position of women; the problem of style and fashion; the sociology of the family; and the contributions and significance of major figure like Goethe, Nietzsche, Michelangelo, and Rembrandt. But the major dimen sions of his social theory are announced in two studies: *On Social Differentia tion: Sociological and Psychological Investigations* (1890), and the weighty two-volume opus, *Introduction to the Moral Sciences: a Critique of Basic Ethical Concepts*. Notwithstanding Simmel's mature criticism of the latter as a "youthful sin," these studies are important for showing the formulation of his central questions and the emergence of his sociology from evolutionary and developmental problematics. The text on social differentiation establishes a fundamental truth that Simmel carries with him the rest of his life, namely, what he calls "the unity of society as reciprocal interaction of its parts." The key concept of "interaction" or *Wechselwirkung*, with its connotations of reci procal (macro) causes and effects brought about by exchanges among individua (micro) units, is already well defined in this work and later becomes a highly nuanced element in Simmel's methodology. It is used in this early context to articulate a theory of social differentiation reminiscent of Durkheim's in *The Division of Labor in Society*, though the Durkheimian evolutionary framework is replaced by autonomous processes of differentiation within and among social groups, operating analogously to the principle of the "conservation of energy." Moreover, Simmel's most urgent problem is not the Durkheimian treatment of social facts as "things," *sui generis*, but rather the protection of individuality, a core value he establishes in this text that is itself a product of social interaction.

The eclecticism and experimentalism of the *Introduction to the Moral Sciences* has tended to diminish its importance. It is fair to say that it has "no recognizable thesis" and offers an "undisciplined reflection on the social" (Köhnke, 1996, pp. 167–8). But it is nevertheless the key early work, for it focuses Simmel's life work and theme around a "double relationship" expressed in the following way: "On the one hand the individual belongs to a whole and is a part of it, while on the other hand s/he is independent and stands opposed to it" (Simmel, 1989, volume 3, p. 178). The overriding concern of the *Introduction* involves answering the questions: how is this double relationship possible, and what are the categories for its analysis? As for J. S. Mill, Simmel's version of the moral sciences encompasses that branch of practical philosophy dealing with ethics and customs or mores; thus, much of his effort leads the reader on a tour through the standard categories: the ought, egoism, altruism, duty, happiness, freedom. But along the way Simmel begins to introduce sociological considerations bearing on the traditional problems of practical philosophy. "With Simmel the formation of *sociological* concepts begins within the framework and thus with the medium of ethics," as Köhnke maintains (1996, p. 397). The basic concepts of social life then start to take shape – individual, group, family, estate, or status order (*Stand*) – as do, most importantly, the forms of interaction and sociation – competition, opposition, super- and subordination, emulation, and the like.

It is with the insertion of this new conceptual language that the venerable "moral sciences" of the nineteenth century give way to the new sociology of the twentieth. In Germany Simmel was the key figure in leading this transformation, as was Durkheim in France. And across the Atlantic it was this Simmelian "interactionist" social perspective that so strongly influenced his American student, Robert Park, and through him led to the formation of the "Chicago School" of American sociology.

## SIMMEL'S SOCIAL THEORY: THE PHILOSOPHY OF MONEY

At the time Simmel was working through issues in ethics and the epistemology of the human sciences, he also began to engage with topics in political economy and models of *Homo economicus*. A paper on the "psychology of money," first delivered in Gustav Schmoller's economics seminar in Berlin, appeared in 1889, and it was followed by brief studies on the role of money in modern culture and in the relationship between the sexes. This work culminated in the seminal volume published in 1900, *The Philosophy of Money*.

Simmel's striking *fin de siècle* title concealed a number of important lines of thought. As "philosophy" his inquiry raised a question about the meaning of "money" as commodity, value, and symbol for the quality of human life. Simmel remarked that he was interested not only in the conditions that produce a money economy, but also in the effects of money and its exchange and use values "upon the inner world – upon the vitality of individuals, upon the linking of their fates, upon culture in general" (Simmel, 1990, p. 54). Such a question cannot be given an exact answer, to be sure, but instead presupposes a method that Simmel referred to as "hypothetical interpretation and artistic reconstruction." In this sense philosophy remains a special form of questioning, whose subject matter is always the "totality of being." Interestingly, however, Simmel's version of philosophical inquiry does not proclaim such a totality. Instead, it proceeds at the level of phenomena that are specific, concrete, limited, and finite. Its investigations are justified by the possibility "of finding in each of life's details the totality of its meaning" (Simmel, 1990, p. 55) – a quintessential Simmelian statement of purpose.

Methodologically, then, for Simmel the "philosophy" of money is distinct from the political economy of the modern capitalist economy, as practiced by Marx and his followers, for

> The attempt is made to construct a new storey beneath historical materialism such that the explanatory value of the incorporation of economic life into the causes of intellectual culture is preserved, while these economic forms themselves are recognized as the result of more profound valuations and currents of psychological or even metaphysical pre-conditions. (Simmel, 1990, p. 56)

In other words, Simmel hopes to uncover the psychological premises upon which modern economic forms must rest. These premises are worked out in terms of the inner valuation of money and the reaction to it as an abstract, impersonal power. The preconditions for the modern economy are found in the depersonalizing norms of calculation and efficiency that encourage us to view the world simply as an "arithmetical problem" having definite solutions. Employing architectonic imagery, Simmel has thus chosen to reinterpret Marx's materialist foundationalism through the medium of a psychologically attuned critique of the modern age. Alternatively, we might say that those aspects of the individual's orientation toward life that Max Weber spoke of as a "spirit" or an "ethos," Simmel tends to treat at the ground level of "psychological preconditions." For Simmel, however, the outcome of such an ordering of relations must be not so much a clearer view of history, but rather a nuanced understanding of the clash between subjective and objective moments in the total life of our evolving civilization.

To reach this understanding and accomplish its purpose *The Philosophy of Money* uses a distinctive perspective informed by juxtaposing "objective" and "subjective" realms of experience, a distinction that becomes central for Simmel's entire theory of culture. In this text the objective forms of the money economy are considered not in order to lay bare the economic substructure of society, but in order to probe what might be called their subjective consequences for the make-up of individuals and the content of social life. The problem is this: there is a contradiction that becomes increasingly evident in the modern age between the simultaneous "increase" in objective (or material) culture and the "decrease" in subjective (or individual) culture. Whereas the former becomes more and more refined, complex, sophisticated, expansive, comprehensive, and domineering, the latter in relation to it becomes cruder, simpler, more trivial, limiting, fragmentary, and anarchic:

> Just as our everyday life is surrounded more and more by objects of which we cannot conceive how much intellectual effort is expended in their production, so our mental and social communication is filled with symbolic terms, in which a comprehensive intellectuality is accumulated, but of which the individual mind need make only minimal use....Every day and from all sides, the wealth of objective culture increases, but the individual mind can enrich the forms and contents of its own development only by distancing itself still further from that culture and developing its own at a much slower pace. (Simmel, 1990, p. 449)

In the face of such a dynamic tendency Simmel then speaks of "the fragmentary life-contents of individuals" and "the insignificance or irrationality of the individual's share" of objective culture. Stated somewhat differently, the material artifacts and technologies we have created are set against ourselves and against human purposes. We lose control of our objective culture, are assaulted and overwhelmed by it, and begin to respond to it in different and opposed ways: with passivity or aggression, fascination or repulsion, immersion or escape. This initial insight into the duality of our experience presents Simmel with his philosophical *and* sociological problem: how is an opposition possible between ourselves and the contents of the world we have created? And what can it mean for the forms of sociation, of individual action in society?

Turning to the first question, the sociology of cultural contradictions is not difficult to conceive: objectification has its root causes in such solid facts as the division of labor; that is, the differentiation of functions and specialization of tasks in the economic order. Indeed, Simmel has already established differentiation as an irreducible general phenomenon and category of social life, whose true home is found in the increasingly complex money economy. But differentiation soon spreads everywhere and "brings about a growing estrangement between the subject and its products," which then "invades even the more intimate aspects of our daily life" (Simmel, 1990, p. 459). While gaining a hold over the life-world through differentiation, the money economy also prepares the way for the subversion of this world, just as it creates the conditions for our self-estrangement. In addition, the fetishism of objects is aligned with the fixation of a psychological dependence upon a quality Simmel refers to as *die Mode* – namely, style or fashion. That which is newly "fashionable" and *au courant* reveals itself in the commanding power of style. The problematic features of economic life are defined not merely by a separation between purportedly "natural" subjects and the material means of production or products of labor, but by the psychological transformation of external forms into a *reified* content. What Simmel thought of as "technological progress" is thus accompanied at the level of individual consciousness by a new interiority or *subjectivism* that renders the ephemeral continuous and the marginal central.

Now the primacy of style, characterized by Simmel at a key juncture in his reasoning as "one of the most significant instances of distancing" (Simmel, 1990, p. 473), is most importantly an indication of the increasingly uneasy awareness of a growing tension within the economy of the ego, or an increasing gulf between the self and objects, the self and others, all of which result from the individual's absorption into the entirely fluid realm of psychological experience. But distancing is also a precondition for sociation and group life. It gives us a starting point for addressing Simmel's second question about the forms of sociation.

One of the great achievements of *The Philosophy of Money* is the way it sets forth a phenomenology of our efforts to cope with the "social-technological mechanism" of the "objective" world, a line of thinking on a par with Freud's later attempt in *Civilization and Its Discontents*. What Simmel is able to do is demonstrate both the opportunities for freedom of the personality on the one hand, and the alternatives for mastery of the world on the other. In the third chapter the *types* of alternatives become quite explicit, and they are subsequently elaborated in some of Simmel's finest essays, such as those on "fashion" and the "metropolis," as well as in his last chapters on sociological topics in the *Fundamental Problems of Sociology* [*Grundfragen der Soziologie*] (see Simmel, 1917, chapter 3; 1971, pp. 294–339): greed or avarice, a life of extravagance, ascetic poverty, cynicism, the blasé attitude or position of complete indifference, reserve, or aversion, the appropriation of "style" in the name of "being different," even conviviality as the "play form" of social interaction – all represent the choice of an ethos, a way of life, occasioned by the intensification and heightening of experience in our material world. In Milan Kundera's language, they are ways of making this "lightness" bearable, of staking out a ground for freedom and personal choice.

For Simmel these psychological alternatives are manifested in two interesting and contrasting ways. First, they are self-referential and reflexive, and they provide a powerful commentary on Simmel's own unique cast of mind and stylistic peculiarities as a "theorist." Second, they recombine in the social types of his sociological analysis and occasional essays: the stranger, adventurer, miser, spendthrift, dandy, coquette, lover, aesthete, and so forth. These figures and the social roles they play signify *possible* responses to the dynamic forces unleashed in the money economy. But there are other responses as well, potentially an even infinite variation. (Parenthetically, Simmel once complained that what counts as sexuality is too limited, a situation modern society may seem determined to remedy!) In one of his last statements on the subject, he gave the idea the following form:

> I should like to think that the efforts of mankind will produce ever more numerous and varied forms for the human personality to affirm itself and to demonstrate the

value of its existence. In fortunate periods, these varied forms may order themselves into harmonious wholes. In doing so, their contradictions and conflicts will cease to be mere obstacles to mankind's efforts: they will also stimulate new demonstrations of the strength of these efforts and lead them to new creations. (Simmel, 1917, p. 103; 1950, p. 84)

Moreover, Simmel tends to view the ideological manifestations of political activity and social movements, such as socialism and feminism, in a similar light. That is, they too arise as a response to the impersonal, disintegrating effects of "money" on associational life.

When precisely a social movement arises, or why one type or direction is chosen over another, are the historical causal questions that Simmel sets off to one side. That is the weakness of his brilliant, process-oriented intellectual tour de force. But the strength of his unconventional analysis is that a "new storey beneath historical materialism" has been constructed and prepared for its new occupant: a general and a formal sociology.

## Sociology: interaction and experience

Simmel's main contributions to systematic sociology are found in two texts, the so-called "major" and the "minor" sociologies: that is, the essays begun in the 1890s and supplemented with later material in the thousand-page opus of 1908, *Sociology: Investigations of the Forms of Sociation*; and the four brief essays penned toward the end of his life and published in 1917 as *Fundamental Problems of Sociology: Individual and Society*. The latter provides a kind of overview of the path Simmel had followed, and in it he distinguishes among three kinds of sociology: general, pure or formal, and philosophical. The distinction can be described in terms of three kinds of problem areas: inquiry into the relationship between individual and society, viewed from the standpoint of the individual or the social; inquiry into the *forms* of interaction among individuals, the reciprocal relations that make up what we call society; and inquiry into the modes and presuppositions of knowledge suggested by the sociological point of view.

These problem areas of the discipline share a number of features. First, they adhere to a conception of society emphasizing its dynamic and process-oriented qualities: "Society exists where a number of individuals enter into interaction [*Wechselwirkung*]," Simmel writes, noting that "interaction always arises on the basis of certain drives or for the sake of certain purposes" (Simmel, 1971, p. 23; 1992, pp. 17–18). Indeed, he argues, "one should properly speak, not of society, but of sociation [*Vergesellschaftung*]. Society merely is the name for a number of individuals, connected by interaction" (Simmel, 1917, p. 14; 1950, p. 10). Society is thus not a reified whole or an observable object that exists *sui generis*, as Durkheim claimed, but a fluid reality composed of willing, acting, conscious individuals who impose a scheme of interpretation on their actions and engagements. It can be viewed as a kind of *a priori*, but only because we are social animals given to sociation and sociability, not because it exists independent of us.

A second commonality is a conception of sociology that "asks what happens to people and by what rules they act, not insofar as they develop comprehensible individual existences in their totality, but insofar as they form groups through interaction and are determined by this group existence" (Simmel, 1917, p. 15; 1950, p. 11, translation altered), a formulation taken up by Louis Wirth and others in the "Chicago School." As the specialized science of society, this sociology therefore "must exclusively investigate these interactions, these kinds and forms of sociation" (Simmel, 1971, p. 25; 1992, p. 19). That is sociology's central task, and it is one Simmel pursued for three decades with perspicacity and seemingly inexhaustible energy in a stream of essays, chapters, and occasional writings. His statement of the task also helps to demarcate the contested boundary between sociology and psychology, an important distinction because of the charges of "psychologism" that have burdened these Simmelian formulations. Whereas sociology's domain is sociation, psychology's is the structure of personality, or the quality Simmel called the irreducible "core of individuality" that makes each person unique.

Third, they share a basic assumption about methodology, namely, the view that sociological inquiry proceeds according to its own canons of knowledge, not according to the nomothetic intentions of the physical sciences. Sociology is essentially a reflexive science, aware of the way knowledge is conditioned by the knowledge-seeker, emphasizing in all domains of life what Simmel calls the "universality of sociation," and using an inductive method. To study sociation is to adopt "a methodology which is wholly different from that for the question of how nature is possible" (Simmel, 1971, p. 8; 1992, p. 45), as Simmel states the case. In contrast to Durkheim's conceptual realism, Simmel thus advocates a thoroughgoing philosophical nominalism that underscores the constructed and purposeful aspects to knowledge in the human sciences.

The chapters of the major or "*grosse*" *Sociology*, as it has been called, are often regarded as the *locus classicus* of Simmel's substantive contribution. They bring together the main outlines of both a general and a pure or formal sociology that proceeds with Euclidean precision from the most elemental of units (the hypothesis of the autonomous individual); to complex interactive units (dyads, triads, groups, organizations, bureaucracy, state); to complex social relationships (subordination, conflict, secrecy, trust), abstract ordering principles ("spatial" relationships), and particular social types (the stranger). Some of Simmel's most insightful studies are found in these investigations of the formal, abstract properties of, say, the "eternal triad" in human relationships, the unusual dynamics of the conspiratorial clique, or the positive functions of intense conflict for group solidarity. Every one of these studies is directed toward advancing our understanding of sociation processes and their typical forms, and all are rich with suggestions for investigating specific actual instances of social life.

Throughout these multifaceted studies it is clear that the most obvious underpinning of Simmel's scientific questioning in the *Sociology* and the *Fundamental Problems of Sociology* is the concept of "interaction," or, as the German word *Wechselwirkung* implies, action that has "reciprocal effects." It is a relational concept that is designed to get at the "objective" aspects of social life which exist outside of any particular individual and are then located between individuals. To speak of an interaction is to characterize a relation between a subject and an object (both of which may be human individuals). The appropriate images for this characterization are spatial, directional, and three-dimensional: movement to and fro, repetitive circular motion, the sweep of a curve, or (one of Simmel's favorites) the spiral movement from one "level" to another. The dynamics of rhythm, pace, and tempo are a part of this Simmelian language, as are the possibilities for either progression or regression, development or implosion, sympathy or antagonism, forming connections or breaking apart, certainty or ambivalence. Ironically, the very range and undecidability of these opposed categories has led critics, starting with Georg Lukács, to place this analysis itself in the "ambivalent" category – a charge that a Simmelian sociologist would say misses the point of Simmel's scientific intentions and ignores the ambivalence inherent in social life.

Summing up, we can say that interaction involves processes like objectification, differentiation and distanciation. Interaction also creates social "forms" – roles, institutions, social structures – and produces social effects, such as integration or marginalization. But this is not the entire story, for it is equally important to recognize, as Nedelmann (1990) has suggested, that Simmel's sociology actually proceeds from a double perspective: on the one side the focus of attention is interaction, and on the other it is "lived experience" or *Erleben*. The potential for this second perspective is already present in the *Philosophy of Money*, where Simmel expresses his interest in understanding the "inner world" and "vitality" of individuals. Then, in his mature sociology, such as the remarkable essay on the metropolis (Simmel, 1971, pp. 324–39), this interest is translated into an effort to grasp the effect of institutional forms produced by interaction on the *Geistesleben* – that is, on the mental, spiritual, and intellectual life of the individual. It is not the structure of the personality, the province of psychology, after all, that is at stake in this perspective, but rather the effort of individuals to integrate the "forms" of the social world, of which they are a part, into their own mental life. It is a matter of developing or choosing one's self, an act that is not merely personal, but social. Along with objectification, therefore, comes the reverse process of internalization of roles, norms, social attitudes, and behaviors – in a word, the process of socialization.

Simmel's sociology thus leaves us with a unique perspective on the fully "socialized" individual as both a cause and an effect: as the agent of interaction, as well as the resultant of the social structure and institutions produced by interaction. The circularity of this account would not have bothered Simmel, for it gave his analysis a secure way to understand sociology's perennial conundrum: the relationship between agency and structure.

## The theory of culture

In his sociology Simmel tends to think of interaction in terms of the "forms" it produces. But he also begins to introduce a vitalistic concept into his thinking, as did contemporaries like Henri Bergson: "Life" expresses itself through interaction, and out of life certain forms emerge that make life itself possible – predictable, secure, bearable, pleasurable, and creative. The difficulty, as Simmel begins to see, is that these forms tend to congeal and rigidify, a concern voiced later by Charles Cooley also. The forms become a constraining "culture" opposed to life, and then set off the eternal struggle between "life" and "form." This insight leads Simmel in the direction of a theory of culture as powerful as that developed by Freud.

The logical dualisms that serve as building blocks for a theory of culture become implicit by the time Simmel writes his last chapter to *The Philosophy of Money*, for in that text two of his most important notions are present: the "objectification of mind," and the growing tension in modernity between "material" and "individual" culture. But it is not until completing some of his last essays, especially "The Concept and Tragedy of Culture" (1911) and "The Conflict in Modern Culture" (1918), that Simmel successfully elaborates the assumptions, arguments, and details of this aspect of his work.

Simmel actually selects a twofold dualism for his point of departure: the Kantian opposition between subject and object, but also the opposition between self-consciousness and the "natural" world without consciousness of itself. "Humans, unlike the animals," he writes in "The Concept and Tragedy of Culture,"

> do not allow themselves simply to be absorbed by the naturally given order of the world. Instead, they tear themselves loose from it, place themselves in opposition to it, making demands of it, overpowering it, then overpowered by it. From this first great dualism springs the never-ending contest between subject and object, which finds its second tribunal within the realm of spirit [*Geist*] itself. (Simmel, 1968, p. 27)

Or as he says later in "The Conflict in Modern Culture": "Whenever life progresses beyond the animal level to that of the spirit, and spirit progresses to the level of culture, an internal contradiction appears. The whole history of culture is the working out of this contradiction" (Simmel, 1971, p. 234). The contradiction between the vital forces of "life" and the timeless forms of "culture" presupposes a process of objectification, which Simmel describes in terms of human mind or spirit projected outside itself, creating "structures" that exist independently of the creative subject, and becoming an autonomous force opposed to that subject. The subject thus becomes "objectified" in this process, which results in a radical and permanent tension – a *Formgegensatz* in Simmel's terminology – between vital, finite life and the fixed, timeless forms it is destined to create as a precondition for its own expression and survival. While the former seem transient, finite, fluctuating, relative to subjects, inward, and immediately experienced, the latter appear to be permanent, timeless, static, objectively valid, external, and mediated by distance. Simmel then announces his major insight: "The idea of culture dwells in the middle of this dualism."

Essentially two senses of the concept of culture seem to follow from this theoretical perspective. The first elaborates the metaphor of culture "as the path of the soul to itself," a formulation that could be read as a comment on an ascetic stance toward life that one also finds discussed in Nietzsche and Freud. Yet against the one-sided criticism of asceticism as repressive, Simmel's idea of culture suggests expression, development, and fulfillment of that which is essentially human: Culture can become

> the completion of the soul ... in which it takes the detour through the formations of the intellectual-historical work of the species: the cultural path of the subjective spirit traverses science and the forms of life, art and state, vocation and knowledge of the world – the path on which it now returns to itself as higher and perfected spirit.

Thus, from this perspective "life" must also be something formed, and the activity of culture can offer it what Simmel calls a "unity of the soul"; that is, the enticing prospect of a "solution to the subject–object dualism" through the promise of setting the preconditions for the pursuit of what could be designated self-development and the cultivation of personality.

In Simmel's view we appear to consist of a bundle of directions for self-development, all having varied potentialities. However, it is also the case that as cultural beings our choices are not arbitrary, but are instead governed by our culturally derived sense of "personal unity." Using Simmel's own peculiar language, we see that "Culture is the way that leads from closed unity through unfolding multiplicity to unfolding unity" (Simmel, 1968, p. 29). Or in more direct phrasing,

> culture exists only if man draws into his development *something that is external to him* ... the perfection of the individual is routed through real and ideal spheres outside of the self. The perfection does not remain a purely immanent process, but is consummated in a unique adjustment and teleological interweaving of subject and object. (Simmel, 1971, p. 230)

Thus, we can say that culture is necessarily dualistic, necessarily objective and subjective, and it makes possible the *process* of forming the self, an "unfolding unity," through reciprocal action between the objective and the subjective.

This conception of culture is rich with paradox, for on the one hand culture requires the perpetuation of an unresolved dualism, while on the other it is thought of as mediating or synthesizing the dialectically separated poles of our existence. Stated somewhat differently, whereas on one level it assumes unresolved difference, on another it urges development through mediative inclusion of the "other." Subjective life, driven toward perfection of its identity, "cannot by itself reach the perfection of culture," yet culture "is always a synthesis" of subjective life and the contents of life that "presupposes the divisibility of elements as an antecedent." Today it is especially modernity that accounts for such otherwise incomprehensible tension and potential confusion, for as Simmel maintains: "Only in an analytically inclined age like the modern could one find in synthesis the deepest, the one and only relationship of form between spirit and world" (Simmel, 1968, pp. 30, 35). We should accurately speak of a *longing* for synthesis and wholeness as most characteristic of the modern.

The clearest depiction of a second sense to the concept of culture comes at the end of Simmel's thinking on the subject in "The Conflict of Modern Culture," where he decides to speak of culture not so much whenever it functions through mediation, but rather

> whenever life produces certain forms in which it expresses and realizes itself: works of art, religions, sciences, technologies, laws, and innumerable others. These forms encompass the flow of life and provide it with content and form, room for play and for order. But although these forms arise out of the life process, because of their unique constellation they do not share the restless rhythm of life, its ascent and descent, its constant renewal, its incessant divisions and reunifications. These forms are cages for the creative life which, however, soon transcends them. They should also house the imitative life, for which, in the final analysis, there is no space left. They acquire fixed identities, a logic and lawfulness of their own [*eigene Logik und Gesetzlichkeit*]; this new rigidity inevitably places them at a distance from the spiritual dynamic which created them and which makes them independent. (Simmel, 1971, p. 375 translation modified)

For Simmel, not capitalism, vocational specialization, or instrumental rationality, but rational culture itself becomes the new "iron cage," employing Weber's well known metaphor from *The Protestant Ethic and the Spirit of Capitalism*. Moreover, this culture also possesses an "internal and lawful autonomy" of the kind Weber assigned to the different life-orders and value-spheres of the world. As a distinctive supralife form, culture is in this way of thinking set squarely against the forces of (creative) life. Culture is not merely the path to self-recognition, but also the dwelling place of repressive order. In one sense culture suggests movement and possibility, in another rigidity and limitation.

Simmel's theory raises this quality of culture that he refers to variously in his later essays as a paradox, crisis, conflict, or tragedy to the conscious level, not in order to abolish or transcend it, as some have supposed, for that would destroy culture and its sources in life, but in order to view cultural paradox as a moment in its own development. Like all of human life, culture has a history too, which shows that in the modern present "we are experiencing a new phase of the old struggle," in Simmel's words; it is "no longer a struggle of a contemporary form, filled with life, against an old, lifeless one, but a struggle of life against form as such, against the principle of form" (Simmel, 1968, p. 12). The peculiar and increasing "formlessness" of modern life is the hallmark of the present, and in agreement with Weber, Simmel believes it has been accompanied by numerous exaggerated expressions of life: endless searches in the avant-garde for originality and heightened experience, strivings for a "new ethic" or a "new religiosity," attempts to sanctify the soul in blasé and cynical personal styles. "Thus arises the typical problematic situation of modern man," Simmel maintains:

his feeling of being surrounded by an innumerable number of cultural elements which are neither meaningless to him nor, in the final analysis, meaningful. In their mass they depress him, since he is incapable of assimilating them all, nor can he simply reject them, since after all, they do belong potentially within the sphere of his cultural development. (Simmel, 1968, p. 44)

However, in Simmel's view it was not always so, for in a rare historical detour he suggests that at the very center of culture, from antiquity to modernity, has been a movement from an assumed "unity of being" (Greek philosophy), to "god" (Christianity), "nature" (the Renaissance), the "self" (the Enlightenment), "society" (the nineteenth century), and finally "life" (modernity), a schematic developmental process that has parallels in Weber's well known and concise critique of the illusory meanings Western culture has assigned to science and the search for knowledge. Just as Weber's modern science has now become disenchanted, or disabused of its innocent pretense, so Simmel's modern culture has surrendered the delusion of unitary meaning. For Western thought to move from Kant's critique of pure reason to Simmel's critique of culture has meant precisely to replace the universal individuality of a transcendental ego, situated in a single and generalizable world of mechanistic properties, with the unique individuality of a determinate subject, dispersed into multiple and particularizing worlds of qualitative variation. Furthermore, Simmel's historic diagnosis of modern culture's paradoxes and tragedies is given an immediacy it would otherwise lack because now our experience has driven the tension between "life" and its "forms" (most importantly including science and knowledge among them) to the greatest extreme yet attained.

In his scientific work Simmel responds in three important ways to the contemporary state of affairs outlined in his theory of culture. In the first place he is intrigued by the many social forces, organized groups, interactions or processes of sociation, sociability, and conviviality (*Geselligkeit*) that aim, as he remarks in his essay on Rodin, "to subordinate the whole of life to a meaningful order" which will serve "that deepest longing of the soul to mould everything that is given in its own image" (quoted in Böhringer and Gründer, 1976, pp. 234–5). This perspective and attendant subject matter can be understood as focused on the attempts in the modern age to recover a lost unity to culture, to find a way of overcoming the paradoxical juxtaposition of life and form. Even the unique concept of "conviviality," as Tönnies noted, was for Simmel precisely the "play form" of reciprocal action or interaction that created a space for "the sense of liberation and relief" indispensable for coping with the conditions of culture (quoted in Coser, 1965, p. 52). But in evaluating the modern search for meaningful order, a healthy metaphysical skepticism often prevents Simmel from doing more than honoring such attempts as humanly understandable and significant efforts from within culture to "solve" the crisis the tension between objective and subjective culture has produced. Genuine solutions lie in the unforeseen future, at the "end" of our history, so to speak. According to Simmel's theory of culture attempts aimed in this direction will lead to further fragmentation and differentiation, to a continuing proliferation of cultural forms, to further tensions between objective and subjective culture.

A second response becomes apparent in the realm of aesthetics, through the quest for "salvation through art" and the experience of conducting one's life as a "work of art." Certainly Simmel's writing on art and artists, such as Rembrandt, Goethe, Rodin, and George, his own authorial experimentation with poetry, and the essay form *sub specie aeternitatis* in the modernist journal of art nouveau, *Jugend*, are inclined in this direction. In addition, so is the aesthetic dimension implicit in the concept of "lived experience" or *Erleben* in his sociology. Indeed, some of Simmel's most provocative formulations appear in connection with the aesthetic dimension of *individual* experience, as distinct from social interaction:

> The problem that afflicts us in all areas, namely, how purely individual existence can be unified, how one can reject consideration of general norms...without descending into anarchy and rootless caprice – this problem has been solved by Rodin's art as art always solves spiritual problems: not in principle, but in individual perceptions [*Anschauungen*]. (Böhringer and Gründer, 1976, p. 233)

Similarly, the closest Simmel ever came to a personal answer to the problem of culture was in his own "individual perceptions," not in a definitive, principled "solution" to the conflict and "tragedy" of culture his analysis disclosed. No such solution existed, for to say that the widespread cultural problem can only be resolved aesthetically is to say that it can and must remain unresolved.

But if Simmel was attracted to the light of aesthetic judgment as a source of illumination, as he most certainly was, then he was also pulled in the direction of the clear air of reflection – caught, as it were, between the imperatives of Kant's first and third critiques. Like Weber and Freud, Simmel also chose to bind himself to the vocation of science, to choose intellect over latent possibility. This was his third response to the ultimate conflicts and tragedy of culture. In one of his very last comments, for instance, he reasoned,

> It is a philistine prejudice that all conflicts and problems are dreamt up merely for the sake of their solution. Both in fact have additional tasks in the economy and history of life, tasks which they fulfill independently of their own solutions. Thus they exist in their own right, even if the future does not replace conflicts with their resolutions, but only replaces their forms and contents with others. In short, the present is too full of contradictions to stand still. This itself is a more fundamental change than the reformations of times past. The bridge between the past and the future of cultural forms seems to be demolished; we gaze into an abyss of unformed life beneath our feet. But perhaps this formlessness is itself the appropriate form for contemporary life. Thus the blueprint of life is obliquely fulfilled. Life is a struggle in the absolute sense of the term which encompasses the relative contrast between war and peace: the absolute peace which might encompass this contrast remains an eternal secret to us. (Simmel, 1971, p. 393)

To speak of the breakdown of cultural tradition and continuity is to return to the paradoxical idea of form's absence as itself a form. This striking version of our acceptance of a formless present and our muted curiosity in the face of mystery may vouchsafe the interpretation of Simmel as a "tragic" and "ambivalent" thinker, trapped by the modern cultural dynamic and unable to penetrate those "eternal secrets" that might lead us into another world. Perhaps in this respect Simmel remained a cultural being, his imagination attuned solely to the rhythms of his own time.

However, in Simmel's defense one should say that the barrier to affirming definitive solutions and a new world, when it arose, was not inability but unwillingness: the other worlds, the alternatives made available in culture, were still for Simmel a part of that unprecedented modern culture he had so carefully dissected in all of its complexity and contradiction. In his critical judgment of those alternatives Simmel surely shed that alleged "ambivalence" that has haunted his reputation as sociologist and philosopher. With good reason he reserved the right, recalling Wittgenstein's well known epigram, to pass over the evaluation of any number of proposed solutions in silence.

The essential achievement of Simmel's theory is to emphasize the dialectical interplay that gives substance, direction, and shape to culture – especially now a modern culture delineated, so to speak, by the struggle between life and form. Simmel is convincing in maintaining that this struggle, considered in the abstract, is inevitable and necessary as a presupposition for culture – a position that separates his analysis from any dialectical syntheses, or the variations on Marx's historical materialism. Yet we can say that it is the very search for resolution and transformation of the dialectical aporia, for reconciliation of life with form, that is most characteristic of the sociology of associative activity in specifically modern culture. Simmel understands this insight, and therefore defends an "empirical" cultural sociology that rests upon his claims about culture's paradoxes. The subject matter for this sociology, in other words, is established by the great refusals to accept the essential opposition between external, material forms and humanity's subjective strivings. We can achieve some measure of judgment, Simmel tells us, by viewing such refusals from a distance, honoring their necessity, but also declining to enlist under the banner of their hopes for reconciling the dualisms of the culture we call our own.

## Woman and female culture

One of the most remarkable and prescient of Simmel's contributions to cultural sociology was his work on woman, gender, and difference. In Germany in the 1890s the women's movement began to gain a following in socialist and liberal circles, with growing numbers of women taking on public roles, participating in organizational activity, entering the universities, and preparing for the professions. As a close observer of social change, Simmel responded with a series of essays that staked out a theoretical position based on his overarching views about society and culture.

Discussion of the "woman question" in the philosophical traditions before Simmel had generally followed one of two possible patterns of thought: either woman was treated as "similar" to man because of a shared basic nature, as argued by Plato; or woman was considered "different" by virtue of differences in biology, psyche, being, or some other factor, as claimed by both Kant and Hegel. Occasionally a writer would articulate a position that combined elements of both views, as did J. S. Mill in "The Subjection of Women." Regardless of the particular orientation, in all of these discussions the major questions were always: similar or different with respect to what goods or values in social life; and what is the relevance of any claimed similarities or differences for social life?

Simmel's approach is a striking instance of the argument from "difference," similar to that of the developmental psychologist Carol Gilligan today. That is, he essentially adopts the view that woman is different in socially important ways, such as having a special relationship to the contents of culture, or having a different "sense of justice." Consider his most comprehensive statement on the issues in "Female Culture" (1911), for instance:

> Frequently the "legal antipathy" of women is stressed: their opposition to legal norms and judgments. However there is no sense in which this necessarily implies an animus against the law itself; instead, it is only against *male* law, which is the only law we have, and for this reason seems to us to be the law as such. In the same way, our historically defined morality, individualized by considerations of both time and place, seems to us to fulfill the conditions of the concept of morality in general. The female "sense of justice," which differs from the male in many respects, would create a different law as well. (Simmel, 1984, p. 68)

However, this "difference" is not understood as a basis for subordination. It is seen instead as an opportunity for developing multiplicity and cultural variation, as a possibility for promoting the emergence of new cultural forms. The reason for this radical perspective is grounded in the logic of Simmel's theory of culture.

Starting from his fundamental distinction between "objective" and "subjective" culture, Simmel links the difference between male and female experience to the process of objectification. The aspects of life that he calls the "cultural capital" of an era are found in its objective culture, and this culture, "with the exception of a very few areas . . . is thoroughly male" (Simmel, 1984, pp. 65, 67). The dichotomy between objective and subjective is then restated in numerous ways in Simmel's writing, but its basic alignment is with a view of woman's difference having to do with notions of differentiation and totality. As Simmel records the idea in one summation, "If there is any sense in which the distinctive psychic quality of woman's nature can be expressed symbolically, it is this: Its periphery is more closely connected with its center and its aspects are more completely integrated into the whole than holds true for the male nature" (Simmel, 1984, p. 73). Now it is not always clear what Simmel wants to infer or conclude from this kind of assertion, or even if he is fully committed to it. There is an experimental quality to such thoughts that may defy our normal expectations for clear and distinct reasoning. But such an experimental claim poses the obvious questions: What social changes occur when women move into the domains of objective culture? If women also create objective culture, is it then a qualitatively different *kind* of culture? Is there, or can there be, such a thing as *female* culture, and if so, what would it be like?

Bearing these qualifications in mind, Simmel nevertheless forges ahead and proposes a number of hypothetical answers to his questions, perhaps surprising to us for their contemporaneity. For instance, he suggests that woman accomplishes something in objective culture men cannot achieve, because of her capacity for empathy, using the example of diagnosis and care in medicine. Or he suggests that woman's unique character and ability can lead to newer forms of knowledge, alluding to the importance of "understanding" in writing history. However, for a contemporary feminist like Marianne Weber, writing a reply to Simmel in the journal *Logos* ("Woman and Objective Culture," 1913), these hypotheses sounded far-fetched, perhaps merely a projection of male needs and a romanticization of woman's difference. Moreover, they still failed to distinguish unambiguously between nature and nurture, between all that is naturally endowed and everything that is socioculturally determined.

Despite these difficulties, Simmel's last word poses an interesting challenge. For in his formulation culture itself is two-sided: it assumes a difference that is gender-specific; its subject is "man" and his choices. But culture also develops through mediative inclusion of the other, of "woman" and her being. This formulation, however, is set forth from within the perspective of objective (male) culture. Is there any other (female) perspective that can be stated in a different language? Consider Simmel's speculative conclusion to "Female Culture," a rare paragraph in which he seems to anticipate the course of the most radical directions of thought in the late twentieth century, especially those challenges to so-called "phallogocentrism" associated with postmodern critics:

> From the standpoint of cultural history, consider the extreme point that the ideal of the independence and equality of women seems to be capable of reaching: an objective female culture parallel to the male and thereby annulling its brutal historical idealization.... Under these circumstances, the male monopolization of objective culture would persist, but with justification. This is because objective culture as a formal principle would qualify as a one-sided male principle. Juxtaposed to it, the female form of existence would present itself as a different form, autonomous on the basis of its ultimate essence, incommensurable on the basis of the standard of the male principle, and with contents that are not formed in the same way. Thus its meaning would no longer turn on an equivalence *within* the general form of objective culture but rather on an equivalence between two modes of existence that have a completely different rhythm. One [male culture] is dualistic, oriented to becoming, knowledge, and volition. As a result, it objectifies the contents of its life out of the process of life in the form of a cultural world. The other [female culture] lies beyond this subjectively constituted and objectively developed dichotomy. For this reason, the contents of its life are not experienced in a form that is external to them. On the contrary, it must search out a perfection that is immanent to them. (Simmel, 1984, pp. 100–1)

Simmel, like modern feminism, does not know what this "immanent perfection" might look like, or what kind of "world" it might create. But the insight of his commentary is to foresee the trajectory of the line of thinking that the argument from *difference* must follow. The world, as he says, is "a form of the contents of consciousness." In this view the argument from difference is all about forming and raising consciousness; once that has taken place, the social world will not be far behind.

## Religion and art

Simmel's writings in the sociology and psychology of religion spanned two decades, from "A Contribution to the Sociology of Religion" of 1898, to the concluding section in "The Conflict of Modern Culture" of 1918. Among this work it was the lengthy essay, *Religion* (1906; 2nd edn 1912), published in Martin Buber's popular multi-volume series on different aspects of modern society, *Die Gesellschaft*, that provided the most sustained discussion of his views.

The subject matter in these writings is not simply the sociology of religion as a field for observing interaction, but more particularly the "lived experience" of the religious person. In contrast to Max Weber's well known essays in the sociology of religion, Simmel's work thus tends to play down comparative historical or institutional questions, while instead investigating the inward and personal aspects of religiosity or "religiousness" – the side of his sociology concerned with "experience." As Phillip Hammond has suggested, in contrast to Weber's "religiously unmusical" self-description we seem in this body of work to be confronted with the "religiously musical" side of Simmel's perceptions (Simmel, 1997, p. vii).

Following the tradition of thought that is also exemplified in William James's *The Varieties of Religious Experience*, Simmel distinguishes between religion as a doctrine or "set of claims," and religion as a "form of life" or a "state of being," agreeing with James that the latter is his primary concern. Both might be said to explore the meaning of Kant's notion that religion is "an attitude of the soul." But unlike James, Simmel explicitly repudiates the mechanistic psychology that views religiosity as a mental entity, instead proposing to see it as "a form according to which the human soul experiences life and comprehends its existence" (Simmel, 1997, pp. 5, 50). "All religiosity," he asserts,

> contains a peculiar admixture of unselfish surrender and fervent desire, of humility and exaltation, of sensual concreteness and spiritual abstraction; this occasions a certain degree of emotional tension, a specific ardor and certainty of the subjective conditions, an inclusion of the subject in a higher order – an order which, at the same time, is felt to be something inward and personal. (Simmel, 1997, p. 104)

Religiosity is thus a type of affective relationship, an aspect of the dialectical struggle between "life" and "form" that Simmel places at the center of his theory of culture. Religion in this sense is not life itself, but a form that emerges out of life and makes an important aspect of our experience possible. For Simmel life's rebellion against form guarantees the renewal of religious experience and the emergence of new forms of the religious life. Religiosity thus provides the essential dynamic of religion as a set of claims. In his important summation,

"Just as cognition does not create causality, but instead causality creates cognition, so religion does not create religiosity, but religiosity creates religion" (ibid., p. 150). Or as Simmel expresses the idea in another passage, the logical sequence the observer must follow is from religiosity to "social phenomena" to "objective religion" (ibid., p. 211).

As in other parts of his thought, one important problem Simmel confronts is framed by the advance of the scientific outlook and the powers of technological civilization: what can be the meaning and experience of religiosity in the modern age, he wants to ask, when we are faced with a withdrawal of the "content" of religion, while the "religious need" – that is, the form called religiousness – remains with us? How are we to understand the reality of a religiosity that exists *independent* of any content, that can be transformed, so to speak, from "a transitive to an intransitive activity" (ibid., p. 23)? Simmel's answer requires that he propose a conjecture:

> The real gravity of the current situation is that not this or that particular dogma but the object of transcendent faith per se is characterized as illusory. What survives is no longer the form of transcendence seeking new fulfillment but something more profound and more desperate: it is a *yearning*, once fulfilled by the idea of transcendence, and now – although it is a concrete reality within the soul – paralyzed by the withdrawal of the content of faith and as if cut off from the path to its own life. (ibid., p. 9)

This observation is congruent with Freud's later theme in *The Future of an Illusion* (1927), and it allows us to understand the modern penchant for experimentation with religiosity. In "The Conflict in Modern Culture," Simmel argues that the modern turn to mysticism and its various forms (such as Zen Buddhism or "New Age" spirituality today) represents an attempt to find a way out of the dilemma. No doubt there are others, though they all may in the last analysis "become equally entangled in contradictions," as Simmel (1997, p. 23) notes.

But there is a second problem for Simmel in this part of his work, for he wants to assess the connection between religiosity and social phenomena. Can there be instructive parallels or analogies between religious conduct and social interaction? Simmel's complex responses take different forms themselves. But in general his reflections on art, subjectivity, inwardness, or reconciliation trace the engagement of the self – especially the contested modern self – with religiosity. Moreover, especially in the longest text, *Religion*, his point is that religiosity is itself a *social* form, observable within other non-religious relationships, serving as a template for appropriate interactions, triggering the search for social unity in a "higher order," or modeling the relationship of the individual to the group. Such passages show Simmel at his best, revealing for him the problems a sociology of religion should pursue:

> We can see, for example, that many human relationships harbor a religious element. The relationship of a devoted child to his parent, of an enthusiastic patriot to his country, of the fervent cosmopolite to humanity; the relationship of the worker

to his insurgent class or of the proud feudal lord to his fellow nobles; the relationship of the subject to his ruler or of the true soldier to his army – all these relationships, with their infinite variety of content, can be seen to share a psychological form. This form has a common tone that can be described only as religious. (Ibid., p. 104)

The interaction between the human being and his God thus encompasses the whole range of possible relationships, both sequentially and simultaneously. In doing so it unmistakably reiterates the behavioral patterns that exist between the individual and his social group. Here we see the same phenomenon of an individual subjected to a supreme power yet permitted a degree of freedom; passive reception that still allows room for a responsive reaction; the self-surrender that does not exclude rebellion; the mixture of reward and punishment; the relationship of a single member to the whole, even though that single member still desires to be a whole himself. One feature of religion in particular can be transposed to the relationship of the individual to the group: that is the humility with which the pious person attributes everything he is and has to God's generosity and sees in divine power the source of his being and strength. For man is not absolutely nothing in relation to God: though only a grain of dust, he is not an utterly insignificant force but is at least a receptacle ready to receive its contents. Thus there are strong similarities between the religious and the sociological forms of existence. (Ibid., p. 157)

In this view not only are there parallels between religious activity and social activity, but the element of religiosity is contained within other, non-religious relationships. By understanding religiosity, we can also grasp the nature of social interactions.

Moreover, for Simmel there is a strong affinity between religion and art, or between the religious life and the artistic life, which then accounts for their historic attraction and repulsion in the great world religions. On the one hand, then, he can envisage an "essential similarity between the form of the religious life and that of art" and postulate "the ultimate similarity of form through which religion always anticipates art and art always stimulates religious sentiment" (ibid., p. 67). The most important reason for this similarity has to do with the process of distanciation at work in both the artistic and religious realms. For both art and religion project their objects into a world "beyond" the empirical here-and-now, Simmel argues, but only in order to draw these objects into the close and immediate orbit of our consciousness. Paradoxically, the distance created between the self and its objects of perception makes possible the subjective possession of these objects and the complete and apparently unmediated identification with them. Of course, in actuality there is a source of mediation in social interaction and group life. Thus, if Rembrandt can be seen as the "painter of the soul," offering a vision of reconciliation for the inner life, as Simmel holds, then it is because these notions of soul, reconciliation, and inner life have meaning and value for us as social beings.

On the other hand art proclaims its autonomy and competition with the religious life: "*l'art pour l'art*" in the rallying cry of the *fin de siècle*. The significance of this challenge for Simmel becomes marked in the essays on art forms and major artists, where in historical and comparative perspective he explores the great dualisms of nature and spirit, content and form, our existence in the life world and the contrasting reality of the work of art. The attraction of *modern* art especially lies in its ability to work through and heighten these age-old dualisms in such a way as to present art as "salvation" from the everyday. Toward the end of his essay on Rodin, for example, Simmel comments,

> Ancient sculpture sought the logic of the body, so to speak, whereas Rodin seeks its psychology. For the essence of modernity as such is psychologism, the lived experience and interpretation of the world in terms of the reactions of our inner life and actually as an inner world, the dissolution of the fixed contents in the fluid elements of the soul, from which all substance has been removed, and whose forms are only forms of motion. Thus the really modern art is music, the most moving of the arts. Thus it was lyric poetry based upon music which most satisfied the longing of the times. Thus landscape painting is the specifically modern achievement of painting, for it is an *état d'âme* and its use of color and composition dispenses with logical structure more than the body and figural composition. (Simmel, 1983, p. 152)

So whereas art in antiquity achieved its goal by freeing us from discontent through a perfection of style that negated the flux of life, Simmel contends, modern art rescues us by grasping the truth of the fluidity, motion, and dissolution of form that we experience. Art is capable of validating our lived experience, a powerful argument for substituting the aesthetic for the religious life, and for Simmel one of the important tendencies at work in modernity.

## PROBLEMS IN SIMMEL'S THOUGHT

The identification and elaboration of important dynamic, dualistic tensions in our experience is one of the most striking aspects of Simmel's thought. His treatment of the category of "life" held in creative tension with "form" is only the most abstract of these dualisms. Surely among the most striking is his exploration of the ways in which individual autonomy and freedom are both opposed to social formations and constraints, but then also authorized and made possible by such formations and constraints. One of the most consequential for modern life is the dynamic interplay between our subjective historical identities and the objectified social-technological forces that challenge those identities, both canceling and reinforcing or reshaping them.

The complexity in this dynamic mode of thinking is one source of the fascination with Simmel. But it is also a contributing source for the questioning of his general approach, method of inquiry, and overall contribution to social theory. This questioning can be reduced to four problem domains: subjectivism, aestheticism, formalism, and ambivalence.

*Subjectivism.* One of the earliest criticisms of Simmel focused attention on the speculative quality of his thinking. To be sure, Simmel was not an "empiricist" in the usual sense of the word, nor did he want to be one. However, neither was he a system-builder whose edifice of thought rested on metaphysical foundations. Avoiding either of these polarities, did he nevertheless have a method of inquiry that could give "systematic coherence" to his approach? Did he provide any guidance at the level of, say, Durkheim in *The Rules of Sociological Method*? For Simmel the answer to such challenges is difficult to formulate, and that difficulty has fed the suspicion among critics that methodological rigor is not among the scientific values promoted in Simmel's work.

*Aestheticism.* Closely related to the charge of subjectivism is the concern that Simmel's distinctive style or manner of thinking – his *Denkart* – is driven and characterized by aesthetic considerations. From this point of view, for example, his version of "political economy" in the *Philosophy of Money* is highly individualized, and notwithstanding an array of brilliant constructions, it lacks the clear conceptual underpinnings and critical edge of Marx's *Capital*, or the explicit analytic categories and systematic intentions of Weber's *Economy and Society*. Instead of merely writing a text, it is as if Simmel wants to compose a dense texture of images that will convey, like a canvass or a score, the essential experience of a phenomenon – in this case "money" as metaphysical power. According to this critical view such results are like a work of art in the hands of a master: admirable for their perfection, originality, and singularity, but not in principle "falsifiable" according to the canons of science.

*Formalism.* Of course, Simmel was also an acknowledged master of "formal" analysis of social interaction. But the difficulty is that such analysis can appear unhistorical and untested by rigorous, substantive comparative applications. It tends to stress only formal properties, rather than investigating historical patterns or developmental logics. Thus, unlike Marx and Weber, Simmel cannot be said to have a comparative historical sociology, or a structural analysis of stratification systems, or a developmental sociology of the modern state. His formal sociology might be viewed as a suggestive heuristic for understanding historical and structural dimensions of a given society, but it is not in itself an analysis, for example, of actual structures or historical patterns of domination.

*Ambivalence.* While often viewed as a diagnostician of the *Zeitgeist*, Simmel has also been accused of reveling in that diagnosis at the expense of developing an unambiguous political position, or making a clear choice about the most desirable path toward a rational future. Simmel's thought is never short on critical perspectives, but in this view those perspectives remain as equally valued possibilities, rather than temporary and questionable positions that must be overcome. His mature thinking thus never connects with transformative action projects, but leaves us instead merely reflecting on the "tragedy" or "fate" or "possibilities" of our times.

Now these four problem areas speak to the provocative and unique character of Simmel's voluminous writings. Better brilliant errors than dull correctness, as Weber once remarked. But in partial defense of Simmel it must be said that many of the charges against him misunderstand or misdirect the tasks he set for himself. Unwilling to pose as a utopian or futurologist, Simmel was content to dissect social life to expose the sinews that made sociability, individuation, and differentiation possible. Content to leave historical and structural problematics to others, he concentrated his efforts on a *general* level of analysis about history, society, economy, or religion *as such*. Not particular histories or particular religions were Simmel's concern, but rather the writing of what we call "history" as an idea and creative act, or the formation of what we call "religion" out of the quality of experience identified as religiosity. For Simmel, then, the loss in specificity of subject matter can be compensated by an unexpected turn, an experimental line of inquiry, a unique depth of understanding. In the last analysis he wanted surprise and experimentation, and it is these qualities that challenge the most earnest criticism.

## SIMMEL'S POSITION IN MODERN SOCIAL THEORY

Returning to Simmel's intellectual and social world of the *fin de siècle*, there was a legendary quality to his public presence in the prewar Berlin of his time. Not many sociologists or philosophers receive the garland of poetic declamation from their students. Simmel was one of the few who did:

> The differences are illusionary;
> Is the flamingo nobler than the stork?
> I sink into my seat painfully
> For the great analyst Geork.
> There I sit in my brown vest,
> And the army of objects envelop me.
> Oh, will the problems never rest,
> The walled-in smoke of indifference encircles me.
> What is the meaning of life? This question
> Is foolish, but it exists nevertheless,
> It needles me for seven thousand days of vexation:
> I sit there in agony, ill-fated, helpless.

So wrote Kurt Hiller in 1911 in the avant-garde expressionist journal, *Die Aktion*, commemorating in doggerel the spell Simmel cast over audiences that included Georg Lukács, Ernst Bloch, and Robert Park. The long shadow of this influence can be seen in their quite varied later work, even in the famous insights about "alienation" and "reification" in Lukács's essays in *History and Class Consciousness* (1922), or the "cultural criticism" advanced by Siegfried Kracauer and members of the early Frankfurt School, as well as the "interactionist" perspectives of the Chicago School of American sociology.

But Simmel never intended to be a founder of a school or movement, in contrast to Durkheim or Marx, and many of those who explicitly borrowed his name, such as Hiller, were marginal figures and outsiders to the academy and the major social and political movements of the time. For the main orthodoxies in social theory and philosophy Simmel seemed to remain a brilliant essayist and wide-ranging intellect, a master of the insightful *aperçu* and the ambiguities of modern life, but a thinker without a philosophical system or a unified, marketable sociological doctrine. It is an interesting comment on the peculiarities of our times to note that it is precisely these alleged deficiencies that have once again made Simmel an engaging presence, even for some an insightful "post-modernist" *avant la lettre*. Simmel, of course, thought he was merely "modern."

With neo-Kantian theory in eclipse during the twentieth century, Simmel's profile in philosophy has retreated into the shadows. But the legacy of his thought has remained strong in several major fields of sociology, where it first attracted attention, especially in the United States, perhaps because the traditions stemming from George Herbert Mead or Robert E. Park bear a certain family resemblance to Simmel's work. Most obviously symbolic interactionism, formal sociology, and conflict sociology all owe a major debt to the Simmelian analysis of interaction processes and patterns of sociation. Indeed, these subject matters and areas of inquiry, represented, for example, by the work of Lewis Coser in conflict theory, are at the core of what was seen for decades as Simmel's unique contribution.

Today, however, a new Simmel has taken the stage. The renaissance of interest in Simmel and his work, some eighty years after his death, is explained by several considerations: renewed interest in cultural theory and analysis, a spate of writings on modernity and its discontents, concern with substantive topics (such as the sociology of emotions, feminism and gender, or the sociology of fashion and art) that Simmel cultivated almost alone, dissatisfaction with ortho-dox sociological empiricism, and the energizing disarray in social theory generally. Among the "classics" Simmel can seem to offer the most sustained, varied, and intriguing discussions of a full range of problems and topics, some of them quite exemplary, that touch on these thematic interests of the present. Apart from the self-sustaining project of pursuing "science for science's sake," as a good Simmelian might put it, what we can hope to find in Simmel's work is an orientation, a series of insights, even a kind of deep programmatic understanding about what is significant in social life that will satisfy our need for clarity about our own situation in the modern world and in sociology. Some have gone even further to find in his work a "research program" for comprehending the "histor-ical anthropology of the modern" (Nolte, 1998). Whether in its weak or strong form, ultimately these orientations are the grounds on which the interest in Simmel's work will be sustained for the foreseeable future.

Simmel was a great raconteur, often lacing lectures and essays with illustrative fables and anecdotes. One of his favorites told the story of the farmer who on his death bed advised his children to search for a treasure he had buried in the fields. They diligently followed his directions, plowing hard and deep, but found no buried treasure. However, the following year the land yielded a three-fold harvest. Like these heirs, we won't find the treasure, Simmel announced, but the world we have cultivated in looking for it will prove many times more fruitful, because such cultivation is the necessary condition for our imagination, intellect, and spirit. And so it is with the promise of Simmel's work. The fable aptly captures the last important legacy of his sociological and philosophical investigations, and suggests the importance of our relation to his science and to him as a cultivator of the intellect and enthusiast for the life of the mind.

## Acknowledgment

The author is indebted to Leon Warshay for his critical comments and helpful suggestions for this essay.

## Bibliography

### Writings of Georg Simmel

*Grundfragen der Soziologie (Individuum und Gesellschaft)*. 1917. Berlin: Göschen.

*The Sociology of Georg Simmel* (translated and edited by K. Wolff). 1950. New York: Free Press.

*Conflict and the Web of Group-affiliations* (translated by K. Wolff and R. Bendix). 1955. New York: Free Press, 1955.

*Georg Simmel 1858–1918* (edited by K. Wolff). 1959. Columbus: Ohio State University Press.

*Essays on Sociology, Philosophy and Aesthetics by Georg Simmel* (edited by K. Wolff). 1959. Columbus: Ohio State University Press.

*The Conflict in Modern Culture and Other Essays* (translated by P. Etzkorn). 1968. New York: Columbia Teachers College Press.

*Georg Simmel on Individuality and Social Forms: Selected Writings* (edited by D. Levine). 1971. Chicago: University of Chicago Press.

*The Problems of the Philosophy of History* (translated by G. Oakes). New York: Free Press.

*Philosophische Kultur: Gesammelte Essais*. 1983. Berlin: Wagenbach.

*Georg Simmel: on Women, Sexuality, and Love* (translated by G. Oakes). 1984. New Haven, CT: Yale University Press.

*Schopenhauer and Nietzsche* (translated by H. Loiskandl et al.). 1986. Amherst: University of Massachusetts Press.

*Einleitung in die Moralwissenschaft: Eine Kritik der ethischen Grundbegriffe. Georg Simmel Gesamtausgabe, volumes 3 and 4*. 1989. Frankfurt: Suhrkamp.

*The Philosophy of Money* (edited and translated by D. Frisby and T. Bottomore). 1990. London: Routledge, 2nd edn.

*Soziologie: Untersuchungen über die Formen der Vergesellschaftung. Georg Simmel Gesamtausgabe, volume 11*. 1992. Frankfurt: Suhrkamp.

*Essays on Religion* (edited and translated by H. J. Helle and L. Nieder). 1997. New Haven, CT: Yale University Press.

### Further reading

Böhringer, H. and Gründer, K. (1976) *Ästhetik und Soziologie um die Jahrhundertwende: Georg Simmel*. Frankfurt: Klostermann.

Coser, L. (ed.) (1965) *Georg Simmel*. Englewood Cliffs, NJ: Prentice Hall.

Frisby, D. (1992) *Sociological Impressionism: A Reassessment of Georg Simmel's Social Theory*, 2nd edn. London: Routledge.

Freud, Sigmund (1927) *The Future of an Illusion*. London: Hogarth Press.

Gassen, K. and Landmann, M. (1993) *Buch des Dankes an Georg Simmel*, 2nd edn. Berlin: Duncker & Humblot.

Habermas, J. (1991) *Texte und Kontexte*. Frankfurt: Suhrkamp.

Kaern, M., Phillips, B. and Cohen, R. (eds) (1990) *Georg Simmel and Contemporary Sociology*. Dordrecht: Kluwer.

Köhnke, K. C. (1996) *Der Junge Simmel in Theoriebeziehungen und sozialen Bewegungen*. Frankfurt: Suhrkamp.

Lukács, Georg (1922) *History and Class Consciousness*. London: Merlin Press (1971).

Nedelmann, B. (1990) On the Concept of "Erleben" in Georg Simmel's Sociology. In M. Kaern et al. (eds), *Georg Simmel and Contemporary Sociology*. Dordrecht: Kluwer, pp. 225–41.

Nolte, P. (1998) Georg Simmels Historische Anthropologie der Moderne: Rekonstruktion eines Forschungsprogramms. *Geschichte und Gesellschaft*, 24, 225–47.

# 8

## Charlotte Perkins Gilman

### CHARLES LEMERT

More than any sociologist of her day, perhaps more than any since, Charlotte Perkins Gilman fearlessly abridged the artificial divide between fact and fiction. Herein lies her abiding witness to all women and men who live their lives between doubt and hope, wherein the disciplined practice of social theory begins. Without fiction, there is no imagination; without imagination, no dreams; without dreams, facts hardly matter. Theories are the ways people use their imagination to talk about the factual realities that hedge their social dreams.

Strictly speaking, a fiction is a fashioning, an imitating, of things the truth of which is not merely, or presently, factual. There would be no progress, not even scientific progress, without these imaginative fashionings after the real. Hence the disputatious role of theory in both practical and scientific life. Many people, ordinary ones and scientists alike, hate theory. Yet they could not live without it. When all is said and done, theory is the more or less disciplined talk by which people make what sense they can of their social worlds. Theory, thus, does its work in the always unsettled space between doubt and promise. Theory seeks, thereby, to describe the possible in order to capture the imagination of others. Whether it tells stories or explains data sets, theory is the work of telling others what one holds to be true about the world. Its hope is to convince others to see things as one sees them, even to invite their participation. This is true, surely, of the most formal scientific theory. But it is pointedly true of theories, like social theories, which cannot help but depend on fiction to find and describe their facts.

Charlotte Perkins Gilman very well understood this perplexingly simple first condition of her craft, which ultimately is the craft of anyone who aims to be socially engaged. Gilman's social theories of the man-made world have endured over time because she seemed to understand without instruction on the subject that, in her day, the factual state of women in the world economy could only be described from some distant standpoint of the social imagination. The arrangements that consign many women to the bourgeois family and the commandments of men were as arbitrary then as they are now. But then there were no theoretical or sociological languages sufficient to their description. Far from being stranger than fiction, the strangeness of the factual is that, in many times and places, reality's finest expressions can only be rendered as fiction.

Among feminist social theorists at the start of the twentieth century, Charlotte Perkins Gilman had no peer because no one saw and spoke with such convincing imagination of the ways Gilded Age capitalism arrogantly structured the lives of women and men. Gilman was a sociologist and a disciplined social thinker. She was not, however, an academic (though she did occasionally write for academic journals like *The American Journal of Sociology*). Her social theory took the form of social criticism of the prevailing foundations of bourgeois social life and its economic arrangements. In books like *Women and Economics* (1898) and *The Home* (1903) – just two of the countless essays, lectures, and books of this kind – she shook the gendered foundations of modern life. In her day, only W. E. B. Du Bois among social critics we read today rivaled Gilman's popularity as a writer. No academic sociologist in the United States came close.

Just the same, to have been a woman in that day, even an intellectual one, meant that if one were to move and shake the public sphere dominated by white males one had to discover some indirect path to the popular imagination. At the end of the nineteenth century, one of the most popular forms of entertainment was the magazine that arrived, usually weekly, at the door of women at homes. This is why the art of fiction was so important to Gilman and other socially conscious women of the time, notably her distant, older relative, Harriet Beecher Stowe – both of them published their best known work in the periodic press. It is, in fact, not entirely implausible to suggest that Gilman's "The Yellow Wallpaper" (1892) did for the social criticism of gender relations what *Uncle Tom's Cabin* had done forty years earlier for race relations. Gilman's disturbing short story of a woman driven mad by the man-made world did not start a war as Abraham Lincoln famously said of Beecher's book in relation to the American Civil War. But for much of the century since its publication in 1892, "The Yellow Wallpaper" did give vent to the outrage of women trapped in a system that exploited their domestic services. Gilman's short fiction was the opening shot of her war of words against the (to use her word) androcentric biases of the world capitalism system. For a full quarter century from this opening blast to the surprising, otherworldly ideas in her feminist utopia, *Herland*, in 1915, Gilman wrote widely read works of fiction. Yet Gilman's fiction always expressed the more studied values of her critical social theory. At every turn, her work gives off, still today, the sweet scent of the long-feared, always inviting, intercourse between the real and the imaginary.

It would be a long time after Gilman quit her public life and work during the First World War before C. Wright Mills, in 1959, would coin the phrase "the sociological imagination." But not even Mills understood what Gilman did about the importance of imagination to social thought. For Mills, the sociological imagination was more a rhetorical hammer used to loosen the grip of academic sociology's empirically narrow and theoretically abstract methods. Mills, of course, urged upon us the notion that sociology always begins in the needs of ordinary people who suffer personal troubles for want of the ability to imagine the larger social structures that are, in most instances, the deeper cause of their sufferings. Mills was one of the first to plant the seeds of formal sociology in the concerns of practical life. But he was not *the* first. More than sixty years before Mills, Gilman saw that social thought was always the imaginative work of bringing into public view the force of social structures in the fate of the troubled individual. Granted, she did not put the idea as succinctly as did Mills. But he, by contrast, never came close to her in plumbing the depths of imagination itself. Gilman's "The Yellow Wallpaper" set a new standard for the use of fiction to tell the truth of the emotional consequences of social and economic structures, much as *Herland* opens possibilities for feminist social criticism that nonfiction writing can never achieve.

## THE PERSON

Imagine, if you will, an educated woman of the working or middle classes – any woman who comes to mind. She is, more often than not, white. She is educated, married with children, well sheltered, with all the necessary provisions and many of the desirable unnecessary ones. Her duty in the social contract with her husband and his world is to care for the children and manage the household. In return, she is offered the honor of being considered a good woman, one who by her domestic labor and sound moral values fulfills the social ideal expected of such a woman. She receives no direct financial compensation. She is left in the home for long hours, sometimes days, with little or no help. The husband, by contrast, enjoys life at work in the wider world. She accompanies him rarely, but entertains his work acquaintances frequently. She is permitted no vocation of her own outside the family circle, save for activities that advance the good name of the householder himself. She feels confined. She very often falls into depression, for which she takes to her room on doctor's orders.

Today it is relatively easy to image such a woman. Many of our mothers or grandmothers experienced just this and knew what it meant to be thus confined. Even though today's economy has put such a life well beyond the expectations of all but a small number of generally quite wealthy families, it is not too difficult for us today to imagine the suffering of the women for whom Charlotte Gilman wrote. They are the paradigm of what is wrong with the so-called traditional family. These are the women who suffered "the problem that has no name" that Betty Friedan would describe for a later generation of women in *The Feminine Mystique* (1963). Gilman was among the first to speak to and for these women. The woman in question was the subject of "The Yellow Wallpaper" – a woman driven to illness, not by the abuse of the man in her life, but by the man-made world. The yellow wallpaper is the nightmarish entanglements of a woman trapped in a system that demands her obedience and denies her participation.

In the 1880s Charlotte Perkins Gilman lived what Betty Friedan would describe in the 1960s for a later generation of women. She was herself a victim of the problem with no name. But Gilman (at the time, Charlotte Stetson) would not succumb to her personal troubles. She had married Walter Stetson, an artist, and a good man, in 1884. Their only child, Katherine, was born the following year. Neither brought wealth to the marriage. Walter respected Charlotte's creative gifts, but his career came first. He was the breadwinner. Her work had to be set aside. The first signs of her depression appeared soon after childbirth. Somehow, even as Charlotte lay ill in 1887, a young woman confined to her own room, Charlotte knew – she just knew – that her illness was not of her own doing. She understood very well that Walter and her physician (the same physician who a generation earlier had been called to the bedside of Harriet Beecher Stowe, for the same "female" illness) were kindly men. The fault was not theirs any more than hers. They too were caught up in the structured relations of bourgeois life in early capitalist America. Though Charlotte Stetson would not find the formal language to describe the system until her first great work of social theory in 1898, *Women and Economics* were already the key words in her personal vocabulary. By courage and personal force, she exercised the sociological imagination to know that what was at stake in a bourgeois woman's life was ultimately an issue of economic structures. Gilman was the sort of person who trusted her feelings long enough to find the words that shaped the intellect that eventually described the structured reality for others. Few social theorists live in such a way that the qualities of their personal lives lead to robust theories of worlds we all inhabit. Gilman did.

The circumstances of Gilman's family of birth were, almost certainly, the source of her feminist sensibilities. She was born on her father's side into one of the nineteenth century's most famously unconventional families. Charlotte's father, Frederick Beecher Perkins, was kin by marriage to the family of Lyman Beecher and his remarkable children. Henry Ward Beecher, the abolitionist; Catharine Beecher, the feminist; Isabella Beecher Hooker, the suffragist; and Harriet Beecher Stowe, the writer – all carried forth their father's reformist values. From childhood, Charlotte witnessed firsthand the worldly work of the Beecher women. Yet what influenced her more was not so much her proximity to the famous family as her painful distance from its, to her, most important member – her father.

Frederick Perkins left his wife, Mary Prescott Perkins, and their two small children in 1869. Charlotte was but nine years old. His abandonment put her, her mother, and her brother at incessant risk of financial ruin. Though Frederick clearly inherited the learning and independence of the Beechers, he utterly lacked the family's deeper sense of personal responsibility. Perkins attended Yale, but dropped out. He studied law, but never practiced it. Eventually, he settled into a stable career as a librarian – first at the Boston Public Library, then (in 1880) as Director of the San Francisco Public Library. He supported the family erratically. He sent money and affection as it pleased him. The economic disaster of the abandonment was severe enough. But its emotional consequences were far the worse. Through her adolescence, Charlotte seized every opportunity to maintain relations with her father, who, true to form, resisted – most hurtfully on one occasion by cutting off her tender affections toward him in an abrupt and cruel letter of rejection.

Only a man damaged by some larger force could behave as harshly as Frederick Perkins did toward his wife and children. And the damage did not end with him. It seldom does in families. Charlotte, like many abandoned children, never stopped longing for her father's affections. It was no accident then that when she in her turn abandoned Walter in 1888 she moved with Katherine (then three) to California – first to Pasadena, then to Oakland, across the Bay from her father. Still, though he was nearby, he kept his distance. Most appalling of all, her father refused to visit his wife, Mary, as she was dying in the late winter of 1893. As she had before, Charlotte covered her pain at this insult added to injury. Her journal entry of March 7, 1898 was stark and false to the events of the day:

> Mother died this morning at 2.10. I lie down at 5.20 & rise at seven – I could not sleep. Get the breakfast and then go to the city, stopping at Dr. Kellogs, an undertakers, & the [San Francisco] Enquirer's Office. Go to father. To Mr. Worcester, lunch at Mrs. Morses, father again, and home.... Father over in the afternoon. (*Diaries*, p. 520)

With rare exceptions, this was a typical journal entry – plain, strict to the facts, devoid of feeling. Though the author of "The Yellow Wallpaper" was a woman of powerful feelings when it came to literary expression, her private journal expunged the emotions she could not bear to embrace directly – and for good reason.

Charlotte had been emotionally starved by *both* parents, though for different reasons. Her mother Mary, in part because of her husband's abandonment, forced herself never to embrace Charlotte. In her personal memoir, *The Living of Charlotte Perkins Gilman*, written late in life, Charlotte recalls her sad search as a child for her mother's love:

> Having suffered so deeply in her own list of early love affairs, and still suffering for lack of a husband's love, [my mother] heroically determined that her baby daughter should not so suffer if she could help it. Her method was to deny the child all expression of affection.... She would not let me caress her, and would not caress, unless I was asleep. This I discovered at last, and then did my best to keep awake till she came to bed, even using pins to prevent dropping off, and sometimes succeeding. Then how rapturously I enjoyed being gathered into her arms, held close and kissed. (Gilman, 1935, pp. 10–11)

Those who have never experienced the effects of emotional deprivation in childhood may find it difficult to believe that the loss of parental affections can have lifelong effects. But clinical records are filled with cases of children thus deprived who never truly give up the search for parental love lost in the earliest years. The brave ones are those who satisfy their desires through good work and positive relations in adult life. Charlotte was brave. Here were the feelings that gave rise to her ideas.

Still, it would be wrong to shrink the whole of Charlotte Gilman's life into the events of early childhood. Her life story turns on any number of contradictions that defy simple explanation. For one thing, "The Yellow Wallpaper" would never have been possible had not Charlotte trained herself, even in childhood, to look hard at the world about her. At the same time, the looking and longing could well have been the cause of the mental illness that struck her down in 1887 and continued to haunt her after. But, also, though Charlotte was intermittently depressed throughout life, she always managed to recoup her energies. Once she had fled her own room of the yellow wallpaper, she was rarely immobilized by the depression. She began her public career in 1888 shortly after leaving Walter for California and her confinement. From then until retirement she worked so productively as to put her more canonical contemporaries, Max Weber and Émile Durkheim, to the test. (And, recall, Weber too suffered a breakdown, but unlike Gilman, his kept him from work for a number of years.)

Over a full quarter century, Charlotte Gilman wrote seven substantial works of social theory, at least four novels, plus countless essays, poems, and short stories. At the height of her powers, Gilman single-handedly wrote and published her own monthly magazine. From 1909 to 1916, *The Forerunner* was an exclusive forum for her ideas. She wrote *every* word of it – all the articles, including some of her best fiction and social criticism, and every jot of copy. For seven years it sold briskly, and helped make Gilman the literary force she was in the years before the First World War.

Yet when she retired *Forerunner* in 1916, the year after she finished *Herland,* she too began to retire. Though she published a few books after, this was the effective end of her life's work. Perhaps something about the Great War depressed her own sense of hope, as it had that of so many other moderns. The political collapse in Europe led to a train of debilitating events from which the world did not recover until well after the Second World War. The twentieth century is often said to have been the most violent in human history because war led to economic failure, which led again to war, then war again and again. Throughout the century that began in such high hopes for human progress, liberal political ideals were never able for more than a few years in the 1920s and then again in the 1950s to sustain the peace upon which the good society depends. This is surely why the First World War dealt such a deadly blow to radical reformers in the United States.

Gilman's own ideals were clearly influenced, as was the thinking of most left liberals at the end of the nineteenth century, by the reformist spirit of the socialist utopians. Edward Bellamy, who wrote *Looking Backward* (1888), was by all odds the most important. (Gilman's own socialist utopia, *Herland,* bears Bellamy's influence.) But there were many other social visionaries, including the social gospel movement with which Anna Julia Cooper and other settlement workers were loosely affiliated. Even the W. E. B. Du Bois of *Souls of Black Folk* (1903) – though true only to his own values – was under the sway of liberal hope that dominated in the first decade or so of the twentieth century. The war brought all this to an end. Gilman was far from alone in losing her way because of the devastating effects of the Great War of 1914.

Still, as significant as world events were to Gilman's early retirement from public work, her ever-complicated story turns again back to the importance of the personal. For her, the personal and the social were never far from each other. So it is also likely that she retired during the years of the First World War in order to enjoy the pleasures of married life to George Houghton Gilman, with whom she left New York after 1922 for the seclusion of his family home in Norwich, Connecticut. But the retirement came only after two decades of worldly success made possible by her second husband's financial and personal security.

Her long and successful marriage to Gilman gave Charlotte much more than the name by which she is known. The second marriage gave her the enduring domestic peace necessary for creative work. She had begun *Women and Economics* in the late summer days of 1897. These were the fresh early days of her romance with Houghton. She married her distant cousin in June 1900. They settled in New York City, there to renew regular relations with her now teenage daughter who had been living with her father. Ironically, she settled comfortably into the very sort of married life she had left in 1888 as a younger woman. In her memoir (Gilman, 1935, p. 381), Charlotte says of her second marriage: "We were married – and lived happily every after. If this were a novel now, here's a happy ending."

Today, it is well understood that the living of a life necessarily includes the retelling of its story and that the retelling cannot be done without a healthy dose of fiction. Few of us, if any, have more than a passing direct recollection of the events of our pasts. If we are to have a life's story to tell our friends and lovers and children we must rely on the stories told us by others. All the stories that compose our life stories cannot help but take poetic liberties with facts no one truly remembers. Charlotte's own life story does indeed read like a novel, which is why her own *The Living of Charlotte Perkins Gilman* very nearly ends with the account of her marriage to Houghton. In a book of twenty-one chapters, she has very little to say of her life after the marriage in 1900. Only four scant chapters account for the thirty-five years she lived after 1900. Indeed, all of the prodigious work of the New York years before the War are reduced to these few, haphazard chapters.

In Charlotte's artful fiction of her life, the drama is condensed into the deprivations of childhood, the depression and the first marriage, the flight for freedom in California, the years of growth and eventual fame. When Houghton enters at the end of the century, Charlotte's life comes to its "happy ending," as she put it – just more than halfway through her seventy-six years. It did not occur to her to finish *The Living of Charlotte Perkins Gilman* until 1935, on the eve of her death, nearly ten years after the first, incomplete draft was written. After Houghton died in 1934, Charlotte (well aware that she too was near death) moved back to California to be with her daughter Kate. Then, insisting on control of death as of her life's story, she took her life on August 17, 1935, preferring, as she said, "chloroform to cancer."

She had found happiness with a man. This charming oddity of her life's story could only be because she found in Houghton what she had lost in childhood. He provided, one might suppose, the loving embraces her parents had withheld. But the path to this man was anything but direct. In her love letters during their courtship, Charlotte's feelings of love for him are referred not to the losses of her childhood, but to the terrible loss of her young womanhood. Still, again, her story turns in a surprising direction. In a letter of Thursday, September 2, 1897, after a long day of work on *Women and Economics*, Charlotte wrote to Houghton: "I think I am taking more comfort with you than I have since the days of Martha Luther – my girl friend of '77–'81" (Hill, 1995, p. 93).

Charlotte's friendship with Martha Luther during late adolescence in Providence, Rhode Island, was the first openly passionate relationship of her life. In *Charlotte Perkins Gilman: the Making of a Radical Feminist: 1860–1896*, Mary A. Hill, Gilman's most accomplished biographer, interprets Charlotte's passion for Martha as a significant passage from the disappointments of childhood to the boldness of her adult feminism:

> Defiance, anger, crying spells – all reflected the intensity of family battle. After all, her self-sacrificing, domestic, and emotionally dependent mother had clashed irreconcilably with her cool, ambitious, independent father. Now these mother–father conflicts erupted once again, this time in herself. To some extent, Martha provided a "lofty" isolated refuge, but the real peace-keeping maneuver, Charlotte decided would be to strengthen her "self" and kill off the inclinations to remain "merely" a woman or to become a mother and a wife. (Hill, 1990, p. 74)

Just how important was the youthful relationship to Martha? And how did it figure, if at all, in her feminism, and especially in the striking platonic lesbianism of *Herland*?

It is not, of course, uncommon for a young woman to hold fast to other women in the developmental search for an independent self. But Charlotte clung to Martha ferociously. Not even Carroll Smith-Rosenberg's (1975) well known argument that nineteenth-century women often petted, kissed, and slept with each other without heteronormal embarrassment quite accounts for Charlotte's devotion to Martha Luther.

Charlotte's matter-of-fact journal entries for the last weeks of October 1881 betray (as in the case of her mother's death) a studied attempt to control otherwise uncontrollable feelings. Late October 1881 brought the end to Martha's passions for Charlotte. Martha accepted Charles Lane's proposal of marriage. Charlotte's diary records the surface of daily life, thus signaling her deeper emotions. The entry for October 17, 1881, is poignant: "Go to Miss Diman's. Miss Alden sick. I tell stories to Louise, who has an ulcerated throat. Home & get work. Go to Martha's all alone. Stay till almost 8. Nice talk. ('No!') Draw letter for guttersnipe. Sew" (*Diaries*, p. 86). "Nice talk" ? – ("No!") Of course not. And who exactly is the guttersnipe? Martha? Her fiance? Gilman, distraught, relaxes her guard in these sharp contradictions to the facts of the day. Then, resorting to form, she takes up work, "Sew." Entries for the two weeks following the 17th make only passing references to her dear friend – with the pointed exception of Thursday, October 27: "Martha there. We take walks & converse. Verily I love the damsel" (*Diaries*, p. 87). Then, on the Tuesday following, November 1, Charlotte writes: "No Abby owing to rain. Study and darn. Martha over. She hath a ring. I have a pain. Give her my blessing. Write to Sam and tell him all about it. Post the same. Note to Abigail. Sew" (*Diaries*, p. 88) Martha hath a ring; Charlotte hath a pain! Though they would continue their now deeply altered friendship for many years, only Charlotte seems to have kept its special importance.

In the chapter of her memoir devoted to her first marriage to Walter in 1884, Charlotte begins with reference to the relationship with Martha:

> Looking back on my uncuddled childhood it seems to me a sad mistake of my heroic mother to withhold from me the petting I so craved, the sufficing comfort of maternal caresses. Denied that natural expression, my first memory of loving any one – not to mention [she names several childhood friends; then continues – CL]. Immeasurably the dearest, was Martha. Martha stayed. We were closely together, increasingly happy together, four of those long years of girlhood. She was nearer and dearer than any one up to that time. This was love, but not sex. (Gilman, 1935, p. 78)

These words were written in 1925, thirty-four years after Martha left her. Still she adds: "This was love, but not sex." Though some speculate that Martha may have been a first lover, it is unlikely that we will ever know. But the speculation is encouraged by the evidence of the years after the break-up of her first marriage – the early California years.

In 1891 Charlotte met and by all reckoning fell in love with Delle Knapp, with whom she lived in Oakland in two rooms of a boarding house, along with Kate and Mary Prescott, who was gravely ill. Charlotte's journals are now filled with references like "Delle spent the night," and her memoir comments on the loss of still another love. "My last love proves even as others" (Gilman, 1935, p. 141). Clearly she loved Delle as she had Martha. But how, and to what effect?

Whether or not Charlotte Gilman enjoyed sexual relations with Martha and Delle, it is clear that they and other women were absolutely central to her efforts to establish an independent and feminist self-understanding. Late in life in her memoir Charlotte was notably defensive about the possibility of a sexual relationship with Martha and oddly silent about the affair with Delle. Why? Why would a woman who could be so shockingly honest about her mental illness, and so sharply disdainful of the marital conventions of the day, wish to cover the sexual feelings of those affairs? Just as the perverse matter-of-factness of her journals belies her true feelings, so the denial of sexual activity at a time in life when it would have made little difference to anyone (certainly not her husband) reveals something unsettled about Gilman's early attractions to women. What?

It may well be that nineteenth-century women, as Carroll Smith-Rosenberg explains, enjoyed physical contact with each other not so much for sexual pleasure as for nurturing shelter from the androcentric world. But this alone does not fully account for the fact that, as in Charlotte's case, there could have been erotic passion in these relationships even when they were not consummated. Then as now, sexual pleasure is polymorphous. And sex is more than pleasure. Sex is a social thing regulated by the needs and purposes of the whole wide social world.

Social historians of sex and sexuality in the Victorian era – notably John D'Emilio, Michel Foucault, and Steven Seidman – explain how industrial capitalism intruded upon mundane patterns of sexuality in order to shape the bourgeois family as the social unit in which labor is reproduced. Control sex; control the family. As Seidman notes in *Romantic Longings* (1991), in the Victorian era the contrast between normal heterosexuality and deviant homosexuality did not exist as we know it today. The control of sexuality was exercised according to a different social ideal of the productive, and reproductive, family. (This, not at all coincidentally, was precisely the defining moment for the bourgeois family Gilman worked to unmask and reform.) In the Victorian Age, says Seidman, sexualities were distinguished by a different social formula: between sex in the family and *all* other forms of sex. The perceived need was to regulate sexual practices in the service of industrial capitalism. Homosexuality was not talked about then as it is today. Homosexuality simply was not the issue. Disciplined families were. Thus, the very sexual practices that in our day would be viewed as homosexual were not, in Gilman's youth, fraught with social trouble as they are now. This may well explain why, when Gilman wrote in 1925 about her youthful affair in 1881, she *did* feel a need to explain the erotic away. Times had changed. Gilman lived on both sides of the historical divide after which homosexuality was born to American political consciousness.

This does not mean, however, that Charlotte's youthful desire for the love of women was any less significant to her feminist consciousness. Surely, as she says, the affair with Martha – like her love for Delle (and others about whom we know even less) – was a "refuge" (her word) that allowed her to work through the emotional deprivations of childhood which led to the fated marriage to Walter. Surely, in our day, we would think of them as lesbian or bisexual relations of one or another kind. But, whatever their sexual nature, these relations gave her courage to brave the losses of childhood and to live on her own in the California years, and thus to prepare for the enduring refuge provided by her marriage to Houghton. Gilman's story is perfect proof of the wisdom of Adrienne Rich's famous 1980 essay. In "Compulsory Heterosexuality and Lesbian Experience," Rich distinguished the *lesbian experience*, which includes the practice of homosexual relations, from the *lesbian continuum*, which includes all "woman identified experience" whether sexual or not. Nearly a full century after Charlotte's painful break-up with Martha, Adrienne Rich described the lesbian continuum as the encompassing possibility that it is (but for which the nineteenth century lacked a social vocabulary). The power available to women in their relations with each other, said Rich (1993, p. 239), "comprises both the breaking of a taboo and the rejection of a compulsory way of life." For Charlotte the lesbian continuum included both those relations that *might* have been sexual and those that clearly were not. Those of the latter kind were, if less acute at the time, more enduring over the years – most specially, her long friendships with Jane Addams, with whom she lived for a while at Hull House, and with Grace Channing, who after the divorce married Walter and helped raise Charlotte's daughter Kate. Without her relations along the lesbian continuum, Charlotte Gilman would not have become the most important feminist social theorist of her day.

In her public life, Gilman worked tirelessly, by writing and lecturing, to accomplish two social goals: get women out of the family into the economy; restructure the bourgeois family itself. Both have come to pass in ways Gilman could not have anticipated. Contrary to Gilman's expectations, we know from writings like Arlie Hochschild's *Second Shift* (1989) that women who attempt simultaneously to maintain career and family suffer impossible burdens. Today, the bourgeois family is much transformed by a rapacious global economy that has drawn most women out of the household to struggle, with or without a domestic partner, just to keep family life afloat. At the same time, as we know from works like Judith Stacey's *Brave New Families* (1990), women are indeed restructuring the traditional family. Women in families they chose (as Kath Weston has put it) are freer and more equal, though more burdened, than in Gilman's time.

After the First World War, Gilman fell out of favor – so completely so that Connecticut College, a leading school for women but a few miles from her home in Norwich, ignored one of the century's most important feminists as though she had never existed. Still, as feminism was reborn after the 1960s, Gilman regained the place of recognition she had earned. It is possible that this great visionary also envisaged the renewal of her ideas. Near the end of her life, Gilman wrote: "This is the woman's century, the first chance for the mother of the world to rise to her full place, her transcendent power to remake humanity, to rebuild the suffering world – and the world waits while she powders her nose..." (Gilman, 1935, p. 331). With a wink at the degrading expectations of the man-made world, Gilman leaves the future open, the sentence dangling on an ellipsis. In much the same way, her public life came to an open end. We know, if she did not, that her ideas anticipated the important outlines of feminist social theory at the end of the twentieth century.

## THE THEORY

It may be for fear of embarrassment that so few theorists comment on the original meaning of the word "theory." According to the *Oxford English Dictionary*, the word derives from the Greek *theoros*: "one who travels in order to see things." Thus, another of the original meanings is, simply, "a spectacle." In our scientific age, these definitions of a very high-minded activity are surprising. They would not have been to Gilman. She was, if not a tourist, certainly a pilgrim who walked her way through her own inner space to get to a fresh view of the spectacle of industrial capitalism and its effects on women. It was not a pretty picture.

Today those with eyes to see can see what Gilman saw behind the debris of a family system crushed, in our time, by a capitalism more cruel than even in Gilman's time – or Marx's for that matter. For those more accustomed to a socialism derived from Marx's painstaking analysis of the evils of the capitalist mode of production, Gilman's progressive socialism might well seem a faint copy of the original. American socialists of the end of the nineteenth century – writers like Henry George, Edward Bellamy, and Gilman herself – understood something of European socialism after Marx. But, for the most part, they developed their ideas in quite independent ways. Perhaps it was the American pragmatism in them that caused these early radicals to attack the selfishness of the industrial bosses with a comparably positive, even evolutionary, principle of human progress. One of the ironies of the Gilded Age is that nearly everyone from the bosses of industry to their radical opponents was caught up in the innocent hopefulness of the new industrial world.

Thus it was that even those, like Gilman, who self-consciously represented social groups oppressed by the dominant social order were alive with hope. W. E. B. Du Bois and Anna Julia Cooper are two of the more astonishing examples. They spoke for the American Negro oppressed by Jim Crow laws in the South and social segregation in the North. Still, in their writings of the last decade of the nineteenth century, both Du Bois and Cooper wrote with surprising confidence in the future of American society. Du Bois, in the most famous chapter of *Souls of Black Folk*, looked to a day when the Negro would be a "coworker in the kingdom of culture." Similarly, Cooper, in *A Voice From the South*, ordained black women who experienced the cruel injustices of the American South as the moral leaders of the day – of a progressive era with "such new and alluring vistas . . . opening out before us."

Gilman, likewise, concluded *Women and Economics* with a word of hope: "When the mother of the race is free, we shall have a better world, by the easy right of birth and by the calm, slow, friendly forces of social evolution" (Gilman, 1898, p. 340). This after 340 pages of relentless criticism of the evil she called the "sexuo-economic relation" at the heart of capitalism. Today readers will not be enchanted by the optimistic coda. Still, like other classic ideas, Gilman's basic feminist principles outlive the cocoon in which they developed.

One of the arguments among feminists at the end of the twentieth century is over the uncertain identity of women caught between family and the workplace. Though the debate has taken many different turns in the last generation, it always returns to the dilemma Gilman tried to resolve by her social criticism of the sexuo-economic relation. She meant, in effect, to complicate the idea of sex – or, in our term, gender. A woman's gender circumstance is always, and necessarily, determined by, but not reducible to, her economic situation. Gilman never thought of Woman in the abstract. For the most part, she resisted the inviting danger of feminist essentialism.

Essentialism abstracts an important feature into a definition. Women are different from men. But their difference in fact may or may not be a difference in kind. Feminist essentialisms tend, one way or another, to claim that a woman's unique nature is a stable, immutable property of her gender. The allure of the essentialist move is the gain of a critical tool made powerful by isolating analytic qualities which may be turned back against arbitrary social arrangements that put those qualities at risk. While meant to sharpen racial, sexual, or gender differences, the problem with essentialisms of all kinds (even strategic ones) is that they don't speak very subtly to the lived reality of women's lives – or for that matter to the lives of those excluded because of their sexual orientation or their race. Essentialisms may be necessary to the polarizing purposes of certain political moments, or the analytic work of theorists, but they are not practical to the experience of real people they are meant to represent. In the vocabulary of our time, Gilman was more interested in the situated knowledge of women's lives. She was a writer and a social critic, a public speaker and an organizer. Her work was with those who do not tolerate abstractions well. In the one surprising instance toward the end of her career where she lapsed into a kind of inadvertent essentialism, she did so almost by the accident of her political and literary purposes. Even then, there was no doctrinal conviction. Gilman wrote about women's lives, as lived.

People live in families, or the hope of families – or, at least, of other forms of intimate association. Yet for their domestic arrangements to survive economically, they must work. Most women (and some men) who live in a world dominated by capitalist greed live with uncertainty doubled. For them the search for intimate association and viable work is hard work and neither can be had without the other. Gilman saw, early in the evolution of modern industrial society, that women had been assigned twice the responsibility for half the pay (if that). This is the sexuo-economic relation. Women must produce and reproduce the family association without which society would fail; and they must do this while held in servile relation to the man-made world.

"Economic progress is almost exclusively male" (Gilman, 1898, p. 8). This is Gilman's opening shot in *Women and Economics*. Among animals, she believed, only the human is so dominated by the male. There is some truth in this. "Queen bee" is a gender slur because it is a biological reality. In her day the continuing backwash of social Darwinianism encouraged the sociobiological gesture in Gilman's early writings. (Lester Ward, the academic sociologist who most influenced her thinking, encouraged Gilman along this line.) Still, Gilman's argument survives her questionable biological claims, which, even today, retain a certain rhetorical force. Gilman equated the female human being with the work horse. Both are servile to a master. "Their labor is the property of another: they work under another will; and what they receive depends not on their labor, but on the power and will of the other" (Gilman, 1898, p. 7).

True to her poetic gifts, Gilman uses a strong comparative figure, but she does not lose sight of the broader economic idea. She aims to show that the relations of men to women are entirely arbitrary to economic convenience. "The labor of women in the house, certainly enables men to produce more wealth than they otherwise could; and in this way women are economic factors in society. But so are horses" (Gilman, 1898, p. 13). The opening allusion to the human female as the work horse of the species sets up the argument that follows. Step by step, with compelling logic, Gilman dismantles each of the then prevailing moral sentiments that served once (and still do in many places) to justify the domestic confinement of bourgeois women. Does not the human female's sexual beauty gain her the natural happiness of marriage? Is it not her nature to sacrifice independence for the sake of home and children? Is she not paid in kind by the support of the breadwinner husband? Do not the children require her attentions? Is not the home the hearth of civilization? The book is a careful exposition of the stupidity of the assumptions that, in her day, would have tempted many to say, in reply to each question: "Well, yes, of course." Gilman's sustained rebuttal of the true womanhood ideal is one of the earliest and still most persuasive exposés of the naturalistic sex role theories that came to dominate social science after the Second World War.

Still, Gilman's thinking was itself a kind of crypto-functionalism. Though her biological figures of speech are a bit heavy-handed for our day, her underlying social theory makes complete sense if we accept that, in the end, Gilman was more a social reformer than a devotee of the principle of social evolution. Her argument is that the fate of the female is necessarily bound to that of the male, as in turn his is to hers. It is not men who are selfish, but the system that makes them so. Greed is at the heart of the economy. "Social life tends to reduce this [self-ishness], which is but a belated individualism; but the sexuo-economic relation fosters and develops it" (Gilman, 1898, p. 338). Here is the sociological imagination at its best. In the normal course of daily life, Gilman is saying, a woman may suffer, but she does not actually see the selfishness of the world behind the men who make her the work horse. The true nature of the relation between the sexes can only be seen in structural perspective. This steady attention to the economic realities is what saves Gilman's ideas from the more naive functionalist thinking that, years later, Talcott Parsons made prominent in American sociology.

Gilman was first and foremost a socialist utopian. Her theories of social evolution served a political ethic more than a scientific concern. Had she been more the Marxist, she might have called for a reversal of the gender relations. But her radicalism was of another kind. She, like Du Bois and Bellamy, Cooper and George, looked to historical progress, not revolution, for a better society. At the end of the twentieth century very few people of certifiable common sense would trust the future for assurance of a better life. Hope, today, is all too realistically hedged by the stark economic realities that have so assaulted family life. Only the most fortunate few enjoy the security of breadwinning, productive labor. For most, the sexuo-economic relation persists, worse perhaps than even Gilman might have imagined.

Still, Gilman's ideas bear consideration because they navigate the waters between gender relations and economic reality with such a keen eye. She had lived at economic risk as a child, and had suffered firsthand the effects of the sexuo-economic relation on her family. Her ideas were always grounded in these experiences. As a result, she looked to a possible future more to understand the present than to predict a necessary outcome. And, just as she held out for the unrequited affections of her despicable father, so she could, at one and the same time, forcefully attack the men who made the androcentric world *and* feel compassion for them.

So we may trace from the sexuo-economic relation of our species not only definite evils in psychic development, bred severally in men and women, and transmitted indifferently to their offspring, but the innate perversion of character resultant from the moral miscegenation of two so diverse souls, – the unfailing shadow and distortion which has darkened and twisted the spirit of man from the beginnings. We have been injured in body and in mind by the two dissimilar traits inherited from our widely separated parents, but nowhere is the injury more apparent than its ill effects upon the moral nature of the race. (Gilman, 1898, p. 339)

She pulls no punches. Nor does she fail to understand that it is the structure of things that causes social evil. If women suffer more acutely, they do not suffer alone. Their men and their children are subject to the same ill moral effects.

When all is said and done, Gilman was a hard-headed realist about the practical consequences of the sexuo-economic relation. It is a curious thing that her phrase has not been reclaimed in this day, when it would seem so apt to the debates over the relative merits of identity and socialist politics. Today, through the contributions of thinkers like Judith Butler and Nancy Fraser, we know that women are not alone in the struggle to find a satisfactory recognition for their social identity, on the one hand, and to gain access to a fair share of economic wealth necessary for a decent life, on the other hand. Men as well as women, people of color as well as whites, heterosexuals as well as homosexuals, struggle with this dilemma. Far from being a postmodern oddity, this is, in many ways, the fundamental dilemma of modern life. Gilman, who lacked all the fancy terms we have today, understood this fundamental fact of life. Men as well as women would benefit from a wholesale transformation of the sexuo-economic relation. Even when she was writing her fiction, or concentrating on specific social issues like the quality of life in the bourgeois home, Gilman understood this. "A home life with a dependent mother, a servant-wife, is not an ennobling influence" (Gilman, 1898, pp. 262–3). When the woman is diminished, so is the man. A good decade before writing this, Charlotte grasped the principle perfectly well in her own life, even in the earliest of her fiction writings, well before she had worked out the theory.

"The Yellow Wallpaper," written six years before *Women and Economics*, remains today her most commanding, and disturbing, picture of the spectacle of the bourgeois family. The story begins innocently enough. The scene is a rented summer cottage, but it was a "cottage" in the grand bourgeois sense of turn-of-the-century retreats that became in our day wealthy suburbs like Newton, Massachusetts, or Greenwich, Connecticut. "Cottage" already signals just what sort of family story this is.

The man in the story condenses the two separate characters of Charlotte's own experience. John is made to be both husband and physician. The unnamed wife is attended by a woman, John's sister – a "perfect and enthusiastic housekeeper" who "hopes for no better profession" (p. 7). There are children. But it is the man – John, the physician husband – who figures as the looming object of the narrator's attentions.

Then, even as the idyllic scene is set, we are warned of something "queer" about the house itself.

> It is very seldom that ordinary people like John and myself secure ancestral halls for the summer.
>
> A colonial mansion, a hereditary estate, I would say a haunted house, and reach the height of romantic felicity – but that would be asking too much of fate!
>
> Still I would probably declare that there is something queer about it.
>
> Else, why should it be let so cheaply? And why have stood so long untenanted? John laughs at me, of course, but one expects that in marriage. (Gilman, 1892, p. 1)

Gilman the author is playing with the incongruity between the outside and inside of things. She uses the excess of the cottage, and its long vacancy, to invite the story's narrative line – that what is off is that this ideal little family will not achieve the felicity of a summer's retreat. The reader's eye is drawn to John by a gentle note of complaint. A woman expects a man to laugh at her. Is male dismissal of female sensibility the queer structure of the arrangement? Does Gilman ask us to think of the house as an icon for the whole of the bourgeois domestic scene – even, perhaps, for the whole of the economic structure that is so delicately hinted at by the pretense of the ironic "cottage"?

The poetic power of a short fiction is that it depends so weightily on the reader's imagination. So few words to say so much. Here the reader is invited by the queer exterior of the cottage to imagine the impending trouble. It is a "beautiful place" with a "delicious garden...never such a garden" (p. 2). But the central figure of the story is the room with ghastly yellow wallpaper:

> dull enough to confuse the eye in following, pronounced enough to constantly irritate and provoke study and when you follow the lame uncertain curves for a little distance they suddenly commit suicide – plunge off at outrageous angles, destroy themselves in unheard of contradictions. (p. 4)

On the exterior, all is delicious. Inside, all is confusing, suicidal, and contradictory.

The deadly interior of the house is, of course, the metonym of the bourgeois woman's confinement. Though the facts of Charlotte's own confinement in 1887 are absent in the fiction, the yellow wallpaper expresses the woman's nightmare. Her own physician, Dr S. Weir Mitchell, was the leading medical specialist in women's illnesses, as they were called. His treatment was the same rest cure which he had earlier prescribed for Harriet Beecher Stowe. The treatment, intended as a relieving ministry, was in fact a harsh imposition the man cannot understand. The woman must refrain from all labor – bed rest, an occasional visit from the children, and, in Charlotte's case, no reading or writing. The rest cure, thus, by depriving her of what she needs most, is bound to fail for most – certainly so for Charlotte.

The woman confined to this absurd contradiction is drawn into the wallpaper itself. The yellow wallpaper – "not arranged on any laws" (p. 3) – comes alive as the emblem of world's work on women.

> Behind that outside pattern the dim shapes get clear, clearer every day.
>
> It is always the same shape, only very numerous.

And it is like a woman stooping down and creeping about behind that pattern. I don't like it one bit. (p. 10)

The woman sees herself in the suicide patterns of the wall. She and contradiction become insanely one and the same. She is one with other women. "Sometimes I think there are a great many women behind [the moving patterns of the wall-paper], and sometimes only one" (p. 15).

It would be easy to miss the importance of what happens next. The woman is driven mad: by the wallpaper; by the domestic arrangement; by the world. But she attacks in self-defense by stripping the paper away sheet by sheet. This cannot be. The man, John, intervenes. But the woman overcomes. The story ends:

"I've got to get out at last," said I, "in spite of you and Jane. And I've pulled off most of the paper, so you can't put me back!"

Now why should that man have fainted? But he did, and right across my path by the wall, so that I had to creep over him every time! (p. 20)

The man faints. The woman escapes. But who is Jane? She is never introduced. Could she be John's sister, the perfect housewife who aspires to nothing more – the true woman, that is, that Charlotte could never be? Or, could Jane be the disturbed self of the woman who must always face her confinement? Is it possible that by this accidental woman Gilman is telling us that women, even when they escape the nightmarish world of the family, must in effect leave behind their very own selves – or, if not their selfhood, the ideal self that the world would impose? At the least, the woman who escapes must leave behind the true woman who remains with John (see Knight, 1992). And, in the image of the swooning husband (a reversal of the hysterical woman image), are we to think that even if she flees, then he is left in the garish room?

The queer house with its deadly room is the problem – not the woman, not even the man. Women, thus, are faced with an impossible choice. If they conform to the gentle absurdity of the man-made world, they are drawn into that world's selfish madness. If they rebel they must leave themselves behind as Charlotte did when she left Walter in order to reinvent herself. Fiction very often leaves the important questions unanswered. But in Gilman's case, Charlotte explains herself by what she became in real life, and by what she wrote in so many words in subsequent writings that made her social program completely obvious.

Woman alone cannot reform herself. Her freedom is freedom for all, even her man, especially her children. "The largest and most radical effect of restoring women to economic independence will be in its result in clarifying and harmonizing the human soul" (Gilman, 1898, pp. 331–2). The human soul demands a structural change in the sexuo-economic relation.

Gilman would play this theme again and again. In *The Home* (1903) she wrote more bitterly of the "domestic mythology," attacking in plain language the pieties of the American home. As to the virtues of home-cooking, for one example, she asks, in effect: but have you ever actually tasted it?

"Home-cooking" is an alluring phrase, but lay aside the allurement ... [and ask] whose home-cooking are we praising? Our own, of course. Which means nothing but that the stomach adapts itself to what it has to live on – unless it is too poisonous.... The long-suffering human system (perhaps toughened by ages of home-cooking) – will adapt itself even to slow death. (Gilman, 1903, pp. 124–5)

Here is but a taste of Gilman's radical, practical socialism at its most cynical best. Why not, she asks, encourage a system in which those expert in tasteful, nutritional cooking prepare the food for the community? Would not all be healthier and happier under such a system?

*The Home* holds up very well today for its relentless practical sneering at the absurd practices of the bourgeois family. The book offers what might be called a countercultural course in home economics. After a brief history of the family, Gilman unmasks the domestic mythology, just as, in *Women and Economics*, she attacked the ideal of true womanhood. "Let us begin," she says (pp. 38–9), starting with the highest of American values about the home, "with that fondly cherished popular idea – 'the privacy of the home.'" No one has privacy at home, least of all the mother. "The mother – poor invaded soul – finds even the bathroom door no bar to hammering little hands" (p. 40). The chapters following continue in this vein, exposing such myths as the home as the housewife's workshop, the lady of the house, and domestic arts, as well as home-cooking.

The more general analytic themes of *Women and Economics* are reconsidered in the closing chapters of *The Home*. As the woman suffers, so too do the boy and girl children – and the men! In passages that anticipate Nancy Chodorow's criticism of sex-role theory in *Reproduction of Mothering* (1978), Gilman unmasks the damage done by the sexuo-economic relation in the home:

The home teaches the boy that women were made for service, domestic service, that the principal cares and labours of life are those which concern the boy, and that his own particular tastes and preferences are of enormous importance. As fast as he gets out of the home and into the school he learns quite other things, getting his exaggerated infant egotism knocked out of him very suddenly, and, as he gets out of school and into business, also into politics, he learns still further the conditions of life. (p. 273)

Though shorn of the theoretical sophistication of Chodorow's book (and perhaps a little too forgiving of the male ego), Gilman brings home the idea that gender differences are produced (and reproduced) in the arbitrary confines of the bourgeois home. Girls become wives and mothers after the example of the mother. Boys become men, full of their own importance, in reaction to the example of the servile mother.

Gilman never turned away from her socialist values. But neither did she come close to a systematic analysis of the capitalist mode of production. She was always clear that the problem at the heart of the sexuo-economic relation was that women were excluded from productive labor. Liberate women, therefore, and you will liberate the world, as she argued in a later work of social criticism,

*The Man-made World*: "The scope of purpose of human life is entirely above and beyond the sex relationship. . . . To develop human life in its true powers we need full equal citizenship for women. . . . An economic democracy must rest on free womanhood; and a free womanhood inevitably leads to an economic democracy" (Gilman, 1911, p. 260). Gilman's last major work of fiction, *Herland*, provides the graphic details of her dream of an economic democracy. Like Bellamy's *Looking Backward*, Gilman's utopia is set stark against the evils of capitalist individualism. Yet, unlike other socialist programs of her day, and unlike her own earlier writings, *Herland* takes a surprising step toward what amounts to a feminist essentialism. Only a world of women, from which all men from the outer world of economic competition are excluded, can be a true economic democracy.

Curiously, unlike "The Yellow Wallpaper" in which the narrator is the suffering woman, the *Herland* story is told in the voice of one Vandyck Jennings, who, more curious still, is a sociologist. Jennings and two male companions from the real world come upon a lost colony of women. The women of Herland are descendants of a small band of female ancestors who, two thousand years before, survived a series of wars and natural disasters. Facing the destruction of the world as it was (by implication, as it still is!), the ancestral mothers rose up against the men who would have kept them as slaves. These women were expressly "white" (p. 56) and otherwise, we are led to believe, remarkably endowed. In particular, they are able to reproduce themselves without benefit of the male sex. Over the centuries the saving remnant of women developed a most peaceful society with a prosperous economy. In Herland social control is exercised by force of personal will, not violence; the needs of all are produced in common, without competition; love (though a markedly sexless love) is shared out of respect, without domination. In a departure from her earlier concepts of sexual equality, Gilman seems to say that only women can bring about this socialist utopia.

The story itself is predictable. The three male visitors are discovered, overcome, and held. Their female captors possess a mystical power over the three men. It is clear that the ability of Herland women to control others by civilized force, not violence, is somehow key to the many virtues of their society. Childcare is shared and thoughtful, education is liberal to the individual's need, economics is practical to the requirements of all. Nothing is out of order in this world without evil.

Nothing, that is, until the men arrive. *Herland's* dramatic interest is sustained by the tantalizing possibility that the men from the outer society will reintroduce the long-lost sexuo-economic ethic. The men themselves are portrayed so as to represent the full range of appalling male habits: sexual appetite, competitiveness, boastful pride. Of the three, only the narrator-sociologist, Vandyck Jennings (despite his name, a caricature of bourgeois idiocy), turns out to be half-plausible as a mate for one of the Herland women. The story comes to its resolution just as Jennings is on the verge of enticing his love to leave Herland, to return with him to the outer world. Then tragic recognition dawns. The risk of discovery and pollution by the world's sexuo-economic values is too great.

The relationship is forbidden. The men are expelled on the not entirely believable trust that they will never betray the way back to Herland. The novel ends, thus, on a tease. Will the corrupt world of poverty, war, and human greed find its way back to Herland, where social evil has been overcome? Will the dream survive?

Just as important as the novel's literary tease is its philosophical tease. Did Gilman change her mind in the end? Is it only women who can maintain an economic democracy? Was she, for all those years, really a closet essentialist? There is no way to know. It is possible that she was led to the appearance of an exaggerated feminist standpoint position by the demands of her genre. A feminist utopia does, after all, require a strong feminist socialism. The free rein of the literary imagination induces a more relaxed attitude toward theoretical principle. On the other hand, by the time Gilman published *Herland* in 1915 she had devoted nearly a quarter century to life and work as a feminist social critic. She knew what she thought. There are few indications in her nonfiction social criticism that she was edging toward a change of heart. *The Man-made World*, written just a few years before *Herland*, held firm to the practical feminist and socialist ideals that had governed Gilman's life work. It is possible she changed her mind; but unlikely. It makes most sense to leave the question open.

One of the considerable strengths of Gilman as a social critic is that she was willing to rethink just about everything. It is, therefore, entirely possible that toward the end she wanted to push her radical ideas to their extreme, not to make a point of principle, but in order to explore still another facet of the troubles women face in the sexuo-economic relation. She had lived as a woman who herself had struggled to escape the compulsory heterosexuality of that relation. Though she remained a woman who loved a man, she very well understood the need women have to escape the man-made world. Her final fiction was, perhaps, a final study of the prospects, if not the realities, of a woman's freedom from that world. *Herland* is not in the end an attack on men. Vandyck Jennings was a plausible partner, just as Walter had been to Charlotte in her youth. The problem the novel, and Gilman's work as whole, seeks to solve is that of the structured relationship between the genders designed by a coercive economic system. She had no settled judgment on this. Nor do we today.

## ASSESSMENT

In her day, Gilman's ideas were quite out of the ordinary. Where the bourgeois values of the Progressive Era coveted capital gain from the rising fortunes of industrial America, Gilman challenged the complicity of capitalist America. Where other white feminists of her own and earlier generations (including her Beecher relatives) narrowed their struggle for women's rights to the right to vote, Gilman identified the suffering of women with the structured whole of societies shaped by the capitalist world system. Where many early feminists like Ellen Key and Margaret Sanger were willing to use the term "feminist" (which came into the culture first in 1910) to further the separate but equal status of women, Gilman challenged the very idea of the women's sphere and called for a complete transformation in gender relations. Where bourgeois people of all kinds held the family as a sacred sphere for women's work, Gilman attacked the bourgeois family as a ridiculous pretense and unmitigated disaster for everyone – men as well as women.

Though not by any means alone in her views, Charlotte Gilman was strikingly the odd woman out of context, even among radicals. Perhaps it was the sharpness of her views that made her the most influential feminist social theorist in the two decades on either side of the end of the nineteenth century. Nancy Cott, in *The Grounding of Modern Feminism* (1987, p. 41), has written:

> Since the 1890s, from California to the East Coast, as a soul stirring speaker and a prolific writer, Gilman had been conveying her critique of the "sexuo-economic" relation that she saw binding women to men, molding women to exaggerate sex-specific characteristics and to rely on men as economic providers. Gilman elevated into a theory of social evolution the changes that perspicacious women saw happening around them; she urged women to move in the direction already pointed out, by leaving their ancient unspecialized home occupation, following the path marked by modern industry and professions, and exercising their full human capabilities in useful work of all sorts.

This was indeed the program that made her famous. Carl Degler thus began his 1956 essay, a foundational study in modern Gilman studies, with the following assessment:

> When Charlotte Perkins Gilman published *Women and Economics* in 1898, the feminist movement in America gained an advocate of uncommon intellectual power and insight. Quickly acclaimed on both sides of the Atlantic [by *Nation* magazine and *The London Chronicle*] for having written "the most significant utterance" on the women's question since Mill, she became the idol of radical feminists and was later judged [by Carrie Chapman Catt] "the most original and challenging mind which the woman movement produced." (Degler 1989, p. 11)

With more reserve, Mari Jo Buhle (1992, p. 270) assesses Gilman's place in history as that of "an analytic bridge between the views of the nineteenth century's woman's movement and the 'scientific' socialist conceptions of woman's advance common to the early twentieth century." Gilman's thinking was, indeed, a bridge to twentieth-century feminism – but it was hardly a scientific socialism. When, after the 1960s, feminism emerged as a force in American, and world, politics, Gilman's ideas returned to favor, but not because of their scientific value.

There are, of course, many ways in which Gilman's thinking is impossible for today's situation. The most prominent of these was her utter blindness to race; not to mention her relative innocence as to the difference made by poverty. She wrote for white, middle-class women – for those, like herself, who bore the brunt of the true womanhood ideal behind the late nineteenth-century bourgeois family. She did not, perhaps could not, see that African-American women, and their families, are differently situated in their domestic lives because the sexuo-economic relation affects them differently (Lanser, 1989). And, even with her impassioned hostility to the capitalist system, she does not seem to have recognized that poverty affects women and their families more harshly than even bourgeois confinement. In these ways, Gilman's thinking is limited.

In other ways, Gilman was way ahead of her times and perfectly suited for today's thinking. Her idea of what later came to be called the sociological imagination still serves well because, as noted, it breaks down abstractions at every turn. She avoided essentialisms, where she did, because she was politically and ethically committed to resolving the troubles women experienced in a family arrangement defined by a false and arbitrary value system. She pursued her work open to all available methods and thus, today, instructs the academically cautious. Because she had lived what she thought, Gilman very well understood the barriers with which social sciences protect themselves from the creative indefiniteness of the literary imagination. Few social critics have written as much good fiction as they have nonfiction and done so with such fine regard for the larger critical issues of the day.

Some may find her fiction too determined by her social values. Others may find her social ideas too indefinite for today's theoretical sophistication. And anyone with sensitivity to the realities of social differences will find her indifference to race a disturbing error of judgment. How could a daughter by marriage of one of the nation's great abolitionist families not imagine that women of color suffered the sexuo-economic relation differently and more severely than white women? Gilman's passions ran deep. Her socialist values were firm. She had a keen eye for political principle and for social theory. Yet she could not see the difference that many, even in her day, realized was the difference at the heart of America's moral sickness. Gilman simply could not entertain thoughts as dark as these. The ones she could were, however, good enough for a lifetime's work, and good enough for us today to appreciate that, whatever the dangers, feminist promises are worth imagining and keeping.

## Bibliography

### Writings of Charlotte Perkins Gilman

The Yellow Wallpaper [1892] and Other Writings (edited by Lynne Sharon Schwartz). New York: Bantam Books (1989).

Women and Economics: a Study of the Economic Relations between Men and Women as a Factor in Social Evolution. 1898. Boston: Small, Maynard & Co. (reprinted New York: Source Book Press, 1970).

The Home: Its Work and Influence. 1903. New York: McClure, Phillips & Co. (reprinted Urbana: University of Illinois Press, 1972).

Human Work. 1904. New York: McClure, Phillips & Co.

The Man-made World or, Our Androcentric Culture. 1911. New York: Charlton Company (reprinted Johnson Reprint Corporation, 1971).

*The Living of Charlotte Perkins Gilman.* 1935. New York: Appleton-Crofts Co. (reprinted Madison: University of Wisconsin Press, 1990).

*Herland* [1915] *and Selected Writings by Charlotte Perkins Gilman* (edited by Barbara Solomon). 1992. New York: Signet.

*The Diaries of Charlotte Perkins Gilman* (edited by Denise Knight), 2 volumes. 1994. Charlottesville: University of Virginia Press.

## Further reading

Bellamy, Edward (1888) *Looking Backward.* New York: Penguin (1960).

Buhle, Mari Jo (1992) Charlotte Perkins Gilman. In Mari Jo Buhle, Paul Buhle, and Dan Georgakas (eds), *Encyclopedia of the American Left.* Urbana: University of Illinois Press, pp. 270–1.

Chodorow, Nancy (1978) *Reproduction of Mothering: Psychoanalysis and the Socialization of Gender.* Berkeley: University of California Press.

Cott, Nancy F. (1987) *The Grounding of Modern Feminism.* New Haven: Yale University Press.

Degler, Carl (1956) Charlotte Perkins Gilman and the Theory and Practice of Feminism. *American Quarterly,* 8, 21–9. Reprinted in Sheryl L. Meyering (ed.), *Charlotte Perkins Gilman: the Woman and Her Work.* Ann Arbor: University of Michigan Research Press (1989), pp. 11–29.

Du Bois, W. E. B. (1903) *Souls of Black Folk.* Chicago: A. C. McClurg (reprinted New York: Bantam, 1989).

Friedan, Betty (1963) *The Feminine Mystique.* New York: W. W. Norton.

Hill, Mary A. (1990) *Charlotte Perkins Gilman: the Making of a Radical Feminist, 1860–1896.* Philadelphia: Temple University Press.

Hill, Mary A. (ed.) (1995) *A Journey Within: the Love Letters of Charlotte Perkins Gilman, 1897–1900.* Lewisburg: Bucknell University Press.

Hochschild, Arlie (1989) *Second Shift.* New York: Avon Books.

Knight, Denise D. (1992) The Reincarnation of Jane: "Through This" – Gilman's Companion to "The Yellow Wallpaper." *Feminist Studies,* 20, 287–302.

Lanser, Susan S. (1989) Feminist Criticism, "The Yellow Wallpaper," and the Politics of Color in America. *Feminist Studies,* 15, 415–41.

Rich, Adrienne (1980) Compulsory Heterosexuality and Lesbian Experience. In Henry Abelove, Michele Aina Barale, and David M. Halperin (eds), *The Lesbian and Gay Studies Reader.* New York: Routledge (1993), pp. 227–54.

Seidman, Steve (1991) *Romantic Longings: Love in America, 1830–1980.* New York: Routledge.

Smith-Rosenberg, Caroll (1975) The Female World of Love and Ritual: Relations between Women in Nineteenth Century America. *Signs,* 1(1).

Stacey, Judith (1990) *Brave New Families.* New York: Basic Books.

# 9

# George Herbert Mead

## Dmitri N. Shalin

## Introduction

George Herbert Mead was trained as a philosopher, taught in a philosophy department, and published primarily in philosophy journals, but his lasting impact was in the field of sociology. The fact that the science of society was still young at the time helps to explain this anomaly. The borderline separating the fledgling discipline from its academic neighbors was still unclear: sociologists did not have much academic turf to protect and felt free to borrow their insights from neighboring fields. The peculiar blend of Romantic idealism and pragmatic activism accomplished by Mead also had something to do with his popularity among social scientists, who found in his life work a model for balancing scholarship and advocacy at a time when America was awash in reform. Finally, it was the bold manner in which Mead married philosophical and sociological idioms that inspired his contemporaries. Mead labored hard to spell out the sociological significance of contemporary philosophical currents and, along with John Dewey, brought a radically sociological imagination to philosophical discourse. While his role in social science is well recognized, Mead's original contribution to philosophy has only recently begun to be fully appreciated (Habermas, 1984; Joas, 1985; Aboulafia, 1986, 1991).

This chapter explores the interfaces between Mead's philosophical and sociological thought, his effort to combine academic pursuits with political engagement, and the impact his work has had on social theory. The discussion draws on Mead's publications, as well as his unpublished papers and correspondence gathered in the Joseph Regenstein Library, University of Chicago (the Mead Papers gathered in this collection are abbreviated below as MP). In his lifetime, Mead published several dozen professional articles and book reviews; they were partially reprinted in 1956 under the title *George Herbert Mead on Social*

*Psychology* (abbreviated thereafter as GHM) and in a 1964 collection *Selected Writings* (SW). Most of Mead's professional writings appeared in print after his death. His lectures on social psychology were published in 1934 as *Mind, Self, and Society* (MSS). More notes on the subject were brought out in 1982 under the heading *The Individual and the Social Self* (TIS). Mead's philosophical writings were collected in the 1938 volume *The Philosophy of the Act* (PA), the 1936 book *Movements of Thought in the Nineteenth Century* (MT), and the 1932 publication *Philosophy of the Present* (PP), based on the lecture series Mead delivered at Berkeley one year before his death.

Mead's life and theoretical corpus have been the subject of several studies which variously inform present discussion (Natanson, 1956; Barry, 1968; Miller, 1973; Joas, 1985; Baldwin, 1986; Shalin, 1984, 1988). Without attempting to do full justice to his numerous contributions, this survey sketches Mead's social theory and places it in historical context. The chapter starts with Mead's biography and intellectual sources, moves on to his social and political theory, and concludes with reflections on Mead's relevance to contemporary social thought.

## THE BIOGRAPHICAL CONTEXT

Mead was born in 1863, at South Hadley, Massachusetts, into a family distinguished by its long roots in New England Puritanism and passionate commitment to Christian values. His father, Hiram Mead, served as a pastor at various South Hadley congregations. In 1869, Hiram moved to Oberlin College, where he was offered a chair in Sacred Rhetoric and Pastoral Theology at the newly established theological seminary. When he died in 1881, at the age of 54, the obituary noted "the quiet, aggressive energy of our brother," his "positiveness of conviction and of self-reliance...modified by delicacy of feeling and gentleness of manner" (*The Oberlin Review*, May 28, 1881, pp. 212–13). Many poor students, the obituary went on, would have had a hard time completing their college work were it not for Hiram Mead's generous help.

Mead's mother, Elizabeth Storrs Billings, a woman noted for her learning and piety, also taught at Oberlin College, and before that, served as a top administrator at Mount Holyoke College. She personally saw to it that the young George would go through his daily regimen of prayer, study, and good works. It was her desire to see her son follow in his father's steps that stirred Mead toward the Christian ministry. Even after Mead began to waver in his faith, he continued to push himself along this path for his mother's sake. "My mother lives in me," Mead wrote to Henry Castle, his college buddy and soul mate, on March 30, 1885 (MP, box 1, folder 1). "Her happiness is bound up in me. I sometimes wonder if it is not my duty to profess Christianity just for the infinite satisfaction it would give her." Shy, studious, and deferential to his parents, Mead seemed perfectly suited to continue the tradition that featured several generations of clergymen on both sides of the family. This must have been his main option when he enroled at Oberlin College, where he took up the classics, rhetoric, and moral philosophy, interlaced with mandatory prayer meetings. But the Christianity Mead imbibed in his formative years was now undergoing rapid changes, struggling to meet the challenges of the late nineteenth century.

German historical criticism, which made its way into the USA midway through the century, raised doubts about the historical veracity of the Bible. These doubts were reinforced by Darwinism, which offered a radically different perspective on the origins of humankind. The downturn in the economic cycle further undermined the appeal of mainstream Protestantism. With rising unemployment and labor unrest, it was harder to sustain its individualistic tenets that predicated personal success on the individual's moral fiber. The mounting economic woes opened the door to socialist doctrine. Throughout the rest of the century, socialism steadily won recruits on US campuses, pushing evangelical Christianity to the left. While mainstream Evangelicals tended to moralize socioeconomic problems by blaming them on assorted personal vices, the Social Gospel movement placed moral issues into a social context and scolded society for its failure to furnish conditions under which every one of its members could thrive. Shaping the human being in the image of God, according to the new evangelicals, meant more than cleansing his soul by prayer; it also required changing the social and economic conditions that corrupted his spirit. "Christian socialists should teach by fact and not by sentiments," explained the Reverend W. D. P. Bliss (quoted in Shalin, 1988, p. 915), "by fact about city gas works, not mere talk about city brotherhood."

These momentous currents intersected at Oberlin College, a Congregationalist institution renowned for its piety and abolitionist sentiments and proud of its place in the forefront of the movement toward socially minded Christianity. *The Oberlin Review*, the campus publication that Mead coedited in his senior year, was among the first in the nation to open its pages to the new teachings. It debated the pros and cons of entering the ministry, pondered the impact of Darwinism on the church doctrine, and urged its readers to take up the Social Gospel, an increasingly influential creed that spurred municipal reform, immigrant surveys, and the social settlement movement.

The new spirit planted the seeds of doubt in Mead's mind about ministry as a vocation. He began to drift away from church teachings, though the process was slow and painful. As late as 1884, Mead confessed to Henry Castle, "I believe Christianity is the only power capable of grappling with evil as it exists now. There can be no doubt of the efficacy of Christ as a remedial agent and so I can speak of him as such. . . . I cannot go out with the world and not work for men. The spirit of a minister is strong with me and I come fairly by it" (MP, April 23 and March 16, 1884, box 1, folder 1). The decision to shun the priesthood was further complicated by his father's untimely death. This tragic occasion placed Mead's family in a precarious financial situation, forcing him to wait on tables in the campus dining hall and sell books door-to-door as a way to offset his tuition costs. Thoughts about the heartache his decision to pursue a secular career might cause his mother terrified the young man. Still, Mead found traditional faith increasingly untenable on intellectual grounds and unappealing as a profession. Indeed, the latter offered less prestige than it once did, as well as fewer financial rewards. Should I choose ministry, explained Mead to his friend (MP, letters to

Henry Castle, March 16 and February 23, 1884, box 1, folder 1), "I shall have to let persons understand that I have some belief in Christianity and my praying be interpreted as a belief in God, whereas I have no doubt that now the most reasonable system of the universe can be formed to myself without a God."

The June 23, 1883, issue of *The Oberlin Review* contained a brief entry on George Mead, who was about to leave Oberlin: "Mead, G. H., Oberlin. Phi Kappa. Essayist at oratorical contest. Has supported himself in part. After graduation will make money, then? Born Feb. 1863." His acutely felt need to support his family led Mead to try his hand as a land surveyor for the Wisconsin Central Railroad Company. This was the first time Mead ventured far beyond the genteel environs of his alma mater and got to see up close the people whom he hoped to teach Christianity. The experience proved unsettling. Mead liked the job, the opportunity to work outdoors, the chance to learn practical skills, but the contacts with the workers on his team left him confused. He was distressed by their callous ways and the little interest they showed in spiritual matters. "The engineer has been drunk off and on and mostly on for the last week," complained Mead to Henry (MP, March 30, 1885, box 1, folder 1), "and between his quarrels with his wife and quarrels with his [fore]man and quarrels with his boarders he has kept himself and the camp in an uproar and has so sickened me that I have about lost my interest in him and creatures of his species....A drunken man howling right outside your tent would destroy the concentration of Socrates and hideousness of the scene seems to slowly close in upon your soul...and yet I ought to find my work and real life interest in working for such men."

Mead also tried to work as a tutor, but the rewards turned out to be equally meager. His charges did not care much for scholastic exercises, and neither did their parents, who were more concerned with the kids helping on the farm than with their progress at school. Mead's failure as a tutor deepened his depression, renewed the doubt about his calling. "I am discouraged Henry. I seem so far off from anything worth living for and I do not see that I gain strength at all by which I can reach anything. My life is spasmodical uneven without purpose. ...Even Christianity looks dreary to me now. I have nothing to offer any woman that would give love an opportunity [to] envigorate my life. It is a sapless dying" (MP, February 8, 1885, box 1, folder 3).

The turning point came in 1887 when Mead joined his friend Henry Castle at Harvard and resumed his secular education. Since his early college years Mead relished philosophical speculations, but he did not see therein any realistic prospects for a career. For one thing, teaching metaphysics was not a common occupation at the time. Also, it appeared to be removed from the burning issues of the day, not a field for someone anxious to serve humanity. But as Mead discovered at Harvard, the academic field was changing fast, drawing its members into a politically charged discourse and publicly minded activism. He could see this in Josiah Royce, perhaps the most influential teacher in Mead's student career, as well as in William James, a highly visible Harvard psychologist and philosopher. The spirit of reform that permeated the country in the 1890s made it respectable for the professorate to engage in social advocacy. Quite a few academics found themselves involved in local and national politics; some toyed with socialism and supported radical reforms.

Mead's decision to pursue an academic career was reinforced by his experience in Germany, where he went in 1888 after winning a prestigious Harvard scholarship that allowed him to pursue doctoral studies abroad. He appeared to have had some help from William James, who took a keen interest in Mead's career, corresponded with Mead's mother, wrote reference letters on Mead's behalf, and was so impressed with the earnest, studious lad that he asked Mead to tutor his children. In Germany, Mead was struck by the active role professors played in public policy debates and the respectability socialism commanded in academic circles. His letters home are brimming with enthusiasm for reforms. He wonders how they could be transplanted to the States, talks about "opening toward everything that is uplifting and satisfying in socialism," urges his friend "to get a hold upon the socialistic literature – and the position of socialism here – in Europe," and deplores in the most sweeping terms American politics: "American political life is horribly idealess.... Our government in ideas and methods belongs so to the past.... We had never had a national legislature in which corrupt motives in the most pecuniary form could be more shamelessly used than in the present" (MP, August 1890, October 21 and 19, 1890, box 1, folder 3). At one point, Mead appeared to be ready to jump into politics himself: "Life looks like such an insignificant affair that two or three or more years of utterly unsuccessful work would not seem to me in the slightest dampening, and the subjective satisfaction of actually doing what my nature asked for of infinitely more importance than anything else.... I mean that I am willing to go into a reform movement which to my eyes may be a failure after all; simply for the sake of the work" (MP, October 19, 1890, box 1, folder 3).

With his political imagination running wild, Mead was neglecting his academic studies. An ambitious thesis on the perception of space and time that he intended to write would never be completed. In 1891, Mead returned to the States, without a degree but with an offer from the University of Michigan to become an instructor in philosophy and physiological psychology. He also brought with him to Ann Arbor his newly wedded wife, Helen Castle, the sister of his dear friend Henry Castle, and the future heiress of the Dole Pineapple fortune. The move to Michigan proved auspicious in one more respect, for there Mead met his lifelong colleague and friend, John Dewey. Already a well established academic, Dewey shared with Mead a puritanic upbringing, a strong desire to do good (his mother used to ask John, "Are you right by Jesus?"), and a passion for social democracy and philosophical discourse. Dewey's encounter with socialism came at about the same time as Mead's. In 1888, Dewey (1969, p. 246) speculated about the "tendency of democracy toward socialism, if not communism" and opined that "there is no need to beat about the bush in saying that democracy is not in reality what it is in name until it is industrial, as well as civil and political...a democracy of wealth is a necessity." The foremost public intellectual of his generation, Dewey would become a role model for Mead, who was struggling to reconcile his secular career with his spiritual longings. That Mead's thinking was still utopian and religiously colored at the time can be gleaned from a rambling letter he wrote in June of 1892 to his parents-in-law: "[I] have been able to follow the connection that has gradually been established between abstract philosophy and daily life. I have learned to see that society advances – men get closer and closer to each other and the Kingdom of Heaven is established on the earth, so far as man becomes more and more organically connected with nature.... [I]t seems to me clearer every day that the telegraph and locomotive are the great spiritual [engines?] of society because they bind man and man so close together, that the interest of the individual must be more completely the interest of all day by day. And America is pushing this spiritualizing of nature [and] is doing more than all in bringing the day when every man will be my neighbor and all life shall be saturated with the divine life" (MP, box 1, folder 3).

Around the time this letter was penned, the University of Chicago invited John Dewey to chair its Philosophy Department. Dewey accepted the offer on the condition that he could bring along his junior colleague. This gave Mead an opportunity to join a premier university in a city famous for its social experimentation. From the fall of 1893 until his death in April of 1931, Mead remained active in city politics. He served as a treasurer for the University of Chicago settlement, helped arbitrate the labor–management dispute in the Chicago garment district strike, and headed the Chicago Educational Association and the Immigrants Protective League of Chicago. In 1918, he was elected president of the City Club, a reform-minded organization of professionals and business people, a high honor that confirmed Mead's standing in the community and sealed his reputation as a public intellectual.

On the academic front, Mead's career was less spectacular. He did not publish enough to reach the top of the academic pecking order. In fact, he did not publish a book during his lifetime. Reasons for this are many. Mead found academic writing to be a painful exercise, so much so that the struggle to commit his ideas to paper would sometimes leave him on the verge of tears. Although Mead generated enough material to fill several volumes, he rarely felt satisfied with what he wrote, continuously reworking his ideas and putting off publication dates. The insights he was trying to communicate required a new theoretical framework, a language that was yet to be invented. "As I look back," Dewey observed on Mead's death (PP, pp. xxxvii, xxxix–xl), "I can see that a great deal of the seeming obscurity of Mr. Mead's expression was due to the fact that he saw something as a problem which had not presented itself at all to other minds. There was no common language because there was no common object of reference.... He was talking about something that the rest of us did not see.... The loss which American philosophy has suffered by Mead's untimely death is increased by the fact that there is every reason to think that he was beginning to get a command of his ideas which made communication to others easier and more effective."

Another trait distinguishing Mead and explaining his relative obscurity was "the combination of great originality and unusual deference to others which marked his personality.... While he was an original thinker, he had no sense of being original. Or if he had such a feeling, he kept it under. Instead of bringing to the front as novelties the problems which were occupying his mind (which they were even as problems), he chose to link them to ideas and movements already current" (Dewey, in PP, p. xxxvi). Indeed, Mead often credited others with insights that were largely his own. His style, deceptively exegetic at times, made many colleagues miss the originality of his thoughts, which came across in Mead's conversations more clearly than in his writing. It was during his lectures on ethics, logic, philosophy, and social psychology that Mead articulated his path-breaking ideas. Soft-spoken, somewhat retiring, but friendly in his demeanor, Mead evoked warm feelings in those who were privileged to know him personally, even though he tended to speak in monotone in the classroom, sometimes repeated himself during lectures, and felt ill at ease with questions in the classroom. Students flocked to his classes. His course on social psychology in particular attracted attention at the university, drawing students from different departments and establishing his reputation as an innovative thinker. At some point, students hired a stenographer to capture his continuously evolving thought. We owe them a debt of gratitude for preserving Mead's ideas for posterity.

## THE INTELLECTUAL SOURCES

Even after Mead embarked on an academic career, he continued to wonder about his true calling and search for discursive props that could satisfy his longing for spiritually meaningful existence. Several intellectual currents making the rounds in his days imprinted themselves on Mead's mind. One was Darwinism, which placed human agency in a broad evolutionary context and demystified reason as a natural phenomenon that belongs to a wide behavioral continuum stretching from the lowest biological forms to the highest ones. John Watson, Mead's colleague at the University of Chicago, radicalized Darwin's premises, vowing to purge psychology from the remnants of spiritualism and to turn it into an exact science of human behavior reducible in its entirety to environmental pressures. Early in the twentieth century, Albert Einstein formulated his relativist physics, which impressed Mead deeply and caused him to rethink his social theory. Important though these developments were in shaping his imagination, they came to Mead filtered through the dual prism of German idealism and American pragmatism – the two intellectual currents that aggressively tackled social issues and passionately advocated responsible being in the world.

Transcendental – or as Mead calls it "Romantic" – idealism is a philosophy that sets itself against dualism and tries to bridge the gap between mind and matter, subject and object, freedom and responsibility. The reality is objective because there are subjects who turn it into an object of their activity – mental activity, that is, for idealists understood reason as primarily an affair of the mind. In and of itself, reality is meaningless, indeterminate; an *a priori* scheme must be imposed on it before it begins to make sense, an *a priori* scheme inherent in the mind. Thus, the subject plays a constitutive role in generating reality. Yet it is only dimly aware of this role, of the fact that reason continuously constructs reality as an objective and meaningful whole. Romantic idealists sought to rectify this situation; they set out to illuminate the transcendental categories humans use to construct their universe, and in the process make humanity realize its responsibility for the world they inhabit.

What Mead found so intriguing about this metaphysics is its sociological underpinnings. "In a very definite sense," he wrote, "we can speak of this philosophy as one which is social in its character" (MT, p. 147). We can see this already in Kant (1951, p. 137), who stipulated that every time the individual makes a generalization, "he disregards the subjective private conditions of his own judgment and reflects upon it from a *universal standpoint* (which he can only determine by placing himself at the standpoint of others)." The rational individual raises a claim on behalf of the entire community whenever he judges something to be the fact. Reason is not idiosyncratic, nor is it compelled by things themselves; it is guided by the spirit of the community, whose logic reason imposes on the outside world. Notice the peculiarly interactionist locution Kant uses to explicate the public nature of reasoning – placing oneself at the standpoint of the other. It thematizes the self which, according to Kant, is the mark of a genuinely human being: "That I am conscious of myself is a thought that already contains a twofold self, the I as subject and the I as object. How it might be possible for the I that I think to be an object . . . is absolutely impossible to explain, even though it is an indubitable fact; it indicates, however, a capacity so highly elevated above sensuous intuition that . . . it has the effect of separating us from all animals, to which we have no reason to attribute the ability to say I to themselves" (Kant, 1983, p. 73). What makes humans unique is that they can grasp themselves as objects without ceasing to be subjects, and they can do so by recourse to *a priori* categories, or, which is the same thing, by assuming the standpoint of the community. Yes, the self as an objective phenomenon is socially constituted. A moral being is a self that places itself in the shoes of other people and follows the golden rule: "Do unto others as you would like others to do unto you." Kant generalized this old biblical injunction into the theory of "categorical imperative," which bids us to do what stands to reason. Act in such a way that the principle underlying your conduct could serve as a law for the entire community, urged Kant, and the community in question would be rational and just. This precept is not only profoundly social, it is also radically democratic in its premise that every individual is a rational being entitled to speak on behalf of the whole community.

To be sure, Kant's thinking was sociological only in its implications. It is the humans' transcendental abilities that constitute society, Kant thought, and not the other way around. The *a priori* categories are universal, unalterable, and inherent in each individual mind; they represent not a particular group or society but the widest possible community – humanity as a whole. Still, the sociological dimension implicit in this philosophy was undeniable, and it came clearly to the fore in Kant's successors. Reality is constructed, Hegel agreed with Kant; things themselves are grasped objectively when they become objects for the mind; but the mind in question is not individual, nor are its *a priori* categories eternal. The flesh and blood person is the mind's immediate locus, but its *a priori* categories are historically emergent and socially derived. This is particularly evident in the case of self, which cannot grasp itself through immediate introspection and which implies a community: "The self perceives itself at the same time that it is perceived by others," contended Hegel (1967, pp. 661, 229). "Self-consciousness exists in itself and for itself... by the very fact that it exists for another self-consciousness; that is to say, it is only by being acknowledged or 'recognized'." As seen from the Hegelian perspective, human history is an ongoing process that gradually brings humanity to self-consciousness, compels it to take stock of its taken-for-granted beliefs, and allows reason to reshape the objective world according to its own consciously chosen rationales.

Romantic idealists made an important discovery: something at the very core of consciousness must remain unconscious if consciousness is to do its job of apprehending objective reality. This unconscious transcendental hideaway is socially and historically emergent. For as long as individuals remain oblivious to the constitutive nature of their *a priori* judgments, the objective world they generate persists in its unyielding thingness. When they stop taking for granted their *a priori* categories and subject them to self-conscious critique, they are bound to disrupt the old structures and, to the extent that new *a priori* beliefs take hold of their minds, bring about a new reality.

These romantic ideas would reverberate throughout the human sciences, engendering new strategies for conceptualizing the bio-psycho-social processes. These strategies aimed at overcoming the dualism and bringing the macro-world directly in touch with the micro-world. The key metaphor of this era was the microcosm recapitulating the macrocosm. It is present in the psychologists' concern for the unconscious, the biologists' discovery of the genetical code, the linguists' preoccupation with the universal grammar, anthropologists' interest in cultural values – everywhere the search was on for an equivalent of the transcendental *a priori* enciphering the larger whole. Romantic idealism left its mark on sociology as well. Feuerbach, Marx, Stirner, Coleridge, Emerson, and other late Romantic thinkers would translate its message into the notions like "species being," "social being," "the self," and kindred concepts undermining the dichotomy of personality and society and re-establishing humans as masters over their fate. "Above all we must avoid postulating 'Society' again as an abstraction vis-a-vis the individual. The individual is *the social being*," wrote Marx (1964, pp. 137–8). "Just as society itself produces *man as man*, so is society *produced* by him. Activity and mind, both in their content and in *their mode of existence*, are social: *social* activity and *social* mind.... Man, much as he may therefore be a *particular* individual...is just as much the totality – the ideal totality – the subjective existence of thought and experienced society for itself."

In Europe, the transcendentalist strategy crystallized into interpretive sociology, with its constructionist agenda and signature attempt to telescope macro-structural phenomena into individual action. "Such concepts as 'state,' 'association,' 'feudalism,' and the like," maintained Weber (1946, p. 55), "designate certain categories of human interaction. Hence it is the task of sociology to reduce those concepts to 'understandable' action, that is, without exception to the actions of participating individual men." The same strategy was realized in Simmel, who linked his famous question "How is society possible?" to the Kantian one, "How is nature possible?" His answer mirrors the transcendentalist logic: "The unity of society is directly realized by its own elements because these elements are themselves conscious and synthesizing units.... The large systems and the super-individual organizations that customarily come to mind when we think of society are nothing but immediate interactions that occur among men constantly, every minute, but that have crystallized as permanent fields, as autonomous phenomena" (Simmel, 1971, p. 7; 1950, p. 10).

A similar strategy was at work in the United States, where Josiah Royce, James Baldwin, Charles Cooley, George Mead, and other minds laboring at the turn of the century sought to appropriate the Romantic legacy. They tackled the problem from a different angle, however. Whereas European sociologists focused on the *a priori* beliefs that motivate conduct and bind together individuals into a social whole, American philosophers and social scientists centered on self-consciousness as a locus of social control and societal change. As Mead (MT, p. 125) put it, "The Romantic philosophy pointed out that the self, while it arises in the human experience, also carries with it the very unity that makes society possible." The *Identitätsphilosophie* (yet another name for transcendental idealism) was interpreted here to mean that reality has to be processed through self-consciousness to emerge as an objective and meaningful whole. Whatever can be said about nature, the famous idealist principle "no object without a subject" sounds almost like a truism when applied to society: the self must identify with a social role before the latter comes to be an objective fact. There would be neither slaves nor masters without individuals acting the part. The structure of social roles found in any given group is inseparable from the structure of selves discernible in its members. The romantic intertwining of self and society had an added appeal to reform-minded Americans because it implied that human agency matters, that the self critically reflecting on its own taken-for-granted beliefs can bring about a more rational society. This activist creed, originally formulated in the aftermath of the French Revolution, fitted well with the Progressive spirit of the time: "When the Revolution came, many institutions which long seemed to be things in themselves, showed that they were nothing but phenomena. And when new constitutions and social orders had to be planned, the spirit of the age emphasized the fact that, at least in the social world, it is the office of human intelligence to impose its own forms upon the phenomena, and to accept no authority but that of the rational self" (Royce, 1919, p. 277).

The last statement belongs to Josiah Royce, the Harvard professor who, in a series of articles published in the 1890s, laid out an agenda that had much to do with Mead's research program. Two of these articles are particularly noteworthy as precursors of Meadian thought, one titled "The External World and the Social Consciousness" (Royce, 1894) and the other "Self-consciousness, Social Consciousness, and Nature" (Royce, 1895). What Royce (1894, p. 531) proposed here was that "neither vividness, nor intrusive resistance to our will, nor peculiarly insistent relation to our muscular experience, nor regular recurrence, suffice to define the notes of externality as we now define them. It is social community that is the true *differentia* of our external world." As an object in our experience, Royce argued, the self submits to this principle as well, for it is social in its origin and substance. Royce credited Romantic idealists in general and Hegel in particular for articulating this insight: "Self-consciousness, as Hegel loved to point out, is, in fact, a mutual affair. . . . I am dependent on my fellows, not only physically, but to the very core of my conscious self-hood, not only for what, physically speaking, I am, but for what I take myself to be. Take away the conscious Alter, and the conscious Ego, so far as in this world we know it, languishes, and languishing dies" (Royce, 1894, p. 532; 1895, p. 468). Along with James Baldwin (1897), Royce speculated about role-playing among children as a mechanism for appropriating self-identity, the relationship between self-consciousness and mental illness, the self's responsibility for its community, and similar subjects that pointed to a fruitful line of inquiry. Mead took it over and pushed it further along than any other scholar of his generation. Much as he was indebted to this tradition, however, Mead transcended it in at least one crucial way: unlike Royce, Mead looked at the dynamics of mind, self, and society not from the idealist but from the pragmatist standpoint. Along with Peirce, James, and Dewey, Mead fastened his intellectual enterprise to "the assumption of the pragmatist that the individual only thinks in order that he may continue an uninterrupted action, that the criterion of the correctness of his thinking is found in his ability to carry on, and that the significant goal of his thinking or research is found not in the ordered presentation of the subject matter but in the uses to which it may be put" (PA, p. 97).

That pragmatism and transcendental idealism are kindred currents goes without saying. The continuity between the two was acknowledged by all principal players in the American pragmatist movement: Charles Peirce, William James, John Dewey, and George Mead. In the words of James (1970, p. 133), pragmatism represents "a new *Identitätsphilosophie* in pluralistic form." Both pragmatists and Romantics stressed agency, responsibility, and the constructed nature of reality, often making it hard to say where romanticism ends and pragmatism begins. There is, of course, one crucial difference, and it has to do with the way each philosophy conceives of human agency. Romantic idealists equate agency with conceptual reasoning continuously perfecting itself throughout the spiritual evolution; pragmatists define reason in post-Darwinian terms as an embodied conduct evolving through biosocial evolution. For Romantic idealists, the transcendental *a priori* is the domain of abstract thought and values; pragmatists transform it into an emotionally charged, biologically grounded, socially informed *a priori* that stands for habit or routine action in which humans are implicated before they can grasp it conceptually. Pragmatists endeavored to reclaim "the universe of nonreflectional experience of our doings, sufferings, enjoyments of the world and of one another" (Dewey, 1916, p. 9). They keep reminding us that "mental processes imply not only mind but that somebody is minding" (PA, p. 69). "The mother minds her baby; she cares for it with affection. Mind is care in the sense of solicitude, anxiety, as well as of active looking after things that need to be tended" (Dewey, 1958, p. 263). Once the cognitive abilities were reconnected to the body, reason lost some of its luster. "Reason, anyway, is a faculty of secondary rank," observed Peirce (1976, p. xxi). "Cognition is but the superficial film of the soul, while sentiment penetrates its substance."

This momentous shift in perspective marked a turning point in the evolution of pragmatism. First articulated by Charles Peirce, pragmatism found a new life in James's *Principles of Psychology* (1890), a widely read volume which tied mental processes to action and brought into wide circulation the concept of social self. Mead and Dewey worked out a similar version of pragmatism in the 1890s, through intense discussions about the nature of the psychical that went back to their Michigan years. Like many of their colleagues at the time, Dewey and Mead sought to find answers to intractable metaphysical problems with the help of psychology, a fledgling discipline that broke away from philosophical discourse while retaining some of its concerns. It was during his preparation for the college course on physiological psychology that Mead realized that "the body and soul are but two sides of the same thing," that "our psychical life can all be read in the functions of our bodies," that "it is not the brain that thinks but our organs insofar as they act together in the processes of life" (MP, letter to the Castle family, June 1892, box 1, folder 3). Dewey came to see mind as minding via his critique of the stimulus–response schema. Of particular interest in this respect is his influential article "The Reflex Arc Concept in Psychology" (Dewey, 1972, volume 5, pp. 100, 106), in which he demolished the notion that stimulus precedes conduct: "In any case, what precedes the 'stimulus' is the whole act, a sensori-motor co-ordination. What is more to the point, the 'stimulus' emerges out of this co-ordination. . . . *Now the response is not only uncertain, but the stimulus is equally uncertain; one is uncertain only in so far as the other is*. The real problem may be equally well stated as either to discover the right stimulus, to constitute the stimulus, or to discover, to constitute, the response." As the last statement shows, pragmatists were fighting their battle on two fronts: they sought to break with the idealist propensity to intellectualize human agency and, at the same time, tried to avoid the reductionist tendency inherent in behaviorism and positivism. The label "physiological psychology" under which pragmatists packaged their discoveries should not mislead us, for this was a nonreductionist, philosophically sophisticated, and, above all, social psychology that they strove to articulate.

Pragmatists were aided in their efforts to steer away from reductionism by the insight into the intimate relationship between reason and community. "The unit of existence is an act," postulated Mead (PA, p. 65), "the act stretches from the stimulus to response," but the act in question, Mead would hasten to add, is itself a part of a larger social undertaking: "What I have attempted to do is to bring rationality back to a certain type of conduct, the type of conduct in which the individual puts himself in the attitude of the whole community to which he belongs. This implies that the whole group is involved in some organized activity and that in this organized activity the action of one calls for the action of the other organisms involved. What we term 'reason' arises when one of the organisms takes into its own response the attitude of the other organisms involved.... When it does so, it is what we term 'a rational being'" (Mead, MSS, p. 334). Dewey took a similar sociological turn. "[M]an is essentially a social being," he claimed from the outset (1969, volume 1, p. 232), "the nonsocial individual is an abstraction arrived at by imagining what man would be if all his human qualities were taken away." To establish human agency as social to the core was important to pragmatists because this placed humans on the same level with society and accorded it a status befitting a truly democratic society. In such a society, individual actions count, each human being is a society in miniature, and the fate of the whole is intertwined with the fate of its individual parts. Here, again, pragmatists revealed their debt to romanticism and its favorite metaphor of man-the-microcosm, which resonated with the progressive creed: "If then, society and the individual are really organic to each other, then the individual is society concentrated ... the localized manifestation of its life ... its vital embodiment. And this is the theory, often crudely expressed, but none the less true in substance, that every citizen is a sovereign, the American theory, a doctrine ... that every man is a priest of God. In conception, at least, democracy approaches most nearly the ideal of all social organization; that in which the individual and society are organic to each other (Dewey, 1969, volume 1, p. 237).

As time wore on, Mead and Dewey would increasingly shun Protestant rhetoric and Romantic shibboleth. In one of his last articles, titled "Royce, James, and Dewey in Their American Setting," Mead distanced himself from his Harvard teachers, whose lofty idealism, he charged, was alien to the pragmatic spirit of America (SW, p. 391). Alas, he overstated his case. Mead and his colleagues owed more to their Romantic predecessors than they were willing to concede. Blended with Protestant yearnings and thoroughly Darwinized, Romantic teaching foreshadowed a theory that sought to explain America to itself and guide the changes ravaging society on the eve of the twentieth century. Pragmatism was the name of this theory, and it found in George Mead "a seminal mind of the very first order" (Dewey, in PP, p. xl), one of its most original interpreters.

## THE THEORETICAL CORPUS

Any attempt to reconstruct Mead's theory faces hurdles. His publications, lecture notes, written fragments, and correspondence give us a good idea about the evolution of his thoughts, but they do not convey a developed theoretical system. It is up to the interpreter to trace the missing links, to recover the systemic features binding together Mead's theoretical corpus.

We also need to bear in mind that Mead was not a professional sociologist. A philosopher by training, he dabbled in physiology, psychology, pedagogy, political theory, and theoretical sociology. His thinking transgressed interdisciplinary boundaries, and this became a handicap once the rationalization process in academia began to favor autonomous disciplines whose practitioners looked askance at their colleagues venturing too far into neighboring fields. If an interest in Mead is now growing, it is in part because the boundaries separating rival academic fields have grown porous and tolerance for alternative research styles is on the rise.

Another problem in reading Mead is his propensity to mingle analytical perspectives. It is one thing to explicate self in the evolutionary perspective, i.e. philogenetically, where any reference to "other selves" is illegitimate, and another to explain how children acquire selves ontogenetically, with a developed human society already in place and other selves lending themselves as the backdrop for conceptualizing the socialization process. A still different approach is called for when behavior is explained *in situ* or sitogenetically, when the researcher confronts fully minded individuals juggling their identities and transcending established norms. Mead often shifts gears, moving briskly between phylogeny, ontogeny, and sitogeny, and in the process confuses his interpreters.

One last difficulty to be mentioned is the unconventional nature of Mead's theory, especially as it evolved in the last two decades of his life, when Mead endeavored to revamp his thoughts in line with the developments in nonclassical physics. This new tack brought Mead into an uncharted territory where he struggled to find language adequate to his insights and to formulate a pragmatist cosmology built on the notion of pansociality. Reconstructing this phase of Mead's thinking is all the more important, given the attention social theorists now pay to neighboring fields and nonclassical perspectives.

While it can hardly do justice to Mead's theory in all its richness and complexity, the following sketch highlights the sociological imagination that distinguishes American pragmatism and its contribution to our understanding of what it means to be human in this world.

## Evolution, relativity, and sociality

Modern evolutionary theory has painted natural history as a process evolving in stages from inchoate blobs of matter to complex mechanical systems to elementary biological forms to higher primates, and then all the way to humans with their self-conscious conduct and rational organizational forms. Social scientists traditionally focus on the tail end of this evolutionary process and model their insights on those of natural science. Mead pretty much stood this approach on its head when he looked at naturalists' discoveries through the social scientist's eye. "The difficulty is found in the fact that the physical scientists present a situation out of which the human animal and his society arose," observed Mead (PA, p. 606). "It has indeed been the procedure of science to explain society in terms of things which are independent of social characters and to represent the social situation as one that has been fortuitous and utterly unessential to its existence of that out of which it has arisen. [Our] undertaking is to work back from the accepted organization of human perspectives in society to the organization of perspectives in the physical world."

What set Mead's imagination off and led him into uncharted waters was the theory of relativity. Its author, Albert Einstein, displayed an uncommon curiosity about the way things appear when sampled from different perspectives. He used to imagine how passing objects would appear to people inside the train and to those gathered on the train station; or else, he would place himself on the edge of a light beam and try to figure out whether the observer stationed on the nearby planet would experience the passing event in the same fashion as the one riding the light beam. Such practice, Mead realized, is a kind of role-taking that marks an intelligent creature simultaneously inhabiting several reference frames: "the relativist is able to hold on to two or more mutually exclusive systems within which the same object appears, by passing from one to the other... as a minded organism he can be in both" (PP, p. 81). This ability to be in several places at once engenders the possibility of different yet equally objective measurements for the same event. Whether light signals emanating from two distant objects were emitted simultaneously cannot be ascertained without the observer being positioned somewhere between the two sources of light. When observers change their positions, the objective reality as measured by the instrument will change as well. The moving body has as many objective readings for its mass, length, and momentum as there are inertial systems in which it is registered.

Relativist phenomena point to the vaguely social manner in which physical things interact with each other. Physical relativity reveals "sociality in nature which has been generally confined to thought," "the social" in its most primitive form (PP, p. 63). Sociality signifies the simultaneous presence in more than one reference frame that alters the character of the event. "Relativity reveals a situation within which the object must be contemporaneously in different systems to be what it is in either.... It is this which I have called the sociality of the present.... Sociality is the capacity to be several things at once" (PP, pp. 63, 49). The fact that a body can have one mass in one inertial system and a different mass in another points to a protosocial situation in which an object enjoys multiple memberships in several systems exerting a cross-pressure on the thing. "I have referred to the increase in mass of a moving body as an extreme case of sociality," wrote Mead (PP, pp. 52–3). A quality that a moving body acquires as a result of its multiple memberships is called "emergent" and the process that brings it into existence "emergence," which Mead defined as "the presence of things in two or more different systems, in such a fashion that its presence in a latter system changes its character in the earlier system or systems to which it belongs" (PP, p. 69). Mead understood that relativist physics appeared to have boosted idealism, but he declined to endorse its subjectivist implications. Neither emergence nor relativity implies subjectivity, he contended; both are natural phenomena requiring no subject; reference frames belong to nature, not consciousness, which appears on the scene belatedly as a by-product of the increasingly more complex relativist phenomena.

The body traversing the mechanical universe does not "choose" among the possibilities it faces, though there is a measure of uncertainty as to where its trajectory will bring it in the end. Nor does it feel pleasure or pain while suffering through its permutations. It is not until the evolutionary process reaches the next stage that the physical body begins to feel its immediate surroundings. The ability to sense one's way around turns the mechanical body into a biological organism, elevates mechanical motion to the level of purposeful conduct, and transforms physical matter into organized environment inhabited by sentient creatures. This crucial step in evolution signifies the beginning of life, which Mead (PP, p. 69) explicated as "a process in which the individual by its action tends to maintain this process both in itself and in later generations, and one which extends beyond what is going on in the organism out into the surrounding world and defines so much of the world as is found in the sweep of these activities as the environment of the individual." Environment is always someone's environment, whether it is a particular individual or the entire species, and when different species appear on the scene, they bring with them an altered environment. There is "a relativity of the organism and its environment, both as to form and content.... Emergent life changes the character of the world just as emergent velocities change the characters of masses" (PA, p. 178; PP, p. 65). As a food object, grass comes into being with certain kinds of animals, while the organism's digestive tract adjusts to the changes in its environment. The important point that sets Mead's approach to evolution apart from Spencer's is that the organism does not simply adapt itself to external stimuli – it picks its stimuli through its sensitivity and action, such as food foraging, nest-building, mating behavior, and similar practices, and through its agency displays a rudimentary intelligence. "Stimuli are means, but the tendency, the impulse, is essential for anything to be a stimulus. This tendency is what marks intelligence. We find it in all stages, perhaps even below life, in crystals.... Intelligence is the selection by the organism of stimuli that will set free and maintain life and aid in rebuilding the form" (TIS, p. 109). Life is relativity brought to a higher level; it signifies a more advanced form of sociality that brings choice into the universe, allows selection between alternative reference frames. It also brings a temporal spread within the organism's purview, which spans the duration of the ongoing act and reflects the organism's ability to foresee the outcome of one's action. A sentient organism favors some reference frames over others, evading those threatening its existence and searching for the ones beneficial to its survival. "Each organism puts its frame of reference on the world" (TIS, p. 115), and in doing so, it maintains, expands, and transforms its environment.

The natural selection process changes its character with the onset of life. Now it features a conflict between competing reference frames favored by species striving to maintain their habitat. A reference frame that organism imposes on the world is called "perspective" – the term Mead borrowed from Alfred Whitehead to describe emergent characteristics that organisms confer on the world through their action and the adaptive changes that the organism undergoes in the process. "The perspective is the world in its relationship to the individual and the individual in his relationship to the world" (PA, p. 115). As species evolve, they bring into the world new perspectives, and as the range of their activity increases, so does their ability to control their environment. This control reaches a qualitatively new stage when the individual succeeds in "getting oneself into the field of one's action," when it emerges as an object within its own field of experience, when it becomes a "self" (TIS, p. 123).

Before the self takes its rightful place as the latest evolutionary emergent alongside mechanism and organism, the living creature must catch its own reflection in other reference frames. Some of this proto-reflexive conduct is already apparent in lower biological forms endowed with senses, yet the animal is unable to switch perspectives or take up a different role at will, nor does it go about its role-playing in a systematic fashion. The animal cannot be another to itself because its biological, physiological, and psychological limitations do not allow it to move in and out of its reference frame. "A perspective can be recognized as such only when lying in the field within which it is no longer a perspective" (PA, p. 607). The ability to leave one's perspective at will and consciously take the role of the other transcends the biological organization of perspectives rooted in heredity. The perspectives must be organized socially for the human being to engage in interaction with oneself, to bring one's action under symbolic control. This breakthrough signifies that the organism has brought within its purview the social process as a whole: "The social organiza-tion of perspectives arises through the individual taking the role of the other within a social act whose various phases are in some sense present in his organism.... [B]y the social mechanism of thought and reflection, the individual transfers himself to another object and organizes the environment from the standpoint of the co-ordinates of that center, he selects another family of dura-tion, another space-time" (PA, p. 610).

Individuals mastering this feat are conscious *and* self-conscious at the same time. They now have what is commonly referred to as mental life, the ability to move freely from one reference frame to another: "It is here that mental life arises – with this continual passing from one system to another, with the occupation of both in passage and with the systematic structure that each involves. It is the realm of continual emergence" (PP, p. 85). This transition presupposes the sociological organization of perspectives, and it signifies the arrival on the evolutionary scene of "minded organisms." In Mead's vocabulary, the term "mind" designates the ability to place oneself in different perspectives in a systematic fashion, to survey oneself from the standpoint of other individuals, to direct one's actions with reference to the social act, and ultimately, to criticize and reconstruct this social act as a whole. "Mind is coterminous with a group. [It] is that part of experience in which the individual becomes an object to itself in the presentation of possible lines of conduct" (TIS, pp. 162, 177). The emergence of mind signifies a new stage in the evolutionary process "when the process of evolution has passed under the control of social reason.... Men in human society have come into some degree of control of the process of evolution out of which they arose" (PA, pp. 508, 511).

To sum up, Mead proposed a cosmology that took the category of the "social" as its fundamental principle. He recast evolution as a process that is accompan-ied by the growth in sociality, by the ability to occupy more than one reference frame or perspective at the same time. He envisioned physical relativity as a primordial form of sociality and conceived of self-consciousness as the highest known evolutionary form of relativity. In this pansocial reckoning, mind and matter are not juxtaposed to each other: the two are perennially evolving sides of the ongoing process of natural evolution: "mind as it appears in the mechanism of social conduct is the organization of perspectives in nature and at least a phase of the creative advance of nature. Nature in its relationship to the organism, and including the organism, is a perspective that is there. A state of mind of the organism is the establishment of simultaneity between the organism and a group of events" (SW, p. 316). This theory suggests "a universe consisting of perspectives. In such a conception the reference of any perspective, as a perspective, is not to an absolute behind the scenes but from one perspective to another" (PA, p. 119). With this daring discursive turn, Mead raised a host of fresh issues and suggested new ways of conceptualizing problems that traditionally occupied social scientists. The new social theory, which Herbert Blumer would later label "symbolic interactionism," brought into one continuum mind, self, and society as three aspects of the same process that calls for a thoroughly sociological treatment and that must be examined in concrete situations.

## Mind, self, and society

Mechanism, organism, and the self are the key evolutionary emergents representing three stages in the development of relativity-cum-sociality. Each stage is ushered in by a set of agents who bring their own perspectives to bear on the world, turning it into an environment or a field of objects peculiar to themselves. "A social organism – that is, a social group of individual organisms – constitutes objects not constituted before.... Wealth, beauty, prestige and various other objects appear in this environment because of its determination by the human social individual, and these are the springs of conduct. The same may, of course, be said of the environment of the biological form. Food, danger, sex, and parenthood are all springs of action and are such because these objects are determined as such by the susceptibilities of the animal forms. Finally, physical objects are at rest or are in motion because of their determination of the here and the there of the percipient event" (PA, p. 201 and MSS, pp. 130). Central among the objects comprising the human environment is the "self" – an emergent property of the human body transformed by social interactions to a point where it grows conscious of its multiple presence in different systems and uses this awareness to conduct itself intelligently. As a minded organism, the self simultaneously inhabits mechanical, biological, and symbolic worlds. While all three are relatively autonomous from each other, they are tied together through multiple feedbacks. Intelligent behavior feeds back into the biological organism: it reshapes its central nervous system, rewires neural connections in the brain, alters the structure of affect. Germs, earthquakes, and interstellar calamities, in turn, remind the minded agents who pride themselves on being the evolution's pinnacle that they are very much a part of the physical and biological realms. All evolutionary domains are tied together by the bonds of sociality. Strictly speaking, there is no reality that is asocial and no minded existence unburdened by the flesh.

Such is the logic underlying Mead's general enterprise. It has several implications for social theory, none more important than this: social theory has to integrate self-conscious humanity with biological corporeality and mechanical physicality in an ecologically sensitive framework that leaves ample room for qualitatively different evolutionary spheres. What are the other features distinguishing this pragmatist approach? It must be *dialectical, decentered, emergent, interactionist* and *process-oriented*.

Like all pragmatists, Mead avoids the dichotomies commonly found in social theory, such as nature and culture, behavior and institution, self and society. He adopts a dialectical strategy that places polar terms on equal footing and renders both contingent on each other. This essentially Romantic strategy makes superfluous questions like "What comes first, self or society?" Each is an abstraction representing a measured linguistic take on the unfractured process: "Human society as we know it could not exist without minds and selves, since all its most characteristic features presuppose the possession of minds and selves by its individual members; but its individual members would not possess minds and selves if these had not arisen within or emerged out of the human social process.... The organization and unification of a social group is identical with the organization and unification of any one of the selves arising within the social process in which that group is engaged" (MSS, pp. 227, 144). Mead follows a similar strategy when he talks about social institutions. He declines to elevate them into a separate realm of social facts. Dialectically understood, an institution is "nothing but an organization of attitudes which we all carry in us.... It makes no difference, over against a person who is stealing your property, whether it is Tom, Dick or Harry. There is an identical response on the part of the whole community under these conditions. We call that the formation of the institution" (MSS, pp. 211, 167). The circle involved in this reasoning is called "hermeneutical." Polar sociological terms are explicated in this circle as flip sides of an ongoing process in which the individual is reproduced as a self-conscious whole while society is generated as a concrete totality of individual perspectives: "The organization of social perspectives in human society takes place through the self, for it is only the organization of a group as the attitude of the individual organism toward itself which gives rise to the self, and it is the activity of the self, so constituted toward and in the group, that is responsible for the peculiar organization of a human community" (PA, p. 625).

The dialectical strategy deployed by Mead results in a characteristically decentered view of consciousness, vaguely reminiscent of Hegel's *Phenomenology of Mind*. Whereas traditional theory locates subjectivity within the organism and juxtaposes to it objective reality on the outside, pragmatist theory disperses consciousness widely and treats mind as a property of social structure. "The locus of mind is not in the individual. Mental processes are fragments of the complex conduct of the individual in and on his environment.... If mind is socially constituted, then the field or locus of any given individual mind must extend as far as the social activity or apparatus of social relations which constitutes it extends; and hence that field cannot be bounded by the skin of the individual organism to which it belongs" (PA, p. 372; MSS, p. 223). Individual mind is not a mental event; it is practical minding in the course of which the individual comes to terms with a larger social act. When the agent places itself in the group perspective and successfully completes a social act, it proves itself to be a mindful, conscious being. When individuals fail in their concerted effort to mesh their action with that of a social group, they open themselves to charges of being mindless or subjective: "The subjectivity does not consist in the experience having the metaphysical nature of consciousness but in its failure to agree with a dominant common perspective which claims the individual.... The objectivity of the perspective of the individual lies in its being a phase of the larger act. It remains subjective in so far as it cannot fall into the larger social perspective" (PA, pp. 610, 548). This is not to suggest that disagreement with the dominant perspective automatically renders the act asocial and the individual involved mindless. The mind embodies group spirit, particularly during the individual's early stages of growth, but if its growth is healthy, mind evolves into a critical, reflective, and reconstructive agency that makes personal experience available to others and compels the group to look at the world in a new way. The affairs of the mind, therefore, are not inherently subjective; mind transcends the individual, it can take up a new perspective at any time. Self-conscious mind is society unto itself in its concrete historical manifestation, and this is precisely why the mind's activity has such a pervasive impact on society. "[T]he whole nature of intelligence is social to the very core," urges Mead (MSS, 141); its immediate locus may be individual, but it reaches as far as society ever extends. Mind's *raison d'être* is to embrace what it is not, which is why it remains open to novelty and serendipity. A decentered mind changes the world by changing itself, by revamping the familiar structure of worn-out perspectives that no longer allow the world to test its potentialities.

Pragmatist social theory zeroes in onto the world's emergent properties. Reality evolves, pragmatists contend, and it never ceases to do so, even at the rudimentary stages of physical evolution: "Things emerge, and emerge in the mechanical order of things, which could not be predicted from what has happened before" (MSS, p. 88). Unsuspected objects appear on the evolutionary scene whenever a new agent is powerful enough to impose on the world its own reference frame. While major evolutionary events are recorded in the annals of science as epoch-making breakthroughs, minor metamorphoses or emergent transformations abound in any given era. This is most notable in the environment populated by self-conscious creatures who are endowed with the extraordinary capacity to change their perspective at will. "The self by its reflexive form announces itself as a conscious organism which is what it is only in so far as it can pass from its own system into those of others, and can thus, in passing, occupy both its own system and that into which it is passing" (PP, p. 82). The self is always on the move, reaching beyond itself, turning into another. At any given moment it is poised to take a quantum leap from one perspective to another and thereby cause an instantaneous – emergent – evolution in its environment. Objective world is the world full of objects brought into existence by self-conscious agency. "There is no self before there is a world, and no world before the self" (TIS, p. 156). This Romantic locution is meant not to mystify but to assert that multiple realities are normal, that ours is the world in the making, that we dwell in what James called "the pluralistic universe" or the universe contingent on our ability to identify with many a universal. A social universal is real when enough individuals generalize their actions in its terms. The new terms bring about a new reality and a new present. "Reality exists in a present" (PP, p. 32), says Mead. An indefinite article in this statement reminds us that there is no absolute time frame to measure the simultaneity of events in nature. With each emergent transformation, a different time structure appears that binds together those involved by a shared sense of the past, with the past understood as "a working hypothesis that has validity in the present within which it works" (PA, p. 96). According to Mead, the past is as hypothetical as the future; it changes with the perspective, with the practical task at hand. "Now the past that is thus constituted is a perspective, and what will be seen in that perspective, and what will be relations between the elements, depends upon the point of reference. There are an infinite number of possible perspectives, each of which will give a different definition to the parts and reveal different relations between them" (PA, p. 99). As the situation runs its course, so does its time structure. A situation has a duration, it endures as long as the agents involved in it keep joining perspectives, sharing a past, and working for a common future. Once the engaged selves assume different guises and adopt alternative time lines, the situation mutates, and so does the reality it engenders. Outside of the time-bound situation, reality remains indeterminate. It takes a quantum of action to salvage it from its indeterminate state, to frame it in definite terms, something that can happen only in the here and the now and that can be grasped only *in situ* and *in actu*.

The pragmatist emphasis on emergent transformations does not imply that pragmatist theory is indifferent to the world's structural properties. Society is very much a structure, according to Mead, and so is the "self as a certain sort of structural process" (MSS, p. 165). Society is comprised of groups, organizations, institutions, and suchlike historical formations that constrain individual action. Each such structural formation revolves around a bundle of privileged perspectives sustained by a power arrangement that reproduces an institutional past in the present and extends the status quo into the future. Recalcitrant individuals unwilling or unable to abide by the existing structure of perspectives will be punished. Yet all these social entities are interactional emergents rather than impenetrable castes. These are emergent universals that have to be brought into being anew with every situational encounter. Individuals are the ones who will ultimately have to choose a perspective and subsume themselves under a social universal. The self's capacity to leap from one universal to another renders social universals fuzzy, makes them appear less as solid "bodies" and more like overlapping "fields." The last term surfaces in Mead's writings, as it does in James and Dewey, who often speculate about "fields of interaction" and "relatively closed fields," and alert us to the changes a thing undergoes "according to the field it enters" (quoted in Shalin, 1986a, pp. 16–17). This is indeed an apt metaphor for the interactionist outlook on social structure. It bids us to look at society as a vast sea of intermeshed fields populated by conscious selves ever ready to make a quantum leap from one symbolic reference frame to another. It is this incessant coming and going, entering and departing, identifying with and dumping the role that is at the heart of social dynamics, as seen from the pragmatist viewpoint. "Membership," correlatively, is more of an achievement than it is an ascription in this pragmatist universe, an on-again/off-again affair, or an "actual occasion" (Alfred Whitehead). Social structure makes itself felt as an ongoing process which ebbs and flows, as group members wander through perspectives and juggle their identities. While the social universe comprised of perspectives is undeniably real, it derives its reality from the particulars who must unlock these perspectives and situate themselves in its time horizons. A towering presence in every individual's experience, society is but a structure of competing time-lines and emerging identities. All power in society is ultimately dependent on the power to universalize the particular and to particularize the universal.

To sum up, Mead's pragmatist theory invites us to look at society as a pluralistic universe at the core of which are perspectives managed by self-conscious individuals. These perspectives are structured, but the structures in question are in flux – they never cease to emerge in the here and now of situational encounters during which humans haggle over the past, present, and future. In this quantum-like world, structure is a processed time or time processing. "You cannot have a process without some sort of a structure, and yet structure is simply something that expresses this process as it takes place" (MT, p.164). Social structure manifests itself in a regime of simultaneities that gives disparate individuals a past to share, a present to grapple with, and a future to strive for. An emergent community thus formed persists as long as a sense of it continues to nourish its members. Intermittent and elusive as this structural process must be, it is the primary focus of interactionist sociology.

## Intelligence, conversation of gestures, and significant symbol

Now we turn to evolutionary social psychology, an important part of Mead's theoretical corpus in which he traces consciousness, language, and self-regarding conduct to their evolutionary precursors. We saw earlier how Mead tackled the problem philosophically by hitching consciousness to relativity: "If we accept those two concepts of emergence and relativity, all I want to point out is that they do answer to what we term 'consciousness,' namely, a certain environment that exists in its relationship to the organism, and in which new characters can arise by virtue of the organism" (MSS, pp. 141, 330). This philosophical insight was fleshed out further, with the substantive input coming from physiology and psychology. One scientific current exerted an especially strong influence over Mead's research agenda: "behaviorism," a radical teaching championed by John Watson, who favored behavior-oriented inquiry over the more traditional, intro-spection-based psychological research. Mead accepted the notion that psychology must approach its subject from the standpoint of behavior, yet he rejected the reductionist strictures prohibiting references to consciousness. In particular, Mead parted company with behaviorists on what qualifies as "stimulus." For Watson, stimulus was an event existing prior to and independent from the response it elicits. Mead cast stimulus as a by-product of an ongoing action, as a phase in the larger act in which the actor selects among many possible perspectives those best answering its current agenda. What is or is not a stimulus cannot be decreed by an outside observer, but must be determined *in situ* and *in actu*, in light of the actor's changing agenda and, in the case of humans, in the broader context of collective behavior. Our social psychology "is behavioristic," explained Mead (MSS, p. 8), "but unlike Watsonian behaviorism it recognizes the parts of the act which do not come to external observation, and it emphasizes the act of the human individual in its natural social situation." In keeping with the behaviorist agenda, however, Mead sought to trace consciousness to animal conduct in its advanced social forms.

Several conditions must be met before instinctive behavior evolves into mindful conduct and the organism seizes itself as an object in its own experience. First of all, a highly sophisticated physiological apparatus has to be in place that enables the organism to delay its immediate response. Second, the cooperation between individual members of the species must reach a high degree of organization, with every member assigned a place in its group and compelled to carry out a part in the larger social act. Third, a prolonged period of infancy is required, during which youngsters practice role-taking, build their sense of self, and learn to measure their conduct by a collective yardstick. Fourth, self-consciousness calls for the forms of communication based on the language of significant symbols. And, fifth, a new regime of managing perspectives has to emerge that separates the sociological principle of organization from the biological one.

Already in graduate school Mead took a keen interest in the physiology of social conduct. He closely followed the developments in brain research and was fascinated with the workings of the central nervous system, in which he saw a biological network uniquely suited for mapping social relations. Its sociological import, Mead surmised, is to be found in the progressively expanding neuron paths that enable the organism to anticipate the future course of action and control its conduct. "[I]t is the function of the central nervous system in the higher forms to connect every response potentially with every other response in the organism.... The central nervous system, in short, enables the individual to exercise conscious control over his behavior. It is the possibility of delayed response which principally differentiates reflective conduct from nonreflective conduct" (PP, p. 125; MSS, p. 117).

Another biological factor favoring humans in their evolutionary ascent is the hand. The versatility that manipulation added to behavior gave humans an edge in the animal kingdom. Along with the hand came tool-making. "Man is essentially a tool-using animal," stressed Mead, "man's hand provides an intermediate contact that is vastly richer in content than that of the jaws or the animal paws.... Man's implements are elaborations and extensions of his hands" (PA, p. 471; MSS, 363). As tool-makers, humans expand their ability to reshape their environment, and to the extent that they master the ultimate tool – symbolic language – they gain control over their own species and affect the direction of evolution itself. "The human hand, backed up, of course, by the indefinite number of actions which the central nervous system makes possible, is of critical importance in the development of human intelligence.... Man's hands have served greatly to break up fixed instincts.... Speech and the hand go along together in the development of the social human being" (MSS, pp. 249, 363, 237). This last point needs to be elaborated further.

Humans are not the only intelligent creatures in the universe. Intelligent behavior is widespread among animals. However, intelligence on the subhuman level differs from what Mead variously calls "social intelligence," "rational intelligence," or "reasoning conduct" found among tool-making animals. At the level of rational intelligence, action is differentiated into several increasingly autonomous phases: "impulse," "perception," "manipulation," and "consummation." Impulse begets image, manipulation tests the percept, purposeful conduct consummates action and satisfies the original drive. It is an impulse – hunger, danger, sexual arousal, or any other drive – that sets the act in motion and makes an object appear in experience. "The starting point of the act is the impulse and not the stimulus" (TIS, p. 114). Impulse converts random events into a definite "situation," turns chaotic reality into "a world in which objects are plans of action" (SW, p. 276). A situation registers in the actor's experience as an "image," "percept," or "perceptual object" that invites "manipulation" – testing of experienced objects via direct contact. Tactile experience either reaffirms the reality of a distant perception or calls it into question, suggesting new perceptual hypotheses. The action's final phase is "consummation" – behavior that appropriates the thing and satisfies the organism's original impulse. "We see what we can reach, what we can manipulate, and then deal with it as we come in contact with it. [The animal's] act is quickly carried to its consummation. The human animal, however, has this implemental stage that comes between the actual consummation and the beginning of the act" (MSS, p, 248). What makes tool-aided behavior so important in the history of intelligence is that it enriches the range of perceptual objects in experience, adds ideas to our mental repertoire, expands time horizons open to the individual, and broadens the spatial properties of the environment within which humans can act: "Ideation extends spatially and temporally the field within which activity takes place" (PP, p. 88). Ideational processes free conduct from its blind reliance on biological drives. The organism that delays its impulsive response and methodically tests its percepts takes a giant step toward rational intelligence. "[R]easoning conduct appears where impulsive conduct breaks down. When the act fails to realize its function, when the impulsive effort to get food does not bring the food, where conflicting impulses thwart each other – here reasoning may come in with a new procedure that is not at the disposal of the biological individual" (MSS, p. 348).

The final step on the road to rational intelligence requires the introduction of symbolic tools into the behavioral repertoire, something that happens to primates involved in complex social interactions. Mead takes great pain to emphasize that this advance implies group behavior. Reason originates in collective behavior implicating the entire community, where every member has a role to play, all roles are potentially interchangeable, and each bit player can, in principle, substitute for the other. On that definition, elaborate social organizations found in insect societies do not qualify as rational. Individual members in such communities are biologically programmed to do their parts – they are physiologically unable to exchange their roles. A honey bee genetically fit to scout a field for pollen cannot collect it, the one that brings it back to the beehive does not know how to process it, the honey-producing specimen would not bear offspring, the queen bee is incapable of defending itself, and the fighting bee can do little more than sting, after which it may die. Mead calls this pole of social differentiation "individual or physiological," and contrasts it with the "personality" or "institutional pole," which presupposes the basic physiological identity of individual members and the fundamental interchangeability of social roles (MSS, pp. 227–34). The latter organizational principle can be traced to collective behavior "in which one organism, in a group of organisms, by its conduct stimulates another to carry out its part in a composite co-operative act.... the individual act [is] a part of the larger social whole to which it in fact belongs, and from which, in a definite sense, it gets its meaning" (PA, p. 189; MSS, p. 8). The various strands of individual conduct implicated in this communal act are, in Mead's vocabulary, "social roles," while the individuals who weave their actions into the tapestry of a group exercise are "personalities" or "social actors." "A person is a personality because he belongs to a community, because he takes over the institutions of that community into his own conduct" (MSS, p. 162). Mindful conduct, then, consists in acting according to a collective script, with every player ready to step in and take the role of other actors in a group: "The evolutionary appearance of the mind and intelligence takes place when the whole social process of experience and behavior is brought within the experience of any one of the separate individuals implicated therein, and when the individual's adjustment to the process is modified and refined by the awareness or consciousness which he thus has of it" (PA, p. 189; MSS, pp. 8, 134).

What makes mind different from other brands of intelligence is that it is mediated by symbolic tools. These tools immensely expand time horizons, give symbol makers a grip on their selves, and turn language users into responsible moral creatures. No matter how smart animals might be, they do not have reason or rational intelligence. Only symbolically mediated conduct can properly be called rational: "Reason is the reference to the relations of things by means of symbols. When we are able to indicate these relations by means of these symbols, we get control of them and can isolate the universal characters of things, and the symbols become significant. No individual or form which has not come into the use of such symbols is rational" (PA, p. 518). Philogenetically, symbolic communication grows from a nonsymbolic one, which Mead characterizes as "the non-significant conversation of gestures." Each participant engaged in this conversation keeps a close watch on everyone else's movement, posturing, facial expression, and other body language signs communicating behavioral attitudes. "Gesture" is the term Mead adopted from the psychologist William Wundt to designate a behavioral act in its early stages, "which serve as the cues or stimuli for the appropriate responses of the other forms involved in the whole social act" (PA, p. 448). Whatever the gesture's social significance, it is not initially available to the actor (the point on which Mead parted company with Wundt). It is only when gestures become transparent to actors themselves that they can be termed "conscious," the conduct involved "rational," and the communication accomplished "conscious conversation of gestures." Mead calls gestures purposefully used to communicate and identical in meaning to all parties involved "significant symbols." The totality of symbols mediating interactions in a society at any given historical stretch is "language." Mead is quick to point out that, from the evolutionary-behavioristic standpoint, meaning is not a subjective event but a social relationship between various components of group behavior: "Meaning is thus a development of something objectively there as a relation between certain phases of the social act; it is not a psychical addition to that act and it is not an 'idea' as traditionally conceived. A gesture by one organism, the resultant of the social act in which the gesture is an early phase, and the response of another organism to the gesture, are the relata in a triple or threefold relationship [that] constitutes the matrix within which the meaning arises, or which develops into the field of meaning.... Language is ultimately a form of behavior and calls for the rationally organized society in which it can properly function" (MSS, p. 76). For all its behavioral grounding, significant symbol is a qualitatively new stage in the evolution of intelligence that coincides with the emergence of thinking and that makes the social organization of perspectives possible. Symbols transformed intelligent behavior peculiar to animals into rational, self-conscious conduct separating human beings from their most developed ancestors.

To summarize, Mead traces rational intelligence and consciousness to the changing physiology, hand manipulation, tool-making, and role-playing that bring into experience a wide array of new perceptual objects with which humans can experiment in a systematic fashion. The most consequential tool that appears along this evolutionary path – significant symbol – weakens the organism's dependence on its biological drives and opens the door to self-conscious social control. A system of significant symbols is language, and "language [is] a principle of social organization that has made the distinctly human society possible" (MSS, p. 260). Symbolic communications bring rationality into the world and turn members of a community into moral creatures responsible for their conduct. "It is as social beings that we are moral beings" (MSS, p. 385). Community-minded, language-mediated, self-referential conduct is socially rational, and society it engenders is rational – human – society.

## Play, game, and the generalized other

Mead is perhaps best known for his theory of the self. His writings on its genesis, structure, and function shift analytical focus from the phylogenetic inquiry to the ontogenetic one, which no longer prohibits references to consciousness, language, and social institutions. Ontogeny deals with children growing up among adult members of their species. While most of what Mead has to say on the subject falls within this theoretical perspective, we should bear in mind how such sociopsychological concepts as "role-taking" and "generalized other" fit into his pragmatist cosmology.

The self is a special case of relativity designating an organism that is aware of its multiple relationships with other things in the pluralistic universe. The body that has reached this evolutionary stage dwells in its multiple perspectives consciously, chooses among affiliations at will, and knows beforehand the role it takes. From the cosmological standpoint, "generalized other [is] the object as

expression of the whole complex of things that make up the environment. . . . The generalized attitude of the other is an assumption of a space that
is absolute over against the relativity of individual organisms" (PA, pp. 193,
310). The generalized other is a totality of perspectives constituting the situation
in someone's experience at any given moment, and role-taking is the mechanism
that allows the individual to explore the otherness of the world by assuming
emotionally charged attitudes and becoming another to oneself. We can see this
most vividly in children engaged in play-acting. The individual takes the role of a
mother, of a dog, of a train; one child claimed to be scrambled eggs! No object is
immune from being enacted by a human fledgling exploring the meaning of
things in their relationship to the self and the self in its relationship to the world.
In infancy and early childhood, all things appear alive in experience; it is only
later that children learn to differentiate between physical and social objects and
reserve role-playing for expressly social occasions: "The physical object is an
abstraction which we make from the social response to nature. We talk to
nature; we address the clouds, the sea, the tree, and objects about us. We later
abstract from that type of response because of what we come to know of such
objects. [Nature] acts as it is expected to act. We are taking the attitude of the
physical things about us, and when we change the situation nature responds in a
different way" (MSS, p. 184). The whole universe arising in experience is, thus,
social through and through. It is in this world that the child "is gradually
building up a definite self which becomes the most important object in his
world" (MSS, p. 369). Unlike objects experienced by intelligent animals, the
self belongs to the realm of signification and implies an elaborate group life in
which the individual takes active part. The following statement captures the
thrust of Mead's theory: "The individual experiences himself as such, not
directly, but only indirectly, from the particular standpoints of other individual
members of the same social group, or from the generalized standpoint of the
social group as a whole to which he belongs. For he enters his own experience as
a self or individual, not directly or immediately, not by becoming a subject to
himself, but only in so far as he first becomes an object to himself just as other
individuals are objects to him or in his experience; and he becomes an object to
himself only by taking the attitudes of other individuals toward himself within a
social environment or context of experience and behavior in which both he and
they are involved" (MSS, p. 138).

Play-acting is the form in which the self grows in ontogenesis. Children
engaged in role-taking accomplish several things. They explore the social structure, find their place in a group, master rule-bound conduct, face punishment for
rule-breaking, learn to negotiate conflicting identities, and discover the meaning
of creativity. Mead singles out two critical stages in this process: "play" and
"game." At the play stage, children act in a way resembling things and people
immediately surrounding them. No partners are necessary for such an exercise,
for all the parts are played by the same person. "The child becomes a generalized
actor-manager, directing, applauding, and criticizing his own roles as well as
those of others" (PA, p. 374). The youngsters commonly address themselves in
the third person or invent "the invisible, imaginary companion which a good

many children produce in their own experience" (MSS, p. 150). At this early stage, the child's sense of self is quite rudimentary, reflecting more or less superficial characteristics of those who stimulate the child's imagination the most. With time, this self begins to exhibit a greater coherence, as the child connects several disparate parts and navigates between them with confidence. "In the play period the child utilizes his own responses to these stimuli which he makes use of in building a self. The response which he has a tendency to make to these stimuli organizes them. He plays that he is, for instance, offering himself something, and he buys it; he gives a letter to himself and takes it away; he addresses himself as a parent, as a teacher; he arrests himself as a policeman" (MSS, pp. 150–1).

The situation changes when imaginary companions are replaced with real partners who interact with a child according to the rules of the game. The self corresponding to this stage is more coherent, internally differentiated, and it is increasingly generalized to reflect the social act as a whole. Playing at being someone does not require a clear-cut time perspective; the past and future are here ill-defined. The game, on the other hand, brings into experience a bigger chunk of environment and offers a far more elaborate time frame where the legitimate past and possible future outcomes are spelled out in vivid details. "The child is one thing at one time and another at another, and what he is at one moment does not determine what he is at another," articulates Mead on the transition from play to game. "He is not organized into a whole. The child has no definite character, no definite personality. . . . But in a game where a number of individuals are involved, then the child taking one role must be ready to take the role of everyone else. . . . The nature of the game is such that every act in the game is determined and qualified by all the other acts. This is expressed by the rules of the game, and implies in each individual a generalized player that is present in every part that is taken" (MSS, pp. 159, 151; PA, p. 374). Game is no longer a childish matter; it is a serious learning exercise modeling responsible conduct in the adult world. The child engaged in game activity "is becoming an organic member of society. He is taking over the morale of that society and is becoming an essential member of it" (MSS, p. 159). A society, after all, is but a series of games adults play, games governed by certain rules, offering tangible stakes, punishing the losers and showering benefits on the winners. To play these high-stake games, humans must learn how to speak the right language, sign themselves in proper terms: "The alley gang has its vocabulary, and so does the club" (TIS, p. 151). Participants in the game also need to know how to juggle identities competing for their attention, to negotiate their membership in various interactional fields, to integrate their disparate selves into a more or less coherent whole, and to bring their action into line with the generalized perspective of the entire community.

"Concrete other," "specific other," "organized other," "generalized other" – these are the terms Mead uses to describe the range of individual and collective others whom we encounter on the road to a full-grown selfhood. The expression "significant other," widely used today, was coined by Harry Stack Sullivan, but it goes back to Mead's concept of a person on whom we model our conduct. The term "generalized other" designates a play team or community of indefinite size whose perspectives have been incorporated into the individual's self. "The organized community or social group which gives to the individual his unity of self may be called 'the generalized other.' The attitude of the generalized other is the attitude of the whole community. . . . It is in the form of the generalized other that the community exercises control over the conduct of its individual members; for it is in this form that the social process or community enters as a determining factor into the individual's thinking" (MSS, p. 154–5). The self fashioned after the generalized other and guided by the group rules is an instrument of social control. By providing its members with selves and minds, society equips them with an ability to criticize their own conduct and to correct their actions accordingly. Self-regarding conduct is by its nature self-critical, the person possessing self-consciousness has a critical attitude built into his or her conduct. "Thus he becomes not only self-conscious but also self-critical; and thus, through self-criticism, social control over individual behavior or conduct operates by virtue of the social origin and basis of such criticism. That is to say, self-criticism is essentially social criticism, and behavior controlled by self-criticism is essentially behavior controlled socially" (MSS, p. 255).

It would be wrong to infer from the above that selfhood turns humans into social robots forever chained to their predetermined identities. Those partaking in numerous symbolic fields are bound to experience a cross-pressure on their identities, which routinely bump against each other and force on the actor tough choices. The conflict is endemic to the social process, and this conflict is inscribed in the selves that emerge in its course. "A highly developed and organized human society is one in which the individual members are interrelated in a multiplicity of different intricate and complicated ways whereby they all share a number of common social interests, yet, on the other hand, are more or less in conflict relative to numerous other interests. . . . Thus, within such a society conflicts arise between different aspects or phases of the same individual self,. . . as well as between different individual selves" (MSS, p. 307). Which particular interest or affiliation wins in any given encounter is problematic; not even the self-conscious individual can be entirely sure how the situation will break out in the end. Self-regarding behavior is creative, either by serendipity or by design. It is also critical and reconstructive; to the extent that self-conscious actions jolt the situation from its original course, they serve not only as an instrument of social control but also as a springboard for social change: "Human society, we have insisted, does not merely stamp the pattern of its organized social behavior upon any one of its individual members, so that this pattern becomes likewise the pattern of the individual's self; it also at the same time, gives him a mind, [and] his mind enables him in turn to stamp the pattern of his further developing self (further developing through his mental activity) upon the structure or organization of human society, and thus in a degree to reconstruct or modify in terms of his self the general pattern of social or group behavior in terms of which his self was originally constituted" (MSS, p. 263).

To conclude, the self is a social structure that appears on the evolutionary scene alongside rational intelligence and symbolic communication. It evolves in stages, beginning with the play stage during which the child tests the otherness of the world by assuming emotionally charged attitudes and imitating animate and inanimate objects, followed by the game stage where the self begins to exhibit a structure reflecting a set of rules. "The game, in other words, requires a whole self, whereas play requires only pieces of the self" (TIS, p. 145). A mature self takes the attitude of the generalized other – a set of privileged perspectives binding together group members. To those who measure their actions by the same generalized other and feel bound by the same reference frame, the emerging structure might appear absolute. Yet this generalized perspective, institutionally privileged though it might be, is relevant only in a given situation and to the present set of participants. The game goes on as long as people keep on playing by its rules; the situation is restructured when those involved take on different disguises and switch to other symbolic fields. While it comes into being within a particular society, the self is not fettered by its symbolic confines. Self-conscious agents criticize the existing perspectives, dump the familiar guises, and conceive new communities endowed with alternative structures of past, present, and future. To understand these dynamics, we need to move beyond phylogeny and ontogeny and immerse ourselves in sitogeny – a theoretical perspective that examines embodied selfhood and the emergent evolution of human society.

## Self, biological individual, and the "I"–"me" dialectics

We saw earlier how human agency gradually emancipates itself from its physical limitations by substituting the social organization of perspectives for the biological one, rational action for impulsive reaction, nonsignificant conversation of gestures for significant communication, and time-conscious conduct for behavior with undifferentiated time-structure. The term "supplementing" is, actually, more appropriate here than "substituting," for the sociological organization of perspectives does not cancel the patterns of sociality found in philogenetically more primitive forms. Although the evolutionary process gives humans the hitherto unknown measure of control over their destiny, it does not turn them into disembodied creatures subsisting in purely symbolic space. The human being is very much a body weighed down by its physical, biological, physiological, and psychological characteristics, all of which exert a continuous influence over individuality and critical reflexivity.

"The line of demarcation between the self and the body is found, then, first of all in the social organization of the act within which the self arises, in its contrast with the physiological organism," maintains Mead (PA, p. 446). Yet he is quick to point out that "the self does not consist simply in the bare organization of social attitudes," that it "is a social entity that must be related to the entire body," that "Walking, writing, and talking are there as physiological processes as well as actions of the self," and that, consequently, it "would be a mistake to assume that a man is a biologic individual plus a reason, if we mean by this definition that he leads two separable lives, one of impulse or instinct, and another of reason" (TIS, p. 148; MSS, pp. 173, 347). Society blends together mechanism, organism, and the self in a complex system of feedbacks that tie together the organizational principles governing perspectives in each evolutionary domain. The question that particularly interested Mead was how the body responds to its selfhood and how the self manages its body. The Freudian solution to the self–body problem gave primacy to unconscious instincts over self-consciousness. Mead, who was very much aware of this solution, rejected it on the ground that Freud underestimated the extent to which the social forces transform our impulsive life. Reason is not just a cipher for immutable drives, a rationalization disguising primordial impulses, nor is society merely a censor reigning in the recalcitrant soma. The societal influence goes far deeper. Society remodels the body's circuits, reshapes the structure of affect, and supplies human agents with symbolic tools that help them mobilize bodily resources for the public good. At the same time, society never obliterates impulses and stamps out emotions. The body or biological individual is a vital link in sociological dynamics.

The biological individual, according to Mead, is the organized group of drives, impulses, and habits that we carry within ourselves and that are variously molded by our group life. Humans excelling in social etiquette have to master the complex machinery of the body to dramatize their social identities. The self abiding by social norms, however, "is very different from the passionate assertive biological individual, that loves and hates and embraces and strikes. *He* is never an object; *his* is a life of direct suffering and action" (MSS, p. 370). It is not that this passionate beast is closed to self-consciousness, although our impulses and gestures are more transparent to outside observers than to ourselves. The point is that impulses and habits are informed by social processes as much as they inform them. The fact that they are amenable to social control does not mean that they can be readily accessed by self-consciousness. "The sets of habits which we have of this sort mean nothing to us; we do not hear the intonations of our speech that others hear unless we are paying particular attention to them. The habits of emotional expression which belong to our speech are of the same sort. We may know that we have expressed ourselves in a joyous fashion but the detailed process is one which does not come back to our conscious selves. There are whole bundles of such habits which do not enter into a conscious self, but which help to make up what is termed the unconscious self" (MSS, p. 163). The biological individual is a creature of impulses and habits, a body unconscious of itself. While the body can exist without a self, the self is fundamentally an embodied experience, an agency that situates itself in the world by mobilizing the organism's semiotic resources. As it signs itself in the flesh, the self gives the body its marching orders, molds it according to a script, and in the process, transforms an indeterminate situation onto an acting stage with distinct spatio-temporal characteristics. An embodied self has a past to claim and the future to strive for, though each is real only in the present where social actors situate themselves with respect to particular reference frames. Once the time structure binding disparate agents into a group has dissipated, the self recedes into the background, the body slips into unconsciousness, and the biological individual takes over. "The biological individual lives in an undifferentiated now; the social reflective individual takes this up into a flow of experience within which stands a fixed past and a more or less uncertain future.... The subject is the biologic individual – never on the scene, and this self adjusted to its social environment, and through this to the world at large, is the object.... Thus the biological individual becomes essentially interrelated with the self, and the two go to make up the personality" (MSS, p. 351, 372–3).

It might seem odd that a theorist who cast the self as a rational process would talk about the "unconscious self." To understand this conceptual twist, we need to remind ourselves that Mead sought to bridge the gap between various evolutionary forms of sociality, that he was a biosocial theorist who took a keen interest in Freud. Mead's views on the subject should also be judged in light of his interest in Romanticism and the subject–object dialectics. We find the direct counterpart to idealism in the theory of "I" and "me," which recast the idealist *a priori* in quasi-naturalistic terms. The transcendental ego, a mysterious realm of paradigmatic preconceptions informing our judgment, turns up in Mead as the unconscious self, biological individual, or "I" – the domain of habituated drives and semi-socialized impulses. What the Romantics called phenomenal self appears in Mead's theory as the conscious self or "me." "The 'I' is the transcendental self of Kant," Mead tells us. "The self-conscious, actual self in social intercourse is the objective 'me' or 'me's'" (SW, p. 141).

The distinction between "I" and "me" serves several strategic functions in the Meadian discourse. It helps square off sociological theory with the notion of indeterminacy, with the fact that our calculated actions routinely produce unanticipated consequences: "However carefully we plan the future it always is different from that which we can previse. [The individual] is never sure about himself, and he astonishes himself by his conduct as much as he astonishes other people" (MSS, pp. 203–4). This distinction biologizes the transcendental *a priori*, which Mead reinterprets as a domain of embodied values and creative drives: "The possibilities of the 'I' belong to that which is actually going on, taking place, and it is in some sense the most fascinating part of our experience. It is there that novelty arises and it is there that our most important values are located" (MSS, p. 204). "Me," by contrast, "is a conventional, habitual individual who is always there. It has to have those habits, those responses that everybody has" (MSS, p. 197). From the sociological standpoint, "me" is an actor obeying common rules. Our "me's" are modeled after conventional roles and historical identities waiting to be claimed as our own. "We are individuals born into a certain nationality, located at a certain spot geographically, and such and such political relations. All of these represent a certain situation which constitutes 'me'; but this necessarily involves a continued action of the organism toward the 'me' in the process within which that lies" (MSS, p. 182). While the "me" is socially scripted, the "I" is not; it represents an improvised response of the body to whatever the situation demands. The resultant self-framing does not always fall within a conventional perspective, though; it can break the established time frame and turn the situation into a stage with action props and time horizons all its own. Whether they stumble on new reference frames or consciously look for alternatives, agents do more than replicate old meanings in the course of interactions. They also express their individuality and imaginatively reconstruct the present situation. Social creativity, according to Mead, flows from "those values which attach particularly to the 'I' rather than to the 'me,' those values which are found in the immediate attitude of the artist, the inventor, the scientist in his discovery, in general in the action of the 'I' which cannot be calculated and which involves a reconstruction of the society, and so of the 'me' which belongs to that society.... To the degree that we make the community in which we live different we all have what is essential to genius, and which becomes genius when the effects are profound" (MSS, pp. 214, 218).

Now, we can see how the "I–me" dialectics advances the Meadian enterprise as a whole. It does so by making make room for the primitive forms of relativity in the world transformed by reason. There is the perennial tension between the biological and sociological imperatives, between the impulsive "I" and the rational "me." For society to maintain its current structure, the "me" has to get a hold of the "I": "The relation between the rational or primarily social side of the self and its impulsive or emotional or primarily anti-social and individual side is such that the latter is, for the most part, controlled with respect to its behavioristic expressions by the former" (MSS, p. 230). Social control works its magic by colonizing the body, compelling it to hide itself under familiar guises, transforming primeval urges into socially acceptable conduct. Self-consciousness is a process that situates the body within its environment by harnessing impulses and mobilizing emotions for public display. Looked at in this perspective, emotions are early warning signals that the body sends to itself as it symbolically traverses numerous references frames, relates itself to others, and evaluates prospective selves. Temporal spread is crucial to understanding human emotions. The more complex the spatio-temporal structure, the richer the organism's emotional life. Intelligence is an emotionally charged agency evaluating its spatio-temporal options in the pluralistic universe.

This is not to say that the rational self always keeps the biological vessel in check. The self weaves its texture from an unyielding stuff, which makes the fit between the body and the self problematic. Having failed to follow the script, the body finds itself in an unfamiliar self, surrounded by an unknown universe, generalizing the other in as yet uncertified fashion. Such experiences are at first accessible to the individual only, but they become part of the public agenda as individual experiences are isolated through symbolic media and incorporated into the communal reality: "This common world is continually breaking down. Problems rise in it and demand solutions. They appear as the exceptions . . . in the experience of individuals and while they have the form of common experiences they run counter to the structure of the common world. The experience of the individuals is precious because it preserves these exceptions. But the individual preserves them in such form that others can experience them, that they may become common experiences" (SW, p. 341).

To recapitulate, Mead undertook a sitogenetic inquiry into the relationship between the body and the self. The question he raised was how the biological organism maintains its selfhood and the conscious self manages its biological agency. His answer to this question was that selfhood is an embodied experience marshaling the semiotic resources of the body with the help of the symbolic stock of society. Whatever feats we accomplish as self-conscious, creative beings, we accomplish because we have bodies, for "only insofar as the self is related to the body is it related to the environment" (TIS, p. 148). The embodied self is a self-conscious body, an organism referenced in a particular perspective, an emotionally engaged subject situated in time and space. Mead distinguished between the "I" and "me" phases of the self, the former representing impulsive, unconscious parts of ourselves, and the latter the rational, self-conscious parts. "Taken together they constitute a personality as it appears in social experience. The self is essentially the social process going on with these two distinguishable phases" (MSS, p. 178). The "I–me" dialectics brings into sociological focus human agency and places embodied subjectivity in its sociohistorical context. It also raises critical questions about the relationship between personal freedom and public necessity and the historical transformation of the pluralistic universe. The last section of this chapter is devoted to these issues.

## Democracy, progressivism, and social reconstruction

Picture a game in which everyone takes part freely, all players follow the generalized other, and no one is barred from trying a particular role. Add to this a provision for revising the rules and inventing new games, and you will get the Meadian blueprint for a humane, democratic community permeated with team spirit and open to continuous improvement. Whatever part the individual plays is illuminated here by the sense of shared purpose and the enjoyment of common products, the sentiments equally prized in a fair game and just society. "It is this that gives joy to creation and belongs to the work of the artist, the research scientist, and the skilled artisan who can follow his article through to its completion. It belongs to co-ordinated efforts of many, when the role of the other in the production is aroused in each worker at the common task, when the sense of team play, *esprit de crops*, inspires interrelated activities. In these situations something of the delight of consummation can crown all intermediate processes. It is unfortunately absent from most labor in modern competitive industrial society" (PA, p. 457).

This statement captures the ambivalence that Mead shared with many contemporaries whose belief in the perfectability of human society was tempered by the keen awareness of its multiple failures. Indeed, Mead's pragmatist cosmology was tailor-made for the Progressive era. It envisioned the pluralistic universe whose inhabitants incessantly multiply perspectives, reinvent their selves, and reconstruct their community for the common good. No society embodies this ideal better than democracy. At its heart is a universal discourse or system of symbols binding individuals into a social whole and transparent to "every citizen of the universe of discourse" (PA, p. 375). Democratic society never stops restructuring its perspectives and broadening its horizons of universality – "'universal' discourse to be universal has to be continuously revised" (MSS, p. 269). Democracy makes its symbolic and material resources available to all its members – it is "responsible for the ordering of its process and structure so that what are common goods in their very nature should be accessible to common enjoyment" (SW, p. 407). Democratic society teaches its members to place themselves in each other's shoes. More than that, it gives everyone a practical chance to experiment with new roles and selves. When it lives up to its promise, democracy approximates what Mead calls "a universal society in which the interests of each would be the interests of all" (PA, p. 466).

The above description should not be taken to mean that the pluralistic universe is devoid of tension, that everything in it hangs together. Local lingos and competing agendas find their place in a democratic society alongside overarching cultural symbols. If attitudes we carry in ourselves clash, it is because institutions of society operate at cross purpose: "Each social institution with the good that it subtends asserts and maintains itself but finds itself in this assertion in conflict with other institutions and their goods" (PA, p. 498). Far from being a threat to the democratic discourse, conflict is its lifeblood. Democratic society does not merely tolerate competing discourses – it encourages and protects them. What makes the tension between perspectives vying for attention in a democratic society constructive is the fact that they are open to criticism. Democratic society teaches its members to use their mind critically, it makes its symbolic resources available to all its members, and it systematically lowers the barriers separating classes and impeding communication across group boundaries. By contrast, nondemocratic societies limit their members' participation in common discourse and zealously police the selves they can rightfully call their own. Castes, estates, classes, cliques – human history abounds in exclusive interactional fields formed around privileged perspectives designed to keep nonmembers at bay. The most insidious in this respect are social configurations based on caste. Superficially, they resemble insect communities whose members are stuck with their parts because they are physiologically outfitted to play them. Ideology that goes with such a society often blames biological differences for the fact that some of its members are barred from particular roles. In reality, social conventions backed by power are primarily responsible for the rigid pattern of role-taking in closed societies. "The development of democratic community implies the removal of castes as essential to the personality of the individual; the individual is not to be what he is in his specific caste or group set over against other groups, but his distinctions are to be distinctions of functional difference which put him in relationship with others instead of separating him" (MSS, p. 318). Like every game, democratic society calls for a division of labor, which poses no immediate threat to social intelligence. As long as every role is there for the taking and no one is shut out of the game, there is ample room for our universal nature to play itself out. Needless to say, American society in the late nineteenth and early twentieth centuries fell short of this democratic ideal.

Mead hammered away at the last point in his political writings. He decried the fact that symbolic means for self-realization were distributed unequally among American citizens. He urged the lowering of economic barriers hampering the disadvantaged. He personally participated in the Chicago immigrants' surveys, documenting their living conditions and educational needs. Immigrants who flooded the country at the turn of the century and supplied much of its labor power, Mead pointed out, were often shortchanged by a system that favored industrial education for future laborers and liberal arts education for well-to-do classes. Mead singled out the factory system for his criticism, charging that the assembly-line technology threatened to reduce universal beings to an appendage in a mechanical process whose overall purpose and ultimate products eluded a machine operator: "The man who tends one of these machines becomes a part of the machine, and when the machine is thrown away the man is thrown away, for he has fitted himself into the machine until he has become nothing but a cog" (quoted in Shalin, 1988, p. 928). Tearing down class barriers, eliminating artificial restrictions, revamping dehumanizing social technologies – such were the causes to which Mead dedicated himself in his political life. Progressivism meant for him a commitment to "the 'democratic ideal' of removing such restrictions," of getting on with social reconstruction and advancing democratic reforms (SW, p. 406). How can the democratic changes be effected? Mead sought the answer to this question in the temporal dynamics of social interactions.

Social change in the pluralistic universe is inextricably linked to its spatio-temporal structure and heavily relies on our ability to fashion disparate actions into a meaningful whole via the continually renewed sense of shared past and future. Each society has its own time horizons, its own unique history that its members recount to themselves and their offspring. When the historical narrative changes, the pluralistic universe slips off its symbolic moorings and expands its familiar confines. "The past that is there for us, as the present is there, stands on the same basis as the world about us that is there.... The histories that have most fastened upon men's minds have been political and cultural propaganda, and every great social movement has flashed back its light to discover a new past" (PA, pp. 94–7). We can pull off this remarkable feat of rediscovering – reinventing – our pasts because society provided us with minds whose locus is not in the head but in the situation implicating the entire group and the generalized other. It is this decentered, time-conscious mind that "frees us from bondage to past or future. We are neither creatures of the necessity of an irrevocable past, nor of any vision given on the Mount" (PP, p. 90). Thanks to its special brand of relativity, rational intelligence not only cushions the effect of biological drives but also delivers humans from the dictate of implacable social norms. Our minds allow us to revise our past, set up a hypothetical future, select suitable means, and appropriate the self that ties all the elements of the situation together in a continual passage from the past to the present and into an indefinite future. The pluralistic universe owes its spatio-temporal structure to self-referential conduct. When the latter undergoes restructuring, the former changes as well: "The relations between social reconstruction and self or personality reconstruction are reciprocal and internal or organic.... In both types of reconstruction the same fundamental material of organized social relations among human individuals is involved, and is simply treated in different ways, or from different angles or points of view, in the two cases, respectively; or in short, social reconstruction and self or personality reconstruction are the two sides of a single process – the process of human social evolution" (MSS, p. 309).

It would be a mistake to conclude from the above that Mead saw reconstruction in society as a purely cognitive affair. Social institutions are ingrained in our emotional habits as much as in logical thinking, which is why social change has to engage both "me" and "I," with the rational "me" pointing the way and the unconscious "I" realizing the imagined future. It takes time for the biological individual to slip into the new self, to change the habits of the heart, which resist the coercion. The new discourse must be backed up by the adjustments in the entire body where our values are sedimented into habits. To achieve its goal, social reconstruction has to mobilize the embodied self, "the individual as embodying the values in himself. . . . We want a full life expressed in our instincts, our natures. Reflective thinking enables us to bring these different values into the realm of possibility" (PA, pp. 625, 463–4). Social reconstruction feeds on emotional substance, it is literally "bodied forth" by the agent redeeming its claim to selfhood in the flesh. Social changes that result in lowering social barriers release emotions conducive to democratic discourse and bring about selves conversant with wider ranging communities: "The breakdown of barriers is something that arouses a flood of emotions, because it sets free an indefinite number of possible contacts to other people which have been checked, held repressed. [The] person does get out of himself, and by doing so makes himself a definite member of a larger community than that to which he previously belonged" (MSS, p. 219).

Despite the confident outlook Mead shared with other progressives, he stayed away from optimistic predictions about the future of democracy; nor did he put a seal of approval on specific forms it ought to take. Such predictions ran contrary to his pragmatist spirit that favored experimentation over doctrinaire social engineering. The future is uncertain, Mead said repeatedly, "there are no fixed or determined ends or goals toward which social progress necessarily moves; and such progress is hence genuinely creative and would not otherwise be progress. . . . The moral question is not the one of setting up a right value against a wrong value; it is a question of finding the possibility of acting so as to take into account as far as possible all the values involved" (MSS, p. 294; PA, p. 465). Still, we can glean the broad outlines of a democratic society he favored from praises he sang to "team work," "universal discourse," "international mindedness," and "the community values of friendship, of passion, of parenthood, of amusement, of beauty, of social solidarity in its unnumbered forms" (SW, p. 311). Whatever helps make the universe of discourse more inclusive is progress. Whoever incorporates the experience of the other into one's own and guides one's actions accordingly is a moral being. Whichever value finds its embodied expression in a democratic community is a concrete universal.

Mead's pragmatic optimism was tempered by the realization that no society can assure the individual a happy life. Meaningful, yes, but not necessarily a happy one. Because the pluralistic universe is forever changing, humans are never completely at home in it: "Human society is not at home in the world because it is trying to change that world and change itself; and, so long as it has failed to so change itself and change its world, it is not at home in it as the physiological and physical mechanism is" (PA, p. 476). What this statement implies is that we cannot lead an authentic life in society as long as we are not trying to change it, yet our concerted efforts to transcend the existing order turn us into spiritual nomads unable to identify completely with any given self. There is no such thing as an authentic self in Mead's social cosmology. Every self we claim as our own will have to be shed, however snugly we might be wrapped into our conventional "me's." The biological individual disguised under a historical mask will sooner or later turn into a corpse, but our dramatic personae will go on, re-enacted by numerous others, eager to step into our shoes: "There is a need for salvation – not the salvation of the individual but the salvation of the self as a social being" (PA, p. 476).

In sum, Mead's social theory called for a continually expanding social universe in which no perspective is foreclosed to its inhabitants, all symbolic resources are distributed equally among its members, and everyone can – and ought to – be an agent of social change. The political system that best approximates this blueprint is democracy. For all its failures, democracy comes closest to realizing the universality of human nature and the creativity of social intelligence. To live up to its promise, democratic society has to keep reinventing itself, and that means re-examining its past, reconstructing its present, and reimagining its future. Social change has a temporal dimension, predicated on the fact that social structure is rooted in a past continually recycled by skilled narrators. When the old historical narrative is revised and the new one finds its way into public discourse, individuals discover a new past, which turns out to be as emergent as the future. "The past is a working hypothesis that has validity in the present within which it works but has no other validity" (PA, p. 96). Social change has a somatic dimension. It requires an alignment between the biological resources of the "I" and the discursive skills of the "me." Social reconstruction is not a teleological process gravitating to some predestined goal; it is an open-ended process whose time horizons are revised by successive generations. The social change that brings down class barriers, levels economic disparities, spreads around symbolic resources, and increases team spirit is progressive. For all the good change brings to society, it does not guarantee happiness and fulfilled selfhood. For transcendence is a distinctly human mode of being in the world and the ultimate form of authenticity available to humanity.

## CONCLUSION

I have pieced together disparate strands of Mead's thought and tried to show them as parts of a vast, unfinished project that will continue to nourish our sociological imagination well into the future. In my closing remarks, I would like to bring into sharper relief a few key insights and unresolved issues in his pragmatist cosmology.

Central to the pragmatist project is the problem of historically situated agency. There are two radical solutions to this problem that Romantic idealists bequeathed to modern social thought. One equates human agency with reason, grammar, norm, or a similar structural principle that disembodies subjectivity and drains agency of its emotional substance. Another approach tends to naturalize and deracinate human agency, reducing the transcendental *a priori* to more or less immutable drives, impulses, and behavioral dispositions. Pragmatists refuse to linguistify or biologize agency. Steering between these two extremes, they conceptualize human agency as a historically situated, fully embodied, emotionally grounded selfhood. Mead acknowledges that the individual is born into a symbolic universe that is already there, but he declines either to dissolve agency into symbolic forms or to reduce it to behavioral drives. There is more to personhood than its symbolic hulk; we are vested in the world with our entire bodies, which are as much a product of society as our beliefs and values. Sociality shapes our neural circuits and affective responses, but our emotional habits and behavioral proclivities feed right back into social structure. Sociological analysis is impoverished when it is preoccupied exclusively with the normative/structural/discursive or the impulsive/affective/behavioral side of the social processes. That is what social pragmatists mean when they say that culture is embodied and body is uncultured – the two must be studied jointly in the context of human society.

While Mead brought into focus the relationship between the biological individual and the self, he might have drawn too sharp a line between conscious and unconscious procesess, between the rational self and the biological individual. This can be gleaned from his belief that animals have no selves, that they know neither past nor future, and that, consequently, "animals have no rights" and "there is no wrong committed when an animal life's is taken away" (MSS, p. 183). An argument can be made that for all their inferior instrumental and symbolic skills, animals are not as different from humans as Mead contended. Since we think not just with our heads but with our entire bodies, rational thinking and emotional intelligence may share considerable evolutionary grounds. Pragmatist sociologists should take a closer look at the continuity of animal and human intelligence. They might want to juxtapose Mead and Freud and reconceptualize the unconscious as historicized, fleshed out, habitualized agency. They also need to re-examine the "I– me" dialectics, and particularly the manner in which the self cares for its body in different cultural settings. The sitogenetic analysis of self–body interactions is a promising line of inquiry that Mead's followers should take seriously.

Mead's social cosmology offers a fresh look at social structure as an emergent event predicated on its members' ability to manage perspectives and process time. This view breaks with the classical theory that casts social structure as something akin to an immovable ether subsisting in absolute space and time and informing individual conduct without being informed by it. In the pragmatist reckoning, social structure is an event unfolding *in situ* where its strategic properties are determined by conscious agents situating themselves across space and time. The self is perceived here as a nonclassically propertied object, a social particle quantum leaping from one interactional field to another. Every time agents assume new disguises and lend emotional substance to their selves, they affect the group's status as a universal, objective, and meaningful whole. This relativist approach renders social structure contingent on the quantum of objectivity supplied to it by self-conscious individuals. The structure of the self evolving in the individual's experience reflects the structure of the community to which this individual belongs, and vice versa, the group structure is encoded in the self-identities of its individual members. Society as a whole transpires here as an emergent system of generalized perspectives held in common by individuals inhabiting the same symbolic niche or environment endowed with emergent spatio-temporal properties by self-conscious agents.

This innovative approach raises questions regarding the relationship between the micro and macro levels of sociological analysis, questions that Mead has not answered adequately. His theory may be seen as positing an over-emergent view of social order that does not do justice to recurrent patterns in social interactions and overarching time sequences. It is true that group perspectives owe their objectivity to self-conscious agents, but the degrees of freedom with which individuals may choose a particular perspective as the basis for self identification vary greatly from one interactional field to another. Societies tend to privilege some perspectives and discourage their members from taking others. Social control mechanisms determine who can raise specific self-claims, under what circumstances, and how such claims can be redeemed and validated. Mead showed that the emergent evolution is built into human agency as it manifests itself on the micro level in concrete situational encounters. He did not explain why certain families of duration become privileged. Neither did he outline the logic that governs the historical evolution of macrostructural patterns. More conceptual work has to be done here. Interactionists need to demonstrate how the emergent time-processing generates relatively stable societal patterns. The gap between macrostructural dynamics and emergent transformations on the micro level is yet to be bridged in interactionist sociology.

The pragmatist emphasis on corporeal selfhood adds a potentially valuable dimension to the theory of social and political institutions. The latter are generally equated with a symbolic code or a normative grammar enciphering relations between individuals in a given organization. The Meadian approach draws attention to the corporeal dimension of social institutions and invites an inquiry into authoritarian emotions, aristocratic demeanor, and the body language of democracy. Indeed, polity affects our entire body. Democracy, in this sense, is an embodied institution. There is more to it than a constitutional system of checks and balances and a list of civil rights. It is also a demeanor, the practical care we take of our own and other people's bodies and selves. The body politic is the politics of the body. The strength of democracy is in civility, which cannot be legislated any more than it can be reduced to a biological drive. Democracy communicates in the flesh; it is a conversation that blends nonsignificant and significant gestures, with each set codifying democratic politics in its own special way. Body language speaks volumes about the body politic and measurably affects the quality of life.

The problem with Mead's political theory is that it does not confront head on the issue of power. Mead tends to blur the distinction between symbolic and economic resources, understates the barriers that market economy places on equitable distribution of resources, and underestimates the extent to which economic, cultural, racial, ethnic, and other divisions subvert the universal nature of intelligence. While he acknowledged the role conflict plays in the pluralistic universe, Mead believed that the cooperation between individuals, groups, and nations is the order of the day, that "revolutions might be carried out by methods which would be strictly constitutional and legal" (SW, pp. 150–1). Alas, Mead might have overdosed on the Progressive era's optimism about the plasticity of human nature and the perfectability of society. His enthusiasm for democracy is infectious, but his take on American political institutions and their democratic promise needs to be complemented by a closer analysis of power, class, and privilege. The pragmatist challenge is to conceptualize the obdurate realities of power that delimit our freedom to assume roles and devise new perspectives.

Finally, I want to single out the ecological dimension of the pragmatist social cosmology. Mead places humans at the pinnacle of evolution and treats self-consciousness as the highest known form of relativity. At the same time, he considers human agency to be an extension of natural phenomena, an emergent product of natural evolution. Although self-referential conduct dramatically alters the way living beings exist in the world, social intelligence does not exempt humans from mechanical laws, nor does it insulate them from biological limitations. For all our fabled reflexivity, we are still suffering, mortal beings. Physical, biological, physiological, psychological, spiritual, and sociological perspectives intersect in our existence, determining our unique mode of being in the world. Selfhood simply designates a new mode of integration of these qualitatively different forms of relativity. Divested from its corporeal substance, the self is just a linguistic fiction, an unsubstantiated discursive claim. By the same token, agents outside their self-conscious reference frames are nothing more than biological entities devoid of rationality and unable to feel oneness with the rest of the world. Our ability to empathize with all creatures, large and small, to place ourselves in the shoes of any other thing, is, indeed, unique. "Is it necessary that that feeling of unity or solidarity should go beyond the society itself to the physical universe which seems to support it?" asks Mead (PA, p. 478). He hesitates to answer this question in the affirmative. As a lapsed Protestant, he probably did not want to be accused of anything like spiritualism and religious exaltation. But our ecological awareness might cause us to reconsider this question and ponder the spiritual implications of Mead's social cosmology.

## Bibliography

### Writings of George Herbert Mead

*Philosophy of the Present.* 1932. Chicago: University of Chicago Press.
*Mind, Self, and Society.* 1934. Chicago: University of Chicago Press.
*Movements of Thought in the Nineteenth Century.* 1936. Chicago: University of Chicago Press.
*The Philosophy of the Act.* 1938. Chicago: University of Chicago Press.
*George Herbert Mead on Social Psychology* (edited by Anselm Strauss). 1956. Chicago: University of Chicago Press.
*Selected Writings: George Herbert Mead* (edited by A. J. Reck). 1964. New York: Bobbs-Merrill.

*The Individual and the Social Self. Unpublished Work of George Herbert Mead* (edited by David L. Miller). 1982. Chicago: University of Chicago Press.

## Further reading

Aboulafia, Mitchell (1986) *The Mediating Self: Mead, Sartre, and Self-determination.* New Haven, CT: Yale University Press.

Aboulafia, Mitchell (1991) *Philosophy, Social Theory, and the Thought of George Herbert Mead.* Albany: State University of New York Press.

Baldwin, James M. (1897) *Social and Ethical Interpretation in Mental Development.* New York: Macmillan.

Baldwin, John (1986) *George Herbert Mead: a Unifying Theory of Sociology.* Beverly Hills, CA: Sage Publications.

Barry, Robert M. (1968) A Man and a City: George Herbert Mead in Chicago. In M. Novak (ed.), *American Philosophy and the Future: Essays for the New Generation.* New York: Charles Scribner's Sons, pp. 173–92.

Dewey, John (1916) *Essays in Experimental Logic.* New York: Dover.

Dewey, John (1934) *Art and Experience.* New York: G. P. Putnam's Sons (1958).

Dewey, John (1969–72) *John Dewey: the Early Works, volumes 1–5.* Carbondale: Southern Illinois University Press.

Dewey, John (1986) Pragmatism and Social Interactionism. *American Sociological Review,* 51, 9–29.

Diner, S. J. (1980) *A City and Its Universities: Public Policy in Chicago, 1892–1919.* Chapel Hill: University of North Carolina Press.

Habermas, Jürgen (1981) *The Theory of Communicative Action. Volume 1, Reason and the Realization of Society.* Boston: Beacon Press (1984).

Hegel, G. W. F. (1967) *The Phenomenology of Mind.* New York: Harper and Row (1967).

James, William (1890) *Principles of Philosophy.* New York: Dover.

James, William (1909) *Essays in Radical Empiricism and Pluralistic Universe.* Gloucester: David McKay (1967).

James, William (1909) *The Meaning of Truth.* Ann Arbor: University of Michigan Press (1970).

Joas, Hans (1985) *G. H. Mead: a Contemporary Reexamination of His Thought.* Cambridge: Polity Press.

Kant, Immanuel (1804) *What Real Progress Has Metaphysics Made in Germany since the Time of Leibniz and Wolf.* New York: Abaris Books Inc. (1983).

Kant, Immanuel (1790) *Critique of Judgment.* New York: Bobbs-Merrill (1951).

Marx, Karl (1844) *The Economic and Philosophic Manuscripts of 1844.* New York: International (1964).

Miller, David L. (1973) *George Herbert Mead: Self, Language and the World.* Austin: University of Texas Press.

Natanson, Maurice (1956) *The Social Dynamics of George H. Mead.* Washington, DC: Public Affairs Press.

Peirce, Charles (1976) *The New Elements of Mathematics.* Atlantic Highlands, NJ: Humanities Press.

Royce, Josiah (1894) The External World and the Social Consciousness. *Philosophical Review,* 3, 513–45.

Royce, Josiah (1895) Self-consciousness, Social Consciousness, and Nature. *Philosophical Review,* 4, 465–85.

Royce, Josiah (1919) *Lectures on Modern Idealism.* New Haven, CT: Yale University Press.

Shalin, Dmitri N. (1984) The Romantic Antecedents of Meadian Social Psychology. *Symbolic Interaction,* 7, 43–65.

Shalin, Dmitri N. (1986a) Pragmatism and Social Interactionism. *American Sociological Review,* 51, 9–29.

Shalin, Dmitri N. (1986b) Romanticism and the Rise of Sociological Hermeneutics. *Social Research,* 53, 77–123.

Shalin, Dmitri N. (1988) Mead, Socialism, and the Progressive Agenda. *American Journal of Sociology,* 93, 913–51.

Simmel, Georg (1908) *George Simmel on Individuality and Social Forms,* edited by D. N. Levine. Chicago: University of Chicago Press (1971).

Simmel, Georg (1950) *The Sociology of Georg Simmel,* translated and edited by K. Wolff. New York: Free Press.

Weber, Max (1926) *From Max Weber: Essays in Sociology.* New York: Oxford University Press (1946).

# 10

# W. E. B. Du Bois

## CHARLES LEMERT

I once had dinner alone in a hotel restaurant in provincial South Korea. After ordering, I left the dining room for a moment. Upon returning, I thought it necessary to explain that I had already been seated. Before I could, the *maître de* said, "Your meal is waiting for you, sir." How could he have known who I was amid so many in a very large restaurant? It took a while before I figured it out. The answer, of course, was that I was the one and only white person in the place. I was easy to spot, perhaps even interesting to follow, as I moved irregularly in violation of local prejudices.

When, just about a century ago, W. E. B. Du Bois wrote so memorably of the color line, he meant to evoke experiences of this kind, though ones very different in their occurrence and meaning. On my side of the color line, such a prejudice is a curiosity. On the side Du Bois had in mind, it is the fundamental fact of life. This is why Du Bois began his most famous book, *The Souls of Black Folk* (1903), as he did:

> Herein lie buried many things which if read with patience may show the strange meaning of being black here at the dawning of the Twentieth Century. This meaning is not without interest to you, Gentle Reader, for the problem of the Twentieth Century is the problem of the color line. I pray you, then, receive my little book in all charity, studying my words with me, forgiving mistake and foible for sake of the faith and passion that is within me, seeking the grain of truth hidden there. (Du Bois, 1903, p. xxxi)

Du Bois wrote in a voice attuned to his purpose. Whites were principal among the gentle readers to whom he had addressed his book, so lovingly composed, but far from gentle in its adventures across the color line. A few paragraphs beyond, he left no doubt which side he was on. "Need I add that I who speak here am bone of the bone and flesh of the flesh of them that live within the Veil?" (p. xxxi). He may have supposed that this coming out was required by the book's declaration of purpose: "Leaving, then, the white world, I have stepped within the Veil, raising it that you may view faintly its deeper recess" (p. xxxi).

Du Bois was thirty-five years old when *The Souls of Black Folk* astonished the world. His education at Fisk, Harvard, and Berlin was behind him. His Harvard doctoral thesis had created a stir of recognition among historians. His now classic urban ethnography, *The Philadelphia Negro* (1899), had also been well received. Du Bois had, thus, given public notice of his intention to write the scientific record of the Negro community in America. At the end of the nineteenth century, most black Americans had been born to mothers or fathers who had been slaves. In those few years of emancipation, other leaders of the race had begun to set the record straight. But none was so supremely qualified as Du Bois to make the facts known. He was, then and ever, the sociologist using science in the service of his politics.

But he was much more than an engaged social scientist. Through the better part of the twentieth century, Du Bois was never far from the center of the politics that shaped the history of the American Negro. In 1998, thirty-five years after Du Bois's death in 1963, Julian Bond was elected chairman of the board of the National Association for the Advancement of Colored People (NAACP). As he took over the leadership of the organization Du Bois helped to found in 1909, Bond recalled a family photograph showing him as a small boy holding the hand of the great man: "I think for people of my age and generation, this was a normal experience – not to have Du Bois in your home, but to have his name in your home, to know about him in your home, to have grown up in this movement. This was table conversation for us" (*The New York Times*, February 28, 1998, p. A1). In the years after its publication in 1903, *Souls* brought Du Bois's name into the homes of black people across the world. He passed quickly beyond mere fame to the higher status Bond describes. For many, he became an icon of racial possibility. There had been moral leaders, poets, race men, political organizers, and intellectuals before him. But no one before had so perfectly combined all these qualities.

For better or worse, Du Bois was well aware of his moral position among American Negroes (the name he fought to dignify by the capital N). He was, perhaps, too insistent upon his moral position. He identified himself with the history of his race by the subtitle he chose for one of four memoirs, *Dusk of Dawn: an Essay toward an Autobiography of a Race Concept* (1940). Today Du Bois is honored as much by criticism of his shortcomings (notably, Reed, 1997; Carby, 1998) as by praise of his genius. In retrospect, it seems odd that anyone could be put forth, or put himself forth, as the embodiment of a people's hopes. That the idea was once entirely reasonable, and is still plausible to many, is measure of the man's stature and accomplishments.

Du Bois must be on the shortlist of men and women of the twentieth century whose influence spread without ceasing as the many years of their lives passed by. Picasso and Borges might head such a list. Joyce just misses. He died relatively young, as did Franklin Roosevelt and Babe Ruth. The list is not long.

Du Bois lived long, and worked hard. He was more famous at the end of life in 1963 than he was at the century's start. In the first decade of the century, Du Bois defied Booker T. Washington's concessions to white power. In the second decade, he became the NAACP's principal spokesman. In the 1920s, he was a leader of the Harlem Renaissance. In the 1930s, he wrote *Black Reconstruction*, still another classic work of scholarship. In the 1940s, after forty years' work in the Pan-African movement, he was recognized as the spiritual leader of blacks the world over. In the 1950s, he defied the American government's indictment of communist conspiracy. In the early 1960s, he traveled the world, quit America altogether, and settled in Ghana to begin work on his life's dream of an *Encyclopedia Africana*. He was 95 when he died, still working. He died, as icons often do, at precisely the right moment – on the eve of the 1963 March on Washington. From the death of Frederick Douglass in 1895 to Martin Luther King Jr's coronation the day after Du Bois's death, no other person of African descent was as conspicuous in the worldwide work of contesting the color line.

Du Bois may well have been a genius. But his accomplishments were born of his work ethic. Most days, for nearly eighty years, Du Bois began his work precisely on schedule at seven-thirty in the morning. Each hour, thereafter, was parsed for a specific task until bed around ten at night. He attributed his longevity to moderation in food and drink, daily exercise, and eight full hours of sleep. Personal discipline was the means to his many accomplishments. He wrote twenty-three books of fiction and nonfiction, of which many endure – three as classics. His articles, essays, and letters are too many to count. Still, his literary work never interfered with his politics. He founded the Niagara Movement, which led to the NAACP, not long after he began organizing the international Pan-African movement. He established and edited three magazines, including *Phylon* and *The Crisis*. He traveled, lectured, while always, somehow, answering his mail. In first six decades of the twentieth century, in the politics of race, there was no debate in which he did not figure.

Du Bois's genius is evident less in the bulk of his work than in its style. Though in person he could be arrogant and difficult, in writing he was refined. It takes a while for some readers of *Souls of Black Folk* to realize the full meaning of the plural *Souls*. Even today, when the famous double consciousness passage trips from every tongue, the subtlety of its underlying idea is easy to miss.

After the Egyptian and Indian, the Greek and the Roman, the Teuton and Mongolian, the Negro is a sort of seventh son, born within the veil, and gifted with second-sight in this American world – a world which yields him no true self-consciousness, but only lets him see himself through the revelation of the other world. It is a peculiar sensation, this double-consciousness, the sense of always looking at one's self through the eyes of others, of measuring one's soul by the tape of a world that looks on in amused contempt and pity. One ever feels his twoness, – an American, a Negro; two souls, two thoughts, two unreconciled strivings; two warring ideals in one dark body, whose dogged strength alone keeps it from being torn asunder. (Du Bois, 1903, pp. 2–3)

This is no mere social psychology of the racial double bind. The American Negro is caught, yes. But by "dogged strength" he overcomes what he "ever feels." He is two at once, always unreconciled. He is, yes, at war within because of the war without. But the struggle is his strength. The "peculiar sensation of always looking at one's self by the tape of the world that looks on in amused contempt and pity" gives the American Negro the "gift of second-sight."

And there is more to this gift than meets the analytic remove of the white eye. The Veil works mysteriously – one might even say, spiritually – on the two souls beyond it, as it does on the white soul before. This is why, in beginning the book, Du Bois offered to lift the Veil for whites, while warning them that, if they go with him who is flesh of the flesh with them within, they will see what they cannot fully understand. The line and the Veil – Du Bois returned again and again to these figures. But he never allowed them to relax into analytic calm. Analysis is for the scientist that Du Bois was. But science moved just one of his souls. His spiritual being energized the other. The two souls, together, made him self-consciously who he was. The color line is the stark exterior of the American Negro's experience. Though a figure of speech, the color line remains an analytic tool, a category serving to divide, classify, and segregate. By contrast, the Veil lends moral uncertainty to the analytic expression. In the early pages of *Souls* the two figures of speech appear side-by-side as if to allow the Veil to unsettle the analytic police work of the color line. From behind the Veil, the Negro ridicules the white world that "looks on in amused contempt and pity" – those, that is, who deploy their pitiful powers to measure the souls of others. The measure taken is nothing beyond its cruel effects, for which, ironically, whites are disadvantaged. They suffer in ignorance. Their color line segregates the terrifying object of white desire. But the line they draw turns out to be a Veil with the reciprocal effect of imposing the blindness upon which their civilization depends. In attempting to cover their eyes, whites are doubly crippled. They are mute as well as blind, even though, everyone knows, we talk all the time about that which we do not wish to see. Whether sexual or economic, white consciousness in the late nineteenth century was wide awake to the facts of life. Burgeoning industrial America could not live without the Negro's laboring powers – powers that exceed field and forge, thus locking imposer and imposed in a darkness only one understood. Thus, the unspeakable corollary to the Negro's gift of second-sight – that moral consciousness encouraged by the secreting Veil – is the apartheid that organizes the singular soul of white folk.

Du Bois, the scientist, respected the mysteries of race. In 1940, nearly forty years after *Souls*, Du Bois wrote in *The Dusk of Dawn* of the white world. As he had done in *Souls*, he wrote here of the mysteries of the color line:

> With the best will the factual outline of a life misses the essence of its spirit. Thus in my life the chief fact has been race – not so much scientific race, as that deep conviction of myriads of men that congenital differences among the main masses of human beings absolutely condition the individual destiny of every member of a group. (Du Bois, 1940, p. 139)

The doubling of consciousness works both ways – to obverse but comparable effect. In weakening the exterior, it strengthens the interior life of black folk. In protecting the fragile culture of white folks, it weakens their souls. On both sides, the Veil determines the destiny of all.

## The Person and the Context

More than any of the great social thinkers who were on stage as the nineteenth century ended, Du Bois was a mover in the global politics of his days. As prominent as Durkheim was to Third Republic French politics, or Weber to late Weimar Germany, or Gilman to American socialism – none so stirred the history of his times as did Du Bois. Few of the others even survived the First World War, which, in its way, killed Durkheim and Weber, while sending Gilman into retirement. Only Freud and Du Bois among this remarkable group survived to expand their work after the Great War.

The First World War changed everything for the hopeful bourgeois peoples who prevailed near the beginning of the twentieth century. In *All Quiet on the Western Front*, the greatest of all novels about that war, Erich Maria Remarque puts these words into the mouth of the generation that had suffered through it: "We will become superfluous even to ourselves, we will grow older, a few will adapt themselves, some others will merely submit, and most will be bewildered; – the years will pass by and in the end we shall fall into ruin." And so, for many, it was. It would be a good quarter century before calm would settle in the West, then only if one ignores the wars throughout its decolonizing empire – Africa, Korea, Vietnam, and Afghanistan; then Africa again and still. Raymond Mon was not far wrong. The twentieth was the "century of total war." Among the rising middle classes, especially in America, the last glimmers of nineteenth-century optimism faded in the shadows. Not even the short run of the 1920s with its white flappers and New Black renaissance in the urban North could revive the simple innocence that had prevailed before the Great War.

Only those social thinkers attuned to the darker, less conscious forces of social evil were able to flourish after the war. Freud and Du Bois were chief among these few – Freud because he believed in the deeper drive toward evil; Du Bois because he knew just how the destiny of the American Negro was necessarily at odds with that of white folk. He knew very well that this war meant opportunity for blacks. It meant the end of the hordes of European immigrant workers coming to serve American industry, which nudged ajar the door of economic opportunity to blacks. Thus began the great wave of migrations to the industrial North. Thereafter, Negro politics and culture were decisively more urban and Northern than rural and Southern. Though the feudal relations of racial production would remain in force in the South until the 1960s, the urban and industrial migrations brought with them a new cultural awareness that would eventually destroy the racial caste system from which so many had fled. For one, the renaissances in South Side Chicago and Harlem, in particular, marked the coming out of black culture into the consciousness of whites. For another, they meant that blacks came to understand their side of the Veil better, and differently. Du Bois's own struggle with these social forces approximated what they meant to the millions who had already come to look to him for guidance.

In 1915, after the Great War had begun, but before the United States had entered it, W. E. B. Du Bois's "leadership position towered above all" (Lewis, 1993, p. 513). In *Souls*, Du Bois had begun the move toward leadership with an essay, "Of Mr. Booker T. Washington and Others," a revision of an earlier, shorter comment on the Principal of the Tuskegee Institute and the leading race man at the turn of the century. The essay was respectful but firm. Du Bois  knew what he was doing by placing it third among the essays in *Souls*. Though his words would not immediately provoke his public rivalry with Washington, the battle began at that moment. The struggle between Du Bois and Washington in the first decade of the twentieth century was, in effect, the beginning of the transformation of a racial politics rooted in the traditions of the feudal South into a politics of the urban and urbane North.

Washington had been born in slavery and educated at the all-Negro Hampton Institute. He directed Tuskegee as the institutional emblem of his famous compromise with white power. Du Bois had been born free in the North and went to Harvard. He became the intellectual emblem of those devoted to the unique moral and cultural contributions of the Negro to American society. The rivalry between Washington and Du Bois is often viewed as one over principles. Indeed it was. But there would have been no philosophical differences had there not been, deeper still, economic realities by which the color line took on its urgency. Hence, the First World War changed things for whites in one way; for blacks in another. Washington's politics were rooted in the convenience of the whites who profited from the feudal traditions of the South. Du Bois's rose on the surge of industrialization in which feudal domination was refracted in the still cruel, but more rational, capitalist world system. Washington dominated Negro politics at the end of the nineteenth century by force of his ability to control. He was as adroit at pulling the strings of black submission as Du Bois was at inspiring resistance to oppression. This difference was Washington's weak hand when faced with Du Bois's more spiritual challenges – and the Great War was the political and economic divide between the two.

To understand the importance of the war to Du Bois's leadership after 1915, one must compare his situation to the conditions of Washington's leadership some twenty years before. Booker T. Washington rose to prominence on the wings of Northern white relief at his 1895 Atlanta Compromise: "that in all things purely social we can be as separate as the fingers, yet one as the hand in all things essential to our mutual progress." Washington's memorable figure of the hand and fingers was for whites balm spread upon the sores of racial trouble. The year after, in 1896, *Plessy* v. *Ferguson* gave legal sanction to the restoration of racial apartheid in the American South. Washington's compromise was a double assurance to whites who feared the freedoms that permitted the social contact attendant upon the practical necessities of their economic contract with black labor. Washington's Tuskegee Institute was flush with white philanthropic payback for the Principal's single-minded devotion to the industrial education of blacks.

In "Of Mr. Booker T. Washington and Others," Du Bois summarized the political and social effects of Washington's 1895 speech: "It startled the nation to hear a Negro advocating such a programme after many decades of bitter complaint; it startled and won the applause of the South, it interested and won the admiration of the North; and after a confused murmur of protest, it silenced if it did not convert the Negroes themselves" (Du Bois, 1903, p. 31). Then, on the point of his differences with Washington, Du Bois continued:

> Mr. Washington distinctly asks that black people give up, at least for the present, three things,–
>     First, political power,
>     Second, insistence on civil rights,
>     Third, higher education of Negro youth,–
> And concentrate all their energies on industrial education, and accumulation of wealth, and the conciliation of the South. The policy has been courageously and insistently advocated for over fifteen years, and has been triumphant for perhaps ten years. As a result of this tender palm-branch, what has been the return? In these years, there have occurred:
>     1. The disfranchisement of the Negro.
>     2. The legal creation of a distinct status of civil inferiority for the Negro.
>     3. The steady withdrawal of aid from institutions for the higher training of the Negro. (Du Bois, 1903, p. 37)

Du Bois was still young when he wrote these words, green to the world of racial politics. Though respectful, he was tough – tough enough to reveal the lie in oversimplifying his doctrine of the talented tenth. Du Bois's commitment to higher education was far more than an elitist ideology of the supremacy of culture over economics. Though it is true that Du Bois felt that the poor must be led by the educated, it is not true that his politics were a mere culturalist reflex to Washington's crude economism.

When it came to racial politics Du Bois understood very well that the color line is always drawn in the factual sands of civil rights, political power, and false economic hopes. He spoke to the terrible misery visited upon the black poor, rejected forever from real economic progress – and rejected as much by Washington's smarmy compromise as by the feudal lords of Jim Crow. That he had staked his position in the cultural politics of racial difference (as Cornel West has put it) does not mean Du Bois had no feel for economic or political justice. Adolph Reed (1997) may think that culture is the realm of elite compromise. But those who share his tiresome view of politics may never have contemplated the contradiction between Du Bois and Washington. The latter was the proponent of the real politics of compromise and economic uplift, and it was Washington who lived the life of luxury as the private cars of Northern philanthropists eased onto the private rail link that led to his mansion at Tuskegee. It was Du Bois, the Northern freeman, who grew up poor (as had Washington); and Du Bois who remained, if not poor, always on the margins of economic security. He lived with the poor, in practice as in the imagination, in a way that the Washington of the

Atlanta Compromise did not. Du Bois's talented tenth doctrine, so often the object of orthodox sneer, was a doctrine of cultural politics founded in fine awareness of the suffering brought down by the political economy of Negro life.

It is true that Booker T. Washington had been born of slavery and that his labor on behalf of poor Negroes in the South was based on his own firm principles. To have built Tuskegee, as he did, is to set one's hands to the hard hewn tools of field and factory. And it is also true that Du Bois, though he never enjoyed the resplendent comforts of Washington's later years, took advantage of a privileged education at Harvard and Berlin. His cultural advantage, more than once, gained him the generosity of white friends who protected him in trouble and sent him to travel abroad. Still, Du Bois never compromised. He died in Ghana and is buried alongside the continuing economic misery of sub-Saharan Africa. The one, Washington, aligned himself with the poor in a racial politics that served the interests of the white and well off. The other, Du Bois, walked and talked with the well off; yet, in the end, it was his photograph that hung in the homes of the poorest blacks. Du Bois earned the respect of the poor because he spoke, and wrote, with feeling for their condition. In his personal style, he could indeed be a mannered snob. But his words, and actions, rang with feeling for the poor with whom he took his stand.

Du Bois's feeling for the poorest of those within the Veil was born less of his own childhood poverty than of the accident of years he spent in adolescence in Tennessee. At the end of high school in 1884, Du Bois had hoped to go straight to Harvard. But for a number of reasons, not excluding race, Du Bois was not admitted on first application. So, in 1885, he began three years of study in the South, at Fisk University in Nashville. Then, for the first time, he experienced life lived fully within the Veil:

> Consider how miraculous it all was to a boy of seventeen, just escaped from a narrow valley: I will and lo! my people come dancing about me, – riotous in color, gay in laughter, full of sympathy, need and pleading; darkly delicious girls – 'colored girls' – sat beside me and actually talked to me while I gazed in tongue-tied silence or babbled in boastful dreams. (Du Bois, 1920, p. 14)

This is how Du Bois remembered those adolescent pleasures many years later. His feelings for those youthful years in black Nashville were undiminished when, even later, he was in his nineties: "Into this world I leapt with enthusiasm. A new loyalty and allegiance replaced my Americanism: hence forward I was a Negro" (Du Bois, 1968, p. 108). To the end of life, he held the Tennessee years as the source of his racial pride – and as the antidote to the first rude, boyhood shock of racial difference.

More important even than the Negro world of Fisk and Nashville was a small village in the far eastern mountains of Tennessee where Du Bois spent the summers of 1886 and 1887 teaching school among the poorest of rural black folk. In his *Autobiography*, written some seventy years after those two college summers, he wrote of this impossibly remote village as though it were still his own:

I have called my community a world, and so its isolation made it. There was among us a but half-awakened common consciousness, sprung from common joy and grief, at burial, birth or wedding; from a common hardship in poverty, poor land and low wages; and, above all, from the sight of the Veil that hung between us and Opportunity. (Du Bois, 1968, p. 120)

These are virtually the same words he had used when he first wrote of this village in *Souls* (p. 48). When he repeated them at the end of life, Du Bois had long been assured of his place in the wider world. The repetition was, thus, a way of giving account of his life's work – a way of saying that, though he had traveled the globe, his life remained in community with the most poor and forgotten.

From those summer days of college in 1886 and 1887, Alexandria, Tennessee, was his spiritual community. Thereafter, Du Bois kept Alexandria, far forgotten by the world, dear among his most special memories of youth. As other stories of the early years faded, those of this one place seemed as special to him at the end of life as at the beginning. Alexandria was, perhaps, an antidote for the lingering poison from his earlier childhood in Massachusetts. Though Great Barrington gave him his start, and was relatively free of racial ugliness, it was also where the sad losses of his life returned. Great Barrington is where his mother endured the miseries of poverty, abandonment, and early death. There, too, he had laid to rest his dear son, Burghardt, dead in infancy because the white hospitals of Atlanta refused him treatment.

But, most of all, this northern, free village was where a white girl's rude dismissal of his party card first taught him the truth of racial differences. It was there, or so he says at the beginning of *Souls* (p. 2), "in the early days of rollicking boyhood that the revelation first bursts upon one, all in a day, as it were." He had done nothing more than join the fun and games of mixed company, when his ease with white children was broken by "one girl, a tall newcomer" unacquainted with local customs. "Then it dawned upon me with a certain suddenness that I was different from the others; or like, mayhap, in heart and life and longing, but shut out from their world by a vast veil" (p. 2). From that moment in childhood, he resolved to live, as he said, "beyond" the Veil. He disdained that little white girl's rejection, just as much as he relished the late adolescent reverie of the "darkly delicious girls" of Nashville.

Why the two types of girls: one white and removed; the others darkly delicious? Hazel Carby (1998, chapter 1) somewhat plausibly suggests that Du Bois may have been like other race men in imagining his adult masculinity as beyond, not just the Veil, but even the frivolity of girlish adolescence. If so, his fully adult recollection of the pleasures of the racial community (written more than thirty years after the first days in Nashville) was also a completely serious adult meditation on the origins of his life work. In his poetic imagination, the two types of girl were, assuredly, figures of the mysterious sexual play at work in racial differences. They were nameless. But a third would appear, fully named and human, as the one most dear to his understanding of the political situation.

The early chapters of *Souls* are, in effect, the manifesto of Du Bois's racial politics. Though *Souls* is a collection of essays, many previously published, they are ordered with purpose. The first four chapters, especially, declare the foundational principles of his vocation. In the first chapter, "Of Our Spiritual Strivings," he announces the double consciousness principle, stated lyrically against the historical fugue of Negro life in America. In the second, "Of the Dawn of Freedom," he scores the facts of life for the Negro American from the hope of Emancipation in 1865, through the rise of Reconstruction and the Freedman's Bureau, and their abandonment in the 1870s, to the beginnings of Jim Crow. In the third chapter, "Of Mr. Booker T. Washington and Others," he joins the philosophical to the political, against the facts of the previous chapter. His argument with Washington was not a matter of personal preference but of historical necessity. Then comes the story of his community. In the fourth chapter, "On the Meaning of Progress," Du Bois completes his manifesto. His criticism of Washington is framed by the historical record – the failure of Reconstruction, and the restoration apartheid in the South – by, as he puts it (p. 49), "the barriers of caste" which Washington had so easily disregarded. Here is Du Bois resetting the clock of racial history in America. Washington's compromise would never do because the backward conditions of Negro life are insufficient by standards ever more rigorous than even those of the feudal South.

Of these opening chapters of *Souls*, none is more poignant, and important, than the fourth. "Of the Meaning of Progress" is surely one of Du Bois's most inventive literary moments. Here he means to call into question the most cherished value of the very Western culture that formed the one of his two souls. Here is the "beyond" of the Veil addressed to his gentle white readers. Here is one of his most elegant theoretical claims posed, not as insistence, but in the surprise of simple stories told of his relationship to poor, isolated Alexandria.

"Of the Meaning of Progress" is irony that sneaks upon the reader. Here, he makes no mention of the easy frivolity of Fisk and Nashville. Du Bois leaps directly to the rural hills where he tells the story of Josie Dowell, the third of the figurative girls in his early life. When he first meets Josie, she is still a child, but "the center of the family: always busy at service, or at home, or berry picking; a little nervous and inclined to scold, like her mother, yet faithful, too, like her father" (p. 45). At first, Josie might seem to be poor kin to the darkly delicious girls he knew in Nashville – perhaps the more bracing antidote to the rejecting white girl of Great Barrington. Yet Du Bois switches the figure of speech. "She had about her a certain fineness, the shadow of an unconscious moral heroism that would willingly give all of life to make life broader, deeper, and fuller for her and hers" (p. 45). Josie, the nervous scold, is in fact the "shadow" of moral heroism. She is double consciousness. She, and her family, "knew that it was a hard thing to dig a living out of a rocky side-hill" (p. 45). Their hardship "awakened common consciousness [of] the Veil that hung between us and Opportunity" (p. 48).

The story breaks off, abruptly. Then it is picked up again, ten years later when Du Bois returns to Alexandria. The Fisk years are long past. Harvard and Berlin are too. His life's work has begun. Every possibility lies ahead. He visits his community, his spiritual home where the gentle reader might reasonably expect some good word of Josie's progress in life. But "Josie was dead, and the gray-haired mother said simply, 'We've had a heap of trouble since you've been away'" (p. 49). Like Josie, his emblem of the Veil's terrible effects, the community Du Bois had taken as his own has disappeared. "My log schoolhouse was gone. In its place stood Progress; and Progress, I understand, is necessarily ugly" (p. 50). The third figurative girl of his childhood had become the measure of liberal culture. But was she, as Carby (1998, p. 20) proposes, the sign of its failure – that is, a play on feminine frailty? Or, was she the beyond in which lay the uncertain hope for racial progress? Carby is too sure of herself. It seems more probable that Du Bois left both possibilities open to the work that lay ahead.

In those ten years much had come to pass. The return visit to Alexandria may have been as early as 1896, the year after Washington's Atlanta Compromise and the year of *Plessy* v. *Ferguson*. If it was 1896, then it was also the year when Du Bois was formulating his theory of the double consciousness (which was first published in 1897). He had returned to "his" community when his own spiritual striving hung in the balance between the formidable possibilities gained by the highest education the world could offer *and* his moral commitment to those whose meager training was the condition of their suffering. The passage of the return was more, much more than mere nostalgia for the terrible intrusion of Progress upon his community. As the coming urban culture advanced on the hillsides from which Josie's family dug out a living, Du Bois turned away from the feelings for those he had lost. He felt sorrow at Josie's death and Alexandria's passing. But he did not give in to sentiment. He asked instead the hard question of the very idea of Progress that lay at the heart of the European civilization that so enriched his other soul.

> My journey was done, and behind me lay hill and dale, and Life and Death. How shall man measure Progress there where the dark-faced Josie lies? How many heartfuls of sorrow shall balance a bushel of wheat? How hard a thing is life to the lowly, and yet how human and real! *And all this life and love and strife and failure, –is it the twilight of the nightfall or the flush of some faint-dawning day?*
>
> Thus sadly musing, I rode to Nashville in the Jim Crow car. (p. 52, emphasis added)

The train from the Cumberland Plateau down to Nashville heads West. In the late afternoon, riders may face the setting sun. Yet, as anyone who has lived in the humid summer heat of the American South knows, the afternoon light can be a deception and a relief. The midday heat lingers, but the thick air sometimes stirs. The light can change tone, breaking bright through the branches. Hence the illusion of which Du Bois wrote. The light could just as well appear to be a dawning as a setting. "Is it," indeed, "the twilight of nightfall or the flush of some faint-dawning day?" The question rose on the beginning of a new century, double-sided and unsure like all else for those then within the Veil. What, then, is the meaning of liberal Progress when measured against the death of Josie – against the passing of the "shadow of moral heroism?"

Nearly forty years later, in the *Dusk of Dawn* (1940), Du Bois would return to this image of the uncertain meaning of the shadows. In the intervening four decades after his sad ride west in the Jim Crow car, Du Bois himself had traveled east to Atlanta, then to New York City, then again to Atlanta, and Europe, and Africa. In 1940 the light, while dusky still, promised a new day. The dusk had become a dawn.

> I have essayed in a half-century three sets of thought centering around the hurts and hesitancies that hem the black man in America. The first of these, "Souls of Black Folk," written thirty-seven years ago, was a cry at midnight thick within the veil, when none rightly knew the coming day. The second, "Darkwater," now twenty years old, was an exposition and militant challenge, defiant with dogged hope. This the third book started to record dimly but consciously that subtle sense of coming day which one feels of early mornings when mist and murk hang low. (Du Bois, 1940, p. xxiv)

Why the switch from dusk to dawn? He wrote in 1940 as the cloud of another war hung over the world, a world still suffering the after-effects of the Great Depression. How could that have been a coming day? Again, the answer lies in the differential consequences of the First World War, which dashed the progressive innocence of whites, while opening – however, slightly – industrial opportunity in the north to blacks.

In 1903, when Du Bois could not yet see the new day, the American Negro suffered the still feudal South and economic margins of the North. Booker T. Washington was the man in charge. Jobs in the industrial North belonged to white immigrants from Europe. In 1914, a million and a quarter Europeans came to America; by 1917, barely a hundred thousand came (Lewis, 1979, p. 21). In that necessary lapse arose an economic opportunity for millions of blacks in America – for, that is, the men and women who would have been the generation of Josie's unborn children. Though it would be years more until Franklin Roosevelt would begin truly to desegregate war mobilization industries during the Second World War, jobs were open to a whole generation as never before. Southern blacks rode the Jim Crows north to work in Chicago, Cincinnati, New York, Philadelphia. Booker T. Washington would die in the first full year of the great migration. His Tuskegee home lay in the lowland just south of the mountains. Tuskegee draws its water from the Tennessee hills of Josie's village as, no doubt, it drew its students from those few of Josie's generation who escaped the hills for the faint promise of a better life at skilled labor. Tuskegee is not far from Montgomery, Alabama, where, on a cold December day forty years after Mr Washington's death, Rosa Parks would lead Martin Luther King Jr, a still very young son of Atlanta's talented tenth, back from his northern education into the rural South of the Civil Rights Movement.

The War of 1914 opened the way for Du Bois and those of his cultured advantages to measure both the facts and the spiritual truths of brothers and sisters like Josie. The valued life would be slow in coming, impossibly far off even today for millions, but the spiritual striving of which Du Bois wrote in 1903 would come to good effect. The color line would ride north on the migrations. When, in the first words of *Souls*, he proclaimed it the problem of the twentieth century, Du Bois was looking far ahead beyond the misery of Josie's sad death, beyond the dusk of his youth, beyond the regional effects of the Veil. He looked to the possible dawn, for him and millions of others – for those especially who gathered in Washington the day after his death in 1963 to dream, not just of interracial hand holding, but of the recognition that the color line was structured deep in the nation, and the world, as a whole. Josie, for him, was not so much a local failure as the emblem of the realities and the promises known only to those with the gift of second sight.

## The Person and His Ideas

All great thinkers come to their ideas in relation to those who went before. Weber makes no sense without Kant, nor Marx without Hegel, nor Durkheim without Montesquieu, nor Gilman without Bellamy. Yet each is more than the sum of the borrowings. So it is with Du Bois – with one difference. He was, if not superior to his contemporaries, much more *sui generis*. He owed his debts, to be sure. But somehow, Du Bois always (perhaps even perversely on occasion) turned his borrowings to his own purposes.

When on rare occasion Du Bois encountered an intellectual peer at close hand, as he did Max Weber in the summer of 1904, it was the other who took the intellectual initiative. The following March, Weber wrote Du Bois, praising *Souls*, offering to take care of a German translation, and seeking his advice (Weber to Du Bois, letter of 30 March 1905, in Du Bois, 1973, pp. 106–7). Du Bois, it seems, did not pursue the translation invitation, just as he seldom acknowledged the influence Weber must have had on him since his student days in Germany. This surely was in part due to Du Bois's isolation and his relative inability to broker comparable deals for those better established in the white world. But it was also his nature to think as he acted – in terms he alone would fashion.

Du Bois's three greatest works all bear the stamp of a thinker who turned the relative isolation of his working conditions to his advantage. His *Philadelphia Negro*, the first great work of American urban ethnography, is often said to be a methodological copy of Charles Booth's earlier classic, *Life and Labour of the People of London* (1889–91). But David Levering Lewis, reading behind the empirical mass of the work, observes (Lewis, 1993, p. 190) that Du Bois thoroughly and remarkably "refined and applied what he borrowed." Hence, Du Bois's most distinctive theoretical conviction: that race never stands alone, apart from the economic realities. *The Philadelphia Negro* appeared fours years before *Souls*, which is itself the work of a man who, apart from the summers in Tennessee, had spent more than a year living among the poor he interviewed in Philadelphia's all black Seventh Ward.

Even today some have trouble seeing what Du Bois saw pretty much on his own. Race makes little sense apart from class. Though, as time went by, Du Bois reformulated this thinking, race for him was always in part a class effect. Later in life, well after the First World War had cleansed nearly everyone of unfettered faith in Progress, he became more the Marxist. To some, *Black Reconstruction* (1935) might appear to be an exercise in class analysis. It was, to be sure, but it was more than that. *Black Reconstruction* endures because no other work of its day, and not many since, examines the facts of economic history in terms of the relations of *racial* production (Roediger, 1991, pp. 11–13).

Not only was he his own man in the way he thought, but Du Bois adapted his thinking to the changing facts of racial politics. At no other point is this more evident than, as always, in the unusual use to which he put his most memorable concept. Where did he get the double consciousness idea at the start of *Souls*? To think about Du Bois is, eventually, to consider this question, for which there is a long list of likely sources: Goethe, Emerson, Herder, Sojourner Truth, William James (see, among others, Gates, 1989, pp. xviii–xxii; Rampersad, 1990, pp. 74–5; Early, 1993, pp. xvii–xxii; Lewis, 1993, pp. 282–3; Lemert, 1994, p. 389; Zamir, 1995). All are possible. Yet, in the end, it hardly makes a difference which might have been uppermost in Du Bois's mind. He thought as few others did, turning everything to his own ends.

Double consciousness is at once borrowed and invented to contain no fewer than three themes at once. As Paul Gilroy rather awkwardly puts it:

> Double consciousness emerges from the unhappy symbiosis between three modes of thinking, being, and seeing. The first is racially particularistic, the second nationalistic in that it derives from the nation state in which the ex-slaves but not-yet-citizens find themselves, rather than from their aspiration towards a nation state of their own. The third is diasporic or hemispheric, sometimes global and occasionally univeralistic. This trio was woven into some unlikely but exquisite patterns in Du Bois's thinking. Things become still more complicated because he self-consciously incorporated his own journeying both inside and outside the veiled world of black America into a narrative structure of the text and the political and cultural critique of the West which it constructed through an extended survey of the post-Civil War history of the American South. (Gilroy, 1993, p. 127)

Du Bois would have sooner not had Gilroy's compliment, with all its unforgiving jargon, had it not been for its basic truth. His thinking was "unlikely but exquisite" – and it was because Du Bois thought from the three points of view at once.

Race, nation, and Africa were always on his mind, from the earliest days. If Africa was not so explicit in the better known early writings, it was there in his 1896 Harvard doctoral thesis on the suppression of the African slave trade (Du Bois, 1898), as it was in the meditations on Alexander Crummel and the sorrow songs at the end of *Souls*. It is all too easy to hear, in the double consciousness lyrics, nothing but the play of race and nation. But Africa too is there, behind the origins of the distinctive black soul, behind the economic hardships that gave voice to the sorrow songs.

It is a long journey, for Du Bois, from birth in 1868 in Great Barrington, Massachusetts, to death and burial in 1963 in Accra, Ghana. At his state funeral in Accra, President Kwame Nkrumah began, "We mourn the death of

Dr. William Edward Burghardt Du Bois, a great son of Africa" (Du Bois, 1970, p. 327). Just a few years before, during a world tour in the year of his ninetieth birthday, he had been celebrated in the capitals of Europe, the Soviet Union, and China. After this he quit all civil relations with the United States and went to Africa. He died a citizen of Ghana – truly a revered son of Africa. But why had he traveled so far? In the answer lies the code to his life's work, and to his social theory.

In 1920, Du Bois published his second intellectual memoir, *Darkwater*. The Great War had ended, leaving the world uncertain. He was fifty-two, and in charge of his own destiny. In the years since *Souls*, Du Bois had helped found the NAACP. He became its most famous spokesman as editor of *Crisis* magazine, which he founded. In 1914, *Crisis* had 33,000 subscribers (Lewis, 1993, p. 474) – not to mention the thousands more to whom the magazine was passed from hand to hand. The number of American Negroes who regularly read the editor's views on every important issue of the day is impossible to know. He was also much in demand as a speaker (and claims to have spoken to 18,000 "human souls" in 1913 alone). Du Bois wrote and spoke less as the scholar, more as the political actor. Mr Washington was gone. If there was a spokesman in the war years, it was Dr Du Bois – who, of course, offered the whites in charge none of the easy comforts of compromise.

But the war years were troubling to Du Bois's own early racial philosophy. By 1920 he, and his many followers, understood that the ideals of the double consciousness – "this longing to attain self-conscious manhood, to merge his double self into a better and truer self" (Du Bois, 1903, p. 3) – would have to be reconsidered. Though thousands of Negroes had joined Du Bois in supporting Woodrow Wilson in 1912, and, after 1914, millions more had served well in industrial work (and many later still in the war effort), little was returned that would promise an end to the longing for "manhood." Thus, as he would say in *Dusk of Dawn* (p. xxiv; quoted above), the memoir of 1920, *Darkwater*, was a "militant challenge, defiant with dogged hope." He took the color line ever more seriously. This is when Africa begins to figure more urgently, if not yet saliently, in Du Bois's thinking. He had long worked with Africa in mind. In 1900 he had participated prominently in the first Pan-African meetings held in Europe. By 1919, as the war was ending, and the first truly international Pan African Congress was convened, Du Bois was a leader among those seeking to unite representatives of the African diaspora. Thereafter, Du Bois thought more and more of Africa.

Gilroy (1993) is surely right to say that Du Bois continued to think from three angles at once. But, just as in *Souls* race and nation were the more prominent of his points of view, then, beginning with *Darkwater* in 1920, Africa came clear in his picture of the racial situation as his American nationalism began to fade.

What, then, is this dark world thinking? It is thinking that as wild and awful as this shameful war was, *it is nothing to compare with that fight for freedom which black and brown and yellow men must and will make unless their oppression and humiliation and insult at the hands of the White World cease. The Dark World is going to submit to its present treatment just as long as it must and not one moment longer.* (Du Bois, 1920, p. 49, original emphasis)

This defiance stands in a bitter essay, sarcastically titled "The Souls of White Folk." He is thinking of race now in relation to the colonized world, and Africa. He speaks less of the "American Negro."

Twenty years later still, in *Dusk of Dawn* (1940), the most upbeat of his first three memoirs, all is clear. His thinking has changed. America is more an object of disappointment than of hope. Where race had been joined to nation, now race was joined to class and the world. Africa had become a way of thinking about the economic misery of blacks in global perspective. Between 1920 and 1940, there were three paths, each importantly connected to the other: culture, Africa, and economics.

> After the [First World War], with most Americans, I was seeking to return to normalcy. I tried three paths, one of which represented an old ideal and ambition, the development of literature and art among Negroes through my own writing and the encouragement of others. The second path was new and had arisen out of war; and that was the development of the idea back of the Pan African Congress. The third idea was quite new, and proved in a way of greater importance in my thinking than the other two; and that was the economic rehabilitation and defense of the American Negro after the change and dislocation of war. (Du Bois, 1940, p. 268)

The defiance is more focused now. These words appear in an essay titled "Revolution."

Du Bois's first path was, of course, that of his important work in the Harlem Renaissance. As editor of *Crisis* he was able to publish Claude McKay, Langston Hughes, Jean Toomer, Countee Cullen, and Jessie Fauset, among others. Though the cultural works of the Renaissance would endure to advance the nation's debt to American Negro culture, both Harlem and *Crisis* would decline with the economic collapse of 1929. As subscriptions to *Crisis* fell below the break-even point, Du Bois lost his hold on power within the NAACP (Marable, 1986, chapters 6 and 7). By 1934, after 24 years, he was terminated from the organization he helped to found. At age 65, he returned to Atlanta University to resume a career as teacher and scholar. The year following, he published what may well be his most important work of empirical scholarship, *Black Reconstruction*, in which the theme was that Reconstruction had failed not because of the cultural unreadiness of the newly freed slaves, but because of economic realities. *Black Reconstruction* was a political economy of race relations. Du Bois's idea of culture, though European in content, was always bound politically to the cultural uplift of the American Negro (tied, that is, to his youthful nationalism). It is not surprising, therefore, that the other two of his interwar years paths converged upon each other. The turn to class and economic realities, encouraged surely by the bitter effects of depression upon his cultural work, led away from the nation to the world – and of course to Africa.

*Dusk of Dawn* is of course a continuing play of light against the darkness introduced in the story of Josie in *Souls*. Nowhere, however, does the figure play with such personal force as it does in his recollection, in *Dusk of Dawn*, of his first sight of Africa:

> When shall I forget the night I first set foot on African soil? I am the sixth generation in descent from forefathers who left this land. The moon was at the full and theaters of the Atlantic lay like a lake. All the long slow afternoon as the sun robed herself in her western scarlet with veils of misty cloud, I had seen Africa afar. Cape Mount – that mighty headland with its twin curves, northern sentinel of the realm of Liberia – gathered itself out of the cloud at half past three and then darkened and grew clear. On beyond flowed the dark low undulating land quaint with palm and breaking sea. The world grew black. Africa faded away, the stars stood forth curiously twisted – Orion in the zenith – the Little Bear asleep and the Southern Cross rising behind the horizon. Then afar, ahead, a lone light shone, straight at the ship's fore. Twinkling lights appear below, around, and rising shadows. "Monrovia," said the Captain. (Du Bois, 1940, pp. 117–18)

Light against the dark, from the beginning – the Veil, the blue sky above the color line, Josie's twilight, darkwater, the dusk of dawn, and now "the world grew black, . . . the twinkling lights appear below, around, and rising shadows." Here at long last is the true reversal of the figure. Here is the true dawn, found in the dusk of Africa, which after 1940 became the measure of the light, white, colonizing world.

Africa dawned for Du Bois in the setting sun of what was left of his liberal nationalism. His faith in America, always drawn in against the color line, eventually disappeared. Neither the advantages of the Great War for the American Negro nor the successes of the Harlem Renaissance were enough to overcome the brutal reality of a world economic system that had dominated since the nineteenth century. He was, perhaps, a little chagrined at his own naive hope that the system could work for good. "It was not until the twentieth century that the industrial situation called not only for understanding but action" (Du Bois, 1940, p. 289). The action had already begun. Apart from his cultural work in the 1920s, Du Bois devoted more energy to the organizational work of four Pan-African congresses: 1919 in Paris; 1921 in London, Brussels, and Paris; 1923 in London, Paris, and Lisbon; and 1927 in New York. But in 1935, *Black Reconstruction* was to be his last great work of science. His turn to action meant Africa.

"I think it was in Africa that I came more clearly to see the close connection between race and wealth" (Du Bois, 1940, p. 129). Race, nation, and Africa were, as Gilroy says, the three structural elements of his thinking – or his soul, really. But Gilroy's scheme (1993, pp. 126–7) does not account for the growing force of Du Bois's spiritual journey to Africa. He gave up on nation, because, in the experience of his life time (which had nearly spanned the three-quarters of a century since Emancipation), the nation had in effect given up on him, on his race (see Roediger, 1991, pp. 111–13). To embrace Africa required him to let go of America, which had promised what it did not deliver.

Though Marx had figured in Du Bois's later thinking, it was just as clear that Marx's own limited ability to envisage the precise global terms of class struggle would in turn limit his appeal to Du Bois. Marx understood that capitalism was a world enterprise, and he understood something about the colonial situation, but he recognized little at all about the racial foundations of the colonial system. Though others would later describe these global relations of racial production, Du Bois was one of the first of the great decolonizing thinkers. When race is considered an economic, as well as a social, thing it must be thought also as a global thing. Hence Africa in the shifting balance of Du Bois's intellectual categories. His Marxism, such as it was, was always something more. That more was not so much Afrocentric as Pan-African. He avoided all essentializing categories. He was thinking, now, of race as a global and economic problem that required action. He was, that is, already a harbinger of the decolonizing thinkers to come (see James, 1998, p. 423).

> Looking at this whole matter of the white race as it confronts the world today, what can be done to make its attitudes rational and consistent and calculated to advance the best interests of the whole world of men? The first point of attack is undoubtedly the economic. The progress of the white world must cease to rest upon the poverty and the ignorance of its own proletariat and of the colored world. (Du Bois, 1940, p. 171)

How, then, did he journey from white New England to Africa? It is plain that he traveled spiritually through Alexandria, Tennessee. "How shall we measure Progress," he asked in his youth, "there where the dark-faced Josie lies?" He had no choice, its seems, but eventually to go to Africa. His own struggle against the color line led him, as it would lead others who came after him, through the dusk of America's oddly confused brand of race-based colonialism to the world, where there where fewer moral deceptions. In Africa, a colony was just that, a colony where few could mistake the true intentions of the whites in charge. Josie came to be the measure of much more than the liberal idealism of Progress. She was, for him, the measure of the structured injustice of the world system itself. She was just that important because whatever else she meant to him in the summer of 1886, she grew, as mythic figures often do, into the archetype of racial suffering. Whatever dawn there would be would be the dawn that rose on the dark-faced Josie. Though he first wrote of Josie at about the same time he wrote Souls, it can be said that the famous double-consciousness ideal was already up against the deeper economic realities that would surface over the years. This is why Du Bois repeated the story of Josie so many times, even in his last years of life. She had taught him, in the deeper workings of his spiritual life, that the American Negro could not for long measure his soul "by the tape of a world that looked on in amused contempt" (Du Bois, 1903, p. 3). By the end, the hard realities of the world economy had made Africa, and the rest of the decolonizing world, the true measure of the failures of white world.

In the end, Du Bois was no longer an American Negro, any more than he was African-American except by spiritual kinship with his fathers and their fathers. He was African and socialist. He called for economic action, for a revolution in the colonial system. As ever, he expressed himself in the idiom of religion, now joined to revolutionary politics (Du Bois, 1968, p. 404):

Awake, awake, put on thy strength, O Zion; reject the meekness of missionaries who teach neither love nor brotherhood, but emphasize the virtues of private profit from capital, stolen from your land and labor. African awake, put on the beautiful robes of Pan-African socialism.

You have nothing to lose but your chains!
You have a continent to regain!
You have human freedom and human dignity to attain!

When Du Bois died in 1963, the great first wave of postcolonial poets and activists were already known around the world: Gandhi, Fanon, Memmi, Cesaire. The wars of colonial liberation were well along. The once hard-sealed global grip of White Progress was slipping, never again to be what it once was.

## ASSESSMENT

Du Bois had his blind spots to be sure. Given his magnificent training in economic and social history, one might say that he was a bit slow in coming to recognize that race was at the foundations of the colonial system, hence at the heart of capitalism and class oppression. But how does one fault someone when he came to the issue well before others? Aimé Cesaire's *Discourse on Colonialism* (1955) and Albert Memmi's *The Colonizer and the Colonized* (1959) would not appear for a good fifteen years and more after Du Bois's first systematic meditations on the colonial system in *Dusk of Dawn*. It would be still another two decades before the first social scientific studies of the capitalist world system appeared, in works like Immanuel Wallerstein's *The Modern World System* (1974, volume 1).

It might be said, too, that Du Bois never touched upon the psychological effects of the colonial experience that so defined Frantz Fanon's *Black Skin, White Masks* (1952) and *The Wretched of the Earth* (1961). That the former student of William James who had proven himself such a fine intuitive psychologist in *Souls of Black Folk* never seems to have thought about Freud, who conceived of the Unconscious as a dark continent, is, simply, a bafflement. Still, criticisms of the sins of omission measure the work against an impossible standard. The fairer question is always: what endures as valuable, hence truly classical, in its own right? Here there can hardly be any question that, apart from the exceptional qualities and ambitions of his life and politics, Du Bois stands alone in two important respects. Better than any other work since, his *Black Reconstruction* uses empirical evidence to demonstrate that, insofar as race is a social construct, it is constructed of economic blocks. While works like David Roediger's *The Wages of Whiteness* begin to take up the empirical demonstration of Du Bois's line, none comes close to the systematic analysis of *Black Reconstruction*. And, though there are important and provocative theoretical discussions of race as a social and economic formation, not even such prominent works as Michael Omi and Howard Winant's *Racial Formation in the United*

*States* (1994) match up against Du Bois's patient teasing of the theory from the historical record.

It is one thing to say that race and class must always be thought in their relationship. It is another actually to do it. Today, we know very well from the important advances of especially queer theory and its affines that, in so far as analytic work demands an artificial setting apart from the empirical contents, analysis itself is a dubious, if necessary, activity. Du Bois, of course, had little patience for the fine points of metatheory. His politics required too much for that. But it also forced him to change his mind, which he did several times through the years.

Yet there is little reason to suppose that the younger Du Bois was of a markedly different intellectual disposition than Du Bois the elder, as (for example) the Durkheim of *Elementary Forms of the Religious Life* (1912) was so beyond himself as to be a virtual stranger to the Durkheim of *Suicide* (1897). The outlines of the economic themes of *Black Reconstruction* were already present in his youth in *Philadelphia Negro* and *Souls*, not to mention his doctoral thesis (1898/1965). It was not just that he changed his mind over the years, which he did, but that he understood from the first, as Gilroy sees, that race, nation, and Africa (plus class, which Gilroy sees less sharply) were part and parcel. Those inclined to say that we today have begun to solve the problem of analytic categories and their relations have only to reflect on the furor attending to each new book of William Julius Wilson, since at least The *Declining Significance of Race* (1987). Wilson insists, as did Du Bois, that race can never stand on its own when the ravages of class disadvantage are as severe as they are today and were in Du Bois's lifetime. All of Du Bois's major works bear examination today – as models of just how courage and steadiness of purpose can produce, over a life's work, the careful explanation of just what the constant shifting of analytic categories against each other looks like.

Beyond the tributes that still can be paid him, the complaint that stands to scrutiny is that Du Bois never even began to see that race and class, even Africa and the world, present themselves differently to men and women. Hazel Carby is absolutely right on this score. But, even she, usually the more astute social theorist, does not quite get to the heart of this problem (probably because she limits herself to *Souls*). Still, Carby gives a good account of the way Du Bois used gender unconsciously "to mediate the relation between his concept of race and his concept of nation" (Carby, 1998, p. 30). She has in mind, to be sure, the figure of Josie but also the grand way he spoke of racial uplift as the work of manhood. She shrewdly describes the way that, for Du Bois, racial manhood was the beyond of feminine sufferings and strivings – as in his subtextual references to Mr Washington "as analogous to his anonymous black mother" (Carby, 1998, pp. 38–9).

It is true that Du Bois, who enjoyed respectful, if also lustful, relations with many women throughout his life, did not think of gender as one of the differentiating conditions of black experience. Yet he would have hardly have survived the political wars in the NAACP without the ministrations of Mary White Ovington, to mention just one of the women with whom he enjoyed tender *and* respectful relations. There were others, of course: his own mother (anything but anonymous) and his dutiful first wife of fifty years, Nina – for whom, both, the gender difference meant confinement to the homes they provided for the boy and the great man. Yet he was blind to gender. Why? Was it only because he was through and through the Victorian gentleman? Or was it that – unlike race and class, even Africa – it was much more difficult for him (for any man?) to think gender seriously in the absence of a feminist culture? To think with these powerful analytic terms is to live with them.

On the other hand, Du Bois might never have so fully thought through the experiences of race and class that made him *the* race man of his times without the real and figurative effects of the experience with Josie. So, here again, one must pause before condemning. Feminist thought, from which has come today's understanding of gender, has itself been troubled, as Judith Butler puts it in *Gender Trouble* (1990). Among much else, gender is about sex, and sex is about the play of differences that no one of right mind – save those stuck in the missionary position – would think to categorize. One of the unexplored curiosities of Du Bois's spiritual infatuation with Josie is his confession late in life that his own first sexual experience was with not one of the darkly delicious girls of Fisk, but Josie's mother (Lewis, 1993, p. 71). Those sad words he took with him in the Jim Crow car back to Nashville and life itself were, thus, the words of innocence lost many times over.

It is possible, of course, to say, as Carby does, that Du Bois's all-too-male attitude toward gender was nothing more than the arrogance of the race man. Or it is possible to say that Josie had such power over him because she, and his experience with her and her family, so powerfully brought home to him all the realities of black experience. He had as little to say about the sexual as about gender differences. But are the silences the same? Or do they make a difference in how one thinks about these things? Here is a dusk, the dawn of which Du Bois did not think through. Yet, one supposes, since they were there below the surface of his recollections of Josie, had he lived in our time, he might have.

## Bibliography

### Writings of W. E. B. Du Bois

*The Suppression of the African Slave Trade to the United States of America, 1638–1870.* 1898. New York: Longmans, Green (reprinted New York: Russell & Russell, 1965).

*The Philadelphia Negro.* 1899. Philadelphia: University of Pennsylvania (reprinted New York: Schocken, 1967).

*The Souls of Black Folk.* 1903. Chicago: A. C. McClurg (reprinted New York: Bantam, 1989).

*Darkwater: Voices within the Veil.* 1920. New York: Harcourt, Brace (reprinted New York: AMS Press, 1969).

*Black Reconstruction in America, 1860–1880.* 1935. New York: Harcourt, Brace (reprinted New York: Atheneum, 1992).

*The Dusk of Dawn: an Essay toward an Autobiography of a Race Concept.* 1940. New York: Harcourt, Brace (reprinted New Brunswick, NJ: Transaction, 1984).

*Color and Democracy: Colonies and Peace*. 1945. New York: Harcourt, Brace.

*The World and Africa*. 1947. New York: Viking (reprinted New York: International Publishers, 1965).

*The Autobiography of W. E. B. Du Bois*. 1968. New York: International Publishers.

*W. E. B. Du Bois Speaks. Speeches and Addresses, 1920–1963* (edited by Philip S. Foner). 1970. New York: Pathfinder.

*The Correspondence of W. E. B. Du Bois/Selections, 1977–1934, volume I* (edited by Herbert Aptheker). 1973. Amherst: University of Massachusetts Press.

## Further reading

Butler, Judith (1990) *Gender Trouble: Feminism and the Subversion of Identity*. New York: Routledge.

Carby, Hazel (1998) *Race Men*. Cambridge, MA: Harvard University Press.

Early, Gerald (1993) *Lure and Loathing*. New York: Penguin.

Gilroy, Paul (1993) *Black Atlantic*. Cambridge, MA: Harvard University Press.

Gates, Henry Louis (1989) Darkly, As through a Veil. Introduction to *Souls of Black Folk*, pp. vii–xxix.

James, C. L. R. (1998) Black Power and Stokely. in Charles Lemert (ed.), *Social Theory*. Boulder, CO: Westview Press, pp. 419–28.

Lemert, Charles (1994) A Classic from the Other Side of the Veil: Du Bois's *Souls of Black Folk*. *Sociological Quarterly*, 35, 385–96.

Lewis, David Levering (1979) *When Harlem Was in Vogue*. New York: Oxford University Press.

Lewis, David Levering (1993) *W. E. B. Du Bois. Biography of a Race, 1868–1919*. New York: Henry Holt. Volume 2 forthcoming.

Marable, Manning (1986) *W. E. B. Du Bois: Black Radical Democrat*. Boston: G. K. Hall.

Omi, Michael and Winant, Howard (1994) *Racial Formation in the United States*. New York: Routledge.

Rampersad, Arnold (1990) *The Art and Imagination of W. E. B. Du Bois*. New York: Schocken.

Reed, Adolph L. Jr (1997) *W. E. B. Du Bois and American Political Thought*. New York: Oxford University Press.

Roediger, David (1991) *The Wages of Whiteness*. London: Verso.

Shamoon, Zamir (1995) *Dark Voices. W. E. B. Du Bois and American Thought, 1888–1903*. Chicago: University of Chicago Press.

Wallerstein, Immanuel (1974) *The Modern World System*. New York: Academic Press.

West, Cornel (1993) The New Cultural Politics of Difference. In *Keeping Faith. Philosophy and Race in America*. New York: Routledge, pp. 3–32.

Wilson, William Julius (1987) *The Declining Significance of Race*. New York: Knopf.

# 11

# Alfred Schutz

## MARY ROGERS

Maurice Natanson (1973, p. 166), first a student and later a colleague and friend of Alfred Schutz (1899–1959), wrote of Edmund Husserl what might also be said of Schutz, namely that his work put him "in the company of those who labor at foundations." Schutz's focus was the "primordial foundation...that makes all understanding possible" (in Grathoff, 1989, p. 212), namely the life-world (*Lebenswelt*) or the world of everyday life. He aimed to show what makes the everyday world possible at all and how it in turn makes understanding possible, including scientific understanding.

Schutz's theorizing goes to the roots of social reality where consciousness moves beyond its own duration and naively grasps its world. For him, that world can be had only in and through mutuality; it is inescapably intersubjective. The world given to consciousness as a taken-for-granted certainty is also marked by multiplicity – its multiplicity of forms and structures, its multiplicity of worlds of experience, its multiplicity of members spanning the past (predecessors), the present (anonymous contemporaries and interacting consociates), and the future (successors). Finally, Schutz shows that to have a world means to make meanings, both the subjective meanings individuals constitute in grasping their own acts and the objective meanings they constitute in interpreting others' subjectively meaningful acts.

Around these core concerns Schutz built up a descriptive framework that delineates the presuppositions not only of members' shared world but also of individuals' biographical situations. He thus took upon himself the goal of philosophically illuminating the coterminous grounds of sociality and individuality. By focusing on the essential connections between social structure and personhood, he carved out theoretical space for illuminating lived experiences of intersubjectivity. Within that space his virtual conversations with Husserl, Max Weber, Max Scheler, Henri Bergson, William James, George Herbert Mead,

Charles Horton Cooley, Talcott Parsons, and other intellectual predecessors and contemporaries gave way to a framework whose analytical power is far-reaching as well as foundational.

## THE PERSON: A MULTIPLICITY OF ROLES

Before we look at some of the notions anchoring Schutz's framework, let us get a preliminary sense of the person who masterminded it. For getting acquainted with Schutz the person, there may be no more instructive source than his correspondence with Aron Gurwitsch (Grathoff, 1989), which spans 1939 to 1959. Schutz, like Gurwitsch, talks about being Jewish, being an immigrant, working in a language that feels alien, finding venues for his essays, and negotiating a career in academic institutions where pecking orders, interpersonal networks, and disciplinary boundaries weigh heavily. Like Gurwitsch, Schutz enjoyed the benefit of a non-employed spouse who typed his manuscripts and also, in his case, letters that he dictated onto tapes. Domestic and international travel pervaded Schutz's life, typically for business but sometimes for vacations and respite.

Schutz mentions 15- and 16-hour days working on various of his papers, particularly on weekends when he found release from the daytime/nighttime bifurcation that marked his weekdays. Nearly all his life Schutz held a full-time position with a banking firm that intensified the challenges of his scholarly work. As early as 1940 Schutz wrote to Gurwitsch, "by night I am a phenomenologist, but by day an executive. At the moment my day life is taking over my night life" (p. 26), a circumstance accounting for letters written at three or so in the morning. In his letters Schutz worries about his son George's eyesight after a horrible accident and about his daughter's and his son's schooling; he mourns the death of his father; he worries at times about his wife Ilse's health and well-being. Schutz also worries about his friend Gurwitsch's job prospects and publishing options. At the same time he delights in and draws sustenance from their friendship.

During the early years of their correspondence these "philosophers in exile" address one another, "Dear Friend Schutz" and "Dear Friend Gurwitsch." For some years they stick with the formal *Sie* before abandoning it for the more personal *Du*. Schutz (p. 119) took the initiative: "Why do we still say 'Sie' to one another? I won't go along with this nonsense any longer!" Several times Schutz (pp. 45, 123, 119) expresses longing for a "heart-to-heart talk" with his friend, whom he describes as his "ideal reader." At one point Schutz's salutation is to "My dear friend and robber of my sleep!" (p. 153). Another salutation finds Schutz addressing Gurwitsch as his "Select and inestimable friend!" (p. 273). In no way did Schutz's ardor preclude wittiness. He closed one letter, "With intersubjective love, your primordi(n)al and egological Alfred" (p. 263). Nor did Schutz's ardor preclude modesty: "You have no idea how much I learn from you, even when you talk about things I am very familiar with" (p. 293).

Unafraid to say in writing what they meant to one another, Schutz and Gurwitsch also confide to one another what they think of other people's work. A spacious seminar room of great minds is gathered together in these letters – Kant, Scheler, Leibniz, Mead, Dewey, James, Sartre, and Husserl, the founder of phenomenology, whose thinking animates both correspondents. Schutz had never formally studied with Husserl any more than with Weber or Bergson, two other major influences on his thinking. As Helmut Wagner (1983, pp. 46–7) describes it, at the behest of his friend Felix Kaufmann and his wife Ilse, Schutz sent Husserl a copy of his *Phenomenology of the Social World* (1932). Kaufmann, who was acquainted with Husserl, suggested that Schutz go to Freiburg to meet him. Schutz went, and he visited Husserl a number of other times before the latter's death in 1938. Husserl's daughter Elizabeth described their bond as "a deep human tie."

Also showing up in these letters are individuals such as sociologist Lewis Coser (a colleague of Gurwitsch at Brandeis University) and philosophers Hannah Arendt, Dorion Cairns, and Marvin Farber. Philosophers of science such as Carl Hempel and Ernest Nagel also make appearances. In these letters one also sees the close bond between Schutz and Natanson taking shape. Schutz comments on the dissertation about Mead's work that earned Natanson a *summa cum laude* and, later, on how he has begun sending his former student manuscripts to edit. One also learns that Schutz and Natanson had even translated Husserl's *Ideas I* and *II* together, though their translation was never published (p. 221).

What these letters disclose is magnanimous spirit, dogged determination, and astonishing stamina (despite worsening health conditions that ended Schutz's life in 1959). Schutz had, to say the least, an enormous appetite for life. For him, that meant multiple roles and responsibilities as well as abiding mutualities. It also meant a habitual inclination to look for "common bases of mutual understanding rather than merely to criticize" (Schutz, in Grathoff, 1978, p. 96).

## MULTIPLICITY AND MUTUALITY

Schutz (1964, p. 137) theorizes a social world that includes not only mundane fare but also "death and dream, vision and art, prophecy and science." Yet he emphasizes that in the "natural attitude" people routinely move from one type of situation to the next with the undisturbed sense that *the* one world is just there as the ever-present stage for their projects. In the world of everyday life the world "out there" is nothing less than certain.

It is also nothing less than replete with multiplicity. People's bodies guarantee the multiplicity of zones wherein they can more or less readily manipulate some part of the social world. Commonsense individuals take for granted, for instance, that some people and things are within reach, others are, for the time being, beyond ready reach, and others remain stubbornly beyond reach for as far ahead as they can see. They also take for granted that some individuals who shaped their world – ancestors, inventors, revolutionaries, prophets, and others – are long since gone from it; that many who will inherit their world are not yet on the scene; that some with whom they share the planet or make their society are entirely unknown to them and others (their consociates) are known in varying degrees of intimacy, anonymity, and intensity.

People in everyday life often leave it for a multiplicity of purposes shaped by the system of relevances currently active within their biographical situation. They step into the world of the theater or religion or dreams or science, and they know how to step back into the world of everyday life when desire or necessity moves them. Commonsense individuals thus move among multiple realities or worlds, typically without undue anxiety or upset. All the while, their lived experiences continuously seal their sense that they inhabit but one world whose certainty lies beyond question and whose reality is straightforward. As Schutz (1967, p. 75) puts it, "instead of discrete experiences, we have everywhere continuity, with horizons opening equally into the past and the future. However diverse the lived experiences may be, they are bound together by the fact that they are *mine*." Schutz calls this experiential continuity a "primal unity." It eventuates alongside the equally essential, double-sided unity of human consciousness and social reality. Bluntly put, Schutz allows no theoretical room for *human* consciousness that is not also *social* consciousness.

Schutz calls the specifically social aspect of our consciousness its Thou-orientation. Without that orientation neither a world nor a self is possible. The *Thou-orientation* involves recognizing another human being as having a life and a consciousness fundamentally like my own. In our actual experiences the Thou-orientation entails more or less recognition of that primal sort, and it may or may not be reciprocated in the face-to-face situation which it presupposes (Schutz, 1967, pp. 163–4). Schutz (1962, p. 57) puts the Thou-orientation at the heart of social reality as well as human consciousness: "since human beings are born of mothers and not concocted in retorts, the experience of the existence of other human beings and of the meaning of their actions is certainly the first and most original empirical observation [a human being] makes."

Out of that observation – the direct, indeed sensuous, observation of social reality – grows a multiplicity of social relationships, both direct and indirect as well as more or less intimate or anonymous. Direct connections with other human beings have, in principle, the form of the *We-relationship* involving not only reciprocal Thou-orientations but also "sympathetic sharing" of one another's lives for however long a time is desirable and possible (Schutz, 1967, p. 164). "In such a relationship," says Schutz (1962, p. 17), "fugitive and superficial as it may be, the Other is grasped as a unique individuality... in its unique biographical situation (although revealed merely fragmentarily)."

The lived We-relationship entails stunning possibilities. It means that I can "keep pace with each moment of [my partner's] stream of consciousness as it transpires," thus making me "better attuned to him [or her] than I am to myself"; it means that whether we join hands or not, we do join glances, eventuating in an "interlocking of glances" and a "thousand-faceted mirroring of each other"; it means that we "witness the literal coming-to-birth of each other's experiences" (Schutz, 1967, pp. 169, 170, 179). In one of my favorite passages Schutz (1967,

p. 178) sketches such possibilities from the standpoint of a partner in a "We" remembering the Other's "you of yesterday":

> When I have a recollection of you, . . . I remember you as you were in the concrete We-relationship with me. I remember you as a unique person in a concrete situation, as one who interacted with me in the mode of "mutual mirroring" described above. I remember you as a person vividly present to me with a maximum of symptoms of inner life, as one whose experiences I witnessed in the actual process of formation. I remember you as one whom I was for a time coming to know better and better. I remember you as one whose conscious life flowed in one stream with my own. I remember you as one whose consciousness was continuously changing in content.

Such memories are contingent. Every lived We also allows for failures to connect or even hurtful disconnection, whether gradual or abrupt. Emphasizing that actual We-relationships *more* or *less* fulfill the possibilities of that social form, Schutz points toward the missteps and lapses that often infiltrate lived We-relationships. He notes, for instance, how people can become more concerned with the We-relationship than with its other participant(s). To that extent they diminish their involvement and become less "genuinely related" to their partners, tending in the extreme to render them "object[s] of thought." By failing to get more and more attuned to their partners, they miss the "higher level of the We-experience" where they can "enrich" their understanding not only of their partners but also of other people (Schutz, 1967, pp. 167, 171). More generally, Schutz illuminates the discontinuous, challenging character of any real-life We:

> In actual life, . . . a marriage or a friendship is made up of many separate events occurring over a long period of time. Some of these events involve face-to-face situations, in others the partners simply exist side by side as contemporaries. To call such social relationships "continuous" is erroneous in the extreme, since discontinuity and repeatability are included in their very definition.

For Schutz, the everyday world rests on and takes shape around the primordial, though often problematic, mutuality of the We-relationship. Common-sense actors routinely and prereflectively live in the "vivid simultaneity of the 'We'." They grasp the Other in the immediacy of his or her current stream of consciousness. To grasp oneself, however, requires retrospective glances at past or just-past experiences. One cannot, in other words, both live within and reflect on one's own experiences. Therefore, Schutz (1962, pp. 174–5) emphasizes,

> In so far as each of us can experience the Other's thoughts and acts in the vivid present whereas either can grasp his [or her] own only as a past by way of reflection, I know more of the Other and [the Other] knows more of me than either of us knows of his own stream of consciousness. This present, common to both of us, is the pure sphere of the "We."

In Schutz's judgment this circumstance regarding knowledge of self and Other offers "a sufficient frame of reference for the foundation of empirical psychology and the social sciences. For all our knowledge of the social world, even of its most anonymous and remote phenomena and of the most diverse types of social communities, is based upon the possibility of experiencing an alter ego in vivid presence" (Schutz, 1962, p. 175). This socially and methodologically consequential circumstance boils down to a foundational mutuality constituted in every We as each participant grasps the Other's Now. Schutz puts it this way: "The alter ego ... is that stream of consciousness whose activities I can seize in their present by my own simultaneous activities." In such mutual seizing, whatever its culturally and biographically specific shape, lie the roots of social life and social structure. As Schutz (1967, p. 171) writes,

> The world of the We is not private to either of us, but is our world, the one common intersubjective world which is right there in front of us. It is only from the face-to-face relationships, from the common lived experience of the world in the We, that the intersubjective world can be constituted.

Thus, the primordial mutuality of the We signals the possibility of roles and statuses, of institutions and various forms of resistance to them, and of socialization and resocialization. Overall, says Schutz, we are joined together by "common influence and work." From such bonds, which vary in intensity and intimacy as well as immediacy, comes all the multiplicity of social reality. Schutz (1962, p. 53) defines *social reality* as

> the sum total of objects and occurrences ... experienced by the common-sense thinking of [people] living their daily lives among their [other people], connected with them in manifold relations of inter-action. It is the world of cultural objects and social institutions into which we are all born, within which we have to find our bearings, and with which we have to come to terms.

Schutz delineates in great detail the thick folds of social reality. He describes how our experiences of other people get more remote and anonymous as we turn toward our mere contemporaries with whom we have no face-to-face contact. Schutz (1967, p. 181) says that such turning entails "pass[age] through one region after another" (eight in all), beginning with our consociates and ending with cultural artifacts that implicitly attest to the subjective meanings of persons unknown to us. Put differently, the world of our mere contemporaries is a web of ideal types, which Schutz (1967, pp. 176ff.) delineates in the only of his books published during his lifetime, namely *The Phenomenology of the Social World.*
To account for our anonymous, mediated connections with all living individuals beyond our consociates, Schutz (1967, p. 177) lays out theoretical scaffolding that describes the "gradual progression from the world of immediately experienced social reality to the world of contemporaries." His concept of *They-orientation* concerns our consciousness of contemporaries; it parallels the Thou-orientation involved in direct, unmediated social relationships (Schutz, 1967, p. 183). Characterizing knowledge of one's contemporaries as "inferential and discursive," Schutz (1967, p. 184) also characterizes it as ideal-typical; that

is, made up of "interpretive schemes for the social world *in general*" (p. 185, emphasis added). Impersonal and anonymous, They-relationships among contemporaries have ideal types as their bedrock:

> Whenever we come upon any ordering of past experience under interpretive schemes, any act of abstraction, generalization, formalization, or idealization, whatever the object involved, there we shall find this process in which a moment of living experience is lifted out of its setting and then, through a synthesis of recognition, frozen into a hard and fast "ideal type." (Schutz, 1967, p. 187)

Overall, Schutz (1967, p. 9) emphasizes that "Living in the world, we live with others and for others, orienting our lives to them." Throughout his work he shows that the "social world is by no means homogeneous but exhibits a multiform structure" (Schutz, 1967, p. 139). That structure conditions the meanings members constitute: "Each of [the social world's] spheres or regions is both a way of perceiving and a way of understanding the subjective experiences of others." Selfhood and sociality are thus conjoined in a "dialectic of intersubjectivity" (Schutz, 1964, p. 145), which takes shape from They-relationships as well as We-relationships. In the end Schutz's corpus shows how thoroughly "They" and "We" are implicated with one another.

## MEANING AND MUTUALITY

Within Schutz's framework making sense means, at root, naming the objects of one's experiences. Such naming involves *typification*, which carries several meanings in Schutz's work. It refers, first, to the application of relevant types to the objects of one's experiences. Such application entails consciousness of similarities between what one has more recently experienced and what one previously experienced, whether firsthand or vicariously. To be conscious of *this* object, one must have already been conscious of objects like it in one or more ways. Those previous objects of one's experiencing thus serve as reference points. Sedimented from one's past experiences, these retentions (expectations built up from one's prior experiences) are themselves typified, or named as this or that type of person or thing.

Language is the storehouse of types and thus the root system of the meanings people constitute. Schutz was passionate about language's role in sense-making. Himself a wielder of English as a second language, Austrian-born Schutz knew, for instance, that "In order to command a language freely as a scheme of expression, one must have written love letters in it; one has to know how to pray and curse in it and how to say things with every shade appropriate to the addressee and the situation" (Schutz, 1964, p. 101). So, too, he understood that "The fringes [of words and sentences] are the stuff poetry is made of; they are capable of being set to music but they are not translatable" (ibid.). Making meaning is thus infinitely more comfortable and certain when one can use the "mother tongue"; that is, when one is linguistically at home. Schutz implies that making sense becomes more difficult the more constrained our vocabularies, the more uncertain our semantics, the more insecure our literacy.

Second, typification concerns the abstractive character of intentionality (or consciousness-of). Schutz and Luckmann (1973, p. 241) stress that the "praxis of everyday life" generally revolves around the "typical repeatability" of objects of experience, not their uniqueness. Thus, individuals abstract from an object those features or characteristics it appears to have in common with objects named in the same way. To that extent they make the object more or less anonymous by suppressing its uniqueness in favor of its commonalities with other objects. Typification thus dovetails with anonymity, which we will consider before long.

Finally, typification refers not only to a process but also to its results. Typifications are categories of typicality that individuals build up, both individually and collectively, as they go about the business of "construct[ing] . . . complex world[s] of experience" (Schutz, 1967, p. 13) for themselves. Schutz (1967, p. 81) emphasized the resourcefulness of sense-makers in the everyday world. He noted that "ordinary" people

> in every moment of [their] lived experience light upon past experiences in the storehouse of [their] consciousness. [They] know about the world and . . . know what to expect. . . . The [person] in the natural attitude "has" . . . a stock of knowledge of physical things and fellow creatures, of social collectives and of artifacts, including cultural objects. He [or she] likewise "has" syntheses of inner experience. Among these are to be found judgment contents (or propositional contents) which are the result of . . . previous acts of judgment. Here also are to be found all products of the activity of the mind and will.

Schutz thus credits the individual's experiences a great deal.

At the same time he points to the stock of knowledge that language undergirds and gives rise to – the lore, guidelines, parables, principles, doctrines, findings, news, and all else that makes up the "cookbook knowledge" whereby we make our way in the world of everyday life. For the most part, Schutz characterizes the individual's stock of knowledge at hand as a hodgepodge. Built up unsystematically, shaped by pragmatic motives, and reflective of the individual's shifting system of relevances, the stock of knowledge at hand is nevertheless generally effective. It lets us get on with our daily affairs without undue puzzlement or upset. It serves our practical purposes, and it promotes taken for grantedness where otherwise there would be distractions from the purposes at hand. Typically, then, our stock of knowledge at hand ensures us a soundly familiar world.

An individual's stock of knowledge at hand takes biographically specific shape, to be sure, but it is also thoroughly social. It is a collective as well as an individual achievement that reflects the intersections of social structure with the individual's life course. Schutz (1964, pp. 120ff.) emphasized that the social stock of knowledge is nonrandomly distributed so as to constitute the broad categories of expert, well informed citizen, and layperson. Knowledge is, then, socially stratified and specialized. Its social shape follows the lines of the various *finite provinces of meaning* Schutz theorized.

Reshaping and extending William James's notion of sub-universes of reality, Schutz devoted considerable theoretical attention to the overlapping but distinct worlds of meaning-compatible experiences. In the course of a day or even an hour people experience any number of these worlds. In fact, Schutz (1970, p. 15) stressed that we actually live simultaneously in several worlds by virtue of how our relevances interplay and overlap. The worlds of dreams, of religion, of theory, of science, of the theater, and so forth each elicit a distinctive "cognitive style." We know by virtue of some sort of "shock" or "leap" – some sort of transitional experience, so to speak – when we are crossing the experiential boundary roughly dividing one finite province of meaning from another. After having seen an engaging film in a theater, for instance, our passage up the aisle and into the lobby represents such a shock. It has gotten dark and begun to rain. These are the first signals that "the" world has gone on without us and has been there all the while we were "away." As we re-enter the world of everyday life, which Schutz deemed the "paramount reality" due to its sheer certitude and overarching givenness, we sustain a measure, however briefly, of strangeness or shock.

Each finite province of meaning entails a distinctive "tension of consciousness" as well as distinctive ways of experiencing time, self, and others. All these aspects of cognitive style involve distinctive typifications, with each province thus ordered by a characteristic vocabulary that enables us to grasp its objects – daydreams, theatrical roles, theorems, heresies, and such – and make sense of our experiences of them. Each province of meaning thus has linguistic boundaries that dovetail with their experiential boundaries. Moving from one to another finite province of meaning means shifting vocabularies as well as making some sort of leap. The two are coterminous experiences.

## SUBJECTIVITY AND INTERSUBJECTIVITY

That finite provinces of meaning are rooted in language means that the world of everyday life remains our home base among them. *Its* commonplace words infiltrate and ultimately anchor other finite provinces of meaning. Their linguistic roots also guarantee finite provinces of meaning an intersubjective dimension. Natanson (in Webb, 1992, p. 284) says that Schutz "was trying to understand how individuals are able to comprehend one another," which made "the problem of intersubjectivity...the central issue of the everyday world" for Schutz. Helmut R. Wagner (1970, p. 30), another of Schutz's students, describes Schutz's theoretical focus this way: "living in the world of everyday life, in general, means living in an interactional involvement with many persons.... The phenomenologically most basic problem here is that of intersubjectivity."

For Schutz (1966, p. 82), "intersubjectivity is not a problem of constitution...but is rather a datum (*Gegebenheit*) of the life-world. It is the fundamental ontological category of human existence." Thus, Schutz set about the task of showing how other people's "interpretations of my situation and mine of theirs codetermine the meaning this situation has for me" (Schutz, 1964, p. 196).

As I make sense of my own experiences, I can never cut myself off from the meanings sedimented in my stock of knowledge, which essentially includes a multiplicity of meanings established by predecessors, mere contemporaries, and consociates as well as by myself. More fundamentally, I cannot forswear language. I cannot, then, leave others behind as I reflect on this or that of my experiences. Schutz (1967, p. 32) was emphatic on this score: "every act of mine through which I endow the world with meaning refers back to some meaning-endowing act...of yours with respect to the same world. Meaning is thus constituted as an intersubjective phenomenon." Each of us inescapably lives in "a shared world of interpretation which carries with it a horizon of expectancies and demands" (Natanson, 1970, p. 40) woven from the stuff of social life as well as the threads of my own experiences.

Yet subjectivity does have an existence resolutely its own. It needs no liberation from the "inter." Instead, implies Schutz, subjectivity always has two sides – the singular and the plural, the unique and the shared, the solitary and the collective. As Natanson (1970, p. 56) reminds us, *subjectivity* means subject-bound. When it is subjects-bound, it amounts to intersubjectivity, which takes shape around the prospect, however fulfilled or not, of two or more subjects coming to terms with and gearing into the world together. It takes shape as two or more persons come to sense that they understand one another enough that they can generally take their mutual understanding for granted.

All the while, Schutz (1967, p. 32) emphasizes that "an action has only one subjective meaning: that of the actor" whose action it is. In the face of widespread attempts – Freudian and otherwise – to inform people about what their actions *really* mean, Schutz aligned himself with interpretive sociology as Weber shaped it. He leaves no theoretical space for "subjective meaning" to denote anything other than whatever meaning subjects assign to their own actions. My experiences remain pre-eminently *mine*, then. The only subjective meaning they can possibly have is what I give them.

Yet Schutz (1964, p. 9) equally emphasizes that "My experience of the world justifies and corrects itself by the experience of the others with whom I am interrelated by common knowledge, common work, and common suffering." The meanings I make grow out of knowledge, work, and suffering that are simultaneously mine alone and ours together. No other human being knows precisely what I know, nor is there anyone whose projects and actions match mine or whose trials and tribulations are identical to my own. Yet I know that great multitudes of people know much of what I know and gear themselves into the world much as I do and feel pain much the way I do. In short, I take for granted that I am far from alone in "the" world or even in "my" world.

At the same time I take for granted that I am capable of understanding the people around me. Schutz (1962, p. 27) reminds us, however, that there is no more than "a mere chance, although a chance sufficient for many practical purposes, that the observer in daily life can grasp the subjective meaning of the actor's acts." The odds may favor us more or less, but we live with no guarantee that we can come to understand what this or that person's action meant. The challenge at hand, after all, is to enter the Other's situation and adopt his or her perspective on or account of the action (Natanson, 1970, p. 100). All the while, though, I have only my own experiences as a point of access to another's experiences. As Schutz (1967, p. 106) puts it, *"everything I know about your conscious life is really based on my knowledge of my own lived experiences,"* including my experiences of your actions.

Schutz (1964, p. 13) theorizes that in the world of everyday life "I am able to understand other people's acts only if I can imagine that I myself would perform analogous acts if I were in the same situation, directed by the same because motives, or oriented by the same in-order-to motives." Thus, understanding others' actions means understanding their situations from retrospective and prospective viewpoints. Such understanding means, then, grasping the background circumstances or antecedent conditions (because motives) or the anticipated outcomes (in-order-to motives) associated with an individual's acts. Understanding another's action thus necessitates what Mead called "taking the role of the other." It requires what Schutz (1962, pp. 11–12) called a *reciprocity of perspectives* whereby, first, I assume that Other and I have interchangeable standpoints in the sense that if we swapped physical places, we would each see things "with the same typicality" that the other had previously experienced; and, second, that despite our different biographical situations Other and I have purposes and relevances that are the same or substantially similar for all practical purposes. Schutz says the reciprocity of perspectives in everyday life revolves around the "structural socialization of knowledge." That knowledge involves familiarity with people's typical purposes in typical situations such as funerals, breakfast buffets, or homeless shelters. Thus what each of us seeks in a typical situation overlaps considerably with what others seek; our *in-order-to motives* dovetail. Our *because motives*, the circumstances we see as having shaped our past actions, are also typically similar by virtue of the social stock of knowledge, including language, that we use to account for those actions.

Schutz (1964, p. 15) thus theorizes that in everyday life

> More or less naively I presuppose the existence of a common scheme of reference for both my own acts and the acts of others. I am interested above all . . . in [others'] intentions, and that means in the in-order-to motives for the sake of which, and in the because motives based on which, they act as they do.

Schutz goes on:

> Convinced that they want to express something by their act or that their act has a specific position within the common frame of reference, I try to catch the meaning which the act in question has, particularly for my co-actors in the social world, and, until presented with counter-evidence, I presume that this meaning for them, the actors, corresponds to the meaning their act has for me.

Such presumption sometimes falters. Commonsense individuals know from their own experiences that the Other sometimes surprises them with "strange" or unfamiliar purposes and relevances. Usually, however, the typicality delineated in and reinforced by the social stock of knowledge prevails, and life proceeds along its well traveled pathways. Although Schutz's theorizing emphasizes this latter state of affairs, he does map out the contours of misunderstanding in everyday life. That theoretical mapping brings us back to the matter of anonymity.

Schutz (1962, p. 27) noted that the more standardized and anonymous an action is, the greater one's chances are of grasping its subjective meaning. Imagine, for instance, a Roman Catholic couple touring a French city on a Sunday morning and passing by a cathedral as parishioners are celebrating Mass together. Even though these tourists are unfamiliar with this specific church and these specific parishioners, they nonetheless recognize the liturgy whereby participants sit, stand, and kneel together at standard junctures, and they deem it not at all strange that the key celebrant is wearing an unusual costume for a contemporary Western man. The passers-by adequately grasp the meaning of what they are seeing; they experience no perplexity.

That scenario contrasts with one involving an intimate We-relationship of some duration. Imagine one partner announcing, "I think we should talk about spending less time with one another. I need more space." Psychobabble aside, such an announcement disrupts the mirroring typical of close, face-to-face relationships. It is likely to leave the listener at least momentarily dumbfounded or at a loss to understand the partner's motives. The more attuned we are to the biographically situated person rather than a *type* of person, the harder it can be to grasp the subjective meaning of his or her actions when they depart from what is typical and familiar in the world we have made together.

As we have seen, alongside lived We-relationships of more or less intimacy or anonymity lie They-relationships with anonymous contemporaries like the people attending Mass in the cathedral. Schutz (1967, p. 185) theorized that "when I am They-oriented, I have 'types' for partners." In general, it is easier to understand types than individuals. Schutz goes on to say why: namely, they are "part of our stock of knowledge" about the social world. We-relationships, however, modify those types and leave us with more singularity and less anonymity to grasp. With more than a little theoretical acumen, Schutz (1967, p. 186) literally underscored that "*The typical and only the typical is homogeneous*, and it is always so. In the typifying synthesis of recognition . . . I abstract the lived experience from its setting . . . and thereby render it impersonal" and anonymous.

Schutz (1962, p. 29) emphasized that

> the general thesis of the reciprocity of perspectives . . . presupposes that both the observed and the observer are sharing a system of relevances sufficiently homogeneous in structure and content for the practical purpose involved. If this is not the case, then a course of action which is perfectly rational from the point of view of the actor may appear as non-rational to the partner or observer and vice versa.

An utterance that momentarily upsets or disorients a partner in a close We-relationship typically reflects at least a short-term disjuncture between the relevances of the speaker and those of the listener. Beyond such relationships the failure to understand – that is, the failure to grasp the subjective meaning of an Other's action – points to a standing divergence between Ego's and Other's systems of relevance. In order to understand the Other, Ego must temporarily set aside his or her own relevances enough to adopt the Other's point of view and thus grasp what she or he meant by a given action or course of action. This challenge of grasping the subjective meanings of people's actions lies at the heart of interpretive sociology and poses methodological challenges in all the social sciences. Schutz addressed this aspect of social-scientific methodology in considerable detail.

## INTERPRETIVE SOCIOLOGY AND CONTEMPORARY SOCIAL THEORY

After serving in the First World War, Schutz studied at the University of Vienna (1918–1921), where he earned his law degree. Thereafter he joined the banking house Reitler & Company as a legal consultant. He worked full-time with that firm nearly the rest of his life – first in Vienna and later in New York after he, Ilse, and their two children escaped the Holocaust and settled there in 1939. By that time Schutz's *Phenomenology of the Social World* had been on scholars' bookshelves for seven years.

That volume grew out of Schutz's postgraduate fascination with Weber's sociology. As Wagner (1983, pp. 14–15) describes it, Schutz was particularly taken with the opening chapter of Weber's *Wirtschaft und Gesellschaft*, which had appeared in 1922. He accepted Weber's "fundamental approach and the core of his methodology" and soon began the project of philosophically undergirding and augmenting Weber's stance. The first chapter of Schutz's book is "The Statement of Our Problem: Max Weber's Basic Methodological Concepts"; its last is "Some Basic Problems of Interpretive Sociology." By elaborating the philosophical foundations of Weber's work, Schutz contributed a great deal to the logic of social inquiry, particularly qualitative methodology.

In all likelihood his teaching let Schutz enlarge those contributions beyond what they would otherwise have been. In the spring of 1943, Schutz offered the first of his courses as a member of the Graduate Faculty of the New School for Social Research, "Introduction to Sociological Theory." That fall he taught the "Theory of Social Action," and the spring of 1944 found him co-teaching a seminar on Mead with Albert Salomon. During the fall of 1944 Schutz taught "Social Groups and Problems of Adjustment," followed in the spring by "Problems of a Sociology of Knowledge." Over the years to come Schutz also offered seminars on "Self and Society," "Problems of a Sociology of Language," and "Methodology of the Social Sciences" (Wagner, 1983, pp. 87–8, 91). These graduate seminars gave him hard-won occasions for interacting with individuals whose systems of relevance revolved around philosophy, social science, and academic We-relationships. His part-time academic work facilitated Schutz's contact with academic contemporaries such as Talcott Parsons and Robert MacIver and connected him with such promising students as Peter L. Berger and Thomas Luckmann as well as Natanson and Wagner. Through it all he managed to complete a number of important papers, many of which extended the social theorizing begun in his 1932 book.

One such paper is pivotal. First published in *Social Research* (summer 1960), "The Social World and the Theory of Social Action" lambasts objectivist, particularly behavioristic, social science. Schutz (1964, p. 3) begins,

> At first sight it is not easily understandable why the subjective point of view should be preferred in the social sciences. Why address ourselves to this mysterious and not too interesting tyrant of the social sciences, called the subjectivity of the actor? Why not honestly describe in honestly objective terms what really happens, and that means speaking our own language, the language of qualified and scientifically trained observers of the social world? And if it be objected that these terms are but artificial conventions..., we could answer that it is precisely this building up of a system of conventions and an honest description of the world which *is* and is alone the task of scientific thought.

Schutz goes on to argue against displacing social reality with a "fictional world" based on scientific methods that illuminate some matters but fail when it comes to intersubjectivity. More generally, Schutz is impatient with social science that revolves around "skillfully and expediently chosen idealizations and formalizations of the social world which are not repugnant to its facts" but do not capture its texture of mutuality and its fabric of meanings.

Such social science ignores "the actor in the social world whose doing and feeling lie at the bottom of the whole system" (Schutz, 1962, p. 6). It thus abandons the *lived* character of social reality. Although he conceded that they have some role to play, Schutz largely inveighed against research methods narrowly concerned with statistical correlations, formal models, and social trends. For him, the most urgent questions in the social sciences center on actors' subjective meanings. Schutz (1964, p. 8) believed that "safeguarding...the subjective point of view is the only but sufficient guarantee that the world of social reality will not be replaced by a fictional non-existing world constructed by the scientific observer."

In one fashion or other such fictional worlds typically fill the pages of journals like the *American Sociological Review* and the *American Political Science Review*. The fare in such journals is far from a balanced mix. Instead, the articles routinely ignore people's lived experiences and subjective meanings. If issues of meaning get raised at all, they most often center on the meaning of this or that blip on the statistical horizon. By contrast, Schutz (1964, p. 13) argued that "social things are only understandable if they can be reduced to human activities; and human activities are only made understandable by showing their in-order-to and because motives." Thus, he insisted that the chief aim of the social sciences is to clarify "what is thought about the social world by those living in it" (Schutz, 1967, p. 222).

With these prognostications Schutz points to a huge methodological paradox, namely that social scientists must act substantially like commonsense actors in order to do their work well. To understand social reality they must, like commonsense members, try to understand the people who constitute it together through their meaningful activities and relationships. If social scientists fail to do that – that is, fail to illuminate sense-making activities in the everyday world – they simultaneously fail to unearth the grounds of their own activities, which always come down to making sense by some means or other. The result is a naive social science that takes for granted what it ought to be analyzing. Schutz sought to defamiliarize such social science by depicting it as a dead-ended pathway into social reality. His theorizing repositions social scientists by revealing their close kinship with common-sense observers. As we will see, ethnomethodologists deploy Schutz's insights along these lines and are among his most significant successors.

Schutz (1967, p. 141) asserted that "the *starting point* of social science is to be found in ordinary social life." In no way did Schutz equate common-sense and scientific sorts of understanding, but he did insist that "the two spheres overlap." The terms of that overlap are types; the bridge between the two spheres is thus typification. In everyday life, says Schutz (1967, p. 187), people typify both people and actions. Their stock of knowledge at hand comprises, in other terms, *personal ideal types* such as childcare worker, golfer, minister, and neighbor intertwined with *course-of-action types* such as tending children, playing golf, preaching, and neighboring. The former category typifies the people who do this, that, or the other thing(s), especially their in-order-to and because motives; the latter typifies their projects and actions.

From these types that pervade the world of everyday life Schutz sees only a short, though significant, step to the types used in the worlds of theory and of social science. He points out, for instance, that common-sense interpretations using course-of-action and personal ideal types have social-scientific parallels not only in role theory but also in the distinction between subjective and objective meanings (Schutz, 1962, p. 149). Like other scientists, social scientists seek the latter type of meanings. What distinguishes their fields of study is that they ultimately seek objective interpretations of subjective meanings.

This definitive circumstance means social scientists need to remain vividly aware of how the meaning of any action necessarily differs for the actor, for the actor's partner in a We-relationship, and for the observer who is not a participant in that relationship (Schutz, 1962, p. 24). We have already seen that lived We-relationships vary enormously in immediacy, intimacy, and intensity so that the "outside" observer and the "inside" participant are more or less dissimilar in their points of view. They cannot make precisely the same objective sense of the actor's subjective meaning. Their respective positions entitle them to differing degrees of familiarity with and knowledge of the actor's relevances, biographical situation, and typical in-order-to and because motives.

To some significant extent social scientists must remain Outsiders, then. No matter how much participant observation, direct observation, ethnographic labor, or other methical work they do, they cannot become full-fledged members of an Other world, which its members are continuously making together and which links their biographical situations together in multiple ways. Social scientists will always remain, at least in part, the Observer (except when lying about or covering up their main in-order-to motive). Participants in their research will use that sort of personal ideal type to typify the social scientist. To some extent they will rely on the course-of-action type "doing research" to account for his or her behavior.

In large measure the social scientist is thus fated to be a perennial outsider. All the while, though, social scientists also remain insiders unable to extricate themselves from the ties of the life-world. Experiencing some familiarity, sharing the language, recognizing some (if not all) of the types of people and action constituting the world of his or her observations, the social scientist draws on the very resources that social science research should illuminate. As Schutz (1967, p. 10) put it, social scientists' data

> are the already constituted meanings of active participants in the social world. It is to these already meaningful data that [their] scientific concepts must ultimately refer: to the meaningful acts of individual men and women, to their everyday experience of one another, to their understanding of one another's meanings, and to their initiation of new meaningful behavior of their own. [Social scientists] will be concerned, furthermore, with the concepts people have of the meaning of their own and others' behavior and the concepts they have of the meaning of artifacts of all kinds. So we see that the data of the social sciences have, while still in the prescientific state, those elements of meaning and intelligible structure which later appear in more or less explicit form with a claim to categorial validity in the interpretive science itself.

In a nutshell, then, insider/outsider social scientists face the standing challenge of developing "methodological devices for attaining objective and verifiable knowledge of a subjective meaning structure" (Schutz, 1962, p. 36). Negotiating the experiential borderland they inhabit as both insiders and outsiders, social scientists intent on representing nonfictional worlds must put into play a logic of inquiry that respects their paradoxical positioning.

Schutz (1967, p. 15) felt that "the man whose thought has penetrated most deeply into the structure of the social world" was Max Weber. In Schutz's (1982, pp. 42–3) judgment the Thou

> stands in the center of Weber's considerations. He intends to comprehend the Thou and his meaning scientifically....However, this Thou is different from all other objects of experience in that it can be understood. Therefore, his comprehension demands a particular method. To exactly formulate this method is the purpose of the main part of this study.

For Schutz (1962, pp. 24–5), that method has its origins in the world of everyday life. Specifically, he theorizes that "the postulate of the 'subjective interpretation of meaning,' as the unfortunate term goes, is not a particularity of Weber's sociology or of the methodology of the social sciences in general but a principle of constructing course-of-action types in common-sense experience." Social scientists *reflectively* pursue what is typically prereflective among common-sense actors, and that difference is significant. Still, though, the two types of actors engage in typifying other actors along the same broad channels. In the end, for example, social scientists can only grasp people in the everyday world as personal ideal types, not as living individuals in their uniqueness, much as common-sense actors can only grasp their mere contemporaries as types who lack unique biographical situations and one-of-a-kind bodies.

Inevitably, such typification does carry the risk of fictionalizing Others and their world. For social scientists committed to minimizing that risk, Schutz (1962, pp. 43–4) laid out three postulates. The *postulate of logical consistency* requires compatibility of one's findings with the principles of formal logic and thus applies to social-scientific findings a criterion that has little applicability to common-sense knowledge. The *postulate of subjective interpretation* requires that social scientists explore the kind of consciousness, including its typical contents, that one must presuppose in order to account for observed actions. The *postulate of adequacy* requires that scientific models of action be formulated so as to make sense to the actors themselves and their consociates "in terms of common-sense interpretation of everyday life." This last postulate ensures close attention to individuals' subjective meanings and others' common-sense inter-pretations of those meanings by requiring that scientific models of action be comprehensible to those whose actions they are supposed to represent. This postulate also stands to make (or keep) social scientists aware of how their own typifications of social reality revolve around "constructs of the second degree" (Schutz, 1962, p. 59) or "second-order constructs" that build on the first-order or common-sense constructs operative in everyday life.

Schutz thus theorized a logic of inquiry capable of lending strength to any methodology that departs from the hegemony of measurement and statistics in the social sciences. In particular, Schutz's stance resonates not only with ethno-methodology but also with other varieties of social theory that have emerged over the past thirty or so years – feminist theory, queer theory, and multicultural social theory in all its far-reaching richness. Let me offer two examples. The first is Dorothy Smith's social theorizing.

Smith (1990, p. 2) observes that "Sociology created...a construct of society that is specifically discontinuous with the world known, lived, experienced, and acted in." Taking off from Schutz's notions about the fictional worlds that social scientists routinely construct, Smith (1990, p. 3) lays out a logic of inquiry that "relies on the insider's knowledge of how the social relations and organization in which she participates work, how they are put together." Smith helped to establish *standpoint theory*, which emphasizes the distinctive slant on a social world that any given social positioning necessarily entails. Smith typically emphasizes women's standpoints as an antidote to the fictionalizing – that is, false universalizing – common among social scientists who often take only men's viewpoints into account.

Renato Rosaldo's theorizing also illuminates the diffuse reach of Schutz's thinking. Trained in anthropology and pursuing work in Chicano/a studies as well, Rosaldo (1993, pp. 169ff.) also emphasizes standpoint as a theoretical line of access to nonfictionalizing methodologies. He cites Schutz as a "key antecedent" to the notions of "subject position" or "positioned subject," which refers to the social location of the experiencing person (Rosaldo, 1993, p. 227). His methodology explicitly problematizes the notion of culture by centering on cultural border zones and implicitly problematizes "home" as much contemporary social theorizing does.

Between the lines of much feminist, queer, and multicultural social theory lie tales about the difficulty many people face making a home for themselves. Much of that theorizing illuminates domestic violence against women and children and elderly men, familial rejection of lesbian daughters and gay sons, hate crimes, and institutionalized biases that systematically deprive racial, sexual, ethnic, and other minorities of the resources necessary to speak with powerful voices in today's postindustrial societies. Schutz wrote rather little about such injustices, though he did write a major paper on "Equality and the Meaning Structure of the Social World" (Schutz, 1964, pp. 226ff.) Schutz (1982, p. 212) had also outlined work on race and sex differentiation, among other things. Yet two of Schutz's essays offer stunning grounds for theorizing about home and thus are key resources for many social theorists today.

"The Stranger: an Essay in Social Psychology" and "The Homecomer" both appeared in the *American Journal of Sociology* (1944 and 1945, respectively). "The Stranger" implies what it means to have a home – to be "accepted or at least tolerated," to feel centered rather than at a loss in one's environment, to experience typicality as "an unquestioned matter of course" and thus as a shelter of taken-for-granted meaning, to know one belongs (Schutz, 1962, pp. 91, 99, 102, 104). "The Homecomer" more explicitly addresses the matter. Home, says Schutz (1962, p. 108), means

> father-house and mother-tongue, the family, the sweetheart, the friends; it means a beloved landscape, "songs my mother taught me," food prepared in a particular way, familiar things for daily use, folkways, and personal habits – briefly, a peculiar way of life composed of small and important elements, likewise cherished.

Schutz goes on to observe that the phrase "to feel at home" expresses "the highest degree of familiarity and intimacy." With such formulations as these Schutz provides theoretical leverage for many of the issues drawing contemporary theorists toward horizons with a multicultural and often postmodernist cast.

A similar generalization might be proffered about Schutz's attention to the body. With renewed and imaginative theorizing about the body in the humanities as well as the social sciences today, Schutz's treatment of the body sets him apart from many of his philosophical and sociological contemporaries. Schutz (1962, p. 148) theorized the body of the Other as an "expressional field" whereby we glean the thoughts, feelings, and motives currently informing the Other's stream of experience. Ego's body is equally central. My body is at the center of my physical world; it is the material basis for "gear[ing] into the outer world" through my work (Schutz, 1962, p. 227). It is also the basis for my "feeling of life," which is what Schutz (1982, p. 77) calls each person's awareness of his or her own body. Schutz (1982, p. 102) also spoke of the "privileged position" somatic experiences occupy and about how touch evokes awareness of the body's boundaries. As with his theorizing about home, Schutz's theorizing about the body gives his work a contemporary feel and, more importantly, substantial relevance today.

## ASSESSMENT

Assessing Schutz's thought seems easy enough until one takes stock of its impact. Except for a few key instances, Schutz's impact has been substantially indirect but dramatically diffuse. His work directly affected Natanson's corpus, which is a stunning achievement bringing together phenomenology, the philosophy of the social sciences, sociology, and much else under the aegis of human experiencing. Schutz's work also shaped the landmark study of Peter Berger and Thomas Luckmann, namely *The Social Construction of Reality: a Treatise on the Sociology of Knowledge* (1967). Berger and Luckmann's masterpiece, itself widely influential, draws on the insights of Weber, Marx, and Durkheim, as well as those of Schutz. To my way of thinking, though, the Schutzian character of this study outweighs its Weberian or other intellectual dimensions. From beginning to end Berger and Luckmann concern themselves with the very questions lending coherence to Schutz's framework. They want to know, for instance, what people's faces *mean* during face-to-face interaction and how two people (A and B) could conceivably launch a sociohistorical world together.

Schutz also directly, though less heavily, influenced Harold Garfinkel, who during the 1960s established ethnomethodology as a major force in the social sciences and beyond. Schutz and Garfinkel corresponded briefly as well as met one another, and the latter's doctoral dissertation (completed under the tutelage of Parsons) incorporates some of Schutz's ideas. Schutz's ideas had a comparable impact on some of Goffman's later work, especially *Frame Analysis: an Essay on the Organization of Experience* (1974). Goffman's twenty-page introduction to this opus revolves around his exploration of James's and Schutz's thinking about experience, meaning, and multiplicity. Goffman's remaining 500-plus pages can be read as a detailed delineation of Schutz's ideas about the social stock of knowledge and, to a lesser extent, any given individual's stock of knowledge at hand. As we saw, Schutz also influenced Dorothy Smith's theorizing. Overall, then, his direct impact on social theorists would seem concentrated in the realms of phenomenology, ethnomethodology, social dramaturgy, and feminist standpoint theory along the lines developed by Natanson, Garfinkel, Goffman, and Smith, respectively.

Yet Schutz's ideas show up across a much wider range of social theory than that, as Rosaldo's work illustrates. For the most part, in fact, it seems that Schutz's influence has been unusually diffuse. Wherever qualitative methodologies are taken seriously, for instance, his ideas have a sound chance of being heard, if only indirectly. For the most part quantitative methods show *how much* is going on in some social world. Quantitative researchers are also good at showing how much one aspect of social reality correlates with other aspects.

All the while quantitative approaches do little to illuminate *what* is going on in a social world. That task is implicitly left to qualitative inquiries, and Schutz's ideas are capable of establishing the root systems of such approaches. Theorizing about human consciousness, experiencing, knowledge, action, taken for grantedness, and intersubjectivity guarantee his relevance to those pursuing qualitative methods. Rosaldo (1993, p. 207) writes that

> the fiction of the uniformly shared culture increasingly seems more tenuous than useful. Although most metropolitan typifications continue to suppress border zones, human cultures are neither necessarily coherent nor always homogeneous. More often than we usually care to think, our everyday lives are crisscrossed by border zones, pockets, and eruptions of all kinds.

I can hear Schutz applauding that formulation. His ideas are as much at work in Rosaldo's volume as anyone else's that Rosaldo invokes. Yet Schutz's name has no place in Rosaldo's index, and he may well have gotten no more than the one citation I have already mentioned.

Overall, then, Schutz's legacy seems to be that of diffuse impact. He launched no identifiable school of thought, and he gathered around him no clear-cut band of disciples. Yet his work gets cited time and time again as social theorists grapple anew with the stubborn question of what it means to share a world while living a life that no one else can have. As social theorists focus their attention on texts and language, discourse and narratives, home and its challenges, bodies and somatic experiences, and much else that Schutz addressed, his impact may well concentrate itself along more decided channels. All the while one does well to bear in mind that impact is a secondary measure of quality. As Schutz himself recognized, connections, contacts, and networks interplay with organizational affiliation as major influences on how much attention and what kind of reception a scholar's ideas get. By and large, those circumstances disadvantaged Schutz.

Until the last several years of his life, Schutz worked only part-time in academe. His part-time affiliation was not with an Ivy League institution, nor was it with the University of Chicago or any of the other centers of lively philosophizing and theorizing. Schutz had no mentor promoting his career, promulgating his ideas, helping him get published, or showing him the ropes of the American academic system. Moreover, Schutz worked in areas of social theory that are hard to define, if only because of their transdisciplinary reach. Nevertheless, he established a name for himself by dint of the powerful framework he built up. Put differently, Schutz's ideas are the main reason he is widely known. His is not a reputation resting to any discernible degree on the advantages common among widely known twentieth-century social theorists.

# Bibliography

## Writings of Alfred Schutz

*Collected Papers I: The Problem of Social Reality* (edited by Maurice Natanson). 1962. The Hague: Martinus Nijhoff.

*Collected Papers II: Studies in Social Theory* (edited by Arvid Brodersen). 1964. The Hague: Martinus Nijhoff.

*Collected Papers III: Studies in Phenomenological Philosophy* (edited by Ilse Schutz). 1966. The Hague: Martinus Nijhoff.

*The Phenomenology of the Social World* (translated by George Walsh and Frederick Lehnert). 1967. Evanston, IL: Northwestern University Press.

*Reflections on the Problem of Relevance* (edited by Richard M. Zaner). 1970. New Haven, CT: Yale University Press.

*The Structures of the Life-World* (with Thomas Luckmann, translated by Richard M. Zaner and H. Tristram Engelhardt Jr). 1973. Evanston, IL: Northwestern University Press.

Husserl and His Influence on Me. 1977. In Don Ihde and Richard M. Zaner (eds), *Interdisciplinary Phenomenology*. The Hague: Martinus Nijhoff, pp. 124–9.

*Life Forms and Meaning Structure* (translated and edited by Helmut R. Wagner). 1982. London: Routledge & Kegan Paul.

## Further reading

Berger, Peter and Luckmann, Thomas (1967) *The Social Construction of Reality*. New York: Doubleday.

Goffman, Erving (1974) *Frame Analysis: an Essay on the Organization of Experience*. New York: Harper and Row.

Grathoff, Richard (1978) *The Theory of Social Action: the Correspondence of Alfred Schutz and Talcott Parsons*. Bloomington: Indiana University Press.

Grathoff, Richard (1989) *Philosophers in Exile: the Correspondence of Alfred Schutz and Aron Gurwitsch, 1939–1959*. Bloomington: Indiana University Press.

Natanson, Maurice (1970) *The Journeying Self: a Study in Philosophy and Social Role*. Reading, MA: Addison-Wesley.

Natanson, Maurice (1973) *Edmund Husserl: Philosopher of Infinite Tasks*. Evanston, IL: Northwestern University Press.

Natanson, Maurice (1986) *Anonymity: a Study in the Philosophy of Alfred Schutz*. Bloomington: Indiana University Press.

Rosaldo, Renato (1993) *Culture and Truth: the Remaking of Social Analysis*. Boston: Beacon Press.

Smith, Dorothy E. (1990) *Texts, Facts, and Femininity: Exploring the Relations of Ruling*. New York: Routledge.

Wagner, Helmut R. (1970) Introduction. In Helmut Wagner (ed.), *Alfred Schutz on Phenomenology and Social Relations*. Chicago: University of Chicago Press, pp. 1–50.

Wagner, Helmut R. (1983) *Alfred Schutz: an Intellectual Biography*. Chicago: University of Chicago Press.

Webb, Rodman B. (1992) The Life and Work of Alfred Schutz: a Conversation with Maurice Natanson. *Qualitative Studies in Education*, 5(4), 283–94.

# 12

## Talcott Parsons

### VICTOR LIDZ

### INTRODUCTION

Talcott Parsons (1902–79) was, and remains, the pre-eminent American sociologist, noted primarily for the broad scope and analytic depth of his theory of human social action. The trends of thought that brought him to leadership in sociological theory were established in his first articles and sustained, through many modifications and elaborations, over fifty years of publication. He published more than ten independent books, including several with collaborators, seven volumes of collected essays, three edited books, and perhaps as many as 100 additional essays. Several of his major writings – *The Structure of Social Action* of 1937, *The Social System* of 1951, *Economy and Society* (with Neil J. Smelser) of 1956, and "On the Concept of Political Power" of 1962 (in Parsons, 1969) – are landmarks in the development of sociological theory. The central force in shaping curricula in sociology at Harvard University from the late 1920s to the mid 1960s, he was the most influential teacher of sociologists in his generation (Fox, 1997). From the 1930s to the early 1970s, he was a mentor to scores of graduate students who later became creative scholars.

Parsons's main concern was to develop a coherent conceptual scheme for sociology that would be applicable in all times and places, would address all aspects of human social organization, and would be open to progressive refinement as the advancing discipline gained in ability to relate theory to empirical knowledge. This concern remained constant throughout his career and provides the unity to theoretical and empirical writings that are otherwise extraordinarily diverse in sources of ideas, topics addressed, and levels of technical elaboration. Parsons's expansive understanding of the mandate for theory in intellectually disciplined or 'scientific' sociology was based on a sophisticated methodology, rooted in his undergraduate and graduate studies of Kant, but modified under the influence of A. N. Whitehead's philosophy of science.

Parsons is often compared to such builders of comprehensive theories as Comte and Spencer, but this mischaracterizes his undertaking. His efforts were focused on developing conceptual schemes or frames of reference to facilitate empirical investigation. Following Whitehead, he viewed establishing frames of reference as logically preliminary to empirical research, including the phase of empirical research that involves generating hypotheses to be tested. He thus regarded his own distinctive contribution as clarifying frames of reference and their consequences for empirical hypotheses and propositional theories (Lidz, in Klausner and Lidz, 1986, chapter 6). He understood that empirical feedback, primarily from the research findings of others, was essential for assessing the value of his conceptual and propositional work. Although most of his conceptual work was highly abstract, and some of it became very complicated, it never had the character of a closed system.

A strong commitment to progressive development of his ideas was a striking characteristic of Parsons's manner of work. He was an astute and persistent critic of his own writings. Never complacent about what he had accomplished, he rarely remained satisfied with particular formulations for more than a brief time. Whenever he returned to a specific topic, even in lectures to undergraduate classes, he endeavored to advance new considerations and new formulations. (He apparently prepared fresh notes for every class and every public presentation.) He undertook new books or major articles with the expectation of developing significantly new theoretical ideas. In second drafts of writings, he typically made major revisions and extensions of ideas he had thought his creative best only weeks or months before.

The strength of Parsons's drive for innovation creates difficulties for scholars who wish to understand, interpret, and critique his theories. While there are a number of fundamental continuities across his writings, he changed important formulations at several points. Subordinate formulations were changed frequently. Writings that introduced changes, especially of technical details, frequently omitted frank justifications for the changes. Interpreting the evolution of Parsons's theory thus requires not only mastery of many difficult writings, but also careful attention to changing conceptual frameworks and shifting details.

## THE PERSON

### Early life and studies

Talcott Parsons was born on December 13, 1902 in Colorado Springs, Colorado, where his father, a Congregational minister by training, served as Professor of English and later Dean of the Faculty at Colorado College. Parsons's parents maintained the ascetic Protestant culture associated with their New England heritage. However, Edward Parsons combined a conservative and disciplined personal manner – he and his wife maintained a teetotaling household – with liberalism on social issues. He held a strong interest in the Social Gospel move-ment and in intellectual matters. Talcott Parsons came to identify with his family connection to the eighteenth-century theologian, Jonathan Edwards, and as an adult also combined an ascetic modesty in personal manners (but not teetotal-ing) with a liberalism on social issues and interpersonal generosity to colleagues and students.

In 1917, Edward Parsons was forced out of Colorado College by trustees who were displeased with his role in reporting improper conduct on the part of the college president. He later became president of Marietta College in Ohio. In the short term, however, he moved his family to New York City, where Talcott Parsons prepared for college at the progressive Horace Mann School. He then attended Amherst College, where his exceptional academic promise became apparent. At Amherst, initially planning to follow an older brother into medi-cine, he studied biology and gained a broad overview of evolutionary theory, comparative anatomy, and physiology that later supported his turn to functional theory in sociology. However, course work in economics resonated with his strong concern for social reform and social justice. Economics at Amherst was dominated by the institutional school, and Parsons gained exposure, through Walton Hamilton, to its latest trends of thought. Parsons studied figures such as Veblen, Commons, Sumner, and Cooley, whose writings addressed the social and institutional aspects of the economy. He also read various American and English economic historians who described the institutional growth of the industrial economy and the many social problems it engendered. He gained sufficient perspective on the institutional school to appreciate that it was largely an out-growth of the German school of historical economics. A course on Kant's *Critique of Pure Reason* with George Brown, a Scottish trained philosopher who emphasized disciplined and critical reading of master texts, influenced Parsons's later tendency to study and restudy selected works by major authors.

After graduating from Amherst in 1924, Parsons matriculated at the London School of Economics (LSE). For a young scholar of economic institutions with sympathy for socialist ideals, the LSE was then a major academic center, and Parsons enrolled with high expectations. Through classes and personal encoun-ters, he came to know several of the LSE luminaries: R. H. Tawney, Morris Ginsberg, Bronislaw Malinowski, and Harold Laski (Parsons, 1977, chapter 1). His participation in Malinowski's seminar left the most favorable impression as well as lasting friendships with E. E. Evans-Pritchard, Meyer Fortes, and Raymond Firth, later major figures in British social anthropology, who also took the seminar. Ginsberg's teaching in sociology was encyclopedic in scope, but made a poor impression. It reified utilitarian concepts and lacked close engagement with specific materials. When an opportunity arose to spend a year in Germany on a fellowship, Parsons gladly accepted the chance to study the German historical school of economics.

Parsons often commented that his assignment to the University of Heidelberg and involvement with the scholarship of Max Weber was serendipitous. He had scarcely known Weber's name. His placement at Heidelberg in 1925 was a chance decision by administrators of the fellowship program. Arriving in

Heidelberg five years after Weber's death, he found that Weber's "ghost" still dominated local social science. Weber's contributions were emphasized in lectures and in informal contacts with faculty. Parsons soon studied *The Protestant Ethic and the Spirit of Capitalism* and was deeply moved by Weber's understanding and analysis of the heritage in which he had been raised (Parsons, 1977, chapter 1). He quickly became immersed in the larger body of Weber's writings, including the comparative studies of religious ethics and civilization, the theoretical schemes of *Economy and Society*, and the methodological essays. He then studied other bodies of scholarship that were essential background to Weber, namely, Rickert and the neo-Kantian movement in historical and social scientific methodology; other key figures in the German historical school of economics, especially Schmoller, Sombart, Below, and Brentano; Mengel and the Austrian marginalist school; and Karl Marx. Methodologically, he was strongly influenced by Weber's writings, the broader neo-Kantian movement, and a second thorough reading of Kant in Karl Jaspers's seminar.

During the 1925–6 academic year, Parsons learned that he could earn a doctorate in Heidelberg without unduly extending his stay in Germany. He focused his studies on the theoretical understanding of the first emergence of modern capitalism and planned a dissertation on the conceptual frameworks needed to interpret and analyze the historical materials. From the outset, the works of Max Weber were to be the centerpiece of his discussion. At the suggestion of his dissertation supervisor, the economic historian and social scientist Edgar Salin, he confined his dissertation to leading figures in the German literature, concentrating on Weber and Sombart.

After his year in Heidelberg, Parsons, extensive notes on his German readings in hand, returned to Amherst to serve as Instructor in Economics for the academic year 1926–7 while writing his doctoral dissertation. He taught a course on sociology as well as courses in economics. In the spring of 1927, he received an appointment as Instructor in the Department of Economics at Harvard for the next fall. His appointment at Harvard brought sufficient economic security that he could marry Helen Walker, whom he had met at LSE. They remained happily married until his death. They had three children, all born in the 1930s: Anne, who became an anthropologist whose interests overlapped with her father's, but whose contributions were cut off by depression and suicide in 1964; Charles, who has become a distinguished philosopher and logician, now professor at Harvard University; and Susan, who has become a bank attorney.

In the summer of 1927, Parsons submitted his doctoral dissertation to Heidelberg. Its German title, according to official records, corresponded to *The Spirit of Capitalism in Weber and Sombart*. He successfully defended the dissertation before a committee of Jaspers, Alfred Weber, and Salin. His doctorate was awarded in 1929 after publication of his two articles on " 'Capitalism' in Recent German Literature: Sombart and Weber" (Parsons, 1991), meeting the requirement of German universities that dissertations be published.

Parsons's appointment at Harvard rested largely on his ability to represent German historical economics. He later said that he regarded himself as a sort of advanced graduate student even though he held faculty title because his German degree had been gained with far less study than was required for American doctorates. He accordingly sat in on the seminars in economic theory of such senior colleagues as Taussig and Schumpeter, and actively exchanged ideas with several junior faculty colleagues (Parsons, 1977, chapter 1). He was aware that his training in German historical economics seemed overly specialized in American settings. To compensate, he studied the rapidly developing American neoclassical economics, its background in Marshall and the British marginalists, and Pareto. He also began to reframe his ongoing research in the terms of American economics, where a synthesis of the institutional and neoclassical approaches would be a significant topic (Camic, Introduction to Parsons, 1991). However, his interests were also open toward sociology. He taught in the undergraduate program on social ethics along with other faculty members who held broad interests in social science and advocated the founding of a sociology department.

## Political values and interests

When Parsons arrived at the LSE, his political views were sympathetic to democratic socialism and optimistic that future economic systems could reduce the inequality and oppressive work conditions of major capitalist systems. However, his intellectual interests were stronger than his ideological tendencies. After a year of study at the LSE, he was disappointed by the lack of intellectual imagination and discipline he had found in the social and economic thought of the British left. In Heidelberg, he encountered in Max Weber's writings the stimulating imagination and uncompromising rigor he had sought. His later political and economic views were likely influenced by Weber's scorn for every strain of utopianism in modern thought. But he did not assimilate the conservatism that predominated in the German academic world.

In his early years at Harvard, if not before, Parsons's residual commitment to socialism gave way to a growing appreciation that markets are needed to institutionalize economic efficiency. He recognized that socialist planning could not substitute for markets without great losses in efficiency and the creation of wealth. This view was strengthened after the Second World War, when studies of the Soviet industrial system demonstrated the inefficiencies of planned economies. By the early 1930s, Parsons looked to better regulation of capitalist production as a more promising path to social improvement than socialism. During the Great Depression, he became a firm supporter of Roosevelt's New Deal, with its emphasis on overcoming the deprivations of poverty and ethnic or racial discrimination. For the rest of his life, he was an adherent of the liberal wing of the Democratic Party and, as an academic, was particularly committed to the freedoms of conscience, speech, publication, and association. He tended to look to expansion of a prosperous middle class as the most effective way to pursue values of social equality. From the mid-1950s to the end of his life, he identified himself as a "Stevenson Democrat" or "academic liberal." Yet he retained a sympathy for the ideals of democratic socialism and opposed the left only when he sensed that it had become authoritarian or radically utopian. His wife Helen's sympathies remained more to the left and more quickly sensitive to new movements, such as the opposition to the Vietnam War.

## THE THEORY

### The Department of Sociology and *The Structure of Social Action*

In 1930, the Russian émigré sociologist, Pitirim Sorokin, who had served in the Kerensky government and later taught at the University of Minnesota, arrived at Harvard to chair a new Department of Sociology. Parsons transferred to the new department expecting a better fit for his long-term interests. However, he soon found himself in frequent conflict with Sorokin, who disparaged his work and obstructed his promotion. He remained an Instructor until 1934 and did not become a tenured associate professor until after *The Structure of Social Action* (*SSA*) had appeared in 1937 and he had been offered a full professorship by the University of Wisconsin. Even then, his promotion occurred only after the intercession of Lawrence J. Henderson, the renowned physiologist who had developed an interest in sociology, taught in the new department, and appreciated Parsons's contributions. Nevertheless, the new departmental setting appears to have liberated Parsons's thought by legitimating his broad interests and shift to conceptual frameworks beyond both neoclassical and institutional economics.

By the mid-1930s, Parsons's main concerns encompassed the relationships between economic and all other social institutions, with a focus on the conceptual and theoretical tools needed to understand this large empirical field. He had translated Weber's *Protestant Ethic and the Spirit of Capitalism* (1930) and focused his scholarship increasingly on Weber rather than other figures in the German school. He had studied the theoretical systems of Alfred Marshall and Vilfredo Pareto and published important articles on their works (Parsons, 1991, chapters 8 and 15). The article on Marshall long remained widely read among economists. He had also begun serious study of the works of Émile Durkheim, whose critique of utilitarian thought provided a key reference point for his own conceptual efforts.

Harvard's new Department of Sociology attracted an exceptionally talented group of graduate students and Parsons soon emerged as its most influential teacher. Within a decade, he had established himself as sociology's most important cultivator of student talent and had placed capable and productive students in leading departments across the country. His postwar status as the central figure in American sociology followed the maturation of his early students' careers when they returned to the universities after military or government service.

The flowering of Parsons's thought in the setting of the new department also involved a significant turn toward the empirical materials of sociology. He initiated a course on comparative institutions, which he then taught many times down to the end of his career. The course was framed in terms of the full scope of Weber's empirical writings. Parsons taught the theory needed for comparative institutional analysis, but during the 1930s and 1940s invited distinguished specialists in many civilizations and historical epochs to teach the empirical materials. He forged intellectual relationships with many of these scholars and studied their writings and other works they cited. His own conceptual schema was affected in its many phases by engagement with empirical materials covered in this course. His writings on the German class structure and the rise of Nazism, the expanding role of professions in American society, the nature of medieval European civilization, or the civilizations of Antiquity were all influenced by the materials of his course on comparative institutional analysis.

Parsons began to formulate the foundations of his own theory in a series of essays that appeared in the early and middle 1930s. These included the essays on Marshall and Pareto, but also three essays that addressed in general terms the sociological elements embedded in economic theory. A 1935 essay entitled "The Place of Ultimate Values in Sociological Theory" was significant in three respects: it was the first major publication in which he addressed sociological theory rather than economic theory as his central topic, thus signaling a shift in his professional identity; it was the first essay to present aspects of the conceptual scheme that later became the core of *SSA*; and it outlined a shrewd and bold argument about the importance of values as structural determinants of social action, staking out a position that Parsons continued to refine throughout his career (Parsons, 1991, chapter 18).

The conceptual scheme to which these essays pointed was presented comprehensively and in greater depth in *SSA* (Parsons, 1937). In *SSA*, Parsons proposed a comprehensive and well integrated frame of reference that departed radically from the empiricism and positivism that were then dominant orientations in American sociology. His conceptual scheme was based initially on a probing evaluation of leading European economists and sociologists of the late nineteenth and early twentieth centuries, particularly Weber, Durkheim, Pareto, and Marshall. The action frame of reference, as Parsons called it, was a careful synthesis of a small number of premises and categories that, he claimed, are fundamental to all sociological understanding. Parsons did not present his frame of reference as a complete or precise theory, but as a thoroughly justified, well balanced set of basic concepts essential to the development of more technical theory. He supported his claims for the action frame of reference empirically with a critical review of the evidence amassed in Weber's comparative studies and in Durkheim's major writings.

As presented in *SSA*, the action frame of reference centers on the notion of the "unit act," a hypothetical entity representing any and all instances of meaningful human social behavior. Parsons specified four essential elements of the unit act: ends, means, norms, and conditions. These four categories of elements (and, in some statements, a category of effort) are essential in the sense that no social action can exist without the presence of at least one instance of each. Every instance of social action, regardless of time, place, or cultural context, necessarily contains exemplars of each category. In developing the idea of the unit act,

Parsons emphasized that the normative elements of social action have the same status as the more familiar elements of ends and means. An emphasis on studying the normative elements of social action, and on understanding the ways in which values and norms, when institutionalized, become structural to society, remained central to Parsons's writings throughout his career.

Parsons limited the scheme of *SSA* to basic concepts in order to concentrate on justifying its premises and essential elements. The justification entailed thorough critiques of the works of Marshall, Pareto, Durkheim, and Weber, but with a focus on the implications for basic premises and concepts. Parsons claimed that his critiques of these four major figures demonstrated that, despite the differences in their intellectual backgrounds, they had "converged" in emphasizing common concepts, which amounted in essence to the action frame of reference. Over the years, his argument has met with much skepticism by scholars who have documented many differences among the works of these theorists, especially Durkheim and Weber. For Parsons's purpose, however, convergence meant principally that the four theorists had agreed that social scientific frames of reference must include normative elements as well as means, ends, and conditions.

Despite the controversies over convergence, Parsons's treatments of all four figures became touchstones for critical evaluations of theoretical works in the social sciences. More than sixty years later, they remain key starting points for critical assessments of the theorists addressed. Due to their rigor, the treatments of Weber and Durkheim remain especially influential, even though a great deal more is now known about the biographies, connections to other scholars, and practical-ideological outlooks of all four figures. Down to the 1960s, *SSA* was the most influential single work in defining the core of the sociological tradition. Yet its aims were concerned less with assessing the writings of other scholars than with establishing the elementary and universal importance of the action frame of reference as a foundation for sociological understanding.

As compared with earlier American theories, Parsons's framework was distinctive in the extent of its emphasis on normative phenomena. Parsons argued that normative elements are necessary for any ongoing social relationships to maintain a degree of social order. In so far as the events of social life exhibit institutional continuity or coherence, the workings of normative elements, e.g. social values (ideals for relationships and institutions) and norms (rules of conduct), are necessary objects of sociological study. The normative components of a social system can be shared by its many participants, and accordingly their goals, and the means they select to pursue their goals, can be regulated by the same standards of conduct. Values and norms constrain or limit actors in their choices of ends or means, and hence are *regulative* in a manner not true of ends or means. Actors who share normative standards are able to develop reciprocal expectations of one another. Concrete expectations often differ according to specialized social roles, but actors in different roles and pursuing different ends may yet agree on the expectations appropriate to each of the parties engaged in common relationships. By focusing on the shared elements of normative order and common grounds of expectation, Parsons was able to analyze the *integration* of social action in a way that is not possible for utilitarian theorists, behaviorists, or other positivists whose theories focus on ends, means, and/or situational conditions as determinants of human behavior.

The methodological foundations of *SSA* are important not only for understanding that work, but because with little change they shaped Parsons's later work as well. Parsons's methodological ideas had sources going back to his early studies of Kant (Bershady, 1973), but were influenced by two senior scholars at Harvard in the 1930s: L. J. Henderson and A. N. Whitehead, a philosopher whose *Science and the Modern World* and *Process and Reality* impressed Parsons (Lidz, in Klausner and Lidz, 1986, chapter 6). For Parsons, Henderson's "approximate definition of fact" as "an empirically verifiable statement about experience" (Parsons often Kantianized the definition by saying "phenomena") "in terms of a conceptual scheme" made an essential point. A fact does not inhere in a phenomenon itself. An event or phenomenon cannot, as Parsons often said, "speak for itself." A fact is a *statement* about a phenomenon. It must be formulated by a person who conceptualizes his or her cognition of the event or phenomenon. Stable statements of facts are not possible without a well ordered conceptual element. To generate and organize many facts about complex events, a carefully framed scheme of concepts is required.

Whitehead emphasized that all elements of scientific knowledge are, by logical necessity, abstract in some degree. He called the empiricist failure to recognize elements of abstraction in all kinds of scientific constructs, even direct statements of fact, the "fallacy of misplaced concreteness." In his view, the relations of scientific knowledge to empirical reality cannot be understood with precision unless the underlying abstractions are clear. He used the term frames of reference to designate the carefully designed modes of abstraction that have guided the most important innovations in science. In *Science and the Modern World* (1925), he demonstrated that the crucial contributions of Galileo, Newton, Lavoisier, Darwin, and others (what we now call the great scientific revolutions) depended on revisions in basic frames of reference. This perspective is in a sense the keystone in the arch of *SSA*'s argument. Parsons was setting out to create a scientific revolution. He sought to establish the frame of reference that would enable sociology to extend and deepen its understanding of social facts. All his major writings are efforts to develop, elaborate, and clarify a central frame of reference for sociology and related disciplines.

## After *The Structure of Social Action*

As Parsons completed *SSA*, he followed the advice of senior colleagues that his next project should be empirical and planned a participant-observer study of medical practice. His underlying interest was in the professional type of role relations. With the debates of the Great Depression years over economic systems as background, Parsons suggested that professional role-relationships are structured in a way that falls between the principle of self-interest in capitalism and the principle of collective interest in socialism (Parsons, 1949, chapter VIII). The professional is expected to act in the interest of the client rather than out of self-interest. Pay for professional services is limited by ethical standards, and was then often modified on a "sliding scale" by what clients could afford, not set at whatever price an openly competitive market would bear. (Today, health insurance rather than the practitioner's sliding scale protects most patients from overwhelming medical costs.) Parsons in fact spent substantial time over more than a year observing several medical practitioners in their work at Harvard Medical School hospitals. As became typical of his later empirical studies, however, the main results were empirically informed theoretical essays. His interests encompassed resolution of theoretical problems with practical and empirical implications, but did not extend to careful reporting of empirical findings.

In the late 1930s, Parsons became a leader among Harvard faculty who organized public opposition to Nazism in Germany and *Bund* activities in America (Gerhardt, 1993). He outspokenly opposed Nazi violations of academic freedom in the German universities and their attacks on many elements of German high culture. Later, he was active in opposing German militarism and expansionism, and became an early proponent of support for Great Britain and preparing the USA for war. His opposition to Nazism remained free of anti-Germanism, however, and he continued in the 1930s and 1940s to acknowledge his intellectual debt to the Kantian and liberal traditions of German culture. During the war years, he wrote a series of notable papers on the causes of Nazism in nineteenth- and twentieth-century German social structure (in Gerhardt, 1993).

Too old for military service during the Second World War, Parsons remained at Harvard, teaching and continuing his research. From 1943 to the end of the war, he taught in a Harvard program to prepare military, intelligence, and diplomatic officers to operate governments in occupied territories, including Germany and Japan. He also consulted with government agencies about matters of wartime policy, but did not become deeply engaged in the war effort as did some of his close Harvard associates. After the war, Parsons worked to promote permanent government funding for the social sciences. The Social Sciences Research Council asked him to prepare a document for use in lobbying Congress to include the social sciences in the mandate of the National Science Foundation. The model was to be the report prepared by Vannevar Bush that had persuaded the Truman administration and the Congress that the nation should continue the public investments in science that had been initiated during the war. Parsons's knowledge, interests, and professional connections seemed to make him an ideal advocate for the social sciences, but his report (in Klausner and Lidz, 1986, chapter 2) was too long, too theoretical, and too turgid for use in lobbying. Viewed as an academic report, however, it discussed an extraordinary range of the applied social science that had been conducted as part of the war effort and outlined many imaginative suggestions about how further development of the same social science techniques would benefit the nation in peacetime.

During the postwar period, Parsons became increasingly active in the American Sociological Association (then the Society). He attended meetings, served on committees, and on several occasions gave well attended and influential talks. In 1949–50, he served as President and later as Secretary. Giving particular attention to opportunities to promote sociological research, he sought out government and foundation support, including for large-scale data collection and archiving of kinds he did not personally do. Developing networks of communication with scholars in Europe, Asia, and elsewhere was another longstanding professional priority. With the first warming of the Cold War in the mid-1960s, he cultivated ties with Soviet, Hungarian, Czechoslovak, and Polish social scientists. He was pleased to learn that informal translations of chapters of *The Social System* circulated underground in the Soviet Union, where means of duplicating texts were strictly controlled.

During the Cold War years, Parsons served on the board of Harvard's Russian Research Center (RRC). He took part in the Harvard administration's early discussions with the Carnegie Foundation and the Department of State to plan the RRC and was later involved in decisions about its initial staffing. At the start, the RRC was directed by Kluckhohn on the basis of his wartime experience in studying closed societies at a distance. Parsons was strongly committed to the idea that, under Cold War conditions, the USA sorely needed more scholarly knowledge of the Soviet Union. He remained on the RRC board until the mid-1960s when his wife, Helen, retired from her long-term role as administrative assistant to the Director.

Parsons's major organizational venture in the postwar period was establishing Harvard's interdisciplinary Department of Social Relations (Nichols, 1998). The department originated in a collaboration among Clyde Kluckhohn in anthropology, Henry A. Murray and Gordon Allport in psychology, and Parsons in sociology. The myth of the department's founding is that each of the principals was hated by his chairman (Sorokin in Parsons's case) and believed his professional advancement was being improperly blocked. Founding a new department was a political coup that created new opportunities for each, especially Parsons, who became the first chairman. (But in fact Parsons had succeeded Sorokin as chair of sociology in 1944.) All of sociology moved into the new department along with the social and cultural anthropologists and the clinical and social psychologists. A curriculum was developed that combined training in each of the several disciplines with interdisciplinary proseminars and requirements that each student take courses in at least one field outside his or her own discipline. Although the department's founding myth captured some truth of the academic politics, the formation of the department was part of a broader interdisciplinary trend in that period. Talented students flocked to the new department and the special opportunities it offered. For more than a decade, the new curriculum was taught with élan and accepted by most students with enthusiasm. The later work of such early social relations students as James Olds, Renee Fox, Robert Bellah, Clifford Geertz, and Neil Smelser shows that the interdisciplinary curriculum had important and enduring effects. Due largely to Parsons's commitment, the benefits were more consistent among sociologists than among anthropologists and particularly psychologists.

## *Toward a General Theory of Action* and *The Social System*

Just as the founding of the Sociology Department had enabled Parsons to write *SSA*, the founding of the Department of Social Relations initiated the period of Parsons's greatest and most self-confident creativity. The new department convened a faculty seminar (including as Visiting Professors Edward A. Shils from the University of Chicago and the psychologist Edward Tolman from the University of California at Berkeley) to develop a manifesto on the importance of interdisciplinary thought to sociology, psychology, and anthropology. The work was published as *Toward a General Theory of Action* (Parsons and Shils, 1951). It included a collaborative statement signed by most of the seminar participants and then their separate contributions. Parsons's contribution, in collaboration with Shils, was a long, dense essay entitled "Values, Motives and the Theory of Action."

This essay presented two cross-cutting dimensions for analyzing differentiation among processes of social action, defined basically in the sense of *SSA*. One dimension pertains to the tendency of ongoing systems of meaningful action to differentiate into three independent but interdependent subsystems: culture, social systems, and personality. This conception of the threefold differentiation of action systems became one of the most famous themes in Parsons's work. The second dimension concerns the differentiation of elements of action into moral-normative, cathectic-affective, and cognitive gradients. The authors argued that cultural, social, and personality systems all differentiate along these three gradients and, indeed, connect with one another independently along each gradient. The conception of this second dimension of differentiation also became a famous theme in Parsons's work. He had used essentially the same triad of concepts, with slightly different terms, in an unpublished working paper prepared in the late 1930s. The earlier document indicates that the triad derived from parallel ideas in Kant, a source not acknowledged in the 1951 publication. The new scheme's emphasis on culture, social system, and personality was widely interpreted as referring, at least approximately, to the domains of anthropology, sociology, and psychology, and thus as legitimating the new department's commitment to interdisciplinary collaboration. The new essay's thorough exploration of the connections between the two dimensions of differentiation produced a far more detailed analytical scheme than Parsons had put forward in *SSA*. The new scheme reached a level of analytical detail that made it more useful for empirical research.

"Values, Motives, and Systems of Action" was quickly followed by *The Social System* (Parsons, 1951), a major work that explored the sociological aspects of the same analytical scheme. Older manuscripts make clear that a work entitled "The Social System" had been in preparation since the early war years. After years of slow progress and dissatisfaction with the results, Parsons rapidly revised and expanded his manuscript after the conceptual scheme of "Values, Motives, and Systems of Action" had crystallized. *The Social System* addressed basic issues of definition and conceptual clarification of the social system and introduced a focused approach to functional analysis of social systems. In chapters that proved highly influential, it discussed processes of socialization and personality development, the classic problems of deviance and social control, and the relations between social systems and cultural belief systems. A particularly successful chapter combined themes from Parsons's earlier observational study of medical practice with his new conception of the social system to discuss the doctor–patient relationship. The resulting discussion became a charter for the early development of medical sociology as a specialty.

The key conceptual-theoretical innovation was a shift in analytical focus from the "unit act" of *SSA* to the "social system." Parsons defined social systems as consisting of interactive *relationships* among individuals. The conceptual framework for sociology was thus based on abstracting the dynamics of interaction from the more comprehensive processes of meaningful human conduct. Sociology became the study of factors of interaction that keep relationships in stable states (equilibria) or force relationships to change. Parsons again identified shared normative standards as a principal basis of stability and continuity in social relationships. However, his normative emphasis was reformulated in more dynamic terms. He now accentuated normative *expectations* that specify general norms (or rules) to particular role relationships and situations of interaction. Individuals who interact hold expectations of one another based on the specific social roles they occupy. Each actor supports his or her expectations of others by using a variety of tactics to sanction the others. The sanctioning tactics may include offering rewards for compliance with expectations and threatening, or actually imposing, punishments for noncompliance. Actual sequences of interaction are outcomes of the expectations and sanctions introduced by each party. Parsons noted that a "double contingency" applies to even the most elementary relationships because decision-making by each party is independent.

One feature of Parsons's conception of social systems runs sharply counter to common intuition. In Parsons's definition, the personalities of individual social actors are not parts of social systems or even societies as large-scale social systems. Rather, personalities are outside social systems because they constitute another class of system of action. Parsons therefore took up the question of how social systems and personality systems relate to one another in the ongoing processes of social action. With his characteristic emphasis on normative elements, he focused on a linkage between the institutional norms of a society and the superegos of individual personalities. He argued that the normative structures of a society and the superegos of its individual actors constitute the *same* moral-normative cultural content, but differently incorporated in the two kinds of system. The normative content is internalized in personalities and institutionalized in social systems. This formulation opened up a way of understanding the relationships between 'social structure' and 'personality' by incorporating dynamic ideas from psychology and psychoanalysis, as well as sociology. Yet it avoided the strong temptation to confound social dynamics with personality dynamics. This was a temptation to which many other theorists, from Malinowksi to Erich Fromm to Abraham Kardiner to Theodor Adorno, had succumbed in one respect or another. Parsons also highlighted a theme of the "institutional integration of motivation," stating that the motivational systems of individual personalities can be coherent and directed to specific goals only in so far as they are supported by social institutions and relationships. Reciprocally, social institutions require concertedly motivated individuals if the responsibilities associated with their constituent social roles are to be fulfilled.

*The Social System* also introduced new formulations in functional analysis. Parsons hypothesized that all social systems, whether mere dyads or entire societies, must manage problems of resource allocation and social integration. Resource allocation involves processes to ensure that role incumbents can command the means necessary to attain expected ends. The nature of the resources in question varies immensely by the type of social relationship in question. Particular kinds of tools, personnel trained in special skills, and financial means are frequently crucial types of resources. Economic markets are the most efficient mechanisms for allocating resources in response to the diverse needs of many units of a society. The need for integration is in the long run as urgent for social systems as the need for resources. Mechanisms of social control are needed to ensure that actors respond to one another's expectations and fulfill role obligations in reciprocal, mutually reinforcing ways. Large-scale social systems require formal methods of social control and dispute resolution, such as courts, legal procedure, and mechanisms of law enforcement. Parsons recognized that processes of resource allocation and processes of social integration often operate in tension or conflict with each other. Resource allocations that support efficiency in the early stages of industrialization, for example, may engender conflicts among social classes that threaten integration of the society. In many societies, the solidarity of traditional family and kin groups has required distribution of financial resources that disperses business capital and undermines family-based enterprise.

Both "Values, Motives, and Systems of Action" and *The Social System* addressed problems of classifying components of action systems, whether motivational patterns of personalities, social relationships, or cultural beliefs. Parsons had long been unsatisfied with the global terms used by sociologists to classify relationships and institutions, especially Ferdinand Toennies's famous contrast between *Gemeinschaft* (person-to-person community) and *Gesellschaft* (impersonal society). He therefore proposed a multidimensional scheme for classifying relationships, which he termed the pattern variables or, occasionally, pattern alternatives. Five dichotomous pattern variables were presented. Two of the variables define choices in actors' orientations to objects in a situation of action. The first is affectivity versus affective neutrality, and defines whether an actor will seek direct gratification or adopt a moral or instrumental stance of renunciation toward the object. The second is self-orientation versus collectivity-orientation, and defines whether the actor pursues his or her personal ends or the ends of a collectivity (e.g. a sports team, research group, or nation) in relating to objects. The third pattern variable is universalism versus particularism, and defines the kind of value-standard to be engaged in the situation. A universalistic standard evaluates an open set of objects in terms of the same criteria, as when a teacher uses the same criteria to grade all students in a class. A particularistic standard invokes different criteria for each kind of relationship between actor and object, e.g. father–son, fellow citizen of a home town (versus an outsider). The fourth and fifth pattern variables concern modalities or characteristics of objects that an actor selects as significant for his conduct in a situation. The fourth pattern variable is ascription versus achievement (later stated as quality versus performance), and defines whether the object is significant for what or who it is or for what it does or can do. A person who obtains a job as a member of the employing family gets it by ascription, while a person who obtains it by prior training gets it by achievement. The fifth pattern variable is specificity versus diffuseness, and defines the scope of the object's significance for the actor. Does an actor relate to another only as a fellow employee, for example, or also as a close friend or family member whose overall well-being is of concern?

All five pattern variables were presented as phenomenological dichotomies. At a given choice-point in a process of action, one term in a pattern variable must be chosen and the other rejected. Together, the five pattern variables were claimed to provide an exhaustive definition of basic alternatives for social action. Few critics have agreed with this claim, although most have agreed that the pattern variables capture basic options facing social actors. As a set, the pattern variables offer a conceptually powerful and elegant alternative to the *Gemeinschaft–Gesellschaft* dichotomy. The combination of affectivity, collectivity-orientation, particularism, ascription, and diffuseness is a multidimensional characterization of *Gemeinschaft*, while the combination of affective neutrality, self-orientation, universalism, achievement, and specificity is a multidimensional characterization of *Gesellschaft*. Parsons, however, noted the importance of various other pattern variable combinations as well. He argued that a number of combinations are helpful in characterizing the functional significance of various institutions within larger systems. The pattern variables have been used in many studies in sociology and political science, and the results confirm their ability to discriminate types of functional significance.

At publication, Parsons presented *The Social System* as an authoritative and carefully considered successor to SSA. In fact, it was creative and filled with suggestive leads for further investigation, but many of its formulations were still provisional. Only months after it appeared, Parsons started work on a new foundation for functional theory, which he called the "four function paradigm." He then used the new functional concepts to reorganize practically the entire theory of social action. Because of the status attributed to *The Social System*, however, many sociologists who had been interested in his earlier work failed to follow the subsequent evolution of his theory. Many sociologists who did encounter parts of his later writing failed to grasp their significance because they continued to rely on *The Social System* for an overview of his theory. When telling critiques of *The Social System* were published, often focusing on its weak chapter on social change, its brilliant but flawed discussion of deviance and social control, or its inadequate presentation of functional analysis, the profession at large was not aware that Parsons's thought had already moved far beyond the criticized formulations.

## The emergence of the four function paradigm

After writing *The Social System*, Parsons's major interest was to refine the concept of *function* in social systems. Building on the notions of allocation and integration, he strove to develop an abstract, generalized, and multidimensional scheme to address basic issues of how social systems are organized. His effort began to bear fruit with *Working Papers in the Theory of Action* (Parsons et al., 1953), which introduced the so-called four function paradigm.

The four function scheme originated in Parsons's collaboration with Robert F. Bales. Bales had conducted laboratory studies of interaction in small groups assigned specific tasks for discussion. To examine issues of leadership, authority, conflict, maintenance of task-focus, and group solidarity, Bales had devised a scheme of sixteen categories to describe types of contribution to group process. He had shown that he could observe groups, record the predominant category of contribution made by each act of a group member, and later analyze the shifting emphases, or "phase movements", among the sixteen categories of group inter-action (Bales, 1950). Bales argued that over time phase movements enable the interaction of group members to address various "needs" of task-oriented groups, e.g. the need for clear coordination to attain specific goals or the need for mutual positive feeling among members. Working together, Parsons and Bales grouped the sixteen categories of interaction process into four more gen-eral categories that appeared to represent fundamental "needs" of the groups.

In their initial formulation, the four 'functional' categories are stated as results of empirical generalization about the needs of groups. They are presented basically as an outcome of empirical studies of a particular kind of group. The four categories were said to demarcate the dimensions of social "space" within which "phase movements" occur. They were designated 'functions' because the phase movements were believed to respond to enduring needs of groups.

A bolder formulation emerged later in *The Working Papers*: namely, that any and every social system needs to handle the same four general "system problems" in order to function. Parsons and colleagues argued that social relationships and institutions – or, more precisely, *aspects* of them – can be classified by how they contribute to managing one or more of the four "system problems." Parsons soon referred to the system problems as "functions." By the 1960s, the notion of function was presented less as a system problem than as an abstract *dimension* of social organization. The resulting "four function paradigm" became an explicit or implicit theoretical frame for practically everything Parsons wrote after the mid-1950s. With the four function paradigm, he approached more closely the goal set early in his career of developing an abstract, formal, and universal ground for sociological analysis and explanation.

The four system problems or functions are:

- *Adaptation*, the processes of gaining generalized control over conditions in the environment of the action system. Often, these processes involve generating new resources or allocating available resources more efficiently among units of the system in order to gain new capabilities for future action.

- *Goal attainment*, the processes of organizing the activities of social units into a concerted effort to achieve a desired change in the system's relationship to its environment. Other collectivities or societies may be principal factors in the environment and predominating over their interests may be a chief goal.
- *Integration*, the processes of adjustment to one another by units of the system. The processes may promote long-term attachment to the system and/or mutual dependence among autonomous units.
- *Pattern maintenance*, the processes of generating long-term commitment to shared values and other principles of action that distinguish the system of reference from other systems.

Particular processes of action may be located on all four dimensions, but generally they are able to specialize on any one dimension only at the expense of capabilities on the other three dimensions. Moreover, strength on one dimension during one phase of action typically requires an ongoing system to develop compensatory strengths on other dimensions during later phases. A system that emphasizes adaptation in one phase might generate strains that require greater emphasis on the integrative dimension soon afterward.

Because the four function paradigm was so abstract, many years of work were needed before Parsons's earlier formulations could be thoroughly assimilated to it. It can be argued that Parsons never completed this task despite a great deal of recasting of earlier ideas. However, the strengths and attractions of the four function paradigm were fundamental. Early "functionalist" theories, including formulations in *The Social System*, were open to the basic criticism that the number of functions was indefinite and empirical analyses often resulted in hypotheses about new functions. Early functional analysis therefore had an *ad hoc* quality that reduced its appeal as a strategy for theory construction. By contrast, the theory of four system problems constituted a definite and *a priori* list of basic functions. The four function paradigm also led to interesting hypotheses about patterns of organization that obtain among social institutions differentiated in terms of function. These hypotheses were gradually clarified as Parsons applied the paradigm to wider ranges of empirical materials.

In the last chapter, the *Working Papers* tentatively proposed that the four functions might be used to represent major dimensions of structural differentiation in society as a whole. This speculative idea forecast much of Parsons's theoretical work over the next two decades. Through that work, a theory of four functionally specialized *subsystems* of society gradually took shape. Each of the four subsystems was treated as a complex set of dynamically interdependent institutions that could in turn be analyzed along the same four functional dimensions. The new theory of societal subsystems (and *sub*subsystems) presented an approach to macrosocial analysis that, although never completely worked out, remains even today more comprehensive and analytically incisive than any alternative scheme.

In outline, the four subsystems of society, as they came to be identified, are:

- The *economy* is the subsystem specialized about the development and allocation of basic resources for use by individuals and collective units of the society. It consists of such institutions as markets for labor and capital, entrepreneurial roles, the legal complexes of property, contract, credit, and employment, and the organizational structure of business firms.
- The *polity* is the subsystem of society specialized about coordination of the pursuit of collective goals. Governmental agencies at all levels, including the administrative, executive, legislative, and judicial arms of public authority, are the primary institutional components of the polity, although Parsons also emphasized various nonpublic organizations and the role of the citizen.
- The *societal community* is the subsystem specialized about the integration of society. Social classes, status groups, ethnic groups, groups that share elements of 'lifestyle', and other groups that maintain diffuse and enduring ties of solidarity contribute to a society's manner of social integration. The dynamically interrelated phenomena of integration and conflict are shaped largely by institutions of class structure, status order, and 'primordial' solidary ties, but also by common law and the informal normative orders of custom or community mores.
- The *fiduciary system* is the subsystem specialized about the transmission (or reproduction), maintenance, and development of a society's enduring values and shared culture. The institutions of religion, family and kinship, and socialization and education are major constituents of the fiduciary system. Following the lead of Max Weber, Parsons emphasized that change in fiduciary systems, notably in religious ethics, have historically been the greatest forces toward long-term and large-scale social change.

The theory of societal subsystems retained Parsons's earlier emphasis on normative order. However, it achieved a new level of analysis of the forms that normative structures assume and the functions they serve in different institutional settings, such as economic exchange, relationships of political authority, solidarity ties among members of a status group, or processes of socialization in family life. Parsons thus opened up a new approach to analyzing modes of articulation between normative orders and practical institutions of societal functioning, e.g. economic markets, political bureaucracies, class structures, or families. His new synthesis transcended in principle (not always in specific empirical discussions) the nineteenth-century dichotomies between normative and interest-driven or ideal and material factors in social causation. Parsons argued that *every* effective social institution embodies an *integration* of normative and interest-driven, ideal and material factors. To be sure, the two dimensions can under practical circumstances be stripped from each other. Relationships must then be formed on either ideal or contrary material grounds, and the pursuit of self-interest may become possible *only* through violation of normative rules. Such situations typically arise during periods of rapid social change and frequent conflict. However, the effective long-term functioning of social institutions depends on a normative regulation of material, interest-driven factors. Under such conditions, the pursuit of self-interest reinforces the controlling normative institutions, as when the ordinary conduct of business requires reliance upon the institutions of property, contract, and employment.

## The Marshall Lectures and Economy and Society

Parsons spent the academic year of 1953–4 at the University of Cambridge in England, where he was invited to deliver the first Marshall Lectures. He knew when he accepted a visiting professorship that Cambridge had not yet made a place for sociology on its faculty, but was considering whether to do so. The social science faculty was dominated by a strong group of economists and economic historians who were skeptical of sociology. Parsons hoped to advance its cause at Cambridge by demonstrating in a new way that the discipline could make significant contributions to economic understanding. The core of this demonstration was to use the four function scheme of the subsystems of society to analyze the relations between economic institutions and other major institutional structures of society.

The Marshall Lectures (Parsons, 1986) started with the idea that Keynes's treatment of the twofold exchange between the aggregate of business firms and the aggregate of households (wages for labor; goods and services for consumer spending) could be treated as a boundary relation between the adaptive and pattern maintenance subsystems of society. Parsons then suggested that each of the four classic factors of economic production, labor, capital, organization, and land, could be treated as an input to the economy from an extra-economic source. Just as labor (meaning a trained and socialized capability to perform economically valuable work) was an input from the pattern maintenance system, so capital (the financial means of controlling and allocating "real" economic resources) was an input from the polity, and organization (the capability to develop innovative relations of production) was an input from the system of social integration. All three of these factors – not only labor – entered the economy through twofold exchange relationships, which Parsons began to call "double interchanges." When viewed in disaggregation, the double interchanges were clearly mediated by complicated, highly differentiated markets. The factor of land Parsons treated as a special case. He used the term "land" to refer to the commitment of resources to economic production rather than to other possible uses, e.g. political or cultural. Land thus represented a factor generated through the specification of general cultural values to the legitimation of economic institutions, activities, and use of resources.

A related conceptual innovation in the Marshall Lectures was to use the four function theory to analyze the economy itself into subsystems (and later *sub*-subsystems). Parsons aligned the double interchanges with the resulting scheme of subsystems of the economy: the labor for wages, goods and services for consumer spending interchange was treated as the boundary relationship of the economy's goal attainment subsystem; the interchanges centering on capital markets were identified as the boundary relationship of the adaptive subsystem; the input of the factor of organization was placed at the economy's integrative subsystem; and markets involving "land" were treated as part of the economy's pattern maintenance function.

An implication of Parsons's treatment of the economy's boundary relationships is that the four subsystems of society are joined together through six double interchanges, each of which is a dynamic mechanism enabling two subsystems to adjust to each other's ongoing operational needs. In addition, each subsystem is regulated internally by a factor that, like "land" in the economy, represents the commitment of resources to a broad type of social process. In sum, by combining the four function theory with the theory of double interchanges, Parsons had developed a model for analyzing the ways in which functionally differentiated institutions adjust to one another's changing operations and requirements. Parsons later suggested that the general equilibrium of a society could be analyzed in these terms. This vision of how social process might be analyzed in relation to institutional structure guided a great deal of Parsons's later work.

While writing the Marshall Lectures, Parsons began a correspondence on many of the key ideas with Neil J. Smelser. Smelser had studied with Parsons as an undergraduate and was then taking courses in economics at Oxford. He was able to relate many of Parsons's Marshallian formulations to then current trends of Keynesian economics. When Smelser returned to Harvard for graduate studies, he collaborated with Parsons in expanding the Marshall Lectures into *Economy and Society* (Parsons and Smelser, 1956). *Economy and Society* achieved greater analytical detail in its use of the four function and double interchange schemes than any of Parsons's other works. It discussed the specific institutions that regulate each kind of market involved in the many boundary processes of the economy and its subsystems. *Economy and Society* thus presents the most thorough demonstration of Parsons's emphasis on the institutional regulation of social process. Smelser (1959) later examined the historical conflicts involved in the growth of the double interchange relationship between businesses and households in eighteenth- and nineteenth-century England.

## Family and socialization

While working on *Economy and Society*, Parsons also continued to collaborate with Bales. *Family, Socialization and Interaction Process* (Parsons and Bales, 1955) discussed the American middle-class family of the postwar era as a social institution. It emphasized the emergence of the "nuclear" family made up of husband, wife, and children as the typical household unit, and as autonomous from extended kinship units in terms of organization and budget. It examined role structures within the family, noting the importance of both gender and generational axes of role differentiation. The core of the book analyzed the structure of the parent–child role relationship as it evolves during the lengthy process of socialization of children. Socialization was presented as a multistaged, highly dynamic process of engaging children in more inclusive social relationships, starting with the mother–baby dyad, then progressing to inclusion of the father, then perhaps other children, then relatives, peers, and eventually others in the local community, and beyond. At the same time, children engage these relationships increasingly at the level of symbolic communication and in terms of affective investment as well as bodily drives and needs. Parental control of the process (the generational axis of role differentiation) is essential to children's internalization of moral-normative standards of conduct as an integral part of their growing reliance on symbolic communication. Parsons argued that parental control requires maintaining a mutually supportive coalition between mother and father and consistency in normative standards when interacting with children.

*Family*... is the most thoroughly developed of Parsons's contributions to the integration of sociological and psychodynamic theory. The work addresses, perhaps more insightfully than any recent study, the profoundly affectual and emotional make-up of relationships in the modern nuclear family, with an erotically based love relationship between parents, the non-erotic love of parents for children, and the love of children for parents that gradually transcends childhood eroticism in favor of more stable affective ties. The emotional intensity of familial relationships often places them under great stress and leaves them highly vulnerable if normative discipline is transgressed or compromised. The family is also portrayed in thoroughly dynamic terms, with emphasis on the rapid change in its role-relationships as children mature, parents grow older, and relations evolve with such entities as business firms, schools, and voluntary associations in the broader community. As a consequence of this broad analysis, Parsons and Bales viewed contemporary American family relationships as highly susceptible to failure, both in terms of divorce and in terms of disturbances in the socialization of children. Their discussion included a number of hypotheses about how disturbed relationships between parents and children might result in emotional illness for the children. *Family*..., along with sections of *The Social System* and his collection of papers, *Social Structure and Personality* (1964), show that Parsons was also among the most creative psychoanalytic theorists of the 1950s and 1960s.

Parsons has been criticized by feminists for his treatment of gender differentiation in the role structure of the family. There is little doubt that he reified the gender roles of the 1950s and did not anticipate later changes. But it should be remembered that when he wrote gender relations were very different from those of today. He did not have the intent of restricting women's roles that his discussion might imply today. His characterization of the emotional and dynamic qualities of family life should not be rejected along with his reification of older gender relationships. As Miriam M. Johnson (1988) has argued, his abstract notion of differentiation in gender roles and in gender-related styles of interaction continues to hold importance for studies of family and gender.

## American society

From the early 1950s, Parsons held the ambition of writing a work on American society that would combine four function macrosocial analysis with an overview of current social scientific knowledge and an interpretation of the society's principal features. In the late 1950s, he wrote several lengthy working papers to try out his ideas. In 1960, he invited Winston White, a student who had just finished his doctorate and whose main interest was the interpretation of American society, to collaborate. Together, Parsons and White drafted several chapters, then reorganized their chapter outline and wrote seven or eight new chapters totaling over six hundred pages. At that point, White left the profession of sociology and Parsons set the project aside. The result has been to leave a large gap in the record of his developing thought.

With the emergence of the four function theory, Parsons had sharpened a theme in his writing that predated even *SSA*. This theme, rooted in Max Weber's comparative studies of civilization, is that shared value orientations are a controlling factor among the many elements that make up institutional orders. Parsons had proposed that social structures can be analyzed into four kinds of elements, values (ideals), norms (rules), collectivities, and roles, that respectively serve pattern maintenance, integrative, goal attainment, and adaptive functions. He also suggested that these elements of structure form what he called a cybernetic hierarchy, a concept he derived from Norbert Wiener (1948). For Wiener, a cybernetic relation involves a well designed regulator controlling or guiding a more powerful mechanism, as when a thermostat controls a furnace or a steering wheel guides a car. Parsons noted that Freud made the same point in comparing the ego's relation to the id with the rider's relation to the horse. Yet Freud had noted that riders can lose control and the horse can become a runaway. Control relationships can break down and the more forceful mechanism can run free, but at the cost of losing guidance. What Parsons proposed is that the relationships among values, norms, collectivities, and roles (or among ideals, practical interests, and material conditions) constitute a series of cybernetic relationships, though ones in which control may be placed at risk under conditions of stress.

The manuscripts on American society emphasize the importance of a value system as a set of cybernetic controls guiding the long-term evolution and general characteristics of a society. Parsons had pronounced his emphasis on values in a number of essays, but had left it to his book on American society to argue the claim in detail. The draft materials address this issue far more thoroughly than any of his published writings. In particular, they spell out the concept of a value system in greater detail. Parsons had in mind a complex system of many factors, themselves hierarchically organized. They extend from abstract religious premises, to religious ethics in Weber's sense, to generalized secular moral beliefs (in American culture, the "law of nature" and "universal human rights"), to ideals of social organization, to more specific values that legitimate the "land" factors in the economy and similar complexes in the other subsystems of society. Parsons argued that the most general elements of a value system tend to be highly stable even over centuries of social change, whereas the more specific elements change under the pressures of social movements or advances in institutional differentiation.

The manuscript portrayed a unity of American values that derives from generalized religious premises he characterized as "instrumental activism." These premises were rooted in the Puritan heritage of early colonial settlers.

Instrumental activism is the belief that everything in the human condition should be mastered by human will and energies and perfected to the extent possible. Its religious dimension is the effort to build "the kingdom of God on earth." But many secular strivings derive their meaning from the same premises of mastery. Athletes who train prodigiously, scholars who study intensely, and entrepreneurs who methodically cultivate their creditworthiness may all be responding to instrumental activism's mandate for self-perfection. At the level of collectivities, business firms, universities, and voluntary associations may all follow the same ideals of mastery and progressive perfection, yet be active in different domains of society and guided by different specific values of achievement. In this manner, Parsons accounted for functional, social class, ethnic, and regional variation in specific value orientations, while also arguing that American society showed a strong consensus around underlying principles of instrumental activism, and had done so since early in its history.

## The polity, power, and symbolic media of interchange

After publishing *Economy and Society*, Parsons wrote a number of essays in the late 1950s and early 1960s that together conceptualize the political subsystem of society (or polity) in terms parallel to his four function analysis of the economy. A notable essay (Parsons, 1969, chapter 9) reinterpreted the findings of then recent survey research on voters and the electoral system in terms of a double interchange between the polity and the integrative subsystem of society. A later essay (Parsons, 1969, chapter 13) presented a four function analysis of the primary subsystems of the polity. The most important essay, "On the Concept of Political Power" (Parsons, 1969, chapter 14), gave a stronger formulation of the double interchange between the polity and the integrative subsystem, presented a radically new concept of power, and opened a new dimension to Parsons's treatment of social process. The essay argued that public politics in modern democracies involve interchanges of both factors of further process and products of process between the polity and the integrative subsystem. The polity receives the factor of "interest demands," or expressions of opinion about needed changes in public policy, from the organized citizenry as a sector of the integrative system. The integrative system receives "policy decisions" as a factor for adjusting the lives of citizens to changing social circumstances. The polity also receives "political support" in the form of votes that, as aggregated under the electoral laws, determine holders of office in a formally binding way. The integrative system then receives "leadership responsibility" as assurance that the well-being of the citizenry will be addressed through political process.

This double interchange shares certain characteristics with the double interchange between business firms and households. As an equilibrium process, it contains significant capabilities to absorb and adjust to social change. It also has capabilities for growth and expansion, as when new types of interest-demands enter the political arena and become sources of more effective political action. Parsons suggested that a well ordered polity is capable of long-term expansion similar to the growth of modern economies. Expansion should benefit the citizenry through increased levels of attainment of the society's collective goals. However, Parsons also noted that polities can experience contractions that reduce the level of effective political activity and harm the collective well-being. He suggested that contractions in public trust can restrict the scope of interest-demands acceptable in the polity and/or of leadership responsibility acceptable among the citizenry, thus precipitating a sort of political depression. He cited McCarthyism as an example of a deflationary force in American politics of the 1950s.

In demonstrating the possibilities for political expansion and contraction, Parsons raised the question of whether political life involves a mediator of process similar to money's role in the general equilibrium of the economy. Keynes had shown imbalances in the circulation of money as wages and as consumer spending to be sources of depression. Parsons hypothesized that political process must have an analogue of money. He therefore proposed that power is a circulating medium for political relationships and a measure of political efficacy, much as money is both a medium of economic exchange and a measure of economic value. If power is viewed as a capacity to make formally binding decisions on behalf of a collectivity, it can be seen as something expended with every political decision, just as money is expended with every purchase. In expending power, officials must anticipate ways of gaining renewed power. Parsons argued that binding decisions issued by public authorities amount to a form of calculated investment designed to attract new power through future electoral support.

The new conception of power departed from ideas long established in political science. In the conventional view, an authority exercises power *over* others and often as means of frustrating their pursuit of individual goals. Power relationships are regarded as zero-sum, such that power of one person is held at the expense of others. Power has also typically been portrayed as a diffuse resource, as in the idea that *any* means of attaining ends over the wishes of others is power. Parsons noted that figures from Machiavelli to Weber to a number of influential contemporaries favored the conventional view. He argued, however, that power is a *specialized* resource that enables duly authorized officers to make binding decisions on behalf of a collectivity, whether the nation, a state, a city, or a private agency or firm. The binding quality of power distinguishes it from other means of pursuing ends, such as expenditures of money or personal influence. Parsons acknowledged that power can be exercised *over* others, as in a binding court decision or military order, but also noted that it is often used impersonally and in some circumstances becomes binding only by aggregation, as when the votes of a majority elect an official. He also argued that power, when properly regulated, can serve the public benefit and bring advantages, including greater power, to the citizenry as well as public officials. Power should not be viewed as intrinsically zero-sum, but as zero-sum only in certain limited circumstances, such as political competition. Finally, Parsons suggested that power, like circulating currency, is a symbolic entity. Previous literature had linked power closely with force, but Parsons argued that actors generally resort to force when their power has been challenged and their ability to command is uncertain (Parsons,

1967, chapter 9). Power is a quality of commands that renders them duly authorized and likely to be obeyed. It is linked to the situated procedures through which it is issued, and its symbolism, as in the forms of court orders, military commands, or legislative enactments, is intrinsic to its efficacy. In this respect, it is like legitimate currency, which derives its value from its precise printed form and the situations of its use.

Parsons's conception of power as a circulating medium overturns a number of long respected but empirically limited preconceptions. It also led him to the more general insight that money is not the only circulating symbolic medium, but one of a class of media. He soon argued that each of the primary subsystems of society must have its own circulating medium. An essay on influence soon followed (Parsons, 1969, chapter 15), treating it as the capacity to persuade and as the circulating medium of the integrative system. Although unsatisfactory in certain respects, the essay capitalized on the body of research on personal influence and reference group relationships by Paul Lazarsfeld, Robert K. Merton, and their colleagues. A few years later, Parsons completed his scheme of media circulating in society with an essay on value-commitments as the medium of the fiduciary system (Parsons, 1969, chapter 16). Although this essay is persuasive in its general argument, it lacked significant bodies of previous empirical research to build upon and accomplished less than the essays on power and influence in guiding future research.

A source of confusion about Parsons's writings on power, influence, and value commitments has been that these media obviously do not circulate in definite quantities in the manner of money. We each have money in our wallets and bank accounts, and can calculate precise quantities of our money, even if its real purchasing power changes over time. Goods and services we buy have definite prices or quantities of money needed for their purchase. Power, influence, and value commitments do not share this precise quantitative form. Public policies are not promulgated by expending specific amounts of "power chits," nor are there definite "power prices" for resolving particular policy issues on behalf of the public. But we do commonly view power, influence, and commitments in quantitative terms. We speak of high officials as exercising a great deal of power, of leaders in a profession as highly influential, or of a person who has taken on too many responsibilities as overcommitted. We understand that systems of authority are built on methodical allocations of power among officials, and we know that a new office, such as Independent Counsel, can affect an entire structure of powers. We expect high officials to have greater power than their formal subordinates. Parsons also seems correct by common intuition when he argues that a public official who expends power to promulgate a major policy is risking his or her future command of power. If the policy proves successful and popular, the official may acquire greater power, but if it fails, he or she will likely lose power.

Parsons believed that differences in quantitative form are functionally related to the kinds of social resources or capacities that the media represent. While power, influence, and commitments have quantitative aspects, their uses would be compromised if, like money, they circulated in definite quantities. We can understand this point easily with respect to commitments. Commitments circulate in the form of promises to undertake courses of action that others can rely upon in planning their own related activities. However, the amount of effort needed to fulfill a commitment often changes with unanticipated circumstances. An actor may know that he or she has made a large commitment, but not know the extent of the effort that will be required to fulfill it. Yet the commitment would be valueless to others if they could not count upon its fulfillment despite changed circumstances.

## The theory of social evolution

In early 1963, Alex Inkeles, then a departmental colleague, asked Parsons to contribute to a new textbook series. Inkeles suggested that Parsons might update *The Social System* in terms of such ideas as the four function paradigm, the double interchanges, and the societal media. Parsons, however, chose to address materials he had been teaching in his course on comparative institutional analysis. He had radically revised the course two years earlier to emphasize a perspective of social evolution. In the proposed book, he planned to analyze a number of historical societies that differed in institutional complexity and in basic cultural pattern. He also hoped to develop a theory of social change that would place the understanding of societies and institutions on the basis of a universal dynamic, comparable to Darwin's theory of natural selection.

Parsons did not complete the social evolution project until after 1970. By then he had written two books, *Societies: Evolutionary and Comparative Perspectives* (1966) and *The System of Modern Societies* (1971). The first book presented a broad typology of primitive, archaic, historic, and "seed bed" societies. The chapter on so-called primitive (nonliterate) societies drew upon a wide range of anthropological materials on Australian, African, South American, and Asian "tribal" peoples. It discussed the religious, kinship, political, and economic institutions of several societies and clarified the general idea of different levels of institutional complexity among nonliterate societies. However, Parsons's discussion of how simpler societies may have evolved into more complex ones did not successfully integrate theoretical analysis with empirical materials.

Parsons presented the archaic type of society by comparing the Egyptian and Mesopotamian civilizations of antiquity. The type is defined in terms of a number of interdependent criteria: craft literacy, central cults where priests monopolize the rituals and interpretation of religious beliefs and mythology, written codes of law, a class system secured by legally codified discriminations among aristocrats, commoners, and slaves, a central administrative apparatus, consolidation of authority around an institution of kingship, intensive agriculture, storehouses for essential goods, local markets for craft and agricultural produce, and concentration of the non-agricultural population in towns. Egyptian and Mesopotamian civilizations both included all of these elements, yet differed in basic ways. Egyptian society emphasized the pattern maintenance and political functions and assimilated religious and political institutions closely to one another in the cult of the divine pharaoh. By contrast, Mesopotamian societies emphasized adaptive and integrative institutions. They gave greater autonomy to extended household units for agricultural and craft production. Their legal systems were more highly developed, their social class systems more flexible, and trade among city-states was more active. Egypt established one unified society that dominated a largely stable territory over thousands of years. Mesopotamian civilization spawned many independent states, endemic rivalry and warfare, mixing of populations through trade and conquest, and repeated rise and fall of empires.

Parsons's discussion of "historic" civilizations covered the classical Chinese, Indian, Islamic, and Roman Empires. All these civilizations extended over vast domains and included populations of many ethnicities. Their cultural foundations rested on religio-philosophical belief systems with transcendental conceptions of sources of value and legitimation for social institutions. Their class systems included honored status groups for the primary interpreters and proponents of the religio-philosophical traditions. Following Max Weber, Parsons carefully analyzed the social make-up and privileged ways of life of these key status groups. The contrasts between the Confucian literati and mandarins in China and the Brahmin priesthood in the Indian caste system, for example, highlight differences between the two civilizations affecting practically every social institution. The Confucians sought worldly honor by cultivating genteel ways of life, participating in the affairs of the patrimonial state, gaining wealth from land rents, and leadership of their extended families. The Brahmins sought to flee everything that represented worldly attachment. In terms of the so-called 'caste system' (a Western term), the Brahmin order was constituted of many independent kinship-based groups that were essentially local in importance, but shared the prestige of priesthood. They typically lived off fees for performing rituals for many other 'caste' groups, and sometimes off land rents or service as literate advisors to ruling households as well. Their positions in the 'caste system' prevented them from participating directly in major economic or political roles and from accumulating wealth or power. Their prestige rested on a monopoly of priestly "magic" and mastery of classic religious writings.

Parsons analyzed each of the major "historic" civilizations in terms of a common set of concepts derived from the four function paradigm. He thus attended to economic production through the organization of agriculture, the crafts, and trade, to political life through institutions of patrimonial authority, administration, territorial control, and military organization, to integrative institutions through class systems, status groups, inter-ethnic relations, and institutions of law, and to religious traditions and cult practices. By using a common scheme to analyze the several "historic" civilizations with their radical differences, Parsons made a significant contribution despite the brevity of his discussion.

Parsons called ancient Greece and Israel the "seed bed" societies because they were not important for their size, wealth, or power, but for effects of their religious and philosophical cultures on later civilizations in a number of epochs. Greek philosophy was the ultimate source of ideals of objective reason that became essential to early Christian theology, Medieval theology, Renaissance philosophy, and Enlightenment rationalism. Greek ideals of the *polis* or autonomous, politically organized city-state, mediated by the Roman republican tradition, became the primary cultural source of late Medieval and Renaissance political ideals and later of modern republican traditions. The Israelite conception of a transcendent, but personal and jealous, God who enters history to reward and punish peoples for their human achievements and failings became the primary source of Christian theodicy and religious ethics. Hebrew sacred writings have become sources of ethical renewal for Western civilization in a number of epochs, but especially during the Reformation. The biblical figures of the later prophets, particularly Isaiah, have been especially important. For sociology, the interesting problem is to understand the mechanisms of social change that enabled elements of ancient cultures to affect basic cultural and social patterns over millennia down to our time.

*The System of Modern Societies* had the primary goal of presenting modern society as a distinctive evolutionary type that first emerged in Western civilization but has grown to have worldwide impact. Parsons first tried to systematize the explanation of why modern society *originated* only in Western civilization. He started by emphasizing that a distinctively dynamic civilization had emerged in the West several centuries before modern institutions. This development began with the fragmentation of Western Roman authority and the emergence of many small, overlapping, yet competing societies, often both tribal and feudal. Medieval civilization then developed through a number of consolidating forces: the Christian religion with a partly universalistic priesthood and church hierarchy; the heritage of Roman *imperium*, with ideals of effective law and authority; a class system centering on an "international" feudal-military nobility; political authority based in fortified manors, but aggregated into hierarchies, albeit unstably, through personalistic feudal ties; agricultural production based in peasant villages; and active commerce and craft production centered in towns and cities.

As early as the eleventh and twelfth centuries, a new European civilization had been created through growth of the monastic orders, literacy, scholarship, systematic theology, and "bureaucratic" organization of the Church; consolidation of large political domains in France, England, Spain, and the Holy Roman Empire; the extension of trade across the continent and to the Near East and Asia; the independence of cities and their cultivation of republican traditions dating to Antiquity; and the rapid evolution of craft production and organized guilds. Through these changes, the European peoples consolidated a civilization distinct in its institutional elements from Antiquity, bounded (except for Spain) against Islamic Asia, Africa, and the Near East, and growing in cultural and technical sophistication. This civilization was then transformed by the cultural movements of the Renaissance, with its elaboration of secular culture in the arts, technology, and moral belief, and the Reformation, with its redirection of fundamental religious beliefs.

Following Weber, Parsons emphasized that the Calvinist ethic of inner-worldly asceticism provided, against a background of other movements in the Reformation, a special impetus to break with traditional institutions and devise new social institutions. The two centuries following the Reformation were a period of intense social conflict and repeated efforts to create new social foundations. The societies where ascetic Protestant sects came to predominate, e.g. Geneva, Holland, England, and the North American colonies, established stringent religious ethics and disciplined social orders. By the eighteenth century, ascetic Protestantism began to accommodate secular as well as religious ethical reasoning. Instead of its original opposition to all worldly activities, it gave rise to recognizably modern elements of what Weber called the "Spirit of Capitalism." A new emphasis was placed on creative entrepreneurship and on efficient use of secular talents, energies, and resources, including financial credit. The economic forces that created the Industrial Revolution were set loose first in England, then in the Low Countries and the USA, and eventually throughout the North and West of Europe. Within decades, the Industrial Revolution produced a growing, and increasingly self-confident "middle class," generating pressures toward democratizing political change and the overturn of aristocracies. Starting with the American and French Revolutions, and proceeding through the nineteenth century, but with a different history in each nation, electoral institutions that enfranchised common citizens and promoted competition among political parties took power away from privileged groups and placed it in the hands of the people's elected representatives.

The USA institutionalized a *combination* of the Industrial and Democratic Revolutions more rapidly and thoroughly than any other society. It also proceeded the most radically in placing a middle class without ascriptive privileges in a prominent position in the class system. Its legal system firmly but flexibly protected new forms of property, contract, and employment. By the first decades of the twentieth century, American society had developed the largest-scale and most efficient industrial system supported by the most highly differentiated occupational structure. These changes were soon complemented by what Parsons called the Educational Revolution, a radical upgrading of popular education. After the mid-twentieth century, a large majority of each population cohort in the USA was completing secondary education and more than half of each cohort was receiving some higher education. At the same time, university-based research and advanced training of personnel in the sciences and other technical fields were transforming the workforce and the economy's capacity for innovation.

In his chapter on American society, Parsons argued that its institutionalization of the Industrial, Democratic, and Educational Revolutions had created a new evolutionary type of society during the nineteenth and twentieth centuries. In the remainder of the book, he discussed the different patterns of institutionalization of such "modernity" among the European nations, the Soviet Union, and Japan, and examined the prospects for its spread, in partial or complete forms, to other societies. In this discussion, Parsons predicted, still early in the Brezhnev regime, that the Soviet Union could not sustain its authoritarian political system in a world where democracies predominate, and hence would give way to more democratic institutions.

Parsons's two small books provide a powerful introduction to comparative and historical analysis in sociology. The evolutionary types of society are presented in comprehensive terms, yet with sharp delineation of their chief institutional elements. The discussions of institutional change, both emergence of more highly developed types and processes of decline of civilizations, are well integrated with the four function paradigm. In these respects, the books importantly advanced the theory of social change. Parsons claimed that he had also outlined a theory of social evolution similar in status to Darwin's theory of evolution. However, he did not develop a concept truly analogous to natural selection, and hence did not create an authentic theory of social evolution. Moreover, he did not really prove that historical change in society is susceptible to analysis in terms of evolution. A view that history is the general category of change for human social action and that evolution involves dynamics that apply only to biological systems (including the human species) is more consistent with the theory of social action.

## The general action system

In a long essay (Parsons, 1970), Parsons used the four function paradigm to reanalyze social action into primary subsystems. The previous classification of culture, social system, and personality was replaced with a scheme that emphasized differentiation and functional alignment among four subsystems. Culture was treated as pattern maintaining due to the effects of core beliefs and values in establishing principles for the entire action system. The social system was treated as integrative due to the effects of attachment, and of normatively established intersubjective reality, among actors who participate in common relationships and milieux. The personality was treated as goal attaining due to the effects of motivational structures in developing *agency* to implement action. Parsons introduced the concept of behavioral organism to stand for the adaptive subsystem. The behavioral organism consists, in this treatment, of the aspects of the individual actor as organism that facilitate physical implementation of action. The senses, the ability to speak, the capacity for coordination of fingers and hands, and the intelligent capabilities of the brain are necessary facilities for human social action.

With the new functional subsystems identified, Parsons proposed a more radical innovation: to treat the four subsystems of action as dynamically related to each other through interchange processes. He identified a symbolic medium for each of the four subsystems: definition of the situation for cultural systems, affect for social systems, performance capacity for personality, and intelligence for the behavioral organism. He justified briefly the proposition that each of the six interfaces between pairs of the subsystems should be viewed as subject to the double contingencies of interchange. He then proposed two pairs of input and output categories for each of the six interchanges. He made clear that his proposals regarding media and interchange categories were tentative and subject to change following critical evaluation.

The essay is one of the boldest of Parsons's technical writings, although its new formulations in fact built upon ideas that he had been developing for a decade in working papers and discussions with research assistants. As the paper's technical appendix notes, some of the formulations were published despite strong arguments in favor of alternatives. The paper also left ambiguous the empirical relationship between processes of the general action system and processes within social systems (including the societal interchange processes) and other subsystems of action. Parsons continued active discussion of alternative formulations for the general action system down to just weeks before his death.

## The American societal community

Throughout the 1970s, Parsons worked intermittently on a lengthy book on the integrative subsystem of American society. His plan for the book had two sources. One was his old commitment to write an interpretive work on American society. The other was a realization that his concepts for analysis of societal integration were comparatively undeveloped, even though he had identified the societal community as the central subject matter of sociology. He accordingly planned a last major book as both a case study of the American societal community and a presentation of concepts for analyzing social integration. After some seven or eight years of intermittent work, Parsons finished a draft of the book, more than 800 typescript pages, the day before leaving on the trip to Germany, during which he died. The manuscript is a rough draft that Parsons would have revised in fundamental ways had he lived. As he left it, it is an unusual combination of abstract theory, general discussion of problems of social integration, summary of historical information, review of data from other sociological studies, and personal reflection.

The general theoretical framework of the manuscript is presented in a chapter on the relations between the societal community and its major environments, including the other three subsystems of society, the societal communities of other nations, and the three nonsocial subsystems of action. Parsons then discussed features of historical experience that have affected the specific institutional patterns of the American societal community: the activistic value system, the multiethnic composition of the population, the traditions of individualism, and the prevailing culturally grounded discomfort with ascriptive class hierarchies. Subsequent chapters address the ethnic and primordial ties of solidarity, the specific forms of class solidarity and cleavage, the principal institutions, such as the law, that protect impersonal, *Gesellschaft*-type relationships, the social foundations for collective action in the relationship between the societal community and polity, and the distinctive protections for individuality and individualism in American society. The final chapter, on individualism, addressing in part themes suggested by Franois Bourricauld (1981), is a fine summary of Parsons's basic lifelong perspective on American society.

## The human condition

Parsons retired from active teaching at Harvard after the spring semester of 1973. In the following academic year, he began to teach courses at the University of Pennsylvania in collaboration with several members of the department who shared his interests. He also joined an informal faculty seminar to discuss new developments in the theory of action. The discussions started with consideration of Parsons's response, in a brief memorandum, to questions that Charles Lidz and the present author had raised about the conception of the behavioral organism as the adaptive subsystem of action. Lidz and Lidz (1976) had argued that the notion of behavioral organism violates the idea of a system *constituted* entirely of meaningful action because it is made up of aspects of the human organism. They had proposed the concept of a behavioral system, constituted by cognitive schemas in the sense of Jean Piaget, as a stronger formulation of the adaptive subsystem of action. Today, they would use the term "mind," in a sense deriving from George Herbert Mead, for the system of cognitive schemas. In his memorandum, Parsons accepted the new proposal, but argued for a need to examine how systems of social action are related to environing systems. Discussion of the memorandum, its implications, and succeeding formulations continued in the faculty seminar for several years. The outcome of these deliberations was Parsons's long essay, "A Paradigm of the Human Condition" (Parsons, 1978, chapter 15). In brief, Parsons argued that the human condition as experienced by actors involves relationships between the system of action and three other systems. In four function terms, systems of action serve the integrative function of the human condition as system. They are placed in three orders of environment: namely, physico-chemical environment (adaptive), the human organic and ecological environment (goal attaining), and a telic or transcendental environment (pattern maintaining). With these system identifications worked out, Parsons suggested tentative terms for subsystems, media, and interchange categories.

The idea of a telic system has been controversial. However, Parsons was not positing that a God or Divine Principle sets the most general pattern or direction for human action, but rather that all systems of action are intrinsically open with respect to ultimate principles. Any given system of action – at the most inclusive level, a civilization – follows specific ultimate principles of action. Its characteristic principles are not the only possible principles, however. In times of cultural stress, as in the Reformation, pressures arise to change them. Yet, Parsons argued, there are limited possibilities for changes of principle. He proposed that Weber's concepts of inner-worldly and other-wordly, mysticism and asceticism, demarcate the dimensions of transcendental possibilities for principles of action. The telic order thus presents the limited possibilities for ultimate principles of action.

Parsons treated action systems as integrative to the human condition because particular systems of action serve to interrelate elements of all three environments (physico-chemical, organic-ecological, and telic) in terms of their own characteristic meaning-patterns. A system of action thus provides the anthropocentric basis of the integration of the human condition, which is different, as Parsons often said, from the fish condition (or horse and ape conditions). Moreover, the human condition has different experiential meaning for Americans, ancient Greeks, premodern Chinese, etc., and for various status groups within any of these societies.

The essay on the human condition was Parsons's last major publication. Commentators have noted that its broad scope and philosophic quality make it a suitable final statement. The essay is also representative of Parsons's work in opening large issues, proposing insightful and suggestive answers, yet leaving significant problems unresolved, some of them affecting basic formulations. Like so much else that Parsons wrote, it leaves a great deal for other social scientists to do.

## Applied writings

Although the distinctive importance of Parsons's work derives from the conceptual schemes he developed, he also wrote many essays on specific empirical problems and matters of social policy. The secondary literature, following the subtitle of his first collection of essays (Parsons, 1949), conventionally divides his writings between contributions to "pure" theory and "applied" essays. But there is actually no sharp division in his thought. Addressing applied problems was for Parsons a way of evaluating the insights produced by his general theory and often resulted in redirection of his theoretical efforts in order to strengthen empirical understanding. Several of his empirical studies animated formulations that he later presented at the level of "pure" theory. Some of the key innovations of *The Social System* grew out of empirical inquiries into processes of socialization and social control and the institutions of medical practice.

Some critics have argued that it was inconsistent for Parsons to write essays on questions of social policy if he prized the objectivity of his theory. Parsons, however, adhered to Max Weber's position that every authentic contribution to empirical knowledge *combines* the pursuit of objectivity with an effort to capture relevance to contemporary practical values (Parsons, 1967, chapter 3). The scientist or scholar seeks to meet the standards of objectivity (in logic and statistical inference, for example) established in his or her discipline when making an argument or demonstration. Yet choices of subject matter and decisions about what problems are important to address necessarily fall back on extra-scientific standards. Such standards are often provided by the political and ideological discourses of the era. Parsons often indicated that the intended value-relevance of his applied writings was grounded in "academic liberalism." He was particularly concerned with the First Amendment freedoms, civil rights, academic freedom, democratic sharing of power, and maintaining world peace. The following discussion addresses only portions of Parsons's applied writings, focusing on essays that convey his social and political views.

In the late 1930s and early 1940s, Parsons wrote several essays that sought to explain the rise of Nazism in Germany (collected in Gerhardt, 1993). His analysis focused on the late but rapid industrialization of Germany and the many social strains its generated, the comparatively late political unification of the nation, the pressures placed on enduring institutions of local *Gemeinschaft*, and the particularly bitter conflicts in the class structure. Unlike most Americans writing on Germany in that era, Parsons expressed his distaste for Nazism without generalizing it to anti-Germanism. He explicitly maintained his respect for German traditions of high culture and scholarship.

At the University of Cambridge in 1953, Parsons found that many English intellectuals believed Joseph McCarthy to be emerging as the "American Hitler." They talked of preparing Europe for the USA's decline into fascism. Parsons wrote an essay entitled "Social Strains in America" (Parsons, 1969, chapter 7) to demonstrate that McCarthyism was a limited political movement with poor prospects for gaining control of the nation. He argued that the social base for McCarthyism was largely in the small towns and in proprietors of small businesses. Groups that had suffered economic decline during the rise of large industry and big government were the base of the movement. They saw trends in the larger society as false to their ways of life and were receptive to McCarthy's extravagant allegations that traitors were common among leaders of big government. Writing before the Senate hearings in which Joseph Welch successfully confronted McCarthy, Parsons argued that the McCarthy movement was a classic "bubble" phenomenon and would disappear rapidly after McCarthy was challenged directly.

At the peak of the Cold War, Parsons wrote essays on American foreign policy in relation to the system of international relations (Parsons, 1967, chapter 14; 1969, chapter 12). At the time, many scholars as well as political leaders advocated uncompromising prosecution of Cold War policies to gain every possible advantage over the Soviet Union as bitter adversary. Parsons, however, argued that the USA and the Soviet Union shared strong interests in limiting conflict to protect against a nuclear "hot war." He emphasized the American interest in developing greater confidence in the international order on the part of the Soviet Union. The constraints imposed on the pursuit of national aims by international institutions might provide important protections against war.

Parsons later participated in the early Pugwash Conferences, where scientists from the USA and Soviet Union started discussions on shared control and destruction of nuclear weapons. In the mid-1960s, with the first thawing of the Cold War, he made contacts with Soviet sociologists at international meetings, visited the Soviet Union to promote professional relationships, and invited Soviet scholars to the USA and Harvard.

With the rise of the Civil Rights movement, Parsons sought to contribute to its cause by clarifying in sociological terms its importance to the nation. His essay "Full Citizenship for the Negro American?" (Parsons, 1969, chapter 11) started with the theoretical question of what part civil rights play in the integrative institutions of modern societies. Parsons also addressed the question historically by examining the major stages in the development of Anglo-American institutions of civil rights. He distinguished three separate complexes of citizenship rights: the legal, involving autonomous courts and equal protection of the laws; the political, involving the franchise and the ability to exercise influence in the political process; and the welfare, involving health, education, and welfare policies to ensure that citizens have the capability to participate effectively in the competitive modern economy.

Parsons also reviewed the historical processes by which various religious, ethnic, and racial groups have gained more complete citizenship rights following earlier exclusion from full community membership. Down to the immigration of

Irish Catholics escaping famine, the USA had been overwhelmingly Protestant and, aside from slaves and small numbers of freed Blacks, white and Anglo-Saxon. From the 1840s to the 1920s, the population became much more diverse with large-scale immigration from Ireland, Central Europe, Scandinavia, Eastern Europe, and Italy. Negative feelings toward new ethnic and religious groups were often strong. Catholics and Jews especially were in many respects excluded from the communities of American life. Parsons traced the social changes that led to the inclusion of these groups on an equal (or nearly equal) basis, often after decades of discrimination and deprivation. He proposed that these processes of inclusion provided in key respects a model for the inclusion of African Americans. He also noted that full inclusion under the protections of legal rights, a process advanced by *Brown* v. *Board of Education* (and after Parsons wrote by the 1960s Civil Rights Acts), created abilities for African Americans to press for recognition of other rights in court. He was optimistic that establishing voting rights for African Americans throughout the country would produce favorable political changes. Political leaders would then have political needs of their own to respond to the interests of African Americans. Parsons predicted that more complicated struggles would follow before African Americans would attain equal status with respect to welfare rights. He doubted that African Americans would achieve complete equality as citizens until they had benefited for a substantial period of time from equal educational opportunities, equal health care, and equal welfare support. Today, his predictions appear largely correct, although the struggle for sufficient welfare rights still faces even greater political obstacles than he had anticipated.

In the late 1960s, Parsons collaborated with Gerald M. Platt on an empirical study of faculty roles in colleges and universities. When the student demonstrations of that time created a crisis in the universities, Parsons and Platt redirected their research into a broad analysis of academic institutions. The resulting book, *The American University* (Parsons and Platt, 1973), is a comprehensive analysis of research universities emphasizing their specialization around producing, preserving, and transmitting intellectually disciplined knowledge. Contrary to common perceptions, Parsons and Platt argued that undergraduate as well as graduate education had been strengthened in scope and quality by the growth of research activities. However, they discussed undergraduate education as a dynamic process involving important elements of personal change. The modern university is ideally a stimulating yet supportive environment that frees students to explore new intellectual and personal interests. Aside from curricular challenges, students often encounter new extracurricular opportunities in the arts, in politics, in moral and religious subcultures, and in community service. Students often enter friendships with people from religious, ethnic, racial, or social class backgrounds different from their own.

Parsons and Platt noted that college students often undergo a great deal of stress when new types of experience challenge their former life-orientations. The stress tends to be especially great for students whose families have not previously experienced higher education, and hence might not understand or support new decisions regarding fields of study, extracurricular interests, political causes, friendships, or future careers. A generation of rapid expansion in higher education had greatly increased the numbers of students who were the first in their families to attend college, and thus probably increased student stress. The expansion of the universities also produced significant institutional dislocations. With larger student bodies, student–faculty relationships had become less personal. The formation of student friendships had become more complicated as student bodies grew more diverse in regional, ethnic, racial, social class, and cultural backgrounds. With larger academic departments, relationships among faculty colleagues also had become more impersonal and often more competitive. The vast growth in administrative structures created difficulties in dealing with students in nonbureaucratic ways, a problem symbolized in the 1960s by student ID numbers and computerization of academic records. The crisis of the 1960s and 1970s had thus been precipitated by rapid change, weakened social integration of university life, and resulting stresses on students.

In response to student demands for change, Parsons and Platt recommended a number of reforms, but warned that the system of higher education should protect its many gains of the postwar years. If the benefits of the Educational Revolution were to be fully preserved, the special institutional make-up of research universities had to be protected. Recalling the damage done to the University of California by state officials reacting to student demands and demonstrations, they noted the dangers to carrying out reforms in a way that might politicize the universities. In terms of both academic freedoms and commitments of public resources, reaction from the right posed a greater threat to the universities than student activism.

Some of the reforms proposed by Parsons and Platt were: to increase the "relevance" of curricula by modestly expanding programs in the arts and in the applied social sciences; to improve university officials' communication with student leaders; to strengthen informal relations between faculty members and students; to add student members to some university committees to ensure attention to student views; and to improve the quality of administrative services for students. However, Parsons and Platt did not expect such changes to have large or rapid consequences. They maintained that the life-stage of "studentry" was intrinsically a time of personal change and stress. During periods of national political turmoil, the stress on students was simply prone to creating problems for universities. Parsons and Platt were confident that over some years the turmoil would abate and university life would be normalized. In the meantime, the principal duty of educators was to protect the freedoms of thought, speech, and association that are essential to academic life.

## CRITIQUES OF PARSONS'S THEORY

From publication of *SSA* to the end of his life, Parsons was a controversial figure who faced substantial professional criticism. The content of the criticism has changed over time, as new perspectives have emerged and often defined their intellectual positions in part by their stances toward Parsons. It would be impossible to review all the significant controversies here, but it is appropriate to comment on several well known ones.

In 1940, Alfred Schutz sent Parsons a laudatory but critical essay he had written on SSA (Grathoff, 1978). Parsons must have been pleased by the respectful discussion of his work, even though some of Schutz's views were in fact quite different from his own. However, Schutz put Parsons in a difficult position by saying that he would publish his essay only if Parsons agreed "in principle" with his criticisms. The difficulty for Parsons was that he could not agree with Schutz's key points. Schutz proposed that the methodology concerning frames of reference and categories of analysis should be presented in the terms of a philosophical epistemology, not as a nonphilosophical, social scientific methodology. He also proposed to revise basic concepts, including subject of action, object of action, rational action, and normative orientation, in terms of his own phenomenological theory. In doing so, he focused almost entirely on face-to-face and person-to-person relationships, leaving aside the institutional and macrosocial analyses that were fundamental to Parsons. The divide between Parsons and Schutz was too wide to be readily bridged, and their correspondence ended in mutual discomfort. However, an impression has lasted in sectors of the profession, unfairly, I believe, that Parsons prevented Schutz from publishing a stringent critique.

In the late 1940s, Robert K. Merton developed the view that theory construction in sociology in its then current condition should concentrate on problems of the "middle range." The middle range was set off against atheoretical descriptive studies of particular settings and against Parsons's research program, which was characterized as "Grand Theory." Merton's account of the value of such middle range concepts as reference groups or the two stage flow of influence was persuasive. He established the scientific validity of his approach, and most sociologists ever since have been more comfortable with a middle range methodology. However, Merton mischaracterized Parsons's approach. Parsons's primary goal was not to develop macroscopic causal generalizations about large-scale institutions or society as a whole (Grand Theory), but to clarify basic premises and categories as antecedents to precise analysis at any level of social organization (Parsons, 1953, chapter 17). Questions of the appropriate frame of reference for sociology, as articulated in SSA, were the distinctive focus of Parsons's methodology. His empirical studies, e.g. discussions of the professions, social control, the family, or processes of socialization, were in actuality middle range as often as macrosocial. In later years, Parsons argued that his debate with Merton had created a false opposition. There had been no need for sociologists to choose between the two approaches. Both he and Merton had made large contributions despite their methodological differences.

In the 1950s and 1960s, Ralf Dahrendorf (1959), Louis Coser (1956), and then others developed the criticism that Parsons's theory could not deal with phenomena of social conflict. They argued that Parsons's focus on systems, functional "contribution" to systems, and the integration of systems obscured the social reality of conflict in a haze of emphasis on social harmony. They proposed that "system theory" requires a complementary "conflict theory" in order to capture the full range of social phenomena. As a corollary of this criticism, they argued that, lacking a theory of conflict, a systems theory could also not come to terms with social change. A complementary conflict theory would thus open systems theory to the analysis of social change as well. However, Parsons's writings exhibit a great deal of attention to empirical conflict and change. Both conflict and change are treated at length in *SSA*, especially in the discussions of Weber's and Pareto's work. Parsons's essays on Germany and the rise of Nazism also deal extensively with conflict and change.

Although Dahrendorf and Coser were particularly critical of *The Social System*, that work, too, treats phenomena of conflict, but primarily in terms of stress or strain in relationships or institutions. The difference is less in perception of conflict than in the ways conflict is conceptualized and linked to change. Dahrendorf and to a degree Coser failed to recognize conflict and change in *The Social System* because of the terms used. Dahrendorf was looking for a Marxian analysis with a focus on conflict among social classes and a direct tie between class conflict and social change. Coser, too, was in part misguided by Marxian preconceptions, but was also disturbed by Parsons's neglect of Simmel's treatment of conflict as a basic social form. Parsons sought to maintain Weber's multidimensional analysis of change in terms of religious ethics, routinization of charisma, rationalization, and bureaucratization as well as conflict among classes and estates. For Parsons, the task was to synthesize these elements of a theory of change in terms of a theory of system dynamics, including strain in relationships and institutions. To accept a bifurcation between system theory and conflict theory would, for Parsons, have been to betray a commitment to developing a unified frame of reference.

During the ideological turmoil of the late 1960s and the 1970s, a number of figures associated with the New Left broadened the conflict theory criticism of Parsons, while also turning it into an ideological attack. In the New Left view, Parsons ignored conflict and change while extolling an ideal of perfect system integration and social harmony because he was a spokesman for the Establishment. The methodology of "value-freedom" was interpreted as a smokescreen to hide blatant partisanship on behalf of the dominant classes and social order. Parsons's status as a senior professor at Harvard was at times cited as sufficient proof of his role as Establishment spokesman. In an influential version of this argument, Alvin Gouldner (1970) stressed the conservatism of L. J. Henderson and the "Pareto Circle" at Harvard as evidence of Parsons's politics. Gouldner's account of Parsons's theoretical work, however, was little more than a caricature. As we have seen, Parsons's political outlook was more ambivalent to the social order of his times and based on specific value-judgments, hardly on a general social harmonism. In a later work, William Buxton (1985) interpreted Parsons's *corpus* as a defense of the "capitalist nation-state." Although Buxton's interpretation is more nuanced than Gouldner's, it overemphasizes the institutional forms of nation-state and capitalism, about which Parsons was in key respects ambivalent. Buxton underemphasizes the institutions of universalistic law, citizen's rights, representative democracy, and competitive elections, which were more important to Parsons's attachment to the American political system.

A thoughtful and penetrating criticism of Parsons's theory of action was developed in the 1950s and 1960s by his former student, Harold Garfinkel. The criticism pertains to the understanding of how normative order regulates the conduct of individual actors. Garfinkel (1967) argued that Parsons greatly underestimated the complexity of subjective processes involved in an actor's judgment regarding how to interpret and whether to observe normative rules. The applicability of specific norms to an actor's conduct in a given social situation rests on many implicit typifications that serve to define the situations – typifications of the social setting, characteristics of the actors, their interests and intentions, their previous experience, and expectable events – all of which Parsons had not explored. To be sure, Parsons himself argued that norms are not self-actualizing. He understood that a set of norms requires the actors in a situation to communicate their expectations to one another, and frequently threats of sanctions as well. Only with the support of give and take regarding expectations and sanctions is a normative order able to regulate actual conduct in the situation. Although Parsons saw the "double contingency" in the normative guidance of actors' conduct, Garfinkel contributed a deeper understanding of the intricate judgment that each actor must use to define the situation and clarify the applicability of norms to his or her own conduct. Parsons himself never grasped Garfinkel's critique or its importance, but a number of his protégés have accepted the need to reconstruct the understanding of how normative orders are actually implemented in interaction.

As we have seen, Parsons consistently maintained that theoretical propositions in sociology must be analytical in form and deal with abstractly conceived aspects or qualities of social objects, not concrete objects. A criticism that Parsons lodged against Weber was that the ideal type method stood halfway between concrete and fully analytic theory. Consistent with his methodology, Parsons built his later theory of subsystems of society in terms of analytic propositions about analytically defined aspects of institutions and relationships. Reinhard Bendix (Bendix and Roth, 1971) criticized Parsons's foundation for system theory by arguing that Weber's ideal type methodology is sharply at odds with Durkheim's functionalism, the precursor of system theory. Bendix had conducted a number of important historical and comparative studies using a modification of Weber's ideal type scheme. He expressed skepticism that analytical schemes based on system theory could be as insightful as an ideal type methodology. Indeed, abstract system theory is difficult to use for original comparative-historical research. Parsons's studies of German social history predate his formal system theory and are basically ideal-typical. His late comparative and historical writings were largely syntheses of evidence developed in previous studies. They used the system theory mainly as an analytical framework for integrating the works of other scholars. Sociologists such as Robert N. Bellah (1957), Neil J. Smelser (1959), S. N. Eistenstadt (1963), and Mark Gould (1987) have successfully used analytic systems theory for historical research, but the respects in which their studies actually transcend ideal type analysis in organizing empirical evidence has perhaps not been fully assessed. Ideal type analysis may be regarded as a proven empirical method in historical sociology, and the intellectually conservative critic may be skeptical of Parsons's claim for the empirical superiority of analytic system theory.

A related consideration pertains to Parsons's stance toward the methods of analysis developed by the German idealist-historicist school. Parsons accepted the method of interpretive understanding or *Verstehen* as it figured in Weber's methodological and empirical writings. He understood that a theory of meaningful social action requires a method of *Verstehen* as its empirical complement. However, he did not perceive the procedures by which historical knowledge is developed to be closely related to theoretical issues in sociology and did not seek himself to advance the methodology of *Verstehen*. He also distanced himself from the German historicists who provided the chief background to Weber's writings on *Verstehen* in a mistaken belief that they had generally insisted on the need for different categories and procedures of understanding for each historical epoch, thereby undermining all grounds for comparative analysis and generalization. On this basis, he failed to build on such contributions as Dilthey's and Simmel's writings on interpretation and historical knowledge. A result is that Parsons tended to invoke knowledge of historical figures without carefully evaluating the formal procedures by which historians had synthesized knowledge of them.

In the 1980s, Parsons's *corpus* received major scholarly evaluations by Jürgen Habermas and Jeffrey Alexander. Habermas (1987) portrayed Parsons's work as the one theoretical system of recent sociology that constitutes essential background to any future general theory. His critical assessment focuses on aspects of the theory of action that are directly relevant to his own theory of communicative action. Of particular interest to Habermas are, first, the conception of social action as a situated process engaging particular actors and, second, the formal system theory. The crux of Habermas's argument is that, contrary to Parsons's claim, these two perspectives were not adequately integrated. Habermas maintains that the two are in fact independent frames of reference, and he appears to argue that in principle the two cannot be authentically integrated. He reviews elements of both formulations in considerable and technical detail. His own interest lies chiefly with the conception of social action, which substantially overlaps with his own theory of communicative action. The system theory, especially its four function version, appears of less value to Habermas, a judgment likely related to his longstanding rejection of German system theory. The present author finds it unfortunate that Habermas focused so much of a frequently penetrating and insightful discussion on one sweeping, and largely forced, conclusion.

Alexander (1983) presents Parsons's work as a culmination of the classical tradition and the pre-eminent contribution since Durkheim and Weber. Alexander provides the most comprehensive and detailed review of Parsons's formulations available in one publication, and thus his study is an indispensable source. He follows the evolution of Parsons's thought through its early, middle, and late stages, and outlines the major late-stage formulations, including the four function paradigm, the double interchanges, and the symbolic media. His discussion focuses particularly on inconsistencies among different presentations of the late system theory and often alleges confusion when the actuality seems to be that Parsons revised or supplemented formulations. He rejects the use of the four function interchange models for systems of action other than social systems, although he does not fully explicate the grounds for doing so. As an overall criticism, he alleges that Parsons's basic formulations overemphasize ideal factors in social organization and underemphasize material factors. This point can be conceded for many – but hardly all – of Parsons's empirical writings, but Alexander does not demonstrate that the criticism applies to the basic frame of reference or chief theoretical propositions. More recently, Alexander has led a "neofunctionalist" movement that strives to build upon the basic thrust of Parsons's functionalism without becoming entangled in its complicated formulations.

## Parsons's Intellectual Legacy

In May 1979, Parsons traveled to Heidelberg for a celebration of the fiftieth anniversary of his doctoral degree. The occasion was a success. He enjoyed the papers presented by a distinguished group of German scholars and his own talk was well received. He and his wife Helen then went to Munich. In an active day at the university, he made two presentations, one a seminar talk and the other a public lecture, both of which were again well received. That evening, he suffered a sudden and massive stroke and was suddenly dead. To have died after a day on which he had lectured twice and engaged students and colleagues in the excitement of recent ideas was a fitting end for the 76-year-old sociologist.

Parsons's legacy can be summarized at three levels. At a first level, his methodology of seeking a scientific revolution by concentrating on the essential ideas of a frame of reference is his most important contribution. His commitment to critical study of frames of reference was complemented by a dedication to establishing technical standards for the evaluation of theoretical work. Despite the volumes that have been written about Parsons's intellectual biases, the chief characteristic of his thought is actually a determination to follow logic and evidence wherever they may lead in refining sociological concepts, ideological attachments and previous theoretical formulations aside. The frequency with which new research persuaded him to overturn previous ideas is a clear index of his attachment to reason. The intensity of Parsons's commitment to fundamental theoretical issues provides a weighty model for future sociologists, particularly in the USA, where empiricist styles of scientific work predominate. The model is all the more powerful because it strikes out against the cultural grain and, in America, will be followed by only a handful of sociologists in any generation. Parsons himself realized that his personal commitment to theoretical work was built on unusual speculative abilities, a dispassionate (affectively neutral) manner of critiquing and evaluating ideas, and the patience to examine and re-examine ideas over years and decades. He understood that only a few could work creatively in this manner.

At a second level, Parsons's legacy consists of major concepts and themes that appear to be enduring contributions: the action frame of reference, the limits of economic theory, normative order and social control, the concept of social system, the idea of functional analysis, the conception of social institutions, the institutional integration of motivation, the professional role relationship, and the basic notion of generalized symbolic media of interchange. These are all fundamental ideas that social scientists today and for the foreseeable future can adopt and modify for their own studies. Many of these ideas are so fundamental to sociological analysis that it is hard to conceive of a sociology that does not make routine use of them. It is also hard to envision a future sociology that will not be strengthened by study of Parsons's writings to learn how he used these ideas and what insights he brought out of them.

At a third level is the Parsonian theory of action as a formally integrated theoretical system. Here we are in the domain of the formal action frame of reference; system theory; the four function paradigm; the primary subsystems of society and their constituent sectors; the symbolic media, double interchanges, and the interchange categories; and the analysis of social institutions as structural elements of society. This theory was projected in bold and methodical terms, albeit with lacunae, oversights, conflicting formulations, and simple mistakes. Despite the many gaps in its presentation, it is a uniquely powerful theory. No other theorist has had Parsons's level of commitment to developing a technically refined theory. No figure since Weber and Durkheim has had his courage to exploit fundamental sociological insights so thoroughly and boldly. The result is that the theory of social action, despite its lacunae, partial formulations, and errors, presents uniquely rich opportunities for scholars who will address its difficulties and undertake its further development.

## Bibliography

### Writings of Talcott Parsons

*The Structure of Social Action*. 1937. New York: McGraw-Hill.
*Essays in Sociological Theory: Pure and Applied*. 1949. Glencoe, IL: Free Press.
*The Social System*. 1951. Glencoe, IL: Free Press.
*Essays in Sociological Theory*, revised edition. 1953. Glencoe, IL: Free Press.
*Social Structure and Personality*. 1964. New York: Free Press.
*Societies: Evolutionary and Comparative Perspectives*. 1966. Englewood Cliffs, NJ: Prentice Hall.
*Sociological Theory and Modern Society*. 1967. New York: Free Press.
*Politics and Social Structure*. 1969. New York: Free Press.
Some Problems of General Theory in Sociology. 1970. In J. C. McKinney and E. A. Tiryakian (eds), *Theoretical Sociology: Perspectives and Developments*. New York: Appleton-Century-Crofts.
*The System of Modern Societies*. 1971. Englewood Cliffs, NJ: Prentice Hall.
*Social Systems and the Evolution of Action Theory*. 1977. New York: Free Press.
*Action Theory and the Human Condition*. 1978. New York: Free Press.
*The Marshall Lectures* (edited by R. Swedberg). 1986. Uppsala: Research Reports from the Department of Sociology, Uppsala University.

*The Early Essays* (edited by C. Camic). 1991. Chicago: University of Chicago Press.

*Family, Socialization and Interaction Process* (with R. F. Bales). 1955. Glencoe, IL: Free Press.

*Working Papers in the Theory of Action* (with R. F. Bales and E. A. Shils). 1953. Glencoe, IL: Free Press.

*The American University* (with G. M. Platt). 1973. Cambridge, MA: Harvard University Press.

*Toward a General Theory of Action* (edited with E. A. Shils). 1951. Cambridge, MA: Harvard University Press.

*Economy and Society* (with N. J. Smelser). 1956. Glencoe, IL: Free Press.

*The Protestant Ethic and the Spirit of Capitalism*, by Max Weber, translated by Talcott Parsons from the original German of 1903–4. 1930. New York: Scribner's.

## Further reading

Alexander, J. C. (1983) *Theoretical Logic in Sociology. Volume 4, The Modern Reconstruction of Classical Thought: Talcott Parsons*. Berkeley, CA: University of California Press.

Bales, R. F. (1950) *Interaction Process Analysis: a Method for the Study of Small Groups*. Cambridge, MA: Addison-Wesley.

Bellah, R. N. (1957) *Tokugawa Religion*. Glencoe, IL: Free Press.

Bendix, R. and Roth, G. (1971) *Scholarship and Partisanship; Essays on Max Weber*. Berkeley, CA: University of California Press.

Bershady, H. J. (1973) *Ideology and Social Knowledge*. Oxford: Basil Blackwell.

Bourricaud, F. (1981) *The Sociology of Talcott Parsons*. Chicago: University of Chicago Press (original French edition 1977).

Buxton, W. (1985) *Talcott Parsons and the Capitalist Nation-state*. Toronto: University of Toronto Press.

Coser, L. A. (1956) *The Functions of Social Conflict*. Glencoe, IL: Free Press.

Dahrendorf, R. (1959) *Class and Class Conflict in Industrial Society*. Stanford, CA: Stanford University Press.

Eisenstadt, S. N. (1963) *The Political Systems of Empires*. New York: Free Press.

Fox, R. (1997) Talcott Parsons, My Teacher. *The American Scholar*, 66, 395–410.

Garfinkel, H. (1967) *Studies in Ethnomethodology*. Englewood Cliffs, NJ: Prentice-Hall.

Gerhardt, U. (ed.) (1993) *Talcott Parsons on National Socialism*. New York: Aldine DeGruyter.

Gould, M. (1987) *Revolution in the Development of Capitalism: the Coming of the English Revolution*. Berkeley: University of California Press.

Gouldner, A. W. (1970) *The Coming Crisis of Western Sociology*. New York: Basic Books.

Grathoff, R. (1978) *The Theory of Social Action: the Correspondence of Alfred Schutz and Talcott Parsons*. Bloomington: University of Indiana Press.

Habermas, J. (1987) *The Theory of Communicative Action. Volume 2, Lifeworld and System: a Critique of Functionalist Reason*. Boston: Beacon Press (originally published in German, 1981).

Johnson, M. M. (1988) *Strong Mothers, Weak Wives: the Search for Gender Equality*. Berkeley: University of California Press.

Klausner, S. Z. and Lidz, V. (1986) *The Nationalization of the Social Sciences*. Philadelphia: University of Pennsylvania Press.

Lidz, C. W. and Lidz, V. (1976) Piaget's Psychology of Intelligence and the Theory of Action. In J. Loubser, R. C. Baum, A. Effrat, and V. Lidz (eds), *Explorations in General Theory in Social Science*, 2 volumes. New York: Free Press, pp. 195–239.

Nichols, L. T. (1998) Social Relations Undone: Disciplinary Divergence and Departmental Politics at Harvard 1946–1970. *The American Sociologist*, 29, 83–107.

Smelser, N. J. (1959) *Social Change in the Industrial Revolution*. Chicago: University of Chicago Press.

Whitehead, A. N. (1925) *Science and the Modern World*. New York: Macmillan.

Wiener, N. (1948) *Cybernetics: Or Control and Communication in the Animal and the Machine*. New York: Wiley.

# Part II
## Contemporary Social Theorists

# 13

# Robert K. Merton

## PIOTR SZTOMPKA

## THE PERSON

Robert King Merton was born on July 4, 1910 in Philadelphia, to a family of working-class Jewish immigrants from Eastern Europe. As a journalist puts it, he started "almost at the bottom of the social structure" (Hunt, 1961, p. 39).

Obviously gifted, from the earliest days he encountered conducive opportunities for his talents to unfold. Close to his Philadelphia home he found the Andrew Carnegie Library, where as a child he spent endless hours, voraciously consuming works in literature, science, and history, and especially biographies and autobiographies (apparently looking for a "role model," as he was to call it later). Since that time he has always remained, to use his own words, "the inveterate loner working chiefly in libraries and in my study at home" (Merton, 1994, p. 16). The Academy of Music, with Leopold Stokowski at the helm, was within walking distance and a place of frequent visits. And later, in the mid-1920s, new institutions were added in the vicinity: the Central Library and the Museum of Art. Thus, outside of formal education at the South Philadelphia High School, young Merton was exposed to a rich educative environment (see Merton, 1994).

There were other opportunities though, having more to do with luck: meeting the right people at the right moments of his life. Among those there were: the librarians at Carnegie Library, who took an interest in the young book addict; George E. Simpson, young sociology instructor at Temple College, who made him a research assistant to the study of the public imagery of Blacks, and thus awoke a lifelong passion for social inquiry; Pitirim A. Sorokin, who after a brief encounter at an American Sociological Association convention encouraged Merton to apply for graduate study at Harvard, and soon after made him his research and teaching assistant, as well as a co-author of his work on social time and a chapter in his monumental *Social and Cultural Dynamics* (1937–41); Talcott Parsons, who pushed his inquisitive mind toward the European founders of sociology – Durkheim, Weber, Marx, Simmel – and taught him analytic skills and conceptual sophistication; George Sarton, who seduced him toward the history of science; and finally a wartime immigrant from Vienna, mathematician-psychologist turned sociologist Paul F. Lazarsfeld, with whom Merton established the long-lasting collaboration at Columbia University and the famous Bureau of Applied Social Research, which they co-directed for several decades.

Let us return to more formal biographical facts. In 1927 Merton entered Temple College at Philadelphia, from which he graduated in 1931. Right after, he won a fellowship for graduate study at Harvard University, and in 1936 defended his doctoral dissertation "Science, Technology and Society in Seventeenth-century England," written under the guidance of George Sarton, and published as a book two years later (Merton, 1938). Here he put forward a hypothesis, akin to Max Weber's famous claim on the link between Protestant ethic and the capitalist economy, arguing for a similar link between Protestant pietism and early experimental science. The "Merton Thesis" has been subjected to criticism, particularly from historians (see Kearney, 1973), and started continuous debates. Some of them have been recently put together in a book by I. Bernard Cohen (1990). Even before his doctoral dissertation, Merton's first influential articles came out in print: "The Unanticipated Consequences of Purposive Social Actions" in 1936 (Merton, 1996, pp. 173–82), and, in 1938, one of his crucial contributions, the article "Social Structure and Anomie" (Merton, 1996, pp. 132–52), starting a whole school in the theory of deviance and becoming a subject of continuing debate for more than half a century. From 1936 to 1939 Merton served as a tutor and instructor at Harvard, and then from 1939 until 1941 he held the positions of professor and chairman at the Department of Sociology at Tulane University in New Orleans. In 1941, choosing between job offers from Harvard and Columbia, Merton moved to Columbia University, where he remained on the faculty of the Sociology Department for 38 years, going through the positions of Assistant Professor, Associate Professor (1944), Full Professor (1947), Chairman (succeeding Paul Lazarsfeld in 1961), Giddings Professor of Sociology (1963), and University Professor (1974). After retirement, from 1979 to 1984 he remained active as a Special Service Professor. He withdrew from teaching in 1984.

Apart from the university, Merton has been much involved in wider academic life, both in the United States and internationally. Among his many official positions are the Presidencies of the American Sociological Association (1956), the Eastern Sociological Society (1968), and the Society for Social Studies of Science (1975). He has held innumerable posts on editorial boards, professional committees, and advising positions to publishing houses. Academic recognition includes membership of the National Academy of Sciences, Academia Europaea, and numerous foreign academies (the Polish Academy of Science was added to this list in 1997). He has received more than twenty honorary doctoral degrees from universities including Yale, Chicago, Harvard, Columbia, Leiden,

Jerusalem, Wales, Ghent, Oxford, and Krakow. He was a Fellow of the Guggenheim Foundation (1962), and the Center for Advanced Studies in Behavioral Science, the Resident Scholar at the Russell Sage Foundation (1979 until the present time), and MacArthur Prize Fellow (1983–8). From the American Sociological Association he received a Career of Distinguished Scholarship award, and in 1994 the President of the United States granted him the highest academic honor: the National Medal of Science.

Married twice, he has a son and two daughters from the first marriage. His son, Robert C. Merton, a professor at Harvard and an eminent specialist in the study of financial markets, won the Nobel Prize in economics in 1997.

## THE SOCIAL CONTEXT

Merton's life covers the major part of twentieth-century American history. Even though he has always been a man of academia, surrounded by and totally devoted to the intellectual community, he has also been touched by the turns of political and economic events. A perfect example of a self-made man, coming from the lowest echelons of class structure and advancing to the narrowest New York elite, as well as to worldwide fame, he could not but recognize the mobility, openness, and democratic virtues of American society making that feat possible. This led him quite early to embrace the liberal-democratic political creed to which he has remained faithful all his life. The experience of the Great Depression raised his sensitivity to social issues, racial discrimination, poverty, deviance, and anomie. And the drama of Stalinist terror, the Nazi ascendance to power and the Second World War, the Holocaust and the Gulag, and other atrocities, brought him to a strong condemnation of totalitarianism. He lived through the defeat of Nazism in 1945 as well as the the final collapse of communism in 1989, which provided happy corroboration of his political commitments.

He reacted to political events with the tools of his academic profession, mostly through research and writing, but was always concerned with the "potentials of relevance" of scientific ideas. He devoted systematic reflection to the role of the intellectual in public bureaucracy (1945), social responsibilities of technologists (1947), and the role of applied social science in the formation of policy (1949). The most "practical" of his own theoretical studies include work on deviance and anomie, racial discrimination, marriage patterns, political "machines," housing, propaganda and the "war-bond drive," and medical education. The most "ideological" of his articles dealt with the destruction of science in Nazi Germany and the defense of the "scientific ethos" (Merton, 1996, pp. 277–85), which for him was a kind of micro-model for the democratic polity. As a co-director of the Bureau of Applied Social Research, he managed and supervised numerous other programs directed at pressing social issues.

As was mentioned above, his most significant social environment was academia. His graduate studies and the beginnings of his professional career coincided with the renaissance of American sociology in the 1930s, with Harvard

University as its most lively center, in Robert Nisbet's metaphor "the Venice" of that time (Coser and Nisbet, 1975, p. 6). His mature career was linked to "the Florence" of American sociology (ibid.) in post-war years, Columbia University. He stayed at Columbia Sociology Department through the peak period of its eminence, in the 1950s and 1960s, to which he himself contributed in considerable measure.

From the "core" of Columbia University, the concentric circles of his "significant others," whom he reciprocally influenced as a highly recognized and esteemed partner, extended to the intellectual, cultural, and artistic community of New York, then Western and Eastern Europe, and eventually an even wider world. He became a true cosmopolitan, maintaining permanent links with international academic communities, not limited by political or ideological biases. One of the founders, in 1948, of the International Sociological Association (ISA), as early as the 1950s he went with the first group of American sociologists to the USSR, paid numerous visits to Poland, Hungary, and Czechoslovakia, visited China, and was always ready to give a generous helping hand to the young apprentices in sociology from those politically exotic parts of the world (here I am happy to record my own personal debt). It would be hard to find a better example of the true "man of the world."

## THE INTELLECTUAL CONTEXT

Merton believed that science develops cumulatively and incrementally by standing "on the shoulders of giants" (Merton, 1965). Hence, the crucial importance of scientific traditions. "I have long argued," Merton says, "that the writings of classical authors in every field of learning can be read with profit time and again, additional ideas and intimations coming freshly into view with each re-reading" (Merton, 1965, p. 45). This is particularly relevant for the adept of a young science like sociology: "the sociologist qua sociologist rather than as historian of sociology, has ample reason to study the works of a Weber, Durkheim, and Simmel and, for that matter, to turn back on occasion to the works of a Hobbes, Rousseau, Condorcet or Saint-Simon" (Merton, 1968, p. 35). But sociology limited to the intepretation of the masters would be sterile. In an attempt to avoid both narrow dogmatism and uncritical novelty, Merton's policy of relating to the masters seems to imply three directives. First is a selective approach; that is, the constant effort to derive from the masters of the past the core of their ideas and to sift it from inevitable marginal contributions, blind alleys, or outright mistakes. Second is reading the masters anew; that is, entering into a sort of critical dialogue with them, reworking their ideas in the light of new perspectives and approaches, later discoveries and experiences, newly acquired data. Third is the injunction to critically enrich, partly supplant, or reject past ideas, if found incomplete, deficient or obsolete: "the founding fathers are honored, not by zealous repetition of their early findings, but by extensions, modifications and, often enough, by rejection of some of their ideas and findings" (Merton, 1968, p. 587).

Merton is quite faithful to this professed policy. Various commentators have noted that he was among the first in his generation of American sociologists to turn their attention to the heritage of European sociology, to have mastered it in depth and to have "assimilated European thought patterns more thoroughly than most of his predecessors" (Coser and Nisbet, 1975, p. 4). But his attitude toward "founding fathers" has never been exegetic or dogmatic. Rather, it has been self-consciously critical, with an emphasis on possible continuities.

Who are those giants "on the shoulders" of which Merton self-consciously places himself? To begin with, there is his pre-eminent indebtedness to Émile Durkheim. In the list of his recognized idols he unfailingly places Durkheim in the forefront, and indicatively Durkheim is quoted more often than any other author in Merton's major volume, *Social Theory and Social Structure* (1968). There is a striking similarity in the dominant orientation of their sociologies: their common attempt to have sociology develop into a reasonably rigorous, "hard" science of a specifically social subject matter, with explanations in terms of identified social factors. Merton's sociology is also in continuity with Durkheim's in terms of common theoretical approach: functional and structural analysis. Finally, there are obvious substantive continuities: from Durkheim's study of suicide, and particularly "anomic suicide," to Merton's analyses of anomie and deviance; and from Durkheim's sociological research on religion, focusing on religious communities, to Merton's sociological analysis of science, undertaking detailed analysis of the structure and functioning of the communities of scholars.

Next in line of Merton's intellectual ancestors comes Karl Marx. In his approach to Marx, Merton rejects dogmatism: "I have long since abandoned the struggle to determine what 'Marxism' is or is not. Instead, I have taken all that I find good in Marxian thought – and that is a considerable amount – and neglected conceptions which do not seem to me to meet tests of validity" (Merton, 1982b, p. 917). Such an approach allows him to follow some Marxian ideas, while remaining far removed from Marxism in the political or ideological sense. Many common methodological and substantive ideas would include the emphasis on sociological, and particularly structural, factors in the explanation of human phenomena; or the focus on contradictions, conflicts, and circularity of social processes. Then, the idea of the existential determination of knowledge, turned into the idea of the social-structural determination of science, has uncontestable Marxian roots.

Third in line of ancestry comes Georg Simmel. There is some commonality in their general approach to sociology: an emphasis on relationships and structures, the "form" or "geometry" of social reality. But Merton's indebtedness to Simmel becomes all the more apparent in the context of conceptual analyses. He reaches some quite similar substantive results. For example, Merton starts from Simmel's hunches in his analysis of patterned interactions, social visibility, and observability (Jaworski, 1990), in-group integration and inter-group conflicts, the completeness, openness, and closedness of groups, reference groups, and several others.

Max Weber has had less influence on Merton's work. To be sure, Merton explicitly identifies Weber as one of his "masters-at-a-distance," but except for the doctoral dissertation on the Puritan ethic and the origins of modern science, and the discussion of bureaucratic structure, it is hard to discover Weberian themes in Merton's work. On the rare occasions when Merton enters the world of Weber's sociology, he mostly accepts Weber's results as given. This is the case with the theory of action, the idea of "value-free" sociology, or the ideal type of bureaucratic organization.

So much for the classics of an earlier time. Among the later twentieth-century masters, some of whom were Merton's contemporaries or even immediate teachers, four names should be mentioned. An important influence on Merton's ideas, particularly in the field of sociology of science, was exerted by George Sarton, at the time of Merton's graduate studies undoubtedly "the acknowledged world dean among historians of science" (Merton, 1985, p. 477). The influence of Sarton can be found at the level of general interests: in science, its development, the operation of scientific communities, and specific techniques for studying historical sources. Apart from that, at the centennial of Sarton's birth, held at the University of Ghent, Merton acknowledged numerous tangible and intangible "gifts" that he received from his mentor; including the conducive microenvironment for the work on his doctoral dissertation, opening the pages of the newly established journal *Isis* for Merton's first publications, and publishing Merton's doctoral thesis in another of Sarton's periodicals, *Osiris* (1938).

Then come the two most influential teachers, under whom, and later with whom, Merton learned and worked: Pitirim Sorokin and Talcott Parsons. It was not entirely a direct and solely positive influence. Merton was apparently not an easy pupil. Admiring his teachers, he did not hesitate to criticize them and to build his own intellectual system partly in opposition to theirs. The case of Sorokin is particularly telling. Having the young Merton collaborate with him on one important chapter of his treatise *Social and Cultural Dynamics* (1937–41) and on an article on "Social Time" (1937), and some thirty years later publicly praising *On the Shoulders of Giants* (1965) as a masterpiece, Sorokin also went so far as to label Merton's paradigm of functional analysis as "a modern variation on Alexandrian or medieval scholasticism in its decaying period. It is heuristically sterile, empirically useless, and a logically cumbersome table of contents" (Sorokin, 1966, pp. 451–2). The same skepticism was expressed toward Merton's theory of reference group: "A multitude of Merton's propositions, especially in his theory of the reference groups, represent a codification of trivialities dressed up as scientific generalizations" (ibid., p. 452). The ambivalence of Sorokin's attitude is beautifully rendered by the personal inscription in one of his books: "To my darned enemy and dearest friend – Robert – from Pitirim."

Another of Merton's teachers is Talcott Parsons. Speaking for his entire generation of Harvard sociologists, Merton remarks: "Talcott was both cause and occasion for our taking sociological theory seriously" (Merton, 1980, p. 70). His influence on steering Merton's interest toward theoretical considerations was certainly immense. But for almost forty years, since a meeting of the ASA in the

1940s, which witnessed their first major, public clash, Parsons's abstract manner of theorizing was a subject of Merton's persistent challenge, leading him to propose in 1945 the notion of a "middle-range theory" (Merton, 1996, pp. 41–50). Similarly, the static and ahistoric "structural functionalism" proposed by Parsons was a subject of Merton's strong critique, contributing to the birth of his own dynamic "functional analysis" in 1949 (ibid., pp. 65–86). But their theoretical debate always stayed within the borders of exemplary civility. As Merton recollects, "I remember the grace with which, some thirty years ago, he responded in a forum of this same Association to my mild mannered but determined criticism of certain aspects of his theoretical orientation" (Merton, 1980, p. 70). Years later Parsons came to acknowledge Merton's "major contribution to the understanding and clarification of the theoretical methodology of what he, I think quite appropriately, called 'functional analysis'" (Parsons, 1975, p. 67), and then saluted him "for his highly creative role in developing the foundations of this challenging intellectual situation" (ibid., p. 80).

Finally, one must recognize Merton's decades-long "improbable collaboration" (Merton, 1994, p. 15) with Paul Lazarsfeld, producing fruit in several co-authored works, as well as in numerous research projects. It is a rare case of basically different styles of research and theorizing supplementing and enriching each other: Merton's focus on discursive, conceptual clarifications and elaborations, and Lazarsfeld's emphasis on turning concepts into operationalized, testable variables. A good example of the collaboration, their common study of friendship formation (Merton, 1954), came as close to real complementarity as could be expected in the case of two strong, independent individualities, with divergent backgrounds, thought patterns and scholarly goals.

## THE WORK

Merton has been a very prolific writer. In his bibliography we find over a dozen books, another dozen edited, or coedited, volumes, and 180 major articles. These numbers continue to grow, as Merton retains his creative powers, and continuously adds new items to his impressive academic output.

There are some characteristic formal traits of his printed work. Most of his formidable output is in the form of extended essays, long articles, introductions, reviews, discussions: sometimes getting so long as to turn imperceptibly into a book, such as the "Shandean postscript" of 290 pages, his favorite *On the Shoulders of Giants* (Merton, 1965), or the "Episodic Memoir" of 150 pages, tracing the development of the sociology of science (Merton, 1979); but most often gathered up in collections, among which *Social Theory and Social Structure* (in its three major editions of 1949, 1957, and 1968), *The Sociology of Science* (1973), *Sociological Ambivalence* (1976), *Social Research and the Practicing Professions* (1982a) and *On Social Structure and Science* (1996) are most significant. Of true "books," in the sense so dear to the humanists and so alien to the natural scientists, he has written only one and only when he had to for formal reasons: his doctoral dissertation.

The thematic range of his interests is very wide: from drug addicts to professionals, from anomie to social time, from friendship formation to role conflicts, from functional analysis to scientific ethos, from medical education to multiple discoveries, from bureaucratic structure to the origins of medieval aphorisms. He seems to pick up various topics, here and there, and then pursue them methodically, meticulously, in depth, sometimes for many years. One of his strongest contributions is insightful concepts. As he identifies new aspects of social life which he finds sociologically significant, he coins neologisms to designate them. A number of these have entered the vocabularies of not only social science but the vernacular of everyday life. Some have already become cases of the process in the history of thought which Merton has identified as "obliteration by incorporation (OBI)," in which "the sources of an idea, finding or concept become obliterated by incorporation in canonical knowledge, so that only a few are still aware of their parentage" (Merton, 1968, pp. 27–8). Merton has also highlighted earlier concepts and terms which had gone largely unregarded, performing what he calls a "cognitive conduit." The list of concepts coined by Merton which entered the canon of contemporary sociology contains manifest and latent functions, dysfunctions, self-fulfilling prophecy, homophily and heterophily, status-sets and role-sets, opportunity structures, anticipatory socialization, reference group behavior, middle-range theories, sociological ambivalence, and others. The supplements to *Oxford English Dictionary* (volumes 1–3) credit ten neologisms to Merton. His theoretical and methodological orientations of functional analysis and structural analysis are widely applied, often without recognition of the authorship. This sort of acceptance is perhaps the strongest proof of Merton's impact on contemporary sociology.

In chronological order one may distinguish a number of phases in his lifelong work (Crothers, 1987, pp. 34–40; Clark, 1990, p. 15). In the 1930s, during his Harvard years, Merton was involved in empirical projects on the homeless of Boston, and prepared his doctoral dissertation on the link between Protestant pietism and the origins of science, to be published in 1938. He also worked on major theoretical articles: "Civilization and Culture" (1936), "The Unanticipated Consequences of Purposive Social Actions" (1936), and "Social Structure and Anomie" (1938). His early interest in European sociology is documented by two review articles: "Recent French Sociology" (1934) and "Durkheim's Division of Labor in Society" (1934). He was to become one of the most cosmopolitan of American sociologists, acquiring a deep knowledge of the European heritage, and long after retirement insisted on his yearly routine of a summer tour of European capitals, savoring their cultural riches and rekindling his vast personal and professional networks of collaborators and friends.

In the 1940s he took part in a number of empirical projects carried out in the Bureau of Applied Social Research, including the study of a radio campaign known as the "war-bond drive," summarized in 1946 in the volume *Mass Persuasion*. Another of his contributions was the reinterpretation of the findings of wartime studies carried out by Samuel Stouffer and his team on the "American soldier," which resulted in an article (with A. Kitt Rossi) on reference groups, published for the first time in 1950 (Merton, 1968, pp. 279–334). The concept of reference group was purged of its early psychological bias, and rephrased in sociological, structural terms. The distinction of normative and comparative reference groups, as well as various subtle permutations of "reference group behavior," have inspired a number of later scholars (Merton, 1968, pp. 335–440). At the same time Merton worked on several methodological and theoretical topics. In 1948 his seminal article "Self-fulfilling prophecy" came out (Merton, 1996, pp. 183–204), and in 1949 his major volume *Social Theory and Social Structure*, including articles on "middle range strategy" and "manifest and latent functions," where the research program of linking empirical research and theoretical reflection, within the framework of so-called functional analysis, was put forward for the first time. It was particularly the idea of middle range theorizing which, despite some criticisms (e.g. Opp, 1970), became widely adopted by sociologists.

In the 1950s his research work was still linked to the Bureau of Applied Social Research, but he also became involved in graduate training, and his lectures and seminars became arenas of conceptual and theoretical developments, unraveled in what he calls "oral publication," only to be published in print much later. The empirical studies of medical education left two products, a methodological volume, *The Focused Interview* (with M. Fiske and P. Kendall, 1956), and a more substantive book, *The Student-Physician* (1957). There are also two theoretical papers, which joined the list of those widely followed and discussed later, and were destined to enter the canon of sociological knowledge: "The Role-set: Problems in Sociological Theory" in 1957 (Merton, 1996, pp. 113–22), where Merton painted a picture of complex and overlapping relationships among social roles and statuses; and "Social Conformity, Deviation and Opportunity-structures" (1959), where he returned after twenty years to the theory of anomie, expanding his argument in considerable measure, only to enrich it even more in 1964 in the article "Anomie, Anomia and Social Interaction: Contexts of Deviant Behavior." The deviant adaptations were shown to result not merely from the condition of anomie, but also from the structurally given, available set of legitimate and illegitimate opportunities for pursuing the chosen goals.

In the 1960s and 1970s Merton returned to his "first love" (Lazarsfeld, 1975, p. 43), namely the sociology of science, a subdiscipline which he initiated, and significantly helped to build and institutionalize. The first sign of a thematic shift came in 1957 when he delivered a presidential lecture to an ASA convention: "Priorities in Scientific Discovery: a Chapter in the Sociology of Science" (Merton, 1996, pp. 286–304). Then a series of essays addressed various problems of the sociology of science: "Singletons and Multiples in Scientific Discovery" in 1961 (Merton, 1996, pp. 305–17); "The Matthew-effect in Science: the Reward and Communication Systems of Science" in 1968, revised in 1988 (Merton, 1996, pp. 318–36); "Insiders and Outsiders: a Chapter in the Sociology of Knowledge" in 1972 (Merton, 1996, pp. 241–66); and others. In 1965, what he called his "prodigal brainchild" appeared under the title *On the Shoulders of Giants*, presenting a number of theoretical points in the sociology of science in the guise of eruditional search for the origins of the medieval metaphor. The story of his favorite subdiscipline came out in 1979 as *The Sociology of Science:*

*an Episodic Memoir*. But in this period he also published crucial statements in general sociological theory: the essay on "structural analysis" in 1975 (Merton, 1996, pp. 101–12), and an earlier study of "sociological ambivalence" (with E. Barber) in 1963 (Merton, 1996, pp. 123–31).

In the 1980s and 1990s Merton has continued his work in various directions. Part of that is devoted to rewriting, polishing, and editing earlier, unpublished manuscripts and preparing collected volumes of essays for print. An example is *Social Research and the Practicing Professions* (1982a). But he also contributed new, original articles of considerable importance: "Client Ambivalences in Professional Relationships" (with V. Merton and E. Barber, 1983), "Socially Expected Durations" (1984), and "The Fallacy of the Latest Word: the Case of Pietism and Science" (1984). At the same time, he started a new *genre* in his work: erudite and dense reminiscences about his collaborators and friends: George Sarton, Talcott Parsons, Florian Znaniecki, Alvin Gouldner, Louis Schneider, Franco Ferrarotti, James Coleman, and Paul Lazarsfeld.

His most recent work returns to the area of the sociology of science with particular emphasis on the fate of scientific concepts and phrases. This starts with the monumental *Social Science Quotations* (Sills and Merton, 1991), and continues with articles on "serendipity," "opportunity structure," "the Matthew Effect," and "the Thomas Theorem," ending with a study of the very term "scientist" as the example of the gendered use of language. In 1994, at the instigation of friends, he turned his reflective focus on himself, and produced the "slight remembrance of things past" titled "A Life of Learning," "orally published" as the C. H. Haskins memorial lecture at Philadelphia (Merton, 1994, reprinted in Merton, 1996, pp. 339–59).

## THE THEORY

From the rich mosaic of Merton's substantive contributions, produced at various levels of generality, in various areas, in various periods of his long career, there emerges a coherent system of ideas. Some of them refer to sociology: its goals, orientation, and methods. Some of them refer to society: its constitution and transformations. And in the background of all that, there is a particular image of science, as a cognitive enterprise, social institution and community of scholars. In my interpretation Merton has given us a comprehensive theory of society. But this is a contentious point, and some commentators see only the multiple, fragmentary contributions of Merton to many sociological problems and complain about the "curious omission" of "a systematic theory or a system of sociology" (Bierstedt, 1981, p. 445). I have entered into extensive debate with Robert Bierstedt on this issue, which for lack of space cannot be summarized here (see Sztompka, 1990, pp. 53–64; Bierstedt, 1990, pp. 67–74).

Two of Merton's formulations come closest to his definition of what sociology is all about. The calling of a sociologist is described as "lucidly presenting claims to logically interconnected and empirically confirmed propositions about the structure of society and its changes, the behavior of man within that structure and the consequences of that behavior" (Merton, 1968, p. 70). And the goal of the whole discipline is characterized as follows: "In the large, sociology is engaged in finding out how man's behavior and fate are affected, if not minutely governed, by his place within particular kinds, and changing kinds, of social structure and culture" (Merton, 1976, p. 184). Thus, clearly the prime subject matter of sociology is conceived as the social structure, and it is to be studied in its multiple and varied aspects: genetic (how it came to be), as well as functional (how it affects behavior); static (how it operates), as well as dynamic (how it changes). The *focus on social structure* appears from the beginning as the defining trait of Merton's sociology. In my reading this is his main focus, but here I differ with some other commentators, who would classify Merton together with Parsons simply as "functionalists" (e.g. Turner, 1974).

It is true that Merton started from an approach he called "functional analysis," but he immediately distanced himself, even by introducing that name, from doctrinaire "functionalism." For him, "the central orientation of functionalism" is "the practice of interpreting data by establishing their consequences for larger structures in which they are implicated" (Merton, 1968, pp. 100–1). In his famous "paradigm for functional analysis" in 1949, he outlined a strikingly open, deeply revised version of functionalism, allowing for the conceptualization of social conflict and social change. Thus, when a quarter century later in 1975 he wrote the important paper "Structural Analysis in Sociology" (Merton, 1996, pp. 101–12), it was not a radical break with functional analysis, but rather its logical extension. Structural analysis was a natural outgrowth of functional analysis, complementing but not at all supplanting it. Merton's own position is explicit: "The orientation is that variant of functional analysis in sociology which has evolved, over the years, into a distinct mode of structural analysis" (Merton, 1976, p. 9). Functional analysis specifies the consequences of a social phenomenon for its differentiated structural context; structural analysis searches for the determinants of the phenomenon in its structural context. Obviously, both orientations refer to the different sides of the same coin; they scrutinize two vectors of the same relationship, between a social phenomenon and its structural setting. There is no opposition of Merton the functionalist to Merton the structuralist; both theoretical orientations have been consolidated into one.

Merton's idea of the social structure, already central for his "functionalist" writings, includes four defining criteria. The focus on relations linking various components of society is clear in the early characterization of social structure: "by social structure is meant that organized set of social relationships in which members of the society or group are variously implicated" (Merton, 1968, p. 216). The emphasis on the patterned, regular, repetitive character of relations is one of the central themes pervading Merton's work, as is the term "patterned," a qualifier he is particularly fond of. As Paul Lazarsfeld noted: "Throughout his writings, this is probably the technical term he uses most often" (Lazarsfeld, 1975, p. 57). The third constitutive criterion of social structure – the idea of a deep, hidden, underlying level (corresponding to the concept of latent functions in functional analysis) – is the only aspect of Merton's approach directly influenced by the "logical-linguistic structuralism" of Claude Lévi-Strauss or Noam

Chomsky. As he puts it: "It is analytically useful to distinguish between manifest and latent levels of social structure" (Merton, 1976, p. 126).

But perhaps most important for Merton's notion of social structure is the fourth criterion, the idea of constraining or facilitating influences exerted by social structure on more concrete, and more directly accessible, social phenomena and events (behaviors, beliefs, attitudes, motivations, etc.). The concept of "structural context," and especially "structural constraint," as limiting the effective field of action, appeared in the early "paradigm for functional analysis," and was developed later: "Behavior is a result not merely of personal qualities, but of these in interaction with the patterned situations in which the individual behaves. It is these social contexts which greatly affect the extent to which the capacities of individuals are actually realized" (Merton, 1982a, p. 174). But the structural context was not conceived only in negative terms, as a limiting constraint, but also as a positive influence, facilitating, encouraging, stimulating certain choices by actors or agents: "the social structure strains the cultural values, making action in accord with them readily possible for those occupying certain statuses within the society and difficult or impossible for others. . . . The social structure acts as a barrier or as an open door to the acting out of cultural mandates" (Merton, 1968, pp. 216–17).

The best example of Merton's structural analysis is his famous theory of anomie. Understood as a structural condition of dissociation between uniform cultural demands of success and the differentiated opportunities for success, anomie is shown to generate various forms of deviant conduct: 'innovation', 'ritualism', 'retreatism' or 'rebellion', depending on the wider structural context within which it appears (Merton, 1938).

Starting from the general framework provided by his functionalist and structuralist orientation, Merton develops a more detailed image of the social structure. There are two traits which endow it with a distinct, unmistakably Mertonian flavor. First, social structure is seen as complex and multidimensional. It covers a plurality of components, elements, and items shaped into various kinds of networks or interlinkages. There are statuses, roles, role-sets, status-sets, norms, values, institutions, collectivities, groups, organizations, interests, etc., and they are depicted as cohering on numerous levels. A related, second property of Merton's idea of social structure is the emphasis on asymmetrical relationships: conflicts, contradictions, dysfunctions, strains, tensions, ambivalence. As Merton emphasizes: "It is fundamental, not incidental to the paradigm of structural analysis that social structures generate social conflict by being differentiated in historically differing extent and kind, into interlocking arrays of social statuses, strata, organizations, and communities that have their own and therefore potentially conflicting as well as common interests and values" (Merton, 1976, pp. 124–5). Merton's core idea is to consider human individuals (and their actions) as structurally located, anchored in the network of social relationships.

Attempting to cope with the immense variety of structural components, Merton proposes the distinction between the social structure in the narrow sense and the cultural structure: "the salient environment of individuals can be usefully thought of as involving the cultural structure, on the one hand, and the social structure, on the other" (Merton, 1968, p. 216). Cultural structure comes to be characterized exclusively in normative terms: as a network of norms, values, roles and institutions. Similarly, the idea of social structure in the narrow sense is gradually enriched with the help of the notion of "opportunity-structure," inspired by the idea of "life-chances," and "vested interests," taken probably from Max Weber and Karl Marx. It is understood as a hierarchically differentiated access to resources, facilities, and valuables (wealth, power, prestige, education, etc.).

The components of social structure at both levels – of social structure proper and of cultural structure – are variously interrelated, both within each level, and across distinct levels. It is, in fact, only the study of those interrelations that reveals the complex quality of the social structure as a relational network. The most important feature of Merton's analysis, which sets him apart from traditional functionalists and other proponents of social equilibrium, consensus, and harmony, is his treatment of integration as problematic and contingent, not as given. The differing degrees of integration span the spectrum, from complete consensus to complete dissensus, with these extreme poles being only analytic possibilities, rarely occurring in empirical reality. And it is striking that, perhaps to counterbalance the bias of "normative functionalism," Merton focuses his analysis on situations closer to the pole of dissensus: various kinds of strains, tensions, contradictions and conflicts in the social structure. He treats them as normal, typical, permanent, and not as pathological disturbances or deviations. Against the predominant stereotype of Merton the functionalist, I believe that his is a conflictual image of society *par excellence*, as distant as can be from the image of a harmonious utopia. Look at some of his central theoretical categories: dysfunction, role-conflict, sociological ambivalence, anomie. All of them refer to the "ugly face" of society, as Ralf Dahrendorf would put it (Dahrendorf, 1968, pp. 129–50).

The image of society underlying Merton's social theory is dynamic, incorporating structurally produced change in and of social structures: "social structures generate both changes within the structure and changes of the structure and . . . these types of change come about through cumulatively patterned choices in behavior and the amplification of dysfunctional consequences resulting from certain kinds of strains, conflicts, and contradictions in the differentiated social structure" (Merton, 1976, p. 125). As the Loomises noted long ago, Merton is "irrevocably committed to a study of the dynamics of social change no less than to stabilities of social structures" (Loomis and Loomis, 1961, p. 315).

There are two types of structural change which fall within the purview of Merton's dynamics. The first type involves the regular "functioning" or everyday "operation" of society. Such changes consist in ongoing adaptive processes which reproduce specified states of a social structure, or at least keep them within the limits which give that structure its identity. The second type of changes involves the "transformation" of society. This consists of the morphogenetic processes that disrupt the existing structure and create a basically new one in its place. The first type of change brings about the reproduction of an old social order; the second type of change brings about the production of a new social order.

The illustrations of Merton's study of adaptive processes are relatively well known. His analyses of the articulation of roles in the role-set and of the social mechanisms of adaptation in status-sets are particularly telling (Merton, 1968, pp. 425, 434). They attempt to face "the general problem of identifying the social mechanisms which serve to articulate the expectations of those in the role-set so that the occupant of a status is confronted with less conflict than would obtain if these mechanisms were not at work" (Merton, 1968, p. 425).

But adaptive processes cover only a part of social dynamics. Changes in social structure reducing inefficiency, conflict, strains, and tensions from what they would otherwise be must be distinguished from the changes of social structure which transform it significantly to produce new structural arrangements. It is rarely recognized that Merton's theory also contributes to this area of social dynamics. In Merton's theoretical orientation, the general scheme of structure-building process can be condensed as follows: under conditions still little under-stood, structural conflict brings about transformations of social structure up to a point when a new structure emerges and the structural conflict is reproduced in a new form. The basic logic underlying the process is that of amplification rather than compensation or, to put it differently, positive rather than negative feed-back.

Merton singles out two general mechanisms of structure-building. The first may be described as the mechanism of accumulated dysfunctions; the second as the mechanism of accumulated innovations. The accumulation of dysfunctions occurs when certain structural elements are dysfunctional for a social system as a whole, or some of its core segments. For example, the unrestrained pattern of egoistic hedonism, if sufficiently widespread, may lead to the disruption of the social system. The larger the number of such dysfunctional elements, and the more dysfunctional each of them, the more likely is the system to break down. Another case appears when some elements are basically functional for a social system, but have some additional, dysfunctional side-effects. For example, the competitive success orientation or "achievement syndrome" may be beneficial for the economy, but at the same time may lead to the neglect of family life and consequent breakdown of family structure. The question now becomes that of the relative weight of the accumulated dysfunctional side-effects, which, passing over a hypothetical threshold, outbalance functional outcomes and lead to institutional breakdown and "basic social change" in the form of replacement of structure. A different and, in Merton's conception, basic and empirically frequent case obtains when certain structures are functional for certain groups or strata in the society and dysfunctional for others. Examples are progressive taxation, social security, apartheid, affirmative action. The net outcome – toward stability or toward change – is then determined by the comparative (relative) power of the diverse groups or strata beneficially or adversely affected by those patterned social arrangements. As groups or strata dysfunctionally affected attain sufficient power, they are likely to introduce structural changes. The final type occurs when some structural elements are functional for certain subsystems and dysfunctional for others. For example, traditional mores or *Gemeinschaft* forms of collectivities, certainly beneficial for the integration of society may often stand in the way of economic modernization, thus becoming dysfunctional for the economic subsystem. The pressure for change here depends on the complex set of historical circumstances determining the relative functional significance of the subsystems dysfunctionally affected. If the dysfunctions touch the subsystems of strategic, core significance – in a modern society the economic institutions, political regime, etc. – structural change is likely.

The alternative mechanism of structure-building is the accumulation of innovations. Here Merton focuses on one selected case: the crescive change of normative structures, particularly through the "institutionalized evasions of institutional rules." Structure-building *via* norm evasion starts from incidents of aberrant behavior by individuals who find the norms too demanding for them, even though generally legitimate. For example, the thief who does not question the legitimacy of the fifth commandment will be outraged if something is stolen from him, and not particularly surprised if caught and sentenced. Some part of evasions from norms remains fully private, invisible, undetected. But when evasions become more widespread, undertaken by a plurality of individuals, repeated on various occasions, the public awareness is apt to be awakened. When villains get identified, the examples of particularly skillful evaders may become the subject of public lore, often tainted with envy. The occurrence of common incentives to evasion among the large collectivities of individuals – coupled with the widespread belief that "everybody does it" and the tendency to imitate successful evaders – accounts for the patterning of evasions: their regular and repeatable character. Tax evasions, cheating on exams, avoidance of customs duties and currency controls, petty theft in business firms, etc., provide familiar examples. But note that, even though rarely sanctioned, the norms are here still accorded some legitimacy. The most crucial phase comes when, as Merton puts it, "A mounting frequency of deviant but 'successful' behavior tends to lessen and, as an extreme potentiality, to eliminate the legitimacy of the institutional norms for others in the system" (Merton, 1968, p. 234). It is only now that his early concept of "institutionalized evasions" fully applies. Institutionalization in this sense is more than the mere patterning, since it involves not only repetition or regularity of behavior but the granting of a degree of legitimacy, widespread acceptance, or even positive sanctioning of evasive behavior.

This leads to the final phase of a structure-building: attaining by evasions the status of sanctioned norms, fully legitimized and embedded in a new normative structure. A cycle of structure-building ends, and of course a next one is opened, as new norms inevitably begin to be evaded, at least by some members of society, and the process of normative change starts to operate again.

A particular implementation of structural orientation is to be found in Merton's sociology of science, the field that comprises the empirical sociology of scientific communities as producing, selecting, and distributing scientific knowledge. Apart from mapping the whole field of this new sociological subdiscipline, Merton has contributed influential ideas to its three focal topics: the scientific ethos, the scientific community, and the origins of modern science.

The analysis of scientific ethos was introduced in the context of penetrating critique of the fate of science under the totalitarian, Nazi regime in Germany. Merton shows that the context functionally indispensable for the proper operation of the system of science is the liberal-democratic order. He believes that the future of science is allied with the spread of the democratic attitude and institutions. The scientific ethos appears as a micro-model of the democratic ethos. It is defined as follows: "The ethos of science is that affectively toned complex of values and norms which is held to be binding on scientists" (Merton, 1968, p. 595). The paramount values are: objectivity, the commitment to the pursuit of knowledge as adequate and as complete as possible; and originality, the commitment to the pursuit of new knowledge. Norms, or "institutional imperatives," define the acceptable or preferred means for realizing those values. There are four of them. "Universalism" requires science to be impersonal. "Communism" requires that scientific knowledge be treated not as private property of its creator, but rather as a common good, to be freely communicated and distributed. "Disinterestedness" demands the subordination of extrinsic interests to the intrinsic satisfaction of finding the truth. "Organized scepticism" requires the scientist to doubt, and then to check whether the doubt is well founded. This is carried out through public criticism by scientists of claimed contributions to scientific knowledge (Merton, 1996, pp. 267–76).

Merton is well aware that this idealized picture of the scientific ethos is rarely found in reality. The most interesting reason for deviance is found in the internal ambivalences and anomie inherent in the ethos itself. Anomic conduct in science derives primarily from the great values placed upon originality, and uniformly so for all working scientists, whereas the opportunities and possibilities of achieving original results are most variable, owing to personal constraints (talents, abilities, competences), as well as to structural constraints (limited resources, underdeveloped scientific culture, unavailable experimental technologies etc.). "In this situation of stress, all manner of adaptive behaviors are called into play, some of these being far beyond the mores of science" (Merton, 1973, p. 323). Examples include outright fraud, the fabrication of data, the denouncing of rivals, aggressive self-assertion, and plagiary.

The other aspect of science that Merton vigorously investigates is the scientific community, a specific type of social organization made up of scientists in their role behavior and mutual, interactive relationships. There are several subsystems that are singled out within the scientific community. The first is the "system of institutionalized vigilance": the examination, appraisal, criticism, and verification of scientific results by academic peers. The second is the "communication system of science": the complex mechanism of scientific publication, making the results visible. Here Merton introduces the biblical metaphor and the concept of the "Matthew Effect," observing that the works published by recognized scholars have much better chances of visibility in the scientific community than equally significant or original contributions by scholars of less renown. Another concept of "obliteration by incorporation" signifies the situation in which both the original source and the literal formulation of an idea are forgotten, owing to its long and widespread use. The notion of "cognitive conduits" refers to the spreading and inheriting of ideas over time. Another subsystem of the scientific community is the evaluation and reward system of science, the complex mechanisms of scientific recognition and reward-allocation, again biased in favor of already recognized scholars. All these processes lead to the emergence of the stratification system of science, the patterned differentiation of scholars according to identifiable criteria. Finally, there is the informal influence system of science: the network of personal ties, acquaintanceships, friendships, and loyalties that cut across other systems and significantly modify their operation. Merton pays ever-growing attention to this elusive domain giving new prominence to the seventeenth-century concept of the "invisible college" (used earlier by D. de Solla Price), as well as the twentieth-century idea of the "thought collective" (introduced by Ludwig Fleck).

The third focus of Merton's concern with science, in fact the earliest in his own research biography, is the historical origins of science and its subsequent development. In his doctoral dissertation (Merton, 1938) he put forward the widely discussed "Merton's Thesis," in some ways parallel to the earlier "Weber's Thesis" concerning the origins of capitalism. Studying the origins of empirical science in seventeenth-century England, Merton observed a linkage between religious commitments and a sustained interest in science. He noted that English scientists in that period were disproportionately ascetic Protestants or Puritans. The values and attitudes characteristic of Puritanism were seen to have had the effect of stimulating scientific research by inviting the empirical and rational quest for identifying the God-given order in the world and for practical applications; just as they legitimized scientific research through religious justification. Once having obtained institutional legitimacy, science largely severed its link with religion, finally to become a counterforce, curbing the influence of religion. But as the first push, religion was seen as crucially important.

## IMPACT

There are various measures that can be applied to evaluate a scholar's impact on his or her discipline. One is the existence of a "school," the wide network of pupils, collaborators, and followers creatively working out the bits and pieces of the master's heritage, as well as the amount of critical evaluation that his work merits. Another is the extent of reception that the work receives, which can be estimated by looking at the number of editions and translations, the time staying in print, and the citation indexes. The third, a bit paradoxical, is the degree to which the concepts and ideas undergo what Merton himself called "obliteration by incorporation," i.e. melt into the accepted, textbook canon of sociology, no longer linked to their originator.

On all three counts Merton ranks very high. As an academic teacher he had the good luck to encounter "successive cohorts of brilliant students" (Merton, 1994, p. 17). It is perhaps not an accident that so many of Merton's students at Columbia found their way into the pages of sociological textbooks: Rose and Lewis Coser, James Coleman, Robert Bierstedt, Peter Blau, Seymour M. Lipset,

Irving L. Horowitz, Alvin Gouldner, Philip Selznick, Louis Schneider, Robin Williams, Alice and Peter Rossi, Jonathan and Steven Cole, Juan Linz, Franco Ferrarotti, Hans L. Zetterberg, Ralf Dahrendorf, and many others. Now, after so many years Merton may be proud "writing papers designed specifically for those honorific volumes known as *Festschriften*. Not, as might be supposed, *Festschriften* in honor of teachers or aged peers but in honor of onetime students" (Merton, 1994, p. 17). The network of close collaborators would embrace other towering figures of twentieth-century sociology: Talcott Parsons, Paul Lazarsfeld, Robert Lynd, C. Wright Mills, Shmuel Eisenstadt. He served innumerable others, freely accepting their manuscripts for reviewing and editing. The number of published books that went through his meticulous editorial grinding exceeds two hundred. There are also hundreds of sociologists worldwide with whom he exchanged correspondence, thoroughly discussing their ideas. The bibliography of writings about Robert Merton amounts to more than four hundred items, including several monographs and collective books.

Most of his own books have gone through a series of printings and multiple foreign editions, with *Social Theory and Social Structure* appearing in almost twenty languages. Some articles are frequently republished in sociological "readers." Most of them are still in print, sometimes half a century after original publication. And the citation indexes are truly impressive. For a period from 1969 to 1989 his Social Science Citation Index count totals 6800, and his Science Citation Index count, 1350 (Clark, 1990, p. 23). This by far exceeds the number of citations to any other living sociologist. Particularly striking is the great number of citations to works published as long as forty or fifty years ago, like *Social Theory and Social Structure* of 1949, or the two famous articles on "unanticipated consequences of social actions" of 1936, and "anomie and social structure" of 1938. Citation data show that the latter "has probably been more frequently cited and reprinted than any paper in sociology" (Cole, 1975, p. 175).

Apart from general sociological theory there are some subdisciplines of sociology whose development was strongly influenced by Merton's contributions. One could mention the sociology of science and the sociology of deviance, where strong Mertonian "schools" are still operating.

## ASSESSMENT

Robert K. Merton certainly belongs to the most influential sociological theorists of the twentieth century. Two kinds of contributions make him a "modern sociological classic": his exemplary style of doing sociology and his substantive contribution to sociological theory.

The most concise characterization of Merton's style of thought may be put in three words: balance, system, and discipline. He has a strong aversion to extremes. The most famous illustration of this is his strategy of "middle range theory," based on the rejection of both narrow empiricism and abstract, scholastic theorizing. The systematic quality of his work is emphasized by the repeated use of what he calls "paradigms," introduced long before, and in meaning different from, Kuhn's, namely as heuristic schemes destined to introduce a measure of order and lucidity into qualitative and discursive sociological analysis, by codifying the results of prior inquiry and specifying the directions of further research. The most famous are his paradigms for functional analysis, for structural analysis, for deviant social behavior, and for the sociology of knowledge. The disciplined quality of Merton's work is self-consciously expressed by his concepts of "disciplined inquiry" and "disciplined eclecticism." The first means "systematic and serious, that is to say, the intellectually responsible and austere pursuit of what is first entertained as an interesting idea" (Merton, 1968, p. xiv). Merton's persistence in tracing the implications and ramifications of his central insights is legendary. Decade after decade he returns to the same themes, each time developing them conceptually and enriching them with new empirical evidence. For example, his major reworkings of the theme of "anomie" came out in 1938, 1949, 1955, 1959, 1964, and 1997. The idea of "disciplined eclecticism" encourages openness and antidogmatism: the critical and systematic adaptation of a plurality of theoretical orientations and theories in solving sociological problems. Thus Merton presents a truly classical model of how sociology should be done, perhaps a needed reminder in the time of a certain methodological anarchy. But of course his contribution is not limited to a methodological model. He applies the model himself, reaching fundamental results, including an original and fruitful image of society.

The preceding analysis of Merton's work was intended to corroborate five claims. First, I believe that despite the dispersed, piecemeal, fragmentary nature of Merton's contributions, they add up to a coherent system of thought. Of course, the system is far from complete: there are many empty spots, many lacunae, many fields of "specified ignorance" (to use his favorite term). But all the islands of enlightenment fit nicely into the overall topography. And the dark or shadowy areas provide the system with strong potentials for elaboration, suggest further problems for fruitful inquiry.

Second, I believe that despite his own research focus on the middle level of generality ("middle range theories"), Merton has unwittingly produced a general theory of society. His contributions add up to a consistent picture of the social world. Third, against the stereotypes identifying Merton as an embodiment of functionalism, I believe that his orientation is and always has been mainly structuralist. Drawing inspiration from Durkheim, he perceives all social phenomena as located in a structural context, interlinked with other phenomena within wider social wholes. Those linkages are of two sorts: causal, when a phenomenon is constrained or facilitated by structural context; and functional, when a phenomenon produces structural effects (functions). "Functional analysis" clearly appears as a specific mode of a more general structural approach pervading Merton's inquiry.

Fourth, he is a conflict theorist *par excellence*. His image of social life is saturated with contradictions, strains, tensions, ambivalence, dysfunctions, and conflicts of all sorts. There is nothing of the tranquil, harmonious, consensual, equilibrated utopia in a human drama as depicted by Merton: with its torment of uncertainty and unintended, latent consequences of any action; with its agony of ambivalence and cross-cutting pressures of norms, roles, and statuses; with its fright of normlessness, or anomie; with its risk of defeat or "self-destroying prophecies."

Fifth, his theory is dynamic in the full sense of the term. As I attempted to illustrate in detail, he not only recognizes various modalities of change, but focuses on structural changes, i.e. those which are structurally generated and structurally consequential. And he not only studies reproductive (or adaptive) processes, but devotes considerable attention to the structure-building through which new, or fundamentally modified, structures are socially constructed.

The structural theory of society – incorporating "social statics" and "social dynamics," "social anatomy" and "social physiology," consensus and conflict, stability and change, reproduction and emergence – provides a fully fledged, multidimensional paradigm for sociology. It is deeply rooted in the classical sociological tradition of the nineteenth century. In fact, Merton synthesizes and extends the classical sociological tradition. He attains balanced, intermediate positions on various traditional issues, unravels entangled premises to reach their rational core, unmuddles the muddle of sociological controversies. This allows him to introduce a further measure of order and systematization to the classical heritage. Merton's determined effort to clarify, codify, consolidate, and organize disparate pieces of sociological wisdom results in a mosaic that is rewarding aesthetically as well as intellectually. The synthesis becomes much more than a summary of earlier ideas: it results in their selective and critical reformulation and cumulation. At many points, novel concepts, insights, and ideas are added to the classical heritage.

Thus, perhaps Merton's most important service to the development of contemporary sociology is the vindication of the classical style of doing sociology and the classical heritage of theoretical ideas. He shows with new vigor that the ideas of the nineteenth-century masters are not at all exhausted or dead. In his work, paradigms of classical thought gain new vitality, as they are shown to be fruitful: both in the explanatory sense, as means of accounting for large areas of social experience and for solving the puzzles confronting men and women in their social life; and in the heuristic sense, as means of raising new questions and suggesting new puzzles for solution.

An important, and only seemingly paradoxical, function of Merton's synthesis is to indicate directions of inquiry that will eventually elaborate and overcome it. Its systematic and lucid quality enables us to perceive not only past and current knowledge but also "the various sorts of failure: intelligent errors and unintelligent ones, noetically induced and organizationally induced foci of interest and blind spots in inquiry, promising lands abandoned, and garden-paths long explored, scientific contributions ignored or neglected by contemporaries,... serendipity lost" (Merton, 1975, p. 336). Ultimately, it leads toward mapping further domains of "specified ignorance": "what is not yet known but needs to be known in order to lay the foundation for still more knowledge" (Merton, 1976, p. 112). It is precisely here that the past and the future of our discipline meet. Merton's work provides a solid bridge from the accomplishments of the classical masters to the future vistas of sociology.

## Bibliography

### Writings of Robert Merton

Social Time: a Methodological and Functional Analysis (with Pitirim A. Sorokin). 1937. *American Journal of Sociology*, 42, 619–29.

Science, Technology and Society in Seventeenth Century England. 1938. In G. Sarton (ed.), *OSIRIS*. Bruges, Belgium: St Catherine Press, pp. 362–632 (reprinted New York: Howard Fertig, 1970 and 1993).

*Mass Persuasion*. 1948. New York: Harper & Brothers.

Friendship as a Social Process: a Substantive and Methodological Analysis (with P. F. Lazarsfeld). 1954. In M. Berger, T. Abel and C. Page (eds), *Freedom and Control in Modern Society*. New York: Van Nostrand, pp. 18–66.

*The Focused Interview* (with M. Fiske and P. L. Kendall). 1956. New York: Free Press.

*The Student-physician: Introductory Studies in the Sociology of Medical Education* (with G. G. Reader and P. L. Kendall). 1957. Cambridge, MA: Harvard University Press.

Social Conformity, Deviation and Opportunity-structure. 1959. *American Sociological Review*, 24(2), 177–89.

*On the Shoulders of Giants*. 1965. New York: Harcourt Brace Jovanovich ("vicennial edition" 1985, Harcourt Brace Jovanovich; "post-Italianate edition" 1993, University of Chicago Press).

*Social Theory and Social Structure*. 1949. New York: Free Press (revised edition 1957; enlarged and revised edition 1968).

*The Sociology of Science: Theoretical and Empirical Investigations* (edited by N. W. Storer). 1973. Chicago: University of Chicago Press.

Thematic Analysis in Science: Notes on Holton's Concept. 1975 *Science*, 188, April 35, 335–8.

*Sociological Ambivalence and Other Essays*. 1976. New York: Free Press.

*Sociology of Science: an Episodic Memoir*. 1979. Carbondale: Southern Illinois University Press.

Remembering the Young Talcott Parsons 1980. *The American Sociologist*, 15 (May), 68–71.

*Social Research and the Practicing Professions* (edited by A. Rosenblatt and T. F. Gieryn). 1982a. Cambridge, MA: ABT Books.

Alvin W. Gouldner: Genesis and Growth of a Friendship. 1982b. *Theory and Society*, 11, 915–38.

George Sarton: Episodic Recollections by an Unruly Apprentice. 1985. *ISIS*, 76, 477–86.

*The Macmillan Book of Social Science Quotations* (edited with D. Sills). 1991. New York: Macmillan.

A Life of Learning. 1994. New York: ACLS Occasional Paper No. 25, 20 pp. (reprinted in *On Social Structure and Science*).

*On Social Structure and Science* (edited by P. Sztompka). 1996. Chicago: University of Chicago Press.

### Further reading

Bierstedt, R. (1981) *American Sociological Theory: a Critical History*. New York: Academic Press.

Bierstedt, R. (1990) Merton's Systematic Theory. In J. Clark, C. Modgil and S. Modgil (eds), *Robert K. Merton: Consensus and Controversy*. London: Falmer Press, pp. 67–74.

Clark, J. (1990) Robert Merton as Sociologist. In J. Clark, C. Modgil and S. Modgil (eds), *Robert K. Merton: Consensus and Controversy*. London: Falmer Press, pp. 13–23.

Clark, J., Modgil C. and Modgil, S. (eds) (1990) *Robert K. Merton: Consensus and Controversy*. London: Falmer Press.

Cohen, I. B. (1990) *Puritanism and the Rise of Modern Science: the Merton Thesis*. New Brunswick, NJ: Rutgers University Press.

Cohen, I. B. (ed.) (1990) *Puritanism and the Rise of Modern Science: The Merton Thesis*. New Brunswick: Rutgers University Press

Cole, S. (1975) The Growth of Scientific Knowledge: Theories of Deviance as a Case Study. In L. A.Coser (ed.), *The Idea of Social Structure: Papers in Honor of Robert K. Merton*. New York: Harcourt Brace Jovanovich, pp. 175–220.

Coser, L. A. (ed.) (1975) *The Idea of Social Structure: Papers in Honor of Robert K. Merton*. New York: Harcourt Brace Jovanovich.

Coser, L. A. and Nisbet, R. (1975) Merton and the Contemporary Mind: an Affectionate Dialogue. In L. A. Coser (ed.), *The Idea of Social Structure: Papers in Honor of Robert K. Merton*. New York: Harcourt Brace Jovanovich, pp. 3–10.

Crothers, C. (1987) *Robert K. Merton: a Key Sociologist*. London: Tavistock.

Dahrendorf, R. (1968) *Essays in the Theory of Society*. Stanford, CA: Stanford University Press.

Gieryn, T. F. (ed.) (1980) *Science and Social Structure: a Festschrift for Robert K. Merton*. New York: New York Academy of Sciences.

Hunt, M. M. (1961) How Does It Come to Be So? Profile of Robert K. Merton. *New Yorker*, 36, pp. 39–63.

Jaworski, G. D. (1990) Robert K. Merton's Extension of Simmel's "Ubersehbar." *Sociological Theory*, 8, 99–105.

Kearney, H. F. (1973) Merton Revisited. *Science Studies*, 3, 72–8.

Lazarsfeld, P. (1975) Working with Merton. In L. A. Coser (ed.), *The Idea of Social Structure: Papers in Honor of Robert K. Merton*. New York: Harcourt Brace Jovanovich, pp. 35–66.

Loomis, C. P. and Loomis, Z. K. (1961) *Modern Social Theories: Selected American Writers*. Princeton, NJ: Van Nostrand.

Mongardini, C. and Tabboni, S. (eds) (1997) *Merton and Contemporary Sociology*. New Brunswick, NJ: Transaction Publishers.

Opp, K. D. (1970) Theories of the Middle Range as a Strategy for the Construction of a General Sociological Theory: a Critique of a Sociological Dogma. *Inquiry*, 2, 243–53.

Parsons, T. (1975) The Present Status of "Structural-Functional" Theory in Sociology. In L. A. Coser (ed.), *The Idea of Social Structure: Papers in Honor of Robert K. Merton*. New York: Harcourt Brace Jovanovich, pp. 67–83.

Sorokin, P. A. (1937–41) *Social and Cultural Dynamics*, 4 volumes. New York: American Books Co.

Sorokin, P. A. (1966) *Sociological Theories of Today*. New York: Harper & Row.

Sztompka, P. (1986) *Robert K. Merton: an Intellectual Profile*. London and New York: Macmillan and St Martin's Press.

Sztompka, P. (1990) R. K. Merton's Theoretical System: an Overview. In L. A. Coser (ed.), *Robert K. Merton: Consensus and Controversy*. London: Falmer Press, pp. 53–64.

Turner, J. H. (1974) *The Structure of Sociological Theory*. Homewood, IL: Dorsey Press.

# 14

## Erving Goffman

### GARY ALAN FINE AND PHILIP MANNING

Erving Goffman has a hold on the sociological imagination. While he was perhaps not as broad or subtle a theorist as Durkheim, Simmel, Marx, or Weber, the images and slogans of this scholar have become an integral part of the discipline. The dramaturgical metaphor has become sociology's second skin. As a consequence, Erving Goffman is arguably the most influential American[1] sociologist of the twentieth century.

While this bald statement would be accepted by many, two additional features are also widely accepted. First, Goffman himself can hardly be considered a conventional social theorist. In his thirty-year academic career Goffman did not attempt to develop an overarching theory of society; nor did he raise issues that speak to transhistorical concerns of social order. While on occasion Goffman referred to other social theorists, such references were typically included in passing, and his work does not contain a systematic confrontation with other sociological theorists. Goffman's work can be characterized equally by those central sociological issues that he did not discuss (or did so only briefly), and those that he explored so brilliantly. Second, Goffman does not easily fit within a specific school of sociological thought. Although he was often linked to the symbolic interactionist perspective, he did not readily accept this label (see Goffman (1969, pp. 136–45) for his account of the limitations of this approach). Further, Goffman did not produce a close-knit school of younger scholars who saw themselves as following his agenda (Grimshaw, 1983, p. 147). Goffman embraced and transformed the ideas of certain important social theorists (Durkheim, Simmel, Blumer, and Hughes, and Schutz), and the work of others, who might be labeled his "students," was profoundly influenced by contact with Goffman (John Lofland, Gary Marx, Harvey Sacks, Eviatar Zerubavel, Carol Brooks Gardner, Emmanuel Schegloff, David Sudnow, and Charles and Marjorie Goodwin). However, it is odd, given Goffman's influence, that there are remarkably few scholars who are continuing his work. In part, this is because Goffman has a signature style, but it is also because Goffman's stylistic approach is not broadly valued in the discipline (Abbott, 1997). This paradox must be at the heart of any analysis of Erving Goffman's theoretical legacy.

## GOFFMAN'S LIFE

Erving Manual Goffman was born in Mannville, Alberta, on June 11, 1922, to Ukrainian Jewish parents. His parents, Max and Ann, were among the 200,000 Ukrainians who migrated to Canada between 1897 and 1914 (Winkin, 1988, p. 16). Along with his sister, Frances, he was brought up in Dauphin, near Winnipeg, where later, in 1937, he attended St John's Technical High School. Winkin (1988) reports that, for unknown reasons, his friends called him "Pookie." Goffman showed an initial interest in chemistry, which he pursued at the University of Manitoba in 1939.

In 1943–4 he worked at the National Film Board in Ottawa, where he met Dennis Wrong, who encouraged Goffman's interest in sociology. Soon after, Goffman enrolled at the University of Toronto, where, under the guidance of C. W. M. Hart and Ray Birdwhistell, he read widely in sociology and anthropology. The writings of Durkheim, Radcliffe-Brown, Warner, Freud and Parsons were particularly important to his intellectual development (Winkin, 1988, p. 25). At Toronto, he also developed a close friendship with the anthropologist Elizabeth Bott.

In 1945 Goffman graduated from Toronto with a degree in sociology and moved to the University of Chicago for graduate work. Winkin reports that he was initially overwhelmed by the transition. This may be a euphemistic way of saying that Goffman's grades were not impressive at the beginning of his graduate career. The University of Chicago was hectic and confusing, a situation exacerbated by the many students relying on funding from the GI Bill. After several difficult years Goffman settled into the routine of graduate life, taking numerous courses, including Everett Hughes's seminar on Work and Occupations, where he first heard the expression "total institution," which became important to his later writing (Burns, 1992, p. 101). For reasons perhaps relating to his steady stream of sarcasm, Goffman earned a nickname from his fellow graduate students: "the little dagger" (Winkin, 1988, p. 28).

Data on Goffman's early years in graduate school are sparse (Winkin, 1999), and apparently he kept to himself during that period, reading voraciously. However, in 1949 Goffman completed his MA thesis, based on a survey research project concerning audience reactions to a then popular radio soap opera. Soon after, he left for the Shetland Islands. From December 1949 to May 1951 Goffman lived on the Island of Unst, where he collected ethnographic data for his doctoral dissertation. Masquerading as an American interested in agricultural techniques, he absorbed as much as he could about everyday life on this small Scottish island, partially overcoming the initial suspicions of the islanders, who thought that he might be a spy (Winkin, 1999).

After leaving the Shetland Islands, Goffman moved to Paris, where he completed a draft of his doctoral dissertation. The following year he returned to Chicago and married the 23-year-old Angelica Choate, whom he had met earlier at the university, where she was an undergraduate majoring in psychology. Their son, Tom, was born the following year.

In 1953 Goffman successfully defended his dissertation. His examiners had mixed reactions to his study: several expected a detailed case study and were dismayed to receive what was, in effect, a general theory of face-to-face interaction (Winkin, 1998). After a brief stretch as a research assistant for Edward Shils, Goffman, his wife, and young son moved to Washington, DC, where in 1955 he began observations at St Elizabeths hospital (Goffman, 1961a). For the next three years Goffman spent time at the hospital, where he was given the position of assistant to the athletic director. This marginal position gave him access to all parts of the institution.

On January 1, 1958, Goffman was invited by Herbert Blumer to teach at the University of California at Berkeley, where he was hired as a visiting assistant professor. During the next four years Goffman progressed rapidly. *The Presentation of Self* was reissued by a prominent publisher in the United States in 1959. This was followed by *Asylums* in 1961 and *Encounters* later that year. He was promoted several times and became a full professor in 1962. In addition to his academic interests, Goffman showed himself to be a shrewd stock market analyst and a keen gambler. Goffman was proud of his stock-picking abilities: later in life he boasted that even though he was one of the highest paid sociologists in the United States, he still earned a third of his income from investments and a third from royalties. By contrast, his gambling abilities remain uncertain: there are reports that he was regularly beaten at poker by colleagues at the university; losses that he accepted with grace and good humor (Marx, 1984). He was a stronger blackjack player, and made frequent visits to casinos in Nevada. Indeed, later he trained, qualified, and worked as a blackjack dealer at the Station Plaza Casino in Las Vegas, where he was promoted to pit boss (Andrea Fontana, personal correspondence). In his published work, particularly in the essay "Where the Action Is," Goffman includes tantalizing hints of an ethnography of gambling and casino life; however, he never published a separate study.

During his stay at Berkeley, his wife, Angelica, had serious mental health problems, which resulted in her suicide in 1964. A parallel may exist between Goffman's academic interests in mental illness and his own personal observations of it at home. Perhaps nowhere is this clearer than in his 1969 essay, "The Insanity of Place," which is, arguably, autobiographical.

In 1966, Goffman spent a sabbatical year at the Harvard Center for International Affairs. At Harvard he developed a friendship with Thomas Schelling, from whom he strengthened his understanding of game theoretic accounts of human behavior. He resigned his position at Berkeley on June 30, 1968 in order to accept a Benjamin Franklin Chair in Sociology and Anthropology at the University of Pennsylvania. His salary at that time was $30,000 a year, setting a new high for a sociology professor. For a variety of reasons (perhaps including salary) Goffman was alienated from his colleagues in sociology, and he spent the first couple of years at the university working out of an office in the Anthropological Museum. The move to Philadelphia did not slow down his research productivity. In 1971 he published *Relations in Public*, in which he brought together many of his ideas about the organization of everyday conduct. Simultaneously he was also working on the book he hoped to be his magnum opus, *Frame Analysis*, eventually published in 1974. Given the long gestation period, the lukewarm reception of the book by the sociological community must have been a disappointment.

In 1981 he married the linguist, Gillian Sankoff, with whom he had a daughter, Alice, in May 1982. On November 20, 1982, he died of stomach cancer, a few weeks after he had to cancel the presentation of his Presidential Address to the American Sociological Association. This paper, "The Interaction Order," was published in the *American Sociological Review* in 1983. The dry humor of the presentation is striking: Goffman added a preface to his speech from his hospital bed, knowing that he would not be able to deliver it in person. The title of the talk was also carefully chosen: this was the title that, in 1953, Goffman had used for the conclusions to his doctoral dissertation. This gesture brought a sense of closure to his intellectual ideas.

## The Social Context

As Goffman's generation is only now passing from the scene as active scholars, the full history of the period in which he was trained is still being written. Despite Goffman's links with a number of academic and research institutions, including the University of Toronto, the Sorbonne, the University of Edinburgh, the National Institutes of Health, the University of California at Berkeley, Harvard University, and the University of Pennsylvania, the one location that has been taken as having more influence on him than all others is the University of Chicago. As a result of a chance meeting, Goffman decided to attend graduate school with Everett Hughes, a fellow Canadian, at the University of Chicago.

While less has been made of Goffman's tenure at Berkeley and at Pennsylvania than is warranted, it was the social scene in Chicago's Hyde Park in the years after the Second World War that had the most lasting and profound impression. Erving Goffman was very much a product of this time and place.

Hyde Park in the late 1940s and early 1950s was a special location for the development of sociology and sociologists. The roster of graduate students from the period reads like a who's who of the creative minds of the discipline. The most extensive set of accounts detailing the intellectual and social life at the University of Chicago in this period are included in *A Second Chicago School?* (Fine, 1995), a collection of essays that depicts the profound influence of the place and period on the development of sociology in the latter half of the twentieth century.

Prior to 1935, Chicago was the dominant sociology program in the United States, and the world. However, by the late 1940s, the development of "the

General Theory of Action" under Talcott Parsons at Harvard and survey research and functional analysis under Paul Lazarsfeld and Robert Merton at Columbia made Cambridge and Morningside Heights strong contenders, perhaps more "cutting edge" than the embattled qualitative tradition at Chicago (Bulmer, 1984; Gusfield, 1995, pp. ix–x; Camic, 1996; Abbott, 1997). Still, Chicago proved to be an intellectually exciting home for many graduate students, even if the changes in the faculty, notably the move of Herbert Blumer to Berkeley, led to misgivings by the university administration (Abbott and Graziano, 1995). Further, despite the stereotypes that have often linked Chicago sociology to the interactionist project, the department was both theoretically and methodologically diverse (Bulmer, 1984; Platt, 1995).

According to Joseph Gusfield (1995, pp. xv–xvi), himself a graduate student in the period, the cohort in which Goffman came of age as a sociologist was a large one, consisting of a high proportion of Jews and veterans. Further, aside from similarities among the members of the cohort, the very size of the cohort contributed to a sense of cohesion and engagement. The Chicago department never had a large faculty. During the late 1940s, the department had fewer than ten faculty and only seven full professors, and, as these were prominent men, several were likely to be on leave at any one time. During the high point of the postwar years over 200 students were registered in either the MA or the PhD programs. Whereas only four PhDs were granted in 1946, by 1954, twenty-eight were awarded. The explosion in the number of graduate students overwhelmed the ability of the faculty to nurture them or even to provide guidance for preliminary exams and doctoral dissertations (Lopata, 1995, p. 365), and provoked irritation or even bitterness toward the structure of the program, especially by graduate students.

As a result, graduate students banded together for social and intellectual support. In 1947, students who had been active previously in union activity formed a student grievance committee that focused on the neglect of students by the faculty (Lopata, 1995, p. 366). The fact that the committee did not achieve many changes (Chicago defined itself as a research university, with teaching graduate students a secondary priority) created graduate student cohesion. In addition, the structure of the department led graduate students to formulate their problems independently from faculty members, leading to scholarly creativity early in their careers. Thus, even Goffman's early work, such as his writings on the significance of class symbols, though clearly influenced by some Chicago faculty and by other graduate students, was also uniquely his own.

However, other factors were at work. One important feature was the geographical ecology of Hyde Park, which helped to form an aggregate of graduate students into a cohesive social group. Gusfield points out that most of the cohort lived within a few blocks of each other, near the somewhat isolated campus, surrounded by a rundown urban area. The campus was a defended neighborhood, circled by a seemingly hostile outside world. Gusfield notes that the many rundown apartment houses made it possible for most graduate students to afford housing close to campus. Students found common hangouts, such as Jimmy's

Bar, the University Tavern, the Tropical Hut eatery, and a wide array of fine bookstores. Gusfield (1995, p. xv) writes:

> The closeness of places, the then-safety of the streets, and the proximity of resid-ence helped us to form friendships and events of solidarity that have been lasting. The classroom spilled over onto the streets and, of course, into the living rooms and kitchens. My wife still remembers the night she thought I had met foul play when a search of the streets at 1:00 A.M. found me and Erving Goffman "talking shop" under a lamp post. During one or two years there was an ongoing softball game in a 57th Street schoolyard. The Social Science building had a daily interdisciplinary coffee hour. There were the frequent parties and, above all, the talk-talk-talk.

The close friendships and networks in which Goffman participated and in which he was an active participant led to sufficient personal respect that he was anointed the "one most likely to succeed."

Although it does not appear that Goffman himself was very active politically, many of his fellow graduate students were involved politically in such causes as civil rights and union activity. His seeming apathy was continually confronted and tested by the commitments of his friends and classmates.

While Goffman's intellectual contributions stand on their own merit, the presence of a powerful social network composed of other prominent sociologists who could promote his work, as well as provide occasional advice, proved beneficial for his future status. Reputation, while grounded in the work itself, is also a function of the social situation (Fine, 1996). The impact of social settings matters in our interpretation of any theorist.

Goffman's years at the University of California at Berkeley (1958–68) were intellectually productive and socially tumultuous. By the early 1960s Berkeley's Department of Sociology was one of the strongest in the United States, situated in a rapidly growing, prestigious state university. In addition to Goffman, the department included such luminaries as Seymour Martin Lipset, Kingsley Davis, Neil Smelser, Nathan Glazer, Reinhard Bendix, John Clausen, David Matza, Philip Selznick, and, of course, Herbert Blumer. As Gary Marx (1984, p. 650) notes, the department drew scholars from the traditions at Harvard, Columbia, and Chicago, and "it was probably the only major school not dominated by one or two powerful intellectual figures and a single methodological or theoretical approach." As the decade progressed, Berkeley became synonymous with stu-dent protest, and the Department of Sociology was one of the centers of protest in this chaotic period (Heirich, 1970; Marx, 1984). While Goffman was by no means part of the radical fringe of the department and rejected political involve-ment (commenting, as Marx (1984, p. 658) reports, "When they start shooting students from the steps of Sproul Hall I guess I'll get involved, but not until then"), his sometimes cynical, always corrosive approach fit well with the spirit of the times. Berkeley in the 1960s, like Chicago in the 1940s and 1950s, was one of the centers for the development of American sociology, and the impressive array of faculty and students, coupled with the protests and debates on campus, had a dramatic effect on Goffman, forcing him to question the very basis by which social actors come to understand and behave towards each other. This theme found its best expression in *Frame Analysis*. Goffman's predilection to view the world as an outsider found considerable support in a community such as Berkeley, an enclave that was self-defined as radical and alienated. Further, one might speculate that the rich and lively street culture found on and around the Berkeley campus provided an impetus for Goffman's analyses of the dynamics of public behavior, given expression in *Behavior in Public Places* and *Relations in Public*.

The University of Pennsylvania was not quite the same intellectual center that Chicago and Berkeley had been, despite the presence of important figures (e.g. Phillip Rieff, Marvin Wolfgang, E. Digby Baltzell); yet even there Goffman was able to create a social environment that supported and enhanced his work. As a Benjamin Franklin Professor, Goffman did not have any specific department responsibilities, and his contacts ranged far afield from the Department of Sociology, incorporating scholars at the Annenberg School of Communication, the Department of Anthropology, and the Department of Linguistics. Indeed, for many of his early years at the University of Pennsylvania, Goffman had only a distant relationship with many colleagues in the Department of Sociology. Perhaps most significant in terms of his social and intellectual development was Goffman's contact with the sociolinguists William Labov and Dell Hymes. Much of Goffman's later work, notably *Gender Advertisements* and *Forms of Talk*, was heavily influenced by communications theory and sociolinguistics.

While it is plausible to contend that Goffman's intellectual eminence would likely have revealed itself in any circumstances, the fact that for much of his career he was surrounded by first-rate scholars in communities of intellectual and social ferment surely contributed to the development of his idiosyncratic vision.

## THE INTELLECTUAL CONTEXT

As noted above, the Department of Sociology at the University of Chicago was small, but intellectually central to the vitality of the discipline. During Goffman's early years as a student in the department, only seven full professors were on staff: Ernest Burgess, Louis Wirth, Herbert Blumer, William F. Ogburn, Robert Hauser, Everett Hughes, and W. Lloyd Warner. Yet, despite the size of the unit, the faculty was remarkably active on a number of important projects. While there was not a mentorship relationship between faculty and students during this period, many students worked with faculty on various projects. Everett Hughes was particularly active in these projects, and worked closely with numerous students (although not, apparently, with Goffman himself). These collaborations produced, among others, studies of the process of aging and medical training (resulting in *Growing Old: the Process of Disengagement* and *Boys in White*). The presence of the National Opinion Research Center (NORC) on campus, having recently moved from the University of Denver, provided a noninteractionist context for large-scale survey research (for other examples of the intellectual context and activities of Chicago in this period see Lopata, 1995, pp. 366–72).

Goffman is a part – a central, defining part – of that group of young scholars who were trained at the University of Chicago in the decade after the Second World War: the "Second Chicago School" (Fine, 1995). These scholars included such subsequently influential and notable figures in the discipline as Joseph Gusfield, Howard Becker, Ralph Turner, Fred Davis, Helena Lopata, and Kurt and Gladys Lang, to name a few. Together, these scholars took a skeptical stance toward the dominant functionalist and quantitative perspective of mid-century American sociology, postulating an alternative, if somewhat hazy, vision. This period represented the flowering of interpretive sociology: a group of scholars that more than their interactionist predecessors were relentlessly empirical, producing a powerful set of detailed, descriptive analyses not found in the substantive analyses of Robert Park, Herbert Blumer, and Everett Hughes. These younger scholars, each in his or her own way, revealed an interest in the power of sudden, dramatic change, a concern with totalitarian control, and a concern with the basis of both community and conformity. The development of theories of collective behavior, race and ethnicity, work and occupations, and deviance, grounded in empirical analyses, set an agenda for research in these areas for decades (see, for example, Snow and Davis, 1995; Wacker, 1995; Galliher, 1995).

At Berkeley, intellectual debates concerned political analysis and language studies. Goffman's mentoring of Gary Marx and John Lofland falls into the first category, his teaching of the future conversational analysts Harvey Sacks, David Sudnow, and Emanuel Schegloff into the second category. Political themes, never explicitly developed in Goffman's own writing, find their echoes in the metaphors of concentration camps in *Asylums*, of passing in race relations in *Stigma*, and in the discussion of espionage in *Strategic Interaction*.

The years at the University of Pennsylvania broadened Goffman's interests in sociolinguistics, nonverbal communication, and the role of implicit meaning in communication systems. Goffman's (1979) analysis of the role of gendered visual communication in magazine advertisements in *Gender Advertisements* could only have been developed in an intellectual context in which the content analysis of media sources was intellectually central and academically legitimate. It is surely not incidental that Goffman's reunion at Annenberg with his early mentor at the University of Toronto, Ray Birdwhistell, certainly was an impetus for his attempt to understand body language. In a similar vein, the sociolinguistic essays found in *Forms of Talk* and in "Felicity's Condition" result from Goffman's interactions with linguists at the University of Pennsylvania. This built on his earlier dialogues, particularly with John Searle, at Berkeley in the early 1960s.

Although it is difficult to trace precisely the intellectual forces that influenced Goffman's distinctive creativity, the intellectual currents at those institutions in which he studied and was employed had a considerable effect on the development of his sociology. Even such a distinctive voice as Goffman's was modulated by the other participants in his academic choruses.

## Goffman's Ideas

As noted, it is notoriously difficult to classify Goffman's style of sociology. Although he was a central figure in American sociology from the early 1960s until his death in 1982, and although he has been adopted by prominent European social theorists interested in the analysis of human agency, Goffman's ideas are difficult to reduce to a number of key themes. A "Goffman school" did not emerge before or after his death. Many sociologists acknowledge an influence, but few consider their work to be a continuation of Goffman's. As Hymes memorably put it, few sociologists have been prepared to pick up Goffman's "golden shovel" (Hymes, 1984, p. 625; quoted by Drew and Wootton, 1988, p. 2).

This observation has led some scholars (Smith, 1989; Williams, 1980) to posit a similarity between Goffman and Georg Simmel. Simmel likened his essayistic ideas to a cash legacy that can be spent or reinvested, with the result that the source is no longer evident in the product. Perhaps something similar has occurred with Goffman's legacy: contemporary sociologists have cashed in their "positions" on Goffman, transforming his work into their own visions. Understood in this way, Goffman emerges as a precursor to ethnomethodology, to structuration theory, to neo-institutionalism, and to both a modernist, critical social theory and a postmodern symbolic interactionism.

Two images of Goffman emerge from this discussion: Goffman can be seen as either a maverick or a transitional figure. Both images account for the absence of a Goffman school. As a maverick, Goffman produced a one-of-a-kind sociology, both stylistically and substantively. Schegloff (1996) recently commented that although several generations of sociologists have admired Goffman's work, there is little sense of what to do with it. As Goffman remarked about himself, his work resists pigeonholing.

Further, as Brown (1977), Atkinson (1989), Fine and Martin (1990), Manning (1991), Smith and Travers (1998), and others have shown, Goffman is a maverick in that his writings can be read as both literature and social science. Although literary figures such as Burke and Pirandello were important to his dramaturgical account of everyday life, Goffman's writing style probably owes more to Everett Hughes.

Not only did he cite literature as source material, Goffman also displayed a deft metaphorical touch. Goffman's work has a literary sensibility that is rare in modern sociology (see Abbott, 1997). Goffman's stylistic devices, however appealing, implicitly question orthodox methodological approaches. What is implicit in his style is often explicit in his prefaces, which defend a Hughesian methodology by criticizing what he sees as the pretensions of quantitative methodology (see, for example, the preface to *Relations in Public*).

Goffman can also be seen as a transitional figure. In this guise he appears as a bridge between generations of Chicago sociology and some of the varied concerns of contemporary sociology. Understood in this way, Goffman is a successor to both Park and Hughes. Particularly from Hughes, Goffman found similarities in apparent differences. Instead of focusing on the obvious differences between the career trajectories of, for example, lawyers and prostitutes, Goffman also looked for telling similarities. Goffman developed a passion for a comparative, qualitative sociology that aimed to produce generalizations about human behavior.

Goffman's ideas have become transitional elements in European theoretical ventures as well. Anthony Giddens (1984) has accorded Goffman a special place in the theory of structuration: seeing a recognition of the interplay of structure and interpretive agency in his analysis. To a lesser extent, Habermas has also attempted to incorporate Goffman into his theory of undistorted communication (see Chriss, 1995). Strong ties also exist between Goffman's and Bourdieu's writing. However, it is worth remembering that Goffman was suspicious of grand theoretical schemes, and his preface to *Frame Analysis* indicated his more modest ambitions. Nevertheless, it is certainly true that new generations are being exposed to Goffman, in some cases for the first time, through the work of these prominent social theorists.

## GOFFMAN'S WORK

We distinguish six components of Goffman's work: (a) his pre-dramaturgical writings, including his graduate work at the University of Chicago; (b) his extended metaphorical investigations, notably *The Presentation of Self* but also his contribution to the study of strategic conduct and game theory; (c) his mature ethnographic work, *Asylums*, and his analysis of the social aspects of mental illness; (d) his sustained inquiry into the organization of everyday behavior, referred to as the "interaction order"; (e) his later investigations into the "framing" of social encounters; and (f) his analysis of language and social interaction. This division is only roughly chronological. Although Goffman's dramaturgical work is linked to the early phase of his career, he retained this interest and it permeates his later work. Similarly, although Goffman is remembered for his early ethnography of St Elizabeths hospital, Goffman also conducted later ethnographic work in Las Vegas and in Philadelphia, where he studied a classical music radio station. Of course, the study of the interaction order is, as Williams (1980) and Manning (1992) point out, the aspect of his work that is present from his doctoral dissertation to his Presidential Address to the American Sociological Association. So, this sixfold classification of Goffman's work must be treated cautiously.

### Pre-dramaturgical writings

Goffman's early writings (1949, 1951, 1952, 1953a, b) produced a nucleus of ideas to which he returned throughout his academic career. His master's thesis is a survey-based project concerning the audience response to a popular radio soap opera, *Big Sister*. In an attempt to extend the research of Lloyd Warner (Warner and Henry, 1948), Goffman interviewed fifty women from the Hyde Park area of

Chicago to discover the typical characteristics of a segment of the soap opera's audience. Goffman attempted to use the Thematic Apperception Test (TAT) to investigate the relation between personality and socioeconomic status. In the course of the research Goffman became critical of the ability of this test to measure responses, and a large segment of the thesis is spent criticizing his own methodology. Smith (1993, p. 11) argued that this line of criticism was essential to the development of Goffman's work:

> It is important to note that [in his master's thesis] Goffman is not engaged in a wholesale critique of positivistic research methods and analytical traditions, but rather [he] presents carefully-formulated criticisms of his own research methods in the light of his original objectives. Goffman shows how, adjudged in the light of its own criteria, the experimental logic of his variable analysis cannot succeed. These discussions also show that Goffman's later (see especially the preface of *Relations in Public*) sharply critical comments on experimental logic and variable analysis were not made in the abstract but have their source in Goffman's firsthand research experience of the deficiencies he describes.

Goffman's first two published papers are quite unlike his master's thesis: both present subtle, almost cynically detached, observations about human conduct. Both are self-consciously literary in their handling of metaphor. "Symbols of Class Status" (1951) explores instrumental manipulations of symbolic representations of class. These manipulations can occur because although symbols represent class status, they do not constitute it. Goffman pointed to the efforts of "curator groups" – or cultural gatekeepers – who protect their group's status symbols from misuse. In a strikingly pre-dramaturgical way, the "Symbols" paper examines the necessary conditions for a persuasive performance to take place. In "On Cooling the Mark Out" (1952), Goffman uses the language of the confidence trick to discuss everyday behavior, suggesting that the world can be understood as competing groups of "con artists" and "marks." The con artist must first steal from the mark, and then "teach" him or her to accept the loss philosophically, without public complaint (ibid., p. 452). This paper contributes to the "sociology of failure." Goffman suggested that people who have failed, by their own standards or those of their group, are "dead people" who nevertheless continue to walk undetected among the living successes (ibid., p. 463).

Goffman's doctoral dissertation, "Communication Conduct in an Island Community," analyzes forms of self-presentation and both verbal and non-verbal interaction among inhabitants of a small island in the Shetlands. The first part of the dissertation served both as an introduction to everyday life on a Scottish island in a community Goffman referred to as "Dixon" and as a justification for the work presented later. Goffman aimed for more than a case study: his goal was to use this material to generate a model of communication strategies in face-to-face interaction. Goffman emphasized that empirical material was not merely a foil for conceptual elaboration; rather, his conceptual elaboration was based on his ethnographic observations (Goffman, 1953a, p. 9).

The dissertation is largely concerned with the analysis of the intersection of ritual and context in everyday life. To this end, Goffman classified the analytic differences between various kinds of social occasion (ibid., pp. 127–35). This in turn enabled him to examine the ways in which people could pay ritual homage to the projections of self evident in all social situations. These rituals, many of which are simply small offerings of appreciation or admiration, make accommodation and integration possible. However, as Williams (1980, p. 231) has commented, accommodation alone may or not be a genuine reflection of concern, and beneath a veneer of politeness, social interaction may be understood as a kind of "cold war" (Williams, 1980, p. 231; Goffman, 1953a, p. 40).

In many ways, the key elements of Goffman's later sociology can all be found in this work: his interest in the interaction order of everyday life, his concern with ethnography and qualitative sociology, and his coolly ironic and self-consciously literary style are all evident (Williams, 1980, p. 210). The still unpublished dissertation remains a key resource for understanding the development of Goffman's ideas.

## Metaphorical investigations

Goffman is justly famous for *The Presentation of Self in Everyday Life*, in which he outlined a theatrical, or "dramaturgical," vocabulary with which to describe everyday social encounters, such as eating in a restaurant, visiting friends, or attending a funeral. However, he used the same strategy, that of extended metaphorical description, in other projects, most notably where he analyzes game-like social situations, and hence it is appropriate to consider them as a single package.

*The Presentation of Self* expanded ideas outlined by Kenneth Burke's "dramatistic" approach (Burke, 1969). As Tom Burns (1992, p. 112) shrewdly observed, Goffman's achievement lay in his ability to pursue "the theatrical metaphor beyond the commonplace notion of 'putting on an act,'" so as to build an "analogical superstructure" that fully exploited the analytical resources of the theatrical metaphor. It is also important to note the work of Harré (1979, pp. 189–231), who has attempted to develop dramaturgical analysis by returning to Burke and retracing Goffman's steps. In so doing, Harré draws our attention to the connection between Goffman's earlier analysis of the social setting and his later analysis (in *Relations in Public*) of the *Umwelt* or surrounding social scene.

*The Presentation of Self* can be thought of as a "handbook" of action, containing six dramaturgical themes: the performance, the team, the region, discrepant roles, communication out of character, and impression management. These themes had been initially explored in Goffman's dissertation, where they were integrated into his ethnographic study of Dixon. In *The Presentation of Self* these themes have been repackaged as general features of social interaction. In a sense, Goffman used his observations of a small Scottish island as building blocks for an ambitious, general theory.

Goffman aimed to provide a persuasive description of familiar events. A person's performance is "given" if it is intended to influence other participants' understanding of the events at hand (Goffman, 1959, pp. 26, 32). Performances consist of elements designed to enhance the audience's sense of "realness." These include a "front": the stage props, appropriate expressions, and attitudes that allow a performer to conjure up a desired self-image. For example, part of what makes a lawyer convincing to a jury is not only the strength of his or her legal argument, but also a professional appearance and appropriate manner. The trial lawyer Fred Barlit reported that when he travels to try a case he is careful to wear different shoes to court every day, so that jurors can believe that he is a home-town lawyer (reported by Couric, 1988, p. 23). Details such as this are necessary for the "dramatic realization" of a performance. In either a discursive or a nondiscursive way, we are all dramaturgically savvy, and hence anxious to distinguish the "given" or "planted" elements of a performance from the unin-tended elements that were unwittingly "given off" by the performer. For ex-ample, a person who wishes to appear scholarly might prominently carry a copy of Wittgenstein's *Philosophical Investigations*. However, if he clearly pronounces the "W" of Wittgenstein, he gives off a rather different impression. As Goffman notes, the key to dramaturgical success is to control the audience's access to information, so that elements of performances that are given are such that audiences believe they were given off.

Goffman's dramaturgical analysis extends to the organization of physical as well as social space, as he describes the "front and "back" stages (or regions) of locations. A public performance is given on a front stage by a "team" of performers who construct a view of the world for the benefit of a public audience. However, in a back stage area, these performers may "knowingly contradict" (Goffman, 1959, p. 114) the impressions that had carefully been publicly presented. Goffman also indicates that these two regions are connected by a "guarded passageway" (such as the double doors found between the kitchen and dining room in many restaurants) so that the public performance cannot be shattered by an inadvertent view of the back stage. This aspect of Goffman's analysis is quite literal: it is more a footnote in the history of architecture than a metaphorical description of familiar experience. Goffman gave the following example: "If the bereaved are to be given the illusion that the dead one is really in a deep and tranquil sleep, then the undertaker must be able to keep the bereaved from the workroom where the corpses are drained, stuffed and painted in preparation for their final performance" (ibid., p. 116).

Manning (1992, pp. 44–8) suggests that Goffman's dramaturgical analysis is underpinned by a "two selves thesis." One self is a public performer with care-fully managed impressions; the second self is a cynical manipulator hidden behind the public performance. Following Park, Goffman noted that the etymo-logy of person is "mask." The two selves thesis explains the common belief that the dramaturgical perspective is a cynical view of social life which implies that all relationships are inauthentic and self-serving.

In other writings Goffman explored alternative metaphorical recastings, most notably a game-theoretic perspective. Although he was knowledgeable of the work in game theory by mathematicians and economists – and frequently cited the seminal text by Von Neuman and Morgenstern (1944) – Goffman's contri-bution to the field was heavily influenced by his friendship with Thomas

chelling, whose own work is not mathematically sophisticated. Goffman's first
efforts at game theory can be traced to his dissertation (Manning, 1992, pp. 64–
71), and his ideas were developed most fully in two books, *Encounters* (1961)
and *Strategic Interaction* (1969).

Although aspects of Goffman's work can be read as contributions to game
theory (see, for example, Collins, 1980, pp. 191–9; Manning, 1992, pp. 56–71),
Goffman generally preferred to emphasize the extent to which game theory is
compatible with the legacy of Chicago Sociology and symbolic interactionism.
He referred to this theoretical merger as "strategic interaction," and his discussion of it (Goffman, 1969, pp. 136–45) contains one of his few public reflections
about the strengths and weaknesses of symbolic interactionism. Goffman's concern about the symbolic interactionism of Mead and Blumer is that its insights
can dissipate into truisms about the importance of meaning and context. His
hope for strategic interaction (which he understood as the addition of Schelling's
work to the symbolic interactionist mix) was that a greater level of specificity
could be achieved. Goffman explained this as follows:

> following the crucial work of Schelling, strategic interaction addresses itself
> directly to the dynamics of interdependence involving mutual awareness; it seeks
> out basic moves and inquires into natural stopping points in the potentially infinite
> cycle of two players taking into consideration their consideration of each other's
> consideration, and so forth. (ibid., p. 137)

Goffman is proposing to transform Blumer's (1969) seminal statement about the
basic tenets of symbolic interactionism. Blumer's focus was on the individual,
definitions of the situation, and the mediation of symbols. Goffman advocated a
focus on the player, basic moves, and the rules governing face-to-face conduct.

Goffman believed that the distinction between a player and a party is often
"easy to neglect" (Goffman, 1969, p. 87), with the consequence that important
distinctions may be missed. Players (or actors) can play for others or for themselves. Players can be "pawns" to be sacrificed for the sake of the game. They can
also be "tokens" who express a position. Goffman (ibid., pp. 87–8) pointed out
that Western diplomacy distinguished between the "nuncio" who can represent a
party but not negotiate for it and the "procurator" who can negotiate but not
represent. To use a contemporary example, car showrooms contain nuncios who
can transmit an offer from a procurator who does not negotiate openly with the
opposing party, who wishes to purchase a car. The role of ambassador combines
the duties of the nuncio and the procurator, but ceremonial constraints prevent
ambassadors from commercial ventures.

According to Goffman (ibid., pp. 11–27), the basic moves of strategic interaction are the "unwitting," the "naive," the "covering," the "uncovering," and,
finally, the "counter-uncovering" move. The unwitting move occurs when the
player is not deliberately acting in the game, as when a person buying a car
engages in small talk during which he reveals that he recently inherited a lot of
money. A naive move is an unwitting move as judged by another player. For
example, a landlord may judge the claim that a potential tenant dislikes pets as

an unwitting move in the game of apartment-renting. A control move is one which will improve a player's standing in a game if accepted by other players. The possible effects of control moves are calculated: "What is essentially involved is not communication but rather a set of tricky ways of sympathetically taking the other into consideration as someone who assesses the environment and might profitably be led into a wrong assessment" (ibid., p. 13).

An example of a primitive control move is camouflage or concealment. More sophisticated control moves involve active misrepresentation (ibid., p. 14). In order to counteract a control move, a player may use an uncovering move. This can involve either spying or an examination of some kind, either of the player or of marks of his or her presence. The interrogator is by design and training the master of the uncovering move (ibid., p. 18). The final basic move is the counter-uncovering move. Goffman gave an instructive example here: instead of presenting an interrogator with a perfect alibi, a suspect may choose to offer one that is wanting and inconclusive, reasoning that a person with nothing to hide would be able to present only a partial alibi, not one that appears to have been specially devised for the contingency of being caught (ibid., p. 20).

Players and moves take place within games, or, as Goffman (1961b, pp. 84–8; 1983) put it, within social worlds or "situated activity systems." These worlds are governed by the normative constraints that govern the interaction order, the uncovering of which was a focus of much of his work. Early in his career, Goffman considered the merits of using Garfinkel's famous "breaching experiments" (Garfinkel, 1967) to identify these constraints, during which participants act in inappropriate ways in an attempt to make rules of conduct transparent. While acknowledging the strength of this approach (1961b, p. 18), Goffman focused instead on the discovery of "rules of irrelevance" which instruct participants about what they should and should not make the focus of their attention during interaction (ibid., pp. 18–31). Clearly, this early contribution signaled the interest in frames explored at length later (Goffman, 1974). Goffman understood throughout his work that social worlds are vulnerable, and that normative rules, though "flimsy," are responsible for our "unshaking sense" of social reality (Goffman, 1961b, p. 72).

## Mature ethnographic work: asylums

In 1955 Goffman began fieldwork at St Elizabeths Hospital in Washington, DC, a large mental hospital with about 7000 patients. Installed as the assistant to the athletics director, Goffman was free to roam the hospital as he wished, without his presence causing undue attention. Only the Superintendent of St Elizabeths was aware of his true purpose.

The choice of St Elizabeths was propitious: the mental hospital provided Goffman with a setting in which he could associate with a sequestered and maligned group – a group that for his academic readers was exotic as well. This site provided him with the opportunity to side with the underdog. Goffman was positioned to snipe at institutionalized authority and, in a Hughesian way, invert traditional hierarchies. Goffman used the opportunity to explore the characteristics of "total institutions," settings in which the time and space of inmates are seemingly controlled completely by staff. Although prisons are the baseline example of the total institution (Goffman, 1961a, p. 20), St Elizabeths, like mental institutions in general, exhibited comparable features.

Hence, St Elizabeths allowed Goffman to collect data for a radically different ethnography. Manning (1998) has referred to *Asylums* as not simply an ethnography of St Elizabeths but an "ethnography of the concept of the total institution." Fine and Martin (1990) gesture to a similar observation when they point out that *Asylums* gives almost no information about the routine operations of St Elizabeths. Goffman does not describe the layout of the hospital; nor does he describe the personnel. There is not even an account of a typical day. Instead, Goffman conveys a "tone of life" – depicting, for instance, the mundane scrounging of cigarettes and food – and in so doing he presents an ethnography less concerned with description than with analysis (Fine and Martin, 1990, p. 93). Goffman's primary goal in *Asylums* is to understand the organization of total institutional life, of which St Elizabeths is an example. In this way, Goffman's aspirations exceed those of the traditional case study.

*Asylums* consists of four essays, each of which was published separately. Unsurprisingly, therefore, there is a certain amount of repetition, as Goffman reworked similar or identical material. The first three essays are interrelated, as they all examine the ordinary experiences of patients (or, as is often the case, inmates) in total institutions. The second essay also considers the "pre-patient" process leading to institutionalization. However, the final essay of *Asylums* is quite different, and sits uncomfortably with the other contributions. This paper is a theoretical examination of professional–client interaction. In it, Goffman isolates the unique elements of psychiatrist–client interaction, in order to show the "grotesque" predicament of the mentally ill (Goffman, 1961a, p. 186). One example Goffman gave of this concerned the treatment of unruly patients. Because staff were unable to punish them for actions that were understood to be linked to a disease, punishments became hidden behind misleading labels. This meant that "solitary confinement" was transformed from an undisguised punishment into a treatment option known as "constructive meditation" (ibid., 82).

Most of *Asylums* deals with the pre-patient and inpatient phases. In the second essay, Goffman offers a subtle account of the process whereby a person who behaves in an unusual way can become a candidate for institutionalization. Although he does not provide a clear account of the empirical basis for his argument, Goffman persuasively discusses the "betrayal funnel" through which unwitting pre-patients discover that the people in whom they have invested the most trust are the same people who report their actions to medical and other personnel. This is an especially painful time for pre-patients, because they witness their families and friends acting strangely around them, hanging up calls when they walk in the room, changing topics when interrupted, and meeting secretly. This informal network of concerned people benignly deceives the pre-patient, refusing to talk to him or her openly, often until they recommend to the pre-patient that a visit to a "doctor" might be helpful, unable even then to avoid this euphemistic reference to a psychiatrist. The unintended consequence of the behavior of concerned friends is that the old adage that "just because you're paranoid doesn't mean they're not out to get you" rings true. Ultimately, pre-patients are passed on to a "circuit of agents" – social workers, various officers of the criminal justice system, psychiatrists, and others – who then assess the viability and desirability of institutionalization. Goffman's analysis can be justly compared to Foucault's (1979) account of the "carceral society" in *Discipline and Punish*.

Once institutionalized, patients are exposed to "batch living" and the tightly controlled life typical of any total institution. The staff has extensive control of time and space, upheld with carefully planned schedules and surveillance devices (Foucault, 1979). The result is "civil death" (Goffman, 1961a, p. 25), or, as Goffman sometimes puts it, a "mortification of self" (ibid., p. 31). New patients at St Elizabeths were quickly transformed from civilian outsiders into hospital products: they were supplied with clothes, familiar names were dropped, and they were disciplined so as to accept the authority of staff members. At St Elizabeths, a "ward system" punished uncooperative patients by limiting them to poor living conditions, from which they could only move gradually to a ward which afforded a degree of comfort.

Over time, St Elizabeths, in common with other total institutions, offered "privileges" to patients who accepted their diminished roles. These consisted of minor rewards, such as cups of coffee or access to newspapers or television. As Goffman trenchantly explained, the consequence of the privilege system "is that cooperativeness is obtained from persons who often have cause to be uncooperative" (ibid., p. 54). An unintended consequence is that patients had a diminished sense of self-worth as they discovered that they were willing to accept trivial rewards in oppressive conditions. In this sense, the total institution had accomplished its mission to be a "forcing house" for changing persons, because outside its walls patients would have been unlikely to cooperate in return for rewards consisting only of taken-for-granted supplies and services.

In different ways and by different means, both the mortification of self and the privilege system undermine the patients' sense of self. In many total institutions, hospital patients, prison or concentration camp inmates, military recruits, neophyte nuns and monks all experience severe attacks on their core conception of self. To use Ralph Turner's (1968) vocabulary, the total institution is able to mount an attack on the person's self-conception, the sense that we have of who we "really" are.

In response to these severe infringements, patients learn to resist the pull of the total institution without directly confronting it, a strategy that, Paul Willis reports in *Learning to Labor*, is also used by rebellious high school boys. Goffman identified four strategies of resistance, which he referred to idiomatically as "playing it cool." The first strategy, "situational withdrawal," involves intensive daydreaming as a means of escaping or absenting oneself from the total institution. In *One Flew Over the Cuckoo's Nest*, Ken Kesey also recognized this practice, as he described patients on a ward pretending collectively to watch a football game on television, becoming for a while completely absorbed in the excitement of the imagined game. The second strategy is to establish an "intransigent line" which if breached triggers uncooperative behavior. This is a means whereby inmates demonstrate a measure of control over their lives by telling themselves (if no one else) that they can only be pushed so far. The intransigent line is always provisional and subject to revision. At its limit, it may involve a hunger strike. Goffman points out that staff members may try to break the intransigent prisoner – in a mental hospital this may take the form of electroshock treatment (ibid., p. 62). The third strategy is colonization, during which inmates play up whatever positive features they can identify in the total institution. Goffman indicates that for inmates with experience of several different total institutions it is simply a matter of reapplying familiar adaptive techniques whereby a home of sorts is made of a restrictive environment. The third essay of *Asylums* contains many examples of "secondary adjustments" – the inmates' ways of challenging institutional authority, thereby giving a human touch to an institutionalized world. The fourth strategy, conversion, involves the inmate's acceptance, or the pretense of acceptance, of the institution's ideology: "the inmate appears to take over the official or staff view of himself and tries to act out the role of the perfect inmate" (ibid., p. 63).

Goffman argued that the similarities between inmate experiences in different total institutions are both "glaring" and "persistent" (ibid., p. 115), such that the apparent antics of the institutionalized mentally ill are misunderstood as symptoms of underlying disorders but better understood as extensively practiced adjustments to trying and threatening circumstances. Goffman made this point forcefully:

> The impression may be given, therefore, that patients throughout the day fitfully engaged in childish tricks and foolhardy gestures to better their lot, and that there is nothing inconsistent between this pathetic display and our traditional notions of mental patients being "ill." I want to state, therefore, that in actual practice almost all of the secondary adjustments I have reported were carried on by the patient with an air of intelligent down-to-earth determination, sufficient, once the full context was known, to make an outsider feel at home, in a community much more similar to others he has known than different from them. (ibid., p. 266)

## The interaction order

In his dissertation, Goffman (1953a, p. 343) used this term to characterize the web of normative beliefs that facilitate communication and social interaction. In this context, it has a functionalist basis and an empirical target. Goffman was not attempting to develop functionalist theory; instead, he wanted to promote the observational study of everyday behavior, and several premises of functionalism were useful for this purpose.

As a result, the concept "interaction order" is purged of an explicit functionalism and is used simply to refer to the study of face-to-face interaction. He then clarified this broad definition by stating that the organization of the interaction order can be understood as "ground rules for a game, the provisions of a traffic code or the rules of syntax of a language" (Goffman, 1983, p. 8). Drew and Wootton (1988, p. 7) remark that this commits Goffman to investigating the "procedures and practices through which people organized, and brought into life, their face-to-face dealings with each other."

Goffman's investigations of the interaction order involve the creation of a vocabulary with which to recast familiar experiences and an empirical inquiry into the applicability of this new vocabulary. However, this empirical inquiry has not been conducted using the mainstream social scientific framework of hypothesis-testing and quantification. In the preface to *Relations in Public*, Goffman acknowledged that his work does not meet the orthodox methodological standards of sociology. However, he was not repentant; instead he criticized sociologists whose work has the appearance of science but lacks explanatory power. Throughout his career, Goffman presented a diverse range of examples for comparison that conform to and exemplify his vocabulary. As a result, Burns (1992, p. 33) refers to Goffman's work as a "sociography" rather than as a sociology, to emphasize the classificatory focus of his research, and to downplay the extent to which it should be judged by the tenets of quantitative social science.

Goffman's exploration of the interaction order consist of four interrelated classificatory inquiries: (a) types of social event; (b) types of audience; (c) levels of commitment; and (d) self-presentation. Throughout his work, but most notably in *Behavior in Public Places*, Goffman classified the types of social event in the interaction order. This classification identified the range of variations in which people find themselves "copresent" with others. To this end, Goffman distinguished a "gathering," a "situation," and a "social occasion" (Goffman, 1963a, pp. 17–19). A gathering occurs when two or more people are in each other's immediate presence. A situation is the "full spatial environment" which begins with "mutual monitoring" (ibid., p. 18). A social occasion, such as a birthday party or a work day at an office, is bounded by space and time, likely to involve props or equipment, and is the background against which situations and gatherings are likely to take place.

In *Behavior in Public Places*, Goffman also analyzed audiences, distinguishing the acquainted from the unacquainted. In *Forms of Talk* (Goffman, 1981a), he also distinguished between a hearer and an overhearer. The acquainted are recognized either "cognitively," as being a particular person and not merely a category of person, or "socially," i.e. the acquainted are recognized in the sense of being welcomed and acknowledged (Goffman, 1963a, pp. 112–13). The acquainted need a reason not to initiate an encounter ("I can't stop, I'm late!"); the opposite holds true for the unacquainted. Goffman considered the circumstances whereby the unacquainted can approach each other. One set of circumstances concerns people who occupy "exposed" social positions, such as police officers, priests, and newsstand vendors, all of whom can be approached for information or even to exchange greetings (ibid., p. 125). There are also people who are considered so "meager in sacred value" that they can be addressed without explanation (ibid., p. 126). Goffman suggests that the old and the very young are examples: they are "open persons" who are exposed to public interaction by virtue of their status as persons and not because of their roles. A third circumstance facilitating interaction among the unacquainted occurs when someone is demonstrably out of role, as when someone is drunk or dressed in an unusual costume. Finally, there are those "non-persons," who are so lacking in social presence – servers of various kinds – that others can freely converse and act *as if* these figures were not present.

In different social events with these audiences, people display different levels of commitment. This commitment or involvement is the person's capacity to give "concerted attention" to the present engagement (ibid., p. 43). This changes during the day, producing an "involvement contour." Goffman distinguished "main" and "side" involvements: the former are claims on the person that he or she is obliged to acknowledge, the latter are activities that can coexist with but must not threaten the focus of the event. Main and side involvements complement each other, in the sense that they allow people to demonstrate respect for group activities while asserting an autonomy from them (Manning, 1992, p. 84).

Self-presentation issues are addressed throughout Goffman's early work, and dramaturgical ideas from his dissertation are recycled in *The Presentation of Self*. Later, in *Relations in Public*, Goffman reconsidered how people appear in social settings, analyzing the different "territories of the self" by which people mark out the space around them. He also considered the "tie-signs" (such as hand-holding) that distinguish groups as a "with" (Goffman, 1971, pp. 194–210; Fine et al., 1984).

Goffman's analysis of the interaction order classifies a broad range of every-day behavior, and draws attention to how people are sensitive to even minor variations to expected conduct. His analysis reveals the stickiness of the web of normative expectations governing mundane interaction. Goffman does not, however, provide anything more than a general account of rule-following prac-tices or socialization processes. The absence of an account of this kind is surprising, especially given his fondness for quoting from etiquette manuals, which are explicitly "how to" guides to middle-class conduct. Goffman was amused by the writings of Emily Post and others, and drew on their work for examples for his own classificatory accounts.

## The framing of social life

Goffman's *Frame Analysis* was published in 1974 after a decade of preparation. It was a project in which Goffman had invested a tremendous amount of time and effort, and the resulting 586-page book was meant to be a major statement of general sociological importance. Unfortunately, the reviews of *Frame Analysis* were mixed and even Goffman's supporters found the book excessively long and repetitive. Nevertheless, the core ideas struck a chord with social scientists and cognitive scientists.

A frame is a way of organizing experiences: it is one of the means whereby people identify the kind of activity that is taking place. For example, the act of kissing someone may be understood romantically, as a gesture of support, as a way of accepting an apology, as an unwanted advance, and so on. Following from the work of Gregory Bateson (1972), Goffman's analysis of frames tried to show how people distinguish these different kinds of activity. The implication is that the procedures to frame something so that it appears real or genuine are the same procedures used to mislead people. To this extent, frame analysis is an extension of Goffman's earlier dramaturgical work (Manning, 1992, p. 120).

*Frame Analysis* is in part a development of ideas from *The Presentation of Self*, but it also bears resemblance to Goffman's study of strategic interaction, particularly the essays in *Encounters* in which social interaction is analyzed as a set of "moves" between "players." Each move preserves or modifies the definition of the situation. This is apparent in Goffman's (1969) account of the work of espionage agents, who constantly evaluate whether their cover has been lost during a mission.

As with other projects, Goffman's frame analysis involves a classificatory vocabulary with which to redescribe the social world. "Frame analysis" is defined as the study of the "organization of experience," each frame of which is a principle of that organization (Goffman, 1974, p. 11). The most fundamental frames are "primary frameworks," which are either "natural" (involving physical events) or "social" (involving human intervention). In either case, the primary framework involves what "really" is happening: a transparent view of reality. For example, two people meeting for a picnic may be understood as using a social framework as a "date," but if the event is cut short by poor weather, the relevant frame is natural. Primary frameworks can be challenged in various ways: by astounding events, deceptions, and miscues that undermine the audience's sense of what is occurring (Goffman, 1974, p. 36). More importantly, primary frameworks can be "keyed" – that is, their meanings can be transformed into something patterned on but independent of the initial frame (ibid., p. 44). Actors recognize that a transformation has taken place, and that the key "unlocks" what is actually occurring. Thus, a key might show us that what appears to be a fight is really just play. These keyings can themselves be rekeyed in a way that requires careful analysis.

In addition to keys there are "fabrications." A frame is fabricated when it is organized so as to mislead others (ibid., p. 83). Fabrications are either "benign" (that is, for the benefit of an audience) or "exploitative" (that is, for the benefit of the fabricator). Keys and fabrications undermine our sense of social life, with the result that frames must be "anchored," so as to persuade people that what appears to be real is real.[2] Together these concepts provide for a construction of interpretations, grounded on, but not limited to, taken-for-granted meanings.

## Language and social interaction

Although Goffman's analysis of talk is given extended treatment in *Forms of Talk* (1981a), similar ideas are aired in the later chapters of *Frame Analysis*, and before that in "The Neglected Situation" (1964). In these works Goffman outlined the general thrust of his argument concerning language and social interaction. Goffman (1964) emphasized that the activity of speaking is social and must be understood as an element of the situation and not as simply a linguistic construction. The appropriate connection between grammar and social interaction remains a fertile area for investigation. Talk cannot be understood merely as the linguistic component of social interaction and analyzed discretely; instead, it must be understood as an inseparable aspect of concerted and coordinated social action.

In the introduction to *Forms of Talk*, Goffman identified three themes of his work on language and social interaction: ritualization, participation frameworks, and embedding. Ritualization refers to the "movements, looks and vocal sounds" that accompany speaking and listening (Goffman, 1981a, p. 2). A participation framework identifies the relationship of each person in an event to that event. For example, a person who overhears an utterance stands in a different relationship to the event from the person to whom the comment was directed. Embedding is the ability to separate the person who speaks from the ownership of the words that are spoken: we can, for example, represent the beliefs of others or quote someone (ibid., pp. 2–4).

These themes are then examined in the five essays that follow. The main themes of this work are captured in one of the essays, concerning a person's "footing" (ibid., pp. 124–59). Goffman defines footing as something concerning a participant's projected self in social interaction. A change in footing occurs when a speaker begins a new alignment to the present interaction (ibid., p. 128). Goffman writes that a "change in footing implies a change in the alignment we take up to ourselves and the others present as expressed in the way we manage the production or reception of an utterance. A change in our footing is another way of talking about a change in our frame for events" (ibid., p. 128). This comment suggests continuity between Goffman's earlier analysis of both frames and the intersection between language and social interaction.

The discussion of footing was introduced with an almost literal example, as Goffman began by discussing an exchange between President Nixon and a female reporter, Helen Thomas. Just after signing a piece of Congressional legislation, Nixon commented on Thomas' clothing, specifically her wearing of "slacks." He asked her to model her clothing for him and the others present by making a pirouette. Then, after attempting to make jokey comments about the relative merits of slacks and "gowns," Nixon asked which was the cheaper item. Thomas replied that they cost the same and Nixon delivered his punchline: "Then change" (ibid., pp. 124–5).

This strip of social interaction exemplifies Goffman's themes. The gendered exchange involves a temporary change of footing in which small talk, with its own tone and content, is marked as a "time-out" from the official business at hand. At the end of the paper, Goffman returned to this example, suggesting that Nixon's change in footing is neither just a display about the "forces" of sexism and presidents nor just a bracketing device marking the end of a ceremony. Rather, Nixon's change in footing was an attempt to demonstrate to the press that he still retained a lively wit and a personal touch, that he was capable of being both the President and an engaging citizen. Goffman ended the paper by speculating that in this exchange Nixon actually lost his footing, because his presentation of self was too wooden and self-conscious, and that even though the members of the press laughed at the proper moment, they did so from Presidential respect and not out of admiration for the man.

Goffman leaves unanswered the question of how he could know that the press interpreted this incident in this way, suggesting only that it should be possible to identify a "structural basis" with which to analyze the cues and markers in the interaction that would confirm his interpretation. This reveals an important difference between Goffman and contemporary conversation analysts, for whom the interest is in precisely the details about which, in this example at least, Goffman only speculated.

## GOFFMAN'S IMPACT

As noted above, Erving Goffman's impact on social theory has been both great and modest. The limits of Goffman's influence are evident in more than the relative absence of younger colleagues who can point to his direct mentoring. More significant is the absence of the style of research and writing that Goffman represented. The form of Goffman's work has not been easy to duplicate. In part this absence refers to the lack of attention that certain of Goffman's primary topics now receive. The analysis of behavior in public places, while it has not entirely disappeared, remains a small field, perhaps because of the perceived "triviality barrier." While creative work is conducted by contemporary scholars such as Lyn Lofland, Carol Brooks Gardner, and Spencer Cahill, the micro-examination of public life has not further developed a set of innovative and powerful concepts as was evident in Goffman's finest work. Likewise, the development of theoretical constructs, explicating the structure of interaction routines, has not advanced much beyond the dramaturgical models that Goffman proposed over a quarter century ago.

Part of these limits of Goffman's impact can be attributed to the daunting perception of his idiosyncratic brilliance. Few wish to place themselves in comparison with this master sociologist, particularly since his approach lacks an easily acquired method. How can one learn to do what Goffman did? Methodological guidelines do not exist. This has the effect of leaving the work both *sui generis* and incapable of imitation. The belief (and perhaps the reality) is that Goffman created a personalistic sociology that was virtually mimic-proof.

Yet this account of the limitations of Goffman's influence is misleading. Nearly all sociologists have been influenced by Goffman's insights. Certainly he had a profound impact in bringing micro-interactionist concerns into the mainstream of the discipline of sociology. As noted above, the important social theorists Anthony Giddens, Jürgen Habermas, Randall Collins, Jeffrey Alexander, and Pierre Bourdieu are all indebted to Goffman's writing, particularly in light of their attempts to create a "seamless" sociology that integrates societal and institutional structures with the agency of individual actors.

Other substantive arenas have also been influenced by Goffman's sensibility and analyses. Part of this importance is reflected in the increasing prominence of qualitative and ethnographic methods, as evidenced by qualitative journals and ethnographic articles in the flagship journals of the discipline. Even though Erving Goffman cannot be considered an exemplary ethnographer – his ethnographic writings were too casual (Fine and Martin, 1990) – the prominence of his writings made a claim that participant observation research could produce rich and persuasive theory. This is exemplified in Goffman's discussion of his research in the Shetland Islands, described in *The Presentation of Self*, and his more elaborate detailing of the strategies of patients in St Elizabeths hospital in *Asylums*. If these were not the most detailed or exemplary ethnographies of the period in methodological terms, they were, along with William Foote Whyte's 1943 *Street Corner Society*, the most influential and among the most widely read. Goffman demonstrated that a cogent example, coupled with a powerful turn of phrase, could encourage the sociological imagination. Further, Goffman's writing style has contributed to a loosening of the rules by which social scientists communicate (Fine, 1988; Fine and Martin, 1990). Goffman's sardonic, satiric, jokey style has served to indicate that other genres and tropes can be legitimate forms of academic writing.

In substantive arenas, Goffman's writings have had repercussions as well. Most notably, *Asylums* provided an impetus for the movement to deinstitutionalize mental patients and to eliminate the large state mental hospitals that often served as warehouses for those who stood outside of societal norms. Whether the massive deinstitutionalization of mental patients contributed to the problem of homelessness, it cannot be doubted that the movement to change the role of the mental hospital was given voice by the searing images found in Goffman's writings.

Goffman's influence is also evident in the usage that various sociologists have made of the concept of frame. The image of a frame as a means of exploring how individuals and groups come to define their environment has been particularly prevalent in the examination of social movements (Snow et al., 1986; Gamson, 1992). In this model, distinct from the usage of frame proposed by Goffman or Gregory Bateson, the actions of social movement participants depend on how they perceive the frameworks in which they are embedded. Frame represents the content of the story by which individuals and groups come to recognize their worlds. This usage does not suggest that a frame represents the kind of reality (an experiment, play, conning) that is being faced, but rather the meaning of the situation. Still, even if the definitions of frame do not accord exactly with that proposed in *Frame Analysis*, this cultural and interactional model of social movements was inspired by Goffman's writing.

Finally, we can trace the concern with the construction of meaning and the phenomenology of reality to Goffman's writings. The increase in interest in symbolic interaction and conversation analysis (the most influential offshoot of ethnomethodology) is in considerable measure an effect of Goffman's emphasis that social interaction is not a given, but is negotiated by participants (Maynard and Zimmerman, 1984; Manning and Ray, 1993). While Goffman was neither the first scholar to make this argument nor the most vigorous proponent of the position, his status as a major social theorist whose works were assigned to generations of graduate students had a unique influence. This constructionist perspective is now a taken-for-granted aspect of sociological thought, even by those whose own research is based upon the assumption that social perspectives converge sufficiently to permit statistical analysis.

## VALUING GOFFMAN

This chapter is not intended to be a paean to a Goffmanian sociology. Yet we repeat, as we began, that Goffman is arguably the most significant American social theorist of the twentieth century; his work is widely read and remains capable of redirecting disciplinary thought. His unique ability to generate innovative and apt metaphors, coupled with the ability to name cogent regularities of social behavior, has provided him an important position in the sociological canon. Further, his sardonic, outsider stance has made Goffman a revered figure – an outlaw theorist who came to exemplify the best of the sociological imagination.

Although Erving Goffman's most influential work was published almost forty years ago, and he died nearly two decades ago, his analyses feel very contemporary: perhaps the first postmodern sociological theorist. Erving Goffman – and his former graduate student colleagues at the University of Chicago in the immediate postwar years – provided models that reoriented sociology. If sociology as a discipline has changed over the past several decades – and it clearly has done so dramatically – it is in considerable measure because of the directions that Erving Goffman suggested that practitioners pursue.

## Acknowledgments

The authors wish to thank George Ritzer, Greg Smith, and Yves Winkin for their help in the preparation of this chapter.

## Notes

1   As we note, Goffman was born in Canada, but his graduate training and employment was in the United States.
2   In an interesting empirical application of this argument, Goffman used a frame analytic perspective to analyze gender. In *Gender Advertisements* (1979) Goffman argued that some male–female rituals are best understood as a keying of parent–child rituals.

## Bibliography

### *Writings of Erving Goffman*

*Some Characteristics of Response to Depicted Experience*. 1949. Unpublished MA thesis, Department of Sociology, University of Chicago.
Symbols of Class Status. 1951. *British Journal of Sociology*, 11, 294–304.

On Cooling the Mark Out: Some Aspects of Adaptation to Failure. 1952. *Psychiatry*, 15(4), 451–63.
*Communication Conduct in an Island Community*. 1953a. Unpublished PhD dissertation, Department of Sociology, University of Chicago.
*The Service Station Dealer: the Man and His Work*. 1953b. Chicago: Social Research Incorporated.
*The Presentation of Self in Everyday Life*. 1959. New York: Anchor.
*Asylums*. 1961a. New York: Anchor.
*Encounters: Two Studies in the Sociology of Interaction*. 1961b. Indianapolis: Bobbs-Merrill.
*Behavior in Public Places: Notes on the Social Organization of Gatherings*. 1963a. New York: Free Press.
*Stigma*. 1963b. Englewood Cliffs, NJ: Prentice Hall.
The Neglected Situation. 1964. *American Anthropologist*, 66(6), 133–6.
*Interaction Ritual: Essays on Face-to-face Behavior*. 1967. New York: Anchor.
*Strategic Interaction*. 1969. Philadelphia: University of Pennsylvania Press.
*Relations in Public: Microstudies of the Public Order*. 1971. New York: Basic Books.
*Frame Analysis: an Essay on the Organization of Experience*. 1974. New York: Harper and Row.
*Gender Advertisements*. 1979. New York: Harper and Row.
*Forms of Talk*. 1981a. Philadelphia: University of Pennsylvania Press.
Reply to Denzin and Keller. 1981b. *Contemporary Sociology*, 10, 60–8.
The Interaction Order. 1983. *American Sociological Review*, 48, 1–17.
On Fieldwork. 1989. *Journal of Contemporary Ethnography*, 18(2), 123–32.

## Further reading

Abbott, Andrew (1997) Of Time and Space: the Contemporary Relevance of the Chicago School. *Social Forces*, 75(4), 1149–82.
Abbott, Andrew and Graziano, Emanuel (1995) Transition and Tradition: Departmental Faculty in the Era of the Second Chicago School. In Gary Alan Fine (ed.), *The Second Chicago School?* Chicago: University of Chicago Press.
Atkinson, Paul (1989) Goffman's Poetics. *Human Studies* 12(1/2), 59–76.
Bateson, Gregory (1972) *Steps toward an Ecology of Mind*. New York: Ballantine.
Berman, Marshall (1972) Weird but Brilliant Light on the Way We Live Now. *New York Times Review of Books*, February 27, 1–2, 10, 12, 14, 16, 18.
Blumer, Herbert (1969) *Symbolic Interactionism*. Englewood Cliffs, NJ: Prentice Hall.
Brown, Richard (1977) *A Poetic for Sociology*. Cambridge: Cambridge University Press.
Bulmer, Martin (1984) *The Chicago School of Sociology*. Chicago: University of Chicago Press.
Burke, Kenneth (1969) *A Grammar of Motive*. Berkeley: University of California Press.
Burns, Tom (1992) *Erving Goffman*. London: Routledge.
Camic, Charles (1996) Three Departments in Search of a Discipline: Localism and Interdisciplinary Interaction in American Sociology, 1890–1940. *Social Research*, 62(4), 1003–33.
Chriss, James (1995) Habermas, Goffman, and Communicative Action: Implications for Professional Practice. *American Sociological Review*, 60(4), 545–65.
Clifford, James (1988) *The Predicament of Culture*. Cambridge, MA: Harvard University Press.
Clough, Patricia (1992) *The End(s) of Ethnography*. Newbury Park, CA: Sage.

Collins, Randall (1980) Erving Goffman and the Development of Modern Social Theory. In Jason Ditton (ed.), *The View From Goffman*. London: Macmillan.

Collins, Randall (1988) Theoretical Continuities in Goffman's Work. In Paul Drew and Anthony Wooton (eds), *Erving Goffman: Exploring the Interaction Order*. Cambridge: Polity Press.

Conrad, Peter and Schneider, Joseph (1980) *Deviance and Medicalization: from Badness to Sickness*. St Louis: C. V. Mosby.

Couric, Emily (1988) *The Trial Lawyers*. New York: St Martin's Press.

Davies, Christie (1989) Goffman's Concept of the Total Institution: Criticisms and Evasions. *Human Studies*, 12 (1/2), 77–95.

Delaney, William P. (1977) The Uses of the Total Institution: a Buddhist Monastic Example. In Robert Gordon and Brett Williams (eds), *Exploring Total Institutions*. Champaign, IL: Stipes.

Denzin, Norman and Keller, C. M. (1981) *Frame Analysis* Reconsidered. *Contemporary Sociology*, 10, 52–60.

Ditton, Jason (ed.) (1980) *The View from Goffman*. London: Macmillan.

Drew, Paul and Wootton, Anthony (eds) (1988) *Erving Goffman: Exploring the Interaction Order*. Cambridge: Polity Press.

Edmondson, Ricca (1984) *Rhetoric and Sociology*. London: Macmillan.

Fine, Gary Alan (1995) A Second Chicago School? The Development of a Postwar American Sociology. In Gary Alan Fine (ed.), *A Second Chicago School?* Chicago: University of Chicago Press.

Fine, Gary Alan (1996) Reputational Entrepreneurs and the Memory of Incompetence: Melting Supporters, Partisan Warriors, and Images of President Harding. *American Journal of Sociology*, 101, 1159–93.

Fine, Gary Alan and Martin, Daniel D. (1990) A Partisan View: Sarcasm, Satire and Irony as in Erving Goffman's *Asylums*. *Journal of Contemporary Ethnography*, 19(1), 89–115.

Fine, Gary Alan, Stitt, Jeffrey, and Finch, Michael (1984) Couple Tie Signs and Interpersonal Threat: a Field Experiment. *Social Psychology Quarterly*, 47, 282–6.

Fish, Stanley (1989) *Doing What Comes Naturally*. Durham, NC: Duke University Press.

Foucault, Michel (1979) *Discipline and Punish: the Birth of the Prison*. New York: Random House.

Galliher, John (1995) Chicago's Two Worlds of Deviance Research: Whose Side Are They On? In Gary Alan Fine (ed.), *The Second Chicago School?* Chicago: University of Chicago Press.

Gamson, William (1992) *Talking Politics*. Cambridge: Cambridge University Press.

Garfinkel, Harold (1967) *Studies in Ethnomethodology*. Englewood Cliffs, NJ: Prentice Hall.

Geertz, Clifford (1988) *Works and Lives: the Anthropologist as Author*. Stanford, CA: Stanford University Press.

Giddens, Anthony (1984) *The Constitution of Society*. Berkeley: University of California Press.

Giddens, Anthony (1987) *Sociology and Modern Social Theory*. Cambridge: Polity Press.

Glaser, Barney (1992) *Basics of Grounded Theory Analysis*. Mill Valley, CA: Sociology Press.

Glaser, Barney and Strauss, Anselm (1967) *The Discovery of Grounded Theory*. New York: Aldine de Gruyter.

Grimshaw, Allan (1983) Erving Goffman: a Personal Appreciation. *Language in Society*, 12(1), 147–8.

Gusfield, Joseph (1995) Preface: the Second Chicago School? In Gary Alan Fine (ed.), *A Second Chicago School?* Chicago: University of Chicago Press.

Hammersley, Martin (1992) *What's Wrong with Ethnography?* London: Routledge.

Harré, Rom (1979) *Social Being: a Theory for Social Psychology.* Oxford: Blackwell.

Heirich, Max (1970) *The Beginning: Berkeley 1964.* New York: Columbia University Press.

Hughes, Everett (1977) *The Growth of an Institution: the Chicago Real Estate Board.* Chicago: University of Chicago Press.

Hymes, Dell (1984) On Erving Goffman. *Theory and Society,* 13(5), 621–31.

Ignatieff, Michael (1983) Life at Degree Zero. *New Society,* January 20, 95–7.

Jameson, Frederic (1976) Review of Frame Analysis. *Theory and Society,* 13, 119–33.

Lopata, Helena Znaniecka (1995) Postscript. In Gary Alan Fine (ed.), *The Second Chicago School?* Chicago: University of Chicago Press.

Manning, Philip (1989) Resemblances. *History of the Human Sciences,* 2(2), 207–33.

Manning, Philip (1991) Drama as Life: the Significance of Goffman's Changing Use of the Theatrical Metaphor. *Sociological Theory,* 9(1), 70–86.

Manning, Philip (1992) *Erving Goffman and Modern Sociology.* Stanford, CA: Stanford University Press.

Manning, Philip (1998) Ethnographic Coats and Tents. In Gregory Smith (ed.), *Goffman's Patrimony: Studies in a Sociological Legacy.* London: Routledge

Manning, Philip and Ray, George (1993) Shyness, Self-confidence and Social Interaction. *Social Psychology Quarterly,* 56(3), 178–92.

Marx, Gary (1984) Role Models and Role Distance: a Remembrance of Erving Goffman. *Theory and Society,* 13(5), 649–62.

Platt, Jennifer (1994) The Chicago School and Firsthand Data. *History of the Human Sciences,* 7(1), 57–80.

Platt, Jennifer (1995) Research Methods and the Second Chicago School. In Gary Alan Fine (ed.), *The Second Chicago School?* Chicago: University of Chicago Press.

Schegloff, Emanuel (1996) Confirming Allusions: toward an Empirical Account of Action. *American Journal of Sociology,* 102, 161–216.

Smith, Gregory (1989) A Simmelian Reading of Goffman. Unpublished PhD dissertation, Department of Sociology, University of Salford, England.

Smith, Gregory (1993) Chrysalid Goffman. Unpublished manuscript.

Smith, Gregory (1994) Snapshots "Sub Specie Aeternitatis": Simmel, Goffman and Formal Sociology. In David Frisby (ed.), *Georg Simmel: Critical Assessments, volume 3.* New York: Routledge.

Smith, Gregory and Travers, Andrew (1998) Goffman's Project and Program: Framing a Sociological Legacy. Unpublished manuscript.

Snow, David A. and Davis, Philip W. (1995) The Chicago Approach to Collective Behavior. In Gary Alan Fine (ed.), *The Second Chicago School?* Chicago: University of Chicago Press.

Snow, David A., Rochford Jr, E. Burke, Worden, Steven K., and Benford, Robert D. (1986) Frame Alignment Processes, Micromobilization and Movement Participation. *American Sociological Review,* 51, 464–81.

Strauss, Anselm and Juliet, Corbin (1990) *Basics of Qualitative Research.* Newbury Park, CA: Sage.

Turner, Ralph (1968) The Self-conception in Social Interaction. In Chad Gordon and Kenneth Gergen (eds), *The Self in Social Interaction.* New York: Wiley.

Verhoeven, J. C. (1993) An Interview with Erving Goffman. *Research Language and Social Interaction,* 26(3), 317–48.

Von Neuman, John and Morgenstern, Oskar (1944) *Theory of Games and Economic Behavior.* Princeton, NJ: Princeton University Press.

Wacker, R. Fred (1995) The Sociology of Race and Ethnicity in the Second Chicago School. In Gary Alan Fine (ed.), *The Second Chicago School?* Chicago: University of Chicago Press.

Warner, W. Lloyd and Henry, W. E. (1948) The Radio Day-time Serial: a Symbolic Analysis. *Genetic Psychology Monograph,* 37.

Weber, Max (1949) *The Methodology of the Social Sciences.* New York: Free Press.

Williams, Robin (1980) Goffman's Sociology of Talk. In Jason Ditton (ed.), *The View from Goffman.* London: Macmillan.

Williams, Robin (1988) Understanding Goffman's Methods. In Paul Drew and Anthony Wootton (eds), *Erving Goffman: Exploring the Interaction Order.* Cambridge: Polity Press.

Willis, Paul (1977) *Learning to Labor.* New York: Columbia University Press.

Winkin, Yves (1988) *Erving Goffman: Les Moments et Leurs Hommes.* Paris: Minuit.

Winkin, Yves (1998) Erving Goffman: What Is a Life? In Gregory Smith (ed.), *Goffman's Patrimony: Studies in a Sociological Legacy.* London: Routledge.

Winkin, Yves (1999) Erving Goffman: a Biography. Unpublished manuscript.

# 15

## Richard M. Emerson

### Karen S. Cook and Joseph Whitmeyer

### The Person

Growing up in Utah within the confines of Mormon culture and community at the base of snow-capped mountains exerted a profound, but little acknowledged, influence on the life and work of Richard Marc Emerson. The mountains he seemed to have always loved were his escape from the closed and somewhat stifling nature of the town in which he was raised. Two themes that emerged subsequently in his work as a sociologist can be traced to these roots: (a) the idea that dependence upon another (or a group) grants them power over you; (b) the notion that the very uncertainty of success brings its own form of motivation. In many ways he was also drawn eventually to sociology by his deep personal understanding of the role of norms, community pressure, hierarchical power relations, and what being an outsider meant in a close-knit town. The lure of the mountains that took hold at a very early age also fed his sociological imagination, and he became an astute first-hand observer of group performance under stressful situations as he joined many mountaineering expeditions during his career, including the first successful American attempt to climb Mount Everest in 1963.

During the last few years of his life he and his wife, Pat, who had studied anthropology and South East Asia, made many trips to Pakistan to live with and study the remote mountain villages to which their treks and mountain expeditions had taken them over the years. Having lost a son, Marc, at the age of 17 in a tragic mountain climbing accident, Dick and Pat had returned on a sabbatical to the mountains of Pakistan to come to terms with their loss and to gain the support of the mountain people they had come to love. In their joint work and in some of his final papers Emerson examined more deeply the nature of these communities, their historical roots as outposts of the vast English empire, and the authority and power relations that had defined these communities in relation to the emergent nation state over time.

A web of intricate social and organizational arrangements made each expedition into the remote mountain villages of Pakistan a job of enormous proportions, especially for lengthy sojourns. Such challenges engaged the full range of talents and skills of Richard Emerson, from the academic and intellectual to the intensely physical. As a member of the elite mountaineering company of the Army during the Second World War, he was able to advance the considerable technical skills he had begun to develop in the mountains of Utah and Wyoming during his youth. He completed his undergraduate degree in sociology with a minor in philosophy at the University of Utah. Later he did graduate work at the University of Minnesota, where he received his MA in 1952 and his PhD in 1955. He was admitted for graduate training at both Harvard and Berkeley, but neither offered the financial assistance that Minnesota did. His master's thesis was entitled " Deviation and Rejection: an Experimental Replication," and was co-directed by Don Martindale, his advisor in sociology, and Stanley Schachter, then a faculty member in psychology at the University of Minnesota.

He was trained in both sociology and psychology, and his PhD thesis was an extensive field and experimental study of the determinants of social influence in face-to-face groups. The field study included an investigation of boy scout troops in what was to be one of his few empirical examinations of social influence outside of the laboratory. Perhaps it was precisely because of the difficulties of collecting data on these boy scouts that he returned to the more controlled environment of the experimental laboratory in much of his subsequent empirical work.

Another significant empirical adventure came when he stepped out of the lab into the "real world" to study social influence, though this time it was to conduct a unique study of group performance among mountain climbers on the 1963 Everest expedition. This research was supported by a National Science Foundation grant entitled "Communication Feedback in Groups under Stress." During this historic expedition, Dick Emerson, one of the strongest team members physically, also served as a field researcher, conducting both experimental and observational research on his colleagues during what amounted to highly complex maneuvers, often at very high altitudes. His mountain climbing friends still complain about the journals they had to keep and even more about the negative feedback they received (in one condition), often during a difficult traverse or climbing exercise. For this unusual and pathbreaking work Richard Emerson received the Hubbard Medal on behalf of the National Geographic Society. The medal was awarded to him at the White House by President Kennedy in 1963 upon his return to the United States from the expedition.

While many academics of his generation moved around during their careers, Emerson served only two institutions during his lifetime. His first job was at the University of Cincinnati, where he joined the faculty in 1955 and was awarded tenure in 1957. He left Cincinnati in 1965 to become a member of the Sociology Department at the University of Washington. His Seattle home overlooked the

Cascade Mountains, where he often climbed with friends and colleagues, the same mountains that later claimed the life of his teenage son. It was at the University of Washington that he completed his first major theoretical papers on social exchange theory, written in 1967 and later published (1972) in a volume on sociological theories in progress. While this work came to fruition at the University of Washington, the earliest seeds of the theory were evident in his PhD thesis and in two of his most influential pieces, on power–dependence relations, published in 1962 and 1964, just before he left the University of Cincinnati. The 1962 paper, entitled "Power–Dependence Relations," became a citation classic in 1981 due to its enormous influence. We trace some of the influence of this work on the social sciences in the section on the intellectual impact of his work.

The tragedy of his life, which began with the death of his son, Marc, followed him throughout his life. He and Pat endured the loss of friends and loved ones, most associated with the tight-knit community of mountain climbers in the Pacific Northwest or with their friends in the remote villages of Pakistan, where the deaths of sherpas were common, but never easy to accept. Willie Unsoeld, close friend, fellow mountaineer, and colleague at the Evergreen State University in Washington, was killed in an avalanche on Mount Rainier. The Unsoelds lost a daughter, Devi, to the mountains and had endured the long recovery of a son who received serious head injuries from a fall while mountain climbing. Despite the certainty of tragedy in the lives of mountain climbers, Emerson continued to climb until his untimely death in 1982. In fact, during the last year of his life he was deeply engaged in planning for a return trip to Pakistan for a long sojourn in remote mountain villages with his wife. In many ways he was just reaching the peak of his career when he died suddenly on the evening before his daughter, Leslie, was to be married in their living room, with the Cascades looming in the background. Cancer surgery a year earlier had taken its toll, but his death was unexpected.

For a career cut short by premature death, the impact of his work can be judged as even more impressive. His collaborative work with Karen Cook at the University of Washington was just beginning to show fruits, and the graduate students they jointly trained, including Mary Gillmore and Toshio Yamagishi, among others, were just beginning their research careers. It is clear that the impact of his work in the social sciences would have been even greater if he had not died in his late fifties.

One gets a clear image of the heart and soul of Richard Emerson in a passage he wrote in the early stages of his career for a book entitled *The New Professors*, by Bowen (1960). In this chapter he writes about his love of mountains:

> Some of the things I appreciate most for sheer beauty are high alpine mountains, their winding valley glaciers, and foreboding corniced ridges. I love to feel them beneath my feet, when climbing, as well as view them as a painter might.... As I ascend the mountain, I can...read from its contours its past and its future, and my climb is placed in grand context. In fact, through the whole experience I am placed in context! And, mind you, people ask me why I climb mountains.

If he had not become a sociologist, he would have become a sculptor, he once admitted. But, whatever his chosen vocation, he would have never given up the mountains he loved and that had been the primary source of his self-worth even as a child.

In this chapter we focus on his academic work and its impact. For the record, he was also a formidable photographer, whose stark photos of sheer mountain ridges, snow-capped peaks at the top of the world, and close-up shots of the mountain people he loved and their villages are mainly unpublished, except for some that appear in various Sierra Club publications. This black and white legacy of unique pictures that chronicle various expeditions and social reality in remote locations may one day also prove to be a significant contribution to social science. Several of these photos hang in the Commons Room in the Department of Sociology at the University of Washington. Before discussing more fully the impact of his scholarly work, we will comment briefly on the social and intellectual context which influenced both the style and content of his research.

## THE SOCIAL AND INTELLECTUAL CONTEXT

Richard Emerson was one of the large number of men who entered academia after the Second World War, supported by the GI Bill, and many in this cohort of scholars are now retiring. As with most of his contemporaries, his graduate training was influenced by the Second World War and the research that had been funded during and following the war. As Cartwright (1979) notes in his review of the development of the field of social psychology, the Second World War had an enormous impact upon the social sciences as researchers attempted to come to terms with the rise of Hitler and the events that precipitated the war. Common topics of research were authoritarianism, styles of leadership, group solidarity, loyalty, conformity and obedience, nationalism, and power. Emerson was influenced by these trends in his own graduate training, which spanned the disciplines of sociology and psychology. In his early career he studied leadership and social influence.

While at the University of Cincinnati he was jointly an assistant professor of sociology and a senior research associate in psychiatry, where he collaborated on a variety of projects on family relations. In this role he developed the Cincinnati Family Relations Inventory. He also participated with many other influential social psychologists in the leadership training that was offered at the National Training Laboratory at Bethel, Maine. Here he was trained not only in the science of leadership, but also in the practice of developing leadership skills. This laboratory was established with funding after the war to determine the factors that promoted the development in society of good leadership. In part, all these efforts nationwide were derivative of the deep political concerns that had emerged during the war over the rise of Hitler, a man who was able to lead a nation to tolerate genocide in the name of nationalism.

For over two decades after the Second World War, the field of social psychology can be said to have been in its heyday. Funding poured into universities, research and training centers in order to produce a science of human behavior and social dynamics. Much of the funding came from military-related sources like ARPA and the Navy (ONR). NIMH and NSF were also strong funding sources for social science of this type. This stream of research carried the academics trained right after the war through the early stages of their careers, which coincided with the expansion of university education in the United States. During the 1950s and 1960s most universities and colleges were in expansionist mode and departments hired many of the PhDs that had been produced as a result of the GI Bill and other efforts to induce students to obtain graduate degrees and become college teachers. This growth was also fueled by the need to educate the "baby-boom" children, the largest cohorts of children the United States had known. The earliest boomers, born just after the war in 1946 and later, began entering higher education in the early 1960s. Emerson's career spanned these events.

Another significant component of the social/intellectual context in which Emerson's work was carried out was the strong emphasis upon sociology as a science and social psychology, in particular, as a scientific subdiscipline. Logical positivism was making inroads into the social sciences in the late 1950s and the early 1960s, with the rising popularity in some sociological circles of the work of Popper (1961), Kuhn (1963), Hempel (1965), and others. This work emphasized the general theoretical strategy of deductive theorizing, the formulation of abstract theoretical principles that could be used along with clearly defined concepts to derive predictions that could be tested empirically. Emerson's training in sociological theory and experimental work in psychology made this form of theory development natural for him. It is most evident in his major theoretical pieces, "Exchange Theory, Parts I and II," written in 1967 and published subsequently in 1972. This formulation is described in greater detail in the section below. Here we will comment only on the general intellectual climate in the social sciences that influenced his work at the time this work was produced. Of course, not all sociologists trained during this same time frame were drawn to deductive theorizing.

Other more specialized influences on his substantive work can be traced to his mentors and the work of his colleagues at Cincinnati and Washington. At Minnesota, Martindale introduced Richard Emerson to general sociological theory and the significant philosophy of social science debates of the time. Stanley Schachter, one of his MA thesis advisors, trained him in experimental methods and the empirical investigation of hypotheses derived from theoretical propositions. As mentioned above, he also worked at Cincinnati on the development of various tools for empirically investigating family relations (i.e. the inventory and computer-based scoring system he helped to develop), and here he was exposed to small groups and leadership training. His contacts with social scientists outside of sociology at the University of Cincinnati were also influential in the development of his theoretical work on power. Alfred Kuhn, an economist at the University of Cincinnati, once informed Karen Cook that he and Richard Emerson had had many productive conversations about theoretical work in the social sciences, the philosophy of science, and general theories of power and exchange as colleagues. Kuhn's major work, *The Study of Society: a Unified Approach*, published in 1963, gives evidence of this cross-fertilization.

At the University of Washington, Emerson was influenced by his colleagues in the sociology department, especially those who were involved with him in the social psychology program, one of the most nationally visible programs in this subfield. The faculty involved with this program included Frank Miyamoto, Otto Larsen, Phillip Blumstein, Robert Leik, David Schmitt, and Robert Burgess. Long conversations over coffee about behaviorism with Bob Burgess and Dave Schmitt drew Emerson's attention to the developments in the empirical invest-igation of human behavior from a behaviorist perspective. During the 1960s behaviorism was growing as a result of the influence of B. F. Skinner (see especially *About Behaviorism*, 1974) and others who were charismatic and very optimistic about the development of a science of behavior. This theoretical development coincided with the growth of interest in the philosophy of social science and with the debate over the importation of natural science models and modes of theorizing into the social sciences. Together, these developments gen-erated widespread optimism in the potential for producing a science of human behavior. It was against this backdrop that Emerson formulated his own theory of social behavior while at the University of Washington.

Certainly Homans was the first social exchange theorist to explore the im-plications of behaviorism for the study of social interaction, but Emerson is noted for his more extensive treatment of behaviorism as the natural foundation for a theory of social exchange. These principles were spelled out in his chapter entitled, "Exchange Theory, Part I. A Psychological Basis for Social Exchange." This piece reflects both the formal deductive theorizing he had come to value and his attempt to provide a more developed micro-level theory of behavior based on the scientific principles of behavior being produced at that time by behaviorists like his colleague Robert Burgess. This informal influence, noted in a footnote in Emerson's chapter, was more formally acknowledged in a paper published by Emerson in a collection of readings on human social behavior edited by Burgess and Bushell (1969). Burgess and Emerson also co-taught for a while the under-graduate lecture class on social psychology at the University of Washington, which stimulated further cross-fertilization of ideas.

In 1972, Karen Cook joined the Department of Sociology at the University of Washington, attracted to the department by the strength of the social psychology program and the opportunity to work with Richard Emerson, whose work she had been exposed to in her own graduate training at Stanford University, where she was influenced by mentors Joseph Berger, Bernard P. Cohen and Morris Zelditch, who also emphasized training in formal theory, deductive models, and experimental methods. In 1973, Cook and Emerson collaborated in the devel-opment of a long-term program of research funded by the National Science Foundation to empirically test propositions derived from Emerson's theory of social exchange, focusing special attention upon the development of a theory of the distribution of power in exchange networks. In addition, Cook and Emerson developed the first computer-based laboratory in sociology for the study of social exchange. This work is described more fully in the theory section. This fruitful collaboration continued until Emerson's death in 1982. Karen Cook continued this program of research with the help of several former students and collaborators, including Mary Gillmore (University of Washington), Toshio Yamagishi (Hokkaido University), Karen A. Hegtvedt (Emory), and, more recently, Jodi O'Brien (Seattle University), Peter Kollock (UCLA), and Joseph Whitmeyer (University of North Carolina-Charlotte).

The collaboration with Karen Cook led to the introduction of more cognitive concepts to the theory of social exchange that Emerson had developed, and a gradual move away from the behavioristic model that had been the hallmark of his original theoretical work. In addition, her work on equity and distributive justice influenced the research by introducing into their joint theoretical work concerns over fairness and equity, returning to some of the normative aspects of social exchange addressed only briefly by Homans and more extensively by Blau. The more behavioral formulation has been subsequently developed and advanced significantly by the work of Linda Molm, trained at the University of North Carolina, primarily by Jim Wiggins, a behaviorist. She has developed a systematic theory of exchange based explicitly upon the behavioral principles originally developed by Emerson, and in a very intensive program of experimental research she has explored the use of power in what she terms "non-negotiated" exchanges. In the development of social exchange theory it is clear that social networks linking the investigators and their collaborators and students have had significant influence. A more complete analysis of the ties among the various actors who subsequently developed Emerson's work is beyond the scope of this chapter. However, it is important to acknowledge that a large part of the social and intellectual context in which a theorist works is social relations, including those with colleagues and students who influence his or her work.

Jonathan Turner (1986) has done a nice job of articulating the specific nature of Emerson's contributions and the intellectual significance of his landmark pieces on power–dependence relations (1962, 1964) and social exchange theory (1972, parts I and II). In his evaluation of exchange theory in the late 1980s Turner argued that Emerson had resolved one of the key difficulties in developing exchange theory to apply across levels of analysis, with the introduction of the idea of connected exchange relations forming networks of exchange. For Turner, this obviated the need to develop ever more complex conceptions of exchange as the nature of the social unit shifted from an individual to a group, organization, or larger social system. In Emerson's theory the "actors" could be individuals or corporate actors involved in networks of exchange (see Cook and Whitmeyer, 1992).

## THE THEORY

Scientists know that, no matter how brilliant their theories, no matter how accurate their explanations, eventually their work will be improved upon and even superseded, no longer consulted directly. The most important scientists have impact not so much through the particular content of their theories, but through changing other scientists' perspectives. They introduce new concepts or reconceptualize old ones in new ways. They fashion new perspectives or ways of looking at familiar phenomena, raising a host of new questions which lead to the rapid development of new theoretical formulations. Their legacy is an approach, concepts, questions.

Richard Emerson is such a scientist, and he contributed much in the way of theory and explanations, but, even more importantly, presented a new way of conceiving and studying an old concept, social power. His approach to social power and social exchange has led to a large program of research and theory development within sociology, and at the same time has informed and enhanced analysis in a variety of substantive areas of social science. Of his specific theoretical formulations, some are still used, some have been modified, and some have been superseded. However, his approach will always be an essential part of social theory.

Emerson's legacy to social theory can be divided into three areas: theoretical approach, theoretical substance, and methodological approach. As with most scientists, during his life he and his collaborators and colleagues were occupied primarily with the second of these, theoretical substance. He worked to develop theories that offered explanations for particular social phenomena, to test these theoretical formulations, and to improve them, based on empirical research. However, in retrospect his legacy in the other two areas has been equally important. Naturally, these three areas – approach, substance, and methodology – are intertwined in his work, and so they are in our description of it.

Emerson's most important contribution is his approach to social power. This approach is distinctive for several reasons. First, he believed that power could be quantified and measured and thus analyzed rigorously, even mathematically. As a result, his analytic theory of power could be tested through experiments. Second, he argued that a theory of power must be based on a conception of the nature of the social relations in which power is embedded. Third, the theory of power should include a behavioral model of the actor. These features of his perspective can be applied more generally than just to social power, but are key to Emerson's approach to power.

Social power is a useful concept. It has been employed by major social thinkers for centuries: Machiavelli, Marx, and Weber, to name just three. Lay people commonly use the term to explain certain social outcomes, whether on the scale of countries or within small informal groups. Nevertheless, its scientific use had been hampered by its lack of formalization and quantification. George Homans, co-pioneer with Peter Blau and Richard Emerson of the exchange perspective in sociology, also discussed power in a deductive framework. However, Emerson took the crucial step of defining power as a quantifiable, measurable concept. This had two beneficial consequences. Theory could become formal and mathematical, with a gain in precision and power over purely verbal reasoning and deduction. In addition, empirical measures of power could be devised so that theoretical inferences could be tested.

The step of formalizing social power was taken in Emerson's 1962 article, "Power–Dependence Relations." The power of actor $A$ over actor $B$ is equated to the dependence of actor $B$ on actor $A$:

$$Pab = Dba \qquad (1)$$

The dependence of $B$ on $A$ in turn is a positive function of the "motivational investment" of $B$ in "goals mediated by" $A$ and a negative function of the "availability of those goals" to $B$ outside the $A$–$B$ relation (Emerson, 1962, p. 32). In this early work, it appears that Emerson takes equation (1) to be a theoretical postulate, with power and dependence considered as at least conceptually distinct, rather than as a definition of power. The fact that Emerson (1964) experimentally tests this equation suggests this as well. However, by 1972, apparently Emerson considered equation (1) to be a *definition* of power ("*Power* is redundant and unnecessary in this scheme, given our conception of dependence"; Emerson, 1972, p. 64). Some subsequent researchers, such as Pfeffer and Salancik (1978) and Molm (1997), likewise have taken equation (1) to be a definition and a measure of power.

Two crucial aspects of equation (1) are that power is a property of a *relation* and that power is a *potential*. A more precise way of stating the first aspect is that an actor's power is not simply a property of that actor, but rather it has a referent, namely the other actor. The second aspect means that power exists prior to behavior and behavioral outcomes. It can therefore affect those outcomes. Moreover, power itself can be affected by other factors, such as aspects of social structure and characteristics of the actors (status, gender, etc.). The analysis of what causes and affects power is separate from and analytically prior to analysis of how power and other factors affect behavior.

An important and influential part of Emerson's power–dependence theory is his identification of *balancing operations*. He calls an exchange relation in which power (and dependence) is unequal *unbalanced*. Then, in view of the two variables that affect dependence, Emerson suggests four possible balancing operations; that is, processes that will make power more equal in unbalanced relations. Suppose $A$ is more powerful than $B$; that is, $Pab > Pba$ and $Dba > Dab$. To balance this relation: (a) $B$ can reduce the level of motivational investment in goals mediated by $A$ ("withdrawal"); (b) $B$ can come up with alternative sources (e.g. actor $C$) for those goals mediated by $A$ ("network extension"); (c) $B$ can attempt to increase $A$'s motivational investment in goals $B$ mediates (e.g. through "status-giving"); and/or (d) $B$ can work to eliminate $A$'s alternative sources for the goals $B$ mediates (e.g. by engaging in coalition formation with other actors, in particular, other suppliers).

It should be noted that Emerson's approach to social power as developed in his 1972 theoretical formulation entails conceiving of social interaction as exchange. Thus this theory falls into two traditions in social science, the study of social power and what is sometimes called exchange theory. In fact, Emerson terms his general approach *social exchange theory*. As Emerson (1972, p. 39) notes, "My initial reason for beginning the work set forth in these two chapters was to formulate a more encompassing (and hopefully enriching) framework around previous work on power–dependence relations."

Emerson then took the methodological step, largely unprecedented in sociology for research on social power, of testing his theoretical propositions with laboratory experiments using human subjects. Such experiments test theory by testing hypotheses derived from the theory for the particular conditions of the laboratory experiment. Laboratory experiments may not be suitable for testing explanations of naturally occurring phenomena (for development of this argument see Zelditch, 1969). However, just as in the physical sciences, they are ideal for *theory*-testing because factors exogenous to the theory can be controlled. Support for hypotheses derived from theoretical principles for specific experimental conditions usually provides unambiguous support for those principles. This is difficult to achieve outside the laboratory, since social processes are rarely isolated in any social context, and thus findings obtained using other methodologies often have alternative interpretations or somewhat ambiguous meaning. (Of course, this can also happen in poorly designed experimental studies.)

Experimental tests of power–dependence theory were possible for two reasons. First, the mathematical definition of dependence allowed it to be created and measured in the laboratory. Second, by conceiving of social interaction as exchange, it was possible to test the theoretical propositions by creating a setting for exchange through experimental design. The theory explicitly applies to exchange with reference to any goals or resources. Thus, experimentally convenient exchange could be used (see also Molm, 1997, on this point). Emerson published his first experimental tests supporting power–dependence theory in 1964.

In a two-part work written in 1967, but published only in 1972, Emerson builds his social exchange theory by extending his analysis of power and dependence in exchange relations in two directions. Part I presents a basis in behavioral psychology for power–dependence theory. In his earlier work, Emerson did little more than assert the relationship between dependence and motivational investment in mediated goals and the availability of alternatives, respectively. Here he derives those relationships from the principles of behaviorism.

"Exchange Theory, Part II: Exchange Relations and Network Structures" contains the crucial extension from exchange relations to exchange networks that is the basis for most of the remaining work of his career. A few definitions are important. An exchange relation is conceived in part I as a "temporal series" containing opportunities for exchange, which, he argued, evoked initiations of exchange that in turn produced or resulted in transactions. An *exchange network* is a set of actors linked together directly or indirectly through exchange relations. An actor is then conceived as "a point where many exchange relations connect" (Emerson, 1972, p. 57). More specifically, two exchange relations between actors A and B (represented as A–B) and between actors B and C (B–C) are *connected* at actor B if they share actor B and if transactions in one relation are somehow related to transactions in the other relation. Note that this is a specialized definition: a connection exists not between actors but between exchange relations. A connection between two exchange relations is either *positive* or *negative*. Suppose two exchange relations are connected. If exchange in one relation is positively related, in frequency or magnitude, to exchange in the other relation, the connection is *positive*. In this case if *A–B* and *B–C* are positively connected exchange relations, for example, an increase in the frequency of *A–B* exchange could result in an increase in the frequency of *B–C* exchange. If exchange in one relation is negatively related, in frequency or magnitude, to exchange in the other relation, the connection is *negative*. In the case in which the *A–B* and *B–C* relations are negatively connected, an increase in the frequency of *A–B* exchange could result in a decrease in the frequency of *B–C* exchange. An example is the situation in which *A* and *C* are alternative dating partners for *B*. Finally, a negatively connected exchange network is *intracategory* if the resources any network member provides could substitute for the resources any other network member provides (such as friendship in a friendship network). A negatively connected network that is not intracategory is *cross-category* (such as a network of heterosexually dating people).

Ironically, given current developments, Emerson considered a move toward economic theory as the basis for his version of exchange theory, which was the strategy Blau had adopted, but he dismissed this idea by arguing that operant psychology provided a more "social" micro-level basis for the theory. The primary reason was that he viewed the social relation as the major focus of the theory (and the social structures created through the formation of exchange relations). That is, the focus was the relatively enduring interactions between particular actors rather than what he viewed as the dominant focus in economics, the transaction in which actors were perfectly interchangeable. This fit with the primary task of developing an approach in which social structure was the major dependent variable. In part I, Emerson (1972, p. 41) states clearly that his purpose is to "address social structure and structural change within the framework of exchange theory."

Before presenting descriptions of what he termed prototypical exchange network structures, Emerson developed several key concepts which define the factors that are significant in understanding exchange relations. These include reciprocity, balance, cohesion, power and power-balancing operations. Reciprocity, for Emerson, was little more than a description of the contingencies intrinsic to all human social exchange, not an explanation. Norms of obligation emerge to reinforce this feature of social exchange, but they are not necessary as an explanation of continued exchange. The reinforcement principles and their link to initiation of exchange provide sufficient explanation for the continuity or extinction of exchange relations in this framework. Balance in an exchange relation is reflected in any difference in initiation probabilities. An exchange relation is balanced if $Dab = Dba$. That is, the relation is balanced if both parties are equally dependent upon the other for exchange (i.e. for resources of value). The concept balance is critical, since it sets the stage for understanding the "balancing operations" Emerson develops to explain changes in exchange relations and networks.

Cohesion represents the "strength" of the exchange relation or its propensity to survive conflict and the costs associated with the impact of what Emerson calls "external events." Relational cohesion is represented in the 1972 chapters as the average dependence of the two actors in the relation. Subsequently, Molm (1985) and others (e.g. Lawler et al., 1988) have come to refer to this concept as average total power (or simply total power). The concept represents how much is at stake in the relation (not the relative power of each actor within the exchange relation, which is treated separately in further developments in the theory). Power is defined straightforwardly in this work as based on dependence, as indicated above, and this definition becomes the basis for specifying the various possible "balancing operations" available to actors in imbalanced exchange relations.

To conclude the 1972 work, Emerson uses these definitions together with the theoretical apparatus he has built involving power, dependence, and balancing processes to predict changes in exchange networks. Examples are as follows. Actors who are weak because they are rivals in a negatively connected network will tend either to specialize or to form a coalition. If they specialize they develop what is effectively a new division of labor. If they form a coalition they have merged to form a "collective actor" in the network, which then must operate as one. Intracategory exchange networks (or networks in which only one dominant type of resource is exchanged, such as approval) will tend to change until they are closed, meaning that social circles get formed and the boundaries are maintained. Such closed social circles, like socially exclusive clubs, are often difficult for new members to penetrate. Under certain circumstances, intracategory networks will tend to become stratified, with closed classes. Here Emerson's theory becomes quite speculative in an effort to examine how networks become stratified, forming classes differentiated by resource magnitude. Both intraclass exchange and interclass exchange are investigated as elements in the emergence of stratified exchange networks. Tentative theoretical principles are developed to explain, for example, the tendency for initiations to "flow upward" in interclass exchange and for transactions within such relations to be initiated from above. Many of these theoretical insights embedded in the text of part II of Emerson's formulation have never been fully developed theoretically or investigated empirically, nor have the rudimentary notions of norm formation and groups as exchange systems been elaborated (an exception is the work of Stolte, 1987).

In 1978 and 1983, Emerson and his colleague Karen Cook, together with former students Mary Gillmore and Toshio Yamagishi in the case of the 1983 paper, published two papers that extend the theory to the analysis of exchange networks and present experimental tests of those extensions (Cook and Emerson, 1978; Cook et al., 1983). From power–dependence theory it follows that, all else being equal, actors who have more alternatives for obtaining their goals will be less dependent on individual partners and thus have more power. Thus, in a negatively connected network, actors who have more partners with whom they can engage in full exchange will have more power. Theoretically, in such cases access to alternatives increases the availability of the resources of value (or goals to be obtained through exchange).

Assuming that to have power is to use it (Emerson, 1972), this proposition can be tested by measuring power use. Use of power in an exchange relation entails

KAREN S. COOK AND JOSEPH WHITMEYER

obtaining terms of exchange more favorable to oneself. Therefore, the more powerful actor in an exchange relation should obtain more favorable terms of exchange. Exchange as operationalized in the 1978 and 1983 experiments consists of negotiating the terms of trade between two parties (or more) for resources of value which are converted into monetary payoffs at the end of the experiment. Assuming actors use their power, the more powerful actor in an exchange relation should obtain a larger share of the valuable resources to be exchanged; that is, receive more points than the partner.

The two experiments in the 1978 paper involve four-actor, fully linked networks. That is, each actor has exchange opportunities with the other three. In the experiment on the balanced network, all linked pairs were equivalent: all could obtain resources of similar value in exchanges with their trading partners (i.e. no actor had resources of greater value than the others). In the experiment on the unbalanced network one of the four actors offered a more valuable resource and thus was the more desirable exchange partner (the transaction was worth a total of 24 units of profit); exchanges between the other actors proffered resources of similar, but lower, value (these transactions were worth a total of eight units of profit). In the unbalanced network, the actor with the more valuable resource was the best alternative for each of his or her partners, thus giving that actor the most power according to the theory. This prediction was supported. Not only did the powerful actor gain significantly more points than his or her partners, but he or she also gained significantly more points than any of the positionally equivalent actors in the balanced network.

The 1983 article is a natural extension of the theory to larger networks, but at the same time enters a new domain. In the 1978 article, the four-actor exchange network was simply the context for tests of predictions from power–dependence theory. In the 1983 article, network structure has become an interesting factor in its own right. The network studied consists of five actors, no longer fully linked, but linked in a ring, so that each actor has only two potential trading partners (see figure 15.1). One of the five exchange relations is not very profitable (the transaction total is worth only eight points, as opposed to a total of 24 units of profit in each of the other four potential trading relations). If we ignore that low-profitability relation (which connects $F_1$ and $F_2$), we have a line (sometimes called "Line 5") of five actors and four exchange relations, $F_1$–$E_1$–$D_1$–$E_2$–$F_2$. Previous theory on social networks had supposed that positional centrality in a network confers the most power, and thus that $D_1$ would be most powerful. However, the authors of this study use power–dependence theory to predict that if such a network is negatively connected, actors $E_1$ and $E_2$ will emerge as the most powerful actors.

The power–dependence reasoning is as follows. In each exchange relation, a partner with no alternatives will be more dependent and therefore less powerful than a partner with more alternatives (or technically a greater availability of resources). Thus, the $F$s will be less powerful than the $E$s. $D_1$ has two alternatives, but since they have weak alternatives from whom they can obtain favorable outcomes, $D_1$ is more dependent on them than they are on $D_1$. As a

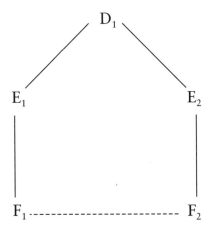

**Figure 15.1**

result, $D_1$ is forced to reduce offers (or demands) down to the level of the *F*s in order to compete. Experimental results supported these general hypotheses.

Note that, as is common in scientific investigation, the experiments reported in the 1978 and 1983 articles were designed to provide clear tests of theory, not to be instances of substantively important exchange phenomena. As a result, many of the substantive features of these experiments are not theoretically crucial. They are operationalizations of theoretical concepts, for which theory therefore makes predictions, which in turn can be evaluated as tests of theory. Thus, exchange is operationalized as coming to agreement on a trade of resources (or profit points); "motivational investment" is operationalized as conversion of points to money (at a constant rate); and negativity is operationalized by allowing each actor only one exchange per round. Many of these aspects of experimental design are not common in natural situations (e.g. one exchange per round), but they instantiate the theoretical concepts in ways easy to control and measure, and therefore permit clear tests of the theory. Thus tested and supported, the theory can then be applied to more complicated natural situations of exchange and exchange networks.

The 1983 paper also inaugurated two general trends in research on exchange networks. First, it presents computer simulation results for four networks: the Line 5, and networks with seven, ten, and thirteen actors. Note again that in order to test the theory of exchange networks, exchange network experiments are designed to focus actors on a single goal: profit maximization. It is easy to embody this goal in simulations by incorporating simple procedures by which simulated actors pursue it. Simulations can thus show whether many actors simultaneously following these procedures produce the results that the theory of exchange networks predicts. Simulation results will thus be valid to the extent that the incorporated procedures match those followed by natural actors.

Second, the paper presents an algorithm for determining the distribution of power in a negatively connected exchange network directly from the network structure. This algorithm is grounded loosely in power–dependence theory. However, application of the algorithm involves only analysis of the network structure and does not use power–dependence theory or models of actor behavior explicitly. This particular algorithm quickly came to be perceived as inadequate. However, many researchers have followed the lead of this paper in seeing it as desirable to have such a structural-level algorithm, and have devised others (see the section on impact for citations to this work).

Emerson's last paper, which he did not complete but which was published in 1987 in an incomplete state, is entitled "Toward a Theory of Value in Social Exchange." However, as he notes and italicizes, "A theory of value must be a theory of actors" (Emerson, 1987, p. 14). This paper attempts to present a more complete model of the (human) actor than that used in his theoretical work of 1962 and 1972. Here he is filling in important remaining lacunae in those theories, just as in his 1972 work he went back and filled in a deductive basis for his 1962 work on power–dependence theory.

Value – that is, the relative importance actors place (behaviorally) on obtaining certain goals or resources – is crucial to both power–dependence theory and its extension into the theory of exchange networks. For example, the first and third of the four balancing operations in a relationship of unequal dependence involve changes of value. Suppose $B$ is more dependent on $A$ than the reverse. $B$ can decrease the value of the goals $A$ mediates or attempt to increase the value to $A$ of the goals $B$ mediates. The values of network members are also integral to the categorization of different types of networks. A *negative* exchange connection exists when two members value a divisible resource provided by a common partner, or when they provide resources that are substitutable to the common partner (a characteristic of the partner's values) and on which the partner satiates. An intracategory network is one in which all network members place similar value on resources available from the other network members.

However, in these theories two important simplifications are made concerning human actors – or, to put it differently, the scope of these theories is limited in two ways. First, the theories of power dependence and exchange networks concern actors interested in only one or perhaps a few goals. Yet human actors are complex, having a variety of different things (goals) they value to different extents, with those values interrelated in complicated ways. A theory of social exchange and social power will become more useful to the extent that it can relax those restrictions and apply to situations in which a fuller panoply of goals is relevant.

Second, in these theories the values of different actors are simply given, without being explained. In 1972 Emerson wrote, and italicized, "In this chapter we will not presume to know the needs and motives of men," followed by "We will see how far we can go on this skimpy basis" (Emerson, 1972, p. 44). Clearly, filling out some of this skimpiness would add to the scope and power of the theory. Understanding how value is created and changed clearly would inform understanding of how and when the first (withdrawal) and third (e.g. status-giving) balancing operations are likely to occur. It would also provide at least partially for a theory of formation and change in the various types of exchange networks.

## The Impact of Emerson's Work

Emerson's influence on contemporary social science falls into two main areas: work stemming from his original formulation of power–dependence theory, and research based on his work on social exchange and exchange networks.

Emerson's work on power and dependence itself has been carried forward in two directions: theoretical investigation of power and more substantive studies of a wide variety of social phenomena. First, his approach has been incorporated into the development of general theory concerning social power. Many power theorists take a more general view, either conceiving of power more broadly or considering social processes in addition to exchange. Thus Emerson's exchange perspective, in which power exists through dependence in an exchange relation, is included alongside other processes, such as persuasion and legitimate authority (see, for example, Wrong, 1988; Coleman, 1990; Friedkin, 1993b).

Second, Emerson's approach has found application in studies of a wide variety of social phenomena. Interactional dynamics in all types of settings frequently involve exchange and power. To the extent that power and power use is responsible for outcomes, Emerson's approach proves useful in analysis and explanation. Substantive areas of study in which it has been applied successfully include marriage and family dynamics, marketing, legal studies, geopolitics, and especially the study of organizations.

Power–dependence theory is a cornerstone of one of the dominant perspectives in organizational studies, known as the *resource dependence* perspective (e.g. Pfeffer and Salancik, 1978). According to this perspective, organizations need a variety of resources from both outside and within the organization. Those entities – individuals, subunits, or other organizations – that exclusively provide the most needed resources will have the most power over or in the organization. This key postulate comes directly from the principle embodied in equation (1), although resource dependence theorists point out that for power actually to be exerted, other elements are also necessary.

Since organizations are not self-sufficient they must engage in exchanges with other organizations and entities in their environments to assure survival. Organizations thus spend much of their time and energy involved in efforts to manage these "strategic dependencies." As Scott (1992, p. 115) argues, "One of the major contributions of the resource dependency perspective is to discern and describe the strategies – ranging from buffering to diversification and merger – employed by organizations to change and adapt to the environment." An early treatment of these strategic options was presented in the work of James D. Thompson (1967) in his influential book, *Organizations in Action*. The application of power–dependence theory to the analysis of organizational exchange and interorganizational relations was pursued by Cook (1977) and subsequently by Cook and Emerson (1984). This work is reflected in more recent developments within the field of organizations. Many of the strategies available to organizations to manage their critical dependencies can be understood in terms of the balancing operations spelled out in power–dependence theory, since the goal is to acquire necessary resources without increasing dependence. Such strategies include, under different circumstances, joint venture, long-term contracting, specialization, consolidation, reduction in production arenas, and vertical integration of various types, among others. As Scott (1992, p. 193) puts it, "Unequal exchange relations can generate power and dependency differences among organizations, causing them to enter into exchange relations cautiously and to pursue strategies that will enhance their own bargaining position."

The work of Emerson and his colleagues has continued to inform research and theory development following the resource dependence perspective on organizations. For example, a recent study (Seabright et al., 1992) of auditor–client relationships found that as the fit between auditor and client declined, the likelihood of this relationship dissolving increased, as the resource dependence perspective predicts. However, the tendency for the relationship to dissolve was attenuated by the development of attachment between the individuals – a development predicted by Emerson and his collaborator Karen Cook. Thus the authors of the study conclude, "We...argue, following theoretical work on social exchange such as Cook (1977) and Cook and Emerson (1978), that attachment is a distinct attribute of interorganizational relationships" (Seabright et al., 1992, p. 153).

Power–dependence theory, as well as its descendent, the theory of exchange networks, has also contributed to the network perspective on organizations. Using power–dependence theory (Emerson, 1962; Cook and Emerson, 1978), Mizruchi (1989) expects and finds that economic dependence and interdependence among businesses leads to similarity in their political behavior. Knoke (1990) points out the parallel between network structures studied in the laboratory and network structures both within and between organizations. He suggests that this parallel should allow theory on exchange networks to help explain power and outcomes in organizational networks, but notes that the complications of the naturally occuring networks have hindered application of the theory thus far.

More recently, various organizational theorists have extended the analysis of networks to the study of organizations and the role of networks more broadly in the economy (see especially Lincoln et al., 1992; Powell, 1990; Sabel, 1991; Gerlach, 1992). Networks are examined as they affect labor practices, informal influence, ethnic enterprises, the organization of business groups, and the networking of companies across national boundaries (see Powell and Smith-Doerr, 1994, for a review). Central to these efforts is the attempt to analyze the relative power of the economic actors in the network and the strategies used to enhance network-wide power or to alter the distribution of power within the network. The focus of attention is on the structural location of the actors in the network and how that influences strategy. Exchange theory and the resource dependence perspective (e.g. Pfeffer and Salancik, 1978) based on power–dependence arguments are commonly used as the framework for analysis in these investigations of economic impact. Other topics of investigation include strategic alliances, collaborative manufacturing enterprises, vertical integration of firms, interlocking directorates, network diffusion of innovative practices, and mergers.

In the field of marketing too, theory has been developed by applying the theoretical ideas of Emerson, Cook, and colleagues to organizations. Cook and Emerson (1978) themselves pointed out the relevance of exchange networks to marketing, noting, for example, that vertically integrated markets and channels of distribution in fact are positively connected networks. A recent example is the work of Anderson et al. (1994), who discuss *business networks*, defined as two or more connected relations between businesses, each business conceived as a collective actor. One of their key propositions is that each firm in a network will develop a *network identity*. This identity has three dimensions: an orientation toward other actors, competence, and power. The last of these, power, is a function of an actor's resources and its network context, following Emerson, Cook, and colleagues. In their examination of two case studies, Anderson et al. note contrasting effects of positive and negative exchange connections. They also point out that connections may switch between positive and negative through time, or even may be simultaneously positive and negative, a point also noted in theoretical work following Emerson and colleagues (Whitmeyer, 1997b). Further exploration of these cases leads Anderson et al. to suggest mechanisms, typically involving network identity, of changes over time in relations and connections in business networks.

In the area of family studies, power–dependence theory has contributed to an understanding of the dynamics of relationships both within families and between family members and outsiders. For example, a recent study of adoption processes analyzing the relationship between birth mothers, adoptive parents, and adoption facilitators suggests that birth mothers may have more power because all other parties are dependent on their decision (Daly and Sobol, 1994). In the study of dating couples, partners, and married people various authors have applied exchange concepts to the analysis of the longevity and quality of such relationships despite the argument that an exchange "logic" does not work in close, personal relations. Michaels et al. (1984), for example, find that exchange outcomes are a more important predictor of relationship satisfaction than are equity concerns. In addition, Sprecher's (1988) research indicates that relationship commitment is affected more by the level of rewards available to partners in alternative relations than by fairness or equity considerations, though there is also evidence in various studies that fairness does matter (see review by Hegtvedt and Cook, forthcoming). A major focus of much of this research is the perceived fairness of the exchanges that occur over time and the symmetry or asymmetry in mutual dependence on the relationship.

Cook and Donnelly (1996) applied the concepts of longitudinal exchange and generalized exchange relations to intergenerational relations both within the family and within the society at large. Relations between generations can be examined as implicit exchange relations in which each generation must determine how to allocate its resources to the next generation, and on what basis. Reciprocity, trust, dependence, power, fairness, and asymmetry in exchange benefits all play a significant role in these determinations. These dynamics are important within families and relate to social issues like long-term care, child care, elder abuse, health care, and the transfer of wealth. Many of these issues also arise at the aggregate level for the society at large in terms of the nature of the relations between the generations, with implications for property law, taxation, welfare policy, social and health services, and education.

Applications of exchange theory in fields like health care are less common, but interesting. Shortell (1977), for example, used exchange theory to analyze the nature of physician referrals under the standard fee-for-service funding regime in place in the health care system at that time. More recently, Grembowski et al. (1998) have examined physician referrals under managed care using an exchange-based model of the nature of the decisions to refer and the network of providers involved in the delivery of health services under different degrees of "managedness." Issues of power and dependence are addressed in this literature at various levels, including the physician–patient relation, the relations between various categories of providers (e.g. physician to physician, primary care provider to specialist, physician to alternative health care provider, and physicians to hospital administrators or other managers within the health care system), and relations between organizational units with involvement in delivery of services (insurance carriers, suppliers of goods and services, other health and community agencies, etc.). Research based on models of exchange and power–dependence principles in the arena of health care holds the promise of providing a more general theory of the processes involved than is currently available. The major shifts that have occurred over the past decade in the delivery of health care have involved significant changes in the distribution of power among the key players in that organizational system (i.e. the shift in power from relatively autonomous physicians to the hospitals in which they practice and the insurers that pay them).

Finally, power–dependence theory has been applied in the geopolitical realm, to relations between states. For example, Jonathan Turner (1995) proposes that ongoing exchange relations between states lead to balancing operations, as suggested by Emerson (1962, 1972). When dependence between states is unequal – that is, trade is imbalanced – the more dependent partner will take steps to reduce the imbalance, perhaps even resorting to coercion.

Emerson's fruitful extension of theory and research into exchange networks has led to the experimental investigation of exchange networks, which has spawned a large body of subsequent research leading in a number of directions. Some of the research looks at social processses in addition to those Emerson investigated. For example, Linda Molm (e.g. 1997) has developed an extensive research program on exchange networks in which network members not only can reward (i.e. confer resource gains on) each other, but also can punish (i.e. impose losses on) each other. As operationalized, punishment consists of taking points away from partners. She also has varied the exchange process by looking at reciprocal exchange, in which partners take turns rewarding or punishing (or not) each other, rather than negotiated exchange, in which partners must come to an agreement about who gets what before the transaction is completed. Emerson's experimental research and much of the work that followed the lead of Cook and Emerson (1978) was restricted to negotiated exchange, though the theoretical formulation Emerson developed was not restricted in this manner.

This point is most clearly demonstrated in the interesting work of Linda Molm (1981, 1987, 1990, 1994, 1997) on reciprocal (or "non-negotiated" exchange).

In her most recent extensive treatment of coercive power in social exchange, Molm (1997) presents the results of a ten-year program of experimental research which indicates the nature of the effects of coercive power in exchange relations. The surprising finding she addresses in this work is the result that coercion is rarely used even by those in positions of power advantage. The primary reason is that the use of punishment power imposes losses upon the exchange partner and raises the cost of the use of power, in terms of both opportunity costs (time better spent in active pursuit of other rewards) and the potential for retaliation. As Molm (1997, p. 138) puts it, in an exchange relation in which one partner uses coercive power to increase exchange benefits, "the coercer pays a price for the rewards obtained." Her work has initiated a more complete examination of the dynamics of exchange processes and the role of strategy in determining the outcomes that were viewed primarily in Emerson's work as structurally induced.

Edward Lawler (e.g. Lawler and Yoon, 1993, 1996), along with colleagues, and others have pursued research that explores in greater depth the notion of an exchange *relation*; that is, a situation of ongoing rather than one-time-only exchange. Lawler builds on the notion, from Emerson's work (1962, 1972; Cook and Emerson, 1978) on power–dependence theory, of *cohesion*, defined as the total dependence (of both partners) in an exchange relation. To this he adds emotional processes, and develops a theory of *commitment* in exchange relations. Not only does this research build on Emerson's work, but it is consistent with the spirit of that work, in its emphasis on an exchange relation as more enduring, and more meaningful for its members, than a simple economic opportunity. A key feature of Lawler's theory of relational exchange is the idea that instrumental exchange relations become transformed over time (based on the nature of the exchange dynamics) in such a way that the relation itself becomes a valued object worthy of commitment. In his studies of gift-giving he examines this transformation and measures it in terms of the emergence of commitment between exchange partners. A second feature that makes this work interesting is that it explicitly incorporates emotions into the theory, an aspect that is distinctly missing in Emerson's early work on exchange, but much less so in the work of the anthropologists who studied more primitive forms of exchange (e.g. Mauss and Malinowski).

Another variant on exchange processes in exchange networks is *generalized exchange*. Under rules of generalized exchange, actors reward actors who are different from the actors who reward them. The prominent existence of such exchange systems in some societies has been described by anthropologists. Inspired by these descriptions, Emerson (1981) himself suggested investigation into generalized exchange, but never had the opportunity to pursue it. It was left to his colleagues and former students (e.g. Gillmore, 1987; Cook and Yamagishi, 1993) to conduct the first experimental investigations of this type of exchange network. One interesting feature of many systems of generalized exchange is that they produce *social dilemmas* through the incentive structures they create for network members. Namely, members do better as individuals by not giving to their partners, but if all refuse to give, they all do worse than if they all gave. Thus, we see investigation of exchange networks extended into the domain of social dilemmas, which is a vast area of research in its own right (see Yamagashi, 1995).

Finally, a considerable body of research continues the experimental study of the effect of network structures on power distributions in exchange networks. Since the late 1980s much of this effort has gone into the development of models to predict accurately the distribution of payoffs among network members given a particular network structure. Most notably, David Willer, Barry Markovsky, John Skvoretz, and their colleagues have developed a series of algorithms for making such predictions for a wide variety of experimental exchange networks, under a variety of experimental rules (e.g. Markovsky et al., 1988, 1993). Nevertheless, this work claims a theoretical basis different from power–dependence theory. It is based on what Willer (1981, 1987) refers to as "elementary theory." Thus, we will not discuss it in further detail in this piece on Emerson's legacy. Another approach to predicting outcomes, called the *expected value model*, has been developed by Noah Friedkin (1992, 1993a). This approach incorporates the notion of actors behaving according to their dependence, and thus has stronger ties to Emerson's approach. As with other algorithms, however, the primary aim of Friedkin's approach has been the accurate prediction of experimental outcomes.

Presumably the rationale behind such model-building efforts is the idea that a model that accurately predicts outcomes somehow must capture the essential processes involved. Nevertheless, this research probably has not moved in the direction Emerson might have anticipated. Recall that Emerson came up with an experimental operationalization of exchange networks as a way of testing analytically derived theory. The concentration on predictive models entails a shift from considering experimental exchange networks simply as an operationally convenient way of testing theoretical points, to considering them as objects of interest in their own right. This shift also means, however, that less attention has been paid to continuing the analytic development of theory concerning power, exchange, and network structure which would be more generally applicable.

One continuation of Emerson's theory of exchange networks that does concentrate on developing more general theory not tied specifically to experimentally operationalized networks is the recent use of microeconomic theory to analyze exchange networks. Cook and Emerson (1978) note the relevance of microeconomic theory for exchange processes, but suggest that equity theory and power–dependence theory provide a more precise analysis of the social interactions in an exchange *relation*. However, in the past few years, theorists have begun to use sophisticated microeconomic theory, in particular game theory and general equilibrium analysis, to analyze the effects of network structure and other factors in exchange networks. In essence, microeconomic models underlying the theory replace the behavioristic models Emerson used to describe basic processes.

Game theory was used to analyze exchange networks first by Bienenstock and Bonacich (1992). Game theory is appropriate for this task, since it is a theoretical apparatus derived for situations in which actors interact strategically in order to maximize some clearly defined interests. A key game theoretic concept is the *core*, defined as the set of all possible outcomes that cannot be improved upon by any coalition of actors, including individual actors and the set of all actors. Bienenstock and Bonacich suggest the *core* as an appropriate solution for exchange networks. One implication is that under many circumstances network structure in negatively connected networks may lead to only a range of power distributions rather than a single power distribution. A subsequent article by Bienenstock and Bonacich (1997) discusses another game theoretic solution concept, the *kernel*. They point out its strong similarity to the concept of *equidependence*, developed from Emerson's theory as a tool for predicting exchange network outcomes by Cook and Yamagishi (1992). According to Bienenstock and Bonacich, one reason to use game theoretic concepts such as the kernel explicitly is that theorists then can take advantage of the large body of work in game theory. For example, they note that the failure of restrictions on information to affect results in some experiments is what would be expected if the kernel describes the experimental subjects' strategies.

General equilibrium analysis is a fundamental tool of modern microeconomics that has been adapted for application to exchange networks by a number of researchers (Marsden, 1983; Whitmeyer, 1994, 1997b; Yamaguchi, 1996). Unlike game theory, which applies to situations involving few actors who thus can act strategically, assumptions of general equilibrium analysis make it most appropriate for market situations; that is, situations involving many actors, all of whom have competitors (Whitmeyer, 1997a). Nevertheless, for analyzing exchange networks it has the merit of yielding a *single* power distribution, which moreover lies within the range of power distributions identified by game theory. Often this single point is sufficient for supporting qualitative theoretical predictions.

Yamaguchi (1996), for example, adapts general equilibrium analysis to exchange networks by assuming that actors are interested not in goods possessed by their partners, but in exchange with those partners itself. A key concept in his approach is that of the *substitutability* of an actor's alternative partners. This is incorporated into his general equilibrium model as the *elasticity of substitution*, denoted $s$. Thus, the model can treat both positively and negatively connected networks, since for $0 < s < 1$ an exchange connection is positive, while for $s > 1$ an exchange connection is negative. Through estimation of $s$, the model can approximate results from experimental networks, both positive and negative. Moreover, the model allows Yamaguchi to explore causes of *centralization*, defined as "agreement between the positions of power and the positions of global centrality." In particular, he is able to develop hypotheses concerning effects of substitutability on centralization.

For the most part, Emerson's deductions concerning balancing operations and thus change in exchange networks have been ignored in subsequent research on exchange networks (with the exception of some work on coalition formation; e.g. Gillmore, 1987; Cook and Gillmore, 1984). This stands in contrast to applications of power–dependence theory in other areas of study, such as organizations, where Emerson's theory of balancing processes has proved useful. This is perhaps because research on exchange networks almost without exception has used experimental exchange networks of short duration and restricted exchange. That is, for reasons of control and logistics, experimental exchange networks have lasted not more than one or at most two hours, and have restricted interaction and domains of exchange. Under such constraints, it is not likely that network members will be able to use balancing processes. However, this may be an area of future research and theoretical development. Other topics currently being investigated include the role of emotions in exchange, the relationship between fairness assessments and strategy in negotiated and non-negotiated exchange, the nature of commitment and solidarity processes, and the emergence of trust in generalized exchange.

## ASSESSMENT OF EMERSON'S LEGACY

Most social theorists die before the full impact of their work is revealed. Emerson was no exception to this rule. While he was alive in 1981 to learn that his 1962 paper on power–dependence relations had become a citation classic, he did not live long enough to accept the invitation to write about this contribution in his own words. This essay completes this unfinished business. Fifteen years after his untimely death it is easier to assess the nature of the impact of the work Emerson began in the early 1960s. In a few words his 1962 and 1964 pieces fundamentally altered the social science view of power. Power viewed as a relational construct based on dependence is now the common view. It is the way we talk about power in most contexts (short of pure violence) at the individual, organizational and societal levels. This is reflected in work on power in friendships, marital partnerships, families, organizational sub-units or departments, organizations and interorganizational relations, governments in relation to citizens or other entities, and international relations. Examples of applications in some of these arenas have been provided in the section on the influence of Emerson's work.

Related to the impact of his work on power is the extent to which theories about social exchange within the field of sociology now draw upon his conception of exchange networks. He was the first exchange theorist in sociology to extend the theory to apply to networks of connected exchange relations. Homans's theoretical work remained primarily at the dyadic and group level. Blau developed an exchange framework that extended into the macro-realm of social life and more complex forms of association, but he did not propose networks as the basis for the extension of exchange concepts beyond the micro-level, as Emerson subsequently did. The significance of this theoretical move, reflected in Turner's assessment discussed earlier in this chapter, is that it connects exchange theory directly to developments in the analysis of social networks (a field that has also expanded greatly in the past two decades) and to the analysis of new forms of organization (see especially Powell and Doerr-Smith, 1994).

## Bibliography

### Writings of Richard M. Emerson

Power–Dependence Relations. 1962. *American Sociological Review*, 27, 31–41.

Power–Dependence Relations: Two Experiments. 1964. *Sociometry*, 27, 282–98.

Operant Psychology and Exchange Theory. 1969. In R. Burgess and D. Bushell (eds), *Behavioral Sociology*. New York: Columbia University Press.

Exchange Theory, Part I. A Psychological Basis for Social Exchange. Exchange Theory, Part II. Exchange Relations and Network Structures. 1972. In J. Berger, M. Zelditch and B. Anderson (eds), *Sociological Theories in Progress, volume 2*. Boston: Houghton Mifflin, pp. 38–87.

Structural Inequality: Position and Power in Network Structures (with John F. Stolte). 1977. In R. Hamblin and J. Kunkel (eds), *Behavioral Theory in Sociology*. New Brunswick, NJ: Transaction, pp. 117–38.

Power, Equity and Commitment in Exchange Networks (with Karen S. Cook). 1978. *American Sociological Review*, 43, 721–39.

Social Exchange Theory. 1981. In Morris Rosenberg and Ralph Turner (eds), *Social Psychology: Sociological Perspectives*. New York: Basic Books, pp. 30–65.

The Distribution of Power in Exchange Networks: Theory and Experimental Results (with K. S. Cook, M. R. Gillmore, and T. Yamagashi). 1983. *American Journal of Sociology*, 89, 275–305.

Exchange Networks and the Analysis of Complex Organizations (with Karen S. Cook). 1984. In Samuel B. Bacharach and E. J. Lawler (eds), *Perspectives on Organizational Sociology: Theory and Research, volume 3*. Greenwich, CT: JAI Press, pp. 1–30.

Toward a Theory of Value in Social Exchange. 1987. In Karen S. Cook (ed.), *Social Exchange Theory*. Newbury Park, CA: Sage, pp. 11–46.

### Further reading

Anderson, James C., Håkansson, Håkan, and Johanson, Jan (1994) Dyadic Business Relationships Within a Business Network Context. *Journal of Marketing*, 58, 1–15.

Blau, Peter (1964) *Exchange and Power*. New York: John Wiley and Sons.

Bienenstock, Elisa Jayne and Bonacich, Phillip (1992) The Core as a Solution to Negatively Connected Exchange Networks. *Social Networks*, 14, 231–43.

Bienenstock, Elisa Jayne and Bonacich, Phillip (1997) Network Exchange as a Cooperative Game. *Rationality and Society*, 9, 37–65.

Bowen, R. O. (1960) *The New Professors*. New York: Holt, Rinehart & Winston.

Cartwright, Dorwin (1979) Contemporary Social Psychology in Historical Perspective. *Sociometry*, 42, 250–8.

Coleman, James S. (1990) *The Structure of Social Theory*. Cambridge, MA: Harvard University Press.

Cook, Karen S. (1977) Exchange and Power in Networks of Interorganizational Relations. *Sociological Quarterly*, 18, 62–82.

Cook, Karen S. (1987) *Social Exchange Theory*. Newbury Park, CA: Sage.

Cook, Karen S. and Donnelly, Shawn (1996) Intergenerational Exchange Relations and Social Justice. In Leo Montada and Melvin J. Lerner (eds), *Current Societal Concerns About Justice*. New York: Plenum Press, pp. 67–83.

Cook, Karen S. and Gillmore, M. R. (1984) Power, Dependence and Coalitions. In Edward J. Lawler (ed.), *Advances in Group Processes, volume 1*. Greenwich, CT: JAI Press, pp. 27–58.

Cook, Karen S. and Whitmeyer, Joseph W. (1992) Two Approaches to Social Structure: Exchange Theory and Network Analysis. In Judith Blake and John Hagan (eds), *Annual Review of Sociology, volume 18*. Palo Alto, CA: Annual Reviews, pp. 109–27.

Cook, Karen S. and Yamagishi, Toshio (1992) Power in Exchange Networks: a Power–Dependence Formulation. *Social Networks*, 14, 245–66.

Daly, Kerry J. and Sobol, Michael P. (1994) Public and Private Adoption: a Comparison of Service and Accessibility. *Family Relations*, 43, 86–93.

Friedkin, Noah E. (1992) An Expected Value Model of Social Power: Predictions for Selected Exchange Networks. *Social Networks*, 14, 213–29.

Friedkin, Noah E. (1993a) An Expected Value Model of Social Exchange Outcomes. In Edward J. Lawler, Barry Markovsky, Karen Heimer, and Jodi O'Brien (eds), *Advances in Group Processes*. Greenwich, CT: JAI Press, pp. 163–93.

Friedkin, Noah E. (1993b) Structural Bases of Interpersonal Influence in Groups: a Longitudinal Case Study. *American Sociological Review*, 58, 861–72.

Gerlach, Michael L. (1992) *Alliance Capitalism: the Social Organization of Japanese Business*. Berkeley: University of California Press.

Gillmore, Mary R. (1987) Implications of Generalized Versus Restricted Exchange. In Karen S. Cook (ed.), *Social Exchange Theory*. Newbury Park, CA: Sage, pp. 170–89.

Grembowski, David, Cook, Karen S., Patrick, Donald, and Roussell, Amy (1998) Managed Care and Physician Referral: a Social Exchange Perspective. *Medical Care Research and Review*, 55, 3–31.

Hegtvedt, Karen A. and Cook, Karen S. (forthcoming). Distributive Justice: Recent Theoretical Developments and Applications. In Lee Hamilton and Joseph Sanders (eds), *Justice, volume 1*. New York: Plenum Press.

Hempel, Carl (1965) *Aspects of Scientific Explanation*. New York: Free Press.

Homans, George C. (1961) *Social Behavior: Its Elementary Forms*. New York: Harcourt, Brace and World.

Knoke, David (1990) *Political Networks: the Structural Perspective*. Cambridge: Cambridge University Press.

Kuhn, Alfred (1963) *The Study of Society: a Unified Approach*. Homewood, IL: Irwin-Dorsey.

Kuhn, Thomas (1964) *The Structure of Scientific Revolutions*. Chicago: University of Chicago Press (2nd edn 1970).

Lawler, Edward J., Ford, Rebecca, and Blegen, Mary A. (1988) Coercive Capability in Conflict: a Test of Bilateral Deterrence versus Conflict Spiral Theory. *Social Psychology Quarterly*, 51, 93–107.

Lawler, Edward J. and Yoon, Jeongkoo (1993) Power and the Emergence of Commitment Behavior in Negotiated Exchange. *American Sociological Review*, 58, 465–81.

Lawler, Edward J. and Yoon, Jeongkoo (1996) Commitment in Exchange Relations: a Test of a Theory of Relational Cohesion. *American Sociological Review*, 61, 89–108.

Lincoln, James R., Gerlach, Michael, and Takashi, Peggy (1992) Keiretsu Networks in the Japanese Economy: a Dyad Analysis of Intercorporate Ties. *American Sociological Review*, 57, 561–85.

Markovsky, Barry, Willer, D., and Patton, T. (1988) Power Relations in Exchange Networks. *American Sociological Review*, 53, 220–36.

Marsden, Peter V. (1983) Restricted Access in Networks and Models of Power. *American Journal of Sociology*, 88, 686–717.

Michaels, James, Edwards, John N., and Acock, Alan C. (1984) Satisfaction in Intimate Relationships as a Function of Inequality, Inequity and Outcomes. *Social Psychology Quarterly*, 47, 347–57.

Mizruchi, Mark S. (1989) Similarity of Political Behavior Among Large American Corporations. *American Journal of Sociology*, 95, 401–24.

Molm, Linda D. (1981) The Conversion of Power Imbalance to Power Use. *Social Psychology Quarterly*, 16, 153–66.

Molm, Linda D. (1985) Relative Effects of Individual Dependencies: Further Tests of the Relation between Power Imbalance and Power Use. *Social Forces*, 63, 810–37.

Molm, Linda D. (1987) Linking Power Structure and Power Use. In Karen S. Cook (ed.), *Social Exchange Theory*. Newbury Park, CA: Sage, pp. 107–29.

Molm, Linda D. (1990) Structure, Action and Outcomes: the Dynamics of Power in Exchange Relations. *American Sociological Review*, 55, 427–47.

Molm, Linda D. (1994) Is Punishment Effective? Coercive Strategies in Social Exchange. *Social Psychology Quarterly*, 57, 75–94.

Molm, Linda D. (1997) *Coercive Power in Social Exchange*. Cambridge: Cambridge University Press.

Molm, Linda D. and Cook, Karen S. (1995) Social Exchange and Exchange Networks. In Karen S. Cook, Gary A. Fine, and James S. House (eds), *Sociological Perspectives on Social Psychology*. Boston: Allyn and Bacon, pp. 209–35.

Pfeffer, Jeffrey and Salancik, Gerald R. (1978) *The External Control of Organizations: a Resource Dependence Perspective*. New York: Harper and Row.

Popper, Karl (1961) *The Poverty of Historicism*. London: Routledge & Kegan Paul.

Powell, Walter W. (1990) Neither Market nor Hierarchy: Network Forms of Organization. In L. L. Cummings and Staw (eds), *Research in Organizational Behaviour, volume 12*. Greenwich, CT: JAI Press, pp. 295–336.

Powell, Walter W. and Doerr-Smith, Laurel (1994) Networks and Economic Life. In Neil Smelser and Richard Swedberg (eds), *The Handbook of Economic Sociology*. Princeton, NJ: Princeton University Press/New York: Russell Sage Foundation, pp. 368–402.

Sabel, Charles F. (1991) Moebius-strip Organizations and Open Labor Markets. In P. Bourdieu and J. S. Coleman (eds), *Social Theory for a Changing Society*. Boulder, CO: Westview Press, pp. 23–54.

Scott, W. Richard (1992) *Organizations: Rational, Natural, and Open Systems*, 3rd edn. Englewood Cliffs, NJ: Prentice Hall.

Seabright, Mark A., Levinthal, Daniel A., and Fichman, Mark (1992) Role of Individual Attachments in the Dissolution of Interorganizational Relationships. *Academy of Management Journal*, 35, 122–60.

Shortell, S. M. (1974) Determinants of Physician Referral Rates: an Exchange Theory Approach. *Medical Care*, 12, 13–31.

Skinner, B. F. (1974) *About Behaviorism*. New York: Vintage Books.

Skvoretz, John and Willer, D. (1993) Exclusion and Power: a Test of Four Theories of Power in Exchange Networks. *American Sociological Review*, 58, 801–18.

Sprecher, Susan (1988) Investment Model, Equity, and Social Support Determinants of Relationship Commitment. *Social Psychology Quarterly*, 51, 57–69.

Stolte, John F. (1987) Legitimacy, Justice and Productive Exchange. In Karen S. Cook (ed.), *Social Exchange Theory*. Newbury Park, CA: Sage, pp. 190–208.

Thibaut, John W. and Kelley, Harold H. (1959) *The Social Psychology of Groups*. New York: John Wiley and Sons.

Thompson, James D. (1967) *Organizations in Action.* New York: McGraw-Hill.

Turner, Jonathan H. (1986) *The Structure of Sociological Theory.* Homewood, IL: Dorsey Press.

Turner, Jonathan H. (1995) *Macrodynamics: toward a Theory on the Organization of Human Populations.* New Brunswick, NJ: Rutgers University Press.

Whitmeyer, Joseph M. (1994) Social Structure and the Actor: the Case of Power in Exchange Networks. *Social Psychology Quarterly,* 57, 177–89.

Whitmeyer, Joseph M. (1997a) Applying General Equilibrium Analysis and Game Theory to Exchange Networks. *Current Research in Social Psychology,* 2, 13–23.

Whitmeyer, Joseph M. (1997b) The Power of the Middleman – a Theoretical Analysis. *Journal of Mathematical Sociology,* 22, 59–90.

Willer, David (1981) The Basic Concepts of Elementary Theory. In David Willer and Bo Anderson (eds), *Networks, Exchange and Coercion: the Elementary Theory and Its Applications.* New York: Elsevier.

Willer, David (1987) The Location of Power in Exchange Networks. *Social Networks* (Special Issue), 10, 187–344.

Wrong, Dennis H. (1988) *Power, Its Forms, Bases, and Uses.* Chicago: University of Chicago Press.

Yamagishi, Toshio (1995) Social Dilemmas. In Karen S. Cook, Gary A. Fine, and James S. House (eds), *Sociological Perspectives on Social Psychology.* Needham Heights, NY: Allyn and Bacon, pp. 311–54.

Yamagishi, T. and Cook, K. S. (1993) Generalized Exchange and Social Dilemmas. *Social Psychology Quarterly,* 56, 235–48.

Yamagishi, T., Gillmore, M. R., and Cook, K. S. (1988) Network Connections and the Distribution of Power in Exchange Networks. *American Journal of Sociology,* 93, 833–51.

Yamaguchi, K. (1996) Power in Networks of Substitutable and Complementary Exchange Relations: a Rational-choice Model and an Analysis of Power Centralization. *American Sociological Review,* 61, 308–22.

Zelditch, Morris (1969) Can You Really Study the Army in the Laboratory. In A. Etzioni (ed.), *A Sociological Reader in Complex Organizations.* New York: Holt, Rinehart and Winston, pp. 428–539.

# 16

## James Coleman

### SIEGWART LINDENBERG

### INTRODUCTION

James Coleman is at present widely considered to be the most prominent sociologist worldwide[1] since Talcott Parsons and Robert Merton. He was born in 1926 in Bedford, Indiana. After a brief interlude as a chemist, he studied sociology at Columbia University in New York from 1951 to 1955, mainly with Merton and Lazarsfeld. Lipset was his thesis advisor. His own assessment of the influence of these three is succinct: "I worked *with* Lipset, worked *for* Lazarsfeld, and *worked to be like* Merton" (Coleman, 1990a, p. 31). "To Robert K. Merton, my teacher" reads the dedication of Coleman's major book, *Foundations of Social Theory*.

After his studies, he became an assistant professor in Chicago for three years and settled as an associate professor for the next fourteen years at the Department of Social Relations of Johns Hopkins University. From 1973 on to his death in 1995, he was professor of sociology at Chicago.

When one presents an author rather than a problem and a problem solution, I believe that it is essential to find a generative key to the work that is being discussed; to find a particular well from which the work, including possible inconsistencies, springs.

There can be more than one key to unlock someone's work but probably there is only a limited number of keys that fit. Coleman's work is so vast and diverse that it is no trivial matter to find one of those fitting keys. He wrote and edited close to thirty books and wrote over 300 articles. How can one find a spring from which it all emerged? If we look at what he said about his own interests and use a considered overview over his work in order to select the most pertinent statements, we can glean two major concerns. First, "a deep concern I have had, since my own high school days, with high schools and with ways to make possible their better functioning" (Coleman, 1961, p. vii). Although this statement was made early on in his career, "the deep concern" stayed within him all his life and drove a good deal of his work. Second, "my major interest is in the way social systems (or subsystems) function."[2] In a subtle way, Coleman indicated by this statement that the functioning of systems was even more important to him than high schools and their improvement. His "major interest" dominated his "deep concern." He even objectified this major interest into sociology's major concern. One year before his death he wrote: "The most formidable task of sociology is the development of a theory that will move from the micro level of action to the macro level of norms, social values, status distribution and social conflict" (Coleman, 1996, p. 348). Lest we miss the message that this task is all about system functioning, he also told us what it was all about: "to discover in real social systems implicit rules and norms, constraints and goals, and the way in which the actions they generate combine and interact to produce system functioning" (ibid.).

For a complete theory of system functioning, we need an equal concern for the macro-to-micro link. Coleman was fully aware of this but, as can be gleaned from his claim about "the most formidable task of sociology," the macro-to-micro link was secondary or at least not as interesting to him. He was quite consistent in this attitude throughout his life as a sociologist. By 1964 (Coleman, 1964a, pp. 37ff) he had distinguished between "explanatory" and "synthetic" theories. The former answer why-questions, whereas the latter answer what-consequence-questions, meaning questions that address the consequences of actions for social phenomena. Even then, in his view, sociology (i.e. his sociology) was (and should be) mainly concerned with synthetic theories.

The combination of his two major interests resulted in a third preoccupation: policy research and institutional innovation, especially in the field of education. The wish to improve the functioning of high schools, combined with the "synthetic" approach, led Coleman to put a great deal of effort into debating how policy research should be done and into theory-driven practical suggestions on how to improve the functioning of the educational system.

An overview of Coleman's work thus falls naturally into these three groups: his work on education, his work on the micro–macro link, and his work on policy research. In all three, the generation of society plays an important role. Education was for him one of the major vehicles for generating an adaptive and just society. The micro–macro link traces the mechanisms by which society is generated; on this basis, policy research helps to create the tools for the purposeful generation of certain societal effects. In my discussion, I will first present Coleman's major contributions in the field of education; then I will turn to his view on policy analysis; finally, I will discuss his "foundations," which mainly deal with the micro–macro link.[3]

## EDUCATION

Coleman's research on education can be divided into three phases. The first phase comprised *The Adolescent Society*; the second phase consisted of the vast research which led to *Equality of Educational Opportunity*; the third phase consisted of his research on private schools and social capital. I will present each phase in some detail.

## The Adolescent Society

The first book Coleman ever wrote on high schools was at once one of his most successful books: *The Adolescent Society* (1961). He investigated 39 classes in ten high schools from communities of different size. The book already combined the three major themes of his overall work: education, system functioning, and policy research. How does a high school function from the students' point of view and what can be done to improve its functioning? The particular puzzle, though, only came out during the research itself, and it is much more specific. In industrial societies, education is of utmost importance and only schools can dampen or erase the effect of accidents of birth by creating equality of opportunity. The major goal of schools is thus to teach children knowledge and cognitive skills. This major goal should be reflected in the value system of schools and in the activities that are rewarded. However, in most schools, from the male students' point of view, it is athletics and, for girls, social success (especially with boys) rather than scholastic achievement that dominate the value system and the social rewards, channeling effort away from scholastic pursuits. While there are important differences between schools concerning value and reward systems, the similarity in values and social rewards is striking, especially in the consistency with which the scholastic achievements rank below non-scholastic characteristics and pursuits. The question which Coleman then asked was: how can this be? Why does the value and reward system of teachers and of the larger society with regard to the major function of schools not find its way into adolescent society in schools?

Although *The Adolescent Society* remains well known even today, many of its most poignant findings have been forgotten. What lingers in the literature is the question of whether Coleman did not overestimate the importance of peer groups and underestimate the importance of the family. I will return to this point below. This overview of Coleman's work gives me the opportunity to refresh the reader's memory with regard to findings and explanations in this book which in my judgment have not lost their importance over time.

Question to the student: "If you could be remembered here at school for one of the three things below, which one would you want it to be? Brilliant student, Athletic star (boys), Leader in activities (girls), Most popular." The answers to this question were compared to the answers by parents to a comparable question ("If your son or daughter could be outstanding in high school in one of the three things listed below, which one would you want it to be?"). Table 16.1 shows the results.

There is a glaring disparity between what parents would like their children to be and the students' own ideal. The difference is most pronounced in the category "brilliant student." For boys, 77 percent of the parents would like them to stand out as a brilliant student, while 68 percent of the boys find their ideal in athletics and in being popular. For the girls, parents are more modest in

**Table 16.1**  How boys and girls want to be remembered and how their parents want them to be outstanding in school (percentages)

|  | Boys | Parents (for boys) | Girls | Parents (for girls) |
|---|---|---|---|---|
| Brilliant student | 32 | 77 | 28 | 54 |
| Athletic star (boys) | 45 | 9 |  |  |
| Leader in activities (girls) |  |  | 38 | 36 |
| Most popular | 23 | 14 | 34 | 10 |

*Source*: compiled from Coleman's *The Adolescent Society*.

their academic expectations, but still a majority would like their daughters to be brilliant students most of all. Girls themselves think differently: 72 percent opt for leader in activities or popularity.

The low standing of academic achievement in the adolescent's value system is corroborated for both boys and girls by the questions about what it takes to belong to the leading crowd and what it takes to be popular. This does not mean that good grades do not contribute to elite standing or to popularity. Rather, it indicates that in most schools investigated, good grades only add to standing when a student also excels in other things. This fact is important because even though it prevents an overall negative correlation of academic success and popularity in school, it means that a good deal of the energies of those who could get high grades are distracted into non-scholastic activities.

There are mainly two things Coleman wants to explain with regard to these findings. First, what determines the value system in schools? A value system for him is the consensual relative evaluation of certain kinds of activities and achievements (sports, scholastic achievement, stirring up excitement, etc.). In particular, what interests him is the rank order of athletics versus scholastic achievements. Second, he wants to explain relevant individual outcomes, i.e. self-esteem and grades.

**THE THEORY OF THE LEADING CROWD** His explanation of the value system is quite ingenious. He focuses on the importance of social rewards and punishments, which he identifies as popularity, respect, acceptance into a crowd, praise, awe, support, and aid on the one hand, and isolation, ridicule, exclusion from a crowd, disdain, discouragement, and disrespect on the other hand. These rewards and punishments operate in the community at large and inside the school. In order to understand how they work in school, Coleman uses the concept of "the leading crowd." Adolescents in schools form a community, and Coleman argues that every community has a leading crowd. Social rewards are tied to the criteria of membership in the leading crowd and thus the crucial question is: what does it take to get into the leading crowd?

**GIRLS** For reasons to be explained later, Coleman offers separate explanations for girls and boys. Let me begin with the *girls*. Coleman's general assumption is that the criteria for membership in the leading crowd depend *not* so much on the values parents hold for their children (such as scholastic versus social achievement) but on the parents' status system. An all-important difference is whether the status of most parents in the community is or is not well established and what criteria the parents use in their own status competition. Where the status of the parents is well established (as in the small town in this study), most students are familiar with the community status system and will more or less reproduce it in school. As a consequence, the leading crowd will largely be a reflection of this status system. If the community is clearly stratified, then family background will play an important role as criterion for membership in the leading crowd. If the status differences are not so large (as in a small farming community), then the criteria of membership in the leading crowd are more based on popular interests of the student body. If the status system of the parents puts considerable emphasis on social achievement for women, then girls in school will also put a great emphasis on social achievements, rather than good grades. There may still be a positive correlation between family background and grades (because of the higher educational level of the elite parents), but high grades will not help to make a girl more popular within the leading crowd. Where parents consider education to belong to the status criteria (also for women), good grades will also belong to the criteria of membership in the leading crowd. In this case, grades will correlate even more highly with family background than in the previous case.

The picture is quite different for communities with high mobility in which the status of parents is not generally known and has to be demonstrated (in the study, these are the larger communities). There are basically two ways for parents to do this, both involving the demonstration of visible status characteristics. First, parents try to demonstrate their status by indications of material success, through ostentatiousness in consumption and the handling of money. Second, parents demonstrate their status by the way they act. Since there is no stable traditional community to reward acting according to traditional norms, status can be demonstrated by acting with self-assuredness and social skill. In such mobile communities, the criteria for membership in the leading crowd in school will then also reflect ostentatiousness, self-assuredness and social skill. Coleman stresses an irony here. Self-assuredness and social skills (in the absence of clear traditional norms) are meant to demonstrate independence, initiative, meeting challenges, and the ability to fascinate other people. Such behavior in school is quite incompatible with doing what you are told. Students in the leading crowd thus have to demonstrate their independence from parents and teachers, take initiative, and "stir up excitement." The irony is that the strong influence of peers on the behavior of students derives from the strong influence of the (mobile) community on the status criteria in school.

**BOYS** In principle, there is no reason to assume that these processes hold only for girls. However, for *boys*, family background is generally much less important a criterion for belonging to the leading crowd than for girls. Why is this so? Coleman's answer to this question also deserves much more attention than it has gotten hitherto. He argues that it is the *system of interscholastic competition* in sports that overshadows the status effect of the community on the membership criteria of the leading crowd. When students compete for grades, they do so individually, so that one student's good grades are a threat to the other students' good grades. However, it is a completely different matter if there is an inter-scholastic competition where excelling also increases the status of those who do not excel. Interscholastic competition allows the *combination* of an internal status differentiation with status equality toward the outside, and it allows the person high on the internal status system to increase everyone's status on the external status system (the one in which the entire school is pitted against other schools or communities). In such a system, the good athlete may be rewarded in three ways for his effort. He is high on the internal status system, he is popular (i.e. others do not begrudge his high status, they like him, and they approve of what he is doing), and he may be high with his school team on the external status system. For this very reason, interscholastic competition offers many more social rewards than scholastic achievement, and drains effort away from the latter. In this way, athletic status can successfully compete with other criteria for member-ship in the leading crowd and reduce their importance.[4]

**REMEDY** Coleman's suggestion of pushing scholastic achievement higher up the rank order of students' priorities is typical of someone interested in the function-ing of systems. He suggests that students be pushed not to achieve better in school individually but to affect the criteria for membership in the leading crowd. Since the school should cut through ascribed criteria of family back-ground and religion, the remedy should be strong enough to cut through these influences. Based on his own research, he could think of no stronger instrument than using the motivating power of interscholastic competition for this purpose. If this competition could be devised to pertain to scholarly matters rather than to sports, then scholarly achievement would become a major criterion for member-ship in the leading crowd. Coleman thereby also rectifies the bad image com-petition has in the public eye as a means to spur learning. It is only individual competition cut loose from intergroup competition which has negative effects, especially when it is tied to arbitrary judgments by teachers who reward the quiet little girl in the front row for always providing the "right" answer. Cole-man specifically suggests the construction of knowledge-related *games*, espe-cially computer games (in 1961!), which could be played between schools. Even if the games were not played between schools but only within schools they would at least remove the often arbitrary judgment by teachers on scholastic achievement. Not much has happened with these suggestions so far, but with present-day information technology, the possibility of introducing interscholas-tic competition on scholastic matters has come a lot closer at hand. What Coleman did not consider was the possibility that competition in scholastic matters might ultimately not bring what sports did even if it involved competi-tion between schools. Scholastic completion may not require *joint* efforts to the same degree that team sports do. One very clever student may win a competition in scholastic matters for the entire school without involving anyone else in the preparation or the competition itself. In team sports, many have to cooperate well and do their best to win the competition. In addition, the entertainment value of sports is likely to be considerably higher for a broad range of people than that of scholastic competition.

## Equality of Educational Opportunity

Based on the success of *The Adolescent Society* (TAS), Coleman was a few years later asked to conduct a large-scale study which resulted in the *Equality of Educational Opportunity* (EEO, 1966). The concern in this study was again with the possibility of the school preparing the student for the requirements of modern society, irrespective of the student's family background (especially his or her racial background). But the focus this time was not on the functioning of the school or part of the school as a system, but on finding facts relevant for social policy: to what extent do schools overcome the inequalities with which children come to school? Do school resources (teacher quality, class size, equipment, expenditure per pupil, etc.) play an important role? The study was truly huge. It involved more than 600,000 students in more than 3,000 elementary and secondary schools. Family background and attitudes of students, the composition of student bodies, and school resources were among the important independent variables, and school achievement (verbal and math scores) was the major dependent variable.

There were many results of this study, but three of them aroused national interest, controversy, and policy changes for quite some time. First, the family background of the students (especially regarding race) plays (statistically speaking) the most important role for student achievement. Second, school inputs have no large effect on student achievement. Third, there is an *asymmetric context effect* on student achievement: weaker students do better among better students but better students are not pulled down by the presence of weaker students. The first and second findings combined constituted a large blow to the expectation that the school operates as the great equalizer of inequalities in opportunity. Family background (mainly race) was much too important and school inputs were much too unimportant for this equalization to occur. These findings also cast some doubt on the meaning of equality of opportunity for both input- and output-based measures of the concept. Because these findings went so much against the grain of equality expectations, they were challenged time and again, leading to various reanalyses. Below, I briefly examine the major criticism.

The third finding was the most consequential and controversial of all. Because most schools were race-segregated, the finding of an asymmetric context effect could be used by advocates of race-integrative policies to suggest bussing black children daily into white schools. There, the asymmetric context effect would do its job and increase the achievement of the black minority students. In this way, the weight of the first and second findings could be partially lifted, and some equality of opportunity could be achieved through schools after all.

Whereas the EEO study deviated greatly in approach from his earlier study on schools, it did show considerably continuity in the substantive findings, even if the focus was different. For example, the research in TAS focused on the question of under what conditions the influence of family background weakens, in favor of peer influence. But this did not imply that family background was deemed unimportant in TAS. To the contrary. Coleman stressed in TAS that, generally speaking, the influence of parents was stronger than that of peers (if measured by the question of whose disapproval would be more difficult to accept: parent's or peer's).[5] This influence was also evidenced in the reproduction of the community status symbols within the school. The strong influence of family background in EEO is thus not in contradiction to TAS, as often assumed.[6] Coleman's theory of community in TAS implied that, unless there are strong countervailing forces at work, inequality in schools is mainly a matter of the status system of the community, including the cumulation of advantages in middle- and upper-class families. Interscholastic sports competition was such a strong countervailing power, but it distracted from scholarly pursuits and thus did not contribute much to the reduction of family and community influence on cognitive achievement.

A similar continuity in findings can be found with regard to the influence of school expenditure on achievement. Coleman claimed in TAS that school expenditure (teachers' salary, school buildings, laboratory equipment, and libraries) does not make a large difference, just as he found years later in EEO.

Where, then, lay the difference between TAS and EEO that is most relevant for the understanding of Coleman's work? In later years, Coleman identified EEO as a "detour" in his own research (Coleman, 1996, p. 19). He was quite dissatisfied, and it is instructive for the understanding of his later development to see why that was so. Uncharacteristically for his earlier approach, Coleman had used a conventional sociological inductive approach in the search for "factors" and their relative weight for the determination of the dependent variable. Thereby, he failed to study the social system of schools and also failed to look at the goals, interests, and constraints of those involved. In short, he did not use an *actor orientation*, as he had done in TAS ("getting inside the lives of those who pass through the schools"); nor did he pay much attention to parents and teachers as actors (something he had done at least to some degree in TAS). In his own terms, EEO, "by largely ignoring the social system of the school, and taking the administrative perspective of the school as delivering services individually to students, may have missed the most important differences between the school environments in which black and white children found themselves" (Coleman, 1996, p. 20). He realized through further research in the 1970s that, even if there was an asymmetric context effect (and that was not sure), it would not work as predicted for bussing because white families fled from urban areas to the suburbs in order to escape the bussing, thereby increasing racial segregation. As a result, he turned against bussing policies and was bitterly attacked for doing so by the advocates of this policy, who had so depended on his prior findings for their own political purposes. In the social context of the 1970s, the social sciences were highly intertwined in political battles, and research on education most of all. If results were politically unacceptable for certain vocal groups, they would be denied and the researcher pursued by these groups. As we will see below, it is this kind of situation that led Coleman to adopt a view on policy research wholly based on revealing mechanisms which could not be easily dragged into a political process of finding the truth. A mechanism-revealing approach must pay close attention to what actors do. The way he had done the EEO research was decidedly not mechanism-revealing, and thus fell prey to a great deal of political controversy.

The failure to take an actor orientation is also responsible for the most cutting and lasting criticism of his study. Had he taken an actor orientation, he would have realized that all three of his major findings may have been strongly affected by the *selection effects* of parents' decision to send their children to certain schools and to be in the company of certain peers.[7] I believe that it was his negative experience with this kind of inductive factor-finding study which cemented his belief that one has to study the functioning of systems, and do so by taking the perspectives of the actors involved. As I discuss below, he spent the last ten years of his life developing analytical tools for this kind of approach.

## Refinement of the theory of community–school relations: social capital

In TAS, Coleman distinguished between two kinds of community: first, the traditional community, with dominant values and a consensual status order; second, the mobile community, without dominant values and without consensual status order. In the latter, status has to be demonstrated by ostentatiousness with regard to consumption and financial power, and by self-assuredness and social skills. Each kind of community affects schools differently, but as a general trend, the first kind of community is vanishing, leaving the dynamics of status achievement of mobile communities and the cumulated advantages of families as the major sources of inequality in school achievement, unless there are strong countervailing forces. Until this point, Coleman had only thought of interscholastic competition as a countervailing force. Now, driven to pay attention to selection effects, Coleman discovered that the strong family influence could itself be a countervailing force.

As part of a study on achievement in public versus private schools (Coleman et al., 1982; Coleman and Hoffer, 1987), Coleman refined the theory of community impact on schools on the basis of what he learned from the critique of the EEO study: that one should not forget that parents often choose schools and that they often do so in order to *increase* the impact of family background on what happens in schools. This kind of choice leads basically to two kinds of communities. A *functional community* "is a community in which social norms and sanctions, including those that cross generations, arise out of the social structure itself, and both reinforce and perpetuate that structure" (Coleman and Hoffer, 1987, p. 7). When parents interact with one another and with their children and when the parents' interaction includes concern for their children, then a functional community will arise. A school becomes part of a functional community when parents of such a community select a particular school for their children and when their children are in the majority in this school. The school, then, is not an "agent" of society (as it is for public schools) but an agent of a community of families. In TAS, Coleman assumed that the only functional communities possible are the traditional (residential) communities, and he observed that they are vanishing. Now he revised this view in the sense that he discovered that special kinds of non-residential communities do not vanish. Religious communities *with common worship* form such a special functional community. The reason status effects do not completely overshadow the value effects in these communities is the very fact that they are not residential communities and thus lack the major locus of status competition between families. The parents may live in very different neighborhoods but they interact through the institution of the church, which creates some closure and dense, at times intergenerational, contact, including contact concerning values, education, and aspirations in life.

Similar values are clearly not enough to create a functional community. Parents who share similar values (including educational philosophies) but do not interact do not come to common evaluations, do not reinforce each other's norms and sanctions and do not have the relevant information for comparative judgments concerning their own children. When these parents choose to send their children to a particular kind of school the school is an agent of the parents and their values, rather than an agent of society at large or an agent of a (functional) community. Teachers and parents have the same values and thus teachers are likely to represent these values. But the effect of this for education is limited by the fact that the only links among parents and between parents and the school are the common values. Parental involvement in the school itself is not subject to social pressure from other parents of the community, and there is generally no reinforcement of the norms and sanctions that come from the community itself. Coleman calls this kinds of community a *value community*.

In sum, Coleman assumes that the traditional residential (functional) community vanishes and that what are left are non-residential religious functional communities, value communities, and the great mass of adults not related to either. For the last, work has become the relevant context of interaction, but it is not intergenerational and thus does not constitute a community that can reach into schools, other than by the effects of cumulated (dis)advantages and status dynamics. In the USA, three kinds of schools can be identified. First, there are religious private schools involved in functional communities. The most frequent of these in the USA is the Catholic school. Second, there are private schools, some religious, some not, involved in value communities (Montessori, Quaker schools, military academies, etc.).[8] Third, there are public schools not involved in any community (heterogeneous parents). The last are by far the largest group of schools in the USA. What relevance do these different types of school have for the achievement of students, and what does this have to do with community?

It is appropriate to answer these questions, especially for children from disadvantaged families, because it is here that the school can make the biggest difference by counteracting the accident of birth. As Coleman had stated in TAS, the traditional functional community creates inequality of achievement inside the school because the parents' status structure will be more or less reproduced in the school and teachers are influenced by it in their attention to and evaluation of students. Teachers follow parents' values more than society's values (if there is a conflict); parental involvement will be relatively high and norms and sanctions are reinforced. However, because of this, status and stigmas from the local community will carry over into school, thus reinforcing the effects of family background that reproduce the community status order in terms of achievement. Children from disadvantaged families are thus confronted with the fact that their lack of support at home is not compensated but matched by the school. By contrast, in religious functional communities, things are different because the community is established mainly on the basis of religion. Because of this, there is a much smaller influence of parental status on the status of the child in school. Given that religious values are both universalistic and achievement-oriented, and that the reinforcement of values and sanctions coming from parents' interaction pertains to these values (i.e. to academic demands), one would predict that children from disadvantaged families would do much better in religious functional community schools than in traditional functional community schools.

How do value communities affect school achievement? Because parents in such communities have made a conscious choice to send their children to a particular school, they are likely to be concerned about how the school functions, and because teachers act as agents of the parents there is no hostility between teachers and parents. Coleman calls common values and norms *social capital*, and thus value communities have some social capital. However, they have only a low level of social capital because the common norms and sanctions are not reinforced through interaction. Thus, in contrast to functional communities, value community schools have few social resources for realizing high academic demands, especially for those who have no parental support in meeting these demands (i.e. for children from disadvantaged families).

TEST A proper test of this theory of community influence on schools is not possible for Coleman because the data were basically known before the theory was formulated. The test of hypotheses should thus be interpreted as a *post hoc* consistency test with the question: is the theory able to make sense of the data? If social capital works the way this theory of community–school relations assumes, then we should find, specifically with regard to the workings of social capital, the following for pupils from disadvantaged families:

1   Schools which are part of a functional community should show systematically higher parental involvement in school than value community schools, which, in turn should show a higher rate of parental involvement than public schools (social pressure argument).
2   Social capital of parents and schools should have a positive effect on achievement if scholastic achievement is a value (norm and sanction reinforcement argument).
3   Even within a functional community school, achievement of pupils should correlate positively with the amount of social capital of the parents (norm and sanction reinforcement argument).

4   Universalistic values and achievement orientation alone will not suffice to counteract the negative effect of the community status order on the achievement of children from disadvantaged families. Only when these values are linked with the social capital of a religious functional community will this impact of the community status order be significantly reduced or eliminated (norm and sanction reinforcement argument).

**RESULTS** Let us have a brief look at the results. Coleman divided the schools into three groups corresponding to the theoretical differentiation made: Catholic schools (generally functional community schools, high social capital), other private schools (generally value community schools, low social capital), and public schools (no intergenerational community, no social capital). The first hypothesis fit. Coleman found parental involvement was highest for Catholic schools, somewhat lower for other private schools, and low for public schools. The second hypothesis is corroborated by a clear superiority of Catholic schools with regard to verbal and math achievement, and also by a good show of verbal achievement in value community schools. Public schools scored the lowest on these measures of achievement. For the third hypothesis, we have to remember that the characteristic feature of the religious functional community (as compared to the value community) is that there is intergenerational interaction via the church. This interaction in turn reinforces norms and sanctions. For this reason, the frequency of the student's church attendance should correlate positively with school achievement, especially if the student is in a functional community school. This hypothesis also fits with the findings. Catholic students who attend church often do considerably better in verbal and math achievement than Catholic students who do not. Conforming to the expectations regarding social capital, this effect is twice as strong for Catholic students in Catholic schools as for those in public schools. The hypothesis was also corroborated in terms of dropout rates. Here the difference is quite dramatic. Of the frequent Catholic church attenders in Catholic schools, only 2.7 percent dropped out. Of the Catholic students who rarely or never attended church and went to a public school, more than 21 percent dropped out of school.

The fourth hypothesis was the most crucial for Coleman's refinement of the theory of the relation between community and school. Common values of teachers and parents are not enough to reduce the impact of the community's status order on achievement. For this effect, it is also necessary that parents and school form a functional community. In order to check this hypothesis, Coleman interprets the Catholic values as universalistic and achievement-oriented, and – together with the social capital assumptions about the Catholic church community – he thus comes to expect students from disadvantaged (i.e. black and Hispanic) families to do much better in Catholic schools than in other private schools (and, of course, in public schools). This is consistent with the findings. If one looks at "deficient" families (especially single-parent families, families with working mothers, families without much communication between parents and children) one finds a result very similar to that for disadvantaged families. Values alone are thus not enough to support high academic demands, especially for children of disadvantaged or deficient families. The reinforcement of norms and sanctions through interaction among parents themselves, among parents and their children, and among parents and teachers makes the crucial difference in whether enough strength is given to values to counteract the effect of the community status order.[9]

Because the test of this social capital theory of community influence on schools was *post hoc*, and because the crucial assumptions on church interaction and on universalistic and achievement-oriented values of Catholics were not directly tested, there is ample room left for empirical work and theoretical refinement of this theory. Indeed, Coleman's studies have spawned considerable research interest in private schools and in social capital.[10] No firm judgment is possible yet.

## POLICY RESEARCH

Coleman had very outspoken views on policy research, and they are well worth going into in some detail. For a good understanding of these views, it is necessary to see how they depend on his conception of social change in the Western world.

### *The Asymmetric Society*

As we have seen, in TAS Coleman's analysis of the relation of community to schools is based on a view that the relevant social change in the Western world is driven by the vanishing of traditional residential communities. Later he qualified this view by pointing to the existence of religious functional communities. But, despite this addition, he kept hammering on the classical theme of a change from *Gemeinschaft* to *Gesellschaft*, and he used this theme to work out the role of sociology in society. On this basis, he then elaborated both his views of policy research and his view of the need for fundamental research.

The theory of change that was underlying his analyses from early on was embellished and elaborated over the years and appeared as a book called *The Asymmetric Society*, which he published in 1982. The major thesis of the book and of later elaborations[11] is an interesting twist on the *Gemeinschaft–Gesellschaft* theme. The crucial distinction in this respect for Coleman is the one between a natural person and a legal person. In many ways, a legal person is constructed in analogy to a natural person before the law. It can own assets, it can have rights, responsibilities, and liabilities, it can enter into contract, it can appear before court, be a plaintiff or a defendant, and it can have legally recognized interests. In short, a legal person is in many ways an actor like a natural person, but it is not of flesh and blood but "corporate." This new kind of actor first appeared in the thirteenth century. Towns became such corporate actors, the church became a corporate actor, trading companies became corporate actors with limited liability, etc. The most serious consequences of its invention for the functioning of society took a long time to show themselves clearly. It was only in the twentieth century that the enormity of the impact of this invention came into full view.

Two developments greatly increased the role of corporate actors in society. First, over time, more and more corporate actors came themselves to be composed of positions rather than of natural persons. Positions can also be seen as legal persons of sorts, but their leeway is limited by the fact that they act as agents of a corporate actor: their rights, obligations, interests, etc., are derived from a corporate actor. Of course, like corporate actors, positions can act only through natural persons, but the legal consequences of acting as an agent of a corporate actor (i.e. as occupant of a position) or as a natural (i.e. private) person are quite different.

The second relevant change had to do with the change in balance between natural persons and corporate actors of the new (i.e. positional) sort. The latter increased greatly in numbers. For example, profit-making corporations in the United States increased by more than 500 percent between 1916 and 1968. This increase outdistanced the increase in natural persons. After the Second World War, corporate actors also greatly increased in size. In addition, corporate and semi-corporate actors of the old style (i.e. those composed of natural persons, such as the family and residential communities) decreased in importance. Productive activity has progressively moved from the family into the modern corporate actor, and thus it also moved away from a neighborhood of families (i.e. residential community). As a consequence, the household and the neighborhood lost much of their importance as foci of social interaction, whereas the corporate actor gained in importance as a focus.

This social change created and continues to create a number of important problems, which are due to the increasing asymmetry between corporate actors and natural persons, especially in terms of power. First, natural persons are increasingly affected by the actions of large corporate actors, but there is little they can do to change the balance of power in their favor. This changed the kind of risks natural persons are exposed to. "Old" risks were mainly due to externalities among natural persons (such as communicable diseases). They are on the decline. The "new" risks are due to behavior of powerful corporate actors that are little concerned about possible negative consequences of their action for natural persons (such as pollution). Second, due to their resources, large corporate actors are able to influence knowledge production and the distribution of information.

This has various consequences. It further reduces the ability of natural persons to take on corporate actors when their interests collide. Via the corporate actors' influence on the mass media and on the content of advertising, there is also an increased inconsistency of norms. For example, in market societies, large corporations stress the legitimacy and importance of spending money on yourself and of self-indulgence in general, which clashes with familial and community norms of caring for others and opposition to self-indulgence.

Third, corporate actors are responsible for only certain aspects of persons, say their learning in school or their safety as employee. They are not responsible for a person as person and thus not concerned with whether the various partial responsibilities add up. Because families and communities become less important, there developed a growing vacuum of responsibility for persons.

As a response to these problems, the state has grown considerably, taking the role of central corporate actor and assuming responsibility for reducing the asymmetry between corporate and natural actors, and for filling the vacuum of responsibility by welfare institutions. This increasing paternalism of the state creates a perverse effect. It decreases the power asymmetry between natural persons and corporate actors, but it increases the power aggrandizement of the state itself.

## The tasks and preconditions of policy research

Against this background, policy research takes on quite a definite profile.[12] First, there is an increasing demand for various kinds of policy research. Corporate actors are purposefully constructed. With their growth, there is an increasing demand for research on the construction of corporate actors, dealing with their proper functioning, their efficiency, their interrelations, etc. Sociology in its various guises (either as sociology proper or under the name of business administration or organization studies) grows in response to this demand. Also, the state, acquiring ever more responsibilities to deal with power imbalances and dependencies, creates a demand for knowledge on how to deal with these responsibilities (sociology, public administration, welfare economics).

Second, the very diagnosis that leads to an understanding of the need for policy research also suggests normative guidelines for what should be done and how it should be done. The guiding normative stance is that policy research should help to redress the asymmetry between corporate actors and natural persons rather than reinforce it, and it should help to suggest how the vacuum of responsibility can be filled.

1   Because of the power balance, it is likely that corporate actors can afford policy research in their favor. Therefore, the information generated by policy research should always be distributed not only to the sponsor of the research but also to the people at whom the policy is directed.

2   Whether or not corporate actors sponsor it, there are some topics of research that should be covered anyway. Policy research should cover the potential perverse effects of state paternalism. How can the interests of natural persons be protected without strengthening the power of the state? This includes research on how to make corporate actors more responsible. Policy research thus includes prominently risk assessment and research into the possibilities of collective decision-making. Policy research should also be done on possible substitutes for the "old" corporate actors (family, church, community). This prominently includes research on socialization and education, on the possibility of age-balanced organizations, on social capital.

3   Most important for the way policy research should be done is Coleman's analysis of the relationship between policy research and legitimacy. Policy research is often used to legitimize a certain political aim. Whoever has the most resources can have research done to support his political aims. For this very reason, it can easily contribute to the asymmetry rather than redress it. Coleman comes to the conclusion that the only way out of the dilemma that

research can be "bought" to bolster a particular political position is that the research itself is done in such a way that it is considered legitimate by conflicting parties. This can only be achieved if the research does not only deal with factors and effects, but also reveals mechanisms by which the factors produce the effects. There can be much controversy about correlations and the significance of coefficients in regression models. But there can be much less controversy when the researcher traces the mechanism leading from certain causes to certain effects under certain conditions. The upshot of this view is that policy research can only be guarded against disabling politicization by being explicitly linked to fundamental research, and a certain kind of fundamental research at that. Here, Coleman's interests in policy research and in the functioning of systems come together. This, then, was one important reason for him to write a book on the foundations of social theory (Coleman, 1990b), i.e. the *foundations of social science as a mechanism-revealing science* in the service of policy research. In the last section of this chapter, I turn to this book, which is very important for rational choice sociology. Before that, I sketch the context within which rational choice sociology developed and the place Coleman took in this development.

## RATIONAL CHOICE SOCIOLOGY

In his research on education, Coleman had been very much interested in detecting the mechanisms by which schools and communities work. However, this research did not focus on making a contribution to the conceptual tools with which a "mechanism-revealing" social science could build its substantive theories. His work on these tools was a separate strand. However, all three strands – education, tools for constructing social theory and policy research – had come together early in Coleman's construction of academic games.[13] As he had found out in TAS, games can create social environments which channel energies devoted to the improvement of knowledge and skills. By introducing the right kind of games one could use them as instruments of social intervention in schools. At the same time, games create a simulated social system and in their construction one would have to anticipate the system's functioning. In addition, by observing games in action, one can discover links between the elements of the games (rules, communication structure, group formation, etc.) and the collective outcomes. Thus games are at once tools for social policy and tools for the detection of system functioning, analogous to experiments in psychology. Coleman was a pioneer in this use of simulation games (see Boocock, 1996). The construction of a system in order to understand it has remained the basic approach throughout his theoretical development.[14] This approach also fed Coleman's development as a rational choice sociologist. How did this paradigm develop?

In the 1960s, the hegemony of functionalism in sociology waned and sociologists began to battle for the successor to the throne. Symbolic interactionism, conflict sociology, exchange theory, systems theory, in their various versions, attacked each other and greatly weakened the prestige sociology had achieved over the years. In addition (or maybe even because of it), a number of economists had broken through the traditional division of labor between sociology and economics and had begun to move into "non-market" areas, especially with regard to the question of how collective decision-making was possible (how one could aggregate individual preferences) and what kinds of institutions would optimally solve problems encountered in collective decision-making. This included studies on voting, political party competition, and coalition formation, constitutions, the supply of public goods, interest groups, bureaucracy, property rights, public policy, and finance. At times this work has been collectively called "the new political economy" or "modern political economics" (see Frey, 1978). The work of Arrow, Downs, Buchanan and Tullock, Hayek, and North is of particular relevance here, but soon political scientists such as Riker (see Riker and Ordeshook, 1973) followed suit. In 1965, the economist Mancur Olson published his *The Logic of Collective Action* and introduced the free-rider problem to the analysis of group behavior, greatly affecting the way interest groups and social movements would be studied from then on.

Through these developments, game theory finally became useful for the analysis of social phenomena on a wider scale, and quickly spread into political science, and later also to sociology and social psychology, especially concerning the study of social dilemmas. As far as sociology was concerned, this "onslaught" by rational choice via economists and political scientists was at first mainly restricted to the area of political sociology, but it exerted considerable pressure on the traditional dividing line between economics and sociology (see Lindenberg, 1985).

From early on, Coleman had followed these developments and was keenly interested. He had come to this interest on account of Homans (see Coleman and Lindenberg, 1989), who made a strong point for viewing social behavior as exchange. But unlike Homans, Coleman did not try to explain exchange behavior by psychological learning theories. He was persuaded that learning theories would not be very useful for the reconstruction of system functioning, whereas a microeconomic approach would. The latter is purposive and has proven its usefulness for the analysis of systems of exchange; the former focuses on conditioning and has been restricted to the analysis of small groups.

In 1964, Coleman published an article that can be seen as the analytical result of his interest in games and the mechanics of system functioning, and, at the same time, as the beginning of the long strand of developing tools for the analysis of social systems. It had the simple title "Collective Decisions" and it dealt with the question of how the economic theory of exchange could be used to explain social order. He argued that sociologists usually take as their starting point social systems in which norms exist. In turn, these norms govern individual behavior. But that says nothing about why there are norms to begin with and how social order can emerge when there are no norms. For this reason, he argued for what he considered to be the opposite, but possibly more fruitful, error: to start with man wholly free, "unsocialized, entirely self-interested, not constrained by norms of a system, but only rationally calculating to further his own self interests" (Coleman, 1964b, p. 167). He held on to this starting point all the way to his *Foundations of Social Theory*.

After 1964, the exchange theory which traces the creation of social order, including norms, rights, systems of authority, and concentration of power, was further worked out in many articles and a number of books. In 1973, he published the book *Mathematics of Collective Action*. One year later, the book *Power and the Structure of Society* appeared. At that time, Coleman's "rational choice" approach remained very much within the realm of what non-market economists did: collective decision-making.

During the early 1970s, the "new political economy" also influenced a number of European sociologists who had earlier been heavily influenced by Homans, most notably Albert, Hummell, Opp, Vanberg, Wippler, and Lindenberg. They developed various versions of rational choice sociology under different names: for example, "individualistic sociology" (see Vanberg, 1975), "structural-individualistic approach" (see Wippler, 1978), "individualistic social science" (see Opp, 1979), "the economic tradition" (see Albert, 1979), and related solutions to the micro–macro problem (see Lindenberg, 1977). In France, Raymond Boudon had been influenced by Lazarsfeld and by Coleman's work on education, and he adopted a rational actor orientation in his research on inequality in education (Boudon, 1974). A number of years later, he developed this into a full-fledged approach to rational action sociology (Boudon, 1981). Substantively, the European versions of rational choice (or rational action, as it was sometimes called) sociology were less formal and more concerned with truly sociological topics than was Coleman's concern with collective decision-making.

In the early 1980s the two developments began to merge. Coleman visited Europe and met with the European rational choice sociologists in a great number of symposia (beginning in 1980 with a symposium on solidarity and trust in Groningen, the Netherlands, and in 1981 with one in Berlin on the micro–macro problem). By then, rational choice sociology was institutionalized in a number of Dutch universities and through the Dutch national science foundation. In 1982, a Dutch–German delegation organized the first rational choice sessions of the International Sociological Association's Meeting (in Mexico), beginning the international institutionalization of rational choice sociology (see Raub, 1982).

Back in the United States, Coleman influenced a number of American scholars, who, quite independently of each other, developed versions of rational choice sociology, including Anthony Oberschall (1973) and Michael Hechter (1983).[15] Hechter also profited from the direct influence of the economic historian Douglas North, who was more sociologically interested than most economists.

The year 1983 was very important for further development. A conference organized by Coleman in Chicago brought many rational choice sociologists together and confronted them with non-market economists and with theorists who were critical of rational choice sociology. The conference papers were later published, along with the heated discussions that followed each presentation (see Lindenberg et al., 1986). This meeting was very important for the establishment of rational choice sociology as a generally recognized approach. Gary Becker, the economist who had done much to push the economic approach into non-market areas, participated at this conference and was asked a few months later by

Coleman whether he would consider a joint appointment in sociology. He accepted and both he and Coleman started in that year a joint faculty seminar on rational choice that became famous far beyond the circles of Chicago academia.

In 1984, a sizable conference on the micro–macro problem followed in Germany (see Alexander et al., 1987), and a few years later, at another rational choice conference in Germany on social institutions (see Hechter et al., 1990), the plan for a journal on rational choice sociology was born. Coleman was willing to carry the burden of editing the journal, and the first issues of *Rationality and Society*, as the journal was called after long deliberation on an appropriate name, appeared in 1989. In the academic year 1991–2, Coleman was president of the American Sociological Association (ASA) and used the ASA meetings of that year as a general forum on the importance of actor-oriented sociology. By then, his magnum opus had appeared and rational choice sociology had changed the discourse among sociologists, even among many of those who would not call themselves rational choice sociologists.

## THE FOUNDATIONS OF SOCIAL THEORY

In 1986, Coleman collected his most relevant articles on collective action and published them under the title *Individual Interests and Collective Action*. The widening of his rational choice sociology into a general approach, however, had to wait until 1990, when his *magnum opus, The Foundations of Social Theory*, appeared.

*The Foundations of Social Theory* is a heavy tome of almost a thousand pages. The various bits and pieces Coleman had worked out earlier are here joined into one architecture. After an introductory chapter on "metatheory," the book presents five parts: I, "elementary actions and relations" (with, among others, a section on actors and resources, interest, and control); II, "structures of action" (with, among others, sections on authority, collective behavior, and norms); III, "corporate action" (with, among others, sections on constitutions and social choice); IV, "modern society" (with, among others, sections on the new corporate actors and on the new social science, akin to arguments from *The Asymmetric Society* but more focused on the relation between policy research and fundamental research); and V, "the mathematics of social action" (with, among others, sections on dynamics of the linear system of action, corporate actors, and collective decisions). This last part is a mathematical treatment of many of the theoretical points made in the book.

Because I have presented the major argument of part IV above, and because it is impossible to go into the mathematics of social action in this review, it is parts I to III which interest us the most. They reflect the "tool" character of the book. Simple tools are developed first, and they help to build more complex tools for the analysis of social systems later. Still driven by the primacy of intervention as the ultimate goal of the social sciences,[16] and, conversely, true to the idea that you only understand a social system if you can construct it, he builds up from micro to macro, from actors to exchange, to systems of exchange and all the way to corporate action. What is the gist of this development?

The *essential elements of actors* considered by Coleman all have to do with what drives interaction among actors, given that each actor strives to increase the realization of his or her interest. Because Coleman is mainly concerned with the micro to macro link, he does not want to assume things which he ultimately wants to explain. Thus, he uses the highly simplified model of microeconomics. "I will use the conception of rationality employed in economics" and "begin with norm-free, self-interested persons as elements of the theory" (Coleman, 1990b, pp.14, 31).

Given this theory of action, Coleman can pinpoint the well from which all social interaction is generated. The basic idea is quite simple, and it represents a reformulation of the classical economic *theory of exchange* (already used by Adam Smith): the natural state is interdependence among actors and this state is a condition of life which keeps returning even though actors keep reducing it. A slightly more technical way to say this is that actors have interests and they control some resources and events, but their world is imperfect because they are not fully in control of those resources and events that can increase the realization of their interests; some of these resources and events are partially or wholly under the control of others. Thus, in order to improve their situation, actors have to exchange control over resources and/or events, i.e. they have to exchange control over things which are of little interest to them for control over things that are of great interest to them. Such voluntary exchange by definition improves the situation of both actors.

Social systems are often generated by the need to facilitate the exchanges which reduce the individual interdependencies (even though such measures may increase the collective interdependencies).[17] What problems does exchange encounter? What solutions to these problems constitute the most important social systems? These two questions guide us easily through the bulk of Coleman's book.

## Control over actions

RIGHTS TO ACT When two people exchange apples for oranges it seems that they exchange physical entities. Often, this view is sufficient. Upon closer inspection, however, it turns out that people do not exchange physical entities, but rights to carry out certain actions. In one society, the exchange implies that each party has the right to use the fruits as he or she sees fit: to consume them or to dispose of them. In another society, the fruits may be subject to certain religious restrictions and therefore the exchange implies only, say, the right to consume, not the right to plant their seeds, or to resell them. For intangible goods this point is even more obvious. To see that not goods but rights are being exchanged is an old but important way to analyze exchange. It presupposes, though, that there are rights. What are they and where do they come from? Here Coleman has developed an original and far-reaching conception. For him, the heart of the matter is *rights to act* in a certain way. To have control over something means that one has the right to do certain things with it.[18] What exactly the control entails depends on the right involved. Ownership of a resource can mean very different things, depending on what rights to act with regard to this resource are connected to it. A local government may not allow a house owner to rent his rooms without permission, a person may not be allowed to sell one of his organs, etc. There are other rights not ordinarily associated with ownership, such as the right to smoke, free speech, or freedom of movement. Rights may change, and thus can be lost and gained without them being exchanged. How can they change? Many rights are legal rights created in the political process. But that process ultimately rests on the broad area of rights not covered by law. For Coleman, such rights rest on consensus, especially the consensus of relevant others. Who are the relevant others? They are those who are powerful enough collectively to enforce a right. Quite contrary to the vast normative discussions on consensual allocation of rights (say by Rawls and Nozick), Coleman puts *given power differences* at the heart of consensus. When one considers power-weighted consensus (as one should, in Coleman's eyes), the question of how rights ought to be distributed is generally unanswerable and only meaningful *within* a system of action in which interests and relative power between actors are given (Coleman, 1990b, p. 53). Thus, rights have a social base, including the power distribution of such a base. But because the allocation of rights to act is so important, and because consensus is often not spontaneously generated, societies will develop structures that deal with the generation and change of such rights and with conflict arising from their allocation.

**INALIENABLE RIGHTS AND AUTHORITY** There is one particular class of rights which create special problems and special solutions. Individuals may or may not have the right of control over a particular class of their own actions. For example, a child may not have the right to decide when to go to school. Conversely, if people have rights of control over many of their own actions, then they can exchange them for something else. The special problem is that actions are inalienable: they remain a part of the person even if the right to control them has been given away. It is through this circumstance that *authority* relations come into existence. To have authority over X is to have the right to control a particular class of X's actions. Because X's actions are inalienable, authority can only exist if X grants the right to control to someone else (provided X has the right to control his own actions, including the right to transfer this right).

An important distinction with regard to authority relations is that between conjoint and disjoint authority. When I grant authority to someone over a certain class of my actions, it may be in a context where I presume the other (for example, a charismatic leader) acts in my interest. This is *conjoint* authority. There is a fundamental limitation to such authority relations, according to Coleman. For an individual, it is not easy to determine for what classes of action authority should be granted. Often, a leader is likely to ask more and an individual is likely to grant more control to the leader than is in the individual's own interest, especially when many other individuals do the same. It may not be easy to fine-tune such decisions and issues of the protection of the individual arise, creating a special problem of asymmetry, as we have seen in the discussion of *The Asymmetric Society*.

In a formal organization, I am likely to grant authority without the presumption that the superordinate acts in my interest. This is *disjoint* authority. Here, I need to be reimbursed for granting this right (say, by wages or salary) because the superordinate has no particular interest in my interests. The defect of this kind of relation, according to Coleman, is, conversely, that the subordinate has no particular interest in the outcome the superordinate wants to achieve. Although he gave away the right to control a certain class of his actions, he is still the one who has to perform these actions. Unless the actions over which control is granted can be closely monitored, individuals are likely to let those actions be governed by their own interests rather than by the outcome desired by the superordinate. This is well known in economics as the *principal–agent problem*. The superordinate, in turn, will try to extend his control over actions of the individual which have not been included in the original exchange. Unless the classes of actions can be very clearly specified, he will probably succeed and this success is likely to lead to the development of structures to protect both principal (superordinate) and agent (subordinate).

## Time asymmetry and trust

Not all exchanges take place instantaneously. Often, a transaction is drawn out in time, such that one party must invest resources (i.e. give away control over resources) long before the other party returns the benefit. For example, in a conjoint authority relation, the control is given away at one point in time and the stream of benefits is drawn out over a longer period of time. Or a company may have to build special machines to make the product that the client wants. If the client pays ahead of time, he does not know whether he will get what he paid for, and if he pays afterwards, the company does not know whether it will recoup its investment. Exchanges which involve such *time asymmetries* involve a special kind of risk: the risk that depends on the performance of another actor. Coleman proposed to use the word *trust* to denote this special kind of risk. It can be expressed in a handy formula. Let $p$ be the probability that the trustee is trustworthy (and $1 - p$ that he is not), let $L$ be the potential loss if he is untrustworthy, and let $G$ be the potential gain if he is trustworthy. Then I will trust the trustee (i.e. I will take the risk of unilateral transfer of control) if $p/1 - p > L/G$.

Many interesting questions are generated by this concept of trust. For example, information on $p$, $L$, and $G$ will have a great impact on whether or not trust is placed, with $p$ often being the least well known quantity. People are likely to have a standard estimate of $p$ which holds for everyone in their system of action about whom they have no particular information. When $L/G$ is large, then a person will trust only if $p$ exceeds the standard estimate, and that may take considerable observation time. Trusting (i.e. close) friendships build up slowly because, in such relationships, the potential loss is quite high compared to the gain, and thus $p$ must be high. A confidence man may achieve very quick trust by convincing someone that he has little to lose and much to gain, i.e. by making $L/G$ appear very low, so that even a slight reduction of the standard estimate of $p$ will still lead to placing trust. Research that has been generated by this conception of trust is growing.[19]

As with the other problems concerning exchange which have been discussed so far, this problem of trust is likely to lead to social structures in which it is to the potential trustee's interest to be trustworthy.

## The impact of size: from relations to structures

As Simmel realized long ago, new problems arise if we move from a dyad to a triad, and new problems arise if we move from a small group to a large group. Heedful of this difference, Coleman moves from dyadic exchange to systems of exchange, from authority relations to systems of authority, from trust relations to systems of trust. The problems arising for the dyads are here confounded by the problems arising from size. I will briefly go into each one of them.

SYSTEMS OF EXCHANGE There may be more than one person offering or demanding a particular good for exchange. In that case, we get competition and indirect exchange; in short, we get markets. One of the major problems of establishing a market is the requirement of pairwise coincidence of wants: B wants something that A has and vice versa. If there is a medium of exchange, this coincidence of wants is not necessary for the exchange and a market can grow. For example, money allows exchange without this coincidence. Coleman discusses some media in non-economic systems of exchange, such as status. However, interesting non-economic systems of exchange can also exist without a particular medium of exchange if the goods exchanged are highly limited in number. The innovative twist he brings to the analysis of these kinds of systems is his particular theory of exchange, which allows a fairly sophisticated analysis of non-economic exchange systems.

The relevant elements of his theory of exchange are two individual-level characteristics (interests and control) and two system-level characteristics (power and value). An example will help. Actors have interests (say, a student wants good grades and free time; the teacher wants serious effort from the student) and they have control over certain resources (say, a student has initial control over his or her own time and effort; the teacher has initial control over grades). Effort can be defined as the proportion of total time a student spends on homework. In a school, there is then an exchange system in which effort is exchanged for grades. This exchange takes place with certain exchange rates. In a perfect market these exchange rates converge to one exchange rate which defines the relative values of effort and grades (values at equilibrium). Note that the exchange rate is a system-level concept; it does not represent the average individual ratio of effort to grades. Power is here conceived of as the value of the resources an actor controls. Thus, although power is assigned to an individual and not to a relation, it is a system-level concept because the value depends on all the others' interest. If the teacher values the effort of some students higher than that of other students, the market is imperfect and the exchange rate is not identical for all students. As a result, the power of students also differs. The power of the teacher is the value of grades. In part V of the *Foundations*, Coleman works out the mathematics of this kind of analysis (and for this example) and I will not go into this here.

Coleman focuses here on the analysis of non-economic exchange systems but, contrary to his treatment of authority and trust, he does not go more deeply into an analysis of problems of exchange systems themselves. Still, his approach to exchange systems has been quite influential. It has been applied in political science (for example, Marsden, 1981; Pappi and Kappelhoff, 1984; König, 1998) and it has helped the development of sophisticated models of influence in collective decision-making (Stokman and Van Oosten, 1994; Yamaguchi, 1996).

**AUTHORITY SYSTEMS** When authority relations are stacked, we get a multi-level authority system. Coleman's concept of rights is very useful here for pointing to a fundamental difference in the way authority systems are organized and function. In a *feudal* authority structure, the layers are indeed stacked. Each subordinate has vested authority in the direct superior. Household members were subject to the authority of the head of the household, the head was subject to the authority of a lord, who, in turn, was subject to the authority of a higher lord, etc., all the way up to the king. The advantage of this structure is that in each link the principal–agent problem is solved by personal loyalty, in which the subordinate identifies with (part of) the interests of the superior. However, the disadvantage is that the span of control is very small. A lord has no authority over members of someone else's household, even though he has authority over the head of the household.

By contrast, a *modern* authority structure involves two important innovations. First, not just one but two rights are transferred to the superior: the right to control a class of actions of the subordinate and the right to delegate this control to someone else. Thus, the boss can delegate authority to a supervisor, so that in fact the subordinate is supervised by someone in whom he or she has not vested authority. This removes all the constraints on the span of control, greatly increasing the power of an organization to act. However, now the principal–agent problem is considerable. If A delegates authority to B, how can she keep B from exercising authority over C mostly for his own interests rather than A's interests? This leads to the second innovation. Rather than authority being vested in individuals, it is vested in positions. The rights and resources belonging to the authority are the property not of a person but of a position.

As a consequence of this combined change from direct to delegated authority and from person to position, a new kind of actor evolved, in whom authority is vested by individuals and who delegates authority to the positions: a *corporate actor*. The importance of this change can – in Coleman's eyes – not be over-estimated. We have seen that Coleman's view of policy research is governed by the asymmetry between natural and corporate actors. Modern society cannot be understood without understanding this asymmetry.

**SYSTEMS OF TRUST** The important point about trust is that it is often the decisive factor in the decision to go through or not to go through with a potentially advantageous exchange between two parties. Without trust the transaction will not go through, and because it would have been potentially advantageous for both, failure to go through is a loss for both. In transaction costs economics, such situations are well analyzed in terms of credible commitments (see Williamson, 1985) through which the probability of default becomes very small. Coleman chose to focus on another mechanism. When these two parties cannot place trust in each other, there may be intermediaries who are trusted by both and who can create an indirect link. Coleman discusses three such links: the advisor, the guarantor, and the entrepreneur. An example of the *advisor* is a lobbyist in Washington, DC, who introduces interested parties (potential trustees) to public officials (potential trustors). The public official trusts the judgment of the lobbyist that he or she has something to gain by being willing to listen to the potential trustee, and therefore he or she is willing to invest some time in the meeting. The *guarantor* is someone who is willing to bear the risk the trustor would otherwise face. The *entrepreneur* is someone who is able to combine the resources of various trustors and deploy them among various trustees. Examples are an investment bank or a political entrepreneur who is able to generate votes for a legislative proposal. Society can be seen as being shot through with such overlapping systems of trust, at times based on special institutions (such as an investment bank), at times based on reputation. These systems of trust are only just beginning to attract wide attention (see, for example, Klein 1997; Hofman et al., 1998).

Coleman also deals with larger systems. In particular, advisory trust can create large systems of trust which characteristically fluctuate in expansion and contraction. In academia such systems are well known. Let there be some well placed advisors who speak highly of X. Others, who trust the judgment of the advisors, repeat their assessment without admitting that they have not formed their own opinion on direct inspection of the performance (say, the publications). Such a reputation can expand quickly and generally lower the requirements for evidence of excellence for jobs, stipends, and research monies. However, this system is precarious. One well placed advisor who asks "Have you really read something by X and found it good? Can anyone really find this work outstanding?" may start a quick process of reputational contraction. A similar process can also be observed for charismatic leaders. Such processes can be analyzed as widespread transfers of control of belief, akin to processes of collective behavior.

*Collective behavior*, such as an escape panic, a bank or stock market panic, a hostile crowd, a rash of sightings of flying saucers, or other fads and fashions, seems to be far removed from rational action. But Coleman analyzes such seemingly irrational group behavior as situations in which many group members transfer large portions of control over their actions (or beliefs) to the various other members and wait for some action of these other members in order to determine what they themselves would do. Coleman discusses different kinds of this behavior and, in my judgment, the analysis is very original and perhaps one the most convincing examples of the usefulness of the concept of transfer of control.

## The role of externalities

When two parties exchange, their actions may generate positive or negative effects on third parties who are not involved in the exchange. Such externalities may also be generated by someone's unilateral actions. Coleman follows the analysis by Ullmann-Margalit (1977) by assuming that it is situations of externalities which create a demand for norms (see also Lindenberg, 1977, 1982). As Ullmann-Margalit did, Coleman focuses mainly on negative externalities. However, he expands on the analysis of norms in a number of ways. First, he defines norms in his own framework as the socially established transfer of the right to control certain of one's own actions to others. A norm concerns some focal action. The most interesting cases involve a focal action which creates a conflict of interest between a target who performs the focal action and others who experience negative side-effects of this action, say from dropping a banana peel on the sidewalk. Norms which regulate such situations Coleman calls "essential norms" (as opposed to "conventional" norms, which coordinate action). The norm takes the right away from the target to do as he pleases and gives the right to control a certain class of his actions to the beneficiaries collectively (of whom the target may or may not be a member). The beneficiaries' right to sanction the target is nothing but the exercise of their right to control (which had been taken away from the target). This transfer of rights to the collectivity of beneficiaries is an important turning point in the construction because it marks the creation of collective actors.

Second, externalities create control interests in the "focal" action among those who experience the externalities. This does not create demand for a norm yet. A control interest only turns into a demand for a norm if (a) an action has similar externalities for many others and (b) no exchanges in rights among dyads can solve the problem (i.e. no individual can acquire the rights of control and a market in rights of control of the action cannot be easily established).

Third, demand for a norm does not mean that a norm will come into existence. What, then, is required for a norm to come into existence? The crucial point is sanctions. If the potential beneficiaries of a norm do not have the capability to apply effective sanctions against the focal action, they cannot really control the focal action of the target. For this reason, Coleman focuses on the conditions for establishing effective sanctions as conditions for the generation of norms. Briefly stated, these conditions come down to the ability to overcome the free-rider problem involved in sanctioning. In turn, this ability depends on social relationships, especially the closure of networks which can create rewards (say approval) for sanctioning which outweigh the costs of sanctioning. Closure provides the strength of consensus necessary for the legitimacy of and the strong approval of sanctioning. In this sense both the social structure and the norms that it can generate can be viewed as social capital, especially when the norms are "conjoint," i.e. when the targets and beneficiaries are the same persons.

Above I discussed the importance of corporate actors in Coleman's view of what drives the most serious problems within modern Western societies and gives direction to policy research. In the *Foundations*, Coleman brings the analysis of *corporate actors* into the general architecture of the micro-to-macro approach. When, due to size or other reasons, a group of individuals has a demand for norms but not the ability to create effective sanctions (and thereby lacks the ability to govern behavior by norms), it may be able to create a *formal constitution* in which the right to control certain classes of actions of individuals is transferred to a collectivity which, in turn, is then clearly identified as a corporate actor with vested authority. There are clear normative consequences of this conception. Constitutions which are established by force are likely to comprise individuals with very heterogeneous power and interests regarding the actions of the corporate actor. In all likelihood, the corporate actor has more authority over some individuals than they would voluntarily grant it. As a response, one could argue that the optimal constitution would be the "conjoint" one, in which targets and beneficiaries are the same individuals. However, Coleman argues, the whole point of this kind of an analysis is that under different circumstances different kinds of constitutions are optimal, since not consensus *per se* is important, but consensus weighted by the power of the actors involved. "A constitution is optimal if in the system that results, rights for each class of actions are allocated in accordance with the interests of those who, postconstitutionally, have power-weighted interests that are stronger than the opposing power-weighted interests" (p. 355).

In this consideration of power for the establishment of constitutions, Coleman's approach is unique, and it is not a matter of taking the side of the strong against the weak but a matter of the criterion used. Coleman rejects collective welfare criteria which are not based on individual choice, and he rejects criteria, such as Pareto optimality, which do not consider interpersonal comparison of utility. The more powerful has a stronger weight in the formation of consensus because others recognize his larger interest in a certain solution. In a way, power has an important effect even without its being used to coerce. Coleman's conceptions of interests, control value, and power lead him directly to the concept of relative power as the characterization of interpersonal comparison and the need for the consideration of interpersonal comparison for the micro-to-macro transition. Constitutions cannot arise and be maintained without reflecting relative power, because the ability to sanction is part and parcel of any collectively held right.

## SUMMARY AND CONCLUSION

The key to Coleman's work can be found in two major concerns and their combination. First, he was concerned with high schools and with ways to improve their functioning. Second, and even more importantly, he was very interested in the development of theory on the functioning of social systems, which for him meant a theory that will move "from the micro level of action to the macro level of norms, social values, status distribution and social conflict." The combination of his two major interests resulted in a third preoccupation: policy research and institutional innovation, especially in the field of education. This review covers all three interests and, for reasons of space, I cannot summarize them here. Suffice it to mention a few highlights. His research on education resulted in interesting theories on the relation of community and social capital to what is going on in schools. It also resulted in the conviction that only an actor-oriented approach can handle the analysis of such complex phenomena as schools and school achievement. The same conclusion drove his view on policy research. In order to keep policy research from being dragged into political battles, it is absolutely necessary to analyze mechanisms which supposedly generate the effect from given conditions. Only such a mechanism-revealing social science can hope to gain enough consensus to stay out of the direct political interests. His *magnum opus*, then, was meant as the foundation for such a mechanism-revealing social science.

There can only be a rough *evaluation* of his work in such an overview. Coleman's work is vast and covers many different areas and, of those, only a few highlights can be mentioned here. His substantive theories of lasting interest are in my view his theory of community, his theory of the asymmetric society, including his elaborations of the concepts of social capital and of trust, and his theory of collective behavior (panics, crazes, etc.). In addition, his insistence that every theory using consensus should consider power-weighted consensus is probably one of the most far-reaching of his substantive suggestions and, at the same time, at present one of the least recognized. His work on rational choice sociology gave a considerable boost to this kind of approach, and it systematized a great number of known pieces into a new architecture.

Of course, there are also some *limitations*. Here, too, I will mention only a few which in my view are of particular importance. First, although many of his substantive theories have been developed in the context of empirical research, they are by and large not well tested yet. Either he developed theory in order to interpret his own findings or he developed it outside the context of empirical research altogether. There is thus ample room left for empirical work on his ideas. Second, his particular kind of rational choice theory led him at times into forced constructions. The insistence on using the "naked" model of rational choice of microeconomics, and the attempt to see all social processes in light of exchanges and the transfer of the right to act, at times severely hampered Coleman in working out his substantive theories. For example, he was of the firm opinion that the design of institutions which could replace the lost functions of primordial orders is one of the prime tasks of policy research. Yet it is hardly possible to describe the functions of primordial orders in the language of his framework, let alone come up with substitutes (see Lindenberg, 1993, 1996, for details). Third, his particular approach to the macro–micro–macro links focuses almost exclusively on the micro–macro connection and pays little attention to the macro–micro link. For this reason, Coleman's theoretical analyses are very much in need of complementary efforts by others. Fourth, his approach only considers exchange. For him people never jointly produce anything. For this reason, the dynamics of cooperation in joint production remains outside his analysis of trust and of the internal and external functioning of corporate actors.

All told, his considerable achievements dwarf the limitations and in my opinion Coleman's place among sociologists of the second half of the twentieth century is likely to remain unequalled.

## Notes

1   This claim can be substantiated by the fact that Coleman in his later life was quoted more than any other living sociologist (see volume 19 of the *International Encyclopedia of the Social Sciences*, 1994). Merton is still alive and active at present but the major period of his contribution to sociology was in the 1940s to the 1960s.

2   Coleman transcript I, p. 361 (in Clark, 1996).

3   Clark's (1996) collection of papers on Coleman is very useful to flesh out many of the aspects covered in this review.

4   Coleman also sees a direct influence of community on the importance of athletics in the fact that adults use interscholastic competition as community entertainment.

5   Boys and girls answered almost identically: 54 percent found parents' disapproval, 43 percent peers' disapproval, and a mere 3 percent teachers' disapproval most difficult to accept; see TAS, p. 5.

6   The difference in research problem in TAS and EEO may have fostered the mistaken idea, often found in the literature (see Kandel, 1996), that Coleman "discovered" the influence of family background in EEO, against his earlier "exaggerated" view of peer influence in TAS.

7   This was forcefully driven home by a number of critics, most notably by Hanushek (1972). See Heckman and Neal (1996) for the broader context of these selection issues in Coleman's study.

8   Within this category, Coleman distinguishes a special subgroup of high-performance schools. I will not go into this finer-grade distinction here.

9   Coleman also finds that the social capital of parents and the school has a bigger impact on achievement of children from disadvantaged families than the per pupil expenditure of that school.

10  For example, Bryk et al. (1993), Schneider and Coleman (1993), Dijkstra and Peschar (1996), and Hofman et al. (1996).

11  Coleman later embellished the arguments in this book in various chapters of his *Foundations of Social Theory*, especially with regard to policy research.

12  There is a great number of publications by Coleman on policy research, but the arguments are most clearly brought together in part IV of his *Foundations of Social Theory*.

13  He is also quite explicit about the importance these games played for his own theoretical development: "It was the development and use of such social-simulation games which led me away from my previous theoretical orientation, of a Durkheimian sort, to one based on purposive action" (Coleman, 1990b, p. 11).

14  The reason computer simulation did not interest Coleman very much is, in his own words, that such simulation draws too much attention to the theory of action and distracts too much from the construction of social theory.

15     Somewhat later, Douglas Heckathorn came to develop an interesting game-theoretic approach to rational choice sociology.

16     The quality criterion of explanations is thus pragmatic: "The explanation is satisfactory if it is useful for the particular kinds of intervention for which it is intended" (Coleman, 1990b, p. 5).

17     This looks like a purely functional (black box) argument, but it is not. Coleman is fully aware that mechanisms need to be specified which translate a demand or need into a structure or rule. When I discuss the emergence of norms below, this point will become clear.

18     At times, Coleman speaks, somewhat confusingly, of the "right to control something," meaning that one has undisputed control over that something.

19     See, for example, Raub and Weesie (1990), Snijders (1996), and Buskens (1999).

# Bibliography

## Writings of James Coleman

*The Adolescent Society.* 1961. Glencoe, IL: Free Press.

*Introduction to Mathematical Sociology.* 1964a. Glencoe, IL: Free Press.

Collective decisions. 1964b. Reprinted in J. S. Coleman, *Individual Interests and Collective Action.* Cambridge: Cambridge University Press (1986), pp.15–32.

*Equality of Educational Opportunity* (with E. Q. Campbell, C. J. Hobson, J. McPartland, A. M. Mood, F. D. Weinfeld, and R. L. York). 1966. Washington, DC: US Government Printing Office.

*The Mathematics of Collective Action.* 1973. London: Heinemann Educational Books.

*The Asymmetric Society.* 1982. Syracuse, NY: Syracuse University Press.

*High School Achievement: Public, Catholic, and Private Schools Compared* (with T. Hoffer and S. Kilgore). 1983. New York: Basic Books.

*Individual Interests and Collective Action.* 1986. Cambridge: Cambridge University Press.

*Approaches to Social Theory* (edited with S. Lindenberg and S. Nowak). 1986. New York: Russell Sage.

*Public and Private High Schools: The Impact of Communities* (with T. Hoffer). 1987. New York: Basic Books.

In Memoriam George Homans (with S. Lindenberg). 1989. *Rationality and Society,* 1, 283ff.

Robert K. Merton as teacher. 1990a. In J. Clark, C. Modgil, and S. Modgil (eds), *Robert K. Merton.* London: Falmer Press, pp. 25–32.

*Foundation of Social Theory.* 1990b. Cambridge, MA: Harvard University Press.

*Parents, Their Children and Schools* (with B. Schneider). 1993. Boulder, CO: Westview Press.

Reflections on Schools and Adolescents. 1996. In J. Clark (ed.), *James S. Coleman.* London/Washington, DC: Falmer Press, pp.17–31.

## Further reading

Albert, H. (1979) The Economic Tradition, Economics as a Research Programme for Theoretical Social Science. In K. Brunner (ed.), *Economics and Social Institutions.* Boston, the Hague, and London: Nijhoff.

Alexander, J. C., Giesen, B., Münch, R. and Smelser, N. J. (eds) (1987) *The Micro Macro Link.* Berkeley: University of California Press.

Boocock, S. S. (1996) Games with Simulated Environments: Educational Innovation and Applied Sociological Research. In J. Clark (ed.), *James S. Coleman*. London and Washington, DC: Falmer Press, pp. 133–46.

Boudon, R. (1974) *Education, Opportunity, and Social Inequality*. New York: Wiley.

Boudon, R. (1981) *The Logic of Social Action*. London: Routledge & Kegan Paul.

Bryk, A. S., Lee, V. E., and Holland, P. B. (1993) *Catholic Schools and the Common Good*. Cambridge, MA: Harvard University Press.

Buskens, V. (1999) *Social Networks and Trust*. Amsterdam: Thesis Publishers.

Clark, J. (ed.) (1996) *James S. Coleman*. London and Washington, DC: Falmer Press.

Dijkstra, A. B. and Peschar, J. L. (1996) Religious Determinants of Academic Attainment in the Netherlands. *Comparative Education Review*, 40, 47–65.

Frey, B. (1978) *Modern Political Economics*. Oxford: Martin Robertson.

Hanushek, E. (1972) *Education and Race*. Cambridge, MA: Ballinger Press.

Hechter, M. (ed.) (1983) *The Microfoundations of Macrosociology*. Philadelphia: Temple University Press.

Hechter, M., Opp, K.-D., and Wippler, R. (eds) (1990) *Social Institutions*. New York: Aldine de Gruyter.

Heckman, J. J. and Neal, D. (1996) Coleman's Contributions to Education: Theory, Research Styles and Empirical Research. In J. Clark (ed.), *James S. Coleman*. London and Washington, DC: Falmer Press, pp. 81–102.

Hoffman, P. T., Postel-Vinay, G., and Rosenthal, J.-L. (1998) What Do Notaries Do? Overcoming Asymmetric Information in Financial Markets: the Case of Paris, 1751. *Journal of Institutional and Theoretical Economics*, 154, 499–530.

Hofman, R., Hofman, W. H. A., Guldenmond, H., and Dijkstra, A. B. (1996) Variation in Effectiveness between Private and Public Schools: the Impact of School and Family Networks. *Educational Research and Evaluation*, 2, 366–94.

Kandel, D. (1996) Coleman's Contribution to Understanding Youth and Adolescence. In J. Clark (ed.), *James S. Coleman*. London and Washington, DC: Falmer Press, pp. 33–46.

Klein, D. B. (ed.) (1997) *Reputation: Studies in the Voluntary Elicitation of Good Conduct*. Ann Arbor: University of Michigan Press.

König, T. (ed.) (1998) Special Issue on Policy Networks. *Journal of Theoretical Politics*, 10(4).

Lindenberg, S. (1977) Individuelle Effekte, kollektive Phänomene und das Problem der Transformation. In K. Eichner and W. Habermehl (eds), *Probleme der Erklärung sozialen Verhaltens*, Meisenheim: Anton Hain, pp. 46–84.

Lindenberg, S. (1982) Sharing Groups: Theory and Suggested Applications. *Journal of Mathematical Sociology*, 9, pp. 33–62.

Lindenberg, S. (1985) Rational Choice and Sociological Theory: New Pressures on Economics as a Social Science. *Journal of Institutional and Theoretical Economics*, 141, 244–55.

Lindenberg, S. (1993) Rights to Act and Beliefs. *Journal of Institutional and Theoretical Economics*, 149, 233–9.

Lindenberg, S. (1996) Constitutionalism versus Relationalism: Two Versions of Rational Choice Sociology. In Jon Clark (ed.), *James S. Coleman*. London and Washington, DC: Falmer Press, pp. 299–312.

Marsden, P. V. (1981) Introducing Influence Processes into a System of Collective Decisions. *American Journal of Sociology*, 86, 1203–35.

Oberschall, A. (1973) *Social Conflict and Social Movements*. Englewood Cliffs, NJ: Prentice Hall.

Olson, M. (1965) *The Logic of Collective Action.* Cambridge, MA: Harvard University Press.

Opp, K. D. (1979) *Individualistische Sozialwissenschaft.* Stuttgart: Enke.

Pappi, F. and Kappelhoff, P. (1984) Abhängigkeit, Tausch und kollektive Entscheidung in einer Gemeindeelite. *Zeitschrift für Soziologie,* 13, 87–117.

Riker, W. H. and Ordeshook, P. C. (1973) *An Introduction to Positive Political Theory.* Englewood Cliffs, NJ: Prentice Hall.

Raub, E. (ed.) (1982) *Theoretical Models and Empirical Analysis.* Utrecht: Explanatory Sociology Publications.

Raub, W. and Weesie, J. (1990) Reputation and Efficiency in Social Interactions: an Example of Network Effects. *American Journal of Sociology,* 96, 626–54.

Snijders, C. (1996) *Trust and Commitment.* Amsterdam: Thesis Publishers.

Stokman, F. N. and Van Oosten, R. (1994) The Exchange of Voting Positions: an Object-oriented Model of Policy Networks. In B. Bueno de Mesquita and F. N. Stokman (eds.) *European Community Decision Making. Models, Applications, and Comparisons.* New Haven, CT: Yale University Press, pp. 105–27.

Ullmann-Margalit, E. (1977) *The Emergence of Norms.* Oxford: Clarendon Press.

Vanberg, V. (1975) *Die zwei Soziologien.* Tübingen: J. C. B. Mohr (Paul Siebeck).

Williamson, Oliver E. (1985) *The Economic Institutions of Capitalism.* New York: Free Press.

Wippler, R. (1978) The Structural–Individualistic Approach in Dutch Sociology. *Netherlands Journal of Sociology,* 14, 135–55.

Yamagushi, K. (1996) Power in Networks of Substitutable and Complementary Exchange Relations: a Rational-choice Model and an Analysis of Power Centralization. *American Sociological Review,* 61, 308–32.

# 17

# Harold Garfinkel

## ANNE RAWLS

## THE THEORY

Since the publication of *Studies in Ethnomethodology* in 1967, Harold Garfinkel has come to be known as the "father" of "ethnomethodology." Garfinkel's theory and corresponding research program have had a widespread influence in the United States, Canada, the UK, Europe, Australia, and Japan. However, despite its acknowledged influence, there remains considerable debate and misunderstanding about what Garfinkel actually meant by ethnomethodology.

For instance, ethnomethodology has often mistakenly been associated with a focus on the individual; Garfinkel is thought to be concerned with the values and beliefs of individual social participants. Another widespread misunderstanding is that Garfinkel's research consists primarily of "breaching experiments" in which persons violate social expectations in order to demonstrate the existence of underlying rules governing social behavior. Others have associated ethnomethodology with a sort of social indeterminacy similar to Baudrillard's postmodernism. Ethnomethodology, however, is not a single research program, nor does it focus on a single social phenomena, whether individual or collective. Ethnomethodology, as elaborated by Garfinkel, involves a complete theoretical reconceptualization of social order and a corresponding multifaceted research program.

The word "ethnomethodology" itself represents a very simple idea. If one assumes, as Garfinkel does, that the meaningful, patterned, and orderly character of everyday life is something people must work constantly to achieve, then one must also assume they have some methods for doing so. If everyday life really exhibits a patterned orderliness, as Garfinkel believes it does, then it is not enough to say that individuals randomly pursuing shared goals will do similar things enough of the time to manifest trends, or patterns, of orderliness in society. Garfinkel argues that members of society must in fact have some shared methods for achieving social order that they use to mutually construct the meaningful orderliness of social situations.

One way of understanding this is by analogy with the idea that in order to make sense by speaking in a language persons have to speak the same language, using the same meanings for words and the same grammatical forms. Another analogy is with the idea that in order to play a game persons have to play by the same rules. It is not possible to play baseball by running downfield with a football. The essential rules of baseball are in important respects constitutive of the game of baseball. Constitutive means that the rules define recognizable boundaries and practices of the game.

There are problems with these analogies because Garfinkel does not think of members' methods in terms of rules or grammars, which are themselves over-simplified conceptualizations of the constitutive features of social practices. In fact, according to Garfinkel the idea that social order is a result of following rules is responsible for many of the classic problems with social theory. But the analogies, nevertheless, help to illustrate what it means to say that the methods used by persons to create the orderliness of ordinary social occasions are con-stitutive of those occasions.

Ethnomethodology, then, is the study of the methods people use for producing recognizable social orders. "Ethno" refers to members of a social or cultural group and "method" refers to the things members routinely do to create and recreate various recognizable social actions or social practices. "Ology," as in the word "sociology," implies the study of, or the logic of, these methods. Thus, ethnomethodology means the study of members' methods for producing recog-nizable social orders.

Ethnomethodology is not itself a method. It is a study of members' methods based on the theory that a faithful dedication to the details of social phenomena will reveal social order. The word ethnomethodology itself does not name a set of research methods any more than the word sociology designates a specific set of research methods. Ethnomethodologists have done their research in many and varied ways. The object of all these research methods, however, is to discover the things that persons in particular situations do, the methods they use, to create the patterned orderliness of social life. Not all research methods are capable of revealing this level of social order. But there are many that can.

Ethnomethodologists generally use methods that require total immersion in the situation being studied. They hold the ideal that they learn to be competent practitioners of whatever social phenomena they are studying. This ideal is referred to by Garfinkel as "unique adequacy." When the subject of research is something that most persons participate in regularly, like ordinary talk, the game of tic tac toe, driving, walking, etc., then unique adequacy can usually be assumed. However, with regard to practices with specialized populations, unique adequacy can be very hard to achieve. An ethnomethodologist pursuing unique adequacy within a specialized population may spend years in a research site becoming a competent participant in its practices, in addition to collecting various sorts of observational, documentary, and audiovisual materials. Ethnomethodologists have taken degrees in law and mathematics, worked for years in science labs, become professional musicians, and worked as truck drivers and in police departments, in an effort to satisfy the unique adequacy requirement.

Ethnomethodology involves a multifaceted focus on the local social orders that are enacted in various situations. The individual persons who inhabit these situations are, as individuals, uninteresting, except in so far as personal characteristics, such as blindness, reveal something about the competencies required to achieve the recognizable production of the local order that is the object of study.

The mistaken identification of ethnomethodology with a specific methodology, and in particular with "breaching experiments," may be due to the fact that in teaching ethnomethodology Garfinkel found it helpful to develop what he refers to as "tutorial exercises," so that students could have first-hand experience of the "phenomenal field properties" of socially constituted phenomena. These tutorial exercises generally involved disrupting the orderly achievement of intelligibility in some way. Students were assigned tutorial tasks which revealed the work involved in the individual and bodily mastery of the various practices constitutive of local orders. For instance, they might be asked to perform ordinary tasks wearing headgear that distorted their vision. The idea was that various tasks and situations that problematize everyday life actions would make students aware of the need for the constant achievement of the social orderliness of local settings. Without an actual experience that revealed the work involved in enacting social reality, Garfinkel found that students had great difficulty in grasping the point of ethnomethodology. The "breaching experiments" were not intended primarily as a research program, although some early research was conducted in this manner, but as a tutorial exercise for students.

Garfinkel's own early research was presented primarily in *Studies in Ethnomethodology*. "Studies," as the 1967 volume has come to be called, consisted of a collection of papers, each of which demonstrated a different theoretical and/or methodological facet of ethnomethodology: accountability, commitment to shared practices, social construction of identity, and the documentary method of interpretation, among them.

"Good Reasons for Bad Clinic Records" reported on a field study of a psychiatric outpatient clinic. The researchers had originally been interested in coding the clinic files. Instead they found that the files were for their purposes "hopelessly incomplete." What interested Garfinkel, however, was that the incompleteness of the files was not random. It reflected a combination of internal clinic practices and concerns for the accountability of those practices to outside agencies. Garfinkel argued that, because of the need for institutional accountability, clinic workers had to carefully manage the information contained in the files. Therefore, it could not be assumed that clinic files and the statistics they generated represent an accurate record of patient histories. They were not designed to do so. Rather, they were designed to meet the institutions' need for internal and external accountability.

Garfinkel's point is not only negative. While the statistical records produced by the clinic cannot be treated as an accurate account of cases, they can be used to show how clinic workers keep the files and why they keep the files the way they do. To a traditionally trained social scientist the clinic files are "bad" files. But they are not bad files from the clinic workers' point of view. They provide just those materials clinic workers need to produce the orderly routines of the clinic day and then account for those routines to the outsiders to whom they are accountable. For the clinic workers there are "good" reasons for these "bad" records. For the ethnomethodologist, the records provide important information regarding the way in which the social order of the clinic is achieved.

In the "Trust" paper Garfinkel elaborated the view that members' methods must be distinguished from the traditional notion of rules. Members' methods remain unspecified and unspecifiable in ways that distinguish them from rules. That is one reason why Garfinkel has objected to the analogy between members' methods and game rules or grammars. Rules and grammars are conceptual simplifications of constitutive features of actual social practices. Members' methods, while instructable and instructably observable, are, according to Garfinkel, not specifiable. Because members must use the same methods in order for recognizable local orders to be produced, there is a certain level of trust about shared methods that is necessary in order for mutual intelligibility to be achieved. This bears a resemblance to Habermas's argument that persons must assume a set of foundational assumptions before they can sit down and reason publicly with one another. The difference is that Habermas refers to a hypothetical set of commitments to the reciprocity of the situation. Garfinkel, on the other hand, underlines the need for all participants to "really" use "just the same" methods for producing recognizable actions.

For instance, if persons find themselves at a particular movie theater where people line up in a particular way, then they must figure out what methods for lining up are being used and line up that way too. Otherwise, they may find out after a great deal of waiting that they have not in fact been in line. That is, they have not been recognizably waiting in line, and the others in the theater will not accept their claim that they have been waiting in line. There will be a moral censure of their activities – "Hey you don't cut in line" – with all the anger and moral outrage that accompanies moral censure. If persons do not produce "just those" actions that are recognized as appropriate for the place they find themselves in, they will find that others do not recognize their actions.

The "Agnes" paper, which explored the practices involved in achieving a recognizable gendered image, has been the subject of much debate. In this paper Garfinkel presents a detailed account of his discussions with a young person who was seeking (and eventually received) a sex change operation. The critics have generally argued over whether or not Garfinkel and the doctors were "taken in" by Agnes, who claimed to be a young woman mistakenly labeled a young man. The question of whether Garfinkel was able to observe Agnes from an "objective" research standpoint, or whether his own beliefs and values influenced what he observed, seems to dominate the discussion.

However, this debate misses the point. What interested Garfinkel was the idea that gender must be socially managed. If Agnes, in being a man who was really a woman, or a man who was pretending to really be a woman, or a woman who had the biology of a man, etc., had to recognizably reproduce actions, expressions of emotion, posture, etc., that were recognizably female, then by watching and talking to Agnes it might be possible to discover the essential features of recognizable actions involved in the social construction of gender. If Agnes was "fooling" anyone, then the performance would, from Garfinkel's standpoint, be *more* valuable as a subject of research, not *less* valuable.

Critics often assume that gender is something biological and that Agnes either "really" had the biology or did not. Garfinkel was assuming something much more radical; that gender is a social production, such that persons who are said to be biologically male can produce recognizably female actions and thereby make the claim that they are female and be believed. The question Garfinkel raises is not the indeterminate biological one of whether Agnes is "really" male or female. The question is how, and in exactly what way, Agnes used members' methods to recognizably reproduce herself or himself socially as a female in each and every particular situation.

Garfinkel's research, understood in this way, is very illuminating. Unlike most of us, Agnes needed a high degree of awareness of how he or she achieved recognition as a gendered being. Agnes is in fact able to talk to Garfinkel at great length about the various ways in which he or she reproduced a recognizably feminine gender. This is one of the earliest discussions of gender as an entirely social phenomenon. Garfinkel could not be "wrong" or "taken in" concerning Agnes's gender, since for Garfinkel gender consists of the ability to produce recognizable social acts, emotions, and bodily forms. The questions of Agnes's "true" biology, or when and whether drugs were involved, make no difference. The point is that Agnes learned what he or she had to do in order to be accepted as "really" female and tried to do those things. Therefore, Agnes is an important source of information about how it is that women reproduce themselves as gendered beings in everyday life.

In the paper "Documentary Methods of Interpretation," Garfinkel argues that persons in everyday life construct carefully documented accounts that gloss the details of social practices in order to warrant claims they make about the orderliness of social events. Garfinkel argues that this common everyday life practice parallels the practices of formal analytic theorizing, which also proceed via documentation and bibliographies. In the very same ways that the everyday life practice of documentary reasoning glosses over the details of practices in producing a documented account, formal analytic reasoning glosses those practices as well.

Garfinkel argues that the documented accounts of both common-sense reasoning and formal analytic theorizing treat conceptual schemes as more important than the contingent details of practices. Because, in his view, social life is organized by the production of recognizable practices, the details of those practices are critical to the understanding of society. Yet the conceptual schemes involved in documented accounts gloss over these details. Therefore, formal analytic theorizing, based as it is on documented accounts, inevitably misses the essential orderliness of society. Where scientific sociology places the clarity of concepts at the heart of its science, Garfinkel blames this same reliance on clear concepts for the "loss of the phenomenon."

Using documentary accounts persons are always able to retrospectively reconstruct a plausible explanation of why something happened that appears to have
predictive power. What Garfinkel argues, however, is that such retrospective
documented accounts bear little or no relationship to how and why events
actually unfolded prospectively in the way that they did. Therefore, when such
accounts are used to predict future social behavior the results are notoriously
inaccurate. In order to know why something happened, Garfinkel argues, one
has to have a carefully detailed prospective account of practices as they unfold.

Garfinkel's argument bears important similarities to C. Wright Mills's argument, in a paper entitled "Situated Actions and the Vocabulary of Motives," that
institutions are not organized prospectively according to rules, but retrospectively according to shared vocabularies of motive. Garfinkel goes farther than
Mills, however, in insisting that social order is constituted not only retrospectively through the enactment of a shared vocabulary of motives (or accounts), but
also prospectively through the enactment of detailed sets of shared practices.
Ethnomethodology seeks to describe the concrete witnessable details of enacted
practices as they unfold over their course, thus avoiding the circularity of
documented accounts.

Since *Studies in Ethnomethodology* swept the discipline in 1967, Garfinkel
has published only five articles: "On Formal Structures of Practical Action" with
Harvey Sacks in 1970, "The Work of a Discovering Science Construed with
Materials from the Optically Discovered Pulsar" with Michael Lynch and Eric
Livingston in 1981, "Evidence for Locally Produced, Naturally Accountable
Phenomena of Order, Logic, Reason, Meaning, Method, etc., in and as of the
Essential Haecceity of Immortal Ordinary Society" (hereafter referred to as
"Parsons's Plenum") in 1988, "Two Incommensurable Asymmetrically Alternate
Technologies of Social Analysis" with Larry Weider in 1992, and "Ethnome-
thodology's Program" in 1996. While few, the articles are very important and
quite illuminating. The bulk of Garfinkel's research, which is extensive, remains
unpublished.

The paper "On Formal Structures of Practical Action," the first to appear after
"Studies," and co-authored with Harvey Sacks, stands as a statement of the joint
theoretical interest of ethnomethodology and conversation analysis. Garfinkel
and Sacks spent several years working closely with one another in the early
1960s when Sacks was developing what would become known as conversational
analysis. "Formal Structures" presents the argument that even the most mundane
of practical actions have formal, observable, structures. While the idea is necessarily pursued differently in studies of conversation *per se*, and studies of
practical activities that involve other sorts of practice along with conversation,
the principle is the same. In order for practices to be mutually intelligible they
must be recognizably produced. This idea that all mutually intelligible ordinary
actions have an observable structure is a distinctive characteristic of ethnomethodology and conversational analysis.

The "Parsons's Plenum" paper, the only mature statement of the relationship
between Garfinkel's work and traditional sociology as represented by Parsons,
stands as a summary statement of concerns that have preoccupied Garfinkel's

later work. Garfinkel argues in that paper that there are two very different assumptions made about the nature of the social world by Parsons and himself. He argues that the assumptions define their respective research programs in essential respects.

According to Garfinkel, Parsons assumed a world in which individual persons, while possessed of a degree of freedom to act according to personal drives and motives, nevertheless come to realize that there are culturally accepted ways for doing most things. Thus individuals, in pursuing their individual interests, will attempt to choose courses of action that are socially acceptable. Furthermore, the very ways in which they interpret their feelings and even their physical needs will be socially constrained. For instance, individuals may have a drive to dominate others. In modern Western society, however, they will, if properly socialized, learn to interpret this drive as an impulse to achieve power or prestige in any of a number of socially acceptable ways.

Furthermore, membership in various subgroups can be expected to influence the choice of goals. For instance, people's religious backgrounds may influence their choice to sublimate an impulse to dominate others. Or the learning of gender roles may influence women to suppress a strong impulse to independence, or conversely influence men to suppress a strong impulse to dependence.

Certainly individuals are constrained by social values. However, if one accepts Parsons's proposal that social order is composed entirely of the relationship between individuals and social constraint, then social order will appear to be merely the net result of general tendencies to comply with norms. In the absence of concrete witnessable patterns of order, evidence of an "underlying social structure" that produces norms and values and constrains persons to follow them depends on the statistical manipulation of large aggregate data sets, as individuals are expected to vary in their degree of compliance. The result, according to Garfinkel, is "Parsons's Plenum": a theoretically constructed world in which order can only be discovered after and as a result of the application of a social scientific method.

Given this initial assumption, the sort of detailed study of particular places and social events advocated by Garfinkel makes no sense. Such studies could not yield evidence of a "plenum" which can only be revealed by large aggregate data sets. However, Garfinkel, for his part, makes the initial assumption that all socially recognizable actions must be produced in orderly and expected ways, and that they display their orderliness in their concrete details. Therefore, he argues, studying concrete practices in the situations in which they are produced gives the researcher immediate access to the process of constructing local orders.

The certainty that order is displayed in the concrete details of enacted practices is not only, or even first, a theoretical assumption, but also something one feels when observing empirically the patterned orderliness of certain social occasions. Social occasions and their practices are often recognizably orderly in ways that the Parsons's Plenum approach cannot account for. The experienced concrete orderliness of such occasions demands a theory that can account for it.

Garfinkel's concern is that the widespread focus of formal analytic theory and methods on aggregating data across large populations is preventing the discovery of the production of social order. The dominant approach in the discipline of sociology to the problem of social order, he says, obscures the very processes of social orderliness that are being sought: the "what more" there is to social order than formal analytic theorizing can ever find.

It is the Parsons's Plenum view of "structure" that leads to the characterization of nonstatistical approaches to sociology, and ethnomethodology in particular, as individualistic "micro" sociologies that are indifferent to the problem of social order. From Garfinkel's perspective, it is Parsons who failed to examine the most fundamental aspects of social order. How are persons able to recognize what the valued courses of action are? How much the same do actions have to be to be recognizable as the same? When persons do not choose valued courses of action how are they sanctioned? In Parsons's system a great deal of behavior that does not fit the norms is possible. For Garfinkel this explains neither the high degree of compliance experienced in everyday life, nor the routine achievement of intelligibility.

Garfinkel does not see himself as examining society at an "individual" or "micro" level, but rather as examining the great classical questions of social order. He interprets Durkheim's immortal society to refer to the local production of order which Garfinkel calls "Immortal Ordinary Society." Society, on this view, does not depend on the tendencies of individuals to more or less comply with social norms. Society is immortal, in that the patterned orderliness of situations outlives the particular persons who staff them. Persons knew, according to Garfinkel, "of just these organizational things that they are in the midst of, that it preceded them and will be there after they leave; the great recurrences of ordinary society, staffed, provided for, produced, observed and observable locally and accountably, in and as of an 'assemblage of Haecceities'."[1]

The classic way of looking at social order places the emphasis on the populations who staff the scenes and thereby appear to create those scenes. The classic demographic questions focus on the characteristics of the individuals who make up the population: gender, race, income, religion, education, etc. Garfinkel's focus on patterned orderliness places the emphasis on the scene and away from the population. From his perspective, the variables are in the scene and not in the population. Any population coming on a particular scene could only recognizably reproduce it by recognizably producing the practices that identify it as a scene of a particular sort. Reconstructing the actor's point of view thus involves taking into account the various contingencies faced by any actor in attempting to produce recognizable practice. It does not involve the perspective of any particular actors. The basic requirements of recognizability must be able to take on the endless contingencies of the actual recognizable reproduction of practices, not the contingencies of individual differences.

In shifting the emphasis from persons to scenes Garfinkel points out that the emphasis was only focused on populations in the first place as a result of looking at the construction of order in the traditional Parsons's Plenum way. Garfinkel claims that the sort of social order that classical thinkers like Durkheim sought does not lie in the characteristics of populations, but in the situated details of practice, and, therefore, cannot be rendered by studies, following Parsons's

Plenum, which create an analytic universe to replace the real one. Neither can they be revealed by traditional studies of the actor's point of view that focus on individual beliefs, values, and perspective. For Garfinkel, the key lies in detailed studies of those shared practices that are essential to the production of local orders.

According to Garfinkel, practitioners of formal analysis know about local orders. But, they don't know what to do with them. They "know" about them only in a special sense: as problems, recurrent irritations, and errors in "measurement" that need to be "controlled" for. They do not know them as social orders. Ethnomethodology recognizes these recurrent irregularities as the achieved orderliness of the "Immortal Ordinary Society." They are Durkheim's "social facts" conceived of not as external and coercive social norms, shared values, collective concepts, or goals, but as the achieved and enacted concrete detail of particular recognizable social practices and their occasions.

Garfinkel rejects the vision, common both to Parsonian structuralism and the poststructural critique, that chaos and contingency are the primary attributes of ordinary social scenes as individual actors struggle against institutional constraint. For Garfinkel, mutually intelligible actions must have recognizably recurrent features and are therefore necessarily orderly.

This insistence on the ongoing production of social order at all mutually intelligible points has been interpreted as evidence that his sociology is conservative because it does not allow the individual actor any room to rebel or create. But Garfinkel does not deny that the individual may have unique or nonconforming thoughts and impulses. In fact, Garfinkel's position allows for a great deal more "rebellion" against institutional values than Parsons, poststructuralism, or postmodernism.

Since formal institutions, and collective concepts and beliefs, have little to do with the production of order and intelligibility, in Garfinkel's view, it is at least theoretically possible for persons to avoid their constraints. It is at the level of enacted practices, or Interaction Orders, that persons must conform to expectations with regard to social practice: if individuals are to achieve mutual intelligibility, they must produce practices that are recognizable to others as practices of a particular sort. While unrecognizable practices may convey various meanings, or have meanings attributed to them, they do not convey a single mutually intelligible meaning. Mutual intelligibility requires the production of shared recognizable practices.

Garfinkel's argument does not deny the reality of institutional constraint. Rather, it adds to the notion of a vague and distant conceptual, or structural, constraint on goals and values an inescapable and ever present constraint on the empirical forms that recognizable concrete actions can take. The message is not that persons should not rebel against social inequities or that social inequality is not of concern to the analyst. The idea is rather that the possibilities for unique expression are even more highly constrained at the interactional level than has been realized. Far from believing that all is well with the status quo, Garfinkel has spent his career warning that many of the most trusted methods, methods presumed to be objective, are themselves shaped in essential ways by constraints on the social practices that constitute the essence of those methods, resulting in "critical" studies biased in favor of the status quo.

## The Person

Harold Garfinkel was born in Newark, New Jersey, on October 29, 1917. His formative years were spent in Newark during the Depression, where his father, Abraham Garfinkel, owned a small business selling household merchandise to immigrant families on the installment plan. The neighborhood in which he was raised consisted of a large Jewish community, at a time when ethnicity was important, and the problem of how to overcome poverty and disadvantage to succeed in the "chosen" country was a pressing one. Many extremely bright young men and women, second- and third-generation immigrants, were struggling not only to find a place in American society, but to formulate that place in their own terms.

For the elder Garfinkel, raising a son during the Depression, employment was the most important concern, and he wanted to be sure that his son learned a trade. Harold, on the other hand, wanted a university education. There was in the family an in-law who was not Jewish and was therefore credited with knowledge about what sorts of professions were viable in the world outside of the Newark Jewish community.

This in-law agreed to give advice with regard to Harold's future. One night at the dinner table he asked Harold what profession he would pursue at a university. Harold, who didn't really want to pursue a profession, recalls that he had been reading an article on surgeons in the *New York Times* and it sounded interesting. He answered that he wanted to become a surgeon. His in-law then told his father, "surgeons and lawyers are driving taxicabs." It was the middle of the Depression (1935). Thereupon, it was decided that Harold would go into the installment business with his father. Courses in business and accounting were germane to the business, however, so it was agreed that Harold would attend the University of Newark, an unaccredited program at the time, majoring in business and accounting during the day, and working in his father's installment business at night.

This early thwarting of the young Garfinkel's plans for a university education had some unpredictably happy results. The courses in accounting, in combination with friends made at the university, had an important and positive influence on the later development of his sociological theory and research. Because the program was unaccredited, the teaching was done primarily by graduate students from nearby universities. In the case of business courses at the University of Newark, the lecturers were quite often graduate students in economics from Columbia. This meant not only that courses were often taught by the best and brightest young minds in the country, but also that in business courses Garfinkel was apt to be taught the theory of business in place of procedure.

According to Garfinkel, his later work on accounts owes as much, or more, to a business course at the University of Newark called the "theory of accounts" as it does to C. Wright Mills and Kenneth Burke, whose social theories of accounts he also studied. The course dealt with double entry bookkeeping and cost accounting. From this course, Garfinkel came to understand that even in setting up an accounting sheet he was theorizing the various categories into which the numbers would be placed. Choosing, for instance, whether to place an item in the debit or assets column was already a decision. Furthermore, that decision was accountable to superiors and other agencies in a variety of complex ways. The course, although a course in accounting, didn't deal with mathematics. "How do you make the columns and figures accountable?" was the big question according to Garfinkel.

These accountants and economists weren't describing events, they were describing "indicators," and unlike the social theorists Garfinkel was to encounter later, they were very frank about it. They didn't pretend that their indicators constituted an underlying order. There are clear connections between this approach to accounting and Garfinkel's later work. The argument of "Good Reasons for Bad Clinic Records," focusing, as it does, on the ways in which clinic workers render the files accountable, is an obvious parallel. So is the much later argument of the "Parsons's Plenum" paper that formal analytic theorizing creates an orderly social world out of "indicators" aggregated across large data sets.

At the University of Newark Harold hung out with a group of Jewish students who were interested in sociology. The group included Melvin Tumin, Herbert McClosky, and Seymour Sarason. According to Garfinkel, Philip Selznick and Paul Lazarsfeld, who were at Columbia at the time, were also known to members of the group. In fact, he recollects that Lazarsfeld taught a course in social statistics at the University of Newark attended by Tumin, McClosky, and Sarason. Students at this unaccredited university were able to take courses, developed by ambitious graduate students, not yet available at more traditional universities.

Discussions with this group turned Garfinkel's interests toward sociology. All the members of the group, along with their friends from Columbia, were later to rise to prominence, a fact that had a very positive influence on Garfinkel's career. Tumin became prominent as an anthropologist at Princeton. McClosky went on to join the political science faculty at Berkeley and helped to introduce survey research to political science. Seymour Sarason went on to join the psychiatry faculty at Yale. Philip Selznick joined the sociology department at UCLA and later went on to Berkeley (where he supported the graduate careers of Sacks, Schegloff, and Sudnow). Lazarsfeld, unknown at the time, went on to establish scientific sociology at Columbia.

By the time Garfinkel graduated from the University of Newark in the summer of 1939 he knew that he could not go into the installment business with his father. He had a professor of insurance, Lawrence Ackerman, in whom he confided. Ackerman told him not to worry; he would help Harold to "get away." A Quaker, Ackerman arranged for Harold to attend a Quaker work camp that summer, building an earthdam for a rural community in Cornelia, Georgia. In that work camp, Garfinkel met a number of idealistic young people from Columbia and Harvard. By the end of the summer he knew he wanted to be a sociologist. At the camp, Morris Mitchell, from the Columbia School of Education, advised him that the sociology department at the University of North Carolina, which placed an emphasis on sociology as an effective means of furthering public service projects, was the place to go.

So, at the end of the summer of 1939 Harold packed his bags and hitchhiked directly from the summer camp in Georgia to the University of North Carolina at Chapel Hill. In the process, he had to make his way across Tennessee and much of Georgia and North Carolina. There were very few cars traveling the road and the trip was a long one. Garfinkel reports spending at least one night in a town jail because he had nowhere else to sleep and the locals generously offered him the jail for the night. Howard W. Odum was chair of the sociology department at North Carolina at the time, a man with a serious commitment to improving the plight of the underprivileged. When Harold showed up on his doorstep, with his bags in hand, he recalls that Odum said to him "You are a New York Jew who has come to the country. I'll support you." Odum admitted Garfinkel to the department on the spot and offered him a graduate fellowship.

At North Carolina Guy Johnson became Harold's mentor and introduced him to the work of W. I. Thomas, whom he says he couldn't stop thinking about. Johnson was a former student of Odum, and his particular expertise was in race relations. Very active in local community associations that dealt with issues of race, Johnson generously made his own early research on race and interracial homicide available to Garfinkel, suggesting that he pursue the subject for his master's thesis. Garfinkel now owned a car, purchased for him by his father, and his fellowship freed him from the need to work, so he was able to visit all the courthouses in a ten county area and dig the information he needed out of the courthouse records. The result was his thesis on interracial homicide.

At North Carolina Garfinkel was introduced to a broad range of theoretical perspectives that shaped the development of ethnomethodology in significant ways. In addition to W. I. Thomas, he studied Florian Znaniecki's *Social Actions*, which he refers to as a highly significant, though much neglected, theoretical work. He was also introduced to the theories of accounts and vocabularies of motive of Kenneth Burke and C. Wright Mills. He studied a broad range of phenomenological philosophy with a fellow student, James Fleming, with whom he discussed courses in the philosophy department that dealt with Husserl, Schutz, and Gurwitsch. Seymour Koch in the psychology department introduced Garfinkel to Lewin and Gestalt psychology. *The Structure of Social Action*, by Talcott Parsons, had been published in 1937 and Harold purchased a first edition from McGraw-Hill that first Christmas at North Carolina. He says that he can still remember sitting in the backyard fingering the book, smelling the newness of its pages. According to Garfinkel it was a "love affair" with sociology from the beginning.

While immersed in the study of sociology at North Carolina, Garfinkel was befriended by a group of five students at the university who challenged Odum's view of sociology. While it seemed to Harold that the great political and social questions of the day were being debated with great energy at North Carolina, these students felt that the "real" debate was going on elsewhere. While Odum was committed to a program of documenting southern folk society, which he believed was the key to generic stable society, the students from New York City and Chicago were dreaming of Parsons at Harvard and Lazarsfeld and Merton at Columbia. It was going to be a scientific sociology, with Parsons, providing for order in ordinary society with grand heroic theories, at its head.

According to Garfinkel, Lazarsfeld was seen as the emissary to the new scientific sociology from Germany. He promised that sociology would become scientific with the use of social statistics and within ten years would be entirely mathematical. The idea was that if economists could make economic affairs accountable with indicators that made up a time series, then a scientific sociology should be able to do the same thing for social behavior in general. Everyone was singing the same chorus of models and modeling, and quantitative methods were the *sine qua non* if you wanted to be taken seriously.

According to Garfinkel, the students "used to worship in the computer room" and could get a PhD by "winding" out associations between variables from a Marchant hand-wound calculator. Students put their numbers into the keyboard and then started to wind the crank. One obtained association took an enormous amount of handwork and, according to Garfinkel, was considered a justifiable numerical account of what was variable in the factors of measurement.

In the sociology department at North Carolina, however, there was one graduate student, James Fleming, who was not taken up with the pursuit of empirical scientific sociology. Fleming was engaged in reading "across the disciplines," looking for the actor's point of view. Znaniecki's book *Social Action*, not the study of the Polish peasant, was the canonical text with regard to the actor's point of view. The most important of Znaniecki's works at the time, according to Garfinkel, the book is now rarely read. As Garfinkel recalls, Fleming believed that there was no major social theorist across the social sciences who was not making provision for the actor's point of view.

The push for a scientific sociology based on statistics turned sociological interest away from the problem of action as Znaniecki had formulated it. According to Garfinkel, Znaniecki was the first to vociferously insist on the adequate description of social action, an issue which became a primary concern of Garfinkel's and remained so throughout his career. The problem facing Znaniecki's theory of social action, however, according to Garfinkel, was what an adequate description of action could consist of, given the ubiquitous insistence on the relevance of the actor's point of view.

Garfinkel's combination of the theory of accounts with the problem of the actor's point of view would provide a novel approach to this problem. His first publication, "Color Trouble," an early effort at an adequate description of accounting practices, exhibits the skeleton of his mature view. It was published in 1939, Garfinkel's first winter at North Carolina.

Garfinkel's graduate career at North Carolina was interrupted by the entry of the United States into the Second World War. After completing his master's thesis, Garfinkel was drafted and assigned to the airforce in 1942, taking with him, as he had into his master's thesis on interracial homicide, his thoughts on Parsons and Znaniecki and his theorizing with regard to accounts. He was by that time also familiar with Husserl, Schutz, and Gurwitsch, and the idea of multiple realities drawn from Schutz (1967). In the airforce, Garfinkel was assigned to designing and teaching strategies for small arms warfare against tanks and rose to the rank of corporal. It was also during the war that Garfinkel married his wife Arlene.

The task of training troops in small arms warfare against tanks was the most ironically appropriate assignment one can think of for the future "father" of ethnomethodology. Garfinkel was given the task of training troops in tank warfare on a golf course on Miami Beach in the complete absence of tanks. Garfinkel had only pictures of tanks from *Life* magazine. The real tanks were all in combat. The man who would insist on concrete empirical detail in lieu of theorized accounts was teaching real troops who were about to enter live combat to fight against only imagined tanks in situations where things like the proximity of the troops to the imagined tank could make the difference between life and death. The impact of this on the development of his views can only be imagined. He had to train troops to throw explosives into the tracks of imaginary tanks; to keep imaginary tanks from seeing them by directing fire at imaginary tank ports. This task posed in a new and very concrete way the problems of the adequate description of action and accountability that Garfinkel had taken up at North Carolina as theoretical issues.

After the war, Garfinkel went on to Harvard to study for his PhD with Talcott Parsons.[2] The relationship between Garfinkel's work and Parsons's social theory, as it developed at Harvard, is an important one. Garfinkel insisted on the adequacy of description and a focus on contingent detail. Parsons relied on conceptual categories and generalization. The clash between their positions would develop into one of the most important theoretical debates of the past several decades. In his doctoral thesis, Garfinkel took on Parsons more or less directly. However, Garfinkel later withdrew from the conceptual debate, maintaining that his position could be demonstrated only empirically, not theoretically.

While pursuing his degree at Harvard, Garfinkel taught for two years at Princeton University.[3] While at Princeton Garfinkel organized a conference with Richard Snyder and Wilbert Moore, funded by the Ford Foundation, called "Problems in Model Construction in the Social Sciences." The idea was to develop interdisciplinary studies in organizational behavior. Garfinkel sought out innovative theorists for this conference, inviting Herbert Simon, Talcott Parsons, Kenneth Burke, Kurt Wolff, Alfred Schutz, and Paul Lazarsfeld. Kurt Wolff was at that time at Ohio State University in a soft money unit called the "Personnel Research Board," a group of industrial psychologists with federal funding to support studies of leadership on submarines and airplanes. When Garfinkel left Princeton in 1952, after receiving his degree from Harvard, Wolff brought him to Ohio for a two-year position.

In Garfinkel's second year on this project the budget was cut, eliminating support for his last six months. At this point, Fred Strodbeck, another classmate from Harvard, who was at Wichita engaged in his jury study project, asked Garfinkel to join the studies he was conducting with Saul Mendlovitz. While Garfinkel was at Wichita the three reported on their work at the American Sociological Association meetings in the summer of 1954. In preparing for this talk, Garfinkel searched for what to call what they found so interesting in their discussions with the jurors. He examined the Yale cross-cultural survey and saw all the "ethnos" – ethnoscience, ethnobotany, etc. – and thought of the jury members' close reasonings with one another as "ethnomethods." The word "methods" was, according to Garfinkel, an extrapolation from Felix Kaufmann, a philosopher, who spoke of the term methodology as the theory of correct decisions in deciding the grounds for action and further inference. Together the two words seemed to apply to what the jurors were doing. Thus, the term "ethnomethodology" was born.

In the fall of 1954 Harold was asked to join the faculty at UCLA. Selznick's earlier move to UCLA turned out to be of particular importance to Garfinkel; it was Selznick along with Tumin who talked the then-chair at UCLA, Leonard Broom, into hiring Harold when Selznick moved from UCLA to Berkeley. UCLA was a joint sociology/anthropology department at the time, and the anthropologists appreciated Garfinkel's attention to interactional detail. This was an unexpectedly lucky move for Garfinkel, as UCLA, which was practically unknown at the time, quickly rose to become one of the top universities nationally. From the very beginning at UCLA Garfinkel used the term ethnomethodology, developed in Wichita, in his seminars.

At UCLA Garfinkel worked with a number of students and colleagues who became prominent proponents of ethnomethodology and conversational analysis. His relationship with Harvey Sacks, who went to UCLA and then to UC Irvine after completing his dissertation with Erving Goffman at Berkeley, was of particular importance. Sacks, along with Emmanuel Schegloff, also from Berkeley, and Gail Jefferson, outlined what has essentially become a new field of conversational studies, referred to as "conversational analysis," within the general parameters of ethnomethodology.

Garfinkel and his wife Arlene, married during the war, lived in Pacific Palisades, California, continuously from 1961. They raised two children and supported one another's intellectual endeavors during 52 plus years of marriage. Arlene Garfinkel's work as a lipid chemist inspired many of Garfinkel's insights into scientists' work. Garfinkel formally retired from UCLA in 1987 but remained active as an emeritus professor.

## THE SOCIAL CONTEXT

Garfinkel grew to maturity at a critical moment in American history. The Depression, the Second World War, and the immediate postwar period were times of sweeping social transition. This social context created a mood of both opportunity and criticism that turned Garfinkel toward an interest in social issues. The Depression was a particularly difficult time for the American working class, whose jobs were eliminated by the failure of industry. During the Depression a new spirit of democracy and anti-elite sentiment swept the nation, and the New Deal placed an emphasis on the problems of the American poor and working classes for the first time. These circumstances led to a heightened political awareness among the working class, and the young Garfinkel found himself caught up in debates over politics, economics, and the possibility of general social transformation going on in the community around him. He dreamed of a university education and a life outside of the Newark Jewish community. They were difficult dreams for a member of an ethnic minority at the time to pursue. Yet Garfinkel's path was criss-crossed by a significant number of others who shared his background. The Depression era had ushered in a time of great intellectual debate within the lower classes that would propel many into the academic, political, and professional realms of society.

With the onset of the Second World War, however, the situation began to change. There were now jobs to be had in industries related to the war effort. In white working-class communities the perception that all was well with America quickly replaced the anxiety of the Depression years. The great majority of the white working class was eager to parlay its new-found job security into upward mobility into the middle class. Race-based government housing and lending programs, begun during the Depression, fueled this interest, enabling the white working class to distance themselves from African-American and ethnic minority communities by building all-white suburbs.

This created a crisis within the working class. The gains made by the working class during the Depression were really very small. Political organs of the working class, like the UAW (United Auto Workers), which had been so strong during the depression, began to wither in the mid-1940s. Even in so strong a union town as Detroit the union was unable to elect a mayor after this period. According to UAW leaders, their political position was weakened by large numbers of the white working class, who simply pretended they had achieved middle-class status, voting middle-class interests.

This wholesale adoption of middle-class values did not penetrate to Jewish and other ethnic minority communities. While they did benefit to some extent from the increase in jobs, the preferential treatment of the white working class during the war and postwar period raised the level of debate over social issues in minority communities to new levels. African-American and Jewish leaders continued to talk about equality and social change throughout the war and postwar years.

Thus, at a time when the majority of white working-class Americans were becoming more politically conservative, the unions that represented the working class, and those Jewish, African American, and other ethnic minorities who were excluded by housing and other forms of discrimination from participation in this exclusive all-white group, became further politicized. Socialism became increasingly popular and labor unions during this time increasingly identified with a socialist or Marxist framework. While it was not the only factor, race and ethnicity played a key role in the determination of political awareness during this period.

This early exposure to the importance of race and ethnicity is reflected in Garfinkel's early writings, in his master's thesis on interracial homicide, and in his first publication "Color Trouble." Both deal with the social production of African-American inequality and demonstrate a clear concern for, and understanding of, the plight of African-Americans, a group whose tenuous relationship to the mainstream Garfinkel well understood. A critical attitude toward the institutions of mainstream American society, political, social, and intellectual, continued to characterize Garfinkel's later studies in ethnomethodology.

In addition to the general social upheaval of the period and the debate it fostered over social issues, the Second World War was a particularly significant time in which to be Jewish in America. Because of the conflict with Hitler's fascist antisemitism, the widespread discrimination against Jews in the United States came to be seen generally for the first time as a social problem. After the war, when Americans realized the extent of German atrocities, an unprecedented effort was made to confront antisemitism. This general sentiment was fueled by the publication of personal records such as the diary of Anne Frank, and first-hand accounts of their arrival at the camps by returning American soldiers. While these efforts may have been more rhetorical than actual, they nevertheless helped to create an atmosphere in which the problems of minorities, and those of the Jewish minority in particular, were discussed.

Within the Jewish community this combination of events created a highly politicized atmosphere, much as a new awareness of postwar segregation and inequality did in the African-American community. Young Jewish men and women, particularly in New York, earnestly discussed politics, the war, and the creation of a Jewish state. When Garfinkel attended the University of Newark, even as a business and accounting student, he found himself continually caught up in these discussions.

This atmosphere of discussion and debate, because of its emphasis on the transformation of the social and political system, resulted, for the first time, in a widespread interest in the discipline of sociology. The social theories of Karl Marx were widely read during this period of wartime antifascism and Marx's antibourgeois stance made his position popular with the working class. Sociology, the efficacy of New Deal social programs, and the future of capitalism were all seriously debated in the 1930s and early 1940s at a time when most universities did not yet have sociology departments. This interest influenced the career choices of many young students, including Garfinkel.

The resulting increase in the demand for courses in sociology forced many universities to open sociology departments, a trend that continued through the 1950s and 1960s. Undergraduate and graduate students alike turned to sociology as a discipline relevant to the social issues of the day. New academic positions were created for those, like Garfinkel, who were attracted to academic life by the social upheaval of the times. Sociology promised to provide solutions to many pressing social problems, and there was room in the thriving new discipline for many innovative young thinkers.

## THE INTELLECTUAL CONTEXT

Critical to an understanding of Garfinkel's work is the fact that he began his graduate education at the University of North Carolina at Chapel Hill prior to the Second World War. He belongs to a generation, educated before the war, who received broad theoretical and methodological training not constrained by scientific sociology as it developed during and immediately after the war.

A tendency to focus on Garfinkel's graduate training at Harvard, overlooking the years he spent at North Carolina, has led to the view that the genesis of his position can be traced to his conflict with Parsons. In fact, it is much more accurate to set the development of Garfinkel's ideas against the intellectual backdrop of the sociology department at North Carolina. Garfinkel went to Harvard with a set of well formulated ideas about the importance of the actor's point of view, the unavoidable character of reflexivity, the importance of adequate description, and a reinterpretation of Mills's theory of accounts, developed at North Carolina. It was the conflict between these already deeply held and well worked out ideas, and Parsons's teaching, that led Garfinkel to develop his mature views.

Sociology, as Garfinkel initially encountered it in the 1930s, was a multifaceted discipline, with many widely divergent theories and methods. The Chicago School, inspired by the work of Robert Park, W. I. Thomas, Charles Horton Cooley, George Herbert Mead, and Florian Znaniecki, was still a dominant force. The perspective of the actor and interaction were serious issues. The work of Karl Marx was actively debated, and Parsons and scientific sociology had not yet come to dominate the discipline.

When Garfinkel arrived at the University of North Carolina as a graduate student in the summer of 1939 he encountered a group of scholars committed to addressing issues of poverty, inequality, and race relations. Both theoretically and methodologically, the department reflected the eclectic nature of the discipline at that time. The graduate training that Garfinkel and others received during this period was broadly theoretical, with a social problems emphasis. Ethnography was an important and widespread methodological tool. Philosophical and epistemological issues concerning the perspective of the actor, the problem of reflexivity, and the validity of knowledge and perception were an important part of the sociological curriculum. There were rumblings about the development of a new scientific sociology, but it had not yet come to pass.

By the time Garfinkel reached Harvard after the war, however, there was a recognized dominant type of sociology considered by most people to be more scientific and valid than the types of sociology that preceded it. Parsons was its acknowledged leader. Znaniecki, the Chicago School, C. Wright Mills, phenomenology, and Marxist sociology all but disappeared for a number of years. Even Max Weber and Émile Durkheim, social theorists championed by Parsons, were for years only interpreted and studied in terms dictated by Parsons.

How and why a combination of statistical methods and Parsonsian structural functionalism came to define the notions of "scientific" and "objective" is an interesting issue. Marx, Weber, Toennies, Simmel, and Mead had not really made use of statistics. Even Durkheim, who introduced the idea that statistical trends might represent underlying social facts in his book *Suicide*, made only very limited use of them. However, by the 1950s the world had changed. The old social order had been, if not radically transformed, at least given that appearance. Miracle drugs, invented to fight infectious diseases, were widely available. The power of the atom had been unleashed on Hiroshima and Nagasaki. Scientific and mathematical challenges directly related to the war had spurred the development of computers.

Novelists in the 1940s and 1950s wrote about a world dominated by technical reason and rational planning, by engineers and their computers. The new technologies seemed to give humans mastery over the universe. In areas of science and philosophy that had yet to make significant "breakthroughs" the assumption was that logic and scientific objectivity were what was needed. The solution, it was said, lay in numbers and the clarity of concepts. When Paul Lazarsfeld moved to the United States from Germany, the social statistics that he advocated were just what an eager population of sociologists, committed to becoming more scientific, wanted.

Other forms of sociology continued to be practiced. Studies focused on interaction continued as a paradigm at the University of Chicago. But in the new intellectual context anything other than the new scientific sociology had to be justified by contrast to the prevailing view. From the early fifties until the late sixties "statistical" sociology with a functional orientation reigned almost unchallenged.

Although dissatisfactions with Parsons's version of scientific sociology emerged quickly – it seemed to present a narrow, politically conservative, view of social issues, incapable of providing the practical advice for solving social problems that young sociologists sought – an initial response to this dissatisfaction was to attempt to perfect the Parsonsian system. The assumption was that the shortcomings were caused by failures in the application of Parsons's system: the statistics were not pure enough, or the concepts not clear enough. For a time, sociology became even more scientific and statistically driven in an attempt to eradicate these problems.

It began to be clear, however, that there were deep theoretical problems involved in the notions of scientific and mathematical clarity when applied to the study of human society. Because human actions are meaningful and involve reflexivity, human intelligibility does not lend itself to "objective" mathematical study. The discipline faced a crisis and sociologists began to search for alternatives. Earlier trends in sociological theorizing, temporarily eclipsed by the new statistically driven scientific theorizing, regained some of their former popularity. Marxist and Weberian approaches to sociology enjoyed a newfound popularity in the 1960s and 1970s. Interactionism and symbolic interactionism became popular. Sociological perspectives influenced by phenomenological philosophy, existentialism, and the philosophy of Wittgenstein also began to gain ground.

Into this social climate stepped Garfinkel, with his emphasis on interactional detail and adequate description. For many young sociologists, Garfinkel provided the first introduction to phenomenology, philosophy, and a new and different appreciation of classical social theory. He was one of the first to argue that phenomenological texts were central to the sociological enterprise. Confronted by a discipline in crisis, Garfinkel and other interactionists, like Herbert Blumer, Erving Goffman, and Howard Becker, seemed for many to have arrived "just in time" to save sociology. Very few students in the 1960s were interested in understanding how to maintain the status quo. They were interested instead in change and challenge; in social movements and revolution; in new ways of thinking that were not so Western, logical, and middle class in emphasis.

Garfinkel challenged the prevailing criteria for adequate research: that studies could be considered scientific only if they aggregated numerically across clear conceptual classifications. In so doing, he challenged the very notion of technical reason that was the driving force behind scientific sociology. He believed that the processes of theoretical and mathematical justification required for acceptance by scientific sociology were logically incompatible with the phenomena of social order. Scientific sociology, as it had emerged in the 1940s and 1950s at Harvard and Columbia, was, according to Garfinkel, obscuring, rather than clarifying, the understanding of social reality.

Garfinkel believed that sociology should be engaged in explaining how phenomena of social order are achieved and recognized by participants in the first place. He assumed a world in which social order was actual, evident, and witnessable in its details. Therefore, the details of social order should be empirically observable without conceptual or theoretical mediation. He argued that social order was to be found in contingencies of local settings, not in generalizations, however conceptually clear.

Ethnomethodology stands as a direct contradiction to the faith in formalism, technical reason, and mathematicized representations of social behavior that came to define postwar sociology. Garfinkel argued that formalism depends on the enactment of social practices which remain unexamined. Even engineers and mathematicians do not work in a pure mathematical vacuum. They must speak to one another. They must create conceptual representations of the domain in which they work. Engineers must imagine the uses to which persons will put the various products they are engaged in producing. These activities involve the use of practices which are in essential respects constitutive of what science, mathematics, and engineering will turn out to be. In fact, according to Garfinkel, no domain of human endeavor is free from this requirement. Ironically, in order to succeed at endeavors based in technical reason, a detailed understanding of those ordinary practices through which persons regularly achieve recognizable and intelligible social practices is required.

## IMPACT

Since the publication of *Studies in Ethnomethodology* in 1967, Harold Garfinkel's work has had an enormous influence on various disciplines in the social sciences and humanities worldwide. Shortcomings with the "scientific" study of human society derived from various interpretations of structural functionalism and positivism in the 1960s and 1970s fueled a search in many disciplines for a new approach. Garfinkel's arguments introduced aspects of the problem of social order and intelligibility that promised to address these concerns. Garfinkel sought to restore both the perspective of the actor and the validity of adequate description of the details of social action. He took seriously the problem of interpretation proposed by hermeneutic philosophy as the alternative to positivism. However, he also and at the same time insisted on the importance of adequate empirical description.

The promise of simultaneously addressing all these issues had great appeal. In addition, Garfinkel's demonstrations of the taken-for-granted constitutive features of members' methods oriented the discipline toward the observation of social practice in a deeper and more detailed way. There has been a subtle shift since the 1960s and 1970s in what counts as adequate description, and Garfinkel played an important part in creating it. The shift crossed disciplinary boundaries and many scholars who would not think of themselves as having been interested in ethnomethodology were nevertheless influenced by Garfinkel's emphasis on members' methods and adequate description.

Researchers began to look for the underbelly of society. Informal orders were discovered everywhere: in formal institutions, in scientific practice, in classroom instruction. Wherever researchers looked there were previously unsuspected levels of detail to be uncovered. While Garfinkel was joined by Goffman and others in leading the discipline toward a more detailed look at interaction and the Interaction Order, it was Garfinkel who moved beyond the problems of self and interpretation to take a serious look at the problem of intelligibility at its most fundamental level.

His argument that even scientific practices and scientific objects are recognizably constructed social orders inspired studies in the sociology of science. His criticisms of technical reason and formalism in the scientific workplace gave rise to studies of practices in mathematics and engineering and the application of computers and other technology in the workplace. Studies of conversation influenced by Garfinkel, Sacks, and Schegloff had an impact on communication studies, semiotics, linguistics, and studies of communication in applied areas such as doctor–patient interaction, intercultural communication, legal reasoning, and various institutional and workplace settings.

Studies of institutional accounting practices, inspired by Garfinkel's theory of accounts, have focused on the generation of records during plea bargaining, on truck drivers' log keeping practices, police record keeping practices, and coroners' decisions with regard to suicide. For many with an interest in social reform his argument pointed toward the organizational production of those statistics which are offered by scientific sociology as representations of the "real" world. If administrators, politicians, and institutional workers all have ongoing organizational reasons for manipulating the generation of statistics, then surely the generation of statistics should be an important topic for a critical social science.

Furthermore, the idea that a social institution that is believed to discriminate by class and race, such as the police, the courts, schools, or a workplace, should be allowed through its own worksite practices to generate statistical accounts that support its own claims not to be discriminating, and that those statistical accounts should be taken as undeniable scientific evidence of social structure, is, in Garfinkel's view, unthinkable. Yet even today the vast majority of the articles published in the *American Sociological Review* use secondary statistical data sets generated by institutional accounts.

From Garfinkel's position, a scientific sociology based on such data can never be politically disinterested. It can only confirm the prevailing views of those institutions that generated its data. That may explain its popularity. Ethnomethodology, on the other hand, generally represented as indifferent to issues of structure and politics, is indifferent only to institutionalized structures of accountability. Ethnomethodology cannot be indifferent to political, ethical, or theoretical critique because that is essentially what it is. Garfinkel seeks to reveal the methods persons use to create the appearance that various "facts" exist independently of those methods.

Ethnomethodologists have also undertaken studies of specific disciplinary methods, such as survey research and focus group interviews. In all these studies the emphasis has been on the practices used to achieve the results in question. How and why do the police arrive at their statistics? How and why do survey researchers code responses to telephone surveys? The details of local practices that comprise the answers to the questions "how" and "why" are, according to Garfinkel, what the resulting statistics and aggregated coding schemes "really" mean. They are the "what more" to social order that is obscured by traditional theory and research.

Garfinkel's insistence that researchers achieve the "unique adequacy" requirement of methods before they attempt to answer these how and why questions has generated many studies that could be considered practical or applied research. Such "hybrid studies," done by outsiders who are also insiders, have as their aim that practitioners in the speciality area being studied will be as interested in the studies as professional sociologists. These studies include research on technical legal reasoning, classroom instruction, the work of mathematical proving, the work of scientific discovery, survey research, policing, doctor–patient interaction, workplace technology, social service delivery, traffic controllers, and jazz musicians.

Many, in fact most, of those who have developed a serious interest in ethnomethodology have also used conversational analysis, developed by Sacks, Schegloff, and Jefferson, as one of their research tools. Many of the practices essential to the constitutive features of any social setting make use of conversation, and there are essential constitutive features of conversation to which practitioners at any worksite must attend. Thus, the constitutive features of talk are inexorably intertwined with the achievement of ordinary practices.

From small beginnings with a handful of graduate students at UCLA, ethnomethodology spread quickly around the world. While several of Garfinkel's students were influential in the spread of ethnomethodology, and colleagues like Sacks and Schegloff also played an important role in promoting the popularity of ethnomethodology, its spread depended heavily on the interest of sociologists who never studied with Garfinkel and who initially knew little about ethnomethodology. Their interest had its origins in a deep dissatisfaction with the state of theory and methods in the discipline.

In recent years an increasing number of sociologists, dissatisfied with the discipline's lack of response to these concerns, have turned to poststructural and postmodern alternatives. It is interesting that while Garfinkel's position offers an important alternative to poststructuralism, it is not generally seen in that light. It is sometimes seen as a counterpart to poststructuralism, with the same indeterminacy and contingency, but rarely as an alternative that addresses the same problems in more satisfactory ways. Ironically, poststructuralists and postmodernists tend to view structure in a Parsons's Plenum sort of way, accepting the individual versus structure dichotomy, while they reject the moral validity of structures. Thus, both sides in the contemporary debate share a conception of structure that Garfinkel rejected. Consequently, his arguments, even though they constitute a profound rejection of structuralism, are not seen as addressed to that debate.

Poststructuralism begins with the understanding that it is against structures that the shared meanings of everyday life are achieved. Meanings are defined in structural opposition either to one another – "up" can only be understood in contrast to "down"' and "black" to "white" – or to institutional structures, as when a person's actions in waiting for a bus to get to work are seen to be defined by the institutions of work, or one's gender role is seen to be defined by the conceptual structure of gender terms in a given society. The essential idea is that "structures," in some fashion or other, impart meaning to everyday language and action. Then, in order to "break out," persons have to "deconstruct" the structures.

The problem is that the result of deconstruction should be a meaningless infinite regress if all shared meaning (and most private meaning) really were produced by relations between persons (or actions) and formal structure. But, in fact, the operation is often quite meaningful and revealing. This is hard to explain from within either the poststructural or the postmodern position. For Garfinkel, however, there are an unlimited number of complex ways of constructing the intelligibility of social action at the local level. When persons rebel against structure, the rebellion is made possible by these underlying endogenously produced intelligibilities. In fact, something like what Garfinkel is articulating seems to be the only explanation for how persons can rebel against structure yet have their language and activities remain mutually intelligible.

From Garfinkel's perspective, the popularity of deconstruction as a method is easy to explain. Poststructuralism is another version of theorized reality. While it is in some respects new, it is also very familiar. It promises novelty without requiring changes in the basic theorized assumptions of sociology as a discipline. In the rush to deconstruct, the social world is once again being theorized, and the interactional practices which are actually constitutive of intelligibility are being overlooked again in favor of an institutionalized view of meaning. Poststructuralism is, from Garfinkel's viewpoint, merely the flip side of structural functionalism: both posit social order and meaning in terms of a constraining relationship between individuals and social structures which threatens individual autonomy. For Garfinkel, on the other hand, the relationship between individuals and social structure is only a secondary phenomenon that needs to be seen against the backdrop of the prior achievement of mutual intelligibility and mutually intelligible practices at a more fundamental level.

Critics often ask why Garfinkel did not himself engage in clarification with regard to issues that have been so consequential for the reception of his work. I believe that his silence is due to a belief that as an argument his position could only be demonstrated theoretically. In Garfinkel's view, theoretical demonstrations depend hopelessly on imagined orders of affairs. Given his commitment to an empirical demonstration of his claims, Garfinkel feels strongly that if the argument cannot be persuasive without being theorized, it must be because the empirical demonstrations still fall somehow short of adequate description. Thus, Garfinkel has consistently met theoretical criticism by attempting to deepen the level of empirical detail in his research, not via theoretical response.[4]

Because he felt that the generic and theorized terminology of mainstream sociology rendered social orders invisible, Garfinkel has been wary of using generic terms and generalizations in his own work. His invention of new words and phrases to express the empirical social relations discovered through his research is part of what makes his work so hard to read. In order to read Garfinkel successfully one must make a commitment to treat his terminology as essential to his argument. In this regard, Garfinkel's writing resembles that of Marx, who, in his attempt to avoid treating mutually dependent social processes as though they were independent entities, constructed sentences in which the subject is also the object of the same sentence. In Garfinkel's case, the attempt to avoid theorized generalities has led to an emphasis on words which attempt to specify the concreteness of things and at the same time to specify the contingency of the various positions in which things are found. Phrases like "as of which," which multiply the propositional relationships between "objects" and the occasions upon which they are socially constructed as such, are common.

The continual emphasis in Garfinkel's work on "just-thisness," "haecceities," "details," "order," and "contingencies" is an attempt not to lose the phenomena through generalization. Trying not to refer to local order phenomena in general terms is linguistically strange. However, the importance of the contingencies of local order phenomena to his argument justifies the attempt.

Garfinkel has opened the way for a new sort of theorizing. Theorizing more broadly conceived does not have to be of the generic, categorizing, plenum sort. There is no reason, in principle, why theorists cannot be faithful to the phenomena; no reason why they have to proceed in generic terms. Garfinkel has shown us the possibility of empirical theorizing and it is in these terms that I want to refer to Garfinkel as one of the great social theorists of the twentieth century. However, he is quite right that contemporary theory has, for the most part, proceeded in terms of categories and generic terms. If I call Garfinkel a theorist, there are sure to be sociologists who will want to reduce his arguments to categories and generic terms. It is essential to note that this understanding of social theory is entirely incompatible with Garfinkel's view.

## ASSESSMENT

Garfinkel's relationship to the discipline of sociology has from the first been both highly significant and extremely ironic. Garfinkel dedicated his life work to uncovering the empirical details of orderly social practices. However, mainstream sociology defined scientific empiricism as the study of abstract conceptual representations of individuals and their normative values, represented in numerical form. Because Garfinkel's work did not fit this definition of empirical, it has been characterized by the discipline as a "micro" sociology focused on individual, contingent, and subjective matters, not on the collective empirical aspects of social structure and intelligibility.

Similarly, many micro sociologists accept a version of sociology that treats conceptual representations as the foundation of social order and meaning. Because they think of "practices" in terms of concepts and ideas, they also reject Garfinkel's claim that in studying concrete witnessable practices he is engaged in empirical research. They argue that Garfinkel is theorizing the relationship between individual concepts and shared symbolic meanings, not engaging in empirical research, as he claims. Consequently, they criticize him for ignoring the infinite regress entailed by representational accounts of meaning.

Because Garfinkel rejects assumptions fundamental to both micro and macro sociology, sociologists from both camps make opposing versions of the same criticism of his work. It is incorrect to assess Garfinkel's work as a conceptual or interpretive exercise. Garfinkel does not set up a relationship between hidden conceptual meanings and their symbolic representations. Ethnomethodology is a thoroughly empirical enterprise devoted to the discovery of social order and intelligibility as witnessable collective achievements. Nor is ethnomethodology indifferent to issues of social structure; only to issues of institutional structure as defined by mainstream sociology.

The keystone of Garfinkel's argument is that local orders exist; that these orders are witnessable in the scenes in which they are produced; and that the possibility of intelligibility is based on the actual existence and detailed enactment of these orders. Because these orders are actual, they can be empirically observed. Because these orders are collective enactments, a focus on individual subjectivity would obscure them.

The characterization of ethnomethodology as an individualistic "micro" sociology is equally wrong. With regard to sociology as a whole, the macro/micro dichotomy is dangerously misleading, tending to portray any approach to sociology that does not focus on aggregations of institutional constraint as trivial. However, with regard to the work of Garfinkel, the distinction is completely meaningless. The dichotomy assumes a distinction between institutionalized and individualistic forms of social behavior that Garfinkel has completely rejected. For Garfinkel, no *social* behavior is individualistic and social institutions only exist as, and are reproduced through, contexts of accountability. His position is neither micro nor macro.

The true irony is that Garfinkel focused on members' methods for achieving recognizable social phenomena because he *did* believe that empirically observable, collectively enacted, social structures existed and were being obscured by conventional methods of research, *not* because he wanted to study individuals. Mainstream sociology focused on statistical indicators of individual tendencies to orient toward normative goals because they *did not* believe that there were social structures that could be observed empirically. They thought they had to aggregate across general concepts to get rid of the details of particular settings and thereby reveal order as a general principle. Garfinkel, on the other hand, believed from the beginning that order was there already in the details of social settings, and that aggregating those details across general concepts was leveling the details of social order to the point of nonrecognition. Focusing on individual interpretation similarly obscures the concrete details of enacted practice.

The misinterpretations of Garfinkel have their origin in the fact that his position conflicts with basic assumptions about the institutional character of social order, and the symbolic and representational nature of meaning; assumptions essential to the macro/micro distinction, which have dominated the discipline since the mid-twentieth century. Parsons popularized an institutional view of social order that left no room for Interaction Order phenomena. In Parsons's wake, Jeffrey Alexander formalized the basic disciplinary assumptions about institutional order, arguing that sociology either took a formal institutionalized collective view (macro) or was individualistic and contingent (micro).

Prior to Parsons, the discipline did not have such a strong bias in favor of institutional order and aggregated indicators. At the end of the nineteenth century close observations of situated events played a central role in social theory and research. Classical sociologists were often exhaustive in their description and documentation of the social processes and practices they were trying to explain. Although there was a tendency to reduce observations to generalizations and ideal types, it was really only in the period after the Second World War, the heyday of positivism, when sociology, and Durkheim in particular, came under fire as idealist and unscientific, that the current situation developed.

Intellectual circles in the 1920s and 1930s were involved in a love affair with positivism and numbers. If sociology came to be considered idealist, it would lose what little institutional support it had achieved. Parsons took it upon himself to save the discipline from the charge of idealism by formulating a sociology amenable to complicated numerical generalizations. The resulting increase in institutional support for the discipline occurred at just the same time that social conditions were creating an interest in arguments and ideas that could properly be said to be sociological. Without Parsons that interest might have turned to existing departments of political science, philosophy, or economics, instead of leading to the creation of new departments of sociology all over the country.

In one sense, Parsons rescued sociology. However, once started, the demand for numerical justification began to drive the discipline. Sociology went from a concern with documenting the details of social order to a concern with becoming more mathematical and generalizable, in order to justify itself as a science.

Mid-century sociology became quite divorced from earlier concerns for adequate description and the accurate representation of the actor's point of view. The beginning of the century concern with the meaning of social actions was almost completely forgotten.

Garfinkel's position preserves those earlier concerns. The difference is that his approach to social order places the emphasis on constitutive local orders, while Parsons and classical sociologists had generally placed it on either institutional or conceptual (representational) orders. Garfinkel's argument is that there is a level of order, below (so to speak) the institutional, or theorized level of order, which constitutes the fundamental intelligibility of social action and language. This is not an order of individual interpretation or conceptual representation, but rather a constitutive order of witnessable enacted practice. Garfinkel and Parsons are talking about two different conceptions of social order, Interaction Orders versus institutional order. For Parsons, only institutional orders and individuals exist, leaving the explanation of social order without any under-pinning of fundamental intelligibility. For Garfinkel, orders at the level of witnessable practice provide a foundation of intelligibility against which institutional contexts of accountability can operate.

Insisting that Interaction Orders are fundamental, or indispensable, to socio-logy has been one of Garfinkel's greatest contributions. As the postmodern crisis makes clear, without an explanation of underlying intelligibility, social orders cannot be given a valid explanation. Because he conceived of social order strictly in institutional terms, Parsons had to invent the plenum in order to display a tendency to orderliness in society. He had to build an elaborate mechanism for displaying a tendency to order, because he believed that society was at any given point not actually ordered. Furthermore, the emphasis he placed on generalization and aggregation obscured the concrete witnessable order of social occasions from his view.

In rejecting this view, Garfinkel does not sacrifice the study of social order. He argues that in focusing on the recognizable production of practices he is studying social order. Mainstream scientific sociology, from his perspective, is studying mathematicized representations of institutionalized typifications, or accounts, not social order. It is in mainstream sociology that individual subjectivity, in the form of operationalized variables, theorized accounts, and individually pro-duced institutional accounts, is to be found, not in ethnomethodology.

For Garfinkel the earlier interest in the actor's point of view, re-emerging in contemporary sociology, was as much a dead end as the focus on institutions. Sociology could not solve its problems by connecting concepts in heads with external symbolic representations. As Wittgenstein argued, representational approaches to meaning are as problematic as trying to explain social order in terms of formal structures. As ethnomethodology developed, the external con-crete witnessable details of enacted practice came to dominate Garfinkel's approach to the problem of intelligibility.

Garfinkel did not give up the actor's point of view, which initially fueled his debate with Parsons. But he transformed it substantially, locating the experien-tial and contingent features of action, originally thought of as belonging to the actor, in the regularities of actual practices. The actor's point of view was transformed into a concern with what populations did in particular settings to achieve the recognizability of particular practices. According to Garfinkel, a population is constituted not by a set of individuals with something in common, but by a set of practices common to particular situations or events: the crowd at the coffee machine, the line at the supermarket, the "gang" at the science lab, and so on.

Instead of talking about the phenomenal properties of experience, Garfinkel began talking about the phenomenal field properties of objects. Thus, in an important sense the actor's point of view and the achieved meaning of social action no longer had to be thought of in connection with individual actors. Because, in Garfinkel's view, intelligibility is achieved in and through the enactment of observable practices, not through interpretive processes in the minds of individual actors, empirical studies of observable practices could reveal the actor's point of view.

Critics argue that the study of local social orders is not sociological because it consists only of a description of what people do and ignores the real social (i.e. institutional) constraints within which those actions took place. The constraint argument is fundamental to sociology; part of the assumption that social order is institutional. The discipline of sociology was, in an important sense, founded on Durkheim's argument that social facts exist as external constraint, rather than as artifacts of the combined psychosocial or biological impulses of a large number of persons. Therefore, when Garfinkel is interpreted as having argued against the existence of external constraint, he is thought to have repudiated the idea of social facts and thus to have rejected sociology as a whole.

However, far from repudiating the idea of external constraint, Garfinkel has reconceptualized it so as to avoid the individual versus society dichotomy and other problems inherent both in the classical theoretical formulation of this issue and in contemporary attempts to reformulate it.

Other critics, from what is sometimes called the "left" of ethnomethodology, and from the postmodern position, argue that ethnomethodology is hopelessly conceptual and theorized, and thus falls victim to its own criticisms of mainstream sociology. Such critics, however, tend to set up a straw man argument. They attribute to ethnomethodology a representational theory of meaning, equating enacted practices with subjective interpretive procedures (often mistakenly equated with the documentary method), and generally render practices in terms of concepts and beliefs. As ethnomethodology treats practices as consisting of their concrete witnessable details, the attribution is incorrect. There is nothing circular in the argument that in order to convey meaning visible concrete actions must be recognizable to others as actions of a sort, and that the constitutive features of what counts and does not count as actions of a sort must therefore be witnessable to participants and available for empirical observation.

For Garfinkel, structure and order are primarily located in local practices, which constitute a primary constraint, with formal institutions acting as a constraint in limited and specific ways via institutional contexts of accountability. According to Garfinkel, "The instructably observable achieved coherent detail of the coherence of objects *is* the fulfillment of Durkheim's promise that the objective reality of social facts is sociology's fundamental principle."[5] Garfinkel has offered a version of external constraint as accountability. Persons are accountable both at the local level for a commitment to a local order of practices, and, at what sociology has generally termed the institutional level, accountable to what Mills (1940) referred to as a shared "vocabulary of motives." Mills argued that persons in institutions do not act by following rules, they act by accounting for what they have done in terms of vocabularies of motive and justification which only retrospectively reference the rules.

In Mills's view, institutional practices bear a peculiar relationship to institutional rules, with rules constituting a context of justification for action, rather than something followed in order to produce the action. According to Mills, social actors examine the desirability of proposed courses of action, asking themselves what people would say if they did a particular thing, or considering how they could explain, or account for, a particular course of action. If a satisfactory explanation can be generated from within the shared vocabulary of motives, then an action can be considered to be in accord with the rules, no matter what form it takes. Therefore, while the rules constrain the practices, in this peculiar way of constraining what will count after the fact as having been a case of following the rules, they are not constitutive of action in its course.

Garfinkel's treatment of accounts goes beyond Mills in proposing a complex network of contexts of accountability at various levels of social organization. In Garfinkel's view persons can be accountable to external institutions, such as government agencies or scientific disciplines, at the same time that they are accountable to the expectations of their colleagues with regard to normal workplace procedures. Persons are constantly accountable for their production of recognizable talk and movements, even while they are managing institutional levels of accountability. Finally, they can also and at the same time be accountable to the properties of natural phenomena, which may refuse to cooperate in producing an accountable display for colleagues.

By extending Mills's theory of accounts in this way Garfinkel is able to consider a wide range of theoretical issues. The theoretical line of argument which Garfinkel's inquiry into "rules" (i.e. instructed action) and accountability develops includes: the classic distinction between traditional and modern rational action (Durkheim, Weber, Toennies, Simmel); the seminal argument of Mills with regard to contexts of accountability; many of the Chicago School studies of organizations and bureaucracies, which revealed the paradox of rules and informal cultures within organizations.

His position also runs parallel to other arguments developed during the 1950s and 1960s regarding the relationship between rules and practice, including: Goffman's study of asylums (1961); similar studies in prisons and psychology by Sykes (1958) and Szasz (1961); labeling theory, which examines the relationship between institutional behavior, the institutional production of statistics, and the beliefs and practices of the populations which staff those organizations; the distinction in philosophy between constitutive and other rules (Warnock, 1958; Searle, 1968); and the extension of this argument into game theory.

Garfinkel's focus on intelligibility also extends a second line of inquiry: attempts by classical social theorists to frame epistemology and intelligibility sociologically (Durkheim, 1915; Weber, 1921; Rawls, 1996). It is important to understand that classical social theorists were philosophers who challenged the limits of their discipline on the issues of epistemology and intelligibility. If, for instance, one begins with Durkheim's theory of the social origins of the categories of the understanding (in *The Elementary Forms*), then one finds Garfinkel continuing the inquiry into the question of intelligibility raised by Durkheim, and extended by Mead, Husserl, Heidegger, Mills, and Schutz, but all but forgotten by both mainstream scientific sociology and its postmodern counterpart.

In the *Elementary Forms of the Religious Life* Durkheim took on the philosophical problem of knowledge. Addressing the differences between Kant and Hume over the origins of human reason, Durkheim argued that the categories of the understanding have their origins in certain concrete social settings. He argued that those social settings supply the concrete experience of general ideas that Hume found the natural world could not supply and Kant had argued must be innate.

Durkheim argued that even key ideas like time, space, force, and causality have a social and not a natural empirical or *a priori* origin. As Durkheim realized, this argument cast the problem of knowledge in an entirely new light. In locating the conditions for intelligibility in the concrete social surroundings of daily life, and in taking the problem of intelligibility as the central problem sociology must address before constructing a theory of social order, Durkheim stands as a direct precursor of Garfinkel. Garfinkel continues to search for the foundations of human intelligibility, reason, and logic in the details of collaborative social practice.

Garfinkel has from the beginning been blessed with a vision of social order that allowed him to see order being produced around him in ordinary events which the rest of us experience as finished products, but which Garfinkel experienced as events produced from patterned details over their course. This is brilliantly evident in his first paper, "Color Trouble." In this paper, we get a picture of Garfinkel as a young student taking a bus home from college. When black passengers are ordered to the back of the bus and won't go, Garfinkel sees something the rest of us would have missed. As the driver engages in his dispute with the black passengers, he is formulating his actions in terms of the excuse he will have to give for being late at the end of the line. He is accountable not for his morals, but for being on time. The longer the dispute takes, the more important will be the acceptability of the account the driver can give, and it will thereby come to pass that color will turn out to be one of the troubles with busses which account for their lateness on certain southern runs.

Garfinkel's description of this incident is masterful, and the essay won an award as one of the best short stories of 1939. More importantly, however, it demonstrates the continuity of vision which has characterized Garfinkel's career as a social thinker. We can imagine Garfinkel sitting in social theory classes at Harvard being confronted with generic categorizations. He recalls that in his first theory class at Harvard the students were told to make up a social theory. The thing was to be purely an invention, an exercise in logic and the generic use of categories. As a young man with a keen sense for the actual unfolding of social order in the everyday world around him, this sort of theorizing, which operated on the assumption that everyday social scenes were not inherently orderly, and that their details were irrelevant, rubbed the wrong way. He quickly realized that his vision of a stable constitutive order of practice stood in contradiction to the received and approved methods of formal analytic theorizing. Through the years Garfinkel has remained true to his vision.

## Notes

1 Haecceities is one of many words that Garfinkel has adopted over the years to indicate the importance of the infinite contingencies in both situations and practices. He has also used the words quiddities, contingencies, and details in this regard. I believe that Garfinkel changes his terminology frequently so as to maintain the open and provisional nature of his arguments. As persons develop a conventional sense for a word he has used, he changes it.
2 His Harvard cohort included Gardner Lindsey, Henry Riecken, David Schneider, David Aberle, Brewster Smith, Duncan MacRae, Bernard Barber, Frank Sutton, James Olds, Fred Strodbeck, Marion Levy, Hans Lucas Taueber, and Renee Fox, any of whom became prominent sociologists and several of whom were instrumental in furthering Garfinkel's career.
3 The faculty at Princeton included Marion Levy and Duncan MacRae, who had been at Harvard with Garfinkel, and Wilbert Moore. Edward Tiryakian, an undergraduate at Princeton for whom Garfinkel served as senior thesis advisor, would later publish Garfinkel's paper, co-authored with Harvey Sacks, "On Formal Structures of Practical Action."
4 Unfortunately, most of these studies remain unpublished.
5 Personal communication.

## Bibliography

### Writings of Harold Garfinkel

Color Trouble. 1939. In Edward O'Brian (ed.), *Best Short Stories of 1939.*
*Studies in Ethnomethodology.* 1967. Englewood Cliffs, NJ: Prentice Hall.
On Formal Structures of Practical Action (with Harvey Sacks). 1970. In Edward Tiryakian and John McKinney (eds), *Theoretical Sociology.* New York: Appleton Century Crofts.
The Work of a Discovering Science Construed with Materials from the Optically Discovered Pulsar (with Michael Lynch and Eric Livingston). 1981.
Evidence for Locally Produced, Naturally Accountable Phenomena of Order, Logic, Reason, Meaning, Method, etc., in and as of the Essential Haecceity of Immortal Ordinary Society. 1988. *Sociological Theory,* 6(1), 103–9.
Two Incommensurable Asymmetrically Alternate Technologies of Social Analysis (with Lawrence Weider). 1992. In Graham Watson and Robert M. Seiler (eds), *Text in Context.* Newbury Park, CA: Sage, pp. 172–206.
Ethnomethodology's Program. 1996. *Social Psychology Quarterly,* 59(1), 5–21.

## Further reading

Baudrillard, Jean (1975) *Mirror of Production*. St Louis: Telos Press.

Baudrillard, Jean (1993) *Symbolic Exchange and Death*. Thousand Oaks, CA: Sage

Becker, Howard (1963) *Outsiders: Studies in the Sociology of Deviance*. New York: Free Press.

Blumer, Herbert (1969) *Symbolic Interaction: Perspective and Method*. Berkeley: University of California Press.

Cooley, Charles Horton (1902) *Human Nature and the Social Order*. New York: Scribner's.

Durkheim, Émile (1912) *The Elementary Forms of The Religious Life*. Chicago: Free Press.

Goffman, Erving (1961) *Asylums*. New York: Anchor Books.

Goffman, Erving (1963) *The Presentation of Self in Everyday Life*. New York: Anchor.

Gurwitsch, Aron (1964) *The Field of Consciousness*. Duquesne, PA: Duquesne University Press.

Habermas, Jürgen (1981) *The Theory of Communicative Action*. Boston: Beacon Press.

Heidegger, Martin (1962) *Being and Time*. London: SCM Press.

Hume, David (1739) *A Treatise of Human Nature*. Oxford: Oxford University Press.

Husserl, Edmund (1962) *Ideas*. New York: Collier Books.

Kant, Immanuel (1929) *Critique of Pure Reason*. New York: St Martin's Press.

Kaufmann, Felix (1944) *Methodology of the Social Sciences*. Oxford: Oxford University Press.

Lewin, Kurt (1938) *The Conceptual Representation and the Measurement of Psychological Forces*. Durham, NC: Duke University Press.

Mead, George Herbert (1934) *Mind, Self, and Society*. Chicago: University of Chicago Press.

Mead, George Herbert (1938) *Philosophy of the Act*. Chicago: University of Chicago Press.

Mills, C. Wright (1940) Situated Action and the Vocabulary of Motives. *American Sociological Review*, 5, 904–93.

Parsons, Talcott (1937) *The Structure of Social Action*. Chicago: Free Press.

Rawls, John (1996) Durkheim's Epistemology: the Neglected Argument. *American Journal of Sociology*, 102(2), 430–82.

Sacks, Harvey, Schegloff, Emmanuel, and Jefferson, Gail (1977) The Simplest Systematics for Turntaking in Conversation. *Language*, 50, 696–735.

Scheff, Thomas (1966) *Being Mentally Ill: a Sociological Theory*. Chicago: Aldine.

Schutz, Alfred (1967) *The Phenomenology of the Social World*. Evanston, IL: Northwestern University Press (originally published in German in 1932).

Searle, John (1968) *Speech Acts*. Berkeley: University of California Press.

Sykes, Gresham (1958) *The Society of Captives*. Princeton, NJ: Princeton University Press.

Szasz, Thomas (1961) *The Myth of Mental Illness: Foundations of a Theory of the Social World*. New York: Harper and Row.

Thomas, W. I. (1927) *The Polish Peasant in Europe and America*. New York: Alfred A. Knopf.

Warnock, Geoffrey J. (1967) *The Philosophy of Perception*. London: Oxford University Press.

Weber, Max (1921) *Economy and Society*. New York: Bedminster Press.

Znaniecki, Florian (1936) *Social Actions*. New York: Farrar and Rinehart.

# 18

## Daniel Bell

### MALCOLM WATERS

Daniel Bell (born 1919) was probably the most famous sociologist of his generation. He was hailed as the prophet of the emergence of a new society, the postindustrial society, and as one of the leading conservative critics of contemporary culture. Bell has been a controversial figure since he suggested in the 1960s that ideological conflicts had disappeared from modern society, but his work has been the spur for a recent flood of writing on the "new society." Bell's intellectual biography begins with an engagement with questions of work, the labor movement, and American capitalism, flowing through to more detailed discussions of political extremism, the new postindustrial society, and the disintegration of culture associated with postmodernism The three works that made Bell famous were *The End of Ideology*, *The Coming of Postindustrial Society*, and *The Cultural Contradictions of Capitalism*.

Daniel Bell's theory is historical and substantive rather than formal and analytic. It proposes that society is organized in three realms. However, Bell is doubtless better known for certain big theoretical ideas about change within each of these realms: the postindustrial society, the end of ideology, and the cultural contradictions of capitalism.

### THE THEORY

The three realms of society are the techno-economic structure (TES; sometimes the "social structure"), the polity, and culture. *Society* is itself one of three superordinate regions (that Bell, confusingly, also describes as "realms"), the others being *nature* and *technology* (Bell, 1991, pp. 3–33). Nature is "a realm outside of man whose designs are reworked by men" (ibid., p. 8). It has two components: the *Umwelt*, the geographical environment, the world of organic and inorganic objects that is open to human intervention; and *physis*, the analytic pattern of natural relationships. Technology is "the instrumental ordering of human experience within a logic of efficient means, and the direction of nature to use its powers for material gain" (ibid., p. 20). It clearly impacts on nature in so far as it opens up possibilities for the transformation of the *Umwelt*, but it also has profound implications for society, creating consumption-based mass societies, elaborately differentiated occupational systems, and synchronized cultures. Bell is a convinced social constructionist, for whom society is "a set of social arrangements, created by men, to regulate normatively the exchange of wants and satisfactions" (ibid., p. 29, italics removed). It is "a social contract, made not in the past but in the present, in which the constructed rules are obeyed if they seem fair and just" (ibid., p. 29).

However, Bell's subdivision of society into three realms is more important. There is some inconsistency in terminology: in *The Winding Passage* (1991, pp. 3–33), the three realms are nature, technology and society, while the three "dimensions" of society are "social" structure, polity, and culture (ibid., p. 31); but in *The Cultural Contradictions of Capitalism* (1979, p. 10), the "techno-economic" structure, polity, and culture are listed as distinct "realms." Further, in *Winding Passage* the latter trinity is said to be a feature of all societies but in *Cultural Contradictions* Bell is agnostic on whether the scheme can be applied generally and reserves it only for modern society (ibid., p. 10). In general though, apart from the single essay in *Winding Passage*, Bell uses the word "realm" for the less abstract societal trinity rather than the more abstract existential trinity, and this is the usage that will be employed here. We can also assume that the three realms are universal aspects of all societies but become separate and autonomous only in modern society.

The *techno-economic structure* (TES) is the realm of economic life, the arena of social arrangements for the production and distribution of goods and services. Such activities imply applications of technology to instrumental ends and result in a stratified occupational system. The axial principle of the modern TES is functional rationality. It consistently drives towards minimizing cost and optimizing output and is therefore regulated by the process that Bell calls *economizing*. So we assess the development of the TES in terms of its level of efficiency, productivity, and productiveness. Indeed, change proceeds along the path of substituting technological processes and social arrangements that are more productive and efficient for those that are less so. *Contra* Weber, who locates the development of bureaucracy in the emergence of the modern state, Bell argues that bureaucracy is the axial structure of the TES. The more that technological functions become specialized, the greater is the need to coordinate these functions and therefore the more elaborate and hierarchical become the organizational arrangements that human beings put in place to accomplish such coordination. The lifeworlds of the TES are, in a terminology that might be traced to Lukács (1968), "reified" worlds in which the individual is subordinated to roles specified in organizational charts. They are also authoritarian worlds that subordinate individual ends to the goals of the organization orchestrated by a technocratic management that recognizes the validity only of the functional and the instrumental (Bell, 1979b, p. 11; 1991, p. 31).

The *polity* is the set of social arrangements that frames a conception of justice and then regulates social conflict within that framework. Justice is elaborated within a set of traditions or a constitution. Regulation is accomplished by applications of power; that is, by the legitimate use of force and, in many societies, by the rule of law. It is therefore a system of societal authority involving the distribution of legitimate power in society. In a modern society, the axial principle specifies that power is legitimated by reference to the consent of the governed. Moreover, this axial principle is egalitarian in so far as it specifies that each person must have a more or less equal voice in providing this consent. Because equality of political participation gives expression to the material and cultural aspirations of all members of society, it extends into other areas of social life via the institution of citizenship that implies equality of access to legal, social and cultural entitlements. The axial structure is a system of representation that allows general consent to be expressed through organized arrangements – that is, political parties, lobby groups, and social movements – that can funnel claims to the center (Bell, 1979b, pp. 11–12).

Bell's version of *culture* is much narrower than the conventional sociological or anthropological definitions that specify it as the overall pattern or shape of life in a society. While recognizing that culture includes the cognitive symbolizations of science and philosophy (ibid., p. 12n), as well as the character structure of individuals (Bell, 1991, p. 31), he restricts his interest in culture to the arena of expressive symbolism: "efforts, in painting, poetry, and fiction, or within the religious forms of litany, liturgy and ritual, which seek to explore and express the meanings of human existence in imaginative form" (Bell, 1979b, p. 12). These expressive symbolizations must always address what Bell regards as the universal and irreducible fundamentals of human existence, the nature and meaning of death, tragedy, heroism, loyalty, redemption, love, sacrifice, and spirituality (Bell, 1979b, p. 12; 1991, p. 31). The axial principle of modern culture is self-expression and self-realization; that is, the value of cultural objects must be assessed against the subjective sentiments and judgments of those who produce and consume them and not against objective standards (Bell, 1979b, p. xvii). The axial structures of modern culture are arrangements for the production and reproduction of meanings and artifacts.

Bell explicitly asserts that, 'there are not simple determinate relations among the three realms' (ibid., p. 12). This is because the direction and the pattern, what he often calls the rhythm, of change in each of them is fundamentally different. In the TES change is linear or progressive, involving an upward curve in production and efficiency. There is no such rule in the polity, where the pattern of change consists in alternation between opposing configurations. People can alternate between the efficiencies of oligarchy and the equalities of democracy, between the expertise of elitism and homogenization of mass society, or between the unifying tendencies of centralization and the localism of confederate systems (Bell, 1991, pp. xx, 31). By contrast, cultural change is recursive. While retaining its past, culture can follow one of two paths in developing upon it. It can follow the additive, developmental and incremental path of tradition, building on well established genres but not stepping outside them. Alternatively, it can engage in indiscriminate mixing and borrowing from several diverse cultural traditions (syncretism).

Because the rhythm of change is different in each realm, each follows its own path through time and thus each has its own separate history. In certain periods of time the particular formations apparent in each of the realms will be synchronized and there will be an accidental unity among them. Bell identifies twelfth-century Europe and the "apogee" of bourgeois society in the last third of the nineteenth century as examples of such periods (ibid., p. xx). However at other times, perhaps at most other times, the realms will be disjunctive; that is, their normative specifications will contradict one another at the level of experience. Disjunction between the realms is a structural source of tension in society and therefore the fulcrum of change. In contradistinction to holistic theories of society, then, Bell's theoretical approach proposes not only that disjunction of the realms is a normal condition of society but also that it is the central feature of contemporary society in particular.

However, the initial pattern of modern society was one of unification between the realms in the formation known as "bourgeois society." It involved a conjunction between individual entrepreneurship and personal economic responsibility in the TES, liberal resistance to the constraints of an enlarged and active state in the polity, and an emphasis on expressing the self, rather than a set of issues prescribed by tradition, in culture. However, a radical hiatus rapidly developed between the TES and culture. At first it involved a contradiction between the disciplinary constraints of work and the quest for a personal sense of the sublime and for emotional excitement in cultural expression. The more the ethic of work disappeared and the more that human labor became subjected to an authoritarian hierarchy, the more cultural tradition was eroded. Social legitimation, as Bell puts it, passed from the sphere of religion to modernism itself, to the cultivation of the individual personality. The economy responded to this demand, mass producing cultural artifacts and images. Modernism turned into a restless search for titillation and novelty, a "rule of fad and fashion: of multiples for the *culturati*, hedonism for the middle classes, pornotopia for the masses. And in the very nature of fashion, it has trivialized the culture" (Bell, 1979b, p. xxvii).

Bell explores this disintegration of modern society through three more specific theoretical accounts, one for each of the realms, for which he is better known than for the general theory. Perhaps the best known of these is Bell's theory of social change called the "postindustrial society." It argues that contemporary societies are or will be going through a shift so that industrial society will give way to a new techno-economic structure that will be as different from industrial society as industrial society is from pre-industrial society. We can perhaps begin by considering the distinctions that Bell makes between these three (1976, pp. 116–19, 126–9). A *pre-industrial society* can be characterized as "a game against nature" that centers on attempts to extract resources from the natural environment. It involves primary-sector industries carried out in a context of limited land supply and climatic and seasonal variation. An *industrial society* is "a game against fabricated nature" centering on the manufacturing and processing of tangible goods by semi-skilled factory workers and engineers.

By contrast, a *postindustrial society* is "a 'game between persons' in which an 'intellectual technology,' based on information, rises alongside of machine technology" (ibid., p. 116). The postindustrial society involves industries from three sectors: the tertiary industries of transportation and utilities; the quaternary industries of trade, finance, and capital exchange; and the quinary industries of health, education, research, public administration, and leisure. Among these, the last is definitive because the key occupations are the professional and technical ones with scientists at the core (ibid., pp. 117–18).

Bell elaborates his ideal-typical construct of the postindustrial society in terms of five dimensions (ibid., pp. 14–33):

- There will be a unilinear progression between industrial sectors (primary through quinary) and a corresponding shift in the labor force toward a *service economy*. Accordingly, "the first and simplest characteristic of a postindustrial society is that the majority of the labor force is no longer engaged in agriculture or manufacturing but in services, which are defined, residually, as trade, finance, transport, health, recreation, research, education, and government" (ibid., p. 15).
- The pre-eminent, although not necessarily the majority of, occupations in the society will be *the professional and technical class*, whose occupations require a tertiary level of education. The core will be scientists and engineers and together they will become a knowledge class that displaces the propertied bourgeoisie.
- *Theoretical knowledge* is the defining "axial principle" of the postindustrial society. The organization of the society around knowledge becomes the basis for social control, the direction of innovation, and the political management of new social relationships. Bell stresses that in a postindustrial society this knowledge is theoretical, rather than traditional or practical, in character. It involves the codification of knowledge into abstract symbolic systems that can be applied in a wide variety of situations.
- The advance of theoretical knowledge allows the *planning of technology*, including forward assessments of its risks, costs, and advantages.
- The society is based on a *new intellectual technology*, the software and the statistical or logical formulae that are entered into computers.

In the paperback edition of this work Bell alters this list of dimensions. The planning dimension is eliminated and seven new characteristics are added (Bell, 1976, pp. xvi–xix):

- Work focuses on an engagement in relationships with other people.
- The expansion of the services sector provides a basis for the economic independence of women that had not previously been available.
- Scientific institutions and their relationship with other institutions are the essential feature of the postindustrial society.

- Situses replace classes. Major conflicts will occur between the four functional situses (scientific, technological, administrative, and cultural) and the five institutional situses (business, government, university and research, social welfare, and military).
- Position will be allocated on the basis of education and skill rather than wealth or cultural advantage.
- Scarcity of goods will disappear in favor of scarcities of information and time.
- Society will follow a cooperative, rather than an individualistic, strategy in the generation and use of information.

However, the core of his proposal is that that there are two "large" dimensions by which one decides whether a social structure has entered a postindustrial phase. These are the centrality of theoretical knowledge (including by implication, the employment of science as a means to technological change) and the expansion of the quinary service sector.

A curious feature of Bell's political sociology is that its central and most controversial idea is not of his own origination. Bell (1988, p. 411) himself notes that the phrase "the end of ideology" was first used by Albert Camus in 1946. It entered sociology in the hands of one of Bell's intellectual confidants, Raymond Aron, who wrote a chapter entitled "The End of the Ideological Age?" for his book attacking Marxism called *The Opium of the Intellectuals* (reprinted in Waxman, 1968, pp. 27–48). Bell selected the theme as the title for a collection of essays on class and politics first published in 1960, but addressed it explicitly only in an epilogue.

Ideology is for Bell a secular religion: "a set of ideas, infused with passion" that "seeks to transform the whole way of life" (Bell, 1988, p. 400). Ideology performs the important function of converting ideas into social levers. It does so precisely by that infusion of passion, by its capacity to release human emotions and to channel their energies into political action, much as religion channels emotional energy into ritual and artistic expression. Ideology was at least partly able to fill the "psychic" gap left by the secularization processes of the nineteenth century by emphasizing the continuity of collective triumph against individual mortality. The political ideologies of the nineteenth century were also strengthened by two important alliances: with a rising class of intellectuals seeking to establish status against lack of recognition by the business bourgeoisie; and with the positive values of science that could measure and indicate progress.

"Today," Bell (1988, p. 402) asserts, "these ideologies are exhausted." He gives three causes: the violent oppression carried out by ruling communist parties against their populations; the amelioration of the worst effects of the capitalist market and the emergence of the welfare state; and the emergence of such new philosophies as existentialism and humanism, which emphasized the stoic-theological ontology of humanity, against such romantic philosophies as Marxism and liberalism, which emphasized the perfectibility of human nature. Bell's conclusion is captured in the following passage:

[O]ut of all this history, one simple fact emerges: for the radical intelligentsia, the old ideologies have lost their "truth" and their power to persuade.

Few serious minds believe any longer that one can set down "blueprints" and through "social engineering" bring about a new utopia of social harmony. At the same time, the older counter-beliefs have lost their intellectual force as well. Few "classic" liberals insist that the State should play no role in the economy, and few serious conservatives...believe that the Welfare State is "the road to serfdom" ...there is today a rough consensus among intellectuals on political issues: the acceptance of the Welfare State; the desirability of decentralized power; a system of mixed economy and of political pluralism. In that sense too the ideological age has ended. (Bell, 1988, pp. 402–3)

Bell is not, it must be stressed, entirely triumphalist about this development. He mourns the spent passions of intellectualized politics and wonders how the energies of the young can be channeled into them. And he also pleads for the retention of utopias as focuses for human aspiration, because without them society is reduced to a meaningless materialism.

Doubtless the most sociologically influential of Bell's arguments about the disintegration of the realms of modern society is his analysis of its cultural contradictions (Bell, 1979b). His general typification of modern culture can be found within his analysis of modernity. He defines modernity thus: "Modernity is individualism, the effort of individuals to remake themselves, and, where necessary, to remake society in order to allow design and choice" (Bell, 1990a, p. 72). It implies the rejection of any "naturally" ascribed or divinely ordained order, of external authority, and of collective authority in favor of the self as the sole point of reference for action. Although not every sociologist would agree with him, Bell adduces that sociology frames five important propositions about modernity (ibid., pp. 43–4):

- that society is constructed out of a social contract between individuals;
- that human beings are dualistic, having an original self and an imposed social self, and therefore face the prospect of self-estrangement or alienation;
- that religion is a superstition that precludes self-awareness;
- that modernity involves an autonomization of the value-spheres of culture (art, morality and justice) which, in particular, involves the differentiation of economics from morality and art from religion;
- that human nature is not universal but that the character of any particular human being is determined by that person's location in social structure (by occupation, ethnicity, gender, etc.).

Under modernity there can be no question about the moral authority of the self. The only question is that of how the self is to be fulfilled – by hedonism, by acquisitiveness, by faith, by the privatization of morality, or by sensationalism.

If bourgeois Protestantism was the privatized–moralistic answer to this question, the shift to a more hedonistic response, Bell argues, could only be confirmed once modernizing changes had also taken place in the realm of social (techno-economic) structure. The transformation of modern culture is due, he now asserts, "singularly" to the emergence of mass consumption and the increased affluence of lower socioeconomic groups (Bell, 1979b, p. 66). The techno-economic changes that made mass consumption possible and desirable began in the 1920s. They were of two types, technological and sociological. A key technological development was the multiplication of human effort by the application of electrical power to manufacturing and to domestic tasks. Others took place in the areas of transportation and the mass media, the latter in the forms of the cinema and radio. The sociological inventions were, for Bell, even more profound. They were: the moving assembly line that reduced the cost of consumer durables, especially cars; the development of advertising and market-ing systems that could cultivate consumer taste; and the extension of consumer credit through installment plans, time payments, personal loans, and the like. These spelt the end of Protestant bourgeois culture.

Bell's critique of modernity centers on the absence of a moral or transcend-ental ethic that is displaced by a mere individualized anxiety. In Puritan com-munities guilt was assuaged by repentance. In mass society anxiety is assuaged by psychotherapy, a process that for Bell is bound to fail because security of identity can only be accomplished within a moral context. This transformation is but one consequence of the contradictions that arise from the cultural develop-ments of modernity. The primary contradiction lies between cultural norms of hedonism and social structural norms of work discipline. But there is also an enormous contradiction within the social structure itself: a good worker delays gratification but a good consumer looks for immediate gratification. Bell con-cludes that this means "One is to be 'straight' by day and a 'swinger' by night"; and then cannot resist an exclamatory protest: "This is self-fulfillment and self-realization!" (ibid., p. 72).

This brings Bell to "an extraordinary sociological puzzle," that of why the cultural movement of modern*ism* that repeatedly attacks and dirempts modern social structure and bourgeois culture should have persisted for more than a century in the face of this contradiction. He defines modernism as: "the self-willed effort of a style and sensibility to remain in the forefront of 'advancing consciousness'" (ibid., p. 46). This attempt can be expressed in terms of several possible descriptions. First, it can be described as *avant garde*, as rejecting elitist cultural traditions in favor of a reinsertion of life into art. Second, it is advers-arial: "The legend of modernism is that of the free creative spirit at war with the bourgeoisie" (ibid., p. 40). Last, it is impenetrable within conventional under-standings and requires intellectual gyrations to be appreciated: "It is willfully opaque, works with unfamiliar forms, is self-consciously experimental, and seeks deliberately to disturb the audience – to shock it, shake it up, even to transform it as if in a religious conversion" (ibid., p. 46). This gives modernism an esoteric appeal, as Bell intones slightly ironically, but it also denies its other claims to being adversarial and *avant garde* – an elitist indulgence can be nothing but privileged. In modernism content and form disappear in favor of medium as the central expression. In art the stress is on paint, its means of application, and substitutes for it; music stresses sounds rather than harmony; poetry emphasizes "breath" and phonemics; literature employs wordplay as against plot or genre; drama promotes action and spectacle at the expense of characterization.

The adversarial "legend," as Bell calls it, has now been extended to order of all kinds. The free, creative spirit of the artist is now at war with "'civilization' or 'repressive tolerance' or some other agency that curtails 'freedom'" (ibid., p. 40). This adversarial strategy has, in general, been highly successful. The modern cultural arena has divorced from the capitalist system that spawned it and has become self-referential. The "hierophants of culture" now construct the audience and in dominating and exploiting it have come to constitute a cultural class. They have grown sufficiently in number to establish group networks and not to be treated as deviant, and they have independent control of the material substructure of artistic expression – galleries, film studios, weekly magazines, universities, and so on. From this lofty salient they sally forth to mount their attacks on crusty tradition:

> Today, each new generation, starting off at the benchmarks attained by the adversary culture of its cultural parents, declares in sweeping fashion that the status quo represents backward conservatism or repression, so that in a widening gyre, new and fresh assaults on the social structure are mounted. (ibid., p. 41)

The emphasis-on-medium and the rage-against-order are two of the three dimensions of contemporary modernism that Bell isolates. However, the third dimension, what he calls "the eclipse of distance" (ibid., pp. 108–19), is the one to which he gives the most attention. The classical fine arts followed two central principles: they were rational in that they organized space and time into a consistent and unified expression; and they were mimetic in that they sought to mirror or represent life and nature. Modernism denies these externalities and emphasizes instead the interior life, rejecting the constraints of the world and glorifying expressions of the self. Bell repeats the terms sensation, simultaneity, immediacy and impact as the syntax of modernism. Against the contemplative character of classical art, each of the artistic modernist movements (Impressionism, post-Impressionism, Futurism, Expressionism, and Cubism) intends:

> on the syntactical level, to break up ordered space; in its aesthetic, to bridge the distance between object and spectator, to "thrust" itself on the viewer and establish itself immediately by impact. One does not interpret the scene; instead, one feels it as a sensation and is caught up by that emotion. (ibid., p. 112)

Bell finds similar syntactical and aesthetic patterns in literature and music. Modern literature seeks to plunge the reader into the maelstrom of the emotions, while music abandons structure in its entirety.

The theory of modernism connects with the three realms argument. The disjunctions between culture and social structure are sustained by a mutual divorce. The cognitive expressions that arise from the social (techno-economic) structure are rapidly reifying and rationalizing human experience: extreme levels of occupational differentiation separate persons from the roles that they occupy; the proliferation of knowledge subcultures prevents the formation of a single expressive tradition that can speak to all; and the mathematization of symbolic representations leaves society without a common cultural language. Modernism is itself complicit in this development because, in rejecting the possibility of a common style, it prevents any claim that it is a culture at all. Modernist culture is differentiating rapidly into a variety of "demesnes," it lacks authoritative centers, it focuses on the instantaneity of the visual, electronic media rather than the permanence of print, and it denies the rationality of the cosmos. The outcome of these dual forces is the diremption of culture as an idea. In an important sense, Bell regards modern society as a society without a culture.

However, if Bell is worried about the effects of modernism then he is positively horrified by the prospects implied by the rise of postmodernism. Bell regards postmodernism as an essentially modernist trend, but as one which carries modernist logic to extremes. Postmodernism substitutes instinctual and erotic justifications for aesthetic and humanistic ones. In the hands of Michel Foucault and Norman O. Brown, "It announced not only the 'de-construction of Man' and the end of the humanist credo, but also the 'epistemological break' with genitality and the dissolution of focussed sexuality into the polymorph perversity of oral and anal pleasures" (Bell, 1990a, p. 69). It legitimated both homosexual liberation and a hippie-rock-drug culture, the latter striking directly at the motivational system that sustains an industrial or postindustrial TES. In a jaundiced phrase, Bell notes that, "the culturati, ever ready, follow[ed] the winds of fashion" (ibid., p. 70), as artists and architects took up the slogan to attack the boundary between high and popular culture. Postmodernist art, architecture, and music emphasize pastiche and playfulness, in Bell's view, at the expense of creativity and genuine style.

> What passes for serious culture today lacks both content and form, so that the visual arts are primarily decorative and literature a self-indulgent babble or con-trived experiment. Decoration, by its nature, no matter how bright and gay, becomes, in its finite and repetitive patterns, mere wallpaper, a receding back-ground incapable of engaging the viewer in the renewable re-visions of perception. Self-referential literature, when both the self and the referent repeat the same old refrains, becomes a tedious bore, like Uno in the circus, showing that he can raise himself on one finger. A culture of re-cycled images and twice-told tales is a culture that has lost its bearings. (ibid., p. 70)

## THE PERSON

Daniel Bell was born in 1919 in the Lower East Side of New York City. Most of his family had chain-migrated from the Bialystok area that lies between Poland and Belarus. His paternal grandfather sold coal in winter and ice in summer from a horse-drawn cart. The family name was Bolotsky, but this was probably an invention only a few generations old, constructed to avoid military service. His father died when he was eight months old and he spent much of his childhood, along with his mother and siblings, with other extended kin, usually maternal sisters. By the age of eleven Bell had a new legal guardian, his paternal uncle Samuel Bolotsky. Samuel was a dentist and upwardly mobile and the name Bolotsky did not fit such a career. So a group of cousins got together to choose new names – some became Ballin, some Ballot, and some Bell.

Not withstanding the latter developments, Bell experienced the full gamut of poor, immigrant Jewish experience: Yiddish as the first language; Hebrew school; ethnic street gangs; petty crime; racketeering; and the public poverty of water-front shacks. By his own supposition, these experiences of poverty predisposed him to become a socialist. When he was thirteen he joined the Young People's Socialist League, one of a number of socialist groups that lived in an uneasy relationship with the Jewish garment-workers' unions. An enduring picture of Bell is that at that tender age he spent long hours in the Ottendorfer branch of the New York Public Library reading avidly on socialism, but also on sociology.

Bell entered the City College of New York as an undergraduate in 1935, majoring in classics. He chose to do so on the advice of a brilliant young communist instructor named Moses Finkelstein, who suggested that ancient history was the best preparation for sociology because one could there examine entire and coherent cultures. After Bell graduated in 1938 he spent a year in graduate school at Columbia University, but without any apparent result. He left, for reasons unexplained, and spent most of the next twenty years working as a journalist. Most of the years of the Second World War were spent at the *New Leader,* a vehicle mainly used by social-democratic supporters of the union movement, first as a staff writer and then as managing editor. From 1948 to 1958 he was a staff writer and then Labor Editor at *Fortune*, the voice of American big business.

Bell's academic career began in 1945, when he accepted a three-year appointment teaching social science at the University of Chicago. Later, during the *Fortune* years, he moonlighted as an adjunct lecturer in sociology at Columbia (1952–6). However, he moved out of journalism permanently in 1958 as an associate professor in the same university. He was awarded a PhD by Columbia in 1960 for a compilation of his published work and was promoted to full professor in 1962. He moved to Harvard in 1969 and was appointed to a prestigious endowed chair as Henry Ford II Professor of Social Sciences in that university in 1980.

Bell is a relentless publisher. By his own count he has written or edited fourteen or so books and a best guess would suggest about 200 articles of a scholarly nature. The articles tend not to be published in sociology journals. He has published an article in the *British Journal of Sociology* (the Hobhouse memorial lecture) but has published only reviews in the *American Journal of Sociology* or the *American Sociological Review*. His preferred outlets are non-refereed, general intellectual journals that are often associated with the New York circle, with other Jewish interests, or with learned societies, including *The Public Interest, Commentary, The Partisan Review, New Leader, Dissent, Daedalus,* and *The American Scholar.*

Bell has also made important contributions to public life. Most of his public service was devoted to insisting on a sociological contribution to planning for the future at the national level. He was *seriatim*: a member of the President's Commission on Technology, Automation and Economic Progress (1964–6) and co-chair of its Panel on Special Indicators; chair of the Commission on the Year 2000, which he founded under the aegis of The American Academy of Arts and Sciences (1964–74); American representative on the OECD's Inter-Futures Project (1976–9); a member of the President's Commission on a National Agenda for the 1980s and chair of its Panel on Energy and Resources; and a member of the National Research Council, Board on Telecommunications and Computers.

In the later years of his career, Daniel Bell has been the recipient of numerous honors, prizes, and visiting lectureships. The most prestigious of these include: Guggenheim Fellowships in 1972 and 1983; the Hobhouse memorial lecture at the University of London, 1977; Vice-President of the American Academy of Arts and Sciences, 1972–5; the Fels lecture at the University of Pennsylvania, 1986; the Suhrkamp lecture at Goethe University, Frankfurt, 1987; the Pitt Professorship in American Institutions and a Fellowship of King's College, Cambridge, 1987–8; the American Academy of Arts and Sciences Talcott Parsons Prize for the Social Sciences, 1992; an American Sociological Association Award for a distinguished career of lifetime scholarship, 1992; and no less than nine honorary doctorates.

## THE SOCIAL CONTEXT

Two aspects of the social context of Bell's youth were to influence his intellectual development: immigrant poverty and the Jewish religion. The impact of the first is perhaps best described by Bell himself:

> I had grown up in the slums of New York. My mother had worked in a garment factory as long as I could remember; my father had died when I was an infant. All around me I saw the "Hoovervilles," the tin shacks near the docks of the East River where the unemployed lived in makeshift houses and rummaged through the garbage scows for food. Late at night I would go with a gang of other boys to the wholesale vegetable markets on the West Side, to swipe potatoes or to pick up bruised tomatoes in the street to bring home, or to eat around the small fires we would make in the street with the broken boxes from the markets. I wanted to know, simply, why this had to be. It was inevitable that I should become a sociologist. (Bell, 1981, p. 532)

Judaism needs no general description here, but Bell experienced it in transition from a traditional, victimized, European context to a somewhat tribal but nevertheless more mobile, secular, and egalitarian American one. Bell declared his own atheism to his Melamud (teacher) at the age of 13. However, throughout his life he has experienced all the torture of the contradiction between being a deep believer in the capacity of religion to provide meaning and simultaneously not being a practising member of any religion. This tension is, according to Bell's friend and mentor, Irving Howe, directly reflected in his sociological output.

> [W]e thought we should know everything. . . . Meyer [Schapiro], I would say, is the ultimate example of the whole idea of range and scope. On a more modest level somebody like Danny Bell lives by the same notion. Behind this is a very profoundly Jewish impulse: namely, you've got to beat the goyim at their own game. So you have to dazzle them a little. (Howe, 1982, p. 284)

Bell's attempt to dazzle was made in the context of a very different America in the post-Second World War period from the society that had preceded it. As Bell himself puts it, the USA "passed from being a nation to becoming a *national society* in which there is not only a coherent national authority, but where the different sectors of the society, that is economy, polity, and culture, are bound together in a cohesive way and where crucial political and economic decisions are now made at the 'center'" (Bell, 1966, p. 69; original italics). Such centralization implies fiscal management by the manipulation of taxation and interest rates. Alongside this national economy there also developed a national polity by the extension of citizenship rights into the socioeconomic arena. The New Deal of the 1930s had ensured that the federal government had begun to assume many of the powers that previously had been vested in the states and the city governments. This process was extended in the 1960s as the government sought to engineer social equality by means of civil rights, anti-discrimination and voter-registration legislation and its enforcement. Such moves were supported by an extension of welfare state provisions, including medicare, social security, welfare payments, housing, environmental protection, and education.

American participation in the global war of 1939–45 and the leading position that the USA took in the victorious alliance in that war had provided a major impetus to centralization. The fact that the USA remained alert to a perceived Soviet military threat during the succeeding "Cold War" created a large, permanent, and centralized military and intelligence establishment. It was accompanied by the development of a national culture centered on the universities and the capacity of their members to move in and out of Washington policy circles. Mass communications, especially television, also contributed to the emergence of a national popular culture in which the sentiments and emotions of a large proportion of the population could simultaneously focus on a single event or entertainment.

American culture was founded in ideas of achievement, "masculine optimism," and progress – the USA had won all its wars, was economically dominant, and had the "biggest" and the "best" of everything material. This led to the notion of American exceptionalism, the idea shared by many citizens of the USA that theirs was an uniquely great and special society, the summit of human evolution and the guardian of crucial human values. By the 1960s, however, unspoken commitment to the American state came under threat from extremisms of the left and the right that recognized threatening international developments: European economic performance began to outstrip America; the USA managed only a doubtful performance in the space race against the USSR; American military adventurism proved less triumphal than in the past, especially in Vietnam; and America was cast in the role of a neocolonial power.

These developments wrought turmoil in university education in the 1960s. It had expanded under the weight of the postwar baby boom and the students were of a generation that had experienced comparative affluence, freedom from exposure to major international conflict, and relative freedom of expression. Many young American men resisted or avoided conscription to military service in Vietnam and many students, especially in the major universities, became politically active. The consequent political mobilization spread over into wider issues, including civil rights and the democratization of universities.

It would be foolhardy to subject Bell's theory to a crude sociology-of-knowledge analysis. Nevertheless, it is difficult to ignore the temporal correspondence between end-of-ideology and the emergence of a consensus-organized national society, between postindustrial society and the rapid expansion of universities, and between cultural contradictions and the value and generational conflicts that appended the Vietnam War. Bell is a substantive theorist and, as an acute social observer, his theoretical development is bound to reflect the social context in this way.

## THE INTELLECTUAL CONTEXT

On attending the City College of New York (CCNY) in 1939, Bell joined a socialist reading group called "Alcove No. 1." Other members, including Meyer Lasky, Irving Kristol, Nathan Glazer, and Irving Howe, were often Trotskyite in their political orientation (although many of these were later to become the core of the neoconservative movement). While finding the members of the group a convenient sounding board for his own democratic socialist commitment, Bell could not accept Trotskyism. Indeed, by 1947 he had rejected socialism entirely, abandoned a book he was writing on the capitalist state, and moved into a job at *Fortune*.

His personal rejection of ideology was linked to an academic interest in its societal rejection. His first monograph (1967), published in 1952, examined the failure of socialism in the USA, and he also worked on the collapse of ideological extremism on the right (1964b). The culmination, of course, was the end-of-ideology essay. This was originally produced for a conference of the *Congress for Cultural Freedom*, a London-based anti-communist intellectual group that, probably unknown to Bell, received some of its income from the CIA (Wald, 1987, p. 351).

However, the bonds of youth remained strong and later crystallized into part of what became known as the "New York Intellectual Circle": "These New York Jewish Intellectuals came together as a self-conscious group, knowing each other, discussing ideas they held in common, differing widely and sometimes savagely, and yet having that sense of kinship which made each of them aware that they were part of a distinctive socio-historical phenomenon" (Bell, 1991, p. 130).

They had a common Jewish immigrant experience, they often spent their early years as socialists if not communists, and they were educationally mobile, often through CCNY and Columbia. In its maturity, the tone of the Circle was distinctly illiberal, refusing to denounce McCarthyism or the American military engagement in Vietnam, opposing affirmative action for blacks and women, standing radically opposed to student protest, and endorsing unquestioning American support for the state of Israel. The Circle was important because it was the integrating point for the national intellectual elite – over 50 per cent of the American intellectual elite lived in New York City and about half of that elite was Jewish (Kadushin, 1974, pp. 22–3). There is little doubt that Bell was a key figure in the Circle, partly by virtue of his contacts with the inner group, and partly because of his editorship of some of the more influential periodicals. However, he has always rejected the label "neoconservative" that Michael Harrington invented for many of its members, even though such authors as Steinfels (1979) always include Bell in the category.

This general intellectual context blended with an emerging sociological intellectualism located in the rapidly expanding universities. At Chicago Bell experienced his first large encounter with academic sociologists. There he team-taught a common course in social science with "an extraordinary group of young thinkers" (Bell, 1991, p. xvii), including David Riesman, Edward Shils, Milton Singer, Barrington Moore, Morris Janowitz, and Philip Rieff. These scholars represent a tradition now, save Bell, largely lost in American sociology, of theorizing long-term societal transformations and the problems they pose for social organization; that is, of doing substantive, general theory that lies between the sterilities of grand theory and empiricism.

The subsequent move to Columbia can be seen as part of the return of the prodigal to Jewish roots. In fact though, the influences there were mixed. Columbia indeed housed the sociological wing of the "New York intellectuals": Philip Selznick, Seymour Martin Lipset, Nathan Glazer, Alvin Gouldner, and Bernard Rosenberg, most of whom were sometime graduate students of Merton and Lazarsfeld. But, for Bell, "the primary influences were Robert McIver and the Horkheimer group, as well as a neglected figure, Alexander von Schelting, who had written a book on Max Weber's *Wissenschaftslehre*, and gave a reading course in Weber's *Wirtschaft und Gesellschaft* that I took" (Bell, personal communication, August 30, 1993). These influences introduced Bell to the Weberian tradition, but it was Weber in the proper guise of historical sociologist rather than Weber as a Parsonsian action theorist.

If one were to seek to locate Bell in relation to the classical triumvirate of founding theoretical ancestors, then, one would say that he is closest to Weber, most opposed to Marx, and most neutral in relation to Durkheim, not withstanding labeling as a Durkheimian (e.g. O'Neill, 1988; Archer, 1990). Otherwise, he is perhaps most influenced by such sociologists of his generation as Aron, Shils, Riesman, and Dahrendorf. However, what really impresses when one reads Bell is not his knowledge of sociological writings in particular but the breadth of his familiarity with the canon of the Western intellectual tradition. He is influenced at least as much by Aristotle, Rousseau, Schumpeter, Nietzsche,

Veblen, Saint-Simon, and Kant, as well as members of the New York Circle, chief among whom he would probably count Howe, Kristol, Trilling, Glazer, and Hook.

However, Bell has seldom been in tune with any dominant sociological intellectual context. When he left Columbia in 1969, American sociology was mainly divided between two hostile camps: the grand theorists led by Talcott Parsons and the positivistic empiricists led by such figures as Hubert M. Blalock and Otis Dudley Duncan. Theoretically weak and empirically inexact, symbolic interactionism had managed to limp on in the sociological imagination, largely by dint of the iconoclastic efforts of such figures as Howard S. Becker and Erving Goffman; and Alfred Schutz had shepherded the influence of European phenomenology into American sociology, although in its new host it mutated into the bizarre and more influential form of ethnomethodology (see Garfinkel).

Bell rejected all these possibilities. He wanted to be a theorist and a generalizer but he found that he could not accept a holistic vision of society that would deny the possibility of contradictory processes and interests and of divergent historical trends. Acutely tuned to shifts in moods and ideas, he found Parsonsian thought to be as inflexible and incommodious in relation to contemporary developments as that of Marx, and he has seldom allowed himself to be impressed by sociological positivism.

## IMPACT

Kadushin's (1974) research on the American intellectual elite in the late 1960s established its membership at about seventy. Daniel Bell was among the top ten of those seventy, along with Noam Chomsky, John Kenneth Galbraith, Norman Mailer, Susan Sontag, and Edmund Wilson (ibid., pp. 30–1). There was no other sociologist in the top ten, although Hannah Arendt and David Riesman were in the top twenty and Edgar Z. Friedenberg, George Lichtheim, Nathan Glazer, Seymour Martin Lipset, Robert K. Merton, Robert Nisbet, and Franz Schurmann could be found lower down, alongside W. H. Auden, Marshall McLuhan and Barrington Moore. The list included neither of the leading theoretical sociologists of the time, Alfred Schutz and Talcott Parsons, nor did it include the leading empirical sociologists, Otis Dudley Duncan, Erving Goffman, and Paul F. Lazarsfeld, or the philosophers of social science, Carl Hempel and Ernest Nagel. Put simply, Kadushin's research confirms the fair estimate that Daniel Bell was probably the most publicly famous sociologist of the postwar generation.

Bell became an important figure not merely because he was read widely but because he has an unusual capacity to bridge academic and public discourse, so that he finds respect and admiration not only among colleagues but also in the elite and the middle mass. Bell fulfills the role of the *Schriftsteller*, the public intellectual *par excellence*. Other sociologists have also fulfilled this role, including, in Bell's own generation, David Riesman, Nathan Glazer, and C. Wright Mills, and in the contemporary context one can identify such figures as Amitai

Etzioni, Anthony Giddens, and Ulrich Beck, but none has been as effective or as famous as Bell. The reason may simply be that Bell is entirely courageous and straightforward. The fame is not accidental but the result of a reflexive, self-conscious, Franklinian effort to compose the self that combines outstanding talent, voluminous reading, a supportive intellectual circle, and a capacity for self-salesmanship.

An assessment of Bell's influence in the academic arena, however, has to be a little more equivocal. In the second half of the twentieth century, sociology has thrown up two figures that can undeniably stand alongside its classical founding theorists. They are Talcott Parsons and Jürgen Habermas. While a fair appraisal of Bell would not unreservedly put him in the same league, he would certainly have a claim to be at the head of the next small group to be considered. Bell's central legacy to sociology is the role he played in fracturing, at the level of general theory, the holistic hegemony, the two variants of the dominant ideology thesis, Marxian and Parsonsian (see Abercrombie et al., 1980). The theory of the three realms is by no means fully developed, but it does provide a conceptual map of the terrain over which sociology stakes its intellectual claim. The leading edge of contemporary theoretical sociology bears a much greater resemblance to Bell than it does to, say, Marx or Parsons.

One of Bell's greatest strengths is his ability to sense shifts in the *Zeitgeist*, to locate them within the Western tradition and to recast them in a provocative and stimulating way. If one had to select the biggest of the big ideas, then it would have to be that of the postindustrial society, the primary example of this capacity and the idea that will always be associated with his name. As Bell himself says, almost with surprise, the phrase "postindustrial society" has passed quickly into the sociological literature (Bell, 1976, p. ix). The argument must be regarded as strongest in its stress on the emergence of the quinary service sector and the development of information as a resource, and perhaps weakest in its claims for a scientocracy and the centrality of universities. These strengths and weaknesses are perhaps reflected in the ways in which sociologists conventionally use the term. Every sociologist knows that "postindustrialization" means the displacement of manufacturing occupations by service occupations, and indeed the description of such jobs as "postindustrial occupations" is common parlance.

The current theoretical fascination is with "New Times," the issue of whether society is entering a new phase that might be after modernity or industrialism. Bell's was the first full-blown example of such theory and it influences much of the current crop and anticipates many of its components. For example, the end-of-ideology thesis anticipates many recent theories of "new" or post-materialist politics (e.g. Inglehart, 1990) because it specifies that politics will be detached from class milieux and refocused on values and lifestyles. Similarly, the idea of the "eclipse of distance" in modernist cultural expression, in which the stress is on simultaneity, impact, sensation, and immediacy, resonates closely with Harvey's (1989) analysis of the postmodern sensibility.

The key contribution of the cultural contradictions argument is an analysis of postmodernism written long before that topic became fashionable. Bell's interpretation is, of course, fundamentally different from those of, say, Lash and Urry

(1987), Harvey (1989), or Crook et al. (1992), in that he views postmodernism as an extreme, perhaps unintended, development of modernism. Nevertheless, each of these three arguments draws on Bell's view that postmodernism involves the disruption and involution of tradition and the cultivation of a mobile, self-gratifying psyche. The theory also anticipates contemporary theories of "detra-ditionalization" (Giddens, 1991; Beck, 1992) that propose that late modernity involves a recasting of modernization as "reflexive modernization." Here individuals are no longer the product of social situations, but are deliberately self-composing in a calculus that compares the self with an idealized goal structure derived from the mass media and expert systems.

Bell's theory of postindustrialization has been appropriated directly in several instances. Two are particularly important. Lyotard's (1984) influential analysis of the postmodern condition draws directly on Bell in so far as he claims that society is moving into a postindustrial age and culture into a postmodern age. However, in Lyotard, the two operate in tandem rather than in contradiction. Postindustrial developments see the commodification of knowledge through the application of new technologies. Lash and Urry's (1994) specification of reflexive accumulation also draws directly on Bell. Here, postindustrialization proliferates cognitive signs, symbols that represent information that becomes the central component of production, displacing material components.

Bell would put himself at some distance from other "New Times" theories. The caveats he places on the postindustrial society thesis, in which, nomenclature notwithstanding, he is not theorizing the emergence of a postindustrial *society* but only a postindustrial, techno-economic structure, and his insistence that postmodernism is only an extreme extension of modernism, confirm this view. But, like it or not, this is exactly where his work has been most influential. Paradoxically, those who reject the notion of New Times in proposing that the current context is best theorized as high modernity or late capitalism (e.g. Habermas, 1981; Jameson, 1984; Giddens, 1991) would find least in common with Bell. The original concepts of postindustrialism and postmodernism that Bell developed have taken on a life of their own. They now center a galaxy of theories that propose that a historical phase shift is under way. They could not be more influential, but it is unlikely that their author would subscribe to the ways in which they are now employed.

## ASSESSMENT

The scale of Bell's impact, it must be stressed, is focused on his substantive commentary on political, societal, and cultural change. This has tended to restrict his reputation as a theorist *per se* because, at least during the twentieth century, successful sociological theorizing has tended to become defined as formal and abstract rather than historical and substantive. To assess Bell's impact as a *theorist*, then, we need to concentrate our assessment on the more formal and abstract elements of the work. These are contained in the three realms argument, which, curiously in view of its quality, is seldom the subject of much serious analysis. As Steinfels (1979, p. 168) avers, the three realms argument "probably deserves more attention from philosophers of social science and theoretically minded sociologists than it appears to have received." This assessment concentrates initially on the three realms argument, and in doing so asks several fundamental questions.

The first might be: "Is society really divided into realms?" It is clear that in complex societies there are quite pronounced boundaries between the networks of social units known as the polity or the economy that are recognized not only by social scientists but by participants, although elsewhere, as in, say, forager societies, the realms are best regarded merely as analytic aspects of a unified society.

A second question might be: "How many realms are there?" The economy and the polity are relatively unproblematic. However, matters become rather more confused when one seeks to categorize the rest, the areas of culture, socialization, leisure, religion, education, community, and kinship. Unlike many others, Bell confines culture to artistic expression and religion. However, in so doing, he omits a whole realm of social life that is focused on domesticity and community, and that both Schutz and Habermas call the lifeworld.

A third question might be: "Are the axes identified appropriately?" The axial patterns of culture are specified tautologically, but there is some confusion about the axes of the TES and the polity. In what has become something of a sociological orthodoxy, Weber locates bureaucratic rationality primarily in the state, but Bell places rationality, bureaucracy, and unequal power firmly in the TES, while addressing the state as the happy sphere of equality and democratic representation. As Weber shows, the primary feature of a state is that it is a system for the allocation of power in hierarchies and that this power can be exercised authoritatively and even arbitrarily.

The last question is: "Are the realms disjunctive?" The general difficulty is that Bell has fallen victim to what Holmwood and Stewart (1991, pp. 42–4) describe as a "horizontal" theoretical fallacy, a view that the contradictory elements of a theory are experienced separately in different parts of society. The contradictions enunciated by Bell lie not between the realms but between the different parts of his theoretical system, which, by implication, might be in need of revision. Society is always unified at the level of human experience. Indeed, modernity is surely one of the success stories of human history in terms of its capacity to survive, prosper, and expand to near-universality. If it was riven by fundamental contradiction it would long since have disintegrated.

Analytic imprecision also weakens the theoretical account of the postindustrial society. First, as Nichols (1975, p. 350) indicates, Bell denies any claim that he is theorizing an end to capitalism and class. However, throughout the book, and particularly in the sections on stratification, it is clear that, in Bell's view, neither society as a whole nor the TES alone will be structured by capital accumulation in the future. This formulation surely must be designed to deny the reality of business power in a claim that is perhaps a little too anti-Marxist. Second, Bell forecasts the development of an enlarged communal state as if it can only happen in some future society. In fact, liberal corporatist states have long existed elsewhere than in the USA that have frequently successfully managed to balance claims within a reasoned political philosophy.

Bell's analysis of culture is the theoretical jewel, a dazzling tour de force, a brilliant demonstration of his humanity, his intellect, his passion, and his sensitivity. The work is challenging, stimulating, informative, and, as one has come to expect from Bell, prescient. Although it has the familiar Bellian problems of repetition, conceptual looseness, and inconsistency, these apparent deficiencies seem to provide him with a freedom to range across the regions of culture with a facility that no other sociologist has remotely accomplished. Nevertheless, the argument is both theoretically and normatively problematic.

Part of the problem is that the theory of culture is an extension of the three realms theory. Everywhere Bell finds radical contradictions between developments that do not really contradict each other at all. The biggest disjunction apparently lies between a culture that celebrates the self and a TES that requires the subordination of the self to discipline. However, an alternative interpretation of these processes is possible. In such an interpretation, the TES requires not self-discipline but merely a non-internalized compliance with rules. It accomplishes this conformity by delivering material gratifications. The individual "economizes" the relative values of wages, promotions, meaningful work, leisure time, overtime, etc. The primary source of commitment in the TES is therefore a radicalized individualism that links firmly to the gratification of the untrammeled self. On this alternative view, the fit between the instrumental worker, the yuppie entrepreneur, the rapacious consumer, and a spectacular, de-hierarchized artistic arena is indissoluble.

Bell's explanation for the rise of modernism is that technology released the demonic self from its religious jail. Several full-blown alternative arguments suggest that the "self," demonic or otherwise, is a modern construction rather than a foundational reality. Foucault (1981), for example, argues that sexuality was not constrained under premodern conditions but was embedded within kinship. For him, bourgeois society "discovered" sexuality and defined its perversities so that it could control it, precisely by means of discipline. For Foucault, as for Giddens (1985), discipline and surveillance are central components of modern societies, institutionalized in schools, prisons, hospitals, universities, and the state as well as factories. Bell tells us that bourgeois culture had long since been defeated by the 1960s, so that there was nothing against which to rebel, but Foucault tells us that there remained a society replete with authoritarian practices, elitist imposts, and bureaucratic controls. If the self strains to express itself against such constraints it is surely a little dismissive to treat that effort as inauthentic or as mere opinionism.

Bell's value-stance on culture is not merely conservative but elitist. His derogations of popular culture and of postmodernism must be read as a claim for not merely authoritative but authoritarian cultural standards. The most liberal reading of Bell's argument would suggest that he is claiming only that cultural standards must be set by knowledgeable experts who have worked through the canon and drawn upon the accumulated wisdom of generations. Three counter-arguments might be offered. First, as a reading of Bourdieu (1984) suggests, expertise is intimately linked to structures of power and class. The operation of systems of expertise acts as a mechanism of closure on access to privilege. Second, while expertise may briefly have been a neutral arbiter of cultural worth, it has long since been commodified, along with that art on which it pronounces. Expert opinion is now directly translatable into monetary values, so that the quality of a cultural object reflects its price, and not vice versa. Third, it is arguable that expertise and a fixation on tradition tend to smother innovation and participation, rather than releasing them.

Perhaps even more than the great sociological theorists of the nineteenth century, Daniel Bell has been the prisoner of his time, his circumstances, and his value-commitments. He appears unable sufficiently to step out of specifically American sociohistorical developments to see his theory generalized and adopted widely. Moreover, this incapacity leads him into fundamental errors about power and class and about the relationship between general cultural standards and individual expression. Notwithstanding these errors, the three realms theory resonates fully into the great sociological traditions and offers a much more accessible and non-determinant framework for the analysis of society than most of the alternatives. A great deal of work needs to be done on the theory, but it would be an investment that would yield rich rewards.

## Bibliography

### Writings of Daniel Bell

Adjusting Men to Machines. 1947. *Commentary*, 79–88.

Twelve Modes of Prediction. 1964a. *Daedalus*, 93, 845–80.

*The New American Right* (editor) (New York, 1955). *The Radical Right: The New American Right Expanded and Updated*. 1964b. Garden City: Anchor.

The Disjunction between Culture and Social Structure. 1965a. *Daedalus*, 94, 208–22.

The Study of the Future. 1965b. *The Public Interest*, 1, 119–30.

*The Reforming of General Education: the Columbia College Experience in Its National Setting*. 1966. New York: Columbia University Press.

*Marxian Socialism in the United States*. 1967. Princeton, NJ: Princeton University Press.

*Towards the Year 2000: Work in Progress* (editor). 1968. Boston: Beacon.

*Confrontation: the Student Revolt and the Universities* (editor with I. Kristol). 1969. New York: Basic Books.

Quo Warranto? Notes on the Governance of the Universities in the 1970s. 1970a. *The Public Interest*, 19, 53–68.

*Work and Its Discontents* (Boston, 1956). 1970b. New York: League for Industrial Democracy.

*Capitalism Today* (editor with I. Kristol). 1970. New York: New American Library.

Religion in the Sixties. 1971. *Social Research*, 38, 447–97.

The Postindustrial Society – a Symposium (with F. Bourricaud, J. Floud, G. Sartori, K. Tominaga, and P. Wiles). 1971. *Survey*, 16, 1–77.

*The Coming of Postindustrial Society: a Venture in Social Forecasting* (New York, 1973). 1976. New York: Basic.

The Social Framework of the Information Society. 1979a. In M. Dertouzos and J. Moses (ed.), *The Computer Age*. Cambridge, MA: MIT Press, pp. 163–211.

*The Cultural Contradictions of Capitalism* (New York, 1976). 1979b. London: Heinemann, 2nd edn.

First Love and Early Sorrows. 1981. *Partisan Review*, 48, 532–51.

*The Crisis in Economic Theory* (editor, with I. Kristol). 1981. New York: Basic Books.

*The Social Sciences since the Second World War*. 1982. New Brunswick, NJ: Transaction.

*The Deficits: How Big? How Long? How Dangerous?* (with L. Thurow). 1985. New York: New York University Press.

The World and the United States in 2013. 1987. *Daedalus*, 116, 1–31.

*The End of Ideology: On the Exhaustion of Political Ideas in the Fifties* (Glencoe, 1965). 1988. Cambridge, MA: Harvard University Press.

American Exceptionalism Revisited: the Role of Civil Society. 1989. *The Public Interest*, 95, 38–56.

*The Third Technological Revolution – and Its Possible Socioeconomic Consequences*. 1990a. Tokyo: Shukan Diamond.

Resolving the Contradictions of Modernity and Modernism.1990b. *Society*, 27, 43–50, 66–75.

The Misreading of Ideology: the Social Determination of Ideas in Marx's Work. 1990c. *Berkeley Journal of Sociology*, 35, 1–54.

*The Winding Passage: Sociological Essays and Journeys* (Boston, 1980). 1991. New Brunswick, NJ: Transaction, 2nd edn.

The Break-up of Space and Time: Technology and Society in a Postindustrial Age. 1992. Paper presented at the American Sociological Association Annual Meeting, Pittsburgh.

Downfall of the Business Giants. 1993. *Dissent*, 316–23.

## Further reading

Abercrombie, N., Hill, S., and Turner, B. (1980) *The Dominant Ideology Thesis*. London: Allen & Unwin.

Archer, M. (1990) Theory, Culture and Postindustrial Society. In M. Featherstone (ed.), *Global Culture*. London: Sage, pp. 207–36.

Badham, R. (1984) The Sociology of Industrial and Postindustrial Societies. *Current Sociology*, 32, 1–141.

Beck, U. (1992) *Risk Society*. London: Sage.

Bloom, A. (1986) *Prodigal Sons*. New York: Oxford University Press.

Bourdieu, P. (1984) *Distinction*. London: Routledge.

Brick, H. (1986) *Daniel Bell and the Decline of Intellectual Radicalism*. Madison: University of Wisconsin Press.

Chernow, R. (1979) The Cultural Contradictions of Daniel Bell. *Change*, 11, 12–17.

Clark, C. (1957) *The Conditions of Economic Progress*. London: Macmillan.

Cooney, T. (1986) *The Rise of the New York Intellectuals*. Madison: University of Wisconsin Press.

Crook, S., Pakulski, J., and Waters, M. (1992) *Postmodernization*. London: Sage.

Dittberner, J. (1979) *The End of Ideology and American Social Thought: 1930–1960*. Ann Arbor: University of Michigan Research Press.

Foote, N. and Hatt, P. (1953) Social Mobility and Economic Advancement. *American Economic Review*, 18, 364–78.

Foucault, M. (1981) *The History of Sexuality volume 1*. Harmondsworth: Penguin.

Frankel, B. (1987) *The Postindustrial Utopians*. Cambridge: Polity Press.

Giddens, A. (1985) *The Nation-state and Violence*. Cambridge: Polity Press.

Giddens, A. (1991) *Modernity and Self-identity*. Cambridge: Polity Press.

Habermas, J. (1981) Modernity vs. Postmodernity. *New German Critique*, 22, 3–14.

Habermas, J. (1983) Neoconservative Culture Criticism in the United States and West Germany. *Telos*, 56, 75–89.

Hagan, R. (1975) Societal Disjunction and Axial Theory: Review Commentary on the Social Theory of Daniel Bell. *Review of Social Theory*, 3, 40–4.

Harvey, D. (1989) *The Condition of Postmodernity*. Oxford: Blackwell.

Hill, R. (1974) The Coming of Postindustrial Society. *The Insurgent Sociologist*, 4, 37–51.

Holmwood, J. and Stewart, A. (1991) *Explanation and Social Theory*. Basingstoke: Macmillan.

Holton, G. (1962) Scientific Research and Scholarship. *Daedalus*, 91, 362–99.

Howe, I. (1982) The Range of the New York Intellectual. In B. Rosenberg and E. Goldstein (ed.), *Creators and Disturbers*. New York: Columbia University Press.

Inglehart, R. (1990) *Culture Shift in Advanced Industrial Society*. Princeton, NJ: Princeton University Press.

Jameson, F. (1984) Postmodernism: Or the Cultural Logic of Late Capitalism. *New Left Review*, 146, 53–92.

Jumonville, N. (1991) *Critical Crossings*. Berkeley: University of California Press.

Kadushin, C. (1974) *The American Intellectual Elite*. Boston: Little Brown.

Kivisto, P. (1981) The Theorist as Seer: the Case of Bell's Postindustrial Society. *Quarterly Journal of Ideology*, 5, 39–43

Kleinberg, B. (1973) *American Society in the Postindustrial Age*. Columbus, OH: Merrill.

Kuhns, W. (1971) *The Postindustrial Prophets*. New York: Harper.

Kumar, K. (1978) *Prophecy and Progress: the Sociology of Industrial and Postindustrial Society*. Harmondsworth: Penguin.

Kumar, K. (1995) *From Postindustrial to Post-modern Society*. Oxford: Blackwell.

Lash, S. and Urry, J. (1987) *The End of Organized Capitalism*. Cambridge: Polity Press.

Lash, S. and Urry, J. (1994) *Economies of Signs and Space*. London: Sage.

Leibowitz, N. (1985) *Daniel Bell and the Agony of Modern Liberalism*. Westport, CT: Greenwood.

Longstaff, S. (1987) Daniel Bell and Political Reconciliation. *Queen's Quarterly*, 94, 660–5.

Lukács, G. (1968) *History and Class Consciousness*. London: Macmillan.

Lyotard, J. (1984) *The Postmodern Condition*. Manchester: Manchester University Press.

Marien, M. (1973) Daniel Bell and the End of Normal Science. *The Futurist*, 7, 262–8.

Miller, S. (1975) Notes on Neo-capitalism. *Theory and Society*, 2, 1–35.

Nichols, T. (1975) The Coming of Postindustrial Society. *Sociology*, 9, 349–52.

O'Neill, J. (1988) Religion and Postmodernism. *Theory, Culture and Society*, 5, 493–508.

Pahl, R. (1975) The Coming of Postindustrial Society. *Sociology*, 9, 347–9.

Rejai, M. (ed.) (1971) *Decline of Ideology?* Chicago: Aldine.

Rose, M. (1991) *The Post-modern and the Postindustrial*. Cambridge: Cambridge University Press.

Ross, G. (1974) The Second Coming of Daniel Bell. In R. Miliband and J. Saville (eds), *The Socialist Register 1974*. London: Merlin, pp. 331–48.

Rule, J. (1971) The Problem with Social Problems. *Politics and Society*, 1, 47–56.

Simons, H. (1988) *Jewish Times*. Boston: Houghton Mifflin.

Stearns, P. (1973) Is There a Postindustrial Society? *Society*, 11, 11–25.

Steinfels, P. (1979) *The NeoConservatives*. New York: Simon & Schuster.

Tilman, R. and Simich, J. (1984) On the Use and Abuse of Thorstein Veblen in Modern American Sociology, II. *American Journal of Economics and Sociology*, 43, 103–28.

Turner, B. (1989) From Postindustrial Society to Postmodern Politics. In J. Gibbins (ed.), *Contemporary Political Culture*. London: Sage, pp. 199–217.

von der Ohe, W., Drabek, T., Hall, R., Hill, R., Lopreato, J., Marcus, P., and Phillips, M., with a reply by Bell, D. (1973) The Coming of Postindustrial Society: a Review Symposium. *Summation*, 3, 60–103.

Wald, A. (1987) *The New York Intellectuals*. Chapel Hill: University of North Carolina Press.

Waters, M. (1996) *Daniel Bell*. London: Routledge.

Waxman, C. (ed.) (1968) *The End of Ideology Debate*. New York: Simon & Schuster.

# 19

# Norbert Elias

## RICHARD KILMINSTER AND STEPHEN MENNELL

> But my whole conviction is that our image
> of and orientation in our social world will
> become very much easier once we realise
> that human beings are not economic in
> one of their pockets, political in another
> and psychological in another, in other
> words that no *real* divisions correspond to
> the traditional divisions.
> *Norbert Elias (1970b, p. 148)*

## INTRODUCTION

Norbert Elias (1897–1990) is most celebrated for his classic work *Über den Prozess der Zivilisation*, first published obscurely in German in 1939, but little known in the anglophone world until the publication of a translation (*The Civilizing Process*) in 1978–82.[1] In this book, Elias traces long-term connections between changes in power balances in society at large and changes in the embodied habitus – or cultural personality makeup – of individual people, among the secular upper classes in Western Europe from the late Middle Ages to the nineteenth century. His work constitutes an endeavor – rare in the history of sociology – to bridge the gap between "micro" and "macro" sociology in a *theoretical-empirical*, rather than merely a conceptual, way. Although it was originally grounded in a study of European history, the theory of civilizing processes points to linked changes in power, behavior, and habitus which can be demonstrated to have been at work elsewhere and in many other periods. In later books and articles, Elias greatly extended the scope of the original theory.

Elias's work constitutes a radical rejection of many of the common assumptions of sociology in the second half of the twentieth century. He conceived of the discipline in the broadest terms, not as just "hodiecentric" (or "present-centered") nor as the study solely of "modern" societies, but as including the study of long-term processes over the whole course of the development of human society. He was hostile to the hegemony of philosophy and what he sometimes called in conversation "philosophoidal" modes of thought in sociology, and told his fellow sociologists to stop making obeisances to the philosophers. His own sociological work is grounded in a *sociological* theory of knowledge and the sciences, rather than in the traditional assumptions of mainstream philosophical epistemology and philosophy of science. This is one of the main ways in which he differs from contemporary "social theorists," who are generally more deferential to philosophy, such as Anthony Giddens, Jeffrey Alexander, and Jürgen Habermas. Elias referred to his way of doing sociology as "process sociology" – it is also commonly referred to as "figurational" sociology – and it involves the rejection of many of the "static polarities" and "false dualities" that pervade sociological thinking.

## LIFE AND TIMES

Perhaps the most striking fact about Norbert Elias's career is how extremely late in life he gained recognition. He published fifteen books, but all of them, except the little-noticed first edition of *Über den Prozess der Zivilisation*, appeared after he reached normal retirement age – indeed most of them when he was in his eighties and nineties. Someone who in 1928 appeared on the same panel of discussants as Ferdinand Toennies, Werner Sombart, and Alfred Weber (Elias, 1929a) – figures whose work we associate with the end of the nineteenth century – thus finally came to seem a very contemporary presence to sociologists at the end of the twentieth century.

Elias was one of the generation of Jewish scholars who fled Germany in 1933 when Hitler came to power. Some of them were immediately able to establish themselves in universities in English-speaking countries; we can only guess how many of them, having escaped with their lives, failed to re-establish themselves as academics. Elias was almost one of the latter group.

He was born on June 22, 1897 in Breslau, the only son of Hermann and Sophie Elias. His father was a businessman, in the textile trade. Although, since the frontier changes at the end of the Second World War, Breslau is now the Polish city of Wrocław, the city was then fully German. At the distinguished *Johannesgymnasium* there, Elias received a first-class, all-round education in the humanities and sciences; he was immersed from an early age in the classics of German literature, Latin and Greek (a reading knowledge of both of which served as a useful research skill into his old age), and French, as well as being given a good grounding in mathematics, physics, and chemistry. Asked in old age whether, as a child, he felt more a member of the Jewish community or of the wider German society, Elias (1994b, p. 10) said that the very question reflected events that have unfolded since then. He knew as a child he was both a German and a Jew, but at the time the two identities did not conflict. There were isolated incidents of antisemitic remarks, but antisemites were people to look down upon. While this may indeed be true of his perceptions as a child, research since his death has revealed that his protestations of never having been involved in politics were not entirely true: from his teenage years he was a leading light in the Zionist youth movement Blau-Weiß (Hackeschmidt, 1997). An early article on antisemitism in Germany (Elias, 1929b) has belatedly come to light.

In 1915, reaching the age when he became eligible for conscription, Elias enlisted in a signals regiment of the German army, and saw action on both the Eastern and Western Fronts in the First World War. He remembered the carnage, especially seeing a comrade killed nearby, and he probably suffered shellshock but could not remember the circumstances. How he came to leave the front and return to Breslau remained a blur, but he served out the war back in his home town as an army medical orderly, and recalled watching a famous surgeon amputating limbs. After the Armistice he enrolled at Breslau University, for some time managing to pursue courses in both medicine and philosophy. He completed the pre-clinical part of the medical training, and always considered that his experience in the dissecting room had left a lasting mark on his understanding of how human beings work as social animals. For nothing he observed – especially dissecting the brain and the musculature of the face – corresponded to the distinction taken for granted in philosophy between the "external" world and the "internal" world of "the mind." But then, to his father's disappointment, he recognized that he could not pursue both disciplines, and dropped medicine in favor of completing his doctoral degree in philosophy.

Elias's student years were a time of enormous political and social instability in Germany after its defeat in the war, the abdication of the Kaiser, and the establishment of the Weimar Republic. Armed left-wing and right-wing militias fought each other in the streets. One of Elias's school-friends, a mild and scholarly youth but apparently suspected of left-wing leanings, was among those killed by the *Freikorps*, a right-wing organization. A little later, Germany experienced the great runaway hyperinflation of 1922–3, which destabilized many aspects of society and in Elias's own case meant that he had for a time to take a job in industry (as export manager for a local manufacturer of iron goods) in order to help support his temporarily financially embarrassed parents.

So, even before the rise of Hitler, Elias had seen a great deal at first hand of war, civil unrest, violent death, and social instability. It is important to bear this in mind as an antidote to a once-common misapprehension about *The Civilizing Process*: Elias did not set out in that *magnum opus* to write a celebration of Western civilization in the popular sense, still less to depict it as the outcome of inevitable "progress." On the contrary, Elias was very conscious of how hard won was the outward show of "civilization," yet how brittle a veneer it remained. That is made abundantly clear at the very end of his life in *The Germans*, in which he describes himself thus: "Standing half-hidden in the background of the studies published here is an eyewitness who has lived for nearly ninety years through the events concerned as they unfolded" (Elias, 1996, p. 1).

Elias wrote his doctoral thesis at Breslau under the neo-Kantian philosopher Richard Hönigswald, from whom he acknowledged that he learned a great deal, even though the relationship ended in their estrangement. The thesis was entitled "Idea and Individual,"[2] and was eventually accepted in January 1924, after a delay of more than a year occasioned by a dispute between student and supervisor. Their dispute concerned a fundamental issue: whether there are any grounds for postulating a notion of truth that is transcendental and independent of human experience and human history. Although he could not then formulate his viewpoint with the precision and clarity that came later, Elias recalled that he had begun at this time to come to the conclusion

> that all that Kant regarded as timeless and given prior to all experience, whether it be the idea of causal connections or of time or of natural and moral laws, together with the words that went with them, had to be learned from other people in order to be present in the consciousness of the individual human being. (Elias, 1994b, p. 91)

Ever afterwards, Elias argued that the whole central tradition of modern Western epistemology, from Descartes through Kant to twentieth-century phenomenology, was misconceived. It was based on asking how a single, *adult*, human mind can know what it knows. Elias called this the model of *homo clausus*, the "closed person," and found it lurking in much of modern sociology (Elias, 1994a, pp. 200–15; 1978, pp. 119ff; Mennell, 1998, pp. 188–93; Kilminster, 1998, chapters 4 and 5). He argued that we must instead think in terms of *homines aperti*, "open people," and in particular of "long lines of generations of people" building up the stock of human knowledge. The crucial point, however, which he developed in *The Civilizing Process* and other later works, was that the image of *homo clausus* corresponded to a *mode of self-experience* that was *not* a human universal but was a social product, particularly of European society from the Renaissance onwards.

The dispute with Hönigswald appears to have influenced Elias's decision, after he had received his doctorate and when his parents' finances had recovered, to resume his studies in Heidelberg not as a philosopher but as a sociologist. Max Weber had died four years earlier, but his circle, centered on his younger brother Alfred and his widow Marianne, was still a dominant presence in Heidelberg. Elias presented his first sociological paper, on the sociology of Gothic cathedrals in France and Germany, at a meeting of Marianne's salon, on the balcony of the Webers' house. Elias had earlier interpolated a semester at Heidelberg (when he also attended a student Zionist conference) during his studies at Breslau, and there had met Karl Jaspers, who introduced him to the work of Max Weber and also encouraged him to write an essay on the notions of *Zivilisation* and *Kultur* in German thought (with special reference to Thomas Mann's essay "Civilization's Literary Man"[3]). Now Elias enrolled as a *Habilitation* student with Alfred Weber, and set out to write a thesis on Florentine society and culture in the transition from pre-scientific to scientific thinking. Alfred Weber was very interested in questions of "civilization" and "culture." He argued that culture could not be reduced to economic relationships or explained in terms of economic interests. It always had to be understood in terms of social behavior, but its pattern of development differed from that of economics, science, and technology; in these there was progress, but in art, religion, and culture in general there were no progressions or regressions – culture was rather to be seen as the self-realization of the soul of a people (Alfred Weber, 1998). Elias's later theory of civilizing processes may be understood as in part an attempt to demonstrate that, *pace* Weber, structured long-term processes can be discovered in "culture movements" too.

Around this time, Elias became friendly with a young *Privatdozent*, Karl Mannheim, four years his senior, who introduced him into the Weber circle. In 1929, when Mannheim became Professor of Sociology at the then quite new University of Frankfurt, Elias went with him as his academic assistant. There were mixed motives for the move: friction had developed between Mannheim and Alfred Weber, making it uncomfortable for Elias as the friend of one and *Habilitation* candidate of the other; and Mannheim promised Elias earlier *Habilitation* than Weber was able to do. And last but not least, as an academic assistant Elias at last received a salary!

At Frankfurt, Elias embarked on a new topic for his *Habilitationsschrift*: a sociological study of life at the court of France in the seventeenth and eighteenth centuries. All the stages of Elias's *Habilitation* – which would give him the rank of *Privatdozent* – were rushed through, except for the inaugural lecture, early in 1933, just as Hitler came to power and shortly before Elias fled into exile. But the thesis was not published until 1969. That is the book known in English as *The Court Society* (1983).

Mannheim headed the Department of Sociology and, as his assistant, Elias was particularly involved in in supervising doctoral dissertations. The department was housed in rented space in a building owned and occupied by the Institut für Sozialforschung – later celebrated as "the Frankfurt School" – of which Max Horkheimer was Director. Relations between the two groups seem to have been polite but distant, although Elias was on good personal terms with Theodor Adorno. There is a degree of thematic similarity between the problems addressed in *The Civilizing Process* and by Horkheimer and Adorno in their *The Dialectic of Enlightenment* (1979) – the relations between control of nature, control of society, and self-control – but also a strikingly symptomatic difference. Horkheimer and Adorno write from within a very traditional philosophical discourse, whereas Elias sets out to turn questions traditionally posed in philosophical terms into empirically researchable socio-historical questions (Bogner, 1987).

Elias stayed long enough in Frankfurt after the Nazis came to power to be able to observe later that the process through which they came to power contained both highly rational *and* very violent elements – the two are not opposites. But, having lost his post and salary in the Nazi takeover of the university, later in 1933 he went into exile in Paris. He then spoke excellent French but little

English. But he failed to secure academic employment. He invested what remained of the money his father had given him in a business making wooden toys. It was not a success; Elias lost all his money, and was effectively destitute. At the urging of his old friend Alfred Glucksmann, who had already emigrated to Cambridge, Elias moved to England in 1935, where he secured a meager stipend from a Dutch Jewish charity.

Although in later years he claimed that *The Civilizing Process* was written in the Reading Room of the British Museum, it is possible that the first volume at least was begun in Paris, where he may have first encountered Lucien Febvre's essay on the origins of the concept of "civilization" (1930), which is cited in *The Civilizing Process*. In the early 1930s he also read Freud's *Civilization and its Discontents* (1930), which he acknowledged as the greatest single intellectual influence on *The Civilizing Process*. Freud's book serves as a reminder that in the 1930s a concern with "culture" and "civilization" was by no means associated with a naive faith in "progress" and its benefits.

The two volumes of *The Civilizing Process* were completed in a white heat of inspiration in London, by 1938 at the latest. The problem was how they were to be published. Elias's parents visited him in London that year, and he tried to persuade them to join him in exile. They refused. All their friends were in Breslau and, said his father, "They can't touch me – I've never broken a law in my life." His father died in Breslau in 1940, and his mother in Auschwitz in 1941. But before that, his father had arranged for *Über den Prozess der Zivilisation* to be printed in Breslau. Before it could actually be published, however, the printer too fled the country. Hermann Elias then surreptitiously arranged for the unbound sheets to be exported to Switzerland, where they were bound and eventually published by Haus zum Falken in 1939. That year, as Bryan Wilson was later wryly to observe, was not the most propitious moment for the publication of a two-volume work, in German, by a Jew, on, of all things, civilization. Few people read it. Among those who did, appreciatively, were Thomas Mann and two prominent reviewers in the Netherlands, both of whom sadly committed suicide when the Germans invaded their country in 1940 (Goudsblom, 1977b, p. 61).

On the publication of *The Civilizing Process*, Elias was awarded a Senior Research Fellowship at the London School of Economics, which was evacuated to Cambridge during the war. He was briefly interned with other "enemy aliens" during 1940, but returned to Cambridge and worked for British Intelligence at the end of the war. Afterwards, he lived in near poverty, scraping a living by teaching extramural lectures. In the early 1950s, with his old friend S. H. Foulkes, he was one of the founders of the Group Analytic school of psychotherapy (Elias, 1969; Pines, 1997). These were years when Elias published almost nothing, however, and the trauma of his mother dying in Auschwitz may be at least part of the explanation for that. Only in 1954, when he was already 57, did he secure his first secure academic post, at the respectable but obscure University College Leicester, soon to be the University of Leicester. There, with Ilya Neustadt, he helped to build up one of the most distinguished departments of sociology in Britain; both Anthony Giddens and John Goldthorpe – among many other notable figures – gained their first teaching posts in the Leicester department. On his retirement in 1962 he served for two years as the first Professor of Sociology at the University of Ghana, and on his return continued to teach part-time at Leicester. These were the years when he published *The Established and the Outsiders* with John Scotson (1994) and began, with Eric Dunning (Elias and Dunning, 1986), to develop in new directions the existing area of the sociology of sport. In 1969, however, *Über den Prozess der Zivilisation* was republished, and in consequence he rapidly became an intellectual celebrity in Germany and the Netherlands (see Elias, 1970b). In the 1970s, he was in demand in both countries as a visiting professor, and gradually abandoned residence in Britain, first for Bielefeld, then for Amsterdam. The 1970s and 1980s were years of unparalleled productivity, in which books and articles that had been gestating for decades finally flowed from his pen. This productivity was considerably aided by the devoted editorial assistance of Michael Schröter. Elias died, still writing at the age of 93, on August 1, 1990.

## INTELLECTUAL CONTEXT AND INFLUENCES

One of the problems which anyone introducing Elias immediately faces is that of situating his highly original work within the theoretical schools, paradigms, and sociological language familiar to mainstream sociologists. The difficulty of "placing" him in the European sociological tradition has always been, as Johan Goudsblom (1977a, pp. 60, 77ff) has pointed out, a problem for commentators. It is difficult to find a place for Elias's sociology of figurations within the paradigms of recent sociology, such as phenomenology, action theory, functionalism, structuration theory, Marxism, Weberianism, poststructuralism, critical realism, rational choice theory, or neopositivism. Elias seems to fall between all stools. Echoes of, and parallels and similarities with, the work of others abound in Elias's figurational sociology, as do concepts and problems common to other traditions of social science, but in a strange way Elias's contribution remains stubbornly unique. How? To answer that question we need to take a brief detour.

Elias did not assign much importance to delineating carefully his intellectual debts and situating himself in relation to other writers and schools, in the detail that we have come to expect and find in the writings of, say, Parsons, Habermas, or Giddens. All this interpretative work of debt assignment and influences in relation to Elias has had to be done by others much later, following up clues in his writings and interviews and drawing on broader knowledge of the state of sociology in Germany in the first quarter of the twentieth century. For many years Elias would avow only one significant intellectual debt. In a footnote to the first volume of *The Civilizing Process* (1994a, p. 249), he acknowledges how much the study owes to the discoveries of Freud, which, he says, is obvious to the reader anyway, so did not need to be pointed out in all instances. Even then, he explicitly stressed the "not inconsiderable *differences* between the whole approach of Freud and that adopted in this study" (our emphasis). Rather than "digressing into disputes at every turn," he continues, it seemed more important "to build a particular intellectual perspective as clearly as possible."

Later, Elias further complicated the issue by challenging the conventional assumption that an "influence" always had to come from a book: "I am extremely conscious of the fact that others have influenced me, that I have learned from others – though not only from books, but also from the events of my age" (quoted by Goudsblom, 1977b, p. 78). He also claimed that, at the time he was writing *The Civilizing Process*, his knowledge of those writers whom we think of today as our sociological ancestors was "extremely deficient" (quoted by Goudsblom, 1977b, p. 78). But this admission has to be taken with a pinch of salt. Even if he did not know these writers in quite the depth that we take for granted today, he nevertheless still participated in the particularly rich sociological culture of Weimar Germany, in which many of these ancestors had already been discussed, absorbed, and processed and areas of enquiry established (see Mannheim, 1953, pp. 209–28; Aron, 1957; Schad, 1972).

The problem-agenda of the generation of Weimar sociologists which included Elias was a remarkably fertile one, set by gifted people such as Max Weber, Simmel, Veblen, Freud, Alfred Weber, Sombart, prominent Marxists such as Lukács, and the more sociologically sympathetic phenomenologists and existentialists, such as Hannah Arendt and Karl Jaspers, in the aftermath of one European war and in the build-up to another. The origins of Elias's sociology lie in the complex political conflicts and alignments of the Weimar period, although the applicability of his insights goes well beyond that. If Elias's work can be placed anywhere it is as a development out of the German *Wissenssoziologie*, to which it bears a family resemblance (Kilminster, 1993).

Having said all that, the question remains: what is the uniqueness of Elias's sociology? Following Goudsblom (1977b, p. 79) again, our view is that the key to answering this question lies in grasping how Elias managed to integrate *through empirical research* many seemingly incompatible perspectives into a "workable synthesis," a single testable model of human interdependence. This enabled him to solve in a preliminary way problems shrewdly posed, but left in the air, by other writers such as those already mentioned. These problems had already been made available, so to speak, in the sociological culture in which Elias participated. To name just a few significant sociological themes, he found, ready-to-hand, discussions of and research into: the conspicuous consumption of elites; "two-front" strata; the monopoly of the means of violence; rationalization; social equalization; competition; social differentiation and integration; the internalization of what is external; the development of civilized self-restraint. All these, and many more, Elias integrated into his sociological synthesis, as concepts or problems requiring solution. In doing so, he did not undertake a great deal of conceptual work to demonstrate how his concepts differed from those developed by other writers in different traditions. For him, the integrity of the synthesis and its empirical extension were everything.

Elias polemicized relentlessly against *homo clausus*. He repeatedly stressed the importance of the long, intergenerational, process of knowledge accumulation that exceeds the scope of the individual knowing subject – the Ego so beloved of the philosophers. At the same time, as has often been pointed out (most recently by van Krieken, 1998, p. 76), he doggedly went his own way and for the most part refused to acknowledge the work of other sociologists. This feature of Elias's thinking and acting perhaps reveals that even he was not immune to one of the self-delusions associated with the *homo clausus* experience, that of self-autarky. As a person, he may have found it hard to admit, even to himself, the extent of his intellectual debts to others. A more charitable gloss on this feature of his character would be that Elias probably genuinely could not see why anyone should be interested in where he had gotten his ideas from – something which, on the other hand, assumes a burning significance for many sociologists today. He did talk about these matters a little, later in his life, in various interviews and in particular in his *Reflections on a Life* (1994b), although somewhat selectively. By and large, he seems to have assumed that people reading *The Civilizing Process* would see that the explanatory power of the "workable synthesis" was everything and would seek to test it further in their own research. Working directly from the sociological model to empirical areas and back again in this high-minded, but unorthodox, way was not without its dangers. It exposed Elias to the risk that readers would find in his books some apparent similarities with the ideas of other sociologists and philosophers but, failing to appreciate the *synthetic* character of his work, accuse him of unacknowledged derivation or lack of originality. Some of the controversy surrounding the belated recognition of his work has arisen from this feature of his approach and his failure to always make this aspect of his way of working clear to his readers.

There is a parallel here with the holistic approach to society found in the work of Elias's colleague and friend of many years, Karl Mannheim, which may illuminate this issue. Perhaps Elias's being out of step with the expectations of the sociological profession regarding the elaborate acknowledgment and documentation of sources of inspiration is also *organically* related to the character of his integrating research strategy. As Kettler and Meja (1995) point out, in his restless attempts to uncover the *Zeitgeist*, Mannheim was open to ideas and inspiration from many sources in his pursuit of a political synthesis. Although Elias's work was not moving in that particular political direction, he did share with Mannheim the idea that the significance of a social event, social grouping or cultural item lies in its relationship with other aspects of the developing social structure as a whole. Subject to the further caveat that Elias would have no truck whatsoever with any talk in a sociological context of spirit (*Geist*), the succinct description given by Kettler and Meja (1995, p. 318) of Mannheim's way of working with concepts and research materials resonates with that of Elias:

> [Mannheim] would subject key concepts to a "change of function." It was unnecessary to criticise others; it was enough to correct and balance what they said by drawing on something said by someone else. All participants were seen as sharing the same condition or expressing the same spirit.

## Reading Elias

There are some further unusual features of Elias's writings which set his work apart from the dominant forms of professional sociology to which we are accustomed. It is worth briefly outlining them as an aid to understanding Elias.

1   For most of his long career, for reasons often beyond his control, Elias was on the periphery of the sociology establishment and thus distanced from it. He therefore felt few of the pressures of the institutionalized world of the academic social sciences. One consequence of this is that his works have an unfamiliar structure and character. The reader will not find the customary beginning with a review of the literature or contemporary debates about the problem or topic addressed. Elias did not work that way. Rather, he always went for the problem or object of inquiry (for example, symbols, scientific establishments, Mozart, time, violence, aging and dying, work, or psychosomatics – to name just a few of the subjects he investigated in his later years), which he would explore in his own way, in his own language of figurational or process sociology.

2   In the later writings in particular, Elias typically lists very few references; indeed, frequently there will only be one, perhaps to an obscure book published many years ago. If one complained to Elias that he had failed to address the contemporary literature, or suggested that he was out of date, he would reply that you had a fetish for the new, that just because a book is old it does not mean that it may not still be the best treatment of a problem. And, conversely, new books did not necessarily represent an advance simply because they were new. It was the intrinsic cognitive worth of the book that counted, not whether it was currently *à la mode* (see Elias, 1987, pp. 117–18). He worked within a very long scientific time scale, detached from current orthodoxies.

3   It is worth mentioning the style of Elias's writings. Wolf Lepenies (1978, p. 63) aptly described their qualities: "a jargon-free concern with clarity, a careful training in sociological observation and a thoroughgoing combination of theoretical discussions with often surprising references to details." Elias was very alert to the subtleties and associations of the language and concepts we employ in sociology. He writes about social processes in a controlled language carefully cleansed of all traces of reification and static metaphysics and highly sensitive to evaluative nuances. Elias will talk of party-establishments when others refer to "the political"; or economic specialists rather than "the economic sphere"; or social specialists for violence control instead of "repressive state apparatuses"; or means of orientation rather than "ideological practice."

4   The more one reads Elias, the more aware one becomes of how he convinces readers not so much by conventional "logical" arguments for this or that position, as by expressing issues (particularly in his articles) in such a way as to provoke people into reflecting upon the categories or assumptions that they routinely employ in dealing with them. As well as containing a theoretical model and empirical materials, *The Civilizing Process* embodies a mode of experiential persuasion which cannot be described as entirely rational. As we read through the picturesque extracts from contemporary documents about

farting, bedroom behavior, spitting, torture, the burning of cats, or whatever, we gain insight *through this experience itself* into our own feelings of shame, repugnance, and delicacy derived from the standards of our own society, representing a later stage of development. Our reactions themselves exemplify the rise in the thresholds of shame, embarrassment, and repugnance which Elias is demonstrating. This effect partly explains why the book is so memorable.

## THE SOCIOLOGICAL IMPERATIVE

For an adequate understanding of Elias, it is essential to appreciate how his sociology developed out of the desire to transcribe philosophical discussions of knowledge, society, culture, and the human condition into a form amenable to empirical sociological investigation. This leaves the status of philosophy ambiguous and disputable. These questions included those traditionally grouped under epistemology, ontology, and ethics (that is, "evaluative" or "normative" questions), which reappear in Elias's works transformed into a sociological idiom. We cannot stress too much the robustly sociological character of Elias's world view. The failure of various commentators to understand this dimension of Elias's work has led to a number of misunderstandings. Readers of Elias need to be prepared for his controversial and uncompromising views about philosophy and his rather sweeping denunciations of its practitioners, which have not won him many friends. He considered that his work presupposed the supersession of philosophy and consistently questioned the authority of philosophers (see Kilminster, 1998, chapter 1).

On the subject of *epistemology,* from as early in his career as when he was a doctoral student under Hönigswald, there were indications in Elias's work that he was moving in the direction of developing a sociological epistemology to replace the traditional philosophical one (Kilminster and Wouters, 1995). This transformed epistemology would relate ways of knowing to the patterns of living together of human beings and remodel the traditional issue of validity (*Geltung*). This realization gathers momentum in his work to a point where he makes a complete break with philosophy, decisively turning his back on the tradition. The failure to grasp this feature of his thinking has sometimes led some commentators to try to pull Elias back into the philosophy from which his life's work was a sustained attempt at emancipation (see, for instance, Maso, 1995); or to criticize him from philosophical positions which he regarded himself as already having moved beyond (Sathaye, 1973).

The neo-Kantian philosophy in which Elias was initially schooled alerted him to key areas of inquiry, including the problem of the historical validity of knowledge, the issue of origins and status of universal categories of thought, and the prevalence of the model of the individual knowing subject in epistemology. The classical German philosophical tradition generally, and neo-Kantianism in particular, thus constituted a point of departure for Elias's transfer of his intellectual energies into a dynamic and historical sociology, which he believed could provide a more inclusive and adequate framework for the solution of those problems. Once Elias had begun to make this break, we would argue, his socio-logical inquiries became *structurally different* from philosophy, despite odd similarities of terminology. For example, philosophical speculations about the "objects" of the different sciences and the so-called "modes of being" postulated by fundamental ontologists and philosophical realists provided the stimulus for Elias to develop a *testable* theory of the levels of integration (physical, chemical, biological, social, etc.) of the social and natural worlds investigated by the different sciences (Elias, 1987). Similarly, discussions of values, value-relevance, and value-freedom in Rickert and Max Weber are recast by Elias as the theory of involvement and detachment, in which the conceptions of "autonomous" and "heteronomous" evaluations play a central role (Elias, 1987; more on this below). Generally, therefore, one finds in Elias a principled avoidance of philo-sophical concepts and the consistent substitution of sociological alternatives which are more amenable to empirical reference. More examples include: "truth" is recast as "reality congruence"; "part/whole" becomes "part-unit/unit"; and "abstractions" are transformed into "symbols at a high level of synthesis."

On the subject of *"evaluative"* or *"normative"* matters, Elias commented very early in his career that "Ethical questions are routinely and very wrongly separated from other scientific questions" (Elias, 1921, p. 140). Furthermore, Elias's total commitment to sociology as a "mission," which comes out clearly in his autobiographical *Reflections on a Life* (1994b), tells us something. He saw sociology as potentially able to assist human beings to orientate themselves in the figurations they form together and to help them to control the unintended social entanglements which threaten to escalate into destructive sequences, such as wars and mass killings. The figurational view of society, and Elias's theories of civilizing processes and established–outsiders relations, are implicitly under-pinned by the perceived imperative of generating knowledge to help groups in achieving greater "mutual identification" and thus to live in controlled antagon-ism with each other. Writers who have failed to grasp this aspect of his work have tended, in their criticisms of Elias, to confuse the technical and normative dimensions of some of Elias's concepts – for example, "civilization" and "civiliz-ing processes" (e.g. Leach, 1986; Bauman, 1988) – when Elias was aware of the normative issue right from the start and had already, to his own satisfaction anyway, transformed the issue and the relevant concepts into a sociological form amenable to empirical investigation (Fletcher, 1997, chapter 8).

It is worth filling in a little more of the background to this aspect of Elias's writings, since it is crucial for an understanding of the "moral" dimension of his work, which could all too easily – in view of the intense commitment of Elias and his followers to empirical research – be assimilated unreflectively into the mode of "value-free," sociological empiricism. The matter can be clarified through examining the links between Elias's thinking and Karl Mannheim's sociological program from the 1920s and 1930s, in the development of which Elias particip-ated. He shared the spirit, if not the last letter, of this intellectual venture. In addition to advocating a "relational" or "perspectival" view of society (echoes of which we find in Elias – see Kilminster, 1993, pp. 88–92), Mannheim's program was at the same time intended to deal with questions normally gathered together under the umbrella of "ethics," "politics," or "evaluative" and "existential" questions. These pertained to the ways in which humankind might achieve greater happiness and fulfillment individually and socially within what Mannheim called "the forms of living together of man" (Mannheim, 1957, p. 43).

In Mannheim's scheme of things, when considering evaluative matters the investigator makes a theoretical move sideways, the intention of this method being to redefine the scope and limits of assertions by politicians, philosophers, and others about the possibilities of human freedom, democracy, and happiness, by showing them to be coming inevitably from differing ideological perspectives. It was only through these one-sided perspectives that access was even possible to knowledge of society, all knowledge being existentially bounded and perspectival. Objectivity is sought by "the translation of perspectives into the terms of another" (Mannheim, 1936, pp. 270–1). Having made these moves, the investigator is then potentially able to evaluate the feasibility or validity of "ethical" or "political" issues in the form in which they were originally raised by the particular politician, party, or ideology. Mannheim refers to this theoretical journey as attaining a new form of "'objectivity'...in a roundabout fashion" (ibid., p. 270). These analytic steps then reach a point where the process "becomes a critique" (ibid., p. 256).

Elias's version of the journey specifies that it is only by a "detour via detachment" that sociologists can hope to gain more adequate knowledge of the structure of social events in which they themselves are also emotionally caught up (Elias, 1987, pp. 105, 106). He integrated a psychoanalytic dimension into the basic perspectivistic insight. He shared the Mannheimian ambition to transcribe so-called ethical and evaluative matters into sociologically manageable terms and thus to put the questions raised philosophically or ideologically on to another level. This position constitutes the pith and marrow of Elias's whole sociological program and is observable sometimes even in the interstices of his work. Consider, for example, the following statement in *The Court Society* on the historians' fear that sociological research threatens to extinguish human freedom and individuality:

> If one is prepared to approach such problems through two-pronged investigations on the theoretical and empirical planes in closest touch with one another, rather than on the basis of preconceived dogmatic positions, the question one is aiming at with words such as "freedom" and "determinacy" *poses itself in a different way.* (Elias, 1983, p. 30, our emphasis)

This "evaluative" intention also pervades the empirical-theoretical presentations that are laid out in *The Civilizing Process*. Elias opens the first volume with a sociogenetic inquiry, typical of the sociology of knowledge, into the origins of the concepts of *Kultur* and *Zivilisation*, which, as we have seen, were both redolent of the covert ideological dimension of Alfred Weber's sociology and other highly charged ideological conflicts at the time over whether civilized behavior was the acme or the nadir of the human social achievement. Among other things, the tacit task of *The Civilizing Process* is to reframe the range, applicability, and realistic usefulness of these two key terms via the sociological inquiry into their genesis in the European civilizing process in general. Significantly, Elias returns to the concepts at the end of volume II (Elias, 1994a, pp. 506ff, 520–4) at a new level and *reposes* the questions about human satisfaction, fulfillment, and constraint embodied more ideologically in the antithesis which partly provided the starting point.

## THE PRINCIPAL WORKS

Elias wrote his first book, which we now know as *The Court Society*, in the Frankfurt years, but it was not published in any form until 1969. It is a sociological study of aristocratic society in France in the century and a half before the Revolution. The reign of Louis XIV (1643–1715) was particularly crucial in completing the process of the "taming of warriors" and transforming some of them into courtiers devoid of independent military power and increasingly the creatures of the king.[4] The courtly nobility were a "two-front stratum" (Simmel's phrase), grouped between the king and the rich bourgeoisie. Elias shows how much of what seems to us the bizarre detail of court ritual can be understood as mechanisms through which the king could manipulate courtiers through tiny expressions of favor and disfavor. The "ethos of rank" became all-pervasive. He shows, for example, how rank determined the courtiers' expenditure, quite regardless of their *income*, and as a result many became impoverished. In an important corrective to the common assumption that bourgeois economic rationality (Max Weber's *Zweckrationalität* or the Frankfurt School's "instrumental rationality") is the characteristic and even unique form of Western rationality, Elias contends that although the extravagance of courtiers appears "irrational" from a bourgeois point of view, it was a manifestation of a "court-rationality" which itself involved a high degree of restraint on short-term effects for longer-term objectives; it was a form of rationality in which prestige and rank, rather than capital and income, were made calculable as instruments of power.

Within the hotbed of faction and intrigue that was the court, courtiers had to develop an extraordinary sensitivity to the status and importance that could be attributed to a person on the basis of fine nuances of bearing, speech, manners, and appearance. Observing, dealing with, relating to, or avoiding people became an art in itself. And self-observation was inextricably bound up in that: greater *self-control* was required. To later sociologists reared on Erving Goffman,[5] that may seem a universal characteristic of human society; in some degree it is – there is no zero-point, as Elias was fond of remarking in this and many other contexts – but Elias argued that this sensitivity was developed in court society to an exceptional *extent* through the competitive struggle for prestige, with vital interests at stake.

The courtly ethos of self-control, Elias argues, is reflected in the literature, drama, and even the French formal gardens of the period. But, above all, it is seen in the philosophy of Descartes and his successors. The image of the person as *homo clausus* so evident in "cogito ergo sum" is not just a philosophical idea but also the characteristic mode of upper class self-experience that had been developing in Europe since the Renaissance and the Reformation (Elias, 1991b). Elias saw his demonstration of the part played by court society in the development of this mode of self-experience as a supplement to, and not necessarily contradictory in all respects to, Max Weber's parallel account in *The Protestant Ethic and the Spirit of Capitalism*. What was needed was a more comprehensive theory of the development of the modern self-image and mode of self-experience, and that is what Elias set out to provide in *The Civilizing Process* and his later writings.

In this complex *magnum opus*, Elias speaks of civilizing processes on two levels.[6] The first is the individual level, and is rather uncontroversial. Infants and children have to acquire through learning the adult standards of behavior and feeling prevalent in their society; to speak of this as a civilizing process is more or less to use another term for "socialization," and ever since Freud and Piaget there has been little dispute that this process possesses structure and sequence. But the second level is more controversial. Where did these standards come from? They have not always existed, nor always been the same. Elias argues it is possible to identify long-term civilizing processes in the shaping of standards of behavior and feeling over many generations within particular cultures. Again, the idea that these standards *change* is not controversial; the controversy is about whether the changes take the form of structured processes of change with a discernible – though unplanned and by no means irreversible – *direction* over time.

The two volumes of *The Civilizing Process* often strike new readers as being about quite different subjects: the first dealing with the history of manners in Western Europe from the late Middle Ages to the Victorian period, the second advancing a detailed model of the process of state formation, again in Europe, since the Dark Ages. The basic idea, and the basic link between the two halves, is that there is a connection between the long-term structural development of societies and long-term changes in people's social character or habitus. (*Habitus* was in fact the word Elias used in German in 1939, but in the English edition of 1978–82 it was translated as "personality makeup"; the concept of "habitus" was later popularized among sociologists by Pierre Bourdieu, who, though a great friend and admirer of Elias's, seems more likely to have picked up the word in the first instance from other writers.) In other words, as the structure of societies becomes more complex, manners, culture, and personality also change in a particular and discernible direction, first among elite groups, then gradually more widely. This is worked out with great subtlety for Western Europe since the Middle Ages.[7]

Elias began the first volume of *The Civilizing Process* by reviewing the accretion of evaluative meanings around the notion of "civilization." The word was derived from *civilité* – the term used by courtiers to denote their own ways of behaving – but by the nineteenth century it had come to have a single general function, as a badge of the West's sense of superiority:

this concept expresses the self-consciousness of the West. . . . It sums up everything in which Western society of the last two or three centuries believes itself superior to earlier societies or "more primitive" contemporary ones. By this term, Western society seeks to describe what constitutes its special character and what it is proud of: the level of *its* technology, the nature of *its* manners, the development of *its* scientific knowledge or view of the world, and much more. (Elias, 1994a, p. 3)

By the nineteenth century, the ways people in the West used the *word* civilization showed that they had largely forgotten the *process* of civilization. Confident of the superiority of their own now seemingly inherent and eternal standards, they wished only to "civilize" the natives of the lands they were now colonizing (or the lower orders of their own societies). They lost awareness that their own ancestors had undergone a learning process, a civilizing process, through which they *acquired* the characteristics now perceived as marks of an imagined *innate* superiority.

In order to retrieve an awareness of this forgotten process from the European past, Elias studied the development of social standards governing eating, nose-blowing, spitting, urinating and defecating, undressing, and sleeping. The reason for investigating these most "natural" or "animalic" facets of behavior was that these are things that by their biological constitution all human beings have to do in any society, culture, or age. Moreover, human infants are born in more or less the same emotional and physical condition at all times and places, and in every society they have to learn how to handle these matters. Therefore, if the way they are handled changes over time, it stands out rather clearly.

Elias's principal sources were French, German, Italian, and English manners books from the Middle Ages to the mid-nineteenth century. In earlier centuries these basic matters of behavior – discussion of which would later cause embarrassment, or at least the humorous sensation of a taboo having been broken – were spoken of openly and frankly, without shame. Then gradually, from the Renaissance, a long-term trend toward greater demands on emotional management in adults becomes apparent: the child has further to travel, so to speak, to attain the adult standard. Codes of behavior become more differentiated, and thresholds of shame and embarrassment advance. Many things become hidden behind the scenes of social life – and also repressed behind the scenes of conscious mental life.

Elias produces evidence to show that this long-term civilizing process cannot be explained away simply by reference to rising levels of material prosperity or to advances in scientific knowledge of health and hygiene, although these were still involved. Moreover, a similar civilizing curve can also be discerned in the development of social standards of self-restraint over resort to the use of *violence*. The explanation is found in the dynamic of social interdependencies. Over a period of many centuries in Europe, chains of social interdependence have grown longer and people have become more subject to more multipolar social constraints. In other words, "more people are forced more often to pay more attention to more other people" (Goudsblom, 1989, p. 722). In the course of this process, the *balance* of the controls by which individual people steer their conduct shifts from the preponderance of external constraints (*Fremdzwänge* –

constraints *by other people*) towards more internalized self-constraints (*Selbstzwänge*). Here the influence of Freud on Elias is evident. But it is not just a matter of *more* self-restraint: rather, the balance tilts toward self-constraint being more *automatic*, more *even* (volatility of mood becomes less than in medieval times), and more *all-embracing* (standards apply more equally in public and private, and to all other people, irrespective of rank, etc.).

In the second volume, Elias puts forward a detailed theory of state formation in Europe, implicitly beginning from Max Weber's definition of the state as an organization which successfully upholds a claim to binding rule-making over a territory, by virtue of commanding a monopoly of the legitimate use of violence. Elias, however, is more interested in the process through which a monopoly of the means of violence – and taxation – is established and extended. That innocent addition – *taxation* – is significant. Elias insisted that Marxist attempts to accord causal primacy to economic "factors" or "forces" or "modes of production" were misleading. The means of production, the means of protection (including attack), and the means of orientation could not be reduced to each other; moreover, in the period of which Elias was talking, the means of violence and the means of production were simply inextricable.

Elias does not regard state-formation as the sole "cause"; indeed, he rejects the use of that concept entirely in this context. State formation, he argues, is only one process interweaving with others to enmesh individuals in increasingly complex webs of interdependence. It interweaves with the division of labor, the growth of trade, towns, the use of money and administrative apparatuses, and increasing population in a spiral process. The internal pacification of territory facilitates trade, which facilitates the growth of towns and division of labor and generates taxes which support larger administrative and military organizations, which in turn facilitate the internal pacification of larger territories, and so on – a cumulative process experienced as a compelling force by people caught up in it. Furthermore, this has long-term effects on people's habitus:

> if in a particular region, the power of central authority grows, if over a larger or smaller area people are *forced* to live at peace with one another, the moulding of the affects and the standards of the demands made upon emotional management are very gradually changed as well (Elias, 1994a, p. 165, our emphasis; translation modified to reflect Elias's later terminology)

According to Elias, the gradually higher standards of habitual self-restraint engendered in people contribute in turn to the upward spiral – being necessary, for example, in the formation of gradually more effective and calculable administration.

## LATER EXTENSIONS

The theory of civilizing processes has provoked much scholarly debate.[8] Meanwhile, Elias extended his original thesis in many directions. What follows is a brief account of a selection of what we judge to be the most important, major extensions and developments of his ideas which he himself undertook, in chronological order. (A number of other works, monographs, and lectures have been omitted.)

In *The Established and the Outsiders: a Sociological Inquiry into Community Problems*, written with John L. Scotson (1965; second edition, 1994), Elias develops, through a detailed piece of empirical research of three neighborhoods in a Leicestershire village, the theory of established–outsider relations, which has a wider application. This theory (which is foreshadowed in *The Civilizing Process* and in early writings such as Elias's 1935 essay on the Huguenots; see Elias, 1998) is designed to provide simpler but more inclusive concepts than class, status, and party, which have dominated Marxian and Weberian approaches to inequality. (These general considerations are set out most clearly in "A Theoretical Essay on Established and Outsider Relations," written by Elias in 1976 and included in the 1994 edition of the book by Elias and Scotson). For Elias, class relations are only one form of social oppression and we should not generalize from their features to all types. The theory of established and outsider relations is conceived as part of the theory of civilizing processes, being particularly useful for understanding the complex dynamics of *varieties* of group oppression and group ascent, and the effects of such social ascendance on social and behavioral codes. In Eliasian language, it enables us to grasp with one concept the changing patterns in the uneven balances of power between many different kinds of interdependent groups in a figuration. These power balances include – in addition to those between economic classes – the relations between men and women, homosexuals and heterosexuals, blacks and whites, parents and children (or, more generally, between older and younger generations), governors and governed, and colonizers and colonized.

According to the theory (which has been applied in a considerable range of empirical research: see works cited in Kranendonk, 1990, pp. 158–69; Mennell, 1998, pp. 125–39), when the power gradient between groups is very steep, outsiders are often stigmatized as unworthy, filthy, shifty, or perhaps childlike, as in the case of whites stigmatizing blacks as Sambo figures. At this stage, images of outsiders are highly fantasy-laden and the attitudes of established toward outsiders are extremely rigid. The differences between the behavior and attitudes of established and outsiders are frequently (wrongly) explained biologically. The "group charisma" of the established is such that power superiority is equated with human merit or the grace of nature or God. Outsiders take into their conscience the view of themselves that the established have formed, and so come to accept that they are unworthy, even inhuman. They come to internalize their own "group disgrace." There is an echo of Freud's "identification with the aggressor" here, the difference being that rather than regarding the phenomenon *individualistically* as a constant in relations between parent and child, or leader and follower, Elias refashions it as symptomatic of a particular *stage* of the shifting power relations between specific interdependent *groups*.

Where the balance of power is becoming more equal, tilting more in favor of the outsiders, then one finds symptoms of rebellion and emancipation, as in the case of the relations between older and younger generations, men and women, homosexuals and heterosexuals, and blacks and whites in recent times. At this stage of the process, images of outsiders become less fantasy-laden and the attitudes of the established groups toward the outsiders more flexible and accommodating. Outsiders begin to develop their own "we-image" and to deny the one imposed by the established. In the early stages of an emancipatory phase there are often calls for separatism (both blacks and women have been through this) and self-help groups form to build new self-images for the rising group (the slogan "black is beautiful" epitomizes this part of the process). As the balance of power becomes *relatively more* equal (not entirely equal) compared with the earlier phase, and outsiders begin to merge with the established to form a new establishment, then more realistic mutual perceptions become possible between groups as the tensions between them diminish.

The three books *Involvement and Detachment* (1987), *Time: an Essay* (1992), and *The Symbol Theory* (1991a) represent major extensions of the theory of civilizing processes to the history of humanity as a whole in the context of biological evolution. These three later works form part of the cluster of Elias's writings on the sociology of knowledge (see, for example, Elias, 1971, 1972, 1974, 1982, 1984), to which he himself, in various interviews, assigned considerable importance. In all of them Elias's very long-term orientation is much to the fore. He also argues in these works, among many other things, that an adequate understanding of social development needs to be integrated into the overall evolutionary process. As he puts it in *The Symbol Theory*:

> The natural constitution of human beings prepares them for learning from others, for living with others, for being cared for by others and for caring for others. It is difficult to imagine how social scientists can gain a clear understanding of the fact that nature prepares human beings for life in society without including aspects of the evolutionary process and of the social development of humankind in their field of vision, (Elias, 1991a, p. 145)

In *Involvement and Detachment* (1987), and in various articles written in the 1970s, Elias developed a sophisticated sociogenetic theory of knowledge and the sciences.[9] In the perspective of the development of human knowledge over the whole history of the species, the "double-bind" relationship between the dangers people faced and the fears they experienced posed formidable initial obstacles to an escape from emotionally charged, fantasy-laden, and "involved" knowledge. Escape can never be complete, but control over social dangers and fears has lagged behind control over natural forces and the fears arising from the human experience of them; and by extension the social sciences remain *relatively* less autonomous and "detached" than the natural sciences. Elias argues that the predominant form of explanation gradually changes across the spectrum from the physical through the biological to the social sciences, with law-like theories becoming less important. The aim of the social scientist should be to construct "process-theories" in five dimensions: the three dimensions of space, plus time and *experience*. As always for Elias, his own substantive sociological investigations stand as exemplars of the pursuit of process theories resting on an image of humankind as "open people."

In *Time: an Essay* (1992) Elias argues that "time" refers not to any universal substance or capacity of the human mind, as philosophers have variously claimed, but to the human social *activity* of *timing*. This activity rests on the human biologically endowed capacity for memory and synthesis, for making connections through the use of symbols. More than any other creatures, humans are orientated by the experience not only of each individual but also of long chains of generations, gradually improving and extending the human means of orientation. It is simply a means of using symbols to connect two or more sequences of changes – physical, biological, or social – using one as a frame of reference for the others. Hence, "time" is not just "subjective"; it has evolved through experience in a long intergenerational learning process.

The social need for timing was much less acute and pervasive in earlier societies than in the more highly organized modern industrial states. Increased differentiation and integration of social functions mean that in modern societies many long chains of interdependence intersect within the individual, requiring constant awareness of time in the coordination of numerous activities. People have to adjust themselves to each other as part of an increasingly intricate mesh of contacts and social necessities, which requires a socially standardized, high-level symbol of timing to enable this to be done with accuracy and predictability. A particularly complex system of self-regulation and an acute individual sensibility with regard to time has developed. The individualization of social time-control thus bears all the hallmarks of a civilizing process.

*The Symbol Theory* (1991a), which turned out to be the last extended work to be completed for publication by Elias prior to his death in August 1990, is an inquiry into the survival value in the evolutionary process of reality-congruent knowledge made possible by the human capacity for symbol making. Part of the task of this book is to look at the human social and biological condition in a detached, non-reductionist, and non-religious way, so as to enable us to develop a more realistic model of humankind as being caught up in the evolutionary process on another level. For Elias, evolutionary theory is not to be identified solely with Darwin's version, which he regards as incomplete and representing an early stage of elaboration. Anticipating the accusations of evolutionary determinism or teleology, he draws the crucial distinction here, as in several other places in this group of writings, between largely irreversible biological *evolution* and potentially reversible social *development*. Unlike processes of biological evolution, it is possible for social processes to go into reverse and return to an earlier stage of their development. (It is in this sense that he acknowledged the possibility of civilizing processes going into reverse as processes of "decivilization": see below.)

Within this broad framework of socio-natural development, which he calls the Great Evolution (Elias, 1987, part III), Elias sees the technical human capacity for communication via symbols to be a unique consequence of the blind inventiveness of nature. Symbols, he insists, are also *tangible* sound patterns of human communication, made possible by the evolutionary biological precondition of the unique and complex vocal apparatus of humans. The capacity of humans to steer their conduct by means of learned knowledge gave them a great evolutionary advantage over other species, which were unable to accomplish this at all or only to a very limited extent.

*The Germans: Power Struggles and the Development of Habitus in the Nineteenth and Twentieth Centuries* (1996) is a late collection of essays and lectures on German social development and national character and the rise of the Nazis, originally published in German in 1989, exactly 50 years after *The Civilizing Process*. The later volume expands and develops the triangular comparison between Britain, France, and Germany which runs through the earlier work, through a detailed analysis of the German case. Elias focuses on the successive historical diminution, through the wars of 1866 and 1914–18, of German territory in the west and east, resulting in the hegemony of Prussia in the German Confederation. This meant that a centralized German nation-state did not emerge with the ease and speed of other European states, such as England and France. The character of the German habitus, personality, and social structure, which combined to produce the rise of Hitler and the Nazi genocides, is best understood in relation to this feature of Germany's past.

The comparatively late unification of Germany occurred under the leadership of the militaristic ruling strata of Prussia. This was a process in the course of which large sections of the middle classes abandoned the humanistic values which had hitherto predominated in their social circles, and adopted instead the militaristic and authoritarian values of the hegemonic Prussians. German society became orientated around a code of honor, in which dueling and the demanding and giving of "satisfaction" occupied pride of place. Elias argues that Germany's unification involved the "brutalization" of much of the middle classes. The code of behavior which they adopted was essentially a warrior code which emphasized the cult of hardness and obedience and unyielding attitudes of contempt for weakness and compromise. Along with these features of the emerging German habitus was a need to submit to a strong state authority and a decided decline in people's ability to empathize with others. Or, in Elias's words, there occurred a contraction in the scope of "mutual identification." Combined with the weakening of the state's monopoly of violence in the Weimar Republic and the consequent escalation of violence and social fears, these preconditions gave rise to a compelling sequential development (a likely, but *not inevitable*, process) which produced a society-wide process of "decivilization," accelerating during the Weimar Republic and culminating in the Second World War and the Holocaust (see Fletcher, 1997).

## Principles of Process Sociology

The central recommendations of Elias's sociology, as a theoretical-empirical research strategy, are set out most systematically and succinctly in *What Is Sociology?* (1978). (The highly stimulating theoretical reflections contained in *The Society of Individuals* (Elias, 1991b) are a good supplement.) These recommendations grew out of a vast amount of research and reflection, some of which we have tried to summarize. Elias states that sociology is about studying real people in the plural in webs of social interdependencies. People are bonded to each other not only economically or politically, but also *emotionally*. (The latter dimension had been a central theme of his work since the beginning. He anticipated the contemporary specialisms of the sociology of emotions and of the body a very long time ago.) Figurational sociology is committed to studying people "in the round," simultaneously in *all* the ways in which they are tied to each other in their social existence. It is best summarized as a dynamic sociology of human bonding and the formation of individuals, which centrally stresses the role of power in human relationships. Primacy is given to the developing structure of the social interdependencies (including local, national, regional, and global dimensions) in which people are actually integrated, not to "the social system" in the abstract, nor to analytically distinguished "spheres" or conditions of social action. As Elias declared, in a polemic against Talcott Parsons: "Why put 'actions' in the center of a theory of society and not the people who act? If anything, societies are networks of human beings in the round, not a medley of disembodied actions" (Elias, 1970a, p. 277).

Since sociologists are part of the figurations which they are seeking to understand and to explain, one of the problems they face is controlling for their wishes, fears, and prejudices ("involvements" in Elias's terminology), which stem from their own enmeshment in the tensions generated by social interdependencies which comprise their society. This problem presents itself simply because there is no place outside the antagonisms and conflicts of the figuration from which to observe it. So, for Elias, the problem of achieving a greater degree of sociological detachment is integral to his theory of knowledge and thus to his sociology (Elias, 1987). It also means that at this stage of the development of the discipline, the cognitive status of sociological texts cannot but be bound up to some degree with the social perspective, location, or position of their authors, and so must be to some degree "involved." So, if standards of detachment and fact orientation ("autonomous evaluations" in Elias's terminology) are only relatively weakly institutionalized in sociology, it is likely that a great deal of sociological output will be more informed by extra-sociological involvements ("heteronomous evaluations"). In other words, under present conditions the inquiries of many sociological practitioners will tell us more about them than about the objects of their investigations. Or to put it another way, their involvement/detachment balance will be tilted towards the former pole.

In summary, Goudsblom (1977a, p. 6) and Mennell (1998, p. 252) have distilled from Elias four principles of process sociology. The fact that readers may initially be suspicious of the simplicity and obviousness of these points may be indicative of the expectations of sophistication and difficulty which sociologists commonly associate with the language of the discipline, particularly its theoretical side.

1   Human beings are interdependent in a variety of ways; they are inextric-
    ably bonded to each other in the social figurations they form with one
    another, including with people they do not know.
2   These figurations are continually in flux, undergoing changes, some rapid
    and ephemeral, others slower and more lasting.
3   The long-term developments taking place in human figurations have been,
    and continue to be, largely unplanned and unforeseen but are nonetheless
    structured.
4   The development of human knowledge (including sociology itself) takes
    place within human figurations and forms one important aspect of their
    overall development.

## SUMMARY AND EVALUATION

The reception of Elias's work and his reputation have varied from country to
country. In the Netherlands and Germany his intellectual standing and reputation are considerable, while in Britain, France, and the USA he is appreciated
only patchily (Mennell, 1998, pp. 278–84).[10] One of the obstacles to the
appreciation of Elias in the USA is that one of prerequisites for making a
successful career in sociology today is the choice of a specialism, say medical,
political, or urban sociology, or perhaps methods. Specialization has gone a very
long way in sociology generally, but particularly far in the USA. With one or two
exceptions, there has been a decline (on both sides of the Atlantic) of the sociological generalist who can cross specialisms and draw things together. This,
however, is precisely the (unfashionable) strength of Elias's perspective.

In the face of the forces of specialization, the synoptic thrust of sociology has
been diverted into the artificial field of "social theory," which tries to accomplish
this aim on a purely conceptual terrain. As a result, "theory" itself has ironically
become yet another specialism. Here, however, the holistic, generalizing, connecting impetus is not carried out in the substantive, theoretical-*empirical* fashion so typical of Elias. Furthermore, the expansion of social theory has tended to
pull sociology back into philosophy, again something upon which Elias had
firmly turned his back (see Kilminster, 1998, part II).

So, it seems, it is hard to find a fertile soil in which Elias's unique brand of
sociology can grow. In the case of Britain, the pattern had already been established. Although Elias lived and worked there for about forty years, scarcely
anyone seemed to have noticed; at any rate, very few took up his work.
Like many other continental social-scientific émigrés, Elias encountered the
inertia of the British traditions of social administration, Fabianism, and empiricism in the service of social reform (Kilminster and Varcoe, 1996, pp. 5–10).
In contrast, the Dutch were from early on receptive to Elias's work. *Über
den Prozess der Zivilisation* was well reviewed in the Netherlands in the
months before the German invasion in 1940, and a major research school
developed there from 1969 onwards under the intellectual leadership of
Johan Goudsblom. The question of why precisely the Netherlands should have

been so much more receptive than Britain or the USA has not yet been fully answered.

There are signs that Elias's intellectual standing generally will continue to rise in the next few decades, with his work carried forward on to a new level. The generation that "discovered" and championed Elias in the early 1970s in Europe is now in mid–late career or approaching retirement. They used Elias's ideas in a wide variety of empirical research (see, for example, Mennell, 1985; Wouters, 1988; Goudsblom, 1992; van Benthem van den Bergh, 1992; Kapteyn, 1996). But this generation of Eliasians, which includes the present authors, is also the embattled one which had to fight to secure his recognition against the social weight of sociology establishments, proliferating paradigm communities, philosophoidal social theorists and politically orientated groups of sociologists (Goudsblom, 1977a, b; Dunning and Mennell, 1979; Dunning, 1987; Korte, 1997; Kilminster, 1998; Mennell, 1998). Sometimes these polemics and defences gave the understandable, but misleading, impression that the Eliasians were a sect. But there are younger people coming up who do not have to fight those battles. As Robert van Krieken (1998, p. 171) has written, there is no further mileage left in "settling questions of whether Elias was right or wrong, or of coming up with the 'correct' interpretation" of aspects of his work. We believe that the next generation can take for granted the nuanced understanding of Elias's work established by the one which preceded them and bring it to bear, along with other perspectives, on the burning issues of their generation. There is evidence that these are emerging as: (a) gender, sexuality, and identity (Klein, 1992; Shilling, 1993; Falk 1994; Tseëlon, 1995; Waldhoff, 1995; Klein and Liebsch 1997; Mellor and Shilling, 1997; Burkitt 1998; Greco, 1998); and (b) the reorientation of a sociological theory specialism bogged down in dualisms and over-abstraction (Burkitt, 1989; Heilbron, 1995; Fletcher, 1997; van Krieken, 1998; also Kilminster 1998). On the latter area, Robert van Krieken has captured the mood:

> There is a powerful tendency among sociologists towards polarisation between structure and action, micro and macro approaches, between historical sociology and ahistorical studies, between rational choice theory and sociological determinism. All the features of Elias's approach – the emphasis on social relations, long-term processes, the interweaving of planned action and unplanned development, the importance of seeing humans as interdependent, the centrality of power in social relations, and the significance of the concept of "habitus" in understanding human conduct – have considerable potential for taking sociological theory beyond these dichotomies, which seem to have rather outlived their usefulness. (van Krieken, 1998, p. 173)

Elias often said that his work was unfinished, simply an early elaboration of problems to be taken further by others. He offered his synthesis as an invitation to others to work empirically and theoretically to confirm or to refute and thus to amend the basic propositions. Our view is that his work is a rich source of inspiration for the sociological imagination.

## Acknowledgments

We are grateful to Eric Dunning and Cas Wouters for their comments on an earlier draft.

## Notes

1   The German text was republished in 1969, and Elias's reputation in Germany and the Netherlands grew rapidly from then onwards. A French translation was published in the early 1970s, but the English version was long delayed and surrounded by confusion when it did appear. The first volume was published under the title *The History of Manners* in 1978. There was then a four-year gap before the appearance of the second, which appeared under two different titles: *State-Formation and Violence* in Britain and the unauthorized *Power and Civility* in the United States. As a consequence, many readers and some reviewers failed to appreciate that the two volumes were inseparable halves of a single work. In 1994, Blackwell published a one-volume edition under the title *The Civilizing Process*, to which it is best to refer, though it reproduces all the textual faults of the earlier English edition.

2   A translation of the first couple of pages of the thesis – enough to give merely the flavour of what Elias wrote – is included in Goudsblom and Mennell (1998, pp. 6–7).

3   See Mann (1983).

4   Elias argued that the taming of warriors was a process of significance not just in European history but in the development of human societies generally, and that it had been relatively neglected by sociologists.

5   Goffman cited the original edition of *Über den Prozess der Zivilisation* in *Asylums* (1961) and *Behavior in Public Places* (1963); that is quite remarkable, considering the obscurity of Elias's work in the early 1960s. (He was probably introduced to the book by Edward Shils in Chicago, where he was a graduate student in the late 1940s.)

6   In fact, especially in his more recent works, such as *Time: an Essay* (1992) and *Humana Conditio* (1985), Elias also spoke of civilizing processes on a third level, that of humanity as a whole. See Mennell (1998, pp. 200–24).

7   *The Civilizing Process* is based entirely on European evidence. It is not so much that it is Euro*centric* as that it is *about* Europe. Elias recognized that one of the most important gaps in his work, and one of the most interesting lines for further research, was the study of equivalent – but in detail no doubt different – civilizing processes in other historic cultures.

8   For a fuller discussion of the controversies, see Mennell (1998), especially chapter 10.

9   Two of his most important essays on knowledge and the sciences were brought together in *Involvement and Detachment* (1987). His many other essays in this field, however, remain scattered between various journals in German or English. For a full discussion, see Mennell (1998, chapters 7 and 8).

10   Two recent signs that American sociologists are coming to regard Elias as a sociologist of the first rank are the inclusion of a selection of his writings in the famous Heritage of Sociology series (Mennell and Goudsblom, 1998) and George Ritzer's extended discussion of his work in the fourth edition of his book *Sociological Theory* (Ritzer, 1996, pp. 511–25).

# Bibliography

## Writings of Norbert Elias

Vom Sehen in der Natur. 1921. *Breslauer Heft*, 8–10 (May–July), 133–44.

Contributions to Discussion on Karl Mannheim, Die Bedeutung der Konkurrenz im Gebiete des Geistigen. 1929a. In *Verhandlungen des Sechsten Deutschen Soziologentages von 17 zu 19 September 1928 in Zürich*. Tübingen, J. C. B. Mohr.

Zur Soziologie des deutschen Antisemitismus. 1929b. *Israelitisches Gemeindeblatt: Offizielles Organ der israelitischen Gemeinden Mannheim und Ludwigshafen*, December 13, 3–6.

*The Established and the Outsiders* (with John L. Scotson). 1965 (2nd edn 1994). London: Sage.

Sociology and Psychiatry. 1969. In S. H. Foulkes and G. Stewart Prince (eds), *Psychiatry in a Changing Society*. London: Tavistock.

Processes of State Formation and Nation-building. 1970a. In *Transactions of the Seventh World Congress of Sociology, Varna. Volume III*. Sofia: International Sociological Association (1972), pp. 274–84.

Interview met Norbert Elias. 1970b. *Sociologische Gids*, 17(2): 133–40. Reprinted as An Interview in Amsterdam. In Johan Goudsblom and Stephen Mennell (eds), *The Norbert Elias Reader: a Biographical Selection*. Oxford: Blackwell, 1998, pp. 141–51.

The Sociology of Knowledge: New Perspectives. 1971. *Sociology*, 5(2/3), 149–68, 355–70.

Theory of Science and History of Science: Comments on a Recent Discussion. 1972. *Economy and Society*, 1(2), 117–33.

The Sciences: towards a Theory. 1974. In Richard Whitley (ed.), *Social Processes of Scientific Development*. London: Routledge.

*What Is Sociology?* 1978. London: Hutchinson.

Scientific Establishments. 1982. In Norbert Elias, Herminio Martins and Richard Whitley (eds), *Scientific Establishments and Hierarchies*. Dordrecht: Reidel.

*The Court Society*. 1983. Oxford: Basil Blackwell.

On the Sociogenesis of Sociology. 1984. *Amsterdams Sociologisch Tijdschrift*, 11(1), 14–52.

*The Loneliness of the Dying*. 1985a. Oxford: Basil Blackwell.

*Humana Conditio: Beobachtungen zur Entwicklung der Menschheit am 40. Jahrestag eines Kriegsendes (8. Mai 1945)*. 1985b. Frankfurt: Suhrkamp.

*Quest for Excitement: Sport and Leisure in the Civilizing Process* (with Eric Dunning). 1986. Oxford: Basil Blackwell.

*Involvement and Detachment*. 1987. Oxford: Basil Blackwell.

*The Symbol Theory*. 1991a. London: Sage.

*The Society of Individuals*. 1991b. Oxford: Blackwell.

*Time: an Essay*. 1992. Oxford: Blackwell.

*The Civilizing Process*. 1994a. Oxford: Blackwell.

*Reflections on a Life*. 1994b. Cambridge: Polity Press.

*The Germans: Power Struggles and the Development of Habitus in the Nineteenth and Twentieth Centuries*. 1996. Cambridge: Polity Press.

The Expulsion of the Huguenots from France. 1998. In Johan Goudsblom and Stephen Mennell (eds), *The Norbert Elias Reader: a Biographical Selection*. Oxford: Blackwell, pp. 19–25.

## Further reading

Aron, Raymond (1957) *German Sociology*. London: Heinemann.

Bauman, Zygmunt (1988) *Modernity and the Holocaust*. Cambridge: Polity Press.

Bogner, Artur (1987) Elias and the Frankfurt School. *Theory, Culture and Society*, 4(2/3), 249–85.

Burkitt, Ian (1989) *Social Selves*. London: Sage.

Burkitt, Ian (1998) Sexuality and Gender Identity: from a Discursive to a Relational Analysis. *Sociological Review*, 46(3), 483–504.

Dunning, Eric (1987) Comments on Elias's "Scenes from the Life of a Knight." *Theory, Culture and Society*, 4(2/3), 366–71.

Dunning, Eric and Mennell, Stephen (1979) "Figurational Sociology": Some Critical Comments on Zygmunt Bauman's "The Phenomenon of Norbert Elias." *Sociology*, 13(3), 497–501.

Falk, Pasi (1994) *The Consuming Body*. London: Sage.

Febvre, Lucien (1930) *Civilization*: Evolution of a Word and a Group of Ideas. In John Rundell and Stephen Mennell (eds), *Classical Readings in Culture and Civilization*. London: Routledge (1998), pp. 160–90.

Fletcher, Jonathan (1997) *Violence and Civilization: an Introduction to the Work of Norbert Elias*. Cambridge: Polity Press.

Freud, Sigmund (1930) *Civilization and Its Discontents*. New York: W. W. Norton (1962).

Goffman, Erving (1961) *Asylums*. Garden City, NY: Doubleday.

Goffman, Erving (1963) *Behavior in Public Places*. New York: Free Press.

Goudsblom, Johan (1977a) *Sociology in the Balance*. Oxford: Basil Blackwell.

Goudsblom, Johan (1977b) Responses to Norbert Elias's work in England, Germany, the Netherlands and France. In Peter Gleichmann, Johan Goudsblom, and Hermann Korte (eds), *Human Figurations: Essays for Norbert Elias*. Amsterdam: Stichting Amsterdams Sociologisch Tijdschrift, pp. 37–97.

Goudsblom, Johan (1989) Stijlen en beschaving. *De Gids*, 152, 720–2.

Goudsblom, Johan (1992) *Fire and Civilization*. London: Allen Lane.

Goudsblom, Johan and Mennell, Stephen (eds) (1998) *The Norbert Elias Reader: a Biographical Selection*. Oxford: Blackwell.

Greco, Monica (1998) *Illness as a Work of Thought: a Foucauldian Perspective on Psychosomatics*. London: Routledge.

Hackeschmidt, Jörg (1997) *Von Kurt Blumenfeld zu Norbert Elias: Die Erfindung einer judischen Nation*. Hamburg: Europäische Verlaganstalt.

Heilbron, Johan (1995) *The Rise of Social Theory*. Cambridge: Polity Press.

Horkheimer, Max and Adorno, Theodor W. (1979) *Dialectic of Enlightenment*. London: New Left Books.

Kapteyn, Paul (1996) *The Stateless Market*. London: Routledge.

Kettler, David and Meja, Volker (1995) *Karl Mannheim and the Crisis of Liberalism: the Secret of These New Times*. New Brunswick, NJ: Transaction Publishers.

Kilminster, Richard (1993) Norbert Elias and Karl Mannheim: Closeness and Distance. *Theory, Culture and Society*, 10(3), 81–114.

Kilminster, Richard (1998) *The Sociological Revolution: from the Enlightenment to the Global Age*. London and New York: Routledge.

Kilminster, Richard and Varcoe, Ian (1996) Introduction: Intellectual Migration and Sociological Insight. In Richard Kilminster and Ian Varcoe (eds), *Culture, Modernity and Revolution: Essays in Honour of Zygmunt Bauman*. London: Routledge.

Kilminster, Richard and Wouters, Cas (1995) From Philosophy to Sociology. Elias and the Neo-Kantians: a Response to Benjo Maso. *Theory, Culture and Society,* 12(3), 81–120.

Klein, Gabriele (1992) *FrauenKoerperTanz: Eine Zivilisationsgeschichte des Tanzes.* Berlin: Quadriga.

Klein, Gabriele and Liebsch, Katherina (eds) (1997) *Zivilisierung des weiblichen Ich.* Frankfurt-am-Main: Suhrkamp.

Korte, Hermann (1997) *Über Norbert Elias: Das Werden eines Wissensschaftlers,* revised edition. Opladen: Leske & Budrich.

Kranendonk, Willem H. (1990) *Society as Process: a Bibliography of Figurational Sociology in the Netherlands.* Amsterdam: Sociologisch Instituut, Universiteit van Amsterdam.

Leach, Edmund (1986) Violence. *London Review of Books,* October 23.

Lepenies, Wolf (1978) Norbert Elias: an Outsider Full of Unprejudiced Insight. *New German Critique,* 15, 57–64.

Mann, Thomas (1983) *Reflections of a Non-political Man.* New York: Frederick Ungar.

Mannheim, Karl (1936) *Ideology and Utopia.* London: Routledge & Kegan Paul.

Mannheim, Karl (1953) German Sociology (1918–1933). In Karl Mannheim, *Essays on the Sociology and Social Psychology.* London: Routledge & Kegan Paul.

Mannheim, Karl (1957) *Systematic Sociology: an Introduction to the Study of Society.* London: Routledge & Kegan Paul.

Maso, Benjo (1995) Elias and the Neo-Kantians: Intellectual Backgrounds of *The Civilizing Process. Theory, Culture and Society,* 12(3), 43–79.

Mellor, Philip and Shilling, Chris (1997) *Re-forming the Body: Religion, Community and Modernity.* London: Sage.

Mennell, Stephen (1985) *All Manners of Food: Eating and Taste in England and France from the Middle Ages to the Present.* Oxford: Blackwell.

Mennell, Stephen (1998) *Norbert Elias: an Introduction.* Dublin: University College Dublin Press.

Mennell, Stephen and Goudsblom, Johan (eds) (1998) *Norbert Elias on Civilization, Power and Knowledge.* Chicago: University of Chicago Press.

Pines, Malcolm (ed.) (1997) Special Section: Centennial Celebration to Commemorate the Birth and Work of Norbert Elias. *Group Analysis,* 30(4), 475–529.

Ritzer, George (1996) *Sociological Theory,* 4th edn. New York: McGraw-Hill.

Sathaye, S. G. (1973) On Norbert Elias's Developmental Paradigm. *Sociology,* 7(1), 117–23.

Schad, Susanne Petra (1972) *Empirical Social Research in Weimar Germany.* The Hague: Mouton.

Shilling, Chris (1993) *The Body and Social Theory.* London: Sage.

Tseëlon, Efrat (1995) *The Masque of Femininity.* London: Sage.

van Benthem van den Bergh, Godfried (1992) *The Nuclear Revolution and the End of the Cold War: Forced Restraint.* London: Macmillan.

van Krieken, Robert (1998) *Norbert Elias.* London: Routledge.

Waldhoff, Hans-Peter (1995) *Fremde und Zivilisierung: Wissenssoziologische Studien über das Verarbeiten von Gefühlen der Fremdheit – Probleme der modernen Peripherie-Zentrums-Migration am türkisch-deutschen Beispiel.* Frankfurt-am-Main: Suhrkamp.

Weber, Alfred (1998) Fundamentals of Culture Sociology: Social Process, Civilizational Process and Culture-movement. In John Rundell and Stephen Mennell (eds), *Classical Readings in Culture and Civilization.* London: Routledge, pp. 191–215.

Wouters, Cas (1988) Etiquette Books and Emotion Management in the Twentieth Century: American Habitus in International Comparison. In Peter N. Stearns and Jan Lewis (eds), *An Emotional History of the United States*. New York: New York University Press, pp. 283–304.

# 20

## Michel Foucault

### Barry Smart

### Introduction: Foucault as a Social Theorist

With all beginnings there is a temptation to simply accept the established discursive order of things, to submit to the agenda which presents itself. But in addressing the issue of Foucault's contribution to social thought – the question of his status as a social theorist and the place, distinctiveness, and significance of his work within social theory – to simply proceed without reflecting on the terms of reference, and the question of their appropriateness, even if only briefly, would be to fail to do justice to the critically reflexive analytic approach Foucault consistently employed in his various studies.

Any attempt to situate Foucault is likely to promote debate, and the identification of Foucault as a social theorist is no exception. As is the case with many of the figures who have been identified as contributors to the discourse of social theory, other claims may be made, other contributions recognized. For example, Marx, Weber, and Simmel are regarded as key social theorists, but their respective works also contribute significantly, in some instances more significantly, to other discursive fields, including political economy (Marx), economic history (Weber), and philosophy and cultural analysis (Simmel). In the case of Foucault, philosophy and history might be acknowledged to have first claim, although the significance for social and cultural analysis of his studies of madness and reason, discipline and punishment, and sexuality and subjectivity is now widely recognized and beyond dispute. In raising these concerns I am trying to draw attention to a number of issues. In reading the work of a particular analyst it is necessary to be aware of the tendency to invoke "the author as the unifying principle in a particular group of writings or statements" (Foucault, 1971, p. 14) and to consider the consequences of so doing. This is a matter on which it is necessary to reflect, a matter with which Foucault was concerned because it had implications for the sources or texts selected for analysis, as well as the "unity" accorded to both the totality of writings ascribed to a particular authorial figure and the individual "works" considered to constitute the author's corpus. In the case of Foucault's various analytic writings, designating the work as "social theory" is not without its problems, for while there is much in Foucault's work that bears significantly on the concerns that lie within the broad discursive field of social theory, there is no direct or sustained attempt to theorize "the social" and no attempt is made to theorize "society," although there are detailed studies of particular social practices. In addition, there are a number of other essays and texts on language, literature and painting which are not generally considered when the figure of Foucault the social analyst is invoked; for example, works on Roussel, Blanchot, and Magritte (Foucault, 1987a, b, 1983a).

When summoned to reflect on his various studies, to account for and order their features, Foucault (1982a) quite deliberately described his practices as "analytical work" rather than as "theory," and when responding to comments on his analysis of relations of power he remarked that it is "not a theory, but rather a way of theorizing practice" (Foucault, 1988d, p. 12). Again, when asked shortly before his death to write a(n) (auto)biographical sketch, he described his enterprise as a *critical history of thought* (Maurice Florence [an alias], 1988). The implication of these remarks is not that Foucault's work has no bearing on social theory, but that the critically reflexive manner in which he conducted his inquiries has significant implications for the practice of social theory, and for the reflective, biographically driven meta-theoretical exercise in hand.

Although, as Foucault remarks, the notion that a proposition derives its "scientific value from its author" has been in decline in the natural, physical, and biological sciences for a considerable time – in some fields since the seventeenth century – in other discursive fields the author function continues to be of importance. Foucault comments on the way in which in literature the author function seems to have become even more important – authors are required to "answer for the unity of the works published in their names;... [to] reveal, or at least display the hidden sense pervading their work;... [and] to reveal their personal lives, to account for their experiences and the real story that gave birth to their writings" (Foucault, 1971, p. 14). Notwithstanding Foucault's methodical attempt in *The Archaeology of Knowledge* (1974) to argue that there are analytically more appropriate principles of unification by which a group of statements may be recognized to warrant the status of a discursive formation than the author function, the latter remains very prominent within social theory.

One of the difficulties encountered in trying to achieve an overview of Foucault's work is his commendable inclination to be prepared to think differently, his readiness to reinterpret earlier studies in the light of subsequently different circumstances and preoccupations, and his willingness to reconstruct or refocus his analyses. Foucault offers a series of (re-)interpretations of the aims and objectives of his work, notable among which are critical reflections in *The Archaeology of Knowledge* (1974) on earlier "disordered" studies; the designation in an inaugural lecture (1971) of the analytic terrain within which his work is to be relocated; reconceptualization of the earlier studies of madness and reason and medicine and the clinic as implicitly posing the question of the articulation and "effects of power and knowledge" (1980), first explicitly addressed in *Discipline and Punish: the Birth of the Prison* (1977b); identification in a subsequent major essay of the question of the subject as "the general theme of my research (1982a, p. 209); and a final refocusing of his work in a preface prepared for the much delayed second volume of *The History of Sexuality*, published shortly before his death, as providing an analysis of the "historicity of forms of experience" through a consideration of "the modality of relation to the self" (Foucault, 1986, pp. 334, 338).

It is ironic that an analyst who sought to problematize the status of the author and who speculated on "the total effacement of the individual characteristics of the writer" (Foucault, 1977a, p. 117) should have so frequently attempted to redefine his work. Far from becoming a matter of indifference, the author-function remains significant and Foucault's tendency to reinterpret his analyses serves as confirmation that the writing subject has not disappeared; indeed, it might be argued that his own work has for some become "a kind of enigmatic supplement of the author beyond his own death" (ibid., p. 120).

## THE THEORY: QUESTIONS OF METHOD AND ANALYSIS

There is no sustained attempt in Foucault's writings to specify or address "the social" as such, but the wide range of questions he posed, the various complex issues and concerns he considered, and the way in which he sought to conduct his analysis of particular institutions and practices have led to his work being widely regarded as central to our understanding of prevailing social conditions. Foucault was certainly not a sociologist, but there is much of relevance and value to sociology in his writings. Equally, there is in his work a great deal that bears significantly on the concerns which lie at the center of contemporary social theory.

In *The Order of Things: an Archaeology of the Human Sciences* (1970), Foucault analyzes the formation of the human sciences within the modern epistemological configuration and identifies the distinguishing features of modern thought. This is one of the early works which is cited in support of the identification of Foucault with structuralism, but his relationship to the problematic unity "structuralism" is more tenuous than some critics have allowed. There is no attempt to uncover elementary structures, as there is with Claude Lévi-Strauss, and there is no conception of a universal unconscious structured like a language, as there is with Jacques Lacan. And while there is an element of potentially misleading structuralist terminology in the first edition of *The Birth of the Clinic*, the analytic superficiality of phrases like "a structural analysis of the signified" is revealed when they are replaced in the second edition by more appropriate references to "an analysis of discourses." If there is a degree of common ground between the early works of Foucault and the analyses of Lévi-Strauss, Lacan, Louis Althusser, and Roland Barthes, respectively, it derives from a shared antipathy toward humanism and existential phenomenology.

In *Madness and Civilization: a History of Insanity in the Age of Reason* (1965), *The Birth of the Clinic: an Archaeology of Medical Perception* (1973), and *Discipline and Punish: the Birth of the Prison* (1977b), respectively, the different ways in which the modern subject has been constituted as an object of knowledge (mad/sane, sick/healthy, delinquent/law-abiding) as a consequence of modern scientific practices such as psychiatry, clinical medicine, and criminal science are carefully documented. Finally, after having published an introductory volume which, among other things, maps out a series of intended studies of the power–knowledge relations constitutive of modern Western sexuality, Foucault reconsidered and then reconfigured the project in the second volume in the series *The History of Sexuality: The Use of Pleasure* (1987c), in order to focus on the ways in which subjects reflect upon and constitute themselves as objects for themselves, as, for example, when individuals "recognize themselves as subjects of pleasure [and]...desire" (Florence, 1988, p. 14).

In contrasting, yet complementary, ways, Foucault's various analyses offer what at one point he describes as a "history of the present" (Foucault, 1977b, p. 31); that is, critical analyses which effectively explore the complex formation of our modernity. For Foucault such a critical and effective history contributes to the transformation of the present by revealing "the accidents, the minute deviations – or conversely, the complete reversals – the errors, the false appraisals, and the faulty calculations that gave birth to those things that continue to exist and have value for us" (Foucault, 1977a, p. 146). By exposing the contingency of modernity, the disorder and heterogeneity of events and processes, and the fragments which have been mistaken for secure foundations, Foucault effectively shows "how that-which-is has not always been; i.e., that the things which seem most evident to us are always formed in the confluence of encounters and chances, during the course of a precarious and fragile history....It means that they reside on a base of human practice and human history; and that since these things have been made, they can be unmade, as long as we know how it was that they were made" (Foucault, 1983b, p. 206). And to learn how things have been made – in particular, how forms of modern subjectivity have been constituted, and associated forms of conduct determined – Foucault argued that it was necessary to analyze not only what he termed "techniques of domination" – for example, the range of disciplinary technologies of power employed in institutions like the asylum, clinic, and prison, and explored in his earlier studies – but also "techniques of the self," that is to say the means by which individuals may exercise "operations on their own bodies, their own souls, their own thoughts, their own conduct, and this in a manner so as to transform themselves" (Foucault and Sennett, 1982, p. 10). In each instance, whether it is disciplinary techniques or what Foucault sometimes called "technologies of the self," it is the *government* of conduct that is analytically central; that is, the ways in which conduct is formed and shaped, guided and directed.

Before we turn in more detail to discuss key features of Foucault's analyses of the "art of governing people in our societies," a discussion that will include consideration of (a) forms of modern rationality, (b) relations of power, and (c) questions of subjectivity, clarification of the analytic methods employed by

Foucault is warranted. Foucault has described several of his earlier studies as archaeologies and he has been credited with making a major contribution to an "archaeology of modernity" (Huyssen, 1984). In some of his later lectures and writings he makes reference to genealogical research and describes how he "tried to get away from the philosophy of the subject, through a genealogy of the modern subject as a historical and cultural reality" (Foucault and Sennett, 1982, p. 9). What are we to make of the notions of "archaeology" and "genealogy" employed by Foucault?

A number of critics of Foucault's earlier studies of madness and reason, medicine and the clinic, and the formation of the human sciences have claimed to find traces of structuralism (White, 1973; Stone, 1983). In *The Archaeology of Knowledge*, a text which outlines the distinctive features of an archaeological method of analysis of discursive formations, Foucault engages with, and attempts to distance his analytic approach from, structuralism. In *The Archaeology of Knowledge* Foucault states that his "aim is not to transfer to the field of history, and more particularly to the history of knowledge (*connaissances*), a structuralist method that has proved valuable in other fields of analysis" (Foucault, 1974, p. 15). While there is an admission that aspects of the analysis of transformations in the field of historical knowledge may not be "entirely foreign to what is called structural analysis," Foucault is adamant that he does not employ the "categories of cultural totalities (whether world-views, ideal-types, the particular spirit of an age)," and that he does not impose on history "the forms of structural analysis" (ibid.). As the imaginary interlocutor introduced by Foucault comments towards the end of the text, "you have been at great pains to dissociate yourself from 'structuralism'" (ibid., p. 199). In *The Archaeology of Knowledge* the question of how social institutions are articulated with discursive formations seems to be put to one side as the analytic approach adopted proceeds to accord discourses autonomy in order to concentrate on demonstrating the rules through which they achieve internal self-regulation. The archaeological approach described has been subjected to criticism on a number of counts, but primarily for rendering virtually incomprehensible the influence that social institutions have on what appear as "autonomous" discursive systems. In so far as archaeology is presented as an end in itself, Foucault is also vulnerable to the charge of effectively foreclosing "the possibility of bringing his critical analyses to bear on his social concerns" (Dreyfus and Rabinow, 1982, pp. xx–xxi). It is with the advent of genealogical research that the call for a more explicitly politically engaged form of critical analysis appears to be answered by Foucault.

A marked shift of analytic focus away from the rules regulating discursive practices and toward the social practices with which discourses are articulated is first signaled in Foucault's (1971) lecture "Orders of Discourse." This text anticipates a subsequent relative marginalization of archaeological analysis and concomitant elevation of genealogy in Foucault's work by placing emphasis on the importance of an analytic (re)turn to the question of the *social* production of discourse and the articulation of discourse and power. In his seminal lecture Foucault delineates the rules of exclusion through which the production of discourse is "controlled, selected, organised and redistributed" (ibid., p. 8). These rules take the form of prohibition, division, and rejection, and the opposition between "true" and "false," and of these it is the last that becomes increasingly important as Foucault's genealogical research proceeds. The principle of exclusion which has increasingly been assimilating the others is that between true and false, an opposition or division with its own complex and uneven history. From classical Antiquity to the present there has been a division differentiating "true discourse from false," a division which Foucault suggests has "never ceased shifting." Instead of an orthodox linear developmental conception of the discovery of knowledge, Foucault promotes the idea that mutations and transformations in knowledge may be regarded as manifestations of forms of the will to truth, and he adds that "this will to knowledge, . . . reliant upon institutional support and distribution, tends to exercise a sort of pressure, a power of constraint upon other forms of discourse" (ibid., p. 11). Implicit in Foucault's remarks on the modern will to knowledge is a concern that subsequently achieves greater prominence in his genealogical researches, namely an analytic focus on the complex articulations between forms of knowledge and relations of power.

Genealogy uncovers the myriad events, "the details and accidents that accompany every beginning" (Foucault, 1977a, p. 144); reveals the dispersions, deviations, and discontinuities that are displaced in the traditional historical analytic pursuit of order, continuity, and secure foundations. Genealogical historical inquiry, what Foucault sometimes terms "effective" history, dispenses with constants and treats everything as having a history. Stability and continuity cannot be assumed; history "becomes 'effective' to the degree that it introduces discontinuity into our very being" (ibid., p. 154). Notwithstanding the emphasis placed on genealogy in Foucault's later writings, archaeology does not disappear; to the contrary, it continues to serve as a methodology for isolating and analysing "local discursivities" in a manner which is complementary to genealogy (Foucault, 1980). As one analyst has remarked, "from the perspective of the production of a knowledge of discursive formations, archaeology remains the indispensable methodology, from the practical polemical and strategic perspective of the use of historical analysis, genealogy holds the key. However, beyond the language of complementarity, genealogy is clearly dominant. It connects the empirical analyses . . . to concerns activated in light of particular contemporary struggles" (Dean, 1994, pp. 33–4).

## Rationality

As stated above, one of the difficulties which arises in attempting to offer a brief overview of Foucault's work is that of giving sufficient attention to the various modifications and shifts of emphasis which affect his analysis. However, there is an associated risk, namely that too much significance may be attached to apparent theoretical shifts, and that evidence of forms of continuity, from what is regarded as the first major work, *Madness and Civilization*, through to the end of his output, may not receive sufficient critical attention. A number of possible lines of continuity in Foucault's work have been identified. A continuous thread extending from *Madness and Civilization* to *Discipline and Punish* has been argued to be present in the form of "an institutional epistemology which correlates the possibility of particular developments in systems of thought to the means of observation and registration afforded by special institutional sites and mechanisms" (Gordon, 1990, p. 12). Another is the "interconnection of questions of governmental rationality and questions of the social organization of subjectivity: the linkage . . . between the macrophysics and the microphysics of power" (ibid., p. 11). With differing degrees of explicitness, evidence of forms of continuity may be found throughout Foucault's work in a general analytic preoccupation with forms of rationality, relations of power, and the constitution of forms of subjectivity.

Whether addressing questions of rationality, power, or subjectivity, Foucault consistently sought to demonstrate that notions of linear development, "reassuring stability," and continuity were problematic. Such a perspective led Foucault to express doubts about the analytic value of "rationalization" conceptualized as a unitary process and to argue instead that "we have to analyze specific rationalities rather than always invoking the progress of rationalization in general" (Foucault, 1982a, p. 210; see also 1981c, p. 226). Foucault's studies of the experiences of madness, illness, death, crime, and sexuality serve as appropriate examples, as they present analyses of "different foundations, different creations, different modifications in which rationalities engender one another, oppose and pursue one another" (Foucault, 1983b, p. 202).

Analysis of prominent aspects of modern rationality constitutes an important element in the work not only of Foucault but also of a number of other theorists, including Max Weber, members of the Frankfurt School, and Jürgen Habermas. However, scope for comparison of the works of Foucault with those of other prominent social theorists is not confined to the question of modern rationality and its consequences. The respective works of Foucault and Weber may be compared on a number of additional counts, including "their studies of forms of domination and techniques of discipline, . . . their writings on methodology and intellectual ethics, [and] their interest in Nietzsche" (Gordon, 1987, p. 293). In turn, other analysts have sought to consider the similarities and differences between the works of Foucault, the Frankfurt School, and Habermas, for the most part in relation to their respective conceptions of relations of power and domination and the influence of Nietzsche's philosophical thought (Hoy, 1981; Dews, 1984; Ingram, 1986).

There are a number of texts in which Foucault has outlined a response to the question of his relationship to aspects of Weber's work and Critical Theory. While Foucault (1988c) has commented that his approach to historical inquiry needs to be differentiated from Weber's "ideal types" analysis, it has been argued that when consideration is given to their substantive historical works differences begin to diminish (Dreyfus and Rabinow, 1982; Gordon, 1987). For example, in the course of an analysis of "world religions" Weber acknowledges that " 'rationalism' may mean very different things" and that "rationalization of life conduct . . . can assume unusually varied forms" (Weber, 1970, p. 293). References such as these to different types of rationalism appear to anticipate Foucault's preference for an "instrumental and relative meaning" for rationalization; that is, for an analytic focus on "specific rationalities" rather than on an assumed general process of rationalization.

Foucault has been interpreted within the tradition of critical theorizing as a critic of reason *in toto*. For example, in an analysis of Foucault's general contribution to our understanding of rationalization, Habermas cautions that "we must be careful not to throw the baby out with the bath water and take flight in a new irrationalism. Foucault visibly falls into that danger" (Habermas, 1986, p. 69). In response to this type of criticism advanced by Habermas and others, Foucault comments that his work provides an analysis of the fragile and precarious history of what "reason perceives as *its* necessity, or rather, what different forms of rationality offer as their necessary being" (Foucault, 1983b, p. 206). Foucault adds that this is not to say that these forms of rationality are irrational, simply that "they reside on a base of human practice and human history" (ibid.). Foucault does not take flight in irrationality, he simply has another agenda; his approach and the questions he poses are quite different from those of Habermas. Elaborating on his thinking about rationality Foucault comments that:

> the central issue of philosophy and critical thought since the eighteenth century has always been, still is, and will, I hope, remain the question, *What* is this Reason that we use? What are its historical effects? What are its limits, and what are its dangers? How can we exist as rational beings, fortunately committed to practicing a rationality that is unfortunately crisscrossed by intrinsic dangers? ... In addition, if it is extremely dangerous to say that Reason is the enemy that should be eliminated, it is just as dangerous to say that any critical questioning of this rationality risks sending us into irrationality.... If intellectuals in general are to have a function, if critical thought itself has a function, and, even more specifically, if philosophy has a function within critical thought, it is precisely to accept this sort of spiral, this sort of revolving door of rationality that refers us to its necessity, to its indispensability, and at the same time to its intrinsic dangers. (Foucault, 1982b, p. 19)

Whereas for the Frankfurt School and Habermas the analytic focus tends to fall on the relationship between rationality and domination, in particular the repressive sociocultural and political consequences of the increasing prominence of instrumental, economic, and administrative reason, for Foucault the problem is posed in quite different terms. Foucault does not identify a particular moment at which "reason bifurcated" into instrumental and moral forms; to the contrary he refers to an "abundance of branchings, ramifications, breaks and ruptures" (Foucault, 1983b, p. 201), and places analytic emphasis on the historically specific forms of rationality through which human subjects became objects of forms of knowledge, and the theoretical, institutional, and economic consequences of subjects speaking "the truth about themselves." One of the ways in which Foucault explored concerns such as these was through studies of the articulation of forms of knowledge with relations of power.

# Power

Although the term is scarcely, if ever, employed in his earlier studies, Foucault claimed in an interview given in 1977 that an analytic interest in the exercise of power, "concretely and in detail – with its specificity, its techniques and tactics" (Foucault, 1980, pp. 115–16) was present in his work all along. Some six years later Foucault sought once more to clarify his approach to the analysis of power relations, this time to correct the impression that he was constructing "a theory of Power." While apparently ready to accept a description of his work as a "microphysics" or an "analytics" of power, Foucault remarked that "I am far from being a theoretician of power. At the limit, I would say that power as an autonomous question, does not interest me" (Foucault, 1983b, p. 207). Notwithstanding such denials, Foucault does offer a series of general observations on power, but rather than attempting to answer the question "what is power and where does it come from," it is the means by which power is exercised and the effects of its exercise with which his analysis is primarily concerned.

Power is conceptualized as a complex strategic situation or relation which produces social realities, practices, and forms of subjectivity, rather than as a property or possession which excludes, represses, masks, or conceals. As Foucault argues in *Discipline and Punish*, power "produces domains of objects and rituals of truth. The individual and the knowledge that may be gained of him belong to this production" (Foucault, 1977b, p. 194). In a series of related texts, Foucault (1979a, 1980) elaborates further on his understanding of power, emphasizing that it is not to be equated with "the sovereignty of the state, the form of the law, or the over-all unity of a domination given at the outset"; instead, power is to be understood "as the multiplicity of force relations immanent in the sphere in which they operate" (Foucault, 1979a, p. 92). Exercised "from innumerable points," power relations are "intentional and nonsubjective" (ibid., p. 94). Relations of power for Foucault are synonymous with sociality. Power is held to be always present in human relations, "whether it be a question of communicating verbally...or a question of a love relationship, an institutional or economic relationship" (Foucault, 1987d, p. 122). Power relations are relations in which influence is exercised over the conduct of free subjects, and as Foucault (1982a, p. 221) puts it, "only in so far as they are free." In brief, subjects have the potential to block, change, overturn, or reverse the relation of guidance, direction, and influence. As I have argued elsewhere, there appears to be an implication here that the subject is, in part at least, responsible for his or her own fate, in so far as there is always the potential to transform a relation of power into an adversarial confrontation (Smart, 1995).

Foucault's clarificatory comments have not resolved matters and his analysis of power relations has remained a source of controversy. For example, Peter Dews (1984, p. 88) suggests that "if the concept of power is to have any critical political import, there must be *some* principle, force or entity which power 'crushes' or 'subdues,' and whose release from this repression is considered desirable. A *purely* positive account of power would no longer be an account of power at all, but simply of the constitutive operation of social systems." Dews proceeds to argue that Foucault does not provide a satisfactory answer to the question of the basis of resistance to power, and concludes by drawing attention to the absence in his work of normative foundations for political critique. A related line of criticism is developed by Charles Taylor (1984, p. 152), who remarks that "Foucault's analyses seem to bring evils to light; and yet he wants to distance himself from the suggestion that would seem inescapably to follow, that the negation of these evils promotes a good." Taylor outlines a range of criticisms in which Foucault's position is described as "incoherent," too ready to equate humanitarianism with a system of control, and too inclined to represent the emergence of new forms of discipline in terms of domination. After having developed further criticisms of Foucault's work for its oversimplification of the complexity of historical events and processes, Taylor argues that a notion of power "*does not make sense* without at least the idea of liberation" (ibid., p. 173). Comparable objections are articulated by Habermas, who asks of Foucault, "Why is struggle preferable to submission? Why ought domination to be resisted?" (Habermas, 1987, p. 284).

What are at issue between Foucault and his critics, what divide them and prevent effective communication and debate, are quite different conceptions, not only of power, but also of truth and freedom. For example, for Taylor, "unmasking" modern forms of power has as its purpose the rescue of "two goods," notably freedom and truth, where "truth...is subversive of power...[and] is on the side of the lifting of impositions" (Taylor, 1984, p. 174). However, the terms employed by Taylor – the equation of power and domination and the idea of a "move toward a greater acceptance of truth – and hence also in certain conditions a move toward greater freedom" (ibid., p. 177) – are not compatible with Foucault's analytics of power. Power is conceptualized as productive and relational by Foucault, it is literally regarded as a "set of actions upon other actions" (Foucault, 1982a, p. 220), and, as I have already noted, is not to be equated with domination. In turn, truth is conceptualized as a historically variable sociocultural "system of ordered procedures for the production, regulation, distribution, circulation and operation of statements," and is considered to be "linked in a circular relation with systems of power" (Foucault, 1980, p. 133). Finally, freedom for Foucault constitutes the (pre)condition for the exercise of power; indeed, he argues that "freedom must exist for power to be exerted" (Foucault, 1982a, p. 221); the freedom to resist must be present, if only as a potential. What is striking about the critical discussion which has developed around Foucault's analytics of power is how frequently criticisms miss their mark because critics have failed to come to terms with the distinctive features of Foucault's analysis (Patton, 1989).

The conception that emerges in *Discipline and Punish*, of the individual as both an effect of power and the element of its articulation, receives clarification and elaboration in Foucault's subsequent discussion, in *The History of Sexuality, Volume 1*, of the development of "bio-power." The two basic forms in which "bio-power," or power over life, is considered to be exercised are disciplines of the body, or an "anatomo-politics of the human body," and a regulation of the species body, or a "bio-politics of the population" (Foucault, 1979a, p. 139). Foucault notes an increasing political and administrative concern, starting in the seventeenth century, to optimize the body's capability, enhance its usefulness, and ensure its docility and integration "into the machinery of production" (ibid., p. 141), followed later by increasing regulation of the species body or population, through interventions in "propagation, births, mortality,...health, life expectancy" (ibid., p. 139) and associated factors and processes. The distinction between two basic forms in which power is exercised over life is developed further in Foucault's (1979b, 1981c) analysis of individualizing and totalizing forms of governmental rationality, an analysis which draws attention to the historical process of the "governmentalization of the state" and its complex consequences. In the course of a series of clarificatory comments on the specificity of power relations, Foucault suggests that the exercise of power consists in "guiding the possibility of conduct and putting in order the possible outcome" (Foucault, 1982a, p. 221) and that, in this respect at least, power constitutes a matter of government. Conceptualizing the exercise of power in these terms – that is, as action upon the actions of "subjects who are faced with a field of possibilities in which several ways of behaving...may be realized" (ibid.) – constitutes an oblique response to the charge that his analysis portrays relations of power as all-pervasive.

Clarification of the exercise of power in terms of government draws attention to the presence of "individual or collective subjects," and serves as an effective response to the criticism that there is a neglect, if not an effective denial, of the active subject, the subject capable of resistance. It is in this setting, namely of a series of responses to questions concerning power, freedom, and governmentality, that Foucault moves once more to reformulate the goal of his work, by stating that the central objective had "not been to analyze the phenomena of power... [but] to create a history of the different modes by which, in our culture, human beings are made subjects" (Foucault, 1982a, p. 208). Three modes of objectification through which human beings are constituted as subjects are identified, notably: (a) particular "human" sciences which objectivize the "speaking subject" (e.g. linguistics), the "productive subject" (e.g. economics), and the "sheer fact of being alive" (e.g. biology); (b) "dividing practices" which constitute subjects as mad/sane, sick/healthy, and criminal/law-abiding; and (c) self-governing practices or "technologies of the self," through which human beings turn themselves into subjects.

## Subjectivity

It is within the final project on sexuality that the question of the subject and technologies of the self become the focus of analytic concern. After the publication of an introductory volume to a planned series on sexuality there is a radical shift of historical and analytic focus away from the Victorian era, the "repressive hypothesis," and a promised subsequent clarification of the modern deployment of sexuality, to a concern with the expression and regulation of pleasures in classical Antiquity, explored in two further, and, as it transpired, final volumes.

To achieve an effective analysis of the subject and subjectivity Foucault argued that a major theoretical shift was necessary, one which would allow the focus of analysis to fall on "the forms and modalities of the relation to self by which the individual constitutes and recognizes himself *qua* subject" (Foucault, 1987c, p. 6). The shift in question led to a radical reorganization of the project around "games of truth," technologies of the self, and the problematization of particular practices, around, that is, "the slow formation, in antiquity, of a hermeneutics of the self" (ibid.). Consequently, the focus in the final volumes on sexuality falls on the different games of truth and error through which human beings historically came to be constituted as desiring subjects, and reflexively experienced themselves as such. The key question articulated is why sexuality became a matter of ethical concern: "how, why and in what forms was sexuality constituted as a moral domain?" (ibid., p. 10).

With this late "abrupt theoretical shift" Foucault moves, according to Dews (1989, p. 39), to "articulate the concepts of subjectivity and freedom in such a way as to avoid any suggestion that such freedom must take the form of the recovery of an authentic 'natural' self." Such a shift of analytic focus to the world of the ancient Greeks also allows Foucault to call into question contemporary assumptions about the "necessary link between ethics and other social or economic or political structures" (Foucault, 1986, p. 350) by placing emphasis on practices of ethical self-construction. However, when the issue of the self-constitution of the subject through technologies of the self is addressed, Foucault is careful to add, by way of clarification, that "these practices are . . . not something that the individual invents by himself. They are patterns that he finds in his culture and which are *proposed, suggested, imposed on him by his culture, his society and his social group*" (Foucault, 1987d, p. 122, emphasis added). While such an observation may seem relatively uncontentious, it does leave open and unanswered the respect(s) in which subjects are, or can be, recognized as active and responsible. To be more precise, and to address directly one of Foucault's later preoccupations, is it really appropriate to talk of creating oneself, and if so on what basis does it become possible "to create oneself"? Foucault takes the view that "the self is not given to us . . . [and] that there is only one practical consequence: we have to create ourselves as a work of art" (Foucault, 1986, p. 351). It is through a process of reflection on similarities and differences between the Greek world and the modern West that the conclusion that the self is not given to us is reached, the argument being that some of our main ethical principles "have been related at a certain moment to an aesthetics of existence" (Foucault, 1986, p. 350). But the idea that there might not be any "necessary link" does not mean that the constitution of the self as a moral subject of action can be considered free of social, economic, or political structures. Foucault's own references to cultural practices which are proposed, suggested, and imposed draw attention to, but neglect to analyze, the social context(s) in which forms of subjectivity are constituted and subjects participate, along with others, in processes of mutual self-development. While the formation of the self through social interaction is briefly acknowledged in Foucault's work – for example, reference is made to individuals transforming themselves through the help of others, and attention is drawn to the importance in the development of care for self of the role of a counsellor, guide, friend, master, "who will tell you the truth" (Foucault, 1987d, p. 118) – no attempt is made to elaborate on or to explore the complex relationships with others that are at the very heart of social life. The analyses outlined by Foucault in *The Use of Pleasure* (1987c), *The Care of the Self* (1988a), and associated texts and interviews introduced another "different line of inquiry in which the modes of relation to the self took precedence" (Foucault, 1986b, p. 338) and the decision to pursue an analysis of "forms of relation to the self" led to questions of ethics becoming an increasingly prominent feature of Foucault's final works (Smart, 1995).

## THE PERSON

The idea that we need to know about the author to understand the intellectual *oeuvre* is one to which Foucault took exception. To be consistent with Foucault's viewpoint it would be more appropriate to subscribe to a line of aesthetic thought traceable to Mallarmé and the modernist movement in the arts, a line of thought which promoted the idea of the autonomy of the work (Eribon, 1992). However, while Foucault (1988d, p. 16) remarked that "my personal life is not at all interesting," many of those interested in his work have been curious about the life of the man.

Foucault grew up in Poitiers, in the French provinces, in the 1930s and 1940s. His family was traditional middle class and nominally Catholic. In 1945, Foucault went to Paris, to one of the most prestigious schools in France, the Lycée Henri-IV, to prepare for the entrance examinations to the École Normale Superieure (ENS), and it was at the Lycée that he first briefly encountered Jean Hyppolite, translator of Hegel's *Phenomenology*, who helped the class to prepare for their philosophy examination, and was introduced to the work of Georges Dumezil. These intellectual figures, along with George Canguilhem, were subsequently acknowledged by Foucault to have exercised a formative influence on his work. Foucault described his time at the ENS as "sometimes intolerable," and accounts of his arguments with fellow students, his attempt at suicide, and his difficulty coming to terms with his homosexuality provide an insight into the difficulties with which he had to cope while pursuing his interests in psychology, psychoanalysis, and psychiatry, and reading the works of Bataille, Blanchot, and Klossowski on "transgression" or the "limit experience." The intellectual environment in which Foucault studied was dominated by phenomenology. However, for the students who attended ENS with Foucault in the years 1946–50 it was the philosophy of Hegel, not Sartre, that was of central importance, and only after reading Hegel, and writing a dissertation on his phenomenology, did Foucault move on to the works of Marx, Heidegger, and Nietzsche. Reflecting on this period in an interview conducted in 1984, Foucault explains the "philosophical shock" of reading Heidegger and subsequently the work of Nietzsche, "the two authors I have read the most" (Foucault, 1988d, p. 250).

On receiving the *agrégation* in 1951 Foucault left the ENS for the Fondation Thiers, where he spent a year doing research before going on to teach at the University of Lille in 1952. In Lille Foucault wrote a book, *Maladie mentale et personnalité* (1954), and a long introductory essay to Ludwig Binswanger's *Le Rêve et l'existence* (1954). In 1955 he left France for Sweden, to escape the constraints of French social and cultural life and to try to find greater personal freedom. Working as a French instructor in the Department of Romance Studies at the University of Uppsala, Foucault was to find intellectual and personal disappointment. From Sweden Foucault moved in 1958 to the University of Warsaw and then to the Institut Français in Hamburg, before returning to France in 1960 with a text, *Folie et déraison: Histoire de la folie a l'âge classique*, which had been researched in France but written in exile. It was a text which constituted the principal thesis for the award to Foucault of the most prestigious French degree, a *doctorat d'état*, the text with which the *oeuvre* associated with the figure of Foucault really begins.

Foucault remained mobile, moving from the University of Clermont-Ferrand, where he taught psychology and philosophy (1960–6), to a philosophy post at the University of Tunis (1966–8), on very briefly, literally a matter of weeks, to the University of Nanterre, and from there to the University of Vincennes, to a tenured professorship in philosophy (1968–70), finally being appointed in 1970 to a chair in the History of Systems of Thought at the most prestigious institution in France, the Collège de France in Paris, where he remained until his death in 1984.

## THE SOCIAL AND INTELLECTUAL CONTEXT

With a thinker as complex as Foucault the task of briefly outlining the social and intellectual contexts in which intellectual interests and affinities developed is daunting. Foucault's intellectual and personal journey from the provincial setting of Poitiers to cosmopolitan Paris, including detours to Uppsala, Warsaw, Hamburg, and Tunis, and periods spent in Brazil, Japan, Canada, and the United States, and in particular California, exposed him to a variety of different cultural practices and a multitude of experiences. Various "events" have been identified as having contributed in different ways to the development of the man and his work – growing up in an "old traditional society," coping with being a student in Paris, living and working in a number of other countries, returning to France in the wake of May 1968 and becoming a prominent figure in the redefinition and extension of the political, to encompass questions of madness, sexuality, imprisonment, and identity, and, of course, learning to live with a sexual orientation that for much of his life necessitated discretion, until his discovery that homosexuality "was an open and visible way of life and culture in New York and San Francisco" (Eribon, 1992, p. 315; see also Macey, 1993; Miller, 1993).

There are traces of many influences in Foucault's analyses, but moving away from the works of particular individuals, it might be argued, as he acknowledged on more than one occasion, that the broader intellectual context in which his thinking initially began to take shape, and in critical response to which his work from *Folie et déraison* (the heavily abridged English translation *Madness and Civilization* was published in 1965) onwards developed, was one which consisted of "Marxism, phenomenology, and existentialism" (Foucault, 1987a, p. 174; see also 1983b). This study, Foucault's first major work, has been argued to be "animated by a critique of Western reason that was not entirely at odds with the anti-scientism of Sartre and Merleau-Ponty" (Poster, 1984, p. 3). However, more significantly, the study presents a form of analysis in which a theoretical shift away from philosophies of consciousness and idealist notions of the subject begins to emerge. As Foucault later remarked, "in *Madness and Civilization* I was trying . . . to describe a locus of experience from the point of view of the history of thought" (Foucault, 1986, p. 336), not from the analytic perspective of existentialism. As such, the text anticipates, albeit at times tangentially, later analytic themes and developments in Foucault's work, including the productive effects of relations of power and the operation of "carceral institutions" (Gordon, 1990).

Existentialism and phenomenology represented only one part of the intellectual context in which Foucault's thinking initially developed; Marxism also exerted a powerful presence. Indeed, in the early 1950s Foucault was a member of the Communist Party, and he is reported to have said that at this time "Marxism as a doctrine made good sense to me" (Eribon, 1992, p. 52). Notwithstanding the influence exerted by Louis Althusser over Foucault, his relationship to Marxism was always somewhat marginal and indirect. When called upon to discuss his intellectual formation in general, and his relationship to Marxism and communism in particular, Foucault remarks that it was through Nietzche and Bataille, rather than Hegelian philosophy, that he found communism – "Thus it was that without knowing Marx very well, refusing Hegelianism, and feeling dissatisfied with the limitations of existentialism, I decided to join the French Communist Party. That was in 1950. A Nietzschean Communist!" (Foucault, 1991, p. 51). Within a very few years Foucault's "feeling of discomfort and uneasiness" with Communist Party political practices caused him to leave the party and immerse himself in his studies, but his name continued to be associated with that of Althusser, and for that matter other major French intellectual figures such as Lévi-Strauss and Lacan, through a wide-ranging theoretical debate over "structuralism" which took place in France during the 1960s.

As I have already noted, Foucault had a rather disparaging view of the notion of structuralism. While there is an admission that some of his earlier works, particularly *The Birth of the Clinic*, might at times have made too "frequent recourse to structural analysis" (Foucault, 1974, p. 16), Foucault generally sought to dissociate himself from structuralism and to question whether those accorded the status "structuralists" had anything more in common than a shared antipathy toward "the theory of the subject" (Foucault, 1991, p. 58). The reservations articulated by Foucault about the idea of structuralism, and the subsequent trajectory of his work, have been cited in support of his inclusion in two other, no less controversially constituted, intellectual formations, notably "poststructuralism" and "postmodernism." While Foucault clearly had reservations about structuralism, and sought to distance his own work from it, there is an acknowledgment that the works considered to exemplify such an approach do at least share a common interest in the question of the subject. In contrast, Foucault has remarked, "I do not understand what kind of problem is common to the people we call post-modern or post-structuralist" (Foucault, 1983b, p. 205). Despite such protestations, Foucault's work has been increasingly identified as "postmodern" (Hoy, 1988; Best and Kellner, 1991).

I have alluded above to merely one aspect of the political context in which the intellectual figure of Foucault was formed; clearly there are other significant features and events to which reference might be made. For example, in terms of historical events which had an impact on theory and politics in France, "May 1968" has assumed considerable significance. Foucault did not participate in the political struggles which took place on the university campuses and in the streets of France during May 1968, as he was working at the University of Tunis at the time, but he has acknowledged that the transformations induced in the intellectual and political climate had a decisive influence upon his work – "it is certain...that without May of '68, I would never have done the things I'm doing today: such investigations as those on the prison, sexuality, etc., would be unthinkable" (Foucault, 1991, p. 140). As well as making possible the study of particular practices and institutions, the events of May 1968 contributed to Foucault's thoughts on the changing status of the intellectual, and the possibility of "reaching a new kind of relationship, a new kind of collaboration between 'intellectuals' and 'non-intellectuals' that would be completely different from the past" (ibid., p. 142).

The question of intellectual activity, or practice, and the associated issue of the role of the intellectual, are explored in a number of Foucault's texts. In a discussion on intellectuals and power which took place in 1972, Foucault argued that the notion of the intellectual as a representative consciousness, as able to speak for others – "to place himself 'somewhat ahead and to the side' in order to express the stifled truth of the collectivity" – could no longer be convincingly sustained. In contrast, the appropriate task for the intellectual identified by Foucault is "to struggle against the forms of power that transform him into its object and instrument in the sphere of 'knowledge', 'truth', 'consciousness', and 'discourse'" (Foucault, 1977b, pp. 207–8). In consequence, the responsibility of the intellectual is no longer assumed to be the provision of knowledge for others, for they are already considered to "*know* perfectly well, without illusion" (Foucault, 1977a, p. 207); rather, the central objective is to challenge the prevailing regime of the production of truth which disqualifies local forms of knowledge as illegitimate (Foucault, 1980).

The conception of the intellectual that emerges from Foucault's intellectual practices and reflections is that of the critical interpreter, a conception which contrasts starkly with the universalizing, legislative ambitions of the modern intellectual. Foucault's conception of intellectual practice has presented great difficulty for readers accustomed to turning to the writings of intellectuals for solutions to social, cultural, and political problems. In Foucault's work it is not solutions or programmatic statements that one finds, but the identification of problems, literally "how and why certain things (behavior, phenomena, processes) became a *problem*" (Foucault, 1988b, p. 16). Throughout his work the emphasis tends to be placed on how and why particular forms of conduct came to be classified, analyzed, and treated, in short problematized, as, for example, "madness," "crime," "sexuality," and so on. In this way Foucault (1988c) sought to question and erode "self-evidentnesses and commonplaces," to contribute to the transformation of existing "ways of perceiving and doing things," and in turn to draw attention to the possibility of constituting new forms of subjectivity.

A critical stand on contemporary issues is taken in Foucault's work, but it is a stand that lays no claim to a universal immanent foundation, a stand that deliberately rejects the legislative ambitions of the universalizing intellectual role for a critical, interpretive, and more specific intellectual practice (Bove, 1980; Smart, 1986). It is a practice which effectively constitutes an "ethic for the intellectual" (Rajchman, 1985, p. 124), "an ethic of responsibility for the truth one speaks, for the political strategies into which these truths enter, and for those ways of relating to ourselves that make us either conformists or resisters to those relations. It is a timely ethic which assists in reclaiming thought's moral responsibilities" (Bernauer, 1992, p. 271), a critical practice which aims to open up new ways of thinking and being.

## IMPACT

In a late reflection on his work Foucault comments that his earlier studies of "asylums, prisons, and so on" deal with "only one aspect of the art of governing people in our societies" (Foucault and Sennett, 1982, p. 10), and that analyses of the government of others need to be complemented by analyses of technologies of self-government. Evidence of the growing significance of a "problematic of government" as an organizing principle and prominent analytic theme can be found in a number of Foucault's later texts, and it is in relation to this broad concern that his work is continuing to have a major impact.

It has been argued that a concept of government occupies a pivotal place in the later Foucault for two reasons: "because it designates a continuity between the micro- and the macro-levels of political analysis, and because it spans the interface between the exercise of power and the exercise of liberty" (Gordon, 1987, p. 296). From the introductory volume on *The History of Sexuality*, where the problematic of government serves to "disarticulate or unde(te)rmine determinate notions of power" (Keenan, 1982, p. 36), Foucault proceeds to use the notion of government as a "guiding thread" in courses of study which address the "formation of a political 'governmentality'," notably liberalism as a governmental technology employed by a state administration to direct the conduct of men (Foucault, 1981a, b), and, turning away from the state and introducing a broader sense of the term, the different modes by which human beings are made subjects; that is, "government of individuals by their own verity" (Foucault, 1982a, p. 240). The problematic of government allows Foucault to avoid the equation of power with the "problematic of the king" and to place emphasis on the direction and guidance of human conduct.

More controversially, it has also been suggested by Colin Gordon that an analytic interest in rationalities of government is not confined to Foucault's later work alone and that there are "complex correlations and precedents" in the earlier "regional histories of normalizing practices," the argument being that institutions of internment analyzed in *Madness and Civilization* constitute an "instrument of a police art of government," and "Bentham's Panopticon, examined in *Discipline and Punish*, is a liberal theorem of political security" (Gordon 1987, pp. 297–8). In the later works analysis of relations of power becomes analytically a question of government, a question of the techniques, procedures, and rationales for guiding, directing, or structuring conduct. In this context government is not to be equated with an institution, or conflated with the state, it is an activity, the contact point "where the way individuals are driven by others is tied to the way they conduct themselves" (Foucault quoted in Keenan, 1982, p. 38). In the broadest of senses the problematic of government encompasses the government of "children, government of souls or of consciences, government of a home, of a State, or of oneself" (ibid., p. 37), and as such it makes possible analysis of the articulation in modern power structures of "individualization techniques, and of totalization procedures" (Foucault, 1982a, p. 213).

In so far as the problematic of government "could concern the relation between self and self, private interpersonal relations involving some form of control or guidance, relations within social institutions and communities and, finally, relations concerned with the exercise of political sovereignty" (Gordon, 1991, pp. 2–3), it has stimulated the development of a rich seam of Foucauldian analyses (Procacci, 1987; Miller and Rose, 1990; Burchell, 1991; Dean, 1992; and the work of *The History of the Present* research network). However, the influence Foucault's work has exercised on contemporary social thought extends beyond the theme of governmental rationality to encompass a wide range of concerns in a growing number of fields of inquiry. If philosophy and history constitute the fields of inquiry closest to Foucault's concerns, his influence nevertheless extends to many other fields, including in particular sociology, anthropology, literary and cultural studies, and feminism. Analysts working in such diverse fields as education, accountancy, architecture, and law have also found in Foucault's project the tools necessary for a series of innovatory studies: for example, on the significance of disciplinary technology in the development of "rational schooling" (Hoskin, 1979) and accounting practices (Hoskin and Macve, 1986); and the "rules of the game" associated with the structuring of space in modern society (Teyssot, 1980; see also Wright and Rabinow, 1982); as well as photography and electronic communications media as potential means of surveillance (Tagg, 1980; Poster, 1990, respectively).

## ASSESSMENT

The impact of Foucault's work on contemporary social thought has already been substantial, and the legacy is still in the making. Whether in relation to social analyses of sexuality, the body and identity, concerns about relations of power, the place and status of intellectual activity in late modern societies, or questions of analytic method and perspective, the influence of Foucault's work continues to be very significant. Foucault sought to problematize, to provoke, to disturb the existing order of things, to challenge the prevailing regime of truth. Without doubt his diagnosis of our modern times has radically transformed the way in which we think about ourselves and our way of life, and it has done so to an extent which bears comparison with the influence exerted by the classical founding figures of modern social thought. Whether future generations will continue to read Foucault and find his analytic tools of value in their attempts to critically understand the history of their present only time will tell, but as one analyst has remarked, "it is difficult to envisage Foucault's work losing its provocation, irrespective of changing critical modes or of the inevitable attempts to institutionalize it" (Bernstein, 1984, p. 15).

## Bibliography

### Writings of Michel Foucault

*Madness and Civilization. A History of Insanity in the Age of Reason.* 1965. New York: Random House.

*The Order of Things: an Archaeology of the Human Sciences.* New York: Random House.

Orders of Discourse. 1971 *Social Science Information,* 10(2).

*The Birth of the Clinic: an Archaeology of Medical Perception.* 1973. London: Tavistock.

*The Archaeology of Knowledge.* 1974. London: Tavistock.

*Language, Counter-memory, Practice: Selected Essays and Interviews,* edited by D. F. Bouchard. 1977a. Oxford: Blackwell.

*Discipline and Punish: the Birth of the Prison.* 1977b. London: Allen Lane.

*The History of Sexuality. Volume 1, An Introduction.* 1979a. London: Allen Lane.

On Governmentality. 1979b. *Ideology and Consciousness,* 6.

*Power/Knowledge: Selected Interviews and Other Writings 1972–1977,* edited by C. Gordon. 1980. Brighton: Harvester Press.

At the Collège de France (i): a Course Summary, translated with an introduction by James Bernauer. 1981a. *Philosophy and Social Criticism,* 8(2).

At the Collège de France (ii): a Course Summary, translated with an introduction by James Bernauer. 1981b. *Philosophy and Social Criticism,* 8(3).

Omnes et Singulatim. In S. M. McMurrin (ed.), *The Tanner Lectures on Human Values, volume 2.* 1981c. London: Cambridge University Press.

The Subject and Power. 1982a. In H. L. Dreyfus and P. Rabinow, *Michel Foucault: Beyond Structuralism and Hermeneutics.* Brighton: Harvester Press.

Space, Knowledge and Power: Interview. 1982b. *Skyline,* March.

Sexuality and Solitude (with R. Sennett). 1982. In *Humanities in Review, volume 1.* Cambridge: Cambridge University Press.

*This Is Not a Pipe.* 1983a. Berkeley: University of California Press.

Structuralism and Post-structuralism: an Interview with Gerard Raulet, *Telos,* 55, 195–211.

*The Foucault Reader,* edited by P. Rabinow. 1986. Harmondsworth: Penguin.

*Death and the Labyrinth – the World of Raymond Roussel.* 1987a. London: The Athlone Press.

*Foucault/Blanchot. Maurice Blanchot: the Thought from Outside.* 1987b. New York: Zone Books.

*The Use of Pleasure. The History of Sexuality, volume 2.* 1987c. London: Penguin.

The Ethic of Care for the Self as a Practice of Freedom – an Interview. 1987d. *Philosophy and Social Criticism*, 12(2/3), 112–31.

*The Care of the Self. The History of Sexuality, volume 3.* 1988a. London: Allen Lane.

On Problematization. 1988b. *History of the Present*, 4.

Questions of Method: an Interview. 1988c. In K. Baynes et al. (eds), *After Philosophy: End or Transformation?* Cambridge, MA: MIT Press.

*Michel Foucault – Politics, Philosophy, Culture. Interviews and Other Writings 1977– 1984*, edited by L. D. Kritzman. 1988d. London: Routledge

(Auto)biography Michel Foucault 1926–1984 (written under the name Maurice Florence). 1988. *History of the Present*, 4.

*Remarks on Marx – Conversations with Duccio Trombadori.* 1991. New York: Semiotext(e).

## Further reading

Bernauer, J. (1992) Beyond Life and Death: on Foucault's Post-Auschwitz Ethic. In T. J. Armstrong (ed.), *Michel Foucault Philosopher*. London: Harvester Wheatsheaf.

Bernstein, M. A. (1984) Street-Foucault. *University Publishing*, Summer.

Best, S. and Kellner, D. (1991) *Postmodern Theory – Critical Interrogations*. London: Macmillan.

Bové, P. (1980) The End of Humanism: Michel Foucault and the Power of Disciplines. *Humanities in Society*, 3, 23–40.

Burchell, G. (1991) Peculiar Interests: Civil Society and Governing "The System of Natural Liberty." In G. Burchill, C. Gordon, and P. Miller (eds), *The Foucault Effect – Studies in Governmentality*. London: Harvester Wheatsheaf.

Dean, M. (1992) A Genealogy of the Government of Poverty. *Economy and Society*, 21(3).

Dean, M. (1994) *Critical and Effective Histories – Foucault's Methods and Historical Sociology*. London: Routledge.

Dews, P. (1984) Power and Subjectivity in Foucault. *New Left Review*, 144.

Dews, P. (1989) The Return of the Subject in Late Foucault. *Radical Philosophy*, 51, 37–41.

Dreyfus, H. L. and Rabinow, P. (1982) *Michel Foucault: Beyond Structuralism and Hermeneutics*. Brighton: Harvester Press.

Eribon, D. (1992) *Michel Foucault*. London: Faber and Faber.

Gordon, C. (1987) The Soul of the Citizen: Max Weber and Michel Foucault on Rationality and Government. In S. Whimster and S. Lash (eds), *Max Weber, Rationality and Modernity*. London: Allen and Unwin.

Gordon, C. (1990) *Histoire de la folie*: an unknown book by Michel Foucault. *History of the Human Sciences*, 3(1), 3–26.

Gordon, C. (1991) Governmental Rationality: an Introduction. In G. Burchell, C. Gordon, and P. Miller (eds), *The Foucault Effect – Studies in Governmentality*. London: Harvester Wheatsheaf.

Habermas J. (1986) *Jürgen Habermas Autonomy and Solidarity Interviews*, edited by P. Dews. London: Verso.

Habermas, J. (1987) *The Philosophical Discourse of Modernity*. Cambridge: Polity Press.

Hoskin, K. (1979) The Examination, Disciplinary Power and Rational Schooling. *History of Education*, 8(2).

Hoskin, K. W. and Macve, R. H. (1986) Accounting and the Examination: a Genealogy of Disciplinary Power. *Accounting, Organizations and Society*, 11(2).

Hoy, D. C. (1981) Power, Repression, Progress: Foucault, Lukes and the Frankfurt School. *Tri Quarterly*, 52, 43–63.

Hoy, D. C. (1988) Foucault: Modern or Postmodern? In J. Arac (ed.), *After Foucault – Humanistic Knowledge, Postmodern Challenges*. New Brunswick, NJ: Rutgers University Press.

Huyssen, A. (1984) Mapping the Postmodern. *New German Critique*, 33.

Ingram, D. (1986) Foucault and the Frankfurt School: a Discourse on Nietzsche, Power and Knowledge. *Praxis International*, 6(3), 311–27.

Keenan, T. (1982) Foucault on Government. Translator's Afterword to Is It Really Important to Think? An Interview with Michel Foucault. *Philosophy and Social Criticism*, 9(1), 29–40.

Macey, D. (1993) *The Lives of Michel Foucault – a Biography*. New York: Pantheon Books.

Miller, J. (1993) *The Passion of Michel Foucault*. New York: Simon & Schuster.

Miller, P. and Rose, N. (1990) Governing Economic Life. *Economy and Society*, 19(1).

Patton, P. (1989) Taylor and Foucault on Power and Freedom. *Political Studies*, 37, 260–76.

Poster, M. (1984) *Foucault, Marxism and History: Mode of Production versus Mode of Information*. Cambridge: Polity Press.

Poster, M. (1990) Foucault and Databases: Participatory Surveillance. In *The Mode of Information: Poststructuralism and Social Context*. Cambridge: Polity Press.

Procacci, G. (1987) Notes on the Government of the Social. *History of the Present*, 3 (Fall).

Rajchman, J. (1985) *Michel Foucault: the Freedom of Philosophy*. New York: Columbia University Press.

Smart, B. (1986) The Politics of Truth and the Problem of Hegemony. In D. C. Hoy (ed.), *Foucault: a Critical Reader*. Oxford: Blackwell.

Smart, B. (1995) The Subject of Responsibility. *Philosophy and Social Criticism*, 21(4).

Stone, L. (1983) Comment on Madness. *New York Review of Books*, March 31, 42–4.

Tagg, J. (1980) Power and Photography – a Means of Surveillance: the Photograph as Evidence in Law. *Screen Education*, 36.

Taylor, C. (1984) Foucault on Freedom and Truth. *Political Theory*, 12(2), 152–83.

Teyssot, G. (1980) Heterotopias and the History of Spaces. *Architecture and Urbanism*, 121.

Weber, M. (1970) *From Max Weber: Essays in Sociology*, edited by H. H. Gerth and C. Wright Mills. London: Routledge & Kegan Paul.

White, H. (1973) Foucault Decoded: Notes from Underground. *History and Theory*, 12, 23–54.

Wright, G. and Rabinow, P. (1982) Spatialization of Power: a Discussion of the Work of Michel Foucault. *Skyline*, March 18.

# 21

# Jürgen Habermas

## WILLIAM OUTHWAITE

Jürgen Habermas, who retired in 1994 from his post as Professor of Philosophy and Sociology at the University of Frankfurt, is the leading representative of the second generation of the neo-Marxist critical theorists often known as the "Frankfurt School" (see Jay, 1973; Bottomore, 1984; Wiggershaus, 1987). Habermas, who studied under Theodor Adorno and Max Horkheimer after their return to Frankfurt from exile in the USA, differs from them in some crucial ways. Like them, he rejected Marxist philosophies of history, in which an account of the development of capitalism and of the rise of the working class is taken to show that the collapse of capitalism and its replacement by socialism are inevitable, or at least extremely probable. Yet he also felt that Adorno and Horkheimer had painted themselves into a pessimistic corner, from which they could only criticize reality, without offering any alternative. Habermas has argued instead throughout his intellectual career for a return to interdisciplinary critical social science of the kind practiced before the Second World War in Horkheimer's Institute of Social Research.

Habermas's mature theory, as he has developed it from the early 1970s, can best be understood as what he would call a "reconstruction" of what is pre-supposed and implied by human communication, cooperation, and debate. In terms of orthodox academic disciplines, there is a theory of communication (linguistics), a theory of communicative action (sociology), and a theory (both descriptive and normative) of morality, politics (including political communica-tion), and law. At the back of all this are substantial elements of a philosophy of science (including, though not confined to, a critique of positivistic social science) and an account of the development of human societies, and in particular of Western modernity, which culminates in a diagnosis of what he sees as the central political problems confronting the advanced capitalist democracies and the world as a whole.

## THE THEORY

The centerpiece of Habermas's developed theorizing is a theory of communicative action grounded in the analysis of linguistic communication. His basic idea is that any serious use of language to make claims about the world, as opposed, for example, to exclamations or the issuing of orders, presupposes the claims that what we say makes sense and is true, that we are sincere in saying it, and that we have the right to say it. These presuppositions can be questioned by our hearers or readers. As Habermas (1981, volume 1, p. 306) shows with the example of a professor asking a seminar participant to fetch a glass of water, even a simple request, understood not as a mere demand but "as a speech act carried out in an attitude oriented to understanding," raises claims to normative rightness, subjective sincerity, and factual practicability which may be questioned. The addressee of the request may reject it as illegitimate ("I'm not your servant"), insincere ("You don't really want one"), or mistaken about the facts of the matter (availability of a source of water).

Only a rational agreement which excluded no one and no relevant evidence or argument would provide, in the last resort, a justification of the claims we routinely make and presuppose in our assertions. This idea gives us, Habermas claims, a theory of truth, anticipated by the American pragmatist philosopher C. S. Peirce, as what we would ultimately come to rationally agree about (Habermas, 1984, p. 107). Moreover, if Habermas is right that moral judgments also have cognitive content and are not mere expressions of taste or disguised prescriptions, it also provides a theory of truth for issues of morality and of legitimate political authority. Moral norms are justified if they are what we would still uphold at the end of an ideal process of argumentation. "When I state that one norm should be preferred to another, I aim precisely to exclude the aspect of arbitrariness: rightness and truth come together in that both claims can only be vindicated discursively, by way of argumentation and a rational consensus" (Habermas, 1984, p. 109). This consensus is of course an idealization; Habermas at one time described it as resulting from what he called an "ideal speech situation." Yet it is counterfactually presupposed, he argues, by our everyday practice of communication, which is made meaningful by the real or hypothetical prospect of ultimate agreement.

The analysis of language-use can thus, Habermas believes, be expanded into a broader theory of communicative action, defined as action oriented by and toward mutual agreement. In social-theoretical terms, this can be contrasted with the models of instrumental or strategic, self-interested action (the model of *Homo economicus* which also largely dominates rational choice theory), normatively regulated action (the model, familiar from functionalism, in which we orient our action to a shared value system), or dramaturgical action, in which our actions are analyzed as a performance, designed to optimize our public image or self-image (Goffman, Garfinkel and others). All these types of action, Habermas claims, can be shown to be parasitic upon communicative action, which incorporates and goes beyond each of them (Habermas, 1981, volume 1, pp. 82–101). The theory of communicative action, then, underpins a communication theory of morality, law, and democracy, and it is these aspects which have dominated Habermas's most recent work.

One of Habermas's best known books is a short and highly compressed text called in English *Legitimation Crisis* (Habermas, 1973a). Here, and in related essays, published in English under the title *Communication and the Evolution of Society* (Habermas, 1976a), he advanced a neo-Marxist theory of historical development and a critique of contemporary advanced or "late" capitalism. Habermas argued that historical materialist explanations of the development of the productive forces needed to be augmented by an account of the evolution of normative structures, understood in a wide sense to include, for example, family forms. In late capitalism, again, a traditional Marxist account of capitalist crisis which focuses on the economic contradictions of the capitalist system needs to be modified to account for the role of the modern interventionist welfare state and the resultant displacement of crisis tendencies from the economic sphere to the political and cultural domains. Instead of the economic crises which remain the fundamental problem, what we experience are incoherent state responses, leading to what Habermas calls rationality crises which weaken state legitimacy; these state interventions also lead to an erosion of individual motivation and a loss of meaning.

In Habermas's subsequent work, grounded in his theory of communicative action, he worked out in more detail both the historical thesis and the diagnosis of contemporary capitalist crises. *The Theory of Communicative Action* (1981) traces the conflict between the rationalization of world views in early modernity, expressed, for example, in secularization and formal law and in the erosion of appeals to traditional authority, and, on the other hand, the restriction of this newly attained sphere, open in principle to rational debate, as market and bureaucratic structures come to dominate the modern world.

Thus, where Max Weber had seen a single, however diverse, rationalization process working its way through economic, political, legal, and religious structures and world views, Habermas stresses the distinction between two kinds of rationalization process. He borrows and modifies the phenomenological philosopher Edmund Husserl's concept of the "lifeworld," the world as it immediately presents itself to us prior to philosophical or scientific analysis. For Habermas, the lifeworld is less a purely cognitive horizon than an environment made up both of attitudes and of practices – a realm of informal culturally grounded understandings and mutual accommodations. In modernity, the systematization of world views and the development of formal reasoning in the law and other spheres involves a rationalization of the lifeworld; the autonomous development of markets and bureaucratic systems represents what he calls its colonization (Habermas, 1981, volume 2, p. 196). In other words, no sooner are human social arrangements opened up to rational discussion with a view to their modification than they are rigidified into the autonomous subsystems analyzed but not criticized by sociological systems theory. In Habermas's model, the "uncoupling" of autonomous market and administrative systems means that the lifeworld becomes "one subsystem among others."

As Max Weber realized, these subsystems become like machines, running independently of their original sources in the moral and political structures of the lifeworld: "economic and bureaucratic spheres emerge in which social relations are regulated only by money and power" (Habermas, 1981, volume 2, p. 154).

Habermas's reconstructive theory of communicative action includes an account of the changing institutional forms which it takes in Europe and North America from around the eighteenth century. This is a two-sided process. On the one hand, more and more areas of social life are prised out of traditional contexts and subjected to rational examination and argument. On the other hand, the expansion of markets and administrative structures leads to what Habermas calls the colonization or hollowing-out of the lifeworld by autonomous subsystems which are removed from rational evaluation, except within their own highly circumscribed terms. Examples of this process can be found in the attempts by welfare state systems to extend legal regulation and monetary calculation right into the private sphere, at the cost of those traces of solidarity which remain; and solidarity, Habermas insists, is a resource which cannot be bought or constrained. More broadly, the differentiation, whose analysis goes back to Kant, of what he calls the "value-spheres" of science, morality, and art facilitates their individual development, but at the cost of their estrangement from each other and from culture as a whole.

Habermas thus follows the tradition of analysis developed by Marx in his theory of alienation, by Max Weber in terms of rationalization and disenchantment (*Entzauberung*), and in György Lukács's concept of reification (*Verdinglichung*). In the early Critical Theorists' critique of instrumental rationality as something inevitably linked to domination, all these motifs come together (Habermas, 1981, volume 1, p. 144). In Habermas's view, however, all these models are insufficiently complex. Marx focuses too one-sidedly on the rationalization of the forces and relations of material production; Max Weber sees societal rationalization too narrowly in terms of patterns of individual purposive-rational action. One needs instead to differentiate between "the rationalization of action orientations and lifeworld structures" and "the expansion of the 'rationality', that is, complexity of action systems" (Habermas, 1981, volume 1, p. 145). Habermas addresses, in other words, the big question of whether we could have had, or can now have, modernity without the less attractive features of capitalism and the bureaucratic nation-state. More tentatively, in *Between Facts and Norms* (1992b) and in more recent volumes of essays, he has begun to reformulate elements of his model of advanced capitalist crisis in the language of his more recent theories (Habermas, 1992b, pp. 384–7).

I have focused in this brief discussion on the theoretical model which Habermas developed from the mid-1970s. His earlier work, however, which he now tends to treat somewhat dismissively, also remains in my view of enormous richness and importance. This is particularly true of *Knowledge and Human Interests* (1968b), which I briefly discuss below, but also of much of the rest of his extremely creative oeuvre (see Müller-Doohm, forthcoming). In some ways, indeed, his most recent work on the state and the public sphere returns, as Habermas has noted himself, to concerns which he had addressed at the beginning of his career and which continue to be central to his thinking.

If Habermas had a single target of attack in his early work, it might best be termed technocratic politics. This he attacked from two directions. One was his influential analysis of the rise and fall of the bourgeois public sphere (Habermas, 1962). The partially realized ideal of independent discussion and rational critique of public affairs which developed in the eighteenth century in Europe and North America mutated in the twentieth century, Habermas argued, into a conception of public opinion as something to be measured and manipulated. These operations in turn relied heavily on an ideology and practice of positivistic social science which Habermas (1963, 1968b) subjected to a philosophical and historical critique; this critique finally underpinned his conception of critical social theory oriented to the critique of ideology.

What might form the basis of this model of critical social science? Habermas (1963) was initially attracted by the idea of conceiving it as an empirically oriented and falsifiable philosophy of history with an emancipatory purpose. He then defined it in more methodological terms as a project combining causal explanation and hermeneutic understanding – a model based on his reading of Freudian psychoanalysis as involving, in essence, the removal of causal obstacles to self-understanding and thus resulting in the patient's liberation from avoidable constraints (Habermas, 1968b). Once we know the real reason, for example, why we are afraid of spiders which we know to be harmless, we are on the way to overcoming our fear. The same sort of model, Habermas argued, underlay the Marxist critique of ideology: once we understand why capitalism appears, misleadingly, as a just system based on agreement and contract, and is presented as such by bourgeois political economy, the way is open to a more accurate and empowering understanding of it as an avoidable system of social exploitation. In other words, Freudian and Marxian thought can be understood as paradigms of critical social science, oriented by and to an interest in emancipation.

Habermas (1973b) then came to feel that the trichotomy of empirical, hermeneutic, and critical sciences was too simplistic, especially in that reflection in the philosophical sense did not necessarily mean emancipation in practice. The truth, in other words, does not necessarily make us free, in the absence of other conditions. And some of the best historical sociology, for example, although it may aid reflection in the first sense, does not really fit Habermas's model of emancipatory science. In place of this model, he developed in the 1970s a more modest account of reconstructive science, exemplified, as noted earlier, by his emergent theory of communicative action and his theory of discourse ethics.

Just as some linguistic theories reconstruct in formal terms our competence as speakers, the theory of communicative action provides a theoretical reconstruction of a practice in which we regularly engage, whether or not we reflect explicitly and theoretically on it. As he put it in an interview (Habermas, 1991a, p. 111), he does not say that people *want* to act communicatively, but that *they have to*....When parents bring up their children, when the living generations appropriate the transmitted wisdom of preceding generations, when individuals and groups cooperate, that is, get along with one another without the costly recourse to violence, they all have to act communicatively. There are elementary social functions that can only be satisfied by means of communicative action.

As we saw above, Habermas (1981) outlined this model in reference both to the traditions of social theory and to the history of Western modernity. He draws in particular on George Herbert Mead's analysis of self–other relations in interaction, and Durkheim's theorization of intersubjectivity and social solidarity in relation to the secularization of religion, what Habermas calls the "linguistification of the sacred," to illustrate some of the social theoretical roots of his own model of communicative action. Habermas goes on to show how Max Weber, who, in *The Protestant Ethic and the Spirit of Capitalism* and in his work as a whole, described the rationalization of the lifeworld in early modernity, also offered an account, complementary to that of Marx, of the reconfinement of human beings in an increasingly rigid and bureaucratized world. As Habermas shows, systematizing the central theme of Western Marxism expressed in Lukács's concept of reification, markets and bureaucratic power relations combine, in varying configurations, to reduce individuals' freedom to act both as individuals and collectively. This means, incidentally, that the postmodern critique of modernity is fundamentally misconceived, since it takes as essential to modernity features found in the capitalist form which it took, but logically separable from it. The task of critical theory, then, is to explore alternative historical and present-day possibilities (Habermas, 1981, volume 2, pp. 374–403).

Shortly after the publication of *The Theory of Communicative Action*, Habermas returned in his writing to the theme of morality which had concerned him in his theory of social evolution and to systematize the ethical principles which underlay that historical model. The American developmental psychologist Lawrence Kohlberg had traced the advance of children's moral reasoning to what Habermas called a post-conventional stage, at which the question of the validity of (often conflicting) moral principles is explicitly addressed. At this point, Habermas argues, ordinary moral reasoning overlaps with philosophical ethics, and this is the situation whch confronts us in the contemporary world, in which, as Max Weber put it, mutually opposed "gods and demons" compete for our allegiance. But where Weber leaves us impaled on the existential dilemmas with nothing to guide us except the imperative to choose in an authentic manner, Habermas insists that one can give compelling reasons in moral argumentation, just as one can in matters of fact.

Once again, it is an ideally informed consensus which would conclusively underwrite, and the more or less conscious pursuit of such a consensus which in practice underwrites, our judgments about justice and, to some extent, even our conceptions of the good. Post-conventional moral reasoning is inevitably a matter of dialogue or discourse, in which principles are justified if they can or could find, for the moment at least, the assent of all those who are or might be affected by them. More formally, according to the principle which Habermas labels U, a norm is morally right if "*All* affected can accept the consequences and the side effects its *general* observance can be anticipated to have for the satisfaction of *everyone's* interests (and these consequences are preferred to those of known alternatives)" (Habermas, 1983, p. 65).

There are strong echoes here, of course, of the Kantian notion of the universalizability of moral judgments, and of John Rawls's modified utilitarian theory of justice, in which inequalities are justified if they are to the benefit of the worst off, but in Habermas's model we also have to choose between alternative bases of moral judgment as well as between alternative applications of them. The same goes, Habermas argues, for the legal principles which abut onto moral ones. Precisely because there are substantial disagreements between alternative legal principles as well as over their interpretation, only the dialogue institutionalized in a functioning democratic state can legitimate the choice between these principles. Habermas's moral universalism is not, then, the arrogant gesture which it sometimes appears to be in the accounts of postmodern or antifoundationalist critics. It is, rather, intended as the only possible response to a situation of radical diversity of views and in which it is practically essential to be able to offer universalistic defenses of fundamental principles: "the concrete, particular moralities rooted in specific forms of life are only acceptable today if they have a universalistic kernel. For they must if it comes down to it (*im Ernstfall*) be able to prevent something like the Shoah happening again. Otherwise they are worth nothing and cannot be justified" (Dews, 1992, p. 226).

At the same time, however, it is not clear how *much* discussion a discourse ethics commits us to, nor how this might best be institutionalized. Communicative action, Habermas insists, is not the same as argumentation; the latter term denotes specific forms of communication – "islands in the sea of praxis" – but the expansion of communicative action at the expense of more authoritarian traditions forms a necessary basis for argumentative discourse to become more widespread. As he put it in another recent work, "What seems to me essential to the degree of liberality of a society is the extent to which its patterns of socialization and its institutions, its political culture, and in general its identity-guaranteeing traditions and everyday practices express a noncoercive form of ethical life in which autonomous morality can be embodied and can take on concrete shape" (Habermas, 1991b, p. 171). Habermas points to the variety of forums in modern societies, ranging from academic symposia to TV debates and parliamentary assemblies, in which specific moral and ethical issues are argued out.

Discourse ethics does not offer, then, a practical solution to concrete moral or ethical issues, so much as a set of recommended practices within which such solutions may be pursued (Habermas, 1983, p. 103). In this of course it resembles democratic theory, which it has also complemented and enriched – notably in its contribution to the conception of deliberative democracy. This to some extent resolves the issue raised in Germany by Albrecht Wellmer and in the USA by a number of critics as to whether discourse ethics should be understood more in relation to politics and the public sphere than in relation to morality in a strict sense. His discourse ethic is, Habermas concedes, necessarily somewhat formal. It is based on a procedure, that of practical discourse, rather than specific ethical prescriptions (Habermas, 1983, p. 103). It draws a sharp distinction between questions of justice and questions of the "good life"; the latter can only be addressed in the context of diverse cultures or forms of life or of individual life-projects (Habermas, 1983, p. 108). On the other hand, a universalistic morality can bridge the division between morality and law, in that both are based, in varying ways, on a relation to discourse. In Habermas's most recent major book, *Between Facts and Norms*, he develops the implications of this model for a theory of law and the democratic state.

Readers of Habermas at the end of the 1980s who were wondering what might be the political implications of his sometimes rather rarefied discussion of moral theory were given an answer in the slogan with which he ended his Tanner Lectures (Habermas, 1988b, p. 279): "A legal system is autonomous only to the extent that the procedures institutionalized for legislation and legal decision guarantee a non-partisan formation of opinion and will and thereby give moral procedural rationality access, as it were, to law and politics. No autonomous law without realized democracy." What Habermas offers in more detail in *Between Facts and Norms* is a full-blown political theory of law and the democratic state. Although law and morality are distinct, both moral and legal norms depend implicitly on what Habermas calls the discourse principle, that those affected by them could agree to them as participants in a rational discourse (Habermas, 1992b, p. 107). Modified to fit the three contexts of morality, law, and political democracy, the intuition embodied in the discourse principle, which aims "to explain the point of view from which norms of action can be *impartially justified*" (Habermas, 1992b, pp. 108–9), underpins the structural relations between them.

Law, especially constitutional law, is crucial for Habermas's argument because it bridges the gap between moral reasoning on the one hand, which can only exhort and rebuke those who ignore it, and political decision-making on the other, which is always at risk of arbitrariness, even when it is democratically legitimated:

> In less complex societies, socially integrating force inheres in the ethos of a form of life, inasmuch as this integral ethical life binds all the components of the lifeworld together, attuning concrete duties to institutions and linking them with motivations. Under conditions of high complexity, moral contents can spread throughout a society along the channels of legal regulation. (Habermas, 1992b, p. 118)

For Habermas, of course, democracy does not simply mean universal suffrage and majority rule. Although, for example, he accepts the legitimacy of majority voting in a system necessarily operating under time constraints, he insists that procedural rules of this kind must themselves be discursively justified. Habermas is at least as much concerned for the extent and quality of public discussion of political issues as for the details of institutional arrangements. In other words, he has returned to issues of the public sphere and public opinion which were the object of one of his first studies, but now armed with a much more substantial normative and empirical theory of the state:

> The rational quality of political legislation does not depend only on how elected majorities and protected minorities work within the parliaments. It depends also on the level of participation and education, on the degrees of information and the precison with which controversial issues are articulated – in short, on the discursive character of non-institutionalized opinon formation in the political public sphere. (Habermas, 1992b, p. 570; cf. Habermas, 1988a, p. 249)

Anyone advancing a theory of the state in the contemporary world has of course to confront issues of globalization and what Habermas (1998a) has termed the "postnational constellation." While Habermas's formal model of the democratic constitutional state (*Rechtsstaat*) was cast very much in traditional nation-state terms, his more informal reflections in interviews and occasional articles have focused on the challenges to state sovereignty posed not simply by the fact of globalization but also by the normative intuitions captured by the notion of a global public opinion or global civil society and political concepts of "cosmopolitan democracy" or "world domestic politics." As Habermas notes in one of his most recent contributions to this topic, a crucial question is "whether political communities can construct a *collective identity* beyond the limits of a nation and thereby satisfy the legitimacy conditions of a postnational democracy" (Habermas, 1998a, p. 136). His tentative answer is that a European federal state, developing a sense of solidarity on the basis of a common European history, albeit one of tension and divison, may serve as a testing ground and a basis for more ambitious experiments in cosmopolitan democracy, just as Europe earlier pioneered a nation-state structure and in large part imposed it on the rest of the world. "Europe's second chance" (Habermas, 1996) should not of course take the form of neocolonial arrogance, but nor should it be missed in a "postcolonial regression into eurocentrism" (Habermas, 1998a, p. 9).

## THE PERSON

Born in 1929, Habermas grew up in the small town of Gummersbach, near Cologne, Germany. He studied philosophy, history, psychology, and German literature at Göttingen, Zurich, and Bonn, where he obtained his doctorate in 1954 with a thesis on Schelling. After some journalistic work he became, in 1956, Adorno's research assistant at the Institute of Social Research in Frankfurt, newly re-established in Germany and the base of what had come to be called the "Frankfurt School." Here he participated in an empirical study on the political awareness of students (Habermas et al., 1961). From 1959 to 1961 he worked on his *Structural Transformation of the Public Sphere* (1962). After a period as Professor of Philosophy at Heidelberg, Habermas returned to Frankfurt in 1964 as Professor of Philosophy and Sociology, where he delivered the inaugural lecture on "Knowledge and Interest" (reprinted in Habermas, 1968b). Also at this time he published the essays entitled *Theory and Practice* (1963), a survey work, *The Logic of the Social Sciences* (1967), and some further essays grouped under the title *Technology and Science as Ideology* (1968).

In 1971 Habermas left Frankfurt for Starnberg, Bavaria, to take up, along with the physicist C. F. von Weizsäcker, the directorship of the newly created Max Planck Institute for the Study of the Conditions of Life in the Scientific-Technical World. Surrounded by some of the most brilliant younger sociologists in the country, many of whom have since become major theorists in their own right, he began to develop the theme of communicative action, which had been present but not particularly prominent in his earlier work, into the centerpiece of his theorizing. He published an enormous amount of material, including the well known *Legitimation Crisis* (1973) and culminating with the *Theory of Communicative Action* (1981). In 1982, he returned to a chair in Philosophy and Sociology at Frankfurt, where he taught until his retirement in 1994.

In the 1980s and 1990s, Habermas developed the implications of his theory of communicative action in three broadly distinct domains. First, he advanced what is generally called a "discourse ethics" or, more precisely, a "discourse theory of morality," in *Moral Consciousness and Communicative Action* (1983), *Justification and Application* (1991), and a number of essays. Second, in the critical history of philosophy, his critique of poststructuralism in *The Philosophical Discourse of Modernity*, based on a series of lectures, was published in 1985, *Postmetaphysical Thinking* in 1988, and *Texte und Kontexte* in 1992. Third, he has developed his moral theory into a theory of politics, law, and the democratic state, with a series of lectures on "Law and Morality" delivered in 1986, *Between Facts and Norms* (1992), and the essays published as *Die Einbeziehung des Anderen* (1996).

The above constitute what Habermas considers his "theoretical" works, but he has also published seven volumes of political writings and, most recently, a further volume of political essays, *Die postnationale Konstellation* (1998). Thus his work in social theory is complemented by a volume of writing on contemporary social and political issues which is itself the subject of at least one book-length study (Holub, 1991). Like Max Weber in Imperial Germany, and Karl Jaspers in the early years of the Federal Republic, he has come to be in some sense the intellectual conscience of the country. Like Weber, he is basically a thinker rather than a man of action, but one who intervenes in political issues when something, as he often puts it, "irritates" him. And although he rejects Weber's doctrine of the value-freedom of science, he insists, like Weber, on the distinction between scholarly and political discourse (Dews, 1986, p. 127).

Habermas has been concerned in particular with three sets of issues, past, present, and future. In the past, or more particularly in current uses of the past, he has repeatedly intervened over issues of the responsibility of Germany and of individual Germans for the Third Reich and the Holocaust. One of his earliest essays was concerned with the philosopher Martin Heidegger's refusal in the 1950s to confront his past as an active Nazi (Habermas, 1953). More recently, in the late 1980s, he initiated what came to be called the Historians'

Dispute (*Historikerstreit*) with an attack on what he saw as a concerted attempt by the West German Right to whitewash the past by historicizing it, relativizing the crimes of the Nazis as one episode among others in a world-historical past which was inevitably often tragic. This "damage settlement" (Habermas, 1987) – a term taken from the insurance industry – was all in order to create a new, confident national consciousness. Most recently, Habermas has intervened in support of the young North American historian Daniel Goldhagen against virulent attacks in Germany on his controversial attempt to demonstrate how widespread was German complicity in the Holocaust.

Of contemporary events which attracted Habermas's active involvement, undoubtedly the most important were the student protests of 1968. Habermas participated very fully in this movement, and although he came to criticize its extremism and had no sympathy for the desperate terrorism which followed its demise, he welcomed its long-term effect in modernizing the political culture of of the Federal Republic. More recently, as noted above, he defended ths liberal and enlightened strand of West German thought against attempts to return to a new (conservative) "obscurity" (Habermas, 1985b). Finally, the reunification of Germany has led Habermas into extended reflections both on Germany itself and on the future of the European nation-state in general. He has been a critical supporter of the European integration process, which he sees as opening up a possible future for a "postnational" world.

## THE SOCIAL CONTEXT

As will be clear from the previous section, Habermas spent the whole of his academic career, with the exception of guest professorships in the USA and elsewhere, in his native country, and he has been crucially concerned with the question which the philosopher Karl Jaspers (1966) made into a book title: where is the Federal Republic going? More concretely, as a member of what has been called the "Hitler Youth generation," drawn as a child into complicity with the most appalling regime of modern times, he was horrified both by the crimes of the Third Reich and by the unwillingness of most of his compatriots to face up to their responsibility for what had happened. For a long time the Nazi period was a taboo subject in schools; major universities conveniently passed over it in their official histories, and the naming of a new university after a leading opponent and victim of Nazism was seen as deeply controversial. Even in communist East Germany, where the history of the Third Reich was at least given the prominence it deserved, issues of personal or collective responsibility were not seriously raised.

The German past is, then, one crucial aspect of the social context of Habermas's life and work. Another was of course something which was common to all the major Western European states in what were called the "thirty glorious years" from the late 1940s to the early 1970s: democratic welfare states, rising prosperity, and full employment. Habermas's response, notably in *Legitimation Crisis* (1973), was to reformulate Marxist crisis theory in a suggestive model of the displacement of crisis tendencies from the economic base to the political and cultural sphere. He had earlier taken up and reformulated the critique of "technocracy," which had been fashionable in the fifties and sixties, concerned to construct a socialist response to the technological determinism deriving from the work of Heidegger, Arnold Gehlen, and Helmut Schelsky. In this context, Habermas also looked into the changing nature of political participation, the public sphere, and civil society – the last of course crucially invigorated in the years around 1968 by "citizen" initiatives and new social movements (Habermas, 1963, 1968b).

Soon after the publication of *Legitimation Crisis*, of course, the age of full employment came to seem lost forever in the aftermath of the first oil price shock of 1973; the political climate shifted to the right, with the rise to power of Ronald Reagan, Margaret Thatcher, and, in West Germany, Helmut Kohl. German neoliberalism was a muted affair compared to that in the USA and UK, but the political background was a good deal nastier, with political terrorism sparking off a peculiarly violent backlash in the "German Autumn" of 1977 and the following years, in which respectable intellectuals were often accused of sympathizing with terrorists. Habermas, and close associates such as Albrecht Wellmer (in Habermas, 1987), attempted to restore some sense of proportion to public debate on these issues.

The Federal Republic, which had muddled through the 1980s more or less effectively under Helmut Kohl's calm and complacent reign as Federal Chancellor, was surprised in the autumn of 1989 by the collapse of its poor sister-state, the German Democratic Republic, along with the other Marxist-Leninist dictatorships in Europe. The "national question" ceased to be the preserve of historians and (mostly right-wing) publicists and rapidly moved to the top of the political agenda. As usual with really important agenda items, it was dealt with perfunctorily, in a technical-fix reunification which left all the important issues unresolved. Habermas (1990) was one of many German intellectuals who argued that a crucial opportunity had been missed to rethink the constitution of the Federal Republic, rather than simply incorporating what were delicately referred to as the "five new states" or the "accession territory." These issues now remain to be confronted, as Habermas rightly insists, on a European and global stage.

## THE INTELLECTUAL CONTEXT

Habermas's thinking emerges from the flexible and interdisciplinary Marxist tradition of what came to be called the "Frankfurt School" of critical theory, based in the early 1930s and again from 1950 in the Institute for Social Research in Frankfurt. As Habermas showed in detail in his *Theory of Communicative Action*, this tradition draws on both Marx and Max Weber, on another non-Marxist, Weber's contemporary Georg Simmel, and on the father of "Western Marxism" (Anderson, 1976), György Lukács. In an autobiographical interview, Habermas recalls reading Lukács for the first time with great excitement but with a sense that his work was no longer directly relevant to postwar societies such as Western Germany. His thinking remained shaped, however, by a Western Marxist agenda emphasizing not just issues of capital and class but the interplay between capitalist exploitation and bureaucratic state rule, and their implications for individual identity and collective political autonomy.

Habermas's relationship to Frankfurt critical theory was somewhat indirect in the early stages of his career. He diverged from the two key members of the Frankfurt School who had returned to Germany, Theodor Adorno and Max Horkheimer, whose interests had become increasingly philosophical, in insisting that a revival of critical theory had once again to engage fully with the social and human sciences. He fully shared, however, Adorno and Horkheimer's concern with the way in which enlightenment, in the form of instrumental rationality, turns from a means of liberation into a new source of enslavement. "Already at that time" (the late 1950s), he has written, "my problem was a theory of modernity, a theory of the pathology of modernity, from the viewpoint of the realization – the deformed realization – of reason in history" (Dews, 1992, p. 187). This involved a working-through of the classics: Marx and Weber, but also Kant, Fichte, and Hegel – and of course ancient Greek thought.

This theoretical emphasis was, however, constantly combined, as in his early volume of essays, *Theory and Practice*, with a concern for the conditions of rational political discussion in modern technocratic democracies. Only the social sciences, broadly conceived, could provide the means to construct a genuinely contemporary critical theory of advanced capitalism, but their own positivistic deformation was itself part of the problem to be overcome. Habermas joined in the "positivism dispute" of the early 1960s in which these issues were battled out in Germany (Adorno, 1966), and devoted the following decade to a detailed historical critique of positivist social science and the elaboration of an alternative model of "reconstructive" science, of which his own theory of communicative action is an example. In *Knowledge and Human Interests* (1968b), Habermas brilliantly showed how positivism had limited our understanding of the natural and the social world and undermined the possibility of critique; this could, however, be reconstructed from the work of Kant, Fichte, Hegel, and Marx and shown to inspire, for example, Freudian pychoanalytic theory and practice. "Critical" sciences such as psychoanalysis or the Marxist critique of ideology, governed by an emancipatory interest in overcoming causal obstacles to self-understanding, bridged the gap between the natural or empirical sciences, oriented to the prediction and control of objectified processes, and the human sciences, oriented to an expansion of mutual understanding.

Earlier critical theory had distinguished itself from more orthodox variants of Marxism by its intense engagement with non-Marxist thought after Marx. Rather than writing off phenomenology, existentialism, or Heidegger's philosophy as a symptom of capitalist crisis, Adorno devoted major studies to Kierkegaard and Husserl, and a substantial part of *Negative Dialectics* (Adorno, 1966) to a discussion of Heidegger. Similarly, though in a more methodological vein, Habermas worked out his own models of critical and reconstructive science – the former in an engagement with Schutzian phenomenological sociology,

Peter Winch's development of Wittgensteinian philosophy into social theory, and Gadamer's Heideggerian philosophical hermeneutics. These, Habermas argued, could be brought into a complementary relation with one another and could then be further augmented by a more materialist reflection on the way in which our understanding of the social world (the common theme of these three currents of thought) is systematically distorted by relations of power and exploitation. In the 1970s, as noted earlier, he developed an idea of reconstructive science, seen as a systematic attempt to isolate the conditions and implications of practices such as linguistic communication and moral reasoning. Here it is linguistic theories of speech pragmatics which provide the paradigm, and social theory the detailed illustration.

Finally, Habermas's discourse ethics has been substantially developed in relation to English-language ethical and political theory. His polemical exchanges with Gadamer and the system theorist Niklas Luhmann have become major documents in their own right. Against Gadamer, he argued that understanding needed to be supplemented by a materialist critique of power and exploitation, which he justified with an appeal to a notion of social theory contrasted with Luhmann's technocratic conception. Habermas has developed his thinking in close contact with others, notably the philosopher Karl-Otto Apel, whose intellectual trajectory in many ways parallels his own. He has also been exceptionally willing to engage with critical discussions of his own work and more recent developments in critical theory in the work of Axel Honneth, Seyla Benhabib, and others – thus giving practical expression to the theoretical and political importance which he attaches to communication and dialogue.

## IMPACT

Habermas came to be recognized relatively early in West Germany as a major social theorist. His standing as a political commentator was helped perhaps by his prominent role in 1968 and the attacks he suffered from both sides of the barricades. Outside the country, he was slower to attract a substantial following, in milieux largely ignorant of the Frankfurt School tradition and its characteristic concerns and modes of approach. Even with the turn to social theory and more politicized social science in the UK in the early 1970s, Habermas was perhaps not Marxist enough for the orthodox, who tended to favor structuralist variants of Marxism, and too Marxist or "theoretical" for others. His impact in the UK and France, for example, came largely as a result of growing interest in his work in the more diverse and pluralistic intellectual milieu of the USA.

In the 1980s and 1990s, however, and despite the somewhat forbidding character of many of his books, his reputation in the English-speaking world grew rapidly. As noted above, Habermas's work has been influential in a whole range of fields, and has become one of the principal reference points for much discussion in social theory and, for example, moral philosophy, legal theory, and theories of international relations. Historians and theorists of culture have also increasingly been influenced by his conception of the public sphere and other elements of his thought (see Calhoun, 1992). Critical theory in the broadest sense has been carried on by contemporaries such as Albrecht Wellmer and a third generation of thinkers including Axel Honneth, Hans Joas, Thomas McCarthy, and Seyla Benhabib – all of whom, in different ways, have responded to issues posed by post-structuralist, postmodernist, and feminist theory, and shown how Habermas's approach can be usefully developed and extended. Habermas's concern with historical sociology and theorizing states and social movements has been carried forward by, for example, Claus Offe and Klaus Eder. In a more speculative vein, Ulrich Beck's influential analysis of modernity in terms of risk again owes a great deal to Habermas. Finally, his discourse ethics and his more recent theorizing about law and the state have attracted enormous interest in areas of analytic moral and legal philosophy previously untouched by Habermasian concerns. This is currently one of the most active areas of research, and to some extent practical ethical and legal argument, which draw directly on Habermas's work, and Habermas has himself been working very substantially in this field.

His opposition to post-structuralism and postmodernism and his occasional polemics with the French philosopher Jean-François Lyotard and others have marked out one of the systematic lines of division in contemporary social theory, concretized to some extent in positions taken in relation to the Enlightenment. For Habermas, this should essentially be seen as a project, incomplete and ambiguous in many ways but no less worthwhile than when it was first articulated in the seventeenth and eighteenth centuries. Thus, while he accepts some of what has been said by postmodernists and others about a certain rigidity in Enlightenment and, more broadly, liberal thinking – as indicated in the title of one of his recent volumes, "The Incorporation of the Other" (Habermas, 1996) – he remains committed to these values and to a universalistic mode of thought and argumentation: again not despite, but precisely because of, the enormous diversity of values and cognitive orientations found in modern societies.

The rise of social theory since the beginning of the 1970s, and more particularly in the 1990s, as a relatively distinct domain of activity and a source of inspiration to the social sciences as a whole, has also been due in considerable part to Habermas's work. He has always been hard to place in disciplinary terms, working on the borders of social theory and philosophy, and always willing to venture into new fields, such as the analysis of language or law, as required by the development of his own work. In short, he has made it possible both to see the contemporary world differently, and to rethink the relations between theories in the social sciences, which are at least one of our main resources in understanding this world.

## ASSESSMENT

Will people still be reading Habermas at the end of the twenty-first century? My feeling is that they should be, for several reasons. First, and irrespective of the direction to be taken by social theory in the century which is just dawning,

Habermas's work documents, more clearly perhaps than that of any other contemporary thinker, the attempt to revitalize the classic propositions of Western Marxism with the aid of some very diverse themes of mid to late twentieth-century social theory. As such, he will surely attract attention from historians of thought as someone who attempted, in the most ambitious theoretical terms, to bring together some at least of the dominant theoretical paradigms of the age and to confront some of its central problems.

The implicit parallel with Hegel's idea of philosophy's mission to grasp "its time" in thought is deliberate: Habermas's mode of theorizing, even when he seems at his most Kantian and formalistic, is to trace a rational line of development through a set of apparently opposed frameworks. This is nowhere clearer than when he attempts, however cautiously and tentatively, to bridge the gaps between empirical and normative issues. As we have seen, for example, his thoroughgoing critique of positivism and ethical subjectivism feeds into an approach to legal and democratic theory which transcends conventional separations between, on the one hand, so-called positive law, where what counts is merely that it has been enacted according to due process, and, on the other hand, an individualistic morality. These are in turn internally related, he argues, to representative democracy and public communication.

Whether or not Habermas is right that one can formally reconstruct theories of all these domains on the basis of an analysis of the preconditions of communication, his basic notion that communication with others is only meaningful if it is driven by the pursuit of rational agreement, and that such agreement is the only legitimate basis of morality and political authority in the modern world, would be widely shared. And if one of the problems of much contemporary social and political theory is that it has little to say about the practical dilemmas with which we are confronted, Habermas offers at least the outlines of a practical political theory as well as a theory of politics.

This is not to say that Habermas will have anything like the massive impact which Hegel exercised over his contemporaries and immediate successors; no present-day thinker could possibly do this in an intellectual world which has become as disaggregated and pluralistic as our own. On the other hand, if, as I suspect, capitalist market economies and capitalist and state bureaucracies continue to dominate the more developed parts of the world in the twenty-first century, critiques of capitalism which still owe much to Marx will no doubt retain their appeal. Habermas was surely right to argue that an adequate theory of the contemporary world must attend to the distinctiveness of advanced capitalism, and in particular of the state forms with which it coexists, and to the issues of culture and identity to which critical theory has been more sensitive than most other Marxist and non-Marxist traditions in social theory. With the eclipse, in the 1980s and 1990s, of more orthodox variants of Marxism, and a certain fusion of horizons between Marxist and non-Marxist approaches in social theory, Habermas's creative synthesis may seem more attractive than ever.

As I noted above, Habermas has continued in his more recent works his analysis of the public sphere and of crisis tendencies in contemporary societies, first addressed in his books of 1962 and 1973. In relation to the public sphere, he has stressed the interplay of public communication at many different levels and the fact that public spheres in modern societies are increasingly mediated and virtual. What this might mean in practice for a political theory of communicative democracy is an issue which clearly requires further exploration. We also badly need a more developed theory of economic, social, and political crises in modern societies, which Habermas is extremely well placed to provide.

What do we *not* get from Habermas? Not much about economics or about culture. These were the two areas which earlier critical theory had attempted to relate – no doubt somewhat too fast and easily, as Axel Honneth (1985) has argued. Habermas's attempt to fill out the dimension of social and political theory restores the center that was missing from much of the work of the first generation of critical theorists, but in a way which leaves the analysis of global political economy and contemporary cultural processes, and the crucial inter-relations between them, to others. To say that Habermas has not done this, however, is not to say that it cannot be done within a recognizably Habermasian framework, and a good deal of recent work in international relations theory has taken this direction. His own work and that of others using a Habermasian approach has also been particularly illuminating in relation to recent discussion of the post-1989 world; thinkers concerned with, for example, the political consequences of globalization for our conceptions of ethics, democracy, citizenship, and (post-) national identity have drawn significantly on Habermas's insights. Habermas would, I think, be happy to feel that he had set up a set of frameworks for use both by himself and by others.

## Bibliography

### Writings of Jürgen Habermas

Mit Heidegger gegen Heidegger denken. 1953. *Frankfurter Allgemeine Zeitung*, July 25 (reprinted in Habermas, 1971, pp. 67–75).

*Student und Politik* (with L. von Friedeburg, C. Oehler, and F. Weltz). 1961. Neuwied/Berlin: Luchterhand.

*Strukturwandel der ffentlichkeit*. 1962. Neuwied/Berlin: Luchterhand (2nd edn, Frankfurt: Suhrkamp, 1989; translated by T. Burger, *The Structural Transformation of the Public Sphere*. Cambridge: Polity Press, 1989).

*Theorie und Praxis*. 1963. Neuwied/Berlin: Luchterhand (translated by J. Viertel, *Theory and Practice*. London: Heinemann, 1974).

*Technik und Wissenschaft als Ideologie*. 1968a. Frankfurt: Suhrkamp (part translated by J. Shapiro, *Toward a Rational Society*. London: Heinemann, 1971).

*Erkenntnis und Interesse*. 1968b. Frankfurt: Suhrkamp (translated by J. Shapiro, *Knowledge and Human Interests*. London: Heinemann, 1971).

*Zur Logik der Sozialwissenschaften*, 2nd edn. 1971. Frankfurt: Suhrkamp (translated by S. W. Nicholsen and J. A. Stark, *On the Logic of the Social Sciences*. Cambridge, MA: MIT Press, 1988).

*Philosophisch–politische Profile*. 1971a. Frankfurt: Suhrkamp (part translated by F. G. Lawrence, *Philosophical–Political Profiles*. London: Heinemann, 1983).

*Theorie der Gesellschaft oder Sozialtechnologie: was leistet die Systemforschung?* (with N. Luhmann). 1971b. Frankfurt: Suhrkamp.

*Legitimationsprobleme im Spätkapitalismus.* 1973a. Frankfurt: Suhrkamp (translated by T. McCarthy, *Legitimation Crisis.* London: Heinemann, 1976).

*Kultur und Kritik.* 1973b. Frankfurt: Suhrkamp.

The Public Sphere. 1974. *New German Critique*, 1(3), 49–55.

*Zur Rekonstruktion des historischen Materialismus.* 1976a. Frankfurt: Suhrkamp (part translated by F. G. Lawrence, *Communication and the Evolution of Society.* Boston: Beacon Press, 1979).

*Stichworte zur "Geistigen Situation der Zeit"* (editor). 1976b. Frankfurt: Suhrkamp (translated by A. Buchwalter, *Observations on the Spiritual Situation of the Age.* Cambridge, MA: MIT Press, 1984).

*Theorie des kommunikativen Handelns*, 2 volumes. 1981. Frankfurt: Suhrkamp (translated by T. McCarthy, *Theory of Communicative Action.* London: Heinemann, 1984).

The Entwinement of Myth and Enlightenment. 1982a. *New German Critique*, 26, 13–20.

Objektivismus in den Sozialwissenschaften. 1982b. In *Zur Logik der Sozialwissenschaften*, 5th edn, p. 549.

*Moralbewußtsein und kommunikatives Handeln.* 1983. Frankfurt: Suhrkamp (translated by C. Lenhardt and S. W. Nicholsen, *Moral Consciousness and Communicative Action.* Cambridge, MA: MIT Press, 1989).

*Vorstudien und Ergänzungen zur Theorie des Kommunikativen Handelns.* 1984. Frankfurt: Suhrkamp.

Modernity – an Incomplete Project. 1985a. In H. Foster (ed.), *Postmodern Culture.* London: Pluto Press.

*Die neue Unübersichtlichkeit.* 1985b. Frankfurt: Suhrkamp (translated by S. W. Nicholsen, *The New Conservatism.* Cambridge: Polity Press, 1989).

*Der philosophische Diskurs der Moderne.* 1985c. Frankfurt: Suhrkamp (translated by F. G. Lawrence, *The Philosophical Discourse of Modernity.* Cambridge, MA: MIT Press, 1987).

*Eine Art Schadensabwicklung. Kleine politische Schriften VI.* 1987. Frankfurt: Suhrkamp.

*Nachmetaphysisches Denken.* 1988a. Frankfurt: Suhrkamp (translated by W. M. Hohengarten, *Postmetaphysical Thinking.* Cambridge: Polity Press, 1992).

Law and Morality. 1988b. *The Tanner Lectures on Human Values*, 8, 217–19.

*Die nachholende Revolution.* 1990. Frankfurt: Suhrkamp.

*Vergangenheit als Zukunft* (edited by M. Heller). 1991a. Zurich: Pendo (2nd edn, Munich: Piper, 1993; translated by M. Pensky, *The Past as Future.* Lincoln: University of Nebraska Press, 1994).

*Erläuterungen zur Diskursethik.* 1991b. Frankfurt: Suhrkamp (translated by C. Cronin, *Justification and Application.* Cambridge, MA: MIT Press, 1993).

*Texte und Kontexte.* 1992a. Frankfurt: Suhrkamp.

*Faktizität und Geltung.* 1992b. Frankfurt: Suhrkamp (translated by W. Rehg, *Between Facts and Norms.* Cambridge: Polity Press, 1996).

*Die Einbeziehung des Anderen.* 1996. Frankfurt: Suhrkamp.

*Die Postnationale Konstellation. Politische Essays.* 1998a. Frankfurt: Suhrkamp.

On the Pragmatics of Communication (edited by M. Cooke). 1998b. Cambridge: Polity Press.

## Further reading

Adorno, T. W. (1966) *Negative Dialektik* (translated by E. B. Ashton, *Negative Dialectics.* London: Routledge, 1973).

Adorno, T. W. et al. (1969) *Der Positivismusstreit in der deutschen Soziologie.* Neuwied: Luchterhand (translated by Glyn Adey, *The Positivist Dispute in German Sociology.* London: Heinemann, 1976).

Anderson, P. (1976) *Considerations on Western Marxism.* London: New Left Books.

Bottomore, T. (1984) *The Frankfurt School.* Chichester: Ellis Horwood.

Calhoun, C. (ed.) (1992) *Habermas and the Public Sphere.* Cambridge, MA: MIT Press.

Dews, P. (ed) (1986) *Habermas, Autonomy and Solidarity.* London: Verso (2nd edn, 1992).

Holub, R. C. (1991) *Jürgen Habermas. Critic in the Public Sphere.* London: Routledge.

Honneth, A. (1985) *Kritik der Macht.* Frankfurt, Suhrkamp (translated by K. Baynes, *Critique of Power.* Cambridge, MA: MIT Press, 1992).

Honneth, A. and Joas, H. (eds) (1988) *Kommunikatives Handeln.* Frankfurt: Suhrkamp (translated by J. Gaines and D. L. Jones, *Communicative Action.* Cambridge: Polity Press, 1991).

Honneth, A. et al. (eds) (1989) *Zwischenbetrachtungen. Im Prozess der Aufklärung.* Frankfurt: Suhrkamp (translated in 2 volumes by W. Rehg, *Philosophical Interventions in the Unfinished Project of the Enlightenment,* and B. Fultner, *Cultural–Political Interventions in the Unfinished Project of the Enlightenment.* Cambridge, MA: MIT Press, 1992).

Jaspers, K. (1966) *Wohin treibt die Bundesrepublik?* Munich: Piper.

Jay, M. (1973) *The Dialectical Imagination. A History of the Frankfurt School and the Institute of Social Research, 1923–1950.* London: Heinemann.

Müller-Doohm, S. (ed.) (forthcoming) *The Interest of Reason. A Retrospective View of the Works of Jürgen Habermas.* Frankfurt: Suhrkamp.

Outhwaite, W. (1994) *Habermas. A Critical Introduction.* Cambridge: Polity Press.

Outhwaite, W. (ed) (1996) *The Habermas Reader.* Cambridge: Polity Press.

Outhwaite, W. (1998) Habermas: Modernity as Reflection. In L. Marcus and B. Cheyette (eds), *Modernity, Culture and "The Jew."* Cambridge: Polity Press.

Thompson, J. B. and Held, D. (eds) (1982) *Habermas. Critical Debates.* London: Macmillan.

White, S. K. (ed.) (1994) *The Cambridge Companion to Habermas.* Cambridge: Cambridge University Press.

Wiggershaus, R. (1987) *Die Frankfurter Schule.* Munich: Piper (translated by Michel Robertson, *The Frankfurt School.* Cambridge: Polity Press, 1993).

# 22

# Anthony Giddens

## CHRISTOPHER G. A. BRYANT AND DAVID JARY

The British sociologist Anthony Giddens has established himself as a theorist of global stature in each of the three main phases of his work: first, as a major interpreter of the classical tradition and its successors; second, as the author of structuration theory, a very influential treatment of agency and structure in which primacy is granted to neither; third, as a commentator on late modernity and globalization.

To an extent equalled, if at all, only by Jürgen Habermas, Giddens's work is distinguished by its comprehensive critical appropriation and imaginative reworking of the main concepts and perspectives of classical and modern theorists. Central to his early and middle work is an incisive critique of functionalism, evolutionism, and historical materialism. His structuration theory has found countless applications throughout the social sciences. The breadth and flair of his coverage of historical and global issues is no less striking. Significantly, he takes issue with currently fashionable conceptions of postmodernity, advancing instead an account of radicalized modernity in which changes characterized as postmodern by recent theorists (including postempiricist epistemology) are treated as already implicit in modernity. Latterly, Giddens has explored the implications of changing conceptions of self-identity, and new sources of risk, in a globalizing society. He has also started to define a new "utopian-realist" politics beyond left and right, a venture attractive to Britain's new Labour government. His cascading arrays of concepts have long caught the attention of social scientists; his reflections on self, society, and politics in a global order are beginning to inform wider publics.

## Introduction: a Global Social Theorist

Giddens is remarkable for the number of his publications, including some thirty-two authored and edited books between 1971 and 1997 (which have been translated into twenty-two languages), and nearly two hundred articles, essays, and reviews in academic journals, books and symposia, and magazines and newspapers. He is also unusual for the scale and scope of his work on three different dimensions. The first of these has to do with substance. Giddens has written on most developments in the social sciences except research design and methods. He has written commentaries on most leading figures, both living and dead, and most schools and traditions of social thought; he has worked on the ontology of the social and the self and has articulated the structuration theory with which his name is now everywhere associated; he has written on class, class societies, and the state; he has paid great attention to features of our own age of late, or "high," modernity and globalization and to their theorization; he has recently taken up issues of self and self-identity; and he currently is helping to specify a politics beyond left and right. In short, he is a world-renowned, a truly global, social theorist – but he is also a participant in debates in areas of special interest throughout the social sciences.

The second dimension is one of level. Giddens's writings range from discussions of fundamental, often somewhat abstruse, metatheoretical problems – as in *New Rules of Sociological Method* (1976a), *Central Problems in Social Theory* (1979) and *The Constitution of Society* (1984) – to very direct and effective books for students. The third dimension pertains to disciplinary range. Giddens is a sociologist who has been interested in anthropology and psychology since his undergraduate days, and who has engaged with developments, and prompted responses from critics, in philosophy, history, geography, linguistics, all the social sciences, management, social work, and psychotherapy.

To all of these can now be added an increasingly visible contribution to public debate in Britain in support of the center-left, including *New Statesman* articles and media appearances.[1]

Giddens would figure in most sociologists' lists of the top ten sociologists in the world today. His reputation extends, however, far beyond sociology. He has been described as Britain's best known social scientist since Keynes, and is well placed to become one of its most influential, having moved from King's College, Cambridge, to the directorship of the London School of Economics just four months before the Labour Party's triumph at the general election of May 1, 1997 after eighteen years in opposition. The new Labour government is dedicated to the "modernization" of Britain and seeks a politics of the "radical center." Quite what these might mean is still being debated and Tony Giddens is pleased to be one of the debaters outside government, but close to it, who is increasingly heard. Others close to the new government have joined the governors of the LSE. But though the *Sunday Times* (July 13, 1997) concluded "new Labour, new LSE," Giddens is anxious to stress that while he personally supports new Labour, the LSE as an institution does not, and must not, have any political alignment.

We will offer an overall comment on Giddens's *oeuvre* in due course but first it may be helpful to say something about his career to date.[2]

## GIDDENS'S CAREER

Anthony Giddens was born in 1938 in Edmonton, north London, the son of a clerk with London Transport. He was educated at a local grammar school, and then Hull University, where he read two nonschool subjects – sociology and psychology. At these he excelled, graduating with first-class honors in 1959. On graduation, he went to the London School of Economics, where he completed an MA thesis entitled "Sport and Society in Contemporary England." In 1961 he started as a lecturer in sociology at Leicester University. At Leicester he taught neither the second-year course in classical sociological theory (apart from three lectures on Simmel) – that was Ilya Neustadt's preserve – nor the third-year course on more recent developments in theory – this was given by Percy Cohen, whose *Modern Social Theory* (1968) is derived from it. Instead, he was primarily responsible for the third-year course in social psychology, in which he chose to link "social personality" to a number of other topics, including socialization, language, attitude formation, identity, institutions, and national character. In this and other courses, including lectures on Durkheim and suicide to a large first-year audience, he impressed not just with what he said but also with how he said it – with exceptional fluency and without notes. It was, it should also be emphasized, a significant time and place in which to make an impact. As T. H. Marshall (1982) and John Eldridge (1990) have each pointed out, Leicester in the late 1950s and the 1960s was one of the seedbeds of British sociology.

We do not wish to make too much of this early experience, but some features are worth noting. For a start, Giddens's version of sociology has always been open to developments in anthropology and psychology. Having been introduced to these in Hull, he found at Leicester a sociology department with an interest in developmental sociology and in-house teaching not only in anthropology but also in psychology. Indeed, it was through in-house psychology courses that Leicester sociology undergraduates first encountered Mead, Becker, and Goffman. Giddens also encountered a remarkable collection of teachers, including Norbert Elias – a key figure in the formation of the Leicester approach to sociology[3] (which is not to say that Elias's influence was necessarily evident to students at the time, as one of us, Chris Bryant, a Leicester graduate, can testify).

Giddens mentioned to us in 1989 that he regarded all his work as one continuous project, which we have called "the making of structuration theory." In addition to their merits as commentary, Giddens's writings prior to *New Rules of Sociological Method* (1976a) have thus also to be seen as part of a larger venture, the critical appropriation of earlier traditions in order to secure a base upon which to build theoretical constructions of his own. Many of those with a special interest in, and respect for, the work of Elias argue that Giddens owes more to Elias in the conception and execution of this undertaking than he acknowledges (on Giddens and Elias, see Kilminster, 1991). Elias, after all, had developed a (con)figurational, or process, sociology which, like Giddens's later structuration theory, sought to overcome the dualism of agency and structure. In particular, Eric Dunning (1994), then and now a teacher at Leicester, has directly challenged our judgment (in Bryant and Jary, 1991) that we had no reason to question Giddens's claim that he never knew enough about Elias's (largely unpublished) work for it to have been a major intellectual influence. He did, however, attend Elias's first-year lecture course, which was organized around the theme of development, in 1961–2, the last time he gave it, and he did read volume 1 of the *The Civilizing Process* both in unpublished translation and later in German (Elias, 1939). Giddens, it should be noted, joined the University of Leicester in 1961 and left in 1969, but, such were their travels, in only four of those eight years were he and Elias in Leicester at the same time. Having said that, Giddens says how impressed he was by the personal example of Elias – the single-minded scholar willing to pursue a large-scale personal project, heedless of distractions, over very many years.

Dunning argues that ours is too individualistic an approach to influence. Elias was, he contends, the major contributant to a departmental culture which influenced Giddens more than he is able or willing to admit. As evidence for this claim, Dunning recalls the debates among the staff between the supporters of developmental sociology led by Elias and their opponents led by Cohen. The opponents supposed Elias to be "championing a regressive return to an old-fashioned and outmoded 'evolutionism' rather than arguing, as he was, for the synthesis of classical and modern themes, concepts and concern" (Dunning, 1994, p. 4). "To his credit," Dunning continues, Giddens "was one of those who grasped Elias's synthesizing aims." But, of itself, that does not indicate any particular debt to Elias. Indeed, Dunning effectively concedes as much with his next remark that, "while at Leicester, Giddens remained – by choice, I think – essentially an aloof outsider." Dunning thinks this helps to explain Giddens's inadequate grasp of Elias's work; we think it suggests that Giddens was his own man from the start.[4]

Giddens taught at Simon Fraser University, near Vancouver, in 1966–7. There he saw how difficult it was for a European Marxist head of department, Tom Bottomore, to cope with students whose radicalism far exceeded his own. In 1967–8 Giddens moved on to the University of California in Los Angeles. Southern California was, he says, a revelation. He tells how a trip to Venice Beach, where he encountered large numbers of strangely attired people engaged in unlikely pursuits, brought home to him how both European structural sociologies and the agenda of the European left had their limitations. Their preoccupations with class, authority, and political party offered little insight into the way of life of the hippies or the course of the anti-Vietnam War movement.

Southern California may have fired his imagination but Giddens would still seem to have felt obliged to take stock of European structural sociologies before moving on intellectually. His *Capitalism and Modern Social Theory* (1971a) and *The Class Structure of the Advanced Societies* (1973) precede the first book to address systematically questions of agency and the microfoundations of social order, *New Rules of Sociological Method* (1976a). Given the early North American experience, however, it is understandable not only that Giddens should, in due course, take up questions of agency, but also that he should eventually seek a politics *Beyond Left and Right* (1994a).

In 1969, Giddens left Leicester for a university lectureship at Cambridge and a fellowship at King's College. He belatedly acquired a doctorate in 1974 and eleven years later became the second holder of the chair of sociology. In 1986, he played a leading role in the establishment of the first new faculty at Cambridge for many decades, Social and Political Sciences, and was appointed its first dean. Giddens remained at Cambridge until 1996, but also made numerous visits to universities and other institutions all over the world. *The Consequences of Modernity* (1990a) originated in lectures given at Stanford University, California, in 1988, and he also greatly valued teaching at the University of California at Santa Barbara before and after the publication of the US edition of his textbook introduction to sociology (1989, 1991).

Between 1975 and 1978, Giddens was the editor for ten books published in the Hutchinson Sociology series, and between 1977 and 1989 he was the editor for over fifty books published in two series by Macmillan. Since 1978, he has been an editor of the journal *Theory and Society*. No doubt this experience stood him in good stead when in 1985 he joined with John Thompson and David Held to found Polity Press. Polity has since become one of the world's leading social science publishers, with well over three hundred titles currently in print, and Giddens has been directly involved with commissioning, editing, and promotion throughout, though, he admits, it is proving harder to keep this going while Director of the LSE.

Giddens's career developed interestingly in the 1990s. From 1989 he had three and a half years with a therapist. The experience deepened his interest in personal life and the emotions, and led to the discussions of the self, identity, love, and sexuality in *Modernity and Self-identity* (1991a) and *The Transformation of Intimacy* (1992b). He has told us how he came to make connections between his personal circumstances and developments in society and culture from the local to the global, and how he came to re-view the latter in light of the former.[5] Giddens's thinking on "dialogic democracy" (presented in *The Transformation of Intimacy* and *Beyond Left and Right*), for example, worked outwards from personal relations to global issues. He also says that therapy gave him the confidence to seek a public role for the first time. It was truly life-transforming; it persuaded him that he could make his future significantly different from his past.

This, then, is the context in which Giddens embarked on the new vein of writing on the human condition in an age of high modernity in the 1990s; increased his intervention in public debates via articles in the press, media appearances, and joint seminars with academics, journalists, politicians, etc.; and, in due course, sought a new job which would provide both a new challenge and an opportunity to promote the public value of social science, inform government, and influence opinion. He obtained the last with his appointment to the directorship of the London School of Economics. Ever the teacher, he has introduced at the LSE a weekly director's lecture (with attendances of up to a thousand students in its first year). It is too soon to say how successful Giddens's directorship will turn out to be, but he has already raised the media profile of the LSE as the place where the issues of the age are addressed and debated.

## THREE PHASES IN THE MAKING OF STRUCTURATION THEORY

It is very generally accepted among sociologists and other social scientists that neither the holy trinity of Marx, Durkheim, and Weber, nor additions to the sainthood like Simmel, provided satisfactory ways of connecting micro- and macro-analysis or agency and structure. The same is generally said about subsequent developments, such as the structural-functionalism and the empirical, even empiricist, inquiry favored by the American mainstream from the 1930s onwards, and the variants of the interpretive tradition which were the principal alternative to the mainstream. The shortcomings of earlier ontologies of the social, and of the self, have thus invited correction, and from the 1970s onwards the numerous writers who have set out to supply it have generated a massive, protracted, and unconcluded debate (Bryant, 1995, chapter 3). It was in 1976, with the appearance of *New Rules of Sociological Method* (1976a) and "Functionalism: *après la lutte*" (1976b), that Giddens first offered his correction, "structuration theory." In terms of the breadth of the response he has generated in different disciplines and in different countries, Giddens is arguably the single most important figure in the whole debate.

Although structuration theory, as such, was only unveiled in 1976, it is possible to view Giddens's work prior to then as, in many ways, a preparation for it; and although its "summation" was published in 1984, in *The Constitution of Society*, it is possible to treat Giddens's work subsequent to then as, in many ways, a further development of it. Indeed, this is how Giddens himself presents it, notwithstanding the transformative consequences of therapy for his writings in the 1990s. It is thus feasible to identify three clear phases in Giddens's writing career. Each is a step in the making of structuration theory and in each works of a particular character predominate.

### Exegesis and commentary

Before 1976, most of Giddens's writings offer critical commentary on a very wide range of writers, schools, and traditions. (The main exception is the work on suicide which extends beyond Durkheim and culminates in *The Sociology of Suicide* (1971b) and Giddens's revised theory of suicide (1977b).) The best known books in this phase are *Capitalism and Modern Social Theory: an Analysis of the Writings of Marx, Durkheim and Max Weber* (1971a) and *The Class Structure of the Advanced Societies* (1973). After publication of *New Rules of Sociological Method* (1976a), commentary is never Giddens's primary activity again – though commentaries continue to appear. He remains, it is generally agreed, a very knowledgeable, perceptive, and stimulating commentator.

In his engagement with the work of others, Giddens is, by his own admission, seeking to go beyond commentary to critical appropriation as a basis from which

;-term project of his own – the making of structuration theory.
mind the early Talcott Parsons (see Sica, 1991).

## turation theory and the duality of structure

⁀ for only a brief account of some of the main features of the
⸺ ₑₐₑₙ briefer indication of some of the criticisms, developments
and applications it has generated.

PRINCIPLES The second period, from 1976 to 1984, is dominated by intensive
work on the elaboration of the principles of structuration theory. It opens with
*New Rules* (1976a), includes *Central Problems in Social Theory* (1979), and
reaches its climax in *The Constitution of Society* (1984). It involves a retreat
from epistemology, on which Giddens had written penetratingly, and an engagement with ontology.

Giddens picked up the term "structuration" from (the French of) Piaget and
Gurvitch, but his usage differs from theirs. With the objective of carrying social
theory beyond classical conceptions, structuration theory makes critical appro-
priations from two main theoretical innovations in mid-twentieth-century
sociology. On one front, Giddens engages with developments in action
theory and social phenomenology. "The characteristic error of the philosophy
of action," according to Giddens (1976a, p. 121), "is to treat the problem of
'production' only, thus not developing any concept of structural analysis at all,"
but he is able to take from action theories (especially from Schutz, Garfinkel,
and the ethnomethodologists) conceptions of "methodical" or "practical" consciousness, which he then deploys against both Durkheim and Parsons. On
another front, Giddens engages with the newer forms of structuralism, with
their roots in linguistics, especially the work of Lévi-Strauss and Althusser.
Although "the limitation of both structuralism and functionalism...is to regard
'reproduction' as a mechanical outcome, rather than as an active constituting
process, accomplished by, and consisting in, the doings of active subjects" (ibid.),
Giddens is able to derive from structuralism the notion of generative rules.
Giddens's claims for the distinctiveness of structuration theory are illustrated
in table 22.1.

Structuration theory attempts to supersede these deficiencies by showing how
"social structures are both constituted by human agency, and yet at the same
time are the very medium of this constitution" (ibid.), and by explaining how
"structures are constituted through action, and reciprocally how action is constituted structurally (Giddens, 1976a, p. 161). This is what is meant by "duality
of structure," the central concept in Giddens's structuration theory, and the
means by which he seeks to avoid a dualism of agency and structure. It is also
to conceive structures not "as simply placing constraints upon human agency,
but as enabling" (ibid.), and to recognize, contrary to Foucault, the omnipresence of a dialectic of control whereby "the less powerful manage resources in
such a way as to exert some control over the more powerful in established power
relationships" (Giddens, 1984, p. 374).

**Table 22.1** Modes of theorizing structure and agency

|  | *Structuralist theories* | *Voluntarist theories* | *Structuration theory* |
|---|---|---|---|
| Characterization of structure | Structures and cultures determine, shape, or heavily constrain. | Structures are the revisable products of free agents. | Structure is the medium and outcome of the conduct it recursively organizes. |
| Characterization of actors/agents | Actors' choices are illusory, marginal, and/or trivial. Actors are cultural dopes, the victims of circumstances or instruments of history. | Actors make real choices. Actors determine. | Actors are knowledgeable and competent agents who refexively monitor their action. |

"To examine the structuration of a social system is to examine the modes whereby that system, through the application of generative rules and resources, is produced and reproduced in social interaction" (Giddens, 1976b, p. 353). Systems, for Giddens, refer to "the situated activities of human agents" (Giddens, 1984, p. 25) and "The patterning of social relations across time-space" (ibid., p. 377). They have an *actual* existence (or a real existence, in the economist's sense of real). Systems display structural properties but are not themselves structures. Structures, by contrast, refer to "systems of generative rules and resources" (Giddens, 1976a, p. 127), or, as Giddens later put it, to "rule-resource sets, implicated in the articulation of social systems" (Giddens, 1984, p. 377). They have only a *virtual* existence, "out of time and out of space" (Giddens, 1976a, p. 127). Structure only exists in the memory of knowledgeable agents and as instantiated in action.

Actors, for Giddens, are never cultural dopes, but knowledgeable and capable agents who reflexively monitor their action. In his stratification model of the actor or agent, Giddens distinguishes between the motivation of action which may be partly unconscious but is not necessarily so, the rationalization of action (agents' articulated reasons for action), and the reflexive monitoring of action (agents' knowledge of what they are doing). Rationalization always involves discursive consciousness, or verbalization; reflexive monitoring involves either or both of discursive consciousness and practical consciousness (unverbalized awareness). Giddens claims that many other theories have ignored practical consciousness, or what actors tacitly know but cannot put in words.

For Giddens, the structuring or "structuration" of social interaction, or social relations, across time and space always involves "three elements: the communication of meaning, the exercise of power, and the evaluative judgement of conduct" (Giddens, 1977c, p. 132) as represented in table 22.2. Taking the top line first, "Structure as signification involves semantic rules; as domination, unequally distributed resources; and as legitimation, moral or evaluative rules" (ibid., p. 133). Rules and resources are the properties of communities and collectivities; the modalities of the middle line have to do with the modes in which actors can draw upon rules and resources in the production of interaction.

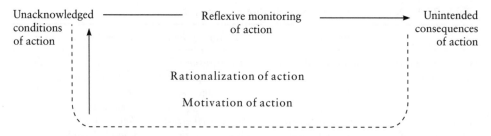

**Figure 22.1**   Stratification model of the agent and consciousness.
*Source*: Modification of combined figures from Giddens (1984, pp. 5 and 7), as in Bryant and Jary (1991, p. 9).

**Table 22.2**   Dimensions of the duality of structure

| *Structure* | Signification | Domination | Legitimation |
|---|---|---|---|
| *(Modality)* | Interpretative scheme | Facility | Norm |
| *Interaction* | Communication | Power | Sanction |

*Source*: Variation on Giddens (1976a, p. 122; 1979, p. 82; 1984, p. 29).

**Table 22.3**   Structures and institutional orders

| | |
|---|---|
| S–D–L | Symbolic orders/modes of discourse |
| D(auth)–S–L | Political institutions |
| D(alloc)–S–L | Economic institutions |
| L–D–S | Legal institutions |

S, signification; D, domination; L, legitimation.
*Source*: Giddens (1984, p. 32).

" 'Interpretative schemes' are the modes of typification incorporated within actors' stocks of knowledge, applied reflexively in the sustaining of communication" (Giddens, 1984, p. 29). Facilities include command over people and resources, and norms include normative expectations of actors.

Rules, both semantic and moral, are the "techniques or generalizable procedures applied in the enactment/reproduction of social practices" (ibid., p. 21). Resources divide into allocative, or material, and authoritative, or nonmaterial; the former derive from dominion over things, the latter from dominion over people. Both are involved in the generation of power, the capacity to do; there is also, however, a dialectic of control, whereby the controlled, and not just the controllers, have an effect on the relation between them and the situation they share. "The most deeply embedded structural properties, implicated in the reproduction of societal totalities" (i.e groups, organizations, collectivities, societies), he calls *structural principles*. Those practices which have the greatest time-space extension within such totalities can be referred to as *institutions*" (ibid., p. 17). Different institutional orders all involve signification, domination, and legitimation, but in different proportions, as table 22.3 shows.

Concern for time-space is one of the most distinctive features of structuration theory, and it has opened up fruitful exchanges with geographers. Drawing on sources as diverse as Heidegger, Lévi-Strauss and the *Annales* historians, Giddens demands that we avoid the sharp distinction between synchrony and diachrony favoured by structuralists and functionalists and that "we...grasp the time-space relations inherent in the constitution of all social interaction" (Giddens, 1979, p. 3). Time-space thus refers not to some framework, or set of coordinates, external to social interaction, but to the ways duration and extent enter into the constitution of social practices. Writing, for example, affords communication at a distance and over time, and clock timing affords the commodification of labor power.

**CRITICISMS** Layder (1994) has pointed out that what Giddens means by "structure" when he refers to the dualism of structure and agency which has bedeviled social science is the notion of pre-given objects or patterned realities. And what Giddens means by "structure" in the duality of structure which graces structuration theory are the rules and resources of the virtual order which are implicated in the reproduction of the actual order or social system. In other words, his resolution of the dualism of agency and structure works by discarding structure as conventionally understood by social scientists and substituting something quite different.

In 1982, Archer complained that structuration theory is unhelpful when trying to account for variations in degrees of voluntarism and determinism and degrees of freedom and constraint. In *The Constitution of Society*, Giddens responds by distinguishing different senses of "constraint" and by reminding us that there are no natural laws of society. He adds that

> The nature of constraint is historically variable, as are the enabling qualities generated by the contextualities of human action. It is variable in relation to the material and institutional circumstances of activity, but also in relation to the forms of knowledgeability that agents possess about those circumstances. (Giddens, 1984, p. 179)

This, however, does not deal with Archer's complaint. Are all these variations historically so contingent that structuration theory can say nothing further about them? Giddens gives a partial answer in terms of structural principles and structural sets. Structural sets, or structures (in the plural), refer to rules and resources which hang together to make a set. Take, for example, the following, very familiar, case of capitalism. The

private property: money: capital: labor contract: profit

items in the set are internally related. One can also move from the set both to (a) the more abstract structural principle of capitalism, or class societies ("the disembedding, yet interconnecting, of state and economic institutions"; Giddens, 1984, p. 183), and (b) the less abstract structure, the rules and resources, which, via the dimensions or axes of structuration (signification, domination, and legitimation), are involved in the institutional articulation of capitalist societies. In assessing what options actors have, much depends on the strength of the internal connectives both within the structural set and between it and the rules and resources upon which actors draw. The options which actors perceive/conceive and enact can vary greatly in number and scope.

Thompson (1989), taking up similar issues, argues that there is more to structures than rules and resources, and the addition is not captured by the notion of structural principles. Instead, it has to do with the connections between, and distributions of, different rules and resources; alternatively, it is about why Giddens's rule-resource sets are setted as they are and what agents can do about them, or with them, other than just reproduce them. Thompson takes as an example Marx's analysis of the capitalist mode of production. It attends to the conditions which make possible capitalist production and exchange, from the circumstances which facilitate the formation of a "free" labor force to the principles and processes involved in the constitution of value and the generation of profit. These cannot, Thompson claims, satisfactorily be "forced into the conceptual mould of structure qua rules and resources" (Thompson, 1989, p. 69).

Both Archer's and Thompson's difficulties are connected to a complex of issues concerning the status of the virtual, voluntarism and determinism, and the nature of constraint. Archer (1982, 1988) has done more than anyone to tease them out. According to Giddens, structure refers to cognitive and moral rules and to allocative and authoritative resources, but it is virtual, not real, in that it exists only in instantiations in action and in memory traces. This amounts to saying structure is real only when it is activated. What Giddens calls rules Archer prefers to call the cultural system. She argues that "Since what is instantiated depends on the power of agency and not the nature of the property [of the rule or constituent of the cultural system], then properties themselves are not differentially mutable" (Archer, 1988, p. 88). In other words, Giddens's rules do not constrain because agents can conform to, modify, or reject them at will. She labels this the "ontological diminution of the cultural system." Giddens's response (1990b) is to say that of course structure, resources as well as rules, differentially enables and constrains, but it does so only as mediated by agents' reasons. Structural constraint cannot enforce like a causal force in nature. Even Marx's wage laborers, forced to sell their labor power, can, and on occasions do, reject one employer's labor contract for another, strike, go slow, and organize politically. Structure is virtual, it turns out, not just because it is out of time and out of space, but also because it does not alone determine. To this we would counter that structure, or better structures, are real (a) because, by Giddens's own admission, they differentially enable and constrain (it is, after all, a realist axiom that something is real if it has real effects), and (b) because, as Archer has pointed out, the differential potentials for enablement and constraint which structures offer have to do not just with agents' different activations of them but also with different properties which inhere in them.

**DEVELOPMENTS AND APPLICATIONS** Giddens's theory of structuration has been developed and applied by a very large number of scholars and researchers around the world in a very wide range of disciplines. We note just two of the developments immediately and will mention some applications later. Stones argues that what is missing from Giddens's theory of structuration is concern for the strategic context of action (Stones, 1991) or, as he now prefers, agent's context analysis (Stones, 1996). Like Cohen (1989), Stones notes how Giddens inclines either to bracket institutional analysis in his treatment of the strategic conduct of knowledgeable agents, or to bracket strategic conduct in his analysis of institutions as chronically reproduced rules and resources. By reworking Giddens's concept of knowledgeability in terms of strategic context, Stones directs attention to the agent's strategic terrain – "the social nexus of interdependencies, rights and obligations, asymmetries of power and the social conditions and consequences of action" (Stones, 1996, p. 98) which make up the perceived and perceivable possibilities of action and their limitations. In effect, Stones seeks a hermeneutically sensitive version of what Parsons (1937) called the conditions of action in his original voluntaristic theory of action. Strategic, or agent's, context analysis, so conceived, affords a critique of action, an examination of its conditions and limits; or, as Stones avers, it allows examination of counterfactual claims that agents could have acted other than they did by treating contexts as neither entirely fixed nor entirely fluid.

Stones indicates that there is potentially more to "knowledgeability" than Giddens himself makes explicit. In a similar vein, Bryant (1991) argues that there is potentially more to Giddens's "dialogical model" of social science application than he was originally able or willing to define. In particular, it overcomes many of the deficiencies of the engineering, enlightenment, and interaction models by aligning a post-empiricist philosophy of social science with the engagement of agents in a reconsideration of their reasons for action. What it does not provide is a rationale for a critical social science. For that one has to turn to the "utopian realism" of *The Consequencies of Modernity* and subsequent works.

Two limitations of Giddens's original theory of structuration remain. On the one hand, it has little to say about the formation and distribution of the unacknowledged and acknowledged conditions of action or about the differential knowledgeability of actors. On the other, it does not elaborate on individual and collective *transformative* projects, and the differential capabilities of actors to see projects through successfully, including the capacity to cope successfully with unintended consequences. Despite these limitations, however, it has proved highly attractive to empirical researchers. Critics such as Stinchcombe (1986) may deplore the self-indulgencies of Giddens's abstract social theory but, ironically, it is the work they consider most arid which researchers have found most useful. Literally dozens of researchers all over the world have applied elements of structuration theory in archaeology, education, geography, management theory, organizational analysis, political science, psychology, and religious studies. Giddens (1991b) has himself commended the use of structuration theory in Burman (1988) on unemployment in Canada, Connell (1987) on gender relations in Australia, and Dandeker (1989) on surveillance, bureaucratic power, and war.

To illustrate applications of Giddens, Bryant and Jary (1996) selected, from a very large number of possibilities: Shotter (1983) in psychology; Carlstein (1981) and Gregson (1986) in geography; Elchardus (1988) on time; Barrett (1988) and Graves (1989) in archaeology; Spybey (1984), Whittington (1992), and Yates and Orlikowski (1992) on management and organizations; Sydow and Windeler (1996) on inter-firm networks; Roberts and Scapens (1985), MacIntosh and Scapens (1990), and Boland (1993) in accountancy; Lee (1992) and Mellor (1993) on religion; and Shilling (1992) on education. Orlikowski (1992) on technology and Scapens and MacIntosh (1996) on accountancy are also worthy of note. DeSanctis and Poole (1994) have also elaborated how, drawing on Giddens, Bourdieu, and others, it is possible to construct "adaptive structuration theory." Most applications draw upon only a small part of Giddens's theory of structuration – principally the few elements outlined above – though no systematic review of the uses of Giddens across disciplines has yet been done.

## Theorizing modernity: the personal and the global in a runaway world

Giddens has always been interested in modernity, as his early *The Class Structure of the Advanced Societies* (1973) confirms – indeed, he has always believed sociology's defining mission to be the analysis of the *modern* world – but it is only after his work on the principles of structuration theory reach their fullest elaboration in *The Constitution of Society* (1984) that he devotes most of his efforts to the analysis of late modernity.

THE CRITIQUE OF HISTORICAL MATERIALISM AND THE INSTITU-TIONAL DIMENSIONS OF MODERNITY The two volumes of *A Contemporary Critique of Historical Materialism* (1981, 1985) provide a link between the second and third phases of Giddens's work. They address the core issues raised by evolutionism and its alternatives and provide new schemata for mapping the historical and contemporary relations between the state and economy in a "globalizing" world. Giddens concludes that:

1  There exists no necessary overall mechanism of social change, no universal motor of history such as class conflict.
2  There are no universal stages, or periodizations, of social development, these being ruled out by intersocietal systems and "time-space edges" (the ever-presence of exogenous variables), as well as by human agency and the inherent "historicity" of societies.
3  Societies do not have needs other than those of individuals, so notions such as adaptation cannot properly be applied to them.
4  Pre-capitalist societies are class-divided, but only with capitalism are there class societies in which there is endemic class conflict, the separation of the

political and economic spheres, property freely alienable as capital, and "free" labor and labor markets.

5  While class conflict is integral to capitalist society, there is no teleology that guarantees the emergence of the working class as the universal class, and no ontology that justifies denial of the multiple bases of modern society represented by capitalism, industrialism, surveillance, and the industrialization of warfare.

6  Sociology, as a subject concerned pre-eminently with modernity, addresses a reflexive reality.

The analysis of premodern, modern, and late modern societies along four partly independent, partly interdependent, dimensions – economic, political, military, and symbolic – none of which has primacy, is, at a minimum, distinctive (though compare Mann, 1986) and instructive. In particular, it attends to features of modernity which sociology has too often ignored: the growth of the administrative power of the state and the industrialization of warfare. It also explores the complex ways in which power figures in time-space distanciation (the stretching of social systems across time-space), including the ways not just nation-states and capitalism but also different types of "locale" – such as cities as "power containers" – exercise domination over both nature and persons. Giddens's critique of historical materialism is one most commentators, Marxist and non-Marxist, respect, even when they differ (see Wright, 1983; Callinicos, 1985; Dandeker, 1990).

A projected third volume which was to have dealt with state socialism and its alternatives never appeared. The defeats suffered by the left in Western Europe from 1979 onwards and the collapse of state socialism in Eastern Europe in 1989 revised Giddens's thinking about possible developments within late modernity and the value of any book focusing on traditional socialist agendas. Instead, *The Consequences of Modernity* (1990a), *Modernity and Self-Identity* (1991a), *The Transformation of Intimacy* (1992b), and *Beyond Left and Right* (1994a) offer striking and perceptive comment on the contemporary human condition, without providing a comprehensive and systematic examination of the economics and politics of late modernity. Reflexivity is the theme which links them all.

**REFLEXIVE MODERNITY** "The reflexivity of modern social life consists in the fact that social practices are constantly examined and reformed in the light of incoming information about those very practices, thus constitutively altering their character" (Giddens, 1990a, p. 38). But, contrary to Enlightenment expectations, knowledge has not led to certitude; instead, reason has lost its foundation, history its direction, and progress its allure. Even so, modernity has not given way to postmodernity but has assumed a new form, that of "radicalized modernity." For both Giddens and Beck (Beck, 1986; Beck et al., 1994) radicalized modernity refers to the new patterns of security and danger, trust and risk, which typify late modern societies; and trust and risk have to do with expectations of what both other people and abstract systems will do. Modernity is radicalized because the intensification of individual and institutional reflexivity in the absence of sure foundations for knowledge has a chronic propensity to "manufacture uncertainty" and generate reordering. It is also radicalized because processes of continuous rationalization are transforming the familiar contours of industrial society.

High modernity involves the disembedding, or lifting out, of social relations, practices, mechanisms, and competencies from their specific, usually local, circumstances of time and space ("locales"), and their extension, thanks to developments in communications, over much wider spans of time and space. The development of expert systems provides one example of the latter; "symbolic tokens" (media which circulate without regard to the characteristics of those who handle them – such as money) provide another. Both expert systems and symbolic tokens depend on trust, not in individuals, but in abstract capacities. "Trust is related to absence in time and space" (Giddens, 1990a, p. 33), and it "operates in environments of risk" (ibid., p. 54). This last is a reminder that living in late modernity is often unsettling and disorienting; it is disturbingly "like being aboard a careering juggernaut" (ibid., p. 53).

Table 22.4 sets out the differences between the conception of postmodernity which Giddens rejects and the conception of radicalized modernity which he endorses. One of the features of the contemporary world acknowledged by both postmodernists and Giddens is the plurality of intellectual formations and cultural spaces, but, *contrary to postmodern theories*, this need not preclude potential convergences, fusions of horizons, larger truths, or agreements on new beginnings. In the fourth row of the radicalized modernity column Giddens emphasizes the possibilities of universal truth claims and systematic knowledge, but he is reluctant to enter further epistemological debate and explain precisely how, given his general acceptance of anti-foundationalist and post-empiricist arguments, these are realizable (Bryant, 1992). There is often a lack of detail in Giddens's epistemological and political thinking. Sometimes this reduces its impact; on the other hand, it adds to the attraction for those who would build on it.

Disoriented or not, men and women in an age of high modernity are not subject to the fate and fortune of their premodern forebears; instead institutional and personal reflexivity, including the calculation of risk, inform social practice and continue to have a bearing on the course of events. Indeed, there is now, according to Giddens, a possibility that "life politics" (the politics of self-actualization) may become more salient than "emancipatory politics" (the politics of inequality); that new social movements may have more social impact than political parties (especially in conditions of "post-scarcity'); and that the reflexive project of the self and changes in gender and sexual relations may lead the way, via the "democratization of democracy," to a new era of "dialogic democracy" in which differences are settled, and practices ordered, through discourse rather than violence, the commands of duly constituted authority, or the separation of the parties.

Giddens's account of the opportunities presented by radicalized modernity is highly generalized. It lacks both justified identification of mediate political groupings – despite an obvious interest in feminism and new social movements

**Table 22.4** A comparison of conceptions of postmodernity and "radicalized modernity"

| Postmodernity | "Radicalized modernity" |
|---|---|
| 1 Understands current transitions in epistemological terms or as dissolving epistemology altogether | 1 Identifies the institutional developments which create a sense of fragmentation and dispersal |
| 2 Focuses upon the centrifugal tendencies of current social transformations and their dislocating character | 2 Sees high modernity as a set of circumstances in which dispersal is dialectically connected to profound tendencies toward global integration |
| 3 Sees the self as dissolved or dismembered by the fragmenting of experience | 3 Sees the self as more than just a site of intersecting forces; active processes of reflective self-identity are made possible by modernity |
| 4 Argues for the contextuality of truth claims or sees them as "historical" | 4 Argues that the universal features of truth claims force themselves upon us in an irresistible way given the primacy of problems of a global kind. Systematic knowledge about these developments is not precluded by the reflexivity of modernity |
| 5 Theorizes powerlessness which individuals feel in the face of globalizing tendencies | 5 Analyzes a dialectic of powerlessness and empowerment, in terms of both experience and action |
| 6 Sees the "emptying" of day-to-day life as a result of the intrusion of abstract systems | 6 Sees day-to-day life as an active complex of reactions to abstract systems, involving appropriation as well as loss |
| 7 Regards coordinated political engagement as precluded by the primacy of contextuality and dispersal | 7 Regards coordinated political engagement as both possible and necessary, on a global level as well as locally |
| 8 Defines postmodernity as the end of epistemology, the individual, ethics | 8 Defines postmodernity as possible transformations moving "beyond" the institutions of modernity |

*Source*: Giddens (1990a, p. 150).

– and careful attention to the principles of structuration theory. Unfortunately, his most recent monograph, *Beyond Left and Right: the Future of Radical Politics* (1994a), does not repair these deficiencies. What it does do is explore the paradox of a political left, for long on the defensive, which had, in many respects, fewer radical inclinations than a market-oriented radical right intent on overthrowing tradition and custom at, it sometimes seemed, any cost. Dismissing without much argument any middle-way "market socialism," Giddens responds to the radicalism of the right by drawing on earlier forms of "philosophic conservatism," in combination with elements of socialist thought to construct a six-point framework for a reconstituted radical politics: (a) repair damaged solidarities; (b) recognize the centrality of life politics; (c) accept that active trust implies generative politics; (d) embrace dialogic democracy; (e) rethink the welfare state; and (f) confront violence.

A RUNAWAY WORLD This is hardly a framework, more an agenda – and arguably an agenda more principled than practical at that. Giddens's "brave new world" (1994b) may be worthy, but is it realistic? It may not all be the "argument-by-mantra" of which Judt (1994, p. 7) complains, but its connections with contemporary political agents and processes in both the state *and* civil society are, to say the least, underspecified. Could it be, however, that this will prove its strength, not its weakness? "There is no single agent, group or movement that, as Marx's proletariat was supposed to do, can carry the hopes of humanity," Giddens (1994a, p. 21) reminds us, "but there are many points of political engagement which offer good cause for optimism." Stop hankering after some new comprehensive, all-connecting, ideologically driven programme, Giddens seems to say, and, in this age of high modernity, do what you can where you can – for there is plenty that you can do in the home, workplace, community, and polity. Tony Blair, for one, is listening. Giddens was a guest at the Britsh Prime Minister's weekend residence, Chequers, on November 1, 1997.

Giddens continues to be fascinated by the notion "of a runaway world," and he chose it for the title of a conference in January 1997, which marked his assumption of the directorship of the LSE and the publication of four volumes of commentary on his work (Bryant and Jary, 1996). The conference asked, in effect, what could be done about, or in, a runaway world when there was great hope but less expectation that the imminent defeat of the Conservative government by new Labour at the ballot box would make a difference.

Giddens often links the image of a runaway world to that of riding a juggernaut (as in *The Consequences of Modernity*, chapter 5, and *Modernity and Self-identity*, chapter 1). We think the juggernaut metaphor has the wrong associations and should be abandoned. Juggernaut, in Hindu mythology, is the name of an idol carried in procession on a huge cart; in the past devotees are said to have thrown themselves in front of it. This ultimate in cultural dopism is plainly incompatible with Giddens's approach to human agency. "Runaway world" is more serviceable, but still presents problems. It suggests a world wholly out-of-control which had formerly been under control – both of which are exaggerations – but it also correctly implies that science, social science, and technology no longer offer the promise of any overall control. Indeed, some technologies – such as industrial processes which pollute, nuclear technology, and genetic engineering – are now as much constituents of a world out-of-control as means of controlling it; they are as much part of the problem, adding to manufactured uncertainty, as part of any solution.

The specter of a runaway world would seem to prompt three alternative responses. First, try to recover, or secure, control; fix the big picture. Second, resign oneself to loss, or absence, of control and retreat to the private and personal. In the circumstances of late modernity, this is more likely to focus on the self than on the soul. Third, go for limited and local control; accept that there is no one big picture, but fix bits of pictures as and when you can for the purposes in hand. In the last of these, positivism gives way to post-positivism, empiricism to post-empiricism, and ideological conviction to pragmatism; we are left as more or less chastened, or more or less emancipated, mourners at what Gray (1995), another contributor to the London conference, calls Enlightenment's wake.

Giddens is cheered, not chastened, by Enlightenment's wake. An age of endings, not just of the millennium but also of modernity and the politics of left and right, also suggests fresh beginnings. The burden of totalizing ambition has been lifted and a world of multiple possibilities beckons. It is interesting to compare his view of these possibilities with Edmund Leach's, because it is Leach's 1968 Reith Lectures for the BBC, *A Runaway World?*, which first planted the idea. Leach argued that developments such as the population explosion and the technological revolution had seemingly led to a runaway world, and "The runaway world is terrifying because we are gradually becoming aware that simple faith in the limitless powers of human rationality is an illusion" (Leach, 1968, p. 78–9). In its place, Leach advocated an evolutionary humanism. Some of its features we would question, but three of Leach's injunctions are worth noting three decades later. First, rethink science along, we would now say, post-empiricist lines. Second, engage with the world to make things happen; men and women can make a difference even if they cannot know all the differences they will make, and even if some of them turn out to be unwelcome. Third, do not be deterred by disorder; the times are always changing, and changing times are always out-of-joint; order is an illusion which affords a sense of security at odds with the inevitability of change. Those who participate in history, instead of looking on, can at least enjoy the present. That way, Leach continues, you can avoid becoming

> a lonely, impotent and terrified observer of a runaway world. A more positive attitude to change will not mean that you will always feel secure, it will just give you a sense of purpose. You should read your Homer. Gods who manipulate the course of destiny are no more likely to achieve their private ambitions than men who suffer the slings and arrows of outrageous fortune; but gods have much more fun. (Leach, 1968, p. 9)

There is a conceit, or perhaps a bravura, in Leach's claim that men and women are, or could be, god-like – except that Leach's gods do not determine the course of history, they just make things happen. What Giddens offers is more a version of men and women condemned to take risks but saved by their potential for dialogue. To put it in Weberian terms, gods might favor an ethic of ultimate conviction, but men and women are better served by an ethic of responsibility.

In Giddens's terms, this is the difference between utopianism and utopian realism, where the latter refers to the combination of realism and idealism in the envisaging of "alternative futures whose very propagation might help them be realised" (Giddens, 1990a, p. 154). Giddens's own utopian realism has at its heart his vision of the possibilities of the more socialized, demilitarized and planetary-caring global order variously articulated within the green, women's, and peace movements, and within the wider democratic movement. Our runaway world could even end up as an agreeable postmodernity (see figure 22.2).

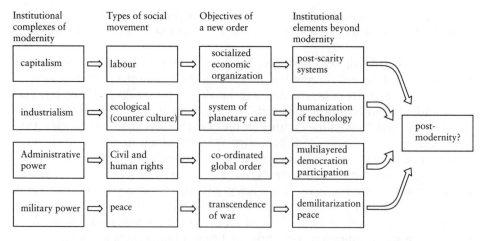

| Institutional complexes of modernity | Types of social movement | Objectives of a new order | Institutional elements beyond modernity |
|---|---|---|---|
| capitalism | labour | socialized economic organization | post-scarity systems |
| industrialism | ecological (counter culture) | system of planetary care | humanization of technology |
| Administrative power | Civil and human rights | co-ordinated global order | multilayered democration participation |
| military power | peace | transcendence of war | demilitarization peace |

post-modernity?

**Figure 22.2**    From modernity to postmodernity: Giddens's scheme.
*Source*: Held (1992, p. 34).

Like Habermas, Giddens presents the possibility of the dialogic, and ultimately democratic, resolution of differences.

## EVALUATING GIDDENS'S OEUVRE

Giddens's commentary on leading figures, schools, and traditions is unsurpassed in volume, range, and consistent quality. It would be a commendable achievement even if he had done nothing else. But, of course, he has. It is arguable that of all the approaches to the agency–structure and macro–micro debates on offer, and they now run into double figures, Giddens's is the most persuasive – not least because of the long list of theorists and theoretical approaches he has critically appropriated.[6] The principles of structuration have also proved useful to an impressive number of researchers in a dauntingly wide range of disciplines. In addition, Giddens has done as much as anyone to make concern for time-space an essential of social theory and empirical research design.

Beginning with *The Consequences of Modernity* (1990a), Giddens has also played a leading role in establishing globalization and its concomitants as one of the biggest topics in contemporary social science. And, whatever the limitations of his more recent work, Giddens has coined, appropriated, and given currency to a host of concepts which can be expected to continue to figure in discourse about late or postmodernity for a long time yet: reflexive and radicalized modernity, institutional reflexivity, detraditionalization, manufactured uncertainty, and global risk environments, emancipatory politics and life politics or the politics of self-actualisation, narratives and projects of the self, the sequestration of experience and ontological security, the democratization of democracy and dialogic democracy, the pure relationship, the transformation of intimacy and confluent love, utopian realism, and many more.

To pay attention to the phases of Giddens's writing career and to aspects of his works is all very proper, but it misses the most important feature of his whole oeuvre – grand synthesis. Craib (1992), a perceptive but not always sympathetic critic, argues that Giddens's oeuvre, whatever its flaws, is probably the best there is at integrating (a) commentary, (b) theorization of the constitution of society and the self, and (c) analysis of premodern, modern, and late modern societies. Craib has his doubts about the feasibility of such grand synthetic ventures, but he also acknowledges that without them sociology could so easily fragment into a host of self-contained and self-absorbed specialities of ever-declining consequence for our understanding of the world at large. Giddens, perhaps more than any other single figure in sociology, is holding the whole discipline together and connecting it to other social sciences.

Having made what we believe to be a formidable case for Giddens, we now want to enter some criticisms of our own. There is, we believe, a pressing need for Giddens to develop further the principles of structuration theory in order to deal more convincingly with the objections raised by critics. The non-appearance of a major systematic treatment of economic and political relations in late modern societies, to fill the gap left by the abandonment of the projected third volume of the contemporary critique of historical materialism, is also a serious omission. The books of the 1990s offer brilliant sketches, countless *aperçus*, engaging prompts, and much else, but are still only a partial remedy. There are also unresolved tensions in Giddens's description of continuities and contingencies in modernity and his depiction of knowledgeable and capable agents in a runaway world.

Giddens has (potentially) provided some of the ingredients for a theory of *late* modernity, such as the focus on the dialogic resolution of issues and the acknowledgment of the continuing importance of traditions (see especially his contribution to Beck et al., 1994). He has also come close to reconsideration of "evolutionary" issues (see Jary, 1991; Craib, 1992), including the role of the aesthetic, the ludic, and perhaps also the religious dimensions of culture (see Tucker, 1993). It would, however, sometimes be more helpful to point up the similarities with Habermas than the differences. The similarities on the dialogic conception of knowledge and the justification of values, and on new social movements, are evident; despite his protestations, there is also the potential for an approach to evolution with some resemblance to Habermas's.

Much of Giddens's recent writing is innovative and speculative – too speculative for many critics. The early Giddens who eschewed judgments in *Capitalism and Modern Social Theory* (1971a) contrasts greatly with the pundit of the 1990s. The close referencing of the early and middle Giddens differs markedly from the light referencing of *The Consequences of Modernity* (1990a) and subsequent books. Rigorous scholarship and analysis have increasingly given way to invention and communication relatively unencumbered by literatures and *systematic* evidence. It would be a pity if Giddens should prove unable to find the time and the will to complete another major work which succeeds more fully in answering doubts about the principles of structuration theory, while at the same time connecting the core of the theory to an analysis of radicalized modernity in which more justified instances of utopian realism inform a thorough examination of its economics and politics – but even without it his achievement has been immense. For the moment, Giddens has other commitments. He wants to secure a brilliant future for the LSE in the difficult circumstances of the chronic underfunding of British universities, and a movement from elite to mass higher education in which greater institutional diversification is inevitable – no mean task. And he wants to contribute prominently and publicly to the fashioning of a politics beyond left and right in which the values of the center-left remain, but the strategies and the policies are rethought – no mean ambition.

## POSTSCRIPT

Since this chapter was written, Giddens "the public intellectual" has become ever more visible. In the autumn of 1998 he published *The Third Way*, an attempt to define a politics beyond left and right for new Labour. Much of the force of Giddens's argument, and much of its appeal to Tony Blair, lies in the claim that socialism and the Old Left have died of exhaustion and maladjustment to a changed world, and their successors, neoliberalism and the New Right, unable to sustain the contradictions of market fundamentalism and conservatism, are now dying too. But what of the successor third way? According to Giddens (1998b, p. 64), "The overall aim of third way politics should be to help citizens pilot their way through the major revolutions of our time: *globalization, transformations in personal life* and our *relationship to nature.*" In all three cases, Giddens argues (with echoes of Saint-Simon) that wise action on our part can make a difference to how these revolutions work themselves out.

Giddens's third way program has as its components the radical center, the new democratic state (the state without external enemies), an active civil society, the democratic family, the new mixed economy, equality as inclusion, positive (enabling) welfare, the social investment state, the cosmopolitan nation, and cosmopolitan democracy. It is notable that Giddens's state still has a lot to do in making social investments, and in regulating capitalism at home and reforming and devising the international institutions to combat market fundamentalism globally. Giddens has discussed the latter with George Soros and is editing a book on it with Will Hutton.

Not all the concepts and ideas in Giddens's version of "the third way" figure in Tony Blair's similarly titled Fabian Society pamphlet, published shortly afterwards (Blair, 1998). In particular, Blair refers disparagingly to the "fundamentalist Left," but it is market fundamentalism and especially the minimal regulation of international capital markets which bothers Giddens more. Giddens's ecological concerns also do not make it into Blair's pamphlet, and nor does his critique of the self-exclusion of the privileged from the social mainstream. Blair's use of Giddens is selective, and his vision is less radical. Be that as it may, third way thinking (recast as the "new center" by Chancellor Schröder in Germany) has made headway in most of the European Union, excluding France.

Giddens also delivered the 1999 Reith Lectures on BBC radio. He took as his title "Runaway World," but omitted any reference to juggernauts. The lectures are prestigious and may have served to make some of his ideas more widely known – especially as three of the five were delivered outside Britain (in Delhi, Hong Kong, and Washington). Each lecture was followed by discussion, and among the questioners were Hillary Clinton and Tony Blair. Audio and video versions of the series were accessible on the World Wide Web, along with an interactive web site. Given that the lectures contained nothing new, the global multimedia were the message.

## Notes

1   Three of these from 1995 have been republished as chapter 13, "Brave New World: the New Context of Politics," of Giddens (1996). We also hazard the suggestion that Giddens (1998a) may prove influential in the definition of a "third-way" political project for Tony Blair's new Labour government. The best piece so far by a journalist on Giddens and his new political role is Boynton's in *The New Yorker* (1997).
2   We have, *inter alia*, drawn on our interviews with Giddens on April 26, 1989 in Cambridge and November 27, 1997 in London.
3   This is not to say that Elias's influence was necessarily evident to students at the time, as one of us, Chris Bryant, a Leicester graduate, can testify.
4   For another view of Elias at Leicester, see Brown (1987).
5   This is, of course, the opposite of C. Wright Mills's (1959) exercise of the sociological imagination, which moves from an examination of "the public issues of social structure" to an enlightening re-view of "the personal troubles of milieu."
6   But like others we sometimes wonder whether Giddens's synthesis sufficiently respects the nuances of the approaches it incorporates – a reservation only reinforced by his recent admission that he hardly ever reads books from cover to cover, he just uses lists of contents and indexes to fillet out the main bits (in the *Guardian*, Higher Education, January 14, 1997).

## Bibliography

### Writings of Anthony Giddens

*Capitalism and Modern Social Theory.* 1971a. Cambridge: Cambridge University Press.
*The Sociology of Suicide* (editor). 1971b. London: Frank Cass.
*Emile Durkheim: Selected Writings* (editor). 1972a. Cambridge: Cambridge University Press.
*Politics and Sociology in the Thought of Max Weber.* 1972b. London: Macmillan.
*The Class Structure of the Advanced Societies.* 1973. London: Hutchinson.
*Positivism and Sociology* (editor). 1974. London: Heinemann.
*New Rules of Sociological Method.* 1976a. London: Hutchinson (2nd edn, 1993).
Functionalism: *après la lutte.* 1976b. *Social Research*, 43, 325–66.
*Studies in Social and Political Theory.* 1977a. London: Hutchinson.
A Theory of Suicide. 1977b. In *Studies in Social and Political Theory*, chapter 9.
Notes on the Theory of Structuration. 1977c. In *Studies in Social and Political Theory*, appendix to chapter 2.
*Durkheim.* 1978. London: Fontana.

*Central Problems in Social Theory: Action, Structure and Contradiction in Social Analysis*. 1979. London: Macmillan.

*A Contemporary Critique of Historical Materialism. Volume 1, Power, Property and the State*, 1981. London: Macmillan (2nd edn, 1995).

*Profiles and Critiques in Social Theory*. 1982a. London: Macmillan.

*Sociology: a Brief but Critical Introduction*. 1982b. London: Macmillan (2nd edn, 1986).

*Classes and the Division of Labour: Essays in Honour of Ilya Neustadt* (editor with G. Mackenzie). 1982. Cambridge: Cambridge University Press.

*The Constitution of Society: Outline of the Theory of Structuration*. 1984. Cambridge: Polity.

*A Contemporary Critique of Historical Materialism. Volume 2, The Nation-state and Violence*. 1985. Cambridge: Polity Press.

*Durkheim on Politics and the State* (editor). 1986. Cambridge: Polity Press.

*Social Theory and Modern Sociology*. 1987. Cambridge: Polity Press.

*Social Theory Today* (editor with J. H. Turner). 1987. Cambridge: Polity Press.

*Sociology*. 1989. Cambridge: Polity Press (2nd edn, 1993; 3rd edn, 1997; US edn, *An Introduction to Sociology*. New York: Norton, 1991).

*The Consequences of Modernity*. 1990a. Cambridge: Polity Press.

Structuration Theory and Sociological Analysis. 1990b. In J. Clark, C. Modgil and S. Modgil (eds), *Anthony Giddens: Consensus and Controversy*. Lewis: Falmer Press, chapter 22.

*Modernity and Self-identity: Self and Society in the Late Modern Age*. 1991a. Cambridge: Polity Press.

Structuration Theory: Past, Present and Future. 1991b. In C. G. A. Bryant and D. W. Jary (eds) *Giddens' Theory of Structuration: a Critical Appreciation*. London: Routledge, chapter 8.

*Human Societies: a Reader*. 1992a. Cambridge: Polity Press (2nd edn, *Sociology: Introductory Readings*, 1997).

*The Transformation of Intimacy: Sexuality, Love and Eroticism in Modern Societies*. 1992b. Cambridge: Polity Press.

*Beyond Left and Right: the Future of Radical Politics*. 1994a. Cambridge: Polity Press.

Brave New World: the New Context of Politics. 1994b. In D. Miliband (ed.), *Reinventing the Left*. Cambridge: Polity Press, chapter 1.

*Politics, Sociology and Social Theory: Encounters with Classical and Contemporary Social Thought*. 1995. Cambridge: Polity Press.

*In Defence of Sociology: Essays, Interpretations and Rejoinders*. 1996. Cambridge: Polity Press.

Centre Left at Centre Stage. 1997. *New Statesman*, special edition, May, 37–9.

After the Left's Paralysis. 1998a. *New Statesman*, May 1, 18–21.

*The Third Way: the Renewal of Social Democracy*. 1998b. Cambridge: Polity Press.

*Runaway World: the 1999 Reith Lectures*. http://news.bbc.co.uk/hi/english/static/events/reith_99.

## Further reading

Archer, M. S. (1982) Morphogenesis versus Structuration: on Combining Structure and Action. *British Journal of Sociology*, 33, 455–88.

Archer, M. S. (1988) *Culture and Agency: the Place of Culture in Social Theory*. Cambridge: Cambridge University Press.

Barrett, J. C. (1988) Fields of Discourse: Reconstituting a Social Archaeology. *Critique of Anthropology*, 7(3), 5–16

Beck, U. (1986) *Risk Society: towards a New Modernity*. London: Sage.

Beck, U., Giddens, A., and Lash, S. (1994) *Reflexive Modernization: Politics, Tradition and Aesthetics in the Modern Order*. Cambridge: Polity Press.

Blair, T. (1998) *The Third Way: New Politics for the New Century*. London: The Fabian Society.

Boland, R. J. (1993) Accounting and the Interpretative Act. *Accounting, Organizations and Society*, 18, 125–40.

Boynton, R. S. (1997) The Two Tonys: Why Is the Prime Minister so Interested in What Anthony Giddens Thinks? *The New Yorker*, October 6, 2–7.

Brown, R. K. (1987) Norbert Elias in Leicester: Some Recollections. *Theory, Culture and Society*, 4, 533–9.

Bryant, C. G. A. (1991) The Dialogical Model of Applied Sociology. In C. G. A. Bryant and D. W. Jary (eds), *Giddens' Theory of Structuration: a Critical Appreciation*, London: Routledge, chapter 7.

Bryant, C. G. A. (1992) Sociology without Philosophy? The Case of Giddens' Structuration Theory. *Sociological Theory*, 10, 137–49.

Bryant, C. G. A. (1995) *Practical Sociology: Postempiricism and the Reconstruction of Theory and Application*. Cambridge: Polity Press.

Bryant, C. G. A. and Jary, D. W. (eds) (1991) *Giddens' Theory of Structuration: a Critical Appreciation*. London: Routledge.

Bryant, C. G. A. and Jary, D. W. (eds) (1996) *Anthony Giddens: Critical Assessments*, 4 volumes. London: Routledge.

Burman, P. (1988) *Killing Time, Losing Ground*. Toronto: Wall and Thompson.

Callinicos, A. (1985) Anthony Giddens – a Contemporary Critique. *Theory and Society*, 14, 133–66.

Carlstein, T. (1981) The Sociology of Structuration in Time and Space: a Timegeographic Assessment of Giddens' Theory. *Svensk Geografisk Arsbok*, 57, 41–57

Cohen, I. J. (1989) *Structuration Theory: Anthony Giddens and the Constitution of Social Life*. London: Macmillan.

Cohen, P. S. (1968) *Modern Social Theory*. London: Heinemann.

Connell, R. W. (1987) *Gender and Power*. Cambridge: Polity Press.

Craib, I. (1992) *Anthony Giddens*. London: Routledge.

Dandeker, C. (1989) *Surveillance, Power and Modernity*. Cambridge: Polity Press.

Dandeker, C. (1990) The Nation-state and the Modern World System. In J. Clark, C. Modgil, and F. Modgil (eds), *Anthony Giddens: Consensus and Controversy*. Lewis: Falmer Press.

DeSanctis, G. and Poole, M. S. (1994) Capturing the Complexity in Advanced Technology Use: Adaptive Structuration Theory. *Organization Science*, 5, 121–47.

Dunning, E. (1994) Towards a Configurational Critique of the Theory of Structuration. Paper presented at the 13th World Congress of Sociology, Bielefeld, Germany.

Elchardus, M. (1988) The Rediscovery of Chronos: the New Role of Time in Sociological Theory. *International Sociology*, 3(1), 35–59.

Eldridge, J. (1990) Sociology in Britain: a Going Concern. In C. G. A. Bryant and H. A. Becker (eds), *What Has Sociology Achieved?* London: Macmillan, chapter 9.

Elias, N. (1939) *The Civilizing Process. Volume I, The History of Manners*. Oxford: Blackwell (1978).

Graves, C. P. (1989) Social Space in the English Medieval Parish Church. *Economy and Society*, 18, 297–322.

Gray, J. (1995) *Enlightenment's Wake: Politics and Culture at the Close of the Modern Age*. London: Routledge.

Gregson, N. (1986) On Duality and Dualism: the Case of Structuration and Time Geography. *Progress in Human Geography*, 10, 184–205.

Held, D. (1992) Liberalism, Marxism and Democracy. In S. Hall, D. Held, D. McGrew, and T. McGrew (eds), *Modernity and its Futures*. Cambridge: Polity Press with Open University Press, chapter 1.

Jary, D. W. (1991) Society as Time Traveller: Giddens on Historical Change, Historical Materialism and the Nation-state in World Society. In C. G. A. Bryant and D. W. Jary (eds), *Giddens' Theory of Structuration: a Critical Appreciation*, London: Routledge, chapter 5.

Jary, D. W. and Jary, J. (1995) The Transformations of Anthony Giddens. *Theory, Culture and Society*, 12(2), 141–60.

Judt, T. (1994) How Much Is Really Left of the Left? *The Times Literary Supplement*, 4773(7), September 23.

Kilminster, R. (1991) Structuration Theory as a World-view. In C. G. A. Bryant and D. W. Jary (eds), *Giddens' Theory of Structuration: a Critical Appreciation*, London: Routledge, chapter 4.

Layder, D. (1994) *Understanding Social Theory*. London: Sage.

Leach, E. (1968) *A Runaway World?* London: BBC.

Lee, R. L. M. (1992) The Structuration of Disenchantment: Secular Agency and the Reproduction of Religion. *Journal for the Theory of Social Behaviour*, 22, 381–402.

MacIntosh, N. B. and Scapens, R. W. (1990) Structuration Theory in Management and Accounting. *Accounting, Organizations and Society*, 15, 455–77.

Mann, M. (1986) *The Sources of Social Power. Volume 1, A History of Power from the Beginning to AD 1760*. Cambridge: Cambridge University Press.

Marshall, T. H. (1982) Introduction to A. Giddens and G. Mackenzie (eds) *Social Class and the Division of Labour: Essays in Honour of Ilya Neustadt*. Cambridge: Cambridge University Press.

Mellor, P. A. (1993) Reflexive Traditions: Anthony Giddens, High Modernity, and the Contours of Contemporary Religiosity. *Religious Studies*, 29, 111–27.

Mills, C. Wright (1959) *The Sociological Imagination*. New York: Oxford University Press.

Orlikowski, W. J. (1992) The Duality of Technology; Rethinking the Concept of Technology in Organization. *Organization Science*, 3, 398–427.

Parsons, T. (1937) *The Structure of Social Action*. New York: McGraw-Hill.

Roberts, J. and Scapens, R. W. (1985) Accounting Systems and Systems of Accounting: Understanding Accounting Practices in Their Organisational Contexts. *Accounting, Organizations and Society*, 10, 443–56.

Scapens, R. W. and MacIntosh, N. B. (1996) Structure and Agency in Management Accounting Research: a Response to Boland's Interpretive Act. *Accounting, Organizations and Society*, 21, 675–90.

Shilling, C. (1992) Reconceptualising Structure and Agency in the Sociology of Education: Structuration Theory and Schooling. *British Journal of Sociology of Education*, 13, 69–87.

Shotter, J. (1983) "Duality of Structure" and "Intentionality" in an Ecological Psychology. *Journal for the Theory of Social Behaviour*, 13, 19–43.

Sica, A. (1991) The California–Massachusetts Strain in Structuration Theory. In C. G. A. Bryant and D. W. Jary (eds), *Giddens' Theory of Structuration: a Critical Appreciation*, London: Routledge, chapter 2.

Spybey, T. (1984) Traditional and Professional Frames of Meaning in Management. *Sociology*, 18, 550–62.

Stinchcombe, A. (1986) Milieu and Structure Updated: a Critique of the Theory of Structuration Theory. *Theory and Society*, 15, 901–14.

Stones, R. (1991) Strategic Context Analysis: a New Research Strategy for Structuration Theory. *Sociology*, 25, 673–95.

Stones, R. (1996) *Sociological Reasoning: towards a Past-modern Sociology*. London: Macmillan.

Sydow, J. and Windeler, A. (1996) Managing Inter-firm Networks: a Structurationist Perspective. In C. G. A. Bryant and D. W. Jary (eds), *Anthony Giddens: Critical Assessments, volume 4*. London: Routledge, chapter 93.

Thompson, J. B. (1989) The Theory of Structuration. In D. Held and J. B. Thompson (eds), *Social Theory of Modern Societies: Anthony Giddens and His Critics*. Cambridge: Cambridge University Press, chapter 3.

Tucker, K. H. (1993) Aesthetics, Play and Cultural Memory: Giddens and Habermas on the Postmodern Challenge. *Sociological Theory*, 11, 194–211.

Whittington, R. (1992) Putting Giddens into Action: Social Systems and Managerial Agency. *Journal of Management Studies*, 29, 693–712.

Wright, E. Olin (1983) Giddens' Critique of Marxism. *New Left Review*, 138, 11–35.

Yates, J. and Orlikowski, W. J. (1992) Genres of Organizational Communication: a Structurational Approach to Studying Communication and Media. *Academy of Management Review*, 17, 299–326.

# 23

## Pierre Bourdieu

### Craig Calhoun

The most influential and original French sociologist since Durkheim, Pierre Bourdieu is at once a leading theorist and an empirical researcher of extraordinarily broad interests and distinctive style. He has analyzed labor markets in Algeria, symbolism in the calendar and the house of Kabyle peasants, marriage patterns in his native Béarne region of France, photography as an art form and hobby, museum goers and patterns of taste, modern universities, the rise of literature as a distinct field of endeavor, and the sources of misery and poverty amid the wealth of modern societies. Bourdieu insists that theory and research are inseparable parts of one sociological enterprise, and refuses to separate them. He has never, accordingly, written a purely abstract theoretical treatise summing up his perspective. Through the course of his writings, however, he has developed a distinctive set of basic themes and concepts. It is on these that we will focus in the present chapter.

## TAKING GAMES SERIOUSLY

A former rugby player, Bourdieu is drawn to the metaphor of games to convey his sense of social life. But by "game" he does not mean mere diversions or entertainments. Rather, he means a serious athlete's understanding of a game. He means the experience of being passionately involved in play, engaged in a struggle with others and with our own limits, over stakes to which we are (at least for the moment) deeply committed. He means intense competition. He means for us to recall losing ourselves in the play of a game, caught in its flow in such a way that no matter how individualistically we struggle we are also constantly aware of being only part of something larger – not just a team, but the game itself. It is worth knowing that rugby (a game of running, passing, kicking, and tackling somewhat like American football, but played with more continuous motion, a bit like soccer) is one of the world's most physically intense games. When Bourdieu speaks of playing, he speaks of putting oneself on the line.

Social life is like this, Bourdieu suggests, except that the stakes are bigger. Not just is it always a struggle; it requires constant improvisation. No game can be understood simply by grasping the rules that define it. It requires not just following rules, but having a "sense" of the game, a sense of how to play.[1] This is a social sense, for it requires a constant awareness of and responsiveness to the play of one's opponent (and in some cases one's teammates). A good rugby (or soccer or basketball) player is constantly aware of the field as a whole, and anticipates the actions of teammates, knowing when to pass, when to try to break free. A good basketball player is not simply one who can shoot, but one who knows when to shoot.

Games are strategic. There are different possible approaches to each contest, and to each moment in the contest. What makes for a good strategy is determined by the rules of the game, of course, but also by assessing one's opponent's strengths and weaknesses – and one's own. Originality or inspiration is only one factor among many in determining the outcome.

Whether a tennis player rushes the net is a complex result of numerous factors, not a simple, conscious decision. Indeed, if it is simply a conscious decision the player is probably already too late. The tennis player has a physical, bodily sense of how strong her own serve was, and an awareness (usually without words) of the shot her opponent is returning; thought and bodily action are not sharply separate. She also has an inclination to rush a lot or a little, to play risky or safe tennis, to be confident in her physical strength and speed or watching for angles or chip shots to throw a stronger opponent off balance. This is partly the result of years of experience, partly the result of coaching and disciplined practice. The coach may even use theory to help analyze the strengths and weaknesses of the player's game; for example, urging her to rush the net a little more, hang back at the baseline a little less. This can be long-term, general advice, or specifically targeted to the opponent the player faces today. Either way, however, the player's actual shots are actions that cannot be reduced to theoretical rules. They are improvisations. Sometimes they are inspired surprises, occasionally disastrous mistakes. But for a good player they are also embodiments of a highly consistent style. This is what Bourdieu terms a "habitus," the capacity each player of a game has to improvise the next move, the next play, the next shot.

We may be born with greater or lesser genetic potentials, but we are not born with a habitus. As the word suggests, this is something we acquire through repetition, like a habit, and something we know in our bodies, not just our minds. A professional basketball player has shot a million free throws before he steps to the line. Some of these have come in practice sessions, designed to allow the player to work on technical skills free from the pressure and chance of a game. But the player's practical experience – and learning – also came in real games, in front of crowds, with the hope of victory and the fear of letting down his teammates on his mind. Whether he has developed a relaxed confidence in his shot and an ability to blot out the noise and waving hands of the arena is also a matter of previous experience. It is part of the player's habitus. And the difference between a great athlete and a mediocre also-ran is often not just physical ability but a hard-to-pin-down mix of confidence, concentration, and ability to rise to the occasion.

The confidence that defines greatness is largely learned, Bourdieu suggests. It is learned in a thousand earlier games. On playgrounds, in high school, and in college, basketball players imagine themselves to be Michael Jordan – but they also learn that they are not. They do not jump as high or float as long; their desperate shots miss when his amazingly often went in. One of the most important points Bourdieu makes is that this is precisely how our very experience of struggling to do well teaches us to accept inequality in our societies. We learn and incorporate into our habitus a sense of what we can "reasonably" expect. I, for example, would *like* to be a great tennis player, but have accepted that I am not. More basically, I have come to regard tennis as a mere recreation. I play it for fun, and sometimes play aggressively, but I do not play it for serious stakes. The games I play more seriously are ones I early learned I was better at, games involving words instead of balls, requiring more speed of thought and less of foot. I play these for greater stakes: my salary, my sense of career accomplishment, my belief that through my work I make a contribution to others. Then there are the games that matter so much to us that most of us play them whether we are good at them or not – love and marriage, raising children and trying to help them prosper, acquiring material possessions, or seeking religious salvation. It is our desire for the stakes of the game that ensures our commitment to it. But we do not invent the games by ourselves; they are the products of history, of social struggles and earlier improvisations, and of impositions by powerful actors with the capacity to say this, and not that, is the right way to make love, create a family, raise children.

To understand any social situation or interaction, Bourdieu suggests, ask what game (or games) the actors are playing. This is closely analogous to distinguishing the different institutional fields of modern life: education, law, family, and so forth. What is at stake in their play? The stakes determine what will count as winning or losing. The game may be literature, for example, and the players seek reputation and immortality (defined as inclusion in the canon of recognized great works). The game may be business, and the players seek wealth. It may be politics and they pursue power. The stakes of different games also shape the ways in which players will attempt to limit the field and preserve its autonomy. Precisely because they care about their literary reputations, therefore, authors of serious books are at pains to distinguish their field from "mere journalism."

Science too is a game, in this only partly metaphorical sense. It is strategic. It has winners and losers. It depends on specific sorts of resources and rules of play. And science has stakes, most notably truth. Scientists do not pursue truth out of simple altruism. It is an interest, not a *dis*interest. Commitment to truth – and to the specifically scientific way of pursuing truth (e.g. by empirical research rather than waiting for divine inspiration) – defines the field of science. But the participants in this field do not simply share peacefully in truth, they struggle over it. They seek to command it; for example, by controlling who gets hired in universities and research institutes, which projects get funded by national science foundations, which kinds of work are published in the most famous journals. They advance competing theories; they attempt to advance competing careers. Science works as a field devoted to truth because it provides players with organized incentives for pursuing their rewards – their victories in the game – by discovering and communicating genuine knowledge. It offers organized disincentives for lying, failure to use good research methods, or refusing to communicate one's discoveries.

The rules of each game are constraints on both the players and the ways in which players get things done. Players usually have to treat them as fixed and unchanging, but in fact they are historically produced. This means that they are subject to continual change, but even more that there is a great deal of investment in the existing organization of fields. When we improvise our actions, we respond to both the social and cultural structures in which we find ourselves and to our own previous experiences. We are able to act only because we have learned from those experiences, but much of what we have learned is how to fit ourselves effectively into existing cultural practices. We are constrained not just by external limits, in other words, but by our own internalization of limits on what we imagine we can do. We cannot simply shed these limits, not only because they are deep within us, but because they are part of our sense of how to play the game. In other words, they are part of the knowledge that enables us to play well, to improvise actions effectively, and maintain our commitment to the stakes of the game.

## Person and Career

No culture prizes intellectuals more than France; in none are intellectuals celebrities of comparable magnitude. Pierre Bourdieu has resented and contested (and profited from and used) this throughout his career. He has challenged the legitimacy of "total intellectuals" with an opinion on every subject and an eye out for the TV cameras. He has offered critical analysis of "the intellectual hit parade," mocking the presentation of scholarship as though it were popular music. He has decried the power wielded by academic mandarins who control university appointments and research institutes. At the same time, Bourdieu has become one of the most prominent French intellectuals of his generation and certainly the most influential and best known social scientist. He has been on the cover of popular magazines, been the subject of television documentaries and news stories, seen his books on bestseller lists, and become a dominant force in parts (though only parts) of the academic world. He has also become an intellectual mandarin himself. Holder of the most prestigious academic appointment in France, a chair at the Collège de France – and indeed, the very chair of sociology first held by Durkheim – he is also the head of a major research center and the editor of two journals. His work is supported by a small army of collaborators and assistants.

Amid all this, Bourdieu has always thought of himself as an outsider, and though it is paradoxical, he has reasons. Paris exerts a power over French intellectual life that far exceeds that of New York, Boston, Chicago, and the San Francisco Bay area combined. The Parisian power structure is dominated by people who combine credentials from a handful of elite institutions with a smooth, urbane cultural style. They fluidly cross the lines of politics, journalism, and the university. Although a disproportionate number of the most creative figures are outsiders by family background, the power structure remains dominated by Parisians of elite class backgrounds. Many have known each other since childhood in a handful of highly selective schools, and quickly recognize and disdain outsiders. Into their midst in the 1950s, an adolescent Pierre Bourdieu came to study in the most elite of the Parisian *grandes écoles*, the École Normale Supérieure (ENS).

Bourdieu's father was the postmaster of Deguin, a small town in the Béarne region of Southwest France.[2] This is the rough French equivalent of coming from Appalachia or a remote part of Idaho. The regional dialect is strong and distinctive; the Béarnaise have resisted homogenizing efforts of the French state for generations. Both brilliant and hard-working, Bourdieu gained admission to a special, highly selective regional high school (the Lycée de Pau) and then to one of Paris's most famous secondary schools, the Lycée Louis-le-Grand. From there he entered the École Normale in 1951. Simply gaining admission to the ENS was a guarantee of membership in France's intellectual power-elite. Students were treated as members of the civil service from the moment they entered, taught to think of themselves as what Bourdieu (1989) later termed "the state nobility." Some who started as outsiders simply assimilated, perhaps especially those whose talents were middle of the pack; Bourdieu excelled and also resisted. So did his ENS contemporaries Jacques Derrida (philosopher and literary scholar, founder of "deconstruction") and Michel Foucault (intellectual historian and cultural critic, possibly the most prominent of all the intellectuals of that generation, though now dead more than a decade). Derrida and Bourdieu graduated at the top of their class at the ENS and both became world famous. But both remained in important ways outsiders to the Parisian intellectual elite. Neither was immediately chosen for major academic positions. Derrida for decades was barred from any of the major chairs of philosophy in France, teaching in a peripheral position even after he was one of the world's most famous and influential scholars. Bourdieu was able to make more of an institutional career only because of fortuitous circumstances.

On the one hand, he was fortunate to be supported early in his career by such powerful figures as Raymond Aron, a distinguished sociologist and journalist. On the other hand, and perhaps even more crucially, an institutional base for the social sciences had been created outside the traditional university structure. The École des Hautes Études en Sciences Sociales (EHESS) had been created (by transformation of an older institution). Bourdieu did not follow the approved path to a regular university appointment – for example, never writing a thesis for the *doctorat d'état*, the special higher degree that was the usual basis for professorships. More than that, he launched strong criticisms of a professorial elite that he thought focused heavily on defending an old intellectual order (and its own power) and minimally on advancing knowledge through research. Bourdieu allied himself with research, with new knowledge, rather than with those who sought instead simply to control the inheritance of old knowledge. This met with predictable disapproval from much of the university elite, but the existence of the EHESS gave Bourdieu an alternative base where he was able in the 1960s to establish a research center and publications program.

Though Bourdieu's writings on the problems of French higher education (especially Bourdieu and Passeron, 1964) influenced the student protests of the 1960s, he was not himself centrally involved in the activism. His approach to politics was more to intervene through producing new knowledge, with the hope that this would help to demystify the way institutions worked, revealing the limits to common justifications and the way in which power rather than simple merit shaped the distribution of opportunities. His views of the educational system reflected the disappointed idealism of one who had invested himself deeply in it, and owed much of his own rise from provincial obscurity to Parisian prominence to success in school. As he wrote in *Homo Academicus*, the famous book on higher education that he began amid the crises of 1968, he was like someone who believed in a religious vocation, then found the church to be corrupt. "The special place held in my work by a somewhat singular sociology of the university institution is no doubt explained by the peculiar force with which I felt the need to gain rational control over the disappointment felt by an 'oblate' [a religious devotee] faced with the annihilation of the truths and values to which he was destined and dedicated, rather than take refuge in feelings of self-destructive resentment" (Bourdieu, 1984, p. xxvi). The disappointment could not be undone, but it could be turned to understanding and potentially, through that understanding, to positive change.

Educational institutions may be central to Bourdieu's concern, but both his sense of disappointment and his critical analyses are more wide-reaching. All the institutions of modernity, including the capitalist market and the state itself, share in a tendency to promise far more than they deliver. They present themselves as working for the common good, but in fact reproduce social inequalities. They present themselves as agents of freedom, but in fact are organizations of power. They inspire devotion from those who want richer, freer lives, and they disappoint them with the limits they impose and the violence they deploy. Simply to attack modernity, however, is to engage in the "self-destructive resentment" Bourdieu seeks to avoid. Rather, the best way forward lies through the struggle to understand, to win deeper truths, and to remove legitimacy from the practices by which power mystifies itself. In this way, one can challenge the myths and deceptions of modernity, enlightenment, and civilization without becoming the enemy of the hopes they offered.

Bourdieu's perspective and approach were both shaped crucially by his fieldwork in Algeria. He studied Kabyle peasant life and participation in a new cash economy that threatened and changed it (Bourdieu and Sayad, 1964). He studied the difficult situation of those who chose to work in the modern economy and found themselves transformed into its "underclass," not even able to gain the full

status of proletarians because of the ethno-national biases of the French coloni-
alists (Bourdieu et al., 1963; Bourdieu, 1972). And during the time of his fieldwork, Bourdieu confronted the violent French repression of the Algerian struggle
for independence. The bloody battle of Algiers was a formative experience for a
generation of French intellectuals who saw their state betray what it had always
claimed was a mission of liberation and civilization, revealing the sheer power
that lay behind colonialism, despite its legitimation in terms of progress.

Bourdieu's formal education had been in philosophy, but in Algeria he remade
himself as a self-taught ethnographer (Honneth et al., 1986, p. 39). It was in
trying to understand Kabyle society that he shaped his distinctive perspective on
the interplay of objective structures and subjective understanding and action.
The experience of fieldwork itself was powerful, and helped to shape Bourdieu's
orientation to knowledge. As an ethnographer, Bourdieu entered into another
social and cultural world, learned to speak an unfamiliar language, and
struggled to understand what was going on, while remaining necessarily in
crucial ways an outsider to it. This helped him to see the importance of combining insider and outsider perspectives on social life. To be altogether an outsider
to Kabylia was certainly to fail to understand it, but in order to grasp it
accurately the ethnographer also had to break with the familiarity of both his
own received categories and those of his informants. His job is neither to impose
his own concepts nor simply to translate those of the people he studies. He must
struggle, as the philosopher Bachelard (an important influence on Bourdieu) put
it, to "win" the facts of his study.

One of the most basic difficulties in such research, Bourdieu came to realize, is
the extent to which it puts a premium on natives' discursive explanations of their
actions. Because the anthropologist is an outsider and starts out ignorant, natives
must explain things to him. But it would be a mistake to accept such explanations as simple truths, not because they are lies but because they are precisely the
limited form of knowledge that can be offered to one who has not mastered
the practical skills of living fully inside the culture (Bourdieu, 1972, p. 2). Unless
he is careful, the researcher is led to focus his attention not on the actual social
life around him but on the statements about it which his informants offer. "The
anthropologist's particular relation to the object of his study contains the mak-
ings of a theoretical distortion inasmuch as his situation as an observer, excluded
from the real play of social activities by the fact that he has no place (except by
choice or by way of a game) in the system observed and has no need to make a
place for himself there, inclines him to a hermeneutic representation of practices,
leading him to reduce all social relations to communicative relations and, more
precisely, to decoding operations" (ibid., p. 1). Such an approach would treat
social life as much more a matter of explicit cognitive rules than it is, and miss
the ways in which practical activity is really generated beyond the determination
of the explicit rules.

In this respect, Bourdieu took the case of anthropological fieldwork to be
paradigmatic for social research more generally. The confrontation with a very
different way of life revealed the need for both outsider and insider perspectives.
Not long after he completed his work in Algeria, Bourdieu challenged himself by

applying the method he was developing to research in his own native region of Béarne. The task, as he began to argue didactically and to exemplify in all his work, was to combine intimate knowledge of practical activity with more abstract knowledge of objective patterns, and, using the dialectical relation between the two, to break with the familiar ways in which people understand their own everyday actions. These everyday accounts always contain distortions and misrecognitions that do various sorts of ideological work. The classic example is gift-giving, which is understood as disinterested, voluntary, and not subject to precise accounting of equivalence, but which people actually do in ways that are more strategic than their self-understanding allows. Bourdieu's project was to grasp the practical strategies people employed, their relationship to the explanations they gave (to themselves as well as to others), and the ways in which people's pursuit of their own ends nonetheless tended to reproduce objective patterns which they did not choose and of which they might even be unaware.

This project was a profound intervention into Bourdieu's intellectual context. French intellectual life in the 1950s and 1960s produced two powerful but opposed perspectives in the human sciences: structuralism and existentialism. The former emphasized the formal patterns underlying all reality (extending ideas introduced to sociology by Durkheim and Mauss); the latter stressed that meaning inhered in the individual experience of being in the world, and especially in autonomous action. The two greatest and most influential figures in French intellectual life of the period were Claude Lévi-Strauss (the structuralist anthropologist) and Jean-Paul Sartre (the existentialist philosopher). Bourdieu's theoretical tastes were closer to Lévi-Strauss, but he saw both as one-sided. If existentialism greatly exaggerated the role of subjective choice, structuralism neglected agency. In a sense, Bourdieu developed an internal challenge to structuralism, incorporating much of its insight and intellectual approach but rejecting the tendency to describe social life in overly cognitive and overly static terms as a matter of following rules rather than engaging in strategic practice.

It is partly for similar reasons that Bourdieu chose not to write an abstract theoretical treatise summarizing his theory. He saw theory as best developed in the task of empirical analysis, and saw this as a practical challenge. Rather than applying a theory developed in advance and in the abstract, he brought his distinctive theoretical habitus to bear on a variety of analytic problems, and in the course of tackling each developed his theoretical resources further. The concepts developed in the course of such work could be transposed from one setting to another by means of analogy, and adapted to each. Theory, like the habitus in general, serves not as a fixed set of rules but as a characteristic mode of improvising (Brubaker, 1992). In an implicit critique of the dominance of philosophy over French social science, Bourdieu held that the real proof that a sociological project has value is to be demonstrated in its empirical findings, not in abstract system-building.

When Bourdieu left Algeria, he received a fellowship to the Institute for Advanced Study in Princeton and followed it with a stay at the University of Pennsylvania. While in the USA, he met the American sociologist Erving

Goffman – another theoretically astute sociologist who refrained from abstract system-building in favor of embedding theory in empirical practice. Goffman had begun to develop a sociology that followed Durkheim's interest in the moral order, but focused on the ways this was reproduced in interpersonal relations by individuals with their own strategic investments in action. Rather than treating individuals as either autonomous or simply socially constructed, for example, Goffman (1959) introduced the element of strategy by writing of the "presentation of self in everyday life." His point was similar to that Bourdieu would stress: to show the element of improvisation and adaptation, rather than simple rule-following, and then to introduce agents as dynamic figures in the social order. Where Bourdieu's favorite metaphor was games, Goffman's was drama, but they shared the sense of social life as a performance that could be played better or worse, and which nearly always tended to the reproduction of social order even when individuals tried to make new and different things happen in their lives.

Goffman encouraged Bourdieu to take a position at the University of Pennsylvania, but Bourdieu felt that if he stayed in the USA he would be unable to develop the kind of critical sociology he wanted to create.[3] It was not simply that he wanted to criticize France rather than the USA, but that he wanted to benefit from inside knowledge while still achieving critical distance. This would present a challenge, but the challenge was itself a source of theoretical insight: "In choosing to study the social world in which we are *involved*, we are obliged to confront, in *dramatized* form as it were, a certain number of fundamental epistemological problems, all related to the question of the difference between practical knowledge and scholarly knowledge, and particularly to the special difficulties involved first in *breaking* with inside experience and then in reconstituting the knowledge which has been obtained by means of this break" (Bourdieu, 1988a, p. 1).

Bourdieu returned to France and took a position in the European Center for Historical Sociology, headed by Raymond Aron. Aron was an important early supporter of Bourdieu's, and made him a deputy in the administration of the Center. The two were never close collaborators, despite initial mutual respect, and they came into increasing conflict as Bourdieu became more critical of French higher education. Aron was a moderate conservative politically, and Bourdieu was aligned with the left. Perhaps more importantly, Aron was a defender of French academia and Bourdieu criticized its role in preserving class inequality (Bourdieu and Passeron, 1964). Things came to a head when student revolt broke out in 1968. Aron suggested that the problem lay primarily with the students and sought to limit – rather than expand – their involvement in the life of the university. Bourdieu was sympathetic to the students, though he thought them naively voluntaristic and inattentive to the deep structures that made for the reproduction of class inequality and the university as an institution (see Bourdieu and Passeron, 1970).[4] He made little public comment on the protests, but he did choose this moment to break with Aron and found his own Center for European Sociology. With him he took a remarkable group of collaborators whom he had attracted, including Luc Boltanski, Jean-Claude Passeron, and Monique de Saint Martin.

Together, this group (and new recruits) conducted a remarkable range of empirical studies. These put the perspective Bourdieu had developed to use in analyzing many different aspects of French social life. In 1975 Bourdieu and his collaborators also founded a new journal, *Actes de la Recherche en Sciences Sociales*. In its pages they not only took up different empirical themes but developed and tried out new ideas and theoretical innovations. *Actes* also translated and introduced work from researchers with cognate interests in other countries.

Almost simultaneously with the founding of his Center, Bourdieu published a kind of manual for doing sociology (Bourdieu et al., 1968). This differed from typical textbooks in presenting not a compilation of facts and a summary of theories, but an approach to sociology as an ongoing effort to "win social facts." Entitled *The Craft of Sociology*, it bypassed abstract codification of knowledge and endeavored to help students acquire the practical skill and intellectual habitus of sociologists. Bourdieu also put his craft to work in an extraordinary series of books and articles. His study (with Passeron) of *Reproduction: In Education, Society, and Culture* was initially the best known in English. It helped to establish a whole genre of studies of how education contributes to the reproduction of social inequality. In theoretical terms, however, Bourdieu's most important work of the period was *Outline of a Theory of Practice* (1972), probably his single most influential work. At almost the same time, he also published his most sustained study of French cultural patterns, *Distinction* (1979), and two books of essays. This remarkable corpus of work was the basis for his election to the chair of sociology in the Collège de France. He has continued his remarkable productivity since then. Among the most important of his books are *Language and Symbolic Power* (1982), *Homo Academicus* (1984), *The State Nobility* (1989), *The Political Ontology of Martin Heidegger* (1988), *The Rules of Art* (1992), and *The Misery of the World* (1993). He has also published several collections of articles, and the noteworthy collaboration with Loïc Wacquant, *An Invitation to Reflexive Sociology* (Bourdieu and Wacquant, 1992), which is among the best overall statements of Bourdieu's perspective on sociology.

In sum, Bourdieu's own educational experience at once gave him fantastic resources – a command of the history of philosophy, multiple languages, and skills in critique and debate – and alienated him from the very institutions that helped, as it were, to make him a star. The resources were not limited to intellectual abilities but included the credentials, connections and sense of the game that enabled him not just to become famous but to create new institutions. The alienation gave Bourdieu the motivation to pioneer a critical approach, rather than a simple affirmation of the status quo.

## FALSE DICHOTOMIES

Bourdieu (1988a) has described one of the central motivations behind his intellectual work as a determination to challenge misleading dichotomies. The broad dualistic outlook of Western thought is expressed in the ubiquitous opposition of mind to body. It also takes the form of specific dichotomies basic to social science: structure/action, objective/subjective, theory/practice. Drawing on Gaston Bachelard and other philosophers critical of this dualistic outlook, Bourdieu set out to transcend it (see the critical discussion in Vandenberghe, 1999). It is crucial, he suggests, not just to see both sides but to see how they are inseparably related to each other. Seemingly fixed objective structures have to be created and reproduced; apparently voluntary subjective actions depend on and are shaped by objective conditions and constraints; knowledge and action constantly inform each other, rather than theory guiding practice by a set of fixed rules. Bourdieu seeks to move sociology beyond the antinomy of social physics (seeing social life as completely external and objective) and social phenomenology (looking at social life through subjective experience) (Bourdieu and Wacquant, 1992, p. 7).

Take the opposition of theory to practice. This is ancient, a central theme as long ago as the philosophical writings of Aristotle. It contrasts knowing to doing, mental to physical activity. This conceptualization has several problems. First, it tends to neglect the kind of non-theoretical knowledge that is implicit in practical skills. Few of us can explain the physics of buoyancy in water, the mechanics of moving muscle and bone, or even the dynamics that make freestyle faster than breaststroke, yet we can swim. In a similar sense, craft workers are able to produce pottery and textiles (among other things) in ways that demonstrate huge amounts of learned knowledge, but which do not depend heavily on putting that knowledge into formal terms, or even into words. This neglect of practical knowledge both reflects and encourages a value judgment that mental work is "better" than physical labor. This was implicit in the class structure of ancient Greece, in which aristocratic men could afford the time for pondering philosophy, while slaves, commoners, and women took care of most material production.

Second, the theory/practice dichotomy encourages the view that practice is the application of theory, a form of rule-following. Behind this is an image of the mind (something distinct from the brain) moving the body like a puppet, giving directions to the muscles as the puppet master pulls strings. Bourdieu (along with a variety of philosophers including especially Wittgenstein) suggests this is misleading. When we perform practical tasks we are not necessarily following rules. Computer models of mental processing commonly suggest something like this because that is the typical nature of a computer program. But human activity involves a combination of discursive awareness and unconscious skill. A "simple" task like buttoning a shirt is not based on consciously following a set of rules (try to articulate what these would be!); rather, it is a practical ability that we learn through the discipline of repetition. We can only do it well when it becomes habitual. The same is true, Bourdieu suggests, not just for such physical tasks but for much more complex social tasks like choosing marriage partners or giving gifts. There *are* rules about such things, but on the basis of careful empirical observation and analysis in both Algeria and France Bourdieu suggests that the rules do not account adequately for what actually goes on. The rules are one part of the story, important to people when they discuss what is desirable, but their practical activity involves a constant adaptation to circumstances that call for going beyond rules. This does not mean that in coming to conclusions about such matters as who makes a good marriage partner people are not drawing on their knowledge. They are making judgments about potential for happiness, economic success, acceptance by their parents, etc. But these judgments are precisely not deductions from scientific theories in the way that, say, an engineer's conclusions that a bridge needs more structural supports may be. Similarly, Bourdieu describes how Kabyle peasants resolve disputes, emphasizing that it is not by rigidly applying formal legal rules, but by making judgments – socially shared through conversation – about what is in accord with justice or honor.

Taking practice seriously implies, third, that we see society through the lens of what social actors are trying to do. Social science is typically built on a totalizing view. This is made possible by the fact that scientists are generally outsiders to the social situations they analyze, and by the fact that they can see how historical events have turned out. This gives the scientists some great advantages. They can know more than most actual social actors about the odds of their choices working out the way they want, and about the unintended consequences of their actions (Merton, 1936). But the scientists need to guard against forgetting the uncertainty under which all real people act. Recall the game analogy. The basketball player with the ball is not concerned with scientific analysis of the probabilities of making a shot from 25 feet. He is concerned with the particular options before him – who is open for a pass, how much time is left on the clock – as well as with his own desire to win and the risk that he will embarrass himself instead of being a hero. Players will respond differently. But all, Bourdieu suggests, respond by acting strategically, not by simply following rules. "To substitute *strategy* for *rule*," he writes, "is to reintroduce time, with its rhythm, its orientation, its irreversibility" (Bourdieu, 1977, p. 9). A good player will not always take the 25-foot shot under similar conditions, but sometimes fake and pass, and sometimes drive for the basket. The key to understanding strategy is not just that the actor wants to accomplish something, but that he or she is trying to do so under conditions of uncertainty. Not only is the future not yet settled, but the actor cannot see the whole of society, the player can only see the game from his or her particular position within it.

Fourth, the traditional idea of theory represents knowledge as passive understanding of the world. The implication is that there is a complete and potentially permanent logical order already existing behind society or culture, and that the task of the sociologist or anthropologist is only to decipher it. Not so, says Bourdieu, partly because every culture is incomplete and contains internal contradictions. It may be relatively structured, but not 100 percent so. As a result, social scientists should not try to represent culture simply as rules that people follow, but as the practical dispositions that enable people to improvise actions where no learned rule fits perfectly. These will not be uniform throughout a society, but will vary with the locations of people's different experiences within it. Those who have more resources (capital) may be better able to realize widely shared values. To take a mundane example, star athletes may be better able to get dates with the prettiest or most popular girls in a high school. It would be a mistake, however, to represent their behavior and luck as though it represented cultural rules from which everyone else deviated. And to grasp the workings of the high school culture, we would need to understand how other people experienced their different social locations, and how this influenced who they thought they could or should date, what they saw as attractive, and so forth. What we would see is a system not simply of rules, but of resources, practical dispositions, and strategies. Our knowledge would also become more critical – we would be aware of the inequalities in the high school in a way that a more conventional cultural theorist might not be, we would see ways in which conventional norms about social attractiveness are in fact a basis of discrimination.

Bourdieu's case is not for an action-centered sociology as opposed to one focused on structure. On the contrary, he seeks to overcome this distinction, which he thinks has limited sociology in the past. His effort is to develop a "genetic structuralism"; that is, a sociology that uses the intellectual resources of structural analysis, but approaches structures in terms of the ways in which they are produced and reproduced through action. Bourdieu had already analyzed dynamics of reproduction in several works of the 1960s, but the most influential statement of his developing theoretical approach came with the publication in 1972 of *Outline of a Theory of Practice*.

Bourdieu starts with the assumption that most social scientists exaggerate "structure" rather than action, because emphasizing the orderly, recurrent, and enduring aspects of social life is what sets "objective" social science apart from everyday "subjective" viewpoints. Every introductory sociology student learns the difference between a personal point of view and a scientific one, between an individual experience or choice and a social pattern in experiences and choices. Students often learn Émile Durkheim's (1895) famous maxim that social facts should be treated as though they were "things" – in other words, hard, objective reality. The facts of social science, Durkheim argued, are external to individuals, endure longer than individual lifetimes, and have coercive power over individuals. The Durkheimian tradition, and these approaches to social facts, remained dominant in French social science when Bourdieu wrote *Outline*.

Bourdieu's first task in *Outline*, thus, is to show the "objective limits of objectivism." Real objectivity in social science starts by breaking with anecdotes and familiar understandings in order to grasp a deeper reality. This is not simply the sum total of the facts that happen to exist (as a purely empiricist view might suggest). Rather, it is the underlying conditions that make possible whatever facts exist. The idea is similar to that involved in grasping the difference between genetics and physical appearance. A man and a woman bring more or less fixed genetic possibilities to the creation of children. But which of these possibilities appear in any specific child is a matter of statistical probabilities. Simply generalizing from the empirical traits of an individual child or even several children may thus be misleading with regard to the underlying pattern of genetic determination. In the same sense, what is "objectively" the deepest "reality" in social life is not the surface phenomena that we see all around us, but the underlying structural features that make these surface phenomena possible. The "objectivist" task of sociology is to grasp these underlying structural features. For example, what are the underlying conditions for the production and distribution of wealth, as distinct from simply its presence or absence among our friends or others we know? But here we see also the limits to pure objectivism. By itself, objectivism cannot make sense of how the underlying conditions of possibility are translated into empirical actuality. This only comes about when they become the bases of human action, which is not altogether objective, but is based on practical subjective knowledge of the social world. Social theory needs, therefore, to study both objective structures and the ways in which human beings act. These are two sides of a dialectical relationship and not simply two distinct phenomena, because the ways in which human beings act are the result of practical dispositions that they develop through their experience of objective structures. This is why most action tends to reproduce structures, and change in social institutions is relatively gradual. If we did not grasp that social action is itself structured, it would be hard to explain why action did not simply dissolve all institutions into chaos.

Objectivist sociology tends to explain the structuring of action only as the result of external forces. We may be pushed in one direction, or constrained from going in another. Our action is governed by force, or by rules, or by obstacles. What this misses, says Bourdieu, is the extent to which social structure is inside each of us because we have learned from the experience of previous actions. We have a practical mastery of how to do things that takes into account social structures. Thus the way in which we produce our actions is already shaped to fit with and reproduce the social structures because this is what enables us to act effectively. But we internalize the social structures as we experience them – not as they exist in some abstract objectivist model. We develop our practical understanding of these structures through our learning of categories that are made available by our culture, but also through our own active development of understanding. On the basis of this combination of experience and cognition, each of us develops a practical disposition to act in certain ways.

> There is action, and history, and conservation or transformation of structures only because there are agents, but agents who are acting and efficacious only because they are not reduced to what is ordinarily put under the notion of individual and who, as socialized organisms, are endowed with an ensemble of dispositions which imply both the propensity and the ability to get into and to play the game. (Bourdieu, 1989b, p. 59)

Bourdieu's stress on the presence of social structure inside the actor is a challenge not only to objectivism, but to most forms of subjectivism. These are mirror images of each other. Subjectivists are prone to two basic errors. First, they are apt to ascribe too much voluntarism to social actors. Focusing on each occasion as though it is an opportunity for creativity and constructing a new reality, they neglect the extent to which people's very abilities to understand and choose and act have been shaped by processes of learning which are themselves objectively structured and socially produced. Second, subjectivist approaches commonly present social life as much less structured, much more contingent, than it really is. As Bourdieu (1989b, p. 47) writes, "If it is good to recall, against certain mechanistic visions of action, that social agents construct social reality, individually and also collectively, we must be careful not to forget, as the interactionists and ethnomethodologists often do, that they have not constructured the categories they put to work in this work of construction." In other words, how we think about reality does shape what it is for us, but how we think about it is a result of what we have learned from our culture and experience, not simply a matter of free will.

Bourdieu draws on sociologists (like George Herbert Mead, Harold Garfinkel, and Erving Goffman) who have paid attention to the ways in which social action shapes social structures, and stressed the ways in which *inter*action even shapes who the actors are and what strategies they pursue. At the same time, he remains sharply critical of philosophers (like Sartre) who write as though individual existence came before society. Bourdieu insists on a dialectic of structure and action, but he also makes it clear that he thinks the crucial first step for social science comes with the discovery of objective structure, and the break with everyday knowledge that this entails.

## WINNING THE SOCIAL FACT

Social life requires our active engagement in its games. It is impossible to remain neutral, and it is impossible to live with the distanced, detached perspective of the outside observer. As a result, all participants in social life have a knowledge of it that is conditioned by their specific location and trajectory in it. That is, they see it from where they are, how they got there and where they are trying to go. Take something like the relations between parents and children. As participants, we see these from one side or the other. They look different at different stages of life and other different circumstances – as, for example, when one's parents become grandparents to one's children. Our engagement in these relationships is powerful, but it is deeply subjective, not objective. We know a lot, but what we know is built into the specific relationships we inhabit and into specific modes of cultural understanding. Much of it is practical mastery of how to be a parent or a child. This is a genuine form of knowledge, but it should not be confused with scientific knowledge.

Our everyday life involvements, Bourdieu suggests, invest us with a great deal of practical knowledge, but require us to misrecognize much of what we and other people do. Misrecognition is not simply error; indeed, in a practical mode of engagement every recognition is also a misrecognition. This is so precisely because we cannot be objective and outside our own relations, we cannot see them from all possible angles. Which aspects of them we understand and how reflects our own practical engagement in them and also the conditions for perpetuating the games in which we are participants. As Bourdieu (1980, p. 68) writes, "Practical faith is the condition of entry that every field tacitly imposes, not only by sanctioning and debarring those who would destroy the game, but by so arranging things, in practice, that the operations of selecting and shaping new entrants (rites of passage, examinations, etc.) are such as to obtain from them that undisputed, pre-reflexive, naive, native compliance with the fundamental presuppositions of the field which is the very definition of doxa." "Doxa" is Bourdieu's term for the taken-for-granted, preconscious understandings of the world and our place in it that shape our more conscious awarenesses. Doxa is more basic than "orthodoxy," or beliefs that we maintain to be correct in the awareness that others may have different views. Orthodoxy is an enforced straightness of belief, like following the teachings of organized religion. Doxa is felt reality, what we take not as beyond challenge but before any possible challenge. But though doxa seems to us to be simply the way things are, it is in fact a socially produced understanding, and what is doxic varies from culture to culture and field to field. In order for us to live, and to recognize anything, we require the kind of orientation to action and awareness that doxa gives. But doxa thus also implies misrecognition, partial and distorted understanding. It was the doxic experience of Europeans for centuries that the world was flat. Thinking otherwise was evidence not of scientific cleverness but of madness.

The ideas of doxa and misrecognition allow Bourdieu a subtle approach to issues commonly addressed through the concept of ideology. Marxist and other analysts have pointed to the ways in which people's beliefs may be shaped to conform with either power structures or the continued functioning of a social order. Ideology is commonly understood as a set of beliefs that is in some degree partial and distorted and serves some specific set of social interests. Thus it is ideological to suggest that individual effort is the basic determinant of where people stand in the class hierarchy. It is not only false, but it serves both to legitimate an unequal social order and to motivate participants. Common use of the notion of ideology, however, tends to imply that it is possible to be without ideology, to have an objectively correct or undistorted understanding of the social world. This Bourdieu rejects. One can shake the effects of specific ideologies, but one cannot live without doxa, and one cannot play the games of life without misrecognition. Misrecognition is built into the very practical mastery that makes our actions effective.

Nonetheless, symbolic power is exercised through the construction of doxa as well as orthodoxy. Every field of social participation demands of those who enter it a kind of preconscious adherence to its way of working. This requires seeing things in certain ways and not others, and this will work to the benefit of some participants more than others. Take the modern business corporation. It seldom occurs to people who work for corporations, or enter into contracts with them, or represent them in court, to question whether they exist. But what is a corporation? It is not precisely a material object, and not a person in any ordinary sense. As the Supreme Court Justice Marshall put it famously, the corporation has "no soul to damn, no body to kick." Yet corporations can own property, make contracts, and sue and be sued in courts of law. Corporations exist largely because they are recognized to exist by a wide range of people, including agents of the legal system and the government. In order to do almost any kind of business in a modern society, one must believe in corporations. Yet they are also in a sense fictions. Behind corporations stand owners and managers – and for the most part, they cannot be held liable for things the corporation "does." To believe in the corporation is to support a system that benefits certain interests much more than others, and yet to not believe in it makes it impossible to carry out effective practical action in the business world. This is how misrecognition works.

In addition to making misrecognition, and doxa, the objects of analysis, Bourdieu wishes to remind us of their methodological significance. It is because ordinary social life requires us to be invested in preconscious understandings that are at least in part misrecognitions that it is a faulty guide to social research. A crucial first step for every sociologist is to break with familiar, received understandings of everyday life. To "win" social facts depends on finding techniques for seeing the world more objectively. This is always a struggle, and one that the researcher must keep in mind throughout every project. It will always be easy to slide back into ways of seeing things that are supported by everyday, doxic understandings – one's own, or those of one's informants. Some of the advantages of statistical techniques, for example, come in helping us to achieve distance on the social life we study. At the same time, however, we need to work to understand the processes by which misrecognition is produced, to grasp that it is not a simple mistake. It is not enough to see the "objective" facts alone. We need to see the game in which they are part of the stakes.

## HABITUS

Participation in social games is not merely a conscious choice. It is something we do prereflectively. We are, in a sense, always already involved. From childhood we are prepared for adult roles. We are asked what we want to be when we grow up and learn that it is right to have an occupation. We are told to sit up straight and speak when spoken to. We experience the reverence our parents show before the church – or before money or fame, depending on the parents. Out of what meets with approval or doesn't, what works or doesn't, we develop a characteristic way of generating new actions, of improvising the moves of the game of our lives. We learn confidence or timidity. But in either case much of the power of the socialization process is experienced in bodily terms, simply as part of who we are, how we exist in the world. This sense is the habitus.

Notoriously difficult to pin down, the term "habitus" means basically the embodied sensibility that makes possible structured improvisation.[5] Jazz musicians can play together without consciously following rules because they have developed physically embodied capacities to hear and respond appropriately to what is being produced by others, and to create themselves in ways which others can hear sensibly and to which others can respond. Or, in Bourdieu's metaphor, effective play of a game requires not just knowledge of rules but a practical sense for the game.[6] If this is a challenge to the static cognitivism of structuralism, it is equally a challenge to the existentialist understanding of subjectivity. Sartre created his famous account of the existential dilemma by positing "a sort of unprecedented confrontation between the subject and the world" (Bourdieu, 1972, p. 73). But this misrepresents how actual social life works, because it leaves completely out of the account the durable dispositions of the habitus. Before anyone is a subject, in other words, he or she is already inculcated with institutional knowledge – recognition and misrecognition.

The habitus appears in one sense as each individual's characteristic set of dispositions for action. There is a social process of matching such dispositions to positions in the social order (as, in another vocabulary, one learns to play the roles that fit with one's statuses). But the habitus is more than this. It is the meeting point between institutions and bodies. That is, it is the basic way in which each person as a biological being connects with the sociocultural order in such a way that the various games of life keep their meaning, keep being played. "Produced by the work of inculcation and appropriation that is needed in order for objective structures, the products of collective history, to be reproduced in the form of the durable, adjusted dispositions that are the condition of their functioning, the *habitus*, which is constituted in the course through which agents partake of the history objectified in institutions, is what makes it possible to inhabit institutions, to appropriate them practically, and so to keep them in activity, continuously pulling them from the state of dead letters, reviving the sense deposited in them, but at the same time imposing the revisions and transformations that reactivation entails" (Bourdieu, 1990, p. 57).[7] Think of an example – say the Christian church, a product of two millennia that still seems alive to members. They experience it as alive, but they also make it live by reinventing it in their rituals, their relations with each other, and their faith. Being brought up in the church helps to prepare members for belief (inculcation), but it is also something they must actively claim (appropriation). The connection between the institution and the person is the very way in which members produce their actions. "Each agent, wittingly or unwittingly, willy nilly, is a producer and reproducer of objective meaning. Because his actions and works are the product of a *modus operandi* of which he is not the producer and has no conscious mastery, they contain an 'objective intention', as the Scholastics put it, which always outruns his conscious intentions" (Bourdieu, 1972, p. 79). To return to an earlier example, each of us reproduces the idea of corporation every time we engage in a transaction with one – owning stock, renting an apartment, going to work – even though that may not be our conscious intention.

Bourdieu emphasizes that habitus is not just a capacity of the individual, but an achievement of the collectivity. It is the result of a ubiquitous "collective enterprise of inculcation." The reason why "strategies" can work without individuals being consciously strategic is that individuals become who they are and social institutions exist only on the strength of this inculcation of orientations to action, evaluation, and understanding. The most fundamental social changes have to appear not only as changes in formal structures but as changes in habitual orientations to action. Bourdieu seeks thus to overcome the separation

of culture, social organization, and embodied individual being that is characteristic of most existing sociology.

## FIELDS AND CAPITAL

As we saw above, one of the ways in which Bourdieu uses the metaphor of
"games" is to describe the different fields into which social activities are organized. Each field, like law or literature, has its own distinctive rules and stakes of
play. Accomplishments in one are not immediately granted the same prestige or
rewards in another. Thus novelists are usually not made judges, and legal writing
is seldom taken as literature. But, although the fields involve different games, it is
possible to make translations between them. To explain this, Bourdieu uses the
concept of capital. His analysis of the differences in forms of capital and
dynamics of conversion between them is one of the most original and important
features of Bourdieu's theory. This describes both the specific kinds of resources
accumulated by those who are winners in the struggles of various fields and the
more general forms of capital – such as money and prestige – that make possible
translations from one to the other. "A capital does not exist and function except
in relation to a field" (Bourdieu and Wacquant, 1992, p. 101). Yet successful
lawyers and successful authors both, for example, seek to convert their own
successes into improved standards of living and chances for their children. To do
so, they must convert the capital specific to their field of endeavor into other
forms. In addition to material property (economic capital), families may accumulate networks of connections (social capital) and prestige (cultural capital) by
the way in which they raise children and plan their marriages. In each case, the
accumulation has to be reproduced in every generation or it is lost.

In short, there are two senses in which capital is converted from one form to
another. One is as part of the intergenerational reproduction of capital. Rich
people try to make sure that their children go to good colleges – which, in fact,
are often expensive private colleges (at least in America). This is a way of
converting money into cultural capital (educational credentials). In this form,
it can be passed on and potentially reconverted into economic form. The second
sense of conversion of capital is more immediate. The athlete with great successes and capital specific to his or her sporting field may convert this into
money by signing agreements to endorse products, or by opening businesses
like car dealerships or insurance agencies, in which celebrity status in the athletic
field may help to attract customers.

Bourdieu's account of capital differs from most versions of Marxism. It is not
backed by a theory of capitalism as a distinct social formation (Calhoun, 1993).
Neither is it the basis for an economic determinism. Bourdieu sees "an economy
of practices" at work insofar as people must always decide how to expend their
effort and engage in strategies that aim at gaining scarce goods. But Bourdieu
does not hold that specifically economic goods are always the main or underlying motivations of action or the basis of an overall system. By conceptualizing
capital as taking many different forms, each tied to a different field of action,

Bourdieu stresses: (a) that there are many different kinds of goods that people pursue and resources that they accumulate; (b) that these are inextricably social, because they derive their meaning from the social relationships that constitute different fields (rather than simply from some sort of material things being valuable in and of themselves); and (c) that the struggle to accumulate capital is hardly the whole story – the struggle to reproduce capital is equally basic and often depends on the ways in which it can be converted across fields.

In addition, Bourdieu shows that fields (such as art, literature, and science) that are constituted by a seeming disregard for or rejection of economic interests nonetheless operate according to a logic of capital accumulation and reproduction. It is common to think of religion, art, and science as basically the opposite of economic calculation and capital accumulation. Even fields like law are constituted not simply by reference to economic capital (however much lawyers may treasure their pay) but by reference to justice and technical expertise in its adjudication. This is crucial, among other reasons, as a basis for the claim of each field to a certain autonomy. This, as Bourdieu (1992, pp. 47ff) has argued, is the "critical phase" in the emergence of a field. Autonomy means that the field can be engaged in the play of its own distinctive game, can produce its own distinctive capital, and cannot be reduced to immediate dependency on any other field.

Bourdieu's most sustained analysis of the development of such a field focuses on the genesis and structure of the literary field. He takes up the late nineteenth-century point at which the writing of "realistic" novels separated itself simultaneously from the broader cultural field and the immediate rival of journalism. His book *The Rules of Art* (1992) focuses equally on the specific empirical case of Gustave Flaubert and his career, and on the patterns intrinsic to the field as such. The emphasis on Flaubert is, among other things, a riposte to and (often implicit) critical engagement with Sartre's famous largely psychological analysis. *The Rules of Art* contests the view of artistic achievement as disinterested, and a matter simply of individual genius and creative impulses. It shows genius to lie in the ability to play the game that defines a field, as well as in aesthetic vision or originality.

Flaubert was the mid-nineteenth-century writer who, more than anyone else with the possible exception of Baudelaire, created the exemplary image of the author as an artistic creator working in an autonomous literary field. The author was not merely a writer acting on behalf of other interests: politics, say, or money. A journalist was such a paid writer, responsible to those who hired him. An author, by contrast, was an artist. This was the key point for Flaubert and for the literary field that developed around and after him. What the artistic field demanded was not just talent, or vision, but a commitment to "art for art's sake." This meant producing works specifically for the field of art.

Writers like Flaubert and Baudelaire made strong claims for the value of their distinctive points of view. This has encouraged the analysis of their products as simply embodiments of their psychological individuality. On the other hand, they wrote "realistic" novels, engaging the social issues of their day, from poverty to the Revolution of 1848. This has encouraged others to focus on the ways in which they reflected one or another side in those issues, interpreting them, for example, as social critics or as voices of the rising middle class. Bourdieu shows how this misses the decisive importance of the creation of a field of literature as art. This meant, first, that when Flaubert or Baudelaire wrote about the issues of their day, they claimed the distinctive authority of artists. Indeed, they helped to pioneer the idea that artists might offer a special contribution to social awareness that reflected precisely their "disinterestedness" – in other words, the fact they they were not *simply* political actors. Second, though, Bourdieu shows that this appearance of distinterestedness is misleading. It is produced to the extent that artists are motivated by interests specific to the artistic field and their place within it, and not merely serving as spokespeople for other social positions. In other words, artists are distinterested in the terms of some other fields precisely because of the extent to which they are interested in the field of art. The autonomy of this field is thus basic to the production of artists in this sense.

Painting as a modern artistic field is defined by the difference between producing "art" for the sake of religion, as in medieval decorations of churches, or for the sake of memory and money, as in some portraiture; and producing art for its own sake (Bourdieu, 1983). The latter approach does not mean that the painter stops wanting food, or fame, or salvation – though he may not consciously recognize how much he is driven by these desires. Rather, what it does is orient his creative work specifically to the field of art, and to the standards of judgment of others in that field. The artist in this sense doesn't just produce more of what the market wants, but endeavors to create works that embody his own distinctive vision and place in the field. He seeks recognition from other artists, and in his work marks off his debts to but also distinctions from them. It is because it becomes a field in this way, oriented to an internal communication and accumulation of specifically artistic capital, that the production of art becomes partially autonomous from popular and even elite tastes. Art may guide tastes (not just be guided by them), or it may operate outside the world of everyday tastes, but it may not be reduced to them. This liberates art from determination by its immediate social context, but it does not liberate artists from all interests in achieving distinction or accumulating capital. On the contrary, they are driven to innovate (rather than just reproducing the masterworks of a previous generation), and to innovate in ways that derive much of their form from the existing state of communication in the art field. The artistic habitus, thus, enables a regulated improvisation, working with the symbolic materials at hand to express at once the artist's original vision and the artist's individual claims on the field of art. Because the art field is autonomous, its works can only be understood by those who master its internal forms of communication. This is why ordinary people find much modern art hard to understand, at least until they take classes or read the guiding statements offered by museum curators. From the mid-nineteenth century, art could become increasingly abstract partly because it was the production not simply of beauty, or of a mirror on the world, but of a communication among artists. This communication was driven simultaneously by the pursuit of distinction and of art for art's sake.

When we set out to understand the "creative project" or distinctive point of view of an artist like Flaubert, therefore, the first thing we need to grasp is his place in and trajectory through the field of art (or the more specific field of literature as art). This, Bourdieu recognizes, must seem like heresy to those who believe in the individualistic ideal of artistic genius. It is one thing to say that sociology can help us understand art markets, but this is a claim that sociology is not just helpful for but crucial to understanding the individual work of art and the point of view of the artist who created it. Bourdieu takes on this task in an analysis simultaneously of Flaubert's career, or his own implicit analysis of it in the novel *Sentimental Education*, and of the genesis and structure of the French literary field. In doing so, he accepts a challenge similar to that Durkheim (1897) took in seeking to explain suicide sociologically: to demonstrate the power of sociology in a domain normally understood in precisely antisociological terms.

The analysis is too complicated to summarize here. At its center lies the demonstration that Flaubert's point of view as an artist is shaped by his objective position in the artistic field and his more subjective position-takings in relation to the development of that field. For example, it is important that Flaubert came from a family that was able to provide him with financial support. This enabled him to participate fully in the ethic (or interest) of art for art's sake, while some of his colleagues (perhaps equally talented) were forced to support themselves by writing journalism for money. This is different from saying simply that Flaubert expressed a middle-class point of view. In fact, it suggests something of why middle- and upper-class people who enter into careers (like art) that are defined by cultural rather than economic capital often become social critics. Their family backgrounds help to buy them some autonomy from the immediate interests of the economy, while their pursuit of distinction in a cultural field gives them an interest in producing innovative or incisive views of the world. In other words, the objective features of an artist's background influence his work not so much directly as indirectly through the mediation of the artistic field.

Within that field, the artist occupies a specific position at any one point in time, and also a trajectory of positions through time. The position of an individual artist is shaped by the network of relationships that connect him to (or differentiate him from) other artists and by his position in the hierarchies of artistic producers defined by both the external market and the internal prestige system of the field. The actual position the artist occupies, however, is only one among a universe of possible positions. He could have made different friends and enemies, could have used his talent better or worse at earlier times, could have traveled abroad rather than staying in Paris. In this sense, the artist's biography (including both the objective resources he starts with and the uses he makes of them) describes a trajectory through the space of objective positions in the field (which itself may be developing and changing). This trajectory is produced partially by choices and by the way the artist played the game, as well as by material factors. At the same time, as we saw in considering the habitus, the way the artist plays the game is itself shaped by the objective circumstances he has experienced. As he sets out to produce any new work, the artist starts from an objective position in the field, and also engages in new "position-takings." That is, he chooses consciously or unconsciously from among the range of possible moves open to him.

In line with Bourdieu's overall approach, what we see here is the deep way in which subjective and objective dimensions of fields and practices are bound up with each other. "Paradoxically," he writes, "we can only be sure of some chance of participating in the author's subjective intention (or, if you like, in what I have called elsewhere his 'creative project') provided we complete the long work of objectification necessary to reconstruct the universe of positions within which he was situated and where what he wanted to do was defined" (Bourdieu, 1992, p. 88). One important way in which the field as a whole shapes the work of a Flaubert, say, is by granting him the freedom to innovate, and to construct a vision of the world that is not immediately constrained by economic logic or political power. In other words, the artist gains his freedom in relation to his broader social context precisely by accepting the determinations that come with investment in the artistic field. "The posts of 'pure' writer and artist, like that of 'intellectual', are institutions of freedom, which are constructed against the 'bourgeoisie' (in the artist's terms) and, more concretely, against the market and state bureaucracies (academies, salons, etc.) through a series of ruptures, partially cumulative, which are often made possible only by a diversion of the resources of the market – hence of the 'bourgeoisie' – and even of state bureau-cracies." That is, the pure writer needs resources from somewhere. "These posts are the end point of all the *collective work* which has led to the constitution of the field of cultural production as a space independent of the economy and politics; but, in return, this work of emancipation cannot be carried out or extended unless the post finds an agent endowed with the required dispositions, such as an indifference to profit and a propensity to make risky investments, as well as the properties which, like income, constitute the (external) conditions of these dispositions" (Bourdieu, 1992, p. 257).

In this sense, the artist is not so much "disinterested" as "differently interested." The illusion of disinterest is produced by the way economic and cultural dimen-sions of modern societies are ideologically opposed to each other. The field of cultural production is defined as the economic world reversed (Bourdieu, 1993, chapter 1). It is one of the central contributions of Bourdieu's theory, however, to show that this is a misrecognition, and the opposition is really between different forms of capital. Directly economic capital operates in a money-based market that can be indefinitely extended. Cultural capital, by contrast, operates as a matter of status, which is often recognized only within specific fields.[8]

Bourdieu situates his logic of multiple fields and specific forms of capital in relation to a more general notion of "the field of power." The field of art thus has its own internal struggles for recognition, power, and capital, but it also has a specific relationship to the overall field of power. Even highly rewarded artists generally cannot convert their professional prestige into the power to govern other institutional domains. By contrast, businesspeople and lawyers are more able to do this. The question is not just who is higher or lower in some overall system, but how different groups and fields relate to each other. Fields that are relatively high in cultural capital and low in economic capital occupy dominated positions within the dominant elite. In other words, university professors, authors, and artists are relatively high in the overall social hierarchy, but we would not get a very complete picture of how they relate to the system of distinctions if we stopped at this. We need to grasp what it means to be in possession of a very large amount of particular kinds of capital (mainly cultural) that trade at a disadvantage in relation to directly economic capital. This translates into a feeling of being dominated even for people who are objectively well off in relation to society as a whole. College professors, for example, don't compare themselves to postmen so much as to their former university classmates who may have gotten lower grades but made more money in business. Similarly, they experience the need to persuade those who control society's purse strings that higher education deserves their support (whereas the opposite is much less often the case; businessmen do not have the same need to enlist the support of college professors – though sometimes it can be a source of prestige to show connections to the intellectual world). This experience of being what Bourdieu has called "the dominated fraction of the dominant class" can have many results. These range from a tendency to be in political opposition to specific tastes that do not put possessors of cultural capital in direct competition with possessors of economic capital. College professors, thus, may prefer old tweed jackets to new designer suits, or old Volvos to new Mercedes as part of their adaptation to the overall position of their field.[9]

## REFLEXIVITY

Analyses of the objective determinants of the tastes of college professors are not in Bourdieu's view simply an idle form of narcissistic self-interest. Rather, it is vital for intellectuals to be clear about their own positions and motivations in order to be adequately self-analytic and self-critical in developing their accounts of the social worlds at large. This is the necessary basis for both public interventions and the best social science itself. Just as an analysis can discern the combination of objective and subjective factors that come to produce the point of view of an author like Flaubert, so analysis can establish the grounds on which scientific production rests.

Bourdieu does not call for the study of the points of view of individual scientists, or a critical uncovering of their personal biases, so much as for the study of the production of the basic perspectives that operate within intellectual fields more broadly. These are collective products. Identifying them is a source of insight into the unconscious cultural structures that shape intellectual orientations. These may be general to a culture or specific to the intellectual field. We saw an example in considering the ways in which anthropologists may be prone to an intellectualist bias in describing action in terms of following cultural rules. This follows not only from the typical self-understanding of intellectuals, but from reliance on discourse with informants as a way of discovering how practices are organized. Grasping how this bias gets produced is a way to improve the epistemic quality of analyses.

Beyond uncovering such possible biases, reflexivity offers the opportunity to see how the organization of the intellectual or academic field as a whole influences the knowledge that is produced within it. A simple example is the way in which the differentiation of disciplines organizes knowledge. Each discipline is predisposed to emphasize those features that are distinctive to it, reinforce its autonomy, and give it special advantage in relation to others. Topics that lie in the interstices may be neglected or relatively distorted. Bourdieu has attempted more systematically to analyze the social space of intellectual work, using a technique called correspondence analysis. This allows him to identify similarities in the products, activities, and relationships of different intellectuals, and graphically represent them as locations in a two or more dimensional space. In his major book on the organization of universities and intellectuals, *Homo Academicus*, he uses this technique to produce an overall picture of social space. This is useful for grasping the battle lines over specific intellectual orientations, and also the conflicts over using knowledge to support or challenge the social order. Law professors, for example, are more likely to be products of private schools and children of senior state officials, and not surprisingly also more likely to be supporters of the state and its elites. Social scientists, more likely to be the children of schoolteachers and professionals, and graduates of Parisian public lycées, tend toward a more critical engagement with the state. Obviously, these are relatively superficial attributes and Bourdieu offers much more detail. Paying attention to these sorts of differentiations among the different disciplines helps us to understand what is at stake when they struggle over intellectual issues – say, whether a new field of study should be recognized with departmental status – and also when their members engage in intellectual production.

Drawing on the example of the literary field, we can see something of what is at stake for Bourdieu here. His reflexivity is not aimed at negative criticism of science, but rather at improving it. He wishes social science to be more scientific, but this depends not simply on imitating natural science but on grasping the social conditions for the production of better scientific knowledge. Mere imitation of natural science (as in some economics) produces objectifications which make no sense of the real world of social practices because they treat social life as though it were solely material life with no room for culture or subjectivity. Bourdieu's analysis helps not only to show the limits of such an approach but to show why it can gain prestige and powerful allies, why it attracts recruits of certain backgrounds, and how it in turn supports the state and business elites. A better social science requires, as we saw earlier, breaking with the received familiarity of everyday social practices in order to grasp underlying truths. It requires reflexively studying the objective limits of objectivism. But it also requires maintaining the autonomy of social science, resisting the temptations to make social science directly serve goals of money or power. Just as literature depends on authors gaining the freedom to produce art for art's sake – with other members of the literary field as its arbiters – so science depends on producing truth for truth's sake, with other scientists as arbiters. This truth can become valuable for a variety of purposes. But just as there is a difference between basic physics and the use of the truths of physics in engineering projects, there is a difference between producing basic sociological knowledge and using this in business or politics. It is especially easy for social scientists to be drawn into an overly immediate relationship to money or power; it is crucial that their first commitment be to the scientific field, because their most valuable contributions to broader public discourse come when they can speak honestly in the name of science. At the same time, truths that social science discovers are likely to make many upholders of the social order uneasy, because they will force more accurate recognitions of the ways in which power operates and social inequality is reproduced.

Bourdieu sees critical social science as politically significant, but he is careful to avoid "short-circuiting" the relationship between scholarly distinction and political voice. He has resisted trading on his celebrity, and kept his interventions to topics where he was especially knowledgeable, such as education or the situation of Algerians in France. More recently, he has written a bestselling polemic about television (1996) and several pointed essays on the ways in which market logic is being introduced into cultural life. His typical goal is to demystify the ways in which seemingly neutral institutions in fact make it harder for ordinary people to learn the truth about the state or public affairs. He has called for an "internationale" of intellectuals (to replace the old Internationale of the working-class movement). In this spirit, he has founded a review of books and intellectual debate, *Libère*, which now appears in half a dozen languages (though, curiously, not English). He has also overcome a longstanding resistance to making public declarations of conscience by signing petitions, in order to work with other leading figures to suggest in the midst of the Yugoslavian wars that there were other options besides passivity and massive high-altitude bombing. The media and the state seemed to suggest, wrote Bourdieu and his colleagues, that there was a simple choice between the NATO military campaign and ignoring the horrors of ethnic cleansing that Milosevic and others had unleashed. Not so, they argued, for there were other possible approaches to stemming the evils, including working more closely with Yugoslavia's immediate neighbors. And it was worth noting that NATO's intervention had actually increased the pace of ethnic cleansing. As Bourdieu (1999) has argued, the categories with which states "think" structure too much of the thinking of all of us in modern society; breaking with them is a struggle, but an important one.

More generally, Bourdieu's mode of intervention has been to use the methods of good social scientific research to expose misrecognitions that support injustice. A prime example is the enormous collective study of "the suffering of the world" produced under his direction (Bourdieu, 1993). This aimed not simply to expose poverty or hardship, but to challenge the dominant points of view that made it difficult for those living in comfort, and especially those running the state, to understand the lives of those who had to struggle most simply to exist. The book thus included both direct attempts to state the truths that could be seen from social spaces of suffering, and examinations of how the views of state officials and other elites prevented them from seeing these truths for themselves. The misrecognition built into the very categories of official knowledge was thus one of its themes. Bourdieu and his colleagues entered the public discourse not simply as advocates, therefore, but specifically as social scientists.

In other cases as well, Bourdieu's interventions into public debate and politics take the form of trying to expose misrecognitions and false oppositions. Worried by the growing dominance of television over popular consciousness, Bourdieu (1998) wrote a short book analyzing its characteristic ways of collapsing the real range of possibilities into false choices and misrecognitions that support certain social interests at the expense of others. Indeed, throughout his work, one of Bourdieu's enduring concerns has been with symbolic violence. By this he means the ways in which people are harmed or held back not by force of arms but by the force of (mis)understanding. The very way in which knowledge is organized for the education of France's most elite students, for example, enshrines certain ways of thinking as right, or as simply "the way to think" (doxa) (see Bourdieu, 1989b, chapter 2). The most powerful forms of symbolic violence are not simply name calling, like saying the poor are lazy or immigrants greedy. Rather, they inhere in the very cognitive structure. Students (Bourdieu has in mind specifically students at France's *grandes écoles*) thus learn to categorize different ways of thinking, different kinds of cultural production, and different social values as higher or lower. It is easier for them later to rebel against a specific classification – say the view that jazz is lower than opera – than to resist the whole project of viewing the world hierarchically. Yet there is nothing intrinsic to the world that requires that all cultural objects be viewed on a scale from higher to lower; this is a specific, culturally reproduced way of thinking. And it is one that systematically encourages support for social hierarchies of other kinds and misrecognition of the actual nature of what people think, or do, or value.

When Bourdieu intervenes in public debates, it is almost always in favor of free exchange. The work and social value of artists, writers, and intellectuals depends on such free exchange – an unhampered and open creativity and communication. It thus depends on maintaining the autonomy of the artistic, literary, and scientific or intellectual fields. Boundaries need to be maintained between serious intellectual pursuit of truth and discourses – however smart – that seek only to use knowledge instrumentally. In this, he has stood clearly against those who would censor intellectual or cultural life in favor of their standards of morality or political expediency (see Bourdieu and Haacke, 1994).

## IMPACT AND ASSESSMENT

Bourdieu's work has had an exceptionally broad, but relatively uneven, impact in sociology.[10] His analyses of the educational structure have been basic to analysis of the role of education in the reproduction of social inequality. His influence over the sociology of education is strong, but in the English-speaking world at least, the impact of his analyses on the study of social stratification generally has been more limited. James Coleman assimilated Bourdieu's concept of cultural capital to Gary Becker's notion of human capital, and called to Bourdieu's discomfort for a social engineering effort to enhance both. Research in social stratification has continued to be predominantly highly objectivist, concerned with descriptions of hierarchies and predictions of patterns of mobility, rather than taking up Bourdieu's challenge to understand the nature of reproduction. This would require a more temporally dynamic, historical approach. It would also require paying attention to cultural as well as material factors, and to the differentiation of fields and problems of the conversion of capital.

Bourdieu's influence on empirical research has been greatest in the sociology of culture. This stems in large part from the range and power of his own empirical studies of forms of artistic production and consumption, and especially of the pursuit of distinction. These have, indeed, played a basic role in creating the contemporary (and highly vibrant) subfield of sociology of culture and have also shaped the broader interdisciplinary field of cultural studies. *Distinction* is easily the best known of these works, and it is extremely widely studied and cited. Somewhat surprisingly, however, there has not been much systematic cross-national research attempting to replicate the study or establish differences in the organization of tastes in different settings. Observers (e.g. Fowler, 1997; Swartz, 1997) have remarked that France may have an unusually tightly integrated cultural hierarchy; it remains for Bourdieu's approach to launch a series of similar empirical studies of anything resembling comparable breadth. Bourdieu himself has done comparative research on similar themes. *The Love of Art* (Bourdieu and Darbel, 1966), for example, focuses on attendance at museums. It is framed by the paradox that state support (and non-profit private organizations) make the great treasures of European art readily accessible to broad populations, most of whom ignore them. The achievement of democratic access is undercut by a widespread perception that the ability to appreciate art is something ineffable, an individual gift, intensely personal. This, Bourdieu and Darbel suggest, is simply a misrecognition underpinning the continued use of art to establish elite credentials in an ostensibly democratic but still highly unequal society. Their study (which looked at six European countries) was one of the earliest in a series of research projects that have established in considerable detail the empirical patterns in the appropriation of culture. Bourdieu did not limit himself to high culture, studying as well the "middlebrow" art form of photography, including that of amateurs (Bourdieu et al. 1965). In this and other research (including *Distinction*), he participated in a broad movement that was basic to the development of cultural studies. This was a challenge to the traditional dichotomy of high versus popular culture. Along with others, Bourdieu helped to debunk the notion that this represented simply an objective distinction inherent in the objects themselves, the nature of their production, or the capacities required to appreciate them. While Bourdieu and other researchers revealed differences in tastes, they showed these to be created by the system of cultural inequality, not reflections of objective differences.

Bourdieu is virtually unique among major theorists in the extent to which he has focused on and been influential through empirical research. Nonetheless, it is probably his theoretical contributions that have had the largest and most general impact in English-language social science. This is an influence that reaches beyond sociology to anthropology, within which he is a comparably major theorist (with the influence of his work on Algeria and especially Kabylia predictably larger and that on France correspondingly reduced). Bourdieu's is probably the single most important theoretical approach to the sociology of culture. More than this, he has helped to bring the study of culture into a central place in sociology. This means paying attention to culture – and struggles over culture – as a crucial part of all social life, not simply approaching cultural objects as a special realm or subfield.

An overall appreciation of Bourdieu's work, however, must resist reading it in fragments: the work on education distinct from that on art and literature, that on power and inequality distinct from that devoted to overcoming the structure/ action antinomy. Bourdieu's key concepts, like habitus, symbolic violence, cultural capital, and field, are useful in themselves, but derive their greatest theoretical significance from their interrelationships. These are best seen not mechanistically, in the abstract, but at work in sociological analysis. The fragments of Bourdieu's work are already exerting an influence, but the whole will have had its proper impact only with a broader shift in the sociological habitus that lies behind the production of new empirical understandings.

Bourdieu's work has been criticized from various perspectives. The most general critical review is that by Jenkins (1992). His grumbling is widely distributed but (aside from complaints about language and French styles in theory) centers on three contentions. First, Bourdieu is somewhat less original than at first appears. This is not an unreasonable point, for Bourdieu's work is indebted to influences (like Goffman and Mauss) that are not always reflected in formal citations. Second, Bourdieu's conceptual framework remains enmeshed in some of the difficulties to which he draws attention and seeks to escape. His invocations of "subjectivism" and "objectivism," for example, are made in the service of encouraging a less binary and more relational approach. Nonetheless, they do tend to reinstitute (if only heuristically) the very opposition they contest. Moreover, Jenkins (1992, p. 113) suggests, Bourdieu's approach entails reifying social structure while developing an abstract model of it; it becomes too cut and dried, too total a system. Third, for Jenkins Bourdieu remains ultimately, and despite disclaimers, a Marxist, and a deterministic one at that. His concept of misrecognition is an epistemologically suspect recourse to the tradition of analyzing ordinary understandings as "false consciousness." This raises the problems that: (a) if ordinary people's consciousness is deeply shaped by misrecognition, their testimony as research subjects becomes dubious evidence; and (b) the claim to have the ability to uncover misrecognition privileges the perspective of the analysts (and may even function to conceal empirical difficulties). Jenkins's reading of Bourdieu is filtered through English-language concerns, theoretical history, and stylistic tastes. Nonetheless, his points are serious and shared with other readers.

Most prominently, despite the "sheep's clothing" of his emphases on culture and action, Bourdieu is held by many critics to be a reductionist wolf underneath. That is, he is charged with adhering to or at least being excessively influenced by one or both of two schools of reductionistic social science: Marxism and rational choice theory. It seems to me clear, for reasons given above (and also elaborated by Bourdieu), that he is not in any strict sense a follower of either of these approaches. He is certainly influenced by Marxism, but also by structuralism, Weber, Durkheim and Durkheimians from Mauss to Goffman, and a variety of other sources. Bourdieu's language of strategy and rational calculation is a different matter. It does not reveal adherence to rational choice theory; indeed, it does not stem from that source but from more general traditions in English philosophy and economics. Nonetheless, Bourdieu is concerned to show that a logic of interest shapes action, even when it is not conscious, and that economies operate in a general sense even in social fields that explicitly deny interest and calculation. "Economies" in this sense mean distributional effects – that social actors enter into interactions with different resources and receive different resources as results of those interactions. That actions cannot be altogether distanced from effects of this kind means, for Bourdieu, that they cannot be removed altogether from interest. This said, Bourdieu has not consistently found ways to express this most general sense of economism without seeming to many readers to espouse a narrower reduction to specifically economic concerns (Jenkins, 1992; Evens, 1999).[11]

The most biting critique of Bourdieu's alleged reductionism has been mounted by Alexander (1995). His attack is partly an attempt to underpin Alexander's own preferred approach to overcoming oppositions of structure and agency, one that would grant culture more autonomy and place a greater emphasis on the capacity of agents to achieve liberation through "authentic communication." Bourdieu, Alexander suggests, tries to make the sociology of knowledge substitute for the analysis of knowledge. That is, he tries to make accounts of how people take positions do the work of analyses of those positions and their normative and intellectual merits. In short, he is a determinist. Moreover, somewhat in common with Jenkins, Alexander sees Bourdieu as covertly accepting too much of the rationalism, structuralism, and Marxism he has argued against:

> Since the early 1960s, Bourdieu has taken aim at two intellectual opponents: structuralist semiotics and rationalistic behaviorism. Against these perspectives, he has reached out to pragmatism and phenomenology and announced his intention to recover the actor and the meaningfulness of her world. That he can do neither . . . is the result of his continuing commitment not only to a cultural form of Marxist thought but to significant strains in the very traditions he is fighting against. The result is that Bourdieu strategizes action (reincorporating behaviorism), subjects it to overarching symbolic codes (reincorporating structuralism), and subjugates both code and action to an underlying material base (reincorporating orthodox Marxism). (Alexander, 1995, p. 130)

Alexander attempts to substantiate this critique by both theoretical argument and (curiously, because he seems to exemplify in more hostile form the very position he decries in Bourdieu) an account of Bourdieu's intellectual development and successive enmities. The latter side of the argument amounts to suggesting that Bourdieu is disingenuous about the sources of his work, but carries little theoretical weight in itself (Alexander's intellectual history is also tendentious). The former side raises a basic issue.

The strengths of Bourdieu's work lie in identifying the ways in which action is interested even when it appears not to be, the ways in which the reproduction of systems of unequal power and resources is accomplished even when it is contrary to explicit goals of actors, and the ways in which the structure of fields and (sometimes unconscious) strategies for accumulating capital shape the content and meaning of "culture" produced within them.[12] Bourdieu's theory is weaker in offering an account of creativity itself and of deep historical changes in the nature of social life or deep differences in cultural orientation. No theoretical orientation provides an equally satisfactory approach to all analytic problems, and certainly none can be judged to have solved them all.

Alexander makes a false start, however, in presenting Bourdieu as simply "fighting against" two specific traditions. His relation to each is more complex, as is his relationship to a range of other theoretical approaches. From the beginning, and throughout his work, Bourdieu has sought precisely to transcend simple oppositions, and has approached different intellectual traditions in a dialectical manner, both criticizing one-sided reliance on any single perspective and learning from many. It is neither surprise nor indictment, for example, that Bourdieu incorporated a great deal of structuralism; it is important to be precise in noting that he challenged the notion that semiotics (or cultural meanings) could adequately be understood autonomously from social forces and practices. Likewise, Bourdieu has labored against the notion that the meanings of behavior are transparent and manifested in purely objective interests or actors' own labels for their behavior. But this does not mean that he has ever sought to dispense with objective factors in social analysis.

It is appropriate to close on a note of contention, not just because Bourdieu has critics but because his theory is critical. It is a contentious, and evolving, engagement with a wide range of other theoretical orientations, problems of empirical analysis, and issues in the social world. Bourdieu's theory is contentious partly because it unsettles received wisdom and partly because it challenges misrecognitions that are basic to the social order – like the ideas that education is meritocratic more than an institutional basis for the reproduction of inequality, or indeed that if the latter is true this is simply something done to individuals rather than something they (each of us) participate in in complex ways. As I have suggested – and, indeed, as Bourdieu himself has indicated – it is also in a strong sense incomplete. It is not a Parsonsian attempt to present a completely coherent system. It does have enduring motifs and recurrent analytic strategies as well as a largely stable but gradually growing conceptual framework. It does not have or ask for closure. Most basically, Bourdieu's theory asks for commitment to creating knowledge – and thus to a field shaped by that interest. This commitment launches the very serious game of social science, which in Bourdieu's eyes has the chance to challenge even the state and its operational categories. In this sense, indeed, the theory that explains reproduction and the social closure of fields is a possible weapon in the struggle for more openness in social life.

## Notes

1 See Taylor (1993) on Bourdieu's account of the limits of rule-following as an explication of action and its relationship to Wittgenstein.

2 Biographical sources on Bourdieu are limited. The best available general discussion of his life and work is Swartz (1997); see also Robbins (1993) and Jenkins (1992). Various articles by Bourdieu's close collaborator Loïc Wacquant provide helpful interpretation; see especially his contributions to Bourdieu and Wacquant (1992). Fowler (1997) situates Bourdieu in relation to cultural theory. The essays in Shusterman (1999) and Calhoun et al. (1993) consider several different aspects of Bourdieu's work.

3 Back in France, Bourdieu was responsible for introducing Goffman's work and arranging the translation of several of his books.

4 In this regard, Bourdieu differed from Alain Touraine, the other most prominent French sociologist of his generation and also a member of Aron's Center. Touraine embraced the student revolt more wholeheartedly and his sociology presented a much more voluntaristic cast. He also broke with Aron and formed his own center (see Colquhoun, 1986).

5 The concept has classical roots, and was revived for sociological use by Norbert Elias as well as Bourdieu; on Elias's version, see Chartier (1988).

6 The notion of "sense" carries, in French as in English, both cognitivist and bodily connotations: to "make sense" and to "sense something." When Bourdieu rewrote and slightly expanded *Outline* in the late 1970s – about the time it was first becoming known in English – he chose the French title *Le sens pratique*. This second version of *Outline* (which has never been comparably influential or as widely read as it deserves) has the English title *The Logic of Practice*, which sacrifices one side of the double meaning.

7 Writing sentences like this is part of Bourdieu's habitus, his connection to the academic game, not least because their very complexity forces us to make the effort to hold several ideas in mind at once, resisting the apparent simplicity of everyday formations. Nonetheless, they do not translate elegantly or read easily.

8 It is not always recognized – but should be – how much this aspect of Bourdieu's theory follows and extends Weber's (1922) analysis of class (economic position) and status.

9 Bourdieu's most sustained analysis of such issues occurs in *Distinction* (1979), a book that attempts "a social critique of the judgement of taste." It is a mixture of empirical analysis of the kinds of tastes characteristic of people at different positions in the French class hierarchy and theoretical argument against those who would legitimate a system of class-based classifications as reflecting a natural order. In other words, Bourdieu shows tastes not to reflect simply greater or lesser "cultivation" or ability to appreciate objective beauty or other virtues, but to be the result of a struggle over classification in which some members of society are systematically advantaged. Lower classes, he contends, make a virtue of necessity, while elites demonstrate their ability to transcend it. The results include working-class preferences for more "realistic" art and comfortable, solid furniture, and elite preferences for more "abstract" art and often uncomfortable or fragile antique furniture.

10 See Bourdieu's (1998) complaints about how he has been understood in translation.

11 Evens's (1999) critique also carries the interesting challenge that Bourdieu has not demonstrated an ability to grasp the radically other, and thus the situated rather

than universal and mutable rather than immutable character of the kind of action and social order he describes.

12 Alexander (1995, p. 152) terms "unconscious strategy" an oxymoron. It is true that the notion invites misunderstanding and confusion, since it is hard to distinguish when it means that results fell into place "as if" there had been a strategy at work, and when it means that actors make a million small choices that add up to a strategy of which they are never consciously aware as such. In any case, Alexander fails himself to consider either of these possibilities clearly. The former is basic to modern economic analysis; the latter is at the heart of the idea of "sense of play," which Bourdieu has argued should replace a mechanistic, rule-following approach to the production of action.

# Bibliography

## Writings of Pierre Bourdieu

*Travail et travailleurs en Algerie* (with A. Darbel, J.-P. Rivet and C. Seibel). 1963. Paris and the Hague: Mouton (translated as *Work and Workers in Algeria*, Stanford, CA: Stanford University Press, 1995).

*Le déracinement, la crise de l'agriculture en Algerie* (with A. Sayed). 1963. Paris: Editions de Minuit.

*The Inheritors: French Students and their Relation to Culture* (with J.-C. Passeron). 1964. Chicago: University of Chicago Press (1979).

*Photography: a Middlebrow Art* (with L. Boltaski, R. Castel, J. C. Chamboredon, and D. Schnapper). 1965. Cambridge: Polity (1990).

*The Love of Art* (with Alain Darbel). 1966. Stanford, CA: Stanford University Press (1990).

*Reproduction: In Education, Culture, and Society* (with J.-C. Passeron). 1967. Beverly Hills, CA: Sage (1971).

*The Craft of Sociology: Epistemological Preliminaries* (with J.-C. Chamboredon and J.-C. Passeron). 1968. New York: Walter de Gruyter (revised edn 1999).

*Outline of a Theory of Practice*, translated by Richard Nice. 1972. Cambridge: Cambridge University Press (1977).

*Distinction*. 1979. London: Routledge and Kegan Paul (1984).

*The Logic of Practice*. 1980. Stanford, CA: Stanford University Press (1990).

*Language and Symbolic Power*. 1982. Cambridge, MA: Harvard University Press (1991).

The Field of Cultural Production, or: The Economic World Reversed. 1983. In *The Field of Cultural Production*. New York: Columbia University Press (1993), pp. 29–73.

*Homo Academicus*. 1984. Stanford, CA: Stanford University Press (1988).

The Forms of Capital. 1986. In John G. Richardson (ed.), *Handbook of Theory and Research in the Sociology of Education*. New York: Greenwood, pp. 241–58.

*The Political Ontology of Martin Heidegger*. 1988a. Stanford, CA: Stanford University Press (1991).

Vive la crise! For Heterodoxy in Social Science. 1988b. *Theory and Society*, 17(5), 773–88.

The Historical Genesis of a Pure Aesthetic. 1989a. In *The Field of Cultural Production*. New York: Columbia University Press (1993), pp. 254–66.

*The State Nobility*. 1989b. Stanford, CA: Stanford University Press (1996).

*In Other Words: Essays towards a Reflexive Sociology*. 1990. Stanford, CA: Stanford University Press.

*Language and Symbolic Power.* 1991. Cambridge, MA: Harvard University Press.

*The Rules of Art: Genesis and Structure of the Literary Field.* 1992. Stanford, CA: Stanford University Press (1996).

*An Invitation to Reflexive Sociology* (with Loïc Wacquant). 1992. Chicago: University of Chicago Press.

*La Misère du Monde* (editor). 1993. Paris: Seuil (translation forthcoming as *The Weight of the World: Social Suffering in Contemporary Society.* Stanford: Stanford University Press).

*Free Exchange* (with Hans Haacke). 1994. Stanford, CA: Stanford University Press (1995).

*On Television.* 1996. New York: New Press (1999).

*Practical Reason: On the Theory of Action.* 1998. Stanford, CA: Stanford University Press.

Rethinking the State: Genesis and Structure of the Bureaucratic Field. 1999. In George Steinmetz (ed.), *State/Culture: State Formation after the Cultural Turn.* Ithaca, NY: Cornell University Press, pp. 53–75.

## Further reading

Alexander, Jeffrey C. (1995) The Reality of Reduction: The Failed Synthesis of Pierre Bourdieu. In *Fin de Siècle Social Theory.* London: Verso, pp. 128–216.

Brubaker, Rogers (1993) Social Theory as Habitus. In C. Calhoun, E. LiPuma, and M. Postone (eds), *Bourdieu: Critical Perspectives.* Chicago: University of Chicago Press, pp. 212–34.

Calhoun, Craig (1993) Habitus, Field, and Capital: The Question of Historical Specificity. In C. Calhoun, E. LiPuma, and M. Postone (eds), *Bourdieu: Critical Perspectives.* Chicago: University of Chicago Press, pp. 61–88.

Calhoun, Craig, LiPuma, Edward, and Postone, Moishe (eds) (1992) *Bourdieu: Critical Perspectives.* Chicago: University of Chicago Press.

Chartier, Roger (1988) Social Figuration and Habitus. In *Cultural History.* Ithaca, NY: Cornell University Press, pp. 71–94.

Colquhoun, Robert (1986) *Raymond Aron: the Sociologist in Society, 1955–1983.* Beverly Hills, CA: Sage.

Dosse, Françlaois (1997) *Structuralism.* 2 volumes. Minneapolis: University of Minnesota Press.

Durkheim, Émile (1895) *The Rules of Sociological Method.* New York: Free Press (1988).

Durkheim, Émile (1897) *Suicide.* New York: Free Press (1988).

Evens, T. M. S. (1999) Bourdieu and the Logic of Practice: Is All Giving Indian-giving or Is "Generalized Materialism" Not Enough? *Sociological Theory,* 17(1), 3–31.

Fowler, Bridget (1997) *Pierre Bourdieu and Cultural Theory: Critical Investigations.* London: Sage.

Goffman, Erving (1959) *The Presentation of Self in Everyday Life.* New York: Anchor.

Harker, Richard, Mahar, Christian, and Wilkes, Chris (eds) (1990) *An Introduction to the Work of Pierre Bourdieu.* New York: St Martins.

Honneth, Axel, Kocyba, Hermann, and Schwibs, Bernd (1986) The Struggle for Symbolic Order: an Interview with Pierre Bourdieu. *Theory, Culture, and Society,* 3(3), 35–51.

Jenkins, Richard (1992) *Pierre Bourdieu.* London: Routledge.

Merton, Robert (1936) The Unintended Consequences of Purposeful Social Action. In Robert Merton, *Sociological Ambivalence*. New York: Free Press (1982).

Robbins, Derrick (1993) *The Work of Pierre Bourdieu: Recognizing Society*. London: Macmillan.

Sayer, Andrew (1999) Bourdieu, Smith and Disinterested Judgment. *The Sociological Review*, 47(3), 403–31.

Shusterman, Richard (ed.) (1999) *The Bourdieu Reader*. Cambridge, MA: Blackwell.

Swartz, David (1997) *Culture and Power: the Sociology of Pierre Bourdieu*. Chicago: University of Chicago Press.

Taylor, Charles (1993) To Follow a Rule. In C. Calhoun, E. LiPuma, and M. Postone (eds), *Bourdieu: Critical Perspectives*. Chicago: University of Chicago Press, pp. 45–60.

Vandenberghe, Frederic (1999) "The Real Is Relational": An Epistemological Analysis of Pierre Bourdieu's Generative Structuralism. *Sociological Theory*, 17(1), 32–67.

Weber, Max (1922) *Economy and Society: an Outline of Interpretive Sociology*. New York: Bedminster Press.

# 24

# Jean Baudrillard

## Douglas Kellner

French theorist Jean Baudrillard is one of the foremost critics of contemporary society and culture, and is often seen as the guru of French postmodern theory. A professor of sociology at the University of Nanterre from 1966 to 1987, Baudrillard took the postmodern turn in the mid-1970s, developing a new kind of social analysis that went beyond the confines of modern social theory. He is ultimately important as a critic of modern society and theory who claims that the era of modernity and the tradition of classical social theory is obsolete, and that we need a novel mode of social analysis adequate to the emerging era of postmodernity.

A prolific author who has written over twenty books, Baudrillard has commented on the most salient sociological phenomena of the contemporary era, including: the erasure of the distinctions of gender, race, and class that structured modern societies in a new postmodern consumer, media, and high tech society; the mutating roles of art and aesthetics; fundamental changes in politics and culture; and the impact of new media, information, and cybernetic technologies in the creation of a qualitatively different social order. For some years a cult figure of postmodern theory, Baudrillard moved beyond the problematic of postmodernism from the early 1980s to the present, and has developed a highly idiosyncratic mode of social and cultural analysis.

In this study, I discuss Baudrillard's thought in relation to the problematic of classical social theory.[1] Baudrillard's 1960s and early 1970s studies of the consumer society and its system of objects drew on classical sociological theory and provided critical perspectives on everyday life in the post-Second World War social order, organized around the production, consumption, display, and use of consumer goods. His work on the political economy of the sign merged semiological and neo-Marxian perspectives, to provide deep insights into the power of consumption and how it was playing a crucial role in organizing contemporary societies around objects, needs, and consumerism. His 1970s studies of the effects of the new communication, information, and media technologies blazed new paths in contemporary social theory and challenged regnant orthodoxies. Baudrillard's claim of a radical break with modern societies was quickly appropriated into the discourse of the postmodern, and he was received as the prophet of postmodernity in avant-garde theoretical circles throughout the world.

Baudrillard proclaimed the disappearance of the subject, political economy, meaning, truth, the social, and the real in contemporary postmodern social formations. This process of dramatic change and mutation, he argued, required entirely new theories and concepts to describe the rapidly evolving social processes and novelties of the present moment. Baudrillard undertook to explore this new and original situation and to spell out the consequences for contemporary theory and practice. For some years, Baudrillard was a cutting-edge, critical social theorist, one of the most stimulating and provocative contemporary thinkers. He became a cult figure and media celebrity of postmodernism during the 1980s, and while he continued to publish books at a rapid rate, a noticeable decline in the quality of his work was apparent. In retrospect, he can be seen as a theorist who has traced in original ways the life of signs and the impact of technology on social and everyday life.

## EARLY WRITINGS: FROM THE SYSTEM OF OBJECTS TO THE CONSUMER SOCIETY

Jean Baudrillard was born in the cathedral town of Reims, France, in 1929. He told interviewers that his grandparents were peasants and his parents became civil servants (Gane, 1993, p. 19). He also claims that he was the first member of his family to pursue an advanced education and that this led to a rupture with his parents and cultural milieu. In 1956, he began working as a professor of secondary education in a French high school (*lyceé*) and in the early 1960s did editorial work for the French publisher Seuil. Baudrillard was initially a Germanist who published essays on literature in *Les temps modernes* in 1962–3 and translated works of Peter Weiss and Bertolt Brecht into French, as well as a book on messianic revolutionary movements by Wilhelm Mühlmann. During this period, he met Henri Lefebvre, whose critiques of everyday life impressed him, and Roland Barthes, whose semiological analyses of contemporary society had lasting influence on his work.

In 1966, Baudrillard entered the University of Paris, Nanterre, and became Lefebvre's assistant, while studying languages, philosophy, sociology, and other disciplines. He defended his "Thèse de Troisième Cycle" in sociology at Nanterre in 1966 with a dissertation on "Le système des objects," and began teaching sociology in October of that year. Opposing French and US intervention in the Algerian and Vietnamese wars, Baudrillard associated himself with the French left in the 1960s. Nanterre was the center of radical politics and the "March 22 movement," associated with Daniel Cohn-Bendit and the *enrageés*, began in the Nanterre sociology department. Baudrillard said later that he was at the center of the events of May 1968, which resulted in massive student uprisings and a general strike that almost drove de Gaulle from power.

During the late 1960s, Baudrillard began publishing a series of books that would eventually make him world famous. Influenced by Lefebvre, Barthes, Georges Bataille, and the French situationists, Baudrillard undertook serious work in the field of social theory, semiology, and psychoanalysis in the 1960s, and published his first book, *The System of Objects*, in 1968, followed by *The Consumer Society* in 1970, and *For a Critique of the Political Economy of the Sign* in 1972. These early publications are attempts, within the framework of critical sociology, to combine the studies of everyday life initiated by Lefebvre (1971, 1991) and the situationists (Debord, 1970) with a social semiology that studies the life of signs in social life. This project, influenced by Barthes (1967, 1972, 1983), centers on the system of objects in the consumer society (the focus of his first two books), and the interface between political economy and semiotics (the nucleus of his third book). Baudrillard's early work was among the first to appropriate semiology to analyze how objects are encoded with a system of signs and meanings that constitute contemporary media and consumer societies. Combining semiological studies, Marxian political economy, and sociology of the consumer society, Baudrillard began his lifelong task of exploring the system of objects and signs which forms our everyday life.

The early Baudrillard described the meanings invested in the objects of everyday life (e.g. the power accrued through identification with one's automobile when driving) and the structural system through which objects were organized into a new modern society (e.g. the prestige or sign value of a new sports car). In his first three books, Baudrillard argued that the classical Marxian critique of political economy needed to be supplemented by semiological theories of the sign. He argued that the transition from the earlier stage of competitive market capitalism to the stage of monopoly capitalism required increased attention to demand management, to augmenting and steering consumption. At this historical stage, from around 1920 to the 1960s, the need to intensify demand supplemented concern with lowering production costs and with expanding production. In this era of capitalist development, economic concentration, new production techniques, and the development of new technologies, accelerated capacity for mass production and capitalist corporations focused increased attention on managing consumption and creating needs for new prestigious goods, thus producing the regime of what Baudrillard has called "sign value."

The result was the now familiar consumer society, which provided the main focus of Baudrillard's early work. In this society, advertising, packaging, display, fashion, "emancipated" sexuality, mass media and culture, and the proliferation of commodities multiplied the quantity of signs and spectacles, and produced a proliferation of "sign value." Henceforth, Baudrillard claims, commodities are not merely to be characterized by use value and exchange value, as in Marx's theory of the commodity; sign value – the expression and mark of style, prestige, luxury, power, and so on – becomes an increasingly important part of the commodity and consumption.

From this perspective, Baudrillard claims that commodities are bought and displayed as much for their sign value as their use value, and that the pheno-menon of sign value has become an essential constituent of the commodity and consumption in the consumer society. This position was influenced by Veblen's notion of "conspicuous consumption" and display of commodities, analyzed in his *Theory of the Leisure Class*, which, Baudrillard argued, has become extended to everyone in the consumer society. For Baudrillard, the entire society is organ-ized around consumption and display of commodities through which individuals gain prestige, identity, and standing. In this system, the more prestigious one's commodities (houses, cars, clothes, and so on), the higher one's standing in the realm of sign value. Thus, just as words take on meaning according to their position in a differential system of language, so sign values take on meaning according to their place in a differential system of prestige and status.

In developing his own theory, Baudrillard criticizes the mainstream view, which conceptualizes consumption in terms of a rational satisfaction of needs, with the aim of maximizing utility. Against this view, he contrasts a "socio-cultural" approach which stresses the ways that society produces needs through socialization and conditioning, and thus manages consumer demand and con-sumption. For Baudrillard, the system of objects is correlated with a system of needs. Although he shares with American theorists such as Packard, Riesman, and Galbraith a critique of the assumption of a free, rational, autonomous ego which satisfies "natural" needs through consumption, he criticizes Galbraith's model of the production of artificial needs and management of consumer demand.

Baudrillard's argument is that critics of the "false," or artificial, needs pro-duced by the consumer society generally presuppose something like true human needs, or a stabilizing principle within human nature that would maintain a harmonious balance and equilibrium were it not for the pernicious artificial needs produced by advertising and marketing. Yet there is no way, Baudrillard claims, to distinguish between true and false needs – at least from the standpoint of the pleasure or satisfaction received from varying goods or activities of consumption. In addition, he maintains that:

> What Galbraith does not see – and this forces him to present individuals as mere passive victims of the system – is the whole social logic of differentiation, the distinguishing processes of class or caste distinctions which are fundamental to the social structure and are given free rein in "democratic" society. In short, there is a whole sociological dimension of difference, status, etc., lacking here, in con-sequence of which all needs are reorganized around an *objective* social demand for signs and differences, a dimension no longer grounding consumption in a function of "harmonious" individual satisfaction. (Baudrillard, 1998, p. 74)

Baudrillard's focus is on the "logic of social differentiation" whereby indivi-duals distinguish themselves and attain social prestige and standing through the purchase and use of consumer goods. He argues that the entire system of production produces a system of needs that is rationalized, homogenized,

systematized, and hierarchized. Rather than an individual commodity (or adver-
tisement) seducing a consumer into purchase (which Baudrillard equates with
the primitive notion of mana), individuals are induced to buy into an entire
system of objects and needs through which one differentiates oneself socially but
is integrated into the consumer society. He suggests that this activity can best be
conceptualized by seeing the objects of consumption as *signs* and the consumer
society as *a system of signs*, in which a specific object, such as a washing machine
or a car, serves as an appliance and acts as an element of prestige and social
differentation. Hence, "need is never so much the need for a particular object as
the 'need' for difference (the *desire for social meaning*)" (Baudrillard, 1998,
pp. 77–8).

In *The Consumer Society*, Baudrillard concludes by valorizing "multiple forms
of refusal" which can be fused in a "practice of radical change" (ibid., p. 183),
and he alludes to the expectation of "violent eruptions and sudden disintegration
which will come, just as unforeseeably and as certainly May 68, to wreck this
white mass" of consumption (ibid., p. 196). On the other hand, Baudrillard also
describes a situation where alienation is so total that it cannot be surpassed,
because "it is the very structure of market society" (ibid., p. 190). His argument
is that in a society where everything is a commodity that can be bought and sold,
alienation is total. Indeed, the term "alienation" originally signified "for sale,"
and in a totally commodified society where everything is a commodity, alienation is ubiquitous. Moreover, Baudrillard posits "the end of transcendence" (a
phrase borrowed from Marcuse), where individuals can perceive neither their
own true needs nor another way of life (ibid., pp. 190ff).

## BAUDRILLARD AND NEO-MARXISM

By 1970, Baudrillard had distanced himself from the Marxist theory of revolution and instead postulated only the possibility of revolt against the consumer
society in an "unforeseeable but certain" form. In the late 1960s, Baudrillard had
associated himself with a group of intellectuals around the journal *Utopie*, which
sought to overcome disciplinary boundaries and, in the spirit of the Situationist
International, to combine reflections on alternative societies, architecture, and
modes of everyday life. Bringing together individuals on the margins of architecture, city planning, cultural criticism, and social theory, Baudrillard and his
associates distanced themselves from other political and theoretical groupings
and developed idiosyncratic and marginal discourse beyond the boundaries of
established disciplines and political tendencies. This affiliation with *Utopie* only
lasted into the early 1970s, but it may have helped to produce in Baudrillard a
desire to work on the margins, to stand aside from current trends and fads, and
to develop his own theoretical positions – although, ironically, Baudrillard
became something of a fad himself, especially in the English-speaking world.

Baudrillard thus had an ambivalent relation to classical Marxism by the early
1970s. On one hand, he carried forward the Marxian critique of commodity
production which delineates and criticizes various forms of alienation,

reification, domination, and exploitation produced by capitalism. At this stage, it appeared that his critique came from the standard neo-Marxian vantage point, which assumes that capitalism is blameworthy because it is homogenizing, controlling and dominating social life, while robbing individuals of their freedom, creativity, time, and human potentialities. On the other hand, he could not point to any revolutionary forces and in particular did not discuss the situation and potential of the working class as an agent of change in the consumer society. Indeed, Baudrillard has no theory of the subject as an active agent of social change whatsoever (thus perhaps following the structuralist and poststructuralist critique of the subject popular at the time). Nor does he have a theory of class or group revolt, or any theory of political organization, struggle, or strategy.

Baudrillard's problematic here is particularly close to the work of the Frankfurt School, especially that of Herbert Marcuse, who had already developed some of the first Marxist critiques of the consumer society (see Kellner, 1984, 1989a). Like Lukács (1971) and the Frankfurt School, Baudrillard employs a mode of thought whereby the commodity and commodification become a totalizing social process that permeates social life. Following the general line of critical Marxism, Baudrillard argues that the process of homogenization, alienation, and exploitation constitutes a process of *reification*, in which objects come to dominate subjects, thereby robbing people of their human qualities and capacities. For Lukács, the Frankfurt School, and Baudrillard, reification – the process whereby human beings become dominated by things and become more thinglike themselves – comes to dominate social life.

In a sense, Baudrillard's work can be read as an account of a higher stage of reification and social domination than that described by the Frankfurt School. Baudrillard goes beyond the Frankfurt School by applying the semiological theory of the sign to describe the world of commodities, media, and the consumer society, and in a sense he takes their theory of "one-dimensional society" to a higher level. Eventually, Baudrillard will take his analysis of domination by signs and the system of objects to even more pessimistic conclusions, where he concludes that the problematic of the "end of the individual" sketched by the Frankfurt School has reached its fruition in the total defeat of the subject by the object world (see below). Yet in his early writings, Baudrillard has a somewhat more active theory of consumption than that of the Frankfurt School's, which generally portrays consumption as a passive mode of social integration. By contrast, consumption in Baudrillard's early writings is itself a kind of labor, "an active manipulation of signs," a way of inserting oneself within the consumer society, and working to differentiate oneself from others. Yet this active manipulation of signs is not equivalent to postulating an active subject which could resist, redefine, or produce its own signs. Thus Baudrillard fails to develop a genuine theory of agency.

Baudrillard's first three works can thus be read in the framework of a neo-Marxian critique of capitalist societies. One could read Baudrillard's emphasis on consumption as a supplement to Marx's analysis of production, and his focus on culture and signs as an important supplement to classical Marxian political economy that adds a cultural and semiological dimension to the Marxian project. But in his 1973 provocation, *The Mirror of Production* (translated into English in 1975), Baudrillard carries out a systematic attack on classical Marxism, claiming that Marxism is but a mirror of bourgeois society, placing production at the center of life, and thus naturalizing the capitalist organization of society.

Although Baudrillard participated in the tumultuous events of May 1968, and was associated with the revolutionary left and Marxism, he broke with Marxism in the early 1970s, but remained politically radical, though unaffiliated, for the rest of the decade. Like many on the left, Baudrillard was disappointed that the French Communist Party did not support the radical 1960s movements, and he also distrusted the official Marxism of theorists like Louis Althusser, whom he found dogmatic and reductive. Consequently, Baudrillard began a radical critique of Marxism, one that would be repeated by many of his contemporaries, who would also take a postmodern turn (see Best and Kellner, 1991, 1997).

Baudrillard argues that Marxism, first, does not adequately illuminate premodern societies, which were organized around symbolic exchange and not production. He also argues that Marxism does not radically enough critique capitalist societies, and calls for a more extreme break. At this stage, Baudrillard turns to anthropological perspectives on premodern societies for hints of more emancipatory alternatives. It is important to note that this critique of Marxism was taken from the left, arguing that Marxism did not provide a radical enough critique of, or alternative to, contemporary productivist societies, capitalist and communist. Baudrillard concluded that the French communist failure to support the May 1968 movements was rooted in part in a conservatism that had roots in Marxism itself. Hence, Baudrillard and others of his generation began searching for more radical critical positions.

*The Mirror of Production* and his next book, *Symbolic Exchange and Death* (1976), a major text finally translated in 1993, are attempts to provide ultra-radical perspectives that overcome the limitations of an economistic Marxist tradition. This ultra-leftist phase of Baudrillard's itinerary would be short-lived, however, though in *Symbolic Exchange and Death* Baudrillard produces one of his most important and dramatic provocations. The text opens with a preface that condenses his attempt to provide a significantly different approach to society and culture. Building on Bataille's principle of excess and expenditure, Marcel Mauss's concept of the gift, and Alfred Jarry's pataphysical desire to exterminate meaning, Baudrillard champions "symbolic exchange" and attacks Marx, Freud, and academic semiology and sociology. Baudrillard argues that in Bataille's claim that expenditure and excess are connected with sovereignty, Mauss's descriptions of the social prestige of gift-giving in premodern society, Jarry's theater, and Saussure's anagrams, there is a break with the logic of capitalist exchange and production, or the production of meaning in linguistic exchange. These cases of "symbolic exchange," Baudrillard believes, break with the logic of production and describe excessive and subversive behavior that provides alternatives to the capitalist logic of production and exchange.

The term "symbolic exchange" was derived from Georges Bataille's notion of a "general economy," where expenditure, waste, sacrifice, and destruction were claimed to be more fundamental to human life than economies of production and utility (Bataille, 1988). Bataille's model was the sun which freely expended its energy without asking anything in return. He argued that if individuals wanted to be truly sovereign (i.e. free from the imperatives of capitalism), they should pursue a "general economy" of expenditure, giving, sacrifice, and destruction to escape determination by existing imperatives of utility.

For Bataille, human beings were beings of *excess*, with exorbitant energy, fantasies, drives, needs, and so on. From this point forward, Baudrillard pre-supposes the truth of Bataille's anthropology and general economy. In a 1976 review of a volume of Bataille's *Complete Works*, Baudrillard writes: "The central idea is that the economy which governs our societies results from a misappropriation of the fundamental human principle, which is a solar principle of expenditure" (Baudrillard, 1987, p. 57). In the early 1970s, Baudrillard took over Bataille's anthropological position and what he calls Bataille's "aristocratic critique" of capitalism, which he now claims is grounded in the crass notions of utility and savings, rather than the more sublime "aristocratic" notion of excess and expenditure. Bataille and Baudrillard presuppose here a contradiction between human nature and capitalism. They maintain that humans "by nature" gain pleasure from such things as expenditure, waste, festivities, sacrifices, and so on, in which they are sovereign and free to expend the excesses of their energy (and thus to follow their "real nature"). The capitalist imperatives of labor, utility, and savings by implication are "unnatural," and go against human nature.

Baudrillard argues that the Marxian critique of capitalism, by contrast, merely attacks exchange value, while exalting use value and thus utility, instrumental rationality, and so forth, thereby

> seeking a *good use* of the economy. Marxism is therefore only a limited petit bourgeois critique, one more step in the banalization of life toward the "good use" of the social! Bataille, to the contrary, sweeps away all this slave dialectic from an aristocratic point of view, that of the master struggling with his death. One can accuse this perspective of being pre- or post-Marxist. At any rate, Marxism is only the disenchanted horizon of capital – all that precedes or follows it is more radical than it is. (Baudrillard, 1987, p. 60)

This passage is highly revealing, and marks Baudrillard's switch to an "aristo-cratic critique" of political economy, deeply influenced by Bataille and Nietzsche. For Bataille and Baudrillard are presenting a version of Nietzsche's "aristocratic," "master morality," where value articulates an excess, overflow, and intensifica-tion of life energies. For some time, Baudrillard would continue to attack the bourgeoisie, capital, and political economy, but from a perspective which valor-izes "aristocratic" expenditure and sumptuary, aesthetic and symbolic values. The dark side of his switch in theoretical and political allegiances is a valorization of sacrifice and death which informs *Symbolic Exchange and Death*.

On the whole, in his mid-1970s work, Baudrillard was extricating himself from the familiar Marxian universe of production and class struggle into a quite different neo-aristocratic and metaphysical world view. Baudrillard seems to assume at this point that precapitalist societies were governed by forms of symbolic exchange similar to Bataille's notion of a general economy. Influenced by Mauss's theory of the gift and countergift, Baudrillard claimed that precapitalist societies were governed by laws of symbolic exchange rather than production and utility. Developing these ideas, Baudrillard sketched a fundamental dividing line in history between symbolic societies – i.e. societies fundamentally organized around symbolic exchange – and productivist societies – i.e. societies organized around production. He thus rejects the Marxian philosophy of history, which posits the primacy of production in all societies, and rejects the Marxian concept of socialism, arguing that it does not break radically enough with capitalist productivism, offering itself merely as a more efficient and equitable organization of production rather than as a completely different sort of society, with a different logic, values, and life activities.

## THE POSTMODERN BREAK

Henceforth, Baudrillard would contrast – in one way or another – his ideal of symbolic exchange to the logic of production, utility, and instrumental rationality which governs capitalist (and socialist) societies. "Symbolic exchange" thus emerges as Baudrillard's "revolutionary" alternative to the values and practices of capitalist society, and stands for a variety of heterogeneous activities in his 1970s writings. For instance, he writes in the *Critique*: "The exchange of looks, the present which comes and goes, are like the air people breathe in and out. This is the metabolism of exchange, prodigality, festival – and also of destruction (which returns to non-value what production has erected, valorized). In this domain, value isn't even recognized" (Baudrillard, 1981, p. 207). He also describes his conception of symbolic exchange in *The Mirror of Production*, where he writes: "The symbolic social relation is the uninterrupted cycle of giving and receiving, which, in primitive exchange, includes the consumption of the 'surplus' and deliberate anti-production" (Baudrillard, 1975, p. 143). The term therefore refers to symbolic or cultural activities which do not contribute to capitalist production and accumulation and which therefore constitute the "radical negation" of productivist society.

At this stage of his thought, Baudrillard stood in a classical French tradition of extolling the "primitive" or premodern over the dissected rationalism of modern society. Baudrillard's defense of symbolic exchange over production and instrumental rationality thus stands in the tradition of Rousseau's defense of the "natural savage" over modern man, Durkheim's posing mechanical solidarities of premodern societies against the abstract individualism and anomie of modern ones, Bataille's valorization of expenditure and the "accursed portion" of premodern societies, or Mauss's or Lévi-Strauss's fascination with the richness of "primitive societies" or "the savage mind." But after deconstructing the modern master thinkers and his own theoretical fathers (Marx, Freud, Saussure, and his French contemporaries) for missing the richness of symbolic exchange,

Baudrillard will eventually question this apparent nostalgia for premodern culture and social forms.

In his mid-1970s work, however, Baudrillard posits another divide in history as radical as the rupture between premodern symbolic societies and modern capitalism. In the mode of classical social theory, he systematically develops distinctions between premodern societies organized around symbolic exchange, modern societies organized around production, and postmodern societies organized around simulation. Against the organizing principles of modern and postmodern society, Baudrillard valorizes the logic of symbolic exchange, as an alternative organizing principle of society. Against modern demands to produce value and meaning, Baudrillard calls for their extermination and annihilation, providing, as examples, Mauss's gift-exchange, Saussure's anagrams, and Freud's concept of the death drive. In all of these instances, there is a rupture with the logic of exchange (of goods, meanings, and libidinal energies) and thus an escape from the logic of production, capitalism, rationality, and meaning. Baudrillard's paradoxical logic of symbolic exchange can be explained as the expression of a desire to liberate himself from modern positions and to seek a revolutionary position outside of modern society. Against modern values, Baudrillard advocates their annihilation and extermination.

It should be noted that Baudrillard's distinction between the logic of production and utility that organized modern societies and the logic of simulation that he believes is the organizing principle of postmodern societies postulates a rupture between modern and postmodern societies as great as the divide between modern and premodern ones. In theorizing the epochal postmodern rupture with modernity, Baudrillard declares the "end of political economy" and of an era in which production was the organizing principle of society. Following Marx, Baudrillard argues that this modern epoch was the era of capitalism and the bourgeoisie, in which workers were exploited by capital and provided a revolutionary force of upheaval. Baudrillard, however, declared the end of political economy and thus the end of the Marxist problematic and of modernity itself:

> The end of labor. The end of production. The end of political economy. The end of the signifier/signified dialectic which facilitates the accumulation of knowledge and of meaning, the linear syntagma of cumulative discourse. And at the same time, the end simultaneously of the exchange value/use value dialectic which is the only thing that makes accumulation and social production possible. The end of the linear dimension of discourse. The end of the linear dimension of the commodity. The end of the classical era of the sign. The end of the era of production. (Baudrillard, 1993a, p. 8)

The discourse of "the end" signifies his announcing a postmodern break or rupture in history. We are now, Baudrillard claims, in a new era of simulation, in which social reproduction (information processing, communication, and knowledge industries, and so on) replaces production as the organizing principle of society. In this era, labor is no longer a force of production but is itself a "one *sign* amongst many" (Baudrillard, 1993a, p. 10). Labor is not primarily productive in this situation, but is a sign of one's social position, way of life, and mode of servitude. Wages too bear no rational relation to one's work and what one produces but to one's place within the system (ibid., pp. 19ff). But, crucially, political economy is no longer the foundation, the social determinant, or even a structural "reality" in which other phenomena can be interpreted and explained (ibid., pp. 31ff). Instead, we live in the "hyperreality" of simulations, in which images, spectacles, and the play of signs replace the logic of production and class conflict as key constituents of contemporary societies.

From now on, capital and political economy disappear from Baudrillard's story, or return in radically new forms. Henceforth, signs and codes proliferate and produce other signs and new sign machines in ever-expanding and spiralling cycles. Technology thus replaces capital in this story, and semiurgy, the proliferation of images, information, and signs, replaces production. His postmodern turn is thus connected to a form of technological determinism and a rejection of political economy as a useful explanatory principle – a move that many of his critics reject (see the studies in Kellner, 1994).

*Symbolic Exchange and Death* and the succeeding studies in *Simulation and Simulacra* (1994a) articulate the principle of a fundamental rupture between modern and postmodern societies and mark Baudrillard's departure from the problematic of modern social theory. For Baudrillard, modern societies are organized around the production and consumption of commodities, while postmodern societies are organized around simulation and the play of images and signs, denoting a situation in which codes, models, and signs are the organizing principles of a new social order where simulation rules. In the society of simulation, identities are constructed by the appropriation of images, and codes and models determine how individuals perceive themselves and relate to other people. Economics, politics, social life, and culture are all governed by the logic of simulation, whereby codes and models determine how goods are consumed and used, politics unfold, culture is produced and consumed, and everyday life is lived.

Baudrillard's postmodern world is also one of radical *implosion*, in which social classes, genders, political differences, and once autonomous realms of society and culture collapse into each other, erasing previously defined boundaries and differences. If modern societies, for classical social theory, were characterized by differentiation, for Baudrillard postmodern societies are characterized by dedifferentiation, or implosion. For Baudrillard, in the society of simulation, economics, politics, culture, sexuality, and the social all implode into each other, such that economics is fundamentally shaped by culture, politics, and other spheres, while art, once a sphere of potential difference and opposition, is absorbed into the economic and political, and sexuality is everywhere. In this situation, differences between individuals and groups implode in a rapidly mutating dissolution of the social and the previous boundaries and structures upon which social theory had once focused.

In addition, his postmodern universe is one of *hyperreality*, in which entertainment, information, and communication technologies provide experiences more intense and involving than the scenes of banal everyday life, as well as the codes and models that structure everyday life. The realm of the hyperreal (media simulations of reality, Disneyland and amusement parks, malls and consumer fantasylands, TV sports, and other excursions into ideal worlds) is more real than real, so that the models, images, and codes of the hyperreal come to control thought and behavior. Yet determination itself is aleatory in a nonlinear world where it is impossible to chart causal mechanisms and logic in a situation in which individuals are confronted with an overwhelming flux of images, codes, and models, any of which may shape an individual's thought or behavior.

In this postmodern world, individuals flee from the "desert of the real" for the ecstasies of hyperreality and the new realm of computer, media, and techno-logical experience. In this universe, subjectivities are fragmented and lost, and a new terrain of experience appears, which for Baudrillard renders previous social theories and politics obsolete and irrelevant. Tracing the vicissitudes of the subject in contemporary society, Baudrillard claims that contemporary subjects are no longer afflicted with modern pathologies like hysteria or paranoia, but exist in "a state of terror which is characteristic of the schizophrenic, an over-proximity of all things, a foul promiscuity of all things which beleaguer and penetrate him, meeting with no resistance, and no halo, no aura, not even the aura of his own body protects him. In spite of himself the schizophrenic is open to everything and lives in the most extreme confusion" (Baudrillard, 1988, p. 27). For Baudrillard, the "ecstasy of communication" means that the subject is in close proximity to instantaneous images and information, in an overexposed and transparent world. In this situation, the subject "becomes a pure screen, a pure absorption and resorption surface of the influence networks" (ibid.).

Thus, Baudrillard's categories of simulation, implosion, and hyperreality com-bine to create a new postmodern condition that requires entirely new modes of social theory and politics to chart and respond to the novelties of the contem-porary era. His style and writing strategies are also implosive, combining mater-ial from strikingly different fields, studded with examples from the mass media and popular culture in a new mode of postmodern theory that effaces all disciplinary boundaries. His writing attempts to simulate the new conditions, capturing its novelties through inventive use of language and theory. Such radical questioning of contemporary theory and the need for new theoretical strategies are thus legitimated for Baudrillard by the radicality of changes in the current era.

For instance, Baudrillard claims that modernity operates with a logic of representation in which ideas represent reality and truth, concepts which are key postulates of modern theory. A postmodern society explodes this epistemo-logy by creating a situation in which subjects lose contact with the real and themselves fragment and dissolve. This situation portends the end of modern theory, which operated with a subject–object dialectic in which the subject was supposed to represent and control the object. In the story of modern philosophy, the philosophic subject attempts to discern the nature of reality, to secure grounded knowledge, and to apply this knowledge to control and dominate the object (nature, other people, ideas, and so on). Baudrillard follows here the poststructuralist critique that thought and discourse could no longer be securely anchored in *a priori* or privileged structures. Reacting against the logic of representation in modern theory, French thought, especially some deconstructionists (Rorty's "strong textualists"), moved into the play of textuality, of discourse, which allegedly referred only to other texts or discourses in which "the real" or an "outside" were banished to the realm of nostalgia.

In a similar fashion, Baudrillard, a "strong simulacrist," claims that in the media and consumer society, people are caught up in the play of images, spectacles, and simulacra, which have less and less relationship to an outside, to an external "reality," to such an extent that the very concepts of the social, political, or even "reality" no longer seem to have any meaning. And the narcoticized and mesmerized (some of Baudrillard's metaphors) media-saturated consciousness is in such a state of fascination with image and spectacle that the concept of meaning itself (which depends on stable boundaries, fixed structures, shared consensus) dissolves. In this alarming and novel postmodern situation, the referent, the behind and the outside, along with depth, essence, and reality, all disappear, and with their disappearance, the possibility of all potential opposition vanishes as well. As simulations proliferate, they come to refer only to themselves: a carnival of mirrors reflecting images projected from other mirrors onto the omnipresent television screen and the screen of consciousness, which in turn refers the image to its previous storehouse of images, also produced by simulatory mirrors. Caught up in the universe of simulations, the "masses" are bathed in a media massage without messages or meaning, a mass age where classes disappear, and politics is dead, as are the grand dreams of disalienation, liberation, and revolution.

Baudrillard claims that henceforth the masses seek spectacle and not meaning. They implode into a "silent majority," signifying "the end of the social" (Baudrillard, 1983b). Baudrillard implies that social theory loses its very object as meanings, classes, and difference implode into a "black hole" of non-differentiation. Fixed distinctions between social groupings and ideologies implode and concrete face-to-face social relations recede as individuals disappear in worlds of simulation – media, computers, virtual reality itself. Social theory itself thus loses its object, the social, while radical politics loses its subject and agency.

Nonetheless, he claims, at this point in his trajectory (i.e. the late 1970s and early 1980s), that refusal of meaning and participation by the masses is a form of resistance. Hovering between nostalgia and nihilism, Baudrillard at once exterminates modern ideas (the subject, meaning, truth, reality, society, socialism, and emancipation) and affirms a mode of symbolic exchange which appears to manifest a nostalgic desire to return to premodern cultural forms. This desperate search for a genuinely revolutionary alternative was abandoned, however, by the early 1980s. Henceforth, he develops yet more novel perspectives on the contemporary moment, vacillating between sketching out alternative modes of thought and behavior and renouncing the quest for political and social change.

In a sense, there is a parodic inversion of historical materialism in Baudrillard. In place of Marx's emphasis on political economy and the primacy of the economic, for Baudrillard it is the model, the superstructure, that generates the real in a situation he denominates the "end of political economy" (Baudrillard,

1993a). For Baudrillard, sign values predominate over use values and exchange values; the materiality of needs and commodity use values to serve them disappear in Baudrillard's semiological imaginary, in which signs take precedence over the real and reconstruct human life. Turning the Marxist categories against themselves, masses absorb classes, the subject of praxis is fractured, and objects come to rule human beings. Revolution is absorbed by the object of critique and technological implosion replaces the socialist revolution in producing a rupture in history. For Baudrillard, in contrast to Marx, the catastrophe of modernity and the eruption of postmodernity is produced by the unfolding of technological revolution. Consequently, Baudrillard replaces Marx's hard economic and social determinism, with its emphasis on the economic dimension, class struggle, and human praxis, with a form of semiological idealism and technological determinism where signs and objects come to dominate the subject.

Baudrillard thus concludes that the "catastrophe has happened," that the destruction of modernity and modern theory, which he noted in the mid-1970s, has been completed by the development of capitalist society itself, that modernity has disappeared and a new social situation has taken its place. Against traditional strategies of rebellion and revolution, Baudrillard begins to champion what he calls "fatal strategies" that push the logic of the system to the extreme in the hopes of collapse or reversal, and eventually adopts a style of highly ironic metaphysical discourse that renounces opposition and the discourse and hopes of progressive social transformation.

## From Pataphysics to Metaphysics and the Triumph of the Object

Baudrillard's thought from the mid-1970s to the present revolves in its own theoretical orbit and provides a set of challenging provocations to modern social theory. During the 1980s, Baudrillard's major works of the 1970s were translated into many languages, and each new book of the 1980s was in turn translated into English and other major languages in short order. Consequently, he became world renowned as one of the master thinkers of postmodernity, one of the major avatars of the postmodern turn. Hence, he became something of an academic celebrity, traveling around the world promoting his work and winning a significant following, though more outside the field of academic social theory than within the discipline of sociology.

At the same time that his work was becoming extremely popular, Baudrillard's own writing became increasingly difficult and obscure. In 1979, Baudrillard published *Seduction* (1990), a curious text that represented a major shift in his thought. The book marks a turning away from the more sociological discourse of his earlier works to a more philosophical and literary discourse. Whereas in *Symbolic Exchange and Death* (1993a) he sketches out ultra-revolutionary perspectives as a radical alternative, taking symbolic exchange as his ideal, he now valorizes seduction as his alternative to production and communicative interaction. Seduction, however, does not undermine, subvert, or transform existing social relations or institutions, but is a soft alternative, a play with appearances, and a game with feminism, that provoked a sharp critical response (see Goshorn in Kellner, 1994).

Baudrillard's concept of seduction is idiosyncratic, and involves games with signs, which oppose seduction as an aristocratic "order of sign and ritual" to the bourgeois ideal of production, while valorizing artifice, appearance, play, and challenge against the deadly serious labor of production. Baudrillard interprets seduction primarily as a ritual and game with its own rules, charms, snares, and lures. His writing at this point becomes dedicated to stylized modes of thought and writing, which introduce a new set of categories – reversibility, the challenge, the duel – that move Baudrillard's thought toward a form of aristocratic aestheticism and metaphysics.

Baudrillard's new metaphysical speculations are evident in *Fatal Strategies* (1983, translated in 1990), another turning point in his itinerary. This text presented a bizarre metaphysical scenario concerning the triumph of objects over subjects within the "obscene" proliferation of an object world so completely out of control that it surpasses all attempts to understand, conceptualize, and control it. His scenario concerns the proliferation and growing supremacy of objects over subjects and the eventual triumph of the object. In a discussion of "ecstasy and inertia," Baudrillard discusses how objects and events in contemporary society are continually surpassing themselves, growing and expanding in power. The "ecstasy" of objects is their proliferation and expansion to the Nth degree, to the superlative; ecstasy as going outside of or beyond oneself; the beautiful as more beautiful than beautiful in fashion, the real more real than the real in television, sex more sexual than sex in pornography. Ecstasy is thus the form of obscenity (fully explicit, nothing hidden) and of the hyperreality described by Baudrillard earlier taken to a higher level, redoubled and intensified. His vision of contemporary society exhibits a careening of growth and excrescence (*croissance et excroissance*), expanding and excreting ever more goods, services, information, messages, or demands – surpassing all rational ends and boundaries in a spiral of uncontrolled growth and replication.

Yet growth, acceleration, and proliferation have reached such extremes, Baudrillard suggests, that the ecstasy of excrescence is accompanied by inertia. For as the society is saturated to the limit, it implodes and winds down into entropy. This process presents a catastrophe for the subject, for not only does the acceleration and proliferation of the object world intensify the aleatory dimension of chance and non-determinacy, but the objects themselves take over in a "cool" catastrophe for the exhausted subject, whose fascination with the play of objects turns to apathy, stupefaction, and an entropic inertia.

In retrospect, the growing power of the world of objects over the subject has been Baudrillard's theme from the beginning, thus pointing to an underlying continuity in his project. In his early writings, he explored the ways that commodities were fascinating individuals in the consumer society and the ways that the world of goods was assuming new and more value through the agency of sign value and the code – which were part of the world of things, the system of objects. His polemics against Marxism were fueled by the belief that sign value and the code were more fundamental than such traditional elements of political economy as exchange value, use value, production, and so on in constituting contemporary society. Then, reflections on the media entered the forefront of his thought: the TV object was at the center of the home in Baudrillard's earlier thinking and the media, simulations, hyperreality, and implosion eventually came to obliterate distinctions between private and public, inside and outside, media and reality. Henceforth, everything was public, transparent, ecstatic and hyperreal in the object world, which was gaining in fascination and seductiveness as the years went by.

So ultimately the subject, the darling of modern philosophy, is defeated in Baudrillard's metaphysical scenario and the object triumphs, a stunning end to the dialectic of subject and object which had been the framework of modern philosophy. The object is thus the subject's fatality and Baudrillard's "fatal strategies" project an obscure call to submit to the strategies and ruses of objects. In "banal strategies," "the subject believes itself to always be more clever than the object, whereas in the other [fatal strategies] the object is always supposed to be more shrewd, more cynical, more brilliant than the subject" (Baudrillard, 1983, pp. 259–60). Previously, in banal strategies, the subject believed itself to be more masterful and sovereign than the object. A fatal strategy, by contrast, recognizes the supremacy of the object and therefore takes the side of the object and surrenders to its strategies, ruses, and rules.

In *The Fatal Strategies* and succeeding writings, Baudrillard seems to be taking social theory into the realm of metaphysics, but it is a specific type of metaphysics, deeply inspired by the pataphysics developed by Alfred Jarry. For Jarry:

> pataphysics is the science of the realm beyond metaphysics.... It will study the laws which govern exceptions and will explain the universe supplementary to this one; or, less ambitiously, it will describe a universe which one can see – must see perhaps – instead of the traditional one.
>
> Definition: pataphysics is the science of imaginary solutions, which symbolically attributes the properties of objects, described by their virtuality, to their lineaments. (Jarry, 1967, p. 131)

Like the universe in Jarry's *Ubu Roi, The Gestures and Opinions of Doctor Faustroll,* and other literary texts – as well as in Jarry's more theoretical explications of pataphysics – Baudrillard's is a totally absurd universe where objects rule in mysterious ways, and people and events are governed by absurd and ultimately unknowable interconnections and predestination (the French playwright Eugene Ionesco is another good source of entry to this universe). Like Jarry's pataphysics, Baudrillard's universe is ruled by surprise, reversal, hallucination, blasphemy, obscenity, and a desire to shock and outrage.

Thus, in view of the growing supremacy of the object, Baudrillard wants us to abandon the subject and to side with the object. Pataphysics aside, it seems that Baudrillard is trying to end the philosophy of subjectivity that has controlled French thought since Descartes by going over completely to the other side. Descartes's *malin genie,* his evil genius, was a ruse of the subject which tried to seduce him into accepting what was not clear and distinct, but over which he was ultimately able to prevail. Baudrillard's "evil genius" is the object itself which is much more malign than the merely epistemological deceptions of the subject faced by Descartes and which constitutes a fatal destiny that demands the end of the philosophy of subjectivity. Henceforth, for Baudrillard, we live in the era of the reign of the object.

## INTO THE 1990S

In the 1980s, Baudrillard posited an "immanent reversal," a reversal of direction and meaning, in which things turn into their opposite. Thus, the society of production was passing over to simulation and seduction; the panoptic and repressive power theorized by Foucault was turning into a cynical and seductive power; the liberation championed in the 1960s was becoming a form of voluntary servitude; sovereignty had passed from the side of the subject to the object; and revolution and emancipation had turned into their opposites, snaring one more and more in the logic of the system, thus trapping individuals in an order of simulation and virtuality. His concept of "immanent reversal" thus provides a perverse form of Horkheimer and Adorno's (1972) dialectic of Enlightenment, where everything becomes its opposite – where Enlightenment becomes domination, where culture becomes culture industry, where democracy becomes a form of mass manipulation, and science and technology become part of an apparatus of domination.

Baudrillard follows this logic and a perverse and nihilistic metaphysics based on this vision into the 1990s, where his thought becomes ever more hermetic, metaphysical, and cynical. During the decade, Baudrillard continued playing the role of academic and media superstar, traveling around the world lecturing and performing in intellectual events. Some of his experiences are captured in the travelogue *America* (1988) and the collections of aphorisms *Cool Memories* (1990a) and *Cool Memories II* (1996a), which combine reflections on his travels and experiences with development of his ideas and perceptions. Retiring from the University of Nanterre in 1987, Baudrillard has subsequently functioned as an independent intellectual, dedicating himself to caustic reflections on our contemporary moment.

During the 1990s, Baudrillard published *The Transparency of Evil* (1993b), *The Gulf War Did Not Take Place* (1995), *The Illusion of the End* (1994b), and *The Perfect Crime* (1996), which continue his excursions into the metaphysics of the object and defeat of the subject. Bringing together reflections which develop his ideas and/or comment on contemporary events, the books continue to postulate a break within history in the space of a postmodern *coupure*, though Baudrillard himself usually distances himself from other versions of postmodern theory.[2]

The 1990s texts continue the fragmentary style and use of short essays, aphorisms, stories, and *aperçus* that Baudrillard began deploying in the 1980s, and often repeat some of the same ideas and stories. They contain few new ideas or perspectives, but are often entertaining, although they can be outrageous and scandalous. These writings can be read as a continual commentary on current social conditions, along with a running dialogue with Marxism and poststructuralist theory. Yet after his fierce polemics of the 1970s against competing models of thought, Baudrillard's dialogue with theory now consists mostly of occasional asides, and his mode of analysis consists of ruminating on contemporary events and trends.

Baudrillard develops in these works "theory fiction," or what he also calls "simulation theory" and "anticipatory theory," to simulate, grasp, and anticipate historical events which he believes outrun all contemporary theory. The current situation, he claims, is more fantastic than the most fanciful science fiction, or theoretical projections of a futurist society. Thus, theory can only attempt to grasp the present on the run and try to anticipate the future. However, Baudrillard has had a particularly poor record as a social and political analyst and forecaster. As a political analyst, he has often been superficial and off the mark. In the essay "Anorexic Ruins," published in 1989, he read the Berlin Wall as a sign of a frozen history, of an anorexic history, in which nothing more can happen, marked by a "lack of events" and the end of history, taking the Berlin Wall as a sign of a stasis between communism and capitalism. Shortly thereafter, rather significant events destroyed the wall that Baudrillard took as eternal and opened up a new historical era.

The Cold War stalemate was long taken by Baudrillard as establishing a frozen history in which no significant change could take place. In his mid-1970s reflections, he presented the Vietnam War as an "alibi" to incorporate China, Russia, and eventually Vietnam into a more rationalized and modernized world economic and political order (Baudrillard, 1983a, pp. 66ff), and in his book on the Gulf War he repeats this claim (Baudrillard, 1995, p. 85), thus failing to see the actual political stakes and reasons for the Vietnam War, as well as the significance of the struggles between capitalist and communist powers. On the whole, Baudrillard sees history as the unfolding of expanding technological rationality, turning into its opposite, as the system incorporates ever more elements, producing an improved technological order, which then becomes irrational through its excesses, its illusions, and its generation of unforeseen consequences. This mode of highly abstract analysis, however, occludes more specific historical determinants that would analyze how technological rationality is constructed and functions and how and why it misfires. It also covers over the disorder and turmoil created by such things as the crises and restructuring of global capitalism, the rise of fundamentalism and ethnic conflict unleashed in part as a response to rationalization and to the breakup of the bipolar world order, or to the passions of identity politics.

Baudrillard's reflections on the Gulf War take a similar position, seeing it as an attempt of the New World Order to further rationalize the world, arguing that the Gulf War really served to bring Islam into the New World Order (Baudrillard, 1995, p. 19). The first study, titled "The Gulf War Will Not Take Place," was initially published a few days before the actual outbreak of military hostilities, and repeats his earlier concept of "weak events" and frozen history. *Pace*

Baudrillard, the war took place, but this did not deter him from publishing studies claiming during the war that it was not "really taking place" and after the war asserting that it "did not take place." Although I have also argued that the "Gulf War" was a media spectacle and not a genuine war (see Kellner, 1992), Baudrillard does not help us to understand much about the event and does not even help us to grasp the role of the media in contemporary political spectacles. Reducing complex events like wars to categories like simulation or hyperreality illuminates the virtual and high-tech dimension to media events, but erases all their concrete determinants. Yet Baudrillardian postmodern categories help us to grasp some of the dynamics of the culture of living in media and computer worlds, where people seem to enjoy immersing themselves in simulated events (witness the fascination of the Gulf War in 1991, the O. J. Simpson trials during 1994–6, the Clinton sex scandals, and various other media spectacles throughout the 1990s, analyzed in Best and Kellner, forthcoming).

In *The Illusion of the End* (1994b), Baudrillard attacks head-on what he sees as current illusions of history, politics, and metaphysics, and gamely tries to explain away his own political misprognoses that we were in a frozen, glacial history stalemated between East and West, that the system of deterrence had frozen history making sure that nothing dramatic could henceforth happen, that the Gulf War couldn't take place, and that we were at the end of history. Baudrillard unleashes his full bag of rhetorical tricks and philosophical analysis to attempt to maintain these hypotheses in the face of the dramatic events of 1989–91, which he claims are in fact "weak events"; events are still on strike, history has indeed disappeared. He continues to argue that we have reached the end of modernity, with its political conflicts and upheavals, its innovations and revolutions, its autonomous and creative subject, and its myths of progress, democracy, Enlightenment, and the like. These myths, these strong ideas, are exhausted, he claims, and henceforth we have a postmodern era in which banal eclecticism, inertial implosion, and eternal recycling of the same become defining features.

In particular, with the collapse of communism, the era of strong ideas, of a conflicted world, of revolution and universal emancipation is over. Communism, in Baudrillard's reading, collapsed of its own inertia, it self-destructed from within, it imploded, rather than perishing in ideological battle or military warfare. With the absorption of its dissidents into power, there is no longer a clash of strong ideas, of opposition and resistance, of critical transcendence. With the embedding of the former communist regimes into the system of the capitalist world market and liberal democracy, the West no longer has an other to battle against, there is no longer any creative or ideological tension, no longer an other or alternative to the Western world.

In general, in Baudrillard's 1990s musings, the postmodern condition is one of absorbing otherness, of erasing difference, of assimilating and imploding all oppositional or negative forces into a viral positivity, in which the positive radiates throughout every interstice of society and culture, irradiating into nullity any negativity, opposition, or difference. It is also an era in which reality itself has disappeared, constituting the "perfect crime" which is the subject of a book of that title (Baudrillard, 1996b). Baudrillard presents himself here as a detective searching for the perpetrator of the "perfect crime," the murder of reality, "the most important event of modern history." His theme is the destruction and disappearance of the real in the realm of information and simulacra, and the subsequent reign of illusion and appearance. In a Nietzschean mode, he suggests that henceforth truth and reality are illusions, that illusions reign, and that therefore we should respect illusion and appearance and give up the illusory quest for truth and reality.

## Concluding Reflections

Baudrillard has never been as influential in France as in the English-speaking world and elsewhere. He is an example of the "global popular," a thinker who has followers and readers throughout the world, though, so far, no Baudrillardian school has emerged. His influence has been largely at the margins of a diverse number of disciplines ranging from social theory to philosophy to art history, and thus it is difficult to gauge his impact on the mainstream of social theory, or any specific academic discipline. He is perhaps most important as part of the postmodern turn against modern society and its academic disciplines. Baudrillard's work cuts across the disciplines and promotes cross-disciplinary thought. He challenges standard wisdom and puts in question received dogma and methods. While his early work on the consumer society, the political economy of the sign, simulation and simulacra, and the implosion of phenomena previously separated can be deployed within critical social theory, much of his post-1980s work quite self-consciously goes beyond the classical tradition and in most interviews of the past decade Baudrillard distances himself from critical social theory, claiming that the energy of critique has dissipated.

Baudrillard thus emerges in retrospect as a transdisciplinary theorist of the fin-de-millennium who produces signposts to the new era of postmodernity and is an important, albeit hardly trustworthy, guide to the new era. In my view, Baudrillard exaggerates the break between the modern and the postmodern, takes future possibilities as existing realities, and provides a futuristic perspective on the present, much like the tradition of dystopic science fiction, ranging from Huxley to cyberpunk. Indeed, I prefer to read Baudrillard's post-1970s work as science fiction which anticipates the future by exaggerating present tendencies, and thus provides early warnings about what might happen if present trends continue. It is not an accident that Baudrillard is an aficionado of science fiction, who has himself influenced a large number of contemporary science fiction writers.

However, in view of his exaggeration of the alleged break with modernity, discerning whether Baudrillard's most recent work is best read as science fiction or social theory is difficult. Baudrillard obviously wants to have it both ways, with social theorists thinking that he provides salient perspectives on contemporary social realities, that Baudrillard reveals what is really happening, that he tells it like it is. Yet more cynical anti-sociologists are encouraged to enjoy

Baudrillard's fictions, his experimental discourse, his games, and play. Likewise, he sometimes encourages cultural metaphysicians to read his work as serious reflections on the realities of our time, while winking a pataphysical aside at those skeptical of such undertakings. Thus, it is undecidable whether Baudrillard is best read as science fiction and pataphysics, or as social theory and cultural metaphysics, and whether his post-1970s work should be read under the sign of truth or fiction.

In retrospect, Baudrillard's early critical explorations of the system of objects and consumer society contain some of his most important contributions to contemporary social theory. His mid-1970s analysis of a dramatic mutation occurring within contemporary societies and the rise of a new logic of simulation which sketched out the effects of media and information on society as a whole is also original and important. But at this stage of his work, Baudrillard falls prey to a technological determinism and semiological idealism, which posits an autonomous technology and play of signs, generating a society of simulation which creates a postmodern break and the proliferation of signs, spectacles, and simulacra. Baudrillard erases autonomous and differentiated spheres of the economy, polity, society, and culture posited by classical social theory, in favor of an implosive theory that also crosses disciplinary boundaries, thus dissolving social theory into a broader form of social critique.

In the final analysis, Baudrillard is perhaps more useful as a provocateur who challenges and puts in question the tradition of classical social theory than as someone who provides concepts and methods that can be applied in social or cultural analysis. He claims that the object of classical theory – modernity – has been surpassed by a new postmodernity and that therefore new theoretical strategies, modes of writing, and forms of theory are necessary. While his work on simulation and the postmodern break from the mid-1970s into the 1980s provides a paradigmatic postmodern theory and analysis of postmodernity that has been highly influential, and that despite its exaggerations continues to be of use in interpreting present social trends, his later work is arguably of more literary and philosophical than sociological interest. Baudrillard thus ultimately goes beyond social theory altogether, into a new sphere and mode of writing that provides occasional insights into contemporary social phenomena and provocative critiques of contemporary and classical social theory, but does not really provide an adequate theory of the present age.

## Notes

1  For my earlier takes on Baudrillard, see Kellner (1989b, 1994, 1995, chapter 8) and Best and Kellner (1991, 1997, chapter 3). Other books on Baudrillard include Frankovits (1984), Gane (1991, 1993), Stearns and Chaloupka (1992), Rojek and Turner (1993), and Genosko (1994).

2  To those who would deny that Baudrillard is a postmodern theorist and has nothing to do with the discourse of the postmodern (e.g. Gane, 1991, 1993), one might note the positive uses of the concept of the postmodern in his most recent books (Baudrillard, 1994b, pp. 23, 27, 31, 34, 36, 107, passim; 1996a, pp. 36, 70, passim). *The*

*Perfect Crime* (Baudrillard, 1996b) does not use the discourse of the postmodern *per se*, but makes ample use of his classic categories of simulation, hyperreality, and implosion to elucidate a new virtual order opposed to the previous order of reality, the murder of which is "the perfect crime" (ibid., pp. 16, 83, 125, 128, passim).

## Bibliography

### Writings of Jean Baudrillard

*The System of Objects*. 1968. London: Verso (1996c).
*The Consumer Society*. 1970. Paris: Gallimard (1998).
*The Mirror of Production*. 1975. St Louis: Telos Press.
*For a Critique of the Political Economy of the Sign*. 1973 St. Louis: Telos Press (1981).
*Simulations*. 1983a. New York: Semiotext(e).
*In the Shadow of the Silent Majorities*. 1983b. New York: Semiotext(e).
The Ecstacy of Communication. 1983c. In Hal Foster (ed.), *The Anti-Aesthetic*. Washington, DC: Bay Press.
When Bataille Attacked the Metaphysical Principle of Economy. *Canadian Journal of Political and Social Theory*, 11(3), 57–62.
*America*. 1988. London: Verso.
*Cool Memories*. 1990a. London: Verso.
*Fatal Strategies*. 1990b. New York: Semiotext(e).
*Symbolic Exchange and Death*. 1993a. London: Sage.
*The Transparency of Evil*. 1993b. London: Verso.
*Simulacra and Simulation*. 1994a. Ann Arbor: University of Michigan Press.
*The Illusion of the End*. 1994b. Oxford: Polity Press.
*The Gulf War Never Happened*. 1995. Oxford: Polity Press.
*Cool Memories II*. 1996a. Oxford: Polity Press.
*The Perfect Crime*. 1996b. London and New York: Verso Books.

### Further Reading

Barthes, Roland (1967) *Elements of Semiology*. London: Jonathan Cape.
Barthes, Roland (1972) *Mythologies*. New York: Hill and Wang.
Barthes, Roland (1983) *The Fashion System*. New York: Hill and Wang.
Bataille, Georges (1988) *The Accursed Share*. New York: Zone Books.
Best, Steven, and Kellner, Douglas (1991) *Postmodern Theory: Critical Interrogations*. London and New York: Macmillan Press and Guilford Press.
Best, Steven, and Kellner, Douglas (1997) *The Postmodern Turn*. New York: Guilford Press.
Best, Steven, and Kellner, Douglas (forthcoming) *The Postmodern Adventure*. New York: Guilford Press.
Debord, Guy (1970) *The Society of the Spectacle*. Detroit: Black and Red.
Frankovits, Alan (ed.) (1984) *Seduced and Abandoned: the Baudrillard Scene*. Glebe, New South Wales: Stonemoss.
Gane, Mike (1991) *Baudrillard. Critical and Fatal Theory*. London: Routledge.
Gane, Mike (ed.) (1993) *Baudrillard Live. Selected Interviews*. London: Routledge.
Genosko, Gary (1994) *Baudrillard and Signs*. London: Routledge.
Horkheimer, Max and Adorno, Theodor (1972) *Dialectic of Enlightenment*. New York: Herder and Herder.

Jarry, Alfred (1963) What Is Pataphysics? *Evergreen Review*, 13, 131–51.

Kellner, Douglas (1984) *Herbert Marcuse and the Crisis of Marxism*. Berkeley: University of California Press.

Kellner, Douglas (1989) *Jean Baudrillard: from Marxism to Postmodernism and Beyond*. Cambridge and Palo Alto, CA: Polity Press and Stanford University Press.

Kellner, Douglas (1992) *The Persian Gulf TV War*. Boulder, CO: Westview Press.

Kellner, Douglas (ed.) (1994) *Jean Baudrillard. A Critical Reader*. Oxford: Basil Blackwell.

Kellner, Douglas (1995) *Media Culture. Cultural Studies, Identity and Politics between the Modern and the Postmodern*. London: Routledge.

Lefebvre, Henri (1971) *Everyday Life in the Modern World*. New Brunswick, NJ: Transaction Books.

Lefebvre, Henri (1991) *Critique of Everyday Life*. London: Verso.

Lukács, Georg (1971) *History and Class Consciousness*. Cambridge, MA: MIT Press.

Pefanis, Julian (1991) *Hetrology and the Postmodern: Bataille, Baudrillard, and Lyotard*, Durham, NC: Duke University Press.

Rojek, Chris and Turner, Bryan (eds) (1993) *Forget Baudrillard*. London: Routledge.

Stearns, William and William Chaloupka (eds) (1992) *The Disappearence of Art and Politics*. New York and London: St Martins Press and Macmillan Press.

# 25

# Judith Butler

## PATRICIA T. CLOUGH

Among feminist philosophers, Judith Butler is distinguished for her treatment of the body, her criticism of the social construction of gender, and her contribution to the development of "queer theory." While Butler's first book, *Subjects of Desire: Hegelian Reflections in Twentieth-century France* (1987), focuses on the criticism of Hegelian philosophy elaborated in the writings of Jacques Derrida, Michel Foucault, Jacques Lacan, and Gilles Deleuze, it was not until the publication of *Gender Trouble: Feminism and the Subversion of Identity* (1990) that Butler's work became central to the heated debates over poststructuralism which characterized intellectual and academic discourses in the last decades of the twentieth century. Butler's poststructural rereadings of feminist theory and psychoanalytic theory – aimed at exposing the presumption of heterosexuality in modern Western philosophy – made *Gender Trouble* an often referred to text. With the publication of *Bodies that Matter: on the Discursive Limits of "Sex"* (1993), Butler became one of the most recognized feminist philosophers of the late twentieth century.

## THE WORK

### Gender, bodies and the matrix of heterosexual desire

Butler's treatment of the sexed body begins as a criticism of the feminist theory of gender. As Butler sees it, the feminist treatment of gender as a social construction of sex leaves sex to the realm of unintelligible nature and, therefore, fails to question how the sexed body is constituted as such. So, Butler asks "what are the constraints by which bodies are materialized as 'sexed,' and how are we to understand the matter of sex and of bodies more generally..." (Butler, 1993,

p. xi). Social constructionism does not offer answers to these questions because social constructionism, Butler argues, typically has not focused on the "process of materialization that stabilizes over time to produce the effect of boundary fixity and surface we call matter" (ibid., p. xi). While Butler's reconsideration of social constructionism begins with a criticism of the feminist theory of gender, her treatment of bodily matter has larger implications for philosophy and social theory.

Butler's treatment of bodily matter is part of the deconstruction of the Subject. It is a rethinking of the way the Subject is figured in modern Western philosophy, especially its Hegelian tradition. In *Subjects of Desire* (1987), Butler rereads Hegelian philosophy through the writings of Derrida, Lacan, Foucault, and Deleuze. She argues that in Hegelian philosophy, the Subject is figured as the origin of thought as well as its end, so that the truth of thought can only be reached in the Subject's final realization of a full self-consciousness of itself. Because Hegelian philosophy makes the Subject a projective figure of coherency, a matter of a unified self-same identity, it also prescribes the Subject's bodily form and thereby excludes different bodily figures or different embodiments of thought. Only some bodies are allowed to matter. Only some bodies are culturally intelligible, and the cultural intelligibility of bodies depends on the exclusion of other bodies, making them unthinkable, abject, even unliveable.

Butler aims to make this exclusion visible and to give philosophical grounds for the possibility of other bodies. She begins by uncovering what she describes as "the regulatory norm of cultural intelligibility," which constitutes bodily matter. She argues that the regulatory norm of cultural intelligibility given in modern Western philosophy is the norm of sexual difference elaborated within a "matrix of heterosexual desire." This norm operates both in the engendering of subject identity and in making gendered subject identity a bodily matter in which there is coherency and continuity among sexual practice, gender, and desire. In other words, the norm of sexual difference within the matrix of heterosexual desire allows for subject identities with only this body with only this desire with only this sexual practice. What are not permitted to "exist," as Butler puts it, are subject identities "in which gender does not follow from sex and those in which the practices of desire do not 'follow' from either sex or gender" (Butler, 1990, p. 17).

In contrast to the treatment of gender as the social construction of sex, Butler argues that gender identities cannot presuppose sexed bodies; sexed bodies and gender identities are constructed at the same time. Genders and sexualities refer to the prior norm of sexual difference in the matrix of heterosexual desire. Butler even argues that the regulatory norm of cultural intelligibility is not only about genders and sexualities. In constituting the cultural intelligibility of bodies, the cultural norm of sexual difference also grounds what is conventionally understood as social reality, personhood, and self-identity.

To treat the historical specificity of the regulatory norm of sexual difference within the matrix of heterosexual desire, Butler makes use of Foucault's genealogical analysis of regimes of sexuality. She draws specifically on Foucault's treatment of the modern regime of sexuality, which, he argues, comes to characterize European society by the end of the eighteenth century, when the incest taboo is articulated in terms of the oedipal crisis, elaborated, most notably, by Sigmund Freud. In *The History of Sexuality* (1980), Foucault argues that Freud's elaboration of oedipality allows for the interpenetration of "the deployment of alliance" and "the deployment of sexuality."

The deployment of alliance, which orders sexual relations before the end of the eighteenth century, refers to the transmission or circulation of wealth in terms of a regulation of licit and illicit sexual partners. By the eighteenth century, the deployment of alliance begins to lose ground to the deployment of sexuality, without, however, the former ever being entirely supplanted by the latter. The deployment of sexuality shifts the regulation of sexual relations to the quality of sensations and pleasures, the control and disciplining of bodies, making the nuclear family central to the operation of the deployment of sexuality. According to Foucault, by the nineteenth century, the family has become the site at which alliance and sexuality are interfaced. The family is where the oedipalization of the incest taboo infuses alliance with sexuality; in the family, Foucault (1980, p. 109) argues, incest "is constantly being solicited and refused . . . an object of obsession and attraction, a dreadful secret and an indispensible pivot."

Drawing on Foucault allows Butler to argue that in the modern regime of sexuality, the oedipal law (of the father or the phallus or *le nom du père*) precedes the constitution of sexed bodies, offering a historically specific regulatory norm of cultural intelligibility. In other words, while the oedipal law is a juridical law, it also is generative as a regulatory ideal or norm. Oedipus generates the desires and the desiring bodies that as law it would seem to forbid. To put this in the deconstructive terms of Butler's criticism of modern Western philosophy, oedipus produces both culturally intelligible subject identities and unintelligible ones; furthermore, the latter are an exclusion constituting the intelligibility of the former. Bodies that are intelligible come to matter in the exclusion of ones which are made unintelligible, abject, and unliveable. As such, oedipus is an agency of power/knowledge which accrues power to itself as law even in the failure of lawfulness; that is, in the constitution of unintelligible bodies. As Butler puts it, echoing Foucault, "desire is manufactured and forbidden as a ritual symbolic gesture whereby the juridical model exercises and consolidates its own power" (Butler, 1990, p. 76).

Yet Butler wants to get closer than Foucault does to the process of engendering subject identity through which individuals also become sexed bodies. To do so, Butler returns to psychoanalysis through Lacan's rereading of Freud. What Lacan offers Butler is an understanding of the compulsion to repeat in unconscious fantasy; she will argue that it is through fantasy that the sexed body materializes along with the construction of a subject identity. It is in the notion of unconscious repetition that Butler also finds a possibility for resistance to the cultural norm of intelligibility – a possibility which Foucault does not offer. But, if Butler returns to psychoanalysis, it is not to forget Foucault. Although she argues that subject identity and the body are materializations or surfaces of unconscious desire in a "phantasmatic field," Butler also argues that it is the historically specific regime of modern sexuality which first makes "the phantasmatic field . . . the very terrain of cultural intelligibility" (Butler, 1993, p. 6).

In returning to psychoanalysis, Butler recognizes that Lacan's rereading of Freud also makes it apparent that the oedipal law of the phallus is not only juridical but also generative. For Lacan, this is because oedipus always fails. As Lacan explains it, with the imposition of the law of the phallus and the initiation of the oedipal crisis, the infant-child is subjected to the symbolic order. Specifically, the infant-child is commanded to give up pre-oedipal attachments and is commanded to do so by fully accepting either a feminine or masculine identity according to the norm of sexual difference and under the threat of castration. But Lacan also suggests that the imposition of the oedipal law of the phallus occurs when the infant-child already has initiated unconscious fantasizing, productive of an imaginary in which lost objects, such as the nourishing milk, have been displaced with fantasmatic objects, such as the mothers's breast or the mother herself, to which the infant's attachment has become passionate or erotic. Borrowing Wendy Brown's terms, Butler argues that it is these pre-oedipal "passionate attachments" which the infant-child elaborates in post-oedipal unconscious fantasy (Butler, 1997a, pp. 6–10).

That is to say, although pre-oedipal unconscious fantasy must be brought into line with the oedipal law of the phallus, post-oedipal unconscious fantasy seems rather to serve in producing a seeming conformity while allowing the refusal of complete adherence to oedipus. Indeed, Lacan suggests that the post-oedipal structure of the individual's unconscious resists oedipus in a fantasmatic elaboration of bisexuality: either there is an unconscious refusal to identify with only masculinity or femininity or there is an unconscious refusal of sexual difference altogether in fantasized hypermasculinity or hyperfemininity. Because oedipus carries with it the threat of castration, the post-oedipal fantasmatic elaboration of bisexuality is as well an elaboration of a denial of castration. So, the fantasmatic resistance to oedipus is a fantasmatic appropriation of phallicity or the phallic embodiment of a unified subject identity.

What makes Lacan's rereading of Freud so important is that it proposes that the subject's identity is only seemingly unified, only seemingly the same as, or one with, the subject's intentionality or conscious self. Even more importantly, the seeming unity of subject identity is itself a production of unconscious fantasy. It is because Lacan's rereading of Freud deeply troubles the notion of a unified subject identity that it has been so important to feminist theorists. In Lacan's rereading of Freud, feminist theorists have seen the possiblity of women's resistance to the feminine identity imposed with oedipus. As Jacqueline Rose (1986, pp. 90–1) has put it, "The unconscious constantly reveals the 'failure' of identity. Because there is no continuity of psychic life, so there is no stability of sexual identity, no position for women (or for men) which is ever simply achieved. . . . Instead . . . there is a resistance to identity at the very heart of psychic life."

Butler draws on various feminist treatments of Lacanian psychoanalysis, such as Rose's, in order to explore how the body is sexed – how the body is "at once a compensatory fantasy and a fetishistic mask" (Butler, 1993, p. 65). But Butler not only shows how the oedipal law of the phallus is a deployment of the norm of sexual difference. She also shows that it is a deployment of a compulsory heterosexuality. Beyond the feminist revision of Lacanian psychoanalysis, Butler shows that the norm of sexual difference is heterosexist.

Butler's argument is that the law of oedipus imposes sexual difference not only by prohibiting an incestuous heterosexual object choice – the mother for the boy and the father for the girl. But, along with this prohibition, let us say even prior to it, there also is a prohibition of the homosexual object choice – for the girl, the mother, and for the boy, the father. As Butler sees it, the loss of the homosexual incestuous object, unlike the loss of the heterosexual incestuous object, is denied completely; what Butler calls "the modality of desire," or what Freud refers to as "the sexual aim," also is denied. For example, in the case of the boy, not only is the father tabooed as an object choice, but the sexual aim or the act toward which the sexual aim tends also is tabooed. Given the norm of sexual difference, the tabooed aim is even figured as feminine; that is, treated as what a male should not desire to do because it is what a female desires to do. Because the losses of the homosexual object and aim are denied, they cannot be grieved and, therefore, cannot be internalized.

Rather than grieved, the loss, Butler argues, is "melancholically incorporated" and thereby kept alive in and as part of the one who cannot grieve. There is an "encrypting" of the loss in the body. It is as if "the body is inhabited or possessed by phantasms of various kinds" (Butler, 1990, p. 68). In the case of the boy, the father and the desire for the father are kept living in deadening the loss onto the infant-child's body, which is thereby made male. The infant-child's body becomes a male body by means of a melancholic incorporation. As Butler puts it, "incorporation literalizes the loss on or in the body and so appears as the facticity of the body, the means by which the body comes to bear 'sex' as its literal truth" (ibid., p. 71).

It is in terms of an oedipalized compulsory heterosexuality that Butler argues that the sexed body is the effect of a fantasmatic melancholic incorporation. The matter of the body is the effect of a literalizing fantasy: "the belief that it is parts of the body, the 'literal penis,' the 'literal vagina,' which cause pleasure and desire – is precisely the kind of literalizing fantasy characteristic of the syndrome of melancholic heterosexuality" (ibid.). The fantasmatic matter of the body even gives the "inside" (of the body) from which "true" or "real" sexuality is imagined to emanate. Butler suggests that through the fantasmatic constitution of the body the interiority of the subject is made from the outside. Or to put it in a more precise way, the fantasmatic constitution of the body makes it a surface of receptivity for all further projected images of socializing instruments and institutions, even though these images will seem to be internal to subjectivity or to come from "inside" the body. This is what Butler argues in *The Psychic Life of Power: Theories in Subjection*, when she proposes that the "melancholic turn" not only constitutes the sexed body. It also constitutes the ego, thereby initiating "a variable boundary between the psychic and the social, a boundary...that distributes and regulates the psychic sphere in relationship to prevailing norms of social regulations" (Butler, 1997a, p. 171).

In treating the interimplication of the psychic sphere and norms of social regulation, Butler not only employs Lacanian psychoanalysis; she also means to give a feminist turn to it by undoing the privilege afforded the phallus in Lacanian psychoanalysis. She rereads Lacan's account of the mirror stage into her treatment of the body as a fantasmatic construction or an "imaginary morphe." Because Lacan argues that the body's unity depends at first on an imaginary projection onto a reflective surface, Butler recognizes that Lacan's rereading of Freud "establishes the morphology of the body as a psychically invested projection" (Butler, 1993, p. 73). But Lacan also argues that the infant-child's subjection to the symbolic order is brought on with oedipus, when finally the pre-oedipal imaginary is subjected to the symbolic and the distinction between "having" the phallus (marked as masculine) and "being" the phallus for the other (marked as feminine) is enforced. Using Lacan's own argument against itself, Butler shows that as transcendental signifier, the phallus is itself an imaginary construct; it presupposes a psychic investment in the penis.

In one of her best known essays, Butler offers "the lesbian phallus" as a figural refusal of the distinction of being and having the phallus, thereby undermining the Lacanian notion of the phallus as the transcendental signifier of the oedipal law. Butler shows the phallus itself to be an imaginary projection or something more like an ideological construct constituted in a regulatory norm of cultural intelligibility. So, Butler treats the oedipal law of the phallus not as a universal law bearing a transcendental signifier of subject identity but as a historically and geopolitically specific ideological narrative of subject identity. Without simply denying oedipus, Butler unmasks its posture as bearer of the transcendental signifier of a universal law.

By reducing oedipus to a norm of cultural intelligibility, Butler undermines the dominance which oedipus obtains in its transcendental and universal posture. In doing so, Butler opens thought to other regulatory psychobiographic forms of the cultural norm of intelligibility – not only those that exist in different cultures at different times, but also those that might come to be in the future. Butler's work is especially aimed at a futurity where subject identity is not dependent on the abjection of others, such as is the case of the norm of sexual difference in the matrix of heterosexual desire.

In all this, Butler means to save the psyche not only from the heterosexism of psychoanalysis but also from the insensitivity to sexual difference in Foucault's genealogy of the regime of modern sexuality. Butler proposes that, while Foucault argues that bodies are materialized according to the regulatory norm of oedipus, he does not explore how oedipus specifies what Butler describes as "modalities of materialization" in terms of sexual difference; he therefore does not recognize that "principles of intelligibility... require and institute a domain of radical unintelligibility" (ibid., p. 35). Foucault does not recognize that bodies which are excluded and made unintelligible haunt the norm of cultural intelligibility and, therefore, all bodies.

Butler argues that it is this haunting which gives the psychic meaning of bodies and makes them a matter of politics. That is to say, because the psyche refers to the domain of radical unintelligibility brought into being with and for the constitution of cultural intelligibility, the psyche gives the possibility of changing the norm in the repetition of fantasy. As Butler puts it:

> If every performance repeats itself to institute the effect of identity, then every repetition requires an interval between the acts, as it were, in which risk and excess threaten to disrupt the identity being constituted. The unconscious is this excess that enables and contests every performance, and which never fully appears within the performance itself. The psyche is not in the body, but in the very signifying process through which that body comes to appear; it is the lapse in repetition as well as its compulsion, precisely what the performance seeks to deny, and that which compels it from the start.... the psyche is the permanent failure of expression, a failure that has its value, for it impels repetition and so reinstates the possibility of disruption. (Butler, 1991, p. 28)

For Butler, the threat of disruption which psychic repetition offers constitutes the possibility for a feminist and queer politics beyond both Lacan's and Foucault's treatments of oedipus. In Lacanian psychoanalysis, there is the possibility of psychic disruption, but it always returns to the law of oedipus; in Foucault, there is a realization that the law is a historically and geopolitically specific regulatory norm, but there is no articulation of the possibility of psychic disruption in relationship to changing the norm itself. For Butler, although the oedipal norm of cultural intelligibility is historically and geopolitically specific, it produces psychic repetition, which, however, is "a crucial resource in the struggle to rearticulate the very terms of symbolic legitimacy and intelligibility" (Butler, 1993, p. 3).

## Performativity, *différance* and power

To specifically address the issues of a feminist and queer politics, Butler first elaborated the possibilities of psychic disruption in terms of the notion of gender performance, her example being "drag." Butler's argument is that because the body is a fantasmatic projection of a psychic repetition, the body renders the relationship of sex, gender, psyche, and subject identity as one of difference; that is, the body, sex, gender, psyche, and subject identity are interimplicated but not reducible one to the other. Each is constituted again and again or repeatedly materialized. The coherency of each is itself a performance; drag shows that the body, sex, and gender are all performed and that they are "falsely naturalized as a unity through the regulatory fiction of heterosexual coherence" (Butler, 1990, p. 137). Drag shows the potential for political change in repetition and the play of differences.

But Butler's critics often fix on the notion of drag, claiming that it presents a "ludic" or trivial response to political exigencies and the political, economic, or material conditions of everyday life (Ebert, 1993). These critics miss the larger philosophical project in which Butler is engaged; that is, the reformulation of bodily matter in terms of a deconstruction of the Subject. In *Bodies that Matter*, Butler argues that in no way is gender performance a matter of play in the trivial sense of choosing a gender at will; performativity is not, Butler argues, "the act by which a subject brings into being what she/he names, but, rather...the reiterative power of discourse to produce the phenomena that it regulates and constrains" (Butler, 1993, p. 2). For Butler, performativity, therefore, is to be thought along the lines suggested by Foucault in his reformulation of power.

For Foucault, power is neither a strength possessed by the individual, nor a structure or institution. Foucault argues instead that power is a process immanent to a field of forces that cannot be represented as such: "power...is the moving substrate of force relations which, by virtue of their inequality, constantly engender states of power but the latter are always local and unstable" (Foucault, 1980, p. 93). While power makes it possible to use its mechanisms as "a grid of intelligibility of the social order," Foucault nonetheless suggests that power is not reducible to the social order, which only retrospectively allows power to be given a name. Butler puts it this way: "power is the name that renders manageable what might be otherwise too unwieldly or complex, and what, in its complexity, might defy the limiting and substantializing ontology presuppposed by the name" (Butler, 1997b, p. 35). Naming is the constitution of an identity which disavows the differences at play in the multiplicity of force fields or the singular, subindividual, finite forces of chance and necessity.

In linking gender performance with Foucault's treatment of power, Butler is not giving a political practice as much as showing how politics arises out of the play of differences which gives the possibility of identity as well as the disidentification with names. In this sense, Butler's rendering of gender performance draws as much on Derrida's treatment of *différance* as it does on Foucault's treatment of power. For Derrida, *différance* refers to the indefinite deferral of identity in the play of differences. But *différance* also refers to the repression or unconscious disvowal of the endless play of differences, when an identity is constituted, including subject identity. To put it another way, *différance* is referred to in order to remember that identity and, therefore, disidentification and change arise out of the play of differences.

In *Excitable Speech: a Politics of the Performative* (1997b), Butler draws both on Foucault's treatment of power and Derrida's treatment of *différance* to discuss hate speech and those attempts made to legislate against speakers using it. To argue against censorship, Butler proposes that the agency of hate speech is not the speaker which the laws against hate speech usually imply. The force of speech to make a difference is in repetition and the possibility of change which repetition gives. For Butler, the subject who speaks hate speech is "clearly responsible" for the speech but not because the subject is the originator of that speech. Butler argues instead that "the speaker renews the linguistic tokens of a community, reissuing and reinvigorating such speech. Responsibility is thus linked with speech as repetition, not as origination" (ibid., p. 39). Butler even suggests that the person named in the speech and who suffers its traumatic effects can be understood in post-Althusserian terms. That is, although a person is hailed and subjected by the hate speech, the hate speech nonetheless allows the person to speak back; indeed, there seems to be a compulsion for the subject to speak the hate speech back and, therefore, to perform it differently.

Hate speech thereby puts the subject for whom it is intended into "linguistic life." As Butler sees it, hate speech is "a founding subordination, and yet the scene of agency" (ibid., p. 38). The subject so named will most likely respond by repeating the hate speech, but for other ends than those for which it was first articulated. In this repetition of hate speech, a counter to it is made possible, without requiring state censorship or returning to the idea of the sovereign freedom of the intentional subject. If censorship is undesirable, Butler argues, it is not only because it is depriving, thereby restricting subjects from certain expression. Censorship also is undesirable because it is formative, constituting subjects or "the domain of the sayable within which I begin to speak at all" (ibid., p. 133).

While Butler's treatment of hate speech relies heavily on Derrida's treatment of the reiterative force in speech, she also insists that speech is a bodily act; not only does speech deflect the body, it also conveys it. Butler, therefore, draws Derrida's treatment of *différance* back to the unconscious, just as she drew Foucault's treatment of power back to it. She argues that Derrida's treatment of reiteration needs to be supplemented. Butler offers to do so with a treatment of "community conventions" which are repeated and enlivened in speech and which are unconsciously embodied in the speaker, who is, therefore, "a repository or the site of an incorporated history" (ibid., p. 152).

Butler turns to Pierre Bourdieu, arguing that his treatment of "habitus" gives an account of how norms or community conventions are embodied in "non-intentional and non-deliberate ways." But Bourdieu's treatment of habitus only shows that social norms are unconsciously embodied, without, however, recognizing that the body is itself unconsciously or fantasmatically constructed in the first place. For Butler, Bourdieu's notion of habitus is therefore limited, but her discussion of it makes clearer what she finds problematic about Derrida's treatment of reiteration; that is, that he locates it at the structural level of the sign. Butler wonders if the compulsion to repeat and the possibility for change which repetition gives are not rather located in the speaker's embodied history or the psychic substrate of the speaker's body, which is a social matter; that is, a materialization of the unconscious repetition of a historically specific norm of cultural intelligibility. This shift in Butler's treatment of the body, drawing Derrida and Foucault back to psychoanalysis, is on behalf of a radical feminist rethinking of the sociality of matter.

## The Person

Judith Butler was born in 1956 in Cleveland, Ohio. It was at synagogue that Butler first realized her interest in philosophy, especially Spinoza and existential philosophy. Because she had trouble behaving in class, Butler was made to take a tutorial with the rabbi. Being in trouble and thinking herself a trouble-maker seemed to enable Butler to "come out" during her high school years, where pre-Stonewall conditions still prevailed. Throughout it all, Butler's interest in philosophy remained.

After a year at Bennington College, she attended Yale, where, at the age of twenty-eight, she received a PhD in Philosophy in 1984. At Yale, her mentor was Maurice Natanson, whose interest in sociology and the social sciences left its mark on Butler's work. She was particularly drawn to the notion of "performative acts" and their sociality, and found Husserl's treatment of "constituting acts" especially suggestive. Along with her engagement with phenomenology, Butler read Hegel, Kant, and writers of the Frankfurt School. Her introduction to feminist theory came by way of a graduate seminar, where she met Nancy Cott. Cott encouraged Butler to go further with feminist theory. She did, and her first examinations of feminist texts dealt with those of Simone de Beauvoir and Monique Wittig.

Not long after completing her graduate study, Butler became one of a small group of scholars who were transforming the character of intellectual life inside and outside the academy. These scholars were publicized in a variety of new interdisciplinary journals which were founded in the late 1970s and early 1980s. Along with national and international conferences, these journals gave these scholars a broad popular appeal, making them intellectual stars. Butler quickly enjoyed and suffered wide public exposure.

Although she is at present the Chancellor's Professor at Berkeley and lives in California with her partner and their child, Butler has been a visiting lecturer at a number of academic institutions and has given innumerable conference papers. She has published five books in all and contributed to a number of edited works. She has been director and active on the board of the International Gay and Lesbian Human Rights Commission.

## INTELLECTUAL CONTEXT

### Feminist theory and psychoanalysis

If, in the early 1970s, feminist theorists had emphasized women's similarity to men in a demand for equality, by the late 1970s, feminist theorists emphasized women's difference from men, as well as women's similarity to each other, based on their shared experiences and identities, especially their experience of mothering and/or their identification with their mothers. Just less than a decade after feminist theorists had insisted on women's equality with men, feminist theorists, such as Nancy Chodorow and Adrienne Rich, turned to a reconsideration of the experiences and institution of motherhood, including the analysis of the deep, unconscious motivations which, as Chodorow proposed, led women to mother.

All through the 1980s, Chodorow's revision of Freudian psychoanalysis was especially influential in the feminist treatment of the family in Western, modern, industrial, capitalist societies and the revaluation of psychosexual reproduction of mother-centered parenting, fixed in the separation of the private and public spheres. But by the late 1980s, the revaluation of woman's experience, along with feminine sexuality, feminine subjectivity, and the feminine psyche, came under criticism for what was referred to as "essentialism." The presumption that all women share the same identity or experiences was profoundly questioned. It was argued instead that behind the essentialism of the feminist theory of gender of the 1970s and early 1980s, there is an unacknowledged standpoint located in the identities and experiences of white, middle-class women of Western Euro-American cultures.

But the feminist treatment of gender was criticized not only in terms of the differences of class, ethnicity, race and nation and their intersection in subject identities. Criticism also came from feminist theorists, who, in the tradition of British cultural studies, developed a post-Althusserian materialist feminism that made more extensive use of Lacan's rereading of Freud. While Chodorow's psychoanalytic approach draws on the object-relations school of ego psychology which revised Freudian psychoanalysis toward the interpersonal relationship of mother and infant/child, Lacan's reading of Freud turns psychoanalysis to the working of unconscious fantasy and the difference or division internal to the subject which unconscious fantasy maintains, and which makes the individual vulnerable to what Althusser referred to as "interpellation" or the individual's subjection to cultural norms.

Many feminist theorists who worked within the post-Althusserian, Lacanian tradition, while concerned with the infant/child/maternal experience, the family, and the private sphere, more often turned their attention to forms of cultural authority and legitimation – such as literature and narrative cinema, which were seen to mediate the private sphere, articulating the discourses of nation-state and civil society onto the individual by interpellating the individual as their subject. In their readings of cultural texts, feminist theorists, such as Jacqueline Rose, Annette Kuhn, Kaja Silverman, Mary Ann Doane, and Teresa de Lauretis, showed that what Althusser referred to as interpellation worked through the oedipalized norm of sexual difference, so that interpellation might better be understood as an engendering subjection of the individual to the symbolic order.

Although focusing on sexual difference in their engagement with Lacanian psychoanalysis, feminist theorists did not challenge, at least not at first, the psychoanalytic presumption of the link between oedipus and unconscious fantasy. Feminist theorists did not thematize the historical or geopolitical specificity of oedipus. How to treat the unconscious in terms of differences other than sexual difference, such as differences of race, class, ethnicity, and nation, was not addressed in early feminist deployments of Lacanian psychoanalysis. But there also was little attention given to "sexual orientation."

In this context, the 1990 publication of Butler's *Gender Trouble* provoked heated debate over "queerness." In reformulating the relationship of sex and gender, Butler not only drew on the various rereadings of Lacan provided by post-Althusserian feminist theorists. She also returned to the French feminists, especially to Luce Irigaray, who had critically engaged Lacan's rereading of Freud. For Butler, Irigaray leads the way in criticizing Lacanian psychoanalysis as part of a feminist deconstruction of Western philosophy.

In *Bodies that Matter* (1993), Butler especially draws on Irigaray's criticism of "phallomorphosis," which uncovers the way in which Western philosophy excludes the body from thought by figuring it as feminine. But even though the feminine is made to figure the body, Irigaray argues that it is a "specular" body; it is not the woman's body that the feminine figures in Western philosophy, but the exclusion of body from rational thought. In Western philosophy, the feminine, Irigaray argues, is of no essence other than that of matter, nature, the irrational. She further proposes that this exclusion of body in the figure of the feminine is a constitutive exclusion, productive of the internal coherence of rationality and the Subject of reason. In the exclusion of the body, not only is thought disembodied but different bodies cannot be imagined at all. In the end, although unmarked and displaced, there is only one body in Western philosophy – the masculine body. For Butler, Irigaray not only offers an understanding of the constitutive exclusion especially operative in the oedipalized norm of sexual difference; she also gives an imagination of different bodies, a future of difference.

## Poststructural criticism and queer theory

At its publication, *Gender Trouble* was not only read as a criticism of the feminist theory of gender; it was also understood as a more general criticism of identity politics and the discourse of gay and lesbian liberation. Butler's work was central to the development of queer theory, a criticism of lesbian/gay theory, in which the accusation of essentialism leveled at early feminist theory is leveled at lesbian/gay theories of identity and experience as well. But even before queer theory was instituted, the taken-for-granted equation of lesbianism with a feminist identity or a woman-identified femininity had been challenged in the "sex debates" of the 1980s, when some lesbian feminists defended sexual practices that had been criticized as male-identified, such as S/M and butch/femme. By then, feminist theorists concerned with questions of race, class, ethnicity, and nation had also begun to refuse the notion of a unified lesbian identity or a uniform lesbian experience.

But queer theory is not just one part of a criticism of feminist theory or gay and lesbian theories of identity and experience. For a number of theorists, such as Diana Fuss, Lee Edelman, Michael Moon, Steven Seidman, Andrew Parker, Michael Warner, and Teresa de Lauretis, queer theory also represents the engagement of lesbian and gay theorists with the debates over poststructuralism. Poststructuralism provided the means for a deconstruction of homosexual identity in terms of the historical specificity of its deployment in relations of power/knowledge. For example, in the same year *Gender Trouble* was published, Eve Kosofsky Sedgwick published *Epistemology of the Closet*, in which she draws on Foucault, among others theorists, to offer a genealogy of the institution in the nineteenth century of the "homo/heterosexual definition." As Sedgwick describes it, the homo/heterosexual definition refers to a "world mapping by which every given person, just as he or she was necessarily assignable to a male or female gender, was now considered necessarily assignable as well to a homo- or a hetero-sexuality" (Sedgwick, 1990, pp. 1–2).

Sedgwick's treatment of the homo/heterosexual definition is not meant to give foundation to an identity politics by which the experiences of lesbians and gays are imagined to offer a standpoint of critical reflection in the production of knowledge. Instead, Sedgwick means to reject a radical distinction between homosexuality and heterosexuality; she offers a "universalizing view" of homosexuality rather than a "minoritizing view." If the latter proposes that the homo/heterosexual definition is important only for a "homosexual minority," the former suggests that it is of "determinant importance in the lives of people across the spectrum of sexuality" (ibid., p. 1). It is a universalizing view of homosexuality that Butler elaborates when she treats sexed bodies in terms of her argument that "there are structures of psychic homosexuality within heterosexual relations, and structures of psychic heterosexuality within gay and lesbian sexuality and relationships" (ibid., p. 121).

But, for Sedgwick, the homo/heterosexual definition is not only a matter of the unconscious fantasies of subject identity. It also is a matter of the fantasmatic configuration which is deployed in relationships of power/knowledge; that is, the homo/heterosexual opposition serves as metaphor for other oppositions, such as "innocence/initiation, natural/artificial, new/old, discipline/terrorism, canonic/noncanonic, wholeness/decadence, urbane/provincial, domestic/foreign, health/illness..." (ibid., p. 11). The homo/heterosexual definition, as Sedgwick sees it, especially contributes to the production and distribution of excusable ignorances and legitimated knowledges; that is, knowledges about which some can easily claim ignorance, but which others are all but forced to embody.

In treating the homo/heterosexual definition, Sedgwick offers a more general proposal that epistemology be displaced by an exploration of the practices of disciplinary knowledge – asking "how certain categorizations work, what enactments they are performing and what relations they are creating rather than what they essentially mean" (ibid., p. 27). For Butler, too, queering the norm of sexual difference within the oedipalized matrix of heterosexual desire demands a shift from epistemology to locating "the problematic (of knowledge) within practices of signification"; this shift, Butler argues, "permits an analysis that takes the epistemological mode itself as one possible and contingent signifying practice" (Butler, 1990, p. 144).

In making epistemology a contingent signifying practice and treating epistemological issues in the politicizing terms of rhetorics, narrative logics, or technical enframements, queer theory draws heavily on poststructural criticism of modern Western philosophy; it especially borrows from the deconstruction of the Subject given as the authorizing and synthesizing figure of rationality and objective knowledge. It is because of its deconstructive aspects that queer theorists joined feminist theorists who already had engaged poststructural criticism in order to uncover the unmarked aspects of the authorized subject of knowledge figured in modern Western philosophy and the discourses of the human sciences. Along with feminist theorists, queer theorists made legible the erased marks of gender, sexuality, ethnicity, class, race, and nation in the figure of authorized subject and, thereby, registered the exclusion of certain subjects from authorized forms of knowledge.

Still, queer theorists refuse essentialism and offer a different understanding of the subject and of knowledge than standpoint epistemologies do. Queer theorists refuse the claim that a more accurate knowledge or a stronger objectivity are possible from the perspective of dominated subjects who have been hitherto excluded from authorizing forms of knowledge. For this reason, queer theorists often support notions of hybridity, especially elaborated by postcolonial theorists in treating patchwork identities in the border crossing cultures of neocolonial diaspora.

All of this also means that queer theorists refuse to name the subject of political agency once and for all; they urge a different view of politics. If, as Butler's work at least suggests, agency must be referred to the play of differences, then politics cannot begin with a definite mapping by the individual subject of its oppression. Neither the individual subject nor the experience of oppression can be the simple origin of politics. Instead, what must be engaged at the start of politics is the reiterative force of difference by which the agency of subject identity and experience are dissimulated. For Butler, *différance* allows for "a democracy to come," as Derrida refers to it. Rather than an identity politics, Butler proposes a politics of "coalition" where it is possible to acknowledge the contradictions involved in coalitions and yet "take action with those contradictions intact" (ibid., p. 15).

## SOCIAL CONTEXT

Butler's work is deeply connected with political, economic, and cultural changes that have occurred in the second half of the twentieth century, and that have seemed to some so profound as to warrant characterization of modern societies as postmodern and, therefore, to require rethinking of the assumptions of modern social theory. Butler is among those intellectuals who have contributed to the reformulation of social theory and who have done so in relationship to the "new" social movements, such as students' movements, women's movements, gay and lesbian liberation movements, race and ethnic pride movements. Linked to the transformations characteristic of postmodernity – decolonization, the transnationalization of capital in neocolonialism and the globalization of telecommunications – the new social movements have raised questions about representation, culture, and identity. In support of struggles against exclusion and contentions over resources for recognition and self-reflexivity, intellectuals connected to the new social movements instigated criticism concerned with the production, circulation, and legitmation of knowledge, and turned modern Western philosophy and the human sciences to reflect on their assumptions. They even raised questions about the assumptions of leftist discourse, often aiming criticism at Marxist theory for its reduction of culture, identity, and representation to the economic.

Throughout the 1970s and the 1980s, there was much writing accompanying the criticism of Western philosophy and the human sciences, which focused on the psychic losses and cultural deprivation due to oppressive relations of domination; a desire was aroused to recover subjugated knowledges hidden in obscure histories and traditions of women, gays, lesbians, persons of color, and of different ethnicities, classes, and nations. And there was a growing sensitivity to the intersection of race, class, gender, ethnicity, sexuality, and nationality that was elaborated in what is often labeled "identity politics." But this focus on culture, representation, and identity was not merely a rejection of political economic analysis. Identity politics seemed instead a register of changes in politics and capitalist economy that were destabilizing that configuration of family and national ideologies, the state and civil society, the public and private spheres long presumed in social theory, especially in the discourse on democracy.

By the late 1970s, it had become more apparent that, in Northern capitalist societies, post-Second World War political economics had been transformed, which profoundly affected Southern and neocolonial nations as well. Keynesian inspired state intervention in market economics through social welfare programs and fiscal and monetary policies was being challenged, while the spatial displacement of the crisis of capital accumulation had led to a transnationalization of capital and the transformation of the Fordist/Taylorist organization of capitalist production into the flexible accumulation or the flexible specialization of neo-Fordism.

Also more apparent were the effects of globalized telecommunications, which not only allowed for outsourcing and subcontracting that supported the just-in-time delivery systems and the small-batch production of a transnational neo-Fordist capitalist production. Telecommunications also promoted the centralization of financial services, permitting instantaneous movements of capital and, therefore, the growing autonomy of the financial system from production. All of this suggested that abstract knowledge or scientific information was displacing labor as central to the accumulation of capital and the creation of wealth. Under such conditions, a distinction between science and technology seemed no longer meaningful and, given the developments in telecommunications, especially the interfacing of teletechnology and computer technology, the distinction between technology and culture also seemed less meaningful, at least in many parts of the world.

All this led some social theorists to argue that representation, culture, and identity had become a matter of a worldwide extension of commodification and the increased alienation of individual subjects due to the pervasiveness of marketing and advertising images that saturate everyday life and obliterate the boundary between the real and the imaginary. Such a view has usually been held by those who would argue for a political economy of the sign to replace or enlarge a more traditional Marxist political economy. But the central place of knowledge or technoscience in transnational, neo-Fordist, capitalist production has also suggested a view of technoscience as the primary agency of power in postmodernity; as such, knowledges became the object of analysis in various cultural studies, offering some indication that the development of telecommunications is driven by something besides capitalism or commodification.

In fact, the globalization of telecommunications made it more apparent that there is a will to record and transmit everything everywhere to everyone all of the time which has been driving the technological developments of capitalist economies from the start. Such a will is visible not only in the development of teletechnology but also in possibilities such as the availability of banks of information about each of us – not only demographics of all sorts but also the more general treatment of individuals as ontologically specific databases of genetic information which can be exchanged among agents that may just as easily be computer programs as people. This will is "the will to truth" which poststructural criticism had treated in relationship to modern Western philosophy and the human sciences.

Perhaps poststructural criticism has been at the center of heated debate over the last decades of the twentieth century because its efforts to deconstruct the authority of modern Western philosophy and the human sciences could be read as both a register and an intervention in the transformation to transnational, neo-Fordist, capitalist production and globalized telecommunications. After all, inside and outside the academy, poststructural criticism caused an intellectual upheaval in arguing that the normative grounds for the truth claims of knowledge, which modern Western philosophy gives the human sciences, are culturally specific; it did this at a time when the "West" was becoming more closely engaged with "the rest" of the world and when simply presuming the universality of the normative grounds of the human sciences was becoming impossible. It was also a time of profound change in the relation of technology, culture, identity, and representation.

But even before poststructural criticism had become a full blown challenge to the presumptions of modern Western philosophy and the human sciences, feminist theory already had gone a long way in undermining the self-assurance of academic discourses. Throughout the 1970s, feminist theorists especially focused their criticism on the configuration of the private and public spheres, in terms of which the function of the woman is given over to the socialization of the infant-child for participation in the nation and the economy. In uncovering the sexual politics of the private sphere and in protesting the exclusion of women from the public sphere, the state, and the economy, feminist theorists initiated debate over culture, identity, and representation.

By the late 1980s, however, feminist theorists themselves were embroiled in a debate over the seeming indifference of early feminist theory to differences of race, class, ethnicity, and nationality. This trouble among feminist theorists resonated with a general debate over identity politics in terms of which different groups claimed that their specific experiences of exclusion and domination gave them a standpoint from which to more adequately understand structures of oppression and domination that shaped identities and experiences. Lesbian and gay theorists also engaged in identity politics; they presumed a standpoint epistemology based on shared experiences of oppression and domination. Nevertheless, by the 1990s, queer theory was receiving a great deal of attention inside and outside the academy, even though it refused identity politics and deployed poststructural criticism, as did postcolonial theory and critical race theory, in rethinking the liberal politics of protesting exclusion in the demand for full participation in the state, the public sphere, and the economy.

In its articulation of the possiblity of a queer politics and queer aesthetics, queer theory registered and fostered a change in the character of lesbian and gay communities. After Stonewall, lesbian and gay communities had gained visibility, as intellectuals, academics, writers, and artists produced works focused on gay and lesbian experiences. There also were lesbian and gay newspapers, journals, productions of mass media and popular literatures. By the 1980s these communities had spawned what Steven Seidman describes as "ethnic models of identity and single-interest group politics inspired by either a liberal assimilationist ideal or, in the case of lesbian-feminism a separatist ideological agenda" (Seidman, 1995, p. 121). When queer theory challenged the unity of homosexual identity or the notion of self-same identity, it challenged the grounds for an ethnic model of identity, single-interest politics, and the liberal assimilationist ideal, on one hand, and separatism, on the other.

The emphasis in queer theory on the performative allowed it to be linked instead with the militant politics of Act-Up and Queer Nation. While Act-Up has supported a confrontational politics of civil disobedience in an effort to obtain services and scientific research for HIV/AIDS, Queer Nation has focused on creating awareness and making visible links between queers situated in various social and institutional settings. Both strategies fit the situation of the post-welfare state; together they promoted negotiation from within government or social institutions, while agitating against them from without.

The militant performative aspects of queer politics especially challenged the notion of representation, because such politics are less about appeals for representation within the state and more about playing with the logics of exposure informing mass media. Queer politics has refused the legitimacy of the configuration of the private and public spheres. In the context of queer politics, not only is private life understood to be political, but public discourses, especially science, are understood to be deployments of power. Indeed, science is understood as a primary agency of power/knowledge and therefore is open to critical revision through direct political action.

For all this, queer theory became a target in the so-called "culture wars" waged by cultural conservatives attempting to reinstate the family as the foundation of democracy by reasserting "family values" against those perceived to have abandoned them, such as queers, feminists, and those engaged in identity politics around race, class, ethnicity, and nation. Queer theory was also implicated in the turn of the culture wars into the so-called "science wars," waged by rightist and leftist critics against intellectuals connected with identity politics, poststructural criticism, and cultural studies of science, who were criticized especially for the argument – no matter how differently elaborated – that science and power are inextricable and that, therefore, the reflexivity of the self-criticism of science must be rethought.

In 1996, when the Sokal affair brought the science wars to public attention, it may very well have marked both the culmination of the long period of critical rethinking of the assumptions of modern Western philosophy and the human sciences and a turn to the normalization of a number of these criticisms. Alan Sokal, a physicist at New York University, wrote an essay which pretended to be a legitimate work of science studies engaging poststructural criticism and feminist theory. It was published in *Social Text*, a journal of leftist cultural criticism. Shortly after the publication of the essay, Sokal announced in another journal that the essay was a hoax which had gone unrecognized as such by the editors of *Social Text* because of their certainty of the political correctness of the cultural studies of science. Sokal, a self-proclaimed leftist and feminist, argued for the necessity of recognizing the possibility of objective knowledge of reality without which leftist politics would be threatened. He thereby produced another version of the usual criticism of poststructuralism: that the insistence on the inextricability of science and power refuses all grounds for judging scientific representation.

Although the Sokal affair brought to a frenzy the anxiety of those leftists who for some time had been proclaiming the excesses of poststructural criticism, feminist theory, queer theory, postcolonial theory, criticial race theory, and the cultural studies of science, ironically it also showed the ongoing relevance of all of these for treating questions raised by the Sokal affair itself – questions about the production and circulation of knowledges, the political interests inherent in doing science and cultural criticism alike, and the relationship of science and the media.

## IMPACT AND ASSESSMENT

Although her work extends social constructionism to the constitution of matter and, therefore, proposes the possiblity of a social theory of materialization, Butler has nevertheless been criticized for ignoring the social and overemphasizing the discursive. Social and political theorists, including some who define themselves as materialist feminists and who draw on the Marxist tradition, have argued that Butler fails to historicize or to give the historical conditions of queer identities or queer theory itself (Benhabib et al., 1995; Hennessy, 1995; Seidman, 1995). More often than not, what is meant by historicizing derives from a contrast between Foucault's approach to the relationship of power/knowledge, upon which Butler draws, and a conjunctural analysis in which linkages between localized practices are thought to be conditioned by and, therefore, to reproduce a social formation such as late capitalism or postmodern capitalism. For the purpose of this comparison, Foucault's approach is described as referring to the linkages of discursive practices belonging only to local arrangements, while his notion of the discursive is reduced to cultural representations distinguishable from the historical, economic, or political relationships underlying cultural representations.

Although this description misrepresents and trivializes the more subtle treatment of discourse and power/knowledge which Foucault gives and which Butler elaborates in her work, it might be worthwhile to consider the centrality of technoscience or abstract theoretical knowledge in neo-Fordist transnational capitalist production as a historical conditioning of a focus on discourse, imaginaries, language, and representation in poststructural criticism generally, and Butler's work especially. Still, Foucault's treatment of discourse and power/knowledge is not merely a historical effect; it is also an intervention and, as such, it gives a new idea of history in the notion of genealogy. In using Foucault's notion of genealogy, Butler historicizes differently than a conjunctural analysis proposes to do. She historicizes the oedipal norm of cultural intelligibility, releasing the potential for change in its reiterative force. In doing so, Butler historicizes agency. She reveals the sociality of agency, which a conjunctural analysis cannot do, since such an analysis assumes an agency behind historical conditions, a revolutionary agency grounded in the intentionality of the human subject.

All this is important for feminist theory and social theory at the end of the twentieth century, when it must be recognized that oedipus and the configuration of national and family ideologies, the state and civil society, the private and public spheres presumed along with oedipus in modern Western philosophy and the human sciences may not be, everywhere or all of the time, the regulative normative ideal of a configuration of social spaces. It follows that the grounds of democratic and scientific representation can only be contingent. For example, in the case of neocolonialist states, it is difficult to ground democratic representation in the configuration of social spaces presumed in modern Western philosophical discourse; after all, women often are made to figure the patriarchal ideology of the nation against capitalist commodification, while they themselves may use their employment in the workforce of a multinational corporation as a site for resisting patriarchal family ideology. Butler offers another example of this complexification of the conditions out of which agency arises. She points to the difference between, on one hand, queers' "coming-out" and thereby naming and discursively constituting homosexuality, and, on the other hand, the military's naming and constituting homosexuality in its prohibiting opportunities for lesbians and gays to name themselves as such. Both examples suggest the need for subtlety in recognizing the impossibility of determining the social conditions of agency and, therefore, of democratic politics. The examples point to the need to attend to the timing of exposures, under- and over-exposure to social situations and media-eventness, where the configuration of the social spaces presumed in the discourse of Western philosophy and the human sciences may no longer exist, or where they may never have been relevant in the first place.

Butler's insistence on the contingency of foundations for normative or ethical judgments is crucial for rethinking democratic and scientific representation in postmodernity. Yet a criticism often leveled against Butler is that she does not even offer normative or ethical foundations for her own resistance to heteronormativity. But Butler's position is that normative and ethical judgments, while necessary to politics and science, are never free from communication or from the labor of cultural translation which those judgments are asked to ground. For this reason, Butler looks for foundations which can move – movable foundations, sensitive to timing as much as to spatial arrangements of the spheres of social life. Butler's work is not anti-foundational as has been argued; rather, it aims to rethink foundations. This is necessary philosophical work, when social theory must be allowed to be touched by the transformations of postmodernity.

# Bibliography

## Writings of Judith Butler

*Subjects of Desire: Hegelian Reflections in Twentieth Century France.* 1987. New York: Columbia University Press.
*Gender Trouble: Feminism and the Subversion of Identity.* 1990. New York: Routledge.
Imitation and Gender Insubordination. 1991. In Diana Fuss (ed.), *inside/out: Lesbian Theories, Gay Theories.* New York: Routledge.
*Bodies that Matter: On the Discursive Limits of "Sex."* 1993. New York: Routledge.
*The Psychic Life of Power: Theories of Subjection.* 1997a. Stanford, CA: Stanford University Press.
*Excitable Speech: a Politics of the Performative.* 1997b. New York: Routledge.

## Further reading

Benhabib, Seyla, et al. (1995) *Feminist Contentions: a Philosophical Exchange.* New York: Routledge.
Clough, Patricia Ticineto (1994) *Feminist Thought: Desire, Power and Academic Discourse.* Oxford: Blackwell.
Ebert, Teresa (1992) Ludic Feminism, the Body, Performance, and Labor: Bringing Materialism Back into Feminist Cultural Studies. *Cultural Critique*, 23, 5–50.
Foucault, Michel (1980) *The History of Sexuality, Volume 1,* translated by Robert Hurley. New York: Vintage.
Hennessy, Rosemary (1995) Queer Visibility in Commodity Culture. In Linda Nicholson and Steven Seidman (eds), *Social Postmodernism, Beyond Identity Politics.* Cambridge: Cambridge University Press, pp. 142–83.
Rose, Jacqueline (1986) *Sexuality in the Field of Vision.* London: Verso.
Sedgwick, Eve Kosofsky (1990) *Epistemology of the Closet.* Berkeley: University of California Press.
Seidman, Steven (1995) Deconstructing Queer Theory. In Linda Nicholson and Steven Seidman (eds), *Social Postmodernism, Beyond Identity Politics.* Cambridge: Cambridge University Press, pp.116–41.

# Index

UNIVERSITY OF WOLVERHAMPTON
LEARNING RESOURCES